The Conscious Reader

The Conscious Reader

SEVENTH EDITION

CAROLINE SHRODES
Late, The Union Institute

HARRY FINESTONE
California State University, Northridge

MICHAEL SHUGRUE
The College of Staten Island of the City University of New York

FONTAINE MAURY BELFORD
The Union Institute

Allyn and Bacon
Boston London Toronto Sydney Tokyo Singapore

Vice President: Eben W. Ludlow
Editorial Assistant: Linda D'Angelo
Marketing Manager: Lisa Kimball
Production Administrator: Rowena Dores
Editorial-Production Service: Lauren Green Shafer
Cover Administrator: Linda Knowles
Composition Buyer: Linda Cox
Manufacturing Buyer: Suzanne Lareau
Text Designer: Denise Hoffman, Glenview Studios
Electronic Composition: Omegatype Typography, Inc.

A Viacom Company
Needham Heights, Massachusetts 02194

Internet: www.abacon.com
America Online: keyword: College Online

Library of Congress Cataloging-in-Publication Data
The conscious reader / [edited by] Caroline Shrodes . . . [et al.]. —
7th ed.
p. cm.
Includes index.
ISBN 0–205–26848-X
1. College readers. I. Shrodes, Caroline.
PE1122.C586 1997
808'.0427—dc21 97–20939
CIP

Credits

Roger Angell, "On the Ball" from *Once More Around the Park: A Baseball Reader.* Copyright © 1991 by Roger Angell. Reprinted with the permission of Ballantine Books, a division of Random House, Inc.

Maya Angelou, "Finishing School" from *I Know Why The Caged Bird Sings.* Copyright © 1969 by Maya Angelou. Reprinted with the permission of Random House, Inc.

continued on next page

Printed in the United States of America
10 9 8 7 6 5 4 3 2 1 RRDV 01 00 99 98 97

Margaret Atwood, "Fiction: Happy Endings" from *Good Bones and Simple Murders.* Copyright © 1983, 1992, 1994 by O. W. Toad, Ltd. A Nan A. Talese Book. Reprinted with the permission of the author and Doubleday, a division of Bantam Doubleday Dell Publishing Group, Inc. "Pornography" from *Chatelaine* (1988). Copyright © 1988 by Margaret Atwood. Reprinted with the permission of the author.

W. H. Auden, "Lullaby" ("Lay Your Sleeping Head") and "The Unknown Citizen" from *W. B. Auden: Collected Poems,* edited by Edward Mendelson. Copyright 1940 and renewed © 1968 by W. H. Auden. Both reprinted with the permission of Random House, Inc.

James Baldwin, "The Discovery of What It Means to Be an American" from *Nobody Knows My Name* (New York: Vintage Books). Copyright © 1961 by James Baldwin, renewed 1989 by Gloria Baldwin Karefa-Smart. Reprinted with the permission of the James Baldwin Estate.

Bruno Bettleheim, "The Child's Need for Magic" from *The Uses of Enchantment.* Originally appeared in *The New Yorker.* Copyright © 1975, 1976 by Bruno Bettleheim. Reprinted with the permission of Alfred A. Knopf, Inc.

Eavan Boland, "When the Spirit Moves" from *The New York Review of Books* (January 12, 1995) 62, no. 1. Copyright © 1995 by Nyrev, Inc. Reprinted with the permission of *The New York Review of Books.*

Jorge Luís Borges, "Borges and Myself" from *The Aleph and Other Stories 1933–1969,* translated by Norman Thomas di Giovanni. Copyright © 1968 by Jorge Luís Borges. English translation copyright © 1968, 1969, 1970 by Emece Editores, S. A. and Norman Thomas Giovanni. Reprinted with the permission of Dutton Signet. a division of Penguin Books USA Inc. "The Web," translated by Alastair Reid, from *The New Yorker* (June 2, 1986). Copyright © 1986 by the Estate of Jorge Luís Borges and Alastair Reid. Reprinted with the permission of The Wylie Agency, Inc.

T. Coraghessan Boyle, "If the River Was Whiskey" from *If the River Was Whiskey.* Copyright © 1989 by T. Coraghessan Boyle. Reprinted with the permission of Viking Penguin, a division of Penguin Books USA Inc.

Ray Bradbury, "Perhaps We Are Going Away." Copyright © 1962 by Peerless Publishing Co., renewed 1990 by Ray Bradbury. Reprinted with the permission of Don Congdon Associates, Inc.

David Bradley, "Harvest Home" from *Family Portraits* by Carolyn Anthony. Copyright © 1989 by David Bradley. Reprinted with the permission of Doubleday, a division of Bantam Doubleday Dell Publishing Group, Inc.

Harold Brodkey, "Reading, the Most Dangerous Game" from *The New York Times Book Review* (November 24, 1985). Copyright © 1985 by Harold Brodkey. Reprinted with the permission of International Creative Management.

Gwendolyn Brooks, "Life for my child is simple, and is good" from *Blacks* (Chicago: Third World Press, 1991). Copyright © 1991 by Gwendolyn Brooks Blakely. Reprinted with the permission of the author.

Lester R. Brown, Christopher Flavin, and Sandra Postel, "Earth Day 2030" from Paul Rothkrug and Robert L. Olson, eds., *Mending the Earth: A World for Our Grandchildren* (Berkeley, Calif.: North Atlantic Books, 1991). Copyright © 1991 by Worldwatch Institute. Reprinted with the permission of Worldwatch Institute.

Victoria Bissell Brown, "Abortion Fight Is Over Choice" from *The Los Angeles Times* (April 1, 1988). Copyright © 1988 by Victoria Bissell Brown.

Art Buchwald, "Leisure Will Kill You" from *Laid Back in Washington.* Copyright © 1978, 1979, 1980, 1981 by Art Buchwald. Reprinted with the permission of The Putnam Publishing Group.

Raymond Carver, "What We Talk About When We Talk About Love" from *What We Talk About When We Talk About Love.* Copyright © 1983 by Raymond Carver. Reprinted with the permission of Alfred A. Knopf, Inc.

John Cheever, "Expelled" from *The New Republic* (October 1, 1930). Reprinted July 19 and 26, 1982. Copyright 1930 by John Cheever. Reprinted with the permission of The Wylie Agency, Inc.

Susan Cheever, "Portrait of My Father" from *Home Before Dark.* Copyright © 1984 by Susan Cheever. Reprinted with the permission of Houghton Mifflin Company. All rights reserved.

Kim Chernin, "The Flesh and the Devil" from *The Obsession: Reflections on the Tyranny of Slenderness,* Copyright © 1981 by Kim Chernin. Reprinted with the permission of HarperCollins Publishers, Inc.

Judith Ortiz Cofer, "Casa: A Partial Remembrance of a Puerto Rican Childhood" from *Prairie Schooner* 63, no. 2 (Fall 1989). Copyright © 1989 by the University of Nebraska Press. Reprinted with the permission of the author and publishers.

Frank Conroy, "Think About It" from *Harper's* (November 1988). Copyright © 1988 by *Harper's Magazine.* All rights reserved. Reproduced from the November issue by special permission.

Aaron Copland, "How We Listen to Music" from *What to Listen for in Music* (New York: McGraw-Hill, 1988). Copyright © 1988 by Aaron Copland. Reprinted with the permission of The Aaron Copland Fund for Music, Inc.

William Cronon, "The Trouble with Wilderness" from *The New York Times Magazine* (August 13, 1995). Adapted from "The Trouble with Wilderness; or, Getting Back to the Wrong Nature" in William Cronon, ed., *Uncommon Ground: Toward Reinventing Nature.* Copyright © 1995 by William Cronon. Reprinted with the permission of W. W. Norton & Company, Inc.

E. E. Cummings, "my father moved through dooms of love" and "i like my body when it is with your" from *Complete Poems 1904–1962,* edited by George J. Firmage. Copyright 1923, 1925, 1940, 1951, 1953, © 1968, 1991 by the Trustees for the E. E. Cummings Trust. Copyright © 1976 by George James Firmage. Reprinted with the permission of Liveright Publishing Corporation.

Annie Dillard, "So This Was Adolescence" from *An American Childhood.* Copyright © 1987 by Annie Dillard. Reprinted with the permission of HarperCollins Publishers, Inc.

E. L. Doctorow, "Ultimate Discourse" from *Esquire* (August 1986). Copyright © 1986 by E. L. Doctorow. Reprinted with the permission of International Creative Management.

Mark Doty, "Tunnel Music" from *Atlantis* (New York: HarperCollins Publishers, 1995). Originally in *The New Yorker* (September 25, 1995). Copyright © 1995 by Mark Doty. Reprinted with the permission of the author.

Rita Dove, "Beauty and the Beast" from *The Yellow House on the Corner* (Pittsburgh: Carnegie-Mellon University Press, 1980). Copyright © 1980 by Rita Dove. Reprinted with the permission of the author.

W. E. B. Du Bois, "On Being Crazy." Reprinted with the permission of Shirley Graham Du Bois.

Alan B. Durning, "Asking How Much Is Enough" from Lester R. Brown, et al., eds., *State of the World 1991.* Copyright © 1991 by Worldwatch Institute. Reprinted with the permission of W. W. Norton & Company, Inc.

Ronald Dworkin, "Life Is Sacred. That's the Easy Part" from *The New York Times Magazine* (May 16, 1993). Copyright © 1993 by The New York Times Company. Reprinted with the permission of *The New York Times.*

Loren Eiseley, "The Hidden Teacher" from *The Unexpected Universe.* Copyright © 1969 by Loren Eiseley. Reprinted with the permission of Harcourt Brace and Company.

Niles Eldredge, "Creationism Isn't Science" from *The New Republic* (April 6, 1981). Copyright © 1981 by The New Republic, Inc. Reprinted with the permission of *The New Republic.*

T. S. Eliot, "The Love Song of J. Alfred Prufrock" from *T. S. Eliot: The Complete Poems and Plays 1909–1962.* Reprinted with the permission of Faber and Faber, Ltd.

Ralph Ellison, "On Becoming a Writer" from *Shadow and Act.* Copyright © 1953, 1964 and renewed 1981, 1992 by Ralph Ellison. Reprinted with the permission of Random House, Inc.

Louise Erdrich, "A Wedge of Shade" from *The New Yorker* (March 6, 1989). Later part of *Tales of Burning Love* (New York: HarperCollins Publishers, 1996). Copyright © 1989 by Louise Erdrich. Reprinted with the permission of the author, c/o Rembar & Curtis, New York.

William Faulkner, "Nobel Prize Award Speech" (editors' title, originally titled "Upon Receiving the Nobel Prize for Literature") from *Essays, Speeches, and Public Letters by William Faulkner.* Copyright 1950 by William Faulkner. "Dry September" from *Collected Stories of William Faulkner.* Copyright 1930 and renewed © 1958 by William Faulkner. Both reprinted with the permission of Random House, Inc.

Grant Fjermedal, "Artificial Intelligence, Surrogate Brains" from *Omni* (October 1986). Copyright © 1986 by Omni Publications International Ltd. Reprinted with the permission of OMNI.

Colin Fletcher, "A Bend in the Road" from *Wilderness Society* Magazine (1988). Copyright © 1988 by Colin Fletcher. Reprinted with the permission of Brandt & Brandt.

E. M. Forster, "Art for Art's Sake" from *Two Cheers for Democracy.* Copyright 1949 by E. M. Forster and renewed © 1977 by Donald Perry. Reprinted with the permission of Harcourt Brace and Company and Edward Arnold, Ltd.

Betty Friedan, "The Quiet Movement of American Men" from *The Second Stage.* Copyright © 1981, 1986 by Betty Friedan. Reprinted with the permission of Simon & Schuster, Inc.

Jane Gallop, "Feminist Accused of Sexual Harassment" from *Art Issues* no. 43 (Summer 1996): 19–22. Copyright © 1996 by Jane Gallop. Reprinted with the permission of the author.

Howard Gardner, "Human Intelligence Isn't What We Think It Is" from *U.S. News & World Report* (March 19, 1984). Copyright © 1984 by U.S. News & World Report. Reprinted with the permission of the publishers.

Henry Louis Gates, Jr., "Talking Back" from Christopher Ricks and Leonard Michaels, eds., *The State of the Language.* Copyright © 1990 by The Regents of the University of California. Reprinted with the permission of the University of California Press.

Ira Glasser, "Artistic Freedom: A Gathering Storm" from *Civil Liberties* 369 (Spring 1990). Copyright © 1990 by American Civil Liberties Union. Reprinted with the permission of American Civil Liberties Union.

Ellen Goodman, "The Company Man" from *At Large.* Copyright © 1981 by The Washington Post Company. Reprinted with the permission of Simon & Schuster, Inc.

Mary Gordon, "A Moral Choice" from *The Atlantic Monthly* (April 1990). Copyright © 1990 by Mary Gordon. Reprinted with the permission of Sterling Lord Literistic.

Greg Graffin, "Anarchy in the Tenth Grade" from *Details* (July 1996). Copyright © 1996 by Advance Magazine Publishers, Inc. Reprinted by permission.

Germaine Greer, "The Stereotype" from *The Female Eunuch.* Copyright © 1970, 1971 by Germaine Greer. Reprinted with the permission of McGraw-Hill, Inc.

Frederick Philip Grove, "The First Day of an Immigrant" from Smara Kamboureli, ed., *Making a Difference* (New York: Oxford University Press, 1996). Reprinted with the permission of A. Leonard Grove, Toronto.

Pete Hamill, "Crack and the Box" from *Esquire* (May 1990). Copyright © 1990 by Pete Hamill. Reprinted with the permission of International Creative Management.

R. C. Harvey, "State of the Art: June 1996" from *The Comics Journal* no. 188 (July 1996). Copyright © 1996 by R. C. Harvey. Reprinted with the permission of the author.

Ernest Hemingway, "Indian Camp" from *In Our Time.* Copyright 1925 by Charles Scribner's Sons, renewed 1953 by Ernest Hemingway. Reprinted with the permission of Scribner, a division of Simon & Schuster, Inc.

Rob Hoerburger, "Gotta Dance" from *The New York Times Magazine,* "About Men" (July 18, 1993). Copyright © 1993 by The New York Times Company. Reprinted with the permission of *The New York Times.*

Garrett Hongo, "Kubota" from *Ploughshares.* Reprinted in *Best American Essays 1991.* Copyright © 1991 by Garrett Hongo. Reprinted with the permission of the author.

Langston Hughes, "Theme for English B" from *The Collected Poems of Langston Hughes,* edited by Arnold Rampersad and David Roessel. Copyright 1949 by Langston Hughes, renewed © 1977 by George Houston Bass. Reprinted with the permission of Alfred A. Knopf, Inc.

Zora Neale Hurston, "How It Feels to Be Colored Me" from *I Love Myself When I'm Laughing,* edited by Alice Walker (New York: The Feminist Press, 1975). Originally in *The World Tomorrow* 11 (May 1928). Copyright 1929 by Zora Neale Hurston, renewed © 1956 by John C. Hurston. Reprinted with the permission of Lucy C. Hurston.

Aldous Huxley, "Conditioning the Children" from *Brave New World.* Copyright 1932 and renewed © 1960 by Aldous Huxley. Reprinted with the permission of HarperCollins Publishers, Inc. and Chatto & Windus, Ltd., on behalf of Mrs. Laura Huxley.

Greg Jones, "The Man on the Moon" from *Buzz* (February 1996). Copyright © 1996 by Buzz, Inc. Reprinted with the permission of the author. All rights reserved.

Franz Kafka, "Letter to His Father" from Max Brod, ed., *Dearest Father: Stories and Other Writings,* translated by Ernst Kaiser and Eithene Wilkins. English translation copyright 1954 and renewed © 1982 by Schocken Books. Reprinted with the permission of Schocken Books, distributed by Pantheon Books, a division of Random House, Inc.

Margo Kaufman, "Who's Educated? Who Knows?" from *The New York Times* (November 1, 1992). Copyright © 1992 by The New York Times Company. Reprinted with the permission of *The New York Times.*

Helen Keller, "Three Days to See." Reprinted with the permission of the American Foundation for the Blind. All rights reserved.

Jamaica Kincaid, "A Small Place" from *A Small Place.* Copyright © 1988 by Jamaica Kincaid. Reprinted with the permission of Farrar, Straus & Giroux, Inc.

Martin Luther King, Jr., "Letter From Birmingham Jail" from *Why We Can't Wait.* Copyright © 1963 by Martin Luther King, Jr., renewed 1991 by Coretta Scott King, Dexter King, Martin Luther King III, Yolanda King and Bernice King. Reprinted with the permission of The Heirs to The Estate of Martin Luther King, Jr., c/o Writers House, Inc.

Peter King, "Of Crumpled Wings and Little Girls" from *The Los Angeles Times* (April 19, 1996). Copyright © 1996 by Times Mirror Company. Reprinted with the permission of the Los Angeles Times Syndicate.

Maxine Hong Kingston, "No Name Woman" from *The Woman Warrior.* Copyright © 1975, 1976 by Maxine Hong Kingston. Reprinted with the permission of Alfred A. Knopf, Inc.

Jonathan Kozol, "Distancing the Homeless" from *Rachel and Her Children: Homeless Families in America.* Copyright © 1988 by Jonathan Kozol. Reprinted with the permission of Crown Publishers, Inc.

Brooke Kroeger, "AIDS and the Girl Next Door" from *Mirabella* (September 1989). Copyright © 1989 by Brooke Kroeger.

D. H. Lawrence, "Give Her a Pattern" from *Phoenix II: Uncollected Papers of D. H. Lawrence,* edited by Roberts and Moore. Copyright © 1959, 1963, 1968 by The Estate of Frieda Lawrence Ravagli. Reprinted with the permission of Viking Penguin, a division of Penguin Books USA Inc.

Li-Young Lee, "Persimmons" from *Rose.* Originally published in *The American Poetry Review.* Copyright © 1986 by Li-Young Lee. Used with the permission of BOA Editions, Ltd.

Ursula K. Le Guin, "Winged: The Creatures on My Mind" from *Harper's* (August 1990). Copyright © 1990 by Ursula K. Le Guin. Reprinted with the permission of the author and the author's agent, Virginia Kidd.

Denise Levertov, "In Mind" from *Poems 1960–1967.* Originally published in Poetry. Copyright © 1963 by Denise Levertov. Reprinted with the permission of New Directions Publishing Corporation.

Mark Levine, "About Face (A Poem Called 'Dover Beach')" from *Debt.* Copyright © 1993 by Mark Levine. Reprinted with the permission of William Morrow & Company, Inc.

Barry Lopez, "Landscape and Narrative" from *Crossing Open Ground* (New York: Charles Scribner's Sons, 1988), originally appeared in *Harper's* (December 1984) under a different title. Copyright © 1984, 1988 by Barry Holstun Lopez. Reprinted with the permission of Sterling Lord Literistic, Inc.

Niccolò Machiavelli, "Of Cruelty and Clemency, and Whether It Is Better to Be Loved or Feared" from *The Prince,* translated by Luigi Ricci, revised by E. R. P. Vincent. Copyright 1935. Reprinted with the permission of Oxford University Press, Ltd.

Nancy Mairs, "On Being a Cripple" from *Plaintext.* Copyright © 1986 by Nancy Mairs. Reprinted with the permission of The University of Arizona Press.

William Maxwell, "What He Was Like" from *All the Days and Nights.* Copyright © 1994 by William Maxwell. Reprinted with the permission of Alfred A. Knopf, Inc.

Rollo May, "The Man Who Was Put in a Cage" from *Psychology and the Human Dilemma.* Copyright 1952 by Rollo May. Reprinted with the permission of W. W. Norton & Company, Inc.

Carson McCullers, "Loneliness...An American Malady" from *The Mortgaged Heart.* Copyright 1940, 1941, 1942, 1945, 1949, 1953, © 1956, 1959, 1963, 1967, 1971 by Floria V. Lasky, Executrix of the Estate of Carson McCullers. "The Sojourner" from *The Ballad of the Sad Cafe and Collected Short Stories.* Copyright 1936, 1941, 1942, 1950, © 1955 by Carson McCullers, renewed © 1979 by Floria V. Lasky. Both reprinted with the permission of Houghton Mifflin Company. All rights reserved.

John McMurtry, "Kill 'Em! Crush 'Em! Eat 'Em Raw!" *Maclean's* (October 1971). Copyright © 1971 by John McMurtry. Reprinted with the permission of the author.

Rigoberta Menchú, "Things Have Happened to Me as in a Movie" from *You Can't Drown the Fire: Latin American Women Writing in Exile,* edited by Alicia Partnoy (San Francisco: Cleis Press, 1988). Copyright © 1988 by Alicia Partnoy. Reprinted with the permission of Cesar Chelala.

Edna St. Vincent Millay, "Love Is Not All" (Sonnet XXX from *Fatal Interview*) from *Collected Poems* (New York: Harper & Row). Copyright 1931 by Edna St. Vincent Millay and renewed © 1958 by Norma Millay Ellis. Reprinted with the permission of Elizabeth Barnett, Literary Executor.

Marianne Moore, "Poetry," "The Student," and "The Mind Is an Enchanting Thing" from *Collected Poems of Marianne Moore.* Copyright 1935, 1941, 1944 and renewed © 1963 by Marianne Moore and T. S. Eliot, © 1969, 1972 by Marianne Moore. Reprinted with the permission of Simon & Schuster, Inc.

Flannery O'Connor, "Everything That Rises Must Converge" from *Everything That Rises Must Converge.* Copyright © 1964, 1965 by The Estate of Flannery O'Connor. Reprinted with the permission of Farrar, Straus & Giroux, Inc.

Tillie Olsen, "I Stand Here Ironing" from *Tell Me a Riddle.* Copyright © 1956, 1957, 1960, 1961 by Tillie Olson. Reprinted with the permission of Delacourt Press/Seymour Laurence, a division of Bantam Doubleday Dell Publishing Group, Inc.

George Orwell, "The Principles of Newspeak" from *Nineteen Eighty-Four.* Copyright 1949 by Harcourt Brace, renewed © 1977 by Sonia Brownell Orwell. Reprinted with the permission of Harcourt Brace and Company, Mark Hamilton as literary executor of the estate of the late Sonia Brownell Orwell, and A. M. Heath & Company, Ltd.

Grace Paley, "The Loudest Voice" from *The Little Disturbances of Man.* Copyright © 1959 by Grace Paley. Reprinted with the permission of Viking Penguin, a division of Penguin Books USA Inc.

Sidney Perkowitz, "Connecting with E. M. Forster" from *The American Prospect* (May–June 1996). Copyright © 1996 by The American Prospect, Inc. Reprinted with the permission of the author and *The American Prospect.*

Noel Perrin, "The Androgynous Man" from *The New York Times Magazine* (February 5, 1984). Copyright © 1984 by The New York Times Company. Reprinted with the permission of *The New York Times.* "Science Fiction: Imaginary Worlds and Real-Life Questions" from *The New York Times Magazine* (April 9, 1989). Copyright © 1989 by Noel Perrin. Reprinted with the permission of the author.

Sylvia Plath, "Daddy" from *Ariel.* Copyright © 1961, 1962, 1963 and renewed 1989, 1990, 1991 by Ted Hughes. Reprinted with the permission of HarperCollins Publishers, Inc. and Faber and Faber, Ltd.

Katherine Anne Porter, "Rope" from *Flowering Judas and Other Stories.* Copyright 1930 and renewed © 1958 by Katherine Anne Porter. Reprinted with the permission of Harcourt Brace & Company.

John Preston, "Medfield, Massachusetts" from *Gay Men Write About Hometowns* (New York: New American Library, 1991). Copyright © 1991 by John Preston. Reprinted with the permission of Curtis Brown, Ltd.

Francine Prose, "Bad Behavior" from *The New York Times* (November 26, 1995). Copyright © 1995 by Francine Prose. Reprinted with the permission of Georges Borchardt, Inc. for the author.

Lawrence Raab, "The Shakespeare Lesson" from *What We Don't Know About Each Other.* Copyright © 1993 by Lawrence Raab. Reprinted with the permission of Viking Penguin, a division of Penguin Books USA Inc.

Bernice Johnson Reagon, "Black Music in Our Hands" from *Sing Out!!* (Winter 1977). Copyright © 1977 by Songtalk Publishing Company. Reprinted with the permission of the author, c/o Songtalk Publishing Company.

Richard Rodriguez, "Heading into Darkness Once Again" from *The Los Angeles Times* (July 21, 1996). Copyright © 1996 by Richard Rodriguez. Reprinted with the permission of Georges Borchardt, Inc. for the author.

Theodore Roethke, "Some Self-Analysis" from Ralph J. Mills, ed., *On the Poet and His Craft: Selected Prose of Theodore Roethke.* Copyright © 1965 by Beatrice Roethke as Administratrix of the Estate of Theodore Roethke. Reprinted with the permission of University of Washington Press. "My Papa's Waltz," "Elegy for Jane: My Student, Thrown by a Horse," and "The Waking" from *The Collected Poems of Theodore Roethke.* Copyright 1942 by Hearst Magazines, Inc. Copyright 1950, 1953 by Theodore Roethke. Reprinted with the permission of Doubleday, a division of Bantam Doubleday Dell Publishing Group, Inc.

Roger Rosenblatt, "What's That to Us?" from *Modern Maturity* (May–June 1996). Copyright © 1996 by Roger Rosenblatt. Reprinted with the permission of the author. "Who Killed Privacy?" from *The New York Times* (January 31, 1993). Copyright © 1993 by The New York Times Co. Reprinted with the permission of *The New York Times.*

Alex Ross, "The Shock of the True" from *The New Yorker* (August 19, 1996). Copyright © 1996 by Alex Ross. Reprinted with the permission of The Robbins Office, Inc. All rights reserved.

Mike Royko, "The Virtue of Prurience" from *Chicago Sun-Times* (April 17, 1983). Copyright © 1983 by Mike Royko. Reprinted with the permission of Sterling Lord Literistic, Inc.

Benjamin Alire Sáenz, "Exiled: The Winds of Sunset Heights," Prologue to *Flowers for the Broken.* Copyright © 1992 by Benjamin Alire Sáenz. Reprinted with the permission of Broken Moon Press.

May Sarton, "The Rewards of Leading a Solitary Life" from *The New York Times* (April 8, 1974). Copyright © 1974 by The New York Times Company. Reprinted with the permission of *The New York Times.*

John Ralston Saul, "Air Conditioning" from *The Doubters Companion.* Copyright © 1994 by John Ralston Saul. Reprinted with the permission of The Free Press, a division of Simon & Schuster, Inc.

Anne Sexton, "Her Kind" from *To Bedlam and Part Way Back.* Copyright © 1960 by Anne Sexton, renewed 1988 by Linda G. Sexton. Reprinted with the permission of Houghton Mifflin Company. All rights reserved.

Leslie Marmon Silko, "Lullaby" from *Storyteller* (New York: Seaver Books, 1981). Copyright © 1981 by Leslie Marmon Silko. Reprinted with the permission of The Wylie Agency, Inc.

Patricia Smith, "Always in the Head" from *Big Towns, Big Talk.* Copyright © 1992 by Patricia Smith. Reprinted with the permission of Zoland Books, Cambridge, Massachusetts.

Aleksandr Solzhenitsyn, "Playing Upon the Strings of Emptiness" from *A Speech at the National Arts Club* in *The New York Times Book Review* (February 7, 1993). Copyright © 1993 by Aleksandr Solzhenitsyn. Reprinted with the permission of the author, c/o Claude Durand, Paris.

Gary Soto, "Black Hair" from *Living Up the Street.* Copyright © 1985 by Gary Soto. Reprinted with the permission of the author.

Wole Soyinka, "Telephone Conversation" from *The Penguin Book of Modern African Poetry* (London: Penguin Books, 1960). Copyright © 1960 by Wole Soyinka. Reprinted with the permission of Brandt & Brandt Literary Agents, Inc.

Shelby Steele, "On Being Black and Middle Class" from *Commentary* (January 1988). Copyright © 1988 by Shelby Steele. Reprinted with the permission of the Carol Mann Agency.

Lincoln Steffens, "I Go to College" from *The Autobiography of Lincoln Steffens.* Copyright 1931 by Harcourt Brace and renewed © 1959 by Peter Steffens. Reprinted with the permission of Harcourt Brace and Company.

John Steinbeck, "The Chrysanthemums" from *The Long Valley.* Copyright 1937 and renewed © 1965 by John Steinbeck. Reprinted with the permission of Viking Penguin, a division of Penguin Books USA Inc.

May Swenson, "Women." Copyright © 1968 by May Swenson, renewed 1996. Reprinted with the permission of The Literary Estate of May Swenson.

Vo Thi Tam, "From Vietnam, 1979" from Joan Morrison and Charlotte Fox Zabusky, eds., *American Mosaic: The Immigrant Experience in the Words of Those Who Lived It* (New York: E. P. Dutton, 1980). Copyright © 1980 by Joan Morrison and Charlotte Fox Zabusky. Reprinted with the permission of the University of Pittsburgh Press.

Studs Terkel, "Miss U.S. A." from *American Dreams: Lost and Found* (New York: Pantheon Books, 1980). Copyright © 1980 by Studs Terkel. Reprinted with the permission of Donadio & Ashworth, Inc.

Audrey Thomas, "Ascension" from *The Wild Blue Yonder.* Copyright © 1989 by Audrey Thomas. Reprinted with the permission of Penguin Books Canada Limited.

Dylan Thomas, "The Force That Through the Green Fuse Drives the Flower" from *The Poems of Dylan Thomas.* Copyright 1939, 1946 by New Directions Publishing Corporation. Reprinted with the permission of New Directions Publishing Corporation and David Higham Associates, London as agents for the Trustees of the Copyrights of Dylan Thomas.

Lewis Thomas, "Humanities and Science" and "Making Science Work" from *Late Night Thoughts on Listening to Mahler's Ninth.* Copyright © 1981 by Lewis Thomas. Reprinted with the permission of Viking Penguin, a division of Penguin Books USA Inc.

Amoja Three Rivers, "Cultural Etiquette: A Guide for the Well-Intentioned" from *Ms.* (November/December 1991). Copyright © 1990, 1991 by Amoja Three Rivers. Reprinted with the permission of the author. Available from Market Wimmin, Auto, WV 24917, $7 ppd.

James Thurber, "The Unicorn in the Garden" from *Fables of Our Time* (New York: Harper & Row, 1940). Copyright 1940 by James Thurber, renewed © 1968 by Rosemary A. Thurber. Reprinted with the permission of The Barbara Hogenson Agency.

Calvin Trillin, "Just How Do You Suppose that Alice Knows?" from *The New Yorker* (November 7, 1994). Copyright © 1994 by Calvin Trillin. Reprinted with the permission of Lescher & Lescher, Ltd.

Alice Walker, "Beauty: When the Other Dancer Is the Self" from *In Search of Our Mothers' Gardens.* Copyright © 1983 by Alice Walker. Reprinted with the permission of Harcourt Brace and Company.

Wendy Wasserstein, "The Man in a Case" from *Orchids* by Anton Chekhov et al. Copyright © 1986 by Wendy Wasserstein. Reprinted with the permission of Alfred A. Knopf, Inc.

Eudora Welty, "Finding a Voice" from *One Writer's Beginnings.* Copyright © 1983, 1984 by Eudora Welty. Reprinted with the permission of Harvard University Press.

John Edgar Wideman, "Father Stories" from *The New Yorker* (August 1, 1994). Copyright © 1994 by John Edgar Wideman. Reprinted with the permission of The Wylie Agency, Inc.

Richard Wilbur, "A Finished Man" from *New and Collected Poems.* Originally published in *The New Yorker* (March 4, 1985). Copyright © 1985 by Richard Wilbur. Reprinted with the permission of Harcourt Brace & Company.

David S. Wilcove, "What I Saw When I Went to the Forest" from *Wilderness* 51, no. 180 (Spring 1989). Copyright © 1989 by David S. Wilcove. Reprinted with the permission of the author.

Nancy Willard, "Questions My Son Asked Me, Answers I Never Gave Him" from *Household Tales of Moon and Water.* Copyright © 1982 by Nancy Willard. Reprinted with the permission of Harcourt Brace and Company.

William Carlos Williams, "The Use of Force" from *The Farmers' Daughters.* Copyright 1938 by William Carlos Williams. Reprinted with the permission of New Directions Publishing Corporation.

Eleanor Wilner, "Emigration" from *Shekhinah* (Chicago: The University of Chicago Press, 1984). Copyright © 1984 by Eleanor Wilner. Reprinted with the permission of the author.

Edward O. Wilson, "Is Humanity Suicidal?" from *The New York Times Magazine* (May 30, 1993). Copyright © 1993 by The New York Times Company. Reprinted with the permission of *The New York Times.*

James Wolcott, "Reborn on the Fourth of July" from *The New Yorker* (July 15, 1996). Copyright © 1996 by James Wolcott. Reprinted with the permission of the author.

Jim Wong-Chu, "Equal Opportunity" from Smara Kamboureli, ed., *Making a Difference.* Copyright © 1996 by Jim Wong-Chu. Reprinted with the permission of the author.

Virginia Woolf, "The Angel in the House" (editors' title, originally titled "Professions for Women") from *The Death of the Moth and Other Essays.* Copyright 1942 by Harcourt Brace and World, renewed © 1971 by Marjorie T. Parsons, Executrix. Reprinted with the permission of Harcourt Brace and Company.

Richard Wright, "The Ethics of Living Jim Crow" from *Uncle Tom's Children.* Copyright 1937 by Richard Wright. Reprinted with the permission of HarperCollins Publishers Inc.

Malcolm X, "A Homemade Education" from *The Autobiography of Malcolm X* by Malcolm X with the assistance of Alex Haley. Copyright © 1964 by Alex Haley and Malcolm X. Copyright © 1965 by Alex Haley and Betty Shabazz. Reprinted with the permission of Random House, Inc.

CONTENTS

Art and Composition

The Search for Self

PERSONAL REMINISCENCES

ESSAYS

FICTION

POETRY

Personal Relationships: Parents and Children

LETTERS AND PERSONAL REMINISCENCES

ESSAYS

FICTION

POETRY

Personal Relationships: Men and Women

ESSAYS

FICTION

POETRY

DRAMA

The Cultural Tradition: Popular Culture

PERSONAL REMINISCENCE

ESSAYS

The Cultural Tradition: Art and Society

PERSONAL REMINISCENCES

ESSAYS

FICTION

POETRY

Science, the Environment, and the Future

ESSAYS

FICTION

POETRY

Freedom and Human Dignity

PERSONAL REMINISCENCES

ESSAYS

FICTION

POETRY

The Examined Life: Education

PERSONAL REMINISCENCES

ESSAYS

FICTION

POETRY

The Examined Life: Personal Values

PERSONAL REMINISCENCES

ESSAYS

FICTION

POETRY

RHETORICAL CONTENTS

The following arrangement of expository essays will suggest ways in which readers can approach the selections. The classifications are not, of course, rigid, and many selections might fit as easily into one category as another.

ANALYSIS

ARGUMENT AND PERSUASION

COMPARISON/CONTRAST

DEFINITION

DICTION AND TONE

IDENTIFICATION

ILLUSTRATION

NARRATION

PREFACE

...the unexamined life is not worth living.

—PLATO, *The Apology*

The academic turmoil of the early 1970s—which may seem remote today—provided the background for the first edition of *The Conscious Reader.* The editors, predisposed to support change, wanted to create a reader that would reflect a multidisciplinary approach to the teaching of writing and would recognize cultural diversity. For the former, we included selections to represent a wide range of academic disciplines and interests from psychology to biology and computer science. For the latter, we chose authors who represent the spectrum of American ethnic cultures and the contribution of minorities and women.

We also wanted to stress our belief in the rational mind, in an era in which university faculties were often inclined to measure relevance by spontaneous response. Unhappy with such a superficial concept of relevance, we compiled a book intended to make readers think, to go beyond reading unconsciously. It occurred to one of us that we could reinforce our belief by giving the book the name it has since held for over twenty years. Today the academic world calls our objective critical reading, but we have never regretted being a little ahead of our time.

Still believing that the development of writing skills depends on the heightening of consciousness, the editors of *The Conscious Reader* invite students to examine and to respond to the basic questions that writers since Plato have posed. The selections included engage our interests by their style and by their focus on issues of universal concern. They reflect the continuity between past and present, serve as a catalyst to self-expression, sharpen our perceptions, and widen our sympathies. Consciousness heightened through reading develops effective writing, and the act of writing fosters self-definition. As we extend awareness by reading, we become increasingly conscious of the reservoir of memories and experiences from which to draw and the variety of forms and techniques that give shape to our writing.

Over two-thirds of the readings in this book are nonfiction prose, primarily exposition or argument. Some of the essays are personal and readily comprehensible and provide models for early writing assignments. Others, more complex, should help students develop the ability to reason abstractly. Although most of the authors included are accomplished literary stylists, others are primarily distinguished for their contributions to popular culture, science, philosophy, or psychology.

We have also included twenty-seven stories and thirty-nine poems. The inclusion of imaginative literature in a composition course needs no special justification. It serves a number of important goals: to enhance the pleasure of reading, to educate the emotions as well as the mind, to stimulate original creative efforts, and to provide vicarious experience with which to test the ideas expressed in essays. The dramatic situations, vivid character portrayals, and verbal compression of fiction and poetry also suggest techniques to enliven student writing. We are convinced more than ever that the most stimulating as well as most economical means of helping students to develop conceptual literacy is to expose them to literate essays and imaginative literature, both of which will arrest their interest and challenge their thinking. In addition, selections by women, minority, and Third World writers add to the book's versatility and its capacity to engage the reader deeply. The book opens with a section on Art and Composition. We have included paintings because we believe that visual art can communicate and inspire not only emotions but ideas as well.

Each selection has a head note and suggestions for discussion and writing to help students explore multiple levels of understanding. The suggestions invite students to pay careful attention to thought and structure and to compare their experience with the vision of life expressed in the selections. Exploring cultural patterns both similar and alien to one's own should encourage a continuing dialectic in classroom discussion as well as in writing.

The thematic groupings represent a convenient division of the book. The readings begin with the search for self and move to consideration of the self in relation to others—parents, friends, and lovers. The next section focuses on culture, including discussions of both popular culture and art and society. The next section explores many facets of the world of science and technology. The readings continue with a variety of statements about our aspirations and failures to ensure a sense of freedom and human dignity for all. The book concludes with several sections on the examined life. The selections mediate between problems of education and human concerns and then return full cycle to the individual's search for meaning and value.

If there is a dominant theme in these readings, it is that neither understanding of the past nor projections of the future can eliminate conflict from our lives and that opposing forces in the self and society are a part of the human condition. Indeed, it is vital that these forces contend. For it is primarily through conscious recognition and expression of these conflicting forces that we may find our way to a tolerance of ambiguity and to an increased freedom of choice.

Acknowledgments

To Margaret Catley-Carson for introducing me to the richness of Canadian literature, John Tallmadge for his guidance in the realm of nature writing, and Don Ellwell for his stalwart research endeavors on behalf of *The Conscious Reader.*

—F. M. B.

To Eve Finestone, who has made the art and composition section possible, and to Anne M. Finestone, Delia Rudiger, and Sarah Caroline Dolan.

—H. F.

Thanks to Jeffrey Topf for editorial assistance.

In memory of Carl A. Barth, Robert C. Farina, and Robert E. Jackson.

—M. F. S.

We wish to thank Eben Ludlow for his patient leadership.

We are grateful to the reviewers for this seventh edition: Cheryl M. Clark, Miami-Dade Community College, Wolfson Campus; Diane Quantic, Wichita State University; Lynn Rasmussen, Northwestern Michigan College; Lou Suarez, Lorain County Community College; Joyce Swofford, Clayton Stage College; Marilyn J. Valentino, Lorain County Community College.

The Conscious Reader

ART AND COMPOSITION

Discussion of art presents certain problems. It is difficult, sometimes impossible, to discover the thought processes of the visual artist or the "argument" of the painting; moreover, students may be unaware of how much the content of the painting derives from traditions of the form. The contemporary artist George Baselitz argues that painting projects no ideas and does not communicate or express publicly any statements, information, or opinions. A number of contemporary artists even find explication of their work repugnant. Nevertheless, the editors believe that painting can communicate and inspire not only emotions but ideas as well. They further believe that ideas relating to the themes of this text, while accounting for only a part of the total meaning or impact of these paintings, will provoke students to think and to write. Therefore, we offer these paintings in the expectation that students and instructors will find them exciting and will see even more in them for discussion or writing than we have suggested.

PAUL GAUGUIN

Self-portrait with Halo (1889)

It was the substantial number of Impressionist paintings that French painter Paul Gauguin (1848–1903) had collected when he was a successful Parisian stockbroker that financed his escape from marriage, fatherhood, and bourgeois respectability while in his mid-thirties. Although he had previously exhibited with the Impressionists, it wasn't until this later age that he devoted himself fully to painting.

Chester Dale Collection, © 1996 Board of Trustees, National Gallery of Art, Washington.

At the same time as he threw himself into the life of the starving bohemian artist in his garret, he began to develop his own theories of painting. He abandoned the Impressionists' careful scientific study of natural light and the ever-changing fragmentation of color it caused. He sought instead to exercise his own intelligence and to express his own response to a subject by creating new forms and assigning his private meaning to colors. His forms became abstract, stylized, and slightly distorted; he applied colors heavily, without modulation, and outlined them with a thick dark brush. He advised a friend,

> *A meter of green is greener than a centimeter. . . . How does that tree look to you? Green? All right, then use green, the greenest on your palette. And that shadow, a little bluish? Don't be afraid. Paint it as blue as you can.*

In Gaugin's personal vocabulary, a Christ became yellow, the soil red, and a pond white.

His flight from the city led him to the provinces of Provence and Brittany, but eventually, like Europeans for centuries, he followed the call of the exotic, the primitive, and the untamed; he sailed for Tahiti and the Marquesas. There Gauguin found the strong bright colors, the simple forms, the decorative patterns of nature and human figures that confirmed the aesthetic he had already established in France. He also found poverty, malnutrition, and syphilis. With the exception of one visit to France, he spent his last twelve years there, creating his great Tahitian masterpieces.

Suggestions for Discussion

1. Why does the painting seem to divide in half? Which half seems to dominate? Examine the forms and lines of Gaugin's face.
2. Describe the multiple symbols. What do they represent? Can you explain the choice of colors? What is the meaning of the halo? Is Gauguin suggesting he should be wearing it? What is suggested by the fact that one apple is red, one green? (Red and green are complementary colors.)
3. What is Gauguin looking at? What is the relationship between the flowers and the snake? What does the direction of his glance tell you about the artist's sense of self?
4. "Art is an abstraction," said Gauguin. How can a self-portrait be an abstraction? What evidence is there that the portrait reflects an introspective person?
5. Compare and contrast this self-portrait with the following one by Frida Kahlo.

Suggestions for Writing

1. Assume you know nothing about Gauguin's life. Write an essay in which you discuss his sense of self, his age, his health, and his values based only on the clues from this self-portrait.
2. How might Gauguin deal with his autobiography in writing rather than in painting? Discuss some differences between the two genres in presenting a self-portrait. What are some of the difficulties and shortcuts of each?

FRIDA KAHLO

Self-Portrait with a Thorn Necklace and Hummingbird (1940)

Frida Kahlo (1907–1954) created her autobiography in her scenes of her own life cycle—from conception and birth to marriage, surgeries, and dreams of her death. These basic subjects are informed by a personal vocabulary. For example, in My Grandparents, My Parents and I *she includes herself both as a naked child and as a fetus painted on her mother's white wedding dress; the portraits of her parents and*

By permission of the Bank of Mexico, in association with the Museum of Diego Rivera and Frida Kahlo and the Technical Committee.

grandparents are set against a desert background of the rocky mountains and cacti of her native Mexico. My Birth *graphically shows the emergence of the fetus; the mother's head is covered by a white sheet and over her hangs a* retablo *(a traditional Mexican painting on tin of a miraculous event usually showing figures against an empty background) of the Virgin as Mother of Sorrows pierced with daggers.*

She was born to a Catholic mother of Indian and Spanish parentage and to an agnostic father, a German Jew of Hungarian origin. She vowed as a teenager to bear a child to the famous Mexican painter Diego Rivera, twenty years her senior, before she had even met him. She did indeed marry him at age twenty-two, after she had been left with a limp from polio and had almost died in a horrifying accident that destroyed much of her body and forced her to abandon her medical studies. As a result she suffered many miscarriages, many operations and hospitalizations, and much pain throughout the remainder of her life. She never did have a child.

Kahlo and Rivera shared a commitment to political action as well as a devotion to "Mexicanidad," a rekindling of pride in indigenous Mexican art and culture that had long been eclipsed by imported colonial values. He was a womanizer, and she eventually took male and female lovers. During 1940, the year of this self-portrait, they were divorced and remarried; they later divorced again. They traveled to the United States for Rivera's commissions, but it was not until 1938 that Kahlo gained recognition, selling four paintings and showing in an exhibition of "Modern Primitives" at the Museum of Modern Art.

Both in narrative paintings and in a large number of self-portraits, Kahlo presents herself by a rather frank rendering of her face with its slight moustache, almond-shaped eyes, and heavy brows, as well as by her choice of costume, accompanying images, and background. Take into account that she had a large collection of native costumes (particularly from Tehauntupec, an ancient matriarchal society), of pre-Columbian jewelry, and of folk art; that she honored the Aztec belief in the animal alter ego; that the dead bird and butterflies signify dead warriors; and that she once took the Nahuatl name Xochitl, or "flower," the sign for artisans.

Suggestions for Discussion

1. How does Kahlo see herself in this portrait? Examine her "costume," her coiffure, her jewels, the pet monkey, and the cat. How realistic is each element? Is the background realistic? What is the effect of the overall composition?
2. What does her expression reveal of herself? Is the portrait realistic or symbolic?

Suggestions for Writing

Write an essay in which you compare Kahlo's self-portrait with that of Gauguin. Organize your essay around one of the following ideas:

1. Compare the two artists' use of color, their sense of design, their expression of the face. Do these elements make one portrait more realistic than the other? Why?
2. Compare the objects in both paintings. What do they mean as symbols? How do we understand their meaning? Are the images universal or personal and private?
3. What does each portrait reveal of its subject? Which one reveals more?

JACOB LAWRENCE

Harriet Tubman (1939–1940)

(One of a series of thirty-one)

Harriet Tubman worked as water girl to field hands. She also worked at plowing, carting, and heaving logs.

The parents of Jacob Lawrence (b. 1917) were part of the African-American migration to the industrial cities of the North following World War I. Born in New Jersey, at age thirteen Lawrence moved to New York City shortly after the flowering of the Harlem Renaissance, when Harlem had become the center for African-American

Hampton University Museum, Hampton, Virginia.

writers, artists, and musicians carving out a cultural identity. Despite the Depression, Harlem was still an exciting place where Lawrence benefited richly from this awakening, from stories and legends told by his family and neighbors, and from his own intensive research at the Schomburg Collection for Research in Black Culture. He received a broad theoretical and practical training in art at WPA art workshops and in art school. In a 1956 interview Lawrence said,

> *I love to tell a story. The history of the United States fascinates me. Right now, I'm reading in it, looking for any episode that suggests a symbol of struggle. The part the Negro has played in all these events has been greatly overlooked. I intend to bring it out. Of course, where the Negro didn't figure, I leave him out. . . . But fear of "propaganda" doesn't worry me. A great purpose of art is to communicate ideas. Color and design are only means to this end.*

To express his ideas, Lawrence turned to narrative painting following in traditions as varied as those of the modern Mexican moralists, of Goya, Breughel, and African art. Many of his series of paintings constitute biographies of heroic figures: Toussaint l'Ouverture, the eighteenth-century liberator of Haiti; Frederick Douglass, an escaped slave who became a writer and an abolitionist editor; Harriet Tubman; and, finally, the white abolitionist John Brown. Other series deal with more generalized subjects: The Migration of the Negro; Hiroshima; Builders, *which celebrates the African-American as worker and craftsperson; and* Eight Sermons of the Creation from the Book of Genesis. *A longtime teacher, Lawrence is presently Professor Emeritus at the University of Washington and an active painter.*

The thirty-one rather small panels of the Harriet Tubman *series tell her story from her childhood as an abused slave and field hand through her frightening escape to the North from where she launched her rescue operation of slaves. Her daring strength became legendary. She advised Frederick Douglass and John Brown, spoke at abolitionist rallies, and was a spy and nurse for the Union army.*

Lawrence provides captions for each painting, but the subject is not always episodic; there is, for example, a lyrical painting of a single cotton plant, a symbol of slavery but a beautiful thing; another of talons covered with eyes and reaching out of the earth to encircle the moon, the searchers who pursued Harriet Tubman as she fled. The painting shown here portrays a woman at work.

Suggestions for Discussion

1. Compare the color tones, paint strokes, and lines used for the woman and for the landscape. How does his technique express the artist's feelings about Harriet Tubman?
2. Is the painting "propaganda"? How does it differ from a poster with its heavy primary colors? If you did not know this was a heroic historical figure, would you understand the "propaganda"? How?

Suggestions for Writing

1. Write a portrait of Harriet Tubman to complement Lawrence's visual portrait.
2. What do you think is the purpose of art? Is it what Lawrence calls "propaganda"?

EDWARD HOPPER

Hotel by a Railroad (1952)

Born in a Hudson River port nearby, Edward Hopper (1882–1967) spent most of his adult life in New York City, leaving it three times for Europe, especially Paris, in his twenties and several times for Mexico in later years. Aside from regular vacations on the coast of New England, he lived and worked in the same small apartment in Greenwich Village from 1913 until his death.

He studied at the New York School of Art under the famous teachers William Merritt Chase and Robert Henri, but supported himself as a commercial artist. It was not until his second one-man show at age forty-two (at the time of his marriage to a fellow painter) that he could afford to give up his work as a magazine illustrator. He continued to lead a quiet life with his wife in their sparsely furnished apartment (he said he did not like clutter). He eventually won innumerable honors and awards,

Hirshhorn Museum and Sculpture Garden, Smithsonian Institution, Gift of Joseph H. Hirshhorn Foundation, 1966. Photo: Lee Stalsworth.

exhibited widely in prestigious shows, had his first retrospective show at the Museum of Modern Art in 1933, others at the Whitney Museum of American Art in 1950 and in 1964.

While he did paint landscapes, seascapes, and villages, Hopper seemed to have been fascinated with the city—its restaurants, its theaters, its offices, its apartments glimpsed through open windows, its empty streets. When he left the city as subject, it was often to study the impermanent elements of travel: trains, filling stations, deserted country roads, hotel lobbies, and motel rooms.

In Paris, Hopper had been fascinated not only by the quality of light in the city itself, but also by the glorious effect of light and the interplay of light and shadow found in Impressionist paintings. The Hopper light, however, as he finally developed it, is sharp, even harsh, a pure white often with a yellow pigment, whether it emanates from the strong midday sun, the melancholy tones of evening, or the artificial light of interiors. It does not soften outlines or cause colors to shimmer; rather, it accentuates angles and permits broad areas of solid color to become emphatic.

Suggestions for Discussion

1. What is the role of light in this painting? What is its source? What does it illuminate? Where is the light stronger? What is the emotional effect of this unequal distribution of light?
2. Examine the composition of the painting. Where are the figures and objects placed? What becomes of the softer, curved lines of the armchair and of the woman's bust as one follows the diagonal axis to the right? Why does the movement seem to be toward the right, from the woman to the furniture with its objects to the man? What happens to this movement when we reach the man?
3. The reflection in the mirror would seem to indicate that this is not a small room. Why, then, do we seem to be on top of the figures? Where are we, the viewers, located? Why do we feel we are in the position of a voyeur?
4. What is the relationship between the two people in the room? Are they comfortable with each other? What is the meaning of the woman's dress? What is the object of her and his attention? How does Hopper establish a tension between the interior and the exterior? Why is so much space devoted to the exterior wall, the railroad track, and the building opposite?

Suggestion for Writing

In an interview, Hopper said, "Great art is the outward expression of the inner life in the artist, and the inner life will result in his personal vision of the world." Write an essay discussing the relevance of this statement to *Hotel by a Railroad.* Is there something personal in this painting? Why has Hopper chosen a hotel room as his setting? What adjectives describe the feeling of the scene? Would a voyeur be welcome in the room?

The Search for Self

For as long as I could remember, I had been transparent to myself, unselfconscious, learning, doing, most of every day. Now I was in my own way; I myself was a dark object I could not ignore. I couldn't remember how to forget myself. I didn't want to think about myself, to reckon myself in, to deal with myself every live-long minute on top of everything else—but swerve as I might, I couldn't avoid it. I was a boulder blocking my own path....

Must I then lose the world forever, that I had so loved? Was it all, the whole bright and various planet, where I had been so ardent about finding myself alive, only a passion peculiar to children, that I would outgrow even against my will?

—ANNIE DILLARD, "So This Was Adolescence"

As I dance, whirling and joyous, happier than I've ever been in my life, another bright-faced dancer joins me.... The other dancer has obviously come through all right, as I have done. She is beautiful, whole and free. And she is also me.

—ALICE WALKER, "Beauty: When the Other Dancer Is the Self"

This crucial day may be the day on which an Algerian taxidriver tells him how it feels to be an Algerian in Paris. It may be the day on which he passes a café terrace and catches a glimpse of the tense, intelligent and troubled face of Albert Camus....

This is a personal day, a terrible day, the day to which his entire sojourn has been tending. It is the day he realizes that there are no untroubled countries in this fearfully troubled world; that if he has been preparing himself for anything in Europe, he has been preparing himself—for America. In short, the freedom that the American writer finds in Europe brings him, full circle, back to himself, with the responsibility for his development where it always was: in his own hands.

—JAMES BALDWIN, "The Discovery of What It Means to Be an American"

PERSONAL REMINISCENCES

ANNIE DILLARD

So This Was Adolescence

Annie Dillard (b. 1945), a contributing editor to *Harper's*, won a Pulitzer Prize in 1975 for *Pilgrim at Tinker Creek*. More recent books are *Living by Fiction, Teaching a Stone to Talk: Expeditions and Encounters, Encounters with Chinese Writers*, and *The Living*. In 1996 *Mornings Like This: Found Poems* and *Modern American Memo* appeared. "So This Was Adolescence" is a section of her 1987 book, *An American Childhood*. In this excerpt Dillard experiences adolescence as an identity crisis. She describes her behavior with graphic imagery and questions whether she might "lose the world forever, that I had so loved."

When I was fifteen, I felt it coming; now I was sixteen, and it hit.

My feet had imperceptibly been set on a new path, a fast path into a long tunnel like those many turnpike tunnels near Pittsburgh, turnpike tunnels whose entrances bear on brass plaques a roll call of those men who died blasting them. I wandered witlessly forward and found myself going down, and saw the light dimming; I adjusted to the slant and dimness, traveled further down, adjusted to greater dimness, and so on. There wasn't a whole lot I could do about it, or about anything. I was going to hell on a handcart, that was all, and I knew it and everyone around me knew it, and there it was.

I was growing and thinning, as if pulled. I was getting angry, as if pushed. I morally disapproved most things in North America, and blamed my innocent parents for them. My feelings deepened and lingered. The swift moods of early childhood—each formed by and suited to its occasion—vanished. Now feelings lasted so long they left stains. They arose from nowhere, like winds or waves, and battered at me or engulfed me.

When I was angry, I felt myself coiled and longing to kill someone or bomb something big. Trying to appease myself, during one winter I whipped my bed every afternoon with my uniform belt. I despised the spectacle I made in my own eyes—whipping the bed with a belt, like a creature demented!—and I often began halfheartedly, but I did it daily after school as a desperate discipline, trying to rid myself and the innocent world of my wildness. It was like trying to beat back the ocean.

Sometimes in class I couldn't stop laughing; things were too funny to be borne. It began then, my surprise that no one else saw what was so funny.

I read some few books with such reverence I didn't close them at the finish, but only moved the pile of pages back to the start, without breathing, and began again. I read one such book, an enormous novel, six times that way—closing the binding between sessions, but not between readings.

On the piano in the basement I played the maniacal "Poet and Peasant Overture" so loudly, for so many hours, night after night, I damaged the piano's keys and strings. When I wasn't playing this crashing overture, I played boogie-woogie, or something else, anything else, in octaves—otherwise, it wasn't loud enough. My fingers were so strong I could do push-ups with them. I played one piece with my fists. I banged on a steel-stringed guitar till I bled, and once on a particularly piercing rock-and-roll downbeat I broke straight through one of Father's snare drums.

I loved my boyfriend so tenderly, I thought I must transmogrify into vapor. It would take spectroscopic analysis to locate my molecules in thin air. No possible way of holding him was close enough. Nothing could cure this bad case of gentleness except, perhaps, violence: maybe if he swung me by the legs and split my skull on a tree? Would that ease this insane wish to kiss too much his eyelids' outer corners and his temples, as if I could love up his brain?

I envied people in books who swooned. For two years I felt myself continuously swooning and continuously unable to swoon; the blood drained from my face and eyes and flooded my heart; my hands emptied, my knees unstrung, I bit at the air for something worth breathing—but I failed to fall, and I couldn't find the way to black out. I had to live on the lip of a waterfall, exhausted.

When I was bored I was first hungry, then nauseated, then furious and weak. "Calm yourself," people had been saying to me all my life. Since early childhood I had tried one thing and then another to calm myself, on those few occasions when I truly wanted to. Eating helped; singing helped. Now sometimes I truly wanted to calm myself. I couldn't lower my shoulders; they seemed to wrap around my ears. I couldn't lower my voice although I could see the people around me flinch. I waved my arm in class till the very teachers wanted to kill me.

I was what they called a live wire. I was shooting out sparks that were digging a pit around me, and I was sinking into that pit. Laughing with Ellin at school recess, or driving around after school with Judy in her jeep, exultant, or dancing with my boyfriend to Louis Armstrong across a polished diningroom floor, I got so excited I looked around wildly for aid; I didn't know where I should go or what I should do with myself. People in books split wood.

When rage or boredom reappeared, each seemed never to have left. Each so filled me with so many years' intolerable accumulation it jammed the space behind my eyes, so I couldn't see. There was no room left even on my surface to live. My rib cage was so taut I couldn't breathe. Every cubic centimeter of atmosphere above my shoulders and head was heaped with last straws. Black hatred clogged my very blood. I couldn't peep, I couldn't wiggle or blink; my blood was too mad to flow.

For as long as I could remember, I had been transparent to myself, unselfconscious, learning, doing, most of every day. Now I was in my own way; I myself was a dark object I could not ignore. I couldn't remember how to forget myself. I didn't want to think about myself, to reckon myself in, to deal with myself every livelong minute on top of everything else—but swerve as I might, I couldn't avoid it. I was a boulder blocking my own path. I was a dog barking between my own ears, a barking dog who wouldn't hush.

So this was adolescence. Is this how the people around me had died on their feet—inevitably, helplessly? Perhaps their own selves eclipsed the sun for so many years the world shriveled around them, and when at last their inescapable orbits had passed through these dark egoistic years it was too late, they had adjusted.

Must I then lose the world forever, that I had so loved? Was it all, the whole bright and various planet, where I had been so ardent about finding myself alive, only a passion peculiar to children, that I would outgrow even against my will?

Suggestions for Discussion

1. What "hit" the author when she was sixteen?
2. How does the metaphor of the tunnel and her movement in it relate to the author's sense of self? How does it relate to her description of what follows?
3. What details of her attitudes and behavior tell you about Annie Dillard's experience of adolescence?
4. What evidence is brought forward that the author was "what they called a live wire"?
5. What does the author mean by being "transparent" to herself? How is that state contrasted with her being in her own way?

6. What images contribute to the reader's understanding of Dillard's sense of crisis?
7. In what sense is Dillard's final questioning a logical conclusion to what has preceded in her narrative?

Suggestions for Writing

1. Recount some of your adolescent experiences and indicate how they related to your sense of self.
2. Draw a portrait of an adolescent you know by examining her/his attitudes and behavior.
3. Compare Dillard's experience of adolescence with that of other writers in this section.

GREG GRAFFIN

Anarchy in the Tenth Grade

Greg Graffin (b. 1965) has been part of the punk group Bad Religion from its inception. He has a master's degree from UCLA in geology, and is presently completing a Ph.D. at Cornell University in evolutionary biology–palentology. He is one of the leading bone tissue paleontologists in the world, and has both given conferences and published papers in this field. In this article Graffin explains why being a punk made him a man.

In 1976, I moved with my mom and brother to the San Fernando Valley in Los Angeles. Like millions of other victims of divorce in the '70s, I had to deal with the fact that my father was now living far away (in Racine, Wisconsin) and that I would not get to see him as much.

This pain was compounded by the bewildering alienation I felt entering the Los Angeles Unified School District, a landscape unlike anything I'd ever experienced in my eleven years of life. I had dark brown, fluffy, wavy hair—unfeatherable, impossible to mold into the cool rock'n'roll hairdos that were so popular. We didn't have a lot of money, so I wore velour kids' shirts from Kmart and corduroys and cheap shoes from Payless. I rode a

Sears ten-speed that was heavy and sluggish and that couldn't jump or skid, and I had a totally uncool powder blue plastic skateboard with noisy, open-bearing wheels. I thought the beach was a place to go swimming, not a symbol for a way of life.

People asked me, "Dude!...Do you party?" It took me about six months to realize it was a synonym for getting high. I did not know what a bong was or why someone would call it bitchin'. All I knew was that there was some weird secret about all this, and I was not one of those who were welcome to the information. Kids moved up the social ladder by revealing their knowledge of rock'n'roll and sharing their covert collections of black beauties, Quaaludes, and joints. If you partook, you were one of them; if not, you were a second-class loser.

I shriveled under this pressure. Unable to compete yet unwilling to shut down, I became friends with a particular class of people labeled geeks, nerds, dorks, wimps, and pussies (or worse, wussies). We hung out together after school and did creative things, but the greatest way to alleviate my suffering was with music. We had an old spinet piano that I would bang on while I sung songs I learned by ear.

I wanted to have a musical identity, like my peers at school, but I wasn't inspired by the bands that formed the fabric of this burnout drug culture: Led Zeppelin, Rush, Kiss, Journey, Foreigner, Styx, Lynyrd Skynyrd. Luckily, by the time I was fourteen I had discovered "Rodney on the Roq" (on station KROQ), and the local bands he played proved there was an entire community of people who used music to share their alienation and confusion. It also proved that you didn't have to be a virtuoso or signed to a major record label in order to be played on the radio. The music he played was gloriously vulgar, and inspiring in its simplicity.

I wanted to be a part of this group of social and musical misfits. I "went punk" at fifteen. I cut my wavy hair very short, dyed it pitch-black, and made my own T-shirts. I was determined to send in a tape to Rodney. I was introduced by a fellow wussy to the guys who would become Bad Religion. By the end of that same year, 1980, we had made our first record and Rodney had played it.

Usually this would make anyone a hero at his high school, but I was seen as the enemy. There were three punkers at school. And all of us got our asses kicked because of our musical preference. This scared me, but at the same time it made me feel powerful. It made me realize how frail most of the conformists really were, how easily they could be pushed to the point where they lost control. I found great solace in the community of other punkers from other schools, all with similar stories of oppression and abuse. We didn't just look different, we thought different. We wanted to confront the people or institutions that seemed unjust instead of establishing an institution from which we could exclude others (which, sadly, is what many punkers really want). I began to feel that there *was* a way to deal with my disillusionment: through questioning and challenging, not conforming and accepting.

This stance made me more insightful about human interaction, but it also made me more cynical and less compassionate toward those who weren't punk, and this definitely hampered my ability to have intimate relationships. We punkers bonded over our collective turmoil, not our individual desires or feelings. Maybe this is why so many of my friends got hooked on hard drugs, and some killed themselves. My punk friends did not practice true understanding, we only exhibited tolerance within our sect.

This shortcoming naturally extended to women. They dressed similarly, had similar hairstyles, and even slam-danced with us boys, but "women's issues" were not on our discussion agenda. Both sexes were too busy being stalwart and tough and equal. I was proud of my egalitarian view. Unfortunately, it gave me an excuse not to address the differences between the sexes. To this day, I am tolerant when women express themselves but bad at understanding their needs. This has interfered with my close friendships with women and undermined my ability to be a good husband.

When I was a teenager, sex was part of punk's shock-value system. Girls walked around in fishnet stockings and ripped-up dresses and it turned me on. We were all just trying to be cool. We were too young to have sex, and without parents around to stop us, it became more an act of rebellion and experimentation than an expression of affection or intimacy. And of course that behavior has come back to haunt me. It's exactly what I'm trying to unlearn now that I want to have a normal, loving relationship.

I got married at twenty-three, to a woman who wasn't punk but who shared some of my views of the world. We met in a college course called "The Intellectual History of the United States." Going to college was not exactly a punk gesture, but I thought it might be a place where dissenting voices were applauded. Yet I found that the university is as replete with the pressure to conform as my high school was. But thanks to my adviser's insistence that I had original research ideas, I was able to continue and receive a master of science in geology. I went on expeditions to the wilds of the western U.S., Mexico, and the lowland rain forests of Bolivia, and I worked for the L.A. County Museum. After that I went on to a Ph.D. program.

Today, I have a more sophisticated view of my surroundings. I own a house, I have insurance, I make financial decisions. I have a four-year-old boy and a girl who's two. I am raising them not to be bullies, not to pick on other kids the way I was picked on. I have no problem being an authority figure to them now, and as they grow up I hope to teach them not to fear authority, but to understand and question its inner logic.

Fatherhood has given me new insights into the world, just as geology, organismic biology, music, and travel do. This plurality insures my individuality. And learning to be an individual was the best gift I got from growing up punk. Last year, more people bought punk-rock records, tapes, CDs, T-shirts, stickers, and concert tickets than ever before. As in any capitalist situation, the punk market is shifting away from its original intent. It is becoming a product category in which selling subcultural mystique is more important than giving a voice to its artists. It's no wonder there are a bunch of "punk police" out there monitoring whether bands like Bad Religion fit their stereotype of authenticity. It is also a shining example of how easy it is to follow the party line and champion a bandwagon mentality—which only motivates me to keep fighting for originality.

For sixteen years now—half my life—I have been a member of this strange subculture, and I have come to realize that there are both liberal and conservative wings of it. It is an inane task to try and define punk universally. A sixteen-year-old girl from an affluent religious family who shows up to church with her green Mohawk and FUCK JESUS shirt is punk. But so is a forty-two-year-old biology professor who claims that Charles Darwin's ideas were wrong. These people have never heard of nor met each other, and yet what links them is their challenge to institutions and to dogmatic thinking. Whether this is genetic or learned is unknown. But I feel a kinship with everyone who shares these traits.

Suggestions for Discussion

1. What was Graffin's original motivation for going punk?
2. Why does being seen as the enemy give Graffin a sense of his own power?
3. Graffin asserts that what links punkers at any age or stage is "their challenge to institutions and to dogmatic thinking." Using this definition can you think of significant historical figures who might be characterized as Punk?

Suggestions for Writing

1. Graffin found a way of "belonging" through establishing a musical identity. What strategies did you employ in high school? What identity did you adopt? Write a first-person account of this experience.
2. The attitudes he developed as a punker later made it difficult for the author to develop appropriate intimate relationships. Are there attitudes you developed as an adolescent that you now struggle to overcome? Try presenting this as you move between different time periods in your life.
3. Graffin feels a special kinship with those who question and challenge, rather than conform and accept. How would you characterize the people with whom you feel a special bond? Write an essay about your intellectual or moral "family."

JORGE LUÍS BORGES

Borges and Myself

Translated by Norman Thomas di Giovanni

Jorge Luís Borges (1899–1986), Argentine poet, short-story writer, essayist, critic, and university professor, was best known for his esoteric short fiction. He received little recognition in America until the publication in 1968 of English translations of *Ficciónes, Labyrinths,* and *The Aleph and Other Stories.* In this short piece the writer speaks of his dual nature, the self who surrenders everything to the creative Borges so that he can weave his tales and poems.

It's to the other man, to Borges, that things happen. I walk along the streets of Buenos Aires, stopping now and then—perhaps out of habit—to look at the arch of an old entranceway or a grillwork gate; of Borges I get news through the mail and glimpse his name among a committee of professors or in a dictionary of biography. I have a taste for hourglasses, maps, eighteenth-century typography, the roots of words, the smell of coffee, and Stevenson's prose; the other man shares these likes, but in a showy way that turns them into stagy mannerisms. It would be an exaggeration to say that we are on bad terms; I live, I let myself live, so that Borges can weave his tales and poems, and those tales and poems are my justification. It is not hard for me to admit that he has managed to write a few worthwhile pages, but these pages cannot save me, perhaps because what is good no longer belongs to anyone—not even the other man—but rather to speech or tradition. In any case, I am fated to become lost once and for all, and only some moment of myself will survive in the other man. Little by little, I have been surrendering everything to him, even though I have evidence of his stubborn habit of falsification and exaggerating. Spinoza held that all things try to keep on being themselves; a stone wants to be a stone and the tiger, a tiger. I shall remain in Borges, not in myself (if it is so that I am someone), but I recognize myself less in his books than in those of others or than in the laborious tuning of a guitar. Years ago, I tried ridding myself of him and I went from myths of the outlying slums of the city to games with time and infinity, but those games are now part of Borges and I will have to turn to other things. And so, my life is a running away, and I lose everything and everything is left to oblivion or to the other man.

Which of us is writing this page I don't know.

Suggestions for Discussion

1. Who is the speaker?
2. What is his relationship to and attitude toward Borges, the writer?
3. With what details are the dual aspects of his personality made clear? Define them.
4. How does he substantiate his belief that he is "fated to become lost once and for all"?
5. On the basis of this brief sketch, what conclusions are you invited to draw about the creative process and about the sources and subject matter of Borges's art?

Suggestions for Writing

1. Read a number of Borges's short stories and analyze the basis of their appeal.
2. The concept of the double appears frequently in literature. Write a sketch of a character in literature (Conrad's "The Secret Sharer," Melville's "Bartleby the Scrivener," Dostoevsky's "The Double," Poe's "William Wilson") who might be described as having a double.
3. Record your daily activities and thoughts for a week, paying no attention to mechanics or organization. Then select one of the journal items for full and logical development.

MAXINE HONG KINGSTON

No Name Woman

Maxine Hong Kingston (b. 1940) was born in Stockton, California, and graduated from the University of California. Her books, *The Woman Warrior* (1976) from which this excerpt has been taken, *China Men* (1980), and *Tripmaster Monkey* (1989), focus on her experiences as a Chinese American. She has won both the National Book Critics Circle and American Book Awards. "No Name Woman" graphically portrays the complex problems of cultural identity and implicitly suggests the author's sense of self.

"You must not tell anyone," my mother said, "what I am about to tell you. In China your father had a sister who killed herself. She jumped into the family well. We say that your father has all brothers because it is as if she had never been born.

"In 1924 just a few days after our village celebrated seventeen hurry-up weddings—to make sure that every young man who went 'out on the road' would responsibly come home—your father and his brothers and your grandfather and his brothers and your aunt's new husband sailed for America, the Gold Mountain. It was your grandfather's last trip. Those lucky enough to get contracts waved good-bye from the decks. They fed and guarded the stowaways and helped them off in Cuba, New York, Bali, Hawaii. 'We'll meet in California next year,' they said. All of them sent money home.

"I remember looking at your aunt one day when she and I were dressing; I had not noticed before that she had such a protruding melon of a stomach. But I did not think, 'She's pregnant,' until she began to look like other pregnant women, her shirt pulling and the white tops of her black pants showing. She could not have been pregnant, you see, because her husband had been gone for years. No one said anything. We did not discuss it. In early summer she was ready to have the child, long after the time when it could have been possible.

"The village had also been counting. On the night the baby was to be born the villagers raided our house. Some were crying. Like a great saw, teeth strung with lights, files of people walked zigzag across our land, tearing the rice. Their lanterns doubled in the disturbed black water, which drained away through the broken bunds. As the villagers closed in, we could see that some of them, probably men and women we knew well, wore white masks. The people with long hair hung it over their faces. Women with short hair made it stand up on end. Some had tied white bands around their foreheads, arms, and legs.

"At first they threw mud and rocks at the house. Then they threw eggs and began slaughtering our stock. We could hear the animals scream their deaths—the roosters, the pigs, a last great roar from the ox. Familiar wild heads flared in our night windows; the villagers encircled us. Some of the faces stopped to peer at us, their eyes rushing like searchlights. The hands flattened against the panes, framed heads, and left red prints.

"The villagers broke in the front and the back doors at the same time, even though we had not locked the doors against them. Their knives dripped with the blood of our animals. They smeared blood on the doors and walls. One woman swung a chicken, whose throat she had slit, splattering blood in red arcs about her. We stood together in the middle of our house, in the family hall with the pictures and tables of the ancestors around us, and looked straight ahead.

"At that time the house had only two wings. When the men came back, we would build two more to enclose our courtyard and a third one to begin a second courtyard. The villagers rushed through both wings, even your grandparents' rooms, to find your aunt's, which was also mine until the men returned. From this room a new wing for one of the younger families would grow. They ripped up her clothes and shoes and broke her combs, grinding them underfoot. They tore her work from the loom. They scattered the cooking fire and rolled the new weaving in it. We could hear them in the kitchen breaking our bowls and banging the pots. They overturned the great waist-high earthenware jugs; duck eggs, pickled fruits, vegetables burst out and mixed in acrid torrents. The old woman from the next field swept a broom through the air and loosed the spirits-of-the-broom over our heads. 'Pig.' 'Ghost.' 'Pig,' they sobbed and scolded while they ruined our house.

"When they left, they took sugar and oranges to bless themselves. They cut pieces from the dead animals. Some of them took bowls that were not broken and clothes that were not torn. Afterward we swept up the rice and sewed it back up into sacks. But the smells from the spilled preserves lasted. Your aunt gave birth in the pigsty that night. The next morning when I went for the water, I found her and the baby plugging up the family well.

"Don't let your father know that I told you. He denies her. Now that you have started to menstruate, what happened to her could happen to you. Don't humiliate us. You wouldn't like to be forgotten as if you had never been born. The villagers are watchful."

Whenever she had to warn us about life, my mother told stories that ran like this one, a story to grow up on. She tested our strength to establish realities. Those in the emigrant generations who could not reassert brute survival died young and far from home. Those of us in the first American generations have had to figure out how the invisible world the emigrants built around our childhoods fit in solid America.

The emigrants confused the gods by diverting their curses, misleading them with crooked streets and false names. They must try to confuse their offspring as well, who, I suppose, threaten them in similar ways—always trying to get things straight, always trying to name the unspeakable. The Chinese I know hide their names; sojourners take new names when their lives change and guard their real names with silence.

Chinese-Americans, when you try to understand what things in you are Chinese, how do you separate what is peculiar to childhood, to poverty, insanities, one family, your mother who marked your growing with stories, from what is Chinese? What is Chinese tradition and what is the movies?

If I want to learn what clothes my aunt wore, whether flashy or ordinary, I would have to begin, "Remember Father's drowned-in-the-well sister?" I cannot ask that. My mother has told me once and for all the useful parts. She will add nothing unless powered by Necessity, a riverbank that guides her life. She plants vegetable gardens rather than lawns; she carries the odd-shaped tomatoes home from the fields and eats food left for the gods.

Whenever we did frivolous things, we used up energy; we flew high kites. We children came up off the ground over the melting cones our parents brought home from work and the American movie on New Year's Day—*Oh, You Beautiful Doll* with Betty Grable one year, and *She Wore a Yellow Ribbon* with John Wayne another year. After the one carnival ride each, we paid in guilt; our tired father counted his change on the dark walk home.

Adultery is extravagance. Could people who hatch their own chicks and eat the embryos and the heads for delicacies and boil the feet in vinegar for party food, leaving only the gravel, eating even the gizzard lining—could such people engender a prodigal aunt? To be a woman, to have a daughter in starvation time was a waste enough. My aunt could not have been the lone romantic who gave up everything for sex. Women in the old China did not choose. Some man had commanded her to lie with him and be his secret evil. I wonder whether he masked himself when he joined the raid on her family.

Perhaps she encountered him in the fields or on the mountain where the daughters-in-law collected fuel. Or perhaps he first noticed her in the market-place. He was not a stranger because the village housed no strangers. She had to have dealings with him other than sex. Perhaps he worked an adjoining field, or he sold her the cloth for the dress she sewed and wore. His demand must have surprised, then terrified her. She obeyed him; she always did as she was told.

When the family found a young man in the next village to be her husband, she stood tractably beside the best rooster, his proxy, and promised before they met that she would be his forever. She was lucky that he was her age and she would be the first wife, an advantage secure now. The night she first saw him, he had sex with her. Then he left for America. She had almost forgotten what he looked like. When she tried to envision him, she only saw the black and white face in the group photograph the men had had taken before leaving.

The other man was not, after all, much different from her husband. They both gave orders: she followed. "If you tell your family, I'll beat you. I'll kill you. Be here again next week." No one talked sex, ever. And she might have separated the rapes from the rest of living if only she did not have to buy her oil from him or gather wood in the same forest. I want her fear to have lasted just as long as rape lasted so that the fear could have been contained. No drawn-out fear. But women at sex hazarded birth and hence lifetimes. The fear did not stop but permeated everywhere. She told the man, "I think I'm pregnant." He organized the raid against her.

On nights when my mother and father talked about their life back home, sometimes they mentioned an "outcast table" whose business they still seemed to be settling, their voices tight. In a commensal tradition, where food is precious, the powerful older people made wrongdoers eat alone. Instead of letting them start separate new lives like the Japanese, who could become samurais and geishas, the Chinese family, faces averted but eyes glowering sideways, hung on to the offenders and fed them left-overs. My aunt must have lived in the same house as my parents and eaten at an outcast table. My mother spoke about the raid as if she had seen it, when she and my aunt, a daughter-in-law to a different household, should not have been living together at all. Daughters-in-law lived with their husbands' parents, not their own; a synonym for marriage in Chinese is "taking a daughter-in-law." Her husband's parents could have sold her, mortgaged her, stoned her. But they had sent her back to her own mother and father, a mysterious act hinting at disgraces not told me. Perhaps they had thrown her out to deflect the avengers.

She was the only daughter; her four brothers went with her father, husband, and uncles "out on the road" and for some years became western men. When the goods were divided among the family, three of the brothers took land, and the youngest, my father, chose an education. After my grandparents gave their daughter away to her husband's family, they had dispensed all the adventure and all the property. They expected her alone to keep the traditional ways, which her brothers, now among the barbarians, could fumble without detection. The heavy, deep-rooted women were to maintain the past against the flood, safe for returning. But the rare urge west had fixed upon our family, and so my aunt crossed boundaries not delineated in space.

The work of preservation demands that the feelings playing about in one's guts not be turned into action. Just watch their passing like cherry blossoms. But perhaps my aunt, my forerunner, caught in a slow life, let dreams grow and fade and after some months or years went toward what persisted. Fear at the enormities of the forbidden kept her desires delicate, wire and bone. She looked at a man because she liked the way the hair was tucked behind his ears, or she liked the question-mark line of a long torso curving at the shoulder and straight at the hip. For warm eyes or a soft voice or a slow walk—that's all—a few hairs, a line, a brightness, a sound, a pace, she gave up family. She offered us up for a charm that vanished with tiredness, a pigtail that didn't toss when the wind died. Why, the wrong lighting could erase the dearest thing about him.

It could very well have been, however, that my aunt did not take subtle enjoyment of her friend, but, a wild woman, kept rollicking company. Imagining her free with sex doesn't fit, though. I don't know any women like that, or men either. Unless I see her life branching into mine, she gives me no ancestral help.

To sustain her being in love, she often worked at herself in the mirror, guessing at the colors and shapes that would interest him, changing them frequently in order to hit on the right combination. She wanted him to look back.

On a farm near the sea, a woman who tended her appearance reaped a reputation for eccentricity. All the married women blunt-cut their hair in flaps about their ears or pulled it back in tight buns. No nonsense. Neither style blew easily into heart-catching tangles. And at their weddings they displayed themselves in their long hair for the last time. "It brushed the backs of my knees," my mother tells me. "It was braided, and even so, it brushed the backs of my knees."

At the mirror my aunt combed individuality into her bob. A bun could have been contrived to escape into black streamers blowing in the wind or in quiet wisps about her face, but only the older women in our picture album wear buns. She brushed her hair back from her forehead, tucking the flaps behind her ears. She looped a piece of thread, knotted into a circle between her index fingers and thumbs, and ran the double strand across her forehead. When she closed her fingers as if she were making a pair of shadow geese bite, the string twisted together catching the little hairs. Then she pulled the thread away from her skin, ripping the hairs out neatly, her eyes watering from the needles of pain. Opening her fingers, she cleaned the thread, then rolled it along her hairline and the tops of her eyebrows. My mother did the same to me and my sisters and herself. I used to believe that the expression "caught by the short hairs" meant a captive held with a depilatory string. It especially hurt at the temples, but my mother said we were lucky we didn't have to have our feet bound when we were seven. Sisters used to sit on their beds and cry together, she said, as their mothers or their slave removed the bandages for a few minutes each night and let the blood gush back into their veins. I hope that the man my aunt loved appreciated a smooth brow, that he wasn't just a tits-and-ass man.

Once my aunt found a freckle on her chin, at a spot that the almanac said predestined her for unhappiness. She dug it out with a hot needle and washed the wound with peroxide.

More attention to her looks than these pullings of hairs and pickings at spots would have caused gossip among the villagers. They owned work clothes and good clothes, and they wore good clothes for feasting the new seasons. But since a woman combing her hair hexes beginnings, my aunt rarely found an occasion to look her best. Women looked like great sea snails—the corded wood, babies, and laundry they carried were the whorls on their backs. The Chinese did not admire a bent back; goddesses and warriors stood straight. Still there must have been a marvelous freeing of beauty when a worker laid down her burden and stretched and arched.

Such commonplace loveliness, however, was not enough for my aunt. She dreamed of a lover for the fifteen days of New Year's, the time for families to exchange visits, money, and food. She plied her secret comb. And sure enough she cursed the year, the family, the village, and herself.

Even as her hair lured her imminent lover, many other men looked at her. Uncles, cousins, nephews, brothers would have looked, too, had they been home between journeys. Perhaps they had already been restraining their curiosity, and they left, fearful that their glances, like a field of nesting birds, might be startled and caught. Poverty hurt, and that was their first reason for leaving. But another, final reason for leaving the crowded house was the never-said.

She may have been unusually beloved, the precious only daughter, spoiled and mirror gazing because of the affection the family lavished on her. When her husband left, they welcomed the chance to take her back from the in-laws; she could live like the little daughter for just a while longer. There are stories that my grandfather was different from other people, "crazy ever since the little Jap bayoneted him in the head." He used to put his naked penis on the dinner table, laughing. And one day he brought home a baby girl, wrapped up inside his brown western-style greatcoat. He had traded one of his sons, probably my father, the youngest, for her. My grandmother made him trade back. When he finally got a daughter of his own, he doted on her. They must have all loved her, except perhaps my father, the only brother who never went back to China, having once been traded for a girl.

Brothers and sisters, newly men and women, had to efface their sexual color and present plain miens. Disturbing hair and eyes, a smile like no other, threatened the ideal of five generations living under one roof. To focus blurs, people shouted face to face and yelled from room to room. The immigrants I know have loud voices, unmodulated to American tones even after years away from the village where they called their friendships out across the fields. I have not been able to stop my mother's screams in public libraries or over telephones. Walking erect (knees straight, toes pointed forward, not pigeon-toed, which is Chinese-feminine) and speaking in an inaudible voice, I have tried to turn myself American-feminine. Chinese communication was loud, public. Only sick people had to whisper. But at the dinner table, where the family members came nearest one another, no one could talk, not the outcasts nor any eaters. Every word that falls from the mouth is a coin lost. Silently they gave and accepted food with both hands. A preoccupied child who took his bowl with one hand got a sideways glare. A complete moment of total attention is due everyone alike. Children and lovers have no singularity here, but my aunt used a secret voice, a separate attentiveness.

She kept the man's name to herself throughout her labor and dying; she did not accuse him that he be punished with her. To save her inseminator's name she gave silent birth.

He may have been somebody in her own household, but intercourse with a man outside the family would have been no less abhorrent. All the village were kinsmen, and the titles shouted in loud country voices never let kinship be forgotten. Any man within visiting distance would have been neutralized as a lover—"brother," "younger brother," "older brother"—one hundred and fifteen relationship titles. Parents researched birth charts probably not so much to assure good fortune as to circumvent incest in a population that has but one hundred surnames. Everybody has eight million relatives. How useless then sexual mannerisms, how dangerous.

As if it came from an atavism deeper than fear, I used to add "brother" silently to boys' names. It hexed the boys, who would or would not ask me to dance, and made them less scary and as familiar and deserving of benevolence as girls.

But, of course, I hexed myself also—no dates. I should have stood up, both arms waving, and shouted out across libraries, "Hey, you! Love me back." I had no idea, though, how to make attraction selective, how to control its direction and magnitude. If I made myself American-pretty so that the five or six Chinese boys in the class fell in love with me, everyone else—the Caucasian, Negro, and Japanese boys—would too. Sisterliness, dignified and honorable, made much more sense.

Attraction eludes control so stubbornly that whole societies designed to organize relationships among people cannot keep order, not even when they bind people to one another from childhood and raise them together. Among the very poor and the wealthy, brothers married their adopted sisters, like doves. Our family allowed some romance, paying adult brides' prices and providing dowries so that their sons and daughters could marry strangers. Marriage promises to turn strangers into friendly relatives—a nation of siblings.

In the village structure, spirits shimmered among the live creatures, balanced and held in equilibrium by time and land. But one human being flaring up into violence could open up a black hole, a maelstrom that pulled in the sky. The frightened villagers, who depended on one another to maintain the real, went to my aunt to show her a personal, physical representation of the break she had made in the "roundness." Misallying couples snapped off the future, which was to be embodied in true offspring. The villagers punished her for acting as if she could have a private life, secret and apart from them.

If my aunt had betrayed the family at a time of large grain yields and peace, when many boys were born, and wings were being built on many houses, perhaps she might have escaped such severe punishment. But the men—hungry, greedy, tired of planting in dry soil, cuckolded—had had to leave the village in order to send food-money home. There were ghost plagues, bandit plagues, wars with the Japanese, floods. My Chinese brother and sister had died of an unknown sickness. Adultery, perhaps only a mistake during good times, became a crime when the village needed food.

The round moon cakes and round doorways, the round tables of graduated size that fit one roundness inside another, round windows and rice bowls—these talismans had lost their power to warn this family of the law: a family must be whole, faithfully keeping the descent line by having sons to feed the old and the dead, who in turn look after the family. The villagers came to show my aunt and her lover-in-hiding a broken house. The villagers were speeding up the circling of events because she was too shortsighted to see that her infidelity had already harmed the village, that waves of consequences would return unpredictably, sometimes in disguise, as now, to hurt her. This roundness had to be made coin-sized so that she would see its circumference: punish her at the birth of her baby. Awaken her to the inexorable. People who refused fatalism because they could invent small resources insisted on culpability. Deny accidents and wrest fault from the stars.

After the villagers left, their lanterns now scattering in various directions toward home, the family broke their silence and cursed her. "Aiaa, we're going to die. Death is coming. Death is coming. Look what you've done. You've killed us. Ghost! Dead ghost! Ghost! You've never been born." She ran out into the fields, far enough from the house so that she could no longer hear their voices, and pressed herself against the earth, her own land no more. When she felt the birth coming, she thought that she had been hurt. Her body seized together. "They've hurt me too much," she thought. "This is gall, and it will kill me." With forehead and knees against the earth, her body convulsed and then relaxed. She turned on her back, lay on the ground. The black well of sky and stars went out and out and out forever; her body and her complexity seemed to disappear, without home, without a companion, in eternal cold and silence. An agoraphobia rose in her, speeding higher and higher, bigger and bigger; she would not be able to contain it; there would be no end to fear.

Flayed, unprotected against space, she felt pain return, focusing her body. This pain chilled her—a cold, steady kind of surface pain. Inside, spasmodically, the other pain, the pain of the child, heated her. For hours she lay on the ground, alternately body and space. Sometimes a vision of normal comfort obliterated reality: she saw the family in the evening gambling at the dinner table, the young people massaging their elders' backs. She saw them congratulating one another, high joy on the mornings the rice shoots came up. When these pictures burst, the stars drew yet further apart. Black space opened.

She got to her feet to fight better and remembered that old-fashioned women gave birth in their pigsties to fool the jealous, pain-dealing gods, who do not snatch piglets. Before the next spasms could stop her, she ran to the pigsty, each step a rushing out into emptiness. She climbed over the fence and knelt in the dirt. It was good to have a fence enclosing her, a tribal person alone.

Laboring, this woman who had carried her child as a foreign growth that sickened her every day, expelled it at last. She reached down to touch the hot, wet, moving mass, surely smaller than anything human, and could feel that it was human after all—fingers, toes, nails, nose. She pulled it up on to her belly, and it lay curled there, butt in the air, feet precisely tucked one under the other. She opened her loose shirt and buttoned the child inside. After resting, it squirmed and thrashed and she pushed it up to her breast. It turned its head this way and that until it found her nipple. There, it made little snuffling noises. She clenched her teeth at its preciousness, lovely as a young calf, a piglet, a little dog.

She may have gone to the pigsty as a last act of responsibility: she would protect this child as she had protected its father. It would look after her soul, leaving supplies on her grave. But how would this tiny child without family find her grave when there would be no marker for her anywhere, neither in the earth nor the family hall? No one would give her a family hall name. She had taken the child with her into the wastes. At its birth the two of them had felt the same raw pain of separation, a wound that only the family pressing tight could close. A child with no descent line would not soften her life but only trail after her, ghost-like, begging her to give it purpose. At dawn the villagers on their way to the fields would stand around the fence and look.

Full of milk, the little ghost slept. When it awoke, she hardened her breasts against the milk that crying loosens. Toward morning she picked up the baby and walked to the well.

Carrying the baby to the well shows loving. Otherwise abandon it. Turn its face into the mud. Mothers who love their children take them along. It was probably a girl; there is some hope of forgiveness for boys.

"Don't tell anyone you had an aunt. Your father does not want to hear her name. She has never been born." I have believed that sex was unspeakable and words so strong and fathers so frail that "aunt" would do my father mysterious harm. I have thought that my family, having settled among immigrants who had also been their neighbors in the ancestral land, needed to clean their name, and a wrong word would incite the kinspeople even here. But there is more to this silence: they want me to participate in her punishment. And I have.

In the twenty years since I heard this story I have not asked for details nor said my aunt's name; I do not know it. People who can comfort the dead can also chase after them to hurt them further—a reverse ancestor worship. The real punishment was not the raid swiftly inflicted by the villagers, but the family's deliberately forgetting her. Her betrayal so maddened them, they saw to it that she would suffer forever, even after death. Always hungry, always needing, she would have to beg food from other ghosts, snatch and steal it from those whose living descendants give them gifts. She would have to fight the ghosts massed at crossroads for the buns a few thoughtful citizens leave to decoy her away from village and home so that the ancestral spirits could feast unharassed. At peace, they could act like gods, not ghosts, their descent lines providing them with paper suits and dresses, spirit money, paper houses, paper automobiles, chicken, meat, and rice into eternity—essences delivered up in smoke and flames, steam and incense rising from each rice bowl. In an attempt to make the Chinese care for people outside the family, Chairman Mao encourages us now to give our paper replicas to the spirits of outstanding soldiers and workers, no matter whose ancestors they may be. My aunt remains forever hungry. Goods are not distributed evenly among the dead.

My aunt haunts me—her ghost drawn to me because now, after fifty years of neglect, I alone devote pages of paper to her, though not origamied into houses and clothes. I do not think she always means me well. I am telling on her, and she was a spite suicide, drowning herself in the drinking water. The Chinese are always very frightened of the drowned one, whose weeping ghost, wet hair hanging and skin bloated, waits silently by the water to pull down a substitute.

Suggestions for Discussion

1. What is the tone of the author's address to Chinese Americans? In what sense does this paragraph logically follow her mother's story?
2. Why must Chinese emigrants try to confuse their offspring as well as "the gods"?
3. How did the author piece together the reasons for her aunt's adultery?
4. With what details does the reader get a picture of the lives of daughters in old China?
5. What does the phrase "taking a daughter-in-law" as a synonym for marriage tell the reader about men–women relationships in old China?
6. With what details do you learn about differing attitudes toward boys and girls?
7. Compare the conjectured and real behavior of the aunt's lover with hers after her ostracism.
8. How did the economy, plagues, floods, and wars affect attitudes toward adultery?

9. Trace the organization of the aunt's story. Compare the way in which it is narrated in the mother's words and in those of the author. What purpose is served by the author's intervening introspections?
10. How does the author account for the aunt's suicide?
11. How does Kingston convey that the story of her aunt was a story "to grow up on"? Kingston speaks of being haunted by the ghost of her aunt. What do her introspections tell you implicitly of her sense of self?

Suggestions for Writing

1. Narrate a story "to grow up on" that tested your "strength to establish realities."
2. The critic John Leonard called the book, in which this is the first chapter, "a poem turned into a sword." Justify this assessment by analyzing the writer's diction and tone.

JUDITH ORTIZ COFER

Casa: A Partial Remembrance of a Puerto Rican Childhood

Judith Ortiz Cofer (b. 1952) is a native of Puerto Rico, although she immigrated to the United States as a small child. Educated in Florida and Georgia, where she still resides, she attended Oxford University, as a Scholar of the English Speaking Union, and the prestigious Bread Loaf Writers' Conference at Middlebury College. A teacher of both English and Spanish at the university level, she has received a number of awards for her poetry, including grants from the Witter Bynner Foundation and the National Endowment for the Arts. Her publications include, among others, *The Line of the Sun* (1989), *Silent Dancing* (1990), *The Latin Deli: Telling the Lives of Latino Women* (1995), *Reaching for the Mainland and Selected New Poems* (1995), and *Terms of Survival* (1995). In this selection she shows the reader how knowledge, of a kind not found in books, is passed from generation to generation through the medium of family storytelling.

At three or four o'clock in the afternoon, the hour of *café con leche,* the women of my family gathered in Mamá's living room to speak of important things and retell familiar stories meant to be overheard by us young girls, their daughters. In Mamá's house (everyone called my grandmother Mamá) was a large parlor built by my grandfather to his wife's exact specifications so that it was always cool, facing away from the sun. The doorway was on the side of the house so no one could walk directly into her living room. First they had to take a little stroll through and around her beautiful garden where prize-winning orchids grew in the trunk of an ancient tree she had hollowed out for that purpose. This room was furnished with several mahogany rocking chairs, acquired at the births of her children, and one intricately carved rocker that had passed down to Mamá at the death of her own mother.

It was on these rockers that my mother, her sisters, and my grandmother sat on these afternoons of my childhood to tell their stories, teaching each other, and my cousin and me, what it was like to be a woman, more specifically, a Puerto Rican woman. They talked about life on the island, and life in *Los Nueva Yores,* their way of referring to the United States from New York City to California: the other place, not home, all the same. They told real-life stories though, as I later learned, always embellishing them with a little or a lot of dramatic detail. And they told *cuentos,* the morality and cautionary tales told by the women in our family for generations: stories that became a part of my subconscious as I grew up in two worlds, the tropical island and the cold city, and that would later surface in my dreams and in my poetry.

One of these tales was about the woman who was left at the altar. Mamá liked to tell that one with histrionic intensity. I remember the rise and fall of her voice, the sighs, and her constantly gesturing hands, like two birds swooping through her words. This particular story usually would come up in a conversation as a result of someone mentioning a forthcoming engagement or wedding. The first time I remember hearing it, I was sitting on the floor at Mamá's feet, pretending to read a comic book. I may have been eleven or twelve years old, at that difficult age when a girl was no longer a child who could be ordered to leave the room if the women wanted freedom to take their talk into forbidden zones, nor really old enough to be considered a part of their conclave. I could only sit quietly, pretending to be in another world, while absorbing it all in a sort of unspoken agreement of my status as silent auditor. On this day, Mamá had taken my long, tangled mane of hair into her ever-busy hands. Without looking down at me and with no interruption of her flow of words, she began braiding my hair, working at it with the quickness and determination that characterized all her actions. My mother was watching us impassively from her rocker across the room. On her lips played a little ironic smile. I would never sit still for *her* ministrations, but even then, I instinctively knew that she did not possess Mamá's matriarchal power to command and keep everyone's attention. This was never more evident than in the spell she cast when telling a story.

"It is not like it used to be when I was a girl," Mamá announced. "Then, a man could leave a girl standing at the church altar with a bouquet of fresh flowers in her hands and disappear off the face of the earth. No way to track him down if he was from another town. He could be a married man, with maybe even two or three families all over the island. There was no way to know. And there were men who did this. Hombres with the devil in their flesh who would come to a pueblo, like this one, take a job at one of the haciendas, never meaning to stay, only to have a good time and to seduce the women."

The whole time she was speaking, Mamá would be weaving my hair into a flat plait that required pulling apart the two sections of hair with little jerks that made my eyes water; but knowing how grandmother detested whining and *boba* (sissy) tears, as she called them, I just sat up as straight and stiff as I did at La Escuela San Jose, where the nuns enforced good posture with a flexible plastic ruler they bounced off of slumped shoulders and heads. As Mamá's story progressed, I noticed how my young Aunt Laura lowered her eyes, refusing to meet Mamá's meaningful gaze. Laura was seventeen, in her last year of high school, and already engaged to a boy from another town who had staked his claim with a tiny diamond ring, then left for Los Nueva Yores to make his fortune. They were planning to get married in a year. Mamá had expressed serious doubts that the wedding would ever take place. In Mamá's eyes, a man set free without a legal contract was a man lost. She believed that marriage was not something men desired, but simply the price they had to pay for the privilege of children and, of course, for what no decent (synonymous with "smart") woman would give away for free.

"María La Loca was only seventeen when *it* happened to her." I listened closely at the mention of this name. María was a town character, a fat middle-aged woman who lived with her old mother on the outskirts of town. She was to be seen around the pueblo delivering the meat pies the two women made for a living. The most peculiar thing about María, in my eyes, was that she walked and moved like a little girl though she had the thick body and wrinkled face of an old woman. She would swing her hips in an exaggerated, clownish way, and sometimes even hop and skip up to someone's house. She spoke to no one. Even if you asked her a question, she would just look at you and smile, showing her yellow teeth. But I had heard that if you got close enough, you could hear her humming a tune without words. The kids yelled out nasty things at her, calling her *La Loca,* and the men who hung out at the bodega playing dominoes sometimes whistled mockingly as she passed by with her funny, outlandish walk. But María seemed impervious to it all, carrying her basket of *pasteles* like a grotesque Little Red Riding Hood through the forest.

María La Loca interested me, as did all the eccentrics and crazies of our pueblo. Their weirdness was a measuring stick I used in my serious quest for a definition of normal. As a Navy brat shuttling between New Jersey and the pueblo, I was constantly made to feel like an oddball by my peers, who made fun of my two-way accent: a Spanish accent when I spoke English, and when I spoke Spanish I was told that I sounded like a *Gringa.* Being the outsider had already turned my brother and me into cultural chameleons. We developed early on the ability to blend into a crowd, to sit and read quietly in a fifth story apartment building for days and days when it was too bitterly cold to play outside, or, set free, to run wild in Mamá's realm, where she took charge of our lives, releasing Mother for a while from the intense fear for our safety that our father's absences instilled in her. In order to keep us from harm when Father was away, Mother kept us under strict surveillance. She even walked us to and from Public School No. 11, which we attended during the months we lived in Paterson, New Jersey, our home base in the states. Mamá freed all three of us like pigeons from a cage. I saw her as my liberator and my model. Her stories were parables from which to glean the *Truth.*

"María La Loca was once a beautiful girl. Everyone thought she would marry the Méndez boy." As everyone knew, Rogelio Méndez was the richest man in town. "But," Mamá continued, knitting my hair with the same intensity she was putting into her story, "this *macho* made a fool out of her and ruined her life." She paused for the effect of her use of the word "macho," which at that time had not yet become a popular epithet for an unliberated man. This word had for us the crude and comical connotation of "male of the species," stud; a *macho* was what you put in a pen to increase your stock.

I peeked over my comic book at my mother. She too was under Mamá's spell, smiling conspiratorially at this little swipe at men. She was safe from Mamá's contempt in this area. Married at an early age, an unspotted lamb, she had been accepted by a good family of strict Spaniards whose name was old and respected, though their fortune had been lost long before my birth. In a rocker Papá had painted sky blue sat Mamá's oldest child, Aunt Nena. Mother of three children, stepmother of two more, she was a quiet woman who liked books but had married an ignorant and abusive widower whose main interest in life was accumulating wealth. He too was in the mainland working on his dream of returning home rich and triumphant to buy the *finca* of his dreams. She was waiting for him to send for her. She would leave her children with Mamá for several years while the two of them slaved away in factories. He would one day be a rich man, and she a sadder woman. Even now her life-light was dimming. She spoke little, an aberration in Mamá's house, and she read avidly, as if storing up spiritual food for the long winters that awaited her in Los Nueva Yores without her family. But even Aunt Nena came alive to Mamá's words, rocking gently, her hands over a thick book in her lap.

Her daughter, my cousin Sara, played jacks by herself on the tile porch outside the room where we sat. She was a year older than I. We shared a bed and all our family's secrets. Collaborators in search of answers, Sara and I discussed everything we heard the women say, trying to fit it all together like a puzzle that, once assembled, would reveal life's mysteries to us. Though she and I still enjoyed taking part in boys' games—chase, volleyball, and even *vaqueros,* the island version of cowboys and Indians involving cap-gun battles and violent shoot-outs under the mango tree in Mamá's backyard—we loved best the quiet hours in the afternoon when the men were still at work, and the boys had gone to play serious baseball at the park. Then Mamá's house belonged only to us women. The aroma of coffee perking in the kitchen, the mesmerizing creaks and groans of the rockers, and the women telling their lives in *cuentos* are forever woven into the fabric of my imagination, braided like my hair that day I felt my grandmother's hands teaching me about strength, her voice convincing me of the power of storytelling.

That day Mamá told how the beautiful María had fallen prey to a man whose name was never the same in subsequent versions of the story; it was Juan one time, José, Rafael, Diego, another. We understood that neither the name nor any of the *facts* were important, only that a woman had allowed love to defeat her. Mamá put each of us in María's place by describing her wedding dress in loving detail: how she looked like a princess in her lace as she waited at the altar. Then, as Mamá approached the tragic denouement of her story, I was distracted by the sound of my Aunt Laura's violent rocking. She seemed on the verge of tears. She knew the fable was intended for her. That week she was going to have her wedding gown fitted, though no firm date had been set for the marriage. Mamá ignored Laura's obvious discomfort, digging out a ribbon from the sewing basket she kept by her rocker while describing María's long illness, "a fever that would not break for days." She spoke of a mother's despair: "that woman climbed the church steps on her knees every morning, wore only black as a *promesa* to the Holy Virgin in exchange for her daughter's health." By the time María returned from her honeymoon with death, she was ravished, no longer young or sane. "As you can see, she is almost as old as her mother already," Mamá lamented while tying the ribbon to the ends of my hair, pulling it back with such force that I just knew I would never be able to close my eyes completely again.

"That María's getting crazier every day." Mamá's voice would take a lighter tone now, expressing satisfaction, either for the perfection of my braid, or for a story well told—it was hard to tell. "You know that tune María is always humming?" Carried away by her enthusiasm, I tried to nod, but Mamá still had me pinned between her knees.

"Well, that's the wedding march." Surprising us all, Mamá sang out, "Da, da, dara...da, da, dara." Then lifting me off the floor by my skinny shoulders, she would lead me around the room in an impromptu waltz—another session ending with the laughter of women, all of us caught up in the infectious joke of our lives.

Suggestions for Discussion

Relate each of the following quotations to the selection you have just read.

1. "It was on these rockers that my mother, her sisters, and my grandmother sat on these afternoons of my childhood to tell their stories, teaching each other, and my cousin and me, what it was like to be a woman, more specifically, a Puerto Rican woman."
2. "Collaborators in search of answers, Sara and I discussed everything we heard the women say, trying to fit it all together like a puzzle that, once assembled, would reveal life's mysteries to us."
3. "We understood that neither the name nor any of the *facts* were important, only that a woman had allowed love to defeat her."

Suggestions for Writing

1. Children learn much of their culture from eavesdropping on the adult world. Describe a time when you had this experience.
2. Cofer distinguishes between "facts" and "themes." Truth in storytelling has far more to do with one than the other. Write a story in which this is manifest.

ALICE WALKER

Beauty: When the Other Dancer Is the Self

Alice Walker (b. 1944) has received numerous awards for her fiction: *The Color Purple* (1982), a best-selling novel, was nominated for the Book Critics Circle Award and received the American Book Award, the Candace Award of the National Coalition of 100 Black Women, and a Pulitzer Prize. She has also published two collections of short stories, *You Can't Keep a Good Woman Down* (1981) and *In Love and Trouble. Possessing the Secret of Joy, To Hell with Dying, Warrior Marks* (1993), *Everyday Use,* and *Alice Walker Banned* (1996) comprise some of her recent publications. *In Search of Our Mother's Gardens: Womanist Prose* (1983) includes this reminiscence of the effect a traumatic injury to her eye had on her self-image.

It is a bright summer day in 1947. My father, a fat, funny man with beautiful eyes and a subversive wit, is trying to decide which of his eight children he will take with him to the county fair. My mother, of course, will not go. She is knocked out from getting most of us ready: I hold my neck stiff against the pressure of her knuckles as she hastily completes the braiding and then be-ribboning of my hair.

My father is the driver for the rich old white lady up the road. Her name is Miss Mey. She owns all the land for miles around, as well as the house in which we live. All I remember about her is that she once offered to pay my mother thirty-five cents for cleaning her house, raking up piles of her magnolia leaves, and washing her family's clothes, and that my mother—she of no money, eight children, and a chronic earache—refused it. But I do not think of this in 1947. I am two and a half years old. I want to go everywhere my daddy goes. I am excited at the prospect of riding in a car. Someone has told me fairs are fun. That there is room in the car for only three of us doesn't faze me at all. Whirling happily in my starchy frock, showing off my biscuit-polished patent-leather shoes and lavender socks, tossing my head in a way that makes my ribbons bounce, I stand, hands on hips, before my father. "Take me, Daddy," I say with assurance; "I'm the prettiest!"

Later, it does not surprise me to find myself in Miss Mey's shiny black car, sharing the back seat with the other lucky ones. Does not surprise me that I thoroughly enjoy the fair. At home that night I tell the unlucky ones all I can remember about the merry-go-round, the man who eats live chickens, and the teddy bears, until they say: that's enough, baby Alice. Shut up now, and go to sleep.

It is Easter Sunday, 1950. I am dressed in a green, flocked, scalloped-hem dress (handmade by my adoring sister, Ruth) that has its own smooth satin petticoat and tiny hot-pink roses tucked into each scallop. My shoes, new T-strap patent leather, again highly biscuit-polished. I am six years old and have learned one of the longest Easter speeches to be heard that day, totally unlike the speech I said when I was two: "Easter lilies / pure and white / blossom in / the morning light." When I rise to give my speech I do so on a great wave of love and pride and expectation. People in the church stop rustling their new crinolines. They seem to hold their breath. I can tell they admire my dress, but it is my spirit, bordering on sassiness (womanishness), they secretly applaud.

"That girl's a little *mess,*" they whisper to each other, pleased.

Naturally I say my speech without stammer or pause, unlike those who stutter, stammer, or, worst of all, forget. This is before the word "beautiful" exists in people's vocabulary, but "Oh, isn't she the *cutest* thing!" frequently floats my way. "And got so much sense!" they gratefully add…for which thoughtful addition I thank them to this day.

It was great fun being cute. But then, one day, it ended.

I am eight years old and a tomboy. I have a cowboy hat, cowboy boots, checkered shirt and pants, all red. My playmates are my brothers, two and four years older than I. Their colors are black and green, the only difference in the way we are dressed. On Saturday nights we all go to the picture show, even my mother; Westerns are her favorite kind of movie. Back home, "on the ranch," we pretend we are Tom Mix, Hopalong Cassidy, Lash LaRue (we've even named one of our dogs Lash LaRue); we chase each other for hours rustling cattle, being outlaws, delivering damsels from distress. Then my parents decide to buy my brothers guns. These are not "real" guns. They shoot "BBs," copper pellets my brothers say will kill birds. Because I am a girl, I do not get a gun. Instantly I am relegated to the position of Indian. Now there appears a great distance between us. They shoot and shoot at everything with their new guns. I try to keep up with my bow and arrows.

One day while I am standing on top of our makeshift "garage"—pieces of tin nailed across some poles—holding my bow and arrow and looking out toward the fields, I feel an incredible blow in my right eye. I look down just in time to see my brother lower his gun.

Both brothers rush to my side. My eye stings, and I cover it with my hand. "If you tell," they say, "we will get a whipping. You don't want that to happen, do you?" I do not. "Here is a piece of wire," says the older brother, picking it up from the roof; "say you stepped on one end of it and the other flew up and hit you." The pain is beginning to start. "Yes," I say. "Yes, I will say that is what happened." If I do not say this is what happened, I know my brothers will find ways to make me wish I had. But now I will say anything that gets me to my mother.

Confronted by our parents we stick to the lie agreed upon. They place me on a bench on the porch and I close my left eye while they examine the right. There is a tree growing from underneath the porch that climbs past the railing to the roof. It is the last thing my right eye sees. I watch as its trunk, its branches, and then its leaves are blotted out by the rising blood.

I am in shock. First there is intense fever, which my father tries to break using lily leaves bound around my head. Then there are chills: my mother tries to get me to eat soup. Eventually, I do not know how, my parents learn what has happened. A week after the "accident" they take me to see a doctor. "Why did you wait so long to come?" he asks, looking into my eye and shaking his head. "Eyes are sympathetic," he says. "If one is blind, the other will likely become blind too."

This comment of the doctor's terrifies me. But it is really how I look that bothers me most. Where the BB pellet struck there is a glob of whitish scar tissue, a hideous cataract, on my eye. Now when I stare at people—a favorite pastime, up to now—they will stare back. Not at the "cute" little girl, but at her scar. For six years I do not stare at anyone, because I do not raise my head.

Years later, in the throes of a mid-life crisis, I ask my mother and sister whether I changed after the "accident." "No," they say, puzzled. "What do you mean?"

What do I mean?

I am eight, and, for the first time, doing poorly in school, where I have been something of a whiz since I was four. We have just moved to the place where the "accident" occurred. We do not know any of the people around us because this is a different county. The only time I see the friends I knew is when we go back to our old church. The new school is the former state penitentiary. It is a large stone building, cold and drafty, crammed to overflowing with boisterous, ill-disciplined children. On the third floor there is a huge circular imprint of some partition that has been torn out.

"What used to be here?" I ask a sullen girl next to me on our way past it to lunch.

"The electric chair," says she.

At night I have nightmares about the electric chair, and about all the people reputedly "fried" in it. I am afraid of the school, where all the students seem to be budding criminals.

"What's the matter with your eye?" they ask, critically.

When I don't answer (I cannot decide whether it was an "accident" or not), they shove me, insist on a fight.

My brother, the one who created the story about the wire, comes to my rescue. But then brags so much about "protecting" me, I become sick.

After months of torture at the school, my parents decide to send me back to our old community, to my old school. I live with my grandparents and the teacher they board. But there is no room for Phoebe, my cat. By the time my grandparents decide there *is* room, and I ask for my cat, she cannot be found. Miss Yarborough, the boarding teacher, takes me under her wing, and begins to teach me to play the piano. But soon she marries an African—a "prince," she says—and is whisked away to his continent.

At my old school there is at least one teacher who loves me. She is the teacher who "knew me before I was born" and bought my first baby clothes. It is she who makes life bearable. It is her presence that finally helps me turn on the one child at the school who continually calls me "one-eyed bitch." One day I simply grab him by his coat and beat him until I am satisfied. It is my teacher who tells me my mother is ill.

My mother is lying in bed in the middle of the day, something I have never seen. She is in too much pain to speak. She has an abscess in her ear. I stand looking down on her, knowing that if she dies, I cannot live. She is being treated with warm oils and hot bricks held against her cheek. Finally a doctor comes. But I must go back to my grandparents' house. The weeks pass but I am hardly aware of it. All I know is that my mother might die, my father is not so jolly, my brothers still have their guns, and I am the one sent away from home.

"You did not change," they say.

Did I imagine the anguish of never looking up?

I am twelve. When relatives come to visit I hide in my room. My cousin Brenda, just my age, whose father works in the post office and whose mother is a nurse, comes to find me. "Hello," she says. And then she asks, looking at my recent school picture, which I did not want taken, and on which the "glob," as I think of it, is clearly visible, "You still can't see out of that eye?"

"No," I say, and flop back on the bed over my book.

That night, as I do almost every night, I abuse my eye. I rant and rave at it, in front of the mirror. I plead with it to clear up before morning. I tell it I hate and despise it. I do not pray for sight. I pray for beauty.

"You did not change," they say.

I am fourteen and baby-sitting for my brother Bill, who lives in Boston. He is my favorite brother and there is a strong bond between us. Understanding my feelings of shame and ugliness he and his wife take me to a local hospital, where the "glob" is removed by a doctor named O. Henry. There is still a small bluish crater where the scar tissue was, but the ugly white stuff is gone. Almost immediately I become a different person from the girl who does not raise her head. Or so I think. Now that I've raised my head I win the boyfriend of my dreams. Now that I've raised my head I have plenty of friends. Now that I've raised my head classwork comes from my lips as faultlessly as Easter speeches did, and I leave high school as valedictorian, most popular student, and *queen,* hardly believing my luck. Ironically, the girl who was voted most beautiful in our class (and was) was later shot twice through the chest by a male companion, using a "real" gun, while she was pregnant. But that's another story in itself. Or is it?

"You did not change," they say.

It is now thirty years since the "accident." A beautiful journalist comes to visit and to interview me. She is going to write a cover story for her magazine that focuses on my latest book. "Decide how you want to look on the cover," she says. "Glamorous, or whatever."

Never mind "glamorous," it is the "whatever" that I hear. Suddenly all I can think of is whether I will get enough sleep the night before the photography session: if I don't, my eye will be tired and wander, as blind eyes will.

At night in bed with my lover I think up reasons why I should not appear on the cover of a magazine. "My meanest critics will say I've sold out," I say. "My family will now realize I write scandalous books."

"But what's the real reason you don't want to do this?" he asks.

"Because in all probability," I say in a rush, "my eye won't be straight."

"It will be straight enough," he says. Then, "Besides, I thought you'd made your peace with that."

And I suddenly remember that I have.

I remember:

I am talking to my brother Jimmy, asking if he remembers anything unusual about the day I was shot. He does not know I consider that day the last time my father, with his sweet home remedy of cool lily leaves, chose me, and that I suffered and raged inside because of this. "Well," he says, "all I remember is standing by the side of the highway with Daddy, trying to flag down a car. A white man stopped, but when Daddy said he needed somebody to take his little girl to the doctor, he drove off."

I remember:

I am in the desert for the first time. I fall totally in love with it. I am so overwhelmed by its beauty, I confront for the first time, consciously, the meaning of the doctor's words years ago: "Eyes are sympathetic. If one is blind, the other will likely become blind too." I realize I have dashed about the world madly, looking at this, looking at that, storing up images against the fading of the light. *But I might have missed seeing the desert!* The shock of that possibility—and gratitude for over twenty-five years of sight—sends me literally to my knees. Poem after poem comes—which is perhaps how poets pray.

on sight

I am so thankful I have seen
The Desert
And the creatures in the desert
And the desert Itself.

The desert has its own moon
Which I have seen
With my own eye.

There is no flag on it.

Trees of the desert have arms
All of which are always up
That is because the moon is up
The sun is up
Also the sky
The stars
Clouds
None with flags.

If there *were* flags, I doubt
the trees would point.
Would you?

But mostly, I remember this:

I am twenty-seven, and my baby daughter is almost three. Since her birth I have worried about her discovery that her mother's eyes are different from other people's. Will she be embarrassed? I think. What will she say? Every day she watches a television program called "Big Blue Marble." It begins with a picture of the earth as it appears from the moon. It is bluish, a little battered-looking, but full of light, with whitish clouds swirling around it. Every time I see it I weep with love, as if it is a picture of Grandma's house. One day when I am putting Rebecca down for her nap, she suddenly focuses on my eye. Something inside me cringes, gets ready to try to protect myself. All children are cruel about physical differences, I know from experience, and that they don't always mean to be is another matter. I assume Rebecca will be the same.

But no-o-o-o. She studies my face intently as we stand, her inside and me outside her crib. She even holds my face maternally between her dimpled little hands. Then, looking every bit as serious and lawyerlike as her father, she says, as if it may just possibly have slipped my attention: "Mommy, there's a *world* in your eye." (As in, "Don't be alarmed, or do anything crazy.") And then, gently, but with great interest: "Mommy, where did you *get* that world in your eye?"

For the most part, the pain left then. (So what, if my brothers grew up to buy even more powerful pellet guns for their sons and to carry real guns themselves. So what, if a young "Morehouse man" once nearly fell off the steps of Trevor Arnett Library because he thought my eyes were blue.) Crying and laughing I ran to the bathroom, while Rebecca mumbled and sang herself off to sleep. Yes indeed, I realized, looking into the mirror. There *was* a world in my eye. And I saw that it was possible to love it: that in fact, for all it had taught me of shame and anger and inner vision, I *did* love it. Even to see it drifting out of orbit in boredom, or rolling up out of fatigue, not to mention floating back at attention in excitement (bearing witness, a friend has called it), deeply suitable to my personality, and even characteristic of me.

That night I dream I am dancing to Stevie Wonder's song "Always" (the name of the song is really "As," but I hear it as "Always"). As I dance, whirling and joyous, happier than I've ever been in my life, another bright-faced dancer joins me. We dance and kiss each other and hold each other through the night. The other dancer has obviously come through all right, as I have done. She is beautiful, whole and free. And she is also me.

Suggestions for Discussion

1. How does the author use detail to portray herself at various ages? To portray her mother?
2. What changes in her personality and view of herself take place in the several age periods that Walker describes?
3. The line "you did not change" recurs. What is its relation to the narrative in the several scenes?
4. What is the significance of the repeated reference to raising her head at various stages of the author's development?
5. How does Walker equate prayer with poetry?
6. How does her daughter's comment on her eye affect her attitude?
7. What does the title signify?

Suggestions for Writing

1. Write a series of short vignettes illustrating how you viewed yourself and/or others viewed you at various stages of your development.
2. Describe the ways in which a traumatic episode in your childhood or that of a person close to you has affected your attitudes or behavior.

ZORA NEALE HURSTON

How It Feels to Be Colored Me

Zora Neale Hurston (1893 or 1903–1960) is now recognized as one of the truly innovative voices in twentieth-century American letters. Born in Florida, she began college while working as a domestic. She was ultimately able to go on to Howard University, a leading center of black scholarship, and to Barnard College where she earned her B.A., and finally to Columbia University where she did graduate work. She was a student of the anthropologist, Franz Boas, who urged her to study Southern Black folklore. In the twenties and thirties she was a major figure in the Harlem Renaissance, but she ultimately died unknown and in poverty. During her career she was a journalist, professor, librarian, folklorist, but above all she was a writer. Five of her books were published during her lifetime, the most prominent being *Mules and Men* (1935), for which she won the Anisfield-Wolf Award, *Their Eyes Were Watching God* (1937), and *Dust Track on a Road* (1942). Since 1985, a number of collections of her work have been published, the most recent being *Mule Bone: A Comedy of Negro Life* (1991), *Collected Essays, Volumes 1 and 2, Complete Short Stories, Complete Plays,* and *Folklore, Memories, and Other Writings* (1995), and *Sweat* (1996). Here we see Hurston, despite her difficult experiences, at her most up-beat and affirmative, refusing the role of victim.

I am colored but I offer nothing in the way of extenuating circumstances except the fact that I am the only Negro in the United States whose grandfather on the mother's side was *not* an Indian chief.

I remember the very day that I became colored. Up to my thirteenth year I lived in the little Negro town of Eatonville, Florida. It is exclusively a colored town. The only white people I knew passed through the town going to or coming from Orlando. The native whites rode dusty horses, the Northern tourists chugged down the sandy village road in automobiles. The town knew the Southerners and never stopped cane chewing when they passed. But the Northerners were something else again. They were peered at cautiously from behind curtains by the timid. The more venturesome would come out on the porch to watch them go past and got just as much pleasure out of the tourists as the tourists got out of the village.

The front porch might seem a daring place for the rest of the town, but it was a gallery seat to me. My favorite place was atop the gate-post. Proscenium box for a born first-nighter. Not only did I enjoy the show, but I didn't mind the actors knowing that I liked it. I usually spoke to them in passing. I'd wave at them and when they returned my salute, I would say something like this: "Howdy-do-well-I-thank-you-where-you-goin'?" Usually the automobile or the horse paused at this, and after a queer exchange of compliments, I would probably "go a piece of the way" with them, as we say in farthest Florida. If one of my family happened to come to the front in time to see me, of course negotiations would be rudely broken off. But even so, it is clear that I was the first "welcome-to-our-state" Floridian, and I hope the Miami Chamber of Commerce will please take notice.

During this period, white people differed from colored to me only in that they rode through town and never lived there. They liked to hear me "speak pieces" and sing and wanted to see me dance the parse-me-la, and gave me generously of their small silver for doing these things, which seemed strange to me for I wanted to do them so much that I needed bribing to stop. Only they didn't know it. The colored people gave no dimes. They deplored any joyful tendencies in me, but I was their Zora nevertheless. I belonged to them, to the nearby hotels, to the county—everybody's Zora.

But changes came in the family when I was thirteen, and I was sent to school in Jacksonville. I left Eatonville, the town of the oleanders, as Zora. When I disembarked from the river-boat at Jacksonville, she was no more. It seemed that I had suffered a sea change. I was not Zora of Orange County any more, I was now a little colored girl. I found it out in certain ways. In my heart as well as in the mirror, I became a fast brown—warranted not to rub nor run.

But I am not tragically colored. There is no great sorrow dammed up in my soul, nor lurking behind my eyes. I do not mind at all. I do not belong to the sobbing school of Negrohood who hold that nature somehow has given them a lowdown dirty deal and whose feelings are all hurt about it. Even in the helter-skelter skirmish that is my life, I have seen that the world is to the strong regardless of a little pigmentation more or less. No, I do not weep at the world—I am too busy sharpening my oyster knife.

Someone is always at my elbow reminding me that I am the granddaughter of slaves. It fails to register depression with me. Slavery is sixty years in the past. The operation was successful and the patient is doing well, thank you. The terrible struggle that made me an American out of a potential slave said "On the line!" The Reconstruction said "Get set!"; and the generation before said "Go!" I am off to a flying start and I must not halt in the stretch to look behind and weep. Slavery is the price I paid for civilization, and the choice was not with me. It is a bully adventure and worth all that I have paid through my ancestors for it. No one on earth ever had a greater chance for glory. The world to be won and nothing to be lost. It is thrilling to think—to know that for any act of mine, I shall get twice as much praise or twice as much blame. It is quite exciting to hold the center of the national stage, with the spectators not knowing whether to laugh or to weep.

The position of my white neighbor is much more difficult. No brown specter pulls up a chair beside me when I sit down to eat. No dark ghost thrusts its leg against mine in bed. The game of keeping what one has is never so exciting as the game of getting.

I do not always feel colored. Even now I often achieve the unconscious Zora of Eatonville before the Hegira. I feel most colored when I am thrown against a sharp white background.

For instance at Barnard. "Beside the waters of the Hudson" I feel my race. Among the thousand white persons, I am a dark rock surged upon, overswept by a creamy sea. I am surged upon and overswept, but through it all, I remain myself. When covered by the waters, I am; and the ebb but reveals me again.

Sometimes it is the other way around. A white person is set down in our midst, but the contrast is just as sharp for me. For instance, when I sit in the drafty basement that is The New World Cabaret with a white person, my color comes. We enter chatting about any little nothing that we have in common and are seated by the jazz waiters. In the abrupt way that jazz orchestras have, this one plunges into a number. It loses no time in circumlocutions, but gets right down to business. It constricts the thorax and splits the heart with its tempo and narcotic harmonies. This orchestra grows rambunctious, rears on its hind legs and attacks the tonal veil with primitive fury, rending it, clawing it until it breaks through to the jungle beyond. I follow those heathen—follow them exultingly. I dance wildly inside myself; I yell within, I whoop; I shake my assegai above my head, I hurl it true to the mark *yeeeeooww!* I am in the jungle and living in the jungle way. My face is painted red and yellow and my body is painted blue. My pulse is throbbing like a war drum. I want to slaughter something—give pain, give death to what, I do not know. But the piece ends. The men of the orchestra wipe their lips and rest their fingers. I creep back slowly to the veneer we call civilization with the last tone and find the white friend sitting motionless in his seat, smoking calmly.

"Good music they have here," he remarks, drumming the table with his fingertips.

Music! The great blobs of purple and red emotion have not touched him. He has only heard what I felt. He is far away and I see him but dimly across the ocean and the continent that have fallen between us. He is so pale with his whiteness then and I am *so* colored.

At certain times I have no race, I am *me*. When I set my hat at a certain angle and saunter down Seventh Avenue, Harlem City, feeling as snooty as the lions in front of the Forty-Second Street Library, for instance. So far as my feelings are concerned, Peggy Hopkins Joyce on the Boule Mich with her gorgeous raiment, stately carriage, knees knocking together in a most aristocratic manner, has nothing on me. The cosmic Zora emerges. I belong to no race nor time. I am the eternal feminine with its string of beads.

I have no separate feeling about being an American citizen and colored. I am merely a fragment of the Great Soul that surges within the boundaries. My country, right or wrong.

Sometimes, I feel discriminated against, but it does not make me angry. It merely astonishes me. How *can* any deny themselves the pleasure of my company! It's beyond me.

But in the main, I feel like a brown bag of miscellany propped against a wall. Against a wall in company with other bags, white, red and yellow. Pour out the contents, and there is discovered a jumble of small things priceless and worthless. A first-water diamond, an empty spool, bits of broken glass, lengths of string, a key to a door long since crumbled away, a rusty knifeblade, old shoes saved for a road that never was and never will be, a nail bent under the weight of things too heavy for any nail, a dried flower or two, still a little fragrant. In your hand is the brown bag. On the ground before you is the jumble it held—so much like the jumble in the bags, could they be emptied, that all might be dumped in a single heap and the bags refilled without altering the content of any greatly. A bit of colored glass more or less would not matter. Perhaps that is how the Great Stuffer of Bags filled them in the first place—who knows?

Suggestions for Discussion

1. When does Hurston cease to be Zora of Orange County, and become a little colored girl?
2. What does the author mean when she says, "Slavery is the price I paid for civilization"? Do you agree with her?

3. Sometimes Zora feels "cosmic," like "a fragment of the Great Soul," "the eternal feminine..." How do these feelings relate to how she understands race?

Suggestions for Writing

1. Hurston describes herself as a "brown bag of miscellany propped against a wall." If someone were to empty the bag that is *you,* what would they find?
2. When did you become aware of how you appeared to the outside world? Did you change because of this? Describe.

JOHN PRESTON

Medfield, Massachusetts

John Preston (1945–1994), who wrote under a variety of pseudonyms, was born in Framingham, Massachusetts, and educated at Lake Forest College. An activist in the Gay Rights movement, he was a social worker, editor of *Advocate,* and from 1976 a full-time writer. *Franny, the Queen of Provincetown* was named Gay Novel of the Year by the *Frontpage,* and a stage adaptation won the Jane Chambers Gay Playwriting Award, both in 1984. His most recent books include *Hometowns* (1991) and *A Member of the Family* (1992). In the piece that follows the author tries to reconcile the sense of identity that his community offers him with the emergence of his identity as a gay man.

Medfield is one of the ancient villages of New England. It was established as a European community in 1649, when pioneers from Dedham moved inland to the location near the headwaters of the Charles River, about twenty-five miles southeast of Boston.

The land on which Medfield was settled had been purchased from Chicatabot, the Sachem of the Neponset nation. He was one of those natives who saw the arrival of the English as, at worst, a neutral event. But it didn't take long for the indigenous people to see that the spread of the Puritan and Pilgrim colonies was threatening their very survival. In 1674, Metacomet, the great leader known to the English as King Philip, organized an alliance of the native nations and led them to battle against the intruders.

The beginning of King Philip's War, as it was called, was fought in the Connecticut Valley. The few communities there were attacked and many of the settlers killed. Within a year Metacomet's warriors were pushing closer to Boston. Medfield was raided on February 19, 1675. Seventeen people were killed and half the buildings were destroyed.

Metacomet was defeated later that winter in a climactic battle in nearby Rhode Island. His campaign was the last serious chance the natives had of sending the English away. Smallpox and other epidemics finished the destruction of the aboriginal nations over the next decades. Medfield's new proprietors, my ancestors, quietly prospered.

When the American Revolution broke out a century later, Medfield was firmly on the side of the rebels. The town meeting communicated regularly with the colonial legislature and the radical Committees of Correspondence, encouraging a strong stance against unfair taxation. When it was apparent that hostilities would break out, the citizens organized a contingent of Minutemen who responded to the call to arms in Concord and Lexington (though they arrived too late to join in the battles).

The Revolution was the last striking event in Medfield's history. Once independence was achieved, Medfield simply became a quintessential Yankee town, the place where I grew up, complete with a phalanx of the white clapboard churches everyone identifies with New England, larded through with extravagant forest parks and with a wealth of substantial wood-frame houses.

When I was born, in 1945, Medfield had fewer than three thousand inhabitants. It was assumed that all of us knew one another. It wasn't just that the population was so small, it was also remarkably stable. Our families had all lived in the same place for so long that it all felt like an extended family. (And there were, in fact, many cousins in town. Not just first cousins, but second and third cousins. We all knew our interlocking heritage at an early age.) The names of all the participants in the colonial and revolutionary events were the same as many of my cousins and classmates and the people in the church my family attended—Harding, Morse, Adams, Lovell, Bullard, Wheelock, and Allen.

We lived our history. When the other kids and I played cowboys and Indians, we did it on the same battlegrounds where our ancestors defeated King Philip. When we studied American history, our teachers taught us the names of the men from Medfield who had fought in the Revolution.

We weren't those for whom this country's history was irrelevant. We weren't left out of the narrative of the white man's ascension. We were, in fact, those for whom American history was written. We were of British ancestry—if not English, then Scots or Irish. We read about people with names that sounded like our own. "Foreign" was, for us, someone of Italian descent. "Alien" was the Roman Catholic church.

As I grew older and came into contact with people from around the state, I discovered a different social criteria. People started to talk about ancestors who'd come from England on the *Mayflower.* I remember going to my mother and asking her if ours had. She looked at me strangely and replied, "Well, whenever any family's lived in a town like ours as long as we have, somebody married somebody who married somebody whose family came over on the *Mayflower.* But, why would you even care?" she asked.

Indeed. Why would anyone look for more than coming from Medfield? There is a story about Yankee insularity that's told in many different forms. A reporter goes up to a lady who's sitting on a bench in a village common and asks her, "If you had the chance to travel to anywhere in the world, where would you go?" The lady looks around her hometown, mystified, and responds, "But why would I go anywhere? I'm already here!" The first times I heard that story, I didn't understand it was a joke. I thought the woman was only speaking the obvious. It's the way we felt about Medfield.

Medfield was a very distinct reality to me. There was even a leftover colonial custom that gave the town a concrete definition. By 1692 the settlements around Boston were growing quickly and their perimeters were hazy because of conflicting land grants and native treaties. The executive power of each town was vested in the Board of Selectmen, three citizens elected by the town meeting to run things between the annual assemblies of the town's voters. The Great and General Court, the romantic name the Commonwealth of Massachusetts still uses for the state legislature, decreed that every five years the selectmen of each town would have to "perambulate the bounds" with the selectmen of its neighbors. The two sets of townspeople had to agree on the markers that separated them.

The requirement for the perambulation stayed on the books until 1973 and even then the rescinding law said, "However, it is enjoyable to keep the old tradition of meeting with the selectmen of adjoining towns for this purpose. It also affords an opportunity to agree to replacement of missing or broken bounds and to discuss subjects of mutual interest." (The Medfield Historical Commission recently reported, "It is also rumored that modern-time selectmen partook of a drink or two at each boundary marker.")

When I was young, I used to walk the bounds of Medfield with the selectmen. The grown-ups' drinking habits weren't important to me, but I was in love with the stones we found with their antiquated signs and the aged oak and maple trees that appeared on the town records as markers between Medfield and Dover, Walpole, Norfolk, and other neighbors.

The living history of the monuments wasn't all I got from these walks. The perambulations gave a firm evidence to just what was my hometown. I was being told that everything on this side of the boundaries was Medfield. Everything on this side of the border was mine.

It's hard to overstate the sense of entitlement that a New England boyhood gave me and my friends. I remember the first time I was taken to Boston. The city seemed large and frightening, at least it did until my mother pointed to the large body of water between Boston and Cambridge and explained that it was the Charles, the same river that separated Medfield from Millis. I realized I couldn't be frightened of someplace that was built on the banks of *my* river.

Even if America wasn't all like Medfield, it certainly acted as though it wanted to be. The new suburban developments that were all the rage in the sixties mimicked the architecture of the buildings that had been standing around our village for centuries. Advertisements for the good life all seemed to take place in our town. Medfield had a wide floodplain to the west, hills to the south, forests to the north. It was the landscape surrounding the "nice people" we saw in magazines and on television. Our lawns were well kept and our trees carefully pruned. A snowstorm was a community event; my mother would make hot chocolate and fresh doughnuts (from scratch) for all the neighborhood children and we'd build snowmen exactly like those pictured on the pages of *The Saturday Evening Post.*

Of course there were blemishes, some of them so well hidden that only those of us inside could see them. There were broken homes and drunken parents. There was economic upheaval as New England's industry migrated to the South after World War II. There were class divisions that were especially apparent to me, since my father's family—he was from Boston's industrial suburbs—was pure working class. We couldn't have been much better off than my aunts and uncles and cousins living in Boston's urban blight, but poverty wasn't as apparent when it was surrounded by beauty like Medfield's. Somerville didn't have Rocky Narrows State Park; Everett didn't have Rocky Woods State Reservation. And, besides, not having a great deal of money had no impact on our status in town. My mother's pedigree made my father's background irrelevant. Her children were of Medfield, and no one ever questioned that.

In fact, we were constantly reminded that our roots were right there on the banks of the Charles. My sisters and brothers and I were continually assaulted by older citizens who would stop us on the street and pinch our cheeks, "Oh, yes, I can see that you must be one of Raymond Blood's family. It's those eyes. Just like his!" My maternal grandfather had died fifteen years before I was born, but townspeople kept on seeing his lineage in my face. He'd been something of a hero in the town, a World War I veteran who'd prospected for gold in Nevada before he'd returned to take over the family's business, selling feed and grain to the small farmers in the region. To be Raymond Blood's grandson was no small matter. The pinches may have been annoying, but the rest of the message was clear: You are from this place.

Medfield was a town where a boy knew what it meant to belong. It was an environment out of which almost any achievement seemed possible. As we grew older, my friends and I picked and chose from the best colleges, dreamed the most extravagant futures, saw ourselves in any situation we could imagine. Our aspirations were the highest possible and they didn't come out of pressure from striving families or a need to escape a stifling atmosphere. We envisioned ourselves however we chose because we felt it was ours, all of it, the entire American Dream. It was so much ours, we took it so much for granted, that we never even questioned it. It was self-evident.

There must have been many ways I was different from the other kids early on. I'm vaguely aware of being too smart, of not being physical enough, of hating sports. I got grief for all those things in the way any group of peers can deliver it, especially in adolescence. I certainly *felt* different. I certainly *knew* I was different. But the difference didn't define itself right away.

As we became teenagers, things happened that actually eased the sense of deviation. There were forces at work that made us more aware of the things that bound us together and made what might have separated us seem less important. Route 128 had been built in a long arc around Boston's suburbs in the fifties. Originally called a highway to nowhere, it was one of the first freeways whose purpose was to create a flow of traffic around centers of population, not between them. One-twenty-eight quickly got another name: "America's Highway of Technology." New companies with names like Raytheon and Northrop and Digital built enormous high-tech plants along 128. They moved the center of the region's economy out of Boston, toward places like Medfield. The town's population doubled, and then doubled again.

By the time we were in high school, we were faced with new classmates with strange accents and different standards. My friends had earned their extra spending money by trapping beavers and muskrats along the tributaries to the Charles and selling their pelts. These new kids didn't know about traps and they didn't think it was important that their new homes in the spreading developments were ruining the animals' habitat. We were used to having fried clams as a special treat at the local drive-up restaurant; they were only angry that there weren't any fast-food chains. They had strange and exotic—and sexual—dances we hadn't even heard of. We stood in the high school auditorium and wondered how they could act that way in public. When they hiked up on Noon Hill, they didn't know that it had been the place from which King Philip had watched Medfield burn. They thought we were backward and quaint that we even cared about such things.

The local kids closed ranks. I'm sure, as I look back now, that the newcomers must have been puzzled when Mike, the captain of every team sport possible, spent time with me, the class brain. They must have wondered just as much why I would pass afternoons with Philip, who didn't even go to Medfield High School but commuted to Norfolk County Agricultural School, the looked-down-upon "aggie" school in Walpole. And why would my (third) cousin Peter, probably the most handsome youth in town, walk home with me so often?

We defied the new standards; we held to our own. We had all been in the Cub Scouts pack that my mother had founded. We had all sat in the same kindergarten. We had all been a part of Medfield. I was one of the group, and they wouldn't deny me.

When I return to my hometown now, I see that, in most ways, we won. People like Mike and Philip and Peter—and my mother and her friends—simply sat it all out. They waited for the newcomers to leave and then for a new wave of them to come in, the waves of migrating suburbanites who can't tell the difference between Medfield and Northfield, Illinois, or Southfield, Michigan, they've changed addresses so often. My family and friends simply stayed, they had never intended to move. Now, my mother is the town clerk, Mike runs the reunions of our high school class, and last I heard Philip took over his father's job as groundsman for the state hospital.

But I had begun to leave while I was still in high school. I had heard rumors about a different life and a different world. Its gateway, my books and magazines told me, was a bus station in a city. I began to travel to Boston more often, supposedly to visit my urban cousins, but I seldom got as far as Somerville. I would stay, instead, in the Greyhound terminal and wait for one of a series of men to come and initiate me. They were traveling salesmen from Hartford, professors from MIT, students from Northeastern.

Eventually I'd travel further to meet them. I took secret trips to New York when I was supposed to be skiing in New Hampshire. I hitchhiked to Provincetown, the fabulous center of the new world into which I was moving. And, with every move, I left more of Medfield behind.

There was really no way I could see to combine my new life and my old. There was a man in Medfield who was whispered about. He belonged to our church and was the target for endless sympathy because he kept entering and leaving the state hospital. And there were two women down the street, nurses, who were so masculine that it was impossible to ignore their deviance from the other norms of the town. But they offered me nothing. I wasn't like the nurses and I never, ever wanted to be like the man who was so continually institutionalized.

In some ways I moved into my new life with great joy. There was real excitement in it, certainly there was great passion. My explorations took me to places as far away as a New England boy could ever imagine. When it came time to pick my college, I chose one in Illinois, the far horizon of my family's worldview, as far away as they could ever conceive of me going.

I also experienced rage over what was happening to me. I was being taken away from Medfield and everything it stood for. I was the one who should have gotten a law degree and come home to settle into comfortable Charles River Valley politics—perhaps with a seat in the Great and General Court? I should have lived in one of those honestly colonial houses on Pleasant Street. I should have walked through the meadows and the hills as long as I wanted, greeted by people I knew, all of us blanketed in our sense of continuity. History had belonged to us. But I was no longer one of them. I had become too different.

There had become a label for me that was even more powerful than the label of being from Medfield, something I don't think I could have ever envisioned being true.

I remember trying to find some way to come back to Medfield. I remember discovering a hairdresser in a Boston bar who had just opened a shop in town. I wanted desperately to fall in love with him and move back and find some way to be of Medfield again. Another time I did fall in love with a truck driver from Providence, a man of as much overstated masculinity as the nurses down the street. Maybe he and I could create a balance that the town could accept. He drank whiskey with my father, fixed cars with our neighbors, and knew all about the Red Sox. Maybe, between the two of us, we had enough that we could stay in Medfield. It didn't work. And, in those days, no one ever thought it would work in any hometown.

I stopped trying to fit my life into Medfield. I turned my back on it. I belonged to a new world now, one that spun around New York, Chicago, San Francisco, Provincetown. I was danced and bedded away from home, into the arms of someplace no one had ever even told me about.

Suggestions for Discussion

1. Why does Preston spend so much time describing the history of Medfield, Massachusetts?
2. What does the author mean when he says, "There had become a label for me that was even more powerful than the label of being from Medfield, something I don't think I could have ever envisioned being true"?
3. Preston, in the end, turns his back on Medfield. "History had belonged to us. But I was no longer one of them. I had become too different." Would he have different options now? Explain.

Suggestions for Writing

1. Describe a situation where, in order to be true to yourself, you had to give up something that mattered to you very much.
2. Preston's piece is in part about continuity, Medfield and its history, and change, his own discovery that he had to leave. What metaphors might represent the continuity and change in your life?

ESSAYS

JAMES BALDWIN

The Discovery of What It Means to Be an American

James Baldwin (1924–1987) was born in New York of Southern, deeply religious, and poor parents. At fourteen, he became a preacher in the Fireside Pentecostal Church in Harlem. His first novel, *Go Tell It on the Mountain* (1953), reflects his experience as a preacher and, together with *Another Country* (1962), a novel about sex and race, established his reputation as a writer. Since the publication of a lengthy essay, *The Fire Next Time* (1962), he has taken a place as an important spokesman for blacks. He has written significant autobiographical essays, and this essay from *Nobody Knows My Name* (1961) examines the ways in which his sojourn in Paris contributed to both his understanding of himself and of America.

"It is a complex fate to be an American," Henry James observed, and the principal discovery an American writer makes in Europe is just how complex this fate is. America's history, her aspirations, her peculiar triumphs, her even more peculiar defeats, and her position in the world—yesterday and today—are all so profoundly and stubbornly unique that the very word "America" remains a new, almost completely undefined and extremely controversial proper noun. No one in the world seems to know exactly what it describes, not even we motley millions who call ourselves Americans.

I left America because I doubted my ability to survive the fury of the color problem here. (Sometimes I still do.) I wanted to prevent myself from becoming *merely* a Negro; or, even, merely a Negro writer. I wanted to find in what way the *specialness* of my experience could be made to connect me with other people instead of dividing me from them. (I was as isolated from Negroes as I was from whites, which is what happens when a Negro begins, at bottom, to believe what white people say about him.)

In my necessity to find the terms on which my experience could be related to that of others, Negroes and whites, writers and non-writers, I proved, to my astonishment, to be as American as any Texas G.I. And I found my experience was shared by every American writer I knew in Paris. Like me, they had been divorced from their origins, and it turned out to make very little difference that the origins of white Americans were European and mine were African—they were no more at home in Europe than I was.

The fact that I was the son of a slave and they were the sons of free men meant less, by the time we confronted each other on European soil, than the fact that we were both searching for our separate identities. When we had found these, we seemed to be saying, why, then, we would no longer need to cling to the shame and bitterness which had divided us so long.

It became terribly clear in Europe, as it never had been here, that we knew more about each other than any European ever could. And it also became clear that, no matter where our fathers had been born, or what they had endured, the fact of Europe had formed us both was part of our identity and part of our inheritance.

I had been in Paris a couple of years before any of this became clear to me. When it did, I, like many a writer before me upon the discovery that his props have all been knocked out from under him, suffered a species of breakdown and was carried off to the mountains of Switzerland. There, in that absolutely alabaster landscape, armed with two Bessie Smith records and a typewriter, I began to try to re-create the life that I had first known as a child and from which I had spent so many years in flight.

It was Bessie Smith, through her tone and her cadence, who helped me to dig back to the way I myself must have spoken when I was a pickaninny, and to remember the things I had heard and seen and felt. I had buried them very deep. I had never listened to Bessie Smith in America (in the same way that, for years, I would not touch watermelon), but in Europe she helped to reconcile me to being a "nigger."

I do not think that I could have made this reconciliation here. Once I was able to accept my role—as distinguished, I must say, from my "place"—in the extraordinary drama which is America, I was released from the illusion that I hated America.

The story of what can happen to an American Negro writer in Europe simply illustrates, in some relief, what can happen to any American writer there. It is not meant, of course, to imply that it happens to them all, for Europe can be very crippling, too; and, anyway, a writer, when he has made his first breakthrough, has simply won a crucial skirmish in a dangerous, unending and unpredictable battle. Still, the breakthrough is important, and the point is that an American writer, in order to achieve it, very often has to leave this country.

The American writer, in Europe, is released, first of all, from the necessity of apologizing for himself. It is not until he *is* released from the habit of flexing his muscles and proving that he is just a "regular guy" that he realizes how crippling this habit has been. It is not necessary for him, there, to pretend to be something he is not, for the artist does not encounter in Europe the same suspicion he encounters here. Whatever the Europeans may actually think of artists, they have killed enough of them off by now to know that they are as real—and as persistent—as rain, snow, taxes or businessmen.

Of course, the reason for Europe's comparative clarity concerning the different functions of men in society is that European society has always been divided into classes in a way that American society never has been. A European writer considers himself to be part of an old and honorable tradition—of intellectual activity, of letters—and his choice of a vocation does not cause him any uneasy wonder as to whether or not it will cost him all his friends. But this tradition does not exist in America.

On the contrary, we have a very deep-seated distrust of real intellectual effort (probably because we suspect that it will destroy, as I hope it does, that myth of America to which we cling so desperately). An American writer fights his way to one of the lowest rungs on the American social ladder by means of pure bull-headedness and an indescribable series of odd jobs. He probably *has* been a "regular fellow" for much of his adult life, and it is not easy for him to step out of that lukewarm bath.

We must, however, consider a rather serious paradox: though American society is more mobile than Europe's, it is easier to cut across social and occupational lines there than it is here. This has something to do, I think, with the problem of status in American life. Where everyone has status, it is also perfectly possible, after all, that no one has. It seems inevitable, in any case, that a man may become uneasy as to just what his status is.

But Europeans have lived with the idea of status for a long time. A man can be as proud of being a good waiter as of being a good actor, and, in neither case, feel threatened. And this means that the actor and the waiter can have a freer and more genuinely friendly relationship in Europe than they are likely to have here. The waiter does not feel, with obscure resentment, that the actor has "made it," and the actor is not tormented by the fear that he may find himself, tomorrow, once again a waiter.

This lack of what may roughly be called social paranoia causes the American writer in Europe to feel—almost certainly for the first time in his life—that he can reach out to everyone, that he is accessible to everyone and open to everything. This is an extraordinary feeling. He feels, so to speak, his own weight, his own value.

It is as though he suddenly came out of a dark tunnel and found himself beneath the open sky. And, in fact, in Paris, I began to see the sky for what seemed to be the first time. It was borne in on me—and it did not make me feel melancholy—that this sky had been there before I was born and would be there when I was dead. And it was up to me, therefore, to make of my brief opportunity the most that could be made.

I was born in New York, but have lived only in pockets of it. In Paris, I lived in all parts of the city—on the Right Bank and the Left, among the bourgeoisie and among *les misérables,* and knew all kinds of people, from pimps and prostitutes in Pigalle to Egyptian bankers in Neuilly. This may sound extremely unprincipled or even obscurely immoral: I found it healthy. I love to talk to people, all kinds of people, and almost everyone, as I hope we still know, loves a man who loves to listen.

This perpetual dealing with people very different from myself caused a shattering in me of preconceptions I scarcely knew I held. The writer is meeting in Europe people who are not American, whose sense of reality is entirely different from his own. They may love or hate or admire or fear or envy this country—they see it, in any case, from another point of view, and this forces the writer to reconsider many things he had always taken for granted. This reassessment, which can be very painful, is also very valuable.

This freedom, like all freedom, has its dangers and its responsibilities. One day it begins to be borne in on the writer, and with great force, that he is living in Europe as an American. If he were living there as a European, he would be living on a different and far less attractive continent.

This crucial day may be the day on which an Algerian taxi-driver tells him how it feels to be an Algerian in Paris. It may be the day on which he passes a café terrace and catches a glimpse of the tense, intelligent and troubled face of Albert Camus. Or it may be the day on which someone asks him to explain Little Rock and he begins to feel that it would be simpler—and, corny as the words may sound, more honorable—to *go* to Little Rock than sit in Europe, on an American passport, trying to explain it.

This is a personal day, a terrible day, the day to which his entire sojourn has been tending. It is the day he realizes that there are no untroubled countries in this fearfully troubled world; that if he has been preparing himself for anything in Europe, he has been preparing himself—for America. In short, the freedom that the American writer finds in Europe brings him, full circle, back to himself, with the responsibility for his development where it always was: in his own hands.

Even the most incorrigible maverick has to be born somewhere. He may leave the group that produced him—he may be forced to—but nothing will efface his origins, the marks of which he carries with him everywhere. I think it is important to know this and even find it a matter for rejoicing, as the strongest people do, regardless of their station. On this acceptance, literally, the life of a writer depends.

The charge has often been made against American writers that they do not describe society, and have no interest in it. Of course, what the American writer is describing is his own situation. But what is *Anna Karenina* describing if not the tragic fate of the isolated individual, at odds with her time and place?

The real difference is that Tolstoy was describing an old and dense society in which everything seemed—to the people in it, though not to Tolstoy—to be fixed forever. And the book is a masterpiece because Tolstoy was able to fathom, and make us see, the hidden laws which really governed this society and made Anna's doom inevitable.

American writers do not have a fixed society to describe. The only society they know is one in which nothing is fixed and in which the individual must fight for his identity. This is a rich confusion, indeed, and it creates for the American writer unprecedented opportunities.

That the tensions of American life, as well as the possibilities, are tremendous is certainly not even a question. But these are dealt with in contemporary literature mainly compulsively; that is, the book is more likely to be a symptom of our tension than an examination of it. The time has come, God knows, for us to examine ourselves, but we can only do this if we are willing to free ourselves of the myth of America and try to find out what is really happening here.

Every society is really governed by hidden laws, by unspoken but profound assumptions on the part of the people, and ours is no exception. It is up to the American writer to find out what these laws and assumptions are. In a society much given to smashing taboos without thereby managing to be liberated from them, it will be no easy matter.

It is no wonder, in the meantime, that the American writer keeps running off to Europe. He needs sustenance for his journey and the best models he can find. Europe has what we do not have yet, a sense of the mysterious and inexorable limits of life, a sense, in a word, of tragedy. And we have what they sorely need: a new sense of life's possibilities.

In this endeavor to wed the vision of the Old World with that of the New, it is the writer, not the statesman, who is our strongest arm. Though we do not wholly believe it yet, the interior life is a real life, and the intangible dreams of people have a tangible effect on the world.

Suggestions for Discussion

1. How does Baldwin's discovery of what it means to be an American relate to his search for identity?
2. How did his Paris sojourn contribute to his sense of self?
3. In what ways did his life in Paris enable him to "find out in what way the *specialness* of my experience could be made to connect me with other people instead of dividing me from them"?

4. How did the Bessie Smith records contribute to Baldwin's search?
5. Compare the attitudes toward writers and toward status of Americans and Europeans.
6. How do the allusions to the Algerian taxi driver, Camus, and the questioner regarding Little Rock relate to Baldwin's understanding of himself and of America?
7. What does the author regard as the responsibility of the writer?
8. What does the author mean when he states that "the interior life is a real life"?

Suggestions for Writing

1. Refer to the text and develop an answer to Question 3.
2. Baldwin believes that America has a "new sense of life's possibilities." What are some of these possibilities?
3. Shelley labeled poets "the potential legislators of the world." Baldwin states that it is the writer, not the statesman, who is our strongest arm in wedding "the vision of the Old World with that of the New." What is your view?

THEODORE ROETHKE

Some Self-Analysis

Theodore Roethke (1908–1963), American poet, taught during the last years of his life at the University of Washington. *The Waking: Poems, 1933–1953* was the winner of the Pulitzer Prize for Poetry in 1953. He received the Bollingen Award for Poetry in 1958. A collected volume, *Words for the Wind,* appeared in 1958, and *The Far Field* was published posthumously in 1964. In this statement, written when he was an undergraduate, Roethke recounts his hopes for the writing course he is taking, assesses his strengths and limitations as a writer, and expresses his faith in himself.

I expect this course to open my eyes to story material, to unleash my too dormant imagination, to develop that quality utterly lacking in my nature—a sense of form. I do not expect to acquire much technique. I expect to be able to seize upon the significant, reject the trivial. I hope to acquire a greater love for humanity in all its forms.

I have long wondered just what my strength was as a writer. I am often filled with tremendous enthusiasm for a subject, yet my writing about it will seem a sorry attempt. Above all, I possess a driving sincerity,—that prime virtue of any creative worker. I write only what I believe to be the absolute truth,—even if I must ruin the theme in so doing. In this respect I feel far superior to those glib people in my classes who often garner better grades than I do. They are so often pitiful frauds,—artificial—insincere. They have a line that works. They do not write from the depths of their hearts. Nothing of theirs was ever born of pain. Many an incoherent yet sincere piece of writing has outlived the polished product.

I write only about people and things that I know thoroughly. Perhaps I have become a mere reporter, not a writer. Yet I feel that this is all my present abilities permit. I will open my eyes in my youth and store this raw, living material. Age may bring the fire that molds experience into artistry.

I have a genuine love of nature. It is not the least bit affected, but an integral and powerful part of my life. I know that Cooper is a fraud—that he doesn't give a true sense of the sublimity of American scenery. I know that Muir and Thoreau and Burroughs speak the truth.

I can sense the moods of nature almost instinctively. Ever since I could walk, I have spent as much time as I could in the open. A perception of nature—no matter how delicate, how subtle, how evanescent,—remains with me forever.

I am influenced too much, perhaps, by natural objects. I seem bound by the very room I'm in. I've associated so long with prosaic people that I've dwarfed myself spiritually. When I get alone under an open sky where man isn't too evident—then I'm tremendously exalted and a thousand vivid ideas and sweet visions flood my consciousness.

I think that I possess story material in abundance. I have had an unusual upbringing. I was let alone, thank God! My mother insisted upon two things,—that I strive for perfection in whatever I did and that I always try to be a gentleman. I played with Italians, with Russians, Poles, and the "sissies" on Michigan Avenue. I was carefully watched, yet allowed to follow my own inclinations. I have seen a good deal of life that would never have been revealed to an older person. Up to the time I came to college then I had seen humanity in diverse forms. Now I'm cramped and unhappy. I don't feel that these idiotic adolescents are worth writing about. In the summer, I turn animal and work for a few weeks in a factory. Then I'm happy.

My literary achievements have been insignificant. At fourteen, I made a speech which was translated into twenty-six languages and used as Red Cross propaganda. When I was younger, it seemed that everything I wrote was eminently successful. I always won a prize when I entered an essay contest. In college, I've been able to get only one "A" in four rhetoric courses. I feel this keenly. If I can't write, what can I do? I wonder.

When I was a freshman, I told Carleton Wells that I knew I could write whether he thought so or not. On my next theme he wrote "You can Write!" How I have cherished that praise!

It is bad form to talk about grades, I know. If I don't get an "A" in this course, it wouldn't be because I haven't tried. I've made a slow start. I'm going to spend Christmas vacation writing. A "B" symbolizes defeat to me. I've been beaten too often.

I do wish that we were allowed to keep our stories until we felt that we had worked them into the best possible form.

I do not have the divine urge to write. There seems to be something surging within,—a profound undercurrent of emotion. Yet there is none of that fertility of creation which distinguishes the real writer.

Nevertheless, I have faith in myself. I'm either going to be a good writer or a poor fool.

Suggestions for Discussion

1. There are a number of paradoxical statements in Roethke's self-analysis, written when he was an undergraduate. Identify and explain.
2. Contrast Roethke's image of himself with what you imagine would be the view of his parents, his instructors, his contemporaries.

Suggestions for Writing

1. Write a statement of your expectations in a course in composition following the format of Roethke's statement. Include an analysis of your strengths and weaknesses, formative influences, sense of present accomplishment, and hopes for the future.
2. In the light of his self-analysis, comment on a selection of Roethke's published poems.

KIM CHERNIN

The Flesh and the Devil

Kim Chernin (b. 1940), a writer and an editor, was educated at the University of California at Berkeley and at Trinity College, Dublin. Through her ground-breaking work in the area of eating disorders, she has become a powerful voice in the feminist movement. In the 1980s she produced, to significant acclaim, six books: *The Obsession: Reflections on the Tyranny of Slenderness* (1981), *In My Mother's House* (1983), *The Hungry Self* (1985), *The Flame Bearers* (1986), *Reinventing Eve* (1987), and *Sex and Other Sacred Games* (1989). Most recently she has written *A Different Kind of Listening* (1994), *Crossing the Border: An Erotic Journey* (1995), and *My Father's Garden: A Daughter's Search for a Spiritual Life* (1996). In this selection she relates American women's preoccupation with their bodies not to narcissism, but to self-rejection.

> *We know that every woman wants to be thin. Our images of womanhood are almost synonymous with thinness.*
>
> —Susie Orbach

> *. . . I must now be able to look at my ideal, this ideal of being thin, of being without a body, and to realize: "it is a fiction."*
>
> —Ellen West

> *When the body is hiding the complex, it then becomes our most immediate access to the problem.*
>
> —Marian Woodman

The locker room of the tennis club. Several exercise benches, two old-fashioned hair dryers, a mechanical bicycle, a treadmill, a reducing machine, a mirror, and a scale.

A tall woman enters, removes her towel; she throws it across a bench, faces herself squarely in the mirror, climbs on the scale, looks down.

A silence.

"I knew it," she mutters, turning to me. "I knew it."

And I think, before I answer, just how much I admire her, for this courage beyond my own, this daring to weigh herself daily in this way. And

I sympathize. I know what she must be feeling. Not quite candidly, I say: "Up or down?" I am hoping to suggest that there might be people and cultures where gaining weight might not be considered a disaster. Places where women, stepping on scales, might be horrified to notice that they had reduced themselves. A mythical, almost unimaginable land.

"Two pounds," she says, ignoring my hint. "Two pounds." And then she turns, grabs the towel and swings out at her image in the mirror, smashing it violently, the towel spattering water over the glass. "Fat pig," she shouts at her image in the glass. "You fat, fat pig...."

Later, I go to talk with this woman. Her name is Rachel and she becomes, as my work progresses, one of the choral voices that shape its vision.

Two girls come into the exercise room. They are perhaps ten or eleven years old, at that elongated stage when the skeletal structure seems to be winning its war against flesh. And these two are particularly skinny. They sit beneath the hair dryers for a moment, kicking their legs on the faded green upholstery; they run a few steps on the eternal treadmill, they wrap the rubber belt of the reducing machine around themselves and jiggle for a moment before it falls off. And then they go to the scale.

The taller one steps up, glances at herself in the mirror, looks down at the scale. She sighs, shaking her head. I see at once that this girl is imitating someone. The sigh, the headshake are theatrical, beyond her years. And so, too, is the little drama enacting itself in front of me. The other girl leans forward, eager to see for herself the troubling message imprinted upon the scale. But the older girl throws her hand over the secret. It is not to be revealed. And now the younger one, accepting this, steps up to confront the ultimate judgment. "Oh God," she says, this growing girl. "Oh God," with only a shade of imitation in her voice: "Would you believe it? I've gained five pounds."

These girls, too, become a part of my work. They enter, they perform their little scene again and again; it extends beyond them and in it I am finally able to behold something that would have remained hidden—for it does not express itself directly, although we feel its pressure almost every day of our lives. Something, unnamed as yet, struggling against our emergence into femininity. This is my first glimpse of it, out there. And the vision ripens.

I return to the sauna. Two women I have seen regularly at the club are sitting on the bench above me. One of them is very beautiful, the sort of woman Renoir would have admired. The other, who is probably in her late sixties, looks, in the twilight of this sweltering room, very much an adolescent. I have noticed her before, with her tan face, her white hair, her fashionable clothes, her slender hips and jaunty walk. But the effect has not been soothing. A woman of advancing age who looks like a boy.

"I've heard about that illness, anorexia nervosa," the plump one is saying, "and I keep looking around for someone who has it. I want to go sit next to her. I think to myself, maybe I'll catch it...."

"Well," the other woman says to her, "I've felt the same way myself. One of my cousins used to throw food under the table when no one was looking. Finally, she got so thin they had to take her to the hospital....I always admired her."

What am I to understand from these stories? The woman in the locker room who swings out at her image in the mirror, the little girls who are afraid of the coming of adolescence to their bodies, the woman who admires the slenderness of the anorexic girl. Is it possible to miss the dislike these women feel for their bodies?

And yet, an instant's reflection tells us that this dislike for the body is not a biological fact of our condition as women—we do not come upon it by nature, we are not born to it, it does not arise for us because of anything predetermined in our sex. We know that once we loved the body, delighting in it the way children will, reaching out to touch our toes and count over our fingers, repeating the game endlessly as we come to knowledge of this body in which we will live out our lives. No part of the body exempt from our curiosity, nothing yet forbidden, we know an equal fascination with the feces we eliminate from ourselves, as with the ear we discover one day and the knees that have become bruised and scraped with falling and that warm, moist place between the legs from which feelings of indescribable bliss arise.

From that state to the condition of the woman in the locker room is a journey from innocence to despair, from the infant's naive pleasure in the body, to the woman's anguished confrontation with herself. In this journey we can read our struggle with natural existence—the loss of the body as a source of pleasure. But the most striking thing about this alienation from the body is the fact that we take it for granted. Few of us ask to be redeemed from this struggle against the flesh by overcoming our antagonism toward the body. We do not rush about looking for someone who can tell us how to enjoy the fact that our appetite is large, or how we might delight in the curves and fullness of our own natural shape. We hope instead to be able to reduce the body, to limit the urges and desires it feels, to remove the body from nature. Indeed, the suffering we experience through our obsession with the body arises precisely from the hopeless and impossible nature of this goal.

Cheryl Prewitt, the 1980 winner of the Miss America contest, is a twenty-two-year-old woman, "slender, bright-eyed, and attractive." If there were a single woman alive in America today who might feel comfortable about the size and shape of her body, surely we would expect her to be Ms. Prewitt? And yet, in order to make her body suitable for the swimsuit event of the beauty contest she has just won, Cheryl Prewitt "put herself through a grueling regimen, jogging long distances down back-country roads, pedaling for hours on her stationary bicycle." The bicycle is still kept in the living room of her parents' house so that she can take part in conversation while she works out. This body she has created, after an arduous struggle against nature, in conformity with her culture's ideal standard for a woman, cannot now be left to its own desires. It must be perpetually shaped, monitored, and watched. If you were to visit her at her home in Ackerman, Mississippi, you might well find her riding her stationary bicycle in her parents' living room, "working off the calories from a large slice of homemade coconut cake she has just had for a snack."

And so we imagine a woman who will never be Miss America, a next-door neighbor, a woman down the street, waking in the morning and setting out for her regular routine of exercise. The eagerness with which she jumps up at six o'clock and races for her jogging shoes and embarks upon the cold and arduous toiling up the hill road that runs past her house. And yes, she feels certain that her zeal to take off another pound, tighten another inch of softening flesh, places her in the school of those ancient wise men who formulated that vision of harmony between mind and body. "A healthy mind in a healthy body," she repeats to herself and imagines that it is love of the body which inspires her this early morning. But now she lets her mind wander and encounter her obsession. First it had been those hips, and she could feel them jogging along there with their own rhythm as she jogged. It was they that had needed reducing. Then, when the hips came down it was the thighs, hidden when she was clothed but revealing themselves every time she went to the sauna, and threatening great suffering now that summer drew near. Later, it was the flesh under the arms—this proved singularly resistant to tautness even after the rest of the body had become gaunt. And finally it was the ankles. But then, was there no end to it? What had begun as a vision of harmony between mind and body, a sense of well-being, physical fitness, and glowing health, had become now demonic, driving her always to further exploits, running farther, denying herself more food, losing more weight, always goaded on by the idea that the body's perfection lay just beyond her present achievement. And then, when she began to observe this driven quality in herself, she also began to notice what she had been thinking about her body. For she would write down in her notebook, without being aware of the violence in what she wrote: "I don't care how long it takes. One day I'm going to get my body to obey me. I'm going to make it lean and tight and hard. I'll succeed in this, even if it kills me."

But what a vicious attitude this is, she realizes one day, toward a body she professes to love. Was it love or hatred of the flesh that inspired her now to awaken even before it was light, and to go out on the coldest morning, running with bare arms and bare legs, busily fantasizing what she would make of her body? Love or hatred?

"You know perfectly well we hate our bodies," says Rachel, who calls herself the pig. She grabs the flesh of her stomach between her hands. "Who could love this?"

There is an appealing honesty in this despair, an articulation of what is virtually a universal attitude among women in our culture today. Few women who diet realize that they are confessing to a dislike for the body when they weigh and measure their flesh, subject it to rigorous fasts or strenuous regimens of exercise. And yet, over and over again, as I spoke to women about their bodies, this antagonism became apparent. One woman disliked her thighs, another her stomach, a third the loose flesh under her arms. Many would grab their skin and squeeze it as we talked, with that grimace of distaste language cannot translate into itself. One woman said to me: "Little by little I began to be aware that the pounds I was trying to 'melt away' were my own flesh. Would you believe it? It never occurred to me before. These 'ugly pounds' which filled me with so much hatred were my body."

The sound of this dawning consciousness can be heard now and again among the voices I have recorded in my notebook, heralding what may be a growing awareness of how bitterly the women of this culture are alienated from their bodies. Thus, another woman said to me: "It's true, I never used to like my body." We had been looking at pictures of women from the nineteenth century; they were large women, with full hips and thighs. "What do you think of them?" I said. "They're like me," she answered, and then began to laugh. "Soft, sensual, and inviting."

The description is accurate; the women in the pictures, and the woman looking at them, share a quality of voluptuousness that is no longer admired by our culture:

> When I look at myself in the mirror I see that there's nothing wrong with me—now! Sometimes I even think I'm beautiful. I don't know why this began to change. It might have been when I started going to the YWCA. It was the first time I saw so many women naked. I realized it was the fuller bodies that were more beautiful. The thin women, who looked so good in clothes, seemed old and worn out. Their bodies were gaunt. But the bodies of the larger women had a certain natural mystery, very different from the false illusion of clothes. And I thought, I'm like them; I'm a big woman like they are and perhaps my body is beautiful. I had always been trying to make my body have the right shape so that I could fit into clothes. But then I started to look at myself in the mirror. Before that I had always looked at parts of myself. The hips were too flabby, the thighs were too fat. Now I began to see myself as a whole. I stopped hearing my mother's voice, asking me if I was going to go on a diet. I just looked at what was really there instead of what should have been there.

What was wrong with it? I asked myself. And little by little I stopped disliking my body.

This is the starting point. It is from this new way of looking at an old problem that liberation will come. The very simple idea that an obsession with weight reflects a dislike and uneasiness for the body can have a profound effect upon a woman's life.

I always thought I was too fat. I never liked my body. I kept trying to lose weight. I just tortured myself. But if I see pictures of myself from a year or two ago I discover now that I looked just fine.

I remember recently going out to buy Häagen Dazs ice cream. I had decided I was going to give myself something I really wanted to eat. I had to walk all the way down to the World Trade Center. But on my way there I began to feel terribly fat. I felt that I was being punished by being fat. I had lost the beautiful self I had made by becoming thinner. I could hear these voices saying to me: "You're fat, you're ugly, who do you think you are, don't you know you'll never be happy?" I had always heard these voices in my mind but now when they would come into consciousness I would tell them to shut up. I saw two men on the street. I was eating the Häagen Dazs ice cream. I thought I heard one of them say "heavy." I thought they were saying: "She's so fat." But I knew that I had to live through these feelings if I was ever to eat what I liked. I just couldn't go on tormenting myself any more about the size of my body.

One day, shortly after this, I walked into my house. I noticed the scales, standing under the sink in the bathroom. Suddenly, I hated them. I was filled with grief for having tortured myself for so many years. They looked like shackles. I didn't want to have anything more to do with them. I called my boyfriend and offered him the scales. Then, I went into the kitchen. I looked at my shelves. I saw diet books there. I was filled with rage and hatred of them. I hurled them all into a box and got rid of them. Then I looked into the ice box. There was a bottle of Weight Watchers dressing. I hurled it into the garbage and watched it shatter and drip down the plastic bag. Little by little, I started to feel better about myself. At first I didn't eat less, I just worried less about my eating. I allowed myself to eat whatever I wanted. I began to give away the clothes I couldn't fit into. It turned out that they weren't right for me anyway. I had bought them with the idea of what my body should look like. Now I buy clothes because I like the way they look on me. If something doesn't fit it doesn't fit. I'm not trying to make myself into something I'm not. I weigh more than I once considered my ideal. But I don't seem fat to myself. Now, I can honestly say that I like my body.

Some weeks ago, at a dinner party, a woman who had recently gained weight began to talk about her body.

"I was once very thin," she said, "but I didn't feel comfortable in my body. I fit into all the right clothes. But somehow I just couldn't find myself any longer."

I looked over at her expectantly; she was a voluptuous woman, who had recently given birth to her first child.

"But now," she said as she got to her feet, "now, if I walk or jog or dance, I feel my flesh jiggling along with me." She began to shake her shoulders and move her hips, her eyes wide as she hopped about in front of the coffee table. "You see what I mean?" she shouted over to me. "I love it."

This image of a woman dancing came with me when I sat down to write. I remembered her expression. There was in it something secretive, I thought, something knowing and pleased—the look of a woman who has made peace with her body. Then I recalled the faces of women who had recently lost weight. The haggard look, the lines of strain around the mouth, the neck too lean, the tendons visible, the head too large for the emaciated body. I began to reason:

There must be, I said, for every woman a correct weight, which cannot be discovered with reference to a weight chart or to any statistical norm. For the size of the body is a matter of highly subjective individual preferences and natural endowments. If we should evolve an aesthetic for women that was appropriate to women it would reflect this diversity, would conceive, indeed celebrate and even love, slenderness in a woman intended by nature to be slim, and love the rounded cheeks of another, the plump arms, broad shoulders, narrow hips, full thighs, rounded ass, straight back, narrow shoulders or slender arms, of a woman made that way according to her nature, walking with head high in pride of her body, however it happened to be shaped. And then Miss America, and the woman jogging in the morning, and the woman swinging out at her image in the mirror might say, with Susan Griffin in *Woman and Nature:*

> And we are various, and amazing in our variety, and our differences multiply, so that edge after edge of the endlessness of possibility is exposed... none of us beautiful when separate but all exquisite as we stand, each moment heeded in this cycle, no detail unlovely....

Suggestions for Discussion

1. Chernin's work led her to the conclusion that America's obsession with thinness has to do with dominating nature, with control. Do you agree? Explain.
2. In their preoccupation with weight women have come to hate their bodies and to derive no sense of pleasure from them, asserts Chernin. With what evidence does she support this statement?

3. Is it possible in our culture to affirm a number of different shapes and sizes Tof women; to see a variety of body types as beautiful? Or are we always going to have an ideal against which all will be measured?

Suggestions for Writing

1. Eating disorders are a major health crisis in our country. Have you, a friend, or a relation ever suffered from one? What was it like? How did you feel about eating? About yourself? Describe.
2. It has been said that Americans are obsessed with their bodies. Write a story built around at least one example of this obsession.

CARSON McCULLERS

Loneliness...An American Malady

Carson McCullers (1917–1967), a Southern writer, was awarded Guggenheim Fellowships in 1942 and in 1946. Her published works include *The Heart Is a Lonely Hunter* (1940), *Reflections in a Golden Eye* (1941), *The Member of the Wedding* (1946), *The Ballad of the Sad Café* (1951), and *Clock Without Hands* (1961). This excerpt from *The Mortgaged Heart* suggests that the way by which we master loneliness is "to belong to something larger and more powerful than the weak, lonely self."

This city, New York—consider the people in it, the eight million of us. An English friend of mine, when asked why he lived in New York City, said that he liked it here because he could be so alone. While it was my friend's desire to be alone, the aloneness of many Americans who live in cities is an involuntary and fearful thing. It has been said that loneliness is the great American malady. What is the nature of this loneliness? It would seem essentially to be a quest for identity.

To the spectator, the amateur philosopher, no motive among the complex ricochets of our desires and rejections seems stronger or more enduring than the will of the individual to claim his identity and belong. From infancy to death, the human being is obsessed by these dual motives. During our first weeks of life, the question of identity shares urgency with the need for milk. The baby reaches for his toes, then explores the bars of his crib; again and again he compares the difference between his own body and the objects around him, and in the wavering, infant eyes there comes a pristine wonder.

Consciousness of self is the first abstract problem that the human being solves. Indeed, it is this self-consciousness that removes us from lower animals. This primitive grasp of identity develops with constantly shifting emphasis through all our years. Perhaps maturity is simply the history of those mutations that reveal to the individual the relation between himself and the world in which he finds himself.

After the first establishment of identity there comes the imperative need to lose this new-found sense of separateness and to belong to something larger and more powerful than the weak, lonely self. The sense of moral isolation is intolerable to us.

In *The Member of the Wedding* the lonely 12-year-old girl, Frankie Addams, articulates this universal need: "The trouble with me is that for a long time I have just been an *I* person. All people belong to a *We* except me. Not to belong to a *We* makes you too lonesome."

Love is the bridge that leads from the *I* sense to the *We,* and there is a paradox about personal love. Love of another individual opens a new relation between the personality and the world. The lover responds in a new way to nature and may even write poetry. Love is affirmation; it motivates the *yes* responses and the sense of wider communication. Love casts out fear, and in the security of this togetherness we find contentment, courage. We no longer fear the age-old haunting questions: "Who am I?" "Why am I?" "Where am I going?"—and having cast out fear, we can be honest and charitable.

For fear is a primary source of evil. And when the question "Who am I?" recurs and is unanswered, then fear and frustration project a negative attitude. The bewildered soul can answer only: "Since I do not understand 'Who I am,' I only know what I am *not.*" The corollary of this emotional incertitude is snobbism, intolerance, and racial hate. The xenophobic individual can only reject and destroy, as the xenophobic nation inevitably makes war.

The loneliness of Americans does not have its source in xenophobia; as a nation we are an outgoing people, reaching always for immediate contacts, further experience. But we tend to seek out things as individuals, alone. The European, secure in his family ties and rigid class loyalties, knows little of the moral loneliness that is native to us Americans. While the European artists tend to form groups or aesthetic schools, the American artist is the eternal maverick—not only from society in the way of all creative minds, but within the orbit of his own art.

Thoreau took to the woods to seek the ultimate meaning of his life. His creed was simplicity and his *modus vivendi* the deliberate stripping of external life to the Spartan necessities in order that his inward life could freely flourish. His objective, as he put it, was to back the world into a corner. And in that way did he discover "What a man thinks of himself, that it is which determines, or rather indicates, his fate."

On the other hand, Thomas Wolfe turned to the city, and in his wanderings around New York he continued his frenetic and lifelong search for the lost brother, the magic door. He too backed the world into a corner, and as he passed among the city's millions, returning their stares, he experienced "That silent meeting [that] is the summary of all the meetings of men's lives."

Whether in the pastoral joys of country life or in the labyrinthine city, we Americans are always seeking. We wander, question. But the answer waits in each separate heart—the answer of our own identity and the way by which we can master loneliness and feel that at last we belong.

Suggestion for Discussion

How does the author establish the connections between loneliness and identity? Between *I* and *We?* Between lack of a sense of identity and fear? Between fear and hatred or destruction?

Suggestions for Writing

1. Develop or challenge Thoreau's belief, "What a man thinks of himself, that it is which determines, or rather indicates, his fate."
2. Develop an essay in which you argue that country life is or is not more conducive to the development of a sense of self than city life.

BRUNO BETTELHEIM

The Child's Need for Magic

Bruno Bettelheim (1903–1990) was born in Vienna and educated at the University of Vienna. Having survived the Nazi holocaust, he became an American psychoanalyst and educator and was director of the remarkable University of Chicago Sonia Shankman Orthogenic School from 1944 to 1973. He wrote many penetrating works on parents and children and the significance of the holocaust. In this excerpt from *The Uses of Enchantment* (1976), the author believes that fairy tales provide answers to the child's pressing questions about his identity and his world.

Myths and fairy stories both answer the eternal questions: What is the world really like? How am I to live my life in it? How can I truly be myself? The answers given by myths are definite, while the fairy tale is suggestive; its messages may imply solutions, but it never spells them out. Fairy tales leave to the child's fantasizing whether and how to apply to himself what the story reveals about life and human nature.

The fairy tale proceeds in a manner which conforms to the way a child thinks and experiences the world; this is why the fairy tale is so convincing to him. He can gain much better solace from a fairy tale than he can from an effort to comfort him based on adult reasoning and viewpoints. A child trusts what the fairy story tells, because its world view accords with his own.

Whatever our age, only a story conforming to the principles underlying our thought processes carries conviction for us. If this is so for adults, who have learned to accept that there is more than one frame of reference for comprehending the world—although we find it difficult if not impossible truly to think in any but our own—it is exclusively true for the child. His thinking is animistic.

Like all preliterate and many literate people, "the child assumes that his relations to the inanimate world are of one pattern with those to the animate world of people: he fondles as he would his mother the pretty thing that pleased him; he strikes the door that has slammed on him." It should be added that he does the first because he is convinced that this pretty thing loves to be petted as much as he does; and he punishes the door because he is certain that the door slammed deliberately, out of evil intention.

As Piaget has shown, the child's thinking remains animistic until the age of puberty. His parents and teachers tell him that things cannot feel and act; and as much as he may pretend to believe this to please these adults, or not to be ridiculed, deep down the child knows better. Subjected to the rational teachings of others, the child only buries his "true knowledge" deeper in his soul and it remains untouched by rationality; but it can be formed and informed by what fairy tales have to say.

To the eight-year-old (to quote Piaget's examples), the sun is alive because it gives light (and, one may add, it does that because it wants to). To the child's animistic mind, the stone is alive because it can move, as it rolls down a hill. Even a twelve-and-a-half-year-old is convinced that a stream is alive and has a will, because its water is flowing. The sun, the stone, and the water are believed to be inhabited by spirits very much like people, so they feel and act like people.

To the child, there is no clear line separating objects from living things; and whatever has life has life very much like our own. If we do not understand what rocks and trees and animals have to tell us, the reason is that we are not sufficiently attuned to them. To the child trying to understand the world, it seems reasonable to expect answers from those objects which arouse his curiosity. And since the child is self-centered, he expects the animal to talk about the things which are really significant to him, as animals do in fairy tales, and as the child himself talks to his real or toy animals. A child is convinced that the animal understands and feels with him, even though it does not show it openly.

Since animals roam freely and widely in the world, how natural that in fairy tales these animals are able to guide the hero in his search which takes him into distant places. Since all that moves is alive, the child can believe that the wind can talk and carry the hero to where he needs to go, as in "East of the Sun and West of the Moon." In animistic thinking, not only animals feel and think as we do, but even stones are alive; so to be turned into stone simply means that the being has to remain silent and unmoving for a time. By the same reasoning, it is entirely believable when previously silent objects begin to talk, give advice, and join the hero on his wanderings. And since everything is inhabited by a spirit similar to all other spirits (namely, that of the child who has projected his spirit into all these things), because of this inherent sameness it is believable that man can change into animal, or the other way around, as in "Beauty and the Beast" or "The Frog King." Since there is no sharp line drawn between living and dead things, the latter, too, can come to life.

When, like the great philosophers, children are searching for the solutions to the first and last questions—"Who am I? How ought I to deal with life's problems? What must I become?"—they do so on the basis of their animistic thinking. But since the child is so uncertain of what his existence consists, first and foremost comes the question "Who am I?"

As soon as a child begins to move about and explore, he begins to ponder the problem of his identity. When he spies his mirror image, he wonders whether what he sees is really he, or a child just like him standing behind this glassy wall. He tries to find out by exploring whether this other child is really, in all ways, like him. He makes faces, turns this way or that, walks away from the mirror and jumps back in front of it to ascertain whether this other one has moved away or is still there. Though only three years old, the child is already up against the difficult problem of personal identity.

The child asks himself: "Who am I? Where did I come from? How did the world come into being? Who created man and all the animals? What is the purpose of life?" True, he ponders these vital questions not in the abstract, but mainly as they pertain to him. He worries not whether there is justice for individual man, but whether *he* will be treated justly. He wonders who or what projects him into adversity, and what can prevent this from happening to him. Are there benevolent powers in addition to his parents? Are his parents benevolent powers? How should he form himself, and why? Is there hope for him, though he may have done wrong? Why has all this happened to him? What will it mean for his future? Fairy tales provide answers to these pressing questions, many of which the child becomes aware of only as he follows the stories.

From an adult point of view and in terms of modern science, the answers which fairy stories offer are fantastic rather than true. As a matter of fact, these solutions seem so incorrect to many adults—who have become estranged from the ways in which young people experience the world—that they object to exposing children to such "false" information. However, realistic explanations are usually incomprehensible to children, because they lack the abstract understanding required to make sense of them. While giving a scientifically correct answer makes adults think they have clarified things for the child, such explanations leave the young child confused, overpowered, and intellectually defeated. A child can derive security only from the conviction that he understands now what baffled him before—never from being given facts which create *new* uncertainties. Even as the child accepts such an answer, he comes to doubt that he has asked the right question. Since the explanation fails to make sense to him, it must apply to some unknown problem—not the one he asked about.

It is therefore important to remember that only statements which are intelligible in terms of the child's existing knowledge and emotional preoccupations carry conviction for him. To tell a child that the earth floats in space, attracted by gravity into circling around the sun, but that the earth doesn't fall to the sun as the child falls to the ground, seems very confusing to him. The child knows from his experience that everything has to rest on something, or be held up by something. Only an explanation based on that knowledge can make him feel he understands better about the earth in space. More important, to feel secure on earth, the child needs to believe that this world is held firmly in place. Therefore he finds a better explanation in a myth that tells him that the earth rests on a turtle, or is held up by a giant.

If a child accepts as true what his parents tell him—that the earth is a planet held securely on its path by gravity—then the child can only imagine that gravity is a string. Thus the parents' explanation has led to no better understanding or feeling of security. It requires considerable intellectual maturity to believe that there can be stability to one's life when the ground on which one walks (the firmest thing around, on which everything rests) spins with incredible speed on an invisible axis; that in addition it rotates around the sun; and furthermore hurtles through space with the entire solar system. I have never yet encountered a prepubertal youngster who could comprehend all these combined movements, although I have known many who could repeat this information. Such children parrot explanations which according to their own experience of the world are lies, but which they must believe to be true because some adult has said so. The consequence is that children come to distrust their own experience, and therefore themselves and what their minds can do for them.

In the fall of 1973, the comet Kohoutek was in the news. At that time a competent science teacher explained the comet to a small group of highly intelligent second- and third-graders. Each child had carefully cut out a paper circle and had drawn on it the course of the planets around the sun; a paper ellipse, attached by a slit to the paper circle, represented the course of the comet. The children showed me the comet moving along at an angle to the planets. When I asked them, the children told me that they were holding the comet in their hands, showing me the ellipse. When I asked how the comet which they were holding in their hands could also be in the sky, they were all nonplussed.

In their confusion, they turned to their teacher, who carefully explained to them that what they were holding in their hands, and had so diligently created, was only a model of the planets and the comet. The children all agreed that they understood this, and would have repeated it if questioned further. But whereas before they had regarded proudly this circle-cum-ellipse in their hands, they now lost all interest. Some crumpled the paper up, others dropped the model in the wastepaper basket. When the pieces of paper had been the comet to them, they had all planned to take the model home to show their parents, but now it no longer had meaning for them.

In trying to get a child to accept scientifically correct explanations, parents all too frequently discount scientific findings of how a child's mind works. Research on the child's mental processes, especially Piaget's, convincingly demonstrates that the young child is not able to comprehend the two vital abstract concepts of the permanence of quantity, and of reversibility—for instance, that the same quantity of water rises high in a narrow receptacle and remains low in a wide one; and that subtraction reverses the process of addition. Until he can understand abstract concepts such as these, the child can experience the world only subjectively.

Scientific explanations require objective thinking. Both theoretical research and experimental exploration have shown that no child below school age is truly able to grasp these two concepts, without which abstract understanding is impossible. In his early years, until age eight or ten, the child can develop only highly personalized concepts about what he experiences.

Therefore it seems natural to him, since the plants which grow on this earth nourish him as his mother did from her breast, to see the earth as a mother or a female god, or at least as her abode.

Even a young child somehow knows that he was created by his parents; so it makes good sense to him that, like himself, all men and where they live were created by a superhuman figure not very different from his parents—some male or female god. Since his parents watch over the child and provide him with his needs in his home, then naturally he also believes that something like them, only much more powerful, intelligent, and reliable—a guardian angel—will do so out in the world.

A child thus experiences the world order in the image of his parents and of what goes on within the family. The ancient Egyptians, as a child does, saw heaven and the sky as a motherly figure (Nut) who protectively bent over the earth, enveloping it and them serenely. Far from preventing man from later developing a more rational explanation of the world, such a view offers security where and when it is most needed—a security which, when the time is ripe, allows for a truly rational world view. Life on a small planet surrounded by limitless space seems awfully lonely and cold to a child—just the opposite of what he knows life ought to be. This is why the ancients needed to feel sheltered and warmed by an enveloping mother figure. To depreciate protective imagery like this as mere childish projections of an immature mind is to rob the young child of one aspect of the prolonged safety and comfort he needs.

True, the notion of a sheltering sky-mother can be limiting to the mind if clung to for too long. Neither infantile projections nor dependence on imaginary protectors—such as a guardian angel who watches out for one when one is asleep, or during Mother's absence—offers true security; but as long as one cannot provide complete security for oneself, imaginings and projections are far preferable to no security. It is such (partly imagined) security which, when experienced for a sufficient length of time, permits the child to develop that feeling of confidence in life which he needs in order to trust himself—a trust necessary for his learning to solve life's problems through his own growing rational abilities. Eventually the child recognizes that what he has taken as literally true—the earth as a mother—is only a symbol.

A child, for example, who has learned from fairy stories to believe that what at first seemed a repulsive, threatening figure can magically change into a most helpful friend is ready to believe that a strange child whom he meets and fears may also be changed from a menace into a desirable companion. Belief in the "truth" of the fairy tale gives him courage not to withdraw because of the way this stranger appears to him at first. Recalling how the hero of many a fairy tale succeeded in life because he dared to befriend a seemingly unpleasant figure, the child believes he may work the same magic.

I have known many examples where, particularly in late adolescence, years of belief in magic are called upon to compensate for the person's having been deprived of it prematurely in childhood, through stark reality having been forced on him. It is as if these young people feel that now is their last chance to make up for a severe deficiency in their life experience; or that without having had a period of belief in magic, they will be unable to meet the rigors of adult life. Many young people who today suddenly seek escape in drug-induced dreams, apprentice themselves to some guru, believe in astrology, engage in practicing "black magic," or who in some other fashion escape from reality into daydreams about magic experiences which are to change their life for the better, were prematurely pressed to view reality in an adult way. Trying to evade reality in such ways has its deeper cause in early formative experiences which prevented the development of the conviction that life can be mastered in realistic ways.

What seems desirable for the individual is to repeat in his life span the process involved historically in the genesis of scientific thought. For a long time in his history man used emotional projections—such as gods—born of his immature hopes and anxieties to explain man, his society, and the universe; these explanations gave him a feeling of security. Then slowly, by his own social, scientific, and technological progress, man freed himself of the constant fear for his very existence. Feeling more secure in the world, and also within himself, man could now begin to question the validity of the images he had used in the past as explanatory tools. From there man's "childish" projections dissolved and more rational explanations took their place. This process, however, is by no means without vagaries. In intervening periods of stress and scarcity, man seeks for comfort again in the "childish" notion that he and his place of abode are the center of the universe.

Translated in terms of human behavior, the more secure a person feels within the world, the less he will need to hold on to "infantile" projections—mythical explanations or fairy-tale solutions to life's eternal problems—and the more he can afford to seek rational explanations. The more secure a man is within himself, the more he can afford to accept an explanation which says his world is of minor significance in the cosmos. Once man feels truly significant in his human environment, he cares little about the importance of his planet within the universe. On the other hand, the more insecure a man is in himself and his place in the immediate world, the more he withdraws into himself because of fear, or else moves outward to conquer for conquest's sake. This is the opposite of exploring out of a security which frees our curiosity.

For these same reasons a child, as long as he is not sure his immediate human environment will protect him, needs to believe that superior powers, such as a guardian angel, watch over him, and that the world and his place within it are of paramount importance. Here is one connection between a family's ability to provide basic security and the child's readiness to engage in rational investigations as he grows up.

As long as parents fully believed that Biblical stories solved the riddle of our existence and its purpose, it was easy to make a child feel secure. The Bible was felt to contain the answers to all pressing questions: the Bible told man all he needed to know to understand the world, how it came into being, and how to behave in it. In the Western world the Bible also provided prototypes for man's imagination. But rich as the Bible is in stories, not even during the most religious of times were these stories sufficient for meeting all the psychic needs of man.

Part of the reason for this is that while the Old and New Testaments and the histories of the saints provided answers to the crucial questions of how to live the good life, they did not offer solutions for the problems posed by the dark sides of our personalities. The Biblical stories suggest essentially only one solution for the asocial aspects of the unconscious: repression of these (unacceptable) strivings. But children, not having their ids in conscious control, need stories which permit at least fantasy satisfaction of these "bad" tendencies, and specific models for their sublimation.

Explicitly and implicitly, the Bible tells of God's demands on man. While we are told that there is greater rejoicing about a sinner who reformed than about the man who never erred, the message is still that we ought to live the good life, and not, for example, take cruel revenge on those whom we hate. As the story of Cain and Abel shows, there is no sympathy in the Bible for the agonies of sibling rivalry—only a warning that acting upon it has devastating consequences.

But what a child needs most, when beset by jealousy of his sibling, is the permission to feel that what he experiences is justified by the situation he is in. To bear up under the pangs of his envy, the child needs to be encouraged to engage in fantasies of getting even someday; then he will be able to manage at the moment, because of the conviction that the future will set things aright. Most of all, the child wants support for his still very tenuous belief that through growing up, working hard, and maturing he will one day be the victorious one. If his present sufferings will be rewarded in the future, he need not act on his jealousy of the moment, the way Cain did.

Like Biblical stories and myths, fairy tales were the literature which edified everybody—children and adults alike—for nearly all of man's existence. Except that God is central, many Bible stories can be recognized as very similar to fairy tales. In the story of Jonah and the whale, for example, Jonah is trying to run away from his superego's (conscience's) demand that he fight against the wickedness of the people of Nineveh. The ordeal which tests his moral fiber is, as in so many fairy tales, a perilous voyage in which he has to prove himself.

Jonah's trip across the sea lands him in the belly of a great fish. There, in great danger, Jonah discovers his higher morality, his higher self, and is wondrously reborn, now ready to meet the rigorous demands of his superego. But the rebirth alone does not achieve true humanity for him: to be a slave neither to the id and the pleasure principle (avoiding arduous tasks by trying to escape from them) nor to the superego (wishing destruction upon the wicked city) means true freedom and higher selfhood. Jonah attains his full humanity only when he is no longer subservient to either institution of his mind, but relinquishes blind obedience to both id and superego and is able to recognize God's wisdom in judging the people of Nineveh not according to the rigid structures of Jonah's superego, but in terms of their human frailty.

Suggestions for Discussion

1. How does Bettelheim distinguish myths from fairy tales? The Bible from fairy tales?
2. Who is Piaget? How has he influenced current thought regarding the way children think and learn?
3. Explain Bettelheim's reference to children as "animistic thinkers." How does this description of them relate to their need for fairy tales?
4. What similarities does the author see between the child and the philosopher? How do they differ?
5. Explain why Bettelheim believes it mistaken to deprive children of fairy tales. How does he relate their need for fairy tales to the difficulties they have in comprehending scientific ideas?

Suggestions for Writing

1. Using one or more fairy tales with which you are familiar, write an essay explaining how magical elements might serve to explain the universe to a child.
2. Write a comparison between a fairy tale and one of the popular children's stories about ordinary life.

ELLEN GOODMAN

The Company Man

Ellen Goodman (b. 1942) was educated at Radcliffe College and pursued a career as a journalist. She was a researcher and reporter for *Newsweek,* a feature writer for the *Boston Globe,* and a syndicated columnist with the Washington Post Writers Group. She has been a Nieman fellow at Harvard University and named columnist of the year by the New England Women's Press Association. In 1980 she won a Pulitzer Prize for distinguished commentary. Her books include, among others, *Turning Points* (1979), *At Large* (1981), a collection of newspaper columns, and *Making Sense* (1989). In this essay she portrays a workaholic whose sense of self is totally based upon his identification with his company.

He worked himself to death, finally and precisely, at 3:00 A.M. Sunday morning.

The obituary didn't say that, of course. It said that he died of a coronary thrombosis—I think that was it—but everyone among his friends and acquaintances knew it instantly. He was a perfect Type A, a workaholic, a classic, they said to each other and shook their heads—and thought for five or ten minutes about the way they lived.

This man who worked himself to death finally and precisely at 3:00 A.M. Sunday morning—on his day off—was fifty-one years old and a vice-president. He was, however, one of six vice-presidents, and one of three who might conceivably—if the president died or retired soon enough—have moved to the top spot. Phil knew that.

He worked six days a week, five of them until eight or nine at night, during a time when his own company had begun the four-day week for everyone but the executives. He worked like the Important People. He had no outside "extracurricular interests," unless, of course, you think about a monthly golf game that way. To Phil, it was work. He always ate egg salad sandwiches at his desk. He was, of course, overweight, by 20 or 25 pounds. He thought it was okay, though, because he didn't smoke.

On Saturdays, Phil wore a sports jacket to the office instead of a suit, because it was the weekend.

He had a lot of people working for him, maybe sixty, and most of them liked him most of the time. Three of them will be seriously considered for his job. The obituary didn't mention that.

But it did list his "survivors" quite accurately. He is survived by his wife, Helen, forty-eight years old, a good woman of no particular marketable skills, who worked in an office before marrying and mothering. She had, according to her daughter, given up trying to compete with his work years ago, when the children were small. A company friend said, "I know how much you will miss him." And she answered, "I already have."

"Missing him all these years," she must have given up part of herself which had cared too much for the man. She would be "well taken care of."

His "dearly beloved" eldest of the "dearly beloved" children is a hard-working executive in a manufacturing firm down South. In the day and a half before the funeral, he went around the neighborhood researching his father, asking the neighbors what he was like. They were embarrassed.

His second child is a girl, who is twenty-four and newly married. She lives near her mother and they are close, but whenever she was alone with her father, in a car driving somewhere, they had nothing to say to each other.

The youngest is twenty, a boy, a high-school graduate who has spent the last couple of years, like a lot of his friends, doing enough odd jobs to stay in grass and food. He was the one who tried to grab at his father, and tried to mean enough to him to keep the man at home. He was his father's favorite. Over the last two years, Phil stayed up nights worrying about the boy.

The boy once said, "My father and I only board here."

At the funeral, the sixty-year-old company president told the forty-eight-year-old widow that the fifty-one-year-old deceased had meant much to the company and would be missed and would be hard to replace. The widow didn't look him in the eye. She was afraid he would read her bitterness and, after all, she would need him to straighten out the finances—the stock options and all that.

Phil was overweight and nervous and worked too hard. If he wasn't at the office, he was worried about it. Phil was a Type A, a heart-attack natural. You could have picked him out in a minute from a lineup.

So when he finally worked himself to death, at precisely 3:00 A.M. Sunday morning, no one was really surprised.

By 5:00 P.M. the afternoon of the funeral, the company president had begun, discreetly of course, with care and taste, to make inquiries about his replacement. One of three men. He asked around: "Who's been working the hardest?"

Suggestions for Discussion

1. What does the phrase "and thought for five or ten minutes about the way they lived" tell the reader about the author's point of view? About her tone?

2. What is the significance of the statement that the man who died was "one of six vice-presidents, and one of three who might...have moved to the top spot"?
3. Why doesn't the author identify the man by name until the end of the third paragraph?
4. Goodman makes statements about Phil, then qualifies them. Cite instances. What is the nature of the qualification? How does this technique add to the characterization? To the tone?
5. What does the brief item on each family member and the company president tell readers about Phil? About themselves?
6. Account for the repetition of Phil's age and the hour of his death.
7. What is the significance of the president's question after the funeral?
8. What is the implicit statement that Goodman makes about workaholics? About large companies?
9. Speculate upon Phil's sense of self.

Suggestions for Writing

1. Make a study of a person you know whose sense of self is based on his or her identification with an institution, a business, a school, or a character in fiction.
2. If you know a workaholic, write a description using incidents and dialogue that illuminate his or her character.

FICTION

ERNEST HEMINGWAY

Indian Camp

Ernest Hemingway (1898–1961), novelist and short story writer, began his career as a reporter and during World War I served with an ambulance unit in France and Italy. After the war he lived in Paris as a correspondent for the Hearst papers. During the Spanish Civil War he went to Spain as a war correspondent. His works include the collections of short stories *In Our Time* (1925), *Men Without Women* (1927), *The Fifth Column and the First 49 Stories* (1938); and the novels *The Sun Also Rises* (1926), *A Farewell to Arms* (1929), *For Whom the Bell Tolls* (1940), and *The Old Man and the Sea* (1952), which was awarded a Pulitzer Prize. In 1954 he received the Nobel Prize for Literature. This is a story of initiation, from the collection *In Our Time,* in which the boy is exposed to a violent birth and death.

At the lake shore there was another rowboat drawn up. The two Indians stood waiting.

Nick and his father got in the stern of the boat and the Indians shoved it off and one of them got in to row. Uncle George sat in the stern of the camp rowboat. The young Indian shoved the camp boat off and got in to row Uncle George.

The two boats started off in the dark. Nick heard the oarlocks of the other boat quite a way ahead of them in the mist. The Indians rowed with quick choppy strokes. Nick lay back with his father's arm around him. It was cold on the water. The Indian who was rowing them was working very hard, but the other boat moved further ahead in the mist all the time.

"Where are we going, Dad?" Nick asked.

"Over to the Indian camp. There is an Indian lady very sick."

"Oh," said Nick.

Across the bay they found the other boat beached. Uncle George was smoking a cigar in the dark. The young Indian pulled the boat way up on the beach. Uncle George gave both the Indians cigars.

They walked up from the beach through a meadow that was soaking wet with dew, following the young Indian who carried a lantern. Then they went into the woods and followed a trail that led to the logging road that ran back into the hills. It was much lighter on the logging road as the timber was cut away on both sides. The young Indian stopped and blew out his lantern and they all walked on along the road.

They came around a bend and a dog came out barking. Ahead were the lights of the shanties where the Indian bark-peelers lived. More dogs rushed out at them. The two Indians sent them back to the shanties. In the shanty nearest the road there was a light in the window. An old woman stood in the doorway holding a lamp.

Inside on a wooden bunk lay a young Indian woman. She had been trying to have her baby for two days. All the old women in the camp had been helping her. The men had moved off up the road to sit in the dark and smoke out of range of the noise she made. She screamed just as Nick and the two Indians followed his father and Uncle George into the shanty. She lay in the lower bunk, very big under a quilt. Her head was turned to one side. In the upper bunk was her husband. He had cut his foot very badly with an ax three days before. He was smoking a pipe. The room smelled very bad.

Nick's father ordered some water to be put on the stove, and while it was heating he spoke to Nick.

"This lady is going to have a baby, Nick," he said.

"I know," said Nick.

"You don't know," said his father. "Listen to me. What she is going through is called being in labor. The baby wants to be born and she wants it to be born. All her muscles are trying to get the baby born. That is what is happening when she screams."

"I see," Nick said.

Just then the woman cried out.

"Oh, Daddy, can't you give her something to make her stop screaming?" asked Nick.

"No. I haven't any anaesthetic," his father said. "But her screams are not important. I don't hear them because they are not important."

The husband in the upper bunk rolled over against the wall.

The woman in the kitchen motioned to the doctor that the water was hot. Nick's father went into the kitchen and poured about half of the water out of the big kettle into a basin. Into the water left in the kettle he put several things he unwrapped from a handkerchief.

"Those must boil," he said, and began to scrub his hands in the basin of hot water with a cake of soap he had brought from the camp. Nick watched his father's hands scrubbing each other with the soap. While his father washed his hands very carefully and thoroughly, he talked.

"You see, Nick, babies are supposed to be born head first but sometimes they're not. When they're not they make a lot of trouble for everybody. Maybe I'll have to operate on this lady. We'll know in a little while."

When he was satisfied with his hands he went in and went to work.

"Pull back that quilt, will you, George?" he said. "I'd rather not touch it."

Later when he started to operate Uncle George and three Indian men held the woman still. She bit Uncle George on the arm and Uncle George said, "Damn squaw bitch!" and the young Indian who had rowed Uncle George over laughed at him. Nick held the basin for his father. It all took a long time.

His father picked the baby up and slapped it to make it breathe and handed it to the old woman.

"See, it's a boy, Nick," he said. "How do you like being an interne?"

Nick said, "All right." He was looking away so as not to see what his father was doing.

"There. That gets it," said his father and put something into the basin.

Nick didn't look at it.

"Now," his father said, "there's some stitches to put in. You can watch this or not, Nick, just as you like. I'm going to sew up the incision I made."

Nick did not watch. His curiosity had been gone for a long time.

His father finished and stood up. Uncle George and the three Indian men stood up. Nick put the basin out in the kitchen.

Uncle George looked at his arm. The young Indian smiled reminiscently.

"I'll put some peroxide on that, George," the doctor said.

He bent over the Indian woman. She was quiet now and her eyes were closed. She looked very pale. She did not know what had become of the baby or anything.

"I'll be back in the morning," the doctor said, standing up. "The nurse should be here from St. Ignace by noon and she'll bring everything we need."

He was feeling exalted and talkative as football players are in the dressing room after a game.

"That's one for the medical journal, George," he said. "Doing a Caesarean with a jack-knife and sewing it up with nine-foot, tapered gut leaders."

Uncle George was standing against the wall, looking at his arm.

"Oh, you're a great man, all right," he said.

"Ought to have a look at the proud father. They're usually the worst sufferers in these little affairs," the doctor said. "I must say he took it all pretty quietly."

He pulled back the blanket from the Indian's head. His hand came away wet. He mounted on the edge of the lower bunk with the lamp in one hand and looked in. The Indian lay with his face toward the wall. His throat had been cut from ear to ear. The blood had flowed down into a pool where his body sagged the bunk. His head rested on his left arm. The open razor lay, edge up, in the blankets.

"Take Nick out of the shanty, George," the doctor said.

There was no need of that. Nick, standing in the door of the kitchen, had a good view of the upper bunk when his father, the lamp in one hand, tipped the Indian's head back.

It was just beginning to be daylight when they walked along the logging road back toward the lake.

"I'm terribly sorry I brought you along, Nickie," said his father, all his post-operative exhilaration gone. "It was an awful mess to put you through."

"Do ladies always have such a hard time having babies?" Nick asked.

"No, that was very, very exceptional."

"Why did he kill himself, Daddy?"

"I don't know, Nick. He couldn't stand things, I guess."

"Do many men kill themselves, Daddy?"

"Not very many, Nick."

"Do many women?"

"Hardly ever."

"Don't they ever?"

"Oh, yes. They do sometimes."

"Daddy?"

"Yes."

"Where did Uncle George go?"

"He'll turn up all right."

"Is dying hard, Daddy?"

"No, I think it's pretty easy, Nick. It all depends."

They were seated in the boat, Nick in the stern, his father rowing. The sun was coming up over the hills. A bass jumped, making a circle in the water. Nick trailed his hand in the water. It felt warm in the sharp chill of the morning.

In the early morning on the lake sitting in the stern of the boat with his father rowing, he felt quite sure that he would never die.

Suggestions for Discussion

1. How is the emotional tension of the story built up by the descriptive details of the journey to the Indian camp and the arrival at the shanties?
2. Inside the hut, what images of sight, sound, and smell take you into the heart of the scene?
3. What is the effect of the rather cold, scientific attitude of the doctor-father? Of his laconic explanations to his son interspersed with details of action? Note the verbs he uses.

4. What do Uncle George and the young Indian observers contribute to the reader's rising sense of horror?
5. How are you prepared for the suicide of the husband?
6. Comment on the irony of the concluding conversation and the significance of the experience in Nick's emotional growth and awareness of life and death.
7. Explain the final sentence.
8. By specific reference to the text, support the view that this is primarily a story of Nick's initiation.

Suggestions for Writing

1. Discuss the story as a commentary on the condition of Indians in rural areas or on reservations today.
2. Write about an early experience in which you learned about birth or death, death or violence.

AUDREY THOMAS

Ascension

Audrey Thomas (b. 1935) is the author of the highly acclaimed novels *Graven Images, Intertidal Life,* which was nominated for the Governer-General Award, and, most recently, *Coming Down from Wa.* She is one of British Columbia's most prestigious and prolific writers. She has done teaching stints in New Hampshire and elsewhere, has lived and traveled extensively in sub-Saharan Africa, but spends most of her time writing in her home in Galiano Island. In this story, taken from the collection *The Wild Blue Yonder,* Thomas uses the metaphor of learning to make bread to describe the protagonist's gradual reconnection to life.

Christine hadn't prayed in fifteen years, but now she prayed in a steady monotone of pleading as she kneaded and turned the bread. Please don't let her die please don't let it happen—knead, knead, then a quarter turn just as Mrs Papoutsia had taught her—please don't let her die. She tried to imagine God as Mrs P must see him, a bearded patriarch in black robes and black beard with a hat like a piece of stove-pipe. Okay, please, for my sake. She hastily, guiltily, corrected herself—I mean for her sake. Knead, turn; knead, turn: for all our sakes, Amen.

When the siren went, Christine was lying on the bed, half-asleep. She thought it was the end of the world, shoved her feet into her slippers, ran downstairs and outside on to the wet grass. One of the volunteers from the south end of the island was just closing the doors of the ambulance. Christine ran across her yard and into the road shouting, "Stop, stop, what's happened?" He waved at her and slapped at his chest, then hurried around the passenger side. The vehicle sped away down the access road and on to the main road south. Wa Wa Wa Wa Wa Wa Wa. She could hear the dreadful sound as the ambulance raced towards the water-taxi.

It couldn't be too serious, Christine thought, or they would have got the helicopter or the Hovercraft. The government wharf was just down below and from time to time, even in the few months she had been on the island, a resident or weekender was taken off white-faced and, even if conscious, *vacant* somehow, as though the easiest way to deal with pain and fear and being in a horizontal and helpless position in full public view (not much public really, only those who lived close by and had heard the helicopter or Hovercraft coming in) was to absent oneself from the body which was causing all the trouble. Christine had seen the weekender who had chopped his finger off taken away like that, the finger in a plastic bag full of ice beside him. The injured man had seemed braver than the people around him, but of course he was in shock. He was a popular man and he put an ad in the local newspaper later on, thanking people for calls and cards and flowers: "Finger and hand reunited and doing fine." She had seen them take away Mr Jenks, the plumber, who had been up on his roof replacing shingles when his foot slipped and he fell off the roof and broke his back.

The faces of the sick or injured were as grey as wasp nests, grey as ashes. And the awful noise. Surely the noise would make one sicker, more frightened? Wa Wa Wa Wa Wa. She could still hear it. The ambulance must be at Smugglers' Cove by now. All along the route people would stop what they were doing, turn to one another or pick up the telephone. Who was it that just went by? "Hello, Muriel, did you hear the ambulance just now?" Christine remembered a poem she had read in second-year university: "The Hound of Heaven." A powerful religious poem by a man half-crazy from despair and opium. But, said her teacher, a man who never lost his faith.

> I fled Him, down the nights and down the days;
> I fled Him, down the arches of the years;...

A shocking poem because she had been brought up, like everybody else she knew, to think of Heaven and Christ in gentler terms. Excess in anything, but especially religious fervour, was frowned upon. "Gentle Jesus meek and mild" was the Christ she knew.

The ambulance sounded like Thompson's Hound of Heaven. But perhaps it wasn't so bad that it made that noise after all—all human terror gathered into the single scream of the ambulance siren. Faint now, but she could still hear it. And Mrs Papoutsia inside.

"Christina," Mrs Papoutsia said. "Nice name. Means golden one. Friends in Greece—lady friends—say, '*chrysomou*'—my golden one. "

"It's Christine, not Christina."

"Same thing."

Christine stood in the wet, winter-logged grass, uncertain what to do. She wanted to go down to the store and find out more but was afraid to seem nosy. "Bread," she thought now, "it's Thursday. She must already have started the bread." Still in her wet slippers she went into Mrs Papoutsia's yard and up the back steps, searched for the key which she knew was hanging on a cup hook under the bathroom window and let herself in. The big black woodstove was still throwing off heat and two large earthenware bowls, covered with clean tea-towels, sat on the warming shelf. The room had the slightly sour smell of yeast and rising bread plus the liquorice smell of oil of anise.

Mrs P's two cats glared at her from the tops of cupboards. They were still shaken by the invasion of strangers and the awful sound.

"It's okay guys," she said, "you can come down." The cats continued to glare.

("What are their names?"

"Perché."

"Both of them?"

"Sure. Perché in Greek mean 'why' and also 'because.' One cat 'why' and the other 'because'." The old lady grinned, showing her gold-capped teeth. "Is joke.")

Christine lifted the heavy bowls down from the top of the stove and set them on the counter. She pulled off the towels and the waxpaper underneath. The dough had risen right up to the top and almost over the edge. She was just in time. She punched the dough down, hard, and it let out a little whoosh of air and a slick-slick sound when the bubbles burst. Christine knew enough about Greek bread by now to know, from the anise, that this was probably Easter bread. Next week Mrs P was going to show her how to make it. But what came after it rose again? Naturally there were no recipe books lying around. It would be a fancy bread, today of all days. It had to be braided and have hard-boiled eggs baked in the centre of it, or were those put in after the bread had baked? Christine looked in the fridge; there was a bowl of six bright red eggs already boiled and dyed. One problem solved at any rate. But did they go in before, or after?

Mrs P could not believe her new neighbour didn't know how to make bread.

"You never?"

"Never ever. I like good bread, but I guess I've always lived where I could get it from a bakery."

"Your mama, no?"

"No. Never. She made good baking-powder biscuits and wonderful pancakes, but we bought our bread. I even remember the name of the bakery because it sponsored a music show on the radio." Christine began to sing, to the "Tales from the Vienna Woods":

The famous Spalding Bakery
A name that stands for quality
We invite you to buy
We invite you to try
Delicious and pure Spalding Bread.

She laughed. "The songs they played were golden oldies—Frank Sinatra, Perry Como, stuff like that. My grandmother must've baked bread though. I remember long cylindrical hinged pans in the back of the kitchen cupboard." Her mother had given the pans to a church sale.

"Your grandmama good woman."

"My mother good woman too. She just didn't bake bread." Sometimes, when she talked with Mrs P she found herself leaving out parts of speech and wondered if the old woman thought she was mocking her.

"Staff of life—bread."

"Is that a Greek saying too? I mean, I've heard it all my life but do people in Greece say it as well?"

"In Bible! Isaiah! You no go to church?"

"I used to. I don't go any more."

"You don't believe?"

"Not any more."

Mrs P snorted. "Belief also staff of life."

"Maybe." The old woman gave her a hard look.

"You have nice voice. Why not join choir here? Not church choir, other one. Thursday night at Activity Centre. Meet people. Lovely to sing."

"I'm not staying long enough," Christine said. "There's no point. "

When Christine came to the island in the New Year she had already made up her mind not be overly friendly with her neighbours, whomever they turned out to be. After all, she was only renting for six months. She'd be gone by Canada Day. Besides, she was there to puzzle out certain things and the fewer complications the better. She had seen the ad in the *Times-Colonist* and answered it on a whim. She made all the arrangements before she told her friends. She also told them not to come and visit. Yeah, sure, they said. You'll get cabin fever in three weeks. You'll be on the phone begging us to come over or you'll be back here every weekend. But they were wrong. It was now the middle of April. She plugged the phone in only once a week, on Sunday mornings, to call her mother in southern Ontario. She did not answer letters, although she might have answered the one letter that never came.

"Where husband?" Mrs Papoutsia said. "Where childrens?"

"No children," Christine replied. "No husband. Not any more. Husband gone." Mrs Papoutsia dipped her cookie in her tea.

"You like nice Greek husband? My son arrange. He knows all Greek mens in Vancouver. He knows Greek mens in Greece."

"No thanks, I'm happy right now the way I am."

"What you do to husband that he leave?"

"What did *I* do! I didn't do anything."

"Hmnph."

Mrs P had a calendar from Greece above the kitchen sink. White stone houses that looked as though they had been dipped in the same powdered sugar she used for her raisin cake, her *kourabiethes*, her sesame turnovers. There were bright geraniums in pots and impossibly blue skies. "April" showed an old-fashioned windmill and two smiling men with a donkey. The simple life. But Christine knew that calendars could lie. She had lived in a city famous for its hanging baskets and old-world charm. Pictures of the teen-age prostitutes never graced the dozens of calendars produced each year.

Michael had been gone for nearly a year and still she couldn't fall asleep right away, no matter how tired she was and still she dreamt of him, strange, disturbing erotic dreams. The first day she got here, after she had unpacked her things, she took her wedding ring out of its velvet-lined box, walked to the end of the government wharf and threw it in. She hoped no fish would swallow it, no fisherman appear at the door one day, wondering if she'd lost something. Their initials were on the inside.

"Listen," Michael said, "there's no nice way of saying this. I'm sorry." At least there were no children, her friends said, it's far worse if there's kids involved.

Christine gave the dough another big *thump*, turned it over to keep it oiled, replaced the paper and towels and put the bowls back on the shelf.

Then she went down the steps and under the house for more wood. She felt she had to finish the bread, keep the fire going, if Mrs Papoutsia was going to have any chance at all, that Mrs P would count on her doing this. The bread was for Greek Easter, only two weeks away. Mrs P was having a big feast for everybody at the North End Hall. Her son was coming over to roast the lamb. When Mrs Papoutsia told her this it sounded like "Roast Lamp."

Had anyone called her son? Emergency numbers plus the son's telephone number and a few other numbers were posted neatly by the telephone. Everything in the small house was neat and tidy. On the window-sill by the back door there were clam shells, oyster shells, even walnut shells full of flower seeds to be planted as soon as the ground dried out a bit more. The little slips of paper identifying them were written in Greek but Christine could recognize a few of them by their shape: marigolds, cornflowers, nasturtiums. Glass jars held bean seeds and tomato seedlings were already sprouting on the front window-sill.

Paper bags were neatly folded in a corner of the cupboard underneath the sink, rubber-bands and twist-ties saved in the kitchen drawer. Everything that could be used again was used again; very little was thrown out. Christine thought of her own untidy life. If something happened to her, her friends and her mother would have a terrible time sorting things out. "I must get a divorce as soon as possible," she thought now, opening the fridge and taking out the cat food. The two cats, both huge grey blue-eyed Persians, were Mrs Papoutsia's big indulgence. That and making breads and cakes. "I must give my life some order." She had taken a leave from teaching, on the grounds of illness. She had been experiencing dizzy spells at work and strange headaches. It was like being hit in the head with a snowball, she told the doctor, a sudden pain and then a dull ache. It scared her. The doctor sent her for tests but they all came back negative. She wept and he offered her a choice of Librium or Valium, "just until you pull yourself together." She declined and answered an ad.

There was quite a crowd at the store, discussing Mrs Papoutsia. She'd had a bad pain in her chest and called the doctor. It was lucky she did, because by the time he arrived with the ambulance she was lying on her bed in great distress.

"Did she call you?" the storekeeper said, noticing Christine.

"My phone was unplugged," she said and felt her face go red. Had she called? Christine imagined the doctor and the paramedics trying to get Mrs Papoutsia's heart to go, thumping it hard the way she had thumped the bread. Thump. Thump. "Where did they take her?" Christina asked. In spite of her shame and embarrassment she had to know. She bought some milk she didn't need and a Kit-Kat bar to give her visit some validity.

"Probably to the Royal Jubilee—if it's a heart attack. The doctor will know."

Christine went back up her path, called the doctor and got his wife. He was with Mrs Papoutsia and they were on their way to Victoria, perhaps even there by now. "She has a son in Vancouver," Christine said, "do you know if he's been called? He runs a delicatessen on Broadway."

"I don't know. Shall I have Jim call you? He'll phone in for messages pretty soon."

Christine left the son's number, which she'd copied down, and also her own. It wasn't time to punch the dough again and then attempt to braid it. She didn't even know what temperature to use. The dough had eggs in it—did that mean a higher or lower temperature? Christine had so far attempted nothing more difficult than round white loaves and something Mrs Papoutsia called "*starénio*," or "peasant bread," which was dark and dense and wonderful spread with Greek honey brought over by the son, who wore the nails of his little fingers very long—to show that he did not work with his hands. He called himself Mr Pappas. Mrs P loved him fiercely but was impatient.

"Father fisherman, grandfather fisherman, good job, *honourable.* Now he wants make sure everybody know he don't work rough work. And change name! Easier for peoples, Mama. No trouble. Papoutsia *easy* name! Pa—poots—see—a." She grinned at Christine. "Husband Dmitri, English 'Jimmy.' His name in English Jimmy Shoes. I, Fotula, Mrs Jimmy Shoes."

Fotula and Dmitri had come to the island every year when the herring were running. Their son, with scuba equipment, dove for octopus. Fotula and Dmitri decided to buy a small lot and build. Now that Dmitri was dead, the son and his wife wanted Fotula to come and live with them but she refused. There were no grandchildren. On the island Mrs P was "Yia yia," "Grandmother" to a couple of dozen little ones. She fed them sweetcakes oozing honey and nuts, wiped their sticky faces, kissed them, rocked them in her rocking chair. They saw her coming and ran to her with their arms outstretched.

"His doorbell play four tunes including Greek anthem. So what? Jimmy good boy but modern. Electric this, electric that. I no like."

Christine had very pointedly kept herself to herself and after a few weeks the neighbours accepted that she really meant it when she said no to morning coffee or afternoon tea, no to darts, no to the garden club, the women's auxiliary to the firehall, no to Scottish country dancing. (Mrs Papoutsia did Scottish country dancing every Tuesday night.) When Christine talked to people she felt that any second now she would crack and fall to pieces right before their eyes. She said she was writing a book and couldn't be disturbed. She was then invited to join the writers' group but declined. It was a book for teaching English as a Second Language, she said, not a creative book at all.

On the third Thursday someone knocked hard on the front door. An old woman stood on the porch, black skirt, black cardigan, black stockings and boots. She smelled of fresh bread and, faintly, of oranges. "Fotula Papoutsia," she said. "Your neighbour. I tell landlord I keep eye. Also clean on Fridays."

"Thank you very much," said Christine, who had been brought up never to be rude to elderly people, "that won't be necessary. I'm fine." The old lady walked right in and put something wrapped in a towel on the kitchen table. Delicious smells came up from under the towel. "Look," said Christine, trying not to sound annoyed. "It's awfully kind of you but—" The red kettle was being filled, the tea cannister taken down from the left-hand cupboard.

"Mr Beldon and me—tea or *kaffes* together Thursdays, bread day. He keep eye on me, my eye on him. You have jam?" She opened the fridge and peered in. "Next time I bring."

Christine took a deep breath. "Mrs Papoutsia, I don't know what your arrangement was with Mr Beldon, but I'm here to be very quiet—no visitors."

"Crazy talk," said the old woman, pouring hot water into the teapot and swirling it around. "Me, I *prefer kaffes*—cof-fee—but Joe he like tea. Come, sit."

A warm loaf, butter, teapot, teacups and saucers. "Sit, eat." When Christine began to cry, Mrs Papoutsia ignored her for a long while, sipped her tea, and buttered slices of bread, looked around the untidy room and muttered foreign words to herself. Finally, "*Andaxi.* Okay. You and me, we talk."

Now Christine felt the old panic returning—Mrs P, her one friend, her support, had been taken away. She was learning to make bread, to understand the mysteries of yeast, of how the milk had to be scalded, the water just the right temperature. When she kneaded and turned, kneaded and turned, kneaded and turned, she felt the anger and hurt leaving her, even if, as yet, it only left for a while, one day a week.

"You can even," said Mrs P, "get yeast out from air. I show you."

On bread-lesson days it was usually dark by the time Christine walked back to her own house, her basket full of Greek food she had sampled during the afternoon. When Mrs Papoutsia told her about the Easter Feast at the North End Hall and had asked—demanded—Christine's help, she had felt strong enough to agree.

"Easy food. Greece not a *fancy* place. Cheese. Olive. *Dolmades,* little pies of spinach, son do the lamp outside. Easter bread—I show you."

Christine dialled the hospital in Victoria. Yes, they had a Mrs Papoutsia in Intensive Care. Her son had just arrived. No, they could tell her nothing if she wasn't kin.

Was she conscious?

"I'm afraid I can't—"

Christine was shouting into the phone. "Well if she *is* conscious could you tell her, could somebody get word to her that Christina—yes, *Christina,* I'm her next-door neighbour—has seen to the bread. The *bread.* That's right. Tell her Christina has seen to the bread."

The son called just as Christine was taking the loaves out of the oven. The braids weren't even but they didn't look half-bad and she had been right to set the coloured eggs in before baking. She carefully put the hot pans on the racks she had already set out. The cats had come down and were watching her with a kind of angry interest. Where was their mistress—what had Christine done with her?

"Hello," Christine said, her own heart bumping loudly against her chest.

"Christina? Jimmy Pappas here. I tried your house then figured you'd be at my mother's."

"How is she?"

"She just slipped away. We lost her about fifteen minutes ago."

"Did she get my message about the bread?"

"She never regained consciousness." She could hear him struggling to keep his voice manly, in charge. "I'll come over tomorrow. Do you think you could feed the cats and keep an eye on things?"

"We'll have to have the Easter Feast," Christine said. "She'd want us to have the Easter Feast."

"Thank you for being such a good friend to her Christina—she often talked about you."

Christine hung up the phone. While the bread cooled she rinsed the pans and bowls and tidied the kitchen. Then she walked around looking at all the framed photographs on the walls: Fotula as a young girl; Fotula in her wedding dress with the six petticoats underneath; Fotula and Dmitri on their fish boat, *The Ariadne*; Fotula with young Dmitri in her arms. In none of the pictures was she smiling but there was a kind of fierce smile implied in the eyes, the mouth, the way she carried herself. A proud woman. Fulfilled.

And then, the most amazing photograph of all—Fotula shaking hands with an astronaut. She was all in black, as usual; he was wearing white. It was the only photograph in which she smiled. The astronaut was smiling too.

"Is that your son?" Christine asked when she first noticed it.

"No. No. Mr. Somebody—I forget name but I have clipping somewhere. I win big prize, go to Ottawa, meet astronauts."

"You won a big prize? Was it a lottery?"

Mrs Papoutsia gave her a look of contempt. "What you mean *lottery?* I enter contest—think up good project to try out in space, project to benefit mankind."

"And?"

"And I win! Make bread in space," I say. "If go to new worlds need staff of life—try make bread in space." Mrs Papoutsia and four others with the same idea had won the contest and been given the royal treatment. That wasn't all—they were to go to Cape Canaveral when the experiment actually went up. Mrs P had been looking forward to it enormously. If it hadn't been for the Challenger she would have gone already.

Christine sat in the rocking chair with one cat on her lap, the other at her feet. She had banked the fire in the stove and shut down the damper. The house smelled wonderful and in spite of her grief and shock Christine couldn't help smiling as she imagined the soul of her friend, fragrant, spicy, lighter than air, gradually rising up through the April skies towards a bright blue heaven.

Suggestions for Discussion

1. Mrs. Papoutsia wins a contest on the basis of her idea that astronauts learn to make bread in space. What does this metaphor suggest to us?
2. Christine speaks of the "Gentle Jesus meek and mild" that she had been brought up to know and the ferocious "Hound of Heaven" that she comes to experience. What does this transition have to do with her own process of healing?
3. What does completing the baking of the Easter bread represent for Christine?

Suggestions for Writing

1. Simple, everyday activities can come to have great symbolic significance for us. Examine your own life and identify one such activity and write a story that makes clear to us what it means to you.
2. Human beings have been described as creatures who have their feet on the earth and their heads in the clouds. Find a metaphor for the earth and the clouds and weave it into a story.
3. This is a story about healing, which happens across generations and cultures. Write a story with this theme, drawn from your own experience if possible.

GARY SOTO

Black Hair

Gary Soto (b. 1952) was born and educated in California, where he is an associate professor in Chicano Studies and English at the University of California at Berkeley. He has published prolifically, both poetry and prose, and has won an impressive series of fellowships and awards. Among these are the Poets' Prize of the Academy of American Poets, the Bess Hopkins Prize for Poetry, a Guggenheim Fellowship, the Levinson Award for Poetry, and the American Book Award from the Before Columbus Foundation. His most recent books are *Pieces of the Heart: New Chicano Fiction* (1993) and *Lesser Evils.* Here we see him as he recounts the grim and almost hopeless life of a young Mexican boy trying to find his way in the world.

There are two kinds of work: One uses the mind and the other uses muscle. As a kid I found out about the latter. I'm thinking of the summer of 1969 when I was a seventeen-year-old runaway who ended up in Glendale, California, to work for Valley Tire Factory. To answer an ad in the newspaper I walked miles in the afternoon sun, my stomach slowly knotting on a doughnut that was breakfast, my teeth like bright candles gone yellow.

I walked in the door sweating and feeling ugly because my hair was still stiff from a swim at the Santa Monica beach the day before. Jules, the accountant and part owner, looked droopily through his bifocals at my application and then at me. He tipped his cigar in the ashtray, asked my age as if he didn't believe I was seventeen, but finally after a moment of silence, said, "Come back tomorrow. Eight-thirty."

I thanked him, left the office, and went around to the chain link fence to watch the workers heave tires into a bin; others carted uneven stacks of tires on hand trucks. Their faces were black from tire dust and when they talked—or cussed—their mouths showed a bright pink.

From there I walked up a commercial street, past a cleaners, a motorcycle shop, and a gas station where I washed my face and hands; before leaving I took a bottle that hung on the side of the Coke machine, filled it with water, and stopped it with a scrap of paper and a rubber band.

The next morning I arrived early at work. The assistant foreman, a potbellied Hungarian, showed me a timecard and how to punch in. He showed me the Coke machine, the locker room with its slimy shower, and also pointed out the places where I shouldn't go: The ovens where the tires were recapped and the customer service area, which had a slashed couch, a coffee table with greasy magazines, and an ashtray. He introduced me to Tully, a fat man with one ear, who worked the buffers that resurfaced the white walls. I was handed an apron and a face mask and shown how to use the buffer: Lift the tire and center, inflate it with a footpedal, press the buffer against the white band until cleaned, and then deflate and blow off the tire with an air hose.

With a paint brush he stirred a can of industrial preserver. "Then slap this blue stuff on." While he was talking a co-worker came up quietly from behind him and goosed him with the air hose. Tully jumped as if he had been struck by a bullet and then turned around cussing and cupping his genitals in his hands as the other worker walked away calling out foul names. When Tully turned to me smiling his gray teeth, I lifted my mouth into a smile because I wanted to get along. He has to be on my side, I thought. He's the one who'll tell the foreman how I'm doing.

I worked carefully that day, setting the tires on the machine as if they were babies, since it was easy to catch a finger in the rim that expanded to inflate the tire. At the day's end we swept up the tire dust and emptied the trash into bins.

At five the workers scattered for their cars and motorcycles while I crossed the street to wash at a burger stand. My hair was stiff with dust and my mouth showed pink against the backdrop of my dirty face. I then ordered a hotdog and walked slowly in the direction of the abandoned house where I had stayed the night before. I lay under the trees and within minutes was asleep. When I woke my shoulders were sore and my eyes burned when I squeezed the lids together.

From the backyard I walked dully through a residential street, and as evening came on, the TV glare in the living rooms and the headlights of passing cars showed against the blue drift of dusk. I saw two children coming up the street with snow cones, their tongues darting at the packed ice. I saw a boy with a peach and wanted to stop him, but felt embarrassed by my hunger. I walked for an hour only to return and discover the house lit brightly. Behind the fence I heard voices and saw a flashlight poking at the garage door. A man on the back steps mumbled something about the refrigerator to the one with the flashlight.

I waited for them to leave, but had the feeling they wouldn't because there was the commotion of furniture being moved. Tired, even more desperate, I started walking again with a great urge to kick things and tear the day from my life. I felt weak and my mind kept drifting because of hunger.

I crossed the street to a gas station where I sipped at the water fountain and searched the Coke machine for change. I started walking again, first up a commercial street, then into a residential area where I lay down on someone's lawn and replayed a scene at home—my Mother crying at the kitchen table, my stepfather yelling with food in his mouth. They're cruel, I thought, and warned myself that I should never forgive them. How could they do this to me.

When I got up from the lawn it was late. I searched out a place to sleep and found an unlocked car that seemed safe. In the backseat, with my shoes off, I fell asleep but woke up startled about four in the morning when the owner, a nurse on her way to work, opened the door. She got in and was about to start the engine when I raised my head up from the backseat to explain my presence. She screamed so loudly when I said "I'm sorry" that I sprinted from the car with my shoes in hand. Her screams faded, then stopped altogether, as I ran down the block where I hid behind a trash bin and waited for a police siren to sound. Nothing. I crossed the street to a church where I slept stiffly on cardboard in the balcony.

I woke up feeling tired and greasy. It was early and a few street lights were still lit, the east growing pink with dawn. I washed myself from a garden hose and returned to the church to break into what looked like a kitchen. Paper cups, plastic spoons, a coffee pot littered on a table. I found a box of Nabisco crackers which I ate until I was full.

At work I spent the morning at the buffer, but was then told to help Iggy, an old Mexican, who was responsible for choosing tires that could be recapped without the risk of exploding at high speeds. Every morning a truck would deliver used tires, and after I unloaded them Iggy would step among the tires to inspect them for punctures and rips on the side walls.

With a yellow chalk he marked circles and Xs to indicate damage and called out "junk." For those tires that could be recapped, he said "goody" and I placed them on my hand truck. When I had a stack of eight I kicked the truck at an angle and balanced them to another work area where Iggy again inspected the tires, scratching Xs and calling out "junk."

Iggy worked only until three in the afternoon, at which time he went to the locker room to wash and shave and to dress in a two-piece suit. When he came out he glowed with a bracelet, watch, rings, and a shiny fountain pen in his breast pocket. His shoes sounded against the asphalt. He was the image of a banker stepping into sunlight with millions on his mind. He said a few low words to workers with whom he was friendly and none to people like me.

I was seventeen, stupid because I couldn't figure out the difference between an F 78 14 and 750 14 at sight. Iggy shook his head when I brought him the wrong tires, especially since I had expressed interest in being his understudy. "Mexican, how can you be so stupid?" he would yell at me, slapping a tire from my hands. But within weeks I learned a lot about tires, from sizes and makes to how they are molded in iron forms to how Valley stole from other companies. Now and then we received a truckload of tires, most of them new or nearly new, and they were taken to our warehouse in the back where the serial numbers were ground off with a sander. On those days the foreman handed out Cokes and joked with us as we worked to get the numbers off.

Most of the workers were Mexican or black, though a few redneck whites worked there. The base pay was a dollar sixty-five, but the average was three dollars. Of the black workers, I knew Sugar Daddy the best. His body carried two hundred and fifty pounds, armfuls of scars, and a long knife that made me jump when he brought it out from his boot without warning. At one time he had been a singer, and had cut a record in 1967 called *Love's Chance,* which broke into the R and B charts. But nothing came of it. No big contract, no club dates, no tours. He made very little from the sales, only enough for an operation to pull a steering wheel from his gut when, drunk and mad at a lady friend, he slammed his Mustang into a row of parked cars.

"Touch it," he smiled at me one afternoon as he raised his shirt, his black belly kinked with hair. Scared, I traced the scar that ran from his chest to the left of his belly button, and I was repelled but hid my disgust.

Among the Mexicans I had few friends because I was different, a *pocho* who spoke bad Spanish. At lunch they sat in tires and laughed over burritos, looking up at me to laugh even harder. I also sat in tires while nursing a Coke and felt dirty and sticky because I was still living on the street and had not had a real bath in over a week. Nevertheless, when the border patrol came to round up the nationals, I ran with them as they scrambled for the fence or hid among the tires behind the warehouse. The foreman, who thought I was an undocumented worker, yelled at me to run, to get away. I did just that. At the time it seemed fun because there was no risk, only a goodhearted feeling of hide-and-seek, and besides it meant an hour away from work on company time. When the police left we came back and some of the nationals made up stories of how they were almost caught—how they out-raced the police. Some of the stories were so convoluted and unconvincing that everyone laughed *mentiras,* especially when one described how he overpowered a policeman, took his gun away, and sold the patrol car. We laughed and he laughed, happy to be there to make up a story.

If work was difficult, so were the nights. I still had not gathered enough money to rent a room, so I spent the nights sleeping in parked cars or in the balcony of a church. After a week I found a newspaper ad for room for rent, phoned, and was given directions. Finished with work, I walked the five miles down Mission Road looking back into the traffic with my thumb out. No rides. After eight hours of handling tires I was frightening, I suppose, to drivers since they seldom looked at me; if they did, it was a quick glance. For the next six weeks I would try to hitchhike, but the only person to stop was a Mexican woman who gave me two dollars to take the bus. I told her it was too much and that no bus ran from Mission Road to where I lived, but she insisted that I keep the money and trotted back to her idling car. It must have hurt her to see me day after day walking in the heat and looking very much the dirty Mexican to the many minds that didn't know what it meant to work at hard labor. That woman knew. Her eyes met mine as she opened the car door, and there was a tenderness that was surprisingly true—one for which you wait for years but when it comes it doesn't help. Nothing changes. You continue on in rags, with the sun still above you.

I rented a room from a middle-aged couple whose lives were a mess. She was a school teacher and he was a fireman. A perfect set up, I thought. But during my stay there they would argue with one another for hours in their bedroom.

When I rang at the front door both Mr. and Mrs. Van Deusen answered and didn't bother to disguise their shock at how awful I looked. But they let me in all the same. Mrs. Van Deusen showed me around the house, from the kitchen and bathroom to the living room with its grand piano. On her fingers she counted out the house rules as she walked me to my room. It was a girl's room with lace curtains, scenic wallpaper of a Victorian couple enjoying a stroll, canopied bed, and stuffed animals in a corner. Leaving, she turned and asked if she could do laundry for me and, feeling shy and hurt, I told her no; perhaps the next day. She left and I undressed to take a bath, exhausted as I sat on the edge of the bed probing my aches and my bruised places. With a towel around my waist I hurried down the hallway to the bathroom where Mrs. Van Deusen had set out an additional towel with a tube of shampoo. I ran the water in the tub and sat on the toilet, lid down, watching the steam curl toward the ceiling. When I lowered myself into the tub I felt my body sting. I soaped a wash cloth and scrubbed my arms until they lightened, even glowed pink, but still I looked unwashed around my neck and face no matter how hard I rubbed. Back in the room I sat in bed reading a magazine, happy and thinking of no better luxury than a girl's sheets, especially after nearly two weeks of sleeping on cardboard at the church.

I was too tired to sleep, so I sat at the window watching the neighbors move about in pajamas, and, curious about the room, looked through the bureau drawers to search out personal things—snapshots, a messy diary, and a high school yearbook. I looked up the Van Deusen's daughter, Barbara, and studied her face as if I recognized her from my own school—a face that said "promise," "college," "nice clothes in the closet." She was a skater and a member of the German Club; her greatest ambition was to sing at the Hollywood Bowl.

After awhile I got into bed and as I drifted toward sleep I thought about her. In my mind I played a love scene again and again and altered it slightly each time. She comes home from college and at first is indifferent to my presence in her home, but finally I overwhelm her with deep pity when I come home hurt from work, with blood on my shirt. Then there was another version: Home from college she is immediately taken with me, in spite of my work-darkened face, and invites me into the family car for a milkshake across town. Later, back at the house, we sit in the living room talking about school until we're so close I'm holding her hand. The truth of the matter was that Barbara did come home for a week, but was bitter toward her parents for taking in boarders (two others besides me). During that time she spoke to me only twice: Once, while searching the refrigerator, she asked if we had any mustard; the other time she asked if I had seen her car keys.

But it was a place to stay. Work had become more and more difficult. I not only worked with Iggy, but also with the assistant foreman who was in charge of unloading trucks. After they backed in I hopped on top to pass the tires down by bouncing them on the tailgate to give them an extra spring so they would be less difficult to handle on the other end. Each truck was weighed down with more than two hundred tires, each averaging twenty pounds, so that by the time the truck was emptied and swept clean I glistened with sweat and my T-shirt stuck to my body. I blew snot threaded with tire dust onto the asphalt, indifferent to the customers who watched from the waiting room.

The days were dull. I did what there was to do from morning until the bell sounded at five; I tugged, pulled, and cussed at tires until I was listless and my mind drifted and caught on small things, from cold sodas to shoes to stupid talk about what we would do with a million dollars. I remember unloading a truck with Hamp, a black man.

"What's better than a sharp lady?" he asked me as I stood sweaty on a pile of junked tires. "Water. With ice," I said.

He laughed with his mouth open wide. With his fingers he pinched the sweat from his chin and flicked at me. "You be too young, boy. A woman can make you a god."

As a kid I had chopped cotton and picked grapes, so I knew work. I knew the fatigue and the boredom and the feeling that there was a good possibility you might have to do such work for years, if not for a lifetime. In fact, as a kid I imagined a dark fate: To marry Mexican poor, work Mexican hours, and in the end die a Mexican death, broke and in despair.

But this job at Valley Tire Company confirmed that there was something worse than field work, and I was doing it. We were all doing it, from foreman to the newcomers like me, and what I felt heaving tires for eight hours a day was felt by everyone—black, Mexican, redneck. We all despised those hours but didn't know what else to do. The workers were unskilled, some undocumented and fearful of deportation, and all struck with an uncertainty at what to do with their lives. Although everyone bitched about work, no one left. Some had worked there for as long as twelve years; some had sons working there. Few quit; no one was ever fired. It amazed me that no one gave up when the border patrol jumped from their vans, baton in hand, because I couldn't imagine any work that could be worse—or any life. What was out there, in the world, that made men run for the fence in fear?

Iggy was the only worker who seemed sure of himself. After five hours of "junking," he brushed himself off, cleaned up in the washroom, and came out gleaming with an elegance that humbled the rest of us. Few would look him straight in the eye or talk to him in our usual stupid way because he was so much better. He carried himself as a man should—with that old world "dignity"—while the rest of us muffed our jobs and talked dully about dull things as we worked. From where he worked in his open shed he would now and then watch us with his hands on his hips. He would shake his head and click his tongue in disgust.

The rest of us lived dismally. I often wondered what the others' homes were like; I couldn't imagine that they were much better than our work place. No one indicated that his outside life was interesting or intriguing. We all looked defeated and contemptible in our filth at the day's end. I imagined the average welcome at home: Rafael, a Mexican national who had worked at Valley for five years, returned to a beaten house of kids who were dressed in mismatched clothes and playing kick-the-can. As for Sugar Daddy, he returned home to a stuffy room where he would read and reread old magazines. He ate potato chips, drank beer, and watched TV. There was no grace in dipping socks into a wash basin where later he would wash his cup and plate.

There was no grace at work. It was all ridicule. The assistant foreman drank Cokes in front of the newcomers as they laced tires in the afternoon sun. Knowing that I had a long walk home, Rudy, the college student, passed me waving and yelling "Hello," as I started down Mission Road on the way home to eat out of cans. Even our plump secretary got into the act by wearing short skirts and flaunting her milky legs. If there was love, it was ugly. I'm thinking of Tully and an older man whose name I can no longer recall fondling one another in the washroom. I had come in cradling a smashed finger to find them pressed together in the shower, their pants undone and partly pulled down. When they saw me they smiled their pink mouths but didn't bother to push away.

How we arrived at such a place is a mystery to me. Why anyone would stay for years is even a deeper concern. You showed up, but from where? What broken life? What ugly past? The foreman showed you the Coke machine, the washroom, and the yard where you'd work. When you picked up a tire, you were amazed at the black it could give off.

Suggestions for Discussion

1. Soto says he cannot imagine any work or any life that could be worse than the one he describes. What makes it so terrible?
2. What does the author mean by "There was no grace at work"? How does this comment relate to how he understands dignity and dullness?
3. As a child Soto imagines a dark fate: "To marry Mexican poor, work Mexican hours, and in the end die a Mexican death, broke and in despair." Why is his experience at the Valley Tire Company even worse?

Suggestions for Writing

1. What is the most disagreeable job you ever had? Why was it so? Describe your workday.
2. In part the protagonist survives by fantasy. How have you used this technique to live through hard times?

DAVID BRADLEY

Harvest Home

David Bradley (b. 1950) was born in Pennsylvania and educated at the University of Pennsylvania and at King's College, London, where he earned an M.A. He is Associate Professor of English at Temple University, and as a writer, he has won the PEN/Faulkner Award and the American Academy of Arts and Letters Award for Literature (1982). His major work is *The Chaneysville Incident* (1981). Recently he has published *On Race and Racism* and *Southeast Asia* (1997). In the account that follows we see him trying to come to grips with the richness of his family heritage and all of the ambiguities therein.

Thanksgiving 1988. In the house my father built my mother and I sit down to dine. A snowy cloth and ivory china give wintry background to browns of turkey and stuffing and gravy, mild yellow of parched corn, mellow orange of candied yams. Amidst those autumnal shades cranberry sauce flares red like flame in fallen leaves, and steam rises like scentless smoke. Head up, eyes open, I chant prefabricated grace (Father, we thank Thee for this our daily bread which we are about to partake of...) and long for the extemporaneous artistry of my father, now almost a decade dead. His blessings—couched in archaic diction ("Harvest Home," he called this holiday) and set in meter measured as a tolling bell—were grounded in a childhood in which daily bread was hoped for, not expected; his grace had gravity, unlike this airy ditty I now mutter.

Still, it seems there is even in this doggerel dogma (...May it nourish our souls and bodies...) an echo of his voice. Hope flutters in me, rises as I come to the end (...in Jesus' name and for His sake...), then hangs, gliding in the silence, as I pause and listen. My mother sits, head bowed, patient and unsurprised; for nine years I have paused so, just short of "amen." What I wait for she has never asked. And I have never before said.

Once there were more of us. For once we were a mighty clan, complete with house and lineage. As we are dark (and sometimes comely), outsiders might expect us to trace that lineage to Africa, but we have benign contempt for those who pin their pride to ancestries dotted by the Middle Passage or *griot*-given claims to Guinean thrones. For what is Africa (spicy groves, cinnamon trees, or ancient dusky rivers?) to a clan that knows, as we know, the precise when and where of our origin: on March 10, 1836, in Seaford, Delaware. Then and there a justice of the peace named Harry L-something (the paper is browned, the ink faded, and ornate script all but undecipherable) certified that a "Col. man by the name of Peter Bradley" was henceforth a freedman. This Peter was our progenitor.

Outsiders might wonder that we do not fix our origin in 1815, the year of Peter's birth. The reason: the slave laws—what oxymoron that!—decreed that a bondsman had right to neither property nor person. Peter could not own a family, for he did not own himself. But on March 10, Peter's master gave Peter to Peter for Peter's birthday; this not only made him, legally, his own man but entitled him to purchase a (black) woman. He could have owned her, and any children he fathered on her. But he did not. Peter wed a free woman; thus the two sons he sired were free from the moment of their birth. But Peter, by that time, was not. For after being given by his master to himself he gave himself to his Master, and became a minister of the gospel.

Such service became a clan tradition. Both Peter's sons became ministers, licensed by the African Methodist Episcopal Zion Church, the first denomination organized by American blacks who chafed at the unequal opportunity offered by the Methodist Episcopal Church. One son was

"M. A."—we do not know his full name, or date of birth. The other was Daniel Francis, born in 1852. Through him our line descends.

Daniel Francis became a minister at the age of nineteen. Although we know nothing of his early assignments, we are sure that they were plentiful, for Zion Methodists followed the dictate of John Wesley that ministers should never stand long in any pulpit, lest they become too powerful. And we know that the Presiding Bishop eventually sent him to Williamsport, Pennsylvania, where he met Cora Alice Brewer. Though in those rigid times, Daniel Francis, at forty-four, would have been called a confirmed bachelor and Cora Alica, at twenty-seven, old enough to be called a spinster, love blossomed into marriage in 1896. The first fruit of the union was a man-child, John, born in 1898. A daughter, Gladys, followed in 1900. More sons, David and Andrew, were born in 1905 and 1906, after the family left Williamsport for Sewickley, Pennsylvania, outside Pittsburgh.

The house came in 1911, when Daniel Francis, who had been reassigned at least five times since Williamsport, was sent to a church called Mt. Pisgah, in the town of Bedford, in the south-central part of Pennsylvania. As Mt. Pisgah had no parsonage, Daniel Francis went ahead of the family to find a place to live. On the train he met a man called Bixler, who offered to sell him an eleven-acre homestead two miles west of Bedford, near the hamlet of Wolfsburg. The price was steep (seven hundred and fifty dollars), the terms usurious (one hundred dollars down, one hundred per year plus annual interest and a widow's dower), but Daniel Francis found both price and terms acceptable, perhaps because there were no other terms at all. And so, in the spring of 1912, our clan took up residence in our first permanent home.

But Daniel Francis did not see the Wolfsburg property as just a home. In early 1915 he announced plans to create what the local weekly, the *Bedford Gazette,* called "an attractive summer resort for those of his race who will gather here from Pittsburgh and Western Pennsylvania." His future plans called for the building of a "large tabernacle for divine services, lectures and entertainments" and in time a normal school for the education of black craftsmen modeled on Tuskegee Institute—Booker T. Washington, Daniel Francis told the *Gazette,* had promised to come to Wolfsburg to speak. Although Booker T. Washington never did appear, a camp meeting was held in August on a sylvan portion of the homestead (christened "Green Brier Grove" in printed advertisements) and the next year a loan from the Bedford County Trust Company liberated the deed from Bixler's clutches and brought Daniel Francis's dream closer to reality. But Zion Methodists, like Wesley, feared empire-building pastors; later that year the bishop kicked Daniel Francis upstairs, appointing him Presiding Elder, the spiritual and financial manager of a group of churches in Pennsylvania and eastern Ohio.

But though the promotion killed a dream, it established our clan's mark of achievement: a successful son is he who follows in his father's footsteps and goes a step further. And though it forced us once again to wander, we never forgot the homestead. Somehow we made mortgage payments. By 1921 the homestead was ours, free and clear. A year later we returned to it. It was not, however, a joyful repatriation. On October 15, 1922, Daniel Francis died of "diabetes mellitus." His first son, John, now at twenty-one our chieftain, paid one hundred dollars for a funeral and secured a permit of removal. We escorted the body of Daniel Francis back to Wolfsburg, he to be buried in Mt. Ross, the local Negro cemetery, we to live.

The homestead did not long save us from wandering. Bedford, which to Daniel Francis seemed prosperous enough to support even black ambitions, soon proved capable of supporting few ambitions at all. White youths who wished to do more than sell hats to each other had to leave, if only to get higher education. Black youths, regardless of ambition, were virtually exiled; Bedford had no place for blacks skilled with pens rather than push brooms, and its small black community offered opportunity for exogamy. Some blacks made do. Bradleys do not make do.

And so we dispersed. Gladys married a man named Caldwell and settled in Cleveland, Ohio. David finished high school, won a scholarship, and went South to college. Andrew, after graduation, attached himself to the local Democratic party—a quixotic alliance, as Bedford blacks were fewer and less powerful than Bedford Democrats—and then went east to Harrisburg, the capital. John, who supported the clan until Andrew's graduation, married and settled in Sewickley, and fathered three daughters. But though we dispersed, the homestead remained—a haven in time of trouble, a gathering place for feasts, a totem signifying that, though we were wanderers, we were not Gypsies.

That is what it signified to outsiders. And so it was that in 1956, our clan's one hundred and twentieth year, the *Gazette,* by then a daily, found our clan of local interest. "The rise of the Bradley family from the enforced degradation of slavery to dignity and high achievement is not unparalleled in the history of the American Negro," wrote reporter Gene Farkas. "But it is certainly one of the more outstanding examples of hard-won Negro accomplishment in the nation and the state. In the annals of Bedford County, the story of the Bradley family is without precedent...for it was from these hills and valleys, from the one-room schoolhouse at Wolfsburg and the old Bedford High School...that the Bradley boys emerged to eminence and respect."

Cosmopolitans and outsiders would have said that it was Andrew who had risen highest; in 1954, he became State Budget Secretary and the first black to sit in the Pennsylvania Governor's Cabinet. But local interest, and perhaps a sense of our clan's traditions—he even used the phrase "the footsteps of his father"—caused Farkas to give more space to David, who in 1948 had been elected an AME Zion General Officer—a step beyond Daniel Francis's final rank of Presiding Elder. Though his new duties called for travel, he was free to fix his base where he chose; David purchased land adjacent to the homestead and built what Farkas called "a modern stone bungalow," in which he housed both his own family and Cora Alice, who spent her days in the spartan familiarity of the homestead but at night enjoyed the sybaritic comforts of indoor plumbing and central heating.

Farkas did a good job for an outsider. Although he did not specifically mention another of David's contributions to the clan, that he alone of the third generation sired a son to carry on the name, the photographs that accompanied the story did depict the lad, David Jr., then six. And though Farkas did give short shrift to John, not mentioning the names of his wife and children (as he did with David and Andrew) and referring to his occupation with a euphemism ("...he has worked for a private family for 25 or 30 years"), in this he only reflected the values of outsiders; men who hold advanced degrees and cabinet posts are commonly deemed more noteworthy than those who held rakes in "private" service. Farkas cannot be blamed for this affront to our dignity. How was he to know that the man so slighted was the chief among us? For the tale as Farkas told it was the tale as we told it to him. Sadly, it was the tale as we were telling it to our children. Except at Harvest Home.

Even when I was too young to comprehend a calendar I knew Harvest Home was coming; I could tell by the smell of my grandmother, Cora Alice. Usually she spent her days in the old homestead crocheting, reading the *Gazette,* and listening in on the party line. But the week before Harvest Home she abandoned leisure, stoked up her big Majestic coal stove, and got busy baking: tangy gingerbread, golden pound cakes, and pies of pumpkin, sweet potato, and mince. In the evening she would come back to the house my father built perfumed with molasses and mace, and I would crawl into her lap and lick surreptitiously at the vestiges of brown sugar that clung to her upper arms. The night before the feast she would not return at all. That would be my signal; I would sneak to my window to keep watch on the homestead a hundred yards away. At last I would see a sweep of headlights. I would press my ear against the gelid glass and listen. The sounds of car doors slammed, greetings shouted, would not satisfy me—I would stand, shivering, until I heard an odd and mighty booming. Then I would know the clan was gathered.

The next afternoon would find us in the rear chamber of the homestead, arrayed around a dark Victorian table with saurian legs and dragon feet. To an outsider the order of our seating might have seemed to loosely reflect Fifties customs—most of the children placed at a separate table and all the men at the main table, while the women served. In fact, it reflected our deep reverence for name and blood. The segregated children had the blood—they were of the fifth generation—but had it through their mothers; none had the name. The women who served—including Cora Alice herself, who, although she presided over the gathering, did so from the sideboard—had the name by marriage. The only woman at table not of the blood was my Uncle Andrew's wife, Gussie, who made it clear she waited on no one. She also smoked and drank in public. (My grandmother had declared her mad; she was left alone.) My cousins—the women of our fourth generation—although they'd lost the name through marriage, had the blood and so had seats. Their husbands had seats only as a courtesy to the chief of a related clan—once a husband tried to displace his wife; Cora Alice took away his plate. The men of the third generation had both blood and name, and so had seats of honor. And I too had a seat of honor: a creaky chair, made tall with cushions, set at the table's foot. For I was David, son of David, the only male of the fourth generation, the only hope for the continuation of the name.

I, of course, did not then understand why I alone among the children had a seat at the table. But I was glad I did. For when all closed eyes and bowed heads to listen to my father bless our gathering in fervent baritone extempore, I could raise my head and look down the table, a virtual continent of sustenance—Great Lakes of gravy, Great Plains of yams, tectonic plates of turkey slices thrust upward by the bulk of the bird itself, which rose like Rushmore. But in the place of the visage of Washington or Lincoln this Rushmore was crowned by a huge dark head with massive jowls, pebbly with beard, a broad flat nose, a gently sloping forehead, grizzled brows: the visage of our clan chief, my Uncle John.

Uncle John was titanic. Below his head was a neck thick with muscle and a broad chest, powerful and deep, on which his huge hands prayerfully rested, the fingers like a logjam. When the food was duly blessed the jam burst. For Uncle John did not eat—he fed. His plate—actually a spare meat platter—was filled and refilled with turkey, potatoes, and stuffing all drenched with tureens of gravy, and garnished with enough corn on the cob to fill a field—once I counted a dozen ears lying ravished by his plate, and always I watched his trench work with apprehension, convinced that one day he would explode.

He made all the noise of an explosion. He did not talk—he roared. He roared with jokes—always corny and often in poor taste—and aphorisms—"You can live forever if you don't quit breathin!"—and responses to conversational gambits—once Uncle Andrew twitted him about his shabby clothing. "Rags to riches! I ain't rich yet!" Uncle John roared, off and on for the next twenty years. Mostly, though, he roared with a laugh as big as he was, so concussive it subsumed all ordinary vibrations. Halfway between a boom and a cackle, Uncle John's laugh was like a bushel of corn husks rustling in a hundred-gallon drum. It was not precisely a pleasant sound, but to me it was a Siren song—or perhaps the call of the wild.

When I was small I would leave my place as soon as I could to go and stand beside him. He would be busy devouring dessert—quarters of pie, one each of pumpkin, sweet potato, mince—like Cronus consuming his children, but would catch me up in the crook of his arm and balance me effortlessly on his knee, where I would sit in greatest contentment, remarkably unoffended by his smell—sweat, smoke, and bay rum (which he used for no good reason, since he rarely shaved). When I grew too big for that I would simply stand beside him while he finished eating. Then we would go to kill his car. He didn't call it that, of course. He termed it "blowing out the pipes" and claimed that without it the car—a spavined station wagon—would never climb the mountains between Bedford and Sewickley. But to me, at six or seven, it seemed like bloody murder.

From the back of the wagon he would take a quart jar of kerosene—he called it "coal oil"—and give it to me to hold while he started the engine, raised the hood, and removed the air cleaner. Then he would take the jar and begin to pour the coal oil into the unsuspecting intake manifold. The engine would pause in shock, then sputter, bark, and bellow at the same time, while from the tail pipe issued gouts of greasy black smoke. Meanwhile Uncle John poured more coal oil into the carburetor, his expression like that of a father administering foul-tasting medicine to an ailing child. When the jar was empty he would leap behind the wheel and pump the throttle; the engine would scream and thrash madly on its mounts, while the smoke from the tail pipe would take on bile-green overtones and show tiny flicks of flame. After a while Uncle John—at some clue known to him alone—would stop pumping. The engine would rattle, almost stop. Then the kerosene would clear through the cylinders; the grateful engine would settle into a smooth, fast idle, and Uncle John would smile.

Years later I marveled at all of this, not because the car survived it, but because we did. For it took no mechanical genius to see that we had toyed with tragedy, that that abused engine could easily have exploded, covering us with burning fuel, shredding us with shrapnel, generally blowing us to Kingdom Come. And I marveled that, even had I known that then—which I of course did not—it would have made no difference. Because then—and now—those dangerous pyrotechnics seemed a fitting prerequisite for what followed. For when the smoke showed clean and white I would sit beside Uncle John as he gently blipped the throttle—helping, he said, the pistons settle down—and recounted chronicles of the clan.

Clan history was nothing new—I heard it every day. But what I heard daily were parables, intended to indoctrinate me with the values and courage that had let us rise up from slavery. At Harvest Home, Uncle John told a different story—unpretentious, earthy, human as an unlimed outhouse. Cora Alice told me about Daniel Francis, after the barn was struck by lightning, burning his hands in the steaming ashes as he searched for nails with which to rebuild. Uncle John told me about my grandfather misjudging the dosage when he wormed the mule. David told me about the Christmas Eve when he, knowing his family was too poor for presents, asked for nothing and cried himself to sleep—but woke to find a hand-carved train, three walnuts, and one incredible orange. Uncle John told me about the time my father had the back of his pants gored by a roving bull. My grandmother and father told me of the glory of my people. Uncle John told me that we *were* people. This was vital. For it was something we were forgetting.

On Harvest Home 1957 I was drummed out of my clan. My crime was lying—a peccadillo, outsiders might say, especially as all children tell lies occasionally, some frequently. But I lied almost constantly, even when there was nothing to be gained. My father said I'd rather crawl up Fib Alley than march down Truth Street; this drove him crazy. For he believed a sterling reputation was some shield against the sanctions society—both American and Bedford County—could bring to bear on a Negro male. He was proud that we were held in high repute and feared what would happen to me—to all of us—were our name to lose its luster because of my lying. He announced that he would break me of it.

But he did not realize how good a liar I'd become—so good I took him in. For a while I told him many obvious lies, let him catch and punish me. Then I tapered off. Catching me less often, he assumed I was lying less. But on that morning he discovered... well, I don't recall exactly what he discovered; some silken web of half-truths I had been spinning out for weeks. He confronted me, hard evidence in his hands, hot fury in his face.

Corporal punishment was not his way. His cat-o'-ninetails was a Calibanian tongue wetted with Prosperian vocabulary, his lashes sad scenarios starring the local sheriff. That morning he seemed so angry I expected J. Edgar Hoover to make a cameo appearance; I could not imagine what salt he would rub into the wounds—I doubt the usual "thou shalt never amount to anything if thou keepest this up" would suffice. But he was too angry for anything like the usual treatment; he simply looked at me coldly and in a frighteningly quiet voice said, "Bradleys don't lie."

That statement rocked me. For I knew—at least I thought I knew—that it was true. My grandmother did not lie. My father surely did not lie. In the Church he had a reputation for truthfulness—and was in some quarters hated for it. His historical writing was marred by a concern for literal truth; he wouldn't say that two and two were four unless he had a picture of both twos and did the arithmetic three times. And God knows he preached what he saw as truth, and practiced what he preached. So I believed him when he said Bradleys did not lie. But I also knew that I did lie.

On any other day the conclusion of the syllogism—that I was not a Bradley—would have disturbed me. But that day was Harvest Home. I sat in my favored place, accepting accolades and choicest bits of feast food—the heel of the bread, the drumstick of the turkey—that all thought were my due, as sole heir to the name, but I knowing in my heart I had no right to them. I could barely eat.

Later, in the car, I only half listened to Uncle John's chronicle, wondering if I could ever explain to him that I had no right to listen at all. But in the midst of my dilemma I detected a variation from an earlier telling. "Wait," I said. "That's not what you said before."

"No," he said easily. "But don't it work out better that way?"

"Well, yeah," I said—and it did work out better—"but it's not the truth."

"Oh yeah," he said. "The truth. Well, truth is funny. Because you never know it all. So you end up makin' things up to fill in the blanks. Everybody does that. But some folks always makes things up that's make folks sound good, make things sound clean and pretty. Trouble is, the truth usually turns out to be whatever makes the most sense. And if you think you got the whole truth, if it don't make sense, you better make a few things up. And even if you're wrong, it makes a better story." He paused, looked at me. I can't imagine what was on my face—amazement, probably, to hear the head of my clan drumming me back into it as firmly as I'd been drummed out. "Now don't you dare ever tell your daddy I said that," he admonished. And then he sent his laughter rustling and booming around the car.

It is interesting to speculate what would have happened if the *Gazette* had done a follow-up on The Bradley Family Twelve Years Later. By 1968 Andrew had served a second term in the cabinet and served there no longer only because the Democrats had lost the Statehouse—he remained a force in the Party, and had had influence with both the Kennedy and Johnson administrations. He had also followed in at least one of Daniel Francis's footsteps, becoming a trustee of Lincoln University, an institution originally dedicated to the education of blacks. David, meanwhile, retraced his father's footsteps even as he stepped beyond; still a General Officer, he was rumored to be a strong candidate for Bishop, the highest office in the Church, and also preached at Mt. Pisgah, which was now too small to pay its own pastor. David Jr. seemed poised to follow. A senior in high school, he had been admitted to the University of Pennsylvania and awarded several national scholarships. Occasionally he too occupied the pulpit of Mt. Pisgah. Such facts could have led a reporter to believe the Bradley family was still upward bound, might even have caused him or her to see a rising track in tragedy; though Cora Alice had died in 1960, her funeral was resplendent with dignitaries: two ministers and a Presiding Elder of the

AME Zion Church, and—the Democrats were then still in power—several state cabinet secretaries and the governor himself. Had such a story been done—it wasn't—the reporter might have written that, after a hundred and thirty-two years of freedom, the Bradleys continued to rise.

To say that, though, the reporter would have had to ignore clippings from the *Gazette* itself—a 1962 story describing the destruction of the Bradley homestead by a fire, photo of the ravished house, its windows like blackened eyes, its clapboard siding stripped away, revealing underlying logs. But to be fair, few reporters would have seen the fire as metaphor. Fewer still would have explored the implications of the fire's aftermath: that for months the house stood unrepaired; that the eventual repairs were minimal; that they were financed by a note cosigned by only David and Andrew; that money to repay the loan was to come from rental of the homestead—to whites. And none, probably, would have understood that the *Gazette*'s account of Cora Alice's funeral reiterated an ancient insult. For although the second paragraph noted the careers of David and Andrew, the clan's chief was not mentioned until the final paragraph, and in passing: "She is survived by another son, John Bradley of Sewickley."

I was only nine when my grandmother died, and so recall little of the pomp and circumstance that surrounded her death. I do recall the lavish spread of ham and turkey and covered dishes brought by neighbors to assuage our grief. I recall that Uncle John ate little. And I recall that at the end of the day I stood beside him on my father's lawn while he looked sadly at the homestead. "I guess that's that," he said, and turned away.

And I do recall my grandmother's final Harvest Home. I remember overhearing my elders in council. The only items on the agenda were her failing health and her refusal to give up her days in the homestead. It was moved and seconded that Uncle Andrew take her to Harrisburg to see a specialist. During discussion the opinion was stated (loudly) that no doctor could cure the fact that my grandmother was ninety years old, but the countermotion ("Let her live the way she wants until she dies") was ruled out of order. The motion carried on a two-to-one vote. Council was adjourned, *sine die.* I remember the meal itself—the mood: heavy, the food: dry, the laughter: absent without leave. And I remember how quiet Uncle John was as he watched my father and Uncle Andrew get my grandmother settled in Uncle Andrew's Chrysler. Mostly I remember how, after my grandmother was driven away, Uncle John went to work with coal oil and a vengeance; I can still hear the sounds he tortured from the engine, the fan belt screaming, the valve lifters chattering like dry bones, the exhaust bellowing like nothing known to man.

Mostly I recall the burning of the house. For if our homestead was once a totem, was it not a totem still? Was not the burning a harbinger of greater doom? For months I would go, sometimes in the dead of night, and circle the hulk of our homestead like a satellite in orbit, pulled down and thrown up simultaneously. In daylight I would peer into the now exposed basement, full of detritus, alive with rats, in darkness sniff the scorched and rotten timber, seeking a message in the rubble and the stench. And when the house was lost to me—repaired and occupied by people my grandmother would have dismissed as poor white trash—I sought a message in the keepsakes of our clan—chipped photographs, browned bills and deeds, yellowed newspaper clippings. When I combined those mementos with my memories I found discrepancies. And when I thought about what made most sense I found a devastating truth: Bradleys did lie.

Most of our lies were common cover-ups of minor moral failures. Others drove to the heart of our history—it seemed doubtful, for example, that Booker T. Washington had ever heard of Daniel Francis. But no lie was as destructive as the one we'd told about my Uncle John.

There are many ways to say it. Then, when clichés were new to me and irony was *terra incognita,* I would have said that Uncle John was our black sheep. Now I say he was the nigger in our woodpile, proof that though Bradley blood flowed in dreamers, power brokers, and preachers, it also flowed in a hewer of wood, a drawer of water, a man content to work in service all his life. This embarrassed us, especially as he was not the least among us; he was the first. And so, while we did not deny him, we denied him his place. We allowed outsiders to see him as a minor footnote to our grand history. And then, made bold by headlines and column inches, tokens Society respects, we had forgotten the rules by which a clan exists and survives. Our junior elders—my father and Uncle Andrew—had rebelled against our rightful leader. This, I decided, was the message of the burned boards and beams of the house of Bradley. Our house had fallen because we had fallen away.

I did not want to fall away. For the years between the burning and my graduation were hard, lonely, desperate years. I needed my people. I needed my clan. I needed my chief. And though I despaired that we had fallen too far from our ways, I hoped that we had not.

I hoped hardest when those years were ending, when to the world outside I seemed poised to take my clan to greater heights. I feared those heights. And so, on the night of my commencement, as my class assembled for its final march, I stood quietly despairing. They chattered about parties and graduation gifts. I wanted only one gift: the presence of my chief. I doubted I would get it. I had sent him an invitation, but Uncle John was almost seventy and Sewickley was more than a hundred mountainous miles away. To make it worse, a violent thunderstorm was raging. Only a fool would make the trip.

But as we marched up to the auditorium door I saw him standing outside the hall, his threadbare coat and tattered sweater soaked with rain, his eyes searching for me in the line of robed seniors. "Who's *that?*" one of my classmates whispered. "My Uncle John," I said. In that moment he saw me. And even in the auditorium they heard, over the pounding of the processional, his booming, rustling laugh.

On Wednesday, September 26, 1979, the *Gazette* recounted the tale of the Bradley clan much as it had in 1956 as part of the page-one obituary of the Reverend David H. Bradley. The burial at Mt. Ross Cemetery would be private, but, later, friends would be received at the Louis Geisel Funeral Home. Memorial services set for the next day, the *Gazette* anticipated, would be appropriately impressive; two AME Zion bishops—mentioned by name—were scheduled to appear. Among the surviving family was listed "John, of Sewickley."

Uncle John was too ill to attend the burial or memorial service, but I prevailed upon the husband of some cousin I did not recall to drive him to the wake, even though his legs were too weak to carry him inside. And so I saw him for the last time when I sat beside him in the car.

He seemed small, shrunken. He joked, but feebly, and when I teased him about the new clothes he was wearing he said, "Rags to riches! Guess I'm gettin' there," but with no force behind it. And he did not even try to laugh. That depressed me, to be honest, more than my father's death, for it told me that my uncle's death would not be long in coming. The death of a father causes grief; the death of a chief causes fear. I was especially fearful. For when he died the chieftainship would descend to me. I was not ready. I was not worthy. And so I sat beside him and cast about for something that would conjure up his laughter.

Inside, I told him, there were two wakes, in adjacent rooms. In our room there was no casket—we'd buried my father that morning. But in the other, in a grand, flower-bedecked coffin lined with crinoline, a rail-thin ancient white lady was laid out. Bedford being a small town, many visitors paid respects in both rooms. Seeing this, the undertaker, to make things more convenient, had opened the doors between the rooms. This caused no problem—until some of my father's ministerial colleagues arrived. Although ignorant of the specific arrangements, they knew just what to do on such sad occasions. Gliding as if on casters, they went to my mother and murmured comfort, then came to give me that two-fisted handshake of condolence before moving on to their next target: the deceased. When they saw no casket they did not panic—they said more comforting words while shaking their heads in sadness, their eyes covertly scanning. Eventually they locked onto the casket in the other room and launched themselves in that direction.

"I should have let them go," I told Uncle John. "But I just couldn't. So I said, 'Gentlemen, please don't go over there. Because if you do you're going to think he suffered a lot more than he did.'" I laughed, hoping that he would laugh too. But his reaction was but a polite chuckle. "Damn," I said. "I should have let them go."

He looked at me and smiled. "Well, don't let it bother you, son. Next time you tell it, you will." And then he did laugh. Not long, but long enough. Not loud, but loud enough.

He died nine months later. I did not attend the funeral. It would have been too quiet. Oh, there would have been sound aplenty—slow hymns, generous lies, even laughter—of a sort. But it would not have been his laughter, a laugh that could shake the earth. And hearing other laughter would have made me know that he and his laugh were gone.

I will never be made to know that, I've decided. I have the right to that decision, for I am clan chief now. I do not have all the wisdom that a chief needs, but I have come to understand some things. I understand that the hypocrisy and hubris that brought our house to ruin were inevitable dangers. For any fool could see that black people in America could not rise on wings of doves. To even think of rising we should have quills of iron, rachises of steel. Of course, we do not have such mighty wings. And so we stiffen our pinfeathers with myths, flap madly, and sometimes gain a certain height.

Suggestions for Discussion

1. Who is the "hero" of the story?
2. What is the significance of the "homestead" to the Bradley family?
3. How is the family misunderstood by those who try to tell its tale? Does the family collaborate in this misunderstanding? Why?
4. Explain the significance of the father's statement, "Bradleys don't lie."
5. Uncle John is both the head of the family and its black sheep. How does the author portray this ambiguity? What are his feelings for his uncle?

Suggestions for Writing

1. Is there a "Harvest Home" equivalent in your family, a time when all generations are gathered together for festivity and celebration? Is it wonderful? Painful? Awkward? Describe it.
2. Who is your favorite relative? Why? What is he or she like? Describe this person in such a way as to enable others to understand why you feel the attachment you do.

POETRY

T. S. ELIOT

The Love Song of J. Alfred Prufrock

Thomas Stearns Eliot (1888–1965) was born in St. Louis, was educated at Harvard University, and studied in Paris and Oxford. He settled in England in 1914 and became a British subject in 1927. His most influential poem, *The Waste Land,* was published in 1922, followed by *The Hollow Men* (1925), *Poems: 1909–1925* (1925), and *Poems: 1909–1935* (1936). His criticism includes *The Use of Poetry and the Use of Criticism* (1933), *Essays Ancient and Modern* (1936), *Notes Toward the Definition of Culture* (1948), and *To Criticize the Critic* (1965). His best-known poetic dramas are *Murder in the Cathedral* (1935), *The Family Reunion* (1939), and *The Cocktail Party* (1950). Prufrock's opposed selves in this dramatic monologue are separated from each other, the one exploring the idea of human involvement and the other observing it in comfortable isolation.

S'io credesse che mia risposta fosse
A persona che mai tornasse al mondo,
Questa fiamma staria senza piu scosse.
Ma perciocche giammai di questo fondo
Non torno vivo alcun, s'i'odo il vero,
Senza tema d'infamia ti rispondo.

["If I believed that my answer would be to one who
would ever return to the world, this flame would
shake no more; but since no one ever returns alive
from this depth, if what I hear is true, I answer you
without fear of infamy."—*Dante's Inferno,* XXVII, 61–66]

Let us go then, you and I,
When the evening is spread out against the sky
Like a patient etherised upon a table;
Let us go, through certain half-deserted streets,

The muttering retreats
Of restless nights in one-night cheap hotels
And sawdust restaurants with oyster-shells:
Streets that follow like a tedious argument
Of insidious intent
To lead you to an overwhelming question...
Oh, do not ask, "What is it?"
Let us go and make our visit.

In the room the women come and go
Talking of Michelangelo.

The yellow fog that rubs its back upon the window-panes,
The yellow smoke that rubs its muzzle on the window-panes
Licked its tongue into the corners of the evening,
Lingered upon the pools that stand in drains,
Let fall upon its back the soot that falls from chimneys,
Slipped by the terrace, made a sudden leap,
And seeing that it was a soft October night,
Curled once about the house, and fell asleep.

And indeed there will be time
For the yellow smoke that slides along the street,
Rubbing its back upon the window-panes;
There will be time, there will be time
To prepare a face to meet the faces that you meet;
There will be time to murder and create,
And time for all the works and days of hands
That lift and drop a question on your plate;
Time for you and time for me,
And time yet for a hundred indecisions,
And for a hundred visions and revisions,
Before the taking of a toast and tea.

In the room the women come and go
Talking of Michelangelo.

And indeed there will be time
To wonder, "Do I dare?" and, "Do I dare?"
Time to turn back and descend the stair,
With a bald spot in the middle of my hair—
[They will say: "How his hair is growing thin!"]
My morning coat, my collar mounting firmly to the chin,
My necktie rich and modest, but asserted by a simple pin—
[They will say: "But how his arms and legs are thin!"]
Do I dare

Disturb the universe?
In a minute there is time
For decisions and revisions which a minute will reverse.

For I have known them all already, known them all:—
Have known the evenings, mornings, afternoons,
I have measured out my life with coffee spoons;
I know the voices dying with a dying fall
Beneath the music from a farther room.
So how should I presume?

And I have known the eyes already, known them all—
The eyes that fix you in a formulated phrase,
And when I am formulated, sprawling on a pin,
When I am pinned and wriggling on the wall,
Then how should I begin
To spit out all the butt-ends of my days and ways?
And how should I presume?

And I have known the arms already, known them all—
Arms that are braceleted and white and bare
[But in the lamplight, downed with light brown hair!]
Is it perfume from a dress
That makes me so digress?
Arms that lie along a table, or wrap about a shawl.
And should I then presume?
And how should I begin?

Shall I say, I have gone at dusk through narrow streets
And watched the smoke that rises from the pipes
Of lonely men in shirt-sleeves, leaning out of windows?...
I should have been a pair of ragged claws
Scuttling across the floors of silent seas.

And the afternoon, the evening, sleeps so peacefully!
Smoothed by long fingers,
Asleep...tired...or it malingers,
Stretched on the floor, here beside you and me.
Should I, after tea and cakes and ices,
Have the strength to force the moment to its crisis?
But though I have wept and fasted, wept and prayed,
Though I have seen my head [grown slightly bald] brought in upon a platter,
I am no prophet—and here's no great matter;
I have seen the moment of my greatness flicker,
And I have seen the eternal Footman hold my coat, and snicker,
And in short, I was afraid.

And would it have been worth it, after all,
After the cups, the marmalade, the tea,
Among the porcelain, among some talk of you and me,
Would it have been worth while,
To have bitten off the matter with a smile,
To have squeezed the universe into a ball
To roll it toward some overwhelming question,
To say: "I am Lazarus, come from the dead.
Come back to tell you all, I shall tell you all"—
If one, settling a pillow by her head,
Should say: "That is not what I meant at all.
That is not it, at all."

And would it have been worth it, after all,
Would it have been worth while,
After the sunsets and the dooryards and the sprinkled streets,
After the novels, after the teacups, after the skirts that trail along the floor—
And this, and so much more?—
It is impossible to say just what I mean!
But as if a magic lantern threw the nerves in patterns on a screen:
Would it have been worth while
If one, settling a pillow or throwing off a shawl,
And turning toward the window, should say:
"That is not it at all,
That is not what I meant, at all."

No! I am not Prince Hamlet, nor was meant to be;
Am an attendant lord, one that will do
To swell a progress, start a scene or two,
Advise the prince; no doubt, an easy tool,
Deferential, glad to be of use,
Politic, cautious, and meticulous;
Full of high sentence, but a bit obtuse;
At times, indeed, almost ridiculous—
Almost, at times, the Fool.

I grow old... I grow old...
I shall wear the bottoms of my trousers rolled.

Shall I part my hair behind? Do I dare to eat a peach?
I shall wear white flannel trousers, and walk upon the beach.
I have heard the mermaids singing, each to each.

I do not think that they will sing to me.

I have seen them riding seaward on the waves
Combing the white hair of the waves blown back
When the wind blows the water white and black.

We have lingered in the chambers of the sea
By sea-girls wreathed with seaweed red and brown
Till human voices wake us, and we drown.

Suggestions for Discussion

1. Who are "you and I"?
2. What evidence can you find in the structural development of the poem to support the view that one self in the dramatic monologue acts out the conflict and the other assumes the role of observer? Cite lines from the poem in which shifts in mood and tone occur. How does the poem achieve dramatic unity?
3. Contrast the images of Prufrock's interior world with those of the external world. How does their recurring juxtaposition illuminate the doubleness of the speaker and contribute to tone? How is sensory experience used to convey the circularity of the dialogue with self? Why are the images of the etherized patient, the staircase, winding streets, cat, and fog especially appropriate dramatic symbols of the speaker's state of mind? Trace the use of sea imagery. How does it function differently in the metaphor of the crab and the vision of the mermaids? How do both relate to theme and tone? What do the allusions to John the Baptist, Lazarus, and Hamlet have in common?
4. Distinguish between the dramatic and the lyric elements. How is the mock heroic used to satirize both speaker and society? Study the effects of repetition on rhythm, tone, and meaning. How do the stanzas and the typographical breaks mark the shifts in tone? Discuss the relationship of tone to syntax, refrain, internal rhyme, diction, tempo, and melody. Comment on the irony in the title.
5. How does time function in the poem? How does the shift in tense from present to present perfect and future provide a key to the poem's resolution? What form does the speaker's recognition take? By what means does the poet evoke sympathy for Prufrock, who is psychically impotent to establish an intimate human relationship? To what do you attribute Prufrock's rejection of human encounter? What part does his self-mockery play in our response to him? Does the poem move beyond pathos and self-mockery?
6. In what respect may the poem be viewed as an expression of a search for self?

Suggestions for Writing

1. Write a character study of Prufrock in which you refer directly to the poem.
2. Write a dialogue in which your interior self is counterpointed against your social self or *persona.*

DYLAN THOMAS

The Force That Through the Green Fuse Drives the Flower

Dylan Thomas (1914–1953) was born in Wales. He was a newspaper reporter for a time and worked for the BBC during World War II. He gained recognition as a lyric poet in his twenties and grew in popularity until his death while on a lecture tour in the United States. His *Collected Poems* appeared in 1953. A collection of his stories, sketches, and essays, *Quite Early One Morning,* was published in 1954; a group of stories and essays, *A Prospect of the Sea,* in 1955; and a verse play, *Under Milk Wood,* in 1954. The poet views natural forces as both destructive and life giving; the poem is an expression of his sense of the energy, both creative and destructive, that runs through all things.

The force that through the green fuse drives the flower
Drives my green age; that blasts the roots of trees
Is my destroyer.
And I am dumb to tell the crooked rose
My youth is bent by the same wintry fever.

The force that drives the water through the rocks
Drives my red blood; that dries the mouthing streams
Turns mine to wax.
And I am dumb to mouth unto my veins
How at the mountain spring the same mouth sucks.

The hand that whirls the water in the pool
Stirs the quicksand; that ropes the blowing wind
Hauls my shroud sail.
And I am dumb to tell the hanging man
How of my clay is made the hangman's lime.

The lips of time leech to the fountain head;
Love drips and gathers, but the fallen blood
Shall calm her sores.
And I am dumb to tell a weather's wind
How time has ticked a heaven round the stars.

And I am dumb to tell the lover's tomb
How at my sheet goes the same crooked worm.

Suggestions for Discussion

1. What images suggest the relationship the poet sees between the world of nature and that of human passions?
2. How does the poet express the sense that the energy that runs through all things is both creator and destroyer? How does the two-line refrain at the end of each stanza relate this theme to the voice of the poet?

Suggestion for Writing

What images depict contrasting forces of life and death? How does the diction convey the sense of sexual energy?

ELEANOR WILNER

Emigration

Eleanor Wilner (b. 1938) was awarded the Juniper Prize for her first book of poetry, *maya* (1979), and in 1991 received a MacArthur Fellowship. Educated at Goucher College and at Johns Hopkins University, where she earned her Ph.D., she is a former editor of the *American Poetry Review,* a contributing editor of *Calyx,* and teaches at the Warren Wilson Program for Writers. Other books include *Gathering the Wind* (1975), a study of the visionary imagination; *Sarah's Choice* (1989); *Otherwise* (1993); and *Shekhinah* (1984), from which this poem was taken. In it we see two poles of the human psyche as metaphorically exemplified by the lives of novelist Charlotte Brontë and her friend Mary Taylor.

There are always, in each of us,
these two: the one who stays,
the one who goes away—
Charlotte, who stayed in the rectory
and helped her sisters die in England;
Mary Taylor who went off to Australia
and set up shop with a woman friend.
"Charlotte," Mary said to her, "you are all
like potatoes growing in the dark."
And Charlotte got a plaque in Westminster

Abbey; Mary we get a glimpse of
for a moment, waving her kerchief
on the packet boat, and disappearing.
No pseudonym for her, and nothing
left behind, no trace
but a wide wake closing.

Charlotte stayed, and paid and paid—
the little governess with the ungovernable
heart, that she put on the altar.
She paid the long indemnity of all
who work for what will never wish them well,
who never set a limit to what's owed
and cannot risk foreclosure. So London
gave her fame, though it could never
sit comfortably with her at dinner—
how intensity palls when it is
plain and small and has no fortune.
When she died with her unborn child
the stars turned east
to shine in the gum trees of Australia,
watching over what has sidetracked evolution,
where Mary Taylor lived
to a great old age, Charlotte's letters in a box
beside her bed, to keep her anger hot.

God bless us everyone until we sicken,
until the soul is like a little child
stricken in its corner by the wall; so there is
one who always sits there under lamplight
writing, staying on, and one
who walks the strange hills of Australia,
far too defiant of convention for the novels
drawn daily from the pen's "if only"—
if only Emily had lived,
if only they'd had money, if only
there had been a man who'd loved them truly...
when all the time there had been
Mary Taylor, whom no one would remember
except she had a famous friend named Charlotte
with whom she was so loving-angry,
who up and left to be a woman
in that godforsaken outpost past
the reach of fantasy, or fiction.

Suggestions for Discussion

1. When Wilner uses the metaphor "…the one who stays, / the one who goes away—" to talk about the nature of the human personality, what does she mean?
2. What do Charlotte Brontë, the novelist, and Mary Taylor, her friend, gain and lose through their respective decisions to stay at home and to leave?
3. What does the author mean when she describes Charlotte as among those "who work for what will never wish them well"? What is the price her work extracts?
4. Australia is described as a "godforsaken outpost past / the reach of fantasy, or fiction." Why would Mary Taylor want to go there? What does she "win" in doing so?

Suggestions for Writing

1. What is the part of us that stays? What is the part that goes away? Are they different for each of us, or essentially the same?
2. London and Australia are metaphors used to describe these different parts of ourselves. What metaphors would serve this function in the United States today?

DENISE LEVERTOV

In Mind

Denise Levertov (b. 1923) was born in England but came to the United States as a young woman. A poet and essayist, her career includes work as an editor, a translator, a professor, with a brief stint in nursing during World War II. She holds four honorary degrees and has won numerous awards for her poetry. These include most recently the Bobst and Shelley Prizes. Author of twenty-one volumes of poetry, current publications include *A Door in the Hive* (1989), *Evening Train* (1992), *New and Selected Essays* (1992), and *Tesserae: Memories and Suppositions* (1996). In the poem that follows she presents portraits of two very different women who inhabit her mind.

There's in my mind a woman
of innocence, unadorned but

fair-featured, and smelling of
apples or grass. She wears

a utopian smock or shift, her hair
is light brown and smooth, and she

is kind and very clean without
ostentation—
        but she has
no imagination.
        And there's a
turbulent moon-ridden girl

or old woman, or both,
dressed in opals and rags, feathers

and torn taffeta,
who knows strange songs—

but she is not kind.

Suggestions for Discussion

1. Each of the women Levertov describes possesses something that the other lacks. Does one woman "make up" for the other?
2. Are the women in Levertov's mind separate women? Or are they both part of the author's secret self, each part of the whole?
3. To which woman figure are you most drawn? Why?

Suggestions for Writing

1. Imagine this poem as a scene in a play. What kind of dialogue would emerge between the two characters?
2. How would you cast the play? Who would role-play each character?
3. Imagine the characters described as men. What would be the masculine equivalents of the two women Levertov describes?

ANNE SEXTON

Her Kind

Anne Sexton (1928–1974) taught and lectured widely, but she was above all a poet. Recipient of three honorary degrees and numerous fellowships, she was also awarded, among others, the Shelley and Pulitzer Prizes. Of her many books the best known are *To Bedlam and Part Way Back* (1960), from which the following poem is taken; *All My Pretty Ones* (1962); *Live or Die* (1966); *Transformations* (1971); and *The Death Notebooks* (1974). In "Her Kind" we see another portrayal of the complex and multiple nature of human personality.

I have gone out, a possessed witch,
haunting the black air, braver at night;
dreaming evil, I have done my hitch
over the plain houses, light by light:
lonely thing, twelve-fingered, out of mind.

A woman like that is not a woman, quite.
I have been her kind.

I have found the warm caves in the woods,
filled them with skillets, carvings, shelves,
closets, silks, innumerable goods;
fixed the suppers for the worms and the elves:
whining, rearranging the disaligned.
A woman like that is misunderstood.
I have been her kind.

I have ridden in your car, driver,
waved my nude arms at villages going by,
learning the last bright routes, survivor
where your flames still bite my thigh
and my ribs crack where your wheels wind.
A woman like that is not ashamed to die.
I have been her kind.

Suggestions for Discussion

1. Why does Sexton choose to describe herself as a witch, a housewife, a martyr? How do these characterizations relate to how society has understood and portrayed women?
2. What characterizes each of the three women in the poem? What kinds of metaphors does Sexton use to describe them?
3. Why is the protagonist described as "not a woman, quite," "misunderstood," "not ashamed to die"?

Suggestions for Writing

1. If you were to think of yourself in terms of a number of different characters or *personae,* what would they be? How would they relate to one another?
2. What are some of the stereotypes our culture has used to describe men? Have these had an impact on how men in our culture behave? Explain.

Personal Relationships: Parents and Children

Sometimes my mother or father would come up with an image, or a fragment of a story, and we would all weave imaginary plots around it. Sometimes we talked about books or movies or the poetry we recited to each other on Sunday afternoons. Often we talked and speculated about other people, our neighbors and friends. No one ever hesitated to be mean—although the insults were usually also pretty funny. We were so mean to each other, in fact, that guests were often astonished and shocked. They didn't catch the undertone of humor in our quick sarcasms, and there were times when we didn't catch it either. Explosions and tears and sudden departures were not at all uncommon. My brothers called our dinner table "the bear garden."

—SUSAN CHEEVER, "Portrait of My Father"
from *Home Before Dark*

She was a child of anxious, not proud, love. We were poor and could not afford for her the soil of easy growth. I was a young mother, I was a distracted mother. There were the other children pushing up, demanding. Her younger sister seemed all that she was not. There were years she did not want me to touch her. She kept too much in herself, her life was such she had to keep too much in herself. My wisdom came too late. She has much to her and probably little will come of it. She is a child of her age, of depression, of war; of fear.

—TILLIE OLSEN, "I Stand Here Ironing"
from *Tell Me a Riddle*

LETTERS AND PERSONAL REMINISCENCES

FRANZ KAFKA

Letter to His Father

Translated by Ernest Kaiser and Eithene Wilkins

Franz Kafka (1883–1924), the German novelist who portrays alienated characters in an absurd world, made little mark during his life but is now considered a major modern writer. Many of his novels have been published posthumously, including *The Trial, The Castle,* and *Amerika.* In the letter, also published posthumously, the author in a legalistic manner indicts himself as well as his father in assessing responsibility for his, Kakfa's, insecurity as a person.

Dearest Father:

You asked me recently why I maintain that I am afraid of you. As usual, I was unable to think of any answer to your question, partly for the very reason that I am afraid of you, and partly because an explanation of the grounds for this fear would mean going into far more details than I could even approximately keep in mind while talking. And if I now try to give you an answer in writing, it will still be very incomplete, because even in writing this fear and its consequences hamper me in relation to you and because [anyway] the magnitude of the subject goes far beyond the scope of my memory and power of reasoning....

Compare the two of us: I, to put it in a very much abbreviated form, a Löwy with a certain basis of Kafkà, which, however, is not set in motion by the Kafka will to life, business, and conquest, but by a Löwyish spur that urges more secretly, more diffidently, and in another direction, and which often fails to work entirely. You, on the other hand, a true Kafka in strength, health, appetite, loudness of voice, eloquence, self-satisfaction, worldly dominance, endurance, presence of mind, knowledge of human nature, a certain way of doing things on a grand scale, of course with all the defects and weaknesses that go with all these advantages and into which your temperament and sometimes your hot temper drive you....

However it was, we were so different and in our difference so dangerous to each other that, if anyone had tried to calculate in advance how I, the slowly developing child, and you, the full-grown man, would stand to each other, he could have assumed that you would simply trample me underfoot so that nothing was left of me. Well, that didn't happen. Nothing alive can be calculated. But perhaps something worse happened. And in saying this I would all the time beg of you not to forget that I never, and not even for a single moment, believe any guilt to be on your side. The effect you had on me was the effect you could not help having. But you should stop considering it some particular malice on my part that I succumbed to that effect.

I was a timid child. For all that, I am sure I was also obstinate, as children are. I am sure that Mother spoilt me too, but I cannot believe I was particularly difficult to manage; I cannot believe that a kindly word, a quiet taking of me by the hand, a friendly look, could not have got me to do anything that was wanted of me. Now you are after all at bottom a kindly and softhearted person (what follows will not be in contradiction to this, I am speaking only of the impression you made on the child), but not every child has the endurance and fearlessness to go on searching until it comes to the kindliness that lies beneath the surface. You can only treat a child in the way you yourself are constituted, with vigor, noise, and hot temper, and in this case this seemed to you, into the bargain, extremely suitable, because you wanted to bring me up to be a strong brave boy....

There is only one episode in the early years of which I have a direct memory. You may remember it, too. Once in the night I kept on whimpering for water, not, I am certain, because I was thirsty, but probably partly to be annoying, partly to amuse myself. After several vigorous threats had failed to have any effect, you took me out of bed, carried me out onto the *pavlatche* and left me there alone for a while in my nightshirt, outside the shut door. I am not going to say that this was wrong—perhaps at that time there was really no other way of getting peace and quiet that night—but I mention it as typical of your methods of bringing up a child and their effect on me. I dare say I was quite obedient afterwards at that period, but it did me inner harm. What was for me a matter of course, that senseless asking for water, and the extraordinary terror of being carried outside were two things that I, my nature being what it was, could never properly connect with each other. Even years afterwards I suffered from the tormenting fancy that the huge man, my father, the ultimate authority, would come almost for no reason at all and take me out of bed in the night and carry me out onto the *pavlatche,* and that therefore I was such a mere nothing for him.

That then was only a small beginning, but this sense of nothingness that often dominates me (a feeling that is in another respect, admittedly, also a noble and fruitful one) comes largely from your influence. What I would have needed was a little encouragement, a little friendliness, a little keeping open of my road, instead of which you blocked it for me, though of course with the good intention of making me go another road. But I was not fit for that. You encouraged me, for instance, when I saluted and marched smartly, but I was no future soldier, or you encouraged me when I was able to eat heartily or even drink beer with my meals, or when I was able to repeat songs, singing what I had not understood, or prattle to you using your own favorite expressions, imitating you, but nothing of this had anything to do with my future. And it is characteristic that even today you really only encourage me in anything when you yourself are involved in it, when what is at stake is your sense of self-importance.

At that time, and at that time everywhere, I would have needed encouragement. I was, after all, depressed even by your mere physical presence. I remember, for instance, how we often undressed together in the same bathing hut. There was I, skinny, weakly, slight; you strong, tall, broad. Even inside the hut I felt myself a miserable specimen, and what's more, not only in your eyes but in the eyes of the whole world, for you were for me the measure of all things. But then when we went out of the bathing hut before the people, I with you holding my hand, a little skeleton, unsteady, barefoot on the boards, frightened of the water, incapable of copying your swimming strokes, which you, with the best of intentions, but actually to my profound humiliation, always kept on showing me, then I was frantic with desperation and all my bad experiences in all spheres at such moments fitted magnificently together....

In keeping with that, furthermore, was your intellectual domination. You had worked your way up so far alone, by your own energies, and as a result you had unbounded confidence in your opinion. For me as a child that was not yet so dazzling as later for the boy growing up. From your armchair you ruled the world. Your opinion was correct, every other was mad, wild, *meshugge,* not normal. With all this your self-confidence was so great that you had no need to be consistent at all and yet never ceased to be in the right. It did sometimes happen that you had no opinion whatsoever about a matter and as a result all opinions that were at all possible with respect to the matter were necessarily wrong, without exception. You were capable, for instance, of running down the Czechs, and then the Germans, and then the Jews, and what is more, not only selectively but in every respect, and finally nobody was left except yourself. For me you took on the enigmatic quality that all tyrants have whose rights are based on their person and not on reason. At least so it seemed to me.

Now where I was concerned you were in fact astonishingly often in the right, which was a matter of course in talk, for there was hardly ever any talk between us, but also in reality. Yet this too was nothing particularly incomprehensible; in all my thinking I was, after all, under the heavy pressure of your personality, even in that part of it—and particularly in that—which was not in accord with yours. All these thoughts, seemingly independent of you, were from the beginning loaded with the burden of your harsh and dogmatic judgments; it was almost impossible to endure this, and yet to work out one's thoughts with any measure of completeness and permanence. I am not here speaking of any sublime thoughts, but of every little enterprise in childhood. It was only necessary to be happy about something or other, to be filled with the thought of it, to come home and speak of it, and the answer was an ironical sigh, a shaking of the head, a tapping of the table with one finger: "Is that all you're so worked up about?" or "I wish I had your worries!" or "The things some people have time to think about!" or "What can you buy yourself with that?" or "What a song and dance about nothing!" Of course, you couldn't be expected to be enthusiastic about every childish triviality, toiling and moiling as you used to. But that wasn't the point. The point was, rather, that you could not help always and on principle causing the child such disappointments, by virtue of your antagonistic nature, and further that this antagonism was ceaselessly intensified through accumulation of its material, that it finally became a matter of established habit even when for once you were of the same opinion as myself, and that finally these disappointments of the child's were not disappointments in ordinary life but, since what it concerned was your person, which was the measure of all things, struck to the very core. Courage, resolution, confidence, delight in this and that, did not endure to the end when you were against whatever it was or even if your opposition was merely to be assumed; and it was to be assumed in almost everything I did....

You have, I think, a gift for bringing up children: you could, I am sure, have been of use to a human being of your own kind with your methods; such a person would have seen the reasonableness of what you told him, would not have troubled about anything else, and would quietly have done things the way he was told. But for me a child everything you shouted at me was positively a heavenly commandment, I never forgot it, it remained for me the most important means of forming a judgment of the world, above all of forming a judgment of you yourself, and there you failed entirely. Since as a child I was together with you chiefly at meals, your teaching was to a large extent teaching about proper behavior at table. What was brought to the table had to be eaten up, there could be no discussion of the goodness of the food—but you yourself often found the food uneatable, called it "this swill," said "that brute" (the cook) had ruined it. Because in accordance with your strong appetite and your particular habit you ate everything fast, hot and in big mouthfuls, the child had to hurry, there was a somber silence at table, interrupted by admonitions: "Eat first, talk afterwards," or "faster, faster, faster," or "there you are, you see, I finished ages ago." Bones mustn't be cracked with the teeth, but you could.

Vinegar must not be sipped noisily, but you could. The main thing was that the bread should be cut straight. But it didn't matter that you did it with a knife dripping with gravy. One had to take care that no scraps fell on the floor. In the end it was under your chair that there were most scraps. At table one wasn't allowed to do anything but eat, but you cleaned and cut your fingernails, sharpened pencils, cleaned your ears with the toothpick. Please, Father, understand me rightly: these would in themselves have been utterly insignificant details, they only became depressing for me because you, the man who was so tremendously the measure of all things for me, yourself did not keep the commandments you imposed on me. Hence the world was for me divided into three parts: into one in which I, the slave, lived under laws that had been invented only for me and which I could, I did not know why, never completely comply with; then into a second world, which was infinitely remote from mine, in which you lived, concerned with government, with the issuing of orders and with annoyance about their not being obeyed; and finally into a third world where everybody else lived happily and free from orders and from having to obey. I was continually in disgrace, either I obeyed your orders, and that was a disgrace, for they applied, after all, only to me, or I was defiant, and that was a disgrace too, for how could I presume to defy you, or I could not obey because, for instance, I had not your strength, your appetite, your skill, in spite of which you expected it of me as a matter of course; this was the greatest disgrace of all. What moved in this way was not the child's reflections, but his feelings....

It was true that Mother was illimitably good to me, but all that was for me in relation to you, that is to say, in no good relation. Mother unconsciously played the part of a beater during a hunt. Even if your method of upbringing might in some unlikely case have set me on my own feet by means of producing defiance, dislike, or even hate in me, Mother canceled that out again by kindness, by talking sensibly (in the maze and chaos of my childhood she was the very pattern of good sense and reasonableness), by pleading for me, and I was again driven back into your orbit, which I might perhaps otherwise have broken out of, to your advantage and to my own. Or it was so that no real reconciliation ever came about, that Mother merely shielded me from you in secret, secretly gave me something, or allowed me to do something, and then where you were concerned I was again the furtive creature, the cheat, the guilty one, who in his worthlessness could only pursue backstairs methods even to get the things he regarded as his right. Of course, I then became used to taking such courses also in quest of things to which, even in my own view, I had no right. This again meant an increase in the sense of guilt.

It is also true that you hardly ever really gave me a whipping. But the shouting, the way your face got red, the hasty undoing of the braces and the laying of them ready over the back of the chair, all that was almost worse for me. It is like when someone is going to be hanged. If he is really hanged, then he's dead and it's all over. But if he has to go through all the preliminaries to being hanged and only when the noose is dangling before his face is told of his reprieve, then he may suffer from it all his life long. Besides, from so many occasions when I had, as you clearly showed you thought, deserved to be beaten, when you were however gracious enough to let me off at the last moment, here again what accumulated was only a huge sense of guilt. On every side I was to blame, I was in debt to you.

You have always reproached me (and what is more either alone or in front of others, you having no feeling for the humiliation of this latter, your children's affairs always being public affairs) for living in peace and quiet, warmth, and abundance, lack for nothing, thanks to your hard work. I think here of remarks that must positively have worn grooves in my brain, like: "When I was only seven I had to push the barrow from village to village." "We all had to sleep in one room." "We were glad when we got potatoes." "For years I had open sores on my legs from not having enough clothes to wear in winter." "I was only a little boy when I was sent away to Pisek to go into business." "I got nothing from home, not even when I was in the army, even then I was sending money home." "But for all that, for all that—Father was always Father to me. Ah, nobody knows what that means these days! What do these children know of things? Nobody's been through that! Is there any child that understands such things today?" Under other conditions such stories might have been very educational, they might have been a way of encouraging one and strengthening one to endure similar torments and deprivations to those one's father had undergone. But that wasn't what you wanted at all; the situation had, after all, become quite different as a result of all your efforts, and there was no opportunity to distinguish oneself in the world as you had done. Such an opportunity would first of all have had to be created by violence and revolution, it would have meant breaking away from home (assuming one had had the resolution and strength to do so and that Mother wouldn't have worked against it, for her part, with other means). But all that was not what you wanted at all, that you termed ingratitude, extravagance, disobedience, treachery, madness. And so, while on the one hand you tempted me to it by means of example, story, and humiliation, on the other hand you forbade it with the utmost severity....

(Up to this point there is in this letter relatively little I have intentionally passed over in silence, but now and later I shall have to be silent on certain matters that it is still too hard for me to confess—to you and to myself. I say this in order that, if the picture as a whole should be somewhat blurred here and there, you should not believe that what is to blame is any lack of evidence; on the contrary, there is evidence that might well make the picture unbearably stark. It is not easy to strike a median position.) Here, it is enough to remind you of early days. I had lost my self-confidence where you were concerned, and in its place had developed a boundless sense of guilt. (In recollection of this boundlessness I once wrote of someone, accurately: "He is afraid the shame will outlive him, even.") I could not suddenly undergo a transformation when I came into the company of other people; on the contrary, with them I came to feel an even deeper sense of guilt, for, as I have already said, in their case I had to make good the wrongs done them by you in the business, wrongs in which I too had my share of responsibility. Besides, you always, of course, had some objection to make, frankly or covertly, to everyone I associated with, and for this too I had to beg his pardon. The mistrust that you tried to instill into me, at business and at home, towards most people (tell me of any single person who was of importance to me in my childhood whom you didn't at least once tear to shreds with your criticism), this mistrust, which oddly enough was no particular burden to you (the fact was that you were strong enough to bear it, and besides, it was in reality perhaps only a token of the autocrat), this mistrust, which for me as a little boy was nowhere confirmed in my own eyes, since I everywhere saw only people excellent beyond all hope of emulation, in me turned into mistrust of myself and into perpetual anxiety in relation to everything else. There, then, I was in general certain of not being able to escape from you.

Suggestions for Discussion

Kafka gave this letter (from which you have only excerpts) to his mother, asking her to give it to his father. Understandably she never did so, but it was found among Kafka's unpublished manuscripts after his death. Although Kafka had asked his friend Max Brod to destroy all unpublished material, Brod did not comply with this request.

1. Study the legalistic manner in which Kafka indicts himself as well as his father. Assuming you were on a jury, evaluate the points for prosecution and defense of both father and son. What would be your final judgment as to responsibility for the boy's insecurity as a person?
2. Study the scenes through which Kafka dramatizes certain moments of special significance in his childhood. In spite of his attempt to be fair, by what means does he enlist sympathy with the child?
3. What seems to be the role of the mother? Why does the boy more closely identify with her and her family than with his father?

Suggestions for Writing

1. Write about a significant moment in your childhood relationship with your parents. What effect may it have had on your self-image?

2. Write on the parents' image versus the child's.
3. Contrast this father with the one portrayed in E. E. Cummings's poem "my father moved through dooms of love."

SUSAN CHEEVER

Portrait of My Father

Susan Cheever (b. 1943) was educated at Brown University. She worked as a journalist before she began writing novels. She also taught creative writing at Hofstra University and has been the recipient of numerous awards and fellowships. Her works include *Looking for Work* (1980), *A Handsome Man* (1981), *And Women* (1987), *Elizabeth Cole* (1989), and the autobiographical *A Woman's Life: The Story of an Ordinary American and her Extraordinary Generation.* Her 1984 biography of her father, famous novelist John Cheever, is titled *Home Before Dark.* By a variety of means—quotations from his journal, statements regarding his philosophy, his contradictions and confusions, his fantasies, and his intimidating qualities—Susan Cheever presents a moving portrait of her father, whom she deeply reveres.

"Susan calls me," my father wrote in his journal in 1952. "It is four or five in the morning. 'I have such awful thoughts, Daddy,' she says. 'I think there is a tiger in the hall and that he will eat me.' She laughs, but she is frightened. It is the hour before light. The dark is troubled for us both. There are no ghosts of men or tigers in the hall, but the dark is hard to bear. There will be great pain and labor before we see this obscurity transformed into sweet morning."

On a cold sunny Monday, about two months before my father died, I checked into New York Hospital and had my own first child, a daughter, Sarah. From the instant I saw her, a tiny red creature bathed in the weird underwater light of the hospital operating room, I loved her with an intensity that life had not prepared me for. As I had grown more pregnant, my father had become sicker. He lost a little every day, and that loss seemed to cast a shadow over all of us. The birth of the baby didn't take away that loss, but it changed everything for me.

My parents drove in to visit me at the hospital the day after she was born. My mother brought a calico mobile, I drank a glass of champagne, and my father's gaunt unbalanced face beamed in at Sarah's plastic bassinet through the transparent wall of the nursery. Her birth seemed to revitalize him. He called the next morning and told me that he felt much better. It was early, but the hospital was already awake. My room was filled with flowers. The cancer was finished, my father had decided. "I've kicked it, Susie," he said. "It's over."

It's a measure of human optimism that we all believed him. For a few weeks it even seemed to be true. He would never be well, of course, but the weakened, wasted father that was left seemed infinitely precious. My first postpregnancy outing was to see him receive the National Medal for Literature at Carnegie Hall. He looked frail, but he spoke with great strength. Afterward my husband and I went backstage. He wasn't there; we found him and the rest of the family ensconced on the banquettes of the Russian Tea Room next door, laughing and eating and ordering more. But early in May, when we took the month-old baby out to visit my parents in Ossining, he looked weaker.

"Make your famous baby noise, John," my mother urged him, and he curled up his lip in a comic high-pitched squeal. Then suddenly he seemed very tired. "Thank you for remembering, dear," he said. That's when I knew he was worse again. As the baby awakened to the world around her that first and last spring, my father waned and faded and grew more absent. The weather stayed warm and sunny. The cherry trees blossomed and shed their pink flowers like a snowfall on the paths in Central Park. The trees turned lush and green. Babies keep odd hours, and often as I watched the sunrise colors well up from the East Side while I fed my daughter, I thought of my father who might be lying awake in his bed in Ossining. In the evening when the baby slept, I called him. By that time, he rarely answered the telephone.

"He won't eat anything," my mother said. Her voice sounded ragged. "Here, Susie, you tell him he has to eat something."

"Hello," my father said in the normal voice that he still managed for telephone hellos and one-word answers.

"Hi, Daddy," I said. "I think you should eat something."

"Yes." His voice had subsided to a grating whisper, and the words were slow and drawn out. Sickness seemed to heighten his sense of social propriety. As his thinking became more chaotic, his manners became more impeccable.

"Shall I call you after dinner?" he said.

"Yes, Daddy." The receiver banged against the telephone as he dropped it.

I remember my father at the head of our family dinner table. First, when there were only three of us, he sat at the end of the plain pine table in the hallway that was the dining room of our apartment on Fifty-ninth Street in New York City.

Later, after we had moved out to Scarborough, he sat at the black modern table next to the window that looked out over the lawns toward Beechwood and the green metal garbage pails behind the estate's big garage. My brother Ben and I sat on opposite sides of the table. At breakfast, before we went to school, Ben would hold a napkin up to his face, slipping food under the bottom edge so that he wouldn't have to look at me. At dinner, nothing like that was allowed. I set the table and my mother cooked and brought the food out in serving dishes and we all sat down and my father said grace.

"Dear Lord, we thank Thee for Thy bounty," he would say while Ben looked longingly at the protection of his napkin. If we children were fighting, as we often were, my father would add a pointed, "And bless this table with peace." And if the dogs were grumbling for scraps under the table, he would also add, "both top and bottom." Then he would say "Amen." My father always said grace. Sometimes he stayed with the short and traditional, sometimes he improvised. Later on, for special occasions, he would base the grace on his favorite quotation, a paraphrase of a line from Jowett's translation of Plato: "Let us consider that the soul of man is immortal, able to endure every sort of good and every sort of evil." Then he would add a paraphrase of the words of the prophet Micah: "So let us live humbly and give thanks unto Our Lord God. Amen."

In the house at Ossining there was a long cherry dining room table with Italian wood and wicker chairs. I always sat on my father's left, with my back to the wall, facing the fireplace with the wing chair in front of it and the long bench next to it that was piled precariously high with galleys of new books and newspapers and magazines: that day's *New York Times*, the local *Ossining Citizen Register, The New Yorker, The New York Review of Books, Newsweek* (when I was working there), *Antaeus*, and sometimes *The Smithsonian* or the *Brown Alumni Monthly*—or anything else that had come in the mail recently enough to have avoided being thrown out. Sometimes at the table my head bumped against the frame of the Piranesi etching that hung on the wall behind me.

I went away to school in 1960, the year my parents bought the house, and Ben went off soon afterward. We three children were rarely there at the same time. When we were, my two brothers sat across from me on the same side of the table. The dogs warmed our feet, sometimes raising themselves for a halfhearted sally after one of the cats. At Christmas vacation, the porch outside would be piled high with snow. In the summer, delicious smells from my mother's flower garden wafted through the open top half of the Dutch door at the end of the room.

The family meal was always served onto our plates by my father from serving platters, and when everyone had said grace and we had all concluded "Amen," my mother would say, "Oh, John, you haven't left yourself anything but the carcass" (if it was a chicken), or "the head" (if it was a fish), or "the tail" (if it was a steak), or "the gristle" (if it was a roast). She was often right. My mother always felt that there wouldn't be enough for her family to eat. Food was so rich and so abundant in our house that even the pets were all overweight. My father, on the other hand, was convinced that somehow he would go hungry—that he would be left out, overlooked, not provided for. He usually managed to make *his* fears seem legitimate, even if it meant heaping our plates to the edges so that there wouldn't be quite enough left for him. "Oh don't worry about me, dear," he would answer my mother. "This is plenty for me." We used to call him Eeyore.

The food, however, was not the main event at our dinner table. Conversation was the main event. Sometimes there was a general discussion of one person's problem: What would I do if Roddy Butler asked me to the dance at the country club? Should Ben major in English at school? Could Fred bring his friend Brad to New Hampshire? Advice, comments, and suggestions came from all quarters. Sometimes it was funny, sometimes it was friendly, sometimes it was harsh or sarcastic. Someone would certainly point out that Roddy had no intention of asking me anywhere, that Ben would be lucky to *pass* English, and that Fred might have trouble keeping his friends if he didn't learn to keep his elbows off the table. There was a lot of joking and very little serious counsel. We learned to make real decisions privately, on our own. My parents' problems were rarely discussed, because that usually ended in tears from my mother or recriminations and sarcasm from my father—and nobody got dessert.

Sometimes my mother or father would come up with an image, or a fragment of a story, and we would all weave imaginary plots around it. Sometimes we talked about books or movies or the poetry we recited to each other on Sunday afternoons. Often we talked and speculated about other people, our neighbors and friends. No one ever hesitated to be mean—although the insults were usually also pretty funny. We were so mean to each other, in fact, that guests were often astonished and shocked. They didn't catch the undertone of humor in our quick sarcasms, and there were times when we didn't catch it either. Explosions and tears and sudden departures were not at all uncommon. My brothers called our dinner table "the bear garden."

"My daughter says that our dinner table is like a shark tank," my father wrote in his journal one day in 1970, between a drunken lunch in honor of his friend Yevtushenko and an evening spent brooding over a bad review of *Bullet Park*. "I go into a spin. I am not a shark, I am a dolphin. Mary is the shark, etc....But what we stumble on is the banality of family situations. Thinking of Susan, she makes the error of daring not to have been invented by me, of laughing at the wrong time and speaking lines I have not written. Does this prove that I am incapable of love or can only love myself? Scotch for breakfast and I do not like these mornings."

By Thanksgiving of 1981, my father was already too sick to eat much. Of course we didn't know how sick. He had had a kidney removed in June, and all summer he had seemed to get better, but in the autumn, as the air cooled and the leaves changed color, he seemed to be weaker again. When Richard Avedon took a picture of him for the cover of *The Dial,* the photograph looked stark and strange. He couldn't ride his bicycle anymore, and so the doctor sent him to a chiropractor. He went twice a week and installed a primitive traction device on Ben's bed upstairs, where he was working then. He wasn't working much, though. *Paradise* had been finished in the spring, and he spent most of his time answering mail and keeping the journal.

My father never quite trusted medicine. On the one hand, he always thought he was fine; at the same time, he always knew he was dying. His perception of physical reality was tenuous at best. Maybe his mother's Christian Science had something to do with it, too. His solution was to stick to small-town doctors and small-town hospitals, where at least he was known and felt comfortable and where it seemed they often told him what he wanted to hear. As a result, when he needed sophisticated diagnosis and expert medical care, he seemed to prefer jolly talk and home remedies. As the pains in his ribs and legs got worse, he was often depressed.

It was the beginning of December by the time he went back into the hospital for some X-rays. The shadows on those heavy plastic sheets showed that cancer had spread from his kidney up to his lungs and down into his legs; and that was why he felt, as he put it, "so lousy." After they saw the X-rays, the doctors told him there was nothing they could do. There was no treatment. The cancer was too far along.

My husband and I were in La Jolla, California, visiting my husband's daughter that week. "It's very bad," my mother said when I called home to see how the X-rays had come out. "It's very bad." Her voice sounded strange. I was sitting on a bed in a hotel room in Southern California. There was a bureau with a few books on it, and my maternity clothes were thrown over a chair. The main street of La Jolla was outside heavily curtained windows.

"They say I'm a dying man," my father said. His voice was still strong, but the laugh in it seemed to fade as I listened. "They say that my bones look moth-eaten." There was an edge of irony to his voice, as if he were talking about someone else. The hotel room had been decorated in Spanish mission style, and the walls and the bedspread were orange. It was the end of the day. Downstairs, people were waiting to meet us for drinks in the Patio Bar. My father told me that my brother Fred would be flying home for the holidays. "Some people will do almost anything to get their children home for Christmas," he said. I leaned back against the headboard, and the ridges of molded wood dug into my spine. A painting of a cowboy hung on the wall. In the distance, I could hear the sound of the sea.

Suggestions for Discussion

1. How does the quotation from her father's journal set the tone for the chapter?
2. What is gained by the juxtaposition of the author's feelings about the birth of her daughter and the declining days of her father? What details sharpen the contrast between the beginning and end of life?
3. In what different contexts are food and the dinner table the subject of discussion? What do these descriptions tell the reader about the writer's father? About the family relationship?
4. What contradictions does the writer see in her father, especially in regard to his attitude toward appearances?
5. Summarize Cheever's relationship with her father.
6. What was the nature of the father–daughter relationship when the latter became a writer?
7. What does the author's description of the setting in the last paragraph contribute to the tone? How does she make the reader know how deeply she cared for her father?

Suggestions for Writing

1. Discuss the banality of family situations.
2. Write a description of someone whose appearance makes a statement about how he or she meets the world. Or write a description of someone whose appearance is very deceptive.
3. Discuss the role that parental expectations play in fostering or inhibiting their children's growth and development.

GARRETT HONGO

Kubota

Garrett Hongo (b. 1951) was born in Hawaii. He received his education at Pomona College and the University of California at Irvine, where he was awarded the M.F.A. He was the founder and artistic director of the Asian Exclusion Act, a theater group, and executive director of the Asian Multi Media Center. A writer, he has been awarded both the Watson and National Endowment for the Arts fellowships, and he has won the Hopwood and Lamont Poetry Prizes. In 1989 he was nominated for the Pulitzer Prize in Poetry. His books include *Yellow Light* (1982), *The River of Heaven* (1988), *The Open Boat* (1993), and *Volcano: A Memoir of Hawaii* (1996). In the reminiscence that follows he opens up for us the heritage of his grandfather's suffering and its impact on him, a young *nisei* boy growing up in post-war America.

On December 8, 1941, the day after the Japanese attack on Pearl Harbor in Hawaii, my grandfather barricaded himself with his family—my grandmother, my teenage mother, her two sisters and two brothers—inside of his home in La'ie, a sugar plantation village on Oahu's North Shore. This was my maternal grandfather, a man most villagers called by his last name, Kubota. It could mean either "Wayside Field" or else "Broken Dreams," depending on which ideograms he used. Kubota ran La'ie's general store, and the previous night, after a long day of bad news on the radio, some locals had come by, pounded on the front door, and made threats. One was said to have brandished a machete. They were angry and shocked, as the whole nation was in the aftermath of the surprise attack. Kubota was one of the few Japanese-Americans in the village and president of the local Japanese language school. He had become a target for their rage and suspicion. A wise man, he locked all his doors and windows and did not open his store the next day, but stayed closed and waited for news from some official.

He was a *kibei,* a Japanese-American born in Hawaii (a U.S. territory then, so he was thus a citizen) but who was subsequently sent back by his father for formal education in Hiroshima, Japan, their home province. *Kibei* is written with two ideograms in Japanese: one is the word for "return" and the other is the word for "rice." Poetically, it means one who returns from America, known as the Land of Rice in Japanese (by contrast, Chinese immigrants called their new home Mountain of Gold).

Kubota was graduated from a Japanese high school and then came back to Hawaii as a teenager. He spoke English—and a Hawaiian creole version of it at that—with a Japanese accent. But he was well liked and good at numbers, scrupulous and hard working like so many immigrants and children of immigrants. Castle & Cook, a grower's company that ran the sugarcane business along the North Shore, hired him on first as a stock boy and then appointed him to run one of its company stores. He did well, had the trust of management and labor—not an easy accomplishment in any day—married, had children, and had begun to exert himself in community affairs and excel in his own recreations. He put together a Japanese community organization that backed a Japanese language school for children and sponsored teachers from Japan. Kubota boarded many of them, in succession, in his own home. This made dinners a silent affair for his talkative, Hawaiian-bred children, as their stern *sensei,* or teacher, was nearly always at the table and their own abilities in the Japanese language were as delinquent as their attendance. While Kubota and the *sensei* rattled on about things Japanese, speaking Japanese, his children hurried through their suppers and tried to run off early to listen to the radio shows.

After dinner, while the *sensei* graded exams seated in a wicker chair in the spare room and his wife and children gathered around the radio in the front parlor, Kubota sat on the screened porch outside, reading the local Japanese newspapers. He finished reading about the same time as he finished the tea he drank for his digestion—a habit he'd learned in Japan—and then he'd get out his fishing gear and spread it out on the plank floors. The wraps on his rods needed to be redone, gears in his reels needed oil, and, once through with those tasks, he'd painstakingly wind on hundreds of yards of new line. Fishing was his hobby and his passion. He spent weekends camping along the North Shore beaches with his children, setting up umbrella tents, packing a rice pot and hibachi along for meals. And he caught fish. *Ulu'a* mostly, the huge surf-feeding fish known on the mainland as the jack crevalle, but he'd go after almost anything in its season. In Kawela, a plantation-owned bay nearby, he fished for mullet Hawaiian-style with a throw net, stalking the bottom-hugging, gray-backed schools as they gathered at the stream mouths and in the freshwater springs. In an outrigger out beyond the reef, he'd try for *aku*—the skipjack tuna prized for steaks and, sliced raw and mixed with fresh seaweed and cut onions, for *sashimi* salad. In Kahaluu and Ka'awa and on an offshore rock locals called Goat Island, he loved to go torching, stringing lanterns on bamboo poles stuck in the sand to attract *kumu'u,* the red goatfish, as they schooled at night just inside the reef. But in La'ie on Laniloa Point near Kahuku, the northernmost tip of Oahu, he cast twelve- and fourteen-foot surf rods for the huge, varicolored, and fast-running *ulu'a* as they ran for schools of squid and baitfish just beyond the biggest breakers and past the low sand flats wadeable from the shore to nearly a half mile out. At sunset, against the western light, he looked as if he walked on water as he came back, fish and rods slung over his shoulders, stepping along the rock and coral path just inches under the surface of a running tide.

When it was torching season, in December or January, he'd drive out the afternoon before and stay with old friends, the Tanakas or Yoshikawas, shopkeepers like him who ran stores near the fishing grounds. They'd have been preparing for weeks, selecting and cutting their bamboo poles, cleaning the hurricane lanterns, tearing up burlap sacks for the cloths they'd soak with kerosene and tie onto sticks they'd poke into the soft sand of the shallows. Once lit, touched off with a Zippo lighter, these would be the torches they'd use as beacons to attract the schooling fish. In another time, they might have made up a dozen paper lanterns of the kind mostly used for decorating the summer folk dances outdoors on the grounds of the Buddhist church during O-Bon, the Festival for the Dead. But now, wealthy and modern and efficient killers of fish, Tanaka and Kubota used rag torches and Colemans and cast rods with tips made of Tonkin bamboo and butts of American-spun fiberglass. After just one good night, they might bring back a prize bounty of a dozen burlap bags filled with scores of bloody, rigid fish delicious to eat and even better to give away as gifts to friends, family, and special customers.

It was a Monday night, the day after Pearl Harbor, and there was a rattling knock on the front door. Two FBI agents presented themselves, showed identification, and took my grandfather in for questioning in Honolulu. He didn't return home for days. No one knew what had happened or what was wrong. But there was a roundup going on of all those in the Japanese-American community suspected of sympathizing with the enemy and worse. My grandfather was suspected of espionage, of communicating with offshore Japanese submarines launched from the attack fleet days before war began. Torpedo planes and escort fighters, decorated with the insignia of the Rising Sun, had taken an approach route from northwest of Oahu directly across Kahuku Point and on toward Pearl. They had strafed an auxiliary air station near the fishing grounds my grandfather loved and destroyed a small gun battery there, killing three men. Kubota was known to have sponsored and harbored Japanese nationals in his own home. He had a radio. He had wholesale access to firearms. Circumstances and an undertone of racial resentment had combined with wartime hysteria in the aftermath of the tragic naval battle to cast suspicion on the loyalties of my grandfather and all other Japanese-Americans. The FBI reached out and pulled hundreds of them in for questioning in dragnets cast throughout the West Coast and Hawaii.

My grandfather was lucky; he'd somehow been let go after only a few days. Others were not as fortunate. Hundreds, from small communities in Washington, California, Oregon, and Hawaii, were rounded up and, after what appeared to be routine questioning, shipped off under Justice Department orders to holding centers in Leuppe on the Navaho reservation in Arizona, in Fort Missoula in Montana, and on Sand Island in Honolulu Harbor. There were other special camps on Maui in Ha'iku and on Hawaii—the Big Island—in my own home village of Volcano.

Many of these men—it was exclusively the Japanese-American men suspected of ties to Japan who were initially rounded up—did not see their families again for more than four years. Under a suspension of due process that was only after the fact ruled as warranted by military necessity, they were, if only temporarily, "disappeared" in Justice Department prison camps scattered in particularly desolate areas of the United States designated as militarily "safe." These were grim forerunners of the assembly centers and concentration camps for the 120,000 Japanese-American evacuees that were to come later.

I am Kubota's eldest grandchild, and I remember him as a lonely, habitually silent old man who lived with us in our home near Los Angeles for most of my childhood and adolescence. It was the fifties, and my parents had emigrated from Hawaii to the mainland in the hope of a better life away from the old sugar plantation. After some success, they had sent back for my grandparents and taken them in. And it was my grandparents who did the work of the household while my mother and father worked their salaried city jobs. My grandmother cooked and sewed, washed our clothes, and knitted in the front room under the light of a huge lamp with a bright three-way bulb. Kubota raised a flower garden, read up on soils and grasses in gardening books, and planted a zoysia lawn in front and a dichondra one in back. He planted a small patch near the rear block wall with green onions, eggplant, white Japanese radishes, and cucumber. While he hoed and spaded the loamless, clayey earth of Los Angeles, he sang particularly plangent songs in Japanese about plum blossoms and bamboo groves.

Once, in the mid-sixties, after a dinner during which, as always, he had been silent while he worked away at a meal of fish and rice spiced with dabs of Chinese mustard and catsup thinned with soy sauce, Kubota took his own dishes to the kitchen sink and washed them up. He took a clean jelly jar out of the cupboard—the glass was thick and its shape squatty like an old-fashioned. He reached around to the hutch below where he kept his bourbon. He made himself a drink and retired to the living room where I was expected to join him for "talk story," the Hawaiian idiom for chewing the fat.

I was a teenager and, though I was bored listening to stories I'd heard often enough before at holiday dinners, I was dutiful. I took my spot on the couch next to Kubota and heard him out. Usually, he'd tell me about his schooling in Japan where he learned judo along with mathematics and literature. He'd learned the *soroban* there—the abacus, which was the original pocket calculator of the Far East—and that, along with his strong, judo-trained back, got him his first job in Hawaii. This was the moral. "Study *ha-ahd,*" he'd say with pidgin emphasis. "Learn read good. Learn speak da kine *good* English." The message is the familiar one taught to any children of immigrants: succeed through education. And imitation. But this time, Kubota reached down into his past and told me a different story. I was thirteen by then, and I suppose he thought me ready for it. He told me about Pearl Harbor, how the planes flew in wing after wing of formations over his old house in La'ie in Hawaii, and how, the next day, after

Roosevelt had made his famous "Day of Infamy" speech about the treachery of the Japanese, the FBI agents had come to his door and taken him in, hauled him off to Honolulu for questioning, and held him without charge for several days. I thought he was lying. I thought he was making up a kind of horror story to shock me and give his moral that much more starch. But it was true. I asked around. I brought it up during history class in junior high school, and my teacher, after silencing me and stepping me off to the back of the room, told me that it was indeed so. I asked my mother and she said it was true. I asked my schoolmates, who laughed and ridiculed me for being so ignorant. We lived in a Japanese-American community, and the parents of most of my classmates were the *nisei* who had been interned as teenagers all through the war. But there was a strange silence around all of this. There was a hush, as if one were invoking the ill powers of the dead when one brought it up. No one cared to speak about the evacuation and relocation for very long. It wasn't in our history books, though we were studying World War II at the time. It wasn't in the family albums of the people I knew and whom I'd visit staying over weekends with friends. And it wasn't anything that the family talked about or allowed me to keep bringing up either. I was given the facts, told sternly and pointedly that "it was war" and that "nothing could be done." "*Shikatta ga nai*" is the phrase in Japanese, a kind of resolute and determinist pronouncement on how to deal with inexplicable tragedy. I was to know it but not to dwell on it. Japanese-Americans were busy trying to forget it ever happened and were having a hard enough time building their new lives after "camp." It was as if we had no history for four years and the relocation was something unspeakable.

But Kubota would not let it go. In session after session, for months it seemed, he pounded away at his story. He wanted to tell me the names of the FBI agents. He went over their questions and his responses again and again. He'd tell me how one would try to act friendly toward him, offering him cigarettes while the other, who hounded him with accusations and threats, left the interrogation room. Good cop, bad cop, I thought to myself, already superficially streetwise from stories black classmates told of the Watts riots and from my having watched too many episodes of *Dragnet* and *The Mod Squad*. But Kubota was not interested in my experiences. I was not made yet, and he was determined that his stories be part of my making. He spoke quietly at first, mildly, but once into his narrative and after his drink was down, his voice would rise and quaver with resentment and he'd make his accusations. He gave his testimony to me and I held it at first cautiously in my conscience like it was an heirloom too delicate to expose to strangers and anyone outside of the world Kubota made with his words. "I give you story now," he once said, "and you learn speak good, eh?" It was my job, as the disciple of his preaching I had then become, Ananda to his Buddha, to reassure him with a promise. "You learn speak good like the Dillingham," he'd say another time, referring to the wealthy scion of the grower family who had once run, unsuccessfully, for one of Hawaii's first senatorial seats. Or he'd then invoke a magical name, the name of one of his heroes, a man he thought particularly exemplary and righteous. "Learn speak dah good Ing-rish like *Mistah Inouye,*" Kubota shouted. "He *lick* dah Dillingham even in debate. I saw on *terre-bision* myself." He was remembering the debates before the first senatorial election just before Hawaii was admitted to the Union as its fiftieth state. "You *tell* story," Kubota would end. And I had my injunction.

The town we settled in after the move from Hawaii is called Gardena, the independently incorporated city south of Los Angeles and north of San Pedro harbor. At its northern limit, it borders on Watts and Compton, black towns. To the southwest are Torrance and Redondo Beach, white towns. To the rest of L.A., Gardena is primarily famous for having legalized five-card draw poker after the war. On Vermont Boulevard, its eastern border, there is a dingy little Vegas-like strip of card clubs with huge parking lots and flickering neon signs that spell out "The Rainbow" and "The Horseshoe" in timed sequences of varicolored lights. The town is only secondarily famous as the largest community of Japanese-Americans in the United States outside of Honolulu, Hawaii. When I was in high school there, it seemed to me that every *sansei* kid I knew wanted to be a doctor, an engineer, or a pharmacist. Our fathers were gardeners or electricians or nurserymen or ran small businesses catering to other Japanese-Americans. Our mothers worked in civil service for the city or as cashiers for Thrifty Drug. What the kids wanted was a good job, good pay, a fine home, and no troubles. No one wanted to mess with the law—from either side—and no one wanted to mess with language or art. They all talked about getting into the right clubs so that they could go to the right schools. There was a certain kind of sameness, an intensely enforced system of conformity. Style was all. Boys wore moccasin-sewn shoes from Flagg Brothers, black A-1 slacks, and Kensington shirts with high collars. Girls wore their hair up in stiff bouffants solidified in hairspray and knew all the latest dances from the slauson to the funky chicken. We did well in chemistry and in math, no one who was Japanese but me spoke in English class or in history unless called upon, and no one talked about World War II. The day after Robert Kennedy was assassinated, after winning the California Democratic primary, we worked on calculus and elected class coordinators for the prom, featuring the 5th Dimension. We avoided grief. We avoided government. We avoided strong feelings and dangers of any kind. Once punished, we tried to maintain a concerted emotional and social discipline and would not willingly seek to fall out of the narrow margin of protective favor again.

But when I was thirteen, in junior high, I'd not understood why it was so difficult for my classmates, those who were themselves Japanese-American, to talk about the relocation. They had cringed, too, when I tried to bring it up during our discussions of World War II. I was Hawaiian-born. They were mainland-born. Their parents had been in camp, had been the ones to suffer the complicated experience of having to distance themselves from their own history and all things Japanese in order to make their way back and into the American social and economic mainstream. It was out of this sense of shame and a fear of stigma I was only beginning to understand that the *nisei* had silenced themselves. And, for their children, among whom I grew up, they wanted no heritage, no culture, no contact with a defiled history. I recall the silence very well. The Japanese-American children around me were burdened in a way I was not. Their injunction was silence. Mine was to speak.

Away at college, in another protected world in its own way as magical to me as the Hawaii of my childhood, I dreamed about my grandfather. Tired from studying languages, practicing German conjugations or scripting an army's worth of Chinese ideograms on a single sheet of paper, Kubota would come to me as I drifted off into sleep. Or I would walk across the newly mown ball field in back of my dormitory, cutting through a street-side phalanx of ancient eucalyptus trees on my way to visit friends off campus, and I would think of him, his anger, and his sadness.

I don't know myself what makes someone feel that kind of need to have a story they've lived through be deposited somewhere, but I can guess. I think about *The Iliad, The Odyssey, The Peloponnesian Wars* of Thucydides, and a myriad of the works of literature I've studied. A character, almost a *topoi* he occurs so often, is frequently the witness who gives personal testimony about an event the rest of his community cannot even imagine. The sibyl is such a character. And Procne, the maid whose tongue is cut out so that she will not tell that she has been raped by her own brother-in-law, the king of Thebes. There are the dime novels, the epic blockbusters Hollywood makes into miniseries, and then there are the plain, relentless stories of witnesses who have suffered through horrors major and minor that have marked and changed their lives. I myself haven't talked to Holocaust victims. But I've read their survival stories and their stories of witness and been revolted and moved by them. My father-in-law, Al Thiessen, tells me his war stories again and again and I listen. A Mennonite who set aside the strictures of his own church in order to serve, he was a Marine codeman in the Pacific during World War II, in the Signal Corps on Guadalcanal, Morotai, and Bougainville. He was part of the island-hopping maneuver MacArthur had devised to win the war in the Pacific. He saw friends die from bombs which exploded not ten yards away. When he was with the 298th Signal Corps attached to the Thirteenth Air Force, he saw plane after plane come in and crash, just short of the runway, killing their crews, setting the jungle ablaze with oil and gas fires. Emergency wagons would scramble, bouncing over newly bulldozed land men used just the afternoon before for a football game. Every time we go fishing together, whether it's in a McKenzie boat drifting for salmon in Tillamook Bay or taking a lunch break from wading the rifles of a stream in the Cascades, he tells me about what happened to him and the young men in his unit. One was a Jewish boy from Brooklyn. One was a foul-mouthed kid from Kansas. They died. And he *has* to tell me. And I *have* to listen. It's a ritual payment the young owe their elders who have survived. The evacuation and relocation is something like that.

Kubota, my grandfather, had been ill with Alzheimer's disease for some time before he died. At the house he'd built on Kamehameha Highway in Hau'ula, a seacoast village just down the road from La'ie where he had his store, he'd wander out from the garage or greenhouse where he'd set up a workbench, and trudge down to the beach or up toward the line of pines he'd planted while employed by the Work Projects Administration during the thirties. Kubota thought he was going fishing. Or he thought he was back at work for Roosevelt, planting pines as a windbreak or soilbreak on the windward flank of the Ko'olau Mountains, emerald monoliths rising out of sea and cane fields from Waialua to Kaneohe. When I visited, my grandmother would send me down to the beach to fetch him. Or I'd run down Kam Highway a quarter mile or so and find him hiding in the cane field by the roadside, counting stalks, measuring circumferences in the claw of his thumb and forefinger. The look on his face was confused or concentrated, I didn't know which. But I guessed he was going fishing again. I'd grab him and walk him back to his house on the highway. My grandmother would shut him in a room.

Within a few years, Kubota had a stroke and survived it, then he had another one and was completely debilitated. The family decided to put him in a nursing home in Kahuku, just set back from the highway, within a mile or so of Kahuku Point and the Tanaka Store where he had his first job as a stock boy. He lived there three years, and I visited him once with my aunt. He was like a potato that had been worn down by cooking. Everything on him—his eyes, his teeth, his legs and torso—seemed like it had been sloughed away. What he had been was mostly gone now and I was looking at the nub of a man. In a wheelchair, he grasped my hands and tugged on them—violently. His hands were still thick and, I believed, strong enough to lift me out of my own seat into his lap. He murmured something in Japanese—he'd long ago ceased to speak any English. My aunt and I cried a little, and we left him.

I remember walking out on the black asphalt of the parking lot of the nursing home. It was heat-cracked and eroded already, and grass had veined itself into the interstices. There were coconut trees around, a cane field I could see across the street, and the ocean I knew was pitching a surf just beyond it. The green Ko'olaus came up behind us. Somewhere nearby, alongside the beach, there was an abandoned airfield in the middle of the canes. As a child, I'd come upon it playing one day, and my friends and I kept returning to it, day after day, playing war or sprinting games or coming to fly kites. I recognize it even now when I see it on TV—it's used as a site for action scenes in the detective shows Hollywood always sets in the islands: a helicopter chasing the hero racing away in a Ferrari, or gun dealers making a clandestine rendezvous on the abandoned runway. It was the old airfield strafed by Japanese planes the day the major flight attacked Pearl Harbor. It was the airfield the FBI thought my grandfather had targeted in his night fishing and signaling with the long surf poles he'd stuck in the sandy bays near Kahuku Point.

Kubota died a short while after I visited him, but not, I thought, without giving me a final message. I was on the mainland, in California studying for Ph.D. exams, when my grandmother called me with the news. It was a relief. He'd suffered from his debilitation a long time and I was grateful he'd gone. I went home for the funeral and gave the eulogy. My grandmother and I took his ashes home in a small, heavy metal box wrapped in a black *furoshiki,* a large silk scarf. She showed me the name the priest had given to him on his death, scripted with a calligraphy brush on a long, narrow talent of plain wood. Buddhist commoners, at death, are given priestly names, received symbolically into the clergy. The idea is that, in their next life, one of scholarship and leisure, they might meditate and attain the enlightenment the religion is aimed at. "*Shaku Shũchi,*" the ideograms read. It was Kubota's Buddhist name, incorporating characters from his family and given names. It meant "Shining Wisdom of the Law." He died on Pearl Harbor Day, December 7, 1983.

After years, after I'd finally come back to live in Hawaii again, only once did I dream of Kubota, my grandfather. It was the same night I'd heard HR 442, the redress bill for Japanese-Americans, had been signed into law. In my dream that night Kubota was "torching," and he sang a Japanese song, a querulous and wavery folk ballad, as he hung paper lanterns on bamboo poles stuck into the sand in the shallow water of the lagoon behind the reef near Kahuku Point. Then he was at a work table, smoking a hand-rolled cigarette, letting it dangle from his lips Bogart-style as he drew, daintily and skillfully, with a narrow trim brush, ideogram after ideogram on a score of paper lanterns he had hung in a dark shed to dry. He had painted a talismanic mantra onto each lantern, the ideogram for the word "red" in Japanese, a bit of art blended with some superstition, a piece of sympathetic magic appealing to the magenta coloring on the rough skins of the schooling, night-feeding fish he wanted to attract to his baited hooks. He strung them from pole to pole in the dream then, hiking up his khaki worker's pants so his white ankles showed and wading through the shimmering black waters of the sand flats and then the reef.

"The moon is leaving, leaving," he sang in Japanese. "Take me deeper in the savage sea." He turned and crouched like an ice racer then, leaning forward so that his unshaven face almost touched the light film of water. I could see the light stubble of beard like a fine, gray ash covering the lower half of his face. I could see his gold-rimmed spectacles. He held a small wooden boat in his cupped hands and placed it lightly on the sea and pushed it away. One of his lanterns was on it and, written in small neat rows like a sutra scroll, it had been decorated with the silvery names of all our dead.

Suggestions for Discussion

1. What do the two renderings of Kubota's name in English, "Wayside Field" and "Broken Dreams," suggest as alternate possibilities for interpretations of his life? What of his death name, "Shining Wisdom of the Law"?
2. Why does no one among Hongo's family and friends want to talk about the evacuation and relocation of the *nisei* (Japanese-Americans) during World War II? Why will Kubota not stop talking about it?
3. How are the stories we are told part of our "making"?

Suggestions for Writing

1. Hongo says of his generation, "We avoided grief.... We avoided strong feelings and dangers of any kind." Does this describe you? Your friends? Explain.
2. "He *has* to tell me. And I *have* to listen. It's a ritual payment the young owe their elders who have survived." Relate this comment to your own experience with someone from a previous generation.

JOHN EDGAR WIDEMAN

Father Stories

John Edgar Wideman (b. 1941) has degrees from the University of Pennsylvania and Oxford University, where he was a Rhodes Scholar. He has taught at the University of Pennsylvania, where he was also director of the Afro-American studies program, and at the University of Wyoming. He is presently affiliated with the University of Massachusetts at Amherst. Honors include, among others, not only the

PEN/Faulkner Award for fiction, a National Book Award nomination, the John Dos Passos Prize for Literature, but being named a member of the Philadelphia Big Five Basketball Hall of Fame. Author of a number of novels, collections of short stories, and articles, his current publications include *All Stories Are True* (1993), *The Stories of John Edgar Wideman* (1992), *Fatheralong: A Meditation on Fathers and Sons, Race and Society* (1994), and *Brothers and Keepers* (1995). The following piece is an effort to memorialize his son, who was lost to him.

One day neither in the past nor in the future, and not at this moment, either, all the people gathered on a high ridge that overlooked the rolling plain of earth, its forests, deserts, rivers unscrolling below them like a painting on parchment. Then the people began speaking, one by one, telling the story of a life—everything seen, heard, and felt by each soul. As the voices dreamed, a vast, bluish mist enveloped the land and the seas below. Nothing was visible. It was as if the solid earth had evaporated. Now there was nothing but the voices and the stories and the mist; and the people were afraid to stop the storytelling and afraid not to stop, because no one knew where the earth had gone.

Finally, when only a few storytellers remained to take a turn, someone shouted: Stop! Enough, enough of this talk! Enough of us have spoken! We must find the earth again!

Suddenly, the mist cleared. Below the people, the earth had changed. It had grown into the shape of the stories they'd told—a shape as wondrous and new and real as the words they'd spoken. But it was also a world unfinished, because not all the stories had been told.

Some say that death and evil entered the world because some of the people had no chance to speak. Some say that the world would be worse than it is if all the stories had been told. Some say that there are no more stories to tell. Some believe that untold stories are the only ones of value and we are lost when they are lost. Some are certain that the storytelling never stops; and this is one more story, and the earth always lies under its blanket of mist being born.

I begin again because I don't want it to end. I mean all these father stories that take us back, that bring us here, where you are, where I am, needing to make sense, to go on if we can and should.

Once, when you were five or six, all the keys to the camp vehicles disappeared. Keys for trucks, vans, rental cars, a school bus, a tractor, boats—the whole fleet necessary each summer to service the business of offering four hundred boys an eight-week escape in the Maine woods. In the innocence of the oasis that your grandfather had created—this gift of water, trees, a world apart—nobody bothered to lock things; keys were routinely left in the ignition for the next driver. Then, one day the keys were gone. For hours, everybody searched high and low. I thought of you as I climbed into the cab of the dump truck to check for a key that might have fallen to the floor or slipped into some crevice or corner of the raw, gasoline-reeking interior. You because countless times I'd hoisted you into the cab, tucked you in the driver's seat. Nothing you enjoyed more than turning a steering wheel, roaring and vrooming engine noise while you whipped the wheel back and forth, negotiating some endless, dramatic highway only you could see. You were fascinated by that imaginary road and the wheels that rolled you there. Even before you could talk, you'd flip your toy trucks and cars on their sides or upside down so you could spin the wheels, growl motor noise.

You never admitted taking the keys, and nobody pressed you very hard after they were found, in a heap in the sand under the boat dock. But, years later, Junie, the head caretaker, mentioned that he'd seen you making your usual early morning rounds from vehicle to vehicle the day the keys were missing, and confided to me a suspicion he had felt then but had kept to himself till you were gone and were unlikely to return for a long time. Turns out your grandfather had been suspicious, too. He didn't miss much that happened in the camp, either, and had observed what Junie had observed. I recall being rather annoyed when your grandfather suggested that I ask you if you might have noticed keys anywhere the day they disappeared. Annoyed and amazed, because you were hardly more than a baby. No reason for you to bother the keys. I'd instructed you never to touch them, and that was one of the conditions you'd promised to honor in return for the privilege of installing yourself behind steering wheels. I trusted you. Questioning my trust insulted us both. Besides, the missing keys implied a plot, a prank, sabotage, some scheme premeditated and methodically perpetrated by older campers or adults, and you were just a kid. You were my son. His grandson. So he gently hinted I might casually check with you, not because you were a suspect but because you had access and had been noticed at the scene, and so perhaps might be able to assist the searchers with a clue.

I don't remember your grandfather's ever mentioning the keys again until we'd lost you and all of us were searching once more for answers. And, since each of us had then begun to understand that answers were not around us, not in the air, and not exclusively in you, but inside us all, when your grandfather repeated ten years later his suspicions about the keys, it sounded almost like a confession, and we both understood that some searches never end.

A small army of adults, stymied, frustrated, turning the camp inside out. A couple of hours of mass confusion, pockets, drawers, memories rifled, conspiracy theories floated, paranoia blossoming, numb searches and re-searches. Minor panic when duplicate keys weren't stashed where they should be; righteous indignation and scapegoating; the buzz, the edge for weeks afterward whenever keys were mentioned, picked up, or set down in the camp office. The morning of the lost keys became one of those incidents, significant or not in themselves, that lend a name, a tone to a whole camp season: the summer of baby goats in the nature lodge, the hurricane summer, the summer a boy was lost for a night on Mt. Katahdin, the summer you-remember-who bit your grandfather's finger, the summer two counsellors from a boys' camp nearby were killed in a highspeed crash late at night, the summer the Israeli nurses swam topless, the summer you left and never returned.

If you'd ambled up on your short, chunky legs and handed me the lost keys, it wouldn't have convinced me you'd taken them. Nor would a confession have convinced me. Nothing you might have said or done could have solved the mystery of the keys. No accident or coincidence would have implicated you. Without a reason, with no motive, no *why,* the idea of your removing the keys remained unthinkable.

You were blond then. Huge brown eyes. Hair on your head of many kinds, a storm, a multiculture of textures: kinky, dead straight, curly, frizzy, ringlets; hair thick in places, sparse in others. All your people, on both sides of the family, ecumenically represented in the golden crown atop your head.

You cried huge tears, too. Heartbreaking, slow, sliding tears that formed gradually in the corners of your dark eyes—gleaming, shapely tears before they collapsed and inched down your cheeks. Big tears, but you cried quietly, almost privately, even though the proof of your unhappiness was smearing your face. Then again, when you needed to, you could bellow and hoot—honking Coltrane explorations of anger, temper, outrage. Most of the time, however, you cried softly, your sobs pinched off by deep, heaving sighs, with a rare, high-pitched, keening wail escaping in spite of whatever was disciplining you to wrap your sorrow so close to yourself.

I'm remembering things in no order, with no plan. These father stories. Because that's all they are.

Your mother said that the story she wishes she could write, but knows is so painful she hesitates to tell it to herself, would be about her, of course, and you, yes, but also about her father, your grandfather: what he built, who he was, his long, special life, how many other lives he touched, the place he created out of nothing, in the woods, along the lake that I'm watching this morning, and that watches me as I write.

It is her father she has returned to all these summers in Maine. What he provided, no strings attached. His gift of water, trees, weather, a world apart, full of surprise, a world unchanging. Summers in Maine were the stable, rooted part of her.

One morning, as I sit on the dock staring at the lake, a man and a boy float past in a small boat. They have turned off the putt-putt outboard motor hanging over the stern and are drifting in closer to the rocky shoreline, casting their fishing lines where the water is blackish green from shadows of tall pines lining the lake. A wake spreads languidly behind the boat, one wing plowing the dark water, its twin unfurling like a bright flag dragged across the surface. No sound except birdsong, the hiss of a fishing line arcing away from the boat, then its plopping like a coin in the bottom of a well. The weather has changed overnight. Wind from the west this morning—a cooling, drying wind lifting the mist before dawn, turning the sky unwaveringly blue at this early hour. A wind shunting away last week's mugginess and humidity, though it barely ruffles the skin of the water in this inlet. Gray bands of different shades and textures stripe the lake's center, panels of a fan lazily unfolding, closing, opening. Later, the west wind will perk up and bring chill gusts, stir a chop into the water. Smooth and quiet now for the man and the boy hunkered down in their boat. They wear baseball caps, layers of shirts and jackets, the same bulky shape twice; one form is larger than the other, and each is a slightly different color, but otherwise the two are identical, down to the way their wrists snap, their lines arc up and away from the boat. The man's lure lands farther away than the boy's each time, in scale with the hunched figures drifting past in the boat.

I will see the boat again, about an hour later, when the water is louder, when ripples driven from the west are forming scalloped waves. The boy, alone then, whips the boat full throttle in tight, spray-sluicing circles, around and around, gouging deep furrows. The nose of the boat high in the air, he hunches over the screaming engine, gunning it in short, sprinting bursts, then in sharp turns, around and around, as if he were trying to escape a swarm of hornets.

The wind is forgetting it's July. I wish for extra insulation under my hooded sweatshirt and nylon windbreaker. Trees are a baffle for the wind and conjure its sound into colder, stronger, arctic messages shuttling through the upper atmosphere. In the same way, your mother's hair when it's long and loose, catching all the colors of light, falling down around her bare shoulders, carries within itself that wind rush of surf crashing far away, the muffled roar of a crowd in a vast, distant stadium.

You'd twist thick clumps of her chestnut hair in your fist, clutch it while she held you and you sucked the thumb of your other hand. For hours. For hours if she'd let you.

Maybe all things happen, including ourselves, long before we see, hear, know they are happening. Memory, then, isn't so much archival as it is a seeking of vitality, harmony, an evocation of a truer, more nearly complete present tense. All of this, of course, relates to personality—the construction of a continuous narrative of self. Our stories. Father stories.

Do you remember your fear of leaves? Of course you do. The teasers in our family would never let you forget.

Once, in Laramie, Wyoming, after dinner, just as a full-moon night was falling and the wide, straight-arrow streets were as empty and still as Long Lake at dawn, I was riding you on my shoulders—a rare moment, the two of us together, away from your mother and brother—when, suddenly you cried out. The street we were on had a ceiling. Branches from trees planted in people's yards hung over fences lining the sidewalk, forming a canopy overhead. I panicked. Thought I'd knocked you against a low branch or you'd got your hair tangled—or, worse, been scratched in the eye or the face. Your fingers dug into my scalp. You didn't want to let go as I tried to unseat you from my shoulders, slide you down into the light from a street lamp to see what was the matter.

You'd given me a couple of good yanks, so I was both mad and scared when I finally pulled you down, cradling you in my arms to get a clear look at your face.

No tears. No visible damage. Yet you were wild-eyed, trembling uncontrollably. The leaves had been after you. Probably not touching you but, worse, a blanket of quivering, rustling, mottled dread suddenly hovering above you. Surrounding you, rendering you speechless. Terrorized beyond words or tears, you'd gripped my hair and kicked my chest. I'd thought you were roughing me up because you wanted to play. Grabbed your wrists and squeezed them tight to hold you as I galloped down the quiet Laramie street, doing my best imitation of the bucking bronco on Wyoming license plates. You were rendered even more helpless with your hands clamped in mine, struggling to free yourself while I thought we were having fun. Your father snorting and braying, jiggedy-jig, jiggedy-jig, suddenly in league with your worst enemy, and nowhere to run, nowhere to hide—he was rushing you to your doom. No wonder your fingers tried to rip my hair out when I released your wrists. Holding on, reining me in, pounding on my skull, fighting back the only way you knew how, short of pitching yourself down from a dizzying height, down, down to the pavement, itself strewn with shadowy leaves.

When I was a kid, I harbored a morbid fear of feathers. Feathers. Not a single feather or a few loose feathers, like the ones I'd stick in my naps to play Indian, but feathers in a bunch, attached to birds who could wriggle them, flutter them, transform them into loose flesh, rotting, molting, the unnatural sign of death-in-life and life-in-death, the zombie, mummy, decaying corpses of movies and my nightmares. Feathers a kind of squirmy skin hanging off the bone, all the more horrible because feathers seemed both dry and sticky with blood.

My feathers, your leaves. One afternoon at the Belmar on Homewood Avenue, in Pittsburgh, in one of those Bible-days epic movies, a man was tortured nearly to death, his bloody body flung off a fortress wall. He landed on a heap of corpses in a ditch. As the camera pans the mangled bodies, the sound of huge wings beating thumps through the Belmar's crackly speakers. After the Technicolor glare of carnage under a desert sun, the camera is blinded an instant by the black swoop of vultures. They land atop the corpses, feathers rippling, glinting as the birds begin their slow-motion, ponderously delicate lope toward the choicest morsels of meat—eyeballs, tongues, exposed guts—toward the not-quite-dead-yet man sprawled on a bed of other victims.

Then a closeup of the man's face. As he spots the vultures and screams, I scream. I know I did. Even though I couldn't hear myself, because everybody in the Belmar joined in one shrieking whoop of fear and disgust. And I never forgot the scene. Never. Never forgot, never forgave. Hated pigeons. They became my scapegoats, or scapebirds. I'd hurt them any chance I got. Trapped one in a box and tormented it. Fully intended to incinerate the crippled one who wound up on the stone steps in the hallway of my dorm freshman year until my roommate shamed me out of it when I asked to borrow his lighter and some fluid and he demanded to know for what.

Pigeons were brown and dirty. They shat everywhere. Spoiled things. Their cooing from the eaves of our roof on Finance Street could startle you awake. They sneaked around, hid in dark corners, carried disease, like rats. Far too many of the useless creatures. I focussed my fear and hate of feathers on them. Went out of my way to cause them difficulties.

Once, I was so angry at your mother's pain I thought I was angry at her. She was sharing out loud for the first time how torn apart she'd felt that summer you never came back. How she feared her father's gift had been blighted forever. Woods, lake, sky a mirror reflecting absence of father, absence of son, the presence of her grief.

I couldn't deal with the pain in her voice, so I made up another story. Presumed to tell her she was letting her pain exclude other ways of trying to make sense, with words, with stories, with the facts as given and the facts as felt, make sense of the enormity of what happens and doesn't happen, the glimmers of it we paste together trying to find peace. One different story would be the day she meets her father again in this place and what he might have to say to her and why he needed to see her and what he might remind her of and why it would need to be here, on a path through the thick pine woods where light can surprise you, penetrating in smoky shafts where it has no business being, where it sparkles, then shifts instantly, gone faster than the noises of creatures in the underbrush you never see. I make up her father, as I'm making up mine. Her father appearing to her in a suit of lights because that, too, could transpire, could redeem, could set us straight in a world where you never know what's going to happen next and often what happens is bad, is crushing, but it's never the worst thing, never the best, it's only the last thing, and not even exactly that, except once, and even then death is not exactly the last thing that happens, because you never know what's going to happen next. For better or worse, cursed and blessed by this ignorance, we invent, fill it, are born with the gift, the need, the weight of filling it with our imaginings. That are somehow as real as we are. Our mothers and fathers and children. Our stories.

I hope this is not a hard day for you. I hope you can muster peace within yourself and deal with the memories, the horrors of the past eight years. It must strike you as strange—as strange as it strikes me—that eight years have passed already. I remember a few days after hearing you were missing and a boy was found dead in the room the two of you had been sharing, I remember walking down toward the lake to be alone, because I felt myself coming apart: the mask I'd been wearing, as much for myself as for the benefit of other people, was beginning to splinter. I could hear ice cracking, great rents and seams breaking my face into pieces, carrying away chunks of numb flesh. I found myself on my knees, praying to a tree. In the middle of some absurdly compelling ritual that I'd forgotten I carried the memory of. Yet there I was on my knees, digging my fingers into the loose soil, grabbing up handfuls, sinking my face into the clawed earth as if it might heal me. Speaking to the roots of a pine tree as if its shaft might carry my message up to the sky, send it on its way to wherever I thought my anguish should be addressed.

I was praying to join you. Offering myself in exchange for you. Take me. Take me. Free my son from the terrible things happening to him. Take me in his place. Let them happen to me. I was afraid you were dying or already dead or suffering unspeakable tortures at the hands of a demon kidnapper. The tears I'd held back were flowing finally, a flood that brought none of the relief I must have believed that hoarding them would earn me when I let go at last. Just wetness burning, clouding my eyes. I couldn't will the spirit out of my body into the high branches of that tree. What felt familiar, felt like prayers beside my bed as a child, or church people moaning in the amen corner, or my mother weeping and whispering *hold on, hold on* to herself as she rocks side to side and mourns, or some naked priest chanting and climbing toward the light on a bloody ladder inside his chest—these memories of what might have been visions of holiness could not change the simple facts. I was a man who had most likely lost his son, and hugging trees and burying his face in dirt and crying for help till breath slunk out of his body wouldn't change a thing.

A desperate, private moment, one of thousands I could force myself to dredge up if I believed it might serve some purpose. I share that one example with you to say that the eight years have not passed quickly. The years are countless moments, many as intense as this one I'm describing to you, moments I conceal from myself as I've hidden them from other people.

Other moments, also countless, when terrible things had to be shared, spoken aloud, in phone calls with lawyers, depositions, interviews, conferences, in the endless conversations with your mother. Literally endless, because often the other business of our lives would seem merely a digression from the dialogue with you, about you. A love story finally, love of you, your brother and sister, since no word except love makes sense of the ever-present narrative our days unfold.

Time can drag like a long string, studded and barbed, through a fresh wound, so it hasn't gone quickly. The moment-to-moment, day-by-day struggles imprint my flesh. But the eight years are also a miracle, a blink of the eye through which I watch myself wending my way from there to here. In this vast house of our fathers and mothers.

Your mother didn't need my words or images to work out her grief. She needed time. Took the time she needed to slowly, gradually, painstakingly unravel feelings knotted in what seemed for a while a hopeless tangle. No choice, really. She's who she is. Can give nothing less than her whole heart to you, to this place, inseparable from all our lives, that her father, your grandfather, provided.

For a while, I guess it must have felt impossible. And still can, I know. She may have doubted her strength, her capacity to give enough, give everything, because everything seemed to be tearing her apart, breaking her down. She needed time. Not healing time, exactly, since certain wounds never heal, but time to change and more time to learn to believe, to understand she could go on, was going on, for better or worse. She could be someone she'd never dreamed she could be. Her heart strong, whole, even as it cracks and each bit demands everything.

The fullness of time. The fullness of time. That phrase has haunted me since I first heard it or read it, though I don't know when or how the words entered my awareness, because they seem to have always been there, like certain melodies, for instance, or visual harmonies of line in your mother's body that I wondered how I'd ever lived without the first time I encountered them, although another recognition clicked in almost simultaneously, reminding me that I'd been waiting for those particular notes, those lines, a very long time. They'd been forming me before I formed my first impressions of them.

The fullness of time. Neither forward nor backward. A space capacious enough to contain your coming into and going out of the world, your consciousness of these events, the wrap of oblivion bedding them. A life, the passage of a life: the truest understanding, measure, experience of time's fullness. So many lives, and each different, each unknowable, no matter how similar to yours, your flesh and not your flesh, lives passing, like yours, into the fullness of time, where each of these lives and all of them together make no larger ripple than yours, all and each abiding in the unruffled innocence of the fullness that is time. All the things that mattered so much to you or them sinking into a dreadful, unfeatured equality that is also rest and peace, time gone: but more, always more, the hands writing, the hands snatching, hands becoming bones, then dust, then whatever comes next, what time takes and fashions of you after the possibilities, permutations, and combinations—the fullness in you—are exhausted, played out for the particular shape the fullness has assumed for a time in you, for you. You are never it but what it could be, then is not: you not lost but ventured, gained, stretched, more, until the dust is particles and the particles play unhindered, unbound, returned to the fullness of time.

I know my father's name, Edgar, and some of his fathers' names, Hannibal, Tatum, Jordan, but I can't go back any further than a certain point, except that I also know the name of a place, Greenwood, South Carolina, and an even smaller community, Promised Land, nearly abutting Greenwood, where my grandfather, who, of course, is your great-grandfather, was born, and where many of his brothers are buried, under sturdy tombstones bearing his name, our name, "Wideman," carved in stone in the place where the origins of the family name begin to dissolve into the loam of plantations owned by white men, where my grandfathers' identities dissolve, where they were boys, then men, and the men they were fade into a set of facts, sparse, ambiguous, impersonal, their intimate lives unretrievable, where what is known about a county, a region, a country and its practice of human bondage, its tradition of obscuring, stealing, or distorting black people's lives, begins to crowd out the possibility of seeing my ancestors as human beings. The powers and principalities that originally restricted our access to the life that free people naturally enjoy still rise like a shadow, a wall between my grandfathers and me, my father and me, between the two of us, father and son, son and father.

So we must speak these stories to one another.

Love.

Suggestions for Discussion

1. How does the telling of stories connect us to time—to the past, the present, and the future?
2. What actually happened to the author's son? What foreshadowing leads us to be prepared for what we come to learn?
3. The author contrasts the beautiful campsite that has been such an important part of the family's life with the torment of the pain the family has endured. How does he do this?

Suggestions for Writing

1. The father is afraid of feathers, the boy of leaves. What frightens you? How is it connected to events in your life?
2. This essay is about connections between fathers and sons across generations, connections that cannot be broken, even by appalling tragedy. What are you connected to in this way?
3. Whatever it is that separates fathers and sons, those boundaries that cannot be crossed, is central to this piece. How have you experienced these boundaries in your own life?

ESSAY

VICTORIA BISSELL BROWN

Abortion Fight Is over Choice

Victoria Bissell Brown teaches American Women's History at San Diego State University. Her portrait of a disagreeing mother and her adolescent daughter and their reconciliation focuses on their respective views of choice.

The local broadcaster announced that after the commercial he would be interviewing a leader in the anti-abortion movement. "Turn it off," I snapped at my daughter, "I can't bear to listen to that."

She gave me the kind of look children in the 1960s gave parents who refused to watch anti-war demonstrations on TV news. That look asked how could I have such a closed mind? How could I be so Establishment? And how could I be so curt, so final, so decisive about what my 13-year-old daughter says she regards as possibly the killing of babies?

Standing there in my kitchen, biscuit dough on my hands, I felt the full force of the abortion backlash. At that moment, my daughter saw me not as a soft-hearted liberal—a political persona I've grown comfortable with—but as a cold-hearted killer, one who sacrifices the unborn in the name of some abstract right to privacy. It was not the fact that she disagreed with me that was so disturbing. She's a teen-ager, she disagrees with me every day. What was so disturbing was the success of the anti-abortion movement at depicting people like me as heartless, amoral abstractionists who care more about rights than about life.

It seems to me that this is where I came in some 20 years ago. Only back then the opponents of abortion laws were the ones who were the heartless killers. Back then, we charged them with caring more about abstract principles than real life. Back then, we were the ones who showed the gruesome pictures—of women butchered on dirty kitchen tables, of women dead from unnecessary infections, of fetuses punctured by coat hangers, of women poisoned from drinking lye.

The movement for abortion rights did not begin and was not fueled by a passion for the right to privacy. That is the principle that convinced the Supreme Court, but the heart of this movement is nothing so anemic as a legalistic principle. The heart of this movement is a deep concern for the lives, the health and the well-being of American women.

That is the point I tried to make to my daughter. As the biscuits cooked and the interview came on the television, we sat and discussed the matter as only a mother and adolescent daughter can. Which is to say that we were alternately snarly and sensitive; there were bursts of honesty as well as of anger; there were questions and accusations; there were tears and occasional smiles. We were momentarily locked in a primal tug of wills over the most primal of issues.

We began, of course, with the fundamentals. "How do you know you're not killing a person?" she asked. Because I know that a 10-week-old fetus cannot survive outside a woman's womb, I know that it has no cognitive abilities. I know that it has no capacity for love or work, I know that it has no relationships or responsibilities. And I weigh that knowledge against the certitude that a pregnant woman is, most definitely, a person with relationships and responsibilities that only she can calculate.

I know that the research on women considering abortions shows that they aren't consumed with the question of privacy rights; they're consumed with the question of responsibilities—to their other children, to their parents, to their employers or teachers, to their husbands or lovers, to themselves, to that embryo. Few women make this decision casually; no women make it because they want to assert their right to privacy. Women decide to abort pregnancies because the ties that bind them in every other corner of their lives take priority over the very tenuous tie that binds them to that very tenuous bit of life in their wombs.

My daughter paid attention to these remarks, but seemed unmoved.

The television interview intruded. "What advice do you give to single women?" asked the interviewer. "We advise chastity," responded the pretty, powdered, softly bow-tied lady on the screen. I looked sideways at my daughter.

"What do you think of that?" I asked her. "Well," she sniffed, "I don't think people should be irresponsible about sex." That answer should have warmed the cockles of my maternal heart, but it didn't. It sounded cold-hearted, abstract—a principle unrelated to real life uttered by one who has yet to experience her first kiss.

My innocent child holds the conviction that women are—or should be—sufficiently in control of their lives so that they could always prevent pregnancy, either through contraception or by simply saying "no." It seems that she is, after all, the daughter of a feminist. This child of the women's movement expects women to be in charge of their lives. After all, her mother had only one child and no abortions—why can't everyone else be similarly well regulated? So great is women's progress (on TV and among the privileged white elite of my daughter's experience) that she simply cannot imagine women as victims of either the law or contraceptive failure or male sexual demands.

In abstract principle, she's right of course. In the best of all possible worlds, women would have the personal socialization and the economic independence that would allow them to say "no," and they would have medical and legal protections against unwanted pregnancies. But we don't live in abstract principle, and this isn't the best of all possible worlds, and despite what the softly bow-tied lady on TV said, making abortion illegal will not decrease premarital—or "irresponsible"—sex. It will only bring back all those couples who "had" to get married and all those women who were maimed or killed by underworld abortionists and all those mothers who abandoned all personal goals and resigned themselves to the vagaries of reproductive chance.

My daughter's eyes glazed over a bit, the way they do when I started sounding like a history professor. This story doesn't end with her throwing her arms around me and swearing her allegiance to my politics. It ends with my husband serving some almost-burned biscuits and my daughter and me making amends at a funny matinee.

She's not going to acquiesce to me on this. She wants the autonomy to make her own choice about abortion. And in that, she is true to the proud tradition of the abortion rights movement.

Suggestions for Discussion

1. What do the rhetorical questions contribute to the mother's sense of her daughter's view of her?
2. What was the nature of the abortion backlash the mother feels in relation to her thirteen-year-old daughter's attitudes?
3. What really disturbed the mother in relation to her teenage daughter?
4. What is the nature of the principle that guided the Supreme Court in its *Roe* v. *Wade* decision?
5. What were the "fundamentals" discussed by mother and daughter?
6. What issues outweigh the question of privacy rights in the research on women considering abortions?
7. In what respect does the mother view the child as naive?
8. How does the mother reconcile her daughter's attitude with her own?

Suggestions for Writing

1. Analyze the character of the mother, the daughter, and the relationship between them.
2. Discuss the significance of "choice" in any aspect of your life or in that of one of your friends or parents.

FICTION

GREG JONES

The Man on the Moon

Greg Jones is a short story writer, novelist, and screenwriter. This story first appeared in *Buzz.*

When I was five and my brother, Brent, was seven, my dad turned in his card at Plumbers Local 1141 in Torrance and bought a stucco rambler down in Costa Mesa so we could grow up near the beach and play baseball in the Orange County little leagues. Dad read in *The Sporting News* that Orange County had produced more major-league ballplayers than any area in the nation. He took the rest of his savings and a V.A. loan and started Farrell & Sons Pipe, expecting that someday, maybe after our major-league careers were over, we'd join the company. He worked long and hard to get his business going but somehow still made time to coach our little-league baseball team. Mom kept the books for Farrell & Sons and served as secretary of the baseball league and she was good at both since, as Dad liked to say, she was born to worry over little things. The business took off and our team won a lot of games, and to celebrate his second successful year, my dad built a new porch across the front of our house with a four-by-four railing so you could sit back and kick up your heels.

On Friday nights after dinner, Dad would sit on the front porch swigging beer and telling stories about his days as a catcher in double-A ball or as a grunt in World War II. One clear night, the three of us sat and studied the craters on the beaming full moon. A pyramid of empty beer cans was growing next to Dad. He leaned back against the porch railing, burped, chuckled, and then said the moon looked like a big-ass smiling jack-o'-lantern. He said the reason the Man on the Moon smiled so much was because there weren't any little boys up there to drive him nuts. He said the Man on the Moon used his huge smile to attract kids. When they came near, he ate them, and when he burped, stars came out of his mouth.

That night in bed, when the moonlight pushed through the shade, I saw the lunatic smile of the Man on the Moon lurking behind my curtains. I huddled under my covers and cried until Brent climbed down from the top bunk and got in bed with me.

"It's OK, Sammy," he whispered. "It's just the silly old Man on the Moon. One of these days, you and me, we're going to fly up there on a magic carpet and play some catch with the Man on the Moon. Cross my heart."

It was about ten years later when Brent left for Mexico. I helped him pack his dilapidated army surplus Jeep—the Road Hog. We loaded his backpack, the green canvas tent we'd shared at Explorer camp, his surfboard, and then I hefted the duffel bag that Dad claimed to have carried in WW II. When I shoved it into the back of the Jeep, a book tumbled from the bag and I picked it up.

"*Leaves of Grass,*" I read from the cover. "Brent, you've got to be the only catcher in baseball history who likes poetry."

"Whitman," he said, swiping the book from my hands, embarrassed. "The man can knock you out with words, Sam." He threw a quick punch at me.

I stepped back and shadow-boxed. "Float like a butterfly, sting like Sam-me!"

"Swat like a gnat," Brent said, and slapped the book against the car before tucking it back into his bag. "The Swan gave me this book," he said. "Show some respect, brother." The Swan was Brent's girlfriend. Her long, lovely neck had earned her the nickname.

"The Swan is divine," I said, bowing. "But poetry? I don't know."

Brent squinted at me as he knelt to test the tire pressure. I could see the sun rising over the house and Mom watching us from the front window. "You throw a wicked fastball, Sam," Brent said, "and you're a grade-A smart-ass. But there's more to it, you know? Take Gallagher's class next year, OK?"

Brent's favorite teacher in high school was his English teacher, Mr. Gallagher, who wore his red hair in a ponytail. He'd once ridden a Harley across the country just to spend a few nights sleeping next to Walt Whitman's grave in Camden, New Jersey.

Brent jumped into the Jeep and snatched his faded Cincinnati Reds baseball cap from the rearview mirror. He pulled the cap on backward over his hair. Then he took a pair of silver mirrored aviator shades from the glove compartment. "Check it out, bro'," he said, wrapping the glasses over his ears. "I'm the Man on the Moon." He made a circle around his face with his hands. "Woooo, woooo," he said, and busted up.

"Shit," I said, shoving my hands in the pockets of my jeans. He could still make me blush by bringing it up.

Brent revved the engine and waved to Mom, who now stood on the front walk with her thin arms crossed over her chest. Dad was at work, as usual. Brent offered me one of his big hands and we shook. "Wish you could go, Sam," he said.

I pushed my hands deep into my pockets. I was signed up to work as a gopher for my dad all summer, and I was pitching American Legion at night. "You be careful," I said. "I hear people drive crazy down there."

"No sweat. You keep hurling smoke!" he yelled. "Wicked smoke!" And as he backed down the driveway he sang out the window, "Sam-wich, Saam-bo, Saaam Hell, Samson and Delilah, Sam the Sham and the Pharaohs, Slinging Sammy Baugh, Brother Smoke Slinging Sam the Man…" Then he popped the clutch and the Jeep bucked down the street.

Brent had been offered a scholarship to play baseball at the University of Arizona, but this was 1969 and he had come up number four in the draft lottery. Mom was all for the college deferment, but Dad had other ideas. The three of them holed up in the dining room one night after dinner, and when they emerged I asked Brent what Dad had said. "When a man is called, he serves," Brent repeated blankly, and saluted.

I told Dad I thought it was a waste of Brent's talent to have him go off to war, but he disagreed. "He'll come back bigger, stronger, and a better man," Dad said. "Ted Williams served. The greatest hitter there ever was. Fought in two wars and played ball till he was 42. The last man to hit .400."

When I asked Mom what she thought, she couldn't even speak. Then the Arizona coach said Brent's scholarship would always be good, no matter how long he was gone, and that sealed it. Brent was due to report to the Marine Corps Recruit Depot in San Diego in early August.

My parents agreed to let Brent and his buddy Chuck go surfing down the coast of Baja before boot camp if he called home every other day and promised to be back by early July. I talked with Brent every time he called. He told me he'd grown a brand-new nose, his had peeled so many times. And the only thing he'd ever seen more perfect than the arching Baja waves was the Swan's neck. He'd paid twenty bucks for a blow job in a dive bar in Tijuana, but couldn't get it up he was so nervous. In Ensenada, a drunk Dodger fan ripped Brent's Reds cap off his head, and Brent had subdued the peckerhead with a swift full nelson. And at the tip of Baja, he'd read Whitman's "Song of the Open Road" out loud by the campfire one night. "I cried when I was done," he said to me. "I'm not afraid to admit it. It's as good a reason as any." He told me he missed me and the Swan and Mom; and that it would be good to get back to a hot shower and Mom's porcupine meatballs and catching some of my heaters in the backyard. "It'll be fine," he said, his voice trailing off, "except then I'll have to go do the John Wayne in Vietnam and probably get my balls blown off."

I answered the phone the first Saturday evening in July, hoping it would be Brent. But it was Chuck. "Sam?" he said.

"The man," I answered. "Where's Brent?"

"You tell me," he said, yawning.

"Where are you, Chuck?"

"Home, man. Jumped in the tub and soaked for an hour this morning. Mom's blueberry pancakes for breakfast. Slept all day in my own bed. I can handle it. Where the hell is Brent, anyway?"

"We haven't heard from him."

"My bet's he went straight to the Swan's. Like gravity, man. Do not pass go."

"He should have called," I said. "Mom gets worried."

"Worry, worry, Sam. You and your mom are two of a kind."

I took my bag of baseballs out to the red dirt pitching mound Brent and I had built at one end of the backyard. The mound rose from the grass to a nice level peak with a regulation rubber plate set in the top. At the other end of the yard Brent had hung a tire from a tree and backed it up with a net so I could throw when he wasn't around to catch for me.

Brent idolized Johnny Bench and had always wanted to be a catcher like Dad; I was tall and slender like my mom, so he decided I had to pitch. After all those years of spanking the leather of Brent's catcher's mitt, I broke into the varsity rotation my sophomore year. Brent was a senior, and we teamed up for an 8-3 record.

I dropped my canvas bag next to the mound, rubbed up a ball, and stretched. Then I began throwing. After I got a rhythm, the game was to put as many balls as possible through the eye of the tire. The sun dropped between the stucco houses. I could smell the ocean in the evening breeze, and when the fog began to roll in with the darkness, Mom turned on the floodlights. I was eager to see Brent, his black Mexican tan, his bleached hair, and hear more stories of Baja. Maybe tomorrow afternoon he and I would be zinging balls back and forth, the thwap of my fastball in his catcher's mitt; his thick legs and chest the perfect frame to work my curve into.

When Mom blinked the lights, I joined her for dinner. We waited quietly in the kitchen, Mom watching the hands on the clock. The phone rang. It was Dad saying he was working late and wouldn't be home for dinner. When Brent didn't show either, Mom and I ate the porcupine meatballs she had fixed in his honor. I ate three helpings to make her feel better.

Monday morning my parents drove to the Costa Mesa police station and filed a missing persons report. That afternoon a policeman came over to interview us. But Dad, who hardly ate any breakfast and paced the kitchen for hours looking at his watch, blew up before the cop got there.

"That kid thinks he's such a big-shot athlete, he probably smarted off to some older guys, got his ass kicked, and now he's afraid to come home bruised up," Dad said. Then he went on about how Brent had quit his job the summer before because he thought he was too good to load pipe scraps in a Dumpster all day. Finally, Dad told Mom that he couldn't tell the police anything more than she could, and he stomped out the door to work.

Chuck and the Swan came over. We drank Cokes and waited quietly in the living room.

The cop had black hair graying at the temples, big weight-lifter arms, and carried himself in the confident manner of an ex-athlete who has nothing to prove. He introduced himself as Jim, and we all took seats around the coffee table.

According to Chuck, he and Brent had driven all night to get home from Ensenada. Brent had dropped him off before daybreak on Saturday morning.

"Did he give any indications that he might have other plans?" Jim asked, opening a small notebook in his lap. "Did he mention Carla, for example?"

"No," Chuck said. "I thought he was headed home. We were burned out."

"Did you buy anything in Mexico?" Jim asked.

"Beer," Chuck said. "Tacos. Shrimp. Gas."

Jim wrote in his notebook. He looked at Chuck. "Other things?"

Chuck stared at him. "We were on a surfing trip," he said, "having fun, you know?"

"Did you get stoned?" Jim asked.

I could see the space between Chuck's freckles turning the same color as his red-orange hair. "Yes," he said.

Jim leaned forward and said patiently, "We're trying to paint a picture here, Chuck."

"We smoked some joints, OK?" he said. "And a Mexican turned us on to some mushrooms one night down near Cabo."

"Did you cross the border—"

"We don't deal," Chuck said. "We didn't bring any back." He threw his hands up. "We had some fun and came home." Chuck stared at the ceiling, then looked at Jim. "Brent has a lot on his mind, you know? One night he asked if I'd ever shot a gun. My grandfather has a farm in Fallbrook, so I said, sure, plenty of times. The guy has never even shot a gun, officer. He just wants to play baseball, man."

"Where on earth could he be?" my mom asked.

"Brent can take care of himself," I said.

"That's why I'm worried," the Swan said. "Three days, and no one has heard from a big guy who can take care of himself." Mom reached over and held her hand.

"He's got a certain way of carrying himself," Chuck explained. "People don't usually mess with him, sir."

Jim finished writing in his notebook and closed it with his big hands. He looked at all of us. "I carry a gun on my hip," he said, "and people mess with me all the time."

A few weeks later I pitched in the backyard until nearly midnight, then I sat on the mound and watched the full moon work its way across the sky. I held a baseball up to it before tossing the ball into my bag. A bag of tiny moons, I thought. I'm chucking tiny moons through a black hole in the middle of the night. Somewhere, I was sure, Brent could see the same moon.

Just a week before, my mom and I had watched an astronaut step onto the moon, walk on it, jump and bound across the gray landscape. A man walking on the moon; it was as strange and hard to believe as my brother disappearing. Maybe it was Brent we had seen on TV inside that shiny silver suit, goofing on all of us. My brother Brent: the Man on the Moon.

"I love you, brother," I said, startled by the sound of my voice. "You know that, though." I tossed my glove in the dirt and lay across the mound on my back. The Man on the Moon was still laughing at me. Laughing at me and Brent and all of us miserable fools. You could stare at the moon all night and have no clue what was going on up there, just like you could share a room with your brother for fifteen years and still not be sure what made him tick. I wanted to crawl out of my skin and fly off into the night, soar right up to the moon, leave my empty body lying there in the backyard like the locust shells Brent and I found clinging to the oak trees in my grandmother's yard when we were kids.

The first day of school that September I wore my hair pulled back in the stub of a ponytail. My baseball coach, Charlie Nelson, was not too pleased. He let me know by grabbing my hair and giving it a few stiff tugs. "Gone fag on me, Sammy?" he said.

"Yes sir," I said. "Care for a hummer?"

He took me into the coaches' locker room and whipped my butt with a lacquered oak paddle he reserved for special offenses. Then he escorted me to the principal's office where we had a long discussion with the principal and my mom that afternoon. They talked about the difficulty of dealing with Brent's disappearance and the effect it was having on me. I twiddled my thumbs.

"Maybe we can sort this out, son," the principal said. "We'd like to help you."

"Find my brother," I said, shrugging. I stared at my feet while they exchanged glances. I could feel the blood turning my ears red. "Look," I said, "there's nothing you can do. And it doesn't matter if Coach doesn't like my hair. I'm not playing baseball anyway."

"We'd like to have you, Sam," Coach Nelson said. "We're counting on you."

I looked the man in the eye. "Coach," I said, "to tell you the truth, I think baseball is probably the most boring, overrated excuse for a sport on earth, next to golf."

My mom and I had always been close, but after Brent was gone I began to spend more time with my dad. I no longer had to stay after school for baseball, so I worked for him as much as he would let me. Like everyone else, Dad rarely mentioned Brent. But my brother was always on my mind, and on our way home I'd drop references into the conversation: "Wonder what Brent would say?" Or, "If Brent's dead, do you think there's a baseball league in heaven?" But Dad would pretend he didn't hear me or mumble something about being tired and hungry.

Then one night we'd barely pulled out of the parking lot when Dad said, "Your brother could have played in the majors, Sam. He had what it takes to do anything he put his mind to." He kept his eyes on the road ahead.

"I know." I stared at the stitching on the seat cover.

"Maybe you'll play again next year," he said. "When things get better."

"Nah," I said, and meant it. "I'd rather work."

Dad turned on the headlights in the dusk. "Alright, Sam," he said.

I came in from pitching one night to find Mom and the Swan sitting next to each other on the couch. I sat in an armchair across from them.

"What's up?" I said. Mom rubbed her eyes with the back of her hands. "I think I'll get ready for bed," she said, getting up quietly and walking to the back of the house.

"She'll get over it," I said to the Swan, punching my fist in my glove. "One of these days."

"I guess we all will," she said. She pushed her brown hair back over one ear. I could see her neck was flushed. She tried to smile. "How have you been, Sam?"

"OK, working mostly," I said. This was the first time I'd been around the Swan alone. It felt strange.

"Some girls were asking about you at the beach the other day. They think you're pretty cute."

"Gimme a break."

"No, really."

"So what?"

"Brent would want us to keep on, don't you think?"

I shrugged and turned sideways, hanging my feet over the arm of the chair. "I used to hate to strike out, drove me crazy. Brent would say, 'Don't look back, brother. Another day, another fastball.' Nothing bothered him."

"Lots of things bothered him, Sam. He hated when people treated him like a jock or talked in movies. He hated getting that draft notice. Brent liked to be in charge. The catcher. Giving the signals."

"Everyone knew you guys would get married."

The Swan laughed. "I'm 17. Why would I want to get married?"

"I thought…"

"I love Brent. And wherever he is, he knows that. But we talked a lot and he knew I wanted to go my own way."

We sat for a while without speaking and then I walked the Swan out to her car. We hugged each other for a moment, my cheek touched her neck, and then a peculiar thing happened: we kissed. It was a kiss, I suppose, of desperation. A long, serious kiss. The Swan slipped her hands around my neck and held my head like a porcelain bowl. Her lips were warm and soft, and when I got hard against her she pushed me away. I sat on the curb with my head in my hands.

"I'm so sorry," she said.

I nodded and waved her away.

Some buddies talked me into going to a party one Saturday night. I had a few beers, and when I saw the long line down the hall to the bathroom, I stepped out back to relieve myself. A couple sat at a picnic table in the shadows. They had their arms wrapped tightly around each other, kissing. I gave a little hoot of encouragement as I crossed the lawn toward a big tree in the back corner of the yard. When they looked up I realized it was Chuck and the Swan.

"Hey," Chuck said, squinting. "Sam?"

"I didn't know," I said. "Sorry."

"It's no big deal," the Swan said.

We were silent for what seemed a long time. "I miss you guys," I said finally.

"Yeah," they both agreed awkwardly.

"Well," I nodded toward the tree, "nature calls."

The next summer my dad and I had dinner at a steak house while Mom was out of town visiting her sister. Afterward, he asked if I wanted to go have a drink. We drove to Newport and sat at a window table in Tug's Tavern, drinking beer and watching the lights of the boats making their way out the channel into the dark ocean. We debated which baseball team was better—Nolan Ryan and the Mets or Don Sutton and the Dodgers. Then Dad asked what I was going to do my senior year.

"Survive," I said. I had lost interest in school, I told him. It was a bunch of rules and regulations, bells and whistles.

"Sam…" he said, looking out the window.

"Another round?" I asked, feeling pretty good.

"Sam, I've decided to leave your mother."

"What for?"

"It's a hard thing to explain, Sammy."

"Why my brother disappeared—*that's* hard to explain."

"There's nothing left between me and your mother."

I peeled the label off my beer bottle, strip by strip, and flicked the tiny rolls of paper on the floor. "Where will you go?"

"I'm moving onto the site. Putting a trailer in back of the plant."

"Cozy."

"I'll be close, Sam. I'm not deserting you."

"What about Mom?"

"She needs you, but she and I… You don't understand. Even before—"

"Please stop."

"Next to Brent, this is the hardest, ever, Sam. I'm sorry."

"Me too."

A police car was parked in front of the house when I came home from work one fall evening. Mom and Jim stood on the front porch talking. I jogged across the yard to join them. "What's going on?" I said hopefully. Jim and I shook hands.

"They found this," Mom said, opening her hand. On her palm was Brent's driver's license. It was scratched and faded and the picture had been cut out of it.

"What else?" I asked.

"That's all," Jim said. "A hitchhiker found it near Barstow."

"Fingerprints?"

"It had been there awhile. In a drainage ditch. No prints."

"So…" I stepped off the porch, shaking my head.

"Sam," Mom said.

"I asked your mother to have dinner with me, Sam. Would you like to join us?"

I looked at Mom, then Jim. "No, thanks. You two go ahead."

The last semester of my senior year I sat in the back of Mr. Gallagher's English class and spoke only when called upon. Brent had been right about Gallagher—he was a colorful guy with lots of charisma. His thing was American literature, and he walked us through Emerson, Thoreau, Hawthorne, Dickinson, Poe, and Twain. But this was only calisthenics for his main man, Whitman. He would crank it up a couple of times a week, pacing in front of the class with his mug of coffee and his red ponytail wagging, as he recited line after line of *Leaves of Grass* from memory. Some kids dozed and others giggled, but I enjoyed listening to the man, his chest rising and falling, and the words rolling off his tongue. Gallagher was into it; he was good, and something about the way he read reminded me of pitching baseballs in my backyard.

One afternoon Gallagher spent the entire class reciting "Song of Myself." By the end of the poem he was in a trance, pacing and reciting, his eyes closed, his voice strange and distant. Then he delivered the final lines:

> I bequeath myself to the dirt to grow from the grass I love,
> If you want me again look for me under your boot-soles.

You will hardly know who I am or what I mean,
But I shall be good health to you nevertheless,
And filter and fibre your blood.

Failing to fetch me at first keep encouraged,
Missing me one place search another,
I stop somewhere waiting for you.

My eyes filled with tears and I put my head down on my desk. When the bell rang, I stayed where I was, waiting for the tears to stop coming. Then I heard Gallagher's voice: "Hey, Sam, you going home today, or should I give you the keys to lock up when your nap's over?" I kept my head glued to the desk. "Sam? You OK, man?" he asked, tugging on my sleeve.

"No," I said. "I don't feel so well." I sat up and wiped my eyes. "Jesus."

Gallagher sat in the desk next to me. "You gonna be all right, friend?"

"Yeah," I said. "Yeah, I guess."

He fixed his blue eyes on me. "Sure?"

"You knew my brother, huh?"

"Brent," Gallagher said. "Sure. Great fellow, your brother. We all miss him."

I nodded my head and stared at my desk.

"Don't worry about him, Sam. It's like old graybeard says," he tapped the picture of Walt Whitman on the cover of my book, "'...somewhere waiting for you.'"

"I'm not. I mean, I know he is."

Gallagher leaned toward me. "Listen, there's a lot of places to be. You know what I'm saying?"

"No," I said. "I'm not sure, really."

"People are heading for the hills, Sam. Colorado, New Mexico, Arkansas, Oregon, Montana. Sleeping in tents and tree houses on Kauai. Crossing the border into Canada, Mexico."

"What are you saying?"

"Unless you want to kill people, there's not much choice."

"You know where my brother is?"

"No, I'm not saying that. But I think I know where your brother was coming from. No matter where he is now, I can tell you that when he was here, I knew, one way or the other, he'd be on down the road."

"He's alive," I whispered.

"Count on it," Gallagher said.

Come summer I got a call from Chuck. "Sam the Man," he said.

"Sam the Warehouse Man," I said. "Load pipe. Unload pipe."

"You still workin' the tire in the backyard?"

"Yeah. It's a habit, I guess."

"How about playing some real ball?"

"It's been a while, Chuck."

"I'm playing on an American Legion team. We've got some players. A good team. A good team that could be very good if we got another pitcher."

"I don't know," I said. "I'm working a lot."

"I'll pick you up after dinner tomorrow."

We won a lot of games that summer and advanced to the AAU southern section playoffs. I won a few on our march to the finals and pitched seven scoreless innings in the championship game, though we lost in extra innings.

After the game, two men approached me in the parking lot. One of them was Jim, still in his cop uniform. He had been coming by our house regularly to visit Mom. The man at his side looked a lot like him, though he was dressed in a golf shirt, jeans, and a baseball cap. "Hey," Jim said. "Nice game."

"Thanks," I shrugged. "We should have won."

"Sam," Jim said, "meet my brother Neal. He coaches baseball at San Diego State."

Neal offered me his hand. His thick forearms and firm handshake were the same as Jim's. "They should have left you in the game," he said. He smiled and made more kind comments about my pitching. He liked my control, the way I was mixing and moving my fastball and curve. Then he asked if I'd let him take me to dinner so we could talk some more baseball. Over a plate of sausage and spaghetti Neal offered me a scholarship to pitch for San Diego State, and I took it. My dad never said a word.

I won a lot of games pitching in college, and after graduation I played minor-league ball for a number of teams in the Giants' organization. I pitched all over the States, met a lot of interesting people, and read plenty of books in hotel rooms, bus stations, and airports. One of my teammates told me I was the only player he ever knew who read poetry and wore a ponytail.

For years, on July 20, the anniversary of the first moon walk, I posted an ad in the local paper wherever I was living, asking after Brent or anyone who had seen him. But I never got a response. My parents never heard from him either.

In my second year of Triple-A ball, my agent asked if I'd be interested in pitching in Japan. "Why not?" I said. I had some pretty good seasons over there, picked up enough language to get by, and found a new hobby—Japanese landscape painting. I'd always loved the delicately stroked black ink drawings of the mountains and valleys and streams, the paths winding away into the foothills, the tiny human figures set against the landscape.

Then I tore the rotator cuff in my shoulder and my arm was shot, and I moved to San Diego and found a job teaching high school English and coaching baseball. I've been doing that a number of years now, and it's a good life, working with the kids.

Lately I've been attending a weekly meeting of painters interested in Japanese ink painting. We meet in a rec center down by the beach with our easels, and afterward, have coffee and talk about our work. The other night, one of the women in the class, Helen—tall with long, black, silver-streaked hair—watched over my shoulder as I painted a desert landscape. Later we sat on a bench by the water and sipped coffee. There was a warm breeze and it was pleasant just to sit with her.

"You know," she said, tilting her head and pushing her hair back over her ear, "there are never any people in your paintings."

"No," I said, smiling. "I guess not."

"How come?"

I shrugged, leaned back on the bench, and rubbed my eyes. It occurred to me that I wanted to kiss Helen. "I have this one idea," I said. "I have a picture in my head. There's a deep, sweeping desert canyon, the walls dotted with scrub trees, cacti, manzanita, and tumbleweeds, with a small stream meandering toward its center. Way down in the heart of the canyon, the stream feeds a round pool of blue water surrounded by tall palms. On a sandy bank beside the pool there are two small boys, barefoot and wearing only shorts, tossing a ball, back and forth, back and forth, not a care in the world."

Suggestions for Discussion

1. How is the man on the moon emblematic of Sam's relationship with his brother?
2. After the disappearance of Brent the family seems to fall apart. Why do you believe this happened?
3. What is your theory of what happened to Brent? On what do you base it?

Suggestions for Writing

1. Write a conclusion to the story that solves the mystery.
2. Choose three images from the story that describe the relationship between the brothers.
3. Why are there never any people in Sam's paintings?

T. CORAGHESSAN BOYLE

If the River Was Whiskey

T. Coraghessan Boyle (b. 1948) has both an M.F.A and a Ph.D. from Iowa University, and presently he is a writer, musician, and professor at the University of California at Los Angeles. Winner of the St. Lawrence and Aga Khan prizes, he is the author of nine books of fiction and autobiography. These include *If the River Was Whiskey* (1989), *East Is East* (1990), *T. Coraghessan Boyle* (1991), *Road to Wellville* (1993), and *The Tortilla Curtain* (1995). The story included here explores the disintegrating relationship between a father and his family.

The water was a heartbeat, a pulse, it stole the heat from his body and pumped it to his brain. Beneath the surface, magnified through the shimmering lens of his face mask, were silver shoals of fish, forests of weed, a silence broken only by the distant throbbing hum of an outboard. Above, there was the sun, the white flash of a faraway sailboat, the weatherbeaten dock with its weatherbeaten rowboat, his mother in her deck chair, and the vast depthless green of the world beyond.

He surfaced like a dolphin, spewing water from the vent of his snorkel, and sliced back to the dock. The lake came with him, two bony arms and the wedge of a foot, the great heaving splash of himself flat out on the dock like something thrown up in a storm. And then, without pausing even to snatch up a towel, he had the spinning rod in hand and the silver lure was sizzling out over the water, breaking the surface just above the shadowy arena he'd fixed in his mind. His mother looked up at the splash. "Tiller," she called, "come get a towel."

His shoulders quaked. He huddled and stamped his feet, but he never took his eyes off the tip of the rod. Twitching it suggestively, he reeled with the jerky, hesitant motion that would drive lunker fish to a frenzy. Or so he'd read, anyway.

"Tiller, do you hear me?"

"I saw a Northern," he said. "A big one. Two feet maybe." The lure was in. A flick of his wrist sent it back. Still reeling, he ducked his head to wipe his nose on his wet shoulder. He could feel the sun on his back now and he envisioned the skirted lure in the water, sinuous, sensual, irresistible, and he waited for the line to quicken with the strike.

The porch smelled of pine—old pine, dried up and dead—and it depressed him. In fact, everything depressed him—especially this vacation. Vacation. It was a joke. Vacation from what?

He poured himself a drink—vodka and soda, tall, from the plastic half-gallon jug. It wasn't noon yet, the breakfast dishes were in the sink, and Tiller and Caroline were down at the lake. He couldn't see them through the screen of trees, but he heard the murmur of their voices against the soughing of the branches and the sadness of the birds. He sat heavily in the creaking wicker chair and looked out on nothing. He didn't feel too hot. In fact, he felt as if he'd been cored and dried, as if somebody had taken a pipe cleaner and run it through his veins. His head ached too, but the vodka would take care of that. When he finished it, he'd have another, and then maybe a grilled swiss on rye. Then he'd start to feel good again.

His father was talking to the man and his mother was talking to the woman. They'd met at the bar about twenty drinks ago and his father was into his could-have-been, should-have-been, way-back-when mode, and the man, bald on top and with a ratty beard and long greasy hair like his father's, was trying to steer the conversation back to building supplies. The woman had whole galaxies of freckles on her chest, and she leaned forward in her sundress and told his mother scandalous stories about people she'd never heard of. Tiller had drunk all the Coke and eaten all the beer nuts he could hold. He watched the Pabst Blue Ribbon sign flash on and off above the bar and he watched the woman's freckles move in and out of the gap between her breasts. Outside it was dark and a cool clean scent came in off the lake.

"Uh huh, yeah," his father was saying, "the To the Bone Band. I played rhythm and switched off vocals with Dillie Richards...."

The man had never heard of Dillie Richards.

"Black dude, used to play with Taj Mahal?"

The man had never heard of Taj Mahal.

"Anyway," his father said, "we used to do all this really outrageous stuff by people like Muddy, Howlin' Wolf, Luther Allison—"

"She didn't," his mother said.

The woman threw down her drink and nodded and the front of her dress went crazy. Tiller watched her and felt the skin go tight across his shoulders and the back of his neck, where he'd been burned the first day. He wasn't wearing any underwear, just shorts. He looked away. "Three abortions, two kids," the woman said. "And she never knew who the father of the second one was."

"Drywall isn't worth a damn," the man said. "But what're you going to do?"

"Paneling?" his father offered.

The man cut the air with the flat of his hand. He looked angry. "Don't talk to me about paneling," he said.

Mornings, when his parents were asleep and the lake was still, he would take the rowboat to the reedy cove on the far side of the lake where the big pike lurked. He didn't actually know if they lurked there, but if they lurked anywhere, this would be the place. It looked fishy, mysterious, sunken logs looming up dark from the shadows beneath the boat, mist rising like steam, as if the bottom were boiling with ravenous, cold-eyed, killer pike that could slice through monofilament with a snap of their jaws and bolt ducklings in a gulp. Besides, Joe Matochik, the old man who lived in the cabin next door and could charm frogs by stroking their bellies, had told him that this was where he'd find them.

It was cold at dawn and he'd wear a thick homeknit sweater over his T-shirt and shorts, sometimes pulling the stretched-out hem of it down like a skirt to warm his thighs. He'd take an apple with him or a slice of brown bread and peanut butter. And of course the orange lifejacket his mother insisted on.

When he left the dock he was always wearing the lifejacket—for form's sake and for the extra warmth it gave him against the raw morning air. But when he got there, when he stood in the swaying basin of the boat to cast his Hula Popper or Abu Relfex, it got in the way and he took it off. Later, when the sun ran through him and he didn't need the sweater, he balled it up on the seat beside him, and sometimes, if it was good and hot, he shrugged out of his T-shirt and shorts too. No one could see him in the cove, and it made his breath come quick to be naked like that under the morning sun.

"I heard you," he shouted, and he could feel the veins stand out in his neck, the rage come up in him like something killed and dead and brought back to life. "What kind of thing is that to tell a kid, huh? About his own father?"

She wasn't answering. She'd backed up in a corner of the kitchen and she wasn't answering. And what could she say, the bitch? He'd heard her. Dozing on the trundle bed under the stairs, wanting a drink but too weak to get up and make one, he'd heard voices from the kitchen, her voice and Tiller's. "Get used to it," she said, "he's a drunk, your father's a drunk," and then he was up off the bed as if something had exploded inside of him and he had her by the shoulders—always the shoulders and never the face, that much she'd taught him—and Tiller was gone, out the door and gone. Now, her voice low in her throat, a sick and guilty little smile on her lips, she whispered, "It's true."

"Who are you to talk?—you're shit-faced yourself." She shrank away from him, that sick smile on her lips, her shoulders hunched. He wanted to smash things, kick in the damn stove, make her hurt.

"At least I have a job," she said.

"I'll get another one, don't you worry."

"And what about Tiller? We've been here two weeks and you haven't done one damn thing with him, nothing, zero. You haven't even been down to the lake. Two hundred feet and you haven't even been down there once." She came up out of the corner now, feinting like a boxer, vicious, her sharp little fists balled up to drum on him. She spoke in a snarl. "What kind of father are you?"

He brushed past her, slammed open the cabinet, and grabbed the first bottle he found. It was whiskey, cheap whiskey, Four Roses, the shit she drank. He poured out half a water glass full and drank it down to spite her. "I hate the beach, boats, water, trees. I hate you."

She had her purse and she was halfway out the screen door. She hung there a second, looking as if she'd bitten into something rotten. "The feeling's mutual," she said, and the door banged shut behind her.

There were too many complications, too many things to get between him and the moment, and he tried not to think about them. He tried not to think about his father—or his mother either—in the same way that he tried not to think about the pictures of the bald-headed stick people in Africa or meat in its plastic wrapper and how it got there. But when he did think about his father he thought about the river-was-whiskey day.

It was a Tuesday or Wednesday, middle of the week, and when he came home from school the curtains were drawn and his father's car was in the driveway. At the door, he could hear him, the *chunk-chunk* of the chords and the rasping nasal whine that seemed as if it belonged to someone else. His father was sitting in the dark, hair in his face, bent low over the guitar. There was an open bottle of liquor on the coffee table and a clutter of beer bottles. The room stank of smoke.

It was strange, because his father hardly ever played his guitar anymore—he mainly just talked about it. In the past tense. And it was strange too—and bad—because his father wasn't at work. Tiller dropped his bookbag on the telephone stand. "Hi, Dad," he said.

His father didn't answer. Just bent over the guitar and played the same song, over and over, as if it were the only song he knew. Tiller sat on the sofa and listened. There was a verse—one verse—and his father repeated it three or four times before he broke off and slurred the words into a sort of chant or hum, and then he went back to the words again. After the fourth repetition, Tiller heard it:

> If the river was whiskey,
> And I was a divin' duck,
> I'd swim to the bottom,
> Drink myself back up.

For half an hour his father played that song, played it till anything else would have sounded strange. He reached for the bottle when he finally stopped, and that was when he noticed Tiller. He looked surprised. Looked as if he'd just woke up. "Hey, ladykiller Tiller," he said, and took a drink from the mouth of the bottle.

Tiller blushed. There'd been a Sadie Hawkins dance at school and Janet Rumery had picked him for her partner. Ever since, his father had called him ladykiller, and though he wasn't exactly sure what it meant, it made him blush anyway, just from the tone of it. Secretly, it pleased him. "I really liked the song, Dad," he said.

"Yeah?" His father lifted his eyebrows and made a face. "Well, come home to Mama, doggie-o. Here," he said, and he held out an open beer. "You ever have one of these, ladykiller Tiller?" He was grinning. The sleeve of his shirt was torn and his elbow was raw and there was a hard little clot of blood over his shirt pocket. "With your sixth-grade buddies out behind the handball court, maybe? No?"

Tiller shook his head.

"You want one? Go ahead, take a hit."

Tiller took the bottle and sipped tentatively. The taste wasn't much. He looked up at his father. "What does it mean?" he said. "The song, I mean—the one you were singing. About the whiskey and all."

His father gave him a long slow grin and took a drink from the big bottle of clear liquor. "I don't know," he said finally, grinning wider to show his tobacco-stained teeth. "I guess he just liked whiskey, that's all." He picked up a cigarette, made as if to light it, and then put it down again. "Hey," he said, "you want to sing it with me?"

All right, she'd hounded him and she'd threatened him and she was going to leave him, he could see that clear as day. But he was going to show her. And the kid too. He wasn't drinking. Not today. Not a drop.

He stood on the dock with his hands in his pockets while Tiller scrambled around with the fishing poles and oars and the rest of it. Birds were screeching in the trees and there was a smell of diesel fuel on the air. The sun cut into his head like a knife. He was sick already.

"I'm giving you the big pole, Dad, and you can row if you want."

He eased himself into the boat and it fell away beneath him like the mouth of a bottomless pit.

"I made us egg salad, Dad, your favorite. And I brought some birch beer."

He was rowing. The lake was churning underneath him, the wind was up and reeking of things washed up on the shore, and the damn oars kept slipping out of the oarlocks, and he was rowing. At the last minute he'd wanted to go back for a quick drink, but he didn't, and now he was rowing.

"We're going to catch a pike," Tiller said, hunched like a spider in the stern.

There was spray off the water. He was rowing. He felt sick. Sick and depressed.

"We're going to catch a pike, I can feel it. I know we are," Tiller said, "I know it. I just know it."

It was too much for him all at once—the sun, the breeze that was so sweet he could taste it, the novelty of his father rowing, pale arms and a dead cigarette clenched between his teeth, the boat rocking, and the birds whispering—and he closed his eyes a minute, just to keep from going dizzy with the joy of it. They were in deep water already. Tiller was trolling with a plastic worm and spinner, just in case, but he didn't have much faith in catching anything out here. He was taking his father to the cove with the submerged logs and beds of weed—that's where they'd connect, that's where they'd catch pike.

"Jesus," his father said when Tiller spelled him at the oars. Hands shaking, he crouched in the stern and tried to light a cigarette. His face was gray and the hair beat crazily around his face. He went through half a book of matches and then threw the cigarette in the water. "Where are you taking us, anyway," he said, "—the Indian Ocean?"

"The pike place," Tiller told him. "You'll like it, you'll see."

The sun was dropping behind the hills when they got there, and the water went from blue to gray. There was no wind in the cove. Tiller let the boat glide out across the still surface while his father finally got a cigarette lit, and then he dropped anchor. He was excited. Swallows dove at the surface, bullfrogs burped from the reeds. It was the perfect time to fish, the hour when the big lunker pike would cruise among the sunken logs, hunting.

"All right," his father said, "I'm going to catch the biggest damn fish in the lake," and he jerked back his arm and let fly with the heaviest sinker in the tackle box dangling from the end of the rod. The line hissed through the guys and there was a thunderous splash that probably terrified every pike within half a mile. Tiller looked over his shoulder as he reeled in his silver spoon. His father winked at him, but he looked grim.

It was getting dark, his father was out of cigarettes, and Tiller had cast the spoon so many times his arm was sore, when suddenly the big rod began to buck. "Dad! Dad!" Tiller shouted, and his father lurched up as if he'd been stabbed. He'd been dozing, the rod propped against the gunwale, and Tiller had been studying the long suffering-lines in his father's face, the grooves in his forehead, and the puffy discolored flesh beneath his eyes. With his beard and long hair and with the crumpled suffering look on his face, he was the picture of the crucified Christ Tiller had contemplated a hundred times at church. But now the rod was bucking and his father had hold of it and he was playing a fish, a big fish, the tip of the rod dipping all the way down to the surface.

"It's a pike, Dad, it's a pike!"

His father strained at the pole. His only response was a grunt, but Tiller saw something in his eyes he hardly recognized anymore, a connection, a charge, as if the fish were sending a current up the line, through the pole, and into his hands and body and brain. For a full three minutes he played the fish, his slack biceps gone rigid, the cigarette clamped in his mouth, while Tiller hovered over him with the landing net. There was a surge, a splash, and the thing was in the net, and Tiller had it over the side and into the boat. "It's a pike," his father said, "goddamnit, look at the thing, look at the size of it."

It wasn't a pike. Tiller had watched Joe Matochik catch one off the dock one night. Joe's pike had been dangerous, full of teeth, a long, lean, tapering strip of muscle and pounding life. This was no pike. It was a carp. A fat, pouty, stinking, ugly mud carp. Trash fish. They shot them with arrows and threw them up on the shore to rot. Tiller looked at his father and felt like crying.

"It's a pike," his father said, and already the thing in his eyes was gone, already it was over, "it's a pike. Isn't it?"

It was late—past two, anyway—and he was drunk. Or no, he was beyond drunk. He'd been drinking since morning, one tall vodka and soda after another, and he didn't feel a thing. He sat on the porch in the dark and he couldn't see the lake, couldn't hear it, couldn't even smell it. Caroline and Tiller were asleep. The house was dead silent.

Caroline was leaving him, which meant that Tiller was leaving him. He knew it. He could see it in her eyes and he heard it in her voice. She was soft once, his soft-eyed lover, and now she was hard, unyielding, now she was his worst enemy. They'd had the couple from the roadhouse in for drinks and burgers earlier that night and he'd leaned over the table to tell the guy something—Ed, his name was—joking really, nothing serious, just making conversation. "Vodka and soda," he said, "that's my drink. I used to drink vodka and grapefruit juice, but it tore the lining out of my stomach." And then Caroline, who wasn't even listening, stepped in and said, "Yeah, and that"—pointing to the glass—"tore the lining out of your brain." He looked up at her. She wasn't smiling.

All right. That was how it was. What did he care? He hadn't wanted to come up here anyway—it was her father's idea. Take the cabin for a month, the old man had said, pushing, pushing in that way he had, and get yourself turned around. Well, he wasn't turning around, and they could all go to hell.

After a while the chill got to him and he pushed himself up from the chair and went to bed. Caroline said something in her sleep and pulled away from him as he lifted the covers and slid in. He was awake for a minute or two, feeling depressed, so depressed he wished somebody would come in and shoot him, and then he was asleep.

In his dream, he was out in the boat with Tiller. The wind was blowing, his hands were shaking, he couldn't light a cigarette. Tiller was watching him. He pulled at the oars and nothing happened. Then all of a sudden they were going down, the boat sucked out from under them, the water icy and black, beating in on them as if it were alive. Tiller called out to him. He saw his son's face, saw him going down, and there was nothing he could do.

Suggestions for Discussion

1. When Tiller describes his father as into his "could-have-been, should-have-been, way-back-when mode," what does he mean? What does this tell us about his father?
2. What is the significance of the river-was-whiskey day in Tiller's relationship with his father?
3. Boyle contrasts the world of nature and the world of human relationships. At several significant points they converge. Why does Tiller want to cry when his father catches a "trash" fish? Why does his father dream Tiller is drowning and he cannot save him?

Suggestions for Writing

1. Describe a moment when you had to face a hard truth about someone you loved.
2. Sometimes things that happen in an instant can change your whole life. Describe one.

WILLIAM CARLOS WILLIAMS

The Use of Force

William Carlos Williams (1883–1963) practiced medicine in Rutherford, New Jersey, the factory town in which he was born. *Selected Poems* appeared in 1949, *Collected Later Poetry* (1950), and *Collected Poems* (1951). His long epic poem, *Paterson,* won the National Book

Award for Poetry in 1950. *Desert Music* appeared in 1954, *Journey to Love* in 1955. He has also written novels, *White Mule* (1937) and *In the Money* (1940); short stories, *Life Along the Passaic* (1938), *Selected Essays* (1954); and an *Autobiography* (1951). He received the Bollingen Award for poetry in 1953. The simple and direct language in this short story heightens the intensity of the feelings of the doctor, parents, and child.

They were new patients to me, all I had was the name, Olson.

Please come down as soon as you can, my daughter is very sick.

When I arrived I was met by the mother, a big startled looking woman, very clean and apologetic who merely said, Is this the doctor? and let me in. In the back, she added. You must excuse us, doctor, we have her in the kitchen where it is warm. It is very damp here sometimes.

The child was fully dressed and sitting on her father's lap near the kitchen table. He tried to get up, but I motioned for him not to bother, took off my overcoat and started to look things over. I could see that they were all very nervous, eyeing me up and down distrustfully. As often, in such cases, they weren't telling me more than they had to, it was up to me to tell them; that's why they were spending three dollars on me.

The child was fairly eating me up with her cold, steady eyes, and no expression to her face whatever. She did not move and seemed, inwardly, quiet; an unusually attractive little thing, and as strong as a heifer in appearance. But her face was flushed, she was breathing rapidly, and I realized that she had a high fever. She had magnificent blonde hair, in profusion. One of those picture children often reproduced in advertising leaflets and the photogravure sections of the Sunday papers.

She's had a fever for three days, began the father and we don't know what it comes from. My wife has given her things, you know, like people do, but it don't do no good. And there's been a lot of sickness around. So we tho't you'd better look her over and tell us what is the matter.

As doctors often do I took a trial shot at it as a point of departure. Has she had a sore throat?

Both parents answered me together, No...No, she says her throat don't hurt her.

Does your throat hurt you? added the mother to the child. But the little girl's expression didn't change nor did she move her eyes from my face.

Have you looked?

I tried to, said the mother, but I couldn't see.

As it happens we had been having a number of cases of diphtheria in the school to which this child went during that month and we were all, quite apparently, thinking of that, though no one had as yet spoken of the thing.

Well, I said, suppose we take a look at the throat first. I smiled in my best professional manner and asking for the child's first name I said, come on, Mathilda, open your mouth and let's take a look at your throat.

Nothing doing.

Aw, come on, I coaxed, just open your mouth wide and let me take a look. Look, I said opening both hands wide, I haven't anything in my hands. Just open up and let me see.

Such a nice man, put in the mother. Look how kind he is to you. Come on, do what he tells you to. He won't hurt you.

At that I ground my teeth in disgust. If only they wouldn't use the word "hurt" I might be able to get somewhere. But I did not allow myself to be hurried or disturbed but speaking quietly and slowly I approached the child again.

As I moved my chair a little nearer suddenly with one catlike movement both her hands clawed instinctively for my eyes and she almost reached them too. In fact she knocked my glasses flying and they fell, though unbroken, several feet away from me on the kitchen floor.

Both the mother and father almost turned themselves inside out in embarrassment and apology. You bad girl, said the mother, taking her and shaking her by one arm. Look what you've done. The nice man...

For heaven's sake, I broke in. Don't call me a nice man to her. I'm here to look at her throat on the chance that she might have diphtheria and possibly die of it. But that's nothing to her. Look here, I said to the child, we're going to look at your throat. You're old enough to understand what I'm saying. Will you open it now by yourself or shall we have to open it for you?

Not a move. Even her expression hadn't changed. Her breaths however were coming faster and faster. Then the battle began. I had to do it. I had to have a throat culture for her own protection. But first I told the parents that it was entirely up to them. I explained the danger but said that I would not insist on a throat examination so long as they would take the responsibility.

If you don't do what the doctor says you'll have to go to the hospital, the mother admonished her severely.

Oh yeah? I had to smile to myself. After all, I had already fallen in love with the savage brat, the parents were contemptible to me. In the ensuing struggle they grew more and more abject, crushed, exhausted while she surely rose to magnificent heights of insane fury of effort bred of her terror of me.

The father tried his best, and he was a big man but the fact that she was his daughter, his shame at her behavior, and his dread of hurting her made him release her just at the critical times when I had almost achieved success, till I wanted to kill him. But his dread also that she might have diphtheria made him tell me to go on, go on though he himself was almost fainting, while the mother moved back and forth behind us raising and lowering her hands in an agony of apprehension.

Put her in front of you on your lap, I ordered, and hold both her wrists.

But as soon as he did the child let out a scream. Don't, you're hurting me. Let go of my hands. Let them go I tell you. Then she shrieked terrifyingly, hysterically. Stop it! Stop it! You're killing me!

Do you think she can stand it, doctor! said the mother.

You get out, said the husband to his wife. Do you want her to die of diphtheria?

Come on now, hold her, I said.

Then I grasped the child's head with my left hand and tried to get the wooden tongue depressor between her teeth. She fought, with clenched teeth, desperately! But now I also had grown furious—at a child. I tried to hold myself down but I couldn't. I know how to expose a throat for inspection. And I did my best. When finally I got the wooden spatula behind the last teeth and just the point of it into the mouth cavity, she opened up for an instant but before I could see anything she came down again and gripped the wooden blade between her molars; she reduced it to splinters before I could get it out again.

Aren't you ashamed, the mother yelled at her. Aren't you ashamed to act like that in front of the doctor?

Get me a smooth-handled spoon of some sort, I told the mother. We're going through with this. The child's mouth was already bleeding. Her tongue was cut and she was screaming in wild hysterical shrieks. Perhaps I should have desisted and come back in an hour or more. No doubt it would have been better. But I have seen at least two children lying dead in bed of neglect in such cases, and feeling that I must get a diagnosis now or never I went at it again. But the worst of it was that I too had got beyond reason. I could have torn the child apart in my own fury and enjoyed it. It was a pleasure to attack her. My face was burning with it.

The damned little brat must be protected against her own idiocy, one says to one's self at such times. Others must be protected against her. It is a social necessity. And all these things are true. But a blind fury, a feeling of adult shame, bred of a longing for muscular release are the operatives. One goes on to the end.

In the final unreasoning assault I overpowered the child's neck and jaws. I forced the heavy silver spoon back of her teeth and down her throat till she gagged. And there it was—both tonsils covered with membrane. She had fought valiantly to keep me from knowing her secret. She had been hiding that sore throat for three days at least and lying to her parents in order to escape just such an outcome as this.

Now truly she was furious. She had been on the defensive before but now she attacked. Tried to get off her father's lap and fly at me while tears of defeat blinded her eyes.

Suggestions for Discussion

1. How do you explain the child's resistance to the doctor?
2. Account for the doctor's statement: "I had already fallen in love with the savage brat, the parents were contemptible to me."
3. How are the doctor's feelings reflected during the struggle? How does he rationalize them?
4. Attempt to recreate the child's relationship with each of her parents.
5. Comment on the use of force. What alternatives did the doctor have?

Suggestion for Writing

Create a scene in which there is interaction between the child and her parents.

FLANNERY O'CONNOR

Everything That Rises Must Converge

Flannery O'Connor (1925–1965), born in Georgia, was educated in Georgia schools and at the University of Iowa. She received the O. Henry Award in 1957 and a Ford Foundation grant in 1959. Her books include the novels *Wise Blood* (1952) and *The Violent Bear It Away* (1960). Her collection of short stories, *Everything That Rises Must Converge,* was published posthumously in 1965. The tension between mother and son is aggravated by the racial conflict and leads to a tragic resolution in which the internal conflict merges with the climax of the racial incident.

Her doctor had told Julian's mother that she must lose twenty pounds on account of her blood pressure, so on Wednesday nights Julian had to take her downtown on the bus for a reducing class at the Y. The reducing class was designed for working girls over fifty, who weighed from 165 to 200 pounds. His mother was one of the slimmer ones, but she said ladies did not tell their age or weight. She would not ride the buses by herself at night since they had been integrated, and because the reducing class was one of her few pleasures, necessary for her health, and *free,* she said Julian could at least put himself out to take her, considering all she did for him. Julian did not like to consider all she did for him, but every Wednesday night he braced himself and took her.

She was almost ready to go, standing before the hall mirror, putting on her hat, while he, his hands behind him, appeared pinned to the door frame, waiting like Saint Sebastian for the arrows to begin piercing him. The hat was new and had cost her seven dollars and a half. She kept saying, "Maybe I shouldn't have paid that for it. No, I shouldn't have. I'll take it off and return it tomorrow. I shouldn't have bought it."

Julian raised his eyes to heaven. "Yes, you should have bought it," he said. "Put it on and let's go." It was a hideous hat. A purple velvet flap came down on one side of it and stood up on the other; the rest of it was green and looked like a cushion with the stuffing out. He decided it was less comical than jaunty and pathetic. Everything that gave her pleasure was small and depressed him.

She lifted the hat one more time and set it down slowly on top of her head. Two wings of gray hair protruded on either side of her florid face, but her eyes, sky-blue, were as innocent and untouched by experience as they must have been when she was ten. Were it not that she was a widow who had struggled fiercely to feed and clothe and put him through school and who was supporting him still, "until he got on his feet," she might have been a little girl that he had to take to town.

"It's all right, it's all right," he said. "Let's go." He opened the door himself and started down the walk to get her going. The sky was a dying violet and the houses stood out darkly against it, bulbous liver-colored monstrosities of a uniform ugliness though no two were alike. Since this had been a fashionable neighborhood forty years ago, his mother persisted in thinking they did well to have an apartment in it. Each house had a narrow collar of dirt around it in which sat, usually, a grubby child. Julian walked with his hands in his pockets, his head down and thrust forward and his eyes glazed with the determination to make himself completely numb during the time he would be sacrificed to her pleasure.

The door closed and he turned to find the dumpy figure, surmounted by the atrocious hat, coming toward him. "Well," she said, "you only live once and paying a little more for it, I at least won't meet myself coming and going."

"Some day I'll start making money," Julian said gloomily—he knew he never would—"and you can have one of those jokes whenever you take the fit." But first they would move. He visualized a place where the nearest neighbors would be three miles away on either side.

"I think you're doing fine," she said, drawing on her gloves. "You've only been out of school a year. Rome wasn't built in a day."

She was one of the few members of the Y reducing class who arrived in hat and gloves and who had a son who had been to college. "It takes time," she said, "and the world is in such a mess. This hat looked better on me than any of the others, though when she brought it out I said, 'Take that thing back. I wouldn't have it on my head,' and she said, 'Now wait till you see it on,' and when she put it on me, I said, 'We-ull,' and she said, 'If you ask me, that hat does something for you and you do something for the hat, and besides,' she said 'with that hat, you won't meet yourself coming and going.'"

Julian thought he could have stood his lot better if she had been selfish, if she had been an old hag who drank and screamed at him. He walked along, saturated in depression, as if in the midst of his martyrdom he had lost his faith. Catching sight of his long, hopeless, irritated face, she stopped suddenly with a grief-stricken look, and pulled back on his arm. "Wait on me," she said. "I'm going back to the house and take this thing off and tomorrow I'm going to return it. I was out of my head. I can pay the gas bill with that seven-fifty."

He caught her arm in a vicious grip. "You are not going to take it back," he said. "I like it."

"Well," she said, "I don't think I ought..."

"Shut up and enjoy it," he muttered, more depressed than ever.

"With the world in the mess it's in," she said, "it's a wonder we can enjoy anything. I tell you, the bottom rail is on the top."

Julian sighed.

"Of course," she said, "if you know who you are, you can go anywhere." She said this every time he took her to the reducing class. "Most of them in it are not our kind of people," she said, "but I can be gracious to anybody. I know who I am."

"They don't give a damn for your graciousness," Julian said savagely. "Knowing who you are is good for one generation only. You haven't the foggiest idea where you stand now or who you are."

She stopped and allowed her eyes to flash at him. "I most certainly do know who I am," she said, "and if you don't know who you are, I'm ashamed of you."

"Oh hell," Julian said.

"Your great-grandfather was a former governor of this state," she said. "Your grandfather was a prosperous landowner. Your grandmother was a Godhigh."

"Will you look around you," he said tensely, "and see where you are now?" and he swept his arm jerkily out to indicate the neighborhood, which the growing darkness at least made less dingy.

"You remain what you are," she said. "Your great-grandfather had a plantation and two hundred slaves."

"There are no more slaves," he said irritably.

"They were better off when they were," she said. He groaned to see that she was off on that topic. She rolled onto it every few days like a train on an open track. He knew every stop, every junction, every swamp along the way, and knew the exact point at which her conclusion would roll majestically into the station: "It's ridiculous. It's simply not realistic. They should rise, yes, but on their own side of the fence."

"Let's skip it," Julian said.

"The ones I feel sorry for," she said, "are the ones that are half white. They're tragic."

"Will you skip it?"

"Suppose we were half white. We would certainly have mixed feelings."

"I have mixed feelings now," he groaned.

"Well let's talk about something pleasant," she said. "I remember going to Grandpa's when I was a little girl. Then the house had double stairways that went up to what was really the second floor—all the cooking was done on the first. I used to like to stay down in the kitchen on account of the way the walls smelled. I would sit with my nose pressed against the plaster and take deep breaths. Actually the place belonged to the Godhighs but your grandfather Chestny paid the mortgage and saved it for them. They were in reduced circumstances," she said, "but reduced or not, they never forgot who they were."

"Doubtless that decayed mansion reminded them," Julian muttered. He never spoke of it without contempt or thought of it without longing. He had seen it once when he was a child before it had been sold. The double stairways had rotted and been torn down. Negroes were living in it. But it remained in his mind as his mother had known it. It appeared in his dreams regularly. He would stand on the wide porch, listening to the rustle of oak leaves, then wander through the high-ceilinged hall into the parlor that opened onto it and gaze at the worn rugs and faded draperies. It occurred to him that it was he, not she, who could have appreciated it. He preferred its threadbare elegance to anything he could name and it was because of it that all the neighborhoods they had lived in had been a torment to him—whereas she had hardly known the difference. She called her insensitivity "being adjustable."

"And I remember the old darky who was my nurse, Caroline. There was no better person in the world. I've always had a great respect for my colored friends," she said. "I'd do anything in the world for them and they'd..."

"Will you for God's sake get off that subject?" Julian said. When he got on a bus by himself, he made it a point to sit down beside a Negro, in reparation as it were for his mother's sins.

"You're mighty touchy tonight," she said. "Do you feel all right?"

"Yes I feel all right," he said. "Now lay off."

She pursed her lips. "Well, you certainly are in a vile humor," she observed. "I just won't speak to you at all."

They had reached the bus stop. There was no bus in sight and Julian, his hands still jammed in his pockets and his head thrust forward, scowled down the empty street. The frustration of having to wait on the bus as well as ride on it began to creep up his neck like a hot hand. The presence of his mother was borne in upon him as she gave a pained sigh. He looked at her bleakly. She was holding herself very erect under the preposterous hat, wearing it like a banner of her imaginary dignity. There was in him an evil urge to break her spirit. He suddenly unloosened his tie and pulled it off and put it in his pocket.

She stiffened. "Why must you look like *that* when you take me to town?" she said. "Why must you deliberately embarrass me?"

"If you'll never learn where you are," he said, "you can at least learn where I am."

"You look like a—thug," she said.

"Then I must be one," he murmured.

"I'll just go home," she said. "I will not bother you. If you can't do a little thing like that for me..."

Rolling his eyes upward, he put his tie back on. "Restored to my class," he muttered. He thrust his face toward her and hissed, "True culture is in the mind, the *mind*," he said, and tapped his head, "the mind."

"It's in the heart," she said, "and in how you do things and how you do things is because of who you *are*."

"Nobody in the damn bus cares who you are."

"I care who I am," she said icily.

The lighted bus appeared on top of the next hill and as it approached, they moved out into the street to meet it. He put his hand under her elbow and hoisted her up on the creaking step. She entered with a little smile, as if she were going into a drawing room where everyone had been waiting for her. While he put in the tokens, she sat down on one of the broad front seats for three which faced the aisle. A thin woman with protruding teeth and long yellow hair was sitting on the end of it. His mother moved up beside her and left room for Julian beside herself. He sat down and looked at the floor across the aisle where a pair of thin feet in red and white canvas sandals were planted.

His mother immediately began a general conversation meant to attract anyone who felt like talking. "Can it get any hotter?" she said and removed from her purse a folding fan, black with a Japanese scene on it, which she began to flutter before her.

"I reckon it might could," the woman with the protruding teeth said, "but I know for a fact my apartment couldn't get no hotter."

"It must get the afternoon sun," his mother said. She sat forward and looked up and down the bus. It was half filled. Everybody was white. "I see we have the bus to ourselves," she said. Julian cringed.

"For a change," said the woman across the aisle, the owner of the red and white canvas sandals. "I come on one the other day and they were thick as fleas—up front and all through."

"The world is in a mess everywhere," his mother said. "I don't know how we've let it get in this fix."

"What gets my goat is all those boys from good families stealing automobile tires," the woman with the protruding teeth said. "I told my boy, I said you may not be rich but you been raised right and if I ever catch you in any such mess, they can send you on to the reformatory. Be exactly where you belong."

"Training tells," his mother said. "Is your boy in high school?"

"Ninth grade," the woman said.

"My son just finished college last year. He wants to write but he's selling typewriters until he gets started," his mother said.

The woman leaned forward and peered at Julian. He threw her such a malevolent look that she subsided against the seat. On the floor across the aisle there was an abandoned newspaper. He got up and got it and opened it out in front of him. His mother discreetly continued the conversation in a lower tone but the woman across the aisle said in a loud voice, "Well that's nice. Selling typewriters is close to writing. He can go right from one to the other."

"I tell him," his mother said, "that Rome wasn't built in a day."

Behind the newspaper Julian was withdrawing into the inner compartment of his mind where he spent most of his time. This was a kind of mental bubble in which he established himself when he could not bear to be a part of what was going on around him. From it he could see out and judge but in it he was safe from any kind of penetration from without. It was the only place where he felt free of the general idiocy of his fellows. His mother had never entered it but from it he could see her with absolute clarity.

The old lady was clever enough and he thought that if she had started from any of the right premises, more might have been expected of her. She lived according to the laws of her own fantasy world, outside of which he had never seen her set foot. The law of it was to sacrifice herself for him after she had first created the necessity to do so by making a mess of things. If he had permitted her sacrifices, it was only because her lack of foresight had made them necessary. All of her life had been a struggle to act like a Chestny without the Chestny goods, and to give him everything she thought a Chestny ought to have; but since, said she, it was fun to struggle, why complain? And when you had won, as she had won, what fun to look back on the hard times! He could not forgive her that she had enjoyed the struggle and that she thought *she* had won.

What she meant when she said she had won was that she had brought him up successfully and had sent him to college and that he had turned out so well—good looking (her teeth had gone unfilled so that his could be straightened), intelligent (he realized he was too intelligent to be a success), and with a future ahead of him (there was of course no future ahead of him). She excused his gloominess on the grounds that he was still growing up and his radical ideas on his lack of practical experience. She said he didn't yet know a thing about "life," that he hadn't even entered the real world—when already he was as disenchanted with it as a man of fifty.

The further irony of all this was that in spite of her, he had turned out so well. In spite of going to only a third-rate college, he had, on his own initiative, come out with a first-rate education; in spite of growing up dominated by a small mind, he had ended up with a large one; in spite of all her foolish views, he was free of prejudice and unafraid to face facts. Most miraculous of all, instead of being blinded by love for her as she was for him, he had cut himself emotionally free of her and could see her with complete objectivity. He was not dominated by his mother.

The bus stopped with a sudden jerk and shook him from his meditation. A woman from the back lurched forward with little steps and barely escaped falling in his newspaper as she righted herself. She got off and a large Negro got on. Julian kept his paper lowered to watch. It gave him a certain satisfaction to see injustice in daily operation. It confirmed his view that with a few exceptions there was no one worth knowing within a radius of three hundred miles. The Negro was well dressed and carried a briefcase. He looked around and then sat down on the other end of the seat where the woman with the red and white canvas sandals was sitting. He immediately unfolded a newspaper and obscured himself behind it. Julian's mother's elbow at once prodded insistently into his rib. "Now you see why I won't ride on these buses by myself," she whispered.

The woman with the red and white canvas sandals had risen at the same time the Negro sat down and had gone further back in the bus and taken the seat of the woman who had got off. His mother leaned forward and cast her an approving look.

Julian rose, crossed the aisle, and sat down in the place of the woman with the canvas sandals. From this position, he looked serenely across at his mother. Her face had turned an angry red. He stared at her, making his eyes the eyes of a stranger. He felt his tension suddenly lift as if he had openly declared war on her.

He would have liked to get in conversation with the Negro and to talk with him about art or politics or any subject that would be above the comprehension of those around them, but the man remained entrenched behind his paper. He was either ignoring the change of seating or had never noticed it. There was no way for Julian to convey his sympathy.

His mother kept her eyes fixed reproachfully on his face. The woman with the protruding teeth was looking at him avidly as if he were a type of monster new to her.

"Do you have a light?" he asked the Negro.

Without looking away from his paper, the man reached in his pocket and handed him a packet of matches.

"Thanks," Julian said. For a moment he held the matches foolishly. A NO SMOKING sign looked down upon him from over the door. This alone would not have deterred him; he had no cigarettes. He had quit smoking some months before because he could not afford it. "Sorry," he muttered and handed back the matches. The Negro lowered the paper and gave him an annoyed look. He took the matches and raised the paper again.

His mother continued to gaze at him but she did not take advantage of his momentary discomfort. Her eyes retained their battered look. Her face seemed to be unnaturally red, as if her blood pressure had risen. Julian allowed no glimmer of sympathy to show on his face. Having got the advantage, he wanted desperately to keep it and carry it through. He would have liked to teach her a lesson that would last her a while, but there seemed no way to continue the point. The Negro refused to come out from behind his paper.

Julian folded his arms and looked stolidly before him, facing her but as if he did not see her, as if he had ceased to recognize her existence. He visualized a scene in which, the bus having reached their stop, he would remain in his seat and when she said, "Aren't you going to get off?" he would look at her as at a stranger who had rashly addressed him. The corner they got off on was usually deserted, but it was well lighted and it would not hurt her to walk by herself the four blocks to the Y. He decided to wait until the time came and then decide whether or not he would let her get off by herself. He would have to be at the Y at ten to bring her back, but he could leave her wondering if he was going to show up. There was no reason for her to think she could always depend on him.

He retired again into the high-ceilinged room sparsely settled with large pieces of antique furniture. His soul expanded momentarily but then he became aware of his mother across from him and the vision shriveled. He studied her coldly. Her feet in little pumps dangled like a child's and did not quite reach the floor. She was training on him an exaggerated look of reproach. He felt completely detached from her. At that moment he could with pleasure have slapped her as he would have slapped a particularly obnoxious child in his charge.

He began to imagine various unlikely ways by which he could teach her a lesson. He might make friends with some distinguished Negro professor or lawyer and bring him home to spend the evening. He would be entirely justified but her blood pressure would rise to 300. He could not push her to the extent of making her have a stroke, and moreover, he had never been successful at making any Negro friends. He had tried to strike up an acquaintance on the bus with some of the better types, with ones that looked like professors or ministers or lawyers. One morning he had sat down next to a distinguished-looking dark brown man who had answered his questions with a sonorous solemnity but who had turned out to be an undertaker. Another day he had sat down beside a cigar-smoking Negro with a diamond ring on his finger, but after a few stilted pleasantries, the Negro had rung the buzzer and risen, slipping two lottery tickets into Julian's hand as he climbed over him to leave.

He imagined his mother lying desperately ill and his being able to secure only a Negro doctor for her. He toyed with that idea for a few minutes and then dropped it for a momentary vision of himself participating as a sympathizer in a sit-in demonstration. This was possible but he did not linger with it. Instead, he approached the ultimate horror. He brought home a beautiful suspiciously Negroid woman. Prepare yourself, he said. There is nothing you can do about it. This is the woman I've chosen. She's intelligent, dignified, even good, and she's suffered and she hasn't thought it *fun*. Now persecute us, go ahead and persecute us. Drive her out of here, but remember, you're driving me too. His eyes were narrowed and through the indignation he had generated, he saw his mother across the aisle, purple-faced, shrunken to the dwarf-like proportions of her moral nature, sitting like a mummy beneath the ridiculous banner of her hat.

He was tilted out of his fantasy again as the bus stopped. The door opened with a sucking hiss and out of the dark a large, gaily dressed, sullenlooking colored woman got on with a little boy. The child, who might have been four, had on a short plaid suit and a Tyrolean hat with a blue feather in it. Julian hoped that he would sit down beside him and that the woman would push in beside his mother. He could think of no better arrangement.

As she waited for her tokens, the woman was surveying the seating possibilities—he hoped with the idea of sitting where she was least wanted. There was something familiar-looking about her but Julian could not place what it was. She was a giant of a woman. Her face was set not only to meet opposition but to seek it out. The downward tilt of her large lower lip was like a warning sign: DON'T TAMPER WITH ME. Her bulging figure was encased in a green crepe dress and her feet overflowed in red shoes. She had on a hideous hat. A purple velvet flap came down on one side of it and stood up on the other; the rest of it was green and looked like a cushion with the stuffing out. She carried a mammoth red pocketbook that bulged throughout as if it were stuffed with rocks.

To Julian's disappointment, the little boy climbed up on the empty seat beside his mother. His mother lumped all children, black and white, into the common category, "cute," and she thought little Negroes were on the whole cuter than little white children. She smiled at the little boy as he climbed on the seat.

Meanwhile the woman was bearing down upon the empty seat beside Julian. To his annoyance, she squeezed herself into it. He saw his mother's face change as the woman settled herself next to him and he realized with satisfaction that this was more objectionable to her than it was to him. Her face seemed almost gray and there was a look of dull recognition in her eyes, as if suddenly she had sickened at some awful confrontation. Julian saw that it was because she and the woman had, in a sense, swapped sons. Though his mother would not realize the symbolic significance of this, she would feel it. His amusement showed plainly on his face.

The woman next to him muttered something unintelligible to herself. He was conscious of a kind of bristling next to him, a muted growling like that of an angry cat. He could not see anything but the red pocketbook upright on the bulging green thighs. He visualized the woman as she had stood waiting for her tokens—the ponderous figure, rising from the red shoes upward over the solid hips, the mammoth bosom, the haughty face, to the green and purple hat.

His eyes widened.

The vision of the two hats, identical, broke upon him with the radiance of a brilliant sunrise. His face was suddenly lit with joy. He could not believe that Fate had thrust upon his mother such a lesson. He gave a loud chuckle so that she would look at him and see that he saw. She turned her eyes on him slowly. The blue in them seemed to have turned a bruised purple. For a moment he had an uncomfortable sense of her innocence, but it lasted only a second before principle rescued him. Justice entitled him to laugh. His grin hardened until it said to her as plainly as if he were saying aloud: Your punishment exactly fits your pettiness. This should teach you a permanent lesson.

Her eyes shifted to the woman. She seemed unable to bear looking at him and to find the woman preferable. He became conscious again of the bristling presence at his side. The woman was rumbling like a volcano about to become active. His mother's mouth began to twitch slightly at one corner. With a sinking heart, he saw incipient signs of recovery on her face and realized that this was going to strike her suddenly as funny and was going to be no lesson at all. She kept her eyes on the woman and an amused smile came over her face as if the woman were a monkey that had stolen her hat. The little Negro was looking up at her with large fascinated eyes. He had been trying to attract her attention for some time.

"Carver!" the woman said suddenly. "Come heah!"

When he saw that the spotlight was on him at last, Carver drew his feet up and turned himself toward Julian's mother and giggled.

"Carver!" the woman said. "You heah me? Come heah!"

Carver slid down from the seat but remained squatting with his back against the base of it, his head turned slyly around toward Julian's mother, who was smiling at him. The woman reached a hand across the aisle and snatched him to her. He righted himself and hung backwards on her knees, grinning at Julian's mother. "Isn't he cute?" Julian's mother said to the woman with the protruding teeth.

"I reckon he is," the woman said without conviction.

The Negress yanked him upright but he eased out of her grip and shot across the aisle and scrambled, giggling wildly, onto the seat beside his love.

"I think he likes me," Julian's mother said, and smiled at the woman. It was the smile she used when she was being particularly gracious to an inferior. Julian saw everything lost. The lesson had rolled off her like rain on a roof.

The woman stood up and yanked the little boy off the seat as if she were snatching him from contagion. Julian could feel the rage in her at having no weapon like his mother's smile. She gave the child a sharp slap across his leg. He howled once and then thrust his head into her stomach and kicked his feet against her shins. "Be-have," she said vehemently.

The bus stopped and the Negro who had been reading the newspaper got off. The woman moved over and set the little boy down with a thump between herself and Julian. She held him firmly by the knee. In a moment he put his hands in front of his face and peeped at Julian's mother through his fingers.

"I see yoooooooo!" she said and put her hand in front of her face and peeped at him.

The woman slapped his hand down. "Quit yo' foolishness," she said, "before I knock the living Jesus out of you!"

Julian was thankful that the next stop was theirs. He reached up and pulled the cord. The woman reached up and pulled it at the same time. Oh my God, he thought. He had the terrible intuition that when they got off the bus together, his mother would open her purse and give the little boy a nickel. The gesture would be as natural to her as breathing. The bus stopped and the woman got up and lunged to the front, dragging the child, who wished to stay on, after her. Julian and his mother got up and followed. As they neared the door, Julian tried to relieve her of her pocketbook.

"No," she murmured, "I want to give the little boy a nickel."

"No!" Julian hissed. "No!"

She smiled down at the child and opened her bag. The bus door opened and the woman picked him up by the arm and descended with him, hanging at her hip. Once in the street she set him down and shook him.

Julian's mother had to close her purse while she got down the bus step but as soon as her feet were on the ground, she opened it again and began to rummage inside. "I can't find but a penny," she whispered, "but it looks like a new one."

"Don't do it!" Julian said fiercely between his teeth. There was a streetlight on the corner and she hurried to get under it so that she could better see into her pocketbook. The woman was heading off rapidly down the street with the child still hanging backward on her hand.

"Oh little boy!" Julian's mother called and took a few quick steps and caught up with them just beyond the lamppost. "Here's a bright new penny for you," and she held out the coin, which shone bronze in the dim light.

The huge woman turned and for a moment stood, her shoulders lifted and her face frozen with frustrated rage, and stared at Julian's mother. Then all at once she seemed to explode like a piece of machinery that had been given one ounce of pressure too much. Julian saw the black fist swing out with the red pocketbook. He shut his eyes and cringed as he heard the woman shout, "He don't take nobody's pennies!" When he opened his eyes, the woman was disappearing down the street with the little boy staring wide-eyed over her shoulder. Julian's mother was sitting on the sidewalk.

"I told you not to do that," Julian said angrily. "I told you not to do that!"

He stood over her for a minute, gritting his teeth. Her legs were stretched out in front of her and her hat was on her lap. He squatted down and looked her in the face. It was totally expressionless. "You got exactly what you deserved," he said. "Now get up."

He picked up her pocketbook and put what had fallen out back in it. He picked the hat up off her lap. The penny caught his eye on the sidewalk and he picked that up and let it drop before her eyes into the purse. Then he stood up and leaned over and held his hands out to pull her up. She remained immobile. He sighed. Rising above them on either side were black apartment buildings, marked with irregular rectangles of light. At the end of the block a man came out of a door and walked off in the opposite direction. "All right," he said, "suppose somebody happens by and wants to know why you're sitting on the sidewalk?"

She took the hand and, breathing hard, pulled heavily up on it and then stood for a moment, swaying slightly as if the spots of light in the darkness were circling around her. Her eyes, shadowed and confused, finally settled on his face. He did not try to conceal his irritation. "I hope this teaches you a lesson," he said. She leaned forward and her eyes raked his face. She seemed trying to determine his identity. Then, as if she found nothing familiar about him, she started off with a headlong movement in the wrong direction.

"Aren't you going on to the Y?" he asked.

"Home," she muttered.

"Well, are we walking?"

For answer she kept going. Julian followed along, his hands behind him. He saw no reason to let the lesson she had had go without backing it up with an explanation of its meaning. She might as well be made to understand what had happened to her. "Don't think that was just an uppity Negro woman," he said. "That was the whole colored race which will no longer take your condescending pennies. That was your black double. She can wear the same hat as you, and to be sure," he added gratuitously (because he thought it was funny), "it looked better on her than it did on you. What all this means," he said, "is that the old world is gone. The old manners are obsolete and your graciousness is not worth a damn." He thought bitterly of the house that had been lost for him. "You aren't who you think you are," he said.

She continued to plow ahead, paying no attention to him. Her hair had come undone on one side. She dropped her pocketbook and took no notice. He stooped and picked it up and handed it to her but she did not take it.

"You needn't act as if the world had come to an end," he said, "because it hasn't. From now on you've got to live in a new world and face a few realities for a change. Buck up," he said, "it won't kill you."

She was breathing fast.

"Let's wait on the bus," he said.

"Home," she said thickly.

"I hate to see you behave like this," he said. "Just like a child. I should be able to expect more of you." He decided to stop where he was and make her stop and wait for a bus. "I'm not going any farther," he said, stopping. "We're going on the bus."

She continued to go on as if she had not heard him. He took a few steps and caught her arm and stopped her. He looked into her face and caught his breath. He was looking into a face he had never seen before. "Tell Grandpa to come get me," she said.

He stared, stricken.

"Tell Caroline to come get me," she said.

Stunned, he let her go and she lurched forward again, walking as if one leg were shorter than the other. A tide of darkness seemed to be sweeping her from him. "Mother!" he cried. "Darling, sweetheart, wait!" Crumpling, she fell to the pavement. He dashed forward and fell at her side, crying, "Mamma, Mamma!" He turned her over. Her face was fiercely distorted. One eye, large and staring, moved slightly to the left as if it had become unmoored. The other remained fixed on him, raked his face again, found nothing and closed.

"Wait here, wait here!" he cried and jumped up and began to run for help toward a cluster of lights he saw in the distance ahead of him. "Help, help!" he shouted, but his voice was thin, scarcely a thread of sound. The lights drifted farther away the faster he ran and his feet moved numbly as if they carried him nowhere. The tide of darkness seemed to sweep him back to her, postponing from moment to moment his entry into the world of guilt and sorrow.

Suggestions for Discussion

1. Trace the steps in the rising action of the story, noting shifts between internal and external action. Study the transitions from one narrative mode to another. How are they effected? What point of view is adopted? What is gained or lost by this device?
2. Characterize the son, distinguishing between his apparent self-image and the individual as you see him.
3. What is the central conflict? What details of setting define the conflict? How is it extended into a larger social area? Comment on the way in which each scene heightens the tension and prepares for the climax.
4. How is your impression of the mother's character created? What is your reaction to the Negro woman's striking of the mother, the son's behavior, and the resulting amnesia? Do you assume that the mother will die? Has the author prepared you for acceptance of the climax, or does it seem contrived? If so, why?
5. What is the central symbol of identity and status in the story? What symbolic elements are used in the description of scene?
6. Find examples of irony and relate them to the controlling purpose of the story.
7. Relate the title to the central theme(s) of the story.

Suggestions for Writing

1. Select one of the above questions for development.
2. The relationship between experience and insight is a central theme of the story. Support this statement by specific references.
3. Compare your view of personal identity with that of your mother and/or father.

WILLIAM MAXWELL

What He Was Like

William Maxwell, Jr. (b. 1908) has degrees from both the University of Illinois and Harvard. After a brief stint as an English professor, he spent his entire professional career as a member of the editorial staff of *The New Yorker.* A writer as well as an editor, he has been the recipient of the American Writer's Award, as well as a grant from the National Institute of Arts and Letters. Among other books, he has written *Over by the River, and Other Stories* (1977), *So Long, See You Tomorrow* (1980), and *All the Days and Nights.*

He kept a diary, for his own pleasure. Because the days passed by so rapidly, and he found it interesting to go back and see how he had occupied his time, and with whom. He was aware that his remarks were sometimes far from kind, but the person they were about was never going to read them, so what difference did it make? The current diary was usually on his desk, the previous ones on a shelf in his clothes closet, where they were beginning to take up room.

His wife's uncle, in the bar of the Yale Club, said, "I am at the age of funerals." Now, thirty-five years later, it was his turn. In his address book the names of his three oldest friends had lines drawn through them. "Jack is dead," he wrote in his diary. "I didn't think that would happen. I thought he was immortal.... Louise is dead. In her sleep.... Richard has been dead for over a year and I still do not believe it. So impoverishing."

He himself got older. His wife got older. They advanced deeper into their seventies without any sense of large changes but only of one day's following another, and of the days being full, and pleasant, and worth recording. So he went on doing it. They all got put down in his diary, along with his feelings about old age, his fear of dying, his declining sexual powers, his envy of the children that he saw running down the street. To be able to run like that! He had to restrain himself from saying to young men in their thirties and forties, "You do appreciate, don't you, what you have?" In his diary he wrote, "If I had my life to live over again—but one doesn't. One goes forward instead, dragging a cart piled high with lost opportunities."

Though his wife had never felt the slightest desire to read his diary, she knew when he stopped leaving it around as carelessly as he did his opened mail. Moving the papers on his desk in order to dust it, she saw where he had hidden the current volume, was tempted to open it and see what it was he didn't want her to know, and then thought better of it and replaced the papers, exactly as they were before.

"To be able to do in your mind," he wrote, "what it is probably not a good idea to do in actuality is a convenience not always sufficiently appreciated." Though in his daily life he was as cheerful as a cricket, the diaries were more and more given over to dark thoughts, anger, resentment, indecencies, regrets, remorse. And now and then the simple joy in being alive. "If I stopped recognizing that I want things that it is not appropriate for me to want," he wrote, "wouldn't this inevitably lead to my not wanting anything at all—which as people get older is a risk that must be avoided at all costs?" He wrote, "Human beings are not like a clock that is wound up at birth and runs until the mainspring is fully unwound. They live because they want to. And when they stop wanting to, the first thing they know they are in a doctor's office being shown an X-ray that puts a different face on everything."

After he died, when the funeral had been got through, and after the number of telephone calls had diminished to a point where it was possible to attend to other things, his wife and daughter together disposed of the clothes in his closet. His daughter folded and put in a suit box an old, worn corduroy coat that she remembered the feel of when her father had rocked her as a child. His wife kept a blue-green sweater that she was used to seeing him in. As for the rest, he was a common size, and so his shirts and suits were easily disposed of to people who were in straitened circumstances and grateful for a warm overcoat, a dark suit, a pair of pigskin gloves. His shoes were something else again, and his wife dropped them into the Goodwill box, hoping that somebody would turn up who wore size-9A shoes, though it didn't seem very likely. Then the two women were faced with the locked filing cabinet in his study, which contained business papers that they turned over to the executor, and most of the twenty-seven volumes of his diary.

"Those I don't know what to do with, exactly," his wife said. "They're private and he didn't mean anybody to read them."

"Did he say so?" his daughter asked.

"No."

"Then how do you know he didn't want anybody to read them?"

"I just know."

"You're not curious?"

"I was married to your father for forty-six years and I know what he was like."

Which could only mean, the younger woman decided, that her mother had, at some time or other, looked into them. But she loved her father, and felt a very real desire to know what he was like as a person and not just as a father. So she put one of the diaries aside and took it home with her.

When her husband got home from his office that night, her eyes were red from weeping. First he made her tell him what the trouble was, and then he went out to the kitchen and made a drink for each of them, and then he sat down beside her on the sofa. Holding his free hand, she began to tell him about the shock of reading the diary.

"He wasn't the person I thought he was. He had all sorts of secret desires. A lot of it is very dirty. And some of it is more unkind than I would have believed possible. And just not like him—except that it *was* him. It makes me feel I can never trust anybody ever again."

"Not even me?" her husband said soberly.

"Least of all, you."

They sat in silence for a while. And then he said, "I was more comfortable with him than I was with my own father. And I think, though I could be mistaken, that he liked me."

"Of course he liked you. He often said so."

"So far as his life is concerned, if you were looking for a model to—"

"I don't see how you can say that."

"I do, actually. In his place, though, I think I would have left instructions that the diaries were to be disposed of unread.... We could burn it. Burn all twenty-seven volumes."

"No."

"Then let's put it back," he said, reaching for the diary. "Put it back in the locked file where your mother found it."

"And leave it there forever?"

"For a good long while. He may have been looking past our shoulders. It would be like him. If we have a son who doesn't seem to be very much like you or me, or like anybody in your family or mine, we can give him the key to the file—"

"If I had a son, the *last* thing in the world I'd want would be for him to read this filth!"

"—and tell him he can read them if he wants to. And if he doesn't want to, he can decide what should be done with them. It might be a help to him to know that there was somebody two generations back who wasn't in every respect what he seemed to be."

"Who was, in fact—"

"Since he didn't know your father, he won't be shocked and upset. You stay right where you are while I make us another of these."

But she didn't. She didn't want to be separated from him, even for the length of time it would take him to go out to the kitchen and come back with a Margarita suspended from the fingers of each hand, lest in that brief interval he turn into a stranger.

Suggestions for Discussion

1. What does the father mean when he writes, "To be able to do in your mind what it is probably not a good idea to do in actuality is a convenience not always sufficiently appreciated"?
2. How well can we truly know another person?
3. What does it mean when the father stops leaving the diary lying around? When he does not destroy it before his death?
4. How much of your own most private self—that is, what you might reveal in a diary—do you actually share with another person?

Suggestions for Writing

1. Write about an incident in which someone is revealed to be very different from the way you had assumed that person to be.
2. Maxwell says, "One goes forward...dragging a cart piled high with lost opportunities." Write about some of the "lost opportunities" one might find in your cart.

TILLIE OLSEN

I Stand Here Ironing

Tillie Olsen (b. 1913) was born in Omaha, Nebraska, but has lived most of her adult life in the San Francisco Bay Area. She worked for a time in manual and clerical jobs but in later years received a number of literary awards: a Stanford University Creative Writing Fellowship, a Ford Foundation grant in literature, and a Radcliffe Institute for Independent Study Fellowship. She is best known for her collection of stories, *Tell Me a Riddle* (1956), from which this story was selected, and *Silences* (1979). The tension of the story lies in the writer's conception of the distance between what might have been and what is.

I stand here ironing, and what you asked me moves tormented back and forth with the iron.

"I wish you would manage the time to come in and talk with me about your daughter. I'm sure you can help me understand her. She's a youngster who needs help and whom I'm deeply interested in helping."

"Who needs help."... Even if I came, what good would it do? You think because I am her mother I have a key, or that in some way you could use me as a key? She has lived for nineteen years. There is all that life that has happened outside of me, beyond me.

And when is there time to remember, to sift, to weigh, to estimate, to total? I will start and there will be an interruption and I will have to gather it all together again. Or I will become engulfed with all I did or did not do, with what should have been and what cannot be helped.

She was a beautiful baby. The first and only one of our five that was beautiful at birth. You do not guess how new and uneasy her tenancy in her now-loveliness. You did not know her all those years she was thought homely, or see her poring over her baby pictures, making me tell her over and over how beautiful she had been—and would be, I would tell her—and was now, to the seeing eye. But the seeing eyes were few or nonexistent. Including mine.

I nursed her. They feel that's important nowadays. I nursed all the children, but with her, with all the fierce rigidity of first motherhood, I did like the books then said. Though her cries battered me to trembling and my breasts ached with swollenness, I waited till the clock decreed.

Why do I put that first? I do not even know if it matters, or if it explains anything.

She was a beautiful baby. She blew shining bubbles of sound. She loved motion, loved light, loved color and music and textures. She would lie on the floor in her blue overalls patting the surface so hard in ecstasy her hands and feet would blur. She was a miracle to me, but when she was eight months old I had to leave her daytimes with the woman downstairs to whom she was no miracle at all, for I worked or looked for work and for Emily's father, who "could no longer endure" (he wrote in his good-bye note) "sharing want with us."

I was nineteen. It was the pre-relief, pre-WPA world of the depression. I would start running as soon as I got off the streetcar, running up the stairs, the place smelling sour, and awake or asleep to startle awake, when she saw me she would break into a clogged weeping that could not be comforted, a weeping I can hear yet.

After a while I found a job hashing at night so I could be with her days, and it was better. But it came to where I had to bring her to this family and leave her.

It took a long time to raise the money for her fare back. Then she got chicken pox and I had to wait longer. When she finally came, I hardly knew her, walking quick and nervous like her father, looking like her father, thin, and dressed in a shoddy red that yellowed her skin and glared at the pockmarks. All the baby loveliness gone.

She was two. Old enough for nursery school they said, and I did not know then what I know now—the fatigue of the long day, and the lacerations of group life in the kinds of nurseries that are only parking places for children.

Except that it would have made no difference if I had known. It was the only place there was. It was the only way we could be together, the only way I could hold a job.

And even without knowing, I knew. I knew the teacher that was evil because all these years it has curdled into my memory, the little boy hunched in the corner, her rasp, "why aren't you outside, because Alvin hits you? that's no reason, go out, scaredy." I knew Emily hated it even if she did not clutch and implore "don't go Mommy" like the other children, mornings.

She always had a reason why we should stay home. Momma, you look sick. Momma, I feel sick. Momma, the teachers aren't there today, they're sick. Momma, we can't go, there was a fire there last night. Momma, it's a holiday today, no school, they told me.

But never a direct protest, never rebellion. I think of our others in their three-, four-year-oldness—the explosions, the tempers, the denunciations, the demands—and I feel suddenly ill. I put the iron down. What in me demanded that goodness in her? And what was the cost, the cost to her of such goodness?

The old man living in the back once said in his gentle way: "You should smile at Emily more when you look at her." What *was* in my face when I looked at her? I loved her. There were all the acts of love.

It was only with the others I remembered what he said, and it was the face of joy, and not of care or tightness or worry I turned to them—too late for Emily. She does not smile easily, let alone almost always as her brothers and sisters do. Her face is closed and sombre, but when she wants, how fluid. You must have seen it in her pantomimes, you spoke of her rare gift for comedy on the stage that rouses a laughter out of the audience so dear they applaud and applaud and do not want to let her go.

Where does it come from, that comedy? There was none of it in her when she came back to me that second time, after I had had to send her away again. She had a new daddy now to learn to love, and I think perhaps it was a better time.

Except when we left her alone nights, telling ourselves she was old enough.

"Can't you go some other time, Mommy, like tomorrow?" she would ask. "Will it be just a little while you'll be gone? Do you promise?"

The time we came back, the front door open, the clock on the floor in the hall. She rigid awake. "It wasn't just a little while. I didn't cry. Three times I called you, just three times, and then I ran downstairs to open the door so you could come faster. The clock talked loud. I threw it away, it scared me what it talked."

She said the clock talked loud again that night I went to the hospital to have Susan. She was delirious with the fever that comes before red measles, but she was fully conscious all the week I was gone and the week after we were home when she could not come near the new baby or me.

She did not get well. She stayed skeleton thin, not wanting to eat, and night after night she had nightmares. She would call for me, and I would rouse from exhaustion to sleepily call back: "You're all right, darling, go to sleep, it's just a dream," and if she still called, in a sterner voice, "now go to sleep, Emily, there's nothing to hurt you." Twice, only twice, when I had to get up for Susan anyhow, I went in to sit with her.

Now when it is too late (as if she would let me hold and comfort her like I do the others) I get up and go to her at once at her moan or restless stirring. "Are you awake, Emily? Can I get you something?" And the answer is always the same: "No, I'm all right, go back to sleep, Mother."

They persuaded me at the clinic to send her away to a convalescent home in the country where "she can have the kind of food and care you can't manage for her, and you'll be free to concentrate on the new baby." They still send children to that place. I see pictures on the society page of sleek young women planning affairs to raise money for it, or dancing at the affairs, or decorating Easter eggs or filling Christmas stockings for the children.

They never have a picture of the children so I do not know if the girls still wear those gigantic red bows and the ravaged looks on the every other Sunday when parents can come to visit "unless otherwise notified"—as we were notified the first six weeks.

Oh it is a handsome place, green lawns and tall trees and fluted flower beds. High up on the balconies of each cottage the children stand, the girls in their red bows and white dresses, the boys in white suits and giant red ties. The parents stand below shrieking up to be heard and the children shriek down to be heard, and between them the invisible wall "Not To Be Contaminated by Parental Germs or Physical Affection."

There was a tiny girl who always stood hand in hand with Emily. Her parents never came. One visit she was gone. "They moved her to Rose Cottage," Emily shouted in explanation. "They don't like you to love anybody here."

She wrote once a week, the labored writing of a seven-year-old. "I am fine. How is the baby. If I write my leter nicly I will have a star. Love" There never was a star. We wrote every other day, letters she could never hold or keep but only hear read—once. "We simply do not have room for children to keep any personal possessions," they patiently explained when we pieced one Sunday's shrieking together to plead how much it would mean to Emily, who loved so to keep things, to be allowed to keep her letters and cards.

Each visit she looked frailer. "She isn't eating," they told us.

(They had runny eggs for breakfast or mush with lumps, Emily said later, I'd hold it in my mouth and not swallow. Nothing ever tasted good, just when they had chicken.)

It took us eight months to get her released home, and only the fact that she gained back so little of her seven lost pounds convinced the social worker.

I used to try to hold and love her after she came back, but her body would stay stiff, and after a while she'd push away. She ate little. Food sickened her, and I think much of life too. Oh she had physical lightness and brightness, twinkling by on skates, bouncing like a ball up and down up and down over the jump rope, skimming over the hill; but these were momentary.

She fretted about her appearance, thin and dark and foreign-looking at a time when every little girl was supposed to look or thought she should look a chubby blonde replica of Shirley Temple. The doorbell sometimes rang for her, but no one seemed to come and play in the house or be a best friend. Maybe because we moved so much.

There was a boy she loved painfully through two school semesters. Months later she told me how she had taken pennies from my purse to buy him candy. "Licorice was his favorite and I brought him some every day, but he still liked Jennifer better'n me. Why, Mommy?" The kind of question for which there is no answer.

School was a worry to her. She was not glib or quick in a world where glibness and quickness were easily confused with ability to learn. To her overworked and exasperated teachers she was an overconscientious "slow learner" who kept trying to catch up and was absent entirely too often.

I let her be absent, though sometimes the illness was imaginary. How different from my now-strictness about attendance with the others. I wasn't working. We had a new baby, I was home anyhow. Sometimes, after Susan grew old enough, I would keep her home from school, too, to have them all together.

Mostly Emily had asthma, and her breathing, harsh and labored, would fill the house with a curiously tranquil sound. I would bring the two old dresser mirrors and her boxes of collections to her bed. She would select beads and single earrings, bottle tops and shells, dried flowers and pebbles, old postcards and scraps, all sorts of oddments; then she and Susan would play Kingdom, setting up landscapes and furniture, peopling them with action.

Those were the only times of peaceful companionship between her and Susan. I have edged away from it, that poisonous feeling between them, that terrible balancing of hurts and needs I had to do between the two, and did so badly, those earlier years.

Oh there are conflicts between the others too, each one human, needing, demanding, hurting, taking—but only between Emily and Susan, no, Emily toward Susan that corroding resentment. It seems so obvious on the surface, yet it is not obvious. Susan, the second child, Susan, golden- and curly-haired and chubby, quick and articulate and assured, everything in appearance and manner Emily was not; Susan, not able to resist Emily's precious things, losing or sometimes clumsily breaking them; Susan telling jokes and riddles to company for applause while Emily sat silent (to say to me later: that was *my* riddle, Mother, I told it to Susan); Susan, who for all the five years' difference in age was just a year behind Emily in developing physically.

I am glad for that slow physical development that widened the difference between her and her contemporaries, though she suffered over it. She was too vulnerable for that terrible world of youthful competition, of preening and parading, of constant measuring of yourself against every other, of envy, "If I had that copper hair," "If I had that skin...." She tormented herself enough about not looking like the others, there was enough of the unsureness, the having to be conscious of words before you speak, the constant caring—what are they thinking of me? without having it all magnified by the merciless physical drives.

Ronnie is calling. He is wet and I change him. It is rare there is such a cry now. That time of motherhood is almost behind me when the ear is not one's own but must always be racked and listening for the child cry, the child call. We sit for a while and I hold him, looking out over the city spread in charcoal with its soft aisles of light. "*Shoogily*," he breathes and curls closer. I carry him back to bed, asleep. *Shoogily.* A funny word, a family word, inherited from Emily, invented by her to say: *comfort.*

In this and other ways she leaves her seal, I say aloud. And startle at my saying it. What do I mean? What did I start to gather together, to try and make coherent? I was at the terrible, growing years. War years. I do not remember them well. I was working, there were four smaller ones now, there was not time for her. She had to help be a mother, and housekeeper, and shopper. She had to set her seal. Mornings of crisis and near hysteria trying to get lunches packed, hair combed, coats and shoes found, everyone to school or Child Care on time, the baby ready for transportation. And always the paper scribbled on by a smaller one, the book looked at by Susan then mislaid, the homework not done. Running out to that huge school where she was one, she was lost, she was a drop; suffering over the unpreparedness, stammering and unsure of her classes.

There was so little time left at night after the kids were bedded down. She would struggle over books, always eating (it was in those years she developed her enormous appetite that is legendary in our family) and I would be ironing, or preparing food for the next day, or writing V-mail to Bill, or tending the baby. Sometimes, to make me laugh, or out of her despair, she would imitate happenings or types at school.

I think I said once: "Why don't you do something like this in the school amateur show?" One morning she phoned me at work, hardly understandable through the weeping: "Mother, I did it. I won, I won; they gave me first prize; they clapped and clapped and wouldn't let me go."

Now suddenly she was Somebody, and as imprisoned in her difference as she had been in anonymity.

She began to be asked to perform at other high schools, even in colleges, then at city and statewide affairs. The first one we went to, I only recognized her that first moment when thin, shy, she almost drowned herself into the curtains. Then: Was this Emily? The control, the command, the convulsing and deadly clowning, the spell, then the roaring, stamping audience, unwilling to let this rare and precious laughter out of their lives.

Afterwards: You ought to do something about her with a gift like that—but without money or knowing how, what does one do? We have left it all to her, and the gift has as often eddied inside, clogged and clotted, as been used and growing.

She is coming. She runs up the stairs two at a time with her light graceful step, and I know she is happy tonight. Whatever it was that occasioned your call did not happen today.

"Aren't you ever going to finish the ironing, Mother? Whistler painted his mother in a rocker. I'd have to paint mine standing over an ironing board." This is one of her communicative nights and she tells me everything and nothing as she fixes herself a plate of food out of the icebox.

She is so lovely. Why did you want me to come in at all? Why were you concerned? She will find her way.

She starts up the stairs to bed. "Don't get me up with the rest in the morning." "But I thought you were having midterms." "Oh, those," she comes back in, kisses me, and says quite lightly, "in a couple of years when we'll all be atom-dead they won't matter a bit."

She has said it before. She *believes* it. But because I have been dredging the past, and all that compounds a human being is so heavy and meaningful in me, I cannot endure it tonight.

I will never total it all. I will never come in to say: She was a child seldom smiled at. Her father left me before she was a year old. I had to work her first six years when there was work, or I sent her home and to his relatives. There were years she had care she hated. She was dark and thin and foreign-looking in a world where the prestige went to blondeness and curly hair and dimples, she was slow where glibness was prized. She was a child of anxious, not proud, love. We were poor and could not afford for her the soil of easy growth. I was a young mother, I was a distracted mother. There were the other children pushing up, demanding. Her younger sister seemed all that she was not. There were years she did not want me to touch her. She kept too much in herself, her life was such she had to keep too much in herself. My wisdom came too late. She has much to her and probably little will come of it. She is a child of her age, of depression, of war, of fear.

Let her be. So all that is in her will not bloom—but in how many does it? There is still enough left to live by. Only help her to know—help make it so there is cause for her to know—that she is more than this dress on the ironing board, helpless before the iron.

Suggestions for Discussion

1. In this story in which the mother speaks of her daughter, who is the listener? What evidence is there that she is speaking to herself as well as to the unnamed listener? How does this technique affect the emotional impact of the story?
2. What is the symbolic and real significance of the title and the opening and concluding allusions to ironing?
3. As you review the chronology of events in the lives of the mother and Emily, how would you characterize the changes in their attitudes, feelings, and behavior?
4. In what respects might it be said that the author portrays two lives that move beyond the personal and reflect a universal phenomenon?
5. What attitude toward life is expressed in the final paragraph?

Suggestions for Writing

1. After stating in your own words the attitude toward life expressed in the last paragraph, discuss your view of it by making reference to your own experience or your observation of others (real or fictional).
2. Rewrite the story of Emily chronologically. What is lost of the author's artistry?
3. Write a monologue in which Emily is the speaker.

LOUISE ERDRICH

A Wedge of Shade

Louise Erdrich (b. 1954), of Chippewa extraction, is a leading voice among Native American writers. Born in Minnesota, she received her B.A. from Dartmouth and her M.A. from the Johns Hopkins University. She has won the Nelson Algren Award, the National Book Critics Circle Award for fiction, and was first on the New York Times Bestseller List with her novels *The Beet Queen* (1986) and *Tracks* (1988). Her most recent books include *Baptism of Desire* (1989), *The Crown of Columbus* (1991), *Bingo Palace* (1995), *The Blue Jay's Dance* (1995), *Grandmother's Pidgeon* (1996), and *Tales of Burning Love* (1996). This short story deals with the intensity of family bonds, and the difficulty of loosening them in order to claim one's own life.

Every place that I could name you, in the whole world around us, has better things about it than Argus, North Dakota. I just happened to grow up there for eighteen years, and the soil got to be part of me, the air has something in it that I breathed. Argus water doesn't taste as good as water in the cities. Still, the first thing I do, walking back into my mother's house, is stand at the kitchen sink and toss down glass after glass.

"Are you filled up?" My mother stands behind me. "Sit down if you are."

She's tall and board-square, French-Chippewa, with long arms and big knuckles. Her face is rawboned, fierce, and almost masculine in its edges and planes. Several months ago, a beauty operator convinced her that she should feminize her look with curls. Now the permanent, grown out in grizzled streaks, bristles like the coat of a terrier. I don't look like her. Not just the hair, since hers is salt-and-pepper and mine is a reddish brown, but my build. I'm short, boxy, more like my Aunt Mary. Like her, I can't seem to shake this town. I keep coming back here.

"There's jobs at the beet plant," my mother says.

This rumor, probably false, since the plant is in a slump, drops into the dim, close air of the kitchen. We have the shades drawn because it's a hot June, over a hundred degrees, and we're trying to stay cool. Outside, the water has been sucked from everything. The veins in the leaves are hollow, the ditch grass is crackling. The sky has absorbed every drop. It's a thin whitish-blue veil stretched from end to end over us, a flat gauze tarp. From the depot, I've walked here beneath it, dragging my suitcase.

We're sweating as if we're in an oven, a big messy one. For a week, it's been too hot to clean much or even move, and the crops are stunted, failing. The farmer next to us just sold his field for a subdivision, but the construction workers aren't doing much. They're wearing wet rags on their heads, sitting near the house sites in the brilliance of noon. The studs of wood stand upright over them, but uselessly—nothing casts shadows. The sun has dried them up, too.

"The beet plant," my mother says again.

"Maybe so," I say, and then, because I've got something bigger on my mind, "Maybe I'll go out there and apply."

"Oh?" She is intrigued now.

"God, this is terrible!" I take the glass of water in my hand and tip some onto my head. I don't feel cooler, though; I just feel the steam rising off me.

"The fan broke down," she states. "Both of them are kaput now. The motors or something. If Mary would get the damn tax refund, we'd run out to Pamida, buy a couple more, set up a breeze. Then we'd be cool out here."

"Your garden must be dead," I say, lifting the edge of the pull shade.

"It's sick, but I watered. And I won't mulch; that draws the damn slugs."

"Nothing could live out there, no bug." My eyes smart from even looking at the yard, which is a clear sheet of sun, almost incandescent.

"You'd be surprised."

I wish I could blurt it out, just tell her. Even now, the words swell in my mouth, the one sentence, but I'm scared, and with good reason. There is this about my mother: it is awful to see her angry. Her lips press together and she stiffens herself within, growing wooden, silent. Her features become fixed and remote, she will not speak. It takes a long time, and until she does you are held in suspense. Nothing that she ever says, in the end, is as bad as that feeling of dread. So I wait, half believing that she'll figure out my secret for herself, or drag it out of me, not that she ever tries. If I'm silent, she hardly notices. She's not like Aunt Mary, who forces me to say more than I know is on my mind.

My mother sighs. "It's too hot to bake. It's too hot to cook. But it's too hot to eat anyway."

She's talking to herself, which makes me reckless. Perhaps she is so preoccupied by the heat that I can slip my announcement past her. I should just say it, but I lose nerve, make an introduction that alerts her. "I have something to tell you."

I've cast my lot; there's no going back unless I think quickly. My thoughts hum.

But she waits, forgetting the heat for a moment.

"Ice," I say. "We have to have ice." I speak intensely, leaning toward her, almost glaring, but she is not fooled.

"Don't make me laugh," she says. "There's not a cube in town. The refrigerators can't keep cold enough." She eyes me the way a hunter eyes an animal about to pop from its den and run.

"O.K." I break down. "I really do have something." I stand, turn my back. In this lightless warmth I'm dizzy, almost sick. Now I've gotten to her and she's frightened to hear, breathless.

"Tell me," she urges. "Go on, get it over with."

And so I say it. "I got married." There is a surge of relief, a wind blowing through the room, but then it's gone. The curtain flaps and we're caught again, stunned in an even denser heat. It's now my turn to wait, and I whirl around and sit right across from her. Now is the time to tell her his name, a Chippewa name that she'll know from the papers, since he's notorious. Now is the time to get it over with. But I can't bear the picture she makes, the shock that parts her lips, the stunned shade of hurt in her eyes. I have to convince her, somehow, that it's all right.

"You hate weddings! Just think, just picture it. Me, white net. On a day like this. You, stuffed in your summer wool, and Aunt Mary, God knows...and the tux, the rental, the groom..."

Her head had lowered as my words fell on her, but now her forehead tips up and her eyes come into view, already hardening. My tongue flies back into my mouth.

She mimics, making it a question, "The groom..."

I'm caught, my lips half open, a stuttering noise in my throat. How to begin? I have rehearsed this, but my lines melt away, my opening, my casual introductions. I can think of nothing that would convince her of how much more he is than the captions beneath the photos. There is no picture adequate, no representation that captures him. So I just put my hand across the table and I touch her hand. "Mother," I say, as if we're in a staged drama, "he'll arrive here shortly."

There is something forming in her, some reaction. I am afraid to let it take complete shape. "Let's go out and wait on the steps, Mom. Then you'll see him."

"I do not understand," she says in a frighteningly neutral voice. This is what I mean. Everything is suddenly forced, unnatural—we're reading lines.

"He'll approach from a distance." I can't help speaking like a bad actor. "I told him to give me an hour. He'll wait, then he'll come walking down the road."

We rise and unstick our blouses from our stomachs, our skirts from the backs of our legs. Then we walk out front in single file, me behind, and settle ourselves on the middle step. A scrubby box-elder tree on one side casts a light shade, and the dusty lilacs seem to catch a little breeze on the other. It's not so bad out here, still hot, but not so dim, contained. It is worse past the trees. The heat shimmers in a band, rising off the fields, out of the spars and bones of houses that will wreck our view. The horizon and the edge of town show through the gaps in the framing now, and as we sit we watch the workers move, slowly, almost in a practiced recital, back and forth. Their headcloths hang to their shoulders, their hard hats are dabs of yellow, their white T-shirts blend into the fierce air and sky. They don't seem to be doing anything, although we hear faint thuds from their hammers. Otherwise, except for the whistles of a few birds, there is silence. Certainly we don't speak.

It is a longer wait than I anticipated, maybe because he wants to give me time. At last the shadows creep out, hard, hot, charred, and the heat begins to lengthen and settle. We are going into the worst of the afternoon when a dot at the end of the road begins to form.

Mom and I are both watching. We have not moved our eyes around much, and we blink and squint to try and focus. The dot doesn't change, not for a long while. And then it suddenly springs clear in relief—a silhouette, lost for a moment in the shimmer, reappearing. In that shining expanse he is a little wedge of moving shade. He continues, growing imperceptibly, until there are variations in the outline, and it can be seen that he is large. As he passes the construction workers, they turn and stop, all alike in their hats, stock-still.

Growing larger yet, as if he has absorbed their stares, he nears us. Now we can see the details. He is dark, the first thing. His arms are thick, his chest is huge, and the features of his face are wide and open. He carries nothing in his hands. He wears a black T-shirt, the opposite of the construction workers, and soft jogging shoes. His jeans are held under his stomach by a belt with a star beaded on the buckle. His hair is long, in a tail. I am the wrong woman for him. I am paler, shorter, un-magnificent. But I stand up. Mom joins me, and I answer proudly when she asks, "His name?"

"His name is Gerry—" Even now I can't force his last name through my lips. But Mom is distracted by the sight of him anyway.

We descend one step, and stop again. It is here we will receive him. Our hands are folded at our waists. We're balanced, composed. He continues to stroll toward us, his white smile widening, his eyes filling with the sight of me as mine are filling with him. At the end of the road behind him, another dot has appeared. It is fast-moving and the sun flares off it twice: a vehicle. Now there are two figures—one approaching in a spume of dust from the rear, and Gerry, unmindful, not slackening or quickening his pace, continuing on. It is like a choreography design. They move at parallel speeds in front of our eyes. Then, at the same moment, at the end of our yard, they conclude the performance; both of them halt.

Gerry stands, looking toward us, his thumbs in his belt. He nods respectfully to Mom, looks calmly at me, and half smiles. He raises his brows, and we're suspended. Officer Lovchik emerges from the police car, stooped and tired. He walks up behind Gerry and I hear the snap of handcuffs, then I jump. I'm stopped by Gerry's gaze, though, as he backs away from me, still smiling tenderly. I am paralyzed halfway down the walk. He kisses the air while Lovchik cautiously prods at him, fitting his prize into the car. And then the doors slam, the engine roars, and they back out and turn around. As they move away there is no siren. I think I've heard Lovchik mention questioning. I'm sure it is lots of fuss for nothing, a mistake, but it cannot be denied—this is terrible timing.

I shake my shoulders, smooth my skirt, and turn to my mother with a look of outrage. "How do you like that?" I try.

She's got her purse in one hand, her car keys out.

"Let's go," she says.

"O.K.," I answer. "Fine. Where?"

"Aunt Mary's."

"I'd rather go and bail him out, Mom."

"Bail," she says. "*Bail?*"

She gives me such a look of cold and furious surprise that I sink immediately into the front seat, lean back against the vinyl. I almost welcome the sting of the heated plastic on my back, thighs, shoulders.

Aunt Mary lives at the rear of the butcher shop she runs. As we walk toward the "House of Meats," her dogs are rugs in the dirt, flattened by the heat of the day. Not one of them barks at us to warn her. We step over them and get no more reaction than a whine, the slow beat of a tail. Inside, we get no answers either, although we call Aunt Mary up and down the hall. We enter the kitchen and sit at the table, which holds a half-ruined watermelon. By the sink, in a tin box, are cigarettes. My mother takes one and carefully puts a match to it, frowning. "I know what," she says. "Go check the lockers."

There are two—a big freezer full of labelled meats and rental space, and another, smaller one that is just a side cooler. I notice, walking past the meat display counter, that the red beacon beside the outside switch of the cooler is glowing. That tells you when the light is on inside.

I pull the long metal handle toward me and the thick door swishes open. I step into the cool, spicy air. Aunt Mary is there, too proud to ever register a hint of surprise. She simply nods and looks away as though I've just been out for a minute, although we've not seen one another in six months or more. She is relaxing on a big can of pepper labelled "Zanzibar," reading a scientific-magazine article. I sit down on a barrel of alum. With no warning, I drop my bomb; "I'm married." It doesn't matter how I tell it to Aunt Mary, because she won't be, refuses to be, surprised.

"What's he do?" she simply asks, putting aside the sheaf of paper. I thought the first thing she'd do was scold me for fooling my mother. But it's odd, for two women who have lived through boring times and disasters, how rarely one comes to the other's defense, and how often they are each willing to take advantage of the other's absence. But I'm benefiting here. It seems that Aunt Mary is truly interested in Gerry. So I'm honest.

"He's something like a political activist. I mean he's been in jail and all. But not for any crime, you see; it's just because of his convictions."

She gives me a long, shrewd stare. Her skin is too tough to wrinkle, but she doesn't look young. All around us hang loops of sausages, every kind you can imagine, every color, from the purple-black of blutwurst to the pale-whitish links that my mother likes best. Blocks of butter and head-cheese, a can of raw milk, wrapped parcels, and cured bacons are stuffed onto the shelves around us. My heart has gone still and cool inside me, and I can't stop talking.

"He's the kind of guy it's hard to describe. Very different. People call him a free spirit, but that doesn't say it either, because he's very disciplined in some ways. He learned to be neat in jail." I pause. She says nothing, so I go on. "I know it's sudden, but who likes weddings? I hate them—all that mess with the bridesmaids' gowns, getting material to match. I don't have girlfriends. I mean, how embarrassing, right? Who would sing 'O Perfect Love'? Carry the ring?"

She isn't really listening.

"What's he do?" she asks again.

Maybe she won't let go of it until I discover the right answer, like a game with nouns and synonyms.

"He—well, he agitates," I tell her.

"Is that some kind of factory work?"

"Not exactly, no, it's not a nine-to-five job or anything…"

She lets the magazine fall, now, cocks her head to one side, and stares at me without blinking her cold yellow eyes. She has the look of a hawk, of a person who can see into the future but won't tell you about it. She's lost business for staring at customers, but she doesn't care.

"Are you telling me that he doesn't…" Here she shakes her head twice, slowly, from one side to the other, without removing me from her stare. "That he doesn't have regular work?"

"Oh, what's the matter, anyway?" I say roughly. "I'll work. This is the nineteen-seventies."

She jumps to her feet, stands over me—a stocky woman with terse features and short, thin points of gray hair. Her earrings tremble and flash—small fiery opals. Her brown plastic glasses hang crooked on a cord around her neck. I have never seen her become quite so instantly furious, so disturbed. "We're going to fix that," she says.

The cooler immediately feels smaller, the sausages knock at my shoulder, and the harsh light makes me blink. I am as stubborn as Aunt Mary, however, and she knows that I can go head to head with her. "We're married and that's final." I manage to stamp my foot.

Aunt Mary throws an arm back, blows air through her cheeks, and waves away my statement vigorously. "You're a little girl. How old is *he?*"

I frown at my lap, trace the threads in my blue cotton skirt, and tell her that age is irrelevant.

"Big word," she says sarcastically. "Let me ask you this. He's old enough to get a job?"

"Of course he is; what do you think? O.K., he's older than me. He's in his thirties."

"Aha, I knew it."

"Geez! So what? I mean, haven't you ever been in love, hasn't someone ever gotten you *right here?*" I smash my fist on my chest.

We lock eyes, but she doesn't waste a second in feeling hurt. "Sure, sure I've been in love. You think I haven't? I know what it feels like, you smart-ass. You'd be surprised. But he was no lazy son of a bitch. Now, listen…" She stops, draws breath, and I let her. "Here's what I mean by 'fix.' I'll teach the sausage-making trade to him—to you, too—and the grocery business. I've about had it anyway, and so's your mother. We'll do the same as my aunt and uncle—leave the shop to you and move to Arizona. I like this place." She looks up at the burning safety bulb, down at me again. Her face drags in the light. "But what the hell. I always wanted to travel."

I'm stunned, a little flattened out, maybe ashamed of myself. "You hate going anywhere," I say, which is true.

The door swings open and Mom comes in with us. She finds a milk can and balances herself on it, sighing at the delicious feeling of the air, absorbing from the silence the fact that we have talked. She hasn't anything to add, I guess, and as the coolness hits, her eyes fall shut. Aunt Mary's too. I can't help it, either, and my eyelids drop, although my brain is conscious and alert. From the darkness, I can see us in the brilliance. The light rains down on us. We sit the way we have been sitting, on our cans of milk and pepper, upright and still. Our hands are curled loosely in our laps. Our faces are blank as the gods'. We could be statues in a tomb sunk into the side of a mountain. We could be dreaming the world up in our brains.

It is later, and the weather has no mercy. We are drained of everything but simple thoughts. It's too hot for feelings. Driving home, we see how field after field of beets has gone into shock, and even some of the soybeans. The plants splay, limp, burned into the ground. Only the sunflowers continue to struggle upright, bristling but small.

What drew me in the first place to Gerry was the unexpected. I went to hear him talk just after I enrolled at the university, and then I demonstrated when they came and got him off the stage. He always went so willingly, accommodating everyone. I began to visit him. I sold lunar calendars and posters to raise his bail and eventually free him. One thing led to another, and one night we found ourselves alone in a Howard Johnson's coffee shop downstairs from where they put him up when his speech was finished. There were much more beautiful women after him; he could have had his pick of Swedes or Yankton Sioux girls, who are the best-looking of all. But I was different, he says. He liked my slant on life. And then there was no going back once it started, no turning, as though it was meant. We had no choice.

I have this intuition as we near the house, in the fateful quality of light, as in the turn of the day the heat continues to press and the blackness, into which the warmth usually lifts, lowers steadily: We must come to the end of something; there must be a close to this day.

As we turn into the yard we see that Gerry is sitting on the porch stairs. Now it is our turn to be received. I throw the car door open and stumble out before the motor even cuts. I run to him and hold him, as my mother, pursuing the order of events, parks carefully. Then she walks over, too, holding her purse by the strap. She stands before him and says no word but simply looks into his face, staring as if he's cardboard, a man behind glass who cannot see her. I think she's rude, but then I realize that he is staring back, that they are the same height. Their eyes are level.

He puts his hand out. "My name is Gerry."

"Gerry what?"

"Nanapush."

She nods, shifts her weight. "You're from that line, the old strain, the ones…" She does not finish.

"And my father," Gerry says, "was Old Man Pillager."

"Kashpaws," she says, "are my branch, of course. We're probably related through my mother's brother." They do not move. They are like two opponents from the same divided country, staring across the border. They do not shift or blink, and I see that they are more alike than I am like either one of them—so tall, solid, dark-haired. They could be mother and son.

"Well, I guess you should come in," she offers. "You are a distant relative, after all." She looks at me. "Distant enough."

Whole swarms of mosquitoes are whining down, discovering us now, so there is no question of staying where we are. And so we walk into the house, much hotter than outside, with the gathered heat. Instantly the sweat springs from our skin and I can think of nothing else but cooling off. I try to force the windows higher in their sashes, but there's no breeze anyway; nothing stirs, no air.

"Are you sure," I gasp, "about those fans?"

"Oh, they're broke, all right," my mother says, distressed. I rarely hear this in her voice. She switches on the lights, which makes the room seem hotter, and we lower ourselves into the easy chairs. Our words echo, as though the walls have baked and dried hollow.

"Show me those fans," says Gerry.

My mother points toward the kitchen. "They're sitting on the table. I've already tinkered with them. See what you can do."

And so he does. After a while she hoists herself and walks out back to him. Their voices close together now, absorbed, and their tools clank frantically, as if they are fighting a duel. But it is a race with the bell of darkness and their waning energy. I think of ice. I get ice on the brain.

"Be right back," I call out, taking the car keys from my mother's purse. "Do you need anything?"

There is no answer from the kitchen but a furious sputter of metal, the clatter of nuts and bolts spilling to the floor.

I drive out to the Superpumper, a big new gas-station complex on the edge of town, where my mother most likely has never been. She doesn't know about convenience stores, has no credit cards for groceries or gas, pays only with small bills and change. She never has used an ice machine. It would grate on her that a bag of frozen water costs eighty cents, but it doesn't bother me. I take the plastic-foam cooler and I fill it for a couple of dollars. I buy two six-packs of Shasta soda and I plunge them in among the uniform cubes of ice. I drink two myself on the way home, and I manage to lift the whole heavy cooler out of the trunk, carry it to the door.

The fans are whirring, beating the air. I hear them going in the living room the minute I come in. The only light shines from the kitchen. Gerry and my mother have thrown the pillows from the couch onto the living-room floor, and they are sitting in the rippling currents of air. I bring the cooler in and put it near us. I have chosen all dark flavors—black cherry, grape, red berry, cola—so as we drink the darkness swirls inside us with the night air, sweet and sharp, driven by small motors.

I drag more pillows down from the other rooms upstairs. There is no question of attempting the bedrooms, the stifling beds. And so, in the dark, I hold hands with Gerry as he settles down between my mother and me. He is huge as a hill between the two of us, solid in the beating wind.

Suggestions for Discussion

1. What does the metaphor "a wedge of shade" have to do with the relationships between the characters in the story?

2. Erdrich uses light and dark, hot and cold, movement and stillness as ways of making us both respond to and understand what is happening in the story. How does she do this? What feelings are evoked? What do we come to know through these metaphors?
3. What reconciles Mom to Gerry?

Suggestions for Writing

1. Metaphors engage us in what is going on without ever becoming explicit about it. Write about a metaphor that expresses something you want to say about a relationship important to you.
2. Write a brief story about what happens in a family when a stranger enters it to stay.

POETRY

E. E. CUMMINGS

my father moved through dooms of love

Edward Estlin Cummings (1894–1963) was an American whose novel *The Enormous Room* (1922) and whose books of poetry *&* and *XLI Poems* (1925) established his reputation as an avant-garde writer interested in experimenting with stylistic techniques. Awarded several important prizes for poetry, he also was Charles Eliot Norton Lecturer at Harvard University in 1952 and published *i: six nonlectures* (1953). The theme of wholeness and reconciliation of opposites in the father's character is implictly expressed in this poem in which images of death, hate, and decay are counterpointed against images that celebrate life and growth.

my father moved through dooms of love
through sames of am through haves of give,
singing each morning out of each night
my father moved through depths of height

this motionless forgetful where
turned at his glance to shining here;
that if (so timid air is firm)
under his eyes would stir and squirm

newly as from unburied which
floats the first who, his april touch
drove sleeping selves to swarm their fates
woke dreamers to their ghostly roots

and should some why completely weep
my father's fingers brought her sleep:
vainly no smallest voice might cry
for he could feel the mountains grow.

Lifting the valleys of the sea
my father moved through griefs of joy;

praising a forehead called the moon
singing desire into begin

joy was his song and joy so pure
a heart of star by him could steer
and pure so now and now so yes
the wrists of twilight would rejoice

keen as midsummer's keen beyond
conceiving mind of sun will stand,
so strictly (over utmost him
so hugely) stood my father's dream

his flesh was flesh his blood was blood:
no hungry man but wished him food;
no cripple wouldn't creep one mile
uphill to only see him smile.

Scorning the pomp of must and shall
my father moved through dooms of feel;
his anger was as right as rain
his pity was as green as grain

septembering arms of year extend
less humbly wealth to foe and friend
than he to foolish and to wise
offered immeasurable is

proudly and (by octobering flame
beckoned) as earth will downward climb,
so naked for immortal work
his shoulders marched against the dark

his sorrow was as true as bread:
no liar looked him in the head;
if every friend became his foe
he'd laugh and build a world with snow.

My father moved through theys of we,
singing each new leaf out of each tree
(and every child was sure that spring
danced when she heard my father sing)

then let men kill which cannot share,
let blood and flesh be mud and mire,
scheming imagine, passion willed,
freedom a drug that's bought and sold

giving to steal and cruel kind,
a heart to fear, to doubt a mind,
to differ a disease of same,
conform the pinnacle of am

though dull were all we taste as bright,
bitter all utterly things sweet,
maggoty minus and dumb death
all we inherit, all bequeath

and nothing quite so least as truth
—i say though hate were why men breathe—
because my father lived his soul
love is the whole and more than all

Suggestions for Discussion

1. Study the verbal juxtapositions that seem antithetical: "dooms of love"; "depths of height"; "griefs of joy." How is the theme of wholeness and reconciliation of opposites in the character of the father implicitly expressed?
2. Cite passages in which the natural imagery of life, love, birth, and rebirth is counterpointed against images of death, hate, and decay.
3. Contrast this father with Kafka's in "Letter to His Father."

SYLVIA PLATH

Daddy

Sylvia Plath (1932–1963) began her career while still a college student by serving as guest editor of *Mademoiselle.* She studied in both the United States and England, taught at Smith College, and then settled in England, where she lived until her suicide. Her poetry is collected in *The Colossus* (1960), *Ariel* (1965), *Crossing the Water* (1971), and *Winter Trees* (1972), and she contributed to such magazines as *Seventeen, The Atlantic,* and *The Nation. The Bell Jar,* her only novel, was written about her late-adolescent attempt at suicide and was published posthumously in 1963 under the pseudonym Victoria Lucas. In "Daddy," the poet as child recalls the past and reinvokes her brutal image of her father.

You do not do, you do not do
Any more, black shoe
In which I have lived like a foot
For thirty years, poor and white,
Barely daring to breath or Achoo.

Daddy, I have had to kill you.
You died before I had time—
Marble-heavy, a bag full of God,
Ghastly statue with one grey toe
Big as a Frisco seal

And a head in the freakish Atlantic
Where it pours bean green over blue
In the waters off beautiful Nauset.
I used to pray to recover you.
Ach, du.

In the German tongue, in the Polish town
Scraped flat by the roller
Of wars, wars, wars.
But the name of the town is common.
My Polack friend

Says there are a dozen or two.
So I never could tell where you
Put your foot, your root,
I never could talk to you.
The tongue stuck in my jaw.

It stuck in a barb wire snare.
Ich, ich, ich, ich
I could hardly speak.
I thought every German was you.
And the language obscene

An engine, an engine
Chuffing me off like a Jew.
A Jew to Dachau, Auschwitz, Belsen.
I began to talk like a Jew.
I think I may well be a Jew.

The snows of the Tyrol, the clear beer of Vienna
Are not very pure or true.
With my gypsy ancestress and my weird luck
And my Taroc pack and my Taroc pack
I may be a bit of a Jew.

I have always been scared of *you*,
With your Luftwaffe, your gobbledygoo.
And your neat moustache
And your Aryan eye, bright blue.
Panzer-man, panzer-man, O You—

Not God but a swastika
So black no sky could squeak through.
Every woman adores a Fascist,
The boot in the face, the brute
Brute heart of a brute like you.

You stand at the blackboard, daddy,
In the picture I have of you,
A cleft in your chin instead of your foot
But no less a devil for that, no not
Any less the black man who

Bit my pretty red heart in two.
I was ten when they buried you.
At twenty I tried to die
And get back, back, back to you.
I thought even the bones would do.

But they pulled me out of the sack,
And they stuck me together with glue.
And then I knew what to do.
I made a model of you,
A man in black with a Meinkampf look

And a love of the rack and the screw.
And I said I do, I do.
So daddy, I'm finally through.
The black telephone's off at the root,
The voice just can't worm through.

If I've killed one man, I've killed two—
The vampire who said he was you
And drank my blood for a year,
Seven years, if you want to know.
Daddy, you can lie back now.

There's a stake in your fat black heart
And the villagers never liked you.
They are dancing and stamping on you.
They always *knew* it was you.
Daddy, daddy, you bastard, I'm through.

Suggestions for Discussion

1. Discuss the theme and mood of the poem. Comment on the relative maturity or insight the narrator has achieved through the distance of time.
2. What may Sylvia Plath's father have had in common with Kafka's father?

THEODORE ROETHKE

My Papa's Waltz

Theodore Roethke (1908–1963), American poet, taught during the last years of his life at the University of Washington. *The Waking: Poems, 1933–1953* was the winner of the Pulitzer Prize for Poetry in 1953. He received the Bollingen Award for Poetry in 1958. A collected volume, *Words for the Wind,* appeared in 1958, and *The Far Field* was published posthumously in 1964. The poet remembers his antic father and his own difficult childhood.

The whiskey on your breath
Could make a small boy dizzy;
But I hung on like death:
Such waltzing was not easy.

We romped until the pans
Slid from the kitchen shelf;
My mother's countenance
Could not unfrown itself.

The hand that held my wrist
Was battered on one knuckle;
At every step I missed
My right ear scraped a buckle.

You beat time on my head
With a palm caked hard by dirt,
Then waltzed me off to bed
Still clinging to your shirt.

Suggestion for Discussion

What images suggest the relationship between the boy and his father?

WILLIAM BUTLER YEATS

A Prayer for My Daughter

William Butler Yeats (1865–1939), the leading poet of the Irish literary revival and a playwright, was born near Dublin and educated in London and Dublin. He wrote plays for the Irish National Theatre Society (later called the Abbey Theatre). For a number of years he served as a senator of the Irish Free State. His volumes of poetry range from *The Wanderings of Oisin* (1889) to *The Last Poems* (1939). *The Collected Poems of W. B. Yeats* appeared in 1933, 1950, and 1956; *The Collected Plays of W. B. Yeats* were published in 1934 and 1952. From his view of a chaotic, threatening world, the poet prays for the harmony and order he considers requisite to the growth of his daughter.

Once more the storm is howling, and half hid
Under this cradle-hood and coverlid
My child sleeps on. There is no obstacle
But Gregory's wood and one bare hill
Whereby the haystack- and roof-levelling wind,
Bred on the Atlantic, can be stayed;
And for an hour I have walked and prayed
Because of the great gloom that is in my mind.

I have walked and prayed for this young child an hour
And heard the sea-wind scream upon the tower,
And under the arches of the bridge, and scream
In the elms above the flooded stream;
Imagining in excited reverie
That the future years had come,
Dancing to a frenzied drum,
Out of the murderous innocence of the sea.

May she be granted beauty and yet not
Beauty to make a stranger's eye distraught,
Or hers before a looking-glass, for such,
Being made beautiful overmuch,
Consider beauty a sufficient end,
Lose natural kindness and maybe

The heart-revealing intimacy
That chooses right, and never find a friend.

Helen, being chosen, found life flat and dull
And later had much trouble from a fool,
While that great Queen, that rose out of the spray,
Being fatherless, could have her way
Yet chose a bandy-leggèd smith for man.
It's certain that fine women eat
A crazy salad with their meat
Whereby the Horn of Plenty is undone.

In courtesy I'd have her chiefly learned;
Hearts are not had as a gift but hearts are earned
By those that are not entirely beautiful;
Yet many, that have played the fool
For beauty's very self, has charm made wise,
And many a poor man that has roved,
Loved and thought himself beloved,
From a glad kindness cannot take his eyes.

May she become a flourishing hidden tree
That all her thoughts may like the linnet be,
And have no business but dispensing round
Their magnanimities of sound.
Nor but in merriment began a chase,
Nor but in merriment a quarrel.
O may she live like some green laurel
Rooted in one dear perpetual place.

My mind, because the minds that I have loved,
The sort of beauty that I have approved,
Prosper but little, has dried up of late,
Yet knows that to be choked with hate
May well be of all evil chances chief.
If there's no hatred in a mind
Assault and battery of the wind
Can never tear the linnet from the leaf.

An intellectual hatred is the worst,
So let her think opinions are accursed.
Have I not seen the loveliest woman born
Out of the mouth of Plenty's horn,
Because of her opinionated mind
Barter that horn and every good

By quiet natures understood
For an old bellows full of angry wind?

Considering that, all hatred driven hence,
The soul recovers radical innocence
And learns at last that it is self-delighting,
Self-appeasing, self-affrighting,
And that its own sweet will is Heaven's will;
She can, though every face should scowl
And every windy quarter howl
Or every bellows burst, be happy still.

And may her bridegroom bring her to a house
Where all's accustomed, ceremonious;
For arrogance and hatred are the wares
Peddled in the thoroughfares.
How but in custom and in ceremony
Are innocence and beauty born?
Ceremony's a name for the rich horn,
And custom for the spreading laurel tree.

Suggestions for Discussion

1. Is the poet imposing on his daughter a conservative ideal of womanhood?
2. What words or images suggest that he might quarrel with the ideas of feminists today?
3. Discuss: "How but in custom and in ceremony / Are innocence and beauty born?"
4. What seems to be the poet's concept of happiness for a woman?

GWENDOLYN BROOKS

"Life for my child is simple, and is good"

Gwendolyn Brooks (b. 1917) is an American poet who grew up in Chicago's slums. Her works, which focus on contemporary black life in the United States, include *A Street in Bronzeville* (1949); *Annie Allen* (1949), which won a Pulitzer Prize; *The Bean Eaters* (1960); *The*

Near Johannesburg Boy and Other Poems (1987), and, most recently, *Report from Part Two* (1996). She also has written a novel and a book for children. In this brief poem the writer sets forth her hopes for her son's joy and growth.

Life for my child is simple, and is good.
He knows his wish. Yes, but that is not all.
Because I know mine too.
And we both want joy of undeep and unabiding things,
Like kicking over a chair or throwing blocks out of a window
Or tipping over an icebox pan
Or snatching down curtains or fingering an electric outlet
Or a journey or a friend or an illegal kiss.
No. There is more to it than that.
It is that he has never been afraid.
Rather, he reaches out and lo the chair falls with a beautiful crash,
And the blocks fall, down on the people's heads,
And the water comes slooshing sloopily out across the floor.
And so forth.
Not that success, for him, is sure, infallible.
But never has he been afraid to reach.
His lesions are legion.
But reaching is his rule.

Suggestions for Discussion

1. Compare Brooks's hopes for her child with those of Yeats for his daughter.
2. What do the joys of "unabiding things" have in common?
3. What oppositions are posed in the poem, and how are they resolved?

NANCY WILLARD

Questions My Son Asked Me, Answers I Never Gave Him

Nancy Willard (b. 1936) received her Ph.D. from the University of Michigan. She has won the Hopwood Award, a Woodrow Wilson Fellowship, and an O. Henry Award for the best short story in 1970. Her publications include *In His Country: Poems* (1966), *Skin of Grace* (1967), *The Carpenter of the Sun: Poems* (1974), *Water Waker* (1990), *The Sorcerer's Apprentice* (1994), *Cracked Corn and Snow Ice Cream: A Family Almanac,* and *Selected Poems* (1996). In this poem Willard responds to her child's questions concerning the nature of his universe with tenderness and whimsy.

1. Do gorillas have birthdays?
Yes. Like the rainbow they happen,
like the air they are not observed.

2. Do butterflies make a noise?
The wire in the butterfly's tongue
hums gold.
Some men hear butterflies
even in winter.

3. Are they part of our family?
They forgot us, who forgot how to fly.

4. Who tied my navel? Did God tie it?
God made the thread: O man, live forever!
Man made the knot: enough is enough.

5. If I drop my tooth in the telephone
will it go through the wires and bite someone's ear?
I have seen earlobes pierced by a tooth of steel.
It loves what lasts.
It does not love flesh.
It leaves a ring of gold in the wound.

6. If I stand on my head
will the sleep in my eye roll up into my head?

Does the dream know its own father?
Can bread go back to the field of its birth?

7. Can I eat a star?
Yes, with the mouth of time
that enjoys everything.

8. Could we xerox the moon?
This is the first commandment:
I am the moon, thy moon.
Thou shalt have no other moons before thee.

9. Who invented water?
The hands of the air, that wanted to wash each other.

10. What happens at the end of numbers?
I see three men running toward a field.
At the edge of the tall grass, they turn into light.

11. Do the years ever run out?
God said, I will break time's heart.
Time ran down like an old phonograph.
It lay flat as a carpet.
At rest on its threads I am learning to fly.

Suggestions for Discussion

1. Since each question is answered, why does the author suggest in her title that she did not answer it?
2. What do the son's questions tell you about him? Note the range of his questions.
3. What do the writer's answers tell you about her? How would you characterize the answers?
4. How does figurative language affect the tone? Describe the tone of the answers. In Question 3 Willard says we "forgot how to fly." What does she mean? The figure of flying is repeated in the last stanza. What is its significance? How does it relate to the question?
5. On the basis of the questions and answers, how would you describe the relationship of mother and son?

Suggestion for Writing

Write your own answer(s) to a hypothetical question you are either asking yourself or someone is asking you.

Personal Relationships: Men and Women

Modern woman isn't really a fool. But modern man is. That seems to me the only plain way of putting it. The modern man is a fool, and the modern young man is a prize fool. He makes a greater mess of his women than men have ever made.

—D. H. LAWRENCE, "Give Her a Pattern"

The men of our civilization have stripped themselves of the fineries of the earth so that they might work more freely to plunder the universe for treasures to deck my lady in. New raw materials, new processes, new machines are all brought into her service. My lady must therefore be the chief spender as well as the chief symbol of spending ability and monetary success. While her mate toils in his factory, she totters about the smartest streets and plushiest hotels with his fortune upon her back and bosom, fingers, and wrists, continuing that essential expenditure in his house which is her frame and her setting, enjoying that silken idleness which is the necessary condition of maintaining her mate's prestige and her qualification to demonstrate it.

—GERMAINE GREER, "The Stereotype"

Her mind only vaguely grasped what he was saying. Her physical being was for the moment predominant. She was not thinking of his words, only drinking in the tones of his voice. She wanted to reach out her hand in the darkness and touch him with the sensitive tips of her fingers upon the face or the lips. She wanted to draw close to him and whisper against his cheek—she did not care what—as she might have done if she had not been a respectable woman.

—KATE CHOPIN, "A Respectable Woman"

ESSAYS

MARY WOLLSTONECRAFT

A Vindication of the Rights of Woman

Mary Wollstonecraft (1759–1797), whose husband was the radical William Godwin and whose daughter became Mrs. Percy Bysshe Shelley, was a schoolteacher, a governess, and a member of a publishing firm. Her *Vindication of the Rights of Woman* (1792) was an extraordinary defense of the rights of eighteenth-century women. This eighteenth-century diatribe against those who would keep women enslaved was written with the wish to persuade women to acquire strength of mind and body.

My own sex, I hope, will excuse me, if I treat them like rational creatures, instead of flattering their *fascinating* graces, and viewing them as if they were in a state of perpetual childhood, unable to stand alone. I earnestly wish to point out in what true dignity and human happiness consists—I wish to persuade women to endeavor to acquire strength, both of mind and body, and to convince them that the soft phrases, susceptibility of heart, delicacy of sentiment, and refinement of taste, are almost synonymous with epithets of weakness, and that those beings who are only the objects of pity and that kind of love, which has been termed its sister, will soon become objects of contempt.

Dismissing, then, those pretty feminine phrases, which the men condescendingly use to soften our slavish dependence, and despising that weak elegancy of mind, exquisite sensibility, and sweet docility of manners, supposed to be the sexual characteristics of the weaker vessel, I wish to show that elegance is inferior to virtue, that the first object of laudable ambition is to obtain a character as a human being, regardless of the distinction of sex; and that secondary views should be brought to this simple touchstone.

This is a rough sketch of my plan; and should I express my conviction with the energetic emotions that I feel whenever I think of the subject, the dictates of experience and reflection will be felt by some of my readers. Animated by this important object, I shall disdain to cull my phrases or polish my style; I aim at being useful, and sincerity will render me unaffected; for, wishing rather to persuade by the force of my arguments, than dazzle by the elegance of my language, I shall not waste my time in rounding periods, or in fabricating the turgid bombast of artificial feelings, which, coming from the head, never reach the heart. I shall be employed about things, not words! and, anxious to render my sex more respectable members of society, I shall try to avoid that flowery diction which has slided from essays into novels, and from novels into familiar letters and conversation.

These pretty superlatives, dropping glibly from the tongue, vitiate the taste, and create a kind of sickly delicacy that runs away from simple unadorned truth; and a deluge of false sentiments and overstretched feelings, stifling the natural emotions of the heart, render the domestic pleasures insipid, that ought to sweeten the exercise of those severe duties, which educate a rational and immortal being for a nobler field of action.

The education of women has, of late, been more attended to than formerly; yet they are still reckoned a frivolous sex, and ridiculed or pitied by the writers who endeavor by satire or instruction to improve them. It is acknowledged that they spend many of the first years of their lives in acquiring a smattering of accomplishments; meanwhile strength of body and mind are sacrificed to libertine notions of beauty, to the desire of establishing themselves—the only way women can rise in the world—by marriage. And this desire making mere animals of them, when they marry they act as such children may be expected to act—they dress; they paint, and nickname God's creatures. Surely these weak beings are only fit for a seraglio!—Can they be expected to govern a family with judgment, or take care of the poor babes whom they bring into the world?

If then it can be fairly deduced from the present conduct of the sex, from the prevalent fondness for pleasure which takes place of ambition, and those nobler passions that open and enlarge the soul; that the instruction which women have hitherto received has only tended, with the constitution of civil society, to render them insignificant objects of desire—mere propagators of fools!—if it can be proved that in aiming to accomplish them, without cultivating their understandings, they are taken out of their sphere of duties, and made ridiculous and useless when the short-lived bloom of beauty is over,* I presume that *rational* men will excuse me for endeavoring to persuade them to become more masculine and respectable.

Indeed the word masculine is only a bugbear: there is little reason to fear that women will acquire too much courage or fortitude; for their apparent inferiority with respect to bodily strength, must render them, in some degree, dependent on men in the various relations of life; but why should it be increased by prejudices that give a sex to virtue, and confound simple truths with sensual reveries?

*A lively writer, I cannot recollect his name, asks what business women turned of forty have to do in the world?

Women are, in fact, so much degraded by mistaken notions of female excellence, that I do not mean to add a paradox when I assert, that this artificial weakness produces a propensity to tyrannize, and gives birth to cunning, the natural opponent of strength, which leads them to play off those contemptible infantine airs that undermine esteem even whilst they excite desire. Let men become more chaste and modest, and if women do not grow wiser in the same ratio, it will be clear that they have weaker understandings. It seems scarcely necessary to say, that I now speak of the sex in general. Many individuals have more sense than their male relatives; and, as nothing preponderates where there is a constant struggle for an equilibrium, without it has naturally more gravity, some women govern their husbands without degrading themselves, because intellect will always govern.

Suggestions for Discussion

1. Why does the author urge women to reject their conventional image of weakness?
2. How does she relate diction and style to the cause of women's rights? The author acknowledges that her feelings are "energetic." How are you made aware of the strength of her conviction? Why is *fascinating* italicized?
3. How does her own use of language affect her purpose and tone?
4. With what details does she convey her view of marriage? How would you characterize her attitude toward members of her own sex?
5. What evidence is there in this brief excerpt that the author is detached from her subject? Deeply involved?
6. According to Wollstonecraft, how does the education of women both reflect and foster the concept of their frivolity and weakness? What does she see as its effect on the family?
7. What causal relationship is established in the last paragraph?
8. How does the concept of self function in the author's argument?
9. What rhetorical devices are used to persuade the reader?

Suggestions for Writing

1. Imagine a dialogue between Mary Wollstonecraft and D. H. Lawrence, whose essay follows. Focus on points of agreement and disagreement.
2. "The first object of laudable ambition is to obtain a character as a human being, regardless of the distinction of sex." Discuss this statement in the light of your reading on the search for self.
3. Defend or refute the comment that the word *masculine,* as applied to women, is "only a bugbear."

D. H. LAWRENCE

Give Her a Pattern

D. H. Lawrence (1885–1930) was a schoolteacher before he turned to writing and became one of the great English novelists of the twentieth century. His best-known novels, which focus on relationships between men and women, include *Sons and Lovers* (1913), *Women in Love* (1920), and *Lady Chatterley's Lover* (1928). He also wrote short stories, essays, poetry, and literary criticism. In "Give Her a Pattern," Lawrence castigates men for not accepting women as real human beings of the feminine sex.

The real trouble about women is that they must always go on trying to adapt themselves to men's theories of women, as they always have done. When a woman is thoroughly herself, she is being what her type of man wants her to be. When a woman is hysterical it's because she doesn't quite know what to be, which pattern to follow, which man's picture of woman to live up to.

For, of course, just as there are many men in the world, there are many masculine theories of what women should be. But men run to type, and it is the type, not the individual, that produces the theory, or "ideal" of woman. Those very grasping gentry, the Romans, produced a theory or ideal of the matron, which fitted in very nicely with the Roman property lust. "Caesar's wife should be above suspicion."—So Caesar's wife kindly proceeded to be above it, no matter how far below it the Caesar fell. Later gentlemen like Nero produced the "fast" theory of woman, and later ladies were fast enough for everybody. Dante arrived with a chaste and untouched Beatrice, and chaste and untouched Beatrices began to march self-importantly through the centuries. The Renaissances discovered the learned woman, and learned women buzzed mildly into verse and prose. Dickens invented the child-wife, so child-wives have swarmed ever since. He also fished out his version of the chaste Beatrice, a chaste but marriageable Agnes. George Eliot imitated this pattern, and it became confirmed. The noble woman, the pure spouse, the devoted mother took the field, and was simply worked to death. Our own poor mothers were this sort. So we younger men, having been a bit frightened of our noble mothers, tended to revert to the child-wife. We weren't very inventive. Only the child-wife must be a boyish little thing—that was the new touch we added. Because young men are definitely frightened of the real female. She's too risky a quantity. She is too untidy, like David's Dora. No, let her be a boyish little thing, it's safer. So a boyish little thing she is.

There are, of course, other types. Capable men produce the capable woman ideal. Doctors produce the capable nurse. Business men produce the capable secretary. And so you get all sorts. You can produce the masculine sense of honor (whatever that highly mysterious quantity may be) in women, if you want to.

There is, also, the eternal secret ideal of men—the prostitute. Lots of women live up to this idea: just because men want them to.

And so, poor woman, destiny makes away with her. It isn't that she hasn't got a mind—she has. She's got everything that man has. The only difference is that she asks for a pattern. Give me a pattern to follow! That will always be woman's cry. Unless of course she has already chosen her pattern quite young, then she will declare she is herself absolutely, and no man's idea of women has any influence over her.

Now the real tragedy is not that women ask and must ask for a pattern of womanhood. The tragedy is not, even, that men give them such abominable patterns, child-wives, little-boy-baby-face girls, perfect secretaries, noble spouses, self-sacrificing mothers, pure women who bring forth children in virgin coldness, prostitutes who just make themselves low, to please the men; all the atrocious patterns of womanhood that men have supplied to woman; patterns all perverted from any real natural fullness of a human being. Man is willing to accept woman as an equal, as man in skirts, as an angel, a devil, a baby-face, a machine, an instrument, a bosom, a womb, a pair of legs, a servant, an encyclopaedia, an ideal, or an obscenity; the one thing he won't accept her as, is a human being, a real human being of the feminine sex.

And, of course, women love living up to strange patterns, weird patterns—the more uncanny the better. What could be more uncanny than the present pattern of the Eton-boy girl with flower-like artificial complexion? It is just weird. And for its very weirdness women like living up to it. What can be more gruesome than the little-boy-baby-face pattern? Yet the girls take it on with avidity.

But even that isn't the real root of the tragedy. The absurdity, and often, as in the Dante–Beatrice business, the inhuman nastiness of the pattern—for Beatrice had to go on being chaste and untouched all her life, according to Dante's pattern, while Dante had a cozy wife and kids at home—even that isn't the worst of it. The worst of it is, as soon as a woman has really lived up to the man's pattern, the man dislikes her for it. There is intense secret dislike for the Eton-young-man girl, among the boys, now that she is actually produced. Of course, she's very nice to show in public, absolutely the thing. But the very young men who have brought about her production detest her in private and in their private hearts are appalled by her.

When it comes to marrying, the pattern goes all to pieces. The boy marries the Eton-boy girl, and instantly he hates the *type.* Instantly his mind begins to play hysterically with all the other types, noble Agneses, chaste Beatrices, clinging Doras, and lurid *filles de joie.* He is in a wild welter of confusion. Whatever pattern the poor woman tries to live up to, he'll want another. And that's the condition of modern marriage.

Modern woman isn't really a fool. But modern man is. That seems to me the only plain way of putting it. The modern man is a fool, and the modern young man a prize fool. He makes a greater mess of his women than men have ever made. Because he absolutely doesn't know *what* he wants her to be. We shall see the changes in the woman-pattern follow one another fast and furious now, because the young men hysterically don't know what they want. Two years hence women may be in crinolines—there was a pattern for you!—or a bead flap, like naked negresses in mid-Africa—or they may be wearing brass armor, or the uniform of the Horse Guards. They may be anything. Because the young men are off their heads, and don't know what they want.

The women aren't fools, but they *must* live up to some pattern or other. They *know* the men are fools. They don't really respect the pattern. Yet a pattern they must have, or they can't exist.

Women are not fools. They have their own logic, even if it's not the masculine sort. Women have the logic of emotion, men have the logic of reason. The two are complementary and mostly in opposition. But the woman's logic of emotion is no less real and inexorable than the man's logic of reason. It only works differently.

And the woman never really loses it. She may spend years living up to a masculine pattern. But in the end, the strange and terrible logic of emotion will work out the smashing of that pattern, if it has not been emotionally satisfactory. This is the partial explanation of the astonishing changes in women. For years they go on being chaste Beatrices or child-wives. Then on a sudden—bash! The chaste Beatrice becomes something quite different, the child-wife becomes a roaring lioness! The pattern didn't suffice, emotionally.

Whereas men are fools. They are based on a logic of reason, or are supposed to be. And then they go and behave, especially with regard to women, in a more-than-feminine unreasonableness. They spend years training up the little-boy-baby-face type, till they've got her perfect. Then the moment they marry her, they want something else. Oh, beware, young women, of the young men who adore you! The moment they've got you they'll want something utterly different. The moment they marry the little-boy-baby-face, instantly they begin to pine for the noble Agnes, pure and majestic, or the infinite mother with deep bosom of consolation, or the perfect business woman, or the lurid prostitute on black silk sheets; or, most idiotic of all, a combination of all the lot of them at once. And that is the logic of reason! When it comes to women, modern men are idiots. They don't know what they want, and so they never want, permanently, what they get. They want a cream cake that is at the same time ham and eggs and at the same time porridge. They are fools. If only women weren't bound by fate to play up to them!

For the fact of life is that women *must* play up to man's pattern. And she only gives her best to a man when he gives her a satisfactory pattern to play up to. But today, with a stock of ready-made, worn-out idiotic patterns to live up to, what can women give to men but the trashy side of their emotions? What could a woman possibly give to a man who wanted her to be a boy-baby-face? What could she possibly give him but the dribblings of an idiot?—And, because women aren't fools, and aren't fooled even for very long at a time, she gives him some nasty cruel digs with her claws, and makes him cry for mother dear!—abruptly changing his pattern.

Bah! men are fools. If they want anything from women, let them give women a decent, satisfying idea of womanhood—not these trick patterns of washed-out idiots.

Suggestions for Discussion

1. Consider the title "Give Her a Pattern" in the light of Lawrence's attitude toward women. As he sketches some of the patterns imposed on women by men through the ages, whom does he regard as villain? Is there any evidence that he regards both men and women as victims of their culture?
2. What details provide the basis for the statement that the one thing man "won't accept her as, is a human being, a real human being of the feminine sex"?
3. Observe the repetition of the charge that modern men are fools. What does Lawrence mean by the statement that women are bound by fate to play up to men? How does he suggest that women are not as great "fools" as men?
4. What is the basis for his fatalistic attitude toward the possibility of real change in relationships between men and women?
5. What relationship does he make between art and nature?
6. How does he lead up to a definition of woman's tragedy?
7. How are comparison and contrast employed to develop his thesis?
8. How do structure, diction, exclamatory sentences, and metaphor contribute to tone and purpose?
9. What rhetorical devices are used to persuade the reader?

Suggestions for Writing

1. Write on modern female stereotypes and the mass media.
2. "Women love living up to strange patterns." What are some of these patterns today?
3. "When it comes to marrying, the pattern goes all to pieces." Can you illustrate?
4. Discuss and illustrate the "terrible logic of emotion" from your own experience.

VIRGINIA WOOLF

The Angel in the House

Virginia Woolf (1882–1941) was an English novelist and critic known for her experimentation with the form of the novel. Her works include *The Voyage Out* (1915), *Night and Day* (1919), *Jacob's Room* (1922), *Mrs. Dalloway* (1925), *To the Lighthouse* (1927), *Orlando: A Biography* (1928), *The Waves* (1931), *The Years* (1937), *Between the Acts* (1941), and several collections of essays. With her husband, Leonard Woolf, she founded the Hogarth Press. Although Woolf was able to overcome certain obstacles to honest writing, she states that women still have "many ghosts to fight, many prejudices to overcome."

When your secretary invited me to come here, she told me that your Society is concerned with the employment of women and she suggested that I might tell you something about my own professional experiences. It is true I am a woman; it is true I am employed; but what professional experiences have I had? It is difficult to say. My profession is literature; and in that profession there are fewer experiences for women than in any other, with the exception of the stage—fewer, I mean, that are peculiar to women. For the road was cut many years ago—by Fanny Burney, by Aphra Behn, by Harriet Martineau, by Jane Austen, by George Eliot—many famous women, and many more unknown and forgotten, have been before me, making the path smooth, and regulating my steps. Thus, when I came to write, there were very few material obstacles in my way. Writing was a reputable and harmless occupation. The family peace was not broken by the scratching of a pen. No demand was made upon the family purse. For ten and sixpence one can buy paper enough to write all the plays of Shakespeare—if one has a mind that way. Pianos and models, Paris, Vienna, and Berlin, masters and mistresses, are not needed by a writer. The cheapness of writing paper is, of course, the reason why women have succeeded as writers before they have succeeded in the other professions.

But to tell you my story—it is a simple one. You have only got to figure to yourselves a girl in a bedroom with a pen in her hand. She had only to move that pen from left to right—from ten o'clock to one. Then it occurred to her to do what is simple and cheap enough after all—to slip a few of those pages into an envelope, fix a penny stamp in the corner, and drop the envelope into the red box at the corner. It was thus that I became a journalist; and my effort was rewarded on the first day of the following month—a very glorious day it was for me—by a letter from an editor containing a cheque for one pound ten shillings and sixpence. But to show you how little I deserve to be called a professional woman, how little I know of the struggles and difficulties of such lives, I have to admit that instead of spending that sum upon bread and butter, rent, shoes and stockings, or butcher's bills, I went out and bought a cat—a beautiful cat, a Persian cat, which very soon involved me in bitter disputes with my neighbours.

What could be easier than to write articles and to buy Persian cats with the profits? But wait a moment. Articles have to be about something. Mine, I seem to remember, was about a novel by a famous man. And while I was writing this review, I discovered that if I were going to review books I should need to do battle with a certain phantom. And the phantom was a woman, and when I came to know her better I called her after the heroine of a famous poem. The Angel in the House. It was she who used to come between me and my paper when I was writing reviews. It was she who bothered me and wasted my time and so tormented me that at last I killed her. You who come of a younger and happier generation may not have heard of her—you may not know what I mean by the Angel in the House. I will describe her as shortly as I can. She was intensely sympathetic. She was immensely charming. She was utterly unselfish. She excelled in the difficult arts of family life. She sacrificed herself daily. If there was chicken, she took the leg; if there was a draught she sat in it—in short she was so constituted that she never had a mind or a wish of her own, but preferred to sympathize always with the minds and wishes of others. Above all—I need not say it—she was pure. Her purity was supposed to be her chief beauty—her blushes, her great grace. In those days—the last of Queen Victoria—every house had its Angel. And when I came to write I encountered her with the very first words. The shadow of her wings fell on my page; I heard the rustling of her skirts in the room. Directly, that is to say, I took my pen in hand to review that novel by a famous man, she slipped behind me and whispered: "My dear, you are a young woman. You are writing about a book that has been written by a man. Be sympathetic; be tender; flatter; deceive; use all the arts and wiles of our sex. Never let anybody guess that you have a mind of your own. Above all, be pure." And she made as if to guide my pen. I now record the one act for which I take some credit to myself, though the credit rightly belongs to some excellent ancestors of mine who left me a certain sum of money—shall we say five hundred pounds a year?—so that it was not necessary for me to depend solely on charm for my living. I turned upon her and caught her by the throat. I did my best to kill her. My excuse, if I were to be had up in a court of law, would be that I acted in self-defense. Had I not killed her she would have killed me. She would have plucked the heart out of my writing. For, as I found, directly I put pen to paper, you cannot review even a novel without having a mind of your own, without expressing what you think to be the truth about human relations, morality, sex. And all these questions, according to the Angel in the House, cannot be dealt with freely and openly by women; they must charm, they must conciliate, they must—to put it bluntly—tell lies if they are to succeed. Thus, whenever I felt the shadow of her wing or the radiance of her halo upon my page, I took up the inkpot and flung it at her. She died hard. Her fictitious nature was of great assistance to her. It is far harder to kill a phantom than a reality. She was always creeping back when I thought I had despatched her. Though I flatter myself that I killed her in the end, the struggle was severe; it took much time that had better have been spent upon learning Greek grammar; or in roaming the world in search of adventures. But it was a real experience; it was an experience that was bound to befall all women writers at that time. Killing the Angel in the House was part of the occupation of a woman writer.

But to continue my story. The Angel was dead; what then remained? You may say that what remained was a simple and common object—a young woman in a bedroom with an inkpot. In other words, now that she had rid herself of falsehood, that young woman had only to be herself. Ah, but what is "herself"? I mean, what is a woman? I assure you, I do not know. I do not believe that you know. I do not believe that anybody can know until she has expressed herself in all the arts and professions open to human skill. That indeed is one of the reasons why I have come here—out of respect for you, who are in process of showing us by your experiments what a woman is, who are in process of providing us, by your failures and successes, with that extremely important piece of information.

But to continue the story of my professional experiences. I made one pound ten and six by my first review; and I bought a Persian cat with the proceeds. Then I grew ambitious. A Persian cat is all very well, I said; but a Persian cat is not enough. I must have a motor car. And it was thus that I became a novelist—for it is a very strange thing that people will give you a motor car if you will tell them a story. It is a still stranger thing that there is nothing so delightful in the world as telling stories. It is far pleasanter than writing reviews of famous novels. And yet, if I am to obey your secretary and tell you my professional experiences as a novelist, I must tell you about a very strange experience that befell me as a novelist. And to understand it you must try first to imagine a novelist's state of mind. I hope I am not giving away professional secrets if I say that a novelist's chief desire is to be as unconscious as possible. He has to induce in himself a state of perpetual lethargy. He wants life to proceed with the utmost quiet and regularity. He wants to see the same faces, to read the same books, to do the same things day after day, month after month, while he is writing, so that nothing may break the illusion in which he is living—so that nothing may disturb or disquiet the mysterious nosings about, feelings round, darts, dashes and sudden discoveries of that very shy and illusive spirit, the imagination. I suspect that this state is the same both for men and women. Be that as it may, I want you to imagine me writing a novel in a state of trance. I want you to figure to yourselves a girl sitting with a pen in her hand, which for minutes, and indeed for hours, she never dips into the inkpot. The image that comes to my mind when I think of this girl is the image of a fisherman lying sunk in dreams on the verge of a deep lake with a rod held out over the water. She was letting her imagination sweep unchecked round every rock and cranny of the world that lies submerged in the depths of our unconscious being. Now came the experience, the experience that I believe to be far commoner with women writers than with men. The line raced through the girl's fingers. Her imagination had rushed away. It had sought the pools, the depths, the dark places where the largest fish slumber. And then there was a smash. There was an explosion. There was foam and confusion. The imagination had dashed itself against something hard. The girl was roused from her dream. She was indeed in a state of the most acute and difficult distress. To speak without figure she had thought of something, something about the body, about the passions which it was unfitting for her as a woman to say. Men, her reason told her, would be shocked. The consciousness of what men will say of a woman who speaks the truth about her passions had roused her from her artist's state of unconsciousness. She could write no more. The trance was over. Her imagination could work no longer. This I believe to be a very common experience with women writers—they are impeded by the extreme conventionality of the other sex. For though men sensibly allow themselves great freedom in these respects, I doubt that they realize or can control the extreme severity with which they condemn such freedom in women.

These then were two very genuine experiences of my own. These were two of the adventures of my professional life. The first—killing the Angel in the House—I think I solved. She died. But the second, telling the truth about my own experiences as a body, I do not think I solved. I doubt that any woman has solved it yet. The obstacles against her are still immensely powerful—and yet they are very difficult to define. Outwardly, what is simpler than to write books? Outwardly, what obstacles are there for a woman rather than for a man? Inwardly, I think, the case is very different; she has still many ghosts to fight, many prejudices to overcome. Indeed it will be a long time still, I think, before a woman can sit down to write a book without finding a phantom to be slain, a rock to be dashed against. And if this is so in literature, the freest of all professions for women, how is it in the new professions which you are now for the first time entering?

Those are the questions that I should like, had I time, to ask you. And indeed, if I have laid stress upon these professional experiences of mine, it is because I believe that they are, though in different forms, yours also. Even when the path is nominally open—when there is nothing to prevent a woman from being a doctor, a lawyer, a civil servant—there are many phantoms and obstacles, as I believe, looming in her way. To discuss and define them is I think of great value and importance; for thus only can the labor be shared, the difficulties be solved. But besides this, it is necessary also to discuss the ends and the aims for which we are fighting, for which we are doing battle with these formidable obstacles. Those aims cannot be taken for granted; they must be perpetually questioned and examined. The whole position, as I see it—here in this hall surrounded by women practising for the first time in history I know not how many different professions—is one of extraordinary interest and importance. You have won rooms of your own in the house hitherto exclusively owned by men. You are able, though not without great labor and effort, to pay the rent. You are earning your five hundred pounds a year. But this freedom is only a beginning; the room is your own, but it is still bare. It has to be furnished; it has to be decorated; it has to be shared. How are you going to furnish it, how are you going to decorate it? With whom are you going to share it, and upon what terms? These, I think, are questions of the utmost importance and interest. For the first time in history you are able to ask them; for the first time you are able to decide for yourselves what the answers should be. Willingly would I stay and discuss those questions and answers—but not tonight. My time is up; and I must cease.

Suggestions for Discussion

1. What are the characteristics of this phantom, the Angel in the House? Do they persist today?
2. Why does the author say she had to kill the Angel?
3. What remaining obstacles to truth did she find? In what ways may women still encounter these obstacles?

4. What are the implications in the concluding paragraph concerning relationships with men?
5. "Ah, but what is 'herself'? I mean, what is a woman?" Discuss these rhetorical questions in relation to purpose and tone.
6. What points of agreement or disagreement might Woolf have with Lawrence?
7. What rhetorical devices are employed to persuade the reader?

Suggestions for Writing

1. Describe an Angel in the House you know.
2. Does this phantom of the Angel still haunt contemporary drama, movies, fiction, advertising?
3. Apply one or more of Woolf's generalizations to a woman poet or writer of fiction.

GERMAINE GREER

The Stereotype

Germaine Greer (b. 1939) is an Australian-born writer and educator, best known as a standard bearer of the women's liberation movement and as the author of the best-selling *The Female Eunuch* (1971), from which this selection is taken, of *Sex and Destiny: The Politics of Human Fertility* (1984), and of *The Change: Women, Aging, and the Menopause* (1993). The stereotype—the Eternal Feminine—sought by women as well as by men, reduces a woman to a cipher and castrates her.

In that mysterious dimension where the body meets the soul the stereotype is born and has her being. She is more body than soul, more soul than mind. To her belongs all that is beautiful, even the very word beauty itself. All that exists, exists to beautify her. The sun shines only to burnish her skin and gild her hair; the wind blows only to whip up the color in her cheeks; the sea strives to bathe her; flowers die gladly so that her skin may luxuriate in their essence. She is the crown of creation, the masterpiece. The depths of the sea are ransacked for pearl and coral to deck her; the bowels of the earth are laid open that she might wear gold, sapphires, diamonds, and rubies. Baby seals are battered with staves, unborn lambs ripped from their mothers' wombs, millions of moles, muskrats, squirrels, minks, ermines, foxes, beavers, chinchillas, ocelots, lynxes, and other small and lovely creatures die untimely deaths that she might have furs. Egrets, ostriches, and peacocks, butterflies and beetles yield her their plumage. Men risk their lives hunting leopards for her coats, and crocodiles for her handbags and shoes. Millions of silkworms offer her their yellow labors; even the seamstresses roll seams and whip lace by hand, so that she might be clad in the best that money can buy.

The men of our civilization have stripped themselves of the fineries of the earth so that they might work more freely to plunder the universe for treasures to deck my lady in. New raw materials, new processes, new machines are all brought into her service. My lady must therefore be the chief spender as well as the chief symbol of spending ability and monetary success. While her mate toils in his factory, she totters about the smartest streets and plushiest hotels with his fortune upon her back and bosom, fingers, and wrists, continuing that essential expenditure in his house which is her frame and her setting, enjoying that silken idleness which is the necessary condition of maintaining her mate's prestige and her qualification to demonstrate it. Once upon a time only the aristocratic lady could lay claim to the title of crown of creation: only her hands were white enough, her feet tiny enough, her waist narrow enough, her hair long and golden enough; but every well-to-do burgher's wife set herself up to ape my lady and to follow fashion, until my lady was forced to set herself out like a gilded doll overlaid with monstrous rubies and pearls like pigeon's eggs. Nowadays the Queen of England still considers it part of her royal female role to sport as much of the family jewelry as she can manage at any one time on all public occasions, although the male monarchs have escaped such showcase duty, which develops exclusively upon their wives.

At the same time as woman was becoming the showcase for wealth and caste, while men were slipping into relative anonymity and "handsome is

> *Taught from infancy that beauty is woman's scepter, the mind shapes itself to the body, and roaming round its gilt cage, only seeks to adorn its prison.*
>
> —MARY WOLLSTONECRAFT, *A Vindication of the Rights of Woman,* 1792.

as handsome does," she was emerging as the central emblem of western art. For the Greeks the male and female body had beauty of a human, not necessarily a sexual, kind; indeed they may have marginally favored the young male form as the most powerful and perfectly proportioned. Likewise the Romans showed no bias towards the depiction of femininity in their predominantly monumental art. In the Renaissance the female form began to predominate, not only as the mother in the predominant emblem of *madonna con bambino*, but as an aesthetic study in herself. At first naked female forms took their chances in crowd scenes or diptychs of Adam and Eve, but gradually Venus claims ascendancy, Mary Magdalene ceases to be wizened and emaciated, and becomes nubile and ecstatic, portraits of anonymous young women, chosen only for their prettiness, begin to appear, are gradually disrobed, and renamed Flora or Primavera. Painters begin to paint their own wives and mistresses and royal consorts as voluptuous beauties, divesting them of their clothes if desirable, but not of their jewelry. Susanna keeps her bracelets on in the bath, and Hélène Fourment keeps ahold of her fur as well!

What happened to women in painting happened to her in poetry as well. Her beauty was celebrated in terms of the riches which clustered around her: her hair was gold wires, her brow ivory, her lips ruby, her teeth gates of pearl, her breasts alabaster veined with lapis lazuli, her eyes as black as jet. The fragility of her loveliness was emphasized by the inevitable comparisons with the rose, and she was urged to employ her beauty in love-making before it withered on the stem. She was for consumption; other sorts of imagery spoke of her in terms of cherries and cream, lips as sweet as honey and skin white as milk, breasts like cream uncurdled, hard as apples. Some celebrations yearned over her finery as well, her lawn more transparent than morning mist, her lace as delicate as gossamer, the baubles that she toyed with and the favors that she gave. Even now we find the thriller hero describing his classy dames' elegant suits, cheeky hats, well-chosen accessories and footwear; the imagery no longer dwells on jewels and flowers but the consumer emphasis is the same. The mousy secretary blossoms into the feminine stereotype when she reddens her lips, lets down her hair, and puts on something frilly.

Nowadays women are not expected, unless they are Paola di Liegi or Jackie Onassis, and then only on gala occasions, to appear with a king's ransom deployed upon their bodies, but they are required to look expensive, fashionable, well-groomed, and not to be seen in the same dress twice. If the duty of the few may have become less onerous, it has also become the duty of the many. The stereotype marshals an army of servants. She is supplied with cosmetics, underwear, foundation garments, stockings, wigs, postiches, and hairdressing as well as her outer garments, her jewels, and furs. The effect is to be built up layer by layer, and it is expensive. Splendor has given way to fit, line, and cut. The spirit of competition must be kept up, as more and more women struggle toward the top drawer, so that the fashion industry can rely upon an expanding market. Poorer women fake it, ape it, pick up on the fashions a season too late, use crude effects, mistaking the line, the sheen, the gloss of the high-class article for a garish simulacrum. The business is so complex that it must be handled by an expert. The paragons of the stereotype must be dressed, coifed, and painted by the experts and the style-setters, although they may be encouraged to give heart to the housewives studying their lives in pulp magazines by claiming a lifelong fidelity to their own hair and soap and water. The boast is more usually discouraging than otherwise, unfortunately.

As long as she is young and personable, every woman may cherish the dream that she may leap up the social ladder and dim the sheen of luxury by sheer natural loveliness; the few examples of such a feat are kept before the eye of the public. Fired with hope, optimism, and ambition, young women study the latest forms of the stereotype, set out in *Vogue, Nova, Queen,* and other glossies, where the mannequins stare from among the advertisements for fabulous real estate, furs, and jewels. Nowadays the uniformity of the year's fashions is severely affected by the emergence of the pert female designers who direct their appeal to the working girl, emphasizing variety, comfort, and simple, striking effects. There is no longer a single face of the year: even Twiggy has had to withdraw into marketing and rationed personal appearances, while the Shrimp works mostly in New York. Nevertheless the stereotype is still supreme. She has simply allowed herself a little more variation.

The stereotype is the Eternal Feminine. She is the Sexual Object sought by all men, and by all women. She is of neither sex, for she has herself no sex at all. Her value is solely attested by the demand she excites in others. All she must contribute is her existence. She need achieve nothing, for she is the reward of achievement. She need never give positive evidence of her moral character because virtue is assumed from her loveliness, and her passivity. If any man who has no right to her be found with her she will not be punished, for she is morally neuter. The matter is solely one of male rivalry. Innocently she may drive men to madness and war. The more trouble she can cause, the more her stocks go up, for possession of her means more the more demand she excites. Nobody wants a girl whose beauty is imperceptible to all but him; and so men welcome the stereotype because it directs their taste into the most commonly recognized areas of value, although they may protest because some aspects of it do not tally with their fetishes. There is scope in the stereotype's variety for most fetishes. The leg man may follow miniskirts, the tit man can encourage see-through blouses and plunging necklines, although the man who likes fat women may feel constrained to enjoy them in secret. There are stringent limits to the variations

> *The myth of the strong black woman is the other side of the coin of the myth of the beautiful dumb blonde. The white man turned the white woman into a weak-minded, weak-bodied, delicate freak, a sex pot, and placed her on a pedestal; he turned the black woman into a strong self-reliant Amazon and deposited her in his kitchen.... The white man turned himself into the Omnipotent Administrator and established himself in the Front Office.*
>
> —ELDRIDGE CLEAVER, "The Allegory of the Black Eunuchs," *Soul on Ice,* 1968.

on the stereotype, for nothing must interfere with her function as sex object. She may wear leather, as long as she cannot actually handle a motorbike: she may wear rubber, but it ought not to indicate that she is an expert diver or waterskier. If she wears athletic clothes the purpose is to underline her unathleticism. She may sit astride a horse, looking soft and curvy, but she must not crouch over its neck with her rump in the air.

Because she is the emblem of spending ability and the chief spender, she is also the most effective seller of this world's goods. Every survey ever held has shown that the image of an attractive woman is the most effective advertising gimmick. She may sit astride the mudguard of a new car, or step into it ablaze with jewels; she may lie at a man's feet stroking his new socks; she may hold the petrol pump in a challenging pose, or dance through woodland glades in slow motion in all the glory of a new shampoo; whatever she does her image sells. The gynolatry of our civilization is written large upon its face, upon hoardings, cinema screens, television, newspapers, magazines, tins, packets, cartons, bottles, all consecrated to the reigning deity, the female fetish. Her dominion must not be thought to entail the rule of women, for she is not a woman. Her glossy lips and mat complexion, her unfocused eyes and flawless fingers, her extraordinary hair all floating and shining, curling, and gleaming, reveal the inhuman triumph of cosmetics, lighting, focusing, and printing, cropping and composition. She sleeps unruffled, her lips red and juicy and closed, her eyes as crisp and black as if new painted, and her false lashes immaculately curled. Even when she washes her face with a new and creamier toilet soap her expression is as tranquil and vacant and her paint as flawless as ever. If ever she should appear tousled and troubled, her features are miraculously smoothed to their proper veneer by a new washing powder or a bouillon cube. For she is a doll: weeping, pouting, or smiling, running or reclining, she is a doll. She is an idol, formed of the concatenation of lines and masses, signifying the lineaments of satisfied impotence.

Her essential quality is castratedness. She absolutely must be young, her body hairless, her flesh buoyant, and *she must not have a sexual organ.* No musculature must distort the smoothness of the lines of her body, although she may be painfully slender or warmly cuddly. Her expression must betray no hint of humor, curiosity, or intelligence, although it may signify hauteur to an extent that is actually absurd, or smoldering lust, very feebly signified by drooping eyes and a sullen mouth (for the stereotype's lust equals irrational submission), or, most commonly, vivacity and idiot happiness. Seeing that the world despoils itself for this creature's benefit, she must be happy; the entire structure would topple if she were not. So the image of woman appears plastered on every surface imaginable, smiling interminably. An apple pie evokes a glance of tender beatitude, a washing machine causes hilarity, a cheap box of chocolates brings forth meltingly joyous gratitude, a Coke is the cause of a rictus of unutterable brilliance, even a new stick-on bandage is saluted by a smirk of satisfaction. A real woman licks her lips and opens her mouth and flashes her teeth when photographers appear: *she* must arrive at the premiere of her husband's film in a paroxysm of delight, or his success might be murmured about. The occupational hazard of being a Playboy Bunny is the aching facial muscles brought on by the obligatory smiles.

So what is the beef? Maybe I couldn't make it. Maybe I don't have a pretty smile, good teeth, nice tits, long legs, a cheeky ass, a sexy voice. Maybe I don't know how to handle men and increase my market value, so that the rewards due to the feminine will accrue to me. Then again, maybe I'm sick of the masquerade. I'm sick of pretending eternal youth. I'm sick of belying my own intelligence, my own will, my own sex. I'm sick of peering at the world through false eyelashes, so everything I see is mixed with a shadow of bought hairs; I'm sick of weighting my head with a dead mane, unable to move my neck freely, terrified of rain, of wind, of dancing too vigorously in case I sweat into my lacquered curls. I'm sick of the Powder Room. I'm sick of pretending that some fatuous male's self-important

> *She was created to be the toy of man, his rattle, and it must jingle in his ears whenever, dismissing reason, he chooses to be amused.*
>
> —MARY WOLLSTONECRAFT, *A Vindication of the Rights of Woman,* 1792.

> *Discretion is the better part of Valerie*
> *though all of her is nice*
> *lips as warm as strawberries*
> *eyes as cold as ice*
> *the very best of everything*
> *only will suffice*
> *not for her potatoes*
> *and puddings made of rice*
>
> —Roger McGough, *Discretion.*

pronouncements are the objects of my undivided attention, I'm sick of going to films and plays when someone else wants to, and sick of having no opinions of my own about either. I'm sick of being a transvestite. I refuse to be a female impersonator. I am a woman, not a castrate.

April Ashley was born male. All the information supplied by genes, chromosomes, internal and external sexual organs added up to the same thing. April was a man. But he longed to be a woman. He longed for the stereotype, not to embrace, but to be. He wanted soft fabrics, jewels, furs, makeup, the love and protection of men. So he was impotent. He couldn't fancy women at all, although he did not particularly welcome homosexual addresses. He did not think of himself as a pervert, or even as a transvestite, but as a woman cruelly transmogrified into manhood. He tried to die, became a female impersonator, but eventually found a doctor in Casablanca who came up with a more acceptable alternative. He was to be castrated, and his penis used as the lining of a surgically constructed cleft, which would be a vagina. He would be infertile, but that has never affected the attribution of femininity. April returned to England, resplendent. Massive hormone treatment had eradicated his beard, and formed tiny breasts: he had grown his hair and bought feminine clothes during the time he had worked as an impersonator. He became a model, and began to illustrate the feminine stereotype as he was perfectly qualified to do, for he was elegant, voluptuous, beautifully groomed, and in love with his own image. On an ill-fated day he married the heir to a peerage, the Hon. Arthur Corbett, acting out the highest achievement of the feminine dream, and went to live with him in a villa in Marbella. The marriage was never consummated. April's incompetence as a woman is what we must expect from a castrate, but it is not so very different after all from the impotence of feminine women, who submit to sex without desire, with only the infantile pleasure of cuddling and affection, which is their favorite reward. As long as the feminine stereotype remains the definition of the female sex, April

> *To what end is the laying out of the embroidered Hair, embared Breasts; vermilion Cheeks, alluring looks, Fashion gates, and artful Countenances, effeminate intangling and insnaring Gestures, their Curls and Purls of proclaiming Petulancies, boulstered and laid out with such example and authority in these our days, as with Allowance and beseeming Conveniency?*
>
> *Doth the world wax barren through decrease of Generations, and become, like the Earth, less fruitful heretofore? Doth the Blood lose his Heat or do the Sunbeams become waterish and less fervent, than formerly they have been, that men should be thus inflamed and persuaded on to lust?*
>
> —ALEX. NICCHOLES, *A Discourse of Marriage and Wiving,* 1615.

Ashley is a woman, regardless of the legal decision ensuing from her divorce. She is as much a casualty of the polarity of the sexes as we all are. Disgraced, unsexed April Ashley is our sister and our symbol.

Suggestions for Discussion

1. How does the author develop the concept that "beauty is woman's scepter"? How does the long series of examples in the first paragraph contribute to purpose and tone?
2. What does the author mean by the stereotype? How does she develop and support her extended definition?
3. In what context does the author invoke the first person? How does its intrusion affect purpose and tone?
4. What purpose is served by the introduction of April Ashley? Do the last two sentences constitute an appropriate summation of what has gone before? Explain.

Suggestion for Writing

Drawing on your own experience and observation, write an essay on stereotypes.

NOEL PERRIN

The Androgynous Man

Noel Perrin (b. 1927), a professor of English and, since 1991, a professor of environmental studies at Dartmouth College, is a frequent contributor to *The New Yorker* and other periodicals. He also practices farming in Vermont. Among his published works are *A Passport Secretly Green* (1961), *First Person Rural: Essays of a Sometime Farmer* (1980), *Third Person Rural: More Essays of a Sometime Farmer* (1981), *Last Person Rural* (1991), and *Solo: Life with an Electric Car* (1992). The writer cites a number of examples to support his view that the androgynous man has a range of choices denied the macho man.

The summer I was 16, I took a train from New York to Steamboat Springs, Colo., where I was going to be assistant horse wrangler at a camp. The trip took three days, and since I was much too shy to talk to strangers, I had quite a lot of time for reading. I read all of "Gone With the Wind." I read all the interesting articles in a couple of magazines I had, and then I went back and read all the dull stuff. I also took all the quizzes, a thing of which magazines were even fuller then than now.

The one that held my undivided attention was called "How Masculine/Feminine Are You?" It consisted of a large number of inkblots. The reader was supposed to decide which of four objects each blot most resembled. The choices might be a cloud, a steam engine, a caterpillar and a sofa.

When I finished the test, I was shocked to find that I was barely masculine at all. On a scale of 1 to 10, I was about 1.2. Me, the horse wrangler? (And not just wrangler, either. That summer, I had to skin a couple of horses that died—the camp owner wanted the hides.)

The results of that test were so terrifying to me that for the first time in my life I did a piece of original analysis. Having unlimited time on the train, I looked at the "masculine" answers over and over, trying to find what it was that distinguished real men from people like me—and eventually I discovered two very simple patterns. It was "masculine" to think the blots looked like man-made objects, and "feminine" to think they looked like natural objects. It was masculine to think they looked like things capable of causing harm, and feminine to think of innocent things.

Even at 16, I had the sense to see that the compilers of the test were using rather limited criteria—maleness and femaleness are both more complicated than *that*—and I breathed a huge sigh of relief. I wasn't necessarily a wimp, after all.

That the test did reveal something other than the superficiality of its makers I realized only many years later. What it revealed was that there is a large class of men and women both, to which I belong, who are essentially androgynous. That doesn't mean we're gay, or low in the appropriate hormones, or uncomfortable performing the jobs traditionally assigned our sexes. (A few years after that summer, I was leading troops in combat and, unfashionable as it now is to admit this, having a very good time. War is exciting. What a pity the 20th century went and spoiled it with high-tech weapons.)

What it does mean to be spiritually androgynous is a kind of freedom. Men who are all-male, or he-man, or 100 percent red-blooded Americans, have a little biological set that causes them to be attracted to physical power, and probably also to dominance. Maybe even to watching football. I don't say this to criticize them. Completely masculine men are quite often wonderful people: good husbands, good (though sometimes overwhelming) fathers, good members of society. Furthermore, they are often so unself-consciously at ease in the world that other men seek to imitate them. They just aren't as free as us androgynes. They pretty nearly have to be what they are; we have a range of choices open.

The sad part is that many of us never discover that. Men who are not 100 percent red-blooded Americans—say, those who are only 75 percent red-blooded—often fail to notice their freedom. They are too busy trying to copy the he-men ever to realize that men, like women, come in a wide variety of acceptable types. Why this frantic imitation? My answer is mere speculation, but not casual. I have speculated on this for a long time.

Partly they're just envious of the he-man's unconscious ease. Mostly they're terrified of finding that there may be something wrong with them deep down, some weakness at the heart. To avoid discovering that, they spend their lives acting out the role that the he-man naturally lives. Sad.

One thing that men owe to the women's movement is that this kind of failure is less common than it used to be. In releasing themselves from the single ideal of the dependent woman, women have more or less incidentally released a lot of men from the single ideal of the dominant male. The one mistake the feminists have made, I think, is in supposing that *all* men need this release, or that the world would be a better place if all men achieved it. It wouldn't. It would just be duller.

So far I have been pretty vague about just what the freedom of the androgynous man is. Obviously it varies with the case. In the case I know best, my own, I can be quite specific. It has freed me most as a parent. I am, among other things, a fairly good natural mother. I like the nurturing role. It makes me feel good to see a child eat—and it turns me to mush to see a 4-year-old holding a glass with both small hands, in order to drink. I even enjoyed sewing patches on the knees of my daughter Amy's Dr. Dentons when she was at the crawling stage. All that pleasure I would have lost if I had made myself stick to the notion of the paternal role that I started with.

Or take a smaller and rather ridiculous example. I feel free to kiss cats. Until recently it never occurred to me that I would want to, though my daughters have been doing it all their lives. But my elder daughter is now 22, and in London. Of course, I get to look after her cat while she is gone. He's a big, handsome farm cat named Petrushka, very unsentimental, though used from kittenhood to being kissed on the top of the head by Elizabeth. I've gotten very fond of him (he's the adventurous kind of cat who likes to climb hills with you), and one night I simply felt like kissing him on the top of the head, and did. Why did no one tell me sooner how silky cat fur is?

Then there's my relation to cars. I am completely unembarrassed by my inability to diagnose even minor problems in whatever object I happen to be driving, and don't have to make some insider's remark to mechanics to try to establish that I, too, am a "Man With His Machine."

The same ease extends to household maintenance. I do it, of course. Service people are expensive. But for the last decade my house has functioned better than it used to because I've had the aid of a volume called "Home Repairs Any Woman Can Do," which is pitched just right for people at my technical level. As a youth, I'd as soon have touched such a book as I would have become a transvestite. Even though common sense says there is really nothing sexual whatsoever about fixing sinks.

Or take public emotion. All my life I have easily been moved by certain kinds of voices. The actress Siobhan McKenna's, to take a notable case. Give her an emotional scene in a play, and within 10 words my eyes are full of tears. In boyhood, my great dread was that someone might notice. I struggled manfully, you might say, to suppress this weakness. Now, of course, I don't see it as a weakness at all, but as a kind of fulfillment. I even suspect that the true he-men feel the same way, or one kind of them does, at least, and it's only the poor imitators who have to struggle to repress themselves.

Let me come back to the inkblots, with their assumption that masculine equates with machinery and science, and feminine with art and nature. I have no idea whether the right pronoun for God is He, She or It. But this I'm pretty sure of. If God could somehow be induced to take that test, God would not come out macho, and not feminismo, either, but right in the middle. Fellow androgynes, it's a nice thought.

Suggestions for Discussion

1. In what ways does the magazine test reflect society's stereotypes of masculine and feminine?
2. What is Perrin's definition of androgyny and why does he believe it to be liberating?
3. What is the writer's view of the strengths and limitations of the completely masculine man? Why are what he calls the "75 percent red-blooded" Americans sad to contemplate?
4. What elements of androgyny discussed by Carolyn Heilbrun does Perrin leave out?

Suggestions for Writing

1. Support or challenge the assumption that "masculine equates with machinery and science, and feminine with art and nature."
2. Drawing upon your own life or your observation of a friend, describe what might be called androgynous experiences.

BETTY FRIEDAN

The Quiet Movement of American Men

Betty Friedan (b. 1921) has been active as a feminist, recorder of the movement, and lecturer at universities and professional associations throughout the world. Her first major book, *The Feminist Mystique* (1963), was critical of women's roles in post–World War II America. Later she brought feminist concerns up to date in *The Second Stage* (1981), from which this selection was taken, and published *The Fountain of Age* (1993). Friedan believes that the women's movement has had a profound effect on men, and she recounts a number of problems, shifts in values, and possible solutions.

It is nothing like the women's movement, and probably never will be. Each man seems to be struggling with it quietly—at twenty-five or thirty-five, or before it is too late, at forty-five or fifty. It is a change not yet fully visible, not clearly identified or understood by the experts and rarely spoken about by men themselves. Nobody is marching. Most men are turned off by the "men's lib" groups, which try to copy women's. With men there is no explosion of anger, no enemy to rage against, no list of grievances or demands for benefits and opportunities clearly valuable and previously denied, as with women. And yet I believe that American men are at the edge of a momentous change in their very identity as men, going beyond the change catalyzed by the women's movement.

It is a deceptively quiet movement, a shifting in direction, a saying "no" to old patterns, a searching for new values, a struggling with basic questions that each man seems to be dealing with alone. He may be going through the same outward motions that have always defined men's lives—making it, or struggling to make it, in the corporate rat race, the office, the plant, college, the ball park; making it with women; getting married; having children. Or he may be deciding not to get married, or thinking in a new way about having children, or no longer really trying to make it in traditional terms. He is not issuing a public statement. He is just grappling with private questions: success, promotion, senior partner, vice-president, $65,000 a year—is that what he really wants out of life? Will he ever get it? What will it be worth? What kind of a man is he anyhow, asking questions like this? Other men are satisfied with their lives, aren't they? But what does he want out of life for himself? How does he fulfill himself as a man?

Asking these questions about himself, he doesn't feel so angry at women. He feels awkward, isolated, confused. Yet he senses that something is happening with men, something large and historic, and he wants to be part of it. He carries the baby in his backpack, shops at the supermarket on Saturday, bakes his own bread with a certain showing-off quality.

It's happened to some men because of the economy: layoffs from jobs that looked secure, as in the auto industry; company takeovers, budget cuts; a dead end suddenly in a career that he had put his all into for years. Or, after sweating it through to the Ph.D., no jobs in his field. Or making it to the top at forty or forty-five—and then having to figure out what to do next—fight off the younger men coming up, or join another company?

Some men just know they don't want to be like their fathers, or like those senior partners, who have heart attacks at fifty—but they don't know what other way there is to be.

It started for many men almost unwillingly, as a response to the women's movement. Women changing their own lives forced men or made it possible for men to change theirs. Some men seem to be making these moves quite independently of women. But they sense, we sense, it's related somehow. The rhetoric of sexual politics that characterized the first stage of the women's movement seemed to demand a hostile stance from the men. But that rhetoric and the response it elicited obscured the real reasons that these changes were threatening to some men, and also obscured the fact that many men supported, and felt a surprising relief about, the women's movement.

At first glance, all it looked like was endless arguments about his doing his share of the housework, the cooking, the cleaning, the dishes, taking out the garbage, scrubbing out the toilet bowl and mopping the kitchen floor without leaving streaks; or about his responsibility for taking care of the children, changing diapers, getting them to bed, into snowsuits, to the park, to the pediatrician. These disputes arose because it was no longer *automatic* that her job was to take care of the house and the kids and all the other details of life, and that his job was to support everyone. Now she was working to support them, too.

But that wasn't the entire issue. Even if she didn't have a job outside the home, she suddenly had to be treated as a person too, as he was. She had a right to her own life and interests. He could help with the kids and the house at night, or on weekends. (The arguments over the housework were worse when she didn't have a job.)

He felt wronged, injured. He had been working so hard to support her and the kids and now he was her "oppressor," a "male chauvinist pig," if he didn't scrub all the pots and pans to boot. "You make dinner," she said. "I'm going to my design class." He felt scared when she walked out like that. If she didn't need him for her identity, her status, her sense of importance, if she was going to get all that for herself, if she could support herself and have a life independent of him, wouldn't she stop loving him? Why would she stay with him? Wouldn't she just leave? So he was supposed to be the big male oppressor, right? How could he admit the big secret—that maybe he needed her more than she needed him? That he felt like a baby when he became afraid she would leave? That he suddenly didn't know what he felt, what he was *supposed* to feel—as a man?

I believe much of the hostility men express toward women comes from their very dependence on our love, from those needy feelings that men aren't supposed to have—just as the excesses of our attacks on our male "oppressors" stemmed from our dependence on men. That old, excessive dependence (which was supposed to be natural in women) made us feel we had to be more independent than any man in order to be able to move at all. Our explosion of rage and our attacks on men, however justified, often masked our own timidity and fear of risking ourselves in a complex, competitive world, in ways never required of us before.

And the more a man pretended to a dominant, cool, masculine superiority he didn't really feel—the more he was forced to carry the burden alone of supporting the whole family against the rough odds of that grim outside economic world—the more threatened and the more hostile he felt.

Sam, an aerospace engineer in Seattle, told me that the period when his wife "tried to be just a housewife" was the worst time in his marriage.

"It was not only her staying home and losing confidence in herself, and the resentment and hostility against me after she joined the consciousness-raising group. It was her loss of confidence in me. If you decide you're going to stay home and be taken care of and you have to depend for everything on this guy, you get afraid—*Can he do it?* It all depended on me, and I was in a constant panic, but I'd say, 'Don't worry.'

"Susie was tired of her job anyhow. It wasn't such a great job—neither is mine if you want to know—but she had an excuse, wanting to stay home with her kids. The pressure was on me, hanging by my fingernails, barely paying the bills each month. But it was crazy. Here I was, not knowing where the next check was coming from after the government contract ran out, suddenly supporting a wife and kids all by myself.

"It's better now that she's working and bringing some money in. But I don't just *help* with the kids now. She has to be at work before I do, so I give them breakfast and get them off to school. The nights she works late, I make dinner, help with the homework, and get everyone to bed. But I don't feel so panicky now—and she isn't attacking me any more."

Phil, a doctor in his thirties who started out to be a surgeon but who now has a small-town family practice in New Jersey, talks to me as he makes pickles, with his kids running around underfoot in the country kitchen that is next to his office.

"I was going to be a surgeon, supercool, in my gleaming white uniform," he says, "the man my mother wanted me to be but I knew I wasn't. So I married a nurse and she stayed home to raise our children, and she was supposed to fulfill herself through my career. It didn't work for either of us. I went through tortures before every operation. I couldn't sleep.

"Then Ellen started turning against me. I always said the children needed her at home, full-time mothering. Maybe because *I* was so scared inside. Maybe she didn't have the nerve to try to do her own thing professionally. All she seemed to want was revenge on me, as if she were locked into some kind of sexual battle against me, playing around, looking elsewhere for true love.

"She got into a women's consciousness-raising group, and I even joined a men's one. At home, I'd grovel, the male chauvinist pig repenting, not letting on how hurt, angry, offended I felt. The worst was when our little girl tried to be as tough as Mummy and went *yuk* at every word I said.

"When Ellen finally got up the nerve to do her own thing—she's a nurse-midwife now—it was a relief. The other stuff stopped. She could come back to being my wife. I'm coming out of this, redefining myself, no longer in terms of success or failure as a doctor (though I still am a doctor) and not as superior or inferior to her. It was a blow to my ego, but what a relief, to take off my surgical mask! I'm discovering my own value in the family.

"Now that I'm not so hurt and angry and afraid that she'll leave me, I can see that it's a hell of a fight for a woman to be seen as a person. I think she's been hiding from herself the fear of accomplishing anything on her own so she made me the villain. Well, I'm happy now to take on the kids while she practices her profession, though every time she goes out of town, I practically wet my pants. I tell my own patients now, the mothers, don't make the kids that dependent on you. That's what my mother did to me. I was so afraid of those messy, needy feelings I couldn't get away from, even as a surgeon. You know, it's as hard for me to feel like a person as it is for her. We couldn't either of us get that from each other."

The change is harder to discern among men because men have a harder time talking about their feelings than women do. They certainly don't talk about their feelings to other men. It's part of the masculine mystique—the definition of man by his "score," competing against other men—that he constantly keep his guard up. And after all, since men have the power and position in society that women are making all the fuss about, why should men want to change unless women make them do so? When men began talking to me about their own new questions (and some refused—which never happened with women—and some just couldn't seem to talk about their feelings, only about abstractions like the economy or the state of the nation), it reminded me of "the problem that has no name" as I heard it from the women I was interviewing for *The Feminine Mystique* twenty years ago, when, each one feeling she was alone, American women were poised unconsciously on the brink of the women's movement.

"Maybe men feel more need to pretend," says a Detroit sales engineer, temporarily laid off, struggling to take "equal responsibility" for the kids and the house, now that his wife has gone to work in a department store. "When I used to see a man on the street with his children on a weekday, I assumed he was unemployed, a loser. Now, it's so common—daddies with their children, at ease. Now, even if a man is unemployed, like I am right now, well, that job is not what makes me a man. I'm not just a breadwinner. I'm a person, I have feelings myself."

With all the attention on the women's movement these past fifteen years, it hasn't been noticed that many of the old bases for men's identity have become shaky. If being a man is defined, for example, as being dominant, superior, as *not-being-a-woman,* that definition becomes an illusion hard to maintain when most of the important work of society no longer requires brute muscular force. The Vietnam war probably was the beginning of the end of the hunter-caveman, gun-toting he-man mystique.

The signs that machismo was dying in the U.S. appeared about the same time as the women's movement emerged in the sixties. The long-haired young men, and their elders imitating them or clubbing them down from repressed envy, began saying they didn't have to be tight-lipped, crewcut or poker-faced like John Wayne to be a man. They didn't have to be all-powerful, superior to everyone in the world, and to napalm all the children in Vietnam and Cambodia and the green leaves off the trees, to prove they were men. They could be sensitive, tender, compassionate, they didn't have to have big muscles, when there were no bears to kill, they could admit they were afraid and they could even cry—and they were still men, their own men.

Books were written such as *The Greening of America,* and hippies played their guitars, chanting "Make love, not war." And the young men said they were not going to live their whole lives for the dollar like their fathers, about the same time as the young women said they were not going to spend their lives as housewife "service stations" like their mothers. How the adventurous good life could be lived on other terms wasn't quite clear. It didn't have to be, while the counterculture was sustained by the allowances from Daddy.

But all that supposedly stopped a while ago, with the end of the Vietnam war, inflation, recession, the job crunch and the energy crisis. Or did it? At the dawn of the eighties, the signs of a quiet, complex, continuing movement among men emerged not just as counterculture, but as shifting currents in the mainstream, converging on the women's movement for the second stage. The men I have been interviewing around the country these past months are not hippies playing games on those allowances from Daddy. They are members of the college classes in which everyone wanted to be a lawyer, a doctor, an MBA. They are the men who fought in Vietnam, or went to graduate school to stay out of the war, or they are assembly-line workers whose line has stopped.

Vietnam was somehow the watershed. If men stop defining themselves by going to war or getting power from jobs woman can't have, what is left? What does it mean to be a man, except not-being-a-woman—being physically superior, able to beat all the other men up? The fact is, when a man admits those "messy, needy feelings" that men as well as women have—and which that brutal, brittle machismo is supposed to hide, but only makes worse—he can't *play* the same kind of man any more.

Tony, who lives now on the Outer Banks of North Carolina, was a pilot in Vietnam when it started for him.

"I was a captain, coming up for major. I had all the medals, could have gone on for twenty years in the Air Force. Sitting up there over Nam, the commander, under heavy fire, the guys screaming into the mikes, the bombers and fighters moving in, me giving the orders, I was caught up in it, crazy-wild, excited. And then I woke up one day and found myself clicking my empty gun at civilians. I knew I had to get out. The next mission, sitting up there, it felt for real, and for the first time, I was frightened. It's so heavy, the medals, the games, and then suddenly realizing that you are dropping napalm on real people."

He "could fly any piece of machinery," so he took a job with an airline. "All I wanted was security," he says. "After one year I was furloughed because the company was having financial difficulties. There was no security. So I came back to this town where I grew up and took a job as a schoolteacher, working with seventh and eighth graders who were reading at the second-grade level. It was the 'reading lab,' the pits, the bottom, and a woman's job. It's the hardest job I've ever done, teaching those kids, and it gets the least respect. Flying a 323,000-pound Lockheed Starlifter can't compare." As a pilot, Tony made $34,000 a year; as a teacher, he makes $12,000.

"But maybe now," he says, "with the ladies moving in and picking up some of the financial slack—my wife works for a florist, and as a waitress, nights—a guy can say 'I'm not going to get much of anywhere, with the money anyhow—how much of it is really going to rub off on me? Why don't I do something really worthwhile from a human point of view?' Now with the ladies out earning, it frees a man from being strapped down to just one job for his whole life. After school, I take out my boat, which I built myself, and if I make some extra money fishing, fine. But there are more important things in life than the dollar bill."

In *Breaktime,* a controversial study of men "living without work in a nine-to-five world," Bernard Lefkowitz reports a 71 percent increase in the number of working-aged men who have left the labor force since 1968 and who are not looking for work. According to Lefkowitz, the "stop-and-go pattern of work" is becoming the predominant pattern, rather than the lifetime jobs and careers men used to pursue both for economic security and for their masculine identity. "In the depression of the 30s," says Lefkowitz, "men were anxious because they were not working. In the 70s, men became anxious because their work was not paying off in the over-all economic security they had expected."

"I thought seriously of killing myself," says a St. Louis man who was forced to resign at the age of fifty when the company he headed was taken over by a large conglomerate. "I saved up the arsenic pills I take for my heart condition. How could I live without that company to run, my office, my staff, six hundred employees, the wheeling and dealing? But then I realized how much of it I'd really hated: the constant worry, getting in at 6 A.M. to read the reports of six vice-presidents, fighting the union to keep wages down, and being hated, knuckling under to people I despised to get accounts. The only good thing was knowing I'd made it to president of a company when my father never got past store clerk. Now I want to work for myself, to live, enjoy the sunsets, and raise begonias. But my kids are gone now, and my wife started her career late, and all she wants is to get ahead in the agency."

It is not only, or even mainly, "losers" making such shifts in values and life style, if not actual jobs. In a *Playboy* survey in 1979, the men from the most oppressed backgrounds were the only group whose main concern was "getting ahead," making more money. The majority of the men polled, age eighteen to forty-nine, valued "personal growth," "self-fulfillment," "love," and "family life" more than making more money and "getting ahead."

But the hold of the old success drive, the competitiveness that always defined men before, hasn't disappeared overnight. It makes for uneasiness, even for men wanting to live by new values.

A young man in Chicago refuses an extra assignment, which would mean working nights and traveling on weekends, on top of his regular job. It doesn't matter that it will probably lead to a big promotion. "We're having another child," he tells his boss, "and I'm committed to sharing the responsibilities at home because my wife's going to law school at night. It hasn't and won't interfere with my job—you were more than satisfied with my last report. But I'm not taking on anything extra. My family is more important to me."

"That man isn't going to get far," his puzzled boss tells a colleague. "Too bad. He was the pick of the litter."

The colleague asks, "What if they all start acting like that? Where are we going to find the men to run the economy, for God's sake, if they all start putting their families first?"

There's a danger today for men and women who may try to get out of their own binds by reversing roles. Exchanging one obsolete model of a half-life for another, they may copy the worst aspects of the old feminine or masculine mystique instead of building from their own enduring, evolving strengths, and liberating their buried feelings or untried potential in the new experiences now open to them until, sharing parenting and work, they create new role models of wholeness.

I've observed men, suppressing their own disenchantment with sterile corporate jobs or bureaucratic professions, watch bemused as some women jump in, eagerly taking courses in "assertiveness training." I've also seen men shaken, threatened and secretly envious when some women, whose identities, after all, do not depend solely on those jobs, move from strengths that must be rooted in their own female experience and *resist* these same dehumanizing corporate practices men have acquiesced in, too long and to no real advantage.

On the other hand, a woman may become uneasy when a man is so intent on dropping out of the rat race that he clearly yearns for a superwoman to support him as she used to yearn for that strong man to take care of her whole life. "My husband wants me to have another child, and he will quit his job altogether and stay home and take care of the kids," a woman in Vermont told me. "Why should that work for him when it didn't work for me? Maybe I don't want him to take over the family that much. I'd resent it, just working to support him."

Beaten, desperate or self-denigrating "inadequate" men, playing into woman's pent-up hunger for power in the world or simply into her own harassed desperation, toy with fantasies that such reversals would be good. "What I need is a wife," she may joke, trying to be superwoman and doing it all herself, not really able yet to give up or share equally her old power in the home and family. But that half-life which made her insecure can also shake his sense of self.

It didn't really work when Phil, in the first flush of liberation from his surgical mask, reversed roles with Ellen. He stayed home full time after they moved to the country, "mothering" their children, cooking and cleaning, even meekly doing all the dishes "including the pots and pans my daughters were supposed to share," while Ellen went off to work. Is there something suspicious about such an excessively repentant male chauvinist pig? "Let her have the bigtime medical career," he urged, with no trace of outward bitterness, as his wife took on acupuncture on top of her new midwife training. "She shouldn't be a nurse any more and take orders from men. She's a natural healer; she's the one who should have gone to medical school. I'll grow our own vegetables and heal myself."

But, in the first place, she didn't make nearly as much money as a nurse as he could as a doctor. And when she came home, the house was never clean enough, the meat loaf wasn't seasoned right, he'd forgotten to put the potatoes in, and she would rush around, tired as she was, doing it all over, making him feel just as guilty as she had in the old days.

"Then I began to feel like a martyr," he says. "Nobody appreciated how hard I worked, taking care of the house and kids all day. Anyhow, she missed that security, the money and all the rest of it, of my being a doctor. Working as much as I want to, with my family practice, and bringing money in again, I don't have to feel guilty if the house isn't all that clean on my shift. And now that they're treating her like a professional at the hospital, she doesn't notice the dust on the window sills so much."

Most men sense they are really dependent on women for security and love and intimacy, just as most women learn, after the old resentment-making imbalances are out of the way, that they are dependent on men for these same qualities. Most husbands will put up with quite a lot to weather their wives' periods of transition as they change their attitudes and redefine their roles (though maybe not quite as much as most wives have always had to put up with from their husbands!).

In a recent lecture on "The Male Sex Role: An Insider's View," sociologist William J. Goode stated that he did not think there was or would be a real masculine backlash to women's demand for equality, though men for a time may both exaggerate and deny the threat to them. Nor did he think that, whatever problems or discomforts might be involved for either sex, women would ever give up the new sense of self-respect and the freedom they now enjoy. "Males will stubbornly resist, but reluctantly adjust: because women will continue to want more equality and will be unhappy if they do not get it; because men on the average will prefer that their women be happy; because neither will find an adequate substitute for the other sex; because neither will be able to find an alternative social system."

Men may feel unjustly threatened by the women's movement because they know they personally didn't create the system or conspire to dominate women. Consciously they aren't even aware of how pervasively the social structure, attitudes and laws give them advantages. Men therefore "assume that their greater accomplishments are actually due to their inborn superiority, so they are more aware of their burdens and responsibilities than their unearned advantages," says Goode. In other words, men notice only the difficulties in their lives. They take the comforts as their due. And because they take their superiority for granted, "men view even small losses of differences, of advantages or opportunities as large threats."

But the change that disturbs men most, Goode says, "is a loss of centrality, a decline in the extent to which they are the center of attention. Boys and grown men have always taken for granted that what they were doing was more important than what the other sex was doing. Women's attention was focused on them." Far more troubling to men than women's demand for equal opportunity and pay is the simple fact that "the center of attention shifts more to women now."

The threat is also somewhat exaggerated because the women now holding the desirable jobs only men had held before are so visible, so different, that the mass media plays them up. Even so, their numbers are still too small to constitute any real threat to men's dominance.

Yet men are right in sensing inexorable forces that are undermining their previous claim to natural superiority. But these threatening forces are not created by women. As Goode reports, "The conditions we now live in are different from those of any prior civilization, and they give less support to men's claim of superiority than any other historical era." More and more, the work is done by specialists and machines. And there is new awareness that in today's complex society the top posts in government and business are not best filled by the stereotypical male but by people, male or female, sensitive to others' needs, adept at obtaining cooperation—in short, with the intuitions and social skills and nurturing qualities once considered feminine.

So *men* envy *women* the women's movement. They envy women the zest and energy with which we approach jobs that hold no novelty or challenge for *them.* These jobs also seem like exciting new challenges to women because we are not saddled with that burdensome mandate to be superior and dominant. We do not yet have the need to suppress feelings of weakness and vulnerability that men have been locked into for so long. As a young man put it to me, after several years of wandering, dropping out of school and trying to find himself, "Every guy I know is in trouble. They can't seem to get it together. They don't know what they want. Only the women seem to be getting it together now."

Whatever a woman does today, she is somehow ahead of where she used to be, of where her mother or older sisters were.

The practical problems remain, emerging more clearly now from the fog of reaction and backlash. As men seek for themselves the liberation that began with the women's movement, both men and women have to confront the conflict between their human needs—for love, for family, for meaning in work and purpose in life—and the demands of the workplace as it is structured today.

A family therapist from Philadelphia, watching his three-year-old learn to throw a ball, talked of the conflict between his own profession and his personal family needs. "I was working at one of the big family-training centers in the country," he said. "There was constant theoretical discussion about getting the father back into the family. But the way our own jobs were set up, you had to work fifty to sixty hours a week. To really get anywhere you had to put in seventy hours, work nights, weekends. You didn't have time for your own family. You were supposed to make the job Number One in your life, and I wouldn't do that. My life is Number One, and my family—my job is only to be a good therapist. To play the office politics and be one of the big guns you had to devote your whole life to it. I started my own practice where I keep my own hours. Most of the other family therapists at the center are now divorced."

Recent managerial studies have shown that the long working hours and the frequent corporate transfers that kept many men from strong daily involvements with their families or with any other fulfilling commitments for interests besides their jobs were not all that necessary for the work of the company. But the long hours and the transfers do serve to keep a man dependent for his very identity, as well as his livelihood, on the corporation—a "company man."

This process is pinpointed in a depth study of executives in a major Connecticut company by Diana Rothbard Margolis published in 1980, *The Managers—Corporate Life in America.* "Security is not all that binds," this study explains. "Beyond the large paychecks, the benefit plans...the corporation controls a trump—the manager's identity. Paradoxically, managers must depend on the corporation for their definition of self precisely because they are moved around so frequently in their jobs.... With interests narrowed by the demands of their [corporate] initiation, a manager's thirst for money, status and security grows until other needs are eclipsed.... For corporation managers, needs usually fulfilled by human relationships become increasingly difficult to satisfy because almost all relationships outside their nuclear family are distant and fleeting. So like half-starved people who in the absence of proteins will fatten themselves on starches, managers and their families hunger for goods money cannot buy, but reach for those it can."

Is it necessary for a man to leave the corporate mainstream to find himself—and his new identity in the family? Might he not be able to turn that corner for himself by acting, along with women, to change those dehumanizing corporate conditions? With productivity declining and absenteeism increasing, corporations will have to come to terms with men's insistence on human terms and meaning in work—which could conceivably strengthen the system, as women's equality is giving new strength to the family.

It seems strange to suggest that there is a new American frontier, a new adventure for men, in this new struggle for wholeness, for openness to feeling, for living and sharing life on equal terms with women, taking equal responsibility for children—the human liberation that began with the women's movement. Unlike the American hero of the past, the new frontier liberates men from the isolating silence of that lonely cowboy. "I'm not just my work now, not just a breadwinner, I can do something just for myself," says Avery. "But to tell you the truth, my fantasies now tend to be in terms of the family. I'd like to take the kids and Judy on the same trip backpacking to Canada I took at nineteen. It's not my fantasy to go off to the South Seas alone like Gauguin."

Men aren't really going to be able to escape, or want to escape, the work world, any more than most women can or want to escape the family. The men in *Breaktime* had to or wanted to go back to work after their unemployment insurance or savings ran out—but on terms now which left them more room to be human, enabled them to use their own abilities and control their own lives more (if not in the job itself, then by reducing the job's importance and putting their main energies into other pursuits). The new statistics showing how frequently men are changing jobs indicate that somehow, even in this turbulent economy, men are taking more control of their own lives instead of being passive robots of the corporation. And new statistics showing for the first time a decline in the number of hours American women spend on housework suggest that when women no longer need all that power and status from the perfectly clean house because they're getting a little more power in the world—they don't let their houses run them.

Instead of being defined by their jobs or careers, more and more young men—and survivors of the midlife crisis—are holding down one or more part-time jobs, like women (taxi driver, teaching one course, waiter, bartender, apartment-house "super" or country caretaker in return for free rent), while "their own thing" may be the cello, ecology, dance, or studying Greek mythology—not for pay at all. Says my young friend David, "I seem to know fewer and fewer men who answer 'What do you do?' in terms of their job. It's 'What is your *shtik?*'"

In the second stage of this struggle that is changing everyone's life, men's and women's needs converge. There are conscious choices now, for men as well as women—to set up their lives in such a way as to achieve a more equitable balance between success in work and gratification in personal life. And here is the missing link, the power that was lacking when women tried to solve these problems by taking it all on themselves as superwomen, the power women did not and will not have, to change the structure of jobs by and for themselves alone. But if young men now need and want self-fulfillment beyond their jobs and the life-grounding women have always had in the family—as much as women now need and want some voice and active power in the world—there will be a new, and sufficient, *combined* force for the second stage.

So this is the other half of Stage Two of the struggle that began with women's movement for equality—men's liberation. Men, it seems, are now seeking new life patterns as much as women are. They envy women's freedom to express their feelings and their private questions and the support they got from each other in those years of the women's movement.

After talking to these men, I wonder about women who struggle so hard to succeed in traditional male roles. A West Point officer, like a number of executives I've met who are dealing with women colleagues as equals for the first time, seemed to have a strange awe, fear, envy almost, of women's power, a sense that women know some secret men don't. (Or maybe, now that women are there, in the man's world, the men are afraid women will discover how hollow men's power can be.)

This is tricky, because there's been so much hypocrisy about the power of women. But the West Point man says, "It always defined women as against men—that we went to war. 'Winners never quit,' 'Quitters never win,' etc. The worst insult was to be called the four- and five-letter words for women's sex. Now the women are in the locker room, too. They have a powerful advantage because they weren't brought up with the black-and-white view of the world: 'If he knocks you down, you're a pussy.' 'He has the courage, so you have to knock him down.' Women aren't stuck with the notion that that kind of courage is necessary, or even possible. They just cast about for ways to do what has to be done, push through the phoniness, the lies, to the concrete reality of it. They know it's not black and white, it's gray. It makes men feel guilty for having believed the lie in the first place, and then for having given up so easily. Men are jealous and afraid of women, maybe envious of their power. It may sound corny, but there is power in women's ability to create life, closeness to life, that men don't have, always chasing power, in the company, in the army.

"Speaking for myself, I need reassurance from women. And now there's all this rhetoric that all the things men bragged about are no good. So men are left with gaping holes in their identity, their equation of life. And now that women feel unfettered ambition is absolutely necessary to get ahead in their own careers, they can't turn around and help men. Men don't like to admit their fear of women, and women don't like to be feared, but the hidden secret is coming out now, and it's freaking people. It's scary to have power over people and be able to control them, the way women do with feelings.

"It seems to me, beginning with the Vietnam war, more and more men are reaching a turning point where if they don't turn the corner and get beyond these black-and-white games, they start to die. Women will make a mistake if they reach that turning point and start to imitate men. Will the women move in and take our place? Men can't be role models for women, not even in the army. We badly need some new role models ourselves."

Suggestions for Discussion

1. What supporting evidence does Friedan provide that American men "are at the edge of a momentous change in their very identity as men"?
2. What questions does the author believe that men are asking?
3. How do dependency and need affect men's attitudes toward women and women's feelings about men?
4. What are some of the signs that "machismo was dying" and what brought about the change?
5. What are the dangers in role reversals?
6. What is sociologist Goode's view of men's response to the women's movement?
7. What is Friedan's suggested solution for the identity problem facing men in the corporate mainstream?
8. How does the author define the second stage of the struggle?
9. How does the West Point man view men's problems?

Suggestions for Writing

1. Compare Friedan's views with those of Noel Perrin in *The Androgynous Man.* Whose analysis seems more valid to you? Draw upon your observation and experience.
2. Read Friedan's book, *The Second Stage,* and try to account for the displeasure expressed by some feminists in its point of view.
3. Discuss any one of the questions above by bringing to bear your observation and experience.
4. Develop a character study of a man (or woman) who is trying to reconcile her or his career goals with a sense of self-fulfillment.

BROOKE KROEGER

AIDS and the Girl Next Door

Brooke Kroeger, a New York City writer, is the author of "Nellie Bly: Daredevil, Reporter, Feminist" (1994). Only by a fluke did "the girl next door" learn that she was HIV-positive and that the source of her infection could not be identified.

There was just no point in joining an AIDS support group for women. What, besides impending death, did she have in common with convicts and heroin addicts? She'd graduated from college and become a professional, a twenty-eight-year-old comer in her field, earning forty thousand dollars a year, the daughter of a respected upper-middle-class family. A gay men's group might have made a better demographic fit. For the time being, no appropriate group exists. Most of the heterosexual men and women with the background to be helpful to her are walking around with the AIDS virus and don't even know it.

But then, neither would she, if not for a series of coincidences that bore the mark of Providence. This is why she has agreed to be interviewed. She thinks there is a message she had better get across. In deference to her family, she asks that her name and any identifying details be excluded from the story.

What makes her story worth telling is that she is utterly ordinary, the girl next door. It was only by a fluke that a doctor would think to suggest that someone with her socioeconomic profile and no symptoms should be tested for AIDS—and that the test would come back HIV-positive.

The story began with a case of fatigue and a stubborn rash in the folds of her groin that would not go away. She would have ignored them both if the raw skin hadn't been so aggravating in the summer heat of 1988. And even though she had good reason to be tired—fourteen-hour, adrenalin-charged workdays would wear anyone out—it felt too much like the mononucleosis of her adolescence. Time for a physical.

The physician examined her carefully. The fatigue was easily explained away. She was working too hard. As for the rash, nylon stockings and relentless humidity made it a common summertime affliction. Still, the rash struck him as meaner than most. He ordered a full blood workup for the new patient.

"So," he said, "it's the 1980s. Tell me about your sex life."

She quickly determined where this conversation might lead, but found the doctor easy to talk to and had no problem answering his questions. She had lost her virginity at twenty, the oldest among her friends, and married the first man she slept with, but divorced him two years later. Depression dulled her very Roman Catholic sensibilities and she "got wild" for about two years. Though she had been celibate for the nine months before the examination, there had been fifteen partners before that. For the most part, they were friends who became lovers or lovers who became friends. There were two one-night stands, but the men were not strangers. Nothing kinky. No violence. No one the least bit exotic. No anal intercourse except for one distasteful, twenty-second attempt while she was married that did not result in penetration or ejaculation. And no condoms; they didn't seem necessary. She knew all these men of the Brooks-Brothers-Suit Brigade. There is, to this day, no reason to think that any of her partners were bisexual or users of intravenous drugs or frequenters of prostitutes. None of them is known to be sick.

The doctor asked her if she would like him to order an AIDS test. He had no particular reason to suggest it, but was mindful of the times. The test would involve nothing more than another entry on the printout of results for which her blood had already been drawn.

She needed only a moment to decide. It *was* the 1980s. Responsible people check their cholesterol and submit to the AIDS test.

"Sure," she said. "Do it."

Over the coming weeks, the test would be repeated twice to confirm its devastating result. From a source that remains unknown, she had contracted the HIV infection. Her most recent tests show that the virus is active. Nevertheless, she feels terrific. She has gained a not-necessarily desired twenty-five pounds since she was diagnosed. She swims everyday, goes horseback riding, foxhunts, plays squash. Her doctor says he thinks the virulence of her rash may have been an indication of a taxed immune system, but this is hindsight. If it weren't for having casually agreed to being tested, she would have walked around for who knows how long oblivious to her infectiousness. There is no published estimate of how many others may be in her situation.

"I could be acting as wild as I was after my divorce or even wilder," she says. "I could be married and giving this to my baby."

The case of Alison Gertz, a twenty-three-year-old New Yorker raised on Park Avenue, is similar to this woman's in that their backgrounds make them atypical of the most common AIDS sufferers in this country, and a cause for concern to the general heterosexual population. What distinguishes the two cases is that Alison Gertz was able to identify the source of her infection: a bartender whom she says she slept with once. He since has died of AIDS.

By the end of May 1989, the Centers for Disease Control (CDC) reported a total of 97,193 cases of AIDS in the United States since 1981, and of that number 56,468 deaths. Heterosexual cases accounted for only 4 percent of that total, or 4,305 cases. To qualify as a heterosexual case, the individual must report specific heterosexual contact with someone who is considered to be at high risk for AIDS—a bisexual, an I.V.-drug user, a hemophiliac, someone who received a blood transfusion before screening began, or someone of African or Caribbean origin (in those countries, AIDS occurs predominantly in heterosexuals).

The woman interviewed for this story is not yet a statistic. There is no national register of people who carry the HIV virus but have not yet developed AIDS. Fewer than thirty states require reporting of those who test HIV-positive and she does not live in one of them. Because the source of her infection is not known, when she does develop AIDS her case will have to be classified as "No Identifiable Risk (NIR)."

Nonetheless, it is presumed that she was infected through sexual contact. Fully 75 percent of AIDS sufferers who have been listed as NIR ultimately are moved to other categories after follow-up studies reveal that they or one of their partners actually belonged to a high-risk group. The source of infection for the other 25 percent remains a mystery.

Jeanette Stehr-Green, M.D., a section chief in AIDS surveillance, CDC, explains why there has been no move at the national level to keep count of those who are HIV-positive but not yet suffering from AIDS. "Many of those who would be HIV-positive are not motivated to get tested," she says, "so there is no way we could count all of them. Many don't know they are at risk. Many are denying their risk. Many may realize their risk but don't feel that getting tested will change anything anyway."

The CDC estimates that the total number of people in the United States who are HIV-positive—from all causes—is somewhere between 1 million and 1.5 million. Working backwards from that figure, Jody Robinson, M.D., a Washington, D.C., physician with a background in immunology, epidemiology, and international medicine, estimates the number of infected heterosexuals to be as high as 400,000 (regardless of how they got the virus). If Dr. Robinson is anywhere near correct—and no one at the CDC is willing to say—then the potential threat to the general heterosexual population could be greater than usually presumed. These infected persons can be assumed to have relations from time to time with people who would have no other risk of infection.

"I think this is a reasonable estimate," says Elizabeth M. Whelan, Ph.D., president of the American Council on Science and Health. "The I.V.-drug-using community is the potential bridge to the general spread of AIDS."

When the woman interviewed for this story asked her doctor if she needed to furnish him with a list of the names and addresses of all her sexual partners, he said, "No, only if you want."

"Only if you want?" she shot back. "ONLY IF YOU WANT? What the f—— is that when someone is out there spreading death?" She thought surely it would be required by law.

The federal government does require any state accepting certain types of federal funds for its AIDS programs to set up partner-notification services. However, it has been left to each state to interpret this requirement. "By definition, the process is voluntary," says Cathy Raevsky, deputy section chief of the Sexually Transmitted Diseases/AIDS Section of the Colorado Health Department's AIDS program, considered to have one of the most aggressive notification systems in the country.

Together, the woman and her doctor drafted a letter, sent without signature, to all the men she had slept with. She located all but one of them. The letter explained that she had contracted the HIV virus and urged that they be tested.

"All of them know how to find me," she says. "You would think that there would have been a letter from at least one of them, even an anonymous one, saying he was HIV-positive and I should be tested. But I've heard nothing and it's been almost a year."

Dr. Robinson has brandished the threat of AIDS to the general, heterosexual population in a series of op-ed page pieces for *The Wall Street Journal, The Washington Post,* the *Chicago Tribune,* the *St. Louis Post-Dispatch* and *The Atlanta Constitution.* His premise is that people should not be lulled into a false sense of security because of their conventional lifestyles or the relatively small number of recorded cases of heterosexual AIDS in this country.

As he explains it, the most efficient means of transmitting the AIDS virus are anal intercourse and inoculation into the vascular system. "This has skewed the sense of this disease in the eyes of the public because of the preponderance of cases who have gotten the disease through these extraordinarily efficient means."

If the median incubation rate for the virus is ten years, and the first cases in this country were only recognized eight years ago in 1981, then it makes sense that the first two waves of infection were among people in those communities in which infection could occur most efficiently—homosexuals, hemophiliacs, heroin addicts. Those who have been infected by somewhat less efficient means—vaginal intercourse—would likely take longer to surface.

For Dr. Robinson the experience with AIDS in Africa serves as a case in point. There, the ratio of infection among heterosexual men and women is 1:1. Here, the ratio is 4:1 men to women. In Africa, he believes, the disease has been spreading longer, even though homosexuality and I.V.-drug use are rare. It is also a place with a high degree of untreated venereal diseases, untreated skin sores, and uncircumcised males—all of which enhance the spread of AIDS infection. In short, if the Africa example is adjusted to the prevailing conditions in this country, it may well mean that the worst is yet to come.

At CDC, however, the view is less alarming for those not already considered to be at risk. Nevertheless, there is cause for concern.

"We are not seeing an explosive increase in heterosexual AIDS," says Mary Chamberland, M.D., a medical epidemiologist with CDC's AIDS program. "But that is not to minimize the problem. In big urban centers, among African-Americans and Hispanics and drug users and prostitutes, it is a big problem. But for most people, heterosexual AIDS is not something that poses a very significant risk.

"But the risk is not zero," she says, "and the woman you have just described is a very good example. It points out the need for education. Everybody does need to take prudent precautions."

Our girl next door has stopped spending time worrying about who her "donor" was. What's important is maintaining a good outlook; eating a high-protein diet; monitoring her T-cell count for signs of a turn in her condition; and deepening her spiritual life, a journey that began long before she discovered her condition. She still spends time with her good friends and they are many. She is someone people like to be with. She has a great sense of humor. She's someone with good values who likes to party.

She is at peace with her situation. It is difficult to imagine the emotional upheavals she has weathered in the past ten months—the shock of discovery, the anxiety attacks, the depression, the suicide attempt. "You don't know me," she says. "But you can't imagine how uncharacteristic my behavior was."

When the test result first came back, she says her reaction was primordial. "My hands and feet went ice cold. I thought I would lose control of my bowels. I stood up and started pacing like an animal in a cage, looking out the window. I kept focusing on the shame. There is so much shame attached to this illness."

Her sister, brother-in-law, and their two children arrived at her apartment, by chance, to spend the weekend.

"I was in complete shock," she says. "When my sister asked what happened at the doctor's office, I told her I was anemic and had to take it easy. I love to eat. We ordered a pizza and I couldn't eat it. Nobody would believe there could be a pizza on the table and I wouldn't eat it. My heart was racing out of my chest. I know now I was having an anxiety attack. The doctor had given me a prescription for Valium. I had never taken it before, not even for a back injury. But I filled it immediately. I needed to get my pulse rate below one hundred. I lost nine pounds getting through that weekend. I thought I was wasting away."

Her sister left; Monday morning she called work and told her boss she had pneumonia. She bought a first-class air ticket on the first possible flight to see her brother.

"It was like a bad Bette Davis movie. It was eight-thirty in the morning and I was slugging Bloody Marys one after the other. And smoking cigarettes. The stewardess didn't know what to make of me. I didn't know how sick I was. I was only dealing with death. Only death."

Her brother calmed her down, got her thinking straight, and put her in touch with a lawyer so she could understand her legal situation. Subsequently her parents and sister were told. The whole family has been a mainstay of support.

But the journey she started toward deepening her religious life stopped cold when her first test result came back. She was severely depressed. She went through a phase of seeing the world as one big germ—compulsively washing her hands, being afraid to touch doorknobs, avoiding hospitals and sick people, fearing any sneeze in her presence.

The worst bout of depression came at Thanksgiving. She attended her tenth high-school reunion and finished the evening with drinking and reminiscing and a 5:30 A.M. breakfast at the home of one of her oldest and dearest friends. She made her confession. The poignance was palpable. The friend and her husband then went upstairs to bed and she remained at the kitchen table with her bottle of Xanax, prescribed by a psychiatrist she had been seeing who had been no help at all. She doesn't recall how many pills she took, but before she passed out, she called her sister, who rushed her to their mother's house and then to a hospital where she spent a week recuperating.

"Until you've done this, you can't imagine the humor," she says. "They treat you like a psychiatric patient because you've tried to kill yourself and they make you have nurses around the clock to make sure you don't try to do it again. I convinced them that I was fine and would not harm myself in order to get them to release me. But I was still clinically depressed, certainly still in danger. That tells you how much faith I have in psychiatrists anymore."

She stayed with her parents for several days, lying in bed, crying, refusing to eat. Her mother would cry with her and that would make her feel worse.

Her mother left an Advent calendar by her bedside. For each day in the countdown to Christmas, there was a verse. She can't remember which one, or what about the experience of reading it every day made the difference, but "something clicked," she says. "I hadn't prayed for three months, but this was perfect, as if it had been written for me. It was loving, forgiving, hopeful.

"And that's when I started getting better," she goes on. "That was my cure. You know, my family has all been praying for a miracle, for a cure, and after this I said, 'This is my cure.' A cure is not only physical, you know. I started feeling and caring and thinking about life again."

She tries not to moralize, knowing how pointless that would be. But she wishes those wild years had never happened, that she had possessed the wisdom at the time to realize how fruitless all the empty activity was. She wishes she had insisted on condoms and spermicides.

"The truth is, I could no more have pulled a condom out of my purse—I couldn't have even raised the question. There is so much pressure from men—so much competition for so few men—women will continue to say yes to men and be too bashful to be cautious. But there is just no dignity in finding out you have AIDS because you were too dignified to ask a man to wear a condom."

As for now, she has taken medical leave from work. It will probably be permanent. She doesn't feel sick in the least and she is not currently undergoing any treatment. A protocol was tried but proved too toxic for her system. Instead of experimenting with other drugs, her doctors think it is best to wait until she may really need them. In the meantime, she concentrates on simplifying her life. She contemplates entering a religious community and hopes to volunteer for an AIDS hotline ("I'm sure I could handle the suicide calls," she jokes). She spends a lot of time with her family.

"I'm not withering away," she says. "Just because it doesn't look like I'm running frantic and busily producing doesn't mean I'm not running frantic and busily producing."

Getting involved with someone, she says, is not in the cards.

"My forever will be a lot shorter than his forever," she says. "And that's not fair."

Neither is AIDS. But that kind of thinking is not part of whom she has become.

Suggestions for Discussion

1. What makes the woman's story worth telling? Why is she called "the girl next door"?
2. What is the significance of the phrase "Brooks-Brothers-Suit Brigade"?
3. Why was the woman astounded when her doctor said "only if you want" when she asked if she needed to furnish him with a list of the names and addresses of all her sexual partners?
4. Trace the varied responses to the condition of "the girl next door."
5. How does she account for her carelessness in her relationships with men?
6. What is her outlook on the future?

Suggestions for Writing

1. What kind of educational program might protect young women from becoming HIV-positive?
2. Describe "a girl next door" among your friends and acquaintances and suggest the ways in which she relates to others.
3. Describe a situation in which "friends became lovers" or in which "lovers became friends."

MARGARET ATWOOD

Fiction: Happy Endings

Margaret Atwood (b. 1939) has lived both in the United States and Europe, but her home is in Toronto. She is best known as the author of the novels *The Edible Woman* (1976); *Surfacing* (1981); *Life Before Man* (1980); *Bodily Harm* (1982); the powerful political thriller, *The Handmaid's Tale* (1986); *Cat's Eye* (1989); *The Robber Bride* (1993); *Morning in a Burned House* (1995); and *Alias Grace: A Novel* (1996). She also has written short stories, television plays, children's books, criticism, and poetry. She did graduate work at Harvard on a Woodrow Wilson Fellowship and has taught at a number of Canadian and American universities. In this understated critique of happy endings, the author comments bitterly upon the relationships of men and women and the vicissitudes of life.

John and Mary meet. What happens next? If you want a happy ending, try A.

A

John and Mary fall in love and get married. They both have worthwhile and remunerative jobs which they find stimulating and challenging. They buy a charming house. Real estate values go up. Eventually, when they can afford live-in help, they have two children, to whom they are devoted. The children turn out well. John and Mary have a stimulating and challenging sex life and worthwhile friends. They go on fun vacations together. They retire. They both have hobbies which they find stimulating and challenging. Eventually they die. This is the end of the story.

B

Mary falls in love with John but John doesn't fall in love with Mary. He merely uses her body for selfish pleasure and ego gratification of a tepid kind. He comes to her apartment twice a week and she cooks him dinner, you'll notice that he doesn't even consider her worth the price of a dinner out, and after he's eaten the dinner he fucks her and after that he falls asleep, while she does the dishes so he won't think she's untidy, having all those dirty dishes lying around, and puts on fresh lipstick so she'll look good when he wakes up, but when he wakes up he doesn't even notice, he puts on his socks and his shorts and his pants and his shirt and his tie and his shoes, the reverse order from the one in which he took them off. He doesn't take off Mary's clothes, she takes them off herself, she acts as if she's dying for it every time, not because she likes sex exactly, she doesn't but she wants John to think she does because if they do it often enough surely he'll get used to her, he'll come to depend on her and they will get married, but John goes out the door with hardly so much as a good-night and three days later he turns up at six o'clock and they do the whole thing over again.

Mary gets run down. Crying is bad for your face, everyone knows that and so does Mary but she can't stop. People at work notice. Her friends tell her John is a rat, a pig, a dog, he isn't good enough for her, but she can't believe it. Inside John, she thinks, is another John, who is much nicer. This other John will emerge like a butterfly from a cocoon, a Jack from a box, a pit from a prune, if the first John is only squeezed enough.

One evening John complains about the food. He has never complained about the food before. Mary is hurt.

Her friends tell her they've seen him in a restaurant with another woman, whose name is Madge. It's not even Madge that finally gets to Mary: it's the restaurant. John has never taken Mary to a restaurant. Mary collects all the sleeping pills and aspirins she can find, and takes them and half a bottle of sherry. You can see what kind of a woman she is by the fact that it's not even whiskey. She leaves a note for John. She hopes he'll discover her and get her to the hospital in time and repent and then they can get married, but this fails to happen and she dies.

John marries Madge and everything continues as in A.

C

John, who is an older man, falls in love with Mary, and Mary, who is only twenty-two, feels sorry for him because he's worried about his hair falling out. She sleeps with him even though she's not in love with him. She met him at work. She's in love with someone called James, who is twenty-two also and not yet ready to settle down.

John on the contrary settled down long ago: this is what is bothering him. John has a steady respectable job and is getting ahead in his field, but Mary isn't impressed by him, she's impressed by James, who has a motorcycle, being free. Freedom isn't the same for girls, so in the meantime Mary spends Thursday evenings with John. Thursdays are the only days John can get away.

John is married to a woman called Madge and they have two children, a charming house which they bought just before the real estate values went up, and hobbies which they find stimulating and challenging, when they have the time. John tells Mary how important she is to him, but of course he can't leave his wife because a commitment is a commitment. He goes on about this more than is necessary and Mary finds it boring, but older men can keep it up longer so on the whole she has a fairly good time.

One day James breezes in on his motorcycle with some top-grade California hybrid and James and Mary get higher than you'd believe possible and they climb into bed. Everything becomes very underwater, but along comes John, who has a key to Mary's apartment. He finds them stoned and entwined. He's hardly in any position to be jealous, considering Madge, but nevertheless he's overcome with despair. Finally he's middle-aged, in two years he'll be bald as an egg and he can't stand it. He purchases a handgun, saying he needs it for target practice—this is the thin part of the plot, but it can be dealt with later—and shoots the two of them and himself.

Madge, after a suitable period of mourning, marries an understanding man called Fred and everything continues as in A, but under different names.

D

Fred and Madge have no problems. They get along exceptionally well and are good at working out any little difficulties that may arise. But their charming house is by the seashore and one day a giant tidal wave approaches. Real estate values go down. The rest of the story is about what caused the tidal wave and how they escape from it. They do, though thousands drown. Some of the story is about how the thousands drown, but Fred and Madge are virtuous and lucky. Finally on high ground they clasp each other, wet and dripping and grateful, and continue as in A.

E

Yes, but Fred has a bad heart. The rest of the story is about how kind and understanding they both are until Fred dies. Then Madge devotes herself to charity work until the end of A. If you like, it can be "Madge," "cancer," "guilty and confused," and "birdwatching."

F

If you think this is all too bourgeois, make John a revolutionary and Mary a counterespionage agent and see how far that gets you. You'll still end up with A, though in between you may get a lustful brawling saga of passionate involvement, a chronicle of our times, sort of.

You'll have to face it, the endings are the same however you slice it. Don't be deluded by any other endings, they're all fake, either deliberately fake, with malicious intent to deceive, or just motivated by excessive optimism if not by downright sentimentality.

The only authentic ending is the one provided here:

John and Mary die. John and Mary die. John and Mary die.

So much for endings. Beginnings are always more fun. True connoisseurs, however, are known to favor the stretch in between, since it's the hardest to do anything with.

That's about all that can be said for plots, which anyway are just one thing after another, a what and a what and a what.

Now try How and Why.

Suggestions for Discussion

1. In the spare language of A there are simple undeveloped declarative sentences. What is the effect on substance and tone?
2. What is the author saying about men–women relationships in B and C? What is the significance of the ending in B and C in which everything continues as in A?
3. What does Atwood mean when she says that plots are "just one thing after another, a what and a what and a what"?
4. In her last sentence the author says "Now try How and Why." What is she saying about plots, about fiction, and about relationships?

Suggestions for Writing

1. In her discussion of Mary and John the author poses a number of problems in men–women relationships. Discuss them drawing on illustrations from your observation or experience.
2. Discuss what you believe to be the major areas of disagreement in marriage.
3. Review a book in which you find an illogical happy ending.

FICTION

NATHANIEL HAWTHORNE

The Birthmark

Nathaniel Hawthorne (1804–1864) was born of New England Puritan stock in Salem, Massachusetts. His first publication, *Twice-Told Tales* (1837), was followed by the novels *The Scarlet Letter* (1850), *The House of the Seven Gables* (1851), and *The Marble Faun* (1860). Other short fiction includes a second series of *Twice-Told Tales* (1842), *Mosses from an Old Manse* (1846), and *The Snow Image and Other Twice-Told Tales* (1851). In "The Birthmark," Aylmer's love for Georgiana deteriorates into self-love and an obsessive sense of his own omnipotence; his faith in science is reduced to an unconscious belief in the possibility of magical exorcism. The opposed forces in his personality become completely separated, and when they cease to contend there is no possibility of a reconciliation between them.

In the latter part of the last century there lived a man of science, an eminent proficient in every branch of natural philosophy, who not long before our story opens had made experience of a spiritual affinity more attractive than any chemical one. He had left his laboratory to the care of an assistant, cleared his fine countenance from the furnace smoke, washed the stain of acids from his fingers, and persuaded a beautiful woman to become his wife. In those days, when the comparatively recent discovery of electricity and other kindred mysteries of Nature seemed to open paths into the region of miracle, it was not unusual for the love of science to rival the love of woman in its depth and absorbing energy. The higher intellect, the imagination, the spirit, and even the heart might all find their congenial aliment in pursuits which, as some of their ardent votaries believed, would ascend from one step of powerful intelligence to another, until the philosopher should lay his hand on the secret of creative force and perhaps make new worlds for himself. We know not whether Aylmer possessed this degree of faith in man's ultimate control over Nature. He had devoted himself, however, too unreservedly to scientific studies ever to be weaned from them by any second passion. His love for his young wife might prove the stronger of the two; but it could only be by intertwining itself with his love of science and uniting the strength of the latter to his own.

Such a union accordingly took place, and was attended with truly remarkable consequences and a deeply impressive moral. One day, very soon after their marriage, Aylmer sat gazing at his wife with a trouble in his countenance that grew stronger until he spoke.

"Georgiana," said he, "has it never occurred to you that the mark upon your cheek might be removed?"

"No, indeed," said she, smiling; but, perceiving the seriousness of his manner, she blushed deeply. "To tell you the truth, it has been so often called a charm that I was simple enough to imagine it might be so."

"Ah, upon another face perhaps it might," replied her husband; "but never on yours. No, dearest Georgiana, you came so nearly perfect from the hand of Nature that this slightest possible defect, which we hesitate whether to term a defect or a beauty, shocks me, as being the visible mark of earthly imperfection."

"Shocks you, my husband!" cried Georgiana, deeply hurt; at first reddening with momentary anger, but then bursting into tears. "Then why did you take me from my mother's side? You cannot love what shocks you!"

To explain this conversation, it must be mentioned that in the centre of Georgiana's left cheek there was a singular mark, deeply interwoven, as it were, with the texture and substance of her face. In the usual state of her complexion—a healthy though delicate bloom—the mark wore a tint of deeper crimson, which imperfectly defined its shape amid the surrounding rosiness. When she blushed it gradually became more indistinct, and finally vanished amid the triumphant rush of blood that bathed the whole cheek with its brilliant glow. But if any shifting motion caused her to turn pale there was the mark again, a crimson stain upon the snow, in what Aylmer sometimes deemed an almost fearful distinctness. Its shape bore not a little similarity to the human hand, though of the smallest pygmy size. Georgiana's lovers were wont to say that some fairy at her birth hour had laid her tiny hand upon the infant's cheek, and left this impress there in token of the magic endowments that were to give her such sway over all hearts. Many a desperate swain would have risked life for the privilege of pressing his lips to the mysterious hand. It must not be concealed, however, that the impression wrought by this fairy sign manual varied exceedingly according to the difference of temperament in the beholders. Some fastidious persons—but they were exclusively of her own sex—affirmed that the bloody hand, as they chose to call it, quite destroyed the effect of Georgiana's beauty and rendered her countenance even hideous. But it would be as reasonable to say that one of those small blue stains which sometimes occur in the purest statuary marble would convert the Eve of Powers to a monster. Masculine observers, if the birthmark did not heighten their admiration, contented themselves with wishing it away, that the world might possess one living specimen of ideal loveliness without the semblance of a flaw. After his marriage,—for he thought little or nothing of the matter before,—Aylmer discovered that this was the case with himself.

Had she been less beautiful,—if Envy's self could have found aught else to sneer at,—he might have felt his affection heightened by the prettiness of this mimic hand, now vaguely portrayed, now lost, now stealing forth again and glimmering to and fro with every pulse of emotion that throbbed within her heart; but, seeing her otherwise so perfect, he found this one defect grow more and more intolerable with every moment of their united lives. It was the fatal flaw of humanity which Nature, in one shape or another, stamps ineffaceably on all her productions, either to imply that they are temporary and finite, or that their perfection must be wrought by toil and pain. The crimson hand expressed the ineludible grip in which mortality clutches the highest and purest of earthly mould, degrading them into kindred with the lowest, and even with the very brutes, like whom their visible frames return to dust. In this manner, selecting it as the symbol of his wife's liability to sin, sorrow, decay, and death, Aylmer's sombre imagination was not long in rendering the birthmark a frightful object, causing him more trouble and horror than ever Georgiana's beauty, whether of soul or sense, had given him delight.

At all the seasons which should have been their happiest he invariably, and without intending it, nay, in spite of a purpose to the contrary, reverted to this one disastrous topic. Trifling as it at first appeared, it so connected itself with innumerable trains of thought and modes of feeling that it became the central point of all. With the morning twilight Aylmer opened his eyes upon his wife's face and recognized the symbol of imperfection; and when they sat together at the evening hearth his eyes wandered stealthily to her cheek, and beheld, flickering with the blaze of the wood fire, the spectral hand that wrote mortality where he would fain have worshipped. Georgiana soon learned to shudder at his gaze. It needed but a glance with the peculiar expression that his face often wore to change the roses of her cheek into a deathlike paleness, amid which the crimson hand was brought strongly out, like a bas relief of ruby on the whitest marble.

Late one night, when the lights were growing dim so as hardly to betray the stain on the poor wife's cheek, she herself, for the first time, voluntarily took up the subject.

"Do you remember, my dear Aylmer," said she, with a feeble attempt at a smile, "have you any recollection, of a dream last night about this odious hand?"

"None! none whatever!" replied Aylmer, starting; but then he added, in a dry, cold tone, affected for the sake of concealing the real depth of his emotion, "I might well dream of it; for, before I fell asleep, it had taken a pretty firm hold of my fancy."

"And you did dream of it?" continued Georgiana hastily; for she dreaded lest a gush of tears should interrupt what she had to say. "A terrible dream! I wonder that you can forget it. Is it possible to forget this one expression?—'It is in her heart now; we must have it out!' Reflect, my husband; for by all means I would have you recall that dream."

The mind is in a sad state when Sleep, the all-involving, cannot confine her spectres within the dim region of her sway, but suffers them to break forth, affrighting this actual life with secrets that perchance belong to a deeper one. Aylmer now remembered his dream. He had fancied himself with his servant Aminadab, attempting an operation for the removal of the birthmark; but the deeper went the knife, the deeper sank the hand, until at length its tiny grasp appeared to have caught hold of Georgiana's heart; whence, however, her husband was inexorably resolved to cut or wrench it away.

When the dream had shaped itself perfectly in his memory Aylmer sat in his wife's presence with a guilty feeling. Truth often finds its way to the mind close muffled in robes of sleep, and then speaks with uncompromising directness of matters in regard to which we practise an unconscious self-deception during our waking moments. Until now he had not been aware of the tyrannizing influence acquired by one idea over his mind, and of the lengths which he might find in his heart to go for the sake of giving himself peace.

"Aylmer," resumed Georgiana, solemnly, "I know not what may be the cost to both of us to rid me of this fatal birthmark. Perhaps its removal may cause cureless deformity; or it may be the stain goes as deep as life itself. Again: do we know that there is a possibility, on any terms, of unclasping the firm grip of this little hand which was laid upon me before I came into the world?"

"Dearest Georgiana, I have spent much thought upon the subject," hastily interrupted Aylmer. "I am convinced of the perfect practicability of its removal."

"If there be the remotest possibility of it," continued Georgiana, "let the attempt be made, at whatever risk. Danger is nothing to me; for life, while this hateful mark makes me the object of your horror and disgust—life is a burden which I would fling down with joy. Either remove this dreadful hand, or take my wretched life! You have deep science. All the world bears witness of it. You have achieved great wonders. Cannot you remove this little, little mark, which I cover with the tips of two small fingers? Is this beyond your power, for the sake of your own peace, and to save your poor wife from madness?"

"Noblest, dearest, tenderest wife," cried Aylmer, rapturously, "doubt not my power. I have already given this matter the deepest thought—thought which might almost have enlightened me to create a being less perfect than yourself. Georgiana, you have led me deeper than ever into the heart of science. I feel myself fully competent to render this dear cheek as faultless as its fellow; and then, most beloved, what will be my triumph when I shall have corrected what Nature left imperfect in her fairest work! Even Pygmalion, when his sculptured woman assumed life, felt not greater ecstasy than mine will be."

"It is resolved, then," said Georgiana, faintly smiling. "And, Aylmer, spare me not, though you should find the birthmark take refuge in my heart at last."

Her husband tenderly kissed her cheek—her right cheek—not that which bore the impress of the crimson hand.

The next day Aylmer apprised his wife of a plan that he had formed whereby he might have opportunity for the intense thought and constant watchfulness which the proposed operation would require; while Georgiana, likewise, would enjoy the perfect repose essential to its success. They were to seclude themselves in the extensive apartments occupied by Aylmer as a laboratory, and where, during his toilsome youth, he had made discoveries in the elemental powers of Nature that had roused the admiration of all the learned societies in Europe. Seated calmly in this laboratory, the pale philosopher had investigated the secrets of the highest cloud region and of the profoundest mines; he had satisfied himself of the causes that kindled and kept alive the fires of the volcano; and had explained the mystery of fountains, and how it is that they gush forth; some so bright and pure, and others with such rich medicinal virtues, from the dark bosom of the earth. Here, too, at an earlier period, he had studied the wonders of the human frame, and attempted to fathom the very process by which Nature assimilates all her precious influences from earth and air, and from the spiritual world, to create and foster man, her masterpiece. The latter pursuit, however, Aylmer had long laid aside in unwilling recognition of the truth—against which all seekers sooner or later stumble—that our great creative Mother, while she amuses us with apparently working in the broadest sunshine, is yet severely careful to keep her own secrets, and, in spite of her pretended openness, shows us nothing but results. She permits us, indeed, to mar, but seldom to mend, and, like a jealous patentee, on no account to make. Now, however, Aylmer resumed these half-forgotten investigations; not, of course, with such hopes or wishes as first suggested them; but because they involved much physiological truth and lay in the path of his proposed scheme for the treatment of Georgiana.

As he led her over the threshold of the laboratory, Georgiana was cold and tremulous. Aylmer looked cheerfully into her face, with intent to reassure her, but was so startled with the intense glow of the birthmark upon the whiteness of her cheek that he could not restrain a strong convulsive shudder. His wife fainted.

"Aminadab! Aminadab!" shouted Aylmer, stamping violently on the floor.

Forthwith there issued from an inner apartment a man of low stature, but bulky frame, with shaggy hair hanging about his visage, which was grimed with the vapors of the furnace. This personage had been Aylmer's underworker during his whole scientific career, and was admirably fitted for that office by his great mechanical readiness, and the skill with which, while incapable of comprehending a single principle, he executed all the details of his master's experiments. With his vast strength, his shaggy hair, his smoky aspect, and the indescribable earthiness that incrusted him, he seemed to represent man's physical nature; while Aylmer's slender figure, and pale, intellectual face, were no less apt a type of the spiritual element.

"Throw open the door of the boudoir, Aminadab," said Aylmer, "and burn a pastil."

"Yes, master," answered Aminadab, looking intently at the lifeless form of Georgiana; and then he muttered to himself, "If she were my wife, I'd never part with that birthmark."

When Georgiana recovered consciousness she found herself breathing an atmosphere of penetrating fragrance, the gentle potency of which had recalled her from her deathlike faintness. The scene around her looked like enchantment. Aylmer had converted those smoky, dingy, sombre rooms, where he had spent his brightest years in recondite pursuits, into a series of beautiful apartments not unfit to be the secluded abode of a lovely woman. The walls were hung with gorgeous curtains, which imparted the combination of grandeur and grace that no other species of adornment can achieve; and, as they fell from the ceiling to the floor, their rich and ponderous folds, concealing all angles and straight lines, appeared to shut in the scene from infinite space. For aught Georgiana knew, it might be a pavilion among the clouds. And Aylmer, excluding the sunshine, which would have interfered with his chemical processes, had supplied its place with perfumed lamps, emitting flames of various hue, but all uniting in a soft, impurpled radiance. He now knelt by his wife's side, watching her earnestly, but without alarm; for he was confident in his science, and felt that he could draw a magic circle round her within which no evil might intrude.

"Where am I? Ah, I remember," said Georgiana, faintly; and she placed her hand over her cheek to hide the terrible mark from her husband's eyes.

"Fear not, dearest!" exclaimed he. "Do not shrink from me! Believe me, Georgiana, I even rejoice in this single imperfection, since it will be such a rapture to remove it."

"O, spare me!" sadly replied his wife. "Pray do not look at it again. I never can forget that convulsive shudder."

In order to soothe Georgiana, and, as it were, to release her mind from the burden of actual things, Aylmer now put in practice some of the light and playful secrets which science had taught him among its profounder lore. Airy figures, absolutely bodiless ideas, and forms of unsubstantial beauty came and danced before her, imprinting their momentary footsteps on beams of light. Though she had some indistinct idea of the method of these optical phenomena, still the illusion was almost perfect enough to warrant the belief that her husband possessed sway over the spiritual world. Then again, when she felt a wish to look forth from her seclusion, immediately, as if her thoughts were answered, the procession of external existence flitted across a screen. The scenery and the figures of actual life were perfectly represented, but with that bewitching yet indescribable difference which always makes a picture, an image, or a shadow so much more attractive than the original. When wearied of this, Aylmer bade her cast her eyes upon a vessel containing a quantity of earth. She did so, with little interest at first; but was soon startled to perceive the germ of a plant shooting upward from the soil. Then came the slender stalk; the leaves gradually unfolded themselves; and amid them was a perfect and lovely flower.

"It is magical!" cried Georgiana. "I dare not touch it."

"Nay, pluck it," answered Aylmer,—"pluck it, and inhale its brief perfume while you may. The flower will wither in a few moments and leave nothing save its brown seed vessels; but thence may be perpetuated a race as ephemeral as itself."

But Georgiana had no sooner touched the flower than the whole plant suffered a blight, its leaves turning coal-black as if by the agency of fire.

"There was too powerful a stimulus," said Aylmer, thoughtfully.

To make up for this abortive experiment, he proposed to take her portrait by a scientific process of his own invention. It was to be effected by rays of light striking upon a polished plate of metal. Georgiana assented; but, on looking at the result, was affrighted to find the features of the portrait blurred and indefinable; while the minute figure of a hand appeared where the cheek should have been. Aylmer snatched the metallic plate and threw it into a jar of corrosive acid.

Soon, however, he forgot these mortifying failures. In the intervals of study and chemical experiment he came to her flushed and exhausted, but seemed invigorated by her presence, and spoke in glowing language of the resources of his art. He gave a history of the long dynasty of the alchemists, who spent so many ages in quest of the universal solvent by which the golden principle might be elicited from all things vile and base. Aylmer appeared to believe that, by the plainest scientific logic, it was altogether within the limits of possibility to discover this long-sought medium; "but," he added, "a philosopher who should go deep enough to acquire the power would attain too lofty a wisdom to stoop to the exercise of it." Not less singular were his opinions in regard to the elixir vitae. He more than intimated that it was at his option to concoct a liquid that should prolong life for years, perhaps interminably; but that it would produce a discord in Nature which all the world, and chiefly the quaffer of the immortal nostrum, would find cause to curse.

"Aylmer, are you in earnest?" asked Georgiana, looking at him with amazement and fear. "It is terrible to possess such power, or even to dream of possessing it."

"O, do not tremble, my love," said her husband. "I would not wrong either you or myself by working such inharmonious effects upon our lives; but I would have you consider how trifling, in comparison, is the skill requisite to remove this little hand."

At the mention of the birthmark, Georgiana, as usual, shrank as if a red-hot iron had touched her cheek.

Again Aylmer applied himself to his labors. She could hear his voice in the distant furnace room giving directions to Aminadab, whose harsh, uncouth, misshapen tones were audible in response, more like the grunt or growl of a brute than human speech. After hours of absence, Aylmer reappeared and proposed that she should now examine his cabinet of chemical products and natural treasures of the earth. Among the former he showed her a small vial, in which, he remarked, was contained a gentle yet most powerful fragrance, capable of impregnating all the breezes that blow across a kingdom. They were of inestimable value, the contents of that little vial; and, as he said so, he threw some of the perfume into the air and filled the room with piercing and invigorating delight.

"And what is this?" asked Georgiana, pointing to a small crystal globe containing a gold-colored liquid. "It is so beautiful to the eye that I could imagine it the elixir of life."

"In one sense it is," replied Aylmer; "or rather, the elixir of immortality. It is the most precious poison that ever was concocted in this world. By its aid I could apportion the lifetime of any mortal at whom you might point your finger. The strength of the dose would determine whether he were to linger out years, or drop dead in the midst of a breath. No king on his guarded throne could keep his life if I, in my private station, should deem that the welfare of millions justified me in depriving him of it."

"Why do you keep such a terrific drug?" inquired Georgiana in horror.

"Do not mistrust me, dearest," said her husband, smiling; "its virtuous potency is yet greater than its harmful one. But see! here is a powerful cosmetic. With a few drops of this in a vase of water, freckles may be washed away as easily as the hands are cleansed. A stronger infusion would take the blood out of the cheek, and leave the rosiest beauty a pale ghost."

"Is it with this lotion that you intend to bathe my cheek?" asked Georgiana, anxiously.

"O, no," hastily replied her husband; "this is merely superficial. Your case demands a remedy that shall go deeper."

In his interviews with Georgiana, Aylmer generally made minute inquiries as to her sensations, and whether the confinement of the rooms and the temperature of the atmosphere agreed with her. These questions had such a particular drift that Georgiana began to conjecture that she was already subjected to certain physical influences, either breathed in with the fragrant air or taken with her food. She fancied likewise, but it might be altogether fancy, that there was a stirring up of her system—a strange, indefinite sensation creeping through her veins, and tingling, half painfully, half pleasurably, at her heart. Still, whenever she dared to look into the mirror, there she beheld herself pale as a white rose and with the crimson birthmark stamped upon her cheek. Not even Aylmer now hated it so much as she.

To dispel the tedium of the hours which her husband found it necessary to devote to the processes of combination and analysis, Georgiana turned over the volumes of his scientific library. In many dark old tomes she met with chapters full of romance and poetry. They were the works of the philosophers of the middle ages, such as Albertus Magnus, Cornelius Agrippa, Paracelsus, and the famous friar who created the prophetic Brazen Head. All these antique naturalists stood in advance of their centuries, yet were imbued with some of their credulity, and therefore were believed, and perhaps imagined themselves to have acquired from the investigation of Nature a power above Nature, and from physics a sway over the spiritual world. Hardly less curious and imaginative were the early volumes of the Transactions of the Royal Society, in which the members, knowing little of the limits of natural possibility, were continually recording wonders or proposing methods whereby wonders might be wrought.

But to Georgiana, the most engrossing volume was a large folio from her husband's own hand, in which he had recorded every experiment of his scientific career, its original aim, the methods adopted for its development, and its final success or failure, with the circumstances to which either event was attributable. The book, in truth, was both the history and emblem of his ardent, ambitious, imaginative, yet practical and laborious life. He handled physical details as if there were nothing beyond them; yet spiritualized them all and redeemed himself from materialism by his strong and eager aspiration towards the infinite. In his grasp the veriest clod of earth assumed a soul. Georgiana, as she read, reverenced Aylmer and loved him more profoundly than ever, but with a less entire dependence on his judgment than heretofore. Much as he had accomplished, she could not but observe that his most splendid successes were almost invariably failures, if compared with the ideal at which he aimed. His brightest diamonds were the merest pebbles, and felt to be so by himself, in comparison with the inestimable gems which lay hidden beyond his reach. The volume, rich with achievements that had won renown for its author, was yet as melancholy a record as ever mortal hand had penned. It was the sad confession and continual exemplification of the shortcomings of the composite man, the spirit burdened with clay and working in matter, and of the despair that assails the higher nature at finding itself so miserably thwarted by the earthly part. Perhaps every man of genius, in whatever sphere, might recognize the image of his own experience in Aylmer's journal.

So deeply did these reflections affect Georgiana that she laid her face upon the open volume and burst into tears. In this situation she was found by her husband.

"It is dangerous to read in a sorcerer's books," said he with a smile, though his countenance was uneasy and displeased. "Georgiana, there are pages in that volume which I can scarcely glance over and keep my senses. Take heed lest it prove detrimental to you."

"It has made me worship you more than ever," said she.

"Ah, wait for this one success," rejoined he, "then worship me if you will. I shall deem myself hardly unworthy of it. But come, I have sought you for the luxury of your voice. Sing to me, dearest."

So she poured out the liquid music of her voice to quench the thirst of his spirit. He then took his leave with a boyish exuberance of gayety, assuring her that her seclusion would endure but a little longer, and that the result was already certain. Scarcely had he departed when Georgiana felt irresistibly impelled to follow him. She had forgotten to inform Aylmer of a symptom which for two or three hours past had begun to excite her attention. It was a sensation in the fatal birthmark, not painful, but which induced a restlessness throughout her system. Hastening after her husband, she intruded for the first time into the laboratory.

The first thing that struck her eye was the furnace, that hot and feverish worker, with the intense glow of its fire, which by the quantities of soot clustered above it seemed to have been burning for ages. There was a distilling apparatus in full operation. Around the room were retorts, tubes, cylinders, crucibles, and other apparatus of chemical research. An electrical machine stood ready for immediate use. The atmosphere felt oppressively close, and was tainted with gaseous odors which had been tormented forth by the process of science. The severe and homely simplicity of the apartment, with its naked walls and brick pavement, looked strange, accustomed as Georgiana had become to the fantastic elegance of her boudoir. But what chiefly, indeed almost solely, drew her attention, was the aspect of Aylmer himself.

He was pale as death, anxious and absorbed, and hung over the furnace as if it depended upon his utmost watchfulness whether the liquid which it was distilling should be the draught of immortal happiness or misery. How different from the sanguine and joyous mien that he had assumed for Georgiana's encouragement!

"Carefully now, Aminadab; carefully, thou human machine; carefully, thou man of clay," muttered Aylmer, more to himself than his assistant. "Now, if there be a thought too much or too little, it is all over."

"Ho! ho!" mumbled Aminadab. "Look, master! look!"

Aylmer raised his eyes hastily, and at first reddened, then grew paler than ever, on beholding Georgiana. He rushed towards her and seized her arm with a grip that left the print of his fingers upon it.

"Why do you come hither? Have you no trust in your husband?" cried he, impetuously. "Would you throw the blight of that fatal birthmark over my labors? It is not well done. Go, prying woman! go!"

"Nay, Aylmer," said Georgiana with the firmness of which she possessed no stinted endowment, "it is not you that have a right to complain. You mistrust your wife; you have concealed the anxiety with which you watch the development of this experiment. Think not so unworthily of me, my husband. Tell me all the risk we run, and fear not that I shall shrink; for my share in it is far less than your own."

"No, no, Georgiana!" said Aylmer, impatiently; "it must not be."

"I submit," replied she, calmly. "And, Aylmer, I shall quaff whatever draught you bring me; but it will be on the same principle that would induce me to take a dose of poison if offered by your hand."

"My noble wife," said Aylmer, deeply moved, "I knew not the height and depth of your nature until now. Nothing shall be concealed. Know, then, that this crimson hand, superficial as it seems, has clutched its grasp into your being with a strength of which I had no previous conception. I have already administered agents powerful enough to do aught except to change your entire physical system. Only one thing remains to be tried. If that fail us we are ruined."

"Why did you hesitate to tell me this?" asked she.

"Because, Georgiana," said Aylmer, in a low voice, "there is danger."

"Danger? There is but one danger—that this horrible stigma shall be left upon my cheek!" cried Georgiana. "Remove it, remove it, whatever be the cost, or we shall both go mad!"

"Heaven knows your words are too true," said Aylmer, sadly. "And now, dearest, return to your boudoir. In a little while all will be tested."

He conducted her back and took leave of her with a solemn tenderness which spoke far more than his words how much was now at stake. After his departure Georgiana became rapt in musings. She considered the character of Aylmer and did it completer justice than at any previous moment. Her heart exulted, while it trembled, at his honorable love—so pure and lofty that it would accept nothing less than perfection nor miserably make itself contented with an earthlier nature than he had dreamed of. She felt how much more precious was such a sentiment than that meaner kind which would have borne with the imperfection for her sake, and have been guilty of treason to holy love by degrading its perfect idea to the level of the actual; and with her whole spirit she prayed that, for a single moment, she might satisfy his highest and deepest conception. Longer than one moment she well knew it could not be; for his spirit was ever on the march, ever ascending, and each instant required something that was beyond the scope of the instant before.

The sound of her husband's footsteps aroused her. He bore a crystal goblet containing a liquor colorless as water, but bright enough to be the draught of immortality. Aylmer was pale; but it seemed rather the consequence of a highly-wrought state of mind and tension of spirit than of fear or doubt.

"The concoction of the draught has been perfect," said he, in answer to Georgiana's look. "Unless all my science have deceived me, it cannot fail."

"Save on your account, my dearest Aylmer," observed his wife, "I might wish to put off this birthmark of mortality by relinquishing mortality itself in preference to any other mode. Life is but a sad possession to those who have attained precisely the degree of moral advancement at which I stand. Were I weaker and blinder, it might be happiness. Were I stronger, it might be endured hopefully. But, being what I find myself, methinks I am of all mortals the most fit to die."

"You are fit for heaven without tasting death!" replied her husband. "But why do we speak of dying? The draught cannot fail. Behold its effect upon this plant."

On the window seat there stood a geranium diseased with yellow blotches which had overspread all its leaves. Aylmer poured a small quantity of the liquid upon the soil in which it grew. In a little time, when the roots of the plant had taken up the moisture, the unsightly blotches began to be extinguished in a living verdure.

"There needed no proof," said Georgiana, quietly. "Give me the goblet. I joyfully stake all upon your word."

"Drink, then, thou lofty creature!" exclaimed Aylmer, with fervid admiration. "There is no taint of imperfection on thy spirit. Thy sensible frame, too, shall soon be all perfect."

She quaffed the liquid and returned the goblet to his hand.

"It is grateful," said she, with a placid smile. "Methinks it is like water from a heavenly fountain; for it contains I know not what of unobtrusive fragrance and deliciousness. It allays a feverish thirst that had parched me for many days. Now, dearest, let me sleep. My earthly senses are closing over my spirit like the leaves around the heart of a rose at sunset."

She spoke the last words with a gentle reluctance, as if it required almost more energy than she could command to pronounce the faint and lingering syllables. Scarcely had they loitered through her lips ere she was lost in slumber. Aylmer sat by her side, watching her aspect with the emotions proper to a man the whole value of whose existence was involved in the process now to be tested. Mingled with this mood, however, was the philosophic investigation characteristic of the man of science. Not the minutest symptom escaped him. A heightened flush of the cheek, a slight irregularity of breath, a quiver of the eyelid, a hardly perceptible tremor through the frame,—such were the details which, as the moments passed, he wrote down in his folio volume. Intense thought had set its stamp upon every previous page of that volume; but the thoughts of years were all concentrated upon the last.

While thus employed, he failed not to gaze often at the fatal hand, and not without a shudder. Yet once, by a strange and unaccountable impulse, he pressed it with his lips. His spirit recoiled, however, in the very act; and Georgiana, out of the midst of her deep sleep, moved uneasily and murmured as if in remonstrance. Again Aylmer resumed his watch. Nor was it without avail. The crimson hand, which at first had been strongly visible upon the marble paleness of Georgiana's cheek, now grew more faintly outlined. She remained not less pale than ever; but the birthmark, with every breath that came and went lost somewhat of its former distinctness. Its presence had been awful; its departure was more awful still. Watch the stain of the rainbow fading out of the sky, and you will know how that mysterious symbol passed away.

"By Heaven! it is well nigh gone!" said Aylmer to himself, in almost irrepressible ecstasy. "I can scarcely trace it now. Success! success! And now it is like the faintest rose color. The lightest flush of blood across her cheek would overcome it. But she is so pale!"

He drew aside the window curtain and suffered the light of natural day to fall into the room and rest upon her cheek. At the same time he heard a gross, hoarse chuckle, which he had long known as his servant Aminadab's expression of delight.

"Ah, clod! ah, earthly mass!" cried Aylmer, laughing in a sort of frenzy, "you have served me well! Matter and spirit—earth and heaven—have both done their part in this! Laugh, thing of the senses! You have earned the right to laugh."

These exclamations broke Georgiana's sleep. She slowly unclosed her eyes and gazed into the mirror which her husband had arranged for that purpose. A faint smile flitted over her lips when she recognized how barely perceptible was now that crimson hand which had once blazed forth with such disastrous brilliancy as to scare away all their happiness. But then her eyes sought Aylmer's face with a trouble and anxiety that he could by no means account for.

"My poor Aylmer!" murmured she.

"Poor? Nay, richest, happiest, most favored!" exclaimed he. "My peerless bride, it is successful! You are perfect!"

"My poor Aylmer," she repeated, with a more than human tenderness, "you have aimed loftily; you have done nobly. Do not repent that, with so high and pure a feeling, you have rejected the best the earth could offer. Aylmer, dearest Aylmer, I am dying!"

Alas! it was too true! The fatal hand had grappled with the mystery of life, and was the bond by which an angelic spirit kept itself in union with a mortal frame. As the last crimson tint of the birthmark—that sole token of human imperfection—faded from her cheek, the parting breath of the now perfect woman passed into the atmosphere, and her soul, lingering a moment near her husband, took its heavenward flight. Then a hoarse, chuckling laugh was heard again! Thus ever does the gross fatality of earth exult in its invariable triumph over the immortal essence which, in this dim sphere of half development, demands the completeness of a higher state. Yet, had Aylmer reached a profounder wisdom, he need not thus have flung away the happiness which would have woven his mortal life of the selfsame texture with the celestial. The momentary circumstance was too strong for him; he failed to look beyond the shadowy scope of time, and, living once for all in eternity, to find the perfect future in the present.

Suggestions for Discussion

1. What do you regard as the forces motivating Aylmer's attitude and behavior?
2. Discuss the multiple ways in which the dream advances the story's development. Justify or challenge the statement that Aylmer's dream marks the climax of the story.
3. Examine the language and imagery with special reference to the birthmark and the varied responses to it. How does the juxtaposition of religious and sexual imagery contribute to characterization, meaning, and tone? What is the function of the animistic detail? How does the contrasting imagery describing Georgiana's chambers and Aylmer's laboratory advance the action?
4. By what means are the polarities between the earthly and the spiritual developed? How are they reflected in the descriptions of Aylmer and Aminadab? What support can you find for the idea that Aminadab is presented as Aylmer's double, representing the submerged aspect of Aylmer's personality (note the significance of Aminadab spelled backward)? How would you define the opposing forces in Aylmer? At what point do they cease to contend? In responding to this question, identify the rising action, climax, falling action, and resolution.
5. What has been gained and lost by the use of the omniscient author point of view? How necessary are the author's interpolations to the reader's

understanding of the story's latent meaning? Note especially the author's comments upon the dream; the expository first paragraph; the passage beginning, "It was the fatal flaw of humanity," and the later one on "the shortcomings of the composite man." (Cf. *Hamlet*, I, iv, 11. 23–38.)

6. Trace the changes that take place in Georgiana's consciousness in the course of the action. If her last words to Aylmer reflect a tragic recognition of what Aylmer has rejected, to what does she remain blind? Discuss the irony in her becoming the instrument of her own fate.
7. Find the examples of the skillful use of foreshadowing. How is suspense maintained? While the reader experiences a mounting sense of impending doom, does he completely surrender his disbelief in the possibility that a miracle might be wrought?

Suggestions for Writing

1. Define the relationship of Aylmer and Georgiana. To what extent is the story dated? Under what circumstances could the action of the story take place today?
2. Discuss "The Birthmark" as a story of moral flaw or of psychological determination. Bring to bear what evidence you can for either point of view by specific allusion to the imagery, setting, and characterizations.

KATE CHOPIN

A Respectable Woman

Kate Chopin (1851–1904) was an early feminist who did not begin to write until her late thirties. Her first novel, *At Fault* (1890), was followed by two volumes of short stories, *Bayou Folk* (1894) and *A Night in Acadie* (1897), and her masterpiece, *The Awakening* (1899). The "respectable woman" undergoes a metamorphosis after her earlier indifference to her husband's friend.

Mrs. Baroda was a little provoked to learn that her husband expected his friend, Gouvernail, up to spend a week or two on the plantation.

They had entertained a good deal during the winter; much of the time had also been passed in New Orleans in various forms of mild dissipation.

She was looking forward to a period of unbroken rest, now, and undisturbed tête-à-tête with her husband, when he informed her that Gouvernail was coming up to stay a week or two.

This was a man she had heard much of but never seen. He had been her husband's college friend; was now a journalist, and in no sense a society man or "a man about town," which were, perhaps, some of the reasons she had never met him. But she had unconsciously formed an image of him in her mind. She pictured him tall, slim, cynical; with eye-glasses, and his hands in his pockets; and she did not like him. Gouvernail was slim enough, but he wasn't very tall nor very cynical; neither did he wear eyeglasses nor carry his hands in his pockets. And she rather liked him when he first presented himself.

But why she liked him she could not explain satisfactorily to herself when she partly attempted to do so. She could discover in him none of those brilliant and promising traits which Gaston, her husband, had often assured her that he possessed. On the contrary, he sat rather mute and receptive before her chatty eagerness to make him feel at home and in face of Gaston's frank and wordy hospitality. His manner was as courteous toward her as the most exacting woman could require; but he made no direct appeal to her approval or even esteem.

Once settled at the plantation he seemed to like to sit upon the wide portico in the shade of one of the big Corinthian pillars, smoking his cigar lazily and listening attentively to Gaston's experience as a sugar planter.

"This is what I call living," he would utter with deep satisfaction, as the air that swept across the sugar field caressed him with its warm and scented velvety touch. It pleased him also to get on familiar terms with the big dogs that came about him, rubbing themselves sociably against his legs. He did not care to fish, and displayed no eagerness to go out and kill grosbecs when Gaston proposed doing so.

Gouvernail's personality puzzled Mrs. Baroda, but she liked him. Indeed, he was a lovable, inoffensive fellow. After a few days, when she could understand him no better than at first, she gave over being puzzled and remained piqued. In this mood she left her husband and her guest, for the most part, alone together. Then finding that Gouvernail took no manner of exception to her action, she imposed her society upon him, accompanying him in his idle strolls to the mill and walks along the batture. She persistently sought to penetrate the reserve in which he had unconsciously enveloped himself.

"When is he going—your friend?" she one day asked her husband. "For my part, he tires me frightfully."

"Not for a week yet, dear. I can't understand; he gives you no trouble."

"No. I should like him better if he did; if he were more like others, and I had to plan somewhat for his comfort and enjoyment."

Gaston took his wife's pretty face between his hands and looked tenderly and laughingly into her troubled eyes. They were making a bit of toilet sociably together in Mrs. Baroda's dressing-room.

"You are full of surprises, ma belle," he said to her. "Even I can never count upon how you are going to act under given conditions." He kissed her and turned to fasten his cravat before the mirror.

"Here you are," he went on, "taking poor Gouvernail seriously and making a commotion over him, the last thing he would desire or expect."

"Commotion!" she hotly resented. "Nonsense! How can you say such a thing? Commotion, indeed! But, you know, you said he was clever."

"So he is. But the poor fellow is run down by overwork now. That's why I asked him here to take a rest."

"You used to say he was a man of ideas," she retorted, unconciliated. "I expected him to be interesting, at least. I'm going to the city in the morning to have my spring gowns fitted. Let me know when Mr. Gouvernail is gone; I shall be at my Aunt Octavie's."

That night she went and sat alone upon a bench that stood beneath a live oak tree at the edge of the gravel walk.

She had never known her thoughts or her intentions to be so confused. She could gather nothing from them but the feeling of a distinct necessity to quit her home in the morning.

Mrs. Baroda heard footsteps crunching the gravel; but could discern in the darkness only the approaching red point of a lighted cigar. She knew it was Gouvernail, for her husband did not smoke. She hoped to remain unnoticed, but her white gown revealed her to him. He threw away his cigar and seated himself upon the bench beside her; without a suspicion that she might object to his presence.

"Your husband told me to bring this to you, Mrs. Baroda," he said, handing her a filmy, white scarf with which she sometimes enveloped her head and shoulders. She accepted the scarf from him with a murmur of thanks, and let it lie in her lap.

He made some commonplace observation upon the baneful effect of the night air at that season. Then as his gaze reached out into the darkness, he murmured, half to himself:

"'Night of south winds—night of the large few stars!
Still nodding night—'"

She made no reply to this apostrophe to the night, which indeed, was not addressed to her.

Gouvernail was in no sense a diffident man, for he was not a self-conscious one. His periods of reserve were not constitutional, but the result of moods. Sitting there beside Mrs. Baroda, his silence melted for the time.

He talked freely and intimately in a low, hesitating drawl that was not unpleasant to hear. He talked of the old college days when he and Gaston had been a good deal to each other; of the days of keen and blind ambitions and large intentions. Now there was left with him, at least, a philosophic acquiescence to the existing order—only a desire to be permitted to exist, with now and then a little whiff of genuine life, such as he was breathing now.

Her mind only vaguely grasped what he was saying. Her physical being was for the moment predominant. She was not thinking of his words, only drinking in the tones of his voice. She wanted to reach out her hand in the darkness and touch him with the sensitive tips of her fingers upon the face or the lips. She wanted to draw close to him and whisper against his cheek—she did not care what—as she might have done if she had not been a respectable woman.

The stronger the impulse grew to bring herself near him, the further, in fact, did she draw away from him. As soon as she could do so without an appearance of too great rudeness, she rose and left him there alone.

Before she reached the house, Gouvernail had lighted a fresh cigar and ended his apostrophe to the night.

Mrs. Baroda was greatly tempted that night to tell her husband—who was also her friend—of this folly that had seized her. But she did not yield to the temptation. Beside being a respectable woman she was a very sensible one; and she knew there are some battles in life which a human being must fight alone.

When Gaston arose in the morning, his wife had already departed. She had taken an early train to the city. She did not return till Gouvernail was gone from under her roof.

There was some talk of having him back during the summer that followed. That is, Gaston greatly desired it; but this desire yielded to his wife's strenuous opposition.

However, before the year ended, she proposed, wholly from herself, to have Gouvernail visit them again. Her husband was surprised and delighted with the suggestion coming from her.

"I am glad, chère amie, to know that you have finally overcome your dislike for him; truly he did not deserve it."

"Oh," she told him, laughingly, after pressing a long, tender kiss upon his lips, "I have overcome everything! you will see. This time I shall be very nice to him."

Suggestions for Discussion

1. How do you learn that Mrs. Baroda is ambivalent about Gouvernail?
2. Why do you think Mrs. Baroda left for the city? What precipitated the move?

3. What details suggest to you that this story was written in an earlier era?
4. What is the significance of the title? Relate it to the theme of the story. Is it used ironically?
5. What are you led to surmise is the relationship of Mrs. Baroda to her husband?
6. What do you think will happen on Gouvernail's next visit? How are you prepared for it?

Suggestion for Writing

Write an essay on Question 4 or 6 above.

JAMES THURBER

The Unicorn in the Garden

James Thurber (1894–1961), American humorist and artist, began contributing in 1927 to *The New Yorker,* in which most of his work first appeared. His humorous essays and short stories are collected in such books as *The Owl in the Attic* (1931), *My Life and Hard Times* (1933), *The Thurber Carnival* (1945), *The Beast in Me* (1948), and *Lanterns and Lances* (1961). He also wrote the short story "The Secret Life of Walter Mitty," several fantasies for children, and with Elliot Nugent, a comedy called *The Male Animal* (1940). "The Unicorn in the Garden," a fable of hostile feelings between husband and wife, ends with a surprise twist.

Once upon a sunny morning a man who sat in a breakfast nook looked up from his scrambled eggs to see a white unicorn with a gold horn quietly cropping the roses in the garden. The man went up to the bedroom where his wife was still asleep and woke her. "There's a unicorn in the garden," he said. "Eating roses." She opened one unfriendly eye and looked at him. "The unicorn is a mythical beast," she said, and turned her back to him. The man walked slowly downstairs and out into the garden. The unicorn was still there; he was now browsing among the tulips. "Here, unicorn," said the man, and he pulled up a lily and gave it to him. The unicorn ate it gravely. With a high heart, because there was a unicorn in his garden, the man went upstairs and roused his wife again. "The unicorn," he said, "ate a lily." His wife sat up in bed and looked at him, coldly. "You are a booby," she said, "and I am going to have you put in the booby-hatch." The man, who had never liked the words "booby" and "booby-hatch," and who liked them even less on a shining morning when there was a unicorn in the garden, thought for a moment. "We'll see about that," he said. He walked over to the door. "He has a golden horn in the middle of his forehead," he told her. Then he went back to the garden to watch the unicorn; but the unicorn had gone away. The man sat down among the roses and went to sleep.

As soon as the husband had gone out of the house, the wife got up and dressed as fast as she could. She was very excited and there was a gloat in her eye. She telephoned the police and she telephoned a psychiatrist; she told them to hurry to her house and bring a strait-jacket. When the police and the psychiatrist arrived they sat down in chairs and looked at her, with great interest. "My husband," she said, "saw a unicorn this morning." The police looked at the psychiatrist and the psychiatrist looked at the police. "He told me it ate a lily," she said. The psychiatrist looked at the police and the police looked at the psychiatrist. "He told me it had a golden horn in the middle of its forehead," she said. At a solemn signal from the psychiatrist, the police leaped from their chairs and seized the wife. They had a hard time subduing her, for she put up a terrific struggle, but they finally subdued her. Just as they got her into the strait-jacket, the husband came back into the house.

"Did you tell your wife you saw a unicorn?" asked the police. "Of course not," said the husband. "The unicorn is a mythical beast." "That's all I wanted to know," said the psychiatrist. "Take her away. I'm sorry, sir, but your wife is as crazy as a jay bird." So they took her away, cursing and screaming, and shut her up in an institution. The husband lived happily ever after.

Moral: Don't count your boobies until they are hatched.

Suggestions for Discussion

1. From what details do you become aware of the hostile feelings between husband and wife?
2. What is Thurber's attitude toward his characters, including the psychiatrist? Refer to the diction, the role of the unicorn, the setting, the details of the action, the twist at the end, the moral, and the drawing.
3. What other "moral" might be appropriate to append to this fable?
4. What evidence can you find that the author is (or is not) detached from his subject?

Suggestions for Writing

1. Write an imaginary description of the events leading up to the situation at the beginning of the fable.
2. Read "The Secret Life of Walter Mitty" and compare situation, tone, and resolution with those of the fable of the unicorn.
3. Write a fable depicting a domestic relationship.

JOHN STEINBECK

The Chrysanthemums

John Steinbeck (1902–1968) wrote novels, short stories, travel sketches, and essays. Born in Salinas, California, he studied at Stanford University. Before he achieved success as a writer, he worked as ranch hand, laborer, and newspaper reporter. Among his novels are *Tortilla Flat* (1935), *Of Mice and Men* (1937), *The Grapes of Wrath* (1939), which was awarded a Pulitzer Prize, and *East of Eden* (1952).

In 1962 he was awarded the Nobel Prize for Literature. Although Elisa's encounter with the tinker in "The Chrysanthemums" leads to her awareness of herself as a woman and of formerly submerged feelings, nothing in her external world has been significantly altered. Her isolation, vitality, and creative energy leave her unfulfilled as a woman.

The high grey-flannel fog of winter closed off the Salinas Valley from the sky and from all the rest of the world. On every side it sat like a lid on the mountains and made of the great valley a closed pot. On the broad, level land floor the gang plows bit deep and left the black earth shining like metal where the shares had cut. On the foothill ranches across the Salinas River, the yellow stubble fields seemed to be bathed in pale cold sunshine, but there was no sunshine in the valley now in December. The thick willow scrub along the river flamed with sharp and positive yellow leaves.

It was a time of quiet and of waiting. The air was cold and tender. A light wind blew up from the southwest so that the farmers were mildly hopeful of a good rain before long; but fog and rain do not go together.

Across the river, on Henry Allen's foothill ranch there was little work to be done, for the hay was cut and stored and the orchards were plowed up to receive the rain deeply when it should come. The cattle on the higher slopes were becoming shaggy and rough-coated.

Elisa Allen, working in her flower garden, looked down across the yard and saw Henry, her husband, talking to two men in business suits. The three of them stood by the tractor shed, each man with one foot on the side of the little Fordson. They smoked cigarettes and studied the machine as they talked.

Elisa watched them for a moment and then went back to her work. She was thirty-five. Her face was lean and strong and her eyes were as clear as water. Her figure looked blocked and heavy in her gardening costume, a man's black hat pulled low down over her eyes, clodhopper shoes, a figured print dress almost completely covered by a big corduroy apron with four big pockets to hold the snips, the trowel and scratcher, the seeds and the knife she worked with. She wore heavy leather gloves to protect her hands while she worked.

She was cutting down the old year's chrysanthemum stalks with a pair of short and powerful scissors. She looked down toward the men by the tractor shed now and then. Her face was eager and mature and handsome; even her work with the scissors was over-eager, over-powerful. The chrysanthemum stems seemed too small and easy for her energy.

She brushed a cloud of hair out of her eyes with the back of her glove, and left a smudge of earth on the cheek in doing it. Behind her stood the neat white farm house with red geraniums close-banked around it as high as the windows. It was a hard-swept looking little house, with hard-polished windows, and a clean mud-mat on the front steps.

Elisa cast another glance toward the tractor shed. The strangers were getting into their Ford coupe. She took off a glove and put her strong fingers down into the forest of new green chrysanthemum sprouts that were growing around the old roots. She spread the leaves and looked down among the close-growing stems. No aphids were there, no sowbugs or snails or cutworms. Her terrier fingers destroyed such pests before they could get started.

Elisa started at the sound of her husband's voice. He had come near quietly, and he leaned over the wire fence that protected her flower garden from cattle and dogs and chickens.

"At it again," he said. "You've got a strong new crop coming."

Elisa straightened her back and pulled on the gardening glove again. "Yes. They'll be strong this coming year." In her tone and on her face there was a little smugness.

"You've got a gift with things," Henry observed. "Some of those yellow chrysanthemums you had this year were ten inches across. I wish you'd work out in the orchard and raise some apples that big."

Her eyes sharpened. "Maybe I could do it, too. I've a gift with things, all right. My mother had it. She could stick anything in the ground and make it grow. She said it was having planters' hands that knew how to do it."

"Well, it sure works with flowers," he said.

"Henry, who were those men you were talking to?"

"Why, sure, that's what I came to tell you. They were from the Western Meat Company. I sold those thirty head of three-year-old steers. Got nearly my own price, too."

"Good," she said. "Good for you."

"And I thought," he continued, "I thought how it's Saturday afternoon, and we might go into Salinas for dinner at a restaurant, and then to a picture show—to celebrate, you see."

"Good," she repeated. "Oh, yes. That will be good."

Henry put on his joking tone. "There's fights tonight. How'd you like to go to the fights?"

"Oh, no," she said breathlessly. "No, I wouldn't like fights."

"Just fooling, Elisa. We'll go to a movie. Let's see. It's two now. I'm going to take Scotty and bring down those steers from the hill. It'll take us maybe two hours. We'll go in town about five and have dinner at the Cominos Hotel. Like that?"

"Of course I'll like it. It's good to eat away from home."

"All right, then. I'll go get up a couple of horses."

She said, "I'll have plenty of time to transplant some of these sets, I guess."

She heard her husband calling Scotty down by the barn. And a little later she saw the two men ride up the pale yellow hillside in search of the steers.

There was a little square sandy bed kept for rooting the chrysanthemums. With her trowel she turned the soil over and over, and smoothed it and patted it firm. Then she dug ten parallel trenches to receive the sets. Back at the chrysanthemum bed she pulled out the little crisp shoots, trimmed off the leaves of each one with her scissors and laid it on a small orderly pile.

A squeak of wheels and plod of hoofs came from the road. Elisa looked up. The country road ran along the dense bank of willows and cottonwoods that bordered the river, and up this road came a curious vehicle, curiously drawn. It was an old spring-wagon, with a round canvas top on it like the cover of a prairie schooner. It was drawn by an old bay horse and a little grey-and-white burro. A big stubble-bearded man sat between the cover flaps and drove the crawling team. Underneath the wagon, between the hind wheels, a lean and rangy mongrel dog walked sedately. Words were painted on the canvas in clumsy, crooked letters. "Pots, pans, knives, sisors, lawn mores. Fixed." Two rows of articles and the triumphantly definitive "Fixed" below. The black paint had run down in little sharp points beneath each letter.

Elisa, squatting on the ground, watched to see the crazy, loose-jointed wagon pass by. But it didn't pass. It turned into the farm road in front of her house, crooked old wheels skirling and squeaking. The rangy dog darted from between the wheels and ran ahead. Instantly the two ranch shepherds flew out at him. Then all three stopped, and with stiff and quivering tails, with taut straight legs, with ambassadorial dignity, they slowly circled, sniffing daintily. The caravan pulled up to Elisa's wire fence and stopped. Now the newcomer dog, feeling out-numbered, lowered his tail and retired under the wagon with raised hackles and bared teeth.

The man on the wagon seat called out. "That's a bad dog in a fight when he gets started."

Elisa laughed."I see he is. How soon does he generally get started?"

The man caught up her laughter and echoed it heartily. "Sometimes not for weeks and weeks," he said. He climbed stiffly down, over the wheel. The horse and the donkey drooped like unwatered flowers.

Elisa saw that he was a very big man. Although his hair and beard were greying, he did not look old. His worn black suit was wrinkled and spotted with grease. The laughter had disappeared from his face and eyes the moment his laughing voice ceased. His eyes were dark, and they were full of the brooding that gets in the eyes of teamsters and of sailors. The calloused hands he rested on the wire fence were cracked, and every crack was a black line. He took off his battered hat.

"I'm off my general road, ma'am," he said. "Does this dirt road cut over across the river to the Los Angeles highway?"

Elisa stood up and shoved the thick scissors in her apron pocket. "Well, yes, it does, but it winds around and then fords the river. I don't think your team could pull through the sand."

He replied with some asperity, "It might surprise you what them beasts can pull through."

"When they get started?" she asked.

He smiled for a second. "Yes. When they get started."

"Well," said Elisa, "I think you'll save time if you go back to the Salinas road and pick up the highway there."

He drew a big finger down the chicken wire and made it sing. "I ain't in any hurry, ma'am. I go from Seattle to San Diego and back every year. Takes all my time. About six months each way. I aim to follow nice weather."

Elisa took off her gloves and stuffed them in the apron pocket with the scissors. She touched the under edge of her man's hat, searching for fugitive hairs. "That sounds like a nice kind of a way to live," she said.

He leaned confidentially over the fence. "Maybe you noticed the writing on my wagon. I mend pots and sharpen knives and scissors. You got any of them things to do?"

"Oh, no," she said quickly. "Nothing like that." Her eyes hardened with resistance.

"Scissors is the worst thing," he explained. "Most people just ruin scissors trying to sharpen'em but I know how. I got a special tool. It's a little bobbit kind of thing, and patented. But it sure does the trick."

"No. My scissors are all sharp."

"All right, then. Take a pot," he continued earnestly, "a bent pot, or a pot with a hole. I can make it like new so you don't have to buy no new ones. That's a saving for you."

"No," she said shortly. "I tell you I have nothing like that for you to do."

His face fell to an exaggerated sadness. His voice took on a whining undertone. "I ain't had a thing to do today. Maybe I won't have no supper tonight. You see I'm off my regular road. I know folks on the highway clear from Seattle to San Diego. They save their things for me to sharpen up because they know I do it so good and save them money."

"I'm sorry," Elisa said irritably. "I haven't anything for you to do."

His eyes left her face and fell to searching the ground. They roamed about until they came to the chrysanthemum bed where she had been working. "What's them plants, ma'am?"

The irritation and resistance melted from Elisa's face. "Oh, those are chrysanthemums, giant whites and yellows. I raise them every year, bigger than anybody around here."

"Kind of a long-stemmed flower? Looks like a quick puff of colored smoke?" he asked.

"That's it. What a nice way to describe them."

"They smell kind of nasty till you get used to them," he said.

"It's a good bitter smell," she retorted, "not nasty at all."

He changed his tone quickly. "I like the smell myself."

"I had ten-inch blooms this year," she said.

The man leaned farther over the fence. "Look. I know a lady down the road a piece, has got the nicest garden you ever seen. Got nearly every kind of flower but no chrysanthemums. Last time I was mending a copper-bottom washtub for her (that's a hard job but I do it good), she said to me, 'If you ever run acrost some nice chrysanthemums I wish you'd try to get me a few seeds.' That's what she told me."

Elisa's eyes grew alert and eager. "She couldn't have known much about chrysanthemums. You can raise them from seed, but it's much easier to root the little sprouts you see there."

"Oh," he said. "I s'pose I can't take none to her, then."

"Why yes you can," Elisa cried. "I can put some in damp sand, and you can carry them right along with you. They'll take root in the pot if you keep them damp. And then she can transplant them."

"She'd sure like to have some, ma'am. You say they're nice ones?"

"Beautiful," she said. "Oh, beautuful." Her eyes shone. She tore off the battered hat and shook out her dark pretty hair. "I'll put them in a flower pot, and you can take them right with you. Come into the yard."

While the man came through the picket gate Elisa ran excitedly along the geranium-bordered path to the back of the house. And she returned carrying a big red flower pot. The gloves were forgotten now. She kneeled on the ground by the starting bed and dug up the sandy soil with her fingers and scooped it into the bright new flower pot. Then she picked up the little pile of shoots she had prepared. With her strong fingers she pressed them into the sand and tamped around them with her knuckles. The man stood over her. "I'll tell you what to do," she said. "You remember so you can tell the lady."

"Yes, I'll try to remember."

"Well, look. These will take root in about a month. Then she must set them out, about a foot apart in good rich earth like this, see?" She lifted a handful of dark soil for him to look at. "They'll grow fast and tall. Now remember this. In July tell her to cut them down, about eight inches from the ground."

"Before they bloom?" he asked.

"Yes, before they bloom." Her face was tight with eagerness. "They'll come right up again. About the last of September the buds will start."

She stopped and seemed perplexed. "It's the budding that takes the most care," she said hesitantly. "I don't know how to tell you." She looked deep into his eyes, searchingly. Her mouth opened a little, and she seemed to be listening. "I'll try to tell you," she said. "Did you ever hear of planting hands?"

"Can't say I have, ma'am."

"Well, I can only tell you what it feels like. It's when you're picking off the buds you don't want. Everything goes right down into your fingertips. You watch your fingers work. They do it themselves. You can feel how it is. They pick and pick the buds. They never make a mistake. They're with the plant. Do you see? Your fingers and the plant. You can feel that, right up your arm. They know. They never make a mistake. You can feel it. When you're like that you can't do anything wrong. Do you see that? Can you understand that?"

She was kneeling on the ground looking up at him. Her breast swelled passionately.

The man's eyes narrowed. He looked away, self-consciously. "Maybe I know," he said. "Sometimes in the night in the wagon there—"

Elisa's voice grew husky. She broke in on him. "I've never lived as you do, but I know what you mean. When the night is dark—why, the stars are sharp-pointed, and there's quiet. Why, you rise up and up! Every pointed star gets driven into your body. It's like that. Hot and sharp and—lovely."

Kneeling there, her hand went out toward his legs in the greasy black trousers. Her hesitant fingers almost touched the cloth. Then her hand dropped to the ground. She crouched low like a fawning dog.

He said, "It's nice, just like you say. Only when you don't have no dinner, it ain't."

She stood up then, very straight, and her face was ashamed. She held the flower pot out to him and placed it gently in his arms. "Here. Put it in your wagon, on the seat, where you can watch it. Maybe I can find something for you to do."

At the back of the house she dug in the can pile and found two old and battered aluminum saucepans. She carried them back and gave them to him. "Here, maybe you can fix these."

His manner changed. He became professional. "Good as new I can fix them." At the back of his wagon he set a little anvil, and out of an oily tool box dug a small machine hammer. Elisa came through the gate to watch him while he pounded out the dents in the kettles. His mouth grew sure and knowing. At a difficult part of the work he sucked his under-lip.

"You sleep right in the wagon?" Elisa asked.

"Right in the wagon, ma'am. Rain or shine I'm dry as a cow in there."

"It must be nice," she said. "It must be very nice. I wish women could do such things."

"It ain't the right kind of a life for a woman."

Her upper lip raised a little, showing her teeth. "How do you know? How can you tell?" she said.

"I don't know ma'am," he protested. "Of course I don't know. Now here's your kettles, done. You don't have to buy no new ones."

"How much?"

"Oh, fifty cents'll do. I keep my prices down and my work good. That's why I have all them satisfied customers up and down the highway."

Elisa brought him a fifty-cent piece from the house and dropped it in his hand. "You might be surprised to have a rival some time. I can sharpen scissors, too. And I can beat the dents out of little pots. I could show you what a woman might do."

He put his hammer back in the oily box and shoved the little anvil out of sight. "It would be a lonely life for a woman, ma'am, and a scarey life, too, with animals creeping under the wagon all night." He climbed over the singletree, steadying himself with a hand on the burro's white rump. He settled himself in the seat, picked up the lines. "Thank you kindly, ma'am," he said. "I'll do like you told me; I'll go back and catch the Salinas road."

"Mind," she called, "if you're long in getting there, keep the sand damp."

"Sand, ma'am?... Sand? Oh, sure. You mean round the chrysanthemums. Sure I will." He clucked his tongue. The beasts leaned luxuriously into their collars. The mongrel dog took his place between the back wheels. The wagon turned and crawled out the entrance road and back the way it had come, along the river.

Elisa stood in front of her wire fence watching the slow progress of the caravan. Her shoulders were straight, her head thrown back, her eyes half-closed, so that the scene came vaguely into them. Her lips moved silently, forming the words "Good-bye—good-bye." Then she whispered. "That's a bright direction. There's a glowing there." The sound of her whisper startled her. She shook herself free and looked about to see whether anyone had been listening. Only the dogs had heard. They lifted their heads toward her from their sleeping in the dust, and then stretched out their chins and settled asleep again. Elisa turned and ran hurriedly into the house.

In the kitchen she reached behind the stove and felt the water tank. It was full of hot water from the noonday cooking. In the bathroom she tore off her soiled clothes and flung them into the corner. And then she scrubbed herself with a little block of pumice, legs and thighs, loins and chest and arms, until her skin was scratched and red. When she had dried herself she stood in front of a mirror in her bedroom and looked at her body. She tightened her stomach and threw out her chest. She turned and looked over her shoulder at her back.

After a while she began to dress, slowly. She put on her newest underclothing and her nicest stockings and the dress which was the symbol of her prettiness. She worked carefully on her hair, pencilled her eyebrows and rouged her lips.

Before she was finished she heard the little thunder of hoofs and the shouts of Henry and his helper as they drove the red steers into the corral. She heard the gate bang shut and set herself for Henry's arrival.

His step sounded on the porch. He entered the house calling "Elisa, where are you?"

"In my room, dressing. I'm not ready. There's hot water for your bath. Hurry up. It's getting late."

When she heard him splashing in the tub, Elisa laid his dark suit on the bed, and shirt and socks and tie beside it. She stood his polished shoes on the floor beside the bed. Then she went to the porch and sat primly and stiffly down. She looked toward the river road where the willow-line was still yellow with frosted leaves so that under the high grey fog they seemed a thin band of sunshine. This was the only color in the grey afternoon. She sat unmoving for a long time. Her eyes blinked rarely.

Henry came banging out of the door, shoving his tie inside his vest as he came. Elisa stiffened and her face grew tight. Henry stopped short and looked at her. "Why—why, Elisa. You look so nice!"

"Nice? You think I look nice? What do you mean by 'nice'?"

Henry blundered on. "I don't know. I mean you look different, strong and happy."

"I am strong? Yes, strong. What do you mean 'strong'?"

He looked bewildered. "You're playing some kind of a game," he said helplessly. "It's a kind of a play. You look strong enough to break a calf over your knee, happy enough to eat it like a watermelon."

For a second she lost her rigidity. "Henry! Don't talk like that. You didn't know what you said." She grew complete again. "I'm strong," she boasted. "I never knew before how strong."

Henry looked down toward the tractor shed, and when he brought his eyes back to her, they were his own again. "I'll get out the car. You can put on your coat while I'm starting."

Elisa went into the house. She heard him drive to the gate and idle down his motor, and then she took a long time to put on her hat. She pulled it here and pressed it there. When Henry turned the motor off she slipped into her coat and went out.

The little roadster bounced along on the dirt road by the river, raising the birds and driving the rabbits into the brush. Two cranes flapped heavily over the willow-line and dropped into the river-bed.

Far ahead on the road Elisa saw a dark speck. She knew.

She tried not to look as they passed it, but her eyes would not obey. She whispered to herself sadly. "He might have thrown them off the road. That wouldn't have been much trouble, not very much. But he kept the pot," she explained. "He had to keep the pot. That's why he couldn't get them off the road."

The roadster turned a bend and she saw the caravan ahead. She swung full around toward her husband so she could not see the little covered wagon and the mismatched team as the car passed them.

In a moment they had left behind them the man who had not known or needed to know what she said, the bargainer. She did not look back.

To Henry, she said loudly, to be heard above the motor, "It will be good, to-night, a good dinner."

"Now you're changed again," Henry complained. He took one hand from the wheel and patted her knee. "I ought to take you in to dinner oftener. It would be good for both of us. We get so heavy out on the ranch."

"Henry," she asked, "could we have wine at dinner?"

"Sure. Say! That will be fine."

She was silent for a while; then she said, "Henry, at those prize fights do the men hurt each other very much?"

"Sometimes a little, not often. Why?"

"Well, I've read how they break noses, and blood runs down their chests. I've read how the fighting gloves get heavy and soggy with blood."

He looked round at her. "What's the matter, Elisa? I didn't know you read things like that." He brought the car to a stop, then turned to the right over the Salinas River bridge.

"Do any women ever go to the fights?" she asked.

"Oh, sure, some. What's the matter, Elisa? Do you want to go? I don't think you'd like it, but I'll take you if you really want to go."

She relaxed limply in the seat. "Oh, no. I don't want to go. I'm sure I don't." Her face was turned away from him. "It will be enough if we can have wine. It will be plenty." She turned up her coat collar so he could not see that she was crying weakly—like an old woman.

Suggestions for Discussion

1. What descriptive details prepare you for Elisa's emotional isolation?
2. The action, rising in emotional intensity to its climax, is developed in four scenes. Describe Elisa's feelings in each scene and attempt to account for them.
3. Discuss the possible symbolic functions of the scissors, the chrysanthemum shoots, the wine, and the fights. How are they related to the complication and resolution of the action?
4. How is the tinker's deception foreshadowed?
5. By what means are we made aware of the change in Elisa's image of herself? How adequately does the story account for Elisa's frustration? Explain the fluctuations in her appearance and mood. By what means are we made aware that her relationship with Henry is not satisfying?

Suggestions for Writing

1. Relate the story to the essay by Germaine Greer, "The Stereotype."
2. Write a character study of Elisa.
3. Portray in narrative form a marital relationship in which there is a failure in communication.

CARSON MCCULLERS

The Sojourner

Carson McCullers (1917–1967), a Southern writer, was awarded Guggenheim fellowships in 1942 and in 1946. Her published works include *The Heart Is a Lonely Hunter* (1940), *Reflections in a Golden Eye* (1941), *The Member of the Wedding* (1946), *The Ballad of the Sad Café* (1951), and *Clock Without Hands* (1961). After a rootless man relives and revisits his past, the experience enables him to acknowledge the waste of his years, the brevity of life, and his need to reorder his relationships with those close to him.

The twilight border between sleep and waking was a Roman one this morning: splashing fountains and arched, narrow streets, the golden lavish city of blossoms and age-soft stone. Sometimes in this semiconsciousness he sojourned again in Paris, or German war rubble, or a Swiss skiing and a snow hotel. Sometimes, also, in a fallow Georgia field at hunting dawn. Rome it was this morning in the yearless region of dreams.

John Ferris awoke in a room in a New York hotel. He had the feeling that something unpleasant was awaiting him—what it was, he did not know. The feeling, submerged by matinal necessities, lingered even after he had dressed and gone downstairs. It was a cloudless autumn day and the pale sunlight sliced between the pastel skyscrapers. Ferris went into the next-door drugstore and sat at the end booth next to the window glass that overlooked the sidewalk. He ordered an American breakfast with scrambled eggs and sausage.

Ferris had come from Paris to his father's funeral which had taken place the week before in his home town in Georgia. The shock of death had made him aware of youth already passed. His hair was receding and the veins in his now naked temples were pulsing and prominent and his body was spare except for an incipient belly bulge. Ferris had loved his father and the bond between them had once been extraordinarily close—but the years had somehow unraveled this filial devotion; the death, expected for a long time, had left him with an unforeseen dismay. He had stayed as long as possible to be near his mother and brothers at home. His plane for Paris was to leave the next morning.

Ferris pulled out his address book to verify a number. He turned the pages with growing attentiveness. Names and addresses from New York, the capitals of Europe, a few faint ones from his home state in the South. Faded, printed names, sprawled drunken ones. Betty Wills: a random love, married now. Charlie Williams: wounded in the Hürtgen Forest, unheard of since. Grand old Williams—did he live or die? Don Walker: a B.T.O. in television, getting rich. Henry Green: hit the skids after the war, in a sanitarium now, they say. Cozie Hall: he had heard that she was dead. Heedless, laughing Cozie—it was strange to think that she too, silly girl, could die. As Ferris closed the address book, he suffered a sense of hazard, transience, almost of fear.

It was then that his body jerked suddenly. He was staring out of the window when there, on the sidewalk, passing by, was his ex-wife. Elizabeth passed quite close to him, walking slowly. He could not understand the wild quiver of his heart, nor the following sense of recklessness and grace that lingered after she was gone.

Quickly Ferris paid his check and rushed out to the sidewalk. Elizabeth stood on the corner waiting to cross Fifth Avenue. He hurried toward her meaning to speak, but the lights changed and she crossed the street before he reached her. Ferris followed. On the other side he could easily have overtaken her, but he found himself lagging unaccountably. Her fair hair was plainly rolled, and as he watched her Ferris recalled that once his father had remarked that Elizabeth had a "beautiful carriage." She turned at the next corner and Ferris followed, although by now his intention to overtake her had disappeared. Ferris questioned the bodily disturbance that the sight of Elizabeth aroused in him, the dampness of his hands, the hard heartstrokes.

It was eight years since Ferris had last seen his ex-wife. He knew that long ago she had married again. And there were children. During recent years he had seldom thought of her. But at first, after the divorce, the loss had almost destroyed him. Then after the anodyne of time, he had loved again, and then again. Jeannine, she was now. Certainly his love for his ex-wife was long since past. So why the unhinged body, the shaken mind? He knew only that his clouded heart was oddly dissonant with the sunny, candid autumn day. Ferris wheeled suddenly and, walking with long strides, almost running, hurried back to the hotel.

Ferris poured himself a drink, although it was not yet eleven o'clock. He sprawled out in an armchair like a man exhausted, nursing his glass of bourbon and water. He had a full day ahead of him as he was leaving by plane the next morning for Paris. He checked over his obligations: take luggage to Air France, lunch with his boss, buy shoes and an overcoat. And something—wasn't there something else? Ferris finished his drink and opened the telephone directory.

His decision to call his ex-wife was impulsive. The number was under Bailey, the husband's name, and he called before he had much time for self-debate. He and Elizabeth had exchanged cards at Christmastime, and Ferris had sent a carving set when he received the announcement of her wedding. There was no reason *not* to call. But as he waited, listening to the ring at the other end, misgiving fretted him.

Elizabeth answered; her familiar voice was a fresh shock to him. Twice he had to repeat his name, but when he was identified, she sounded glad. He explained he was only in town for that day. They had a theater engagement, she said—but she wondered if he would come by for an early dinner. Ferris said he would be delighted.

As he went from one engagement to another, he was still bothered at odd moments by the feeling that something necessary was forgotten. Ferris bathed and changed in the late afternoon, often thinking about Jeannine: he would be with her the following night. "Jeannine," he would say, "I happened to run into my ex-wife when I was in New York. Had dinner with her. And her husband, of course. It was strange seeing her after all these years."

Elizabeth lived in the East Fifties, and as Ferris taxied uptown he glimpsed at intersections the lingering sunset, but by the time he reached his destination it was already autumn dark. The place was a building with a marquee and a doorman, and the apartment was on the seventh floor.

"Come in, Mr. Ferris."

Braced for Elizabeth or even the unimagined husband, Ferris was astonished by the freckled red-haired child; he had known of the children, but his mind had failed somehow to acknowledge them. Surprise made him step back awkwardly.

"This is our apartment," the child said politely. "Aren't you Mr. Ferris? I'm Billy. Come in."

In the living room beyond the hall, the husband provided another surprise; he too had not been acknowledged emotionally. Bailey was a lumbering red-haired man with a deliberate manner. He rose and extended a welcoming hand.

"I'm Bill Bailey. Glad to see you. Elizabeth will be in, in a minute. She's finishing dressing."

The last words struck a gliding series of vibrations, memories of the other years. Fair Elizabeth, rosy and naked before her bath. Half-dressed before the mirror of her dressing table, brushing her fine, chestnut hair. Sweet, casual intimacy, the soft-fleshed loveliness indisputably possessed. Ferris shrank from the unbidden memories and compelled himself to meet Bill Bailey's gaze.

"Billy, will you please bring that tray of drinks from the kitchen table?"

The child obeyed promptly, and when he was gone Ferris remarked conversationally, "Fine boy you have there."

"We think so."

Flat silence until the child returned with a tray of glasses and a cocktail shaker of Martinis. With the priming drinks they pumped up conversation: Russia, they spoke of, and the New York rain-making, and the apartment situation in Manhattan and Paris.

"Mr. Ferris is flying all the way across the ocean tomorrow," Bailey said to the little boy who was perched on the arm of his chair, quiet and well behaved. "I bet you would like to be a stowaway in his suitcase."

Billy pushed back his limp bangs. "I want to fly in an airplane and be a newspaperman like Mr. Ferris." He added with sudden assurance, "That's what I would like to do when I am big."

Bailey said, "I thought you wanted to be a doctor."

"I do!" said Billy. "I would like to be both. I want to be a atom-bomb scientist too."

Elizabeth came in carrying in her arms a baby girl.

"Oh, John!" she said. She settled the baby in the father's lap. "It's grand to see you. I'm awfully glad you could come."

The little girl sat demurely on Bailey's knees. She wore a pale pink crepe de Chine frock, smocked around the yoke with rose, and a matching silk hair ribbon tying back her pale soft curls. Her skin was summer tanned and her brown eyes flecked with gold and laughing. When she reached up and fingered her father's horn-rimmed glasses, he took them off and let her look through them a moment. "How's my old Candy?"

Elizabeth was very beautiful, more beautiful perhaps than he had ever realized. Her straight clean hair was shining. Her face was softer, glowing and serene. It was a madonna loveliness, dependent on the family ambiance.

"You've hardly changed at all," Elizabeth said, "but it has been a long time."

"Eight years." His hand touched his thinning hair self-consciously while further amenities were exchanged.

Ferris felt himself suddenly a spectator—an interloper among these Baileys. Why had he come? He suffered. His own life seemed so solitary, a fragile column supporting nothing amidst the wreckage of the years. He felt he could not bear much longer to stay in the family room.

He glanced at his watch. "You're going to the theater?"

"It's a shame," Elizabeth said, "but we've had this engagement for more than a month. But surely, John, you'll be staying home one of these days before long. You're not going to be an expatriate, are you?"

"Expatriate," Ferris repeated. "I don't much like the word."

"What's a better word?" she asked.

He thought for a moment. "Sojourner might do."

Ferris glanced again at his watch, and again Elizabeth apologized. "If only we had known ahead of time—"

"I just had this day in town. I came home unexpectedly. You see, Papa died last week."

"Papa Ferris is dead?"

"Yes, at Johns Hopkins. He had been sick there nearly a year. The funeral was down home in Georgia."

"Oh, I'm so sorry, John. Papa Ferris was always one of my favorite people."

The little boy moved from behind the chair so that he could look into his mother's face. He asked, "Who is dead?"

Ferris was oblivious to apprehension; he was thinking of his father's death. He saw again the outstretched body on the quilted silk within the coffin. The corpse flesh was bizarrely rouged and the familiar hands lay massive and joined above a spread of funeral roses. The memory closed and Ferris awakened to Elizabeth's calm voice.

"Mr. Ferris's father, Billy. A really grand person. Somebody you didn't know."

"But why did you call him *Papa* Ferris?"

Bailey and Elizabeth exchanged a trapped look. It was Bailey who answered the questioning child. "A long time ago," he said, "your mother and Mr. Ferris were once married. Before you were born—a long time ago."

"Mr. Ferris?"

The little boy stared at Ferris, amazed and unbelieving. And Ferris's eyes, as he returned the gaze, were somehow unbelieving too. Was it indeed true that at one time he had called this stranger, Elizabeth, Little Butterduck during nights of love, that they had lived together, shared perhaps a thousand days and nights and—finally—endured in the misery of sudden solitude the fiber by fiber (jealousy, alcohol and money quarrels) destruction of the fabric of married love?

Bailey said to the children, "It's somebody's suppertime. Come on now."

"But Daddy! Mama and Mr. Ferris—I—"

Billy's everlasting eyes—perplexed and with a glimmer of hostility—reminded Ferris of the gaze of another child. It was the young son of Jeannine—a boy of seven with a shadowed little face and knobby knees whom Ferris avoided and usually forgot.

"Quick march!" Bailey gently turned Billy toward the door. "Say good night now, son."

"Good night, Mr. Ferris." He added resentfully, "I thought I was staying up for the cake."

"You can come in afterward for the cake," Elizabeth said. "Run along now with Daddy for your supper."

Ferris and Elizabeth were alone. The weight of the situation descended on those first moments of silence. Ferris asked permission to pour himself another drink and Elizabeth set the cocktail shaker on the table at his side. He looked at the grand piano and noticed the music on the rack.

"Do you still play as beautifully as you used to?"

"I still enjoy it."

"Please play, Elizabeth."

Elizabeth rose immediately. Her readiness to perform when asked had always been one of her amiabilities; she never hung back, apologized. Now as she approached the piano there was the added readiness of relief.

She began with a Bach prelude and fugue. The prelude was as gaily iridescent as a prism in a morning room. The first voice of the fugue, an announcement pure and solitary, was repeated intermingling with a second voice, and again repeated within an elaborated frame, the multiple music, horizontal and serene, flowed with unhurried majesty. The principal melody was woven with two other voices, embellished with countless ingenuities—now dominant, again submerged, it had the sublimity of a single thing that does not fear surrender to the whole. Toward the end, the density of the material gathered for the last enriched insistence on the dominant first motif and with a chorded final statement the fugue ended. Ferris rested his head on the chair back and closed his eyes. In the following silence a clear, high voice came from the room down the hall.

"Daddy, how *could* Mama and Mr. Ferris—" A door was closed.

The piano began again—what was this music? Unplaced, familiar, the limpid melody had lain a long while dormant in his heart. Now it spoke to him of another time, another place—it was the music Elizabeth used to play. The delicate air summoned a wilderness of memory. Ferris was lost in the riot of past longings, conflicts, ambivalent desires. Strange that the music, catalyst for this tumultuous anarchy, was so serene and clear. The singing melody was broken off by the appearance of the maid.

"Miz Bailey, dinner is out on the table now."

Even after Ferris was seated at the table between his host and hostess, the unfinished music still overcast his mood. He was a little drunk.

"*L'improvisation de la vie humaine,*" he said. "There's nothing that makes you so aware of the improvisation of human existence as a song unfinished. Or an old address book."

"Address book?" repeated Bailey. Then he stopped, noncommittal and polite.

"You're still the same old boy, Johnny," Elizabeth said with a trace of the old tenderness.

It was a Southern dinner that evening, and the dishes were his old favorites. They had fried chicken and corn pudding and rich, glazed candied sweet potatoes. During the meal Elizabeth kept alive a conversation when the silences were overlong. And it came about that Ferris was led to speak of Jeannine.

"I first knew Jeannine last autumn—about this time of the year—in Italy. She's a singer and she had an engagement in Rome. I expect we will be married soon."

The words seemed so true, inevitable, that Ferris did not at first acknowledge to himself the lie. He and Jeannine had never in that year spoken of marriage. And indeed, she was still married—to a White Russian money-changer in Paris from whom she had been separated for five years. But it was too late to correct the lie. Already Elizabeth was saying: "This really makes me glad to know. Congratulations, Johnny."

He tried to make amends with truth. "The Roman autumn is so beautiful. Balmy and blossoming." He added, "Jeannine has a little boy of six. A curious trilingual little fellow. We go to the Tuileries sometimes."

A lie again. He had taken the boy once to the gardens. The sallow foreign child in shorts that bared his spindly legs had sailed his boat in the concrete pond and ridden the pony. The child had wanted to go in to the puppet show. But there was not time, for Ferris had an engagement at the Scribe Hotel. He had promised they would go to the guignol another afternoon. Only once had he taken Valentin to the Tuileries.

There was a stir. The maid brought in a white-frosted cake with pink candles. The children entered in their night clothes. Ferris still did not understand.

"Happy birthday, John," Elizabeth said. "Blow out the candles."

Ferris recognized his birthday date. The candles blew out lingeringly and there was the smell of burning wax. Ferris was thirty-eight years old. The veins in his temples darkened and pulsed visibly.

"It's time you started for the theater."

Ferris thanked Elizabeth for the birthday dinner and said the appropriate good-byes. The whole family saw him to the door.

A high, thin moon shone above the jagged, dark skyscrapers. The streets were windy, cold. Ferris hurried to Third Avenue and hailed a cab. He gazed at the nocturnal city with the deliberate attentiveness of departure and perhaps farewell. He was alone. He longed for flight-time and the coming journey.

The next day he looked down on the city from the air, burnished in sunlight, toylike, precise. Then America was left behind and there was only the Atlantic and the distant European shore. The ocean was milky pale and placid beneath the clouds. Ferris dozed most of the day. Toward dark he was thinking of Elizabeth and the visit of the previous evening. He thought of Elizabeth among her family with longing, gentle envy and inexplicable regret. He sought the melody, the unfinished air, that had so moved him. The cadence, some unrelated tones, were all that remained; the melody itself evaded him. He had found instead the first voice of the fugue that Elizabeth had played—it came to him, inverted mockingly and in a minor key. Suspended above the ocean the anxieties of transience and solitude no longer troubled him and he thought of his father's death with equanimity. During the dinner hour the plane reached the shore of France.

At midnight Ferris was in a taxi crossing Paris. It was a clouded night and mist wreathed the lights of the Place de la Concorde. The midnight bistros gleamed on the wet pavements. As always after a transocean flight the change of continents was too sudden. New York at morning, this midnight Paris. Ferris glimpsed the disorder of his life: the succession of cities, of transitory loves; and time, the sinister glissando of the years, time always.

"*Vite! Vite!*" he called in terror. "*Dépéchez-vous.*"

Valentin opened the door to him. The little boy wore pajamas and an outgrown red robe. His grey eyes were shadowed and, as Ferris passed into the flat, they flickered momentarily.

"*J'attends Maman.*"

Jeannine was singing in a night club. She would not be home before another hour. Valentin returned to a drawing, squatting with his crayons over the paper on the floor. Ferris looked down at the drawing—it was a banjo player with notes and wavy lines inside a comicstrip balloon.

"We will go again to the Tuileries."

The child looked up and Ferris drew him closer to his knees. The melody, the unfinished music that Elizabeth had played came to him suddenly. Unsought, the load of memory jettisoned—this time bringing only recognition and sudden joy.

"Monsieur Jean," the child said, "did you see him?"

Confused, Ferris thought only of another child—the freckled, family-loved boy. "See who, Valentin?"

"Your dead papa in Georgia." The child added, "Was he okay?"

Ferris spoke with rapid urgency: "We will go often to the Tuileries. Ride the pony and we will go into the guignol. We will see the puppet show and never be in a hurry any more."

"Monsieur Jean," Valentin said. "The guignol is now closed."

Again, the terror, the acknowledgment of wasted years and death. Valentin, responsive and confident, still nestled in his arms. His cheek touched the soft cheek and felt the brush of the delicate eyelashes. With inner desperation he pressed the child close—as though an emotion as protean as his love could dominate the pulse of time.

Suggestions for Discussion

1. In *The Mortgaged Heart* McCullers suggests that the way by which we master loneliness is "to belong to something larger and more powerful than the weak, lonely self." How is this belief developed in her short story?
2. What do the descriptions in the opening four paragraphs tell you about Ferris? In particular, try to account for his emotional response to the names in his address book.
3. From the moment Ferris catches a glimpse of Elizabeth on the sidewalk outside the restaurant to his flight to Paris and his taxi ride across the city, the reader gains an understanding of Elizabeth and of their relationship. What details clarify your knowledge of Elizabeth? Of Ferris?
4. What is Ferris's response to his evening at the Baileys? How does the playing of the fugue and the second piece he couldn't identify affect Ferris?
5. Why does Ferris lie to Elizabeth about his relationship with Jeannine and Valentin?
6. How are you prepared for Ferris's new relationship with Valentin?
7. What is the meaning of the last sentence? Relate it to what has gone before in Ferris's life.

Suggestions for Writing

1. Discuss the McCullers quotation in Question 1.
2. Write a narrative growing out of your observation or experience about the effects of divorce on the former mates and/or the children.

LESLIE MARMON SILKO

Lullaby

Leslie Marmon Silko (b. 1948) received her B.A. from the University of New Mexico; she has taught both there and at the University of Arizona. She grew up on the Laguna Pueblo Reservation, where she presently lives. In addition to having won the Pushcart and Chicago

Review Poetry Prizes, she has been awarded fellowships from the National Endowment for the Arts and, in 1983, the MacArthur Foundation. Among her recent books are *Storyteller* (1981), *The Delicacy and Strength of Lace* (1986), *Almanac of the Dead* (1991), and *Yellow Woman and Beauty of the Spirit: Essays on Native American Life Today* (1996).

The sun had gone down but the snow in the wind gave off its own light. It came in thick tufts like new wool—washed before the weaver spins it. Ayah reached out for it like her own babies had, and she smiled when she remembered how she had laughed at them. She was an old woman now, and her life had become memories. She sat down with her back against the wide cottonwood tree, feeling the rough bark on her back bones; she faced east and listened to the wind and snow sing a high-pitched Yeibechei song. Out of the wind she felt warmer, and she could watch the wide, fluffy snow fill in her tracks, steadily, until the direction she had come from was gone. By the light of the snow she could see the dark outline of the big arroyo a few feet away. She was sitting on the edge of Cebolleta Creek, where in the springtime the thin cows would graze on grass already chewed flat to the ground. In the wide, deep creek bed where only a trickle of water flowed in the summer, the skinny cows would wander, looking for new grass along winding paths splashed with manure.

Ayah pulled the old Army blanket over her head like a shawl. Jimmie's blanket—the one he had sent to her. That was a long time ago and the green wool was faded, and it was unraveling on the edges. She did not want to think about Jimmie. So she thought about the weaving and the way her mother had done it. On the tall wooden loom set into the sand under a tamarack tree for shade. She could see it clearly. She had been only a little girl when her grandma gave her the wooden combs to pull the twigs and burrs from the raw, freshly washed wool. And while she combed the wool, her grandma sat beside her spinning a silvery strand of yarn around the smooth cedar spindle. Her mother worked at the loom with yarns dyed bright yellow and red and gold. She watched them dye the yarn in boiling black pots full of beeweed petals, juniper berries, and sage. The blankets her mother made were soft and woven so tight that rain rolled off them like birds' feathers. Ayah remembered sleeping warmly on cold windy nights, wrapped in her mother's blankets on the hogan's sandy floor.

The snow drifted now, with the northwest wind hurling it in gusts. It drifted up around her black overshoes—old ones with little metal buckles. She smiled at the snow which was trying to cover her little by little. She could remember when they had no black rubber overshoes; only the high buckskin leggings that they wrapped over their elkhide moccasins. If the snow was dry or frozen, a person could walk all day and not get wet; and in the evenings the beams of the ceiling would hang with lengths of pale buckskin leggings drying out slowly.

She felt peaceful remembering. She didn't feel cold any more. Jimmie's blanket seemed warmer than it had ever been. And she could remember the morning he was born. She could remember whispering to her mother, who was sleeping on the other side of the hogan, to tell her it was time now. She did not want to wake the others. The second time she called to her, her mother stood up and pulled on her shoes; she knew. They walked to the old stone hogan together, Ayah walking a step behind her mother. She waited alone learning the rhythms of the pains while her mother went to call the old woman to help them. The morning was already warm even before dawn and Ayah smelled the bee flowers blooming and the young willow growing at the springs. She could remember that so clearly, but his birth merged into the births of the other children and to her it became all the same birth. They named him for the summer morning and in English they called him Jimmie.

It wasn't like Jimmie died. He just never came back, and one day a dark blue sedan with white writing on its doors pulled up in front of the boxcar shack where the rancher let the Indians live. A man in a khaki uniform trimmed in gold gave them a yellow piece of paper and told them that Jimmie was dead. He said the Army would try to get the body back and then it would be shipped to them; but it wasn't likely because the helicopter had burned after it crashed. All of this was told to Chato because he could understand English. She stood inside the doorway holding the baby while Chato listened. Chato spoke English like a white man and he spoke Spanish too. He was taller than the white man and he stood straighter too. Chato didn't explain why; he just told the military man they could keep the body if they found it. The white man looked bewildered; he nodded his head and left. Then Chato looked at her and shook his head, and then he told her, "Jimmie isn't coming home anymore," and when he spoke, he used the words to speak of the dead. She didn't cry then, but she hurt inside with anger. And she mourned him as the years passed, when a horse fell with Chato and broke his leg, and the white rancher told them he wouldn't pay Chato until he could work again. She mourned Jimmie because he would have worked for his father then; he would have saddled the big bay horse and ridden the fence lines each day, with wire cutters and heavy gloves, fixing the breaks in the barbed wire and putting the stray cattle back inside again.

She mourned him after the white doctors came to take Danny and Ella away. She was at the shack alone that day they came. It was back in the days before they hired Navajo women to go with them as interpreters. She recognized one of the doctors. She had seen him at the children's clinic at Cañoncito about a month ago. They were wearing khaki uniforms and they waved papers at her and a black ball-point pen, trying to make her understand their English words. She was frightened by the way they looked at the children, like the lizard watches the fly. Danny was swinging on the tire swing on the elm tree behind the rancher's house, and Ella was toddling around the front door, dragging the broomstick horse Chato made for her. Ayah could see they wanted her to sign the papers, and Chato had taught her to sign her name. It was something she was proud of. She only wanted them to go, and to take their eyes away from her children.

She took the pen from the man without looking at his face and she signed the papers in three different places he pointed to. She stared at the ground by their feet and waited for them to leave. But they stood there and began to point and gesture at the children. Danny stopped swinging. Ayah could see his fear. She moved suddenly and grabbed Ella into her arms; the child squirmed, trying to get back to her toys. Ayah ran with the baby toward Danny; she screamed for him to run and then she grabbed him around his chest and carried him too. She ran south into the foothills of juniper trees and black lava rock. Behind her she heard the doctors running, but they had been taken by surprise, and as the hills became steeper and the cholla cactus were thicker, they stopped. When she reached the top of the hill, she stopped to listen in case they were circling around her. But in a few minutes she heard a car engine start and they drove away. The children had been too surprised to cry while she ran with them. Danny was shaking and Ella's little fingers were gripping Ayah's blouse.

She stayed up in the hills for the rest of the day, sitting on a black lava boulder in the sunshine where she could see for miles all around her. The sky was light blue and cloudless, and it was warm for late April. The sun warmth relaxed her and took the fear and anger away. She lay back on the rock and watched the sky. It seemed to her that she could walk into the sky, stepping through clouds endlessly. Danny played with little pebbles and stones, pretending they were birds' eggs and then little rabbits. Ella sat at her feet and dropped fistfuls of dirt into the breeze, watching the dust and particles of sand intently. Ayah watched a hawk soar high above them, dark wings gliding; hunting or only watching, she did not know. The hawk was patient and he circled all afternoon before he disappeared around the high volcanic peak the Mexicans called Guadalupe.

Late in the afternoon, Ayah looked down at the gray boxcar shack with the paint all peeled from the wood: the stove pipe on the roof was rusted and crooked. The fire she had built that morning in the oil drum stove had burned out. Ella was asleep in her lap now and Danny sat close to her, complaining that he was hungry; he asked when they would go to the house. "We will stay up here until your father comes," she told him, "because those white men were chasing us." The boy remembered then and he nodded at her silently.

If Jimmie had been there he could have read those papers and explained to her what they said. Ayah would have known then, never to sign them. The doctors came back the next day and they brought a BIA policeman with them. They told Chato they had her signature and that was all they needed. Except for the kids. She listened to Chato sullenly; she hated him when he told her it was the old woman who died in the winter, spitting blood; it was her old grandma who had given the children this disease. "They don't spit blood," she said coldly. "The whites lie." She held Ella and Danny close to her, ready to run to the hills again. "I want a medicine man first," she said to Chato, not looking at him. He shook his head. "It's too late now. The policeman is with them. You signed the paper." His voice was gentle.

It was worse than if they had died: to lose the children and to know that somewhere, in a place called Colorado, in a place full of sick and dying strangers, her children were without her. There had been babies that died soon after they were born, and one that died before he could walk. She had carried them herself, up to the boulders and great pieces of the cliff that long ago crashed down from Long Mesa; she laid them in the crevices of sandstone and buried them in fine brown sand with round quartz pebbles that washed down the hills in the rain. She had endured it because they had been with her. But she could not bear this pain. She did not sleep for a long time after they took her children. She stayed on the hill where they had fled the first time, and she slept rolled up in the blanket Jimmie had sent her. She carried the pain in her belly and it was fed by everything she saw: the blue sky of their last day together and the dust and pebbles they played with; the swing in the elm tree and broomstick horse choked life from her. The pain filled her stomach and there was no room for food or for her lungs to fill with air. The air and the food would have been theirs.

She hated Chato, not because he let the policeman and doctors put the screaming children in the government car, but because he had taught her to sign her name. Because it was like the old ones always told her about learning their language or any of their ways: It endangers you. She slept alone on the hill until the middle of November when the first snows came. Then she made a bed for herself where the children had slept. She did not lie down beside Chato again until many years later, when he was sick and shivering and only her body could keep him warm. The illness came after the white rancher told Chato he was too old to work for him anymore, and Chato and his old woman should be out of the shack by the next afternoon because the rancher had hired new people to work there. That had satisfied her. To see how the white man repaid Chato's years of loyalty and work. All of Chato's fine-sounding English talk didn't change things.

It snowed steadily and the luminous light from the snow gradually diminished into the darkness. Somewhere in Ceboletta a dog barked and other village dogs joined with it. Ayah looked in the direction she had come, from the bar where Chato was buying the wine. Sometimes he told her to go on ahead and wait; and then he never came. And when she finally went back looking for him, she would find him passed out at the bottom of the wooden steps to Azzie's Bar. All the wine would be gone and most of the money too, from the pale blue check that came to them once a month in a government envelope. It was then that she would look at his face and his hands, scarred by ropes and the barbed wire of all those years, and she would think, this man is a stranger; for forty years she had smiled at him and cooked his food, but he remained a stranger. She stood up again, with the snow almost to her knees, and she walked back to find Chato.

It was hard to walk in the deep snow and she felt the air burn in her lungs. She stopped a short distance from the bar to rest and readjust the blanket. But this time he wasn't waiting for her at the bottom step with his old Stetson hat pulled down and his shoulders hunched up in his long wool overcoat.

She was careful not to slip on the wooden steps. When she pushed the door open, warm air and cigarette smoke hit her face. She looked around slowly and deliberately, in every corner, in every dark place that the old man might find to sleep. The bar owner didn't like Indians in there, especially Navajos, but he let Chato come in because he could talk Spanish like he was one of them. The men at the bar stared at her, and the bartender saw that she left the door open wide. Snowflakes were flying inside like moths and melting into a puddle on the oiled wood floor. He motioned to her to close the door, but she did not see him. She held herself straight and walked across the room slowly, searching the room with every step. The snow in her hair melted and she could feel it on her forehead. At the far corner of the room, she saw red flames at the mica window of the old stove door; she looked behind the stove just to make sure. The bar got quiet except for the Spanish polka music playing on the jukebox. She stood by the stove and shook the snow from her blanket and held it near the stove to dry. The wet wool smell reminded her of newborn goats in early March, brought inside to warm near the fire. She felt calm.

In past years they would have told her to get out. But her hair was white now and her face was wrinkled. They looked at her like she was a spider crawling slowly across the room. They were afraid; she could feel the fear. She looked at their faces steadily. They reminded her of the first time the white people brought her children back to her that winter. Danny had been shy and hid behind the thin white woman who brought them. And the baby had not known her until Ayah took her into her arms, and then Ella had nuzzled close to her as she had when she was nursing. The blonde woman was nervous and kept looking at a dainty gold watch on her wrist. She sat on the bench near the small window and watched the dark snow clouds gather around the mountains; she was worrying about the unpaved road. She was frightened by what she saw inside too: the strips of venison drying on a rope across the ceiling and the children jabbering excitedly in a language she did not know. So they stayed for only a few hours. Ayah watched the government car disappear down the road and she knew they were already being weaned from these lava hills and from this sky. The last time they came was in early June, and Ella stared at her the way the men in the bar were now staring. Ayah did not try to pick her up; she smiled at her instead and spoke cheerfully to Danny. When he tried to answer her, he could not seem to remember and he spoke English words with the Navajo. But he gave her a scrap of paper that he had found somewhere and carried in his pocket; it was folded in half, and he shyly looked up at her and said it was a bird. She asked Chato if they were home for good this time. He spoke to the white woman and she shook her head. "How much longer?" he asked, and she said she didn't know; but Chato saw how she stared at the boxcar shack. Ayah turned away then. She did not say good-bye.

She felt satisfied that the men in the bar feared her. Maybe it was her face and the way she held her mouth with teeth clenched tight, like there was nothing anyone could do to her now. She walked north down the road, searching for the old man. She did this because she had the blanket, and there would be no place for him except with her and the blanket in the old adobe barn near the arroyo. They always slept there when they came to Cebolleta. If the money and the wine were gone, she would be relieved because then they could go home again; back to the old hogan with a dirt roof and rock walls where she herself had been born. And the next day the old man could go back to the few sheep they still had, to follow along behind them, guiding them, into dry sandy arroyos where sparse grass grew. She knew he did not like walking behind old ewes when for so many years he rode big quarter horses and worked with cattle. But she wasn't sorry for him; he should have known all along what would happen.

There had not been enough rain for their garden in five years; and that was when Chato finally hitched a ride into the town and brought back brown boxes of rice and sugar and big tin cans of welfare peaches. After that, at the first of the month they went to Ceboletta to ask the postmaster for the check; and then Chato would go to the bar and cash it. They did this as they planted the garden every May, not because anything would survive the summer dust, but because it was time to do this. The journey passed the days that smelled silent and dry like the caves above the canyon with yellow painted buffaloes on their walls.

He was walking along the pavement when she found him. He did not stop or turn around when he heard her behind him. She walked beside him and she noticed how slowly he moved now. He smelled strong of woodsmoke and urine. Lately he had been forgetting. Sometimes he called her by his sister's name and she had been gone for a long time. Once she had found him wandering on the road to the white man's ranch, and she asked him why he was going that way; he laughed at her and said, "You know they can't run that ranch without me," and he walked on determined, limping on the leg that had been crushed many years before. Now he looked at her curiously, as if for the first time, but he kept shuffling along, moving slowly along the side of the highway. His gray hair had grown long and spread out on the shoulders of the long overcoat. He wore the old felt hat pulled down over his ears. His boots were worn out at the toes and he had stuffed pieces of an old red shirt in the holes. The rags made his feet look like little animals up to their ears in snow. She laughed at his feet; the snow muffled the sound of her laugh. He stopped and looked at her again. The wind had quit blowing and the snow was falling straight down; the southeast sky was beginning to clear and Ayah could see a star.

"Let's rest awhile," she said to him. They walked away from the road and up the slope to the giant boulders that had tumbled down from the red sandrock mesa throughout the centuries of rainstorms and earth tremors. In a place where the boulders shut out the wind, they sat down with their backs against the rock. She offered half of the blanket to him and they sat wrapped together.

The storm passed swiftly. The clouds moved east. They were massive and full, crowding together across the sky. She watched them with the feeling of horses—steely blue-gray horses startled across the sky. The powerful haunches pushed into the distances and the tail hairs streamed white mist behind them. The sky cleared. Ayah saw that there was nothing between her and the stars. The light was crystalline. There was no shimmer, no distortion through earth haze. She breathed the clarity of the night sky; she smelled the purity of the half moon and the stars. He was lying on his side with his knees pulled up near his belly for warmth. His eyes were closed now, and in the light from the stars and the moon, he looked young again.

She could see it descend out of the night sky: an icy stillness from the edge of the thin moon. She recognized the freezing. It came gradually, sinking snowflake by snowflake until the crust was heavy and deep. It had the strength of the stars in Orion, and its journey was endless. Ayah knew that with the wine he would sleep. He would not feel it. She tucked the blanket around him, remembering how it was when Ella had been with her; and she felt the rush so big inside her heart for the babies. And she sang the only song she knew to sing for babies. She could not remember if she had ever sung it to her children, but she knew that her grandmother had sung it and her mother had sung it:

The earth is your mother,
  she holds you.
The sky is your father,
  he protects you.
Sleep,
sleep.
Rainbow is your sister,
  she loves you.
The winds are your brothers,
  they sing to you.
Sleep,
sleep.
We are together always
We are together always
There never was a time
when this
was not so.

Suggestions for Discussion

1. Silko's story is in part about the different ways we have to say good-bye to the people we love and to parts of our life. What has Ayah lost? And how?
2. Why does the author call the story "Lullaby"? To whom is the lullaby sung and for what reason? What do the words of the lullaby tell us about the worldview of the Navajo?
3. How does Ayah's connection with her own past parallel her connection with the natural world?

Suggestions for Writing

1. Think of a lullaby or nursery rhyme that has special meaning for you. Use it as the focal point of a story about yourself.
2. Write a lullaby or a sleep/comfort song that describes what you find peaceful and reassuring.
3. Outline the plot of a western movie from the perspective of Ayah.

RAYMOND CARVER

What We Talk About When We Talk About Love

Raymond Carver (1939–1988) was born in Clatskaine, Oregon, and lived in the Pacific Northwest until his death. He received a number of honors including a Guggenheim Fellowship, National Endowment for the Arts grants, and the Mildred and Harold Strauss Living Award. Four collections of his short stories have been published: *Will You Please Be Quiet, Please* (1976), nominated for the National Book Award; *What We Talk About When We Talk About Love* (1981); *Cathedral* (1984), nominated for the National Book Critics Circle Award; and *The Stories of Raymond Carver* (1985). Although two couples are seated around the kitchen table drinking gin, the primary focus is on Mel and to a lesser degree his second wife, Terri. In Mel's reminiscences about his personal and professional life and in his behavior, he expresses differing and perhaps contradictory views of love.

My friend Mel McGinnis was talking. Mel McGinnis is a cardiologist, and sometimes that gives him the right.

The four of us were sitting around his kitchen table drinking gin. Sunlight filled the kitchen from the big window behind the sink. There were Mel and me and his second wife, Teresa—Terri, we called her—and my wife, Laura. We lived in Albuquerque then. But we were all from somewhere else.

There was an ice bucket on the table. The gin and the tonic water kept going around, and we somehow got on the subject of love. Mel thought real love was nothing less than spiritual love. He said he'd spent five years in a seminary before quitting to go to medical school. He said he still looked back on those years in the seminary as the most important years in his life.

Terri said the man she lived with before she lived with Mel loved her so much he tried to kill her. Then Terri said, "He beat me up one night. He dragged me around the living room by my ankles. He kept saying, 'I love you, I love you, you bitch.' He went on dragging me around the living room. My head kept knocking on things." Terri looked around the table. "What do you do with love like that?"

She was a bone-thin woman with a pretty face, dark eyes, and brown hair that hung down her back. She liked necklaces made of turquoise, and long pendant earrings.

"My God, don't be silly. That's not love, and you know it," Mel said. "I don't know what you'd call it, but I sure know you wouldn't call it love."

"Say what you want to, but I know it was," Terri said. "It may sound crazy to you, but it's true just the same. People are different, Mel. Sure, sometimes he may have acted crazy. Okay. But he loved me. In his own way maybe, but he loved me. There was love there, Mel. Don't say there wasn't."

Mel let out his breath. He held his glass and turned to Laura and me. "The man threatened to kill me," Mel said. He finished his drink and reached for the gin bottle. "Terri's a romantic. Terri's of the kick-me-so-I'll-know-you-love-me school. Terri, hon, don't look that way." Mel reached across the table and touched Terri's cheek with his fingers. He grinned at her.

"Now he wants to make up," Terri said.

"Make up what?" Mel said. "What is there to make up? I know what I know. That's all."

"How'd we get started on this subject, anyway?" Terri said. She raised her glass and drank from it. "Mel always has love on his mind," she said. "Don't you, honey?" She smiled, and I thought that was the last of it.

"I just wouldn't call Ed's behavior love. That's all I'm saying, honey," Mel said. "What about you guys?" Mel said to Laura and me. "Does that sound like love to you?"

"I'm the wrong person to ask," I said. "I didn't even know the man. I've only heard his name mentioned in passing. I wouldn't know. You'd have to know the particulars. But I think what you're saying is that love is an absolute."

Mel said, "The kind of love I'm talking about is. The kind of love I'm talking about, you don't try to kill people."

Laura said, "I don't know anything about Ed, or anything about the situation. But who can judge anyone else's situation?"

I touched the back of Laura's hand. She gave me a quick smile. I picked up Laura's hand. It was warm, the nails polished, perfectly manicured. I encircled the broad wrist with my fingers, and I held her.

"When I left, he drank rat poison," Terri said. She clasped her arms with her hands. "They took him to the hospital in Santa Fe. That's where we lived then, about ten miles out. They saved his life. But his gums went crazy from it. I mean they pulled away from his teeth. After that, his teeth stood out like fangs. My God," Terri said. She waited a minute, then let go of her arms and picked up her glass.

"What people won't do!" Laura said.

"He's out of the action now," Mel said. "He's dead."

Mel handed me the saucer of limes. I took a section, squeezed it over my drink, and stirred the ice cubes with my finger.

"It gets worse," Terri said. "He shot himself in the mouth. But he bungled that too. Poor Ed," she said. Terri shook her head.

"Poor Ed nothing," Mel said. "He was dangerous."

Mel was forty-five years old. He was tall and rangy with curly soft hair. His face and arms were brown from the tennis he played. When he was sober, his gestures, all his movements, were precise, very careful.

"He did love me though, Mel. Grant me that," Terri said. "That's all I'm asking. He didn't love me the way you love me. I'm not saying that. But he loved me. You can grant me that, can't you?"

"What do you mean, he bungled it?" I said.

Laura leaned forward with her glass. She put her elbows on the table and held her glass in both hands. She glanced from Mel to Terri and waited with a look of bewilderment on her open face, as if amazed that such things happened to people you were friendly with.

"How'd he bungle it when he killed himself?" I said.

"I'll tell you what happened," Mel said. "He took this twenty-two pistol he'd bought to threaten Terri and me with. Oh, I'm serious, the man was always threatening. You should have seen the way we lived in those days. Like fugitives. I even bought a gun myself. Can you believe it? A guy like me? But I did. I bought one for self-defense and carried it in the glove compartment. Sometimes I'd have to leave the apartment in the middle of the night. To go to the hospital, you know? Terri and I weren't married then, and my first wife had the house and kids, the dog, everything, and Terri and I were living in this apartment here. Sometimes, as I say, I'd get a call in the middle of the night and have to go in to the hospital at two or three in the morning. It'd be dark out there in the parking lot, and I'd break into a sweat before I could even get to my car. I never knew if he was going to come up out of the shrubbery or from behind a car and start shooting. I mean, the man was crazy. He was capable of wiring a bomb, anything. He used to call my service at all hours and say he needed to talk to the doctor, and when I'd return the call, he'd say, 'Son of a bitch, your days are numbered.' Little things like that. It was scary, I'm telling you."

"I still feel sorry for him," Terri said.

"It sounds like a nightmare," Laura said. "But what exactly happened after he shot himself?"

Laura is a legal secretary. We'd met in a professional capacity. Before we knew it, it was a courtship. She's thirty-five, three years younger than I am. In addition to being in love, we like each other and enjoy one another's company. She's easy to be with.

"What happened?" Laura said.

Mel said, "He shot himself in the mouth in his room. Someone heard the shot and told the manager. They came in with a passkey, saw what had happened, and called an ambulance. I happened to be there when they brought him in, alive but past recall. The man lived for three days. His head swelled up to twice the size of a normal head. I'd never seen anything like it, and I hope I never do again. Terri wanted to go in and sit with him when she found out about it. We had a fight over it. I didn't think she should see him like that. I didn't think she should see him, and I still don't."

"Who won the fight?" Laura said.

"I was in the room with him when he died," Terri said. "He never came up out of it. But I sat with him. He didn't have anyone else."

"He was dangerous," Mel said. "If you call that love, you can have it."

"It was love," Terri said. "Sure, it's abnormal in most people's eyes. But he was willing to die for it. He did die for it."

"I sure as hell wouldn't call it love," Mel said. "I mean, no one knows what he did it for. I've seen a lot of suicides, and I couldn't say anyone ever knew what they did it for."

Mel put his hands behind his neck and tilted his chair back. "I'm not interested in that kind of love," he said. "If that's love, you can have it."

Terri said, "We were afraid. Mel even made a will out and wrote to his brother in California who used to be a Green Beret. Mel told him who to look for if something happened to him."

Terri drank from her glass. She said, "But Mel's right—we lived like fugitives. We were afraid. Mel was, weren't you, honey? I even called the police at one point, but they were no help. They said they couldn't do anything until Ed actually did something. Isn't that a laugh?" Terri said.

She poured the last of the gin into her glass and waggled the bottle. Mel got up from the table and went to the cupboard. He took down another bottle.

"Well, Nick and I know what love is," Laura said. "For us, I mean," Laura said. She bumped my knee with her knee. "You're supposed to say something now," Laura said, and turned her smile on me.

For an answer, I took Laura's hand and raised it to my lips. I made a big production out of kissing her hand. Everyone was amused.

"We're lucky," I said.

"You guys," Terri said. "Stop that now. You're making me sick. You're still on the honeymoon, for God's sake. You're still gaga, for crying out loud. Just wait. How long have you been together now? How long has it been? A year? Longer than a year?"

"Going on a year and a half," Laura said, flushed and smiling.

"Oh, now," Terri said. "Wait awhile."

She held her drink and gazed at Laura.

"I'm only kidding," Terri said.

Mel opened the gin and went around the table with the bottle.

"Here, you guys," he said. "Let's have a toast. I want to propose a toast. A toast to love. To true love," Mel said.

We touched glasses.

"To love," we said.

Outside in the backyard, one of the dogs began to bark. The leaves of the aspen that leaned past the window ticked against the glass. The afternoon sun was like a presence in this room, the spacious light of ease and generosity. We could have been anywhere, somewhere enchanted. We raised our glasses again and grinned at each other like children who had agreed on something forbidden.

"I'll tell you what real love is," Mel said. "I mean, I'll give you a good example. And then you can draw your own conclusions." He poured more gin into his glass. He added an ice cube and a sliver of lime. We waited and sipped our drinks. Laura and I touched knees again. I put a hand on her warm thigh and left it there.

"What do any of us really know about love?" Mel said. "It seems to me we're just beginners at love. We say we love each other and we do, I don't doubt it. I love Terri and Terri loves me, and you guys love each other too. You know the kind of love I'm talking about now. Physical love, that impulse that drives you to someone special, as well as love of the other person's being, his or her essence, as it were. Carnal love and, well, call it sentimental love, the day-to-day caring about the other person. But sometimes I have a hard time accounting for the fact that I must have loved my first wife too. But I did, I know I did. So I suppose I am like Terri in that regard. Terri and Ed." He thought about it and then he went on. "There was a time when I thought I loved my first wife more than life itself. But now I hate her guts. I do. How do you explain that? What happened to that love? What happened to it, is what I'd like to know. I wish someone could tell me. Then there's Ed. Okay, we're back to Ed. He loves Terri so much he tries to kill her and he winds up killing himself." Mel stopped talking and swallowed from his glass. "You guys have been together eighteen months and you love each other. It shows all over you. You glow with it. But you both loved other people before you met each other. You've both been married before, just like us. And you probably loved other people before that too, even. Terri and I have been together five years, been married for four. And the terrible thing, the terrible thing is, but the good thing too, the saving grace, you might say, is that if something happened to one of us—excuse me for saying this—but if something happened to one of us tomorrow, I think the other one, the other person, would grieve for a while, you know, but then the surviving party would go out and love again, have someone else soon enough. All this, all of this love we're talking about, it would just be a memory. Maybe not even a memory. Am I wrong? Am I way off base? Because I want you to set me straight if you think I'm wrong. I want to know. I mean, I don't know anything, and I'm the first one to admit it."

"Mel, for God's sake," Terri said. She reached out and took hold of his wrist. "Are you getting drunk? Honey? Are you drunk?"

"Honey, I'm just talking," Mel said. "All right? I don't have to be drunk to say what I think. I mean, we're all just talking, right?" Mel said. He fixed his eyes on her.

"Sweetie, I'm not criticizing," Terri said.

She picked up her glass.

"I'm not on call today," Mel said. "Let me remind you of that. I am not on call," he said.

"Mel, we love you," Laura said.

Mel looked at Laura. He looked at her as if he could not place her, as if she was not the woman she was.

"Love you too, Laura," Mel said. "And you, Nick, love you too. You know something?" Mel said. "You guys are our pals," Mel said.

He picked up his glass.

Mel said, "I was going to tell you about something. I mean, I was going to prove a point. You see, this happened a few months ago, but it's still going on right now, and it ought to make us feel ashamed when we talk like we know what we're talking about when we talk about love."

"Come on now," Terri said. "Don't talk like you're drunk if you're not drunk."

"Just shut up for once in your life," Mel said very quietly. "Will you do me a favor and do that for a minute? So as I was saying, there's this old couple who had this car wreck out on the interstate. A kid hit them and they were all torn to shit and nobody was giving them much chance to pull through."

Terri looked at us and then back at Mel. She seemed anxious, or maybe that's too strong a word.

Mel was handing the bottle around the table.

"I was on call that night," Mel said. "It was May or maybe it was June. Terri and I had just sat down to dinner when the hospital called. There'd been this thing out on the interstate. Drunk kid, teenager, plowed his dad's pickup into this camper with this old couple in it. They were up in their mid-seventies, that couple. The kid—eighteen, nineteen, something—he was DOA. Taken the steering wheel through his sternum. The old couple, they were alive, you understand. I mean, just barely. But they had everything. Multiple fractures, internal injuries, hemorrhaging, contusions, lacerations, the works, and they each of them had themselves concussions. They were in a bad way, believe me. And, of course, their age was two strikes against them. I'd say she was worse off than he was. Ruptured spleen along with everything else. Both kneecaps broken. But they'd been wearing their seatbelts and, God knows, that's what saved them for the time being."

"Folks, this is an advertisement for the National Safety Council," Terri said. "This is your spokesman, Dr. Melvin R. McGinnis, talking." Terri laughed. "Mel," she said, "sometimes you're just too much. But I love you, hon," she said.

"Honey, I love you," Mel said.

He leaned across the table. Terri met him halfway. They kissed.

"Terri's right," Mel said as he settled himself again. "Get those seatbelts on. But seriously, they were in some shape, those oldsters. By the time I got down there, the kid was dead, as I said. He was off in a corner, laid out on a gurney. I took one look at the old couple and told the ER nurse to get me a neurologist and an orthopedic man and a couple of surgeons down there right away."

He drank from his glass. "I'll try to keep this short," he said. "So we took the two of them up to the OR and worked like fuck on them most of the night. They had these incredible reserves, those two. You see that once in a while. So we did everything that could be done, and toward morning we're giving them a fifty–fifty chance, maybe less than that for her. So here they are, still alive the next morning. So, okay, we move them into the ICU, which is where they both kept plugging away at it for two weeks, hitting it better and better on all the scopes. So we transfer them out to their own room."

Mel stopped talking. "Here," he said, "let's drink this cheapo gin the hell up. Then we're going to dinner, right? Terri and I know a new place. That's where we'll go, to this new place we know about. But we're not going until we finish up this cut-rate, lousy gin."

Terri said, "We haven't actually eaten there yet. But it looks good. From the outside, you know."

"I like food," Mel said. "If I had it to do all over again, I'd be a chef, you know? Right, Terri?" Mel said.

He laughed. He fingered the ice in his glass.

"Terri knows," he said. "Terri can tell you. But let me say this. If I could come back again in a different life, a different time and all, you know what? I'd like to come back as a knight. You were pretty safe wearing all that armor. It was all right being a knight until gunpowder and muskets and pistols came along."

"Mel would like to ride a horse and carry a lance," Terri said.

"Carry a woman's scarf with you everywhere," Laura said.

"Or just a woman," Mel said.

"Shame on you," Laura said.

Terri said, "Suppose you came back as a serf. The serfs didn't have it so good in those days," Terri said.

"The serfs never had it good," Mel said. "But I guess even the knights were vessels to someone. Isn't that the way it worked? But then everyone is always a vessel to someone. Isn't that right? Terri? But what I liked about knights, besides their ladies, was that they had that suit of armor, you know, and they couldn't get hurt very easy. No cars in those days, you know? No drunk teenagers to tear into your ass."

"Vassals," Terri said.

"What?" Mel said.

"Vassals," Terri said. "They were called vassals, not vessels."

"Vassals, vessels," Mel said, "what the fuck's the difference? You knew what I meant anyway. All right," Mel said. "So I'm not educated. I learned my stuff. I'm a heart surgeon, sure, but I'm just a mechanic. I go in and I fuck around and I fix things. Shit," Mel said.

"Modesty doesn't become you," Terri said.

"He's just a humble sawbones," I said. "But sometimes they suffocated in all that armor, Mel. They'd even have heart attacks if it got too hot and they were too tired and worn out. I read somewhere that they'd fall off their horses and not be able to get up because they were too tired to stand with all that armor on them. They got trampled by their own horses sometimes."

"That's terrible," Mel said. "That's a terrible thing, Nicky. I guess they'd just lay there and wait until somebody came along and made a shish kebab out of them."

"Some other vessel," Terri said.

"That's right," Mel said. "Some vassal would come along and spear the bastard in the name of love. Or whatever the fuck it was they fought over in those days."

"Same things we fight over these days," Terri said.

Laura said, "Nothing's changed."

The color was still high in Laura's cheeks. Her eyes were bright. She brought her glass to her lips.

Mel poured himself another drink. He looked at the label closely as if studying a long row of numbers. Then he slowly put the bottle down on the table and slowly reached for the tonic water.

"What about the old couple?" Laura said. "You didn't finish that story you started."

Laura was having a hard time lighting her cigarette. Her matches kept going out.

The sunshine inside the room was different now, changing, getting thinner. But the leaves outside the window were still shimmering, and I stared at the pattern they made on the panes and on the Formica counter. They weren't the same patterns, of course.

"What about the old couple?" I said.

"Older but wiser," Terri said.

Mel stared at her.

Terri said, "Go on with your story, hon. I was only kidding. Then what happened?"

"Terri, sometimes," Mel said.

"Please, Mel," Terri said. "Don't always be so serious, sweetie. Can't you take a joke?"

"Where's the joke?" Mel said.

He held his glass and gazed steadily at his wife.

"What happened?" Laura said.

Mel fastened his eyes on Laura. He said, "Laura, if I didn't have Terri and if I didn't love her so much, and if Nick wasn't my best friend, I'd fall in love with you. I'd carry you off, honey," he said.

"Tell your story," Terri said. "Then we'll go to that new place, okay?"

"Okay," Mel said. "Where was I?" he said. He stared at the table and then he began again.

"I dropped in to see each of them every day, sometimes twice a day if I was up doing other calls anyway. Casts and bandages, head to foot, the both of them. You know, you've seen it in the movies. That's just the way they looked, just like in the movies. Little eye-holes and nose-holes and mouth-holes. And she had to have her legs slung up on top of it. Well, the husband was very depressed for the longest while. Even after he found out that his wife was going to pull through, he was still very depressed. Not about the accident, though. I mean, the accident was one thing, but it wasn't everything. I'd get up to his mouth-hole, you know, and he'd say no, it wasn't the accident exactly but it was because he couldn't see her through his eye-holes. He said that was what was making him feel so bad. Can you imagine? I'm telling you, the man's heart was breaking because he couldn't turn his goddamn head and *see* his goddamn wife."

Mel looked around the table and shook his head at what he was going to say.

"I mean, it was killing the old fart just because he couldn't *look* at the fucking woman."

We all looked at Mel.

"Do you see what I'm saying?" he said.

Maybe we were a little drunk by then. I know it was hard keeping things in focus. The light was draining out of the room, going back through the window where it had come from. Yet nobody made a move to get up from the table to turn on the overhead light.

"Listen," Mel said. "Let's finish this fucking gin. There's about enough left here for one shooter all around. Then let's go eat. Let's go to the new place."

"He's depressed," Terri said. "Mel, why don't you take a pill?"

Mel shook his head. "I've taken everything there is."

"We all need a pill now and then," I said.

"Some people are born needing them," Terri said.

She was using her finger to rub at something on the table. Then she stopped rubbing.

"I think I want to call my kids," Mel said. "Is that all right with everybody? I'll call my kids," he said.

Terri said, "What if Marjorie answers the phone? You guys, you've heard us on the subject of Marjorie? Honey, you know you don't want to talk to Marjorie. It'll make you feel even worse."

"I don't want to talk to Marjorie," Mel said. "But I want to talk to my kids."

"There isn't a day goes by that Mel doesn't say he wishes she'd get married again. Or else die," Terri said. "For one thing," Terri said, "she's bankrupting us. Mel says it's just to spite him that she won't get married again. She has a boyfriend who lives with her and the kids, so Mel is supporting the boyfriend too."

"She's allergic to bees," Mel said. "If I'm not praying she'll get married again, I'm praying she'll get herself stung to death by a swarm of fucking bees."

"Shame on you," Laura said.

"Bzzzzzzz," Mel said, turning his fingers into bees and buzzing them at Terri's throat. Then he let his hands drop all the way to his sides.

"She's vicious," Mel said. "Sometimes I think I'll go up there dressed like a beekeeper. You know, that hat that's like a helmet with the plate that comes down over your face, the big gloves, and the padded coat? I'll knock on the door and let loose a hive of bees in the house. But first I'd make sure the kids were out, of course."

He crossed one leg over the other. It seemed to take him a lot of time to do it. Then he put both feet on the floor and leaned forward, elbows on the table, his chin cupped in his hands.

"Maybe I won't call the kids, after all. Maybe it isn't such a hot idea. Maybe we'll just go eat. How does that sound?"

"Sounds fine to me," I said. "Eat or not eat. Or keep drinking. I could head right on out into the sunset."

"What does that mean, honey?" Laura said.

"It just means what I said," I said. "It means I could just keep going. That's all it means."

"I could eat something myself," Laura said. "I don't think I've ever been so hungry in my life. Is there something to nibble on?"

"I'll put out some cheese and crackers," Terri said.

But Terri just sat there. She did not get up to get anything.

Mel turned his glass over. He spilled it out on the table.

"Gin's gone," Mel said.

Terri said, "Now what?"

I could hear my heart beating. I could hear everyone's heart. I could hear the human noise we sat there making, not one of us moving, not even when the room went dark.

Suggestions for Discussion

1. In what respects does the setting for the discussion between the two couples affect the dialogue?
2. Characterize each of the participants by referring to their behavior, their expressions of love, and their attitudes toward love. For example, how do Terri and Mel differ in their views of love?
3. What to Mel is both the "terrible thing" and the "saving grace" about love?
4. What is the significance of Mel's story about the elderly couple whom he treated in the hospital? Why does he use vulgar language in describing their relationship? Mel has earlier described love as carnal and sentimental. How adequate are those adjectives in describing the love of the elderly couple?
5. Why is Mel's story of the elderly couple troubling to Nick and Laura? How do you know?
6. Note the changes in Mel's statements about love. To what extent are his differing statements of attitude affected by his drinking? By his earlier years in the seminary? By his profession as a cardiologist?
7. Are there discrepancies between Mel's views and his behavior? Why do you think he is a pill taker?

Suggestions for Writing

1. You have read a number of writers on the meaning of love. Drawing upon these readings, and your experience and observation, develop in either narrative or expository form your feelings and thoughts about love.
2. Interview a number of your contemporaries. What appears to be their sense of the meaning of love? To what extent is their behavior consonant with their attitude?

KATHERINE ANNE PORTER

Rope

Katherine Anne Porter (1890–1980), American short story writer, novelist, and critic, was born in Texas and educated in convent schools in Texas and New Orleans. She was a visiting lecturer at numerous colleges and universities and lived and traveled in Mexico, Germany, and France. Her books include *Flowering Judas* (1930); *Noon-Wine* (1937); *Pale Horse, Pale Rider* (1939); critical essays, *The Days Before* (1952); and a novel, *Ship of Fools* (1962). In "Rope," the frustration of husband and wife, expressed in displaced anger, is followed by an expression of the more enduring ties of a shared life.

On the third day after they moved to the country he came walking back from the village carrying a basket of groceries and a twenty-four-yard coil of rope. She came out to meet him, wiping her hands on her green smock. Her hair was tumbled, her nose was scarlet with sunburn; he told her that already she looked like a born country woman. His gray flannel shirt stuck to him, his heavy shoes were dusty. She assured him he looked like a rural character in a play.

Had he brought the coffee? She had been waiting all day long for coffee. They had forgot it when they ordered at the store the first day.

Gosh, no, he hadn't. Lord, now he'd have to go back. Yes, he would if it killed him. He thought, though, he had everything else. She reminded him it was only because he didn't drink coffee himself. If he did he would remember it quick enough. Suppose they ran out of cigarettes? Then she saw the rope. What was that for? Well, he thought it might do to hang clothes on, or something. Naturally, she asked him if he thought they were going to run a laundry. They already had a fifty-foot line hanging right before his eyes. Why, hadn't he noticed it, really? It was a blot on the landscape to her.

He thought there were a lot of things a rope might come in handy for. She wanted to know what, for instance. He thought a few seconds, but nothing occurred. They could wait and see, couldn't they? You need all sorts of strange odds and ends around a place in the country. She said, yes, that was so; but she thought just at that time when every penny counted, it seemed funny to buy more rope. That was all. She hadn't meant anything else. She hadn't just seen, not at first, why he felt it was necessary.

Well, thunder, he had bought it because he wanted to, and that was all there was to it. She thought that was reason enough, and couldn't understand why he hadn't said so, at first. Undoubtedly it would be useful, twenty-four yards of rope, there were hundreds of things, she couldn't think of any at the moment, but it would come in. Of course. As he had said, things always did in the country.

But she was a little disappointed about the coffee, and oh, look, look, look at the eggs! Oh, my, they're all running! What had he put on top of them? Hadn't he known eggs mustn't be squeezed? Squeezed, who had squeezed them, he wanted to know. What a silly thing to say. He had simply brought them along in the basket with the other things. If they got broke it was the grocer's fault. He should know better than to put heavy things on top of eggs.

She believed it was the rope. That was the heaviest thing in the pack, she saw him plainly when he came in from the road, the rope was a big package on top of everything. He desired the whole wide world to witness that this was not a fact. He had carried the rope in one hand and the basket in the other, and what was the use of her having eyes if that was the best they could do for her?

Well, anyhow, she could see one thing plain: no eggs for breakfast. They'd have to scramble them now, for supper. It was too damned bad. She had planned to have steak for supper. No ice, meat wouldn't keep. He wanted to know why she couldn't finish breaking the eggs in a bowl and set them in a cool place.

Cool place! if he could find one for her, she'd be glad to set them there. Well, then, it seemed to him they might very well cook the meat at the same time they cooked the eggs and then warm up the meat for tomorrow. The idea simply choked her. Warmed-over meat, when they might as well have had it fresh. Second best and scraps and makeshifts, even to the meat! He rubbed her shoulder a little. It doesn't really matter so much, does it, darling? Sometimes when they were playful, he would rub her shoulder and she would arch and purr. This time she hissed and almost clawed. He was getting ready to say that they could surely manage somehow when she turned on him and said, if he told her they could manage somehow she would certainly slap his face.

He swallowed the words red hot, his face burned. He picked up the rope and started to put it on the top shelf. She would not have it on the top shelf, the jars and tins belonged there; positively she would not have the top shelf cluttered up with a lot of rope. She had borne all the clutter she meant to bear in the flat in town, there was space here at least and she meant to keep things in order.

Well, in that case, he wanted to know what the hammer and nails were doing up there? And why had she put them there when she knew very well he needed that hammer and those nails upstairs to fix the window sashes? She simply slowed down everything and made double work on the place with her insane habit of changing things around and hiding them.

She was sure she begged his pardon, and if she had had any reason to believe he was going to fix the sashes this summer she would have left the hammer and nails right where he put them; in the middle of the bedroom floor where they could step on them in the dark. And now if he didn't clear the whole mess out of there she would throw them down the well.

Oh, all right, all right—could he put them in the closet? Naturally not, there were brooms and mops and dustpans in the closet, and why couldn't he find a place for his rope outside her kitchen? Had he stopped to consider there were seven God-forsaken rooms in the house, and only one kitchen?

He wanted to know what of it? And did she realize she was making a complete fool of herself? And what did she take him for, a three-year-old idiot? The whole trouble with her was she needed something weaker than she was to heckle and tyrannize over. He wished to God now they had a couple of children she could take it out on. Maybe he'd get some rest.

Her face changed at this, she reminded him he had forgot the coffee and had bought a worthless piece of rope. And when she thought of all the things they actually needed to make the place even decently fit to live in, well, she could cry, that was all. She looked so forlorn, so lost and despairing he couldn't believe it was only a piece of rope that was causing all the racket. What *was* the matter, for God's sake?

Oh, would he please hush and go away, and *stay* away, if he could, for five minutes? By all means, yes, he would. He'd stay away indefinitely if she wished. Lord, yes, there was nothing he'd like better than to clear out and never come back. She couldn't for the life of her see what was holding him, then. It was a swell time. Here she was, stuck, miles from a railroad, with a half-empty house on her hands, and not a penny in her pocket, and everything on earth to do; it seemed the God-sent moment for him to get out from under. She was surprised he hadn't stayed in town as it was until she had come out and done the work and got things straightened out. It was his usual trick.

It appeared to him that this was going a little far. Just a touch out of bounds, if she didn't mind his saying so. Why the hell had he stayed in town the summer before? To do a half-dozen extra jobs to get the money he had sent her. That was it. She knew perfectly well they couldn't have done it otherwise. She had agreed with him at the time. And that was the only time so help him he had ever left her to do anything by herself.

Oh, he could tell that to his great-grandmother. She had her notion of what had kept him in town. Considerably more than a notion, if he wanted to know. So, she was going to bring all that up again, was she? Well, she could just think what she pleased. He was tired of explaining. It may have looked funny but he had simply got hooked in, and what could he do? It was impossible to believe that she was going to take it seriously. Yes, yes, she knew how it was with a man: if he was left by himself a minute, some woman was certain to kidnap him. And naturally he couldn't hurt her feelings by refusing!

Well, what was she raving about? Did she forget she had told him those two weeks alone in the country were the happiest she had known for four years? And how long had they been married when she said that? All right, shut up! If she thought that hadn't stuck in his craw.

She hadn't meant she was happy because she was away from him. She meant she was happy getting the devilish house nice and ready for him. That was what she had meant, and now look! Bringing up something she had said a year ago simply to justify himself for forgetting her coffee and breaking the eggs and buying a wretched piece of rope they couldn't afford. She really thought it was time to drop the subject, and now she wanted only two things in the world. She wanted him to get that rope from underfoot, and go back to the village and get her coffee, and if he could remember it, he might bring a metal mitt for the skillets, and two more curtain rods, and if there were any rubber gloves in the village, her hands were simply raw, and a bottle of milk of magnesia from the drugstore.

He looked out at the dark blue afternoon sweltering on the slopes, and mopped his forehead and sighed heavily and said, if only she could wait a minute for *anything*, he was going back. He had said so, hadn't he, the very instant they found he had overlooked it?

Oh, yes, well...run along. She was going to wash windows. The country was so beautiful! She doubted they'd have a moment to enjoy it. He meant to go, but he could not until he had said that if she wasn't such a hopeless melancholiac she might see that this was only for a few days. Couldn't she remember anything pleasant about the other summers? Hadn't they ever had any fun? She hadn't time to talk about it, and now would he please not leave that rope lying around for her to trip on? He picked it up, somehow it had toppled off the table, and walked out with it under his arm.

Was he going this minute? He certainly was. She thought so. Sometimes it seemed to her he had second sight about the precisely perfect moment to leave her ditched. She had meant to put the mattresses out to sun, if they put them out this minute they would get at least three hours, he must have heard her say that morning she meant to put them out. So of course he would walk off and leave her to it. She supposed he thought the exercise would do her good.

Well, he was merely going to get her coffee. A four-mile walk for two pounds of coffee was ridiculous, but he was perfectly willing to do it. The habit was making a wreck of her, but if she wanted to wreck herself there was nothing he could do about it. If he thought it was coffee that was making a wreck of her, she congratulated him: he must have a damned easy conscience.

Conscience or no conscience, he didn't see why the mattresses couldn't very well wait until tomorrow. And anyhow, for God's sake, were they living in the house, or were they going to let the house ride them to death? She paled at this, her face grew livid about the mouth, she looked quite dangerous, and reminded him that housekeeping was no more her work than it was his: she had other work to do as well, and when did he think she was going to find time to do it at this rate?

Was she going to start on that again? She knew as well as he did that his work brought in the regular money, hers was only occasional, if they depended on what *she* made—and she might as well get straight on this question once for all!

That was positively not the point. The question was, when both of them were working on their own time, was there going to be a division of the housework, or wasn't there? She merely wanted to know, she had to make her plans. Why, he thought that was all arranged. It was understood that he was to help. Hadn't he always, in summers?

Hadn't he, though? Oh, just hadn't he? And when, and where, and doing what? Lord, what an uproarious joke!

It was such a very uproarious joke that her face turned slightly purple, and she screamed with laughter. She laughed so hard she had to sit down, and finally a rush of tears spurted from her eyes and poured down into the lifted corners of her mouth. He dashed towards her and dragged her up to her feet and tried to pour water on her head. The dipper hung by a string on a nail and he broke it loose. Then he tried to pump water with one hand while she struggled in the other. So he gave it up and shook her instead.

She wrenched away, crying for him to take his rope and go to hell, she had simply given him up: and ran. He heard her high-heeled bedroom slippers clattering and stumbling on the stairs.

He went out around the house into the lane; he suddenly realized he had a blister on his heel and his shirt felt as if it were on fire. Things broke so suddenly you didn't know where you were. She could work herself into a fury about simply nothing. She was terrible, damn it: not an ounce of reason. You might as well talk to a sieve as that woman when she got going. Damned if he'd spend his life humoring her! Well, what to do now? He would take back the rope and exchange it for something else. Things accumulated, things were mountainous, you couldn't move them or sort them out or get rid of them. They just lay around and rotted. He'd take it back. Hell, why should he? He wanted it. What was it anyhow? A piece of rope. Imagine anybody caring more about a piece of rope than about a man's feelings. What earthly right had she to say a word about it? He remembered all the useless, meaningless things she bought for herself: Why? because I wanted it; that's why! He stopped and selected a large stone by the road. He would put the rope behind it. He would put it in the tool-box when he got back. He'd heard enough about it to last him a life-time.

When he came back she was leaning against the post box beside the road waiting. It was pretty late, the smell of broiled steak floated nose high in the cooling air. Her face was young and smooth and fresh looking. Her unmanageable funny black hair was all on end. She waved to him from a distance, and he speeded up. She called out that supper was ready and waiting, was he starved?

You bet he was starved. Here was the coffee. He waved it at her. She looked at his other hand. What was that he had there?

Well, it was the rope again. He stopped short. He had meant to exchange it but forgot. She wanted to know why he should exchange it, if it was something he really wanted. Wasn't the air sweet now, and wasn't it fine to be here?

She walked beside him with one hand hooked into his leather belt. She pulled and jostled him a little as he walked, and leaned against him. He put his arm clear around her and patted her stomach. They exchanged wary smiles. Coffee, coffee for the Ootsum-Wootsums! He felt as if he were bringing her a beautiful present.

He was a love, she firmly believed, and if she had had her coffee in the morning, she wouldn't have behaved so funny... There was a whippoorwill still coming back, imagine, clear out of season, sitting in the crab-apple tree calling all by himself. Maybe his girl stood him up. Maybe she did. She hoped to hear him once more, she loved whippoorwills... He knew how she was, didn't he?

Sure, he knew how she was.

Suggestions for Discussion

1. Think of the multiple uses of rope and determine the ways in which the title serves as a metaphor for the quarrel and the bond between husband and wife. What does the phrase "enough rope" connote? How might it relate to the story?
2. What is the purpose of the indirect approach to the narrative through a third-person narrator? Is it more or less effective than if told from the point of view of husband or wife? Account for the frequent questions and their effect.
3. With what details are the character of husband and wife revealed?
4. What are the ostensible and real causes of the quarrel? Is the mechanism of displacement at work? Explain.

5. How do you learn of the husband and wife's economic situation?
6. How serious was the husband's threat to go away? How did the wife respond?
7. Account for the shift in tone on the husband's return. What other changes in tone do you find?
8. What does the introduction of the whippoorwill add to the resolution of the story?
9. Why was the wife particularly incensed at the time the husband asked if they were "going to let the house ride them to death"?
10. What effect is achieved by referring to the characters as husband and wife rather than as Dan and Mary or other proper names?
11. In what sense is this a story of affirmation?

Suggestions for Writing

1. Retell the story from the wife's or the husband's point of view.
2. Discuss the mechanism of displacement in human relationships. Account for it and illustrate it.
3. Argue for or against the idea that the title "Rope" is symbolic of the relationship. If you were to retitle the story, what title would you give it and why?

POETRY

WILLIAM SHAKESPEARE

William Shakespeare (1564–1616) is generally acknowledged to be the greatest playwright in the English language. He was born in Stratford-upon-Avon, England. By 1592 he had become an actor and playwright in London, and in 1599 he helped establish the famous Globe Theatre. In addition to the sonnets, his works include historical plays, comedies such as *A Midsummer Night's Dream,* and tragedies such as *Macbeth, Hamlet, King Lear,* and *Othello.* The self-doubt in Sonnet 29 is resolved with the poet's thoughts of his love. In Sonnet 116 the poet attests to the inviolability and permanence of love.

When in Disgrace with Fortune and Men's Eyes

(Sonnet 29)

When, in disgrace with fortune and men's eyes,
I all alone beweep my outcast state,
And trouble deaf heaven with my bootless cries,
And look upon myself and curse my fate;
Wishing me like to one more rich in hope,
Featured like him, like him with friends possessed,
Desiring this man's art, and that man's scope,
With what I most enjoy contented least;
Yet in these thoughts myself almost despising,
Haply I think on thee, and then my state,
Like to the lark at break of day arising
From sullen earth, sings hymns at heaven's gate;
For thy sweet love remembered such wealth brings
That then I scorn to change my state with kings.

Let Me Not to the Marriage of True Minds

(Sonnet 116)

Let me not to the marriage of true minds
Admit impediments. Love is not love
Which alters when it alteration finds,
Or bends with the remover to remove:
Oh, no! it is an ever-fixed mark,
That looks on tempests and is never shaken;
It is the star to every wandering bark,
Whose worth's unknown, although his height be taken.
Love's not Time's fool, though rosy lips and cheeks
Within his bending sickle's compass come;
Love alters not with his brief hours and weeks,
But bears it out even to the edge of doom.
If this be error and upon me proved,
I never writ, nor no man ever loved.

Suggestions for Discussion

1. How does the imagery in each of the sonnets contribute to its unity?
2. How does dramatic understatement at the end of the second of the two sonnets reinforce the theme?

WILLIAM BLAKE

The Clod and the Pebble

The Garden of Love

William Blake (1757–1827), poet and artist, illustrated his poems with his own engravings. His works include *Songs of Innocence* (1789), *Songs of Experience* (1794), *The Marriage of Heaven and Hell* (1790), *The Gates of Paradise* (1793), and *Visions of the Daughters of*

Albion (1793). The poems that follow suggest some of the contradictions inherent in concepts of love.

The Clod and the Pebble

"Love seeketh not Itself to please,
  Nor for itself hath any care,
But for another gives its ease,
  And builds a Heaven in Hell's despair."

So sung the Clod of Clay,
  Trodden with the cattle's feet,
But a Pebble in the brook
  Warbled out these metres meet:

"Love seeketh only Self to please,
  To bind another to its delight,
Joys in another's loss of ease,
  And builds a Hell in Heaven's Despite."

The Garden of Love

I went to the Garden of Love,
And I saw what I never had seen:
A Chapel was built in the midst,
Where I used to play on the green.

And the gates of this Chapel were shut,
And "Thou shalt not" writ over the door:
So I turned to the Garden of Love
That so many sweet flowers bore;

And I saw it was filled with graves,
And tomb-stones where flowers should be;
And Priests in black gowns were walking their rounds,
And binding with briars my joys and desires.

Suggestion for Discussion

Both of Blake's poems suggest some of the contradictions inherent in concepts of "love." What are they and what seems to be the poet's conclusion?

W. H. AUDEN

Lay Your Sleeping Head, My Love

Wystan Hugh Auden (1907–1973), English poet educated at Oxford University, was early recognized as a leader of the poets of his generation. His poetry collections include *The Orators* (1932), *The Double Man* (1941), *The Shield of Achilles* (1955), *Homage to Clio* (1960), *About the House* (1965), and *The Age of Anxiety* (1947), which won a Pulitzer Prize in 1948. His autobiography, *Certain World: A Commonplace Book,* was published in 1970. Auden also experimented with drama, and his criticism was collected in *The Dyer's Hand* in 1963. In 1967 he was made a fellow of Christ College, Oxford. The writer speaks of the threats to love in this poem that weaves back and forth between the present and future, the concrete and abstract.

Lay your sleeping head, my love,
Human on my faithless arm;
Time and fevers burn away
Individual beauty from
Thoughtful children, and the grave
Proves the child ephemeral:
But in my arms till break of day
Let the living creature lie,
Mortal, guilty, but to me
The entirely beautiful.

Soul and body have no bounds:
To lovers as they lie upon
Her tolerant enchanted slope
In their ordinary swoon,
Grave the vision Venus sends
Of supernatural sympathy,
Universal love and hope;
While an abstract insight wakes
Among the glaciers and the rocks
The hermit's sensual ecstasy.
Eye and knocking heart may bless,

Certainty, fidelity
On the stroke of midnight pass
Like vibrations of a bell,
And fashionable madmen raise
Their pedantic boring cry:
Every farthing of the cost,
All the dreaded cards foretell,
Shall be paid, but from this night
Not a whisper, not a thought,
Not a kiss nor look be lost.

Beauty, midnight, vision dies:
Let the winds of dawn that blow
Softly round your dreaming head
Such a day of sweetness show
Eye and knocking heart may bless,
Find the mortal world enough;
Noons of dryness see you fed
By the involuntary powers,
Nights of insult let you pass
Watched by every human love.

Suggestions for Discussion

1. What images are employed by the speaker to suggest the hazards of love?
2. Account for the movement from present to future and from particular to general.

EDNA ST. VINCENT MILLAY

Love Is Not All

Edna St. Vincent Millay (1892–1950), American poet, wrote "Renascence," her first major poem, while she was still in college. Her early works such as *A Few Figs from Thistles* (1920) exhibited a cynical flippancy that deepened into bitter disillusionment in later works such as

The Harp-Weaver and Other Poems (1923), a Pulitzer Prize selection, and *The Buck in the Snow* (1928). In this sonnet the poet exalts the power of love.

Love is not all; it is not meat nor drink
Nor slumber nor a roof against the rain,
Nor yet a floating spar to men that sink
And rise and sink and rise and sink again;
Love can not fill the thickened lung with breath,
Nor clean the blood, nor set the fractured bone;
Yet many a man is making friends with death
Even as I speak, for lack of love alone.
It well may be that in a difficult hour,
Pinned down by pain and moaning for release,
Or nagged by want past resolution's power,
I might be driven to sell your love for peace,
To trade the memory of this night for food.
It well may be. I do not think I would.

Suggestion for Discussion

What are the apparent limitations of love?

E. E. CUMMINGS

i like my body when it is with your

E. E. Cummings (1894–1962) was an American whose book *The Enormous Room* (1922) and whose poetry *&* and *XLI Poems* (1925) established his reputation as an avant-garde writer interested in experimenting with stylistic techniques. Awarded several important prizes for poetry, he was also Charles Eliot Norton Lecturer at Harvard University in 1952 and wrote *i: six nonlectures* (1953). The repetitions and typography as well as the sensory detail contribute to Cummings's expression of joy in physical love.

i like my body when it is with your
body. It is so quite new a thing.
Muscles better and nerves more.
i like your body. i like what it does,
i like its hows. i like to feel the spine
of your body and its bones, and the trembling
-firm-smooth ness and which i will
again and again and again
kiss, i like kissing this and that of you,
i like, slowly stroking the, shocking fuzz
of your electric fur, and what-is-it comes
over parting flesh.... And eyes big love-crumbs,

and possibly i like the thrill

of under me you so quite new

Suggestions for Discussion

1. Account for the appeal of the poem.
2. How do the repetitions and the typography contribute to the poem's effectiveness? What distinguishes this poem from prose?

MAY SWENSON

Women

May Swenson (1919–1989) was an American poet best known for *Another Animal* (1954), *A Cage of Spines* (1958), *To Mix with Time* (1963), *Poems to Solve* (1966), and *Half Sun Half Sleep* (1967). She won numerous prizes and grants, including Guggenheim, Ford Foundation, and Rockefeller Foundation fellowships, the National Institute of Arts and Letters Award, and the Shelley Award. The poet's anger is reflected in the pedestal and rocking horse metaphors.

Women
should be
pedestals
moving
pedestals
moving
to the
motions
of men
Or they
should be
little horses
those wooden
sweet
oldfashioned
painted
rocking
horses
the gladdest things in the toyroom
The
pegs
of their
ears
so familiar
and dear
to the trusting
fists
To be chafed
feelingly
and then
unfeelingly
To be
joyfully
ridden
rockingly
ridden until
the restored
egos dismount and the legs stride away
Immobile
sweetlipped
sturdy
and smiling
women
should always
be waiting
willing
to be set
into motion
Women
should be
pedestals
to men

Suggestions for Discussion

1. How does the central metaphor define the author's point of view? How does it contribute to tone?
2. How does the second extended metaphor contribute to purpose and tone?
3. How do alliteration and repetition function in the poem?
4. Comment on the function of the verbs and adjectives in creating mood and tone.

Suggestion for Writing

Using the same title, write an ironic sketch or poem.

CALVIN TRILLIN

Just How Do You Suppose that Alice Knows?

Calvin Trillin (b. 1935) was educated at Yale and has spent his entire career as a writer and humorist in all genres, and as a food critic. A staff writer for *Time, The Nation,* and most significantly, *The New Yorker* (since 1963), he has published prolifically. His most recent books include *The Tummy Trilogy* (1994), *Too Soon to Tell* (1995), *Deadline Poet: My Life as a Doggerelist* (1995), and *Messages from My Father* (1996). He was nominated for the National Book Award for *Alice Let's Eat.* This poem is a tongue-in-cheek commentary on women's ways of knowing.

Just how do you suppose that Alice knows
So much about what's au courant in clothes?
You wouldn't really think that she's the sort
To know much more than whether skirts are short
Or long again, or somewhere in between.
She's surely not the sort who would be seen
In front-row seats at Paris fashion shows.
In fact, she looks at that sort down her nose.
For her to read a fashion mag would seem
As out of synch as reading *Field & Stream.*
Biographies are what she reads instead.
And yet she has, in detail, in her head
Whose indigos are drawing "ooh"s and "oh"s.
Just how do you suppose that Alice knows?

We're leaving, and I'll ask her, once we've gone,
"What *was* that thing that whatzername had on?
It lacked a back. The front was sort of lined
With gauzy stuff. It seemed to be the kind
Of frock that might be worn by Uncle Meyer
If he played Blanche in 'Streetcar Named Desire.'"
And Alice knows. She knows just who designed
The rag and why some folks are of a mind

To buy this *schmattameister's* frilly things
For what a small Brancusi usually brings.
She mentions something newly chic this year.
To me it looked like antique fishing gear.
I'm stunned, as if she'd talked in Urdu prose.
Just how do you suppose that Alice knows?

She gets no E-mail info on design.
(She's au courant but, so far, not on-line.)
No fashion maven tells her what is kitsch.
She goes to no symposium at which
She learns why some designer's models pose
As Navajos or folks from U.F.O.s.
I know that women have no special gene
Providing knowledge of the fashion scene,
The way that men all have, without a doubt,
The chromosome for garbage-taking-out.
And yet she's fashion-conscious to her toes.
Does she divine these things? Does she osmose
What's in the air concerning hose and bows?
Just how do you suppose that Alice knows?

Suggestions for Discussion

1. Trillin poses the question of women's apparently innate knowledge of fashion. Do you have a theory which might offer an answer?
2. This poems exhibits one of the classic feminine stereotypes. Do you find it true of the women you know? Do you find it offensive?
3. How would you describe the tone of the poem? How does Trillin achieve his comic effect? Does his style remind you of anyone else's?

Suggestions for Writing

1. Choose a classic male stereotype and portray it ironically.
2. Trillin uses a great many allusions to enrich the impact of his poem. Come up with a topic that interests you and see how many relevant references you can find to strengthen the effect you are trying to achieve.
3. The question of how we know what we know is very rich. Write a story about how someone comes to know something.

DRAMA

WENDY WASSERSTEIN

The Man in a Case

Wendy Wasserstein (b. 1950) has a B.A. from Mount Holyoke and graduate degrees from the City University of New York and Yale University. Widely considered to be one of the most accomplished of contemporary playwrights, she has won the Joseph Jefferson and Dramalogue awards for *Uncommon Women* (1978), and the Toni, Pulitzer, and New York Drama Critics awards for *The Heidi Chronicles* (1989). This selection based on a play by Chekhov parodies a courtship between two not quite so young Russians at the end of the nineteenth century. *An American Daughter* opened in 1997.

Characters

BYELINKOV
VARINKA

A SMALL GARDEN IN THE VILLAGE OF MIRONITSKI. 1898.

BYELINKOV *is pacing. Enter* VARINKA *out of breath.*

BYELINKOV: You are ten minutes late.

VARINKA: The most amazing thing happened on my way over here. You know the woman who runs the grocery store down the road. She wears a black wig during the week, and a blond wig on Saturday nights. And she has a daughter who married an engineer in Moscow who is doing very well thank you and is living, God bless them, in a three-room apartment. But he really is the most boring man in the world. All he talks about is his future and his station in life. Well, she heard we were to be married and she gave me this basket of apricots to give to you.

BYELINKOV: That is a most amazing thing!

VARINKA: She said to me, Varinka, you are marrying the most honorable man in the entire village. In this village he is the only man fit to speak with my son-in-law.

BYELINKOV: I don't care for apricots. They give me hives.

VARINKA: I can return them. I'm sure if I told her they give you hives she would give me a basket of raisins or a cake.

BYELINKOV: I don't know this woman or her pompous son-in-law. Why would she give me her cakes?

VARINKA: She adores you!

BYELINKOV: She is emotionally loose.

VARINKA: She adores you by reputation. Everyone adores you by reputation. I tell everyone I am to marry Byelinkov, the finest teacher in the county.

BYELINKOV: You tell them this?

VARINKA: If they don't tell me first.

BYELINKOV: Pride can be an imperfect value.

VARINKA: It isn't pride. It is the truth. You are a great man!

BYELINKOV: I am the master of Greek and Latin at a local school at the end of the village of Mironitski.

(VARINKA *kisses him)*

VARINKA: And I am to be the master of Greek and Latin's wife!

BYELINKOV: Being married requires a great deal of responsibility. I hope I am able to provide you with all that a married man must properly provide a wife.

VARINKA: We will be very happy.

BYELINKOV: Happiness is for children. We are entering into a social contract, an amicable agreement to provide us with a secure and satisfying future.

VARINKA: You are so sweet! You are the sweetest man in the world!

BYELINKOV: I'm a man set in his ways who saw a chance to provide himself with a small challenge.

VARINKA: Look at you! Look at you! Your sweet round spectacles, your dear collar always starched, always raised, your perfectly pressed pants always creasing at right angles perpendicular to the floor, and my most favorite part, the sweet little galoshes, rain or shine, just in case. My Byelinkov, never taken by surprise. Except by me.

BYELINKOV: You speak about me as if I were your pet.

VARINKA: You are my pet! My little school mouse.

BYELINKOV: A mouse?

VARINKA: My sweetest dancing bear with galoshes, my little stale babka.

BYELINKOV: A stale babka?

VARINKA: I am not Pushkin.

BYELINKOV (*Laughs*): That depends what you think of Pushkin.

VARINKA: You're smiling. I knew I could make you smile today.

BYELINKOV: I am a responsible man. Every day I have for breakfast black bread, fruit, hot tea, and every day I smile three times. I am halfway into my translation of the *Aeneid* from classical Greek hexameter into Russian alexandrines. In twenty years I have never been late to school. I am a responsible man, but no dancing bear.

VARINKA: Dance with me.

BYELINKOV: Now? It is nearly four weeks before the wedding?

VARINKA: It's a beautiful afternoon. We are in your garden. The roses are in full bloom.

BYELINKOV: The roses have beetles.

VARINKA: Dance with me!

BYELINKOV: You are a demanding woman.

VARINKA: You chose me. And right. And left. And turn. And right. And left.

BYELINKOV: And turn. Give me your hand. You dance like a school mouse. It's a beautiful afternoon! We are in my garden. The roses are in full bloom! And turn. And turn. (*Twirls* VARINKA *around*)

VARINKA: I am the luckiest woman!

(BYELINKOV *stops dancing*)

Why are you stopping?

BYELINKOV: To place a lilac in your hair. Every year on this day I will place a lilac in your hair.

VARINKA: Will you remember?

BYELINKOV: I will write it down. (*Takes a notebook from his pocket*) Dear Byelinkov, don't forget the day a young lady, your bride, entered your garden, your peace, and danced on the roses. On that day every year you are to place a lilac in her hair.

VARINKA: I love you.

BYELINKOV: It is convenient we met.

VARINKA: I love you.

BYELINKOV: You are a girl.

VARINKA: I am thirty.

BYELINKOV: But you think like a girl. That is an attractive attribute.

VARINKA: Do you love me?

BYELINKOV: We've never spoken about housekeeping.

VARINKA: I am an excellent housekeeper. I kept house for my family on the farm in Gadyatchsky. I can make a beetroot soup with tomatoes and aubergines which is so nice. Awfully awfully nice.

BYELINKOV: You are fond of expletives.

VARINKA: My beet soup, sir, is excellent!

BYELINKOV: Please don't be cross. I too am an excellent housekeeper. I have a place for everything in the house. A shelf for each pot, a cubby for every spoon, a folder for favorite recipes. I have cooked for myself for twenty years. Though my beet soup is not outstanding, it is sufficient.

VARINKA: I'm sure it's very good.

BYELINKOV: No. It is awfully, awfully not. What I am outstanding in, however, what gives me the greatest pleasure, is preserving those things which are left over. I wrap each tomato slice I haven't used in a wet cloth and place it in the coolest corner of the house. I have had my shoes for seven years because I wrap them in the galoshes you are so fond of. And every night before I go to sleep I wrap my bed in quilts and curtains so I never catch a draft.

VARINKA: You sleep with curtains on your bed?

BYELINKOV: I like to keep warm.

VARINKA: I will make you a new quilt.

BYELINKOV: No. No new quilt. That would be hazardous.

VARINKA: It is hazardous to sleep under curtains.

BYELINKOV: Varinka, I don't like change very much. If one works out the arithmetic the final fraction of improvement is at best less than an eighth of value over the total damage caused by disruption. I never thought of marrying till I saw your eyes dancing among the familiar faces at the headmaster's tea. I assumed I would grow old preserved like those which are left over, wrapped suitably in my case of curtains and quilts.

VARINKA: Byelinkov, I want us to have dinners with friends and summer country visits. I want people to say, "Have you spent time with Varinka and Byelinkov? He is so happy, now that they are married. She is just what he needed."

BYELINKOV: You have already brought me some happiness. But I never was a sad man. Don't ever think I thought I was a sad man.

VARINKA: My sweetest darling, you can be whatever you want! If you are sad, they'll say she talks all the time, and he is soft-spoken and kind.

BYELINKOV: And if I am difficult?

VARINKA: Oh, they'll say he is difficult because he is highly intelligent. All great men are difficult. Look at Lermontov, Tchaikovsky, Peter the Great.

BYELINKOV: Ivan the Terrible.

VARINKA: Yes, him too.

BYELINKOV: Why are you marrying me? I am none of these things.

VARINKA: To me you are.

BYELINKOV: You have imagined this. You have constructed an elaborate romance for yourself. Perhaps you are the great one. You are the one with the great imagination.

VARINKA: Byelinkov, I am a pretty girl of thirty. You're right, I am not a woman. I have not made myself into a woman because I do not deserve that honor. Until I came to this town to visit my brother I lived on my family's farm. As the years passed I became younger and younger in fear that I would never marry. And it wasn't that I wasn't pretty enough or sweet enough, it was just that no man ever looked at me and saw a wife. I was not the woman who would be there when he came home. Until I met you I thought I would lie all my life and say I never married because I never met a man I loved. I will love you, Byelinkov. And I will help you to love me. We deserve the life everyone else has. We deserve not to be different.

BYELINKOV: Yes. We are the same as everyone else.

VARINKA: Tell me you love me.

BYELINKOV: I love you.

VARINKA (*Takes his hands*): We will be very happy. I am very strong. (*Pauses*) It is time for tea.

BYELINKOV: It is too early for tea. Tea is at half past the hour.

VARINKA: Do you have heavy cream? It will be awfully nice with apricots.

BYELINKOV: Heavy cream is too rich for teatime.

VARINKA: But today is special. Today you placed a lilac in my hair. Write in your note pad. Every year we will celebrate with apricots and heavy cream. I will go to my brother's house and get some.

BYELINKOV: But your brother's house is a mile from here.

VARINKA: Today it is much shorter. Today my brother gave me his bicycle to ride. I will be back very soon.

BYELINKOV: You rode to my house by bicycle! Did anyone see you?

VARINKA: Of course. I had such fun. I told you I saw the grocery store lady with the son-in-law who is doing very well thank you in Moscow, and the headmaster's wife.

BYELINKOV: You saw the headmaster's wife!

VARINKA: She smiled at me.

BYELINKOV: Did she laugh or smile?

VARINKA: She laughed a little. She said, "My dear, you are very progressive to ride a bicycle." She said you and your fiancé Byelinkov must ride together sometime. I wonder if he'll take off his galoshes when he rides a bicycle.

BYELINKOV: She said that?

VARINKA: She adores you. We had a good giggle.

BYELINKOV: A woman can be arrested for riding a bicycle. That is not progressive, it is a premeditated revolutionary act. Your brother must be awfully, awfully careful on behalf of your behavior. He has been careless—oh so careless—in giving you the bicycle.

VARINKA: Dearest Byelinkov, you are wrapping yourself under curtains and quilts! I made friends on the bicycle.

BYELINKOV: You saw more than the headmaster's wife and the idiot grocery woman.

VARINKA: She is not an idiot.

BYELINKOV: She is a potato-vending, sausage-armed fool!

VARINKA: Shhhh! My school mouse. Shhh!

BYELINKOV: What other friends did you make on this bicycle?

VARINKA: I saw students from my brother's classes. They waved and shouted, "Anthropos in love! Anthropos in love!!"

BYELINKOV: Where is that bicycle?

VARINKA: I left it outside the gate. Where are you going?

BYELINKOV (*Muttering as he exits):* Anthropos in love, anthropos in love.

VARINKA: They were cheering me on. Careful, you'll trample the roses.

BYELINKOV (*Returning with the bicycle*): Anthropos is the Greek singular for man. Anthropos in love translates as the Greek and Latin master in love. Of course they cheered you. Their instructor, who teaches them the discipline and contained beauty of the classics, is in love with a sprite on a bicycle. It is a good giggle, isn't it? A very good giggle! I am returning this bicycle to your brother.

VARINKA: But it is teatime.

BYELINKOV: Today we will not have tea.

VARINKA: But you will have to walk back a mile.

BYELINKOV: I have my galoshes on. (*Gets on the bicycle*) Varinka, we deserve not to be different. (*Begins to pedal. The bicycle doesn't move*)

VARINKA: Put the kickstand up.

BYELINKOV: I beg your pardon.

VARINKA (*Giggling*): Byelinkov, to make the bicycle move, you must put the kickstand up.

(BYELINKOV *puts it up and awkwardly falls off the bicycle as it moves*)

(*Laughing*) Ha ha ha. My little school mouse. You look so funny! You are the sweetest dearest man in the world. Ha ha ha!

(*Pause*)

BYELINKOV: Please help me up. I'm afraid my galosh is caught.

VARINKA (*Trying not to laugh*): Your galosh is caught! (*Explodes in laughter again*) Oh, you are so funny! I do love you so. (*Helps* BYELINKOV *up*) You were right, my pet, as always. We don't need heavy cream for tea. The fraction of improvement isn't worth the damage caused by the disruption.

BYELINKOV: Varinka, it is still too early for tea. I must complete two stanzas of my translation before late afternoon. That is my regular schedule.

VARINKA: Then I will watch while you work.

BYELINKOV: No. You had a good giggle. That is enough.

VARINKA: Then while you work I will work too. I will make lists of guests for our wedding.

BYELINKOV: I can concentrate only when I am alone in my house. Please take your bicycle home to your brother.

VARINKA: But I don't want to leave you. You look so sad.

BYELINKOV: I never was a sad man. Don't ever think I was a sad man.

VARINKA: Byelinkov, it's a beautiful day, we are in your garden. The roses are in bloom.

BYELINKOV: Allow me to help you on to your bicycle. (*Takes* VARINKA'S *hand as she gets on the bike*)

VARINKA: You are such a gentleman. We will be very happy.

BYELINKOV: You are very strong. Good day, Varinka.

(Varinka pedals off. BYELINKOV, *alone in the garden, takes out his pad and rips up the note about the lilac, strews it over the garden, then carefully picks up each piece of paper and places them all in a small envelope as lights fade to black)*

Suggestions for Discussion

1. Varinka and Byelinkov have very different approaches to life. How would you characterize them?
2. Imagine three different situations and decide how the two protagonists would respond to each of them.
3. Does this couple have a future? What might give us reason to hope? To doubt?

Suggestions for Writing

1. Translate this turn-of-the-century Russian couple into a turn-of-the-century North American couple, one hundred years later.
2. One might characterize this couple as a male "realist" and a female "romantic." Switch the roles, and write a love story about a male romantic and a female realist.
3. Describe a courtship ritual as it takes place between couples twenty years old, forty years old, sixty years old.

The Cultural Tradition: Popular Culture

I wince when I'm called a former beauty queen or Miss U.S.A.

—STUDS TERKEL, "Miss U.S.A."

"How can I go to work," I yelled, "when I've got so much leisure time on my hands?"

—ART BUCHWALD, "Leisure Will Kill You"

In short, television works on the same imaginative and intellectual level as psychoactive drugs.

—PETE HAMILL, "Crack and the Box"

The trouble is, people nowadays simply assume that they have the right to know about everyone—and indeed, in the course of events, that they *will* know about everyone, and everyone will know about them.

—ROGER ROSENBLATT, "Who Killed Privacy?"

I believe that Black musicians/artists have a responsibility to be conscious of their world and to let their consciousness be heard in their songs.

—BERNICE REAGON, "Black Music in Our Hands"

Violence as art is a last-ditch attempt at the Sublime.

—ALEX ROSS, "The Shock of the True"

Only Hollywood in the nineties could arrange such a pain-free, upbeat Armageddon.

—JAMES WOLCOTT, "Reborn on the Fourth of July"

PERSONAL REMINISCENCE

STUDS TERKEL

Miss U.S.A.

Studs Terkel (b. 1912), long associated with radio station WFMT in Chicago, won the Pulitzer Prize for General Non-Fiction in 1985. He gained fame as an oral historian with the publication of *Division Street* (1966), *Hard Times* (1970), *Working* (1974), and *American Dreams: Lost and Found* (1980), from which the following selection is taken. More recent books include *The Good War* (1985), an oral history of World War II; *The Great Divide: Second Thoughts on the American Dream* (1991); *How Blacks and Whites Think and Feel About the American Obsession* (1992); and *Coming of Age* (1995). In "Miss U.S.A.," Terkel interviews Emma Knight, a perceptive and outspoken former beauty queen.

Emma Knight, Miss U.S.A., 1973. She is twenty-nine.

I wince when I'm called a former beauty queen or Miss U.S.A. I keep thinking they're talking about someone else. There are certain images that come to mind when people talk about beauty queens. It's mostly what's known as t and a, tits and ass. No talent. For many girls who enter the contest, it's part of the American Dream. It was never mine.

You used to sit around the TV and watch Miss America and it was exciting, we thought, glamorous. Fun, we thought. But by the time I was eight or nine, I didn't feel comfortable. Soon I'm hitting my adolescence, like fourteen, but I'm not doing any dating and I'm feeling awkward and ugly. I'm much taller than most of the people in my class. I don't feel I can compete the way I see girls competing for guys. I was very much of a loner. I felt intimidated by the amount of competition females were supposed to go through with each other. I didn't like being told by *Seventeen* magazine: Subvert your interests if you have a crush on a guy, get interested in what he's interested in. If you play cards, be sure not to beat him. I was very bad at these social games.

After I went to the University of Colorado for three and a half years, I had it. This was 1968 through '71. I came home for the summer. An agent met me and wanted me to audition for commercials, modeling, acting jobs. Okay. I started auditioning and winning some.

I did things actors do when they're starting out. You pass out literature at conventions, you do print ads, you pound the pavements, you send out your resumés. I had come to a model agency one cold day, and an agent came out and said: "I want you to enter a beauty contest." I said: "No, uh-uh, never, never, never. I'll lose, how humiliating." She said: "I want some girls to represent the agency, might do you good." So I filled out the application blank: hobbies, measurements, blah, blah, blah. I got a letter: "Congratulations. You have been accepted as an entrant into the Miss Illinois-Universe contest." Now what do I do? I'm stuck.

You have to have a sponsor. Or you're gonna have to pay several hundred dollars. So I called up the lady who was running it. Terribly sorry, I can't do this. I don't have the money. She calls back a couple of days later: "We found you a sponsor, it's a lumber company."

It was in Decatur. There were sixty-some contestants from all over the place. I went as a lumberjack: blue jeans, hiking boots, a flannel shirt, a pair of suspenders, and carrying an axe. You come out first in your costume and you introduce yourself and say your astrological sign or whatever it is they want you to say. You're wearing a banner that has the sponsor's name on it. Then you come out and do your pirouettes in your one-piece bathing suit, and the judges look at you a lot. Then you come out in your evening gown and pirouette around for a while. That's the first night.

The second night, they're gonna pick fifteen people. In between, you had judges' interviews. For three minutes, they ask you anything they want. Can you answer questions? How do you handle yourself? Your poise, personality, blah, blah, blah. They're called personality judges.

I thought: This will soon be over, get on a plane tomorrow, and no one will be the wiser. Except that my name got called as one of the fifteen. You have to go through the whole thing all over again.

I'm thinking: I don't have a prayer. I'd come to feel a certain kind of distance, except that they called my name. I was the winner, Miss Illinois. All I could do was laugh. I'm twenty-two, standing up there in a borrowed evening gown, thinking: What am I doing here: This is like Tom Sawyer becomes an altar boy.

I was considered old for a beauty queen, which is a little horrifying when you're twenty-two. That's very much part of the beauty queen syndrome: the young, untouched, unthinking human being.

I had to go to this room and sign the Miss Illinois-Universe contract right away. Miss Universe, Incorporated, is the full name of the company. It's owned by Kayser-Roth, Incorporated, which was bought out by Gulf & Western. Big business.

I'm sitting there with my glass of champagne and I'm reading over this contract. They said: "Oh, you don't have to read it." And I said: "I never sign anything that I don't read." They're all waiting to take pictures, and I'm sitting there reading this long document. So I signed it and the phone rang and the guy was from a Chicago paper and said: "Tell me, is it Miss or Ms.?" I said: "It's Ms." He said: "You're kidding." I said: "No, I'm not." He wrote an article the next day saying something like it finally happened: a beauty queen, a feminist. I thought I was a feminist before I was a beauty queen, why should I stop now?

Then I got into the publicity and training and interviews. It was a throwback to another time where crossed ankles and white gloves and teacups were present. I was taught how to walk around with a book on my head, how to sit daintily, how to pose in a bathing suit, and how to frizz my hair. They wanted curly hair, which I hate.

One day the trainer asked me to shake hands. I shook hands. She said: "That's wrong. When you shake hands with a man, you always shake hands ring up." I said: "Like the pope? Where my hand is up, like he's gonna kiss it?" Right. I thought: Holy mackerel! It was a very long February and March and April and May.

I won the Miss U.S.A. pageant. I started to laugh. They tell me I'm the only beauty queen in history that didn't cry when she won. It was on network television. I said to myself: "You're kidding." Bob Barker, the host, said: "No, I'm not kidding." I didn't know what else to say at that moment. In the press releases, they call it the great American Dream. There she is, Miss America, your ideal. Well, not my ideal, kid.

The minute you're crowned, you become their property and subject to whatever they tell you. They wake you up at seven o'clock next morning and make you put on a negligee and serve you breakfast in bed, so that all the New York papers can come in and take your picture sitting in bed, while you're absolutely bleary-eyed from the night before. They put on the Kayser-Roth negligee, hand you the tray, you take three bites. The photographers leave, you whip off the negligee, they take the breakfast away, and that's it. I never did get any breakfast that day. (Laughs).

You immediately start making personal appearances. The Jaycees or the chamber of commerce says: "I want to book Miss U.S.A. for our Christmas Day parade." They pay, whatever it is, seven hundred fifty dollars a day, first-class air fare, round trip, expenses, so forth. If the United Fund calls and wants me to give a five-minute pitch on queens at a luncheon, they still have to pay a fee. Doesn't matter that it's a charity. It's one hundred percent to Miss Universe, Incorporated. You get your salary. That's your prize money for the year. I got fifteen thousand dollars, which is all taxed in New York. Maybe out of a check of three thousand dollars, I'd get fifteen hundred dollars.

From the day I won Miss U.S.A. to the day I left for Universe, almost two months, I got a day and a half off. I made about two hundred fifty appearances that year. Maybe three hundred. Parades, shopping centers, and things. Snip ribbons. What else do you do at a shopping center? Model clothes. The nice thing I got to do was public speaking. They said: "You want a ghost writer?" I said: "Hell, no, I know how to talk." I wrote my own speeches. They don't trust girls to go out and talk because most of them can't.

One of the big execs from General Motors asked me to do a speech in Washington, D.C., on the consumer and the energy crisis. It was the fiftieth anniversary of the National Management Association. The White House, for some reason, sent me some stuff on it. I read it over, it was nonsense. So I stood up and said: "The reason we have an energy crisis is because we are, industrially and personally, pigs. We have a short-term view of the resources available to us; and unless we wake up to what we're doing to our air and our water, we'll have a dearth, not just a crisis." Oh, they weren't real pleased. (Laughs.)

What I resent most is that a lot of people didn't expect me to live this version of the American Dream for myself. I was supposed to live it their way.

When it came out in a newspaper interview that I said Nixon should resign, that he was a crook, oh dear, the fur flew. They got very upset until I got an invitation to the White House. They wanted to shut me up. The Miss Universe corporation had been trying to establish some sort of liaison with the White House for several years. I make anti-Nixon speeches and get this invitation.

I figured they're either gonna take me down to the basement and beat me up with a rubber hose or they're gonna offer me a cabinet post. They had a list of fifteen or so people I was supposed to meet. I've never seen such a bunch of people with raw nerve endings. I was dying to bring a tape recorder but thought if you mention the word "Sony" in the Nixon White House, you're in trouble. They'd have cardiac arrest. But I'm gonna bring along a pad and paper. They were patronizing. And when one of 'em got me in his office and talked about all the journalists and television people being liberals, I brought up blacklisting, *Red Channels*, and the TV industry. He changed the subject.

Miss Universe took place in Athens, Greece. The junta was still in power. I saw a heck of a lot of jeeps and troops and machine guns. The Americans were supposed to keep a low profile. I had never been a great fan of the Greek junta, but I knew darn well I was gonna have to keep my mouth shut. I was still representing the United States, for better or for worse. Miss Philippines won. I ran second.

At the end of the year, you're run absolutely ragged. That final evening, they usually have several queens from past years come back. Before they crown the new Miss U.S.A., the current one is supposed to take what they call the farewell walk. They call over the PA: Time for the old queen's walk. I'm now twenty-three and I'm an old queen. And they have this idiot farewell speech playing over the airwaves as the old queen takes the walk. And you're sitting on the throne for about thirty seconds, then you come down and they announce the name of the new one and you put the crown on her head. And then you're old.

As the new one is crowned, the reporters and photographers rush on the stage. I've seen photographers shove the girl who has just given her reign up thirty seconds before, shove her physically. I was gone by that time. I had jumped off the stage in my evening gown. It is very difficult for girls who are terrified of this ending. All of a sudden (snaps fingers), you're out. Nobody gives a damn about the old one.

Miss U.S.A. and remnants thereof is the crown stored in the attic in my parents' home. I don't even know where the banners are. It wasn't me the fans of Miss U.S.A. thought was pretty. What they think is pretty is the banner and crown. If I could put the banner and crown on that lamp, I swear to God ten men would come in and ask it for a date. I'll think about committing an axe murder if I'm not called anything but a former beauty queen. I can't stand it any more.

Several times during my year as what's-her-face I had seen the movie *The Sting*. There's a gesture the characters use which means the con is on: they rub their nose. In my last fleeting moments as Miss U.S.A., as they were playing that silly farewell speech and I walked down the aisle and stood by the throne, I looked right into the camera and rubbed my finger across my nose. The next day, the pageant people spent all their time telling people that I hadn't done it. I spent the time telling them that, of course, I had. I simply meant: the con is on. (Laughs.)

Miss U.S.A. is in the same graveyard that Emma Knight the twelve-year-old is. Where the sixteen-year-old is. All the past selves. There comes a time when you have to bury those selves because you've grown into another one. You don't keep exhuming the corpses.

If I could sit down with every young girl in America for the next fifty years, I could tell them what I liked about the pageant. I could tell them what I hated. It wouldn't make any difference. There're always gonna be girls who want to enter the beauty pageant. That's the fantasy: the American Dream.

Suggestions for Discussion

1. What sequence of events led Emma Knight to win the title of Miss U.S.A.?
2. Describe her life as Miss U.S.A.

3. What evidence does she show of her interest in politics? In women's rights?
4. For what reasons does she signal "the con is on" at the end of her reign?

Suggestions for Writing

1. Explain why Emma Knight believes there will always be "girls who want to enter the beauty pageant." Do you agree?
2. Describe a contest in which you were a participant. Use details that the casual observer would not know.

ESSAYS

ART BUCHWALD

Leisure Will Kill You

Art Buchwald (b. 1925), the nationally syndicated columnist, won the Pulitzer Prize in 1982 for his humorous, critical writings. Among his more than two dozen books are *The Buchwald Stops Here* (1978), *You Can Fool All of the People All of the Time* (1986), *While Reagan Slept* (1987), *Lighten Up, George* (1991), and *Laid Back in Washington* (1981), from which the following droll selection is taken. A memoir, *Leaving Home,* was published in 1993.

This country is producing so much leisure equipment for the home that nobody has any leisure time anymore to enjoy it. A few months ago I bought a television tape recorder to make copies of programs when I was out of the house.

Last week I recorded the Nebraska–Oklahoma football game. When I came home in the evening, I decided to play it back. But my son wanted to play "Baseball" on the TV screen with his Atari Computer. We finished four innings when my wife came in the room and asked me if I would like to listen to the Vienna Opera on our hi-fi stereo set. I told her I was waiting to finish the baseball match so I could watch the football game I had recorded.

She said if I watched the football game for three hours, I would miss *Love Boat.* I told her I would record *Love Boat* and we could watch it later in the evening. She protested that *Casablanca* was showing on Channel 5 at 11:30 and she wanted to see it again.

"Don't worry," I assured her, "we can watch *Love Boat* late Saturday and *Casablanca* on Sunday morning when we get up."

"But if we watch *Casablanca* tomorrow morning when can we see the instant Polaroid movies you took of Ben yesterday afternoon?"

"We'll see them after we play backgammon on the new table."

"If we do that," my daughter said, "we won't be able to see the Washington Redskins–New York Giants football game."

"I'll record the Redskins–Giants football game and we'll watch it while *60 Minutes* is on the air. We can see *60 Minutes* at 11 o'clock."

"But," my son said, "you promised to play the pinball machine with me at 11."

"Okay, we'll play pinball at 11 and watch *60 Minutes* at midnight."

My wife said, "Why don't we listen to the Vienna Opera while we're eating and then we can save an hour to play computer golf?"

"That's good thinking," I said. "The only problem is I've rented a TV tape for *Cleopatra* and that runs for three hours."

"You could show it on Monday night," she suggested.

"I can't do that. I have to return the tape Monday afternoon or be charged for it another week. I have an idea. I won't go to work Monday morning and we'll watch it then."

"I was hoping to use our Jacuzzi Monday morning," my wife said.

"Okay, then I'll tape *Cleopatra* and you can see it Monday afternoon."

"I'm using the set Monday afternoon," my son said, "to play digital hockey on the TV screen."

"You can't do that," I said. "I have to watch the *Today* show in the afternoon if I'm going to watch *Cleopatra* in the morning."

"Why can't you watch the *Today* show at dinnertime?" my wife asked.

"Because the Wolfingtons are coming over to hear me play 'Tea for Two' on the electric organ."

"I thought we might play computer bridge at dinner," my wife said.

"We'll play it after my encore," I assured her.

"Then when will we see *Monday Night Football?*" my son wanted to know.

"Tuesday," I said.

"Does that mean you're not going to work on Tuesday?" my wife asked.

"How can I go to work," I yelled, "when I've got so much leisure time on my hands?"

Suggestions for Discussion

1. Explain Buchwald's observation that our "country is producing so much leisure equipment for the home that nobody has any leisure time anymore to enjoy it." Do you agree? State your reasons.
2. Discuss whether or not the conflicts that Buchwald sets up in this short essay are realistic, believable, and resolvable.
3. Suggest solutions to the conflicts Buchwald identifies.
4. Discuss Buchwald's use of exaggeration and accumulated detail to give humor to his essay.

Suggestions for Writing

1. Identify and discuss dangers to the individual and to the family posed by excessive amounts of leisure.
2. Depict a busy scene in your own home.

PETE HAMILL

Crack and the Box

Pete Hamill, editor in chief of the New York *Daily News* is the author of eight novels, including *Loving Women* (1990) and *Snow in August* (1997). In the essay that follows, Hamill argues that "television works on the same imaginative and intellectual level as psychoactive drugs." In 1994 he published *A Drinking Life: A Memoir,* and in 1996 *Piecework.*

One sad rainy morning last winter, I talked to a woman who was addicted to crack cocaine. She was twenty-two, stiletto-thin, with eyes as old as tombs. She was living in two rooms in a welfare hotel with her children, who were two, three, and five years of age. Her story was the usual tangle of human woe: early pregnancy, dropping out of school, vanished men, smack and then crack, tricks with johns in parked cars to pay for the dope. I asked her why she did drugs. She shrugged in an empty way and couldn't really answer beyond "makes me feel good." While we talked and she told her tale of squalor, the children ignored us. They were watching television.

Walking back to my office in the rain, I brooded about the woman, her zombielike children, and my own callous indifference. I'd heard so many versions of the same story that I almost never wrote them anymore; the sons of similar women, glimpsed a dozen years ago, are now in Dannemora or Soledad or Joliet; in a hundred cities, their daughters are moving into the same loveless rooms. As I walked, a series of homeless men approached me for change, most of them junkies. Others sat in doorways, staring at nothing. They were additional casualties of our time of plague, demoralized reminders that although this country holds only 2 percent of the world's population, it consumes 65 percent of the world's supply of hard drugs.

Why, for God's sake? Why do so many millions of Americans of all ages, races, and classes choose to spend all or part of their lives stupefied? I've talked to hundreds of addicts over the years; some were my friends. But none could give sensible answers. They stutter about the pain of the world, about despair or boredom, the urgent need for magic or pleasure in a society empty of both. But then they just shrug. Americans have the money to buy drugs; the supply is plentiful. But almost nobody in power asks, *Why?* Least of all, George Bush and his drug warriors.

William Bennett talks vaguely about the heritage of sixties permissiveness, the collapse of Traditional Values, and all that. But he and Bush offer the traditional American excuse: It Is Somebody Else's Fault. This posture set the stage for the self-righteous invasion of Panama, the bloodiest drug arrest in world history. Bush even accused Manuel Noriega of "poisoning our children." But he never asked *why* so many Americans demand the poison.

And then, on that rainy morning in New York, I saw another one of those ragged men staring out at the rain from a doorway. I suddenly remembered the inert postures of the children in that welfare hotel, and I thought: *television.*

Ah, no, I muttered to myself: too simple. Something as complicated as drug addiction can't be blamed on television. Come on.... but I remembered all those desperate places I'd visited as a reporter, where there were no books and a TV set was always playing and the older kids had gone off somewhere to shoot smack, except for the kid who was at the mortuary in a coffin. I also remembered when I was a boy in the forties and early fifties, and drugs were a minor sideshow, a kind of dark little rumor. And there was one major difference between that time and this: television.

We had unemployment then; illiteracy, poor living conditions, racism, governmental stupidity, a gap between rich and poor. We didn't have the all-consuming presence of television in our lives. Now two generations of Americans have grown up with television from their earliest moments of consciousness. Those same American generations are afflicted by the pox of drug addiction.

Only thirty-five years ago, drug addiction was not a major problem in this country. There were drug addicts. We had some at the end of the nineteenth century, hooked on the cocaine in patent medicines. During the placid fifties, Commissioner Harry Anslinger pumped up the budget of the old Bureau of Narcotics with fantasies of reefer madness. Heroin was sold and used in most major American cities, while the bebop generation of jazz musicians got jammed up with horse.

But until the early sixties, narcotics were still marginal to American life; they weren't the $120-billion market they make up today. If anything, those years have an eerie innocence. In 1955 there were 31,700,000 TV sets in use in the country (the number is now past 184 million). But the majority of the audience had grown up without the dazzling new medium. They embraced it, were diverted by it, perhaps even loved it, but they weren't *formed* by it. That year, the New York police made a mere 1,234 felony drug arrests; in 1988 it was 43,901. They confiscated ninety-seven *ounces* of cocaine for the entire year; last year it was hundreds of pounds. During each year of the fifties in New York, there were only about a hundred narcotics-related deaths. But by the end of the sixties, when the first generation of children *formed* by television had come to maturity (and thus to the marketplace), the number of such deaths had risen to 1,200. The same phenomenon was true in every major American city.

In the last Nielsen survey of American viewers, the average family was watching television seven hours a day. This has never happened before in history. No people has ever been entertained for seven hours a *day.* The Elizabethans didn't go to the theater seven hours a day. The pre-TV generation did not go to the movies seven hours a day. Common sense tells us that this all-pervasive diet of instant imagery, sustained now for forty years, must have changed us in profound ways.

Television, like drugs, dominates the lives of its addicts. And though some lonely Americans leave their sets on without watching them, using them as electronic companions, television usually absorbs its viewers the way drugs absorb their users. Viewers can't work or play while watching television; they can't read; they can't be out on the streets, falling in love with the wrong people, learning how to quarrel and compromise with other human beings. In short they are asocial. So are drug addicts.

One Michigan State University study in the early eighties offered a group of four- and five-year-olds the choice of giving up television or giving up their fathers. Fully one third said they would give up Daddy. Given a similar choice (between cocaine or heroin and father, mother, brother, sister, wife, husband, children, job), almost every stone junkie would do the same.

There are other disturbing similarities. Television itself is a consciousness-altering instrument. With the touch of a button, it takes you out of the "real" world in which you reside and can place you at a basketball game, the back alleys of Miami, the streets of Bucharest, or the cartoony living rooms of Sitcom Land. Each move from channel to channel alters mood, usually with music or a laugh track. On any given evening, you can laugh, be frightened, feel tension, thump with excitement. You can even tune in *MacNeil/Lehrer* and feel sober.

But none of these abrupt shifts in mood is *earned.* They are attained as easily as popping a pill. Getting news from television, for example, is simply not the same experience as reading it in a newspaper. Reading is *active.* The reader must decode little symbols called words, then create images or ideas and make them connect; at its most basic level, reading is an act of the imagination. But the television viewer doesn't go through that process. The words are spoken to him by Dan Rather or Tom Brokaw or Peter Jennings. There isn't much decoding to do when watching television, no time to think or ponder before the next set of images and spoken words appears to displace the present one. The reader, being active, works at his or her own pace; the viewer, being passive, proceeds at a pace determined by the show. Except at the highest levels, television never demands that its audience take part in an act of imagination. Reading always does.

In short, television works on the same imaginative and intellectual level as psychoactive drugs. If prolonged television viewing makes the young passive (dozens of studies indicate that it does), then moving to drugs has a certain coherence. Drugs provide an unearned high (in contrast to the earned rush that comes from a feat accomplished, a human breakthrough earned by sweat or thought or love).

And because the television addict and the drug addict are alienated from the hard and scary world, they also feel they make no difference in its complicated events. For the junkie, the world is reduced to him and the needle, pipe, or vial; the self is absolutely isolated, with no desire for choice. The television addict lives the same way. Many Americans who fail to vote in presidential elections must believe they have no more control over such a choice than they do over the casting of *L.A. Law.*

The drug plague also coincides with the unspoken assumption of most television shows: Life should be *easy.* The most complicated events are summarized on TV news in a minute or less. Cops confront murder, chase the criminals, and bring them to justice (usually violently) within an hour. In commercials, you drink the right beer and you get the girl. *Easy!* So why should real life be a grind? Why should any American have to spend years mastering a skill or a craft, or work eight hours a day at an unpleasant job, or endure the compromises and crises of a marriage? Nobody *works* on television (except cops, doctors, and lawyers). Love stories on television are about falling in love or breaking up; the long, steady growth of a marriage—its essential *dailiness*—is seldom explored, except as comedy. Life on television is almost always simple: good guys and bad, nice girls and whores, smart guys and dumb. And if life in the real world isn't that simple, well, hey, man, have some dope, man, be happy, feel good.

The doper always whines about how he *feels;* drugs are used to enhance his feelings or obliterate them, and in this the doper is very American. No other people on earth spend so much time talking about their feelings; hundreds of thousands go to shrinks, they buy self-help books by the millions, they pour out intimate confessions to virtual strangers in bars or discos. Our political campaigns are about emotional issues now, stated in the simplicities of adolescence. Even alleged statesmen can start a sentence, "I feel that the Sandinistas should..." when they once might have said, "I *think....*" I'm convinced that this exaltation of cheap emotions over logic and reason is one by-product of hundreds of thousands of hours of television.

Most Americans under the age of fifty have now spent their lives absorbing television; that is, they've had the structures of drama pounded into them. Drama is always about conflict. So news shows, politics, and advertising are now all shaped by those structures. Nobody will pay attention to anything as complicated as the part played by Third World debt in the expanding production of cocaine; it's much easier to focus on Manuel

Noriega, a character right out of *Miami Vice,* and believe that even in real life there's a Mister Big.

What is to be done? Television is certainly not going away, but its addictive qualities can be controlled. It's a lot easier to "just say no" to television than to heroin or crack. As a beginning, parents must take immediate control of the sets, teaching children to watch specific television *programs,* not "television," to get out of the house and play with other kids. Elementary and high schools must begin teaching television as a subject, the way literature is taught, showing children how shows are made, how to distinguish between the true and the false, how to recognize cheap emotional manipulation. All Americans should spend more time reading. And thinking.

For years, the defenders of television have argued that the networks are only giving the people what they want. That might be true. But so is the Medellín cartel.

Suggestions for Discussion

1. Explain Hamill's observation that we live in a "time of plague."
2. Discuss the ties he sees between television and drug addiction. Do you agree or disagree with his conclusions? Why?
3. Comment on Hamill's assertion that "television works on the same imaginative and intellectual level as psychoactive drugs."
4. What recommendations does he make? Do you find them sound? Explain.

Suggestions for Writing

1. Explore the power of television viewing on your life and/or on the lives of others you know. You might keep a log for a week or more to ascertain what and when you watch.
2. Write a response to Hamill's controversial assertions.

ROGER ROSENBLATT

Who Killed Privacy?

Roger Rosenblatt (b. 1940), essayist, television commentator, and playwright, is the author of *Children of War* (1992), *Life Itself: Abortion in the American Mind* (1992), and *The Man in the Water* (1993). In the following essay he argues that "people nowadays simply assume that they have the right to know about everyone."

I don't know about you, but my life has not been significantly improved by watching any of the three versions of the Amy Fisher story (one version fewer than the story of Jesus), or by learning of the doings of "Dallas" in the palace, or by seeing Fergie topless or Woody humorless, or even—hard as this may be to swallow—by photographs surreptitiously taken of Chelsea Clinton's cat, Socks. I could, if need be, spend the rest of my days without learning one more fact about Socks or any of those other subjects. (I guess the royals aren't subjects.) I am out of things, of course. This is the age where everything is known, everything told.

"If I had to choose my place of birth," Rousseau exclaimed in a fit of nonsense, "I would have chosen a state in which everyone knew everyone else, so that neither the obscure tactics of vice nor the modesty of virtue could have escaped public scrutiny and judgment." Jean-Jacques, say bonjour to Ron Galella.

I really ought not to sound too above it all, because I do not in the least understand this general lust for publicity, this death, this murder and suicide of private life. Socks's father had it right. "The boom mike," the President complained with a forced smile, "has done what 12 years of the Reagan–Bush Supreme Court couldn't do to abolish the right to privacy." Here is precisely what puzzles me: Privacy in our time has not only been invaded; it's been eagerly surrendered. Do people no longer see themselves as private beings? What do *you* think, Socks?

It's difficult to tell the manifestations of this phase or phenomenon or whatever it is from the causes. Technology, for instance, offers both. Bill Clinton's reference to the boom mike is quaint compared with the new spying and surveillance devices that have made a multimillion-dollar industry of what used to be the obscure tactics of vice. A recent science magazine bears an advertisement for a book called "How to Eavesdrop on

Your Neighbor," a twist on the Welcome Wagon. An Atlanta mail-order house offered Listenaider, which amplifies nearby sounds and is designed to look like a Walkman. With Mail Inspector one may spray envelopes to read their contents. With a Tracman vehicle tracking system, anybody may follow anybody else's car.

Also available is a voice changer that alters one's telephone voice; this is useful, its makers say, for a man who wishes to pretend he has a secretary. A monitor phone permits one to spy on another room of one's own house; a scanner, to listen in on the police and fire departments. With several devices on the premises, a wife could listen in on her husband disguising his voice as his secretary's, and contact the police.

Since there are as many debugging devices produced as those that bug, one may envision a small, idiotic universe in which everyone spies or thwarts spies in an area the size of an embassy bedroom; but in fact this world of perpetual mutual observation is wide. Businesses spend loads of time and money looking in on competing businesses. Trinet America and its parent company, American Business Information Inc. of Omaha, recently brought out a computer program called "Lists-on-Disk" which, for a license that costs $750 a year, issues factual information on 9.2 million private and public businesses—type, location, number of employees, ownership, revenues and so forth.

When companies are not poking around about one another, they always have us. The Lotus Development Corporation offered and then withdrew something called "Marketplace: Households," a CD-ROM containing essential information on 120 million citizens, things like marital status, income, buying habits—information readily compiled from one of the large credit bureaus, Equifax Inc. Though "Marketplace: Households" was removed from the market, *The New York Times* wrote that "such programs will not go away" because they offer gold mines for small businesses. In any case, what used to be deemed private information on practically everyone has been available for the taking for years, thanks to financial organizations like TRW, which, in spite of frequent citations for harmful inaccuracies, continues to offer data on credit cards, personal loans and tax liens on more than 170 million Americans, including, almost certainly, you.

As business goes, so goes the United States Government. In 1990 Congress proposed legislation that would allow Federal agencies wider latitude than ever in sharing confidential financial information obtained from banks. Under the Right to Financial Privacy Act of 1978, such information cannot be exchanged unless a customer is notified first. Under the new legislation, no prior notification would be necessary; the law would permit agencies to share information on deposits, mortgages and other loans. This bill must have looked especially interesting in the light of Congress's check-kiting scandal of 1991, during which several Congressmen protested reporters' inquiries on the grounds that their privacy was being violated.

The fact is, most people are no longer shocked by the devices or the impulses of public exposure, and in many contexts are happy to contribute to the exposure themselves. See the television shows of Oprah, Donahue and Geraldo, which were once the refuges for nymphomaniacal nuns with eating disorders and now provide lecterns for Presidential candidates. Video telephones are newly for sale, which will be successful only if everyone wants to be seen as well as heard, since a gizmo at one end requires another at another. The entire presumption of private life has been turned on its head. Liz Smith observed astutely, and with equal amusement and irritation, that her province of gossip is regularly raided by front-page news.

The age of grievance, too, is both a cause and effect of this atmosphere. For the past 30 years or so, people have tended to see themselves, and have tended to be seen, as members of interest groups (racial, national, sexual) and not as individuals, making every life both political and potentially publishable; the leap between a private complaint and a public cause is semiautomatic. Multiculturalism insists that everybody is a class of being, as do other bad current ideas. The practice of "outing" homosexuals implies contradictorily that homosexuals have a right to private choice but not to private lives.

My own guess is that television has had more to do with hastening the death of privacy than anything else—not television shows per se, but camcorders, those home TV cameras owned by seemingly everyone. There used to be a sweet kind of shyness displayed by ordinary people whenever they appeared on television. I remember how passers-by used to look at themselves on television monitors in the NBC window at Rockefeller Center—how, tickled with the sight of themselves, they would point, giggle and blush. No more. With the advent of camcorders, everybody is on television, is a TV "personality," taking exposure in stride.

It is astonishing, and heartbreaking, to watch parents of children who were caught in a fire or a crossfire appearing before local TV news cameras mere moments after a tragedy. They are ready for their appearance, even if they have never been on television before, because they know how it is done, how one is to pose, look and speak.

If ordinary citizens do not feel uncomfortable about airing their lives in this way, it should hardly be surprising that celebrities, who live to be noticed, are eager to disclose the details of their brutalized childhoods and bestial "relationships." La Toya Jackson, Patti Davis, Roseanne tell more than anyone wants to know about life with father and mother. What the principals won't reveal the media will. Magic Johnson goes public about his HIV. But the earth would have continued to spin without anyone knowing that Arthur Ashe had AIDS; that was the press's doing. Ashe was endangering no one. The fact that he is a public figure does not deprive him of the right to personal anguish. It was moving, if anachronistic, to hear Anthony Perkins's family announce that the circumstances leading to the actor's death by AIDS were nobody's business.

I wonder, incidentally, if AIDS itself does not, in some atmospheric way, contribute to the sense that people are no longer safe as private entities—if the terrible omnipresence of the pandemic doesn't reinforce the idea that everyone in the world is helplessly exposed.

With AIDS or any serious communicable disease the question of what is or is not private gets complicated, as several school boards and distraught families have learned. But the non-right to privacy has been extended to genetic diseases as well. The March of Dimes Birth Defect Foundation conducted a survey asking if someone other than the patient—an insurance company, an employer—has the right to know if that patient has a genetic defect. Fifty-seven percent of the respondents said yes.

Things also get more problematic when it comes to revelations about political candidates, especially the Presidential variety, where the issue becomes one of "What do we have here?" No one deeply cared if Bill Clinton or George Bush had a G(J)ennifer, because it seemed clear to most voters that the ability of both men to govern was not impaired by their alleged scandals. Yet Gary Hart's boaty fling seemed to indicate a person out of control, so a distinction was drawn.

To give exposure its due, if there were not this tendency to shout private news, sexual harassment would still be a dirty little secret. And it is at least arguable that the men's movement, sans grunts and howls, has encouraged a useful unlocking of spirits. Without the climate of revelation there might have been no Pentagon papers or Watergate, either—though there is a difference between privacy and secrecy. The camcorder has valuable applications, too, as the nation discovered through Rodney King.

The trouble is, people nowadays simply assume that they have the right to know about everyone—and indeed, in the course of events, that they *will* know about everyone, and everyone will know about them. This suggests the possibility of two interesting aftereffects:

People will behave better as a result of the continual prospect of public exposure. People will abjure the interior life, and live only in the open.

To the first proposition, I bravely offer the observation: Who knows? In the 45,000 or so years the species has been around, people have improved incrementally by learning to get along a little better in masses, so perhaps the exposed life is a first evolutionary step toward more companionable communities. Perhaps.

But if the penalty for achieving community involves the forfeiture of thinking of ourselves as private beings, we're in a fix. Robert Warshow once asked: "How shall we regain the use of our experience in the world of mass culture?" He was considering the natural opposition of culture and democracy. It is possible that the publicizing of private lives is an extension of the old democratizing impulse to make everybody equal—by exposing them equally. Yet the idea that it is somehow more egalitarian, thus more American, to dry every life on the line undermines individualism, that other basic notion of the Republic.

Privacy is more difficult to cultivate than publicity because it involves being alone with oneself. John V. Kelleher, professor emeritus of Irish studies at Harvard, used to quote an Old Irish maxim: "Strife is better than loneliness." And privacy requires both. Maybe that's what's at the bottom of this intense desire to know and tell all—a fear of keeping one's own company, of Emersonian self-reliance, which is dreaded in direct proportion to an increase of state power or the power of other institutions over one's life. The more I open myself to the State of New York or to the Ajax Corporation the less I think of myself in control of my destiny, the less I seek that control, the less I am.

Private thoughts are more complicated and confused than public announcements, thus usually more true. Praising Elizabeth Bishop's "power of reticence," Octavio Paz complained that "20th-century poetry has become garrulous. We are drowning not in a sea but in a swamp of words. We have forgotten that poetry is not in what words say but in what is said between them, that which appears fleetingly in pauses and silences. In the poetry workshops of universities there should be a required course for young poets: learning to be silent." Ralph Ellison made a variation on the same point in "Invisible Man," where the narrator admires Louis Armstrong for playing the blues in the breaks between the notes—private space felt by him alone. Earl (the Pearl) Monroe played basketball like that. When the defenders were down, the Pearl was up; he played the game in his own imagined air.

I know it sounds paradoxical, but the killing of privacy is, in some fundamental way, a supremely antisocial act. Everybody goes public, and who cares? Who sympathizes? On the other hand, the person who nurtures and preserves a private existence encourages the respect and imitation of others. Under the best circumstances a general decorum ensues; people feel more comfortable with one another for the walls they erect and defend. Civilizations are made of such interacting privacies, since civilizations tend to rely more on communion than communication.

Out of our private gropings and self-inspections grow our imaginative values—private language, imagery, memory. In the caves of the mind one bats about to discover a light entirely of one's own which, though it should turn out to be dim, is still worth a life.

Suggestions for Discussion

1. Discuss Rosenblatt's criticism of the "general lust for publicity, this death, this murder and suicide of private life." Comment on the language of his critique.
2. Explain the "age of grievance" to which he refers.
3. Give examples to show that "most people are no longer shocked by the devices or the impulses of public exposure, and in many contexts are happy to contribute to the exposure themselves."

Suggestions for Writing

1. Give three or four examples of startling revelations about people that you have observed on television. Would you feel comfortable revealing such personal information about yourself? Discuss.
2. Discuss Rosenblatt's assertion that for the past thirty years or so, "people have tended to see themselves, and have tended to be seen, as members of interest groups (racial, national, sexual) and not as individuals." What examples can you offer to support or refute his observation?

BERNICE REAGON

Black Music in Our Hands

Bernice Reagon, the editor of *Black American Culture and Scholarship* (1985), grew up in Albany, Georgia, and attended Albany State College and Spelman College before earning her doctorate in Black history and music from Howard University in 1975. Having served as a director of the Washington, D.C., Black Repertory Company and as consultant in Black music to the Smithsonian Institution, she asserts the importance of "Black music that functions in relation to the people and community who provide the nurturing compost that makes its creation and continuation possible."

In the early 1960s, I was in college at Albany State. My major interests were music and biology. In music I was a contralto soloist with the choir, studying Italian arias and German lieder. The Black music I sang was of three types:

(1) Spirituals sung by the college choir. These were arranged by such people as Nathaniel Dett and William Dawson and had major injections of European musical harmony and composition. (2) Rhythm 'n' Blues, music done by and for Blacks in social settings. This included the music of bands at proms, juke boxes, and football game songs. (3) Church music; gospel was a major part of Black church music by the time I was in college. I was a soloist with the gospel choir.

Prior to the gospel choir, introduced in my church when I was twelve, was many years' experience with unaccompanied music—Black choral singing, hymns, lined out by strong song leaders with full, powerful, richly ornate congregational responses. These hymns were offset by upbeat, clapping call-and-response songs.

I saw people in church sing and pray until they shouted. I knew *that* music as a part of a cultural expression that was powerful enough to take people from their conscious selves to a place where the physical and intellectual being worked in harmony with the spirit. I enjoyed and needed that experience. The music of the church was an integral part of the cultural world into which I was born.

Outside of church, I saw music as good, powerful sounds you made or listened to. Rhythm and blues—you danced to; music of the college choir—you clapped after the number was finished.

The Civil Rights Movement changed my view of music. It was after my first march. I began to sing a song and in the course of singing changed the song so that it made sense for that particular moment. Although I was not consciously aware of it, this was one of my earliest experiences with how my music was supposed to *function.* This music was to be integrative of and consistent with everything I was doing at that time; it was to be tied to activities that went beyond artistic affairs such as concerts, dances, and church meetings.

The next level of awareness came while in jail. I had grown up in a rural area outside the city limits, riding a bus to public school or driving to college. My life had been a pretty consistent, balanced blend of church, school, and proper upbringing. I was aware of a Black educated class that taught me in high school and college, of taxi cabs I never rode in, and of people who used buses I never boarded. I went to school with their children.

In jail with me were all these people. All ages. In my section were women from about thirteen to eighty years old. Ministers' wives and teachers and teachers' wives who had only nodded at me or clapped at a concert or spoken to my mother. A few people from my classes. A large number of people who rode segregated city buses. One or two women who had been drinking along the two-block stretch of Little Harlem as the march went by. Very quickly, clashes arose: around age, who would have authority, what was proper behavior?

The Albany Movement was already a singing movement, and we took the songs to jail. There the songs I had sung because they made me feel good or because they said what I thought about a specific issue did something. I would start a song and everybody would join in. After the song, the differences among us would not be as great. Somehow, making a song required an expression of that which was common to us all. The songs did not feel like the same songs I had sung in college. This music was like an instrument, like holding a tool in your hand.

I found that although I was younger than many of the women in my section of the jail, I was asked to take on leadership roles. First as a song leader and then in most other matters concerning the group, especially in discussions, or when speaking with prison officials.

I fell in love with that kind of music. I saw that to define music as something you listen to, something that pleases you, is very different from defining it as an instrument with which you can drive a point. In both instances, you can have the same song. But using it as an instrument makes it a different kind of music.

The next level of awareness occurred during the first mass meeting after my release from jail. I was asked to lead the song that I had changed after the first march. When I opened my mouth and began to sing, there was a force and power within myself I had never heard before. Somehow this music—music I could use as an instrument to do things with, music that was mine to shape and change so that it made the statement I needed to make—released a kind of power and required a level of concentrated energy I did not know I had. I liked the feeling.

For several years, I worked with the Movement eventually doing Civil Rights songs with the Freedom Singers. The Freedom Singers used the songs, interspersed with narrative, to convey the story of the Civil Rights Movement's struggles. The songs were more powerful than spoken conversation. They became a major way of making people who were not on the scene feel the intensity of what was happening in the south. Hopefully, they would move the people to take a stand, to organize support groups or participate in various projects.

The Georgia Sea Island Singers, whom I first heard at the Newport Festival, were a major link. Bessie Jones, coming from within twenty miles of Albany, Georgia, had a repertoire and song-leading style I recognized from the churches I had grown up in. She, along with John Davis, would talk about songs that Black people had sung as slaves and what those songs meant in terms of their struggle to be free. The songs did not sound like the spirituals I had sung in college choirs; they sounded like the songs I had grown up with in church. There I had been told the songs had to do with worship of Jesus Christ.

The next few years I spent focusing on three components: (1) The music I had found in the Civil Rights Movement. (2) Songs of the Georgia Sea Island Singers and other traditional groups, and the ways in which those songs were linked to the struggles of Black peoples at earlier times. (3) Songs of the church that now sounded like those traditional songs and came close to having, for many people, the same kind of freeing power.

There was another experience that helped to shape my present-day use of music. After getting out of jail, the mother of the church my father pastored was at the mass meeting. She prayed, a prayer I had heard hundreds of times. I had focused on its sound, tune, rhythm, chant, whether the moans came at the proper pace and intensity. That morning I heard every word that she said. She did not have to change one word of prayer she had been praying for much of her Christian life for me to know she was addressing the issues we were facing at that moment. More than her personal prayer, it felt like an analysis of the Albany, Georgia, Black community.

My collection, study, and creation of Black music has been, to a large extent, about freeing the sounds and the words and the messages from casings in which they have been put, about hearing clearly what the music has to say about Black people and their struggle.

When I first began to search, I looked for what was then being called folk music, rather than for other Black forms, such as jazz, rhythm and blues, or gospel. It slowly dawned on me that during the Movement we had used all those forms. When we were relaxing in the office, we made up songs using popular rhythm and blues tunes; songs based in rhythm and blues also came out of jails, especially from the sit-in movement and the march to Selma, Alabama. "Oh Wallace, You Never Can Jail Us All" is an example from Selma. "You Better Leave Segregation Alone" came out of the Nashville Freedom Rides and was based on a bit by Little Willie John, "You Better Leave My Kitten Alone." Gospel choirs became the major musical vehicle in the urban center of Birmingham, with the choir led by Carlton Reese. There was also a gospel choir in the Chicago work, as well as an instrumental ensemble led by Ben Branch.

Jazz had not been a strong part of my musical life. I began to hear it as I traveled north. Thelonious Monk and Charlie Mingus played on the first SNCC benefit at Carnegie Hall. I heard of and then heard Coltrane. Then I began to pick up the pieces that had been laid by Charlie Parker and Coleman Hawkins and whole lifetimes of music. This music had no words. But, it had power, intensity, and movement under various degrees of pressure; it had vocal texture and color. I could feel that the music knew how it felt to be Black and Angry. Black and Down, Black and Loved, Black and Fighting.

I now believe that Black music exists in every place where Black people run, every corner where they live, every level on which they struggle. We have been here a long while, in many situations. It takes all that we have created to sing our song. I believe that Black musicians/artists have a responsibility to be conscious of their world and to let their consciousness be heard in their songs.

And we need it all—blues, gospel, ballads, children's games, dance, rhythms, jazz, lovesongs, topical songs—doing what it has always done. We need Black music that functions in relation to the people and community who provide the nurturing compost that makes its creation and continuation possible.

Suggestions for Discussion

1. Analyze the careful structure of Reagon's essay.
2. Discuss the levels of awareness about music that the author describes. What examples does she use to illustrate each?
3. Discuss her assertion that music is "tied to activities that" go "beyond artistic affairs." Are her examples convincing? Explain.

Suggestions for Writing

1. Describe the special significance of certain music to your life.
2. Compare and contrast Bernice Reagon's essay with Aaron Copland's "How We Listen to Music."

JOHN MCMURTRY

Kill 'Em! Crush 'Em! Eat 'Em Raw!

John McMurtry (b. 1939) is a professor of philosophy at the University of Guelph in Canada. He is the author of *The Global Market as an Ethical System* (1996). A former college linebacker and a player for the Calgary Stampeders in the Canadian Football League, McMurtry examines in this essay the widespread violence in football.

A few months ago my neck got a hard crick in it. I couldn't turn my head; to look left or right I'd have to turn my whole body. But I'd had cricks in my neck since I started playing grade-school football and hockey, so I just ignored it. Then I began to notice that when I reached for any sort of large book (which I do pretty often as a philosophy teacher at the University of Guelph) I had trouble lifting it with one hand. I was losing the strength in my left arm, and I had such a steady pain in my back I often had to stretch out on the floor of the room I was in to relieve the pressure.

A few weeks later I mentioned to my brother, an orthopedic surgeon, that I'd lost the power in my arm since my neck began to hurt. Twenty-four hours later I was in a Toronto hospital not sure whether I might end up with a wasted upper limb. Apparently the steady pounding I had received playing college and professional football in the late fifties and early sixties had driven my head into my backbone so that the discs had crumpled together at the neck—"acute herniation"—and had cut the nerves to my left arm like a pinched telephone wire (without nerve stimulation, of course, the muscles atrophy, leaving the arm crippled). So I spent my Christmas holidays in the hospital in heavy traction and much of the next three months with my neck in a brace. Today most of the pain has gone, and I've recovered most of the strength in my arm. But from time to time I still have to don the brace, and surgery remains a possibility.

Not much of this will surprise anyone who knows football. It is a sport in which body wreckage is one of the leading conventions. A few days after I went into hospital for that crick in my neck, another brother, an outstanding football player in college, was undergoing spinal surgery in the same hospital two floors above me. In his case it was a lower, more massive herniation, which every now and again buckled him so that he was unable to lift himself off his back for days at a time. By the time he entered the hospital for surgery he had already spent several months in bed. The operation was successful, but, as in all such cases, it will take him a year to recover fully.

These aren't isolated experiences. Just about anybody who has ever played football for any length of time, in high school, college or one of the professional leagues, has suffered for it later physically.

Indeed, it is arguable that body shattering is the very *point* of football, as killing and maiming are of war. (In the United States, for example, the game results in 15 to 20 deaths a year and about 50,000 major operations on knees alone.) To grasp some of the more conspicuous similarities between football and war, it is instructive to listen to the imperatives most frequently issued to the players by their coaches, teammates and fans. "Hurt 'em!" "Level 'em!" "Kill 'em!" "Take 'em apart!" Or watch for the plays that are most enthusiastically applauded by the fans. Where someone is "smeared," "knocked silly," "creamed," "nailed," "broken in two," or even "crucified." (One of my coaches when I played corner linebacker with the Calgary Stampeders in 1961 elaborated, often very inventively, on this language of destruction: admonishing us to "unjoin" the opponent, "make 'im remember you" and "stomp 'im like a bug.") Just as in hockey, where a fight will bring fans to their feet more often than a skillful play, so in football the mouth waters most of all for the really crippling block or tackle. For the kill. Thus the good teams are "hungry," the best players are "mean," and "casualties" are as much a part of the game as they are of a war.

The family resemblance between football and war is, indeed, striking. Their languages are similar: "field general," "long bomb," "blitz," "take a shot," "front line," "pursuit," "good hit," "the draft" and so on. Their principles and practices are alike: mass hysteria, the art of intimidation, absolute command and total obedience, territorial aggression, censorship, inflated insignia and propaganda, blackboard maneuvers and strategies, drills, uniforms, formations, marching bands and training camps. And the virtues they celebrate are almost identical: hyper-aggressiveness, coolness under fire and suicidal bravery. All this has been implicitly recognized by such jock-loving Americans as media stars General Patton and President Nixon, who have talked about war as a football game. Patton wanted to make his Second World War tank men look like football players. And Nixon, as we know, was fond of comparing attacks on Vietnam to football plays and drawing coachly diagrams on a blackboard for TV war fans.

One difference between war and football, though, is that there is little or no protest against football. Perhaps the most extraordinary thing about the game is that the systematic infliction of injuries excites in people not concern, as would be the case if they were sustained at, say, a rock festival, but a collective rejoicing and euphoria. Players and fans alike revel in the spectacle of a combatant felled into semi-consciousness, "blindsided," "clotheslined" or "decapitated." I can remember, in fact, being chided by a coach in pro ball for not "getting my hat" injuriously into a player who was already lying helpless on the ground. (On another occasion, after the Stampeders had traded the celebrated Joe Kapp to BC, we were playing the Lions in Vancouver and Kapp was forced on one play to run with the ball. He was coming "down the chute," his bad knee wobbling uncertainly, so I simply dropped on him like a blanket. After I returned to the bench I was reproved for not exploiting the opportunity to unhinge his bad knee.)

After every game, of course, the papers are full of reports on the day's injuries, a sort of post-battle "body count," and the respective teams go to work with doctors and trainers, tape, whirlpool baths, cortisone and morphine to patch and deaden the wounds before the next game. Then the whole drama is reenacted—injured athletes held together by adhesive, braces and drugs—and the days following it are filled with even more feverish activity to put on the show yet again at the end of the next week. (I remember being so taped up in college that I earned the nickname "mummy.") The team that survives this merry-go-round spectacle of skilled masochism with the fewest incapacitating injuries usually wins. It is a sort of victory by ordeal: "We hurt them more than they hurt us."

My own initiation into this brutal circus was typical. I loved the game from the moment I could run with a ball. Played shoeless on a green open field with no one keeping score and in a spirit of reckless abandon and laughter, it's a very different sport. Almost no one gets hurt and it's rugged, open and exciting (it still is for me). But then, like everything else, it starts to be regulated and institutionalized by adult authorities. And the fun is over.

So it was as I began the long march through organized football. Now there was a coach and elders to make it clear by their behavior that beating other people was the only thing to celebrate and that trying to shake someone up every play was the only thing to be really proud of. Now there were severe rule enforcers, audiences, formally recorded victors and losers, and heavy equipment to permit crippling bodily moves and collisions (according to one American survey, more than 80 percent of all football injuries occur to fully equipped players). And now there was the official "given" that the only way to keep playing was to wear suffocating armor, to play to defeat, to follow orders silently and to renounce spontaneity for joyless drill. The game had been, in short, ruined. But because I loved to play and play skillfully, I stayed. And progressively and inexorably, as I moved through high school, college and pro leagues, my body was dismantled. Piece by piece.

I started off with torn ligaments in my knee at 13. Then, as the organization and the competition increased, the injuries came faster and harder. Broken nose (three times), broken jaw (fractured in the first half and dismissed as a "bad wisdom tooth," so I played with it for the rest of the game), ripped knee ligaments again. Torn ligaments in one ankle and a fracture in the other (which I remember feeling relieved about because it meant I could honorably stop drill-blocking a 270-pound defensive end). Repeated rib fractures and cartilage tears (usually carried, again, through the remainder of the game). More dislocations of the left shoulder than I can remember (the last one I played with because, as the Calgary Stampeder doctor said, it "couldn't be damaged any more"). Occasional broken or dislocated fingers and toes. Chronically hurt lower back (I still can't lift with it or change a tire without worrying about folding). Separated right shoulder (as with many other injuries, like badly bruised hips and legs, needled with morphine for the games). And so on. The last pro game I played—against the Winnipeg Blue Bombers in the Western finals in 1961—I had a recently dislocated left shoulder, a more recently wrenched right shoulder and a chronic pain center in one leg. I was so tied up with soreness I couldn't drive my car to the airport. But it never occurred to me or anyone else that I miss a play as a corner linebacker.

By the end of my football career, I had learned that physical injury—giving it and taking it—is the real currency of the sport. And that in the final analysis the "winner" is the man who can hit to kill even if only half his limbs are working. In brief, a warrior game with a warrior ethos into which (like almost everyone else I played with) my original boyish enthusiasm had been relentlessly taunted and conditioned.

In thinking back on how all this happened, though, I can pick out no villains. As with the social system as a whole, the game has a life of its own. Everyone grows up inside it, accepts it and fulfills its dictates as obediently as helots. Far from ever questioning the principles of the activity, people simply concentrate on executing these principles more aggressively than anybody around them. The result is a group of people who, as the leagues become of a higher and higher class, are progressively insensitive to the possibility that things could be otherwise. Thus, in football, anyone who might question the wisdom or enjoyment of putting on heavy equipment on a hot day and running full speed at someone else with the intention of knocking him senseless would be regarded simply as not really a devoted athlete and probably "chicken." The choice is made straightforward. Either you, too, do your very utmost to efficiently smash and be smashed, or you admit incompetence or cowardice and quit. Since neither of these admissions is very pleasant, people generally keep any doubts they have to themselves and carry on.

Of course, it would be a mistake to suppose that there is more blind acceptance of brutal practices in organized football than elsewhere. On the contrary, a recent Harvard study has approvingly argued that football's characteristics of "impersonal acceptance of inflicted injury," an overriding "organization goal," the "ability to turn oneself on and off" and being, above all, "out to win" are of "inestimable value" to big corporations. Clearly, our sort of football is no sicker than the rest of our society. Even its organized destruction of physical well-being is not anomalous. A very large part of our wealth, work and time is, after all, spent in systematically destroying and harming human life. Manufacturing, selling and using weapons that tear opponents to pieces. Making ever bigger and faster predator-named cars with which to kill and injure one another by the million every year. And devoting our very lives to outgunning one another for power in an ever more destructive rat race. Yet all these practices are accepted without question by most people, even zealously defended and honored. Competitive, organized injuring is integral to our way of life, and football is simply one of the more intelligible mirrors of the whole process: a sort of colorful morality play showing us how exciting and rewarding it is to Smash Thy Neighbor.

Now it is fashionable to rationalize our collaboration in all this by arguing that, well, man *likes* to fight and injure his fellows and such games as football should be encouraged to discharge this original-sin urge into less harmful channels than, say, war. Public-show football, this line goes, plays the same sort of cathartic role as Aristotle said stage tragedy does: without real blood (or not much), it releases players and audience from unhealthy feelings stored up inside them.

As an ex-player in the seasonal coast-to-coast drama, I see little to recommend such a view. What organized football did to me was make me *suppress* my natural urges and re-express them in an alienating, vicious form. Spontaneous desires for free bodily exuberance and fraternization with competitors were shamed and forced under ("If it ain't hurtin' it ain't helpin'") and in their place were demanded armored mechanical moves and cool hatred of all opposition. Endless authoritarian drill and dressing-room harangues (ever wonder why competing teams can't prepare for a game in the same dressing room?) were the kinds of mechanisms employed to reconstruct joyful energies into mean and alien shapes. I am quite certain that everyone else around me was being similarly forced into this heavily equipped military precision and angry antagonism, because there was always a mutinous attitude about full-dress practices, and everybody (the pros included) had to concentrate incredibly hard for days to whip themselves into just one hour's hostility a week against another club. The players never speak of these things, of course, because everyone is so anxious to appear tough.

The claim that men like seriously to battle one another to some sort of finish is a myth. It only endures because it wears one of the oldest and most propagandized of masks—the romantic combatant. I sometimes wonder whether the violence all around us doesn't depend for its survival on the existence and preservation of this tough-guy disguise.

As for the effect of organized football on the spectator, the fan is not released from supposed feelings of violent aggression by watching his athletic heroes perform it so much as encouraged in the view that people-smashing is an admirable mode of self-expression. The most savage attackers, after all, are, by general agreement, the most efficient and worthy players of all (the biggest applause I ever received as a football player occurred when I ran over people or slammed them so hard they couldn't get up). Such circumstances can hardly be said to lessen the spectators' martial tendencies. Indeed it seems likely that the whole show just further develops and titillates the North American addiction for violent self-assertion.... Perhaps, as well, it helps explain why the greater the zeal of U.S. political leaders as football fans (Johnson, Nixon, Agnew), the more enthusiastic the commitment to hard-line politics. At any rate there seems to be a strong correlation between people who relish tough football and people who relish intimidating and beating the hell out of commies, hippies, protest marchers and other opposition groups.

Watching well-advertised strong men knock other people round, make them hurt, is in the end like other tastes. It does not weaken with feeding and variation in form. It grows.

I got out of football in 1962. I had asked to be traded after Calgary had offered me a $25-a-week-plus-commissions off-season job as a clothing-store salesman. ("Dear Mr. Finks:" I wrote. [Jim Fink was then the Stampers' general manager.] "Somehow I do not think the dialectical subtleties of Hegel, Marx and Plato would be suitably oriented amidst the environmental stimuli of jockey shorts and herringbone suits. I hope you make a profitable sale or trade of my contract to the East.") So the Stampeders traded me to Montreal. In a preseason intersquad game with the Alouettes I ripped the cartilages in my ribs on the hardest block I'd ever thrown. I had trouble breathing and I had to shuffle-walk with my torso on a tilt. The doctor in the local hospital said three weeks rest, the coach said scrimmage in two days. Three days later I was back home reading philosophy.

Suggestions for Discussion

1. Explain why McMurtry gave up professional football.
2. What conclusions does he draw about the language used to describe football? Do you think the language is merely colorful or contributes to a climate of violence? Give specific examples from his essay or from your own experience.
3. Discuss the author's conclusion that football is "a sort of colorful morality play showing us how exciting and rewarding it is to Smash Thy Neighbor."

Suggestions for Writing

1. Describe the positive and negative effects of your own participation in football or another sport.
2. Write about whether or not you would encourage your own children to participate in a contact sport.

ROB HOERBURGER

Gotta Dance!

Rob Hoerburger, an editor of the *New York Times Magazine*, writes about dancing, "something that most of my life I had feared would bring me ridicule."

I walked into the confessional a repentant sinner and walked out a dancer. The priest who heard my sins half-jokingly suggested that for my penance I join the church's production of *West Side Story*, which he was directing. I was 27 at the time and hadn't performed on a stage since fourth grade, but I figured at the very least I could help out with the lights.

Instead, I ended up with the featured role of Riff, the leader of the Jets, mostly because of a lucky break (as in the ankle of the actor originally cast), and the usual dearth of male bodies in community-theater productions. After months of rehearsal, I was comfortable enough with the dialogue and the singing, but the dancing—and *West Side Story* is *mostly* dancing—petrified me. Right up to opening night, I was never sure which foot I would land on.

My anxiety was born of some taboo I had long ago internalized about dancing not being masculine. The typical after-school and after-supper pastimes for boys in my suburban neighborhood were baseball and football. Forget that dancing can actually develop the timing and coordination needed to play second base, or that dancers have physiques that gym rats only dream about. Any parent signing his or her son up for dance class instead of (or even in addition to) Little League was practically subject to child-abuse charges—because invariably that boy would be subject to the cruel taunts of his peers.

This unspoken prohibition was especially painful because secretly I loved to dance. Sports were O.K., but there were many nights when I would forgo the pickup game of baseball on the street, throw on some Motown and whirl around my room for a few hours. But always behind closed doors. Now here I was about to make a public spectacle of myself, and in *West Side Story* no less.

Most of the other men in the cast expressed similar anxiety, but we got a reprieve in that the choreography de-emphasized the more balletic turns in favor of macho posturing and finger-snapping and the climbing of fences. When the steps did get a little more complicated, I took the choreographer's advice to "show a lot of attitude" and chalked the rest up to the power of prayer. And I vowed to get better.

But childhood taboos die hard. It took me a year and a half to summon the courage to enroll in a dance class in Manhattan. As I signed my name for a year's worth of lessons, a lifetime of aversion—my own and my friends'—to dancing in public flashed through my head. I thought of linebackers in high school who took and gave poundings on the football field but sweated through the box step at the prom. And I knew firefighters and fleet-footed detectives who had been in shootouts who cowered at the sight of a wood floor with a strobe light above it. Even after John Travolta gyrated through *Saturday Night Fever,* tough guys still didn't dance.

I had been assured that there would be other men in the class, but when I arrived for the first one I was surrounded by leggy women in tights and tutus. The only other man was the instructor, Jeff, a former Broadway dancer who had been in *A Chorus Line* early in its run. He wore makeup and several earrings. Would I have felt more comfortable if he looked like Cal Ripken? Probably, but then I didn't have time to dwell on it, because I was immediately barraged with not only new steps but a new language ("plié," "relevé," "jazz third") and lessons in attire. ("This is not aerobics," Jeff would say, casting gentle aspersions at my jock wear—sneakers and sweats, which I clung to as the last bastions of my maleness.)

I tried to hide in the back lines, but in dance studios even the support beams have mirrors. I heard my name a lot in those first weeks: "Keep your shoulders down." "Other hand." "Watch your head." Yet every time I was tempted to quit, I also heard Jeff's words of encouragement: "If you get only 25 percent of the routine, I'll be happy" or "Just showing up is the victory."

Eventually the routines seemed less tyrannical, and I started to relax. I even compromised on my attire—retaining my Nike T-shirt but trading the sweats and sneakers for black satin jazz pants and jazz shoes. ("Now those," Jeff said, "have style.") And the benefits of the class were instantaneous—walking to my train after each session, I felt a kind of honorable exhaustion, having coaxed into consciousness muscles I hadn't even known existed. It was the same sense of physical satisfaction that I'd felt hitting a bases-clearing double or finishing a half-marathon.

My lessons were interrupted when the next show came along: *Man of La Mancha,* which required me to age 30 years but hardly afforded me an opportunity to show off my new steps. When the show finished its run, I returned to the studio, only to find Jeff out sick and the class being taught by a drill-sergeant substitute. She demanded that each dancer cross the floor individually while she exhorted, "Kick that leg higher—and now *sell* it." Under Jeff's kid-gloves tutelage, I had imagined myself as Fred Astaire, but now, under this magnifying glass, I turned back into Fred Flintstone—

stumbling, clumsy, self-conscious, as if all the inhibitions I had been whittling away suddenly gathered themselves back into an intractable whole. On my third or fourth solo flight across the floor I kept going into the locker room, up the stairs and out the door.

Jeff's absence turned out to be permanent—his illness was forcing him to retire—and the studio closed soon after that, a victim of the economy's own failing health. Then I got word of a cast call for a local production of *South Pacific*, a show whose feats are primarily vocal, at least for the men. Reluctantly, I auditioned and made the male chorus. It looked as if my dancing days would be indefinitely deferred.

The men did have one big number—*There Is Nothin' Like a Dame*—which basically involved animated marching. Posture and expression were key, and, because Jeff had emphasized these in class, I had no trouble picking up the routine. The choreographer even singled me out to demonstrate a couple of steps, and the other men—most of whom had never danced on stage before and were wearing the same long faces I did during *West Side Story*—were saying things like "Obviously you've done this before." Now I was being celebrated for something that most of my life I had feared would bring me ridicule.

After much fine-tuning and many weeks of rehearsal, the other men came around, and by the time the show opened there was a buzz about *There Is Nothin' Like a Dame.* The women in the show had three times as many dance numbers and their steps were much fancier. But the novelty appeal of "men who can move" ran high, and when we successfully executed a kickline at the end of the song we brought down the house.

At moments like that, and the many since I've had dancing in public and private, I remember that trip to the confession booth, and realize that dance has in fact become a kind of physical and psychic redemption. But it isn't penance anymore.

Suggestions for Discussion

1. Discuss Hoerburger's anxiety "about dancing not being masculine," an anxiety shared by most of the other men in the cast of an amateur production of *West Side Story.* How does he overcome his anxiety?
2. In what ways has dancing become "a kind of physical and psychic redemption" for the author?

Suggestions for Writing

1. Discuss your psychological responses to certain sports or other kinds of physical activity. Were you afraid you might be injured? Anxious to succeed? Worried about competing successfully? Concerned about your

image? How did you overcome your negative responses and reinforce positive ones?

2. Research and write brief biographical sketches of five major modern dancers.

ROGER ANGELL

On the Ball

Roger Angell (b. 1920) has long been associated with *The New Yorker* as writer and editor. He writes about baseball in this essay from the collection *Once More Around the Park* (1991).

It weighs just over five ounces and measures between 2.86 and 2.94 inches in diameter. It is made of a composition-cork nucleus encased in two thin layers of rubber, one black and one red, surrounded by 121 yards of tightly wrapped blue-gray wool yarn, 45 yards of white wool yarn, 53 more yards of blue-gray wool yarn, 150 yards of fine cotton yarn, a coat of rubber cement, and a cowhide (formerly horsehide) exterior, which is held together with 216 slightly raised red cotton stitches. Printed certifications, endorsements, and outdoor advertising spherically attest to its authenticity. Like most institutions, it is considered inferior in its present form to its ancient archetypes, and in this case the complaint is probably justified; on occasion in recent years it has actually been known to come apart under the demands of its brief but rigorous active career. Baseballs are assembled and hand-stitched in Taiwan (before this year the work was done in Haiti, and before 1973 in Chicopee, Massachusetts), and contemporary pitchers claim that there is a tangible variation in the size and feel of the balls that now come into play in a single game; a true peewee is treasured by hurlers, and its departure from the premises, by fair means or foul, is secretly mourned. But never mind: any baseball is beautiful. No other small package comes as close to the ideal in design and utility. It is a perfect object for a man's hand. Pick it up and it instantly suggests its purpose; it is meant to be thrown a considerable distance—thrown hard and with precision. Its feel and heft are the beginning of the sport's critical dimensions; if it were a fraction of an inch larger or smaller, a few centigrams heavier or lighter, the game of baseball would be utterly different. Hold a baseball in your hand. As it happens, this one is not brand-new. Here, just to one side of the curved surgical welt of stitches, there is a pale-green grass smudge, darkening on one edge almost to black—the mark of an old infield play, a tough grounder now lost in memory. Feel the ball, turn it over in your hand; hold it across the seam or the other way, with the seam just to the side of your middle finger. Speculation stirs. You want to get outdoors and throw this spare and sensual object to somebody or, at the very least, watch somebody else throw it. The game has begun.

Thinking about the ball and its attributes seems to refresh our appreciation of this game. A couple of years ago, I began to wonder why it was that pitchers, taken as a group, seemed to be so much livelier and more garrulous than hitters. I considered the possibility of some obscure physiological linkage (the discobologlottal syndrome) and the more obvious occupational discrepancies (pitchers have a lot more spare time than other players), but then it came to me that a pitcher is the only man in baseball who can properly look on the ball as being his instrument, his accomplice. He is the only player who is granted the privilege of making offensive plans, and once the game begins he is (in concert with his catcher) the only man on the field who knows what is meant to happen next. Everything in baseball begins with the pitch, and every other part of the game—hitting, fielding, and throwing—is reflexive and defensive. (The hitters on a ball team are referred to as the "offense," but almost three quarters of the time this is an absolute misnomer.) The batter tapping the dirt off his spikes and now stepping into the box looks sour and glum, and who can blame him, for the ball has somehow been granted in perpetuity to the wrong people. It is already an object of suspicion and hatred, and the reflex that allows him occasionally to deflect that tiny onrushing dot with his bat, and sometimes even to relaunch it violently in the opposite direction, is such a miraculous response of eye and body as to remain virtually inexplicable, even to him. There are a few dugout flannel-mouths (Ted Williams, Harry Walker, Pete Rose) who can talk convincingly about the art of hitting, but, like most arts, it does not in the end seem communicable. Pitching is different. It is a craft ("the crafty portsider...") and is thus within reach.

The smiling pitcher begins not only with the advantage of holding his fate in his own hands, or hand, but with the knowledge that every advantage of physics and psychology seems to be on his side. A great number of surprising and unpleasant things can be done to the ball as it is delivered from the grasp of a two-hundred-pound optimist, and the first of these is simply to transform it into a projectile. Most pitchers seem hesitant to say so, but if you press them a little they will admit that the prime ingredient in their intense personal struggle with the batter is probably fear. A few pitchers in the majors have thrived without a real fastball—junk men like Eddie Lopat and Mike Cuellar, superior control artists like Bobby Shantz and Randy Jones, knuckleballers like Hoyt Wilhelm and Charlie Hough—but almost everyone else has had to hump up and throw at least an occasional no-nonsense hard one, which crosses the plate at eighty-five miles per hour or better, and thus causes the hitter to—well, to *think* a little. The fastball sets up all the other pitches in the hurler's repertoire—the curve, the slider, the sinker, and so on—but its other purpose is to intimidate. Great fastballers like Bob Gibson, Jim Bunning, Sandy Koufax, and Nolan Ryan have always run up high strikeout figures because their money pitch was almost untouchable, but their deeper measures of success—twenty-victory seasons and low earned-run averages—were due to the fact that none of the hitters they faced, not even the best of them, was immune to the thought of what a 90-mph missile could do to a man if it struck him. They had been ever so slightly distracted, and distraction is bad for hitting. The intention of the pitcher has almost nothing to do with this; very few pitches are delivered with intent to maim. The bad dream, however, will not go away. Walter Johnson, the greatest fireballer of them all, had almost absolute control, but he is said to have worried constantly about what might happen if one of his pitches got away from him. Good hitters know all this and resolutely don't think about it (a good hitter is a man who can keep his back foot firmly planted in the box even while the rest of him is pulling back or bailing out on an inside fastball), but even these icy customers are less settled in their minds than they would like to be, just because the man out there on the mound is hiding that cannon behind his hip. Hitters, of course, do not call this fear. The word is "respect."

It should not be inferred, of course, that major-league pitchers are wholly averse to hitting batters, or *almost* hitting batters. A fastball up around the Adam's apple not only is a first-class distracter, as noted, but also discourages a hitter from habitually leaning forward in order to put more of his bat on a dipping curve or a slider over the outer rim of the plate. The truth of the matter is that pitchers and batters are engaged in a permanent private duel over their property rights to the plate, and a tough, proud hurler who senses that the man now in the batter's box has recently had the better of things will often respond in the most direct manner possible, with a hummer to the ribs. Allie Reynolds, Sal Maglie, Don Drysdale, Early Wynn, and Bob Gibson were cold-eyed lawmen of this stripe, and the practice has by no means vanished, in spite of strictures and deplorings from the high chambers of baseball. Early this year, Lynn McGlothen, of the Cards, routinely plunked the Mets' Del Unser, who had lately been feasting on his pitches, and then violated the ancient protocol in these matters by admitting intent. Dock Ellis, now a Yankee but then a Pirate, decided early in the 1974 season that the Cincinnati Reds had somehow established dominance over his club, and he determined to set things right in his own way. (This incident is described at length in a lively new baseball book, *Dock Ellis in the Country of Baseball*, by Donald Hall.) The first Cincinnati batter of the game was Pete Rose, and the first pitch from Ellis was at his head—"not actually to *hit* him," Ellis said later, but as a "*message* to let him know that he was going to be hit." He then hit Rose in the side. The next pitch hit the next Red batter, Joe Morgan, in the kidney. The third batter was Dan Driessen, who took Ellis's second pitch in the back. With the bases loaded, Dock now threw four pitches at Tony Perez (one behind his back), but missed with all of them, walking in a run. He then missed Johnny Bench (and the plate) twice, whereupon Pirate manager Danny Murtaugh came out to the mound, stared at Ellis with silent surmise, and beckoned for a new pitcher.

Hitters can accept this sort of fugue, even if they don't exactly enjoy it, but what they do admittedly detest is a young and scatter-armed smoke-thrower, the true wild man. One famous aborigine was Steve Dalkowski, an Oriole farmhand of the late nineteen fifties and early sixties who set records for strikeouts and jumpy batters wherever he played. In one typical stay with a Class D league, he threw 121 strikeouts and gave up 129 walks and 39 wild pitches, all in the span of 62 innings. Dalkowski never made it to the majors, but, being a legend, he is secure for the ages. "Once I saw him work a game in the Appalachian League," a gravel-voiced retired coach said to me not long ago, "and nothing was hit *forward* for seven innings—not even a foul ball." An attempt was once made to clock Dalkowski on a recording device, but his eventual mark of 93.5 mph was discounted, since he threw for forty minutes before steering a pitch into the machine's recording zone.

Better-known names in these annals of anxiety are Rex Barney, a briefly flaring Brooklyn nova of the nineteen forties, who once threw a no-hit game but eventually walked and wild-pitched his way out of baseball; Ryne Duren, the extremely fast and extremely nearsighted reliever for the Yankees and other American League clubs in the fifties and sixties, whose traditional initial warm-up pitch on his being summoned to the mound was a twelve-foot-high fastball to the foul screen; and a pair of rookies named Sandy Koufax and Bob Feller. Koufax, to be sure, eventually became a superb control artist, but it took him seven years before he got his great stuff entirely together, and there were times when it seemed certain that he would be known only as another Rex Barney. Sandy recalls that when he first brought his boyish assortment of fiery sailers and bouncing rockets to spring-training camp he had difficulty getting in any mound work, because whenever he picked up his glove all the available catchers would suddenly remember pressing appointments in some distant part of the compound. Feller had almost a career-long struggle with *his* control and four times managed to lead his league simultaneously in walks and in strikeouts. His first appearance against another major-league club came in an exhibition game against the Cardinals in the summer of 1936, when he was seventeen years old; he entered the game in the fourth inning, and eventually struck out eight batters in three innings. but when his searing fastball missed the plate it had the batters jumping around in the box like roasting popcorn. Frank Frisch, the St. Louis player-manager, carefully observed Feller's first three or four deliveries and then walked down to the end of the dugout, picked up a pencil, and removed himself from the Cardinal lineup.

The chronically depressed outlook of major-league batters was pushed to the edge of paranoia in the nineteen-fifties by the sudden and utterly unexpected arrival of the slider, or the Pitcher's Friend. The slider is an easy pitch to throw and a hard one to hit. It is delivered with the same motion as the fastball, but with the pitcher's wrist rotated approximately ninety degrees (to the right for a right-hander, to the left for a southpaw), which has the effect of placing the delivering forefinger and middle finger slightly off center on the ball. The positions of hand, wrist, and arm are almost identical with those that produce a good spiral forward pass with a football. The result is an apparent three-quarter-speed fastball that suddenly changes its mind and direction. It doesn't break much—in its early days it was slightingly known as the "nickel curve"—but a couple of inches of lateral movement at the plateward end of the ball's brief sixty-foot-six-inch journey can make for an epidemic of pop-ups, foul balls, and harmless grounders. "Epidemic" is not an exaggeration. The slider was the prime agent responsible for the sickening and decline of major-league batting averages in the two decades after the Second World War, which culminated in a combined average of .237 for the two leagues in 1968. A subsequent crash program of immunization and prevention by the authorities produced from the laboratory a smaller strike zone and a lowering of the pitcher's mound by five inches, but the hitters, while saved from extermination, have never regained their state of rosy-cheeked, pre-slider good health.

For me, the true mystery of the slider is not its flight path but the circumstances of its discovery. Professional baseball got under way in the eighteen-seventies, and during all the ensuing summers uncounted thousands of young would-be Mathewsons and Seavers spent their afternoons flinging the ball in every conceivable fashion as they searched for magic fadeaways and flutter balls that would take them to Cooperstown. Why did eighty years pass before anybody noticed that a slight cocking of the wrist would be sufficient to usher in the pitchers' Golden Age? Where were Tom Swift and Frank Merriwell? What happened to American Know-How? This is almost a national disgrace. The mystery is deepened by the fact that—to my knowledge, at least—no particular pitcher or pitching coach is given credit for the discovery and propagation of the slider. Bob Lemon, who may be the first man to have pitched his way into the Hall of Fame with a slider, says he learned the pitch from Mel Harder, who was an elder mound statesman with the Indians when Lemon came up to that club, in 1946. I have also heard some old-timers say that George Blaeholder was throwing a pretty fair slider for the St. Louis Browns way back in the nineteen-twenties. But none of these worthies ever claimed to be the Johnny Appleseed of the pitch. The thing seemed to generate itself—a weed in the bullpen that overran the field.

The slider has made baseball more difficult for the fan as well as for the batter. Since its action is late and minimal, and since its delivery does not require the easily recognizable armsnap by the pitcher that heralds the true curve, the slider can be spotted only by an attentive spectator seated very close to home plate. A curve thrown by famous old pretzel-benders like Tommy Bridges and Sal Maglie really used to *curve;* you could see the thing break even if you were way out in the top deck of Section 31. Most fans, however, do not admit the loss. The contemporary bleacher critic, having watched a doll-size distant slugger swing mightily and tap the ball down to second on four bounces, smiles and enters the out in his scorecard. "Slider," he announces, and everybody nods wisely in agreement.

The mystery of the knuckleball is ancient and honored. Its practitioners cheerfully admit that they do not understand why the pitch behaves the way it does; nor do they know, or care much, which particular lepidopteran path it will follow on its way past the batter's infuriated swipe. They merely prop the ball on their fingertips (not, in actual fact, on the knuckles) and launch it more or less in the fashion of a paper airplane, and then, most of the time, finish the delivery with a faceward motion of the glove, thus hiding a grin. Now science has confirmed the phenomenon. Writing in *The American Journal of Physics,* Eric Sawyer and Robert G. Watts, of Tulane University, recently reported that wind-tunnel tests showed that a slowly spinning baseball is subject to forces capable of making it swerve a foot or more between the pitcher's mound and the plate. The secret, they say, appears to be the raised seams of the ball, which cause a "roughness pattern" and an uneven flow of air, resulting in a "nonsymmetric lateral force distribution and...a net force in one direction or another."

Like many other backyard baseball stars, I have taught myself to throw a knuckleball that moves with so little rotation that one can almost pick out the signature of Charles S. Feeney in midair; the pitch, however, has shown disappointingly few symptoms of last-minute fluttering and has so far proved to be wonderfully catchable or hittable, mostly by my wife. Now, at last, I understand the problem. In their researches, Sawyer and Watts learned that an entirely spinless knuckler is *not* subject to varying forces, and thus does not dive or veer. The ideal knuckler, they say, completes about a quarter of a revolution on its way to the plate. The speed of the pitch, moreover, is not critical, because "the magnitude of the lateral force increases approximately as the square of the velocity," which means that the total lateral movement is "independent of the speed of the pitch."

All this has been perfectly understood (if less politely defined) by any catcher who has been the battery mate of a star knuckleballer, and has thus spent six or seven innings groveling in the dirt in imitation of a bulldog cornering a nest of field mice. Modern catchers have the assistance of outsized gloves (which lately have begun to approach the diameter of tea trays), and so enjoy a considerable advantage over some of their ancient predecessors in capturing the knuckler. In the middle nineteen-forties, the receivers for the Washington Senators had to deal with a pitching staff that included *four* knuckleball specialists—Dutch Leonard, Johnny Niggeling, Mickey Haefner, and Roger Wolff. Among the ill-equipped Washington catchers who tried to fend off almost daily midafternoon clouds of deranged butterflies were Rick Ferrell and Jake Early; Early eventually was called up to serve in the armed forces—perhaps the most willing inductee of his day.

The spitball was once again officially outlawed from baseball in 1974, and maybe this time the prohibition will work. This was the third, and by far the most severe, edict directed at the unsanitary and extremely effective delivery, for it permits an umpire to call an instantaneous ball on any pitch that even looks like a spitter as it crosses the plate. No evidence is required; no appeal by the pitcher to higher powers is permissible. A subsequent spitball or imitation thereof results in the expulsion of the pitcher from the premises, *instanter,* and an ensuing fine. Harsh measures indeed, but surely sufficient we may suppose, to keep this repellent and unfair practice out of baseball's shining mansion forever. Surely, and yet... Professional pitchers have an abiding fondness for any down-breaking delivery, legal or illegal, that will get the job done, and nothing, they tell me, does the job more effectively or more entertainingly than a dollop of saliva or slippery-elm juice, or a little bitty dab of lubricating jelly, applied to the pitching fingers. The ball which is sent off half wet and half dry, like a dilatory schoolboy, hurries innocently toward the gate and its grim-faced guardians, and at the last second darts under the turnstile. Pitchers, moreover, have before them the inspiring recent example of Gaylord Perry, whose rumored but unverified Faginesque machinations with K-Y Jelly won him a Cy Young Award in 1972 and led inevitably to the demand for harsher methods of law enforcement. Rumor has similarly indicted other highly successful performers, like Don Drysdale, Whitey Ford and Bill Singer. Preacher Roe, upon retiring from the Dodgers, in 1954, after an extended useful tenure on the mound at Ebbets Field, published a splendidly unrepentant confession, in which he gave away a number of trade secrets. His favorite undryer, as I recall, was a full pack of Juicy Fruit gum, and he loaded up by straightening the bill of his cap between pitches and passing his fingers momentarily in front of his face—now also illegal, alas.

It may be perceived that my sympathies, which lately seemed to lie so rightly on the side of the poor overmatched hitters, have unaccountably swung the other way. I admit this indefensible lapse simply because I find the spitter so enjoyable for its deviousness and skulking disrespect. I don't suppose we should again make it a fully legal pitch (it was first placed outside the pale in 1920), but I would enjoy a return to the era when the spitter was treated simply as a misdemeanor and we could all laugh ourselves silly at the sight of a large, outraged umpire suddenly calling in a suspected wetback for inspection (and the pitcher, of course, *rolling* the ball to him across the grass) and then glaring impotently out at the innocent ("Who—*me?*") perpetrator on the mound. Baseball is a hard, rules-dominated game, and it should have more room in it for a little cheerful cheating.

All these speculations, and we have not yet taken the ball out of the hands of its first friend, the pitcher. And yet there is always something more. We might suddenly realize, for instance, that baseball is the only team sport in which the scoring is not done with the ball. In hockey, football, soccer, basketball, lacrosse, and the rest of them, the ball or its equivalent actually scores or is responsible for the points that determine the winner. In baseball, the score is made by the base runner—by the man down there, just crossing the plate—while the ball in most cases, is a long way off, doing something quite different. It's a strange business, this unique double life going on in front of us, and it tells us a lot about this unique game. A few years ago, there was a suddenly popular thesis put forward in some sports columns and light-heavyweight editorial pages which proposed that the immense recent popularity of professional football could be explained by the fact that the computerlike complexity of its plays, the clotted and anonymous masses of its players, and the intense violence of its action constituted a perfect Sunday parable of contemporary urban society. It is a pretty argument, and perhaps even true, especially since it is hard not to notice that so many professional football games, in spite of their noise and chaos, are deadeningly repetitious, predictable, and banal. I prefer the emotions and suggestions to be found in the other sport. I don't think anyone can watch many baseball games without becoming aware of the fact that the ball, for all its immense energy and unpredictability, very rarely escapes the control of the players. It is released again and again—pitched and caught, struck along the ground or sent high in the air—but almost always, almost instantly, it is recaptured and returned to control and safety and harmlessness. Nothing is altered, nothing has been allowed to happen. This orderliness and constraint are among the prime attractions of the sport; a handful of men, we discover, can police a great green country, forestalling unimaginable disasters. A slovenly, error-filled game can sometimes be exciting, but it never seems serious, and is thus never truly satisfying, for the metaphor of safety—of danger subdued by skill and courage—has been lost. Too much civilization, however, is deadly—in this game, a deadly bore. A deeper need is stifled. The ball looks impetuous and dangerous, but we perceive that in fact it lives in a slow, guarded world of order, vigilance, and rules. Nothing can ever happen here. And then once again the ball is pitched—sent on its quick, planned errand. The bat flashes, there is a new, louder sound, and suddenly we see the ball streaking wild through the air and then bounding along distant and untouched in the sweet green grass. We leap up, thousands of us, and shout for its joyful flight—free, set free, free at last.

Suggestions for Discussion

1. How does thinking about the ball and its attributes refresh our appreciation of the game?
2. Distinguish among the fastball, slider, knuckleball, and spitball.
3. Discuss Angell's fascination with pitchers.

Suggestions for Writing

1. Write about a baseball game that exemplifies the notion of "danger subdued by skill and courage."
2. Write a brief sketch of a pitcher you admire.
3. Discuss the significance of the ball in another sport.

R. C. HARVEY

State of the Art: June 1996

R. C. Harvey is the author of *The Art of the Funnies* and *The Art of the Comic Book.* In the following essay he discusses the state of the art of cartooning.

It's better than you might think. But if you think that, then it's probably worse. In some ways, the state of the art of cartooning is better today than it's ever been. But in most respects, the medium is blighted, and the prospects for the future are bleak.

Magazine cartooning has all but perished. Where once great national magazines—*Collier's, Saturday Evening Post, Parade, Saturday Review of Literature,* and *Look*—published single panel gag cartoons by the score with every weekly issue, now only *The New Yorker* holds forth. And the economics of publishing that magazine have dictated a lower weekly page count than in William Shawn's heyday, and that means fewer cartoons. (And *New Yorker* cartoons are increasingly lifeless: the comedy, such as it is, resides in the captions, and the pictures add little or nothing to this essentially verbal humor. The art of blending word and picture for comic impact languishes here.)

While the newsstands are littered these days with monthly magazines that publish a few cartoons apiece, the magazines serve a vast array of special interests, and the very variety inhibits any proliferation of cartoons. Magazine gag cartoonists work entirely "on spec": they crank out cartoons and peddle them door-to-door at magazines in the speculation that they'll sell one here and there as they go along. No guarantees. In the rollicking days of yesteryear, a cartoonist could produce a dozen "general interest" cartoons with the expectation of selling many of them at one or another of a dozen "general interest" magazines (*Collier's*, etc.).

Today, a cartoonist must produce cartoons about skiing for the monthly skiing magazine, about fishing for the fishing magazine, about wind surfing for the wind surfing magazine, and so on; and if he can't sell his wind surfing cartoons at that magazine, the chances are that no other magazine will take them. In short, the percentages are against the magazine cartoonist: it simply doesn't pay to spend much time on special interest cartoons.

Unless the special interest is sex. Only "men's magazines" appear in sufficient number to provide a viable market for freelance cartoonists working wholly on spec. But even here the prospects are waning as gynecological photography flourishes.

The evaporation of magazine markets for cartoons is a critical fact in the health of the medium because magazine cartooning used to offer newcomers the best avenue of access to the profession. Aspiring cartoonists could work at home—wherever they lived—creating cartoons in their spare time and submitting them to editors by mail. As they gained in skill and proficiency, they sold more cartoons; the more cartoons they sold, the more time they could afford to spend cartooning—until, at last, they abandoned their day jobs to become full-time cartoonists. And some—Mort Walker, Johnny Hart, Charles Schulz, Hank Ketcham, Randy Glasbergen—eventually became nationally syndicated comic strip cartoonists.

I can't think of any circumstance today that is similar. Given the number of cartoonist clubs and societies around the country, there are doubtless plenty of cartoonists. They tend not to be full-time cartoonists—or, even, full-time cartoonists in their spare time; they dabble at cartooning (fondly, very often with great skill) while earning their bread at other commercial art jobs. Dabbling may be the best they'll ever do. What, after all, can they aspire to? Where can they cartoon these days?

Magazine cartooning has all but disappeared, as I said. And newspapers, that other great venue for cartoonists of yore, have turned outright hostile to comics. What cartoonist in his right mind would aspire to produce drawings that will be published at the size of postage stamps?

This, perhaps, does not constitute a problem: there will never be a shortage of newspaper cartoonists because (according to that hoary commonplace of popular culture) no cartoonist is, by definition, in his right mind. And those that come to their senses—Bill Watterson, Gary Larson, Berke Breathed—seem to leave the field.

Sorry: pardon my momentary lapse into glib flippery.

Even in newspapers, we can find excellent work: Pat Brady with *Rose Is Rose,* for instance, is doing imaginative work of startling brilliance. So is Bill Holbrook in *Fastrack* and Wiley Miller in *Non Sequitur.*

And even though syndicates have pooh-poohed story strips for years, Jim Scancarelli with *Gasoline Alley,* Lynn Johnston with *For Better or For Worse,* and Stan Lee and his brother Larry with *Spider-Man* fly in the face of conventional wisdom and consistently demonstrate the popularity and viability of the continuity strip (while working in quarters so cramped that it is nearly impossible to swing a pen or brush let alone a wrench, a frying pan, or a fist).

Still, the miserable size begrudgingly afforded newspaper comic strips encourages a proliferation of non-art offerings—*Dilbert, Cathy,* and *Drabble,* for instance, which can survive reproduction at the tiniest dimension imaginable. And because of the modest artistic attainments of their creators, such strips rely on verbal gyrations to elicit laughter instead of blending words and pictures in the best traditions of the art form.

And when the National Cartoonists Society confers its highest award, the Reuben, on Garry Trudeau, who does not draw much and who is, therefore, more writer than cartoonist, the newspaper bias against cartooning receives the imprimatur of approval from the very profession that the practices of newspaper editors have been systematically emasculating for years.

The editorial cartoonist has been faring somewhat better in the newspaper. Editorial cartoons still get a decent allotment of space, for one thing. And for a while, the number of editorial cartoonists seemed on the rise. Many more newspapers had editorial cartoonists on staff than in bygone years. (Not as many as in the early years of the century, perhaps; but more than, say, thirty years ago. Or so it seemed.) But the trend to comedy instead of commentary still infects the field with an eviscerating contagion.

Editors would rather that their editorial cartoonists tell jokes. Editors might be wonderfully courageous on their editorial pages when dealing exclusively in words, but they seem curiously hesitant about words when they're combined with pictures in editorial cartoons. They don't want to offend readers. Apparently readers are not offended by words alone—only by words in combination with pictures. (Or perhaps editors harbor an insidious suspicion: their readers don't really read at all—except the grocery store advertisements. But they do look at pictures. So why are editors so chintzy with space for comic strips? You see? If we pause to think, most of the so-called rationale that permeates newspaper editorial offices goes up in a belch of smoke.)

In any event, editors have discovered that the best way to avoid offending readers (or nonreaders) with cartoons that they might look at is to publish cartoons that are simply funny on topical matters without making any "editorial comment." And because cartoonists by nature are tempted to tell jokes with their verbal-visual blends, they easily fall into the comfortable habit of avoiding commentary: they thereby please their editors and themselves.

But as social or political forces for reform, their cartoons aren't too powerful.

Exceptions abound here, too. But the trend to comedy pablum is alive and well.

Of the print venues for cartoonists, only comic books seem in any way vibrant. To begin with, the comic book format offers the cartoonist more ways of constructing dramatic verbal-visual narratives than any of the other print media. The format permits great variation in layout and panel composition for effect; and the number of pages afforded a cartoonist can be adjusted (at least a little) to suit the demands of his story. Moreover, the comic book industry seems, at the moment, more hospitable to creative endeavor than other genre.

The comic book industry may be staggering about wildly. The direct market is still suffering from the violent restructuring forced on it by Marvel's draconian greed. Comic shops and alternate publishers are dropping like flies. Or so they say.

But if the doom-sayers are to be believed, there would be no comic shops or alternate publishers this summer at all. The most dire predictions of last year had the industry on the ropes in a few months, DOA by the end of the year.

Yet here we are.

I don't mean to suggest that the industry is financially healthy; I suspect it is, at best, only borderline ambulatory. It's certainly not as vigorous as it was a few years ago. But then, it never was, was it?

The vigor of the industry is not our topic, of course. We're examining the state of the *art,* not the state of the industry. But the economic health of the industry bears directly on the state of the art: in a capitalist economy, no art flourishes without accompanying financial well being. Take Marvel.

Marvel seems sick-unto-dying: having cut itself off from the rest of the industry by creating an exclusive distribution universe of its own, it is now slowly expiring in the magnificent splendor of its isolation. Incidentally, the marketing principle at work in the minds of Marveliers flies in the face of the accumulated wisdom of shopping mall experts. Why do you suppose that malls are routinely peppered with at least a half dozen shoe stores, all of which become roaringly successful? Because shoppers know they are more likely to find what they want if they have an array of choices. And all the shoe stores profit from the clustering as shoppers go from one to another. Yeah, I know: comic books aren't shoes. But maybe we could learn something from these pedestrian enterprises.

Actually, it's probably too late for Marvel. Marvel has become but the toy of a rich man, just another chip in the stack in front of him as he gambles in the corporate marketplace. For him, the production of comic books is doubtless little different than the production of sausages. As a consequence, I see little evidence in the House of Ideas of anything but sausages. Link sausages. Sausagelike, its comic books are endlessly repetitive and therefore lifeless not to mention directionless and uninspired.

In contrast, DC seems a dynamo of innovation and creativity. DC, which I once said stood for "Dull Comics," is actually producing adventurous material (*Sandman* and some Vertigo and Paradox titles). And some of its books are drawn in different graphic styles (different from the otherwise prevailing Imagery, that is). Moreover, DC has found a way to make blockbuster movies out of comic book superheroes—something Marvel has been vainly hacking away at for decades.

But the state of the art of the comic book is defined these days less by the state of the Big Two than it ever was before. And that, it seems to me, is the good news this summer.

Consider, in this, the twentieth year of the *Journal,* that two decades ago there weren't nearly as many publishers of comic books as there are today. Twenty years ago, the state of the art was determined almost solely by the health and inclination of the two biggest comic book publishers. Today, that is no longer entirely the case.

Even with the collapse of smaller publishing endeavors in recent months, there are more publishers of comic books today than there were twenty years ago. Granted, that the unstable market situation (the complexities of distribution and the marginal reliability of some comics shops) demands good management if a publisher is to succeed. In the flush years of wild investor speculation or the black-and-white glut of a decade ago, no management at all seemed necessary: just put out the product, and the buyers will be there to snap it up.

But the need for good management is scarcely a sign of industry-wide weakness; it would seem, rather, quite the reverse. "Management"—particularly "good management"—implies maturity in the market and the industry: maturity implies longevity, or, at least, the kind of stability that lends itself to management.

Maybe that's just a trick of semantics, a linguistic sleight of hand. Be that as it may, we have more publishers of comic book material these days than we have had since the heydays of the Golden Age. And even if 90% of everything is unadulterated crapola, the more product there is, the more sheer quantity there is in the remaining 10%.

More importantly, however, more publishers means more opportunity for cartoonists. And the more cartoonists there are, the greater the likelihood for individual—even idiosyncratic—expression in the medium.

Frank Miller, Erik Larsen, Sergio Aragonés, Donna Barr, Jim Woodring, Mike Mignola, Paul Chadwick, Roberta Gregory—just a few of those who draw and write their own material and do so with a distinctive and often innovative flair, exploiting format as well as adding new subject matters to the inventory.

Twenty years ago, such individual work would not have much chance for publication.

Individual expression may not be socially or politically significant. Erik Larsen is not Thomas Nast. Sin City is not the Tweed Ring. But if creating comic books is satisfying for the cartoonist seeking artistic fulfillment, then the state of the art is healthy.

And if the dilemmas faced by such characters as Concrete and Bitchy Bitch engage our sympathy or evoke a response in simple human terms, then the state of the art is Art. And I think that is increasingly the case in comic books.

Not high art yet by any means. But the outlook is not so bleak in comic books as it seems elsewhere in the world of cartooning for print. After all, any medium that has room for Erik Larsen to explore the varieties of flatulent hilarity to be found in a supervillain named Backfire is a medium of enlightened opportunity.

Suggestions for Discussion

1. Why does Harvey believe that the comic book industry is "more hospitable to creative endeavor than other genre"?
2. Contrast Marvel and DC.
3. Discuss Harvey's claim that cartoons aren't powerful "social or political forces for reform."

Suggestions for Writing

1. Analyze three editorial cartoons.
2. Discuss the work of a leading comic book cartoonist whose work you know and admire.

ALEX ROSS

The Shock of the True

Alex Ross, a regular contributor to *The New Yorker,* writes about the American fascination with gruesome crime.

"True crime" is the name that has attached itself to journalistic and literary accounts of exceptional human ghastliness. The term became a standard publishing category in the nineteen-eighties, distinct from long-standing genres of mystery and crime literature. In its basic guise, true crime takes the form of those slim, brightly colored paperbacks sold in the finer airports and sleazier bookstores, with titles like *Toxic Love, Savage Vengeance,* and *The Eyeball Killer.* In more cultivated hands, it touches a thanatoid poetical note—*In Cold Blood, The Executioner's Song, Midnight in the Garden of Good and Evil.* The uncontested titan of the type is *Helter Skelter,* the life of Charles Manson as told by his prosecutor, which was reissued last year in a special twenty-fifth-anniversary edition. If, as Matthew Arnold boasted, culture aspires to reveal the best that has been thought and known in the world, true crime desires to reveal the worst.

The name is new, the genre is not. These books may look like so much scattered sediment on the contemporary plain, but they will soon form a neat geological layer, crushed over many older layers. Readers have been devouring hastily printed accounts of mayhem and disaster since the invention of the popular press. "There is no spectacle we so eagerly pursue, as that of some uncommon and grievous calamity," Edmund Burke wrote in 1757. William Bolitho, the once widely read author of *Murder for Profit,* declared nearly two centuries later, "We have a need for the sight of life and death as for salt. We wage-slaves live continually in incompletion and inexplicability; we strain for a sight of stars and mud." Violence has always been one of the chief indices by which any society measures its fall from grace or its hope for redemption. The first big event after man's expulsion from paradise was Cain's senseless bludgeoning of Abel.

Still, this dank little corner of the bookstore raises some fresh questions. How true is true crime? How and why are its particular truths chosen? The shock of the real is the main selling point: even the laziest true-crime hack, armed with evidence of stupefying acts, can outdo all the chic young writers and hip directors who think themselves daring for their gore. But facts, somehow, do not always suffice. These books freely re-create scenes witnessed by only the dead and the mad. They touch the border where fantasy turns to fact, where the unimaginable becomes trite. They generalize portentously from freak events. They invite fascination to overcome disgust: you want to put them down but can't. And, sometimes, they give people dangerous ideas. More than most cultural pursuits, true crime is very much at the mercy of its audience.

The roots of true crime go back at least as far as Daniel Defoe, who in 1725 published a "True and Genuine Account of the Life and Actions of the late Jonathan Wild; not made up of Fiction and Fable, but taken from his own Mouth, and Collected from Papers of his own Writing." Wild was the long-reigning mastermind of criminal London, whose fame grew through the circulation of newspapers, periodicals, pamphlets, and songs: he passed into myth in *The Beggar's Opera.* But Defoe's "true and genuine account" mixed fact and fiction, despite all the vehement protestations of the title. Well into the next century, crime tended to serve other genres, particularly political satire, rather than hold interest in its own right. It was Thomas De Quincey, the brilliant and bizarre Romantic essayist best known for his "Confessions of an English Opium-Eater," who liberated the form in his sequence of essays "On Murder Considered as One of the Fine Arts."

At first, De Quincey's "On Murder" followed the conventions of high-minded satire. It imagined a Society of Connoisseurs in Murder, which appraised vicious acts according to strict aesthetic criteria. (The apparent target was Burke's treatise on "The Sublime and Beautiful," which observed man's terror before the majesty of nature. If the monstrous in nature can assume philosophical grandeur, why not the monstrous in man?) But De Quincey found more to savor in the bare facts of favorite cases than his roundabout conceit allowed him to show. In an 1854 Postscript, he added a methodical hypnotic narrative of various killings carried out by a yellow-haired sailor named John Williams. In those forty-odd pages, true crime blossomed. There is a cool sketch of the character of the villain, balancing his dandyish charm against an inner viciousness ("His eyes seemed frozen and glazed, as if their light were all converged upon some victim lurking in the far background"); there is a look into the doomed home of innocents ("[Marr] was a stout, fresh-colored young man of twenty-seven, in some slight degree uneasy from his commercial prospects, but still cheerful"); there is a heightening of suspense through close inspection of ominous detail ("The cry of *past one o'clock*...commencing a few seconds after one, lasted intermittingly for ten or thirteen minutes").

At the climactic moment, De Quincey suddenly withdraws his omniscient gaze: "Let us leave the murderer alone with his victims. For fifty minutes let him work his pleasure. The front door, as we know, is now fastened against all help. Help there is none." He then pieces together the scene of the crime through the wild gaze of a servant girl who had stepped out to buy oysters. The style is almost cinematic in its quick-cut juxtaposition of criminal and innocent points of view. Admittedly, the real-time narrative also includes some outlandish De Quinceyan touches: citations of Shelley and Wordsworth, baroque exclamations of horror, invocations of the sublime, and a delirious fantasy sequence in which Sailor Williams escapes his second crime, flees to America, and becomes President of the United States. (But no, the poor man hesitates for ninety seconds and ends up hanging himself in jail.)

By the end of the nineteenth century, the establishment of police forces in London, New York, and other major cities had pushed crime rates—notably the rates for homicides—steadily down. But the advance of mass media created an ever-growing hunger for tales of gruesome crime: far-flung cases were marshalled to form something like a continuous procession of atrocities. The so-called Jack the Ripper murders, in the late eighteen-eighties, were an international sensation, launching a true-crime cottage industry that still thrives. Absolutely nothing was known of the man responsible; letters signed with the name "Jack the Ripper" were probably a sick hoax. What mattered most was the lurid consistency of the crimes: whoever committed them knew how to paint nightly horrors for the morning paper. The interplay between mass media and mass murder settled into an established routine in Victorian London.

Oscar Wilde's trial and humiliation, in 1895, intensified the public's interest in courtroom spectacles, but cases more brutal and common than Wilde's sated that interest in later years. A growing Anglo-American true-crime market absorbed titles like F. Tennyson Jesse's *Murder and Its Motives* (1924), Edmund Pearson's *Studies in Murder* (1924), and William Roughead's *Malice Domestic* (1928). Roughead, a Scots criminal historian, boasted a distinguished readership that included Joseph Conrad and Henry James. That these courtroom procedurals satisfied a particular kind of craving was borne out by nearly identical fan letters Roughead had received from his famous admirers: "I haven't sat down yet properly to the feast, but am looking forward to it. I know the taste of some of your dishes" (Conrad); "I devoured the tender Blandy [a female poisoner] in a single feast; I thank you most kindly for having anticipated so handsomely my appetite" (James).

William Bolitho's *Murder for Profit* (1926) surveys the field of violent crime from a loftier vantage point. This serial biography of five notorious murderers owes its extravagant, sometimes supercilious style to an older generation but also sounds rather modern in its weary suspicion of psychiatric nostrums. Bolitho was a South African journalist who earned modest fame in the twenties, before dying from appendicitis. His sardonic attacks on Fascism undercut some intellectuals' early admiration for Mussolini—notably Hemingway's. The criminal protagonists of *Murder for Profit* are painted with De Quinceyan relish, but there is also deadly scorn for the penitentiaries that bred them, the neighbors who overlooked them, the legal pedants who wrangled over their mental state, and the mob that applauded their ultimate destruction. The final chapter is a devastating account of the crimes and times of Fritz Haarmann, who killed several dozen adolescent boys in Weimar Germany while working as a police informer. Bolitho's apocalyptic vision of mass murder serving a murderous state is curiously prescient.

Such grandiose cynicism went out of fashion after the Second World War. A scary rise in the crime rate seemed to push writers toward a more earnest exploration of individual cases. *In Cold Blood,* Truman Capote's prose reënactment of the random slaughter of a Kansas family, began a new wave in true crime: the book-length investigation of an archetypal tragedy, observed with a flat analytic gaze and reported in exhaustive detail. Two of Capote's techniques have been much imitated: first, the habit of factual embroiderment, which he justified by calling his book a "nonfiction novel"; second, the narrative of childhood trauma and discontent, which ultimately renders the two young killers as sympathetic subjects. Like Norman Mailer after him, Capote wanted to apply shocks of real-life violence while retaining the novelist's right to dissect the psyche. But the docudrama style, impressive in the hands of its originators, has had a dubious fallout in contemporary crime literature and tabloid television, where it often smacks of either poverty of invention or disrespect for the dead. Rhapsodies of criminal psychology, delving into shady, half-imagined mental zones, raise a similar discomfort. However sober-minded their medical sources, they carry a poisonous trace of fantasy and titillation.

Helter Skelter, the perennial true-crime best-seller, is a peculiarly satisfying hybrid of the genre, because it mixes Capote's total immersion with Bolitho's lordly contempt. Vincent Bugliosi, the legendary Los Angeles district attorney who convicted Charles Manson, tells his own story with an unaffected swagger and treats what he did not see with scrupulous care. The result is a very deft fusion of solid storytelling and prosecutorial ire.

But a different kind of doubt surfaces here: the book's case against Manson is too strong for its own good. Bugliosi faced something less than an open-and-shut case; he had to place Manson's spirit at the two murder scenes from which he had been absent in person. And so the jury was asked to consider Manson's hallucinogenic babblings as cold conspiratorial intent. "Helter Skelter," the Beatles' song about a children's playground slide, became the smoking gun in a vast plot to incite race war and anarchy. Bugliosi aggrandized a savage con man into the arch-conspirator of the age; Manson, naturally, admired him in return. The author deserves thanks for insuring that Manson will undoubtedly never leave jail, but the book that maintains his infamy also maintains his fame.

Most true-crime books now flooding the shelves are simpler and stupider. Some of them carry on the nonfiction-novel techniques that Capote claimed to have pioneered. Others stick to journalistic reportage. The quality of the writing varies enormously, from the tensely stylish to the borderline moronic. If it seems as though a literary pursuit has devolved into a cheap industry, it should be remembered that much of this material has actually moved onward and upward from grisly police-news columns, detective magazines, and other instant literature. What follows is an unsystematic anatomy of the genre's current traits and tics, virtues and sins, absurdities and accidental truths.

Fatal Death. Titles speak volumes. Earlier in the century, true-crime titles still echoed the high facetious tone of De Quincey's "On Murder Considered as One of the Fine Arts." William Roughead's popular crime anthologies were given titles like *Reprobates Reviewed, Rascals Revived,* and *Tales of the Criminous.* Joe McGinniss's *Fatal Vision* (1983) started a fashion for sullen, solemn two-word formulas. Now true-crime titles seem to be pounded out by the same wordsmiths who baptize straight-to-video movies starring Corey Haim. The St. Martin's True Crime Library, easily identifiable by the bloody handprint on the spine, offers *Lethal Lolita, Bad Blood,* and *Unanswered Cries.* One recent presentation brings you up to date on those two English boys who kidnapped and killed a toddler. David James Smith's book was originally published in England as *The Sleep of Reason.* The heavy allusion to Rousseau ("childhood is the sleep of reason") was apparently considered too much for tender American minds, for they got *Beyond All Reason* in hardback and *Fatal Innocence* in paperback.

It was a dark and eerie night. True crime likes to zoom in slowly and incrementally on the fatal scene. *Helter Skelter* begins, "It was so quiet, one of the killers would later say, you could almost hear the sound of ice rattling in cocktail shakers in the homes way down the canyon." Tim Cahill's voyage inside the mind of John Wayne Gacy, *Buried Dreams,* starts with this: "One of the neighbors was wakened from her sleep by screams in the night: faint, high-pitched screams that drifted across the neatly mowed lawns and seemed to come from the house beyond a hedge she could see from her back door." (The elegance of this sentence resides in the purring suburban blandness of its nouns, except the scream.) Jonathan Coleman's *Exit the Rainmaker,* by contrast, begins in broad daylight: "It was the sort of fine spring morning when you feel the urge to hop into a red convertible, flip on the radio, and drive forever." (True crime does not always deal in horrific violence. *Rainmaker* is the story of a well-liked community-college president who one day simply vanishes from his life, mailing gnomic notes to his family and friends. He commits a sort of bloodless murder of himself, and moves to El Paso.)

Scenery of the crime. One major seduction of the genre is its surrounding décor, its societal bric-a-brac. Like a good episode of *Cops,* these books provide vivid, unexpected cross-sections of daily American life. Violent death has a way of lighting up a workaday environment, setting its ordinariness in bold relief. (Edmund Burke observed that many people are drawn to London's glory only when it catches fire.) But the scene setter should be wary of giving out too much information. Coleman's story of the Rainmaker, after its bracing start, immediately gets lost in statistics: "It was a Wednesday, May 19, 1982. Twenty-five miles south of Washington, D.C., a tall man with china-blue eyes was preparing to leave his twenty-three-room Georgian house shortly before eight." Just because Coleman wrote it down in his little notebook doesn't mean that we need to read it. Jack Olsen's *Charmer,* the tale of a man who picks up women in singles bars and kills them, contains this intoxicating evocation of a typical night out: "Women emitted clouds of pheromones while demurely nursing five-dollar drinks like Sex on the Beach, made of peach schnapps, vodka, cranberry, and orange juice; Smith & Wesson, a blend of Kahlúa, Coke, vodka and cream; and Electric Watermelon, made of vodka, sweet-and-sour mix, 7-Up and the melon liqueur Midori." Only Bret Easton Ellis is allowed to write sentences like that.

The fiend in our midst. The invisibility of the higher class of killer—John Wayne Gacy, well-liked organizer of the Polish Day parade in Chicago; Charles Manson, wacky pal of L.A. rock stars—relies heavily on the blissful inattention of the general public. Amateur detectives, professional hysterics, and mindless crowds are always ready to run down scapegoats (the Polish Jew who was hounded in the Jack the Ripper case, for example), but they habitually overlook the lunatics next door. True crime is plentifully stocked with neighbors who hear gunshots and go back to sleep (Manson), accept a "bad meat" explanation for a terrible stench (Dahmer), smile good morning at someone carrying a bucket of blood downstairs (Haarmann), and share books on ominous subjects ("He borrowed my books on Ted Bundy and Charles Manson and didn't return them," complains the killer's roommate in *Charmer*). These all-unseeing, all-unknowing neighbors are often harshly judged by true-crime writers; Bolitho accuses them of "corporate stupidity," even of unconscious complicity in the crimes. Here, perhaps, he judges too much: after all, a sound relationship with one's neighbors depends on a careful balance of knowledge and ignorance, and the kind of mind that would readily believe in a serial killer living next door does not rest easily at night.

Victims. Every few days, someone covering the O. J. Simpson case would murmur, "Overlooked in all this is the other victim, Ron Goldman"; then, for seven-tenths of a second, we would see footage of Goldman modelling menswear or appearing as a contestant on "Studs." This had the effect of saying, "Let's take a moment to overlook Ron Goldman." All crime stories have trouble recovering respect for the dead. Brief biographical sketches of the victims, written to ease a guilty conscience and heighten suspense, do not suffice. William Bolitho, averse to all hypocrisy, openly derided his killers' targets, as in this telegraphic description of a Fritz Haarmann victim: "Wilhelm Apel, aged 16. A dreamy, romantic schoolboy. His father reproached him with cigarette-smoking; he did not come home." A new book by the prolific true-crime writer Jack Olsen indicates a recent trend toward sharpened sensitivity. His *Salt of the Earth* is a clumsily affecting nonfiction saga whose victims dominate the plot. Olsen writes of a family struggling to overcome the terrible legacy of violent crime, and he makes sure the murderous stranger who precipitates the principal catastrophe remains a dim, marginal presence. Set in bleak California and Pacific Northwest landscapes, the book has the makings of grand pathos. If only it didn't contain sentences like this: "The cronies were as close as twins and combined muscle and strength with hearts of mush."

What on earth were they thinking? One early voyage inside a killer's mind was George Crabbe's poem about the sadistic fisherman Peter Grimes, which attempted to show how "a man of feeling so dull should yet become insane, should be of so horrible a nature." The mental stumble from dullness into horror does not always generate great poetry, or even intelligible prose, but it remains one of the chief lures of true crime. Writers long to show not only the lurid particulars of a diseased mind but also the general type of mind inclined to murder: and so they help themselves to vague descriptive categories or "profiles" fashionable in criminal psychology. Tim Cahill's *Buried Dreams* wallows for many pages in John Wayne Gacy's suspiciously elaborate account of his own multiple-personality disorder. Even if it were genuine, the disorder would fail to explain why any one personality took the leap into violence. The search for a definite "criminal type" has advanced very little since the days of the criminologist Cesare Lombroso, who argued that madmen can be recognized by the shape of their skulls.

Detectives. These cases are often ones in which an unspectacular intellect has managed to elude capture by disposing of people no one cares about, like prostitutes or male hustlers. The killer is usually caught by accident, if at all, when a routine investigation stumbles upon horror. Nonetheless, authors make working-class heroes of the homicide detectives, cartoonishly antithetical to the monsters they track. "Albert worked with men who were very strong practising Christians," David James Smith writes of one police angel. "He was not obligated to go to work that Sunday but, Albert being Albert, it was the kind of thing he'd do." In Olsen's *Salt of the Earth,* the detective Tom Pszonka is "on a personal crusade to jail every criminal in the Pacific Northwest," and has "already dispatched one with a single shot." (It's a fine marksman who can jail a criminal with a single shot.) Two other officers are, reassuringly, "family men with a special abhorrence of pedophiles."

The butler did it. A growing subgenre of true crime is devoted to the reopening of famous murder cases, recent or ancient: the murders ascribed to Richard III, the possible poisoning of Napoleon, even the circumstances surrounding the stabbing of Christopher Marlowe. Some of these writers avail themselves of apparent advances in the science of forensics. Hugh Thomas's *The Murder of Adolf Hitler* microscopically analyzes the dental records and photographed remains of Hitler, Eva Braun, and other Nazis. It concludes that Hitler was strangled by his valet, and that Eva escaped alive, leaving a corpse dressed up as her own, with an insertion of fake dental work. Some of the initial dental inferences seem plausible, but an elementary scientific principle has been ignored in the development of the final hypothesis: when several explanations seem to fit the facts, it is wise to choose the simplest, most elegant solution, and not one that is tortuous, counterintuitive, and harebrained. (Having speculated that Eva Braun escaped alive, Thomas shows amazingly little curiosity about what then became of her.) But the field has seen a recent counterrevolution: various representatives of a New Levelheadedness are announcing with great fanfare that the obvious is true. Vincent Bugliosi's latest prosecutorial bestseller, *Outrage,* is a bombastic but thoroughly persuasive argument for O. J. Simpson's guilt. Bugliosi is also working on a book about the J. F. K. assassination, fingering Lee Harvey Oswald. Gerald Posner made the same daring case in "Case Closed," while Jim Fisher once again convicted Bruno Hauptmann in *The Lindbergh Case.*

Young-adult true crime. Another subgenre of true crime links up with the punkish subculture of aestheticized violence—the friendly folks who have given us coffee-table books of autopsy photographs, exhibitions of paintings by John Wayne Gacy, serial-killer trading cards, Amok Books in Los Angeles, certain novels of Bret Easton Ellis and Dennis Cooper, a Manson composition sung by Axl Rose, the pretentious gore of movies like

Seven, and so on. Though this brand of murder chic worries many, it usually amounts to little more than an adolescent urge to consternate the elders. One undelightful release from St. Martin's Press explores the world of the Wisconsin killer Ed Gein, who was the inspiration for *Psycho* and *The Silence of the Lambs.* An address for the Ed Gein Fan Club's merchandising department is appended in the back, along with an annotated rock-and-roll discography. The author writes sunnily of one Gein-influenced band: "Macabre are so monomaniacally obsessed with death, so cartoonishly nihilistic, you just know they've got to be having fun."

Books don't kill people, readers do. The question of a cultural incentive to murder, brought to full boil by Bob Dole last summer, has been simmering for centuries. Gilles de Rais, a comrade of Joan of Arc's who went mad and turned his castle into a slaughterhouse of kidnapped children, read Suetonius's *Twelve Caesars* and took inspiration from the bloody experiments of Caligula. It seems that some crimes are so ghastly that we can hardly conceive of people inventing them out of thin air, and conclude that they must have gotten their ideas from somewhere. The English had a debate on the subject of evil books thirty years ago, at the time of the still infamous Moors murders. Here there was little question that the particularly horrid Ian Brady, killer of three, had made a close study of some works in his library—most notably *Justine,* by the Marquis de Sade. He was also an avid filmgoer, and styled himself after Harry Lime in *The Third Man.* Conservatives contemplated banning *Justine* but not *The Third Man.*

Bully pulpit. The lust to kill is often accompanied by an urge to use the media as a captive audience for eccentric intellectual and religious pronouncements. The Unabomber is only the most recent and verbose example. But the question of a murderer's oratory acquires a very different significance when words themselves become the weapon. Like Professor Moriarty, and like the killer in Agatha Christie's *Curtain,* Charles Manson talked others into killing for him. The problem of homicidal speech is also at the core of the case of Joe Hunt, the mastermind of the Billionaire Boys Club. As a huge, mesmerizing new book by Randall Sullivan (*The Price of Experience*) makes clear, Hunt is a peculiarly odious phenomenon: a sleek amoralist who convinced his rich, feckless preppie pals to slide from financial scams into cold-blooded murder under the spell of sub-Nietzschean philosophizing. He was not so clever as to avoid some obvious mistakes—he drafted a plan for the perfect crime, then left it at the scene—but he also managed to get all the charges in his second murder trial dismissed. Conducting his own defense, he stumped lawyers and charmed jurors. In some ways he is worse than Dahmer or Bundy, for his corruption is still spreading.

Why do they write this stuff? Ostentatiously, true-crime writers suppress fears that their work reveals a fundamentally morbid frame of mind. Robert Ressler, the F. B. I. psychologist who coined the phrase "serial killer," gives his memoirs the ambitious title *Whoever Fights Monsters,* alluding to Nietzsche's famous quip "Whoever fights monsters should see to it that in the process he does not become a monster." Needless to say, Ressler lets no abyss look into him. On this same question, Emlyn Williams, a chronicler of the Moors murders, defensively asks, "Who expects savor from a story of noisome evil?" No right-thinking person, except maybe Henry James. "The proper study of mankind is man," Williams ventures further. "And man cannot be ignored because he has become vile. Woman neither." The Ripper expert Philip Sugden hears imaginary voices wondering why he has devoted his life to a destroyer of women. He answers majestically, "Some would have it that those who read or write about the murders are misogynists. I am not a misogynist. Nor, for that matter, is any serious student of the case personally known to me." Well, there you have it! Whether we admit it or not, our motives for reading this material and their motives for writing it are murky and complex. Whoever fights monsters should take care not to turn into a charlatan.

In the end, true crime reveals few useful truths about violence in society. Street crime in the inner city and minority neighborhoods, which accounts for most of the steep rise in homicide rates during the past three decades, figures nowhere in these books. It is true that the isolated, spectacular outbursts of suburban psychosis they like to depict are certifiably on the rise, according to sober statistical studies. But the numbers remain negligible next to the anonymous mass of urban homicides. Serial killers, pedophiles, and the like are the suburbs' heavily overworked bogeymen. We choose to pay attention to them because of their quality, not their quantity. It has often been observed that certain élite criminals develop a close, electric relationship with the media. Peter Kürten, the Vampire of Düsseldorf, told a crowd of journalists after his capture in 1930, "The sensational reports in certain scandal sheets turned me into the man who stands before you today." Manson likes to say the same thing, and in your heart you know he's right.

Is it all evidence of a society gone mad and plunging toward chaos? Perhaps instead it is evidence of a society more and more terminally bored, coddled and protected from real threat, distant from living death. True-crime mayhem is perhaps a lateral reorganization, a consolidation, a downsizing of evil. Never in the history of the great white American suburb has so much murder been committed for so many by so few. The phenomenon is even more visible in England, which has long had astonishingly low homicide rates and astonishingly rich annals of multiple murder. True-crime books are, perhaps, evidence not of growing viciousness but of growing pacifism, of a progressively more relaxed national brain, which needs progressively bigger shocks to seize its attention. The shocks are not events, nor are they media pseudo-events; they are what the French philosopher Jean-François Lyotard calls occurrences—episodes to contradict the deepening suspicion that nothing is actually happening. Occurrences serve to enliven true crime, real life, and fake art. They explode across the screen of one of Quentin Tarantino's movies in order to contradict the suspicion that the actors are merely chattering about old TV shows. Tragedy is comedy plus blood. Violence as art is a last-ditch attempt at the Sublime.

Burke saw it coming. "Chuse a day," he wrote, more than two centuries ago, "on which to represent the most sublime and affecting tragedy we have; appoint the most favourite actors; spare no cost upon the scenes and decorations; unite the greatest efforts of poetry, painting and music; and when you have collected your audience, just at the moment when their minds are erect with expectation, let it be reported that a state of high rank is on the point of being executed in the adjoining square; in a moment the emptiness of the theatre would demonstrate the comparative weakness of the imitative arts, and proclaim the triumph of the real sympathy." True-crime writers endlessly restage that old scene of the public hanging. Their nobler impulse is to insist on the full, world-wrecking reality of violence, the multiple consequences of actions, the fallout of fantasy. But they are caught in a nasty paradox: to the degree that they stay true to their subject, they transcribe a murderer's vision of the world. Notwithstanding all moralistic protests, they have given up the moral advantage. They cannot quite control the sympathy of the milling crowd, which might lie with the executed or with the executioner. They promise the truth, the whole truth: very well, so help us God.

Suggestions for Discussion

1. Explain the meaning of the term "true crime."
2. What "non-fiction novel" techniques did Truman Capote introduce?
3. Explain Ross's emphasis on the "shock of the real."

Suggestion for Writing

Chronicle a "true crime" that you have recently followed.

JAMES WOLCOTT

Reborn on the Fourth of July

James Wolcott, a film critic for *The New Yorker,* analyzes the appeal and achievement of the popular film *Independence Day.*

In Susan Sontag's 1965 essay "The Imagination of Disaster," a standard text in the aesthetics of schlock, she observes that one of the "primitive gratifications" of science-fiction films is "the depiction of urban disaster on a colossally magnified scale." This *Independence Day* delivers, and how. The latest (unacknowledged) remake of H. G. Wells's novel *The War of the Worlds,* it razes more real estate and bowls more fireballs through tunnels than any alien-invasion movie ever. Mass hysteria has never looked more massive or hysterical. But it isn't the size of the blasts that "sells" the movie; it's the iconography of the targets. Instead of incapacitating countries by K.O.'ing hydroelectric dams or utility plants, this alien armada set on conquering Earth leaves the Statue of Liberty face down in the river, and the Empire State Building, which survived King Kong, is blown to bits. The trailer—probably the most successful trailer in movie history—featured what they call in porno the movie's "money shot": the White House itself exploding.

More than just a big summer movie, *Independence Day* is a mega metaphenomenon—a pseudo event in which the audience prides itself on being part of the hype. You not only enjoy the movie, you enjoy yourself enjoying the movie, which is sprinkled with cute pop-cult references to *Top Gun, Lawrence of Arabia, The X-Files, Alien, 2001: A Space Odyssey, Dr. Strangelove, E. T., Star Wars,* and *Close Encounters of the Third Kind.* What makes the movie "meta" is not only its self-awareness but the fact that it doesn't mean anything beyond itself. Other alien-invasion films tapped into nocturnal anxieties about nuclear doom (*The Day the Earth Stood Still*), soulless conformity (*Invasion of the Body Snatchers*), the bogeyman (*The Thing*). *Independence Day* has no subtext. It's all *uber*text.

Unlike so many current action films, this one isn't a frantic narrative jumble. It's structured like a classic three-act play, each day representing an act: July 2nd–arrival; July 3rd–aftermath; July 4th–counterattack. The first intimation that company's coming—a shadow crossing the stiff American flag planted on the moon—has a ceremonial majesty rare in this kind of expensive junk. And the flag is relevant. In the original *War of the Worlds,* published in 1898, England was the battleground of the Martian attack. But this has been the American century, America is the only superpower now, and an attack on Earth becomes ipso facto an attack on the American way (our cars, our cheeseburgers). Americans take their heritage so much for granted that perhaps only a non-native can fake the fervor of defending the homeland. Born and raised in Germany, the film's director, Roland Emmerich, pictures America through the lens of an awe-struck tourist: postcard images of the Iwo Jima memorial and the Statue of Liberty depict an idealism so intact, a country bathed in such bountiful light, that the effect is ironic, enshrining, like Steven Spielberg's making the suburban tract in *E. T.* look like the little town of Bethlehem. The spaceships first enter the earth's atmosphere in a Biblical cloud of fire, and a shadow creeps up the seated figure of Abraham Lincoln on his marble throne as darkness eclipses the skylines of New York, Los Angeles, etc. The spaceships themselves are city-size disks—cities poised above cities, with a strip of sky sandwiched between.

Meanwhile, the free world fidgets. As President Whitmore, Bill Pullman deploys a politician's smile so "sincere" that it seems to be hurting his fillings. Like Michael Douglas in *The American President,* Pullman has neoliberal hair and a lightweight demeanor. President Whitmore is clearly intended to be a Clintonesque figure—young, vital, empathetic, and dogged by leadership doubts. A fighter pilot in the Gulf War, Whitmore is accused of being a gutless wonder in office. When he addresses the nation, expressing the hope that these Darth Vader spheroids have come in peace, he doesn't invite them to the next G7 summit, but that's the general drift. Then, as he learns of their evil intentions, he urges a calm, orderly withdrawal from the cities (translation: *Run for your lives!*). Escaping from the burning capital on Air Force One, the President clenches his jaw. These goons from another galaxy have finally got on the fighting side of him. Forget the idea that the country is in flabby decline: the populist message of *Independence Day* is that America is still a scrappy, defiant, can-do country; the spirit of 1776 lies dormant in our collective genes. The President himself, proud, determined, and mourning his dead wife (Mary McDonnell) for what seems like all of two minutes, straps on a helmet and takes to the air to lead the freedom forces. There's no dramatic ploy too shameless for this movie to try.

When Sontag deplored the "moral simplification" of sci-fi films, she couldn't have anticipated how much hip flair a square format would accommodate in the postmodern era. *Independence Day,* lingering over wedding bands and service uniforms, honoring duty, patriotism, and the power of prayer ("I haven't spoken to God since your mother died," one character apologizes), is so red-blooded and true-blue retro macho that it becomes a vague put-on, italicizing the attitudes it promotes until they seem unreal. Unreal, but not absurd: the movie makes it clear that, at crunch time, only do-gooders can get the job done. As in *Forrest Gump,* where Boy Scout virtues took on a beatitude through Tom Hanks's carefully folded-in performance, the counterculture is portrayed here as a pagan tribe of silly, deluded deadbeats. With a spaceship hovering over Los Angeles, assorted hippies, U. F. O. buffs, and hedonists welcome the aliens by turning a high-rise rooftop into an open-air club and partying like it's 1999. When the bottom hatch of the ship begins to open, emitting blue light, the revellers cup their faces upward like the cosmic beholders in *Close Encounters*—only to be obliterated by the death ray. Foolish earthlings!

Every alien-invasion movie features a high-level conference of politicians, scientists, and military hotheads bickering over strategy as the news from outside grows ever grimmer. ("They've taken out Seattle, sir.") Here the role of scientist is assumed by Jeff Goldblum, reprising his geek elegance from *Jurassic Park* and *The Fly*: he adjusts his glasses like a true thinker. As Goldblum's father, Judd Hirsch overplays as ripely as Goldblum underplays, shuffling across the screen like an old man making his way to the bathroom, and doing lovable-cranky, clogged-artery Jewish shtick. Military derring-do is exemplified by Will Smith, TV's *Fresh Prince,* as a Marine fighter pilot who captures the first alien with a punch to the head (*thump:* "Welcome to Earth"). The brother has no fear. When Smith and Goldblum share a spacecraft on a near-suicide mission to the alien mother ship, wisecracking in the face of extinction, they show how the soldier and the scientist—and, more important, the black and the Jew—can bond; they're the Cornel West and Michael Lerner of extraterrestrial *tikkun.* (Also bucking for glory is Randy Quaid, making Popeye faces as an alien abductee looking for payback.)

Like so many productions, *Independence Day* has third-act problems. The pace drags. The dogfights between the tattered air force of the allies and the alien fighters become a confusing swarm of gnats. The movie, lacking any brainstorms of its own, mimics *War of the Worlds* to the very end. In Wells's novel, the Martians fall prey to infection, their immune systems laid waste by bacterial strains long assimilated by humankind but new to them; in *Independence Day,* it's a *computer* virus that proves their undoing. The difference between these two wars of the worlds is in the emotional aftereffects. The narrator in Wells's novel staggers through a deathscape in which piles of Martians are beset by birds and dogs in a blackened pit. At the end of *Independence Day,* millions are dead, entire cities are destroyed, spaceships smolder like downed zeppelins (nice shot of one banked behind the pyramids), nuclear detonations have released radioactive fallout—and the battered survivors stand around grinning as if they'd just won a volleyball game. They couldn't be more gee-whiz. There's no weight to what has happened—no hint of hard, scavenger times ahead. Only Hollywood in the nineties could arrange such a pain-free, upbeat Armageddon.

Suggestions for Discussion

1. How does *Independence Day* depict "urban disaster on a colossally magnified scale"?
2. Discuss the structure of *Independence Day* as a classic three-act play.

Suggestions for Writing

1. Analyze a popular science fiction film of your choice.
2. Compare *Independence Day* with *The War of the Worlds* by H. G. Wells.
3. Review one of the other science fiction films discussed in Wolcott's essay.

The Cultural Tradition: Art and Society

The memory is a living thing—it too is in transit. But during its moment, all that is remembered joins, and lives—the old and the young, the past and the present, the living and the dead.

—EUDORA WELTY, "Finding a Voice"

In this sense fiction became the agency of my efforts to answer the questions, Who am I, what am I, how did I come to be? What shall I make of the life around me, what celebrate, what reject, how confront the snarl of good and evil which is inevitable?

—RALPH ELLISON, "On Becoming a Writer"

Works of art, in my opinion, are the only objects in the material universe to possess internal order, and that is why, though I don't believe that only art matters, I do believe in Art for Art's sake.

—E. M. FORSTER, "Art for Art's Sake"

PERSONAL REMINISCENCES

EUDORA WELTY

Finding a Voice

Eudora Welty (b. 1909), the preeminent Southern novelist and short story writer, has published *Delta Wedding* (1946); *Losing Battles* (1970); *The Optimist's Daughter* (1972), for which she won the Pulitzer Prize; *Collected Stories* (1980); and *Eudora Welty's Photographs* (1989). She was awarded the Presidential Medal of Freedom in 1980 and the National Medal of Arts in 1987. In the following excerpt from her reminiscence, *One Writer's Beginnings* (1985), she explores the source of one of the characters she has created.

What discoveries I've made in the course of writing stories all begin with the particular, never the general. They are mostly hindsight: arrows that I now find I myself have left behind me, which have shown me some right, or wrong, way I have come. What one story may have pointed out to me is of no avail in the writing of another. But "avail" is not what I want; freedom ahead is what each story promises—beginning anew. And all the while, as further hindsight has told me, certain patterns in my work repeat themselves without my realizing. There would be no way to know this, for during the writing of any single story, there is no other existing. Each writer must find out for himself, I imagine, on what strange basis he lives with his own stories.

I had been writing a number of stories, more or less one after the other, before it belatedly dawned on me that some of the characters in one story were, and had been all the time, the same characters who had appeared already in another story. Only I'd written about them originally under different names, at different periods in their lives, in situations not yet interlocking but ready for it. They touched on every side. These stories were all related (and the fact was buried in their inceptions) by the strongest ties—identities, kinships, relationships, or affinities already known or remembered or foreshadowed. From story to story, connections between the characters' lives, through their motives or actions, sometimes their dreams, already existed: there to be found. Now the whole assembly—

some of it still in the future—fell, by stages, into place in one location already evoked, which I saw now was a focusing point for all the stories. What had drawn the characters together there was one strong strand in them all: they lived in one way or another in a dream or in romantic aspiration, or under an illusion of what their lives were coming to, about the meaning of their (now) related lives.

The stories were connected most provocatively of all to me, perhaps, through the entry into my story-telling mind of another sort of tie—a shadowing of Greek mythological figures, gods and heroes that wander in various guises, at various times, in and out, emblems of the characters' heady dreams.

Writing these stories, which eventually appeared joined together in the book called *The Golden Apples,* was an experience in a writer's own discovery of affinities. In writing, as in life, the connections of all sorts of relationships and kinds lie in wait of discovery, and give out their signals to the Geiger counter of the charged imagination, once it is drawn into the right field.

The characters who go to make up my stories and novels are not portraits. Characters I invent along with the story that carries them. Attached to them are what I've borrowed, perhaps unconsciously, bit by bit, of persons I have seen or noticed or remembered in the flesh—a cast of countenance here, a manner of walking there, that jump to the visualizing mind when a story is underway. (Elizabeth Bowen said, "Physical detail cannot be invented." It can only be chosen.) I don't write by invasion into the life of a real person: my own sense of privacy is too strong for that; and I also know instinctively that living people to whom you are close—those known to you in ways too deep, too overflowing, ever to be plumbed outside love—do not yield to, could never fit into, the demands of a story. On the other hand, what I do make my stories out of is the *whole* fund of my feelings, my responses to the real experiences of my own life, to the relationships that formed and changed it, that I have given most of myself to, and so learned my way toward a dramatic counterpart. Characters take on life sometimes by luck, but I suspect it is when you can write most entirely out of yourself, inside the skin, heart, mind, and soul of a person who is not yourself, that a character becomes in his own right another human being on the page.

It was not my intention—it never was—to invent a character who should speak for me, the author, in person. A character is in a story to fill a role there, and the character's life along with its expression of life is defined by that surrounding—indeed is created by his own story. Yet, it seems to me now, years after I wrote *The Golden Apples,* that I did bring forth a character with whom I came to feel oddly in touch. This is Miss Eckhart, a woman who has come from away to give piano lessons to the young of

Morgana. She is formidable and eccentric in the eyes of everyone, is scarcely accepted in the town. But she persisted with me, as she persisted in spite of herself with the other characters in the stories.

Where did the character of Miss Eckhart come from? There was my own real-life piano teacher, "eligible" to the extent that she swatted my hands at the keyboard with a fly-swatter if I made a mistake; and when she wrote "Practice" on my page of sheet music she made her "P" as Miss Eckhart did—a cat's face with a long tail. She did indeed hold a recital of her pupils every June that was a fair model for Miss Eckhart's, and of many another as well, I suppose. But the character of Miss Eckhart was miles away from that of the teacher I knew as a child, or from that of anybody I did know. Nor was she like other teacher-characters I was responsible for: my stories and novels suddenly appear to me to be full of teachers, with Miss Eckhart different from them all.

What the story "June Recital" most acutely shows the reader lies in her inner life. I haven't the slightest idea what my real teacher's life was like inside. But I knew what Miss Eckhart's was, for it protruded itself well enough into the story.

As I looked longer and longer for the origins of this passionate and strange character, at last I realized that Miss Eckhart came from me. There wasn't any resemblance in her outward identity: I am not musical, not a teacher, nor foreign in birth; not humorless or ridiculed or missing out in love; nor have I yet let the world around me slip from my recognition. But none of that counts. What counts is only what lies at the solitary core. She derived from what I already knew for myself, even felt I had always known. What I have put into her is my passion for my own life work, my own art. Exposing yourself to risk is a truth Miss Eckhart and I had in common. What animates and possesses me is what drives Miss Eckhart, the love of her art and the love of giving it, the desire to give it until there is no more left. Even in the small and literal way, what I had done in assembling and connecting all the stories in *The Golden Apples*, and bringing them off as one, was not too unlike the June recital itself.

Not in Miss Eckhart as she stands solidly and almost opaquely in the surround of her story, but in the making of her character out of my most inward and most deeply feeling self, I would say I have found my voice in my fiction.

Of course any writer is in part all of his characters. How otherwise would they be known to him, occur to him, become what they are? I was also part Cassie in that same story, the girl who hung back, and indeed part of most of the main characters in the connected stories into whose minds I go. Except for Virgie, the heroine. She is right outside me. She is powerfully like Miss Eckhart, her co-equal in stubborn and passionate feeling, while more expressive of it—but fully apart from me. And as Miss Eckhart's powers shrink and fade away, the young Virgie grows up more rampant, and struggles into some sort of life independent from all the rest.

If somewhere in its course your work seems to you to have come into a life of its own, and you can stand back from it and leave it be, you are looking then at your subject—so I feel. This is how I came to regard the character of Virgie in *The Golden Apples.* She comes into her own in the last of the stories, "The Wanderers." Passionate, recalcitrant, stubbornly undefeated by failure or hurt or disgrace or bereavement, all the while heedlessly wasting of her gifts, she knows to the last that there is a world that remains out there, a world living and mysterious, and that she is of it.

Inasmuch as Miss Eckhart might have been said to come from me, the author, Virgie, at her moments, might have always been my subject.

Through learning at my later date things I hadn't known, or had escaped or possibly feared realizing, about my parents—and myself—I glimpse our whole family life as if it were freed of that clock time which spaces us apart so inhibitingly, divides young and old, keeps our living through the same experiences at separate distances.

It is our inward journey that leads us through time—forward or back, seldom in a straight line, most often spiraling. Each of us is moving, changing, with respect to others. As we discover, we remember; remembering, we discover; and most intensely do we experience this when our separate journeys converge. Our living experience at those meeting points is one of the charged dramatic fields of fiction.

I'm prepared now to use the wonderful word *confluence,* which of itself exists as a reality and a symbol in one. It is the only kind of symbol that for me as a writer has any weight, testifying to the pattern, one of the chief patterns, of human experience.

Here I am leading to the last scenes in my novel, *The Optimist's Daughter:*

> She had slept in the chair, like a passenger who had come on an emergency journey in a train. But she had rested deeply.
>
> She had dreamed that she *was* a passenger, and riding with Phil. They had ridden together over a long bridge.
>
> Awake, she recognized it: it was a dream of something that had really happened. When she and Phil were coming down from Chicago to Mount Salus to be married in the Presbyterian Church, they came on the train. Laurel, when she travelled back and forth between Mount Salus and Chicago, had always taken the sleeper. She and Phil followed the route on the day train, and she saw it for the first time.
>
> When they were climbing the long approach to a bridge after leaving Cairo, rising slowly higher until they rode above the tops of bare trees, she looked down and saw the pale light widening and the river bottoms opening out, and then the water appearing, reflecting the low, early sun. There were

two rivers. Here was where they came together. This was the confluence of the waters, the Ohio and the Mississippi.

They were looking down from a great elevation and all they saw was at the point of coming together, the bare trees marching in from the horizon, the rivers moving into one, and as he touched her arm she looked up with him and saw the long, ragged, pencil-faint line of birds within the crystal of the zenith, flying in a V of their own, following the same course down. All they could see was sky, water, birds, light, and confluence. It was the whole morning world.

And they themselves were a part of the confluence. Their own joint act of faith had brought them here at the very moment and matched its occurrence, and proceeded as it proceeded. Direction itself was made beautiful, momentous. They were riding as one with it, right up front. It's our turn! she'd thought exultantly. And we're going to live forever.

Left bodiless and graveless of a death made of water and fire in a year long gone, Phil could still tell her of her life. For her life, any life, she had to believe, was nothing but the continuity of its love.

She believed it just as she believed that the confluence of the waters was still happening at Cairo. It would be there the same as it ever was when she went flying over it today on her way back—out of sight, for her, this time, thousands of feet below, but with nothing in between except thin air.

Of course the greatest confluence of all is that which makes up the human memory—the individual human memory. My own is the treasure most dearly regarded by me, in my life and in my work as a writer. Here time, also, is subject to confluence. The memory is a living thing—it too is in transit. But during its moment, all that is remembered joins, and lives—the old and the young, the past and the present, the living and the dead.

As you have seen, I am a writer who came of a sheltered life. A sheltered life can be a daring life as well. For all serious daring starts from within.

Suggestions for Discussion

1. Discuss her observation that the "characters who go to make up my stories and novels are not portraits. Characters I invent along with the story that carries them."
2. Why did she "come in touch" with the character of Miss Eckhart?
3. Explain her use of the word *confluence.*

Suggestions for Writing

1. Document her observation that "each of us is moving, changing, with respect to others."
2. Use your memory to recreate a scene or character of significance.

RALPH ELLISON

On Becoming a Writer

Ralph Ellison (1914–1994), the distinguished American writer, was born in Oklahoma City. In the 1930s he was a student at the Tuskegee Institute, which granted him an honorary Ph.D. in Human Letters in 1963. He held honorary degrees from other American universities and has been a visiting professor of writing in many of them. He was Emeritus Professor of English at New York University. He is best known for *The Invisible Man* (1952). His other works include *Going to the Territory* (1986) and *Shadow and Act* (1964), a collection of essays from which is taken the following reminiscence of becoming aware of what it means to be an "American Negro."

In the beginning writing was far from a serious matter; it was a reflex of reading, an extension of a source of pleasure, escape, and instruction. In fact, I had become curious about writing by way of seeking to understand the aesthetic nature of literary power, the devices through which literature could command my mind and emotions. It was not, then, the *process* of writing which initially claimed my attention, but the finished creations, the artifacts, poems, plays, novels. The act of learning writing technique was, therefore, an amusing investigation of what seemed at best a secondary talent, an exploration, like dabbling in sculpture, of one's potentialities as a "Renaissance Man." This, surely, would seem a most unlikely and even comic concept to introduce here; and yet, it is precisely because I come from where I do (the Oklahoma of the years between World War I and the Great Depression) that I must introduce it, and with a straight face.

Anything and everything was to be found in the chaos of Oklahoma; thus the concept of the Renaissance Man has lurked long within the shadow of my past, and I shared it with at least a half dozen of my Negro friends. How we actually acquired it I have never learned, and since there is no true sociology of the dispersion of ideas within the American democracy, I doubt if I ever shall. Perhaps we breathed it in with the air of the Negro community of Oklahoma City, the capital of that state whose Negroes were often charged by exasperated white Texans with not knowing their "place." Perhaps we took it defiantly from one of them. Or perhaps I myself picked it up from some transplanted New Englander whose shoes I had shined on a Saturday afternoon. After all, the most meaningful tips do not always come in the form of money, nor are they intentionally extended. Most likely, however, my friends and I acquired the idea from some book or some idealistic Negro teacher, some dreamer seeking to function responsibly in an environment which at its most normal took on some of the mixed character of nightmare and of dream.

One thing is certain, ours was a chaotic community, still characterized by frontier attitudes and by that strange mixture of the naive and sophisticated, the benign and malignant, which makes the American past so puzzling and its present so confusing; that mixture which often affords the minds of the young who grow up in the far provinces such wide and unstructured latitude, and which encourages the individual's imagination—up to the moment "reality" closes in upon him—to range widely and, sometimes, even to soar.

We hear the effects of this in the Southwestern jazz of the 30's, that joint creation of artistically free and exuberantly creative adventurers, of artists who had stumbled upon the freedom lying within the restrictions of their musical tradition as within the limitations of their social background, and who in their own unconscious way have set an example for any Americans, Negro or white, who would find themselves in the arts. They accepted themselves and the complexity of life as they knew it, they loved their art and through it they celebrated American experience definitively in sound. Whatever others thought or felt, this was their own powerful statement, and only non-musical assaults upon their artistic integrity—mainly economically inspired changes of fashion—were able to compromise their vision.

Much of so-called Kansas City jazz was actually brought to perfection in Oklahoma by Oklahomans. It is an important circumstance for me as a writer to remember, because while these musicians and their fellows were busy creating out of tradition, imagination, and the sounds and emotions around them, a freer, more complex, and driving form of jazz, my friends and I were exploring an idea of human versatility and possibility which went against the barbs or over the palings of almost every fence which those who controlled social and political power had erected to restrict our roles in the life of the country. Looking back, one might say that the jazzmen, some of whom we idolized, were in their own way better examples for youth to follow than were most judges and ministers, legislators and governors (we were stuck with the notorious Alfalfa Bill Murray). For as we viewed these pillars of society from the confines of our segregated community we almost always saw crooks, clowns, or hypocrites. Even the best were revealed by their attitudes toward us as lacking the respectable qualities to which they pretended and for which they were accepted outside by others, while despite the outlaw nature of their art, the jazzmen were less torn and damaged by the moral compromises and insincerities which have so sickened the life of our country.

Be that as it may, our youthful sense of life, like that of many Negro children (though no one bothers to note it—especially the specialists and "friends of the Negro" who view our Negro-American life as essentially nonhuman) was very much like that of Huckleberry Finn, who is universally so praised and enjoyed for the clarity and courage of his moral vision. Like Huck, we observed, we judged, we imitated and evaded as we could the dullness, corruption, and blindness of "civilization." We were undoubtedly comic because, as the saying goes, we weren't supposed to know what it was all about. But to ourselves we were "boys," members of a wild, free, outlaw tribe which transcended the category of race. Rather we were Americans born into the forty-sixth state, and thus, into the context of Negro-American post–Civil War history, "frontiersmen." And isn't one of the implicit functions of the American frontier to encourage the individual to a kind of dreamy wakefulness, a state in which he makes—in all ignorance of the accepted limitations of the possible—rash efforts, quixotic gestures, hopeful testings of the complexity of the known and the given?

Spurring us on in our controlled and benign madness was the voracious reading of which most of us were guilty and the vicarious identification and empathetic adventuring which it encouraged. This was due, in part, perhaps to the fact that some of us were fatherless—my own father had died when I was three—but most likely it was because boys are natural romantics. We were seeking examples, patterns to live by, out of a freedom which for all its being ignored by the sociologists and subtle thinkers, was implicit in the Negro situation. Father and mother substitutes also have a role to play in aiding the child to help create himself. Thus we fabricated our own heroes and ideals catch-as-catch-can; and with an outrageous and irreverent sense of freedom. Yes, and in complete disregard of ideas of respectability or the surreal incongruity of some of our projections. Gamblers and scholars, jazz musicians and scientists, Negro cowboys and soldiers from the Spanish-American and First World Wars, movie stars and stunt men, figures from the Italian Renaissance and literature, both classical and popular, were combined with the special virtues of some local bootlegger, the eloquence of some Negro preacher, the strength and grace of some local athlete, the ruthlessness of some businessman-physician, the elegance in dress and manners of some head-waiter or hotel doorman.

Looking back through the shadows upon this absurd activity, I realize now that we were projecting archetypes, recreating folk figures, legendary heroes, monsters even, most of which violated all ideas of social hierarchy and order and all accepted conceptions of the hero handed down by cultural, religious, and racist tradition. But we, remember, were under the intense spell of the early movies, the silents as well as the talkies; and in our community, life was not so tightly structured as it would have been in the traditional South—or even in deceptively "free" Harlem. And our imaginations processed reality and dream, natural man and traditional hero, literature and folklore, like maniacal editors turned loose in some frantic film-cutting room. Remember, too, that being boys, yet in the play-stage of our development, we were dream-serious in our efforts. But serious nevertheless, for *culturally* play is a preparation, and we felt that somehow the human ideal lay in the vague and constantly shifting figures—sometimes comic but always versatile, picaresque, and self-effacingly heroic—which evolved from our wildly improvisatory projections: figures neither white nor black, Christian nor Jewish, but representative of certain desirable essences, of skills and powers, physical, aesthetic, and moral.

The proper response to these figures was, we felt, to develop ourselves for the performance of many and diverse roles, and the fact that certain definite limitations had been imposed upon our freedom did not lessen our sense of obligation. Not only were we to prepare but we were to perform—not with mere competence but with an almost reckless verve; with, may we say (without evoking the quaint and questionable notion of *négritude*) Negro-American style? Behind each artist there stands a traditional sense of style, a sense of the felt tension indicative of expressive completeness; a mode of humanizing reality and of evoking a feeling of being at home in the world. It is something which the artist shares with the group, and part of our boyish activity expressed a yearning to make any and everything of quality *Negro-American;* to appropriate it, possess it, recreate it in our own group and individual images.

And we recognized and were proud of our group's own style wherever we discerned it, in jazzmen and prize-fighters, ballplayers, and tap dancers; in gesture, inflection, intonation, timbre, and phrasing. Indeed, in all those nuances of expression and attitude which reveal a culture. We did not fully understand the cost of that style, but we recognized within it an affirmation of life beyond all question of our difficulties as Negroes.

Contrary to the notion currently projected by certain specialists in the "Negro problem" which characterizes the Negro-American as self-hating and defensive, we did not so regard ourselves. We felt, among ourselves at least, that we were supposed to be whoever we would and could be and do anything and everything which other boys did, and do it better. Not defensively, because we were ordered to do so; nor because it was held in the society at large that we were naturally, as Negroes, limited—but because we demanded it of ourselves. Because to measure up to our own standards was the only way of affirming our notion of manhood.

Hence it was no more incongruous, as seen from our own particular perspective in this land of incongruities, for young Negro Oklahomans to project themselves as Renaissance men than for white Mississippians to see themselves as ancient Greeks or noblemen out of Sir Walter Scott. Surely our fantasies have caused far less damage to the nation's sense of reality, if for no other reason than that ours were expressive of a more democratic ideal. Remember, too, as William Faulkner made us so vividly aware, that the slaves often took the essence of the aristocratic ideal (as they took Christianity) with far more seriousness than their masters, and that we, thanks to the tight telescoping of American history, were but two generations from that previous condition. Renaissance men, indeed!

I managed, by keeping quiet about it, to cling to our boyish ideal during three years in Alabama, and I brought it with me to New York, where it not only gave silent support to my explorations of what was then an unknown territory, but served to mock and caution me when I became interested in the Communist ideal. And when it was suggested that I try my hand at writing it was still with me.

The act of writing requires a constant plunging back into the shadow of the past where time hovers ghostlike. When I began writing in earnest I was forced, thus, to relate myself consciously and imaginatively to my mixed background as American, as Negro-American, and as a Negro from what in its own belated way was a pioneer background. More important, and inseparable from this particular effort, was the necessity of determining my true relationship to that body of American literature to which I was most attracted and through which, aided by what I could learn from the literatures of Europe, I would find my own voice and to which I was challenged, by way of achieving myself, to make some small contribution, and to whose composite picture of reality I was obligated to offer some necessary modifications.

This was no matter of sudden insight but of slow and blundering discovery, of a struggle to stare down the deadly and hypnotic temptation to interpret the world and all its devices in terms of race. To avoid this was very important to me, and in light of my background far from simple. Indeed, it was quite complex, involving as it did, a ceaseless questioning of all those formulas which historians, politicians, sociologists, and an older generation of Negro leaders and writers—those of the so-called "Negro Renaissance"—had evolved to describe my group's identity, its predicament, its fate, and its relation to the larger society and the culture which we share.

Here the question of reality and personal identity merge. Yes, and the question of the nature of the reality which underlies American fiction and thus the human truth which gives fiction viability. In this quest, for such it soon became, I learned that nothing could go unchallenged; especially that feverish industry dedicated to telling Negroes who and what they are, and which can usually be counted upon to deprive both humanity and culture of their complexity. I had undergone, not too many months before taking the path which led to writing, the humiliation of being taught in a class in sociology at a Negro college (from Park and Burgess, the leading textbook in the field) that Negroes represented the "lady of the races." This contention the Negro instructor passed blandly along to us without even bothering to wash his hands, much less his teeth. Well, I had no intention of being bound by any such humiliating definition of my relationship to American literature. Not even to those works which depicted Negroes negatively. Negro-Americans have a highly developed ability to abstract desirable qualities from those around them, even from their enemies, and my sense of reality could reject bias while appreciating the truth revealed by achieved art. The pleasure which I derived from reading had long been a necessity, and in the *act* of reading, that marvelous collaboration between the writer's artful vision and the reader's sense of life, I had become acquainted with other possible selves; freer, more courageous and ingenuous and, during the course of the narrative at least, even wise.

At the time I was under the influence of Ernest Hemingway, and his description, in *Death in the Afternoon*, of his thinking when he first went to Spain became very important as translated in my own naïve fashion. He was trying to write, he tells us,

> and I found the greatest difficulty aside from knowing truly what you really felt, rather than what you were supposed to feel, and had been taught to feel, was to put down what really happened in action; what the actual things were which produced the emotion that you experienced....

His statement of moral and aesthetic purpose which followed focused my own search to relate myself to American life through literature. For I found the greatest difficulty for a Negro writer was the problem of revealing what he truly felt, rather than serving up what Negroes were supposed to feel, and were encouraged to feel. And linked to this was the difficulty, based upon our long habit of deception and evasion, of depicting what really happened within our areas of American life, and putting down with honesty and without bowing to ideological expediencies the attitudes and values which give Negro-American life its sense of wholeness and which render it bearable and human and, when measured by our own terms, desirable.

I was forced to this awareness through my struggles with the craft of fiction; yes, and by my attraction (soon rejected) to Marxist political theory, which was my response to the inferior status which society sought to impose upon me (I did not then, now, or ever *consider* myself inferior).

I did not know my true relationship to America—what citizen of the U.S. really does?—but I did know and accept how I felt inside. And I also knew, thanks to the old Renaissance Man, what I expected of myself in the matter of personal discipline and creative quality. Since by the grace of the past and the examples of manhood picked willy-nilly from the continuing-present of my background, I rejected all negative definitions imposed upon me by others, there was nothing to do but search for those relationships which were fundamental.

In this sense fiction became the agency of my efforts to answer the questions, Who am I, what am I, how did I come to be? What shall I make of the life around me, what celebrate, what reject, how confront the snarl of good and evil which is inevitable? What does American society *mean* when regarded out of my *own* eyes, when informed by my *own* sense of the past and viewed by my *own* complex sense of the present? How, in other words, should I think of myself and my pluralistic sense of the world, how express my vision of the human predicament, without reducing it to a point which would render it sterile before that necessary and tragic—though enhancing—reduction which must occur before the fictive vision can come alive? It is quite possible that much potential fiction by Negro-Americans fails precisely at this point: through the writers' refusal (often through provincialism or lack of courage or through opportunism) to achieve a vision of life and a resourcefulness of craft commensurate with the complexity of their actual situation. Too often they fear to leave the uneasy sanctuary of race to take their chances in the world of art.

Suggestions for Discussion

1. Discuss the significance to Ellison of his Oklahoma experience.
2. What distinction does Ellison make between "the process of writing" and "the finished creations, the artifacts, poems, plays, novels"?
3. Describe his use of literature to relate himself to American life.

Suggestions for Writing

1. Discuss a piece of fiction that has helped you "answer the questions, who am I, what am I, how did I come to be?"
2. Relate the importance of where you "come from" to your understanding of yourself.

ESSAYS

AARON COPLAND

How We Listen to Music

Aaron Copland (1900–1990) studied music in the United States and France. His French teacher, Nadia Boulanger, was the first to conduct his Symphony for Organ and Orchestra in 1925. Much of Copland's work reflects the influence of American jazz and folk music: for example, in *John Henry* (1940) and in his well-known ballets *Billy the Kid* (1938), *Rodeo* (1942), and *Appalachian Spring* (1944). His major symphonic works are *El Salon Mexico* (1936) and *The Third Symphony;* he also has written music for films. Copland has remained a major influence in contemporary music and was awarded the National Medal for Arts in 1986. He has also written about music for the general public. This essay from *What to Listen for in Music* (1939, 1957) provides a defense for the difficulty of contemporary music and explains the obligations of the intelligent listener.

We all listen to music according to our separate capacities. But, for the sake of analysis, the whole listening process may become clearer if we break it up into its component parts, so to speak. In a certain sense we all listen to music on three separate planes. For lack of a better terminology, one might name these: (1) the sensuous plane, (2) the expressive plane, (3) the sheerly musical plane. The only advantage to be gained from mechanically splitting up the listening process into these hypothetical planes is the clearer view to be had of the way in which we listen.

The simplest way of listening to music is to listen for the sheer pleasure of the musical sound itself. That is the sensuous plane. It is the plane on which we hear music without thinking, without considering it in any way. One turns on the radio while doing something else and absent-mindedly bathes in the sound. A kind of brainless but attractive state of mind is engendered by the mere sound appeal of the music.

You may be sitting in a room reading this book. Imagine one note struck on the piano. Immediately that one note is enough to change the atmosphere of the room—providing that the sound element in music is a powerful and mysterious agent, which it would be foolish to deride or belittle.

The surprising thing is that many people who consider themselves qualified music lovers abuse that plane in listening. They go to concerts in order to lose themselves. They use music as a consolation or an escape. They enter an ideal world where one doesn't have to think of the realities of everyday life. Of course they aren't thinking about the music either. Music allows them to leave it, and they go off to a place to dream, dreaming because of and apropos of the music yet never quite listening to it.

Yes, the sound appeal of music is a potent and primitive force, but you must not allow it to usurp a disproportionate share of your interest. The sensuous plane is an important one in music, a very important one, but it does not constitute the whole story.

There is no need to digress further on the sensuous plane. Its appeal to every normal human being is self-evident. There is, however, such a thing as becoming more sensitive to the different kinds of sound stuff as used by various composers. For all composers do not use that sound stuff in the same way. Don't get the idea that the value of music is commensurate with its sensuous appeal or that the loveliest sounding music is made by the greatest composer. If that were so, Ravel would be a greater creator than Beethoven. The point is that the sound element varies with each composer, that his usage of sound forms an integral part of his style and must be taken into account when listening. The reader can see, therefore, that a more conscious approach is valuable even on this primary plane of music listening.

The second plane on which music exists is what I have called the expressive one. Here, immediately, we tread on controversial ground. Composers have a way of shying away from any discussion of music's expressive side. Did not Stravinsky himself proclaim that his music was an "object," a "thing," with a life of its own, and with no other meaning than its own purely musical existence? This intransigent attitude of Stravinsky's may be due to the fact that so many people have tried to read different meanings into so many pieces. Heaven knows it is difficult enough to say precisely what it is that a piece of music means, to say it definitely, to say it finally so that everyone is satisfied with your explanation. But that should not lead one to the other extreme of denying to music the right to be "expressive."

My own belief is that all music has an expressive power, some more and some less, but that all music has a certain meaning behind the notes and that the meaning behind the notes constitutes, after all, what the piece is saying, what the piece is about. The whole problem can be stated quite simply by asking, "Is there a meaning to music?" My answer to that would be, "Yes." And "Can you state in so many words what the meaning is?" My answer to that would be, "No." Therein lies the difficulty.

Simple-minded souls will never be satisfied with the answer to the second of these questions. They always want music to have a meaning, and the more concrete it is the better they like it. The more the music reminds them of a train, a storm, a funeral, or any other familiar conception the more expressive it appears to be to them. This popular idea of music's meaning—stimulated and abetted by the usual run of musical commentator—should be discouraged wherever and whenever it is met. One timid lady once confessed to me that she suspected something seriously lacking in her appreciation of music because of her inability to connect it with anything definite. That is getting the whole thing backward, of course.

Still, the question remains, How close should the intelligent music lover wish to come to pinning a definite meaning to any particular work? No closer than a general concept, I should say. Music expresses, at different moments, serenity or exuberance, regrets or triumph, fury or delight. It expresses each of these moods, and many others, in a numberless variety of subtle shadings and differences. It may even express a state of meaning for which there exists no adequate word in any language. In that case, musicians often like to say that it has only a purely musical meaning. They sometimes go further and say that *all* music has only a purely musical meaning. What they really mean is that no appropriate word can be found to express the music's meaning and that, even if it could, they do not feel the need of finding it.

But whatever the professional musician may hold, most musical novices still search for specific words with which to pin down their musical reactions. That is why they always find Tschaikovsky easier to "understand" than Beethoven. In the first place, it is easier to pin a meaning-word on a Tschaikovsky piece than on a Beethoven one. Much easier. Moreover, with the Russian composer, every time you come back to a piece of his it almost always says the same thing to you, whereas with Beethoven it is often quite difficult to put your finger right on what he is saying. And any musician will tell you that that is why Beethoven is the greater composer. Because music which always says the same thing to you will necessarily soon become dull music, but music whose meaning is slightly different with each hearing has a greater chance of remaining alive.

Listen, if you can, to the forty-eight fugue themes of Bach's *Well Tempered Clavichord.* Listen to each theme, one after another. You will soon realize that each theme mirrors a different world of feeling. You will also soon realize that the more beautiful a theme seems to you the harder it is to find any word that will describe it to your complete satisfaction. Yes, you will certainly know whether it is a gay theme or a sad one. You will be able, in other words, in your own mind, to draw a frame of emotional feeling around your theme. Now study the sad one a little closer. Try to pin down the exact quality of its sadness. Is it pessimistically sad or resignedly sad; is it fatefully sad or smilingly sad?

Let us suppose that you are fortunate and can describe to your own satisfaction in so many words the exact meaning of your chosen theme.

There is still no guarantee that anyone else will be satisfied. Nor need they be. The important thing is that each one feel for himself the specific expressive quality of a theme or, similarly, an entire piece of music. And if it is a great work of art, don't expect it to mean exactly the same thing to you each time you return to it.

Themes or pieces need not express only one emotion, of course. Take such a theme as the first main one of the *Ninth Symphony,* for example. It is clearly made up of different elements. It does not say only one thing. Yet anyone hearing it immediately gets a feeling of strength, a feeling of power. It isn't a power that comes simply because the theme is played loudly. It is a power inherent in the theme itself. The extraordinary strength and vigor of the theme results in the listener's receiving an impression that a forceful statement has been made. But one should never try to boil it down to "the fateful hammer of life," etc. That is where the trouble begins. The musician, in his exasperation, says it means nothing but the notes themselves, whereas the nonprofessional is only too anxious to hang on to any explanation that gives him the illusion of getting closer to the music's meaning.

Now, perhaps, the reader will know better what I mean when I say that music does have an expressive meaning but that we cannot say in so many words what that meaning is.

The third plane on which music exists is the sheerly musical plane. Besides the pleasurable sound of music and the expressive feeling that it gives off, music does exist in terms of the notes themselves and of their manipulation. Most listeners are not sufficiently conscious of this third plane....

Professional musicians, on the other hand, are, if anything, too conscious of the mere notes themselves. They often fall into the error of becoming so engrossed with their arpeggios and staccatos that they forget the deeper aspects of the music they are performing. But from the layman's standpoint, it is not so much a matter of getting over bad habits on the sheerly musical plane as of increasing one's awareness of what is going on, in so far as the notes are concerned.

When the man in the street listens to the "notes themselves" with any degree of concentration, he is most likely to make some mention of the melody. Either he hears a pretty melody or he does not, and he generally lets it go at that. Rhythm is likely to gain his attention next, particularly if it seems exciting. But harmony and tone color are generally taken for granted, if they are thought of consciously at all. As for music's having a definite form of some kind, that idea seems never to have occurred to him.

It is very important for all of us to become more alive to music on its sheerly musical plane. After all, an actual musical material is being used. The intelligent listener must be prepared to increase his awareness of the musical material and what happens to it. He must hear the melodies, the rhythms, the harmonies, the tone colors in a more conscious fashion. But above all he must, in order to follow the line of the composer's thought, know something of the principles of musical form. Listening to all of these elements is listening on the sheerly musical plane.

Let me repeat that I have split up mechanically the three separate planes on which we listen merely for the sake of greater clarity. Actually, we never listen on one or the other of these planes. What we do is to correlate them—listening in all three ways at the same time. It takes no mental effort, for we do it instinctively.

Perhaps an analogy with what happens to us when we visit the theater will make this instinctive correlation clearer. In the theater, you are aware of the actors and actresses, costumes and sets, sounds and movements. All these give one the sense that the theater is a pleasant place to be in. They constitute the sensuous plane in our theatrical reactions.

The expressive plane in the theater would be derived from the feeling that you get from what is happening on the stage. You are moved to pity, excitement, or gayety. It is this general feeling, generated aside from the particular words being spoken, a certain emotional something which exists on the stage, that is analogous to the expressive quality in music.

The plot and plot development is equivalent to our sheerly musical plane. The playwright creates and develops a character in just the same way that a composer creates and develops a theme. According to the degree of your awareness of the way in which the artist in either field handles his material you will become a more intelligent listener.

It is easy enough to see that the theatergoer never is conscious of any of these elements separately. He is aware of them all at the same time. The same is true of music listening. We simultaneously and without thinking listen on all three planes.

In a sense, the ideal listener is both inside and outside the music at the same moment, judging it and enjoying it, wishing it would go one way and watching it go another—almost like the composer at the moment he composes it; because in order to write his music, the composer must also be inside and outside his music, carried away by it and yet coldly critical of it. A subjective and objective attitude is implied in both creating and listening to music.

What the reader should strive for, then, is a more *active* kind of listening. Whether you listen to Mozart or Duke Ellington, you can deepen your understanding of music only by being a more conscious and aware listener—not someone who is just listening, but someone who is listening *for* something.

Suggestions for Discussion

1. According to Copland, on what different levels do we listen to music?
2. Why does Copland believe that listening to music as an escape is an inadequate response to it?

3. Does Copland believe that a musical composition can have meaning? Does he believe it possible to state that meaning easily?
4. How, according to Copland, is the meaning of a musical composition related to its expressive power? What boundaries does Copland place on the expressive power of music? Explain his use of Bach in this regard.
5. What for Copland are significant differences between Tschaikovsky and Beethoven? Why does he consider Beethoven the greater composer?
6. What are the elements of the third plane of music? How do professional musicians and listeners of music differ about this third plane? What criticism does Copland make of musicians? What obligation does the intelligent listener have to this plane?
7. Explain Copland's analogy between the elements in music and in drama. What important differences exist for the audience in its response to both forms of art?
8. Contrast E. M. Forster's position with Copland's in the matter of meaning in the arts. Can you account for their different points of view?

Suggestions for Writing

1. Listen to a composition by Bach and to one by Duke Ellington and, insofar as you can, discuss the music on all three levels.
2. Summarize the arguments of Copland and Mannes about the problems of responding to art. Which of these essays do you find most helpful for your own response? Explain your position in detail.

MIKE ROYKO

The Virtue of Prurience

Mike Royko (1932–1997) was born in Chicago. He attended Wright Junior College, the University of Illinois, and Northwestern University. He received an honorary doctor of letters degree from Lake Forest College in 1981. Following service in the air force during the Korean War, he spent two years as night editor of the City News Bureau of Chicago, a traditional training ground for reporters. He later joined the *Chicago Daily News* as a general assignment reporter and soon became a rewriteman. In 1962 he was assigned a weekly government and political column, "County Beat." It was his tough, cynical, and knowledgeable observations mostly about Chicago and its citizens that led to his 1972 Pulitzer. His commentary, "Mike Royko," which ranged from City Hall to the White House, first appeared in September 1963 in the *Daily News.* His insight and experiences provided material for many books including *Boss: Richard J. Daley of Chicago.*

My first right-wing endeavor—helping get a book banned—has failed miserably. I now can appreciate how frustrating life in our permissive society must be for such grim-lipped groups as the Moral Majority.

Normally, I don't favor censorship and have never before tried to get anything banned. But several months ago, I joined in a crusade that was being led by Bill and Barbara Younis of Hannibal, N.Y.

Bill and Barbara are parents of an 18-year-old high school senior, and they became alarmed when they discovered that their daughter was being required to read a book they considered vulgar.

They went to the school superintendent and demanded that the book be removed from the reading list. He refused.

So they asked friends and neighbors to sign petitions supporting them, and they demanded that the school board ban the book.

That's when I found out about it. A reporter from that part of New York called to ask me what I thought of the censorship efforts.

I responded by dropping the phone, shouting, "Hot damn, yowee!" and dancing gleefully around my office.

I reacted that way because it is a book that I wrote about 12 years ago. It is called "Boss" and is about Mayor Richard J. Daley, power, and Chicago politics.

Before long, there were news stories about the censorship efforts of the Younises, and my phone started ringing with calls from other writers.

One of them said:

"You slick devil, how did you ever pull that off?"

I'm just lucky, I guess.

"Well, I don't get it. My last book was so torrid and lurid that I blushed while writing it. And there hasn't even been a hint from anybody about banning it."

You're just unlucky, I guess.

Another writer called and said: "This is so unfair. In my last book, George did it with Lucy, Lucy did it with Wally, Wally did it with Evelyn, Evelyn did it with George, George did it with Wally, Lucy did it with Sally, and then they all did it together."

Sounds exhausting.

"What I don't understand, is why you, but not me. I mean, I could really use a break like that."

Maybe I just live right.

What they were talking about was the tremendous commercial value of being banned. By anyone, anywhere, just as long as you are banned. It works this way:

If you can get a book banned in, say, Minneapolis, and there is a great furor about it, the book will suddenly become a best-seller next door in St. Paul. Sure, you won't sell any books in Minneapolis. But for every book you don't sell in Minneapolis, you'll sell 10 in St. Paul.

That's all part of the forbidden-fruit syndrome. Tell people they can't have or do something, and they immediately want to do it.

With this in mind, I called my publisher and said: "Get those presses rolling. We're going to sell a ton."

He said: "Not yet. You haven't been banned yet. And just being threatened with censorship isn't enough. You've got to be tossed off the shelves."

So I got on the phone and called Mr. and Mrs. Younis.

"Your book is vulgar," they said. "It is filled with swear words."

I know. That's the way Chicago politicians talk, so I quoted them. But you're right. It's vulgar. Shocking.

"You agree?"

Hell… I mean, heck, yes. And I'm behind you 100 percent.

"You are?"

Of course I am. I think what you're doing is terrific. And if I were there, I'd sign your petition.

"You would?"

Darn right. I don't want 18-year-olds reading words like (bleep) and (censored) and (deleted). Who ever heard of 18-year-olds being exposed to such language?

"Would you send us a letter expressing your support?"

Of course. I'll do more than that. I'll write a column urging that my book be banned.

And I did.

Since then, I've been thumbing through travel folders, real-estate brochures for tropical hideaways, yachting magazines, and girlie magazines, anticipating life as a rich and censored author.

Nothing ever works out.

The school board set up a three-member committee to review the book and the Younises' complaint.

Then a hearing was held. Mr. and Mrs. Younis, bless them, came to the hearing and said things like: "It's got the kind of language you see painted on bridges. Books like this encourage young ladies to become prostitutes."

That's dynamite stuff. Would you want your daughter to read a book that would encourage her to enter the employ of a brothel? I should hope not.

Despite this, the committee ruled that the book would remain on the reading list.

Mr. and Mrs. Younis have now removed three of their four children from the school system and say they will send them to private schools.

A noble effort, but it doesn't do me much good. As the school superintendent said:

"We made our decision, and it was a good one. There is nothing wrong with that book."

Doggone busybody.

Suggestions for Discussion

1. What is the tone of Royko's essay? How does he achieve the right tone? Is it appropriate to the subject of the essay? Explain its title.
2. Why are fellow authors jealous of Royko? What examples of their works does he use? How are those works different from his? Should the book about George and Lucy and the others be banned? Explain.
3. What is "the forbidden-fruit syndrome"?
4. What serious issue does Royko suggest in his description of the Younis couple?
5. Why is censorship a danger to human freedom? Are there instances in which censorship might safely be imposed?

Suggestions for Writing

1. Royko says, "Tell people they can't have or do something, and they immediately want to do it." Write an essay illustrating this comment. Explain why you think Royko's observation about people may be accurate.
2. Write an essay in which you discuss a play, movie, poem, painting, or novel that you think should be banned. Explain your reasons. If you don't believe in banning anything, explain why, giving your reasons carefully.

E. M. FORSTER

Art for Art's Sake

Edward Morgan Forster (1879–1970) was a British novelist educated at King's College, Cambridge. He lived for a time in Italy, was a member of the Bloomsbury Group of writers and artists in London, and spent the major part of his life in Cambridge. His works include *Where Angels Fear to Tread* (1905), *A Room with a View* (1908), and *A Passage to India* (1924). In this essay from *Two Cheers for Democracy* (1951), Forster explains the importance of art as a source of comfort and order in a troubled society.

I believe in art for art's sake. It is an unfashionable belief, and some of my statements must be of the nature of an apology. Sixty years ago I should have faced you with more confidence. A writer or a speaker who chose "Art for Art's Sake" for his theme sixty years ago could be sure of being in the swim, and could feel so confident of success that he sometimes dressed himself in aesthetic costumes suitable to the occasion—in an embroidered dressing-gown, perhaps, or a blue velvet suit with a Lord Fauntleroy collar; or a toga, or a kimono, and carried a poppy or a lily or a long peacock's feather in his mediaeval hand. Times have changed. Not thus can I present either myself or my theme to-day. My aim rather is to ask you quietly to reconsider for a few minutes a phrase which has been much misused and much abused, but which has, I believe, great importance for us—has, indeed, eternal importance.

Now we can easily dismiss those peacock's feathers and other affectations—they are but trifles—but I want also to dismiss a more dangerous heresy, namely the silly idea that only art matters, an idea which has somehow got mixed up with the idea of art for art's sake, and has helped to discredit it. Many things besides art, matter. It is merely one of the things that matter, and high though the claims are that I make for it, I want to keep them in proportion. No one can spend his or her life entirely in the creation or the appreciation of masterpieces. Man lives, and ought to live, in a complex world, full of conflicting claims, and if we simplified them down into the aesthetic he would be sterilised. Art for art's sake does not mean that only art matters and I would also like to rule out such phrases as, "The Life of Art," "Living for Art," and "Art's High Mission." They confuse and mislead.

What does the phrase mean? Instead of generalising, let us take a specific instance—Shakespeare's *Macbeth,* for example, and pronounce the words, "*Macbeth* for *Macbeth*'s *sake.*" What does that mean? Well, the play has several aspects—it is educational, it teaches us something about legendary Scotland, something about Jacobean England, and a good deal about human nature and its perils. We can study its origins, and study and enjoy its dramatic technique and the music of its diction. All that is true. But *Macbeth* is furthermore a world of its own, created by Shakespeare and existing in virtue of its own poetry. It is in this aspect *Macbeth* for *Macbeth*'s sake, and that is what I intend by the phrase "art for art's sake." A work of art—whatever else it may be—is a self-contained entity, with a life of its own imposed on it by its creator. It has internal order. It may have external form. That is how we recognise it.

Take for another example that picture of Seurat's which I saw two years ago in Chicago—"*La Grande Jatte.*" Here again there is much to study and to enjoy: the pointillism, the charming face of the seated girl, the nineteenth-century Parisian Sunday sunlight, the sense of motion in immobility. But here again there is something more; "*La Grande Jatte*" forms a world of its own, created by Seurat and existing by virtue of its own poetry: "*La Grande Jatte*" *pour "La Grande Jatte": l'art pour l'art.* Like *Macbeth* it has internal order and internal life.

It is to the conception of order that I would now turn. This is important to my argument, and I want to make a digression, and glance at order in daily life, before I come to order in art.

In the world of daily life, the world which we perforce inhabit, there is much talk about order, particularly from statesmen and politicians. They tend, however, to confuse order with orders, just as they confuse creation with regulations. Order, I suggest, is something evolved from within, not something imposed from without; it is an internal stability, a vital harmony, and in the social and political category, it has never existed except for the convenience of historians. Viewed realistically, the past is really a series of *dis*orders, succeeding one another by discoverable laws, no doubt, and certainly marked by an increasing growth of human interference, but disorders all the same. So that, speaking as a writer, what I hope for today is a disorder which will be more favourable to artists than is the present one, and which will provide them with fuller inspirations and better material conditions. It will not last—nothing lasts—but there have been some advantageous disorders in the past—for instance, in ancient Athens, in Renaissance Italy, eighteenth-century France, periods in China and Persia—and we may do something to accelerate the next one. But let us not again fix our hearts where true joys are not to be found. We were promised a new order after the first world war through the League of Nations. It did not come, nor have I faith in present promises, by whomsoever endorsed.

The implacable offensive of Science forbids. We cannot reach social and political stability for the reason that we continue to make scientific discoveries and to apply them, and thus to destroy the arrangements which were based on more elementary discoveries. If Science would discover rather than apply—if, in other words, men were more interested in knowledge than in power—mankind would be in a far safer position, the stability statesmen talk about would be a possibility, there could be a new order based on vital harmony, and the earthly millennium might approach. But Science shows no signs of doing this: she gave us the internal combustion engine, and before we had digested and assimilated it with terrible pains into our social system, she harnessed the atom, and destroyed any new order that seemed to be evolving. How can man get into harmony with his surroundings when he is constantly altering them? The future of our race is, in this direction, more unpleasant than we care to admit, and it has sometimes seemed to me that its best chance lies through apathy, uninventiveness, and inertia. Universal exhaustion might promote that Change of Heart which is at present so briskly recommended from a thousand pulpits. Universal exhaustion would certainly be a new experience. The human race has never undergone it, and is still too perky to admit that it may be coming and might result in a sprouting of new growth through the decay.

I must not pursue these speculations any further—they lead me too far from my terms of reference and maybe from yours. But I do want to emphasize that order in daily life and in history, order in the social and political category, is unattainable under our present psychology.

Where is it attainable? Not in the astronomical category, where it was for many years enthroned. The heavens and the earth have become terribly alike since Einstein. No longer can we find a reassuring contrast to chaos in the night sky and look up with George Meredith to the stars, the army of unalterable law, or listen for the music of the spheres. Order is not there. In the entire universe there seem to be only two possibilities for it. The first of them—which again lies outside my terms of reference—is the divine order, the mystic harmony, which according to all religions is available for those who can contemplate it. We much admit its possibility, on the evidence of the adepts, and we must believe them when they say that it is attained, if attainable, by prayer. "O thou who changest not, abide with me," said one of its poets. "*Ordina questo amor, o tu che m'ami,*" said another: "Set love in order thou who lovest me." The existence of a divine order, though it cannot be tested, has never been disproved.

The second possibility for order lies in the aesthetic category, which is my subject here: the order which an artist can create in his own work, and to that we must now return. A work of art, we are all agreed, is a unique product. But why? It is unique not because it is clever or noble or beautiful or enlightened or original or sincere or idealistic or useful or educational—it may embody any of those qualities—but because it is the only material object in the universe which may possess internal harmony. All the others have been pressed into shape from outside, and when their mold is removed they collapse. The work of art stands up by itself, and nothing else does. It achieves something which has often been promised by society, but always delusively. Ancient Athens made a mess—but the *Antigone* stands up. Renaissance Rome made a mess—but the ceiling of the Sistine got painted. James I made a mess—but there was *Macbeth.* Louis XIV—but there was *Phedre.* Art for art's sake? I should just think so, and more so than ever at the present time. It is the one orderly product which our muddling race has produced. It is the cry of a thousand sentinels, the echo from a thousand labyrinths; it is the lighthouse which cannot be hidden: *c'est le meilleur témoignage que nous puissions donner de notre dignité. Antigone* for *Antigone*'s sake, *Macbeth* for *Macbeth*'s, "*La Grande Jatte*" pour "*La Grande Jatte.*"

If this line of argument is correct, it follows that the artist will tend to be an outsider in the society to which he has been born, and that the nineteenth century conception of him as a Bohemian was not inaccurate. The conception erred in three particulars: it postulated an economic system where art could be a full-time job, it introduced the fallacy that only art matters, and it overstressed idiosyncracy and waywardness—the peacock-feather aspect—rather than order. But it is a truer conception than the one which prevails in official circles on my side of the Atlantic—I don't know about yours: the conception which treats the artist as if he were a particularly bright government advertiser and encourages him to be friendly and matey with his fellow citizens, and not to give himself airs.

Estimable is mateyness, and the man who achieves it gives many a pleasant little drink to himself and to others. But it has no traceable connection with the creative impulse, and probably acts as an inhibition on it. The artist who is seduced by mateyness may stop himself from doing the one thing which he, and he alone, can do—the making of something out of words or sounds or paint or clay or marble or steel or film which has internal harmony and presents order to a permanently disarranged planet. This seems worth doing, even at the risk of being called uppish by journalists. I have in mind an article which was published some years ago in the London *Times,* an article called "The Eclipse of the Highbrow," in which the "Average Man" was exalted, and all contemporary literature was censured if it did not toe the line, the precise position of the line being naturally known to the writer of the article. Sir Kenneth Clark, who was at that time director of our National Gallery, commented on this pernicious doctrine in a letter which cannot be too often quoted. "The poet and the artist," wrote Clark, "are important precisely because they are not average men; because in sensibility, intelligence, and power of invention they far exceed the average." These memorable words, and particularly the words "power of invention," are the Bohemian's passport. Furnished with it, he slinks about society, saluted now by a brickbat and now by a penny, and accepting either of them with equanimity. He does not consider too anxiously what his relations with society may be, for he is aware of something more important than that—namely the invitation to invent, to create order, and he believes he will be better placed for doing this if he attempts detachment. So round and round he slouches, with his hat pulled over his eyes, and maybe with a louse in his beard, and—if he really wants one—a peacock's feather in his hand.

If our present society should disintegrate—and who dare prophesy that it won't?—this old-fashioned and démodé figure will become clearer: the Bohemian, the outsider, the parasite, the rat—one of those figures which have at present no function either in a warring or a peaceful world. It may not be dignified to be a rat, but many of the ships are sinking, which is not dignified either—the officials did not build them properly. Myself, I would sooner be a swimming rat than a sinking ship—at all events I can look around me for a little longer—and I remember how one of us, a rat with particularly bright eyes called Shelley, squeaked out, "Poets are the unacknowledged legislators of the world," before he vanished into the waters of the Mediterranean.

What laws did Shelley propose to pass? None. The legislation of the artist is never formulated at the time, though it is sometimes discerned by future generations. He legislates through creating. And he creates through his sensitiveness and power to impose form. Without form the sensitiveness vanishes. And form is as important today, when the human race is trying to ride the whirlwind, as it ever was in those less agitating days of the past, when the earth seemed solid and the stars fixed, and the discoveries of science were made slowly, slowly. Form is not tradition. It alters from generation to generation. Artists always seek a new technique, and will continue to do so as long as their work excites them. But form of some kind is imperative. It is the surface crust of the internal harmony, it is the outward evidence of order.

My remarks about society may have seemed too pessimistic, but I believe that society can only represent a fragment of the human spirit, and that another fragment can only get expressed through art. And I wanted to take this opportunity, this vantage ground, to assert not only the existence of art, but its pertinacity. Looking back into the past, it seems to me that that is all there has ever been: vantage grounds for discussion and creation, little vantage grounds in the changing chaos, where bubbles have been blown and webs spun, and the desire to create order has found temporary gratification, and the sentinels have managed to utter their challenges, and the huntsmen, though lost individually, have heard each other's calls through the impenetrable wood, and the lighthouses have never ceased sweeping the thankless seas. In this pertinacity there seems to me, as I grow older, something more and more profound, something which does in fact concern people who do not care about art at all.

In conclusion, let me summarise the various categories that have laid claim to the possession of Order.

(1) The social and political category. Claim disallowed on the evidence of history and of our own experience. If man altered psychologically, order here might be attainable: not otherwise.

(2) The astronomical category. Claim allowed up to the present century, but now disallowed on the evidence of the physicists.

(3) The religious category. Claim allowed on the evidence of the mystics.

(4) The aesthetic category. Claim allowed on the evidence of various works of art, and on the evidence of our own creative impulses, however weak these may be or however imperfectly they may function. Works of art, in my opinion, are the only objects in the material universe to possess internal order, and that is why, though I don't believe that only art matters, I do believe in Art for Art's Sake.

Suggestions for Discussion

1. Why does Forster make clear that the belief in art for art's sake does not mean a belief that only art matters?
2. Where does art stand, for Forster, in the list of things that matter?
3. Explain Forster's phrase, "*Macbeth* for *Macbeth*'s sake." How does he use it to explain his main argument?
4. Explain Forster's comparison of the order of art with order in life. How does this comparison function in his argument?
5. What does Forster mean by claiming that a work of art is a unique product?
6. Examine Forster's categories that have laid claim to the possession of order. Why does he reject all but the religious and aesthetic categories?

Suggestions for Writing

1. Write a paper explaining Forster's defense of art.
2. Obviously, many people feel differently from Forster about the autonomy of art. In Marxist countries, for example, art is often considered to be a servant of the state. Write a paper in which you argue for or against Forster's position.

IRA GLASSER

Artistic Freedom: A Gathering Storm

Ira S. Glasser (b. 1938) was born in Brooklyn and studied mathematics at Queens College (New York City) and at Ohio State University. He was associate editor and then editor of *Current Magazine* from 1962 to 1967 and briefly lectured in mathematics at Sarah Lawrence College. He was the New York director of the American Civil Liberties Union until becoming its executive director in 1978. Since 1974 he has also served as director of the Asian American Legal Defense and Education Fund. The New York Association of Black School Supervisors gave him their Martin Luther King, Jr., Award in 1971. He contributes articles to various professional journals as well as a column for *Civil Liberties,* the publication of the ACLU. In 1991 he published *Visions of Liberty,* written to commemorate the 200th anniversary of the Bill of Rights. He is also the coauthor of *Doing Good,* (1978). This essay, the subject of one of his columns, demonstrates why Glasser and the ACLU regard the rising tendency to censorship in the late eighties and early nineties as a serious threat to First Amendment rights.

The roots of current efforts to curb freedom of artistic expression reach back to the early 1980s, when religious fundamentalists and other authoritarians attempted to censor books, films and television. Libraries, museums, schools, theaters, television stations, bookstores and video shops all came under sustained pressure to restrict the display or availability of images and words felt to offend various self-appointed monitors of morality and taste.

This censorship movement found powerful allies in government. Attorney General Edwin Meese enthusiastically joined the crusade, heading up a Presidential commission convened to establish a behavioral link between vaguely defined "pornography" and sex crimes (a link that has eluded social scientists for decades), and to establish a rationale for prosecuting the purveyors of "offensive" artworks.

Today, we are reaping the harvest of those earlier efforts: a climate in which artistic expression—from rock music lyrics to unconventional imagery in photography, to political symbolism in paintings and sculpture, to unique cinematic visions of reality—is under sustained assault. Today, artistic freedom is threatened across the country by escalating (if more refined) pressure from private groups, new censorship laws, and politically-inspired funding cuts.

For example, in 1985 Tipper Gore's Parents' Music Resource Center (PMRC) pressured record companies to label song lyrics that allegedly encourage sex, suicide, drugs, alcohol and belief in "the occult." The Recording Industry Association of America, feeling the heat from the PMRC, agreed to support "warning" labels. Today, retail outlets around the country are using such labels to decide what records to sell, and to whom. Hastings, the nation's eighth largest book and music store chain, places "18 for Purchase" stickers on 74 rock albums and refuses to sell them to underage consumers. The other large chains are similarly restricting record sales, according to what criteria no one knows. One chain recently decided not to stock labeled records at all. Obviously, these actions on the part of the large chains, which dominate record sales nationwide, are bound to engender self-censorship tendencies in composers and recording artists—who need the chains to gain access to their market.

Predictably, these retail labeling practices, combined with the recording industry's drift toward self-censorship, are now prompting politicians to begin introducing laws that *require* labeling.

In December 1989, the Pennsylvania legislature passed a bill banning the sale to minors of "sexually explicit" albums, unless the album covers bear a day-glo label that reads: "WARNING: May contain explicit lyrics descriptive of or advocating one or more of the following: suicide, incest, bestiality, sadomasochism, sexual activity in a violent context, murder, morbid violence, illegal use of drugs or alcohol. PARENTAL ADVISORY." Retailers caught selling such material without a label are subject to a $300 fine and 90 days in jail. The state representative who introduced the bill was quoted recently as saying that his intent is not to censor song lyrics, but to label them "just as we do for corn flakes and pesticides and many other things."

Similar legislation has been introduced in Missouri, Virginia, Arizona, Iowa, New Mexico, Illinois, Oklahoma, Delaware, Kansas and Florida. The Missouri bill adds nudity and adultery to the danger zone; Florida includes books and magazines and would prohibit the sale of labeled materials to minors. Maryland would also label racist and anti-Semitic content in music lyrics (presumably, local prosecutors would identify the guilty lyrics). The state representative who introduced the Missouri bill has sent a copy of it to his counterparts in 35 states, encouraging them to duplicate his effort. One wonders, if it is acceptable to label records, whether labels on books are next.

In some states, prosecutors are not waiting for these new censorship proposals to become law. For example, the ACLU represented an Alabama retailer whose record store was raided in June 1988; 25 rap music tapes were confiscated and he was arrested, under the state's obscenity law. The day before the raid, the store owner had sold a rap cassette containing lyrics that were "offensive" to an undercover police officer. This was the first case in which recorded music was the basis for an obscenity prosecution.

The store owner was convicted in municipal court and fined $500. He then requested a jury trial, as was his right under Alabama law. At the trial, held this February, the ACLU presented a music critic and linguist as expert witnesses to argue that such obscenity convictions would have a widespread chilling effect on artists. On February 22, the jury overturned the conviction. We regard it as a hopeful sign that the people of Alabama would chafe so readily at the threat of prosecutors deciding what music they can and cannot hear.

The visual arts are also under assault. Only a few weeks into 1990, the city of New Haven, Connecticut ordered the dismantling of an exhibition of Vietnam War photographs on the grounds that they were "too explicit." In November 1989, in Washington, D.C. a black artist's outdoor portrait of Jesse Jackson as blond, blue-eyed and white-skinned, was attacked with sledgehammers by a group of offended black men. A painting that depicts the late Chicago Mayor Harold Washington in women's underwear, when exhibited last year at the Art Institute of Chicago, provoked offended city aldermen to call out the police to literally arrest the painting and remove it from the premises. The ACLU is suing the city for damages and injunctive relief on behalf of the artist, to whom the painting was later returned in a damaged condition.

Another controversy at the Art Institute of Chicago last summer, surrounding the display of a sculpture by "Dread" Scott Tyler that invited viewers to trod upon an American flag spread out on the floor, ultimately led to the enactment of new city, state and federal bans on flag desecration! Senator Robert Dole (R-KA) said at the time, "I don't know much about art, but I know desecration when I see it."

The flag issue did not go away. On June 21, 1989, the U.S. Supreme Court handed down its anxiously awaited decision in the flag burning case, *Texas v. Johnson.* The Texas statute that banned flag-burning as part of a political protest, said the Court, was unconstitutional under the First Amendment. Ironically, the decision ignited a firestorm that raged so out of control as to underscore the total insignificance of the conflagration Gregory Johnson had visited upon the 1984 Republican convention in Dallas.

Let's amend the Constitution, said President Bush one week after the decision. And so commenced a campaign to attach to the First Amendment an exception that would allow enactment of a law prohibiting "desecration" of the American flag. With great haste and nearly without dissent,

Congress passed "sense of the Congress" resolutions condemning the Supreme Court decision.

Mercifully, the proposed constitutional amendment did not pass. But a new federal law prohibiting "desecration" of the flag did. That law has now been declared unconstitutional by two federal courts, and appeals are on the way to the U.S. Supreme Court. If the Supreme Court upholds the lower court decisions, that could recharge efforts to amend the Constitution. And while proponents of flag desecration laws are primarily interested in restricting political expression, if such laws are allowed to stand there will be no way to limit their sweep through the arts.

Censorship of visual images has also been enabled by federal funding restrictions. Last summer, Senator Jesse Helms, outraged by two exhibits underwritten by the National Endowment for the Arts (NEA), one of them featuring homoerotic photographs by Robert Mapplethorpe, introduced a federal law that would have broadly restricted NEA funding of "offensive" art. The mere introduction of the Helms bill had an immediate censorious effect: The Corcoran Gallery in Washington cancelled its plans to mount the Mapplethorpe exhibit that had been the object of Helms' wrath. Congress rejected the initial Helms bill but enacted legislation that prohibits funding of "obscene" art, seems to define all homoerotic art as *per se* obscene, and establishes a regime of surveillance over artistic expression.

To even *read* the restrictions and guidelines that the new law imposes on the NEA is to be chilled! The law establishes a federal commission to review the NEA's grant-making process; requires the NEA to give Congress 30 days notice of its intention to award further grants to the institutions responsible for the Mapplethorpe exhibit, so that Congress may review the plan; and puts Congress on record as disavowing the previous NEA grants to those institutions, as well as the NEA fellowship awarded to painter Andres Serrano, who created a work thought to defame the Christian religion.

The very first application of the guidelines realized their potential for being wielded as a political weapon. Prior to enactment of the law, a small New York City gallery called Artists' Space had obtained a $10,000 NEA grant to help mount a show dealing with AIDS. After the new legislation took effect, the gallery director reported to the NEA that the show's catalogue and some of its imagery might be controversial. Incoming NEA chair John Frohnmeyer responded by threatening to withdraw the grant entirely, on the grounds that an essay in the catalogue criticized public officials—including Senator Helms. Said Frohnmeyer: "Political discourse ought to be in the political arena and not in a show sponsored by the Endowment."

One of the most disturbing things about current efforts to corral expression in the arts and in popular culture is that such efforts are increasingly broad-based.

For example: In the early 1980s, some feminists and legal scholars began to argue that pornography is a type of civil rights violation and gained passage of local ordinances broadly outlawing images that "denigrate" women. The ACLU challenged these laws and helped strike them down in court.

Interestingly, these laws are founded on the same reasoning that the Meese Commission on Pornography used to advocate the shutting down of bookstores and video shops, and prosecution of their owners for trafficking in "obscene" materials.

Similar efforts to categorize speech that "denigrates" as a civil rights violation are now occurring on numerous college and university campuses. As deeply troubling as the resurgence of racial tensions among students is, it is also troubling that the regulations and policies being devised by universities to respond to these tensions echo the standards of Jesse Helms. The original Helms law would have prohibited grants of NEA funds for artistic expression that "denigrates, debases or reviles a person, group or class of citizens on the basis of race, creed, sex, handicap or national origin," or that "denigrates any religion or non-religion."

Thus, it turns out that overbroad campus regulations intended to protect minorities and women from racial and sexual harassment are lending a veil of legitimacy to the efforts of people like Jesse Helms, whose targets are unconventional art. Similarly, restrictions on rock lyrics are now not only rationalized on the grounds that the music presumably encourages drug use, promiscuity and violence, but also because its content is presumably racist, sexist, anti-Semitic and/or homophobic. Wrote Tipper Gore, on the op-ed page of the *Washington Post* January 8, 1990: "Words like 'bitch' and 'nigger' are dangerous. Racial and sexual epithets, whether screamed across a street or camouflaged by the rhythms of a song, turn people into objects less than human... [w]e must raise our voices in protest and put pressure on those who not only reflect this hatred but also package, polish, promote, and market it."

Another, and inevitable, twist of fate is the fact that campus rules prohibiting racist speech are being turned against minority students themselves and their kinfolk in the arts. Recently, a student group at Columbia University tried to invoke campus rules against racist speech to bar an appearance on campus by a controversial member of the black rap group, Public Enemy, who had made some allegedly anti-Semitic remarks last summer.

Permitting restraints on expression in one area only fuels efforts to restrain it in another. Censorship is as indivisible as the First Amendment itself. That is why the ACLU challenges *all* censorship—whether it is an attempt to prohibit "unpatriotic" uses of the flag, racist speech on campuses, sexually explicit rock lyrics, the banning of films or NEA funding for certain artistic expression.

Suggestions for Discussion

1. What is the major point that Glasser makes in this essay? Explain his assertion that "censorship is as indivisible as the First Amendment itself."
2. Discuss the various areas of art that, according to Glasser, have been intimidated by the threat of censorship. What common thread does he see running through the movement to censor art?
3. Even in this short discussion, Glasser enables us to see how complex and ambiguous the issues of censorship become. Discuss these ambiguities and complexities in several of the examples cited.

Suggestions for Writing

1. The Mapplethorpe and Serrano works are the ones most frequently cited in the controversy over funding by the National Endowment for the Arts. Write an essay in which you explain why. (You will need to do some library research if you are not familiar with the works.) Make some personal commentary on these controversies.
2. Why does the American Civil Liberties Union oppose censorship in any form? Do you agree with their position? Use Glasser's remarks as a basis for your conclusions.
3. Why does one find opposing political movements (for example, the feminist movement and religious fundamentalism) sometimes in agreement over censorship? How would they answer Glasser's comments? Write an essay explaining this issue and make a personal comment on it.

MARGARET ATWOOD

Pornography

Margaret Atwood was born in 1939 in Ottawa, Canada, and was educated at Victoria College of the University of Toronto, Radcliffe College, and Harvard University. She has taught at universities in Canada, Europe, and the United States and is writer-in-residence at the University of Toronto. Her novels include *Bodily Harm* (1982), *The Handmaid's Tale* (1986), *Cat's Eye* (1989), *Alias Grace* (1996); and *The Robber Bride* (1994). She has also written a controversial study of

Canadian literature, *Survival* (1972), and compiled *The New Oxford Book of Canadian Verse in English* (1983). Her *Selected Poems*, originally published in 1976, has appeared in several editions, the latest in 1992. In this essay, she attempts to explain clearly why pornography is intolerable and why discussions of banning it have created much confusion.

When I was in Finland a few years ago for an international writers' conference, I had occasion to say a few paragraphs in public on the subject of pornography. The context was a discussion of political repression, and I was suggesting the possibility of a link between the two. The immediate result was that a male journalist took several large bites out of me. Prudery and pornography are two halves of the same coin, said he, and I was clearly a prude. What could you expect from an Anglo-Canadian? Afterward, a couple of pleasant Scandinavian men asked me what I had been so worked up about. All "pornography" means, they said, is graphic depictions of whores, and what was the harm in that?

Not until then did it strike me that the male journalist and I had two entirely different things in mind. By "pornography," he meant naked bodies and sex. I, on the other hand, had recently been doing the research for my novel *Bodily Harm*, and was still in a state of shock from some of the material I had seen, including the Ontario Board of Film Censors' "outtakes." By "pornography," I meant women getting their nipples snipped off with garden shears, having meat hooks stuck into their vaginas, being disemboweled; little girls being raped; men (yes, there are some men) being smashed to a pulp and forcibly sodomized. The cutting edge of pornography, as far as I could see, was no longer simple old copulation, hanging from the chandelier or otherwise: it was death, messy, explicit and highly sadistic. I explained this to the nice Scandinavian men. "Oh, but that's just the United States," they said. "Everyone knows they're sick." In their country, they said, violent "pornography" of that kind was not permitted on television or in movies; indeed, excessive violence of any kind was not permitted. They had drawn a clear line between erotica, which earlier studies had shown did not incite men to more aggressive and brutal behavior toward women, and violence, which later studies indicated did.

Some time after that I was in Saskatchewan, where, because of the scenes in *Bodily Harm*, I found myself on an open-line radio show answering questions about "pornography." Almost no one who phoned in was in favor of it, but again they weren't talking about the same stuff I was, because they hadn't seen it. Some of them were all set to stamp out bathing suits and negligees, and, if possible, any depictions of the female body whatsoever. God, it was implied, did not approve of female bodies, and sex of any kind, including that practised by bumblebees, should be shoved back into the dark, where it belonged. I had more than a suspicion that *Lady Chatterley's Lover,* Margaret Laurence's *The Diviners,* and indeed most books by most serious modern authors would have ended up as confetti if left in the hands of these callers.

For me, these two experiences illustrate the two poles of the emotionally heated debate that is now thundering around this issue. They also underline the desirability and even the necessity of defining the terms. "Pornography" is now one of those catchalls, like "Marxism" and "feminism," that have become so broad they can mean almost anything, ranging from certain verses in the Bible, ads for skin lotion and sex texts for children to the contents of Penthouse, Naughty '90s postcards and films with titles containing the word *Nazi* that show vicious scenes of torture and killing. It's easy to say that sensible people can tell the difference. Unfortunately, opinions on what constitutes a sensible person vary.

But even sensible people tend to lose their cool when they start talking about this subject. They soon stop talking and start yelling, and the name-calling begins. Those in favor of censorship (which may include groups not noticeably in agreement on other issues, such as some feminists and religious fundamentalists) accuse the others of exploiting women through the use of degrading images, contributing to the corruption of children, and adding to the general climate of violence and threat in which both women and children live in this society; or, though they may not give much of a hoot about actual women and children, they invoke moral standards and God's supposed aversion to "filth," "smut" and deviated *perversion,* which may mean ankles.

The camp in favor of total "freedom of expression" often comes out howling as loud as the Romans would have if told they could no longer have innocent fun watching the lions eat up Christians. It too may include segments of the population who are not natural bedfellows: those who proclaim their God-given right to freedom, including the freedom to tote guns, drive when drunk, drool over chicken porn and get off on videotapes of women being raped and beaten, may be waving the same anticensorship banner as responsible liberals who fear the return of Mrs. Grundy, or gay groups for whom sexual emancipation involves the concept of "sexual theatre." *Whatever turns you on* is a handy motto, as is *A man's home is his castle* (and if it includes a dungeon with beautiful maidens strung up in chains and bleeding from every pore, that's his business).

Meanwhile, theoreticians theorize and speculators speculate. Is today's pornography yet another indication of the hatred of the body, the deep mind-body split, which is supposed to pervade Western Christian society? Is it a backlash against the women's movement by men who are threatened by uppity female behavior in real life, so like to fantasize about women done up like outsize parcels, being turned into hamburger, kneeling at their feet in slavelike adoration or sucking off guns? Is it a sign of collective impotence, of a generation of men who can't relate to real women at all but have to make do with bits of celluloid and paper? Is the current flood just a result of smart marketing and aggressive promotion by the money men in what has now become a multibillion-dollar industry? If they were selling movies about men getting their testicles stuck full of knitting needles by women with swastikas on their sleeves, would they do as well, or is this penchant somehow peculiarly male? If so, why? Is pornography a power trip rather than a sex one? Some say that those ropes, chains, muzzles and other restraining devices are an argument for the immense power female sexuality still wields in the male imagination: you don't put these things on dogs unless you're afraid of them. Others, more literary, wonder about the shift from the 19th-century Magic Women or Femme Fatale image to the lollipop-licker, airhead or turkey-carcass treatment of women in porn today. The proporners don't care much about theory: they merely demand product. The anti-porners don't care about it in the final analysis either: there's dirt on the street, and they want it cleaned up, now.

It seems to me that this conversation, with its *You're-a-prude/You're-a-pervert* dialectic, will never get anywhere as long as we continue to think of this material as just "entertainment." Possibly we're deluded by the packaging, the format: magazine, book, movie, theatrical presentation. We're used to thinking of these things as part of the "entertainment industry," and we're used to thinking of ourselves as free adult people who ought to be able to see any kind of "entertainment" we want to. That was what the First Choice pay-TV debate was all about. After all, it's only entertainment, right? Entertainment means fun, and only a killjoy would be antifun. What's the harm?

This is obviously the central question: *What's the harm?* If there isn't any real harm to any real people, then the antiporners can tsk-tsk and/or throw up as much as they like, but they can't rightfully expect more legal controls or sanctions. However, the no-harm position is far from being proven.

(For instance, there's a clear-cut case for banning—as the federal government has proposed—movies, photos and videos that depict children engaging in sex with adults: real children are used to make the movies, and hardly anybody thinks this is ethical. The possibilities for coercion are too great.)

To shift the viewpoint, I'd like to suggest three other models for looking at "pornography"—and here I mean the violent kind.

Those who find the idea of regulating pornographic materials repugnant because they think it's Fascist or Communist or otherwise not in accordance with the principles of an open democratic society should consider that Canada has made it illegal to disseminate material that may lead to hatred toward any group because of race or religion. I suggest that if pornography of the violent kind depicted these acts being done predominantly to Chinese, to blacks, to Catholics, it would be off the market immediately, under the present laws. Why is hate literature illegal? Because whoever made the law thought that such material might incite real people to do real awful things to other real people. The human brain is to a certain extent a computer: garbage in, garbage out. We only hear about the extreme cases (like that of American multimurderer Ted Bundy) in which pornography has contributed to the death and/or mutilation of women and/or men. Although pornography is not the only factor involved in the creation of such deviance, it certainly has upped the ante by suggesting both a variety of techniques and the social acceptability of such actions. Nobody knows yet what effect this stuff is having on the less psychotic.

Studies have shown that a large part of the market for all kinds of porn, soft and hard, is drawn from the 16-to-21-year-old population of young men. Boys used to learn about sex on the street, or (in Italy, according to Fellini movies) from friendly whores, or, in more genteel surroundings, from girls, their parents, or, once upon a time, in school, more or less. Now porn has been added, and sex education in the schools is rapidly being phased out. The buck has been passed, and boys are being taught that all women secretly like to be raped and that real men get high on scooping out women's digestive tracts.

Boys learn their concept of masculinity from other men: is this what most men want them to be learning? If word gets around that rapists are "normal" and even admirable men, will boys feel that in order to be normal, admirable and masculine they will have to be rapists? Human beings are enormously flexible, and how they turn out depends a lot on how they're educated, by the society in which they're immersed as well as by their teachers. In a society that advertises and glorifies rape or even implicitly condones it, more women get raped. It becomes socially acceptable. And at a time when men and the traditional male role have taken a lot of flak and men are confused and casting around for an acceptable way of being male (and, in some cases, not getting much comfort from women on that score), this must be at times a pleasing thought.

It would be naïve to think of violent pornography as just harmless entertainment. It's also an educational tool and a powerful propaganda device. What happens when boy educated on porn meets girl brought up on Harlequin romances? The clash of expectations can be heard around the block. She wants him to get down on his knees with a ring, he wants her to get down on all fours with a ring in her nose. Can this marriage be saved?

Pornography has certain things in common with such addictive substances as alcohol and drugs: for some, though by no means for all, it induces chemical changes in the body, which the user finds exciting and pleasurable. It also appears to attract a "hard core" of habitual users and a penumbra of those who use it occasionally but aren't dependent on it in any way. There are also significant numbers of men who aren't much interested in it, not because they're undersexed but because real life is satisfying their needs, which may not require as many appliances as those of users.

For the "hard core," pornography may function as alcohol does for the alcoholic: tolerance develops, and a little is no longer enough. This may account for the short viewing time and fast turnover in porn theatres. Mary Brown, chairwoman of the Ontario Board of Film Censors, estimates that for every one mainstream movie requesting entrance to Ontario, there is one porno flick. Not only the quantity consumed but the quality of explicitness must escalate, which may account for the growing violence: once the big deal was breasts, then it was genitals, then copulation, then that was no longer enough and the hard users had to have more. The ultimate kick is death, and after that, as the Marquis de Sade so boringly demonstrated, multiple death.

The existence of alcoholism has not led us to ban social drinking. On the other hand, we do have laws about drinking and driving, excessive drunkenness and other abuses of alcohol that may result in injury or death to others.

This leads us back to the key question: what's the harm? Nobody knows, but this society should find out fast, before the saturation point is reached. The Scandinavian studies that showed a connection between depictions of sexual violence and increased impulse toward it on the part of male viewers would be a starting point, but many more questions remain to be raised as well as answered. What, for instance, is the crucial difference between men who are users and men who are not? Does using affect a man's relationship with actual women, and, if so, adversely? Is there a clear line between erotica and violent pornography, or are they on an escalating continuum? Is this a "men versus women" issue, with all men secretly siding with the proporners and all women secretly siding against? (I think not; there *are* lots of men who don't think that running their true love through the Cuisinart is the best way they can think of to spend a Saturday night, and they're just as nauseated by films of someone else doing it as women are.) Is pornography merely an expression of the sexual confusion of this age or an active contributor to it?

Nobody wants to go back to the age of official repression, when even piano legs were referred to as "limbs" and had to wear pantaloons to be decent. Neither do we want to end up in George Orwell's *1984*, in which pornography is turned out by the State to keep the proles in a state of torpor, sex itself is considered dirty and the approved practise is only for reproduction. But Rome under the emperors isn't such a good model either.

If all men and women respected each other, if sex were considered joyful and life-enhancing instead of a wallow in germ-filled glop, if everyone were in love all the time, if, in other words, many people's lives were more satisfactory for them than they appear to be now, pornography might just go away on its own. But since this is obviously not happening, we as a society are going to have to make some informed and responsible decisions about how to deal with it.

Suggestions for Discussion

1. Identify the following in the essay: D. H. Lawrence's *Lady Chatterley's Lover,* Margaret Laurence's *The Diviners,* Mrs. Grundy, the Marquis de Sade.
2. Summarize Atwood's major argument against pornography. What action does she believe society should take against it?
3. How do the Scandinavian countries deal with pornography? How do they define it?
4. Is Atwood too pessimistic about the ability of people who watch or read pornography to resist translating it into action by themselves?

Suggestions for Writing

1. Write a paper in which you express your agreement or disagreement with Atwood's definition of pornography.
2. Does Atwood's position result in censorship? Are you opposed to censorship? Write a paper in which you discuss censorship and pornography as defined by Atwood.
3. Is pornography an issue for women or is it important to both sexes? Write a paper in which you explain your opinion.

NOEL PERRIN

Science Fiction: Imaginary Worlds and Real-Life Questions

Noel Perrin (b. 1927), a professor of English and, since 1991, a professor of environmental studies at Dartmouth College, is a frequent contributor to *The New Yorker* and other periodicals. He also practices farming in Vermont. Among his published works are *A Passport*

Secretly Green (1961), *First Person Rural: Essays of a Sometime Farmer* (1980), *Third Person Rural: More Essays of a Sometime Farmer* (1981), *Last Person Rural* (1991), and *Solo: Life with an Electric Car* (1992). This personal account of his role in making science fiction respectable at Dartmouth also claims that it is an art form demanding serious consideration.

Fourteen years ago I began to teach a course in science fiction at Dartmouth College. Spaceships figured in the reading, along with faster-than-light travel, telepathic robots and in one story some bright orange aliens who rather resembled tennis balls on legs.

Not all my colleagues in the English department were embarrassed by the new course, just most. Say, 25 out of 30. In general, they knew just enough about science fiction—without, perhaps, having read any except those two special cases, *Brave New World* and *Nineteen Eighty-four*—to know that it was a formula genre, like the murder mystery, and not worthy of attention in the classroom. But they were powerless to stop the new course, or at least it would have taken a concerted effort. I was chairman of the department at the time, and my last year in office I spent such credit as I had left on getting the science fiction course approved.

Why did I want a science fiction course? It is not self-evident that Dartmouth students need to hear about tennis-ball-shaped aliens. Was I maybe pandering to popular taste, as chairmen often do when they want to build enrollment? (If so, it worked. About 160 students signed up that first year, and still more would have if we hadn't quickly closed the course.)

If I was pandering, it certainly wasn't conscious. I wanted the course for what seemed to me the very highest of reasons. I thought that the most important questions of the 20th century got more attention in works of science fiction than anywhere else. Fairly often they even got answers.

Some of these questions are quite specific. What might it feel like to live in the age after a nuclear war? Just how possible will it be, perhaps in the not so distant future, to turn all work over to robots? Since we can splice genes, what kind of creatures will we make of ourselves? Others are as broad as questions can get. What is the good life for human beings? What are our duties, if any, to other life-forms? If we can, should we abolish death? (That's a genuine issue. Some scientists think a form of immortality is no more than a century away.)

Philosophers once used to ask some of the same questions. A few of them still do. But to most philosophers the broad questions seem naïve, the product of an outdated metaphysics, and the narrow ones demand a range of technical knowledge most philosophers don't have.

More recently, novelists pondered many of the more metaphysical issues—until both they and critics realized that literature is self-referential and not much of a guide to the real world. Mainstream fiction now mostly flows in more private directions.

But science fiction, immensely sophisticated about technology, has stayed naïve about metaphysics—naïve in the sense that most science fiction writers continue to suppose that questions of value can be meaningfully discussed. (I suppose that, too. If I didn't, I would probably resign my job.) In fact, science fiction has become the chief refuge for metaphysics. It is where you go in literature if you want to hear people openly and seriously talking about meaning, and especially meaning in a world increasingly made and controlled by ourselves.

That is the main reason I wanted a science fiction course, but it is not the only one. There is also the question of literary merit. I support as much as any of my colleagues the notion that a genre needs to have attained a high level of distinction before it deserves to be taught in a course. I also think science fiction has attained that level. But it is not amazing that most professors of English failed to perceive that in 1975.

To begin with, though science fiction was well out of its infancy in 1975—was in fact about a hundred years old—it still seemed new. For example, with rare exceptions, it attained the dignity of being published in hard cover only in the 1960's. More serious science fiction was (and is) hard to distinguish from a couple of seedy cousins. If you were to pose the three for a group picture, you would put science fiction in the middle, clean-faced and intelligent. On one side, wearing stage armor, would be the sword-and-sorcery novel. On the other, holding a couple of laser pistols and wearing a gaudy helmet, space opera. Both these genres *are* formulaic, derivative, unworthy of being taught. And both are so interactive with science fiction that they can sometimes inhabit the same book. But science fiction is a much more serious genre, which, instead of trafficking in pure fantasy, attempts to be scientifically and logically responsible to the real universe.

Frank Herbert's *Dune,* for example, is part sword-and-sorcery—though in his case I prefer the politer name of heroic fantasy. There are witches in the book, prophecies, much hand-to-hand combat. But the book is also full of spaceships, personal atomic weapons and advanced ecology, and is partly science fiction.

Or take Larry Niven and Jerry Pournelle's book *The Mote in God's Eye,* once described by Robert A. Heinlein, one of the eminences of the field, as possibly the finest science fiction novel he'd ever read. The half of the book devoted to the alien creatures called Moties is indeed major science fiction. But the other half! That takes place aboard a starship of the Imperial Space Navy (I can see my colleagues grinning at the very name), and it reeks of space opera.

I doubt if any of my colleagues had read or even heard of *The Mote in God's Eye* in 1975. But they had certainly picked up on its vibes, as one would have said back then. They knew about space opera, and they erroneously thought that no science fiction existed without it.

In fact, enough science fiction of high literary quality, pure and unmixed with either space opera or fantasy, already existed to fill two or three courses. Easy to assert, hard to prove. What I shall do is name a few of the ones I actually used. The one that gave me the most private amusement was a novella written back in 1909. The author, an Englishman, had been reading H. G. Wells and had been so put off by what he saw as Wells's mindless faith in technology that he wrote his own work of science fiction as a riposte. Thus it came about that in the spring of 1975 one member of the department was teaching E. M. Forster's *Passage to India* in the 20th-century British novel course while I was simultaneously teaching *The Machine Stops* by the same E. M. Forster in the new science fiction course. It fitted in nicely. Just as Forster had written in response to Wells, so Arthur C. Clarke much later was moved to answer Forster in "The City and the Stars"; and that brooding novel—it deals with earthly immortality—was also in the course.

But there are not a lot of Huxleys, Orwells and Forsters who once or twice in their lives come trailing clouds of respectability into science fiction. Most of the good work (and virtually all of the bad) is by people who start out in science fiction, and who, along with all their books, were invisible to my colleagues in 1975. Such were three of the other works I taught.

The star of the course was undoubtedly Walter Miller's extraordinary novel, *A Canticle for Leibowitz.* It's the best and wisest of all novels about the world after a nuclear war, and also the most exhilarating to read. You didn't know a novel about a radioactive world *could* be exhilarating? You haven't read *Canticle* then.

Then I had Samuel R. Delany's story "We, in Some Strange Power's Employ, Move on a Rigorous Line." It's about employees of the one great power company that serves the whole planet, maybe 60 years from now, when the remotest Tibetan village is guaranteed access to electricity. It's also about what constitutes the good life, and about destiny, and about ambition. It operates on more levels that William Empson could have counted, including one on which the story plays off Spenser's *Faerie Queene,* though so unobtrusively that no Dartmouth student has yet noticed. Mr. Delany is the first major black science fiction writer to emerge, not that I knew that in 1975. I just knew that he had written a classic story.

And I also taught Ursula K. Le Guin's *Left Hand of Darkness,* a novel that goes so far beyond either feminism or male chauvinism as to leave people attached to either gender gasping in the dust. One way I know the book's power is that it has consistently stimulated good papers from students—some of the best papers I have ever got in any course.

A book focused on sex and gender is, of course, bound to be deeply interesting to 20-year-olds. I mean, even more interesting than to the rest of us. But *Left Hand* does more than speculate on what human beings would be like if all of us belonged to both sexes and were likely to be active in a male phase one month and female the next. It tells a heroic story. It develops rounded characters, most of them two-sexed inhabitants of the planet Gethen, but one a male visitor from Earth. (His nickname among Gethenians is "the pervert.") It brings a whole imagined world into plenary existence. There is nothing of formula here. There is high literature.

Three student generations have passed since those books were picked. (Not that I mean to claim pioneer status for the course. The first regular science fiction course seems to have been given at Colgate University in 1962.) If much good literature was available back then, vastly more is now. The late 20th century has been the golden age of science fiction.

In this country, writer after fine writer has emerged. I think of Michael Bishop, whose novella *Death and Designation Among the Asadi* gives so powerful a sense of what it would really be like to encounter—and not to understand—an alien intelligence that one understands even Columbus differently after reading it. I think of Alice Sheldon, the woman who wrote as James Tiptree, Jr. Her depiction of life aboard a United Nations starship in the novella *A Momentary Taste of Being* is to the Niven-Pournelle account of the Imperial Space Navy as a real horse is to a child's drawing. I think of Judith Moffett, who just two or three years ago turned from a successful career as a poet to a still more successful one as a writer of science fiction. Her first novel, *Pennterra,* the only work of Quaker science fiction I know, already establishes her as a presence in the field. It's as interesting ecologically as literarily.

Meanwhile, translation of major work from other parts of the world has proceeded rapidly. The most impressive examples have come from the Soviet Union and its satellites. Science fiction has its Borges in the person of Stanislaw Lem of Poland. I'm thinking especially of *The Cyberiad,* his mock-epic about cybers—that is, cybernetic beings, or robots. Mr. Lem's elaborate fantasies are less *outré* than the reader first supposes. In the real world, computer science students at the Massachusetts Institute of Technology are already wondering—as he has in this fiction—whether it will constitute murder when someone first unplugs a self-aware robot.

Among the Eastern Europeans, I particularly admire Arkady and Boris Strugatsky, Russian brothers whose jointly written novels dominate Soviet science fiction and are among the best in the world. If American publishers had the decency to keep them in print, I would always have had one in the course—most often, probably, *Roadside Picnic,* despite the bad translation in which it comes to us. The concept of the book is wonderful—that at some point a few years hence a group of aliens pauses briefly on Earth without our ever noticing and carelessly leaves a little debris behind when they go, like sandwich bags and soda cans after a picnic. We, like, ants, find it. And it is as mysterious to us as a soda can to an ant, which doesn't even know what Nutrasweet *is,* let alone its risks.

In 1989 I don't suppose that more than half the department is embarrassed by the existence of the course. Maybe less. But not many of my colleagues see it as important, either. I no longer teach the course. (I burn out on any course after a few years—13 with science fiction is my record for longevity.) The department's response has been to "bracket" the course. It will stay in the catalogue, but for now at least it will not be taught.

I admit that some of my colleagues' literary misgivings have been justified. Not about the books, but about me. I have found the metaphysics too tempting. Once a colleague came across a copy of my final exam. There was a perfectly decent question or two about narrational mode and so on, but there was also a question that asked simply, "If it were in your power to air-condition this planet, would you?"

Of course I can see why a literary theorist might shudder at such an exam. And I would be perfectly happy to have the department hire a replacement who would deal with science fiction in more rigorous and analytical ways. Such is the power of the genre that the metaphysics would come through anyway.

Suggestions for Discussion

1. What is Perrin's basic argument for including a course in science fiction in the English department curriculum? Does he make a good case? How?
2. What distinction does Perrin make between science fiction on one hand and the sword-and-sorcery novel and space opera on the other? With what works of space opera are you familiar?
3. Discuss Perrin's reasons for describing works by Miller, Delany, Le Guin, and others as profound works of fiction. Have you read any of the works he mentions? Does his description of them make you want to read them? Why?
4. What is the tone of this essay? How does Perrin establish it? Why does he disparage his final examination question that he quotes?
5. Discuss Perrin's statement that if he did not believe questions of value can be meaningfully discussed, he would give up teaching.

Suggestions for Writing

1. Write a paper in which you explain whether you think a work of science fiction has significance as literature. Notice how Perrin presents his evaluations and attempt to follow his example in your own essay.
2. Write an essay in which you discuss the proposition that what Perrin calls sword-and-sorcery works and space opera are not serious works of literature. Use as many examples, including film, as you think necessary to persuade your reader.

E. L. DOCTOROW

Ultimate Discourse

E. L. Doctorow (b. 1931), born in New York City, graduated with honors in philosophy from Kenyon College and has received two honorary doctorate degrees. He has worked as an editor in publishing and as a member of the English faculty at Sarah Lawrence College, Yale University, University of California, Irvine, and since 1982 has been a professor at New York University. He has received numerous honors, including the National Book Critics Circle Award for *Ragtime* (1975). He has served as director of the Authors Guild and is a member of the American Academy and the Institute for Arts and Letters. Among his works are *The Book of Daniel* (1971), *Drinks Before Dinner* (1979), *Loon Lake* (1980), and *Billy Bathgate* (1988). In 1990 he won the National Book Critics Circle Award and the PEN/Faulkner Award and was elected to the American Academy and Institute of Arts and Letters. In this brief essay he explains why fiction occupies a significant place in our lives.

When I was a boy everyone in my family was a good storyteller, my mother and father, my brother, my aunts and uncles and grandparents; all of them were people to whom interesting things seemed to happen. The events they spoke of were of a daily, ordinary sort, but when narrated or acted out they took on great importance and excitement as I listened.

Of course, when you bring love to the person you are listening to, the story has to be interesting, and in one sense the task of a professional writer who publishes books is to overcome the terrible loss of not being someone the reader knows and loves.

But apart from that, the people whose stories I heard as a child must have had a very firm view of themselves in the world. They must have been strong enough as presences in their own minds to trust that people would listen to them when they spoke.

I know now that everyone in the world tells stories. Relatively few people are given to mathematics or physics, but narrative seems to be within everyone's grasp, perhaps because it comes of the nature of language itself.

The moment you have nouns and verbs and prepositions, the moment you have subjects and objects, you have stories.

For the longest time there would have been nothing but stories, and no sharper distinction between what was real and what was made up than between what was spoken and what was sung. Religious arousal and scientific discourse, simple urgent communication and poetry, all burned together in the intense perception of a metaphor—that, for instance, the sun was a god's chariot driven across the heavens.

Stories were as important to survival as a spear or a hoe. They were the memory of the knowledge of the dead. They gave counsel. They connected the visible to the invisible. They distributed the suffering so that it could be borne.

In our era, even as we separate the functions of language, knowing when we speak scientifically we are not speaking poetically, and when we speak theologically we are not speaking the way we do to each other in our houses, and even as our surveys demand statistics, and our courts demand evidence, and our hypotheses demand proof—our minds are still structured for storytelling.

What we call fiction is the ancient way of knowing, the total discourse that antedates all the special vocabularies of modern intelligence.

The professional writer of fiction is a conservative who cherishes the ultimate structures of the human mind. He cultivates within himself the universal disposition to think in terms of conflict and its resolution, and in terms of character undergoing events, and of the outcome of events being not at all sure, and therefore suspenseful—the whole thing done, moreover, from a confidence of narrative that is grounded in our brains as surely as the innate talent to construe the world grammatically.

The fiction writer, looking around him, understands the homage a modern up-to-date world of nonfiction specialists pays to his craft—even as it isolates him and tells him he is a liar. Newsweeklies present the events of the world as installments in a serial melodrama. Weather reports on television are constructed with exact attention to conflict (high-pressure areas clashing with lows), suspense (the climax of tomorrow's prediction coming after the commercial), and the consistency of voice (the personality of the weathercaster). The marketing and advertising of product-facts is unquestionably a fictional enterprise. As is every government's representations of its activities. And modern psychology, with its concepts of *sublimation, repression, identity crisis, complex,* and so on, proposes the interchangeable parts for the stories of all of us; in this sense it is the industrialization of storytelling.

But nothing is as good at fiction as fiction. It is the most ancient way of knowing but also the most modern, managing when it's done right to burn all the functions of language back together into powerful fused revelation. Because it is total discourse it is ultimate discourse. It excludes nothing. It will express from the depth and range of its sources truths that no sermon or experiment or news report can begin to apprehend. It will tell you without shame what people do with their bodies and think with their minds. It will deal evenhandedly with their microbes or their intuitions. It will know their nightmares and blinding moments of moral crisis. You will experience love, if it so chooses, or starvation or drowning or dropping through space or holding a hot pistol in your hand with the police pounding on the door. This is the way it is, it will say, this is what it feels like.

Fiction is democratic, it reasserts the authority of the single mind to make and remake the world. By its independence from all institutions, from the family to the government, and with no responsibility to defend their hypocrisy or murderousness, it is a valuable resource and instrument of survival.

Fiction gives counsel. It connects the present with the past, and the visible with the invisible. It distributes the suffering. It says we must compose ourselves in our stories in order to exist. It says if we don't do it, someone else will do it for us.

Suggestions for Discussion

1. Doctorow suggests that storytelling is basic to everyone, a universal activity. How does he distinguish between the stories people tell to their loved ones and those authors write for publication?
2. What does Doctorow say is the origin of the urge to tell stories? Explain his assertion that storytelling fuses the elements of religion, science, and poetry.
3. Although the fused elements became separate in modern times, how does fiction remain fundamental to all activity? How, for example, is it used by representatives of government and business and by professional psychologists?
4. Doctorow says that "nothing is as good at fiction as fiction." Explain his reasons for this assertion.

Suggestions for Writing

1. Doctorow not only calls fiction the "ultimate discourse," but he says that it is also democratic. Write an essay in which you explain both of these assertions. Do you agree? Why?
2. Doctorow states that fiction "says we must compose ourselves in our stories in order to exist. It says if we don't do it, someone else will do it for us." Explain what he means by these remarks, particularly by the last sentence.

ALEKSANDR SOLZHENITSYN

Playing Upon the Strings of Emptiness

Aleksandr Solzhenitsyn (b. 1918), a Russian writer, was born in Kislovodsk, grew up in Rostov, and studied mathematics at the university there. During World War II he rose to the rank of captain in the Soviet artillery and was decorated for bravery. While still serving on the German front in 1945, he was arrested for criticizing Stalin and sentenced to eight years in prison where he became familiar with other political prisoners. His novel *One Day in the Life of Ivan Denisovich* (1962) was published through the intervention of Nikita Khrushchev. Its publication made the author famous. As his subsequent novels, *The First Circle* (1964) and *Cancer Ward* (1966), were regarded as too critical of the Soviet Union, he was censored and expelled from the Union of Soviet Writers. He was awarded the Nobel Prize for Literature in 1970, but, wishing to remain in the Soviet Union, he refused it. Since he also refused to remain silent about Soviet repression, he was arrested and forcibly deported in 1974. Soon after, he accepted his Nobel Prize. He is perhaps best known for *The Gulag Archipelago* (1973), which records the prison operations of Soviet totalitarianism from 1918 to 1956. After many years of exile in the United States, Solzhenitsyn returned to Russia after the overturn of the government of the Soviet Union. In 1993 he received the medal of honor of the National Arts Club. His wife received the award on his behalf and read his acceptance speech, printed here, translated by his sons, Ignat and Stephan. The reader, aware of the author's experience with repression in the Soviet Union, should not be surprised by the conservatism of his position in this speech.

There is a long-accepted truth about art that "style is the man" ("*le style est l'homme*"). This means that every work of a skilled musician, artist or writer is shaped by an absolutely unique combination of personality traits, creative abilities and individual, as well as national, experience. And since such a combination can never be repeated, art (but I shall here speak primarily of literature) possesses infinite variety across the ages and among different peoples. The divine plan is such that there is no limit to the appearance of ever new and dazzling creative talents, none of whom, however, negate in any way the works of their outstanding predecessors, even though they may be 500 or 2,000 years removed. The unending quest for what is new and fresh is never closed to us, but this does not deprive our grateful memory of all that came before.

No new work of art comes into existence (whether consciously or unconsciously) without an organic link to what was created earlier. But it is equally true that a healthy conservatism must be flexible both in terms of creation and perception, remaining equally sensitive to the old and to the new, to venerable and worthy traditions, and to the freedom to explore, without which no future can ever be born. At the same time the artist must not forget that creative *freedom* can be dangerous, for the fewer artistic limitations he imposes on his own work, the less chance he has for artistic success. The loss of a responsible organizing force weakens or even ruins the structure, the meaning and the ultimate value of a work of art.

Every age and every form of creative endeavor owes much to those outstanding artists whose untiring labors brought forth new meanings and new rhythms. But in the 20th century the necessary equilibrium between tradition and the search for the new has been repeatedly upset by a falsely understood "avant-gardism"—a raucous, impatient "avant-gardism" at any cost. Dating from before World War I, this movement undertook to destroy all commonly accepted art—its forms, language, features and properties—in its drive to build a kind of "superart," which would then supposedly spawn the New Life itself. It was suggested that literature should start anew "on a blank sheet of paper." (Indeed, some never went much beyond this stage.) Destruction, thus, became the apotheosis of this belligerent avant-gardism. It aimed to tear down the entire centuries-long cultural tradition, to break and disrupt the natural flow of artistic development by a sudden leap forward. This goal was to be achieved through an empty pursuit of novel forms as an end in itself, all the while lowering the standards of craftsmanship for oneself to the point of slovenliness and artistic crudity, at times combined with a meaning so obscured as to shade into unintelligibility.

This aggressive impulse might be interpreted as a mere product of personal ambition, were it not for the fact that in Russia (and I apologize to those gathered here for speaking mostly of Russia, but in our time it is impossible to bypass the harsh and extensive experience of my country), in

Russia this impulse and its manifestations preceded and foretold the most *physically* destructive revolution of the 20th century. Before erupting on the streets of Petrograd, this cataclysmic revolution erupted on the pages of the artistic and literary journals of the capital's bohemian circles. It is there that we first heard scathing imprecations against the entire Russian and European way of life, the calls to sweep away all religions or ethical codes, to tear down, overthrow, and trample all existing traditional culture, along with the self-extolment of the desperate innovators themselves, innovators who never did succeed in producing anything of worth. Some of these appeals literally called for the destruction of the Racines, the Murillos and the Raphaels, "so that bullets would bounce off museum walls." As for the classics of Russian literature, they were to be "thrown overboard from the ship of modernity." Cultural history would have to begin anew. The cry was "Forward, forward!"—its authors already called themselves "futurists," as though they had now stepped over and beyond the present, and were bestowing upon us what was undoubtedly the genuine art of the Future.

But no sooner did the revolution explode in the streets, than those "futurists" who only recently, in their manifesto entitled "A Slap in the Face of Public Taste," had preached an "insurmountable hatred toward the existing language"—these same "futurists" changed their name to the "Left Front," now directly joining the revolution at its leftmost flank. It thus became clear that the earlier outbursts of this "avant-gardism" were no mere literary froth, but had very real embodiment in life. Beyond their intent to overturn the entire culture, they aimed to uproot life itself. And when the Communists gained unlimited power (their own battle cry called for tearing the existing world "down to its foundations," so as to build a new Unknown Beautiful World in its stead, with equally unlimited brutality) they not only opened wide the gates of publicity and popularity to this horde of so-called "avant-gardists," but even gave some of them, as to faithful allies, power to administrate over culture.

Granted, neither the ragings of this pseudo-"avant-garde" nor its power over culture lasted long; there followed a general coma of all culture. We in the U.S.S.R. began to trudge, downcast, through a 70-year-long ice age, under whose heavy glacial cover one could barely discern the secret heartbeat of a handful of great poets and writers. These were almost entirely unknown to their own country, not to mention the rest of the world, until much later. With the ossification of the totalitarian Soviet regime, its inflated pseudoculture ossified as well, turning into the loathsome ceremonial forms of so-called "socialist realism." Some individuals have been eager to devote numerous critical analyses to the essence and significance of this phenomenon. I would not have written a single one, for it is outside the bounds of art altogether: the *object* of study, the style of "socialist realism," never existed. One does not need to be an expert to see that it consisted of nothing more than servility, a style defined by "What would you care for?" or "Write whatever the Party commands." What scholarly discussion can possibly take place here?

And now, having lived through these 70 lethal years inside Communism's iron shell, we are crawling out, though barely alive. A new age has clearly begun, both for Russia and for the whole world. Russia lies utterly ravaged and poisoned; its people are in a state of unprecedented humiliation, and are on the brink of perishing physically, perhaps even biologically. Given the current conditions of national life, and the sudden exposure and ulceration of the wounds amassed over the years, it is only natural that literature should experience a pause. The voices that bring forth the nation's literature need time before they can begin to sound once again.

However, some writers have emerged who appreciate the removal of censorship and the new, unlimited artistic freedom mostly in one sense: for allowing uninhibited "self-expression." The point is to *express* one's own perception of one's surroundings, often with no sensitivity toward today's ills and scars, and with a visible emptiness of heart; to express the personality of an author, whether it is significant or not; to express it with no sense of responsibility toward the morals of the public, and especially of the young; and at times thickly lacing the language with obscenities which for hundreds of years were considered unthinkable to put in print, but now seem to be almost in vogue.

The confusion of minds after 70 years of total oppression is more than understandable. The artistic perception of the younger generations finds itself in shock, humiliation, resentment, amnesia. Unable to find in themselves the strength fully to withstand and refute Soviet dogma in the past, many young writers have now given in to the more accessible path of pessimistic relativism. Yes, they say, Communist doctrines were a great lie; but then again, absolute truths do not exist anyhow, and trying to find them is pointless. Nor is it worth the trouble to strive for some kind of higher meaning.

And in one sweeping gesture of vexation, classical Russian literature—which never disdained reality and sought the truth—is dismissed as next to worthless. Denigrating the past is deemed to be the key to progress. And so it has once again become fashionable in Russia to ridicule, debunk, and toss overboard the great Russian literature, steeped as it is in love and compassion toward all human beings, and especially toward those who suffer. And in order to facilitate this operation of discarding, it is announced that the lifeless and servile "socialist realism" had in fact been an organic continuation of full-blooded Russian literature.

Thus we witness, through history's various thresholds, a recurrence of one and the same perilous anti-cultural phenomenon, with its rejection of and contempt for all foregoing tradition, and with its mandatory hostility toward whatever is universally accepted. Before, it burst in upon us with the fanfares and gaudy flags of "futurism"; today the term "post-modernism" is applied. (Whatever the meaning intended for this term, its lexical makeup involves an incongruity: the seeming claim that a person can think and experience *after* the period in which he is destined to live.)

For a post-modernist, the world does not possess values that have reality. He even has an expression for this: "the world as text," as something secondary, as the text of an author's work, wherein the primary object of interest is the author himself in his relationship to the work, his own introspection. Culture, in this view, ought to be directed inward at itself (which is why these works are so full of reminiscences, to the point of tastelessness); it alone is valuable and real. For this reason the concept of play acquires a heightened importance—not the Mozartian playfulness of a Universe overflowing with joy, but a forced playing upon the strings of emptiness, where an author need have no responsibility to anyone. A denial of any and all ideals is considered courageous. And in this voluntary self-delusion, "post-modernism" sees itself as the crowning achievement of all previous culture, the final link in its chain. (A rash hope, for already there is talk of the birth of "conceptualism," a term that has yet to be convincingly defined in terms of its relationship to *art,* though no doubt this too will duly be attempted. And then there is already *post-avant-gardism;* and it would be no surprise if we were to witness the appearance of a "post-post-modernism," or of a "post-futurism.") We could have sympathy for this constant searching, but only as we have sympathy for the suffering of a sick man. The search is doomed by its theoretical premises to forever remaining a secondary or ternary exercise, devoid of life or of a future.

But let us shift our attention to the more complex flow of this process. Even though the 20th century has seen the more bitter and disheartening lot fall to the peoples under Communist domination, our whole world is living through a century of spiritual illness, which could not but give rise to a similar ubiquitous illness in art. Although for other reasons, a similar "post-modernist" sense of confusion about the world has also arisen in the West.

Alas, at a time of an unprecedented rise in the material benefits of civilization and ever-improving standards of living, the West, too, has been undergoing an erosion and obscuring of high moral and ethical ideals. The spiritual axis of life has grown dim, and to some lost artists the world has now appeared in seeming senselessness, as an absurd conglomeration of debris.

Yes, world culture today is of course in crisis, a crisis of great severity. The newest directions in art seek to outpace this crisis on the wooden horse of clever stratagems—on the assumption that if one invents deft, resourceful new methods, it will be as though the crisis never was. Vain hopes. Nothing worthy can be built on a neglect of higher meanings and on a relativistic view of concepts and culture as a whole. Indeed, something greater than a phenomenon confined to art can be discerned shimmering here beneath the surface—shimmering not with light but with an ominous crimson glow.

Looking intently, we can see that behind these ubiquitous and seemingly innocent experiments of rejecting "antiquated" tradition there lies a deep-seated hostility toward any spirituality. This relentless cult of novelty, with its assertion that art need not be good or pure, just so long as it is new, newer, and newer still, conceals an unyielding and long-sustained attempt to undermine, ridicule and uproot all moral precepts. There is no God, there is no truth, the universe is chaotic, all is relative, "the world as text," a text any post-modernist is willing to compose. How clamorous it all is, but also—how helpless.

For several decades now, world literature, music, painting and sculpture have exhibited a stubborn tendency to grow not higher but to the side, not toward the highest achievements of craftsmanship and of the human spirit but toward their disintegration into a frantic and insidious "novelty." To decorate public spaces we put up sculptures that estheticize pure ugliness—but we no longer register surprise. And if visitors from outer space were to pick up our music over the airwaves, how could they ever guess that earthlings once had a Bach, a Beethoven and a Schubert, now abandoned as out of date and obsolete?

If we, the creators of art, will obediently submit to this downward slide, if we cease to hold dear the great cultural tradition of the foregoing centuries together with the spiritual foundations from which it grew—we will be contributing to a highly dangerous fall of the human spirit on earth, to a degeneration of mankind into some kind of lower state, closer to the animal world.

And yet, it is hard to believe that we will allow this to occur. Even in Russia, so terribly ill right now, we wait and hope that after the coma and a period of silence, we shall feel the breath of a reawakening Russian literature, and that we shall witness the arrival of fresh new forces—of our younger brothers.

Suggestions for Discussion

1. Explain the writer's point that God provides the opportunity for many skilled, original, and diverse artists. How does he relate this occurrence to the tradition of literature? What does he mean by "healthy conservatism"?

2. What distinguishes twentieth-century literature from the tradition of the past?
3. What is Solzhenitsyn's reaction to "avant-gardism"? Why does he believe that this art movement differs from any other art movement in previous times? Why does he regard the "avant-garde" as destructive?
4. What is the tone of this speech? Is it suited to the subject? Does Solzhenitsyn distinguish between the literature of the West and that of Russia? According to the author, what role did communism play in the development of twentieth-century literature?
5. Discuss the author's use of the term "post-modernism." How does he trace the rise of post-modernism to the loss of spirituality in the West?

Suggestions for Writing

1. Write a paper in which you attempt to summarize and evaluate the author's conservative hostility to twentieth-century literature.
2. T. S. Eliot's essay "Tradition and the Individual Talent" makes several points similar to the one made in this speech. Write a paper in which you compare and contrast the arguments of both authors. (You will find the other essay in the *Collected Essays* of T. S. Eliot.)

EAVAN BOLAND

When the Spirit Moves

Eavan Boland (b. 1944 or 1945) was born in Dublin and educated in London and New York before graduating from Trinity College, Dublin. She played a central role in founding Arlen House, a feminist publishing company in Dublin, and has published many volumes of poetry, including *Object Lesson, Night Seed, In Her Own Language* and *Outside History: Selected Poems*, 1980–1990. She won the America/Ireland Fund Literary Award and, in 1994, the Lannan Literary Award for Poetry. This essay, an adaptation of a speech at a conference on religion and poetry, discusses the implications of numerous 1985 sightings of the enshrined Virgin Mary moving.

Asked to take part in a conference on "the writer and religion," I found the subject so wide and the implications of it so broad that the only way I could bring it into focus was to start by being both local and personal. I will begin here with a story which is both odd and true and which, for me, raises just a few of the questions that are at the heart of the subject.

The summer of 1985 was warm and fine in Ireland. The good weather meant that the evenings were often clear and sunny and, because Ireland is so far north, the light at midsummer lasts until an hour or so before midnight. I remember that clearly, because my children were not yet teen-agers and they could ride their bicycles and stay out with their friends much later than usual. When the day was over, there were tell-tale streaks of orange and light pink in the sky—the rhyming sky of the shepherd's delight. And so the pattern of warm evenings and changed habits continued. Therefore instead of staying in and watching August rain and lamenting a lost summer, or reading newspaper headlines about a spoiled harvest—all of which can be common summer experiences in Ireland—it was possible to go out and drive or visit friends or work in the garden.

All this has a bearing on the story. Because in West Cork, along the seaboard, the weather was also fine. In the town of Kinsale, which is a summer resort on that coast, there were more tourists than usual. This is one of the beautiful parts of Ireland and indeed, without being tribal, one of the beautiful parts of Europe. Surrounding it are small towns, villages, and farms. The terrain is fairly flat, without some of the Gulf Stream warmth which produces the dramatic palms and tropical branches of certain parts of Kerry further west.

This is what happened there. And this is how it stirred almost the whole of Ireland during that summer. Traveling back by car on one of those fine evenings, a woman stopped at a grotto which contained a statue of Our Lady. Ireland, which in the Republic at least has sustained a largely Catholic culture, had celebrated what was called a Marian year in 1950: a year, that is, in which Our Lady was honored as the Mother of Christ. The result of the celebrations was that hundreds of small grottoes and statues and shrines to Our Lady remained scattered around the countryside as continuing places of worship. This one was just outside the village of Ballinspittle, perhaps ten miles from Kinsale. It was eloquently set in the recess of a hillside, about thirty feet above the road. And on one of those sunny evenings, in late July, when travel in a car, or a visit to the places which contained such a grotto, must have seemed like a pleasant and appropriate summer diversion, a woman saw that statue of the Virgin Mary move.

Within not weeks, but days, someone reported a similar phenomenon. Then another. Then another. Then more and at different shrines. Subheadlines of the *Irish Times*, second leaders on the evening news, whole radio programs, and finally television documentaries were devoted to the phenomenon. A woman had seen a statue move in a city church. Another had seen the Virgin reach out her hand. Another saw her move as if to step down from her shrine.

Then the headlines gave way, at least in the urban press, to analysis. Sociologists, psychologists, psychiatrists began to be featured on television. They explained that this was not unusual, that in times of stress, of hardship and recession, this sort of thing had been observed widely. By this time the summer evenings were getting shorter but the clear, warm hours before dark, and just after it, were filled with literally hundreds of cars, visitors, couples, and whole families converging on any place along the seaboard, but especially near Kinsale, where this had been observed. In an outpouring of insistence and longing, men and women with accents which were not so often features of the urban Dublin news programs described what they had seen, and they could not be shaken from their stories.

Then the explanations grew less frequent. The outrage and suspicion of the Catholic clergy, disowning and warning against these visions, became less emphatic. The journalistic silly season passed. The evenings grew colder. The rain returned. Suddenly, as quickly as it had come, the phenomenon was over. No statues moved. No sociologists talked. Normality returned.

I remember that summer clearly. I remember driving down the Dublin roads, where the luburnum and lilac filled the verges with yellow and violet, and listening to my car radio. Something seemed to have happened that was not faith, and could not be called religion; that was short of hysteria and yet by no means rational. From the safety of a cosmopolitan city, which Dublin has finally become—with fast cars and fast food and a limited concentration span—I could hear, to use Joyce's phrase, "the batsqueak" of another Ireland. Through the statistics of debt and unemployment, and Northern violence, I could hear the elegy and anger break out one last time, lamenting a simpler time and a surer one.

I did not believe that the statues had moved. But I did not believe the sociologists either. I knew enough about the unreason of Irish history to respect and even be in some awe of what had taken place on, those fierce and unaccountable evenings, in the long light hours, in small towns and farmlands where television cameras hardly ever reached, and where political scientists usually never went, except briefly at election time. And I was troubled.

As I listened to disc jockeys and radio broadcasters speaking jovially or contemptuously, whichever way you viewed it, of the faith and hallucination of those who saw those statues move, I turned back in my own mind to what I exactly thought of it all. On the one hand I could treat it—and I was tempted to—as simply a viral strain of Irish history breaking out again: a summer fever of doubt and need and image-making, all bound in with the old rituals and the once familiar certainties. On the other hand, long after that summer was over I continued to think about what had happened, turning it over in my mind. Since I lived in Dublin, I heard more of the skepticism and muted contempt which a place of purported sophistication has for a simpler region than anything which might indicate sympathy with what had happened.

And yet I was moved. I could not completely share in the cynicism of a capital city. During those weeks, I had driven, as I've said, with the car radio on, from leafy road to city center, from new shopping complex to concert hall. I had turned the car toward and away from all those amenities and derivations which a capital city prides itself on. I had passed tire signs, Coke signs, fast food restaurants, garages selling new imports—and all the time I had the car radio on. All the time I had been listening to those reports from the seaboard, taking in those messages of an older Ireland. While the summer gathered heat and intensity and then began to wane and cool, an old wound had broken open: some human longing for faith and need.

Long after it was all forgotten this remained with me. However remote I felt from the participants of those events, however removed by region and belief and history, I was still in some degree affected by what had happened. If nothing else, that outbreak of an old mode of perception made me begin to look more inquiringly at those things we thought of as new. And one of the things I began to measure, without even being conscious of it, was a distance between ways of seeing. After all, those people in the farms and at the crossroads had spoken, for a brief moment that summer, of vision. Maybe a vision of impossible things. But vision all the same. I had grown up as an Irish poet in a country where the distance between vision and imagination was not quite as wide as in some other countries. As late as the eighteenth century, when the English poets were in coffee houses, publishing stylish magazines, and making couplets into epigrams, the Irish poets were storming against history, lamenting the loss of their language, and writing of The Aisling, the vision of a maiden who was both Ireland and destiny: a muselike figure found in a dark time.

But of course that was all far in the past. The twentieth century had produced literature in Ireland which kept a tense distance from the sources of faith. And for good reason. Irish writing had suffered a terrible censorship in the twentieth century. Yet despite that, I began, in my own mind anyway, to look afresh at some of those changes and adjustments that had divided us from the culture of belief in Ireland. I had seen those changes increase as I grew older.

Now I began to look at the anomalies and contrasts around me much more closely. Just as the capital city had changed from the small, insular town I had found as a young poet, so the writer's life had similarly changed. Then I had started writing in a closed, post-Revival world, where the shadows of the national upheaval and the intense effort to make a literary movement were still evident. Now we lived a life as writers which was more cosmopolitan, more open, which had more travel, and more exchange. And always, whenever an old life changes into a new one, or so it seemed to me, there was a belief on the part of those who lived that new life that they were more rational, less prone to the hysterias and superstition which marked the old one.

Certainly one of the ways we defined ourselves as Irish writers—although perhaps not openly or articulately—was in the distance we had made and kept from those dark forces which had collected at the crossroads, and which saw the images of an old faith move and shimmer and reach out toward affirmation in the dying light. The Irish censorship, which I just spoke of, had been a savage affair. It had lasted from 1929 right into the 1960s. I began writing at the very end of it, but many of the older writers I know—mostly novelists—had been injured and isolated by it. It had kept out of the reach of Irish readers not only the writings of their own countrymen and women, but also the good and experimental work of other countries. And the engines of that censorship were, in some sense, just those collective forces of unreason which collected at the seaboards, drove their cars through small towns and into open fields, and worshiped a moving statue. But in the case of the censorship they were those forces having found voices, laws, and power. Every writer's nightmare.

In Ireland then, writers considered themselves at some distance from such forces. Not always, but often, faith was cast as unreason. The faithless and skeptical world of the writer was cast as the force of rationality and light. In opposing the censorship I understood that shorthand. But I was troubled. I had been moved by the need, the raw expectation and hunger of those who saw the statues move. I believed, in common with many others, that these were the hallucinations of a bad summer: a summer of recession and political instability. But I did not like the superiority that the capital city, and in some senses the writing world, assumed about it. And I began to seriously think about whether writers were as innocent of that superstition as they claimed.

It is certainly true that writers take a stance at some variance from organized religion. This, of course, has not always been true. But since the Romantic movement, and of course I'm speaking now, and will from now on, really exclusively about poetry, the emphasis has been on an individual imagination defined against, rather than in terms of, any orthodoxy. The decline of faith is a backdrop to the poems of Shelley, Tennyson, Hopkins. Despite the fact that Yeats spoke with real bitterness about having been brought up in a secular household, where his father was a follower of Huxley and Darwin, the emphasis of the individual poet has been, in the last hundred years, more on decline than on faith. Therefore, inevitably, the act of the individual imagination, in poetry anyway, is seen as free from superstition and prejudice, and so committed to individual exploration that it escapes the hysteria of collective superstition. Of course there is substance in all this. Of course the individual imagination is a subversive force, and far less likely, for the very reason that it stands alone, to be the accomplice of a collective suppression. Nevertheless it seems to me that in the opposition between imagination and faith which we inherit from Romanticism—at least as poets—imagination has become an article *of* faith. And I want to challenge this.

Obviously one of the things which the conference I attended was considering is whether the relation between religion and literature is valuable or dangerous. Not surprisingly, the answer may well be that it is both. As an Irish poet, my view is neither clear nor straightforward. The Republic of Ireland has had a powerfully Catholic history. To the ritualistic emphasis of the Irish past, to the vitality of a speech which shadows faith, I owe something, as any Irish person would. But to the intervention of religion in civil expression I also, like all other Irish writers and citizens, owe one of the worst censorships in Europe. But the issue of religion and literature, in my own case, goes well beyond Ireland and Irish affairs and therefore I set it out here briefly, so as to summarize something of my doubts about what is lost and what is gained in that relation.

I inherited, as an Irish poet—and as all Irish writers do—a duality of cultural reference. It is one of the inevitabilities of a colonial past. Behind me, on the one hand, was the ruined language of my own country, the dispersal of the Bardic orders, and the loss of one kind of history which was a direct result of colonial oppression. To adapt Yeats's phrase, Irish "was my native language but it was not my mother tongue." Therefore when I was a young poet, when I lifted my pen to write a poem, that pen described an arc of tensions and contradictions which reflected the ambiguity of the Irish experience. Among those tensions was the fact that I also, as an Irish poet, looked to the British nineteenth century.

The contradictions of that dual awareness were added to by other, far more subjective ones. When I left college I married, I had two young children, I went to live in the suburbs. I found that I now considered the past not as an abstract presence, but as an urgent reference point. And yet it was increasingly hard to have any kind of dialogue with a poetic past. I lived an ordinary life among down-to-earth routines. I lifted a child; I left a milk bottle out on the step. And yet I felt two things very strongly: I felt, however ordinary those routines, that I stood at the lyric center of my experience, and that I wished to make a visionary claim for that experience. Nevertheless, in some sense I felt obstructed from doing so. Some shadow fell between me and my sense that I could get from that historic-poetic past the sanction I needed, both for my subject matter and the claim I wished to make for it in formal terms.

And so I wrote my poems, and increasingly was drawn into speculation about a past tradition, and where exactly the authority of the poet came from, and what it was within that historic tradition which seemed to me to have prescribed an inflationary spiral of subject matter in poetry, so that the ordinary day I lived was not easily included or made welcome there.

Everything I am saying now is telescoped, rushed, gathered into a shorthand, and I hope you will bear with me. These issues are so wide and important they should not be issued in telegrams as I am doing now. But I will say that gradually I came to the belief—and of course I am using the widest terms once again—that what had gone wrong was exactly what the conference I attended was to address: I felt that a relation between religion and literature had failed in a particular way. In that difficult time for me, when I tried to discover why my life was not named in a past tradition I loved, I had the illusion that I might find one moment which was instructive of all the exclusions and obstructions within that tradition. There never, of course, is such a moment. Nevertheless, I came to settle on the figure of Matthew Arnold, the British poet and critic who in the mid-nineteenth century in England restated the destiny of poetry in his criticism. Here is one of the things he said:

> We should conceive of poetry worthily, and more highly than it has been the custom to conceive of it. We should conceive of it as capable of higher uses, and called to higher destinies, than those which in general men have assigned to it hitherto. More and more mankind will discover that we have to turn to poetry to interpret life for us, to console us, to sustain us. Without poetry our science will appear incomplete; and most of what now passes with us for religion and philosophy will be replaced by poetry.

In his Oxford lectures on poetry Matthew Arnold expanded this view in this way:

> There is not a creed which is not shaken, not an accredited dogma which is not shown to be questionable, not a received tradition which does not threaten to dissolve. Our religion has materialized itself in the fact, in the supposed fact; it

> has attached its emotion to the fact and now the fact is failing it. But for poetry the idea is everything; the rest is a world of illusion, of divine illusion. Poetry attaches its emotion to the idea; the idea is the fact. The strongest part of our religion today is its unconscious poetry.

To me these statements summarize a danger in the relation between religion and literature—although once again let me emphasize I make these remarks from the viewpoint of a poet. Arnold lived in a time when the edifice of faith was cracking, when doubt was replacing it as a communal possession. He lived when the Church was being challenged and when its most rigid tenets were in the process of being set aside. In these words, as he sets out his views, a boundary has shimmered and dissolved. The line between religion and poetry has given way. And what comes forth, monstrous to my eyes anyway, is neither religion nor poetry, but the religion of poetry.

And this brings up the irony of the relation. Those men and women at the crossroads in Ireland were not sensible, were not logical. They may not have seen what they thought they saw. They may not have known why they needed to see it. But they were, as Eliot said, reverting to a psychological habit which may no longer be supported, but is still part of human history.

What I found poignant and memorable about the account of that summer, and the images and accents of those people, is that they stayed with me not as harbingers of unreason, but as voices of the disenfranchised. Their brief moment of hallucination and insistence only proved that they were cut off from a hinterland of faith which would once, centuries before, have been their entitlement. And which, in countries like Ireland, remained long after its occasion had passed in the rest of Europe. In their attempt to make sacred a time and a country that were resolutely being defined as secular, they were testifying to an enormous loss and a true deprivation.

I think it is, right to ask whether literature has registered that loss exactly; whether it has written it down as a communal one. Or whether it has merely responded to it by denoting the imagination as a sacred place, and forgetting or dismissing the communal aspect of it all.

The events at the crossroads then were expressions of a communal will. But in its individual insistence, Matthew Arnold's argument seems to me much more insidious. Even the most ardent secularists of this century and the last, even those who would lament what happened at the Irish crossroads, who would regard it as primitive, unwise, an omen of the dark ages, have not always been able to resist the temptation held out by Arnold which, for all its eloquence, is still a call to faith and unreason. His argument that the imagination is a sacramental force and that the poem can usurp some of the functions of religion has been profoundly influential on poetry in this century. In a time of lost power it makes a claim for increased privileges for the artist. The irony of this, to me anyway, is that it brings us back to something more primitive again. To invest, as Arnold does, the imagination with sacramental force restores to poetry not its religious force, but its magical function.

Even those who most widely dispute the connection between religion and literature do not always set aside this old connection. But it is a dangerous one. And I think it should be a subtext here of the discussion about religion and literature, because magic and expression are older even than that, and have profoundly influenced that later conjunction. Poetry, of course, has always had a connection with magic. In the oldest societies they were part and parcel of each other. But magic, in my view, is the most inferior of the past associations of poetry, and ironically remains as the most inferior of all present temptations for the poet. Magic, after all, is the search for control over an unruly environment: that control is achieved, so history tells us, by secret words known only to a few men. When these associations—which are so primitive and so recurring—are carried into the act of poetry, strange things can happen.

To begin with, the man or woman writing ceases to be human and becomes "a poet." Words cease to be what they mean and become what they do: Do they rhyme, do they elide, does this vowel go with that consonant? The momentum of the poem is guided and obstructed by the demand that it be "poetic." Experience itself is sifted so that the "poetic" bits are winnowed out in case they contaminate the final product. And the best you achieve is a decorative simplification of life based on a dread of it.

In this tension, this debate between literature and religion, I am reminded of a beautiful phrase which William Yeats used when he looked out on the Clare-Galway border from his own tower in the west of Ireland. He spoke there about "a community bound together by imaginative possessions." It is an eloquent phrase and he used it in the context of a National Theatre. He intended it to be a phrase of celebration and regret, and a way of noting those things which are gained and lost in the small communities which exist in rural parts.

His phrase could serve on both sides of the argument about what distance, or closeness, should exist between literature and religion. The old argument which writers have justifiably made against organized religion is that it did not bind together the communal possessions of a people; that in fact it distorted them with false and automatic meanings. But in the great drive which has existed since the nineteenth century, which is there in the rhetoric of Matthew Arnold—a move to insist on the sacramental qualities of the creative imagination—I believe the writer is in fact turning away from the priestly superstitions only to take on the mantle of the priest. It is a maneuver which has narrowed the scope of poetry and confined the debate about its importance. In an age like our own, when poets are turning in on themselves more and more, when they are engaged in a painful debate about the nature of their audience, this old tendency to consider the poetic imagination as an abstract of the privileges of faith has not been helpful.

It seems to me right, then, that in our age and our time, the relation between religion and literature should be looked at with vigilance and fear and inquiry. The ominous injustice to Salman Rushdie, the events in Turkey two years ago, the prescriptions laid on subject matter by non-artistic agendas, all of these are true threats to imaginative freedom. They argue for a distance between the established tenets of religion and the working freedoms of the artist. And I support that.

Nevertheless I think we have to confront the fact that any such distance is not unambiguous. When I listened on those evenings to those stories of faith and image-making, those hallucinations of the supernatural, I also envied a world which once existed for the writer, and now was gone: of faith and grace and surrender.

It does not seem to me to be enough to propose cold, clear distances between literature and religion without looking at the fact that over the last century, while the relation between literature and religion has failed, the rise of the religion of literature, the hubris of the imagination and its sanctity has been an undercurrent of a great deal of the analysis and discussion of art. If a writer, whether man or woman, has a doubt and a dread about the relation of literature and religion then I support that. But not if, at the same time, they are constructing an image of the writer which accrues to the imagination the old privileges of magic and control; the old status of arbiter of reality.

There is a hysteria in religion; I come from a country which has seen it in many aspects over the last century. It is there in the censorship Irish writers endured. It is there in the fact that the Irish attorney general would not allow a teen-age girl, who had been raped and was pregnant, to leave the country two years ago to have an abortion. It is there in the killings that happened, in the various names of faith, for twenty-five years in Ireland. And it was there nine years ago on those summer nights, under painted statues, at the end of summer, when a whole nation held its breath and observed a return—of the raw hunger for certainty and grace and escape.

But there is a hysteria that is latent in a certain view of the imagination as well. And yet the irony of the summer of 1985 was that the roads and distances were filled with men and women who were not merely caught in the grip of a religious excess, but of an imaginative one as well. The sources of their imaginative fervor are mysterious and may well be corrupt. But they have a source in the communal imagination, in that community of possession and re-statement which Yeats wrote about. The separation between religion and imagination needs to be discriminating and exact. And it comes, as all such separations do, when the individual imagination breaks with an orthodoxy. When it is able to say, to use Joyce's phrase, "non serviam." In Ireland that has been a painful choice. For those who wish to keep a vigil for expression and freedom, it is also a necessary one. But I see no point at all in taking from religion its old powers of suppression and authority, and transferring them to the imagination of the artist.

Suggestions for Discussion

1. Summarize Boland's ambivalent attitude toward the relationship between religion and poetry in Ireland.
2. What is the significance of the outbreak of visions, in the summer of 1985, of moving statutes of the Virgin Mary? Was the Catholic Church friendly or hostile in its reaction? How did secular commentators explain the visions?
3. Explain Boland's mentions of Irish censorship. Why does she believe that Ireland was particularly susceptible to censorship?
4. Boland refers to Matthew Arnold's beliefs about religion and poetry. How does she respond to Arnold and to other English writers of the nineteenth century?
5. What does Boland envision as the ideal relationship between Irish religion and Irish poetry?

Suggestions for Writing

1. Boland refers to the Irish poet Yeats several times. Why is Yeats an important figure for her?
2. Write an essay (after some research) on the impact of English colonialism on the development of Irish writing and thought.
3. Write an essay explaining Boland's use of the visions of the Virgin Mary.

ROGER ROSENBLATT

What's That to Us?

Roger Rosenblatt (b. 1940) was born in New York City. He holds graduate degrees from Harvard University and honorary degrees from several other universities. He has been editor of *The New Republic,* columnist for the *Washington Post,* and contributing editor of the *New York Times Magazine.* He has published a number of books and won numerous journalistic honors. In this short essay, he argues that the traditional canon of English literature is, because of its high quality, meaningful for students from many different backgrounds.

The food was wrong. The medicines were wrong. The clothing was wrong. We took the wrong exercise. We learned the wrong trades. We used the wrong words. One of the more irritating parts of growing older is that you come to find out that everything you did in your youth was wrong. Oh, yes. Our education. Our education was terribly wrong.

How gratifying, then, to be sitting in a movie theater and watching *Sense and Sensibility.* I thought "The hell it was"—the "it" being the education of my over-50 generation, which was a literary education, which was an English literary education, composed of the observations of obsolete Europeans. Extreme multiculturalists declare that the travails of a bunch of DWEMs (dead white European males), or in the case of *Sense and Sensibility,* DWEFs, were none of our business. They say that the curriculum ought to allow for every ethnic group to study its own lit. But we studied English lit., which usually consisted of the efforts of oddly costumed people to keep money or get money, so that they could live happily forever, bowing and curtseying to one another, drinking tea, riding horses, and wailing on the moors. "What's that to us?" the multiculturalists want to know. The question is not entirely a stupid one.

In the late 1960s, when the question was born in universities, I was teaching in a distinguished university whose distinguished English department taught not one black American author. The survey course in American literature not only overlooked the more minor writers like Paul Laurence Dunbar and James Weldon Johnson, it did not include indisputably first-class writers like Richard Wright, Ralph Ellison and James Baldwin. A group of black students, upset at this omission, came to me and asked if I would teach them these writers. I told them that I knew as little about the subject as they did, but that I did know how to plumb a text, and if they were willing to attempt the discovery together, I was their man.

We met as a noncredit seminar for a year, and learned much about African-American writers and, in the process, about America. Amiri Baraka/LeRoi Jones said that a black man who emerges from his own room in America's house, knows the whole house. And so my students and I learned a lot about the whole house of our country—I more than they, who had been living in that special room. But the joy of that course, which soon grew into a large lecture course for credit and became part of the curriculum, was that we were studying black writers as an enrichment of the old canon. Indeed, they justified the stability of the old canon by adding a particular experience to the general, which, no matter how remote it might appear, pertained to black and white, and everyone else, together.

Watching *Sense and Sensibility,* I rediscovered the value of the old canon. I was not alone. My fellow audience members were as ethnically diverse as any urban audience in America, yet we sat together—Latinos, Asians, African-Americans, Jews, Irish, Italians, and maybe a few English descendants as well, all laughing and weeping in the right spots at people and circumstances wholly removed from contemporary experience. This was my education, as it was for most of the readers of this magazine (I assume that *Modern Maturity* may not be given to anyone underage; that is, under age 50). Our standard syllabus could certainly have been improved, with such additions as black writers, but it was quite strong at the core.

Up to a few years ago, a literary education meant the reading of such books as *Great Expectations.* Ethnically diverse though we were, we older generations had no trouble seeing ourselves as laboring boys or as haughty wards, living in draughty manses or traipsing about the brooding English hills. American Pips and Estellas came in every color. It was no hardship to project ourselves into the life of an English prince or a pauper or a housekeeper or a mad young man storming about in a storm. It never occurred to us that merely because our forefathers happened to come from the bogs or from the shtetl or from shacks in the South that we could be denied our noble birthright or our place on the British throne.

Three reasons for this easy acceptance by association occurred to me as I walked out of *Sense and Sensibility.* One was the attitude of the English themselves, they who created English lit. They might be an island, but they saw themselves as the world, and they built up a navy to prove the point. No Englishman ever worried about being out of it. They *were* it—at least until the Empire struck out. The supreme self-confidence that could be so unattractive in international matters, leading, for example, to their remarkable habit of seizing and subjugating every foreign country they landed in, also enabled them in the arts to speak for all human experience with persuasive authority.

Second, they were good; English literature was/is very good stuff. (The reason my lecture course grew from a seminar was that the material we were reading was very good stuff.) Since the English tongue (or a version of it) was also America's, we were bound to go for English literature no matter what it was like. Luckily for us, most of English lit. was the top of the line. Chaucer, Shakespeare, Donne, Marvell, Milton, Swift, Pope, Johnson, Wordsworth, Keats, and George Eliot, and Jane Austen—you don't get much better than those boys and girls. It was no strain at all to accept the English monarchy as one's own, as long as Shakespeare taught it to speak.

But the third reason, which is probably the most important as regards the value of our archaic, out-of-date education, is that we *wanted* to be dead Englishmen; that is, we gladly gave ourselves over to being people other than whom we were. Keats called this capacity in Shakespeare that of "negative capability"—the ability to translate oneself into a character so wholeheartedly that the self was negated. We older-timers were more than happy to negate ourselves to become Heathcliff, Becky Sharp, Ebenezer Scrooge, or the ladies of *Sense and Sensibility* because by that imaginative leap we ourselves entered into the creative process.

The trouble with extreme multiculturalism, to my way of thinking, has nothing at all to do with its content. Books and stories I've read by Bharati Mukherjee, Oscar Hijuelos, N. Scott Momaday, Richard Rodriguez, and Amy Tan, not to mention Wright, Ellison and Baldwin, are as good as anything written about Hampshire manses and Yorkshire moors. The trouble lies in the attitude adopted by people who argue for multicultural education as a political issue. Instead of seeing the value of the self negated, they want the self pampered and pandered to. They want literature to come to them. They have the queer idea that education has self-esteem as its primary purpose. Self-esteem played a part in the black students' approaching me originally, but the pleasure lay in our esteem of the authors. I like the question, "What's that to us?" because the answer was, and should be, "Nothing."

Great writers do not write to make readers feel good about themselves. More often they write to make us feel troubled about ourselves. But they really do not take much account of us at all. They simply, and not at all simply, beckon us to their world. The test of a good book is whether it is worth negating the self to enter it. The excessive individualism that has poisoned America in recent years, and of which extreme multiculturalism is a by-product, has led to the worst of all things in art and education—dullness. Individualism carried to extremes not only breaks the social contract, it tends to look the same in every manifestation: "I am proud, I am sensitive, I am misunderstood, I am alone."

The touching beauty of the audience in which I sat at *Sense and Sensibility* is that we were not alone. Together we were eager to become that strange remote past we saw on the screen, which was also our strange remote present. We were there; the story was ours. And when, in the end, Edward Ferrars tells Elinor Dashwood that he is not married, as she had feared, but is free to marry her, and Elinor, who has been so brave and "sensible" throughout, bursts into a tearful, joyful laugh, we all left the theater, mounted up, rode home to our estates and felt like queens and kings of the perfectly green hills.

Suggestions for Discussion

1. What is Rosenblatt's defense of the canon of English literature?
2. Explain Rosenblatt's major disagreement with the concept of multiculturalism in relation to literature. What is Rosenblatt's response to the question, "What's that to us?" Explain why you agree or disagree with his response.
3. What conclusion does Rosenblatt draw from his seminar on African-American writers in the 1960s?

Suggestions for Writing

1. Write an essay in which you agree or disagree with Rosenblatt's position on literature.
2. Write an essay explaining the meaning of the term *negative capability.*

FICTION

WILLA CATHER

The Sculptor's Funeral

Willa Cather (1873–1947) was born in Virginia and grew up in Nebraska. On leaving the University of Nebraska, where as an undergraduate she had written for a Lincoln newspaper, she worked in Pittsburgh as a reporter and then as a teacher, and wrote her first collection of stories, *The Troll Garden* (1905). Her works include *My Antonia* (1918), *A Lost Lady* (1923), *The Professor's House* (1925), *Death Comes for the Archbishop* (1927), and *Sapphira and the Slave Girl* (1940), which dealt with her native Virginia. She celebrated the frontier spirit, whether of art or of action. However, in this story, she shows how small-town intolerance and demands for conformity are inimical to artistic impulses and creativity.

A group of the townspeople stood on the station siding of a little Kansas town, awaiting the coming of the night train, which was already twenty minutes overdue. The snow had fallen thick over everything; in the pale starlight the line of bluffs across the wide, white meadows south of the town made soft, smoke-coloured curves against the clear sky. The men on the siding stood first on one foot and then on the other, their hands thrust deep into their trousers pockets, their overcoats open, their shoulders screwed up with the cold; and they glanced from time to time toward the southeast, where the railroad track wound along the river shore. They conversed in low tones and moved about restlessly, seeming uncertain as to what was expected of them. There was but one of the company who looked as though he knew exactly why he was there; and he kept conspicuously apart; walking to the far end of the platform, returning to the station door, then pacing up the track again, his chin sunk in the high collar of his overcoat, his burly shoulders drooping forward, his gait heavy and dogged. Presently he was approached by a tall, spare, grizzled man clad in a faded Grand Army suit, who shuffled out from the group and advanced with a certain deference, craning his neck forward until his back made the angle of a jackknife three-quarters open.

"I reckon she's a-goin' to be pretty late agin tonight, Jim," he remarked in a squeaky falsetto. "S'pose it's the snow?"

"I don't know," responded the other man with a shade of annoyance, speaking from out an astonishing cataract of red beard that grew fiercely and thickly in all directions.

The spare man shifted the quill toothpick he was chewing to the other side of his mouth. "It ain't likely that anybody from the East will come with the corpse, I s'pose," he went on reflectively.

"I don't know," responded the other, more curtly than before.

"It's too bad he didn't belong to some lodge or other. I like an order funeral myself. They seem more appropriate for people of some repytation," the spare man continued, with an ingratiating concession in his shrill voice, as he carefully placed his toothpick in his vest pocket. He always carried the flag at the G.A.R. funerals in the town.

The heavy man turned on his heel, without replying, and walked up the siding. The spare man shuffled back to the uneasy group. "Jim's ez full ez a tick, ez ushel," he commented commiseratingly.

Just then a distant whistle sounded, and there was a shuffling of feet on the platform. A number of lanky boys of all ages appeared as suddenly and slimily as eels wakened by the crack of thunder; some came from the waiting-room, where they had been warming themselves by the red stove, or half asleep on the slat benches; others uncoiled themselves from baggage trucks or slid out of express wagons. Two clambered down from the driver's seat of a hearse that stood backed up against the siding. They straightened their stooping shoulders and lifted their heads, and a flash of momentary animation kindled their dull eyes at that cold, vibrant scream, the worldwide call for men. It stirred them like the note of a trumpet; just as it had often stirred the man who was coming home to-night, in his boyhood.

The night express shot, red as a rocket, from out the eastward marsh lands and wound along the river shore under the long lines of shivering poplars that sentineled the meadows, the escaping steam hanging in grey masses against the pale sky and blotting out the Milky Way. In a moment the red glare from the headlight streamed up the snow-covered track before the siding and glittered on the wet, black rails. The burly man with the dishevelled red beard walked swiftly up the platform toward the approaching train, uncovering his head as he went. The group of men behind him hesitated, glanced questioningly at one another, and awkwardly followed his example. The train stopped, and the crowd shuffled up to the express car just as the door was thrown open, the spare man in the G.A.R. suit thrusting his head forward with curiosity. The express messenger appeared in the doorway, accompanied by a young man in a long ulster and traveling cap.

"Are Mr. Merrick's friends here?" inquired the young man.

The group on the platform swayed and shuffled uneasily. Philip Phelps, the banker, responded with dignity: "We have come to take charge of the body. Mr. Merrick's father is very feeble and can't be about."

"Send the agent out here," growled the express messenger, "and tell the operator to lend a hand."

The coffin was got out of its rough box and down on the snowy platform. The townspeople drew back enough to make room for it and then formed a close semicircle about it, looking curiously at the palm leaf which lay across the black cover. No one said anything. The baggage man stood by his truck, waiting to get at the trunks. The engine panted heavily, and the fireman dodged in and out among the wheels with his yellow torch and long oilcan, snapping the spindle boxes. The young Bostonian, one of the dead sculptor's pupils who had come with the body, looked about him helplessly. He turned to the banker, the only one of that black, uneasy, stoop-shouldered group who seemed enough of an individual to be addressed.

"None of Mr. Merrick's brothers are here?" he asked uncertainly.

The man with the red beard for the first time stepped up and joined the group. "No, they have not come yet: the family is scattered. The body will be taken directly to the house." He stooped and took hold of one of the handles of the coffin.

"Take the long hill road up, Thompson, it will be easier on the horses," called the liveryman as the undertaker snapped the door of the hearse and prepared to mount to the driver's seat.

Laird, the red-bearded lawyer, turned again to the stranger: "We didn't know whether there would be any one with him or not," he explained. "It's a long walk, so you'd better go up in the hack." He pointed to a single battered conveyance, but the young man replied stiffly: "Thank you, but I think I will go up with the hearse. If you don't object," turning to the undertaker, "I'll ride with you."

They clambered up over the wheels and drove off in the starlight up the long, white hill toward the town. The lamps in the still village were shining from under the low, snow-burdened roofs; and beyond, on every side, the plains reached out into emptiness, peaceful and wide as the soft sky itself, and wrapped in a tangible, white silence.

When the hearse backed up to a wooden sidewalk before a naked, weather-beaten frame house, the same composite, ill-defined group that had stood upon the station siding was huddled about the gate. The front yard was an icy swamp, and a couple of warped planks, extending from the sidewalk to the door, made a sort of rickety footbridge. The gate hung on one hinge, and was opened wide with difficulty. Steavens, the young stranger, noticed that something black was tied to the knob of the front door.

The grating sound made by the casket, as it was drawn from the hearse, was answered by a scream from the house; the front door was wrenched open, and a tall, corpulent woman rushed out bareheaded into the snow and flung herself upon the coffin, shrieking: "My boy, my boy! And this is how you've come home to me!"

As Steavens turned away and closed his eyes with a shudder of unutterable repulsion, another woman, also tall, but flat and angular, dressed entirely in black, darted out of the house and caught Mrs. Merrick by the shoulders, crying sharply: "Come, come, mother; you mustn't go on like this!" Her tone changed to one of obsequious solemnity as she turned to the banker: "The parlour is ready, Mr. Phelps."

The bearers carried the coffin along the narrow boards, while the undertaker ran ahead with the coffin rests. They bore it into a large, unheated room that smelled of dampness and disuse and furniture polish, and set it down under a hanging lamp ornamented with jingling glass prisms and before a "Rogers group" of John Alden and Priscilla, wreathed with smilax. Henry Steavens stared about him with the sickening conviction that there had been some horrible mistake, and that he had somehow arrived at the wrong destination. He looked painfully about over the clover-green Brussels, the fat plush upholstery; among the hand-painted china plaques and panels, and vases, for some mark of identification, for something that might once conceivably have belonged to Harvey Merrick. It was not until he recognized his friend in the crayon portrait of a little boy in kilts and curls hanging above the piano, that he felt willing to let any of these people approach the coffin.

"Take the lid off, Mr. Thompson; let me see my boy's face," wailed the elderly woman between her sobs. This time Steavens looked fearfully, almost beseechingly into her face, red and swollen under its masses of strong, black, shiny hair. He flushed, dropped his eyes, and then, almost incredulously, looked again. There was a kind of power about her face—a kind of brutal handsomeness, even, but it was scarred and furrowed by violence, and so coloured and coarsened by fiercer passions that grief seemed never to have laid a gentle finger there. The long nose was distended and knobbed at the end, and there were deep lines on either side of it; her heavy, black brows almost met across her forehead, her teeth were large and square, and set far apart—teeth that could tear. She filled the room; the men were obliterated, seemed tossed about like twigs in an angry water, and even Steavens felt himself being drawn into the whirlpool.

The daughter—the tall, raw-boned woman in crêpe, with a mourning comb in her hair which curiously lengthened her long face—sat stiffly upon the sofa, her hands, conspicuous for their large knuckles, folded in her lap, her mouth and eyes drawn down, solemnly awaiting the opening of the coffin. Near the door stood a mulatto woman, evidently a servant in the house, with a timid bearing and an emaciated face pitifully sad and gentle. She was weeping silently, the corner of her calico apron lifted to her eyes, occasionally suppressing a long, quivering sob. Steavens walked over and stood beside her.

Feeble steps were heard on the stairs, and an old man, tall and frail, odorous of pipe smoke, with shaggy, unkempt grey hair and a dingy beard, tobacco stained about the mouth, entered uncertainly. He went slowly up to the coffin and stood rolling a blue cotton handkerchief between his hands, seeming so pained and embarrassed by his wife's orgy of grief that he had no consciousness of anything else.

"There, there, Annie, dear, don't take on so," he quavered timidly, putting out a shaking hand and awkwardly patting her elbow. She turned with a cry, and sank upon his shoulder with such violence that he tottered a little. He did not even glance toward the coffin, but continued to look at her with a dull, frightened, appealing expression, as a spaniel looks at the whip. His sunken cheeks slowly reddened and burned with miserable shame. When his wife rushed from the room, her daughter strode after her with set lips. The servant stole up to the coffin, bent over it for a moment, and then slipped away to the kitchen, leaving Steavens, the lawyer, and the father to themselves. The old man stood trembling and looking down at his dead son's face. The sculptor's splendid head seemed even more noble in its rigid stillness than in life. The dark hair had crept down upon the wide forehead; the face seemed strangely long, but in it there was not that beautiful and chaste repose which we expect to find in the faces of the dead. The brows were so drawn that there were two deep lines above the beaked nose, and the chin was thrust forward defiantly. It was as though the strain of life had been so sharp and bitter that death could not at once wholly relax the tension and smooth the countenance into perfect peace—as though he were still guarding something precious and holy, which might even yet be wrested from him.

The old man's lips were working under his stained beard. He turned to the lawyer with timid deference: "Phelps and the rest are comin' back to set up with Harve, ain't they?" he asked. "Thank 'ee, Jim, thank 'ee." He brushed the hair back gently from his son's forehead. "He was a good boy, Jim; always a good boy. He was ez gentle ez a child and the kindest of 'em all—only we didn't none of us ever onderstand him." The tears trickled slowly down his beard and dropped upon the sculptor's coat.

"Martin, Martin. Oh, Martin! come here," his wife wailed from the top of the stairs. The old man started timorously: "Yes, Annie, I'm coming." He turned away, hesitated, stood for a moment in miserable indecision; then reached back and patted the dead man's hair softly, and stumbled from the room.

"Poor old man, I didn't think he had any tears left. Seems as if his eyes would have gone dry long ago. At his age nothing cuts very deep," remarked the lawyer.

Something in his tone made Steavens glance up. While the mother had been in the room, the young man had scarcely seen any one else; but now, from the moment he first glanced into Jim Laird's florid face and bloodshot eyes, he knew that he had found what he had been heartsick at not finding before—the feeling, the understanding that must exist in some one, even here.

The man was red as his beard, with features swollen and blurred by dissipation, and a hot, blazing blue eye. His face was strained—that of a man who is controlling himself with difficulty—and he kept plucking at his beard with a sort of fierce resentment. Steavens, sitting by the window, watched him turn down the glaring lamp, still its jangling pendants with an angry gesture, and then stand with his hands locked behind him, staring down into the master's face. He could not help wondering what link there could have been between the porcelain vessel and so sooty a lump of potter's clay.

From the kitchen an uproar was sounding; when the dining-room door opened, the import of it was clear. The mother was abusing the maid for having forgotten to make the dressing for the chicken salad which had been prepared for the watchers. Steavens had never heard anything in the least like it; it was injured, emotional, dramatic abuse, unique and masterly in its excruciating cruelty, as violent and unrestrained as had been her grief of twenty minutes before. With a shudder of disgust the lawyer went into the dining room and closed the door into the kitchen.

"Poor Roxy's getting it now," he remarked when he came back. "The Merricks took her out of the poorhouse years ago; and if her loyalty would let her, I guess the poor old thing could tell tales that would curdle your blood. She's the mulatto woman who was standing in here a while ago, with her apron to her eyes. The old woman is a fury; there never was anybody like her for demonstrative piety and ingenious cruelty. She made Harvey's life a hell for him when he lived at home; he was so sick ashamed of it. I never could see how he kept himself so sweet."

"He was wonderful," said Steavens slowly, "wonderful; but until tonight I have never known how wonderful."

"That is the true and eternal wonder of it, anyway; that it can come even from such a dung heap as this," the lawyer cried, with a sweeping gesture which seemed to indicate much more than the four walls within which they stood.

"I think I'll see whether I can get a little air. The room is so close I am beginning to feel rather faint," murmured Steavens, struggling with one of the windows. The sash was stuck, however, and would not yield, so he sat down dejectedly and began pulling at his collar. The lawyer came over, loosened the sash with one blow of his red fist and sent the window up a few inches. Steavens thanked him, but the nausea which had been gradually climbing into his throat for the last half hour left him with but one desire—a desperate feeling that he must get away from this place with what was left of Harvey Merrick. Oh, he comprehended well enough now the quiet bitterness of the smile that he had seen so often on his master's lips!

He remembered that once, when Merrick returned from a visit home, he brought with him a singularly feeling and suggestive bas-relief of a thin, faded old woman, sitting and sewing something pinned to her knee; while a full-lipped, full-blooded little urchin, his trousers held up by a single gallus, stood beside her, impatiently twitching her gown to call her attention to a butterfly he had caught. Steavens, impressed by the tender and delicate modelling of the thin, tired face, had asked him if it were his mother. He remembered the dull flush that had burned up in the sculptor's face.

The lawyer was sitting in a rocking-chair beside the coffin, his head thrown back and his eyes closed. Steavens looked at him earnestly, puzzled at the line of the chin, and wondering why a man should conceal a feature of such distinction under that disfiguring shock of beard. Suddenly, as though he felt the young sculptor's keen glance, he opened his eyes.

"Was he always a good deal of an oyster?" he asked abruptly. "He was terribly shy as a boy."

"Yes, he was an oyster, since you put it so," rejoined Steavens. "Although he could be very fond of people, he always gave one the impression of being detached. He disliked violent emotion; he was reflective, and rather distrustful of himself—except, of course, as regarded his work. He was surefooted enough there. He distrusted men pretty thoroughly and women even more, yet somehow without believing ill of them. He was determined, indeed, to believe the best, but he seemed afraid to investigate."

"A burnt dog dreads the fire," said the lawyer grimly, and closed his eyes.

Steavens went on and on, reconstructing that whole miserable boyhood. All this raw, biting ugliness had been the portion of the man whose tastes were refined beyond the limits of the reasonable—whose mind was an exhaustless gallery of beautiful impressions, and so sensitive that the mere shadow of a poplar leaf flickering against a sunny wall would be etched and held there forever. Surely, if ever a man had the magic word in his fingertips, it was Merrick. Whatever he touched, he revealed its holiest secret; liberated it from enchantment and restored to it its pristine loveliness, like the Arabian prince who fought the enchantress spell for spell. Upon whatever he had come in contact with, he had left a beautiful record of the experience—a sort of ethereal signature; a scent, a sound, a colour that was his own.

Steavens understood now the real tragedy of his master's life; neither love nor wine, as many had conjectured; but a blow which had fallen earlier and cut deeper than these could have done—a shame not his, and yet so unescapably his, to hide in his heart from his very boyhood. And without—the frontier warfare; the yearning of a boy, cast ashore upon a desert of newness and ugliness and sordidness, for all that is chastened and old, and noble with traditions.

At eleven o'clock the tall, flat woman in black crêpe entered and announced that the watchers were arriving, and asked them "to step into the dining-room." As Steavens rose, the lawyer said dryly: "You go on—it'll be a good experience for you, doubtless; as for me, I'm not equal to that crowd tonight; I've had twenty years of them."

As Steavens closed the door after him he glanced back at the lawyer, sitting by the coffin in the dim light, with his chin resting on his hand.

The same misty group that had stood before the door of the express car shuffled into the dining room. In the light of the kerosene lamp they separated and became individuals. The minister, a pale, feeble-looking man with white hair and blond chin-whiskers, took his seat beside a small side table and placed his Bible upon it. The Grand Army man sat down behind the stove and tilted his chair back comfortably against the wall, fishing his quill toothpick from his waistcoat pocket. The two bankers, Phelps and Elder, sat off in a corner behind the dinner table, where they could finish their discussion of the new usury law and its effect on chattel security loans. The real estate agent, an old man with a smiling, hypocritical face, soon joined them. The coal and lumber dealer and the cattle shipper sat on opposite sides of the hard coal-burner, their feet on the nickelwork. Steavens took a book from his pocket and began to read. The talk around him ranged through various topics of local interest while the house was quieting down. When it was clear that the members of the family were in bed, the Grand Army man hitched his shoulders and, untangling his long legs, caught his heels on the rounds of his chair.

"S'pose there'll be a will, Phelps?" he queried in his weak falsetto.

The banker laughed disagreeably, and began trimming his nails with a pearl-handled pocketknife.

"There'll scarcely be any need for one, will there?" he queried in his turn.

The restless Grand Army man shifted his position again, getting his knees still nearer his chin. "Why, the ole man says Harve's done right well lately," he chirped.

The other banker spoke up. "I reckon he means by that Harve ain't asked him to mortgage any more farms lately, so as he could go on with his education."

"Seems like my mind don't reach back to a time when Harve wasn't bein' edycated," tittered the Grand Army man.

There was a general chuckle. The minister took out his handkerchief and blew his nose sonorously. Banker Phelps closed his knife with a snap. "It's too bad the old man's sons didn't turn out better," he remarked with reflective authority. "They never hung together. He spent money enough on Harve to stock a dozen cattle farms and he might as well have poured it into Sand Creek. If Harve had stayed at home and helped nurse what little they had, and gone into stock on the old man's bottom farm, they might all have been well fixed. But the old man had to trust everything to tenants and was cheated right and left."

"Harve never could have handled stock none," interposed the cattle-man. "He hadn't it in him to be sharp. Do you remember when he bought Sander's mules for eight-year olds, when everybody in town knew that Sander's father-in-law give 'em to his wife for a wedding present eighteen years before, an' they was full-grown mules then."

Every one chuckled, and the Grand Army man rubbed his knees with a spasm of childish delight.

"Harve never was much account for anything practical, and he shore was never fond of work," began the coal and lumber dealer. "I mind the last time he was home; the day he left, when the old man was out to the barn helpin' his hand hitch up to take Harve to the train, and Cal Moots was patchin' up the fence, Harve, he come out on the step and sings out, in his ladylike voice: 'Cal Moots, Cal Moots! please come cord my trunk.'"

"That's Harve for you," approved the Grand Army man gleefully. "I kin hear him howlin' yet when he was a big feller in long pants and his mother used to whale him with a rawhide in the barn for lettin' the cows get foundered in the cornfield when he was drivin' 'em home from pasture. He killed a cow of mine that-a-way onct—a pure Jersey and the best milker I had, an' the ole man had to put up for her. Harve, he was watchin' the sun set acrost the marshes when the anamile got away; he argued that sunset was oncommon fine."

"Where the old man made his mistake was in sending the boy East to school," said Phelps, stroking his goatee and speaking in a deliberate, judicial tone. "There was where he got his head full of trapesing to Paris and all such folly. What Harve needed, of all people, was a course in some first-class Kansas City business college."

The letters were swimming before Steavens's eyes. Was it possible that these men did not understand, that the palm of the coffin meant nothing to them? The very name of their town would have remained forever buried in the postal guide had it not been now and again mentioned in the world in connection with Harvey Merrick's. He remembered what his master had said to him on the day of his death, after the congestion of both lungs had shut off any probability of recovery, and the sculptor had asked his pupil to send his body home. "It's not a pleasant place to be lying while the world is moving and doing and bettering," he had said with a feeble smile, "but it rather seems as though we ought to go back to the place we came from in the end. The townspeople will come in for a look at me; and after they have had their say I shan't have much to fear from the judgment of God. The wings of the Victory, in there"—with a weak gesture toward his studio—"will not shelter me."

The cattleman took up the comment. "Forty's young for a Merrick to cash in; they usually hang on pretty well. Probably he helped it along with whisky."

"His mother's people were not long-lived, and Harvey never had a robust constitution," said the minister mildly. He would have liked to say more. He had been the boy's Sunday-school teacher, and had been fond of him; but he felt that he was not in a position to speak. His own sons had turned out badly, and it was not a year since one of them had made his last trip home in the express car, shot in a gambling house in the Black Hills.

"Nevertheless, there is no disputin' that Harvey frequently looked upon the wine when it was red, also variegated, and it shore made an oncommon fool of him," moralized the cattleman.

Just then the door leading into the parlor rattled loudly and everyone started involuntarily, looking relieved when only Jim Laird came out. His red face was convulsed with anger, and the Grand Army man ducked his head when he saw the spark in his blue, bloodshot eye. They were all afraid of Jim; he was a drunkard, but he could twist the law to suit his client's needs as no other man in all western Kansas could do; and there were many who tried. The lawyer closed the door gently behind him, leaned back against it and folded his arms, cocking his head a little to one side. When he assumed this attitude in the courtroom, ears were always pricked up, as it usually foretold a flood of withering sarcasm.

"I've been with you gentlemen before," he began in a dry, even tone, "when you've sat by the coffins of boys born and raised in this town; and, if I remember rightly, you were never any too well satisfied when you checked them up. What's the matter, anyhow? Why is it that reputable young men are as scarce as millionaires in Sand City? It might almost seem to a stranger that there was some way something the matter with your progressive town. Why did Ruben Sayer, the brightest young lawyer you ever turned out, after he had come home from the university as straight as a die, take to drinking and forge a check and shoot himself? Why did Bill Merrit's son die of the shakes in a saloon in Omaha? Why was Mr. Thomas's son, here, shot in a gambling-house? Why did young Adams burn his mill to beat the insurance companies and go to the pen?"

The lawyer paused and unfolded his arms, laying one clenched fist quietly on the table. "I'll tell you why. Because you drummed nothing but money and knavery into their ears from the time they wore knickerbockers;

because you carped away at them as you've been carping here tonight, holding our friends Phelps and Elder up to them for their models, as our grandfathers held up George Washington and John Adams. But the boys, worse luck, were young and raw at the business you put them to; and how could they match coppers with such artists as Phelps and Elder? You wanted them to be successful rascals; they were only unsuccessful ones—that's all the difference. There was only one boy ever raised in this borderland between ruffianism and civilization, who didn't come to grief, and you hated Harvey Merrick more for winning out than you hated all the other boys who got under the wheels. Lord, Lord, how you did hate him! Phelps, here, is fond of saying that he could buy and sell us all out any time he's a mind to; but he knew Harve wouldn't have given a tinker's damn for his bank and all his cattle farms put together; and a lack of appreciation, that way, goes hard with Phelps.

"Old Nimrod, here, thinks Harve drank too much; and this from such as Nimrod and me!

"Brother Elder says Harve was too free with the old man's money—fell short in filial consideration, maybe. Well, we can all remember the very tone in which brother Elder swore his own father was a liar, in the county court; and we all know that the old man came out of that partnership with his son as bare as a sheared lamb. But maybe I'm getting personal, and I'd better be driving ahead at what I want to say."

The lawyer paused a moment, squared his heavy shoulders, and went on: "Harvey Merrick and I went to school together, back East. We were dead in earnest, and we wanted you all to be proud of us some day. We meant to be great men. Even I, and I haven't lost my sense of humour, gentlemen, I meant to be a great man. I came back here to practise, and I found you didn't in the least want me to be a great man. You wanted me to be a shrewd lawyer—oh, yes! Our veteran here wanted me to get him an increase of pension, because he had dyspepsia; Phelps wanted a new country survey that would put the widow Wilson's little bottom farm inside his south line; Elder wanted to lend money at 5 percent a month, and get it collected; old Stark here wanted to wheedle old women up in Vermont into investing their annuities in real-estate mortgages that are not worth the paper they are written on. Oh, you needed me hard enough, and you'll go on needing me; and that's why I'm not afraid to plug the truth home to you this once.

"Well, I came back here and became the damned shyster you wanted me to be. You pretend to have some sort of respect for me; and yet you'll stand up and throw mud at Harvey Merrick, whose soul you couldn't dirty and whose hands you couldn't tie. Oh, you're a discriminating lot of Christians! There have been times when the sight of Harvey's name in some Eastern paper has made me hang my head like a whipped dog; and, again, times when I liked to think of him off there in the world, away from all this hogwallow, doing his great work and climbing the big, clean up-grade he'd set for himself.

"And we? Now that we've fought and lied and sweated and stolen, and hated as only the disappointed strugglers in a bitter, dead little Western town know how to do, what have we got to show for it? Harvey Merrick wouldn't have given one sunset over your marshes for all you've got put together, and you know it. It's not for me to say why, in the inscrutable wisdom of God, a genius should ever have been called from his place of hatred and bitter waters; but I want this Boston man to know that the drivel he's been hearing here tonight is the only tribute any truly great man could ever have from such a lot of sick, side-tracked, burnt-dog, land-poor sharks as the here-present financiers of Sand City—upon which town may God have mercy!"

The lawyer thrust out his hand to Steavens as he passed him, caught up his overcoat in the hall, and had left the house before the Grand Army man had had time to lift his ducked head and crane his long neck about at his fellows.

Next day Jim Laird was drunk and unable to attend the funeral services. Steavens called twice at his office, but was compelled to start East without seeing him. He had a presentiment that he would hear from him again, and left his address on the lawyer's table; but if Laird found it, he never acknowledged it. The thing in him that Harvey Merrick had loved must have gone underground with Harvey Merrick's coffin; for it never spoke again, and Jim got the cold he died of driving across the Colorado mountains to defend one of Phelps's sons who had got into trouble out there by cutting government timber.

Suggestions for Discussion

1. Discuss the details Cather uses to characterize the small Kansas town to which the dead sculptor's body is brought for burial. Why is Steavens repelled by the furnishings in the house of Merrick's mother?
2. The sculptor's mother is overcome by grief. Steavens is repelled by her outburst of emotion. Why? Explain how Cather arranges details so that we will agree with Steavens.
3. How does Cather contrast Mrs. Merrick with her daughter? What function do both characters have in the story?
4. Why does Cather portray Jim Laird as a heavy drinker? What is his function in the story?
5. What was the real tragedy of the dead sculptor's life? How had it affected his work?

6. What is the theme of Cather's story? Why does she use the long speech by Laird to express it?

Suggestion for Writing

Cather's view of the artist as somehow alienated from his society is illustrated in this story. Write a paper dealing with the issue, using examples of well-known artists. You might make this a research project by investigating the life of Beethoven, Mozart, Baudelaire, or Poe. What about the relation of the artists to society in other cultures; for example, China, India, or Bali?

POETRY

MARIANNE MOORE

Poetry

Marianne Moore (1877–1972) was born in Missouri, graduated from Bryn Mawr College, taught at an Indian school, worked in the New York Public Library, edited *The Dial* between 1925 and 1929 and was a distinguished resident of Brooklyn Heights. Her first collection of poems was published in 1921, her *Collected Poems* in 1951. Among her works are *Predilection* (1955), a volume of critical essays, a poetic translation of La Fontaine's *Fables* (1954), and the volume of poetry *Tell Me, Tell Me* (1967). In the following poem, as she appears to put poetry in its place and dismisses high-flown theories about art, she affirms the power of the genuine article and the real significance of poetry.

I, too, dislike it: there are things that are important beyond all this fiddle,
  Reading it, however, with a perfect contempt for it, one discovers in
  it after all, a place for the genuine.
    Hands that can grasp, eyes
    that can dilate, hair that can rise
      if it must, these things are important not because a

high-sounding interpretation can be put upon them but because they are
  useful. When they become so derivative as to become unintelligible,
  the same thing may be said for all of us, that we
    do not admire what
    we cannot understand: the bat
      holding on upside down or in quest of something to

eat, elephants pushing, a wild horse taking a roll, a tireless wolf under
  a tree, the immovable critic twitching his skin like a horse that feels a flea,
      the base-
  ball fan, the statistician—
    nor is it valid
      to discriminate against "business documents and

school-books"; all these phenomena are important. One must make a
distinction
however: when dragged into prominence by half poets, the result is not
poetry,
nor till the poets among us can be
"literalists of
the imagination"—above
insolence and triviality and can present

for inspection, "imaginary gardens with real toads in them," shall we have
it. In the meantime, if you demand on the one hand,
the raw material of poetry in
all its rawness and
that which is on the other hand
genuine, you are interested in poetry.

Suggestions for Discussion

1. Why does the poet, on one hand, refer to poetry as "all this fiddle" and, on the other, find in it "a place for the genuine"?
2. What does the poet list as the important parts of poetry? Why does she dismiss the unintelligible in poetry?
3. Moore wants poets to become "'literalists of the imagination.'" Relate this phrase to her belief that the poets must create "'imaginary gardens with real toads in them.'"

Suggestions for Writing

1. Write a paper in which you compare the view of poetry in this poem with the view that poetry is a romantic outburst of pure emotion. What arguments would you use in defense of either position?
2. Rewrite the poem in prose sentences in a paragraph. Write a comment on what you have done with the poem. How have you changed it? Does your change effect a change in defining the piece as a poem?

RITA DOVE

Beauty and the Beast

Rita Dove (b. 1952), born in Akron, Ohio, and educated at Miami University in Oxford, Ohio, was appointed the first black poet laureate of the United States in 1993. She has an M.F.A. from the University of Iowa and holds honorary degrees from a number of universities. She is a Commonwealth Professor of English at the University of Virginia. Her books of poetry include *The Yellow House on the Corner* (1980); *Museum* (1983); *Thomas and Beulah* (1987), for which she won the Pulitzer Prize; *Grace Notes* (1989); and *Selected Poems* (1993). She has also written a play, a collection of short stories, *Fifth Sunday* (1985), and a novel, *Through the Ivory Gate* (1992). A verse drama, *The Darker Face of the Earth,* appeared in 1994 and 1996. "Beauty and the Beast" illustrates how the artist transforms an ever-popular fairy tale into a statement on the human condition.

Darling, the plates have been cleared away,
the servants are in their quarters.
What lies will we lie down with tonight?
The rabbit pounding in your heart, my

child legs, pale from a life of petticoats?
My father would not have had it otherwise
when he trudged the road home with our souvenirs.
You are so handsome it eats my heart away...

Beast, when you lay stupid with grief
at my feet, I was too young to see anything
die. Outside, the roses are folding
lip upon red lip. I miss my sisters—

they are standing before their clouded mirrors.
Gray animals are circling under the windows.
Sisters, don't you see what will snatch you up—
the expected, the handsome, the one who needs us?

Suggestions for Discussion

1. Who is the speaker in this poem? Try to put together the characteristics of the speaker from suggestions in the poem to describe the nature of the person speaking.
2. Why does the speaker refer to the Beast as lying "stupid with grief / at my feet"? The speaker asks several other questions in the poem. How are they related to each other?

Suggestion for Writing

Write an essay in which you compare and contrast the events of the fairy tale with the remarks of the speaker in the poem. Summarize clearly the significance of the speaker's statements and questions to the Beast and to her sisters.

LI-YOUNG LEE

Persimmons

Li-Young Lee (b. 1957) was born in Jakarta, Indonesia, of Chinese parents. His father, a political prisoner for one year, fled Indonesia with his family in 1959. They arrived in the United States in 1964, after living in Hong Kong, Macao, and Japan. Li-Young Lee studied at the University of Pittsburgh, the University of Arizona, and SUNY at Brockport. He and his family live in Chicago where he works as an artist. His poems in *Rose,* of which this is one, deal lyrically with the relations between parents and children, men and women, and the creation of art through painting or poetry.

In sixth grade Mrs. Walker
slapped the back of my head
and made me stand in the corner
for not knowing the difference
between *persimmon* and *precision.*
How to choose

persimmons. This is precision.
Ripe ones are soft and brown-spotted.

Sniff the bottoms. The sweet one
will be fragrant. How to eat:
put the knife away, lay down newspaper.
Peel the skin tenderly, not to tear the meat.
Chew the skin, suck it,
and swallow. Now, eat
the meat of the fruit,
so sweet,
all of it, to the heart.

Donna undresses, her stomach is white.
In the yard, dewy and shivering
with crickets, we lie naked,
face-up, face-down.
I teach her Chinese.
Crickets: *chin chin.* Dew: I've forgotten.
Naked: I've forgotten.
Ni, wo: you and me.
I part her legs,
remember to tell her
she is beautiful as the moon.

Other words
that got me into trouble were
fight and *fright, wren* and *yarn.*
Fight was what I did when I was frightened,
fright was what I felt when I was fighting.
Wrens are small, plain birds,
yarn is what one knits with.
Wrens are soft as yarn.
My mother made birds out of yarn.
I loved to watch her tie the stuff;
a bird, a rabbit, a wee man.

Mrs. Walker brought a persimmon to class
and cut it up
so everyone could taste
a *Chinese apple.* Knowing
it wasn't ripe or sweet, I didn't eat
but watched the other faces.

My mother said every persimmon has a sun
inside, something golden, glowing,
warm as my face.

Once, in the cellar, I found two wrapped in newspaper,
forgotten and not yet ripe.
I took them and set both on my bedroom windowsill,
where each morning a cardinal
sang, *The sun, the sun.*

Finally understanding
he was going blind,
my father sat up all one night
waiting for a song, a ghost.
I gave him the persimmons,
swelled, heavy as sadness,
and sweet as love.

This year, in the muddy lighting
of my parents' cellar, I rummage, looking
for something I lost.
My father sits on the tired, wooden stairs,
black cane between his knees,
hand over hand, gripping the handle.
He's so happy that I've come home.
I ask how his eyes are, a stupid question.
All gone, he answers.

Under some blankets, I find a box.
Inside the box I find three scrolls.
I sit beside him and untie
three paintings by my father:
Hibiscus leaf and a white flower.
Two cats preening.
Two persimmons, so full they want to drop from the cloth.

He raises both hands to touch the cloth,
asks, *Which is this?*

This is persimmons, Father.

Oh, the feel of the wolftail on the silk,
the strength, the tense
precision in the wrist.
I painted them hundreds of times
eyes closed. These I painted blind.
Some things never leave a person:
scent of the hair of one you love,
the texture of persimmons,
in your palm, the ripe weight.

Suggestions for Discussion

1. Discuss the way Lee uses the difficulties he had with English words (*persimmon/precision, fight/fright, wren/yarn*) to create the ideas for this poem.
2. In what ways does the poem reveal the relations between members of the narrator's family? Between the two young lovers? What special bond exists between the narrator in the poem and his father?
3. What statements does the father make about the nature of art in the final stanza of the poem? In the seven-line stanza before the end of the poem?
4. Why has the poet chosen the persimmon as the title for this poem?

Suggestions for Writing

1. Write a paper explaining the structure of the poem. What are its parts? How does the poet help the reader discover them?
2. Write two paragraphs summarizing the poet's ideas on the art of poetry.

MARK DOTY

Tunnel Music

Mark Doty, who lives in Provincetown on Cape Cod, published *Turtle, Swan* (1987), *Bethlehem in Broad Daylight* (1991), *My Alexandria* (1993), for which he won the National Book Critics Circle Award for poetry in 1994, and *Atlantis* (1995). He has received fellowships from the National Endowment for the Arts, the Massachusetts Artist Foundation, and the Vermont Council on the Arts. He teaches at Sarah Lawrence College and in the Vermont College M.F.A. Writing Program. The following poem illustrates his considerable gifts as a lyric poet.

Times Square, the shuttle's quick chrome
flies open and the whole car floods with
—what is it? Infernal industry, the tunnels
under Manhattan broken into hell at last?

Guttural churr and whistle and grind
of the engines that spin the poles?

Enormous racket, ungodly. What it is
is percussion: nine black guys

with nine lovely and previously unimagined
constructions of metal ripped and mauled,
welded and oiled: scoured chemical drums,
torched rims, unnameable disks of chrome.

Artifacts of wreck? The end of industry?
A century's failures reworked, bent,
hammered out, struck till their shimmying
tumbles and ricochets from tile walls:

anything dinged, busted or dumped
can be beaten till it sings.
A kind of ghostly joy in it, though
this music's almost unrecognizable,

so utterly of the coming world it is.

Suggestions for Discussion

1. What is the setting for the action in the poem? Who are the participants? Do both elements combine in a meaningful experience?
2. How does the language of the poem incorporate the sounds of the "tunnel music"?
3. Explain how the last three lines of the poem express the meaning of the music.

Suggestion for Writing

Write an essay in which you discuss the various sounds of the language in the poem. How does the author achieve percussive sound?

Science, the Environment, and the Future

Darwin's dice have rolled badly for Earth. It was a misfortune for the living world in particular, many scientists believe, that a carnivorous primate and not some more benign form of animal made the breakthrough.

—EDWARD O. WILSON, "Is Humanity Suicidal?"

So the creationists distort. An attack on some parts of Darwin's views is equated with a rejection of evolution.

—NILES ELDREDGE, "Creationism Isn't Science"

A generation of research has revealed that when natural landscapes are chopped into little pieces, ecological processes go awry and species go extinct.

—DAVID S. WILCOVE, "What I Saw When I Went to the Forest"

And beyond the rich, rolling, ancient panorama of rising, interlocking ridges I saw—spread vividly out before my mind's unhappy eye—our modern panorama of Los Angeles and the Love Canal, Beirut and Chernobyl, Ethiopia and the East Bronx.

—COLIN FLETCHER, "A Bend in the Road"

ESSAYS

FRANCIS BACON

Idols of the Mind

Sir Francis Bacon (1561–1626) was a lawyer, essayist, philosopher, and statesman. Among his best-known works are *The Advancement of Learning* (1605), *The New Organum* (1620), and *The New Atlantis* (1627). He is considered the originator of modern scientific induction because of his insistence on observation and experimentation as a means to knowledge. In "Idols of the Mind," from *The New Organum,* Bacon illustrates those habits of thought that inhibit human understanding and the spirit of scientific inquiry.

XXIII

There is a great difference between the Idols of the human mind and the Ideals of the divine. That is to say, between certain empty dogmas, and the true signatures and marks set upon the works of creation as they are found in nature.

XXXVIII

The idols and false notions which are now in possession of the human understanding, and have taken deep root therein, not only so beset men's minds that truth can hardly find entrance, but even after entrance obtained, they will again in the very instauration of the sciences meet and trouble us, unless men being forewarned of the danger fortify themselves as far as may be against their assaults.

XXXIX

There are four classes of Idols which beset men's minds. To these for distinction's sake I have assigned names,—calling the first class *Idols of the Tribe;* the second, *Idols of the Cave;* the third, *Idols of the Market Place;* the fourth, *Idols of the Theater.*

XL

The formation of ideas and axioms by true induction is no doubt the proper remedy to be applied for the keeping off and clearing away of idols. To point them out, however, is of great use; for the doctrine of Idols is to the Interpretation of Nature what the doctrine of the refutation of Sophisms is to common Logic.

XLI

The Idols of the Tribe have their foundation in human nature itself, and in the tribe or race of men. For it is a false assertion that the sense of man is the measure of things. On the contrary, all perceptions as well of the sense as of the mind are according to the measure of the individual and not according to the measure of the universe. And the human understanding is like a false mirror, which, receiving rays irregularly, distorts and discolors the nature of things by mingling its own nature with it.

XLII

The Idols of the Cave are the idols of the individual man. For everyone (besides the errors common to human nature in general) has a cave or den of his own, which refracts and discolours the light of nature; owing either to his own proper and peculiar nature; or to his education and conversation with others; or to the reading of books, and the authority of those whom he esteems and admires; or to the differences of impressions, accordingly as they take place in a mind preoccupied and predisposed or in a mind indifferent and settled; or the like. So that the spirit of man (according as it is meted out to different individuals) is in fact a thing variable and full of perturbation, and governed as it were by chance. Whence it was well observed by Heraclitus that men look for sciences in their own lesser worlds, and not in the greater or common world.

XLIII

There are also Idols formed by the intercourse and association of men with each other, which I call Idols of the Market Place, on account of the commerce and consort of men there. For it is by discourse that men associate; and words are imposed according to the apprehension of the vulgar. And therefore the ill and unfit choice of words wonderfully obstructs the understanding. Nor do the definitions or explanations wherewith in some things learned men are wont to guard and defend themselves, by any means set the matter right. But words plainly force and overrule the understanding, and throw all into confusion, and lead men away into numberless empty controversies and idle fancies.

XLIV

Lastly, there are Idols which have immigrated into men's minds from the various dogmas of philosophies, and also from wrong laws of demonstration. These I call Idols of the Theater; because in my judgment all the received systems are but so many stage-plays, representing worlds of their own creation after an unreal and scenic fashion. Nor is it only of the systems now in vogue, or only of the ancient sects and philosophies, that I speak; for many more plays of the same kind may yet be composed and in like artificial manner set forth; seeing that errors the most widely different have nevertheless causes for the most part alike. Neither again do I mean this only of entire systems, but also of many principles and axioms in science, which by tradition, credulity, and negligence have come to be received.

But of these several kinds of Idols I must speak more largely and exactly, that the understanding may be duly cautioned.

XLV

The human understanding is of its own nature prone to suppose the existence of more order and regularity in the world than it finds. And though there be many things in nature which are singular and unmatched, yet it devises for them parallels and conjugates and relatives which do not exist. Hence the fiction that all celestial bodies move in perfect circles; spirals and dragons being (except in name) utterly rejected. Hence too the element of Fire with its orb is brought in, to make up the square with the other three which the sense perceives. Hence also the ratio of density of the so-called elements is arbitrarily fixed at ten to one. And so on of other dreams. And these fancies affect not dogmas only, but simple notions also.

XLVI

The human understanding when it has once adopted an opinion (either as being the received opinion or as being agreeable to itself) draws all things else to support and agree with it. And though there be a greater number and weight of instances to be found on the other side, yet these it either neglects and despises, or else by some distinction sets aside and rejects; in order that by this great and pernicious predetermination the authority of its former conclusions may remain inviolate. And therefore it was a good answer that was made by one who when they showed him hanging in a temple a picture of those who had paid their vows as having escaped shipwreck, and would have him say whether he did not now acknowledge the power of the gods,—"Aye," asked he again, "but where are they painted that were drowned after their vows?" And such is the way of all superstition, whether in astrology, dreams, omens, divine judgments, or the like; wherein men, having a delight in such vanities, mark the events where they are fulfilled, but where they fail, though this happen much oftener, neglect and pass them by. But with far more subtlety does this mischief insinuate itself into philosophy and the sciences; in which the first conclusion colors and brings into conformity with itself all that come after, though far sounder and better. Besides, independently of that delight and vanity which I have described, it is the peculiar and perpetual error of the human intellect to be more moved and excited by affirmatives than by negatives; whereas it ought properly to hold itself indifferently disposed towards both alike. Indeed in the establishment of any true axiom, the negative instance is the more forcible of the two.

XLVII

The human understanding is moved by those things most which strike and enter the mind simultaneously and suddenly, and so fill the imagination; and then it feigns and supposes all other things to be somehow, though it cannot see how, similar to those few things by which it is surrounded. But for that going to and fro to remote and heterogeneous instances, by which axioms are tried as in the fire, the intellect is altogether slow and unfit, unless it be forced thereto by severe laws and overruling authority.

XLVIII

The human understanding is unquiet; it cannot stop or rest, and still presses onward, but in vain. Therefore it is that we cannot conceive of any end or limit to the world; but always as of necessity it occurs to us that there is something beyond. Neither again can it be conceived how eternity has flowed down to the present day; for that distinction which is commonly received of infinity in time past and in time to come can by no means hold; for it would thence follow that one infinity is greater than another, and that infinity is wasting away and tending to become finite. The like subtlety arises touching the infinite divisibility of lines, from the same inability of thought to stop. But this inability interferes more mischievously in the discovery of causes: for although the most general principles in nature ought to be held merely positive, as they are discovered, and cannot with truth be referred to a cause; nevertheless the human understanding being unable to rest still seeks something prior in the order of nature. And then it is that in struggling toward that which is further off it falls back upon that which is more nigh at hand; namely, on final causes: which have relation clearly to the nature of man rather than to the nature of the universe; and from this source have strangely defiled philosophy. But he is no less an unskilled and shallow philosopher who seeks causes of that which is most general, than he who in things subordinate and subaltern omits to do so.

XLIX

The human understanding is no dry light, but receives an infusion from the will and affections; whence proceed sciences which may be called "sciences as one would." For what a man had rather were true he more readily believes. Therefore he rejects difficult things from impatience of research; sober things, because they narrow hope; the deeper things of nature, from superstition; the light of experience, from arrogance and pride, lest his mind should seem to be occupied with things mean and transitory; things not commonly believed, out of deference to the opinion of the vulgar. Numberless in short are the ways, and sometimes imperceptible, in which the affections color and infect the understanding.

L

But by far the greatest hindrance and aberration of the human understanding proceeds from the dullness, incompetency, and deceptions of the senses; in that things which strike the sense outweigh things which do not immediately strike it, though they be more important. Hence it is that speculation commonly ceases where sight ceases; insomuch that of things invisible there is little or no observation. Hence all the working of the spirits enclosed in tangible bodies lies hid and unobserved by men. So also all the more subtle changes of form in the parts of coarser substances (which they commonly call alteration, though it is in truth local motion through exceedingly small spaces) is in like manner unobserved. And yet unless these two things just mentioned be searched out and brought to light, nothing great can be achieved in nature, as far as the production of works is concerned. So again the essential nature of our common air, and of all bodies less dense than air (which are very many), is almost unknown. For the sense by itself is a thing infirm and erring; neither can instruments for enlarging or sharpening the senses do much; but all the truer kind of interpretation of nature is effected by instances and experiments fit and apposite; wherein the sense decides touching the experiment only, and the experiment touching the point in nature and the thing itself.

LI

The human understanding is of its own nature prone to abstractions and gives a substance and reality to things which are fleeting. But to resolve nature into abstractions is less to our purpose than to dissect her into parts; as did the school of Democritus, which went further into nature than the rest. Matter rather than forms should be the object of our attention, its configurations and changes of configuration, and simple action, and law of action or motion; for forms are figments of the human mind, unless you will call those laws of action forms.

LII

Such then are the idols which I call *Idols of the Tribe;* and which take their rise either from the homogeneity of the substance of the human spirit, or from its preoccupation, or from its narrowness, or from its restless motion, or from an infusion of the affections, or from the incompetency of the senses, or from the mode of impression.

LIII

The *Idols of the Cave* take their rise in the peculiar constitution, mental or bodily, of each individual; and also in education, habit, and accident. Of this kind there is a great number and variety; but I will instance those the pointing out of which contains the most important caution, and which have most effect in disturbing the clearness of the understanding.

LIV

Men become attached to certain particular sciences and speculations, either because they fancy themselves the authors and inventors thereof, or because they have bestowed the greatest pains upon them and become most habituated to them. But men of this kind, if they betake themselves to philosophy and contemplations of a general character, distort and color them in obedience to their former fancies; a thing especially to be noticed in Aristotle, who made his natural philosophy a mere bond-servant to his logic, thereby rendering it contentious and well nigh useless. The race of chemists again out of a few experiments of the furnace have built up a fantastic philosophy, framed with reference to a few things; and Gilbert also, after he had employed himself most laboriously in the study and observation of the lodestone, proceeded at once to construct an entire system in accordance with his favourite subject.

LVI

There are found some minds given to an extreme admiration of antiquity, others to an extreme love and appetite for novelty; but few so duly tempered that they can hold the mean, neither carping at what has been well laid down by the ancients, nor despising what is well introduced by the moderns. This however turns to the great injury of the sciences and philosophy; since these affectations of antiquity and novelty are the humors of partisans rather than judgments; and truth is to be sought for not in the felicity of any age, which is an unstable thing, but in the light of nature and experience, which is eternal. These factions therefore must be abjured, and care must be taken that the intellect be not hurried by them into assent.

LVIII

Let such then be our provision and contemplative prudence for keeping off and dislodging the *Idols of the Cave,* which grow for the most part either out of the predominance of a favourite subject, or out of an excessive tendency to compare or to distinguish, or out of partiality for particular ages, or out of the largeness or minuteness of the objects contemplated. And generally let every student of nature take this as a rule—that whatever his mind seizes and dwells upon with peculiar satisfaction is to be held in suspicion, and that so much the more care is to be taken in dealing with such questions to keep the understanding even and clear.

LIX

But the *Idols of the Market Place* are the most troublesome of all: idols which have crept into the understanding through the alliances of words and names. For men believe that their reason governs words; but it is also true that words react on the understanding; and this it is that had rendered philosophy and the sciences sophistical and inactive. Now words, being commonly framed and applied according to the capacity of the vulgar, follow those lines of division which are most obvious to the vulgar understanding. And whenever an understanding of greater acuteness or a more diligent observation would alter those lines to suit the true divisions of nature, words stand in the way and resist the change. Whence it comes to pass that the high and formal discussions of learned men end oftentimes in disputes about words and names; with which (according to the use and wisdom of the mathematicians) it would be more prudent to begin, and so by means of definitions reduce them to order. Yet even definitions cannot cure this evil in dealing with natural and material things; since the definitions themselves consist of words, and those words beget others: so that it is necessary to recur to individual instances, and those in due series and order; as I shall say presently when I come to the method and scheme for the formation of notions and axioms.

LX

The idols imposed by words on the understanding are of two kinds. They are either names of things which do not exist (for as there are things left unnamed through lack of observation, so likewise are there names which result from fantastic suppositions and to which nothing in reality corresponds), or they are names of things which exist, but yet confused and ill-defined, and hastily and irregularly derived from realities. Of the former kind are Fortune, the Prime Mover, Planetary Orbits, Element of Fire, and like fictions which owe their origin to false and idle theories. And this class of idols is more easily expelled, because to get rid of them it is only necessary that all theories should be steadily rejected and dismissed as obsolete.

But the other class, which springs out of a faulty and unskillful abstraction, is intricate and deeply rooted. Let us take for example such a word as *humid;* and see how far the several things which the word is used to signify agree with each other; and we shall find the word *humid* to be nothing else than a mark loosely and confusedly applied to denote a variety of actions which will not bear to be reduced to any constant meaning. For it both signifies that which easily spreads itself round any other body; and that which in itself is indeterminate and cannot solidify; and that which readily yields in every direction; and that which easily divides and scatters itself; and that which easily unites and collects itself; and that which readily flows and is put in motion; and that which readily clings to another body and wets it; and that which is easily reduced to a liquid, or being solid easily melts. Accordingly when you come to apply the word—if you take it in one sense, flame is humid; if in another, air is not humid; if in another, fine dust is humid; if in another, glass is humid. So that it is easy to see that the notion is taken by abstraction only from water and common and ordinary liquids, without any due verification.

There are however in words certain degrees of distortion and error. One of the least faulty kinds is that of names of substances, especially of lowest species and well-deduced (for the notion of *chalk* and of *mud* is good, of *earth* bad); a more faulty kind is that of actions, as *to generate, to corrupt, to alter;* the most faulty is of qualities (except such as are the immediate objects of the sense) as *heavy, light, rare, dense,* and the like. Yet in all these cases some notions are of necessity a little better than others, in proportion to the greater variety of subjects that fall within the range of the human sense.

LXI

But the *Idols of the Theater* are not innate, nor do they steal into the understanding secretly, but are plainly impressed and received into the mind from the play-books of philosophical systems and the perverted rules of demonstration. To attempt refutations in this case would be merely inconsistent with what I have already said: for since we agree neither upon principles nor upon demonstrations there is no place for argument. And this is so far well, inasmuch as it leaves the honor of the ancients untouched. For they are no wise disparaged—the question between them and me being only as to the way. For as the saying is, the lame man who keeps the right road outstrips the runner who takes a wrong one. Nay it is obvious that when a man runs the wrong way, the more active and swift he is the further he will go astray.

But the course I propose for the discovery of sciences is such as leaves but little to the acuteness and strength of wits, but places all wits and understandings nearly on a level. For as in the drawing of a straight line or a perfect circle, much depends on the steadiness and practice of the hand, if it be done by aim of hand only, but if with the aid of rule or compass, little or nothing; so is it exactly with my plan. But though particular confutations would be of no avail, yet touching the sects and general divisions of such systems I must say something; something also touching the external signs which show that they are unsound; and finally something touching the causes of such great infelicity and of such lasting and general agreement in error; that so the access to truth may be made less difficult, and the human understanding may the more willingly submit to its purgation and dismiss its idols.

LXII

Idols of the Theater, or of Systems, are many, and there can be and perhaps will be yet many more. For were it not that now for many ages men's minds have been busied with religion and theology; and were it not that civil governments, especially monarchies, have been averse to such novelties, even in matters speculative; so that men labor therein to the peril and harming of their fortunes—not only unrewarded, but exposed also to contempt and envy; doubtless there would have arisen many other philosophical sects like to those which in great variety flourished once among the Greeks. For as on the phenomena of the heavens many hypotheses may be constructed, so likewise (and more also) many various dogmas may be set up and established on the phenomena of philosophy. And in the plays of this philosophical theater you may observe the same thing which is found in the theater of the poets, that stories invented for the stage are more compact and elegant, and more as one would wish them to be, than true stories out of history.

LXVII

A caution must also be given to the understanding against the intemperance which systems of philosophy manifest in giving or withholding assent; because intemperance of this kind seems to establish Idols and in some sort to perpetuate them, leaving no way open to reach and dislodge them.

This excess is of two kinds: the first being manifest in those who are ready in deciding, and render sciences dogmatic and magisterial: the other in those who deny that we can know anything, and so introduce a wandering kind of inquiry that leads to nothing: of which kinds the former subdues, the latter weakens the understanding. For the philosophy of Aristotle, after having by hostile confutations destroyed all the rest (as the Ottomans serve their brothers), has laid down the law on all points; which done, he proceeds himself to raise new questions of his own suggestion, and dispose of them likewise; so that nothing may remain that is not certain and decided: a practice which holds and is in use among his successors.

LXVIII

So much concerning the several classes of Idols, and their equipage: all of which must be renounced and put away with a fixed and solemn determination, and the understanding thoroughly freed and cleansed; the entrance into the kingdom of man, founded on the sciences, being not much other than the entrance into the kingdom of heaven, whereinto none may enter except as a little child.

Suggestions for Discussion

1. Bacon names the four idols he is going to discuss. They can be represented diagramatically as follows:

of Tribe	of Cave	of Market Place	of Theater

   Relate each aphorism to one of the idols Bacon has named. How does each aphorism apply to or illustrate an idol?

2. In discussing the idols of the market place Bacon deals with nonexistent and ill-defined things. Why does he separate the two? He rapidly disposes of the first category with a number of short examples. The second he divides into three degrees of distortion. What are the degrees? Why does Bacon deal with ill-defined things more precisely than with nonexistent things?
3. For almost every division or subdivision Bacon provides an example or illustration. List at least one example for each. Which are the most important examples? Which divisions have no examples? Why?
4. The language of the aphorisms often has an archaic flavor. Examples: *instauration, whence.* What elements other than archaic words contribute to this flavor? What examples are no longer meaningful to a modern reader?
5. Bacon frequently uses vivid imagery. The concept of "idols of the mind" is imagistic. Discuss some of the images and show how they function to support his arguments in the aphorisms.

Suggestions for Writing

1. Select one of the idols and define it in your own words. Using contemporary illustrations, write an essay (approximately 500 words) to apply the idol to your own world.
2. You may wish to write a paper on some idols of the American mind. Follow Bacon's idols as a guide and try to classify your categories as Bacon does.

ALAN B. DURNING

Asking How Much Is Enough

Alan B. Durning graduated with honors from Oberlin College and Conservatory from which he holds degrees in philosophy and music. He is a senior researcher at the Worldwatch Institute in Washington, D.C., investigating global problems. Among the papers he has either written or co-authored are "Action at the Grassroots: Fighting Poverty and Environmental Issues" (1988), "Poverty and the Environment: Reversing the Downward Spiral" (1989), and "Apartheid's Environmental Toll" (1990). He also contributes to various periodicals on these issues. This selection appeared in the *San Francisco Chronicle* (March 13, 1991) and is an excerpt from the Worldwatch Institute's 1991 "State-of-the-World Report."

Early in the age of affluence that followed World War II, an American retailing analyst named Victor Lebow proclaimed, "Our enormously productive economy...demands that we make consumption our way of life, that we convert the buying and use of goods into rituals, that we seek our spiritual satisfaction, our ego satisfaction, in consumption.... We need things consumed, burned up, worn out, replaced and discarded at an ever increasing rate."

Americans have responded to Lebow's call, and much of the world has followed.

Consumption has become a central pillar of life in industrial lands and is even embedded in social values. Opinion surveys in the world's two largest economies—Japan and the United States—show consumerist definitions of success becoming ever more prevalent.

In Taiwan, a billboard demands "Why Aren't You a Millionaire Yet?" The Japanese speak of the "new three sacred treasures": color television, air conditioning and the automobile.

The affluent life-style born in the United States is emulated by those who can afford it around the world. And many can: the average person today is 4.5 times richer than were his or her great-grandparents at the turn of the century.

Needless to say, that new global wealth is not evenly spread among the earth's people. One billion live in unprecedented luxury; 1 billion live in destitution. Even American children have more pocket money—$230 a year—than the half-billion poorest people alive.

Overconsumption by the world's fortunate is an environmental problem unmatched in severity by anything but perhaps population growth. Their surging exploitation of resources threatens to exhaust or unalterably disfigure forests, soils, water, air and climate.

Ironically, high consumption may be a mixed blessing in human terms, too. The time-honored values of integrity of character, good work, friendship, family and community have often been sacrificed in the rush to riches.

Thus, many in the industrial lands have a sense that their world of plenty is somehow hollow—that, hoodwinked by a consumerist culture, they have been fruitlessly attempting to satisfy what are essentially social, psychological and spiritual needs with material things.

Of course, the opposite of overconsumption—poverty—is no solution to either environmental or human problems. It is infinitely worse for people and bad for the natural world too. Dispossessed peasants slash-and-burn their way into the rain forests of Latin America, and hungry nomads turn their herds out onto fragile African rangeland, reducing it to desert.

If environmental destruction results when people have either too little or too much, we are left to wonder how much is enough. What level of consumption can the earth support? When does having more cease to add appreciably to human satisfaction?

Answering these questions definitively is impossible, but for each of us in the world's consuming class, asking is essential nonetheless. Unless we see that more is not always better, our efforts to forestall ecological decline will be overwhelmed by our appetites.

In simplified terms, an economy's total burden on the ecological systems that undergird it is a function of three factors: the size of the population, average consumption and the broad set of technologies—everything from mundane clothesline to the most sophisticated satellite communications system—the economy uses to provide goods and services.

Changing agricultural patterns, transportation systems, urban design, energy uses and the like could radically reduce the total environmental damage caused by the consuming societies, while allowing those at the bottom of the economic ladder to rise without producing such egregious effects.

Japan, for example, uses a third as much energy as the Soviet Union to produce a dollar's worth of goods and services, and Norwegians use half as much paper and cardboard apiece as their neighbors in Sweden, though they are equals in literacy and richer in monetary terms.

Some guidance on what the earth can sustain emerges from an examination of current consumption patterns around the world.

For three of the most ecologically important types of consumption—transportation, diet and use of raw materials—the world's people are distributed unevenly over a vast range. Those at the bottom clearly fall below the "too little" line, while those at the top, in what could be called the cars-meat-and-disposables class, clearly consume too much.

About 1 billion people do most of their traveling, aside from the occasional donkey or bus ride, on foot, many of them never going more than 500 miles from their birthplaces. Unable to get to jobs easily, attend school or bring their complaints before government offices, they are severely hindered by the lack of transportation options.

The massive middle class of the world, numbering some 3 billion, travels by bus and bicycle. Mile for mile, bikes are cheaper than any other vehicles, costing less than $100 new in most of the Third World and requiring no fuel.

The world's automobile class is relatively small: only 8 percent of humans, about 400 million people, own cars. Their cars are directly responsible for an estimated 13 percent of carbon dioxide emissions from fossil fuels worldwide, along with air pollution, acid rain and a quarter-million traffic fatalities a year.

Car owners bear indirect responsibility for the far-reaching impacts of their chosen vehicle. The automobile makes itself indispensable: cities sprawl, public transit atrophies, shopping centers multiply, workplaces scatter. As suburbs spread, families start to need a car for each driver.

One-fifth of American households own three or more vehicles, more than half own at least two, and 65 percent of new American houses are built with two-car garages.

Today, working Americans spend nine hours a week behind the wheel. To make these homes-away-from-home more comfortable, 90 percent of new cars have air conditioning, doubling their contributions to climate change and adding emissions of ozone-depleting chlorofluorocarbons.

Some in the auto class are also members of a more select group: the global jet set. Although an estimated 1 billion people travel by air each year, the overwhelming majority of trips are taken by a small group. The 4 million Americans who account for 41 percent of domestic trips, for example, cover five times as many miles a year as average Americans.

Furthermore, because each mile traveled by air uses more energy than one traveled by car, jetsetters consume six-and-a-half times as much energy for transportation as other car-class members.

The global food consumption ladder has three rungs. At the bottom, the world's 630 million poorest people are unable to provide themselves with a healthy diet, according to the latest World Bank estimates.

On the next rung, the 3.4 billion grain eaters of the world's middle class get enough calories and plenty of plant-based protein, giving them the healthiest basic diet of the world's people. They typically receive less than 20 percent of their calories from fat, a level low enough to protect them from the consequences of excessive dietary fat.

The top of the ladder is populated by the meat eaters, those who obtain close to 40 percent of their calories from fat. These 1.25 billion people eat three times as much fats per person as the remaining 4 billion, mostly because they eat so much red meat. The meat class pays the price of its diet in high death rates from the so-called diseases of affluence—heart disease, stroke and certain types of cancer.

The earth also pays for the high-fat diet. Indirectly, the meat-eating quarter of humanity consumes nearly 40 percent of the world's grain—grain that fattens the livestock they eat. Meat production is behind a substantial share of the environmental strains induced by the present global agricultural system, from soil erosion to overpumping of underground water.

In the extreme case of American beef, producing 2 pounds of steak requires 10 pounds of grain and the energy equivalent of 2 gallons of gasoline, not to mention the associated soil erosion, water consumption, pesticide and fertilizer runoff, groundwater depletion and emissions of the greenhouse gas methane.

Beyond the effects of livestock production, the affluent diet rings up an ecological bill through its heavy dependence on long-distance transport. North Europeans eat lettuce trucked from Greece and decorate their tables with flowers flown in from Kenya. Japanese eat turkey from the United States and ostrich from Australia.

One-fourth of the grapes eaten in the United States are grown 5,500 miles away, in Chile, and the typical mouthful of American food travels 1,000 miles from farm field to dinner plate.

Processing and packaging add further resource costs to the way the affluent eat. Extensively packaged foods are energy gluttons, but even seemingly simple foods need a surprising amount of energy to prepare: ounce for ounce, getting canned corn to the consumer takes 10 times the energy of providing fresh corn in season. Frozen corn, if left in the freezer for much time, takes even more energy.

To be sure, canned and frozen vegetables make a healthy diet easy even in the dead of winter; more of a concern are the new generation of microwave-ready instant meals. Loaded with disposable pans and multilayer packaging, their resource inputs are orders of magnitude larger than preparing the same dishes at home from scratch.

In raw material consumption, the same pattern emerges.

In the throwaway economy, packaging becomes an end in itself, disposables proliferate, and durability suffers. Four percent of consumer expenditures on goods in the United States goes for packaging—$225 a year.

Likewise, the Japanese use 30 million "disposable" single-roll cameras each year, and the British dump 12.5 billion diapers. Americans toss away 180 million razors annually, enough paper and plastic plates and cups to feed the world a picnic six times a year, and enough aluminum cans to make 6,000 DC-10 airplanes.

Where disposability and planned obsolescence fail to accelerate the trip from cash register to junk heap, fashion sometimes succeeds. Most clothing goes out of style long before it is worn out; lately, the realm of fashion has even colonized sports footwear. Kevin Ventrudo, chief financial officer of California-based L.A. Gear, which saw sales multiply 50 times in four years, told the Washington Post, "If you talk about shoe performance, you only need one or two pairs. If you're talking fashion, you're talking endless pairs of shoes."

In transportation, diet and use of raw materials, as consumption rises on the economic scale, so does waste—both of resources and of health. Bicycles and public transit are cheaper, more efficient and healthier transport options than cars. A diet founded on the basics of grains and water is gentle to the earth and the body.

And a lifestyle that makes full use of raw materials for durable goods without succumbing to the throwaway mentality is ecologically sound while still affording many of the comforts of modernity.

Suggestions for Discussion

1. How are luxury and poverty both bad for the state of the world's environment, according to Durning?
2. Discuss the opening quotation that increased consumption has become the most significant goal in America and other industrialized countries. Relate this to the Taiwan billboard and the Japanese version of the "new three sacred treasures."
3. Why is more consumption not always the better goal for consumers? What factors determine what is better?
4. Discuss Durning's comments on both the inequities and consequences of excessive use of fuel, consumption of food, and the "throwaway" economy.

Suggestions for Writing

1. Durning makes certain assumptions about eating and what foods are best for people. Write a short research paper in which you either confirm or

contradict his statements. In order to write this paper, you will have to study the consequences of eating certain foods.

2. Write a paper in which you discuss "throwaway" consumption. Give explicit examples with which you are familiar. Do you agree with Durning's assertions? Would you be willing personally to give up throwaway consumption?

GRANT FJERMEDAL

Artificial Intelligence

Grant Fjermedal has written *Magic Bullets: A Revolution in Cancer Treatment* (1984) and *The Tomorrow Makers: A Brave New World of Living Brain Machines* (1986). This essay, published in *Omni*, an excerpt from *The Tomorrow Makers*, presents in dramatic fashion the choice that people one day may be able to make between dying or continuing to live forever by transferring one's capacity for thinking from one's brain to a machine.

I'm sure that Hans Moravec is at least as sane as I am, but he certainly brought to mind the classic mad scientist as we sat in his fifth-floor office at Carnegie-Mellon University on a dark and stormy night. It was nearly midnight, and he mixed for each of us a bowl of chocolate milk and Cheerios, with slices of banana piled on top.

Then, with banana-slicing knife in hand, Moravec, the senior research scientist at Carnegie-Mellon's Mobile Robot Laboratory, outlined for me how he could create a robotic immortality for Everyman, a deathless universe in which life would go on forever. By creating computer copies of our minds and transferring, or downloading, this program into robotic bodies, Moravec explained, humans could survive for centuries.

"You are in an operating room. A robot brain surgeon is in attendance.... Your skull but not your brain is anesthetized. You are fully conscious. The surgeon opens your braincase and peers inside." This is how Moravec described the process in a paper he wrote called "Robots That Rove." The robotic surgeon's "attention is directed at a small clump of about one hundred neurons somewhere near the surface. Using high-resolution 3-D nuclear-magnetic-resonance holography, phased-array radio encephalography, and ultrasonic radar, the surgeon determines the three-dimensional structure and chemical makeup of that neural clump. It writes a program that models the behavior of the clump and starts it running on a small portion of the computer sitting next to you."

That computer sitting next to you in the operating room would in effect be your new brain. As each area of your brain was analyzed and simulated, the accuracy of the simulation would be tested as you pressed a button to shift between the area of the brain just copied and the simulation. When you couldn't tell the difference between the original and the copy, the surgeon would transfer the simulation of your brain into the new, computerized one and repeat the process on the next area of your biological brain.

"Though you have not lost consciousness or even your train of thought, your mind—some would say soul—has been removed from the brain and transferred to a machine," Moravec said, "In a final step your old body is disconnected. The computer is installed in a shiny new one, in the style, color, and material of your choice."

As we sat around Moravec's office I asked what would become of the original human body after the downloading. "You just don't bother waking it up again if the copying went successfully," he said. "It's so messy. Humans have got so many problems that you might just want to leave it retired. You don't take your junker car out if you've got a new one."

Moravec's idea is the ultimate in life insurance: Once one copy of the brain's contents has been made, it will be easy to make multiple backup copies, and these could be stashed in hiding places around the world, allowing you to embark on any sort of adventure without having to worry about aging or death. As decades pass into centuries you could travel the globe and then the solar system and beyond—always keeping an eye out for the latest in robotic bodies into which you could transfer your computer mind.

If living forever weren't enough, you could live forever several times over by activating some of your backup copies and sending different versions of yourself out to see the world. "You could have parallel experiences and merge the memories later," Moravec explained.

In the weeks and months that followed my stay at Carnegie-Mellon, I was intrigued by how many researchers seemed to believe downloading would come to pass. The only point of disagreement was *when*—certainly a big consideration to those of us still knocking around in mortal bodies. Although some of the researchers I spoke with at Carnegie-Mellon, MIT, and Stanford and in Japan thought that downloading was still generations away, there were others who believed achieving robotic immortality was imminent and seemed driven by private passions never to die.

The significance of the door Moravec is trying to open is not lost on others. Olin Shivers, a Carnegie-Mellon graduate student who works closely with Moravec as well as with Allen Newell, one of the founding fathers of artificial intelligence, told me, "Moravec wants to design a creature, and my professor Newell wants to design a creature. We are all, in a sense, trying to play God."

At MIT I was surprised to find Moravec's concept of downloading given consideration by Marvin Minsky, Donner Professor of Science and another father of artificial intelligence. Minsky is trying to learn how the billions of brain cells work together to allow a person to think and remember. If he succeeds, it will be a big step toward figuring out how to join perhaps billions of computer circuits together to allow a computer to receive the entire contents of the human mind.

"If a person is like a machine, once you get a wiring diagram of how he works, you can make copies," Minsky told me.

Although Minsky doesn't think he'll live long enough to download (he's fifty-seven now), he would consider it. "I think it would be a great thing to do," he said. "I've spent a long time learning things, and I'd hate to see it all go away."

Minsky also said he would have no qualms about waving good-bye to his human body and taking up residence within a robot. "Why not avoid getting sick and things like that?" he asked. "It's hard to see anything against it. I think people will get fed up with bodies after a while. Then you'll have another population problem: You'll have all the people of the past, as well as the new ones."

Another believer is Danny Hillis, one of Minsky's Ph.D. students and the founding scientist of Thinking Machines, a Cambridge-based company that is trying to create the kind of computer that might someday receive the contents of a brain. During my research several computer scientists would point to Hillis's connection machine as an example of a new order of computer architecture, one that's comparable to the human brain. (Hillis's connection machine doesn't have one large central processing unit as other computers do but a network of 64,000 small units—roughly analogous in concept, if not in size, to the brain's network of 40 billion neuronal processing units.)

"I've added up the things I want to do in my life, and it's about fifteen hundred years' worth of stuff," Hillis, now twenty-eight, told me one day as we stood out on the sixth-floor sun deck of the Thinking Machines building. "I enjoy having a body as much as anyone else does, but if it's a choice between downloading into a computer—even one that's stuck in a room someplace—and still being able to think versus just dying, I would certainly take that opportunity to think."

Gerald J. Sussman, a thirty-six-year-old MIT professor and a computer hacker of historic proportions, expressed similar sentiments. "Everyone would like to be immortal. I don't think the time is quite right, but it's close. I'm afraid, unfortunately, that I'm in the last generation to die."

"Do you really think that we're that close?" I asked.

"Yes," he answered, which reminded me of something Moravec had written not too long ago: "We are on a threshold of a change in the universe comparable to the transition from nonlife to life."

Suggestions for Discussion

1. Summarize the major thesis of this brief essay. Is it one that you take seriously? Explain your response.
2. What method does Fjermedal use to develop his essay? What is its tone? Is there an element of ambiguity in the tone?
3. Define the term *downloading.*
4. Explain the significance of the quotation in the last paragraph.
5. How close does this essay come to what we think of as science fiction?

Suggestions for Writing

1. Write an essay in which you describe a world inhabited by surrogate brains. What would be the advantages, disadvantages of such a world? Is it one that you would want to inhabit? Explain your response to this question.
2. Using this essay and others in this text, write a paper examining the directions of research in the fields of computer science.

EDWARD O. WILSON

Is Humanity Suicidal?

Edward O. Wilson (b. 1929) was born in Birmingham, Alabama, and educated at the University of Alabama and Harvard. The Frank B. Baird, Jr., Professor of Science at Harvard, he has taught at many universities in the United States and abroad and holds a number of honorary degrees. Having won many prizes for his research, he also was awarded the Pulitzer Prize for General Non-Fiction in 1979, demonstrating that he belongs to that limited number of distinguished scientists who also write extremely well. He is a member of the National Academy of Science, a Fellow of the American Academy of Arts and

Science, and an honorary member of the Royal Society of London. In "Is Humanity Suicidal?" Wilson states what human beings must do to avoid the eventual disappearance of the species *Homo sapiens* on earth.

Imagine that on an icy moon of Jupiter—say, Ganymede—the space station of an alien civilization is concealed. For millions of years its scientists have closely watched the earth. Because their law prevents settlement on a living planet, they have tracked the surface by means of satellites equipped with sophisticated sensors, mapping the spread of large assemblages of organisms, from forests, grasslands and tundras to coral reefs and the vast planktonic meadows of the sea. They have recorded millennial cycles in the climate, interrupted by the advance and retreat of glaciers and scattershot volcanic eruptions.

The watchers have been waiting for what might be called the Moment. When it comes, occupying only a few centuries and thus a mere tick in geological time, the forests shrink back to less than half their original cover. Atmospheric carbon dioxide rises to the highest level in 100,000 years. The ozone layer of the stratosphere thins, and holes open at the poles. Plumes of nitrous oxide and other toxins rise from fires in South America and Africa, settle in the upper troposphere and drift eastward across the oceans. At night the land surface brightens with millions of pinpoints of light, which coalesce into blazing swaths across Europe, Japan and eastern North America. A semicircle of fire spreads from gas flares around the Persian Gulf.

It was all but inevitable, the watchers might tell us if we met them, that from the great diversity of large animals, one species or another would eventually gain intelligent control of Earth. That role has fallen to *Homo sapiens,* a primate risen in Africa from a lineage that split away from the chimpanzee line five to eight million years ago. Unlike any creature that lived before, we have become a geophysical force, swiftly changing the atmosphere and climate as well as the composition of the world's fauna and flora. Now in the midst of a population explosion, the human species has doubled to 5.5 billion during the past 50 years. It is scheduled to double again in the next 50 years. No other single species in evolutionary history has even remotely approached the sheer mass in protoplasm generated by humanity.

Darwin's dice have rolled badly for Earth. It was a misfortune for the living world in particular, many scientists believe, that a carnivorous primate and not some more benign form of animal made the breakthrough. Our species retains hereditary traits that add greatly to our destructive impact. We are tribal and aggressively territorial, intent on private space beyond minimal requirements and oriented by selfish sexual and reproductive drives. Cooperation beyond the family and tribal levels comes hard.

Worse, our liking for meat causes us to use the sun's energy at low efficiency. It is a general rule of ecology that (very roughly) only about 10 percent of the sun's energy captured by photosynthesis to produce plant tissue is converted into energy in the tissue of herbivores, the animals that eat the plants. Of that amount, 10 percent reaches the tissue of the carnivores feeding on the herbivores. Similarly, only 10 percent is transferred to carnivores that eat carnivores. And so on for another step or two. In a wetlands chain that runs from marsh grass to grasshopper to warbler to hawk, the energy captured during green production shrinks a thousandfold.

In other words, it takes a great deal of grass to support a hawk. Human beings, like hawks, are top carnivores, at the end of the food chain whenever they eat meat, two or more links removed from the plants; if chicken, for example, two links, and if tuna, four links. Even with most societies confined today to a mostly vegetarian diet, humanity is gobbling up a large part of the rest of the living world. We appropriate between 20 and 40 percent of the sun's energy that would otherwise be fixed into the tissue of natural vegetation, principally by our consumption of crops and timber, construction of buildings and roadways and the creation of wastelands. In the relentless search for more food, we have reduced animal life in lakes, rivers and now, increasingly, the open ocean. And everywhere we pollute the air and water, lower water tables and extinguish species.

The human species is, in a word, an environmental abnormality. It is possible that intelligence in the wrong kind of species was foreordained to be a fatal combination for the biosphere. Perhaps a law of evolution is that intelligence usually extinguishes itself.

This admittedly dour scenario is based on what can be termed the juggernaut theory of human nature, which holds that people are programmed by their genetic heritage to be so selfish that a sense of global responsibility will come too late. Individuals place themselves first, family second, tribe third and the rest of the world a distant fourth. Their genes also predispose them to plan ahead for one or two generations at most. They fret over the petty problems and conflicts of their daily lives and respond swiftly and often ferociously to slight challenges to their status and tribal security. But oddly, as psychologists have discovered, people also tend to underestimate both the likelihood and impact of such natural disasters as major earthquakes and great storms.

The reason for this myopic fog, evolutionary biologists contend, is that it was actually advantageous during all but the last few millennia of the two million years of existence of the genus *Homo*. The brain evolved into its present form during this long stretch of evolutionary time, during which people existed in small, preliterate hunter-gatherer bands. Life was precarious and short. A premium was placed on close attention to the near future and early reproduction, and little else. Disasters of a magnitude that occur only once every few centuries were forgotten or transmuted into myth. So today the mind still works comfortably backward and forward for only a few years, spanning a period not exceeding one or two generations. Those in past ages whose genes inclined them to short-term thinking lived longer and had more children than those who did not. Prophets never enjoyed a Darwinian edge.

The rules have recently changed, however. Global crises are rising within the life span of the generation now coming of age, a foreshortening that may explain why young people express more concern about the environment than do their elders. The time scale has contracted because of the exponential growth in both the human population and technologies impacting the environment. Exponential growth is basically the same as the increase of wealth by compound interest. The larger the population, the faster the growth; the faster the growth, the sooner the population becomes still larger. In Nigeria, to cite one of our more fecund nations, the population is expected to double from its 1988 level to 216 million by the year 2010. If the same rate of growth were to continue to 2110, its population would exceed that of the entire present population of the world.

With people everywhere seeking a better quality of life, the search for resources is expanding even faster than the population. The demand is being met by an increase in scientific knowledge, which doubles every 10 to 15 years. It is accelerated further by a parallel rise in environment-devouring technology. Because Earth is finite in many resources that determine the quality of life—including arable soil, nutrients, fresh water and space for natural ecosystems—doubling of consumption at constant time intervals can bring disaster with shocking suddenness. Even when a nonrenewable resource has been only half used, it is still only one interval away from the end. Ecologists like to make this point with the French riddle of the lily pond. At first there is only one lily pad in the pond, but the next day it doubles, and thereafter each of its descendants doubles. The pond completely fills with lily pads in 30 days. When is the pond exactly half full? Answer: on the 29th day.

Yet, mathematical exercises aside, who can safely measure the human capacity to overcome the perceived limits of Earth? The question of central interest is this: Are we racing to the brink of an abyss, or are we just gathering speed for a takeoff to a wonderful future? The crystal ball is clouded; the human condition baffles all the more because it is both unprecedented and bizarre, almost beyond understanding.

In the midst of uncertainty, opinions on the human prospect have tended to fall loosely into two schools. The first, exemptionalism, holds that since humankind is transcendent in intelligence and spirit, so must our species have been released from the iron laws of ecology that bind all other species. No matter how serious the problem, civilized human beings, by ingenuity, force of will and—who knows—divine dispensation, will find a solution.

Population growth? Good for the economy, claim some of the exemptionalists, and in any case a basic human right, so let it run. Land shortages? Try fusion energy to power the desalting of sea water, then reclaim the world's deserts. (The process might be assisted by towing icebergs to coastal pipelines.) Species going extinct? Not to worry. That is nature's way. Think of humankind as only the latest in a long line of exterminating agents in geological time. In any case, because our species has pulled free of old-style, mindless Nature, we have begun a different order of life. Evolution should now be allowed to proceed along this new trajectory. Finally, resources? The planet has more than enough resources to last indefinitely, if human genius is allowed to address each new problem in turn, without alarmist and unreasonable restrictions imposed on economic development. So hold the course, and touch the brakes lightly.

The opposing idea of reality is environmentalism, which sees humanity as a biological species tightly dependent on the natural world. As formidable as our intellect may be and as fierce our spirit, the argument goes, those qualities are not enough to free us from the constraints of the natural environment in which our human ancestors evolved. We cannot draw confidence from successful solutions to the smaller problems of the past. Many of Earth's vital resources are about to be exhausted, its atmospheric chemistry is deteriorating and human populations have already grown dangerously large. Natural ecosystems, the wellsprings of a healthful environment, are being irreversibly degraded.

At the heart of the environmentalist world view is the conviction that human physical and spiritual health depends on sustaining the planet in a relatively unaltered state. Earth is our home in the full, genetic sense, where humanity and its ancestors existed for all the millions of years of their evolution. Natural ecosystems—forests, coral reefs, marine blue waters—maintain the world exactly as we would wish it to be maintained. When we debase the global environment and extinguish the variety of life, we are dismantling a support system that is too complex to understand, let alone replace, in the foreseeable future. Space scientists theorize the existence of a virtually unlimited array of other planetary environments, almost all of which are uncongenial to human life. Our own Mother Earth, lately called Gaia, is a specialized conglomerate of organisms and the physical environment they create on a day-to-day basis, which can be destabilized and turned lethal by careless activity. We run the risk, conclude the environmentalists, of beaching ourselves upon alien shores like a great confused pod of pilot whales.

If I have not done so enough already by tone of voice, I will now place myself solidly in the environmentalist school, but not so radical as to wish a turning back of the clock, not given to driving spikes into Douglas firs to prevent logging and distinctly uneasy with such hybrid movements as ecofeminism, which holds that Mother Earth is a nurturing home for all life and should be revered and loved as in premodern (paleolithic and archaic) societies and that ecosystematic abuse is rooted in androcentric—that is to say, male-dominated—concepts, values and institutions.

Still, however soaked in androcentric culture, I am radical enough to take seriously the question heard with increasing frequency: Is humanity suicidal? Is the drive to environmental conquest and self-propagation embedded so deeply in our genes as to be unstoppable?

My short answer—opinion if you wish—is that humanity is not suicidal, at least not in the sense just stated. We are smart enough and have time enough to avoid an environmental catastrophe of civilization-threatening dimensions. But the technical problems are sufficiently formidable to require a redirection of much of science and technology, and the ethical issues are so basic as to force a reconsideration of our self-image as a species.

There are reasons for optimism, reasons to believe that we have entered what might someday be generously called the Century of the Environment. The United Nations Conference on Environment and Development, held in Rio de Janeiro in June 1992, attracted more than 120 heads of government, the largest number ever assembled, and helped move environmental issues closer to the political center stage; on November 18, 1992, more than 1,500 senior scientists from 69 countries issued a "Warning to Humanity," stating that overpopulation and environmental deterioration put the very future of life at risk. The greening of religion has become a global trend, with theologians and religious leaders addressing environmental problems as a moral issue. In May 1992, leaders of most of the major American denominations met with scientists as guests of members of the United States Senate to formulate a "Joint Appeal by Religion and Science for the Environment." Conservation of biodiversity is increasingly seen by both national governments and major landowners as important to their country's future. Indonesia, home to a large part of the native Asian plant and animal species, has begun to shift to land-management practices that conserve and sustainably develop the remaining rain forests. Costa Rica has created a National Institute of Biodiversity. A pan-African institute for biodiversity research and management has been founded, with headquarters in Zimbabwe.

Finally, there are favorable demographic signs. The rate of population increase is declining on all continents, although it is still well above zero almost everywhere and remains especially high in sub-Saharan Africa. Despite entrenched traditions and religious beliefs, the desire to use contraceptives in family planning is spreading. Demographers estimate that if the demand were fully met, this action alone would reduce the eventual stabilized population by more than two billion.

In summary, the will is there. Yet the awful truth remains that a large part of humanity will suffer no matter what is done. The number of people living in absolute poverty has risen during the past 20 years to nearly one billion and is expected to increase another 100 million by the end of the decade. Whatever progress has been made in the developing countries, and that includes an overall improvement in the average standard of living, is threatened by a continuance of rapid population growth and the deterioration of forests and arable soil.

Our hopes must be chastened further still, and this is in my opinion the central issue, by a key and seldom-recognized distinction between the nonliving and living environments. Science and the political process can be adapted to manage the nonliving, physical environment. The human hand is now upon the physical homeostat. The ozone layer can be mostly restored to the upper atmosphere by elimination of CFCs, with these substances peaking at six times the present level and then subsiding during the next half century. Also, with procedures that will prove far more difficult and initially expensive, carbon dioxide and other greenhouse gases can be pulled back to concentrations that slow global warming.

The human hand, however, is not upon the biological homeostat. There is no way in sight to micromanage the natural ecosystems and the millions of species they contain. That feat might be accomplished by generations to come, but then it will be too late for the ecosystems—and perhaps for us. Despite the seemingly bottomless nature of creation, humankind has been chipping away at its diversity, and Earth is destined to become an impoverished planet within a century if present trends continue. Mass extinctions are being reported with increasing frequency in every part of the world. They include half the freshwater fishes of peninsular Malaysia, 10 birds native to Cebu in the Philippines, half the 41 tree snails of Oahu, 44 of the 68 shallow-water mussels of the Tennessee River shoals, as many as 90 plant species growing on the Centinela Ridge in Ecuador, and in the United States as a whole, about 200 plant species, with another 680 species and races now classified as in danger of extinction. The main cause is the destruction of natural habitats, especially tropical forests. Close behind, especially on the Hawaiian archipelago and other islands, is the introduction of rats, pigs, beard grass, lantana and other exotic organisms that outbreed and extirpate native species.

The few thousand biologists worldwide who specialize in diversity are aware that they can witness and report no more than a very small percentage of the extinctions actually occurring. The reason is that they have facilities to keep track of only a tiny fraction of the millions of species and a sliver of the planet's surface on a yearly basis. They have devised a rule of thumb to characterize the situation: that whenever careful studies are made of habitats before and after disturbance, extinctions almost always come to light. The corollary: the great majority of extinctions are never observed. Vast numbers of species are apparently vanishing before they can be discovered and named.

There is a way, nonetheless, to estimate the rate of loss indirectly. Independent studies around the world and in fresh and marine waters have revealed a robust connection between the size of a habitat and the amount of biodiversity it contains. Even a small loss in area reduces the number of species. The relation is such that when the area of the habitat is cut to a tenth of its original cover, the number of species eventually drops by roughly one-half. Tropical rain forests, thought to harbor a majority of Earth's species (the reason conservationists get so exercised about rain forests), are being reduced by nearly that magnitude. At the present time they occupy about the same area as that of the 48 conterminous United States, representing a little less than half their original, prehistoric cover; and they are shrinking each year by about 2 percent, an amount equal to the state of Florida. If the typical value (that is, 90 percent area loss causes 50 percent eventual extinction) is applied, the projected loss of species due to rain forest destruction worldwide is half a percent across the board for all kinds of plants, animals and microorganisms.

When area reduction and all the other extinction agents are considered together, it is reasonable to project a reduction by 20 percent or more of the rain forest species by the year 2020, climbing to 50 percent or more by midcentury, if nothing is done to change current practice. Comparable erosion is likely in other environments now under assault, including many coral reefs and Mediterranean-type heathlands of Western Australia, South Africa and California.

The ongoing loss will not be replaced by evolution in any period of time that has meaning for humanity. Extinction is now proceeding thousands of times faster than the production of new species. The average life span of a species and its descendants in past geological eras varied according to group (like mollusks or echinoderms or flowering plants) from about 1 to 10 million years. During the past 500 million years, there have been five great extinction spasms comparable to the one now being inaugurated by human expansion. The latest, evidently caused by the strike of an asteroid, ended the Age of Reptiles 66 million years ago. In each case it took more than 10 million years for evolution to completely replenish the biodiversity lost. And that was in an otherwise undisturbed natural environment. Humanity is now destroying most of the habitats where evolution can occur.

The surviving biosphere remains the great unknown of Earth in many respects. On the practical side, it is hard even to imagine what other species have to offer in the way of new pharmaceuticals, crops, fibers, petroleum substitutes and other products. We have only a poor grasp of the ecosystem services by which other organisms cleanse the water, turn soil into a fertile living cover and manufacture the very air we breathe. We sense but do not fully understand what the highly diverse natural world means to our esthetic pleasure and mental well-being.

Scientists are unprepared to manage a declining biosphere. To illustrate, consider the following mission they might be given. The last remnant of a rain forest is about to be cut over. Environmentalists are stymied. The contracts have been signed, and local landowners and politicians are intransigent. In a final desperate move, a team of biologists is scrambled in an attempt to preserve the biodiversity by extraordinary means. Their assignment is the following: collect samples of all the species of organisms quickly, before the cutting starts; maintain the species in zoos, gardens and laboratory cultures or else deep-freeze samples of the tissues in liquid nitrogen, and finally, establish the procedure by which the entire community can be reassembled on empty ground at a later date, when social and economic conditions have improved.

The biologists cannot accomplish this task, not if thousands of them came with a billion-dollar budget. They cannot even imagine how to do it. In the forest patch live legions of species: perhaps 300 birds, 500 butterflies, 200 ants, 50,000 beetles, 1,000 trees, 5,000 fungi, tens of thousands of bacteria and so on down a long roster of major groups. Each species occupies a precise niche, demanding a certain place, an exact microclimate, particular nutrients and temperature and humidity cycles with specified timing to trigger phases of the life cycle. Many, perhaps most, of the species are locked in symbioses with other species; they cannot survive and reproduce unless arrayed with their partners in the correct idiosyncratic configurations.

Even if the biologists pulled off the taxonomic equivalent of the Manhattan Project, sorting and preserving cultures of all the species, they could not then put the community back together again. It would be like unscrambling an egg with a pair of spoons. The biology of the microorganisms needed to reanimate the soil would be mostly unknown. The pollinators of most of the flowers and the correct timing of their appearance could only be guessed. The "assembly rules," the sequence in which species must be allowed to colonize in order to coexist indefinitely, would remain in the realm of theory.

In its neglect of the rest of life, exemptionalism fails definitively. To move ahead as though scientific and entrepreneurial genius will solve each crisis that arises implies that the declining biosphere can be similarly manipulated. But the world is too complicated to be turned into a garden. There is no biological homeostat that can be worked by humanity; to believe otherwise is to risk reducing a large part of Earth to a wasteland.

The environmentalist vision, prudential and less exuberant than exemptionalism, is closer to reality. It sees humanity entering a bottleneck unique in history, constricted by population and economic pressures. In order to pass through to the other side, within perhaps 50 to 100 years, more science and entrepreneurship will have to be devoted to stabilizing the global environment. That can be accomplished, according to expert consensus, only by halting population growth and devising a wiser use of resources than has been accomplished to date. And wise use for the living world in particular means preserving the surviving ecosystems, micromanaging them only enough to save the biodiversity they contain, until such time as they can be understood and employed in the fullest sense for human benefit.

Suggestions for Discussion

1. Wilson's essay begins by imagining that at the space station of an alien civilization the environmental history of our planet has been secretly tracked. What advantage does he gain in using this introductory device?
2. Explain Wilson's statement in the fourth paragraph: "Darwin's dice have rolled badly for Earth." What does he mean when he states later in the essay, "It is possible that intelligence in the wrong kind of species was foreordained to be a fatal combination for the biosphere"?
3. Who are the "exemptionalists"? What do they believe about humans' ability to control the environment? How does Wilson interpret their beliefs?
4. What is the "environmentalist world view"? To which school of belief does Wilson belong? Why?
5. According to the author, what can humankind do to save itself from extinction?

Suggestions for Writing

1. Write a paper explaining the difficulties we face in trying to protect the rain forests. Why is it necessary for us to attempt to do so?
2. Is Wilson optimistic about the future of human beings on earth? Write a paper carefully explaining his position. Do you agree? Explain your own position on the issue.

NILES ELDREDGE

Creationism Isn't Science

Niles Eldredge (b. 1925), born in Brooklyn, New York, and educated as an undergraduate and graduate at Columbia University, is the curator of the Department of Invertebrates at the American Museum of Natural History in New York. The author of a number of books, including *Time Frame* (1985), *Life Pulse* (1987), and *Miner's Canary* (1991), he is a scientist deeply concerned about Darwinism and other theories of evolution that derive from Charles Darwin's *On the Origin of Species* (1859). Following the publication of Darwin's book, a violent argument ensued between science and religion that appeared to come to a close after the Scopes Trial in 1925. In recent years, however, with the rise of fundamentalist religion in the United States, an argument has flowered that creationism has as much validity as a theory as Darwin's theory of evolution. Eldredge attempts to show in this essay why the two theories are not equal and how the zeal of creationists is undermining the teaching of science in the schools.

Despite this country's apparent modernism, the creationist movement once again is growing. The news media proclaimed a juryless trial in California as "Scopes II" and those who cling to the myth of progress wonder how the country could revert to the primitive state it was in when Darrow and Bryan battled it out in the hot summer of 1925 in Dayton, Tennessee. But the sad truth is that we have not progressed. Creationism never completely disappeared as a political, religious, and educational issue. Scopes was convicted of violating the Tennessee statute forbidding the teaching of the evolutionary origins of mankind (although in fact he was ill and never really did teach the evolution segment of the curriculum). The result was a drastic cutback in serious discussion of evolution in many high school texts until it became respectable again in the 1960s.

Although technological advances since 1925 have been prodigious, and although science news magazines are springing up like toadstools, the American public appears to be as badly informed about the real nature of science as it ever was. Such undiluted ignorance, coupled with the strong anti-intellectual tradition in the US, provides a congenial climate for creationism to leap once more to the fore, along with school prayer, sex education, Proposition 13, and the other favorite issues of the populist, conservative movement. Much of the success of recent creationist efforts lies in a prior failure to educate our children about science—how it is done, by whom, and how its results are to be interpreted.

Today's creationists usually cry for "equal time" rather than for actually substituting the Genesis version of the origin of things for the explanations preferred by modern science. (The recent trial in California is an anachronism in this respect because the plaintiff simply affirmed that his rights of religious freedom were abrogated by teaching him that man "descended from apes"). At the heart of the creationists' contemporary political argument is an appeal to the time-honored American sense of fair play. "Look," they say, "evolution is only a theory. Scientists cannot agree on all details either of the exact course of evolutionary history, or how evolution actually takes place." True enough. Creationists then declare that many scientists have grave doubts that evolution actually has occurred—a charge echoed by Ronald Reagan during the campaign, and definitely false. They argue that since evolution is only a theory, why not, in the spirit of fair play, give equal time to equally plausible explanations of the origin of the cosmos, of life on earth, and of mankind? Why not indeed?

The creationist argument equates a biological, evolutionary system with a non-scientific system of explaining life's exuberant diversity. Both systems are presented as authoritarian, and here lies the real tragedy of American science education: the public is depressingly willing to see merit in the "fair play, equal time" argument precisely because it views science almost wholly in this authoritarian vein. The public is bombarded with a constant stream of oracular pronouncements of new discoveries, new truths, and medical and technological innovations, but the American education system gives most people no effective choice but to ignore, accept on faith, or reject out of hand each new scientific finding. Scientists themselves promote an Olympian status for their profession; it's small wonder that the public has a tough time deciding which set of authoritarian pronouncements to heed. So why not present them all and let each person choose his or her own set of beliefs?

Of course, there has to be some willingness to accept the expertise of specialists. Although most of us "believe" the earth is spherical, how many of us can design and perform an experiment to show that it must be so? But to stress the authoritarianism of science is to miss its essence. Science is the enterprise of comparing alternative ideas about what the cosmos is, how it works, and how it came to be. Some ideas are better than others, and the criterion for judging which are better is simply the relative power of different ideas to fit our observations. The goal is greater understanding of the natural universe. The method consists of constantly challenging received ideas, modifying them, or, best of all, replacing them with better ones.

So science is ideas, and the ideas are acknowledged to be merely approximations to the truth. Nothing could be further from authoritarianism—dogmatic assertions of what is true. Scientists deal with ideas that appear to be the best (the closest to the truth) given what they think they know about the universe at any given moment. If scientists frequently act as if their ideas *are* the truth, they are simply showing their humanity. But the human quest for a rational coming-to-grips with the cosmos recognizes imperfection in observation and thought, and incorporates the frailty into its method. Creationists disdain this quest, preferring the wholly authoritarian, allegedly "revealed" truth of divine creation as an understanding of our beginnings. At the same time they present disagreement among scientists as an expression of scientific failure in the realm of evolutionary biology.

To the charge that "evolution is *only* a theory," we say "all science is theory." Theories are ideas, or complex sets of ideas, which explain some aspect of the natural world. Competing theories sometimes coexist until one drives the other out, or until both are discarded in favor of yet another theory. But it is true that one major theory usually holds sway at any one time. All biologists, including biochemists, molecular geneticists, physiologists, behaviorists, and anatomists, see a pattern of similarity interlocking the spectrum of millions of species, from bacteria to timber wolves. Darwin finally convinced the world that this pattern of similarity is neatly explained by "descent with modification." If we imagine a genealogical system where an ancestor produces one or more descendants, we get a pattern of progressive similarity. The whole array of ancestors and descendants will share some feature inherited from the first ancestor; as each novelty appears, it is shared only with later descendants. All forms of life have the nucleic acid RNA. One major branch of life, the vertebrates, all share backbones. All mammals have three inner ear bones, hair, and mammary glands. All dogs share features not found in other carnivores, such as cats. In other words, dogs share similarities among themselves in addition to having general mammalian features, plus general vertebrate features, as well as anatomical and biochemical similarities shared with the rest of life.

How do we test the basic notion that life has evolved? The notion of evolution, like any scientific idea, should generate predictions about the natural world, which we can discover to be true or false. The grand prediction of evolution is that there should be one basic scheme of similarities interlocking all of life. This is what we have consistently found for over 100 years, as thousands of biologists daily compared different organisms. Medical experimentation depends upon the interrelatedness of life. We test drugs on rhesus monkeys and study the effects of caffeine on rats because we cannot experiment on ourselves. The physiological systems of monkeys are more similar to our own than to rats. Medical scientists know this and rely on this prediction to interpret the significance of their results in terms of human medicine. Very simply, were life not all interrelated, none of this would be possible. There would be chaos, not order, in the natural world. There is no competing, rational biological explanation for this order in nature, and there hasn't been for a long while.

Creationists, of course, have an alternative explanation for this order permeating life's diversity. It is simply the way the supernatural creator chose to pattern life. But any possible pattern could be there, including chaos—an absence of any similarity among the "kinds" of organisms on earth—and creationism would hold that it is just what the creator made. There is nothing about this view of life that smacks of prediction. It tells us nothing about what to expect if we begin to study organisms in detail. In short, there is nothing in this notion that allows us to go to nature to test it, to verify or reject it.

And there is the key difference. Creationism (and it comes in many guises, most of which do not stem from the Judeo-Christian tradition) is a belief system involving the supernatural. Testing an idea with our own experiences in the natural universe is simply out of bounds. The mystical revelation behind creationism is the opposite of science, which seeks rational understanding of the cosmos. Science thrives on alternative explanations, which must be equally subject to observational and experimental testing. No form of creationism even remotely qualifies for inclusion in a science curriculum.

Creationists have introduced equal-time bills in over 10 state legislatures, and recently met with success when Governor White of Arkansas signed such a bill into law on March 19 (reportedly without reading it). Creationists also have lobbied extensively at local school boards. The impact has been enormous. Just as the latest creationist bill is defeated in committee, and some of their more able spokesmen look silly on national TV, one hears of a local school district in the Philadelphia environs where some of the teachers have adopted the "equal time" or "dual model" approach to discussing "origins" in the biology curriculum on their own initiative. Each creationist "defeat" amounts to a Pyrrhic victory for their opponents. Increasingly, teachers are left to their own discretion, and whether out of personal conviction, a desire to be "fair," or fear of parental reprisal, they are teaching creationism along with evolution in their biology classes. It is simply the path of least resistance.

Acceptance of equal time for two alternative authoritarian explanations is a startling blow to the fabric of science education. The fundamental notion a student should get from high school science is that people can confront the universe and learn about it directly. Just one major inroad against this basic aspect of science threatens all of science education. Chemistry, physics, and geology—all of which spurn biblical revelation in favor of direct experience, as all science must—are jeopardized every bit as much as biology. That some creationists have explicitly attacked areas of geology, chemistry, and physics (in arguments over the age of the earth, for example) underscores the more general threat they pose to all science. We must remove science education from its role as authoritarian truthgiver. This view distorts the real nature of science and gives creationists their most potent argument.

The creationists' equal-time appeal maintains that evolution itself amounts to a religious belief (allied with a secular humanism) and should not be included in a science curriculum. But if it is included, goes the argument, it must appear along with other religious notions. Both are authoritarian belief systems, and neither is science, according to this creationist ploy.

The more common creationist approach these days avoids such sophistry and maintains that both creationism and evolution belong in the realm of science. But apart from some attempts to document the remains of Noah's Ark on the flanks of Mt. Ararat, creationists have been singularly unsuccessful in posing testable theories about the origin, diversity, and distribution of plants and animals. No such contributions have appeared to date either in creationism's voluminous literature or, more to the point, in the professional biological literature. "Science creationism" consists almost exclusively of a multipronged attack on evolutionary biology and historical geology. No evidence, for example, is presented in favor of the notion that the earth is only 20,000 years old, but many arguments attempt to poke holes in geochemists' and astronomers' reckoning of old Mother Earth's age at about 4.6 billion years. Analysis of the age of formation of rocks is based ultimately on the theories of radioactive decay in nuclear physics. (A body of rock is dated, often by several different means, in several different laboratories. The results consistently agree. And rocks shown to be roughly the same age on independent criteria (usually involving fossils) invariably check out to be roughly the same age when dated radiometrically. The system, although not without its flaws, works.) The supposed vast age of any particular rock can be shown to be false, but not by quoting Scripture.

All of the prodigious works of "scientific creationism" are of this nature. All can be refuted. However, before school boards or parent groups, creationists are fond of "debating" scientists by bombarding the typically ill-prepared biologist or geologist with a plethora of allegations, ranging from the second law of thermodynamics (said to falsify evolution outright) to the supposed absence of fossils intermediate between "major kinds." No scientist is equally at home in all realms of physics, chemistry, geology, and biology in this day of advanced specialization. Not all the proper retorts spring readily to mind. Retorts there are, but the game is usually lost anyway, as rebuttals strike an audience as simply another set of authoritarian statements they must take on faith.

Although creationists persist in depicting both science and creationism as two comparable, monolithic belief systems, perhaps the most insidious attack exploits free inquiry in science. Because we disagree on specifics, some of my colleagues and I are said now to have serious doubts that evolution has occurred. Distressing as this may be, the argument actually highlights the core issue raised by creationism. The creationists are acknowledging that science is no monolithic authoritarian belief system. But even though they recognize that there are competing ideas within contemporary biology, the creationists see scientific debate as a sign of weakness. Of course, it really is a sign of vitality.

Evolutionary theory since the 1940s (until comparatively recently) has focused on a single coherent view of the evolutionary process. Biologists of all disciplines agree to a remarkable degree on the outlines of this theory, the so-called "modern synthesis." In a nutshell, this was a vindication of Darwin's original position: that evolution is predominantly an affair of gradual progressive change. As environmental conditions changed, natural selection (a culling process similar to the "artificial" selection practiced by animal breeders) favored those variants best suited to the new conditions. Thus evolutionary change is fundamentally adaptive. The modern synthesis integrated the newly arisen science of genetics with the Darwinian view and held that the entire diversity of life could be explained in these simple terms.

Some biologists have attacked natural selection itself, but much of the current uproar in evolutionary biology is less radical in implication. Some critics see a greater role for random processes. Others, like me, see little evidence of gradual, progressive change in the fossil record. We maintain that the usual explanation—the inadequacy of the fossil record—is itself inadequate to explain the non-change, the maintenance of status quo which lasts in some cases for 10 million years or more in our fossil bones and shells. In this view, change (presumably by natural selection causing adaptive modifications) takes place in bursts of a few thousand years, followed usually by immensely longer periods of business as usual.

Arguments become heated. Charges of "straw man," "no evidence," and so on are flung about—which shows that scientists, like everyone, get their egos wrapped up in their work. They believe passionately in their own ideas, even if they are supposed to be calm, cool, dispassionate, and able to evaluate all possibilities evenly. (It is usually in the collective process of argument that the better ideas win out in science; seldom has anyone single-handedly evinced the open-mindedness necessary to drop a pet idea.) But nowhere in this *sturm und drang* has any of the participants come close to denying that evolution has occurred.

So the creationists distort. An attack on some parts of Darwin's views is equated with a rejection of evolution. They conveniently ignore that Darwin merely proposed one of many sets of ideas on *how* evolution works. The only real defense against such tactics lies in a true appreciation of the scientific enterprise—the trial-and-error comparison of ideas and how they seem to fit the material universe. If the public were more aware that scientists are expected to disagree, that what a scientist writes today is not the last word, but a progress report on some very intensive thinking and investigation, creationists would be far less successful in injecting an authoritarian system of belief into curricula supposedly devoted to free, open rational inquiry into the nature of natural things.

Suggestions for Discussion

1. Eldredge refers to the Scopes II trial in California. What was the first Scopes trial in Tennessee about? What issues about evolution were raised in 1925 by the trial, and how are they relevant today?
2. What does Eldredge have to say about the relationship between the populist–conservative movement and creationism? How do you define *creationism?*
3. Explain Eldredge's response to the claim that since Darwinian evolution is only a theory, equal time in the schools should be given to the proponents of creationism.
4. For Eldredge, what are the dangers of accepting the authoritarianism of science? What does he believe the real function of the scientific enterprise to be? How do creationists, according to Eldredge, misunderstand the meaning of the constant debates raging in the scientific community?
5. What causes one major scientific theory to predominate for a given period of time? Summarize Eldredge's explanation of why Darwin's theory has held the support of scientists for such a long period.
6. Why does Eldredge believe that creationism does not lend itself to testing? What is the significance of testing theories?
7. For Eldredge, what is the most significant danger of the struggle by creationists for equal time in the schools? How do creationists take advantage, according to Eldredge, of scientific authoritarianism? Why does Eldredge believe that debates among scientists are a sign of vitality?
8. Summarize Eldredge's description of recent debates among evolutionists and his claim that these debates are distorted by creationists.

Suggestions for Writing

1. Write a paper in which you explain how one may believe in God without accepting the position of the creationists. Document your argument with examples.

2. Do you believe that creationists should be allowed equal time with biologists in the schools? If you do, explain your position.
3. Write a paper in which you summarize Eldredge's position and contrast it with arguments by a creationist. State why you agree with one side of the argument or the other.

DAVID S. WILCOVE

What I Saw When I Went to the Forest

David S. Wilcove, who received a Ph.D. in biology from Princeton University in 1985, is a staff ecologist for the Wilderness Society and the author of numerous scientific publications and popular articles on the conservation of biological diversity. For a series published by the Wilderness Society called *On National Policies for the Forest of the Future,* he has contributed a volume, *Protecting Biological Diversity.* In this essay he narrates his firsthand experience of the dangers to the forest ecosystem created by the timber industry's practice of clearing too rapidly.

"The penalty of an ecological education," Aldo Leopold wrote, "is that one lives alone in a world of wounds." Wounds I was prepared to see when I went to the Pacific Northwest, but not the mutilated and hemorrhaging patient that is the old-growth forest. Now, half a year later when I look back on my trip, I find myself alternating between two very different sets of feelings: a sense of wonder and affection for the forest itself—for its complexity, its antiquity, and, of course, its beauty—and a sense of sadness and anger for what we are doing to it. I make no apologies for my shifting moods. Schizophrenia of this sort is common among ecologists.

There were two of us from The Wilderness Society—Chief Forester Barry Flamm and I—who together traveled from San Francisco to Seattle, visiting the old-growth forests and meeting the people who study them, defend them, manage them, and destroy them. What follows is a summary of my experiences—a blending, I hope, of ecological awe and environmentalist outrage, beginning with a small plane buzzing over the Willamette National Forest in south-central Oregon.

It looked for all the world as though some alien force had attacked the land with a giant cookie-cutter. As far as the eye could see, there were clearcuts, each one crisply excised from the surrounding forest. The most recent of them still showed signs of the fires used to dispose of the slash: charred earth and all too often a fringe of dead trees where the flames had escaped into the forest. In death, the needles of the burned trees had turned bright orange, creating a grotesque and incongruous burst of New England autumn color in a landscape that was otherwise green. A quick pass over some of the private forestlands fringing the Willamette confirmed what we already suspected: outside the public lands, the old growth was simply gone. In its stead were acre upon acre of young Douglas-fir trees. They were a young and exuberant lot, these saplings, but in aggregate about as exciting as a cornfield. As the little plane bobbed and weaved its way back to the airstrip, I found myself wishing it were thirty years earlier, when we had more old-growth and more time to protect it.

Spokesmen from the timber industry are fond of pointing out how much of the old-growth is already "locked up" in parks, wilderness areas, and research natural areas. Whether or not their numbers are accurate is almost irrelevant, because simple numbers cannot begin to convey the complexity and variety of the old-growth ecosystem or the subtle changes in species composition and stand structure that are caused by nuances of topography, elevation, exposure, and history. To lump a Sitka spruce forest in the Coast Range with a mid-elevation Douglas-fir forest in the Cascades is to ignore the senses and overrule the mind, for the two forests look, sound, and smell very differently. As near as I can tell, the easiest and safest generality to make about old-growth is that all of it seems to be disappearing rapidly.

Nor do acreage figures reflect the on-going fragmentation of the old-growth ecosystem. A generation of research has revealed that when natural landscapes are chopped into little pieces, ecological processes go awry and species go extinct. It can be an insidiously slow process, as the sensitive species wink out one after the other over a period of decades or even centuries. The fact that young spotted owls have had abysmal success in establishing themselves in new territories is indicative of the old-growth fragmentation that already has occurred. The spotted owl, of course, has attracted the lion's share of attention, and it may well be the first to go. And if the logging continues unabated, other species will follow.

Consider, for example, the Vaux's swift. It is not a bird one hears much about, and despite my fondness for it, I must admit that it isn't much to look at. The field guides accurately but heartlessly describe this small, brown, almost tailless bird as "a cigar with wings." Like all swifts, it is a creature of the air, invariably seen streaking across the sky, its long, stiff wings beating furiously as it runs down some hapless insect. Vaux's swifts are not particularly fussy about where they forage, and during my trip I often saw them hawking insects over open fields and small towns. But when it comes time to nest, they seek out large fire-hollowed snags. There they cement their saucer-shaped nests against the inner walls, using their own saliva as the glue. Snags of this sort occur in old-growth forests, but not in the young, intensively managed stands that are rapidly replacing the old-growth.

About two centuries ago, an identical problem faced the chimney swift, a close relative of the Vaux's swift, which inhabits eastern North America. As the settlers began felling the primeval forests of the East, some of the chimney swifts began nesting in dormant chimneys, an adaptive response that may have spared them a rather grim fate. Unfortunately, Vaux's swifts have not caught on to the trick as quickly as their eastern counterparts, and relatively few of them now nest in chimneys. It has become a race between natural selection, which is pushing the swifts away from the snags and into the chimneys, and the loggers, who are destroying the forests where the birds currently reside. There is a third possibility, however: our own species could voluntarily leave enough old growth for the swifts to continue living as they have for thousands of years.

Swifts and snags. It's easy to rhapsodize about swifts—their aeronautical prowess stirs our terrestrial imaginations—but by devoting so much attention to them we may be doing an injustice to the snags. To portray a snag as simply a condominium for swifts is to overlook its multi-faceted talents, such as the center of a termite civilization, a place where a long-eared bat can pass the time of day, or the feeding grounds for fungal filaments. Part of the elegance of the old-growth ecosystem lies in the fact that linkages between the living forest and the dead trees are so strong. Even the word "old growth" expresses this fact: strictly speaking, the term *ought* to be an oxymoron—"old" implying stasis or even decay, and "growth" implying youth, vigor, and change—but it isn't. Seeing the old-growth forests and thinking about these linkages brought to mind the issue of old-growth "management."

Most of the scientists I met, whether in the Forest Service or academia, were respectful of the complexity of the old-growth ecosystem. They were trying to find ways to juggle rotation times, cutting patterns and the like, not with any confidence that we can have our old-growth cake and eat it, too, but out of concern for what would assuredly happen to the forests without their input. Yet here and there in the forestry literature one occasionally encounters papers that purport to show how old-growth conditions can be recreated by intensively managing second-growth stands: the "you tell us what you want and we'll take our chainsaws into the woods and create it" mentality. I do not question the sincerity of the authors of these papers, but I find their self-confidence nothing short of astounding.

Despite considerable training as an ecologist, I am not entirely confident of my ability to manage that quarter-acre collection of crab grass and dandelions that masquerades as my front lawn, much less an ancient, complex assemblage of plants and animals, individual trees of which were around when King John was forced to consider the Magna Carta.

Politically astute conservationists tend to avoid emphasizing the importance of the spotted owl in the old-growth matrix. The issue, they rightly point out, is not survival of an owl, but survival of an entire ecosystem, and until the public realizes this, the timber industry will have the upper hand. Yet I am nevertheless compelled to talk about the spotted owl. For a simple reason: I like owls. And I have always wanted to see a spotted owl, even before it bore the weight of the old-growth ecosystem upon its fluffy brown shoulders.

My own encounter with the spotted owl was, like most momentous events in birdwatching, a breathlessly sedate event. We hiked into a large and undisturbed section of old-growth forest within the Willamette National Forest and began hooting like a spotted owl. Within a few minutes, an honest-to-goodness spotted owl answered back. Unfortunately, it did not call long enough for us to get a bearing on its location, and all we could ascertain was that it was somewhere very close, perhaps even watching us.

We tried all manner of owl calls but could not get the bird to hoot back. Either it recognized a phony when it heard one or had no interest in defending its turf from an intruding owl. Finally, with nothing to lose we fanned out into the forest, walking quietly and scanning the trees. While scrambling over a log, I glanced ahead and noticed a Buddha-shaped object sitting in a small yew tree. A closer look through my binocular confirmed it: a spotted owl. In what I thought was a calm voice, but one which probably sounded delirious, I beckoned for the others to come quickly. I was afraid the wily creature would slip away before they had a chance to see it.

I needn't have worried. That bird had no intention of flying away. As we crept closer, snapping twigs underfoot, stumbling, and otherwise making all the noise that people make when they try to slip silently through the forest, the owl just yawned, stretched its wings, and dozed off. The sounds of our cameras, our whispered "oohs and aahs," our presence just a few feet away—none of this seemed to faze it in the least. This, I was told, is fairly typical of spotted owls. Why, we wondered, are they so fearless, even trusting, of the very species that seems hell-bent on driving them to extinction?

The answer came to me when a vole darted across a log, behind and out of view of the owl. Instantly, the owl swiveled its head and glared in the direction of the vole. Apparently the sound of cameras clicking and humans whispering meant nothing to the bird. But the sound of a rodent's feet scurrying across the forest floor—now *that* was a sound worth hearing.

I realized then that spotted owls are neither fearless nor trusting of humans. They are simply oblivious to them. Their world revolves around what for countless generations have been the essentials for survival in the old-growth forest: expertise in the art of capturing voles and flying squirrels, fear of great horned owls, knowledge of the right hoots and whistles for attracting a mate. A fear of humans? My guess is that natural selection hasn't had time to get around to that particular lesson, not when there have been so many other pressing issues to resolve.

Had we been slower in our assault on old growth, logging the trees over the course of millennia rather than decades, the spotted owls, the Vaux's swifts, and all of the other inhabitants might have found a way to coexist with us. But it didn't happen that way because we turned out to be as competent at cutting down trees as spotted owls are at capturing voles. Perhaps, in a rather perverse way, it is a measure of our own success as a species that we have destroyed so much of the old growth in such a short span of time. If so, a better measure will surely be our willingness to save what little is left.

There is some irony in the fact that when I finally saw a spotted owl, it was perched in a Pacific yew tree. For years, foresters have shunned the small, slow-growing yew as a worthless "weed" tree. It isn't replanted on logged sites, it has no place in the managed forest. Only recently have we discovered that the bark of the Pacific yew contains a chemical that combats cancerous tumors, causing medical researchers to engage in a frenzied search for yew trees in the old-growth forests. I am not suggesting that we will derive fabulous pharmaceutical compounds from spotted owls, long-eared bats, Vaux's swifts, or big, old snags. But I am suggesting that each of them has important things to teach us, lessons we will never learn at the rate we're going.

Suggestions for Discussion

1. The author obviously believes that preservation of "old-growth" forests is a much more complicated matter than that of the protection of Vaux's swifts and spotted owls. Yet he devotes much of his essay to those two species. Why? What important argument does he make by stressing the need to save these birds?
2. Wilcove says that the very term "old growth" ought to be an oxymoron, and yet it is not. What is an oxymoron? What point does Wilcove make here about ecosystems?
3. Three of the essays on conservation are highly personal and familiar. Which are they? Why is this kind of essay effective in presenting an argument for the environmental movement?

Suggestions for Writing

1. What are some examples, other than those in this essay, of species that have been destroyed as people have, so to speak, tamed nature? Write an essay in which you argue for or against the inevitability of this extinction.
2. If you do not understand what Wilcove means by "ecosystems," do some research and then consider the importance to civilization of maintaining them. Write an essay in which you describe the dangers of such destruction.

URSULA K. LE GUIN

Winged

The Creatures on My Mind

Ursula K. Le Guin (b. 1929) was born in Berkeley, California, and holds a B.A. from Radcliffe College and an M.A. from Columbia University. She has been a visiting lecturer and writer in residence at many universities in the United States and abroad. Her career as a writer of fiction, including science fiction, has been a distinguished one. Among her works are *Planet of Exile* (1967), *The Left Hand of Darkness* (1969), *The Farthest Shore* (1972), *The Compass Rose* (1982), and *Always Coming Home* (1985). She has also written numerous short stories, poems, criticism, and screenplays and has received numerous awards, including the National Book Award. This deeply personal essay shows by example how we can become more aware of and sensitive to other species that we tend to ignore.

I. The Beetle

When I stayed for a week in New Orleans, out near Tulane, I had an apartment with a balcony. It wasn't one of those cast-iron-lace showpieces of the French Quarter, but a deep, wood-railed balcony made for sitting outside in privacy, just the kind of place I like. But when I first stepped out on it, the first thing I saw was a huge beetle. It lay on its back directly under the light fixture. I thought it was dead, then saw its legs twitch and twitch again. No doubt it had been attracted by the light the night before, and had flown into it, and damaged itself mortally.

Big insects horrify me. As a child I feared moths and spiders, but adolescence cured me, as if those fears evaporated in the stew of hormones. But I never got enough hormones to make me easy with the large, hard-shelled insects: wood roaches, June bugs, mantises, cicadas. This beetle was a couple of inches long; its abdomen was ribbed, its legs long and jointed; it was dull reddish brown; it was dying. I felt a little sick seeing it lie there twitching, enough to keep me from sitting out on the balcony that first day.

Next morning, ashamed of my queasiness, I went out with the broom to sweep it away. But it was still twitching its legs and antennae, still dying. With the end of the broom handle I pushed it very gently a little farther toward the corner of the balcony, and then I sat to read and make notes in the wicker chair in the other corner, turned away from the beetle because its movements drew my eyes. My intense consciousness of it seemed to have something to do with my strangeness in that strange city, New Orleans, and my sense of being on the edge of the tropics—a hot, damp, swarming, fetid, luxuriant existence—as if my unease took the beetle as its visible sign. Why else did I think of it so much? I weighed maybe two thousand times what it weighed, and lived in a perceptual world utterly alien from its world. My feelings were quite out of proportion.

And if I had any courage or common sense, I kept telling myself, I'd step on the poor damned creature and put it out of its misery. We don't know what a beetle may or may not suffer, but it was, in the proper sense of the word, in agony, and the agony had gone on two nights and two days now. I put on my leather-soled loafers. But then I couldn't do it. It would crunch, ooze, squirt under my shoe. Could I hit it with the broom handle? No, I couldn't. I have had a cat with leukemia put down, and have stayed with a cat while he died; I think that if I were hungry, if I had reason to, I could kill for food, wring a chicken's neck, as my grandmothers did, with no more guilt and no less fellow feeling than they. My inability to kill this creature had nothing ethical about it, and no kindness in it. It was mere squeamishness. It was a little rotten place in me, like the soft brown spots in fruit; a sympathy that came not from respect but from loathing. It was a responsibility that would not act. It was guilt itself.

On the third morning the beetle was motionless, shrunken, dead. I got the broom again and swept it into the gutter of the balcony among dry leaves. And there it still is in the gutter of my mind, among dry leaves, a tiny dry husk, a ghost.

II. The Sparrow

In the humid New England summer the small cooling plant ran all day, making a deep, loud noise. Around the throbbing machinery was a frame of coarse wire net. I thought the bird was outside that wire net, then I hoped it was, then I wished it was. It was moving back and forth with the regularity of the trapped: the zoo animal that paces twelve feet east and twelve feet west and twelve feet east and twelve feet west, hour after hour; the heartbeat of the prisoner in the cell before the torture; the unending recurrence; the silent, steady panic. Back and forth, steadily fluttering between two wooden uprights just above a beam that supported the wire screen: a sparrow, ordinary, dusty, scrappy. I've seen sparrows fighting over territory till the feathers fly, and fucking cheerfully on telephone wires, and in winter gathering in trees in crowds like dirty little Christmas ornaments and talking all together like noisy children, chirp, charp, chirp, charp! But this sparrow was alone, and back and forth it went in terrible silence, trapped in wire and fear. What could I do? There was a door to the wire cage, but it was padlocked. I went on. I tell you I felt that bird beat its wings right here, here under my breastbone in the hollow of my heart. I said in my mind, Is it my fault? Did I build the cage? Just because I happened to see it, is it my sparrow? But my heart was low already, and I knew now that I would be down, down like a bird whose wings won't bear it up, a starving bird.

Then on the path I saw the man, one of the campus managers. The bird's fear gave me courage to speak. "I'm so sorry to bother you," I said. "I'm just visiting here at the librarians' conference—we met the other day in the office. I didn't know what to do, because there's a bird that got into the cooling plant there, inside the screen, and it can't get out." That was enough, too much, but I had to go on. "The noise of the machinery, I think the noise confuses it, and I didn't know what to do. I'm sorry." Why did I apologize? For what?

"Have a look," he said, not smiling, not frowning.

He turned and came with me. He saw the bird beating back and forth, back and forth in silence. He unlocked the padlock. He had the key.

The bird didn't see the door open behind it. It kept beating back and forth along the screen. I found a little stick on the path and threw it against the outside of the screen to frighten the bird into breaking its pattern. It went the wrong way, deeper into the cage, toward the machinery. I threw another stick, hard, and the bird veered and then turned and flew out. I watched the open door, I saw it fly.

The man and I closed the door. He locked it. "Be getting on," he said, not smiling, not frowning, and went on his way, a man with a lot on his mind, a hardworking man. But did he have no joy in it? That's what I think about now. Did he have the key, the power to set free, the will to do it, but no joy in doing it? It is his soul I think about now, if that is the word for it, the spirit, that sparrow.

III. The Gull

They were winged, all the creatures on my mind.

This one is hard to tell about. It was a seagull. Gulls on Klatsand Beach, on any North Pacific shore, are all alike in their two kinds: white adults with black wingtips and yellow bills; and yearlings, adult-sized but with delicately figured brown features. They soar and cry, swoop, glide, dive, squabble, and grab; they stand in their multitudes at evening in the sunset shallows of the creek mouth before they rise in silence to fly out to sea, where they will sleep the night afloat on waves far out beyond the breakers, like a fleet of small white ships with sails furled and no riding lights. Gulls eat anything, gulls clean the beach, gulls eat dead gulls. There are no individual gulls. They are magnificent flyers, big, clean, strong birds, rapacious, suspicious, fearless. Sometimes as they ride the wind I have seen them as part of the wind and the sea, exactly as the foam, the sand, the fog is part of it all, all one, and in such moments of vision I have truly seen the gulls.

But this was one gull, an individual, for it stood alone near the low-tide water's edge with a broken wing. I saw first that the left wing dragged, then saw the naked bone jutting like an ivory knife up from blood-rusted feathers. Something had attacked it, something that could half tear away a wing, maybe a shark when it dove to catch a fish. It stood there. As I came nearer, it saw me. It gave no sign. It did not sidle away, as gulls do when you walk toward them, and then fly if you keep coming on. I stopped. It stood, its flat red feet in the shallow water of a tidal lagoon above the breakers. The tide was on the turn, returning. It stood and waited for the sea.

The idea that worried me was that a dog might find it before the sea did. Dogs roam that long beach. A dog chases gulls, barking and rushing, excited; the gulls fly up in a rush of wings; the dog trots back, maybe a little hangdog, to its owner strolling far down the beach. But a gull that could not fly and the smell of blood would put a dog into a frenzy of barking, lunging, teasing, torturing. I imagined that. My imagination makes me human and makes me a fool; it gives me all the world and exiles me from it. The gull stood waiting for the dog, for the other gulls, for the tide, for what came, living its life completely until death. Its eye looked straight through me, seeing truly, seeing nothing but the sea, the sand, the wind.

Suggestions for Discussion

1. This essay has a subtitle, "The Creatures on My Mind." What do the creatures under reflection have in common? How do they determine the organization of the essay?
2. What is the underlying idea that binds these reflections together? What conclusions based on her experiences does the author suggest? What do these conclusions have in common?
3. How does the language of the reflections express the author's concerns? Is this a formal or an informal essay?
4. What is the connection between this essay and the others in its section? How do you respond to its very personal nature?
5. In what way are the author's conclusions unusual?

Suggestions for Writing

1. Many of us have had experiences with creatures in nature similar to those of the author. Write an essay in which you describe such an experience and in which you draw some conclusions based on it.
2. Keep a journal for one week in which you record your observations of birds or insects. You should try to examine the degree to which you either sympathize with or are repelled by them. Attempt to draw some conclusions about the world of nature from your own observations.

COLIN FLETCHER

A Bend in the Road

Colin Fletcher (b. 1922), born in Cardiff, Wales, studied at the West Buckland School in North Devon, England. He served in the Royal Marine Commandos, eventually becoming captain, from 1940 until 1947. He has been a manufacturer's representative, a farmer, and a road builder in Africa; he has worked in Canada for mining companies during the summer; he has worked as head janitor in a San Francisco hospital; and since 1958 he has been a writer, living in California. His books include *The Thousand-Mile Summer* (1964),

The Man Who Walked Through Time (1968), *The Complete Walker III* (1984), and *The Secret Worlds of Colin Fletcher* (1989). He has also written *Learn of the Green World* (1991), which is an audiotape. This essay expresses an environmentalist's concern for the subtle way that development destroys the delicate balance between countryside and neighborhood.

When we contemplate such rents in the fabric as Los Angeles and the Love Canal, Beirut and Chernobyl, Ethiopia and the East Bronx, most of us tend to bleat about politicians or multi-nationals or drug cartels or other handy breeds of "them." Indictments of this kind are easy and exculpating and slightly titillating; but perhaps we should be looking closer to home.

A hundred yards from my house there is a bend in our little county road. The road is narrow and the bend is blind, and vehicles are apt to swing around it in wide, dangerous trajectories. If you are driving and if you have any sense, you slow down and sound your horn. If you are walking you hug the outside sweep of the bend, between the blacktop and the chain-link fence, close to the red fire hydrant; but if it is a good day, inside and outside your skin, you look beyond these tokens of "shruburbia" and discern curving harmonies.

The harmonies of the place were once far more resonant. At this bend, the road cuts through a notch between our valley's main southern slope and a hill-capped spur that geologic chance has thrust out from it. This notch or gap or saddle was once a room-sized patch of level ground, probably somewhat open, as such places tend to be. Grass grew, and a few small bushes, but the trees stood back. To the right, though, the slope was heavily wooded, and to the left a fringe of live oaks masked the outlier hill's steep-sided dome. East and west, the saddle commanded vistas: down-valley to a glimpse of ocean; up-valley into a rich and rolling panorama of rising, interlocking ridges.

Once upon a time, this saddle held a peripherally pivotal place in valley life. Band-tailed pigeons and robins and other birds, journeying along the valley's flank from feeding place to feeding place, swept through in dense, swooshing flocks. Tule elk and black-tailed deer, traveling to and from their own feeding and sleeping and breeding places, also funnelled through. And predators passed by on their wider excursions: bobcats and foxes and coyotes and mountain lions and black and grizzly bears—but not, at that time, men. The predators surely recognized the saddle as a natural place for an ambush; and after every successful strike the turkey vultures, or buzzards, that for hours had been in holding patterns above the dome of the outlier hill—floating on updrafts focused by its steep slopes—moved in to fulfill their role as garbage collectors.

For many, many years, this life continued at its slow, rhythmic pace. Animal populations waxed and waned. From time to time fire swept through the saddle; but afterward the vegetation resprouted and resumed its recurring program of succession.

When the first men appeared, nothing really changed. The men came only rarely to the saddle, passing by on their hunting and seed-gathering forays. They too knew a good ambush site when they saw one, and they duly lay in wait, flintheaded arrows ready, for the deer and elk, for the band-tailed pigeons and for any quail unwise enough to cross the open space. Or perhaps they set traps. But the men made just one more predator—and a rare and rather inefficient one, at that—so they disturbed no balances. And they altered the saddle, physically, not at all. It remained a beautiful, curving, harmonious place.

For many more years this state of affairs continued. The life-form cycles—of vegetation and birds and beasts, including humans—rolled on. Down decades and centuries, human hunting techniques improved only marginally, if at all, so men still disturbed no balances.

Then, little more than two centuries ago, a new, paler tribe of people came up from the south.

At first no newcomers visited this obscure saddle on the flanks of a long, outlying valley. They began, though, to kill off the local bears, both grizzly and black, and soon there were no bears visiting the saddle. The new tribe of men killed off the mountain lions, too, and before long the lions became rare, and most of the survivors lived deep in the forests. The newcomers established one of their red-roofed adobe missions at the mouth of the valley, and strove to change the habits of the darker and earlier people. Soon, these earlier humans rarely visited the saddle, either.

Then one day a party of pale newcomer land surveyors rode up into the saddle to mark a boundary of one of the vast estates into which they were dividing the whole countryside. They came to the saddle because the boundary happened to cut directly through it and then slant up a slope of the outlier hill. That first day, the men probably approached the saddle from the west, up a steep wooded gully, but certain local relics suggest that at some point they, the land surveyors, cut the first road to the saddle, angling it up at a gentler grade than the gully offered. Perhaps they just followed a deer trail. If it was not the surveyors who cut this road, then it was probably the men who in due course came to fence the boundary line. Anyway, a process had begun.

Within a few years, a different pale-faced tribe took over control of the land, and soon their homes began to dot the valley floor and flanks. Before long they cleared outlying fire roads to protect their houses from the summer brush fires. One of these dirt fire roads followed the line of the surveyors' road up to the saddle and pushed out beyond it. Because the hillside was steep, the upper side of the widened road now cut deep into it, above and below the saddle. The road therefore sliced more severely into the saddle's southern flank, sheering off almost half the root system of a live oak that grew there. For the first time, the curving harmony of the place suffered a serious wound.

Before long, someone built a cabin along the rough and ready road, half a mile beyond the saddle. Naturally, he improved his access road. In doing so he sliced off a little more from the saddle's flank, a little more from the live oak's root system. About this time—no more than fifty years ago—some local horseback riders cut a narrow bridle trail clear around the slope of the domed outlier hill. Soon, around on the plunging and friable far side of the hill, the trail crumbled away; but its useless, deep-cut beginning and ending remained, converging at the saddle as two stark and angular wounds in its once curving harmonies.

Down in the valley, the buildings grew more dense—and spread outward. Someone else built a house a little way down the fire road. A few more years, and the land around the saddle was subdivided. A dirt road was cut up the side of the outlier hill to the obvious building site at its summit—now leveled in readiness for a house. Down at the saddle, the road bisected the termini of the bridle trail, where the curves had once met in harmony. Soon, when a couple of people decided to build four or five houses along the old fire road and sell them, the county widened the road and blacktopped it. Saddle and live oak suffered further degradation.

Power poles now went in along the road. One pole stood on the lip of the saddle, so sited that to anyone standing there it rose stage center in the rich and rolling panorama of rising, interlocking ridges. The new houses needed a booster pump for their water supply, and the pump needed a meter, so two boxes appeared a few feet above the saddle, opposite the power pole. Access to the boxes was up a flight of wooden steps, set in a shallow cleft in the road embankment. Steps and gully were both reasonably discreet, but you could not pretend that they did anything to mend the tatters of the old harmonies.

This was the state of affairs when, thirteen years ago, I bought, from its second owner, the house nearest the saddle, just a hundred yards down the road.

At that time, the country around the saddle was, by shruburban standards, a quiet and reasonably harmonious place. Flocks of band-tailed pigeons—though probably smaller than when Indians lay waiting for them—still swooshed through the saddle. So, at certain seasons, did the robins. Spring and summer, quail families struttled querulously abroad. Deer sometimes glided through the oaks and skittered across the road. At night, raccoons roamed, and a pair of foxes often came to the water tub at the end of my veranda. Once or twice a year I would look out my picture window at the flank of the outlier hill and see a bobcat strolling across an open grassy patch just above three fire-charred fence posts that still survived from the original Spanish estate line.

In the years since I moved in, nothing dramatic has happened, really. Nothing at all, in fact, except natural events in the advance of what we label progress.

The county, for example, has applied normal civilized maintenance to the road. Periodically, it has resurfaced the blacktop. Because there was space to spare on one side of the saddle, the blackness tended to creep outward over what was once a room-sized grassy patch. The county also executed its annual spraying of roadside vegetation and tidy-up grading of ditches and embankments. Such deeds no doubt helped maintain the road—as much as they did anywhere else.

Meanwhile, five or six additional houses were built along our road. None stood within sight of the saddle, but because of them the saddle suffered a further series of improvements. Most of them were minor. Each was regarded by at least some of us locals as useful or even necessary.

All our homes face a severe fire hazard, and some years ago our excellent fire department installed a roadside hydrant on the level ground of the original saddle. At first it was painted bright yellow, then red.

About this time, a new house went in barely two hundred feet above the saddle—not for the owner to live in but for rental. Trees screen it, though, and the only obvious impact on the saddle comes when its renters are a rowdy bunch.

Soon afterward, a Midwesterner bought the subdivision that embraced the whole of the domed outlier hill, and although he was not yet ready to build he installed across the line of the saddle—which was the only place you could gain motorized access to "his" hill—an ugly galvanized chain link fence with an ugly galvanized gate. Somehow, the fence lay even more heavily on the saddle than the bulldozed road and bridle trail. It was possible, though, to hope that it lay less permanently.

Then the water company upgraded its booster pump and meter. It also tore down the flight of weathered wooden access steps, hacked its shallow cleft into a deep and angular trench, and installed a modern gray concrete stairway equipped with an equally soulless metal-pipe hand rail.

Soon, the electric company improved our supply—and the power pole that stood stage center in the panorama of rising, interlocking ridges became a kingpin in the upgraded local system. Seven lines now fed in and out of this pole, and its crown sprouted a wild assortment of gadgetry, including two extra cross arms festooned with massive double-dish porcelain insulators and a big gray metal transformer, unlovely as a garbage can. Sullen gray plastic or metal shields shrouded support stays and parts of the main pole. And so that no one, sober or otherwise, could possibly run into this repulsive, cobwebbed monstrosity—which even in Los Angeles would have stood out as a monument to ugliness—it bore at human eye level a pair of garish metal reflector strips that glittered by day and at night, in approaching headlights, glowed like evil rectangular eyes.

By this time, Friday-night teeny-boppers had bopped the gate in the new chain link fence and would drive up to the now-leveled summit of the hill and there—or, when it got crowded, down at the saddle, just inside the felled gate—they would, until the sheriffs arrived, bop their radios up to max and strew the place with beer cans and bottles and audio tapes and fragments of female underwear and condoms.

All these changes, you will note, had "utility" as an excuse. In somebody's eyes, anyway.

Then, a few years ago, the absentee Midwesterner sold "his" hill to a man with other homes on other continents, and this new man bulldozed the flat on the hill's summit flatter and bigger, and erected there a large and angular house, soon known locally as "the powerhouse," that probably had Frank Lloyd Wright executing at least one turn in his grave—and then another turn when he saw the matching power gate that this man built down in the saddle, across his newly blacktopped access road. For the gate was also a power gate—one that could be opened and closed remotely, from the house—and this stark erection (stout sliding ironwork, painted off-white; two massive, ill-proportioned, off-white pillars; square box housing the machinery) stood dead center in what had once been a saddle. A friend of mine seeing it for the first time, said, "You know, it's difficult to imagine anyone putting up such a gate outside anything except a prison." Dead center on his pretentious gate, our new neighbor wired a cheap red plastic sign: "Beware of Dog." And once a week, on the day when all of us put out our offerings for the modern garbage disposers, he put out a galvanized garbage can so battered that its lid would not fit properly and the wind and passing animals often left a ring of refuse lying around it, there in the once beautiful, curving and harmonious saddle, beside the still-standing galvanized chain-link fence, midway between the red fire hydrant and the angular off-white gate complex, opposite the mutilated live oak roots and the water company's cement-and-metal stairway, in the lee of the grotesque, spider-webbed power pole.

A spin-off from the gate complex has been that local teeny-boppers, barred from the hill's summit, now favor the roadside space outside it as a small-scale substitute where they can—for short interludes, before one of us neighbors has time to summon the sheriff—at least max car radios and spread a little miscellaneous litter.

Yet I have to say that in spite of all the degradations our little enclave beyond the saddle remains, by modern standards, a quiet and relatively harmonious place. Band-tailed pigeons, and robins at their season, still swoosh through the saddle. Quail families still stroll. Buzzards still soar above the hill on its daily updrafts. Hawks, too. Raccoons still roam at night, I think, and deer still glide and skitter—though less freely since the powerhouse dweller extended his chain-link fence and girdled his garden with electrified wires. It is a long time, though, since the foxes visited my veranda. And I have not glimpsed a bobcat since the powerhouse went up. The saddest fact, it seems to me, is that the saddle, where most of our improvements seem to have focused—the saddle that was once the local jewel—has become our bleakest corner. What is even sadder, perhaps, is that few people seem to recognize quite what has happened—or even in some cases, to recognize that our bend in the road was once a saddle. For my part, I guess I had begun to resign myself—though by no means happily—to the slow toll exacted by "progress."

But one day last week as I walked along the road toward the bend I saw something lying on the blacktop, out in the middle of the road, midway between the water company's concrete stairway and the power pole. When I reached it, I saw that it was a white paper bag, and that something even whiter, and gooey, was oozing out of it. Carefully, I picked the bag up. It bore the insignia of a famous fast food dispensary. I pulled the mouth of the bag open, peered: several french fries; a plastic knife and fork; such unconsumed portions of a melting ice cream stick as had not already oozed out onto the blacktop; and four pennies.

I stood there for a moment, studying what I had found. In itself it was nothing, of course. Just a small sample of typical modern litter. But I stood for a long moment—dangerously, there in the middle of the blacktop, just beyond the bend around which vehicles are now apt to swing in wide trajectories; stood there in what had once been a beautiful saddle; stood there looking down at the unsavory little sample that had been jettisoned without thought; looking down in particular at the now-sticky pennies that someone could not be bothered to keep. Then I raised my eyes.

I found myself looking out over the red fire hydrant and the battered garbage can with its fringe of refuse, looking over and beyond the galvanized chain-link fence, looking through the gross and repulsive spider web of the power pole, with the off-white shape of the hideous gate complex tucked in at the left edge of my vision. And beyond the rich, rolling, ancient panorama of rising, interlocking ridges I saw—spread vividly out before my mind's unhappy eye—our modern panorama of Los Angeles and the Love Canal, Beirut and Chernobyl, Ethiopia and the East Bronx. Beyond them I perceived larger rents that we have torn in the fabric: polluted oceans, raped rainforests, the ozone rift. In that instant of looking I did not need mundane logical bridges to connect those vivid distant vistas with the tattered remnant rags of the saddle in which I stood, or with the paper bag still clutched in my hand and its attendant little pool of ice cream lying white and sticky on the blacktop at my feet. It was a short journey from one to the other, as the canker creeps.

Suggestions for Discussion

1. This essay begins and ends with what the author considers outrageous violations of the environment. What do these examples have in common? Are they all equally significant as disasters? Name other examples.
2. What is the emotional effect of the brief history of the valley and the hill above before it began to be transformed into a "neighborhood"?
3. The author is clearly conscious of and sensitive to the negative results of land development. How aware are you of similar events in your own neighborhood? If you live in a city, do you see examples of the ill effects of development?
4. How does the author organize his argument against development? What is the tone of this essay? How does the last episode of finding food in the road contribute to the tone?

Suggestions for Writing

1. Write an essay in which you describe the deterioration of a neighborhood or countryside with which you are familiar. Explain, if possible, the causes for deterioration. Are the causes often obscure or disguised?
2. Opponents of development cite the destruction of the environment as their primary concern. However, opponents of the environmental movement complain that environmentalists are insensitive to the loss of jobs that occurs when development is blocked. They also regard the environmental movement as white and middle-class. Write an essay in which you discuss these opposing views. Prepare for your essay by following newspaper and television debates on this issue.

LESTER R. BROWN

Earth Day 2030

Lester R. Brown (b. 1934) was born in New Jersey. He attended Rutgers University, where he received a master's degree in agriculture, and Harvard University, where he was awarded a master's in public administration. He holds honorary doctoral degrees from numerous universities and has won several international prizes. Since 1974 Brown has been president of the World Watch Institute in Washington, D.C. He has written and edited many books, including *In the Human Interest* (1974), *By Bread Alone* (1974), and *Full House* (1994). He was a MacArthur Foundation Fellow in 1986 and was named to the Rutgers University Hall of Fame in 1990. In 1991, with Christopher Flavin and Sandra Postel, Brown edited *Saving the Planet,* from which the following essay is taken. It displays his grasp of the complexities of environmental issues.

On April 22nd, millions of people around the world celebrated Earth Day 1990. Marking the 20th anniversary of the original Earth Day, this event came at a time when public concern about the environmental fate of the planet has soared to unprecedented heights.

Threats such as climate change and ozone depletion underscore the fact that ecological degradation has reached global proportions. Meanwhile, the increasing severity and spread of more localized problems—including soil erosion, deforestation, water scarcity, toxic contamination, and air pollution—are already beginning to slow economic and social progress in much of the world.

Governments, development agencies, and people the world over have begun to grasp the need to reverse this broad-based deterioration of the environment. But what has resulted so far is a flurry of fragmented activity—a new pollution law here, a larger environment staff there—that lacks any coherent sense of what, ultimately, we are trying to achieve.

Building an environmentally stable future requires some vision of what it would look like. If not coal and oil to power society, then what? If forests are no longer to be cleared to grow food, then how is a larger population to be fed? If a throwaway culture leads inevitably to pollution and resource depletion, how can we satisfy our material needs?

In sum, if the present path is so obviously unsound, what picture of the future can we use to guide our actions toward a global community that can endure?

A sustainable society is one that satisfies its needs without jeopardizing the prospects of future generations. Unfortunately, few models of sustainability exist today. Most developing nations have for the past several decades aspired to the automobile-centered, fossil-fuel-driven economics of the industrial West. However, from the regional problems of air pollution to the global threat of climate change, it is clear that these societies are far from durable; indeed, they are rapidly bringing about their own demise.

Describing the shape of a sustainable society is a risky proposition. Ideas and technologies we can't now foresee obviously will influence society's future course. Yet just as any technology of flight must abide by the basic principles of aerodynamics, so must a lasting society satisfy some elementary criteria. With that understanding and the experience garnered in recent decades, it is possible to create a vision of a society quite different from, indeed preferable to, today's.

Time to get the world on a sustainable path is rapidly running out. We believe that if humanity achieves sustainability, it will do so within the next 40 years. If we have not succeeded by then, environmental deterioration and economic decline will be feeding on each other, pulling us down toward social decay and political upheaval. At such a point, reclaiming any hope of a sustainable future might be impossible. Our vision, therefore, looks to the year 2030, a time closer to the present than is World War II.

Whether Earth Day 2030 turns out to be a day to celebrate lasting achievements or to lament missed opportunities is largely up to each one of us as individuals, for in the end, it is individual values that drive social change. Progress toward sustainability thus hinges on a collective deepening of our sense of responsibility to the earth and to our offspring. Without a reevaluation of our personal aspirations and motivations, we will never achieve an environmentally sound global community.

Begin with the Basics

In attempting to sketch the outlines of a sustainable society, we need to make some basic assumptions. First, our vision of the future assumes only existing technologies and foreseeable improvements in them. This clearly is a conservative assumption: 40 years ago, for example, some renewable energy technologies on which we base our model didn't even exist.

Second, the world economy of 2030 will not be powered by coal, oil, and natural gas. It is now well accepted that continuing heavy reliance on fossil fuels will cause catastrophic changes in climate. The most recent scientific evidence suggests that stabilizing the climate depends on eventually cutting annual global carbon emissions to some two billion tons per year, about one-third the current level. Taking population growth into account, the world in 2030 will therefore have per-capita carbon emissions about one-eighth the level found in Western Europe today.

The choice then becomes whether to make solar or nuclear power the centerpiece of energy systems. We believe nuclear power will be rejected because of its long list of economic, social, and environmental liabilities. The nuclear industry has been in decline for over a decade. Only 94 plants remain under construction; most will be completed in the next few years. Safety concerns and the failure to develop permanent storage for nuclear waste have disenchanted many citizens.

It is possible scientists could develop new nuclear technologies that are more economical and less accident-prone. Yet this would not solve the waste dilemma. Nor would it prevent the use of nuclear energy as a stepping stone to developing nuclear weapons. Trying to stop this in a plutonium-based economy with thousands of operating plants would require a degree of control incompatible with democratic political systems. Societies are likely to opt instead for diverse, solar-based systems.

The third major assumption is about population size. Current United Nations projections have the world headed for nearly nine billion people by 2030. This figure implies a doubling or tripling of the populations of Ethiopia, India, Nigeria, and scores of other countries where human numbers are already overtaxing natural support systems. But such growth is inconceivable. Either these societies will move quickly to encourage smaller families and bring birthrates down or rising death rates from hunger and malnutrition will check population growth.

The humane path to sustainability by the year 2030 therefore requires a dramatic drop in birthrates. As of this year, 13 European countries had stable or declining populations; by 2030, most countries are likely to be in that category. We assume a population 40 years from now of at most eight billion that will be either essentially stable or declining slowly toward a number the earth can comfortably support.

Dawn of a Solar Age

In many ways, the solar age today is where the coal age was when the steam engine was invented in the 18th century. At that time, coal was used to heat homes and smelt iron ore, but the notion of using coal-fired steam engines to power factories or transportation systems was just emerging. Only a short time later, the first railroad started running and fossil fuels began to transform the world economy.

Many technologies have been developed that allow us to harness the renewable energy of the sun effectively, but so far these devices are only in limited use. By 2030 they will be widespread and much improved. The pool of renewable energy resources we can tap is immense: The annual influx of such accessible resources in the United States is estimated at 250 times the country's current energy needs.

The mix of energy sources will reflect the climate and natural resources of particular regions. Northern Europe, for example, is likely to rely heavily on wind and hydropower. Northern Africa and the Middle East may instead use direct sunlight. Japan and the Philippines will tap their abundant geothermal energy. Southeast Asian countries will be powered largely by wood and agricultural wastes, along with sunshine. Some nations—Norway and Brazil, for example—already obtain more than half of their energy from renewables.

By 2030, solar panels will heat most residential water around the world. A typical urban landscape may have thousands of collectors sprouting from rooftops, much as television antennas do today. Electricity will come via transmission lines from solar thermal plants located in desert regions of the United States, North Africa, and central Asia. This technology uses mirrored troughs to focus sunlight onto oil-filled tubes that convey heat to a turbine and generator that then produce electricity. An 80-megawatt solar thermal plant built in the desert east of Los Angeles in 1989 converted an extraordinary 22 percent of incoming sunlight into electricity—at a third less than the cost of power from new nuclear plants.

Power will also come from photovoltaic solar cells, a semiconductor technology that converts sunlight directly into electricity. Currently, photovoltaic systems are less efficient than and four times as expensive as solar thermal power, but by 2030 their cost will be competitive. Photovoltaics will be a highly decentralized energy source found atop residential homes as well as adjacent to farms and factories.

Using this technology, homeowners throughout the world may become producers as well as consumers of electricity. Indeed, photovoltaic shingles have already been developed that turn roofing material into a power source. As costs continue to decline, many homes are apt to get their electricity from photovoltaics; in sunny regions residents will sell any surplus to the utility company.

Wind power, an indirect form of solar energy generated by the sun's differential heating of the atmosphere, is already close to being cost-competitive with new coal-fired power plants. Engineers are confident they can soon unveil improved wind turbines that are economical not just in California's blustery mountain passes, where they are now commonplace, but in vast stretches of the U.S. northern plains and many other areas. Forty years from now the United States could be deriving 10 to 20 percent of its electricity from the wind.

Small-scale hydro projects are likely to be a significant source of electricity, particularly in the Third World, where the undeveloped potential is greatest. As of this year hydropower supplied nearly one-fifth of the world's electricity. By 2030 that share should be much higher, although the massive dams favored by governments and international lending agencies in the late 20th century will represent a declining proportion of the total hydro capacity.

Living plants provide another means of capturing solar energy. Through photosynthesis, they convert sunlight into biomass that can be burned or converted to liquid fuels such as ethanol. Today, wood provides 12 percent of the world's energy, chiefly in the form of firewood and charcoal in developing countries. Its use will surely expand during the next 40 years, although resource constraints will not permit it to replace all of the vast quantities of petroleum in use today.

Geothermal energy taps the huge reservoir of heat that lies beneath the earth's surface, making it the only renewable source that does not rely on sunlight. Continuing advances will allow engineers to use previously unexploitable, lower-temperature reservoirs that are hundreds of times as abundant as those in use today. Virtually all Pacific Rim countries, as well as those along East Africa's great Rift and the Mediterranean Sea, will draw on geothermal resources.

Nations in what now is called the Third World face the immense challenge of continuing to develop their economies without massive use of fossil fuels. One option is to rely on biomass energy in current quantities but to step up replanting efforts and to burn the biomass much more efficiently, using gasifiers and other devices. Another is to turn directly to the sun, which the Third World has in abundance. Solar ovens for cooking, solar collectors for hot water, and photovoltaics for electricity could satisfy most energy needs.

In both industrial and developing nations, energy production inevitably will be much more decentralized, breaking up the utilities and huge natural gas, coal, and oil industries that have been a dominant part of the economic scene in the late 20th century. Indeed, a world energy system based on the highly efficient use of renewable resources will be less vulnerable to disruption and more conducive to market economics.

Efficient in All Senses

Getting total global carbon emissions down to two billion tons a year will require vast improvements in energy efficiency. Fortunately, many of the technologies to accomplish this feat already exist and are cost-effective. No technical breakthroughs are needed to double automobile fuel economy, triple the efficiency of lighting systems, or cut typical home heating requirements by 75 percent.

Automobiles in 2030 are apt to get at least 100 miles per gallon of fuel, four times the current average for new cars. A hint of what such vehicles may be like is seen in the Volvo LCP 2000, a recently developed prototype automobile. It is an aerodynamic four-passenger car that weighs half as much as today's models. Moreover, it has a highly efficient and clean-burning diesel engine. With the addition of a continuously variable transmission and a flywheel energy storage device, this vehicle will get 90 miles to the gallon.

Forty years from now, Thomas Edison's revolutionary incandescent light bulbs may be found only in museums—replaced by an array of new lighting systems, including halogen and sodium lights. The most important new light source may be compact fluorescent bulbs that use 18 watts rather than 75 to produce the same amount of light.

In 2030, homes are likely to be weather-tight and highly insulated, greatly reducing the need for heating and cooling. Some superinsulated homes in the Canadian province of Saskatchewan are already so tightly built that it doesn't pay to install a furnace. Homes of this kind use one-third as much energy as do modern Swedish homes, or one-tenth the U.S. average. Inside, people will have appliances that are on average three to four times as efficient as those in use today.

Improving energy efficiency will not noticeably change lifestyles or economic systems. A highly efficient refrigerator or light bulb provides the same service as an inefficient one—just more economically. Gains in energy efficiency alone, however, will not reduce fossil-fuel-related carbon emissions by the needed amount. Additional steps to limit the use of fossil fuels are likely to reshape cities, transportation systems, and industrial patterns, fostering a society that is more efficient in all senses.

By the year 2030, a much more diverse set of transportation options will exist. The typical European or Japanese city today has already taken one step toward this future. Highly developed rail and bus systems move people efficiently between home and work: in Tokyo only 15 percent of commuters drive cars to the office. The cities of 2030 are apt to be crisscrossed by inexpensive, street-level light-rail systems that allow people to move quickly between neighborhoods.

Automobiles will undoubtedly still be in use four decades from now, but their numbers will be fewer and their role smaller. Within cities, only electric or clean hydrogen-powered vehicles are likely to be permitted, and most of these will be highly efficient "city cars." The energy to run them may well come from solar power plants. Families might rent efficient larger vehicles for vacations. The bicycle will also play a major role in getting people about, as it already does in much of Asia as well as in some industrial-country towns and cities—in Amsterdam, the Netherlands and Davis, California, bike-path networks encourage widespread pedaling. There are already twice as many bikes as cars worldwide. In the bicycle-centered transport system of 2030, the ratio could easily be 10 to 1.

Forty years from now, people will live closer to their jobs, and much socializing and shopping will be done by bike rather than in a one-ton automobile. Computerized delivery services may allow people to shop from home—consuming less time as well as less energy. Telecommunications will substitute for travel as well. In addition, a world that allows only two billion tons of carbon emissions cannot be trucking vast quantities of food and other items thousands of miles, which is apt to encourage more decentralization of agriculture, allowing local produce suppliers to flourish.

The automobile-based modern world is now only about 40 years old, but with its damaging air pollution and traffic congestion it hardly represents the pinnacle of human social evolution. Although a world where cars play a minor role may be hard to imagine, our grandparents would have had just as hard a time visualizing today's world of traffic jams and smog-filled cities.

Nothing to Waste

In the sustainable, efficient economy of 2030, waste reduction and recycling industries will have largely replaced the garbage collection and disposal companies of today. The throwaway society that emerged during the late 20th century uses so much energy, emits so much carbon, and generates so much air pollution, acid rain, water pollution, toxic waste, and rubbish that it is strangling itself. Rooted as it is in planned obsolescence and appeals to convenience, it will be seen by historians as an aberration.

A hierarchy of options will guide materials policy in the year 2030. The first priority, of course, will be to avoid using any nonessential item. Second will be to reuse a product directly—for example, refilling a glass beverage container. The third will be to recycle the material to form a new product. Fourth, the material can be burned to extract whatever energy it contains, as long as this can be done safely. The option of last resort will be disposal in a landfill.

In the sustainable economy of 2030, the principal source of materials for industry will be recycled goods. Most of the raw material for the aluminum mill will come from the local scrap collection center, not from the bauxite mine. The steel mills of the future will feed on worn-out automobiles, household appliances, and industrial equipment. Paper and paper products will be produced at recycling mills, with recycled paper moving through a series, of uses, from high-quality bond to newsprint and, eventually, into cardboard boxes. Industries will turn to virgin raw materials only to replace any losses in use and recycling.

The effect on air and water quality will be obvious. For example, steel produced from scrap reduces air pollution by 85 percent, cuts water pollution by 76 percent, and eliminates mining wastes altogether. Making paper from recycled material reduces pollutants entering the air by 74 percent and the water by 35 percent. It also reduces pressures on forests in direct proportion to the amount recycled.

The economic reasons for such careful husbanding of materials will by 2030 seem quite obvious. Just 5 percent as much energy is needed to recycle aluminum as to produce it from bauxite ore. For steel produced entirely from scrap, the saving amounts to roughly two-thirds. Newsprint from recycled paper takes 25 to 60 percent less energy to make than that from wood pulp. Recycling glass saves up to a third of the energy embodied in the original product.

Societies in 2030 may also have decided to replace multi-sized and -shaped beverage containers with a set of standardized ones made of durable glass that can be reused many times. These could be used for fruit juices, beer, milk, and soda pop.

One of the cornerstones of a sustainable society will likely be its elimination of waste flows at the source. Industry will have restructured manufacturing processes to slash wastes by a third or more from 1990 levels. Food packaging, which in 1986 cost American consumers more than American farmers earned selling their crops, will have been streamlined. Food items buried in three or four layers of packaging will be a distant memory.

As recycling reaches its full potential over the next 40 years, households will begin to compost yard wastes rather than put them out for curbside pickup. A lost art in many communities in 1990, composting will experience a revival. Garbage flows will be reduced by one-fifth or more, and gardeners will have a rich source of humus.

In addition to recycling and reusing metal, glass, and paper, a sustainable society must also recycle nutrients. In nature, one organism's waste is another's sustenance. In cities, however, human sewage has become a troublesome source of water pollution. Properly treated to prevent the spread of disease and to remove contaminants, sewage will be systematically returned to the land in vegetable-growing greenbelts around cities, much as this is done in Shanghai and other Asian cities today.

Other cities will probably find it more efficient to follow Calcutta's example and use treated human sewage to fertilize aquacultural operations. A steady flow of nutrients from human waste can help nourish aquatic life, which in turn is consumed by fish.

How to Feed Eight Billion

Imagine trying to meet the food, fuel, and timber needs of eight billion people—nearly three billion more than the current population—with 960 billion fewer tons of topsoil (more than twice the amount of all U.S. cropland) and one billion fewer acres of trees (an area more than half the size of the continental United States).

That, in a nutshell, will be the predicament faced by society in 2030 if current rates of soil erosion and deforestation continue unaltered for the next 40 years. It is a fate that can only be avoided through major changes in land use.

Of necessity, societies in 2030 will be using the land intensively; the needs of a population more than half again as large as today's cannot be met otherwise. But, unlike the present, tomorrow's land-use patterns would be abiding by basic principles of biological stability: nutrient retention, carbon balance, soil protection, water conservation, and preservation of species diversity. Harvests will rarely exceed sustainable yields.

Meeting food needs will pose monumental challenges, as some simple numbers illustrate. By 2030, assuming cropland area expands by 5 percent between now and then and that the population grows to eight billion, cropland per person will have dropped to a third less than we have in today's inadequately fed world. Virtually all of Asia, and especially China, will be struggling to feed its people from a far more meager base of per-capita cropland area.

In light of these constraints, the rural landscapes of 2030 are likely to exhibit greater diversity than they do now. Variations in soils, slope, climate, and water availability will require different patterns and strains of crops grown in different ways to maximize sustainable output. For example, farmers may adopt numerous forms of agroforestry—the combined production of crops and trees—to provide food, biomass, and fodder, while also adding nutrients to soils and controlling water runoff.

Also, successfully adapting to changed climates resulting from greenhouse warming, as well as to water scarcity and other resource constraints, may lead scientists to draw on a much broader base of crop varieties. For example, a greater area will be devoted to salt-tolerant and drought-resistant crops.

Efforts to arrest desertification, now claiming 15 million acres each year, may by 2030 have transformed the gullied highlands of Ethiopia and other degraded areas into productive terrain. Much of the sloping land rapidly losing topsoil will be terraced, protected by shrubs or nitrogen-fixing trees planted along the contour.

Halting desertification also depends on eliminating overgrazing. The global livestock herd in 2030 is likely to be much smaller than today's three billion. It seems inevitable that adequately nourishing a human population 60 percent larger than today's will preclude feeding a third of the global grain harvest to livestock and poultry, as is currently the case. As meat becomes more expensive, the diets of the affluent will move down the food chain to greater consumption of grains and vegetables, which will also prolong lifespans.

A Healthy Respect for Forests

Forests and woodlands will be valued more highly and for many more reasons in 2030 than is the case today. The planet's mantle of trees, already a third smaller than in pre-agricultural times and shrinking by more than 27 million acres per year now, will be stable or expanding as a result of serious efforts to slow deforestation and to replant vast areas.

Long before 2030, the clearing of most tropical forests will have ceased. Since most of the nutrients in these ecosystems are held in the leaves and biomass of the vegetation rather than in the soil, only activities that preserve the forest canopy are sustainable. While it is impossible to say how much virgin tropical forest would remain in 2030 if sustainability is achieved, certainly the rate of deforestation will have had to slow dramatically by the end of this decade. Soon thereafter it will come to a halt.

Efforts to identify and protect unique parcels of forest will probably have led to a widely dispersed network of preserves. But a large portion of tropical forests still standing in 2030 will be exploited in a variety of benign ways by people living in and around them. Hundreds of "extractive reserves" will exist, areas in which local people harvest rubber, resins, nuts, fruits, medicines, and other forest products.

Efforts to alleviate the fuel wood crisis in developing countries, to reduce flooding and landslides in hilly regions, and to slow the buildup of carbon dioxide may spur the planting of an additional 500 million acres or so of trees. Many of these plantings will be on private farms as part of agroforestry systems, but plantations may also have an expanded role. Cities and villages will turn to managed woodlands on their outskirts to contribute fuel for heating, cooking, and electricity. This wood will substitute for some portion of coal and oil use and, since harvested on a sustained-yield basis, will make no net contribution of carbon dioxide to the atmosphere.

Restoring and stabilizing the biological resource base by 2030 depends on a pattern of land ownership and use far more equitable than today's. Much of the degradation now occurring stems from the heavily skewed distribution of land that, along with population growth, pushes poor people into ever more marginal environments. Stewardship requires that people have plots large enough to sustain their families without abusing the land, access to means of using the land productively, and the right to pass it on to their children.

No matter what technologies come along, the biochemical process of photosynthesis, carried out by green plants, will remain the basis for meeting many human needs, and its efficiency can only be marginally improved. Given that humanity already appropriates an estimated 40 percent of the earth's annual photosynthetic product on land, the urgency of slowing the growth in human numbers is obvious. The sooner societies stabilize their populations, the greater will be their opportunities for achieving equitable and stable patterns of land use that can meet their needs indefinitely.

Economic Progress in a New Light

The fundamental changes that are needed in energy, forestry, agriculture, and other physical systems cannot occur without corresponding shifts in social, economic, and moral character. During the transition to sustainability, political leaders and citizens alike will be forced to reevaluate their goals and aspirations and to adjust to a new set of principles that have at their core the welfare of future generations.

Shifts in employment will be among the most visible as the transition gets under way. Moving from fossil fuels to a diverse set of renewable energy sources, extracting fewer materials from the earth and recycling more, and revamping farming and forestry practices will greatly expand opportunities in new areas. Job losses in coal mining, auto production, and metals prospecting will be offset by gains in the manufacture and sale of photovoltaic solar cells, wind turbines, bicycles, mass transit equipment, and a host of technologies for recycling materials.

Since planned obsolescence will itself be obsolete in a sustainable society, a far greater share of workers will be employed in repair, maintenance, and recycling activities than in the extraction of virgin materials and production of new goods.

Wind prospectors, energy-efficiency auditors, and solar architects will be among the professions booming from the shift to a highly efficient, renewable-energy economy. Numbering in the hundreds of thousands today, jobs in these fields may collectively total in the millions worldwide within a few decades. Opportunities in forestry will expand markedly.

As the transition to a more environmentally sensitive economy progresses, sustainability will gradually eclipse growth as the focus of economic policy making. Over the next few decades, government policies will encourage investments that promote stability and endurance at the expense of those that simply expand short-term production.

As a yardstick of progress, the gross national product (GNP) will be seen as a bankrupt indicator. By measuring flows of goods and services, GNP undervalues the qualities a sustainable society strives for, such as durability and resource protection, and overvalues planned obsolescence and waste. The pollution caused by a coal-burning power plant, for instance, raises GNP by requiring expenditures on lung disease treatment and the purchase of a scrubber to control emissions. Yet society would be far better off if power were generated in ways that did not pollute the air in the first place.

National military budgets in a sustainable world will be a small fraction of what they are today. Moreover, sustainability cannot be achieved without a massive shift of resources from military endeavors into energy efficiency, soil conservation, tree planting, family planning, and other needed development activities. Rather than maintaining large defense establishments, governments may come to rely on a strengthened U.N. peacekeeping force.

A New Set of Values

Movement toward a lasting society cannot occur without a transformation of individual priorities and values. Throughout the ages, philosophers and religious leaders have denounced materialism as a path to human fulfillment. Yet societies across the ideological spectrum have persisted in equating quality of life with increased consumption.

Because of the strain on resources it creates, materialism simply cannot survive the transition to a sustainable world. As public understanding of the need to adopt simpler and less consumptive lifestyles spreads, it will become unfashionable to own fancy new cars, clothes, and the latest electronic devices. The potential benefits of unleashing the human energy now devoted to producing, advertising, buying, consuming, and discarding material goods are enormous.

As the amassing of personal and national wealth becomes less of a goal, the gap between haves and have-nots will gradually close, eliminating many societal tensions. Ideological differences may fade as well, as nations adopt sustainability as a common cause, and as they come to recognize that achieving it requires a shared set of values that includes democratic principles, freedom to innovate, respect for human rights, and acceptance of diversity. With the cooperative tasks involved in repairing the earth so many and so large, the idea of waging war could become an anachronism.

The task of building a sustainable society is an enormous one that will take decades rather than years. Indeed, it is an undertaking that will easily absorb the energies that during the past 40 years have been devoted to the Cold War. The reward in the year 2030 could be an Earth Day with something to celebrate: the achievement of a society in balance with the resources that support it, instead of one that destroys the underpinnings of its future.

Suggestions for Discussion

1. What assumptions about the future does the author make as he looks forward to the year 2030?
2. Name and discuss some specific changes in our attitudes and practices that we will have to make if we are to survive the struggle to control the environment.
3. Is the author optimistic about the future? Is he practical or reasonable in assuming that we will make the changes he proposes?

Suggestions for Writing

1. Choose one of the environmental problems we face in the future and summarize the author's solutions. Do you agree with them?
2. Write an essay in which you defend or reject the optimism of the author.

WILLIAM CRONON

The Trouble with Wilderness

William Cronon (b. 1954), born in New Haven, Connecticut, is a well-known historian. He was educated at the University of Wisconsin, at Yale University, and at Oxford University. Cronon has taught at Yale and is now the Frederick Jackson Turner Chair of history, geography, and environmental studies at the University of Wisconsin. His works include *Nature's Metropolis, Chicago,* and *The Great West* (1991), which won the Bancroft Prize in 1992. He was one of the editors of *Under an Open Sky: Rethinking America's Western Past* (1992). In this essay, Cronon argues persuasively for a realistic rather than a romantic view of the wilderness.

Preserving wilderness has for decades been a fundamental tenet—indeed, a passion—of the environmental movement, especially in the United States. For many Americans, wilderness stands as the last place where civilization, that all-too-human disease, has not fully infected the earth. It is an island in the polluted sea of urban-industrial modernity, a refuge we must somehow recover to save the planet. As Henry David Thoreau famously declared, "In Wildness is the preservation of the World."

But is it? The more one knows of its peculiar history, the more one realizes that wilderness is not quite what it seems. Far from being the one place on earth that stands apart from humanity, it is quite profoundly a human creation—indeed, the creation of very particular human cultures at very particular moments in human history. It is not a pristine sanctuary where the last remnant of an endangered but still transcendent nature can be encountered without the contaminating taint of civilization. Instead, it is a product of that civilization. As we gaze into the mirror it holds up for us, we too easily imagine that what we behold is nature when in fact we see the rejection of our own longings and desires. Wilderness can hardly be the solution to our culture's problematic relationship with the nonhuman world, for wilderness is itself a part of the problem.

To assert the unnaturalness of so natural a place may seem perverse: we can all conjure up images and sensations that seem all the more hauntingly real for having engraved themselves so indelibly on our memories. Remember this? The torrents of mist shooting out from the base of a great waterfall in the depths of a Sierra Nevada canyon, the droplets cooling your face as you listen to the roar of the water and gaze toward the sky through a rainbow that hovers just out of reach. Or this: Looking out across a desert canyon in the evening air, the only sound a lone raven calling in the distance, the rock walls dropping away into a chasm so deep that its bottom all but vanishes as you squint into the amber light of the setting sun. Remember the feelings of such moments, and you will know as well as I do that you were in the presence of something irreducibly nonhuman, something profoundly Other than yourself. Wilderness is made of that too.

And yet: what brought each of us to the places where such memories became possible is entirely a cultural invention.

For the Americans who first celebrated it, wilderness was tied to the myth of the frontier. The historian Frederick Jackson Turner wrote the classic academic statement of this myth in 1893, but it had been part of American thought for well over a century. As Turner described the process, Easterners and European immigrants, in moving to the wild lands of the frontier, shed the trappings of civilization and thereby gained an energy, an independence and a creativity that were the sources of American democracy and national character. Seen this way, wilderness became a place of religious redemption and national renewal, the quintessential location for experiencing what it meant to be an American.

Those who celebrate the frontier almost always look backward, mourning an older, simpler world that has disappeared forever. That world and all its attractions, Turner said, depended on free land—on wilderness. It is no accident that the movement to set aside national parks and wilderness areas gained real momentum just as laments about the vanishing frontier reached their peak. To protect wilderness was to protect the nation's most sacred myth of origin.

The decades following the civil war saw more and more of the nation's wealthiest citizens seeking out wilderness for themselves. The passion for wild land took many forms: enormous estates in the Adirondacks and elsewhere (disingenuously called "camps" despite their many servants and amenities); cattle ranches for would-be roughriders on the Great Plains; guided big-game hunting trips in the Rockies. Wilderness suddenly emerged as the landscape of choice for elite tourists. For them, it was a place of recreation.

In just this way, wilderness came to embody the frontier myth, standing for the wild freedom of America's past and seeming to represent a highly attractive natural alternative to the ugly artificiality of modern civilization. The irony, of course, was that in the process wilderness came to reflect the very civilization its devotees sought to escape. Ever since the 19th century, celebrating wilderness has been an activity mainly for well-to-do city folks. Country people generally know far too much about working the land to regard unworked land as their ideal.

There were other ironies as well. The movement to set aside national parks and wilderness areas followed hard on the heels of the final Indian wars, in which the prior human inhabitants of these regions were rounded up and moved onto reservations so that tourists could safely enjoy the illusion that they were seeing their nation in its pristine, original state—in the new morning of God's own creation. Meanwhile, its original inhabitants were kept out by dint of force, their earlier uses of the land redefined as inappropriate or even illegal. To this day, for instance, the Blackfeet continue to be accused of "poaching" on the lands of Glacier National Park, in Montana, that originally belonged to them and that were ceded by treaty only with the proviso that they be permitted to hunt there.

The removal of Indians to create an "uninhabited wilderness" reminds us just how invented and how constructed the American wilderness really is. One of the most striking proofs of the cultural invention of wilderness is its thoroughgoing erasure of the history from which it sprang. In virtually all its manifestations, wilderness represents a flight from history. Seen as the original garden, it is a place outside time, from which human beings had to be ejected before the fallen world of history could properly begin. Seen as the frontier, it is a savage world at the dawn of civilization, whose transformation represents the very beginning of the national historical epic. Seen as sacred nature, it is the home of a God who transcends history, untouched by time's arrow. No matter what the angle from which we regard it, wilderness offers us the illusion that we can escape the cares and troubles of the world in which our past has ensnared us. It is the natural unfallen antithesis of an unnatural civilization that has lost its soul, the place where we can see the world as it really is, and so know ourselves as we really are—or ought to be.

The trouble with wilderness is that it reproduces the very values its devotees seek to reject. It offers the illusion that we can somehow wipe clean the slate of our past and return to the tabula rasa that supposedly existed before we began to leave our marks on the world. The dream of an unworked natural landscape is very much the fantasy of people who have never themselves had to work the land to make a living—urban folk for whom food comes from a supermarket or a restaurant instead of a field, and for whom the wooden houses in which they live and work apparently have no meaningful connection to the forests in which trees grow and die. Only people whose relation to the land was already alienated could hold up wilderness as a model for human life in nature, for the romantic ideology of wilderness leaves no place in which human beings can actually make their living from the land.

We live in an urban-industrial civilization, but too often pretend to ourselves that our real home is in the wilderness. We work our nine-to-five jobs, we drive our cars (not least to reach the wilderness), we benefit from the intricate and all too invisible networks with which society shelters us, all the while pretending that these things are not an essential part of who we are. By imagining that our true home is in the wilderness, we forgive ourselves for the homes we actually inhabit. In its flight from history, in its siren song of escape, in its reproduction of the dangerous dualism that sets human beings somehow outside nature—in all these ways, wilderness poses a threat to responsible environmentalism at the end of the 20th century.

Do not misunderstand me. What I criticize here is not wild nature, but the alienated way we often think of ourselves in relation to it. Wilderness can still teach lessons that are hard to learn anywhere else. When we visit wild places, we find ourselves surrounded by plants and animals and landscapes whose otherness compels our attention. In forcing us to acknowledge that they are not of our making, that they have little or no need for humanity, they recall for us a creation far greater than our own. In wilderness, we need no reminder that a tree has its own reasons for being, quite apart from us—proof that ours is not the only presence in the universe.

We get into trouble only if we see the tree in the garden as wholly artificial and the tree in the wilderness as wholly natural. Both trees in some ultimate sense are wild; both in a practical sense now require our care. We need to reconcile them, to see a natural landscape that is also cultural in which city, suburb, countryside and wilderness each has its own place. We need to discover a middle ground in which all these things, from city to wilderness, can somehow be encompassed in the word "home." Home, after all, is the place where we live. It is the place for which we take responsibility, the place we try to sustain so we can pass on what is best in it (and in ourselves) to our children.

Learning to honor the wild—learning to acknowledge the autonomy of the other—means striving for critical self-consciousness in all our actions. It means that reflection and respect must accompany each act of use, and means we must always consider the possibility of nonuse. It means looking at the part of nature we intend to turn toward our own ends and asking whether we can use it again and again and again—sustainably—without diminishing it in the process. Most of all, it means practicing remembrance and gratitude for the nature, culture and history that have come together to make the world as we know it. If wildness can stop being (just) out there and start being (also) in here, if it can start being as humane as it is natural, then perhaps we can get on with the unending task of struggling to live rightly in the world—not just in the garden, not just in the wilderness, but in the home that encompasses them both.

Suggestions for Discussion

1. Cronon suggests that most Americans' conventional attitudes toward the wilderness are mistaken. Summarize these attitudes.
2. What examples does Cronon give to make the reader understand the profound effect that the wilderness has on him?
3. Discuss William Jackson Turner's remarks about the meaning of the wilderness.
4. In what ways have European Americans and Easterners omitted Native Americans from our consideration of the wilderness?
5. Summarize Cronon's final definition of wilderness.

Suggestions for Writing

1. Write an essay in which you explain how the wilderness became a playground for the wealthy.
2. Does this brief essay assist you in understanding the significance of the wilderness? Write an essay in which you explain Cronon's point of view.

JOHN RALSTON SAUL

Air Conditioning

John Ralston Saul, named by the *Utne Reader* "as one of the great visionaries of our times," holds a Ph.D. from King's College, London, has run a Paris-based investment firm, and has worked as an oil executive. He writes extensively about North Africa and Southeast Asia. Saul has published *The Paradise Eater, Voltaire's Bastards, The Unconscious Civilization,* and *The Doubter's Companion* (1994), which includes his rather humorous definition of one of the perils of civilization.

An efficient and widely used method for spreading disease.

One of the keys to the revolution in architecture and planning which struck Western cities after the Second World War was the gradual realization by engineers and architects that systems of forced air could heat and cool large numbers of people in a cost-effective manner.

This removed one of the major restrictions on the size of buildings. If windows needn't be opened then neither depth nor height had to be limited. Once heated or cooled, the air could be endlessly recycled through buildings.

This revolution was soon being applied in the air. Before the arrival of the Jumbo Jet, most commercial planes expelled air continually and took in fresh air, which then had to be brought to cabin temperature. With the Jumbo, fuel savings were chosen over air quality. Passengers, from first-class to steerage and smoking to non-smoking, began travelling across the Atlantic in a classless fog. Fifty per cent of the air was recycled. After a few hours in the plane, passengers began to feel as if they were breathing dead air. It was as if each airplane contained a single pair of lungs shared among three to four hundred bodies.

By the early 1980s, standard frequent-flyer rhetoric referred to air travel as exhausting. People began to notice that working in large office towers was far more draining than in buildings where windows could be opened. Then a dramatic incident focused attention. A group of old American veterans staying in a hotel to attend a convention began to die, as if struck by a plague. It was explained that legionnaires' disease was the result not of recycled air but of defective recycling.

There were more common experiences which weren't fatal. People began to expect that following one flight out of every two or three they would fall sick. Sometimes they merely caught a cold; increasingly it was a virulent strain of what was called the flu. But these flus could bring on vomiting, dangerous temperatures and exhaustion. They often killed the elderly or fragile. In fact, they seemed to come in international waves which changed character each season. Every few months there would be a mutation in the type of virulence. The planes made these flu strains instantly international. And the office towers then spread them around in each city. What passengers didn't know was that some airlines were cutting back further on the fresh air quota in order to save money in the hard times brought on by DEREGULATION and the DEPRESSION.

Modern hospitals were also being built with these air-flow systems and it soon became common knowledge that hospitals were places in which you caught things. The hard-learned medical lessons of physical isolation clarified in the nineteenth and early twentieth centuries seemed to have been forgotten.

Much of modern medicine is based upon controlling diseases by controlling movements. Now there were new and unexpected waves of viral diseases. Small epidemics in fact. One year it would be viral pneumonia. The next there would be a line of executives struck by ill-defined symptoms which exhausted them, sometimes for several years.

Air-conditioning also became a clear example of the inflexibility of modern industry and of technocratic structures generally. Economics seemed to be painfully linear. Every hour of work lost to a company through sickness is also money lost. It is common during the winter in places with moderate climates to find that 20 to 30 per cent of office workers are home sick. There seemed to be no room for applied thought which used practical observation in order to re-evaluate earlier policies.

This absurd rigidity is reminiscent of the old European colonial armies in the tropics. Well into the twentieth century British soldiers in India wore heavy clothing to protect them from the sun. In addition, a flat metal cross wrapped in cloth was placed beneath their jacket. This cross ran down the spine and over the shoulders. It was meant to stop the rays. Regiments functioned with permanently elevated levels of soldiers in hospital suffering from heat prostration. Attempts to bring in light clothing were resisted by most of the General Staff, who argued that the army would be decimated by the sun. When the change was at last introduced, and the hospital beds emptied, the Staff was amazed.

In manufacturing circles it is widely known that the least advanced area of aeronautics engineering is air treatment. In public, the press officers busily deny there is a problem. The number of formal complaints, they insist, are "statistically insignificant." But then airline industry organizations don't compile data on these sorts of complaints. In 1993 American government officials investigated the case of a flight attendant with tuberculosis who seemed to have infected twenty-three other crew over a short period of time. TB is spread by airborne bacteria. Uncirculated air was therefore a likely factor. However, the mechanism of general DENIAL kept turning.

Corporations inquiring whether windows can be made to open in office towers are told by architects and the construction industry that this is impossible, or only for a significant extra charge, plus long-term air-management costs. In spite of thousands of books about management and competitiveness, many of which talk about getting the most out of executives and other employees through leadership, training and encouragement of individual talents, there seems to be no calculus for integrating the costs of sick-leave into those of air-conditioning.

In truth, the only barrier to airplanes taking in a constant stream of fresh air, cooling it and then expelling it is the absence of pressure from passengers, the airlines' employees and the airlines. The case of office towers is even simpler. The air-conditioning system is rarely mentioned by companies when they build, buy or rent. Nothing prevents them from demanding air-conditioning systems limited to small areas—less than a floor—and which constantly take in and expel air. Nothing, that is, except the inability of our system to integrate widely recognized medical costs with those of engineering

Suggestions for Discussion

1. How does the metaphor of the British colonial soldiers in India, acting to avoid heat prostration, resemble the present popular attitude toward air conditioning?
2. What are the health dangers associated with air conditioning? Is it possible to avoid these dangers?
3. Discuss the changes in the attitude of architects toward open office windows and air conditioning.

Suggestions for Writing

1. Explain how the development of the Jumbo Jet changed the air quality in aviation travel.
2. Write an essay in which you balance the benefits and ill effects of air conditioning. Is there a practical solution to the dangers of air conditioning?

FICTION

ALDOUS HUXLEY

Conditioning the Children

Aldous Huxley (1894–1963) was born in England and educated at Oxford. He is the author of many novels including *Point Counter Point* (1928) and the anti-utopian *Brave New World* (1932). He also wrote essays, short stories, poetry, and plays. After he moved to Southern California, he became increasingly interested in Hindu philosophy and mysticism. *The Doors of Perception* (1954) describes his experience with hallucinogenic drugs. This brief selection from *Brave New World* describes without comment painful experiments to condition the minds of newborn infants.

The D.H.C.[1] and his students stepped into the nearest lift and were carried up to the fifth floor.

INFANT NURSERIES. NEO-PAVLOVIAN CONDITIONING ROOMS, announced the notice board.

The Director opened a door. They were in a large bare room, very bright and sunny; for the whole of the southern wall was a single window. Half a dozen nurses, trousered and jacketed in the regulation white viscose-linen uniform, their hair aseptically hidden under white caps, were engaged in setting out bowls of roses in a long row across the floor. Big bowls, packed tight with blossom. Thousands of petals, ripeblown and silkily smooth, like the cheeks of innumerable little cherubs, but of cherubs, in that bright light, not exclusively pink and Aryan, but also luminously Chinese, also Mexican, also apoplectic with too much blowing of celestial trumpets, also pale as death, pale with the posthumous whiteness of marble.

The nurses stiffened to attention as the D.H.C. came in.

"Set out the books," he said curtly.

In silence the nurses obeyed his command. Between the rose bowls the books were duly set out—a row of nursery quartos opened invitingly each at some gaily coloured image of beast or fish or bird.

[1]Director of Hatcheries and Conditioning.

"Now bring in the children."

They hurried out of the room and returned in a minute or two, each pushing a kind of tall dumb-waiter laden, on all its four wire-netted shelves with eight-month-old babies, all exactly alike (a Bokanovsky Group, it was evident) and all (since their caste was Delta) dressed in khaki.

"Put them down on the floor."

The infants were unloaded.

"Now turn them so that they can see the flowers and books."

Turned, the babies at once fell silent, then began to crawl towards those clusters of sleek colors, those shapes so gay and brilliant on the white pages. As they approached, the sun came out of a momentary eclipse behind a cloud. The roses flamed up as though with a sudden passion from within; a new and profound significance seemed to suffuse the shining pages of the books. From the ranks of the crawling babies came little squeals of excitement, gurgles and twitterings of pleasure.

The Director rubbed his hands. "Excellent!" he said. "It might almost have been done on purpose."

The swiftest crawlers were already at their goal. Small hands reached out uncertainly, touched, grasped, unpetaling the transfigured roses, crumpling the illuminated pages of the books. The Director waited until all were happily busy. Then, "Watch carefully," he said. And, lifting his hand, he gave the signal.

The Head Nurse, who was standing by a switchboard at the other end of the room, pressed down a little lever.

There was a violent explosion. Shriller and ever shriller, a siren shrieked. Alarm bells maddeningly sounded.

The children started, screamed; their faces were distorted with terror.

"And now," the Director shouted (for the noise was deafening), "now we proceed to rub in the lesson with a mild electric shock."

He waved his hand again, and the Head Nurse pressed a second lever. The screaming of the babies suddenly changed its tone. There was something desperate, almost insane, about the sharp spasmodic yelps to which they now gave utterance. Their little bodies twitched and stiffened; their limbs moved jerkily as if to the tug of unseen wires.

"We can electrify that whole strip of floor," bawled the Director in explanation. "But that's enough," he signaled to the nurse.

The explosions ceased, the bells stopped ringing, the shriek of the siren died down from tone to tone into silence. The stiffly twitching bodies relaxed, and what had become the sob and yelp of infant maniacs broadened out once more into a normal howl of ordinary terror.

"Offer them the flowers and the books again."

The nurses obeyed; but at the approach of the roses, at the mere sight of those gaily-coloured images of pussy and cock-a-doodle-doo and baa-baa black sheep, the infants shrank away in horror; the volume of their howling suddenly increased.

"Observe," said the Director triumphantly, "observe."

Books and loud noises, flowers and electric shocks—already in the infant mind the couples were compromisingly linked; and after two hundred repetitions of the same or a similar lesson would be wedded indissolubly. What man has joined, nature is powerless to put asunder.

"They'll grow up with what the psychologists used to call an 'instinctive' hatred of books and flowers. Reflexes unalterably conditioned. They'll be safe from books and botany all their lives." The Director turned to his nurses. "Take them away again."

Still yelling, the khaki babies were loaded on to their dumb-waiters and wheeled out, leaving behind them the smell of sour milk and a most welcome silence.

Suggestions for Discussion

1. Summarize the Pavlovian experiment demonstrated on the children. Do the doctor and the student observers regard the experiment as cruel? Explain their attitude.
2. What details in the selection would you regard as contributing to the anti-utopian atmosphere? How does Huxley employ imagery in the details?

Suggestion for Writing

Write a story that describes a method of controlling human behavior. You may wish to place the events in a utopian, an anti-utopian, or a completely ordinary setting.

POETRY

WALT WHITMAN

When I Heard the Learn'd Astronomer

Walt Whitman (1819–1892), regarded by many as the greatest American poet, was born on Long Island, New York. He was a printer, a journalist, and a nurse during the Civil War. Strongly influenced by Ralph Waldo Emerson, he published *Leaves of Grass* in 1855 at his own expense. He added sections to new editions over the years. By the time of his death, he had become a major influence on younger poets who were moved by his experiments in free verse and by his transcendental ideas. In "When I Heard the Learn'd Astronomer," impatient with explanations of abstract science, he turns instead to silent contemplation of nature which, he implies, provides a profounder insight than do the "charts and diagrams" of science.

When I heard the learn'd astronomer,
When the proofs, the figures, were ranged in columns before me,
When I was shown the charts and diagrams, to add, divide, and measure
    them,
When I sitting heard the astronomer where he lectured with much applause
    in the lecture-room,
How soon unaccountable I became tired and sick,
Till rising and gliding out I wander'd off by myself,
In the mystical moist night-air, and from time to time,
Look'd up in perfect silence at the stars.

Suggestions for Discussion

1. Notice that this poem is contained in one sentence. How does Whitman organize the sentence to lead to the climax of the last line?
2. What is the poet's attitude toward the scientist? Why does he reject the scientific method of looking at nature? Why is his response "unaccountable"?
3. What is the significance of the phrase "perfect silence" in the last line?

Suggestion for Writing

Write an essay in which you explain not only the idea in the poem but how the idea is developed. Your essay should consider how a prose statement of the idea would differ.

Freedom and Human Dignity

"Liberty consists in being able to do anything which is not harmful to another or to others...."

"The Declaration of the Rights of Man,"
Paris, August 27, 1789

I believe that man will not merely endure: he will prevail. He is immortal, not because he alone among creatures has an inexhaustible voice but because he has a soul, a spirit capable of compassion and sacrifice and endurance.

—WILLIAM FAULKNER, "Nobel Prize Award Speech," 1949

Tell me, then, whether you agree with and assent to my first principle, that neither injury nor retaliation nor warding off evil by evil is ever right.

—PLATO, "The *Crito*"

Was he free? Was he happy? The question is absurd: Had anything been wrong, we should certainly have heard.

—W. H. AUDEN, "The Unknown Citizen"

PERSONAL REMINISCENCES

W. E. B. DU BOIS

On Being Crazy

William Edward Burghardt Du Bois (1868–1963) was born in Massachusetts. In the course of his life he became a major influence on American blacks. By 1903 he had written *The Souls of Black Folk,* which stated his major objections to the attitudes found in the writings of Booker T. Washington, the most influential black figure in the early twentieth century. In 1909 Du Bois helped found the National Association for the Advancement of Colored People. He edited *Crisis,* the magazine of the NAACP, and also founded the influential quarterly *Phylon* at Atlanta University. In this brief sketch (1907), Du Bois, in a series of conversations, touches ironically on the insanity of the relations between blacks and whites in the early days of the twentieth century. It might be instructive to consider just how different the relations between the races are today.

It was one o'clock and I was hungry. I walked into a restaurant, seated myself, and reached for the bill of fare. My table companion rose.

"Sir," said he, "do you wish to force your company on those who do not want you?"

No, said I, I wish to eat.

"Are you aware, sir, that this is social equality?"

Nothing of the sort, sir, it is hunger—and I ate.

The day's work done, I sought the theatre. As I sank into my seat, the lady shrank and squirmed.

I beg pardon, I said.

"Do you enjoy being where you are not wanted?" she asked coldly.

Oh no, I said.

"Well you are not wanted here."

I was surprised. I fear you are mistaken, I said, I certainly want the music, and I like to think the music wants me to listen to it.

"Usher," said the lady, "this is social equality."

"No, madame," said the usher, "it is the second movement of Beethoven's Fifth Symphony."

After the theatre, I sought the hotel where I had sent my baggage. The clerk scowled.

"What do you want?"

Rest, I said.

"This is a white hotel," he said.

I looked around. Such a color scheme requires a great deal of cleaning, I said, but I don't know that I object.

"We object," said he.

Then why, I began, but he interrupted.

"We don't keep niggers," he said, "we don't want social equality."

Neither do I, I replied gently, I want a bed.

I walked thoughtfully to the train. I'll take a sleeper through Texas. I'm a little bit dissatisfied with this town.

"Can't sell you one."

I only want to hire it, said I, for a couple of nights.

"Can't sell you a sleeper in Texas," he maintained. "They consider that social equality."

I consider it barbarism, I said, and I think I'll walk.

Walking, I met another wayfarer, who immediately walked to the other side of the road, where it was muddy. I asked his reason.

"Niggers is dirty," he said.

So is mud, said I. Moreover, I am not as dirty as you—yet.

"But you're a nigger, ain't you?" he asked.

My grandfather was so called.

"Well then!" he answered triumphantly.

Do you live in the South? I persisted, pleasantly.

"Sure," he growled, "and starve there."

I should think you and the Negroes should get together and vote out starvation.

"We don't let them vote."

We? Why not? I said in surprise.

"Niggers is too ignorant to vote."

But, I said, I am not so ignorant as you.

"But you're a nigger."

Yes, I'm certainly what you mean by that.

"Well then!" he returned, with that curiously inconsequential note of triumph. "Moreover," he said, "I don't want my sister to marry a nigger."

I had not seen his sister, so I merely murmured, let her say no.

"By God, you shan't marry her, even if she said yes."

But—but I don't want to marry her, I answered, a little perturbed at the personal turn.

"Why not!" he yelled, angrier than ever.

Because I'm already married and I rather like my wife.

"Is she a nigger?" he asked suspiciously.
Well, I said again, her grandmother was called that.
"Well then!" he shouted in that oddly illogical way.
I gave up.
Go on, I said, either you are crazy or I am.
"We both are," he said as he trotted along in the mud.

Suggestions for Discussion

1. Why has Du Bois chosen these specific scenes for his conversations with white people?
2. In what way is the final conversation different from those preceding it?
3. Discuss some of the examples of Du Bois's use of irony.

Suggestion for Writing

Write an essay in which you examine the areas of racism dealt with in this selection from today's perspective. What significant differences would you find? What similarities? In what way is "On Being Crazy" relevant for our time?

RICHARD WRIGHT

The Ethics of Living Jim Crow

A major American black writer, Richard Wright (1908–1960) wrote stories, novels, an autobiography, and other books about America's racial problems. His best-known works are *Native Son* (1940), *Black Boy* (1945), and *White Man, Listen* (1957). The following autobiographical account of his education in race relations in a totally segregated South is from *Uncle Tom's Children* (1938).

I

My first lesson in how to live as a Negro came when I was quite small. We were living in Arkansas. Our house stood behind the railroad tracks. Its skimpy yard was paved with black cinders. Nothing green ever grew in that yard. The only touch of green we could see was far away, beyond the tracks, over where the white folks lived. But cinders were good enough for me and I never missed the green growing things. And anyhow cinders were fine weapons. You could always have a nice hot war with huge black cinders. All you had to do was crouch behind the brick pillars of a house with your hands full of gritty ammunition. And the first woolly black head you saw pop out from behind another row of pillars was your target. You tried your very best to knock it off. It was great fun.

I never fully realized the appalling disadvantages of a cinder environment till one day the gang to which I belonged found itself engaged in a war with the white boys who lived beyond the tracks. As usual we laid down our cinder barrage, thinking that this would wipe the white boys out. But they replied with a steady bombardment of broken bottles. We doubled our cinder barrage, but they hid behind trees, hedges, and the sloping embankments of their lawns. Having no such fortifications, we retreated to the brick pillars of our homes. During the retreat a broken milk bottle caught me behind the ear, opening a deep gash which bled profusely. The sight of blood pouring over my face completely demoralized our ranks. My fellow-combatants left me standing paralyzed in the center of the yard, and scurried for their homes. A kind neighbor saw me and rushed me to a doctor, who took three stitches in my neck.

I sat brooding on my front steps, nursing my wound and waiting for my mother to come from work. I felt that a grave injustice had been done me. It was all right to throw cinders. The greatest harm a cinder could do was leave a bruise. But broken bottles were dangerous; they left you cut, bleeding, and helpless.

When night fell, my mother came from the white folks' kitchen. I raced down the street to meet her. I could just feel in my bones that she would understand. I knew she would tell me exactly what to do next time. I grabbed her hand and babbled out the whole story. She examined my wound, then slapped me.

"How come yuh didn't hide?" she asked me. "How come yuh awways fightin'?"

I was outraged, and bawled. Between sobs I told her that I didn't have any trees or hedges to hide behind. There wasn't a thing I could have used as a trench. And you couldn't throw very far when you were hiding behind the brick pillars of a house. She grabbed a barrel stave, dragged me home, stripped me naked, and beat me till I had a fever of one hundred and two. She would smack my rump with the stave, and, while the skin was still smarting, impart to me gems of Jim Crow wisdom. I was never to throw cinders any more. I was never to fight any more wars. I was never, never, under any conditions, to fight *white* folks again. And they were absolutely right in clouting me with the broken milk bottle. Didn't I know she was working hard every day in the hot kitchens of the white folks to make money to take care of me? When was I ever going to learn to be a good boy? She couldn't be bothered with my fights. She finished by telling me that I ought to be thankful to God as long as I lived that they didn't kill me.

All that night I was delirious and could not sleep. Each time I closed my eyes I saw monstrous white faces suspended from the ceiling, leering at me.

From that time on, the charm of my cinder yard was gone. The green trees, the trimmed hedges, the cropped lawns grew very meaningful, became a symbol. Even today when I think of white folks, the hard, sharp outlines of white houses surrounded by trees, lawns, and hedges are present somewhere in the background of my mind. Through the years they grew into an overreaching symbol of fear.

It was a long time before I came in close contact with white folks again. We moved from Arkansas to Mississippi. Here we had the good fortune not to live behind the railroad tracks, or close to white neighborhoods. We lived in the very heart of the local Black belt. There were black churches and black preachers; there were black schools and black teachers; black groceries and black clerks. In fact, everything was so solidly black that for a long time I did not even think of white folks, save in remote and vague terms. But this could not last forever. As one grows older one eats more. One's clothing costs more. When I finished grammar school I had to go to work. My mother could no longer feed and clothe me on her cooking job.

There is but one place where a black boy who knows no trade can get a job, and that's where the houses and faces are white, where the trees, lawns, and hedges are green. My first job was with an optical company in Jackson, Mississippi. The morning I applied I stood straight and neat before the boss, answering all his questions with sharp yessirs and nosirs. I was very careful to pronounce my *sirs* distinctly, in order that he might know that I was polite, that I knew where I was, and that I knew he was a *white* man. I wanted that job badly.

He looked me over as though he were examining a prize poodle. He questioned me closely about my schooling, being particularly insistent about how much mathematics I had had. He seemed very pleased when I told him I had had two years of algebra.

"Boy, how would you like to try to learn something around here?" he asked me.

"I'd like it fine, sir," I said, happy. I had visions of "working my way up." Even Negroes have those visions.

"All right," he said. "Come on."

I followed him to the small factory.

"Pease," he said to a white man of about thirty-five, "this is Richard. He's going to work for us."

Pease looked at me and nodded.

I was then taken to a white boy of about seventeen.

"Morrie, this is Richard, who's going to work for us."

"Whut yuh sayin' there, boy!" Morrie boomed at me.

"Fine!" I answered.

The boss instructed these two to help me, teach me, give me jobs to do, and let me learn what I could in my spare time.

My wages were five dollars a week.

I worked hard, trying to please. For the first month I got along O.K. Both Pease and Morrie seemed to like me. But one thing was missing. And I kept thinking about it. I was not learning anything and nobody was volunteering to help me. Thinking they had forgotten that I was to learn something about the mechanics of grinding lenses, I asked Morrie one day to tell me about the work. He grew red.

"Whut yuh tryin' t' do, nigger, get smart?" he asked.

"Naw; I ain't tryin t' git smart," I said.

"Well, don't, if yuh know whut's good for yuh!"

I was puzzled. Maybe he just doesn't want to help me, I thought. I went to Pease.

"Say, are yuh crazy, you black bastard?" Pease asked me, his gray eyes growing hard.

I spoke out, reminding him that the boss had said I was to be given a chance to learn something.

"Nigger, you think you're *white,* don't you?"

"Naw, sir!"

"Well, you're acting mighty like it!"

"But, Mr. Pease, the boss said..."

Pease shook his fist in my face.

"This is a *white* man's work around here, and you better watch yourself!"

From then on they changed toward me. They said good-morning no more. When I was just a bit slow in performing some duty, I was called a lazy black son-of-a-bitch.

Once I thought of reporting all this to the boss. But the mere idea of what would happen to me if Pease and Morrie should learn that I had "snitched" stopped me. And after all the boss was a white man, too. What was the use?

The climax came at noon one summer day. Pease called me to his workbench. To get to him I had to go between two narrow benches and stand with my back against a wall.

"Yes, sir," I said.

"Richard, I want to ask you something," Pease began pleasantly, not looking up from his work.

"Yes, sir," I said again.

Morrie came over, blocking the narrow passage between the benches. He folded his arms, staring at me solemnly.

I looked from one to the other, sensing that something was coming.

"Yes, sir," I said for the third time.

Pease looked up and spoke very slowly.

"Richard, *Mr.* Morrie here tells me you called me *Pease.*"

I stiffened. A void seemed to open up in me. I knew this was the showdown.

He meant that I had failed to call him Mr. Pease. I looked at Morrie. He was gripping a steel bar in his hands. I opened my mouth to speak, to protest, to assure Pease that I had never called him simply *Pease,* and that I had never had any intentions of doing so, when Morrie grabbed me by the collar, ramming my head against the wall.

"Now, be careful, nigger!" snarled Morrie, baring his teeth. "*I* heard yuh call 'im *Pease!*" 'N' if yuh say yuh didn't yuh're callin' me a *lie,* see?" He waved the steel bar threateningly.

If I had said: No, sir, Mr. Pease, I never called you *Pease,* I would have been automatically calling Morrie a liar. And if I had said: Yes, sir, Mr. Pease, I called you *Pease,* I would have been pleading guilty to having uttered the worst insult that a Negro can utter to a southern white man. I stood hesitating, trying to frame a neutral reply.

"Richard, I asked you a question!" said Pease. Anger was creeping into his voice.

"I don't remember calling you *Pease,* Mr. Pease," I said cautiously. "And if I did, I sure didn't mean…"

"You black son-of-a-bitch! You called me *Pease,* then!" he spat, slapping me till I bent sideways over a bench. Morrie was on top of me, demanding:

"Didn't yuh call 'im *Pease?* If yuh say yuh didn't, I'll rip yo' gut string loose with this bar, yuh black granny dodger! Yuh can't call a white man a liar 'n' git erway with it, you black son-of-a-bitch!"

I wilted. I begged them not to bother me. I knew what they wanted. They wanted me to leave.

"I'll leave," I promised. "I'll leave right *now.*"

They gave me a minute to get out of the factory. I was warned not to show up again, or tell the boss.

I went.

When I told the folks at home what had happened, they called me a fool. They told me that I must never again attempt to exceed my boundaries. When you are working for white folks, they said, you got to "stay in your place" if you want to keep working.

II

My Jim Crow education continued on my next job, which was portering in a clothing store. One morning, while polishing brass out front, the boss and his twenty-year-old son got out of their car and half dragged and half kicked a Negro woman into the store. A policeman standing at the corner looked on, twirling his night-stick. I watched out of the corner of my eye, never slackening the strokes of my chamois upon the brass. After a few minutes, I heard shrill screams coming from the rear of the store. Later the woman stumbled out, bleeding, crying, and holding her stomach. When she reached the end of the block, the policeman grabbed her and accused her of being drunk. Silently, I watched him throw her into a patrol wagon.

When I went to the rear of the store, the boss and his son were washing their hands at the sink. They were chuckling. The floor was bloody and strewn with wisps of hair and clothing. No doubt I must have appeared pretty shocked, for the boss slapped me reassuringly on the back.

"Boy, that's what we do to niggers when they don't want to pay their bills," he said, laughing.

His son looked at me and grinned.

"Here, hava cigarette," he said.

Not knowing what to do, I took it. He lit his and held the match for me. This was a gesture of kindness, indicating that even if they had beaten the poor old woman, they would not beat me if I knew enough to keep my mouth shut.

"Yes, sir," I said, and asked no questions.

After they had gone, I sat on the edge of a packing box and stared at the bloody floor till the cigarette went out.

That day at noon, while eating in a hamburger joint, I told my fellow Negro porters what had happened. No one seemed surprised. One fellow, after swallowing a huge bite, turned to me and asked:

"Huh! Is tha' all they did t' her?"

"Yeah. Wasn't tha' enough?" I asked.

"Shucks! Man, she's a lucky bitch!" he said, burying his lips deep into a juicy hamburger. "Hell, it's a wonder they didn't lay her when they got through."

III

I was learning fast, but not quite fast enough. One day, while I was delivering packages in the suburbs, my bicycle tire was punctured. I walked along the hot, dusty road, sweating and leading my bicycle by the handlebars.

A car slowed at my side.

"What's the matter, boy?" a white man called.

I told him my bicycle was broken and I was walking back to town.

"That's too bad," he said. "Hop on the running board."

He stopped the car. I clutched hard at my bicycle with one hand and clung to the side of the car with the other.

"All set?"

"Yes, sir," I answered. The car started.

It was full of young white men. They were drinking. I watched the flask pass from mouth to mouth.

"Wanna drink, boy?" one asked.

I laughed as the wind whipped my face. Instinctively obeying the freshly planted precepts of my mother, I said:

"Oh, no!"

The words were hardly out of my mouth before I felt something hard and cold smash me between the eyes. It was an empty whisky bottle. I saw stars, and fell backwards from the speeding car into the dust of the road, my feet becoming entangled in the steel spokes of my bicycle. The white men piled out and stood over me.

"Nigger, ain' yuh learned no better sense'n tha' yet?" asked the man who hit me. "Ain' yuh learned t' say *sir* t' a white man yet?"

Dazed, I pulled to my feet. My elbows and legs were bleeding. Fists doubled, the white man advanced, kicking my bicycle out of the way.

"Aw, leave the bastard alone. He's got enough," said one.

They stood looking at me. I rubbed my shins, trying to stop the flow of blood. No doubt they felt a sort of contemptuous pity, for one asked:

"Yuh wanna ride t' town now, nigger? Yuh reckon yuh know enough t' ride now?"

"I wanna walk," I said, simply.

Maybe it sounded funny. They laughed.

"Well, walk, yuh black son-of-a-bitch!"

When they left they comforted me with:

"Nigger, yuh sho better be damn glad it wuz us yuh talked t' tha' way. Yuh're a lucky bastard, 'cause if yuh'd said tha' t' somebody else, yuh might've been a dead nigger now."

IV

Negroes who had lived South know the dread of being caught alone upon the streets in white neighborhoods after the sun has set. In such a simple situation as this the plight of the Negro in America is graphically symbolized. While white strangers may be in these neighborhoods trying to get home, they can pass unmolested. But the color of a Negro's skin makes him easily recognizable, makes him suspect, converts him into a defenseless target.

Late one Saturday night I made some deliveries in a white neighborhood. I was pedaling my bicycle back to the store as fast as I could, when a police car, swerving toward me, jammed me into the curbing.

"Get down and put up your hands!" the policemen ordered.

I did. They climbed out of the car, guns drawn, faces set, and advanced slowly.

"Keep still!" they ordered.

I reached my hands higher. They searched my pockets and packages. They seemed dissatisfied when they could find nothing incriminating. Finally, one of them said:

"Boy, tell your boss not to send you out in white neighborhoods after sundown."

As usual, I said:

"Yes, sir."

V

My next job was a hall-boy in a hotel. Here my Jim Crow education broadened and deepened. When the bell-boys were busy, I was often called to assist them. As many of the rooms in the hotel were occupied by prostitutes, I was constantly called to carry them liquor and cigarettes. These women were nude most of the time. They did not bother about clothing, even for bell-boys. When you went into their rooms, you were supposed to take their nakedness for granted, as though it startled you no more than a blue vase or a red rug. Your presence awoke in them no sense of shame, for you were not regarded as human. If they were alone, you could steal sidelong glimpses at them. But if they were receiving men, not a flicker of your eyelids could show. I remember one incident vividly. A new woman, a huge, snowy-skinned blonde, took a room on my floor. I was sent to wait upon her. She was in bed with a thick-set man; both were nude and uncovered. She said she wanted some liquor and slid out of bed and waddled across the floor to get her money from a dresser drawer. I watched her.

"Nigger, what in hell you looking at?" the white man asked me, raising himself upon his elbows.

"Nothing," I answered, looking miles deep into the blank wall of the room.

"Keep your eyes where they belong, if you want to be healthy!" he said.

"Yes, sir."

VI

One of the bell-boys I knew in this hotel was keeping steady company with one of the Negro maids. Out of a clear sky the police descended upon his home and arrested him, accusing him of bastardy. The poor boy swore he had had no intimate relations with the girl. Nevertheless, they forced him to marry her. When the child arrived, it was found to be much lighter in complexion than either of the two supposedly legal parents. The white men around the hotel made a great joke of it. They spread the rumor that some white cow must have scared the poor girl while she was carrying the baby. If you were in their presence when this explanation was offered, you were supposed to laugh.

VII

One of the bell-boys was caught in bed with a white prostitute. He was castrated and run out of town. Immediately after this all the bell-boys and hall-boys were called together and warned. We were given to understand that the boy who had been castrated was a "mighty, mighty lucky bastard." We were impressed with the fact that next time the management of the hotel would not be responsible for the lives of "trouble-makin' niggers." We were silent.

VIII

One night, just as I was about to go home, I met one of the Negro maids. She lived in my direction, and we fell in to walk part of the way home together. As we passed the white night-watchman, he slapped the maid on her buttock. I turned around, amazed. The watchman looked at me with a long, hard, fixed-under stare. Suddenly he pulled his gun and asked:

"Nigger, don't yuh like it?"

I hesitated.

"I asked yuh don't yuh like it?" he asked again, stepping forward.

"Yes, sir," I mumbled.

"Talk like it, then!"

"Oh, yes, sir!" I said with as much heartiness as I could muster.

Outside, I walked ahead of the girl, ashamed to face her. She caught up with me and said:

"Don't be a fool! Yuh couldn't help it!"

This watchman boasted of having killed two Negroes in self-defense.

Yet, in spite of all this, the life of the hotel ran with an amazing smoothness. It would have been impossible for a stranger to detect anything. The maids, the hall-boys, and the bell-boys were all smiles. They had to be.

IX

I had learned my Jim Crow lessons so thoroughly that I kept the hotel job till I left Jackson for Memphis. It so happened that while in Memphis I applied for a job at a branch of the optical company. I was hired. And for some reason, as long as I worked there, they never brought my past against me.

Here my Jim Crow education assumed quite a different form. It was no longer brutally cruel, but subtly cruel. Here I learned to lie, to steal, to dissemble. I learned to play that dual role which every Negro must play if he wants to eat and live.

For example, it was almost impossible to get a book to read. It was assumed that after a Negro had imbibed what scanty schooling the state furnished he had no further need for books. I was always borrowing books from men on the job. One day I mustered enough courage to ask one of the men to let me get books from the library in his name. Surprisingly, he consented. I cannot help but think that he consented because he was a Roman Catholic and felt a vague sympathy for Negroes, being himself an object of hatred. Armed with a library card, I obtained books in the following manner: I would write a note to the librarian, saying: "Please let this nigger boy have the following books." I would then sign it with the white man's name.

When I went to the library, I would stand at the desk, hat in hand, looking as unbookish as possible. When I received the books desired I would take them home. If the books listed in the note happened to be out, I would sneak into the lobby and forge a new one. I never took any chances guessing with the white librarian about what the fictitious white man would want to read. No doubt if any of the white patrons had suspected that some of the volumes they enjoyed had been in the home of a Negro, they would not have tolerated it for an instant.

The factory force of the optical company in Memphis was much larger than that in Jackson, and more urbanized. At least they liked to talk, and would engage the Negro help in conversation whenever possible. By this means I found that many subjects were taboo from the white man's point of view. Among the topics they did not like to discuss with Negroes were the following: American white women; the Ku Klux Klan; France, and how Negro soldiers fared while there; French women; Jack Johnson; the entire northern part of the United States; the Civil War; Abraham Lincoln; U.S. Grant; General Sherman; Catholics; the Pope; Jews; the Republican Party; slavery; social equality; Communism; Socialism; the 13th and 14th Amendments to the Constitution; or any topic calling for positive knowledge or manly self-assertion on the part of the Negro. The most accepted topics were sex and religion.

There were many times when I had to exercise a great deal of ingenuity to keep out of trouble. It is a southern custom that all men must take off their hats when they enter an elevator. And especially did this apply to us blacks with rigid force. One day I stepped into an elevator with my arms full of packages. I was forced to ride with my hat on. Two white men stared at me coldly. Then one of them very kindly lifted my hat and placed it upon my armful of packages. Now the most accepted response for a Negro to make under such circumstances is to look at the white man out of the corner of his eye and grin. To have said: "Thank you!" would have made the white man *think* that you *thought* you were receiving from him a personal service. For such an act I have seen Negroes take a blow in the mouth. Finding the first alternative distasteful, and the second dangerous, I hit upon an acceptable course of action which fell safely between these two poles. I immediately—no sooner than my hat was lifted—pretended that my packages were about to spill, and appeared deeply distressed with keeping them in my arms. In this fashion I evaded having to acknowledge his service, and, in spite of adverse circumstances, salvaged a slender shred of personal pride.

How do Negroes feel about the way they have to live? How do they discuss it when alone among themselves? I think this question can be answered in a single sentence. A friend of mine who ran an elevator once told me:

"Lawd, man! Ef it wuzn't fer them polices 'n' them ol' lynch-mobs, there wouldn't be nothin' but uproar down here!"

Suggestions for Discussion

1. Analyze Wright's sketch in terms of (a) structure, (b) progression and unity in nine segments, (c) expository-narrative style, and/or (d) themes.
2. How does Wright's title contribute to the development of the major themes of the sketch? Why does he use *ethics* and *living?*
3. Discuss his use of personal experiences to illustrate his themes.

4. Discuss his use of violence in the sketch. Is it believable? Significant? Explain.

Suggestions for Writing

1. Analyze the motivation behind an incident of discrimination that you have observed or experienced.
2. Analyze the dramatic irony in the last line and its climactic effect as the final comment on the whole sketch.

BENJAMIN ALIRE SÁENZ

Prologue to *Exiled: The Winds of Sunset Heights*

Benjamin Alire Sáenz, born in Las Cruces in southern New Mexico, teaches at the University of Texas in El Paso. He holds an M.A. from the University of Louvain in Belgium and from the University of Texas at El Paso. He also has a Ph.D. from Stanford University where he was granted a Stegner Fellowship. He has published in numerous journals and magazines. His first book of poems, *Calendar of Dust,* won the Before Columbus Foundation American Book Award in 1992. Sáenz was the winner of the 1993 Lannan Poetry Fellowship. This prologue records the anger that a native-born Chicano, living near the border, feels over the frequent harassment by the border patrol.

That morning—when the day was new, when the sun slowly touched the sky, almost afraid to break it—that morning I looked out my window and stared at the Juárez Mountains. Mexican purples—burning. I had always thought of them as sacraments of belonging. That was the first time it happened. It had happened to others, but it had never happened to me. And when it happened, it started a fire, a fire that will burn for a long time.

As I walked to school, I remember thinking what a perfect place Sunset Heights was: turn of the century houses intact; remodeled houses painted pink and turquoise; old homes tastefully gentrified by the aspiring young;

the rundown Sunset Grocery store decorated with the protest art of graffiti on one end and a plastic-signed "Circle K" on the other.

This was the edge of the piece of paper that was America, the border that bordered the University—its buildings, its libraries; the border that bordered the freeway—its cars coming and going, coming and going endlessly; the border that bordered downtown—its banks and businesses and bars; the border that bordered the border between two countries.

The unemployed poor from Juárez knocking on doors and asking for jobs—or money—or food. Small parks filled with people whose English did not exist. The upwardly mobile living next to families whose only concern was getting enough money to pay next month's rent. Some had lived here for generations, would continue living here into the next century; others would live here a few days. All this color, all this color, all this color beneath the shadow of the Juárez Mountains. Sunset Heights: a perfect place with a perfect name, and a perfect view of the river.

After class, I went by my office and drank a cup of coffee, sat and read, and did some writing. It was a quiet day on campus, nothing but me and my work—the kind of day the mind needs to catch up with itself, the kind of uneventful day so necessary for living. I started walking home at about three o'clock, after I had put my things together in my torn backpack. I made a mental note to sew the damn thing. *One day everything's gonna come tumbling out—better sew it.* I'd made that mental note before.

Walking down Prospect, I thought maybe I'd go for a jog. I hoped the spring would not bring too much wind this year. The wind, common desert rain; the wind blew too hard and harsh sometimes; the wind unsettled the desert—upset things, ruined the calmness of the spring. My mind wandered, searched the black asphalt littered with torn papers; the chained dogs in the yards who couldn't hurt me; the even bricks of all the houses I passed. I belonged here, yes. I belonged. Thoughts entered like children running through a park. This year, maybe the winds would not come.

I didn't notice the green car drive up and stop right next to me as I walked. The border patrol interrupted my daydreaming: "Where are you from?"

I didn't answer. I wasn't sure who the agent, a woman, was addressing.

She repeated the question in Spanish, "*¿De dónde eres?*"

Without thinking, I almost answered her question—in Spanish. A reflex. I caught myself in midsentence and stuttered in a nonlanguage.

"*¿Dónde naciste?*" she asked again.

By then my mind had cleared, and quietly I said: "I'm a U.S. citizen."

"Were you born in the United States?"

She was browner than I was. I might have asked her the same question. I looked at her for awhile—searching for something I recognized.

"Yes," I answered.

"Where in the United States were you born?"

"In New Mexico."

"Where in New Mexico?"

"Las Cruces."

"What do you do?"

"I'm a student."

"And are you employed?"

"Sort of."

"Sort of?" She didn't like my answer. Her tone bordered on anger. I looked at her expression and decided it wasn't hurting anyone to answer her questions. It was all very innocent, just a game we were playing.

"I work at the University as a teaching assistant."

She didn't respond. She looked at me as if I were a blank. Her eyes were filling in the empty spaces as she looked at my face. I looked at her for a second and decided she was finished with me. I started walking away. "Are you sure you were born in Las Cruces?" she asked again.

I turned around and smiled, "Yes, I'm sure." She didn't smile back. She and the driver sat there for awhile and watched me as I continued walking. They drove past me slowly and then proceeded down the street.

I didn't much care for the color of their cars.

"Sons of bitches," I whispered, "pretty soon I'll have to carry a passport in my own neighborhood." I said it to be flippant; something in me rebelled against people dressed in uniforms. I wasn't angry—not then, not at first, not really angry. In less than ten minutes I was back in my apartment playing the scene again and again in my mind. It was like a video I played over and over—memorizing the images. Something was wrong. I was embarrassed, ashamed because I'd been so damned compliant like a piece of tin foil in the uniformed woman's hand. Just like a child in the principal's office, in trouble for speaking Spanish. "I should have told that witch exactly what I thought of her and her green car and her green uniform."

I lit a cigarette and told myself I was overreacting. "Breathe in—breathe out—breathe in—breathe out—no big deal—you live on a border. These things happen—just one of those things. Just a game..." I changed into my jogging clothes and went for a run. At the top of the hill on Sunbowl Drive, I stopped to stare at the Juárez Mountains. I felt the sweat run down my face. I kept running until I could no longer hear *Are you sure you were born in Las Cruces?* ringing in my ears.

School let out in early May. I spent the last two weeks of that month relaxing and working on some paintings. In June I got back to working on my stories. I had a working title, which I hated, but I hated it less than the actual stories I was writing. It would come to nothing; I knew it would come to nothing.

From my window I could see the freeway. It was then I realized that not a day went by when I didn't see someone running across the freeway or walking down the street looking out for someone. They were people who looked not so different from me—except that they lived their lives looking over their shoulders.

One Thursday, I saw the border patrol throw some men into their van—throw them—as if they were born to be thrown like baseballs, like rings in a carnival ringtoss, easy inanimate objects, dead bucks after a deer hunt. The illegals didn't even put up a fight. They were aliens, from somewhere else, somewhere foreign, and it did not matter that the "somewhere else" was as close as an eyelash to an eye. What mattered was that someone had once drawn a line, and once drawn, that line became indelible and hard and could not be crossed.

The men hung their heads so low that they almost scraped the littered asphalt. Whatever they felt, they did not show; whatever burned did not burn for an audience. I sat at my typewriter and tried to pretend I saw nothing. *What do you think happens when you peer out windows? Buy curtains.*

I didn't write the rest of the day. I kept seeing the border patrol woman against a blue sky turning green. I thought of rearranging my desk so I wouldn't be next to the window, but I thought of the mountains. No, I would keep my desk near the window, but I would look only at the mountains.

Two weeks later, I went for a walk. The stories weren't going well that day; my writing was getting worse instead of better; my characters were getting on my nerves—I didn't like them—no one else would like them either. They did not burn with anything. I hadn't showered, hadn't shaved, hadn't combed my hair. I threw some water on my face and walked out the door. It was summer; it was hot; it was afternoon, the time of day when everything felt as if it were on fire. The worst time of the day to take a walk. I wiped the sweat from my eyelids; it instantly reappeared. I wiped it off again, but the sweat came pouring out—a leak in the dam. Let it leak. I laughed. A hundred degrees in the middle of a desert afternoon. Laughter poured out of me as fast as my sweat. I turned the corner and headed back home. I saw the green van. It was parked right ahead of me.

A man about my height got out of the van and approached me. Another man, taller, followed him. "*¿Tienes tus papeles?*" he asked. His gringo accent was as thick as the sweat on my skin.

"I can speak English," I said. I started to add: *I can probably speak it better than you,* but I stopped myself. No need to be aggressive, no need to get any hotter.

"Do you live in this neighborhood?"

"Yes."

"Where?"

"Down the street."

"Where down the street?"

"Are you planning on making a social visit?"

He gave me a hard look—cold and blue—then looked at his partner. He didn't like me. I didn't care. I liked that he hated me. It made it easier.

I watched them drive away and felt as hot as the air, felt as hot as the heat that was burning away the blue in the sky.

There were other times when I felt watched. Sometimes, when I jogged, the green vans would slow down, eye me. I felt like prey, like a rabbit who smelled the hunter. I pretended not to notice them. I stopped pretending. I started noting their presence in our neighborhood more and more. I started growing suspicious of my own observations. Of course, they weren't everywhere. But they *were* everywhere. I had just been oblivious to their presence, had been oblivious because they had nothing to do with me; their presence had something to do with someone else. I was not a part of this. I wanted no part of it. The green cars and the green vans clashed with the purples of the Juárez Mountains. Nothing looked the same. I never talked about their presence to other people. Sometimes the topic of the *Migra* would come up in conversations. I felt the burning; I felt the anger, would control it. I casually referred to them as the Gestapo, the traces of rage carefully hidden from the expression on my face—and everyone would laugh. I hated them.

When school started in the fall, I was stopped again. Again I had been walking home from the University. I heard the familiar question: "Where are you from?"

"Leave me alone."

"Are you a citizen of the United States?"

"Yes."

"Can you prove it?"

"No. No, I can't."

He looked at my clothes: jeans, tennis shoes, and a casual California shirt. He noticed my backpack full of books.

"You a student?"

I nodded and stared at him.

"There isn't any need to be unfriendly—"

"I'd like you to leave me alone."

"Just doing my job," he laughed. I didn't smile back. *Terrorists. Nazis did their jobs. Death squads in El Salvador and Guatemala did their jobs, too.* An unfair analogy. An unfair analogy? Yes, unfair. I thought it; I felt it; it was no longer my job to excuse—someone else would have to do that, someone else. The Juárez Mountains did not seem purple that fall. They no longer burned with color.

In early January I went with Michael to Juárez. Michael was from New York, and he had come to work in a home for the homeless in South El Paso. We weren't in Juárez very long—just looking around and getting gas. Gas was cheap in Juárez. On the way back, the customs officer asked us to declare our citizenship. "U.S. citizen," I said. "U.S. citizen," Michael followed. The customs officer lowered his head and poked it in the car. "What are you bringing over?"

"Nothing."

He looked at me. "Where in the United States were you born?"

"In Las Cruces, New Mexico."

He looked at me a while longer. "Go ahead," he signaled.

I noticed that he didn't ask Michael where he was from. But Michael had blue eyes; Michael had white skin. Michael didn't have to tell the man in the uniform where he was from.

That winter, Sunset Heights seemed deserted to me. The streets were empty like the river. One morning, I was driving down Upson Street toward the University, the wind shaking the limbs of the bare trees. Nothing to shield them—unprotected by green leaves. The sun burned a dull yellow. In front of me, I noticed two border patrol officers chasing someone, though that someone was not visible. One of them put his hand out, signaling me to slow down as they ran across the street in front of my car. They were running with their billy clubs in hand. The wind blew at their backs as if to urge them on, as if to carry them.

In late January, Michael and I went to Juárez again. A friend of his was in town, and he wanted to see Juárez. We walked across the bridge, across the river, across the line into another country. It was easy. No one there to stop us. We walked the streets of Juárez, streets that had seen better years, that were tired now from the tired feet that walked them. Michael's friend wanted to know how it was that there were so many beggars. "Were there always so many? Has it always been this way?" I didn't know how it had always been. We sat in the Cathedral and in the old chapel next to it and watched people rubbing the feet of statues; when I touched a statue, it was warmer than my own hand. We walked to the marketplace and inhaled the smells. Grocery stores in the country we knew did not have such smells. On the way back we stopped in a small bar and had a beer. The beer was cold and cheap. Walking back over the bridge, we stopped at the top and looked out at the city of El Paso. "It actually looks pretty from here, doesn't it?" I said. Michael nodded. It did look pretty. We looked off to the side—down the river—and for a long time watched the people trying to get across. Michael's friend said it was like watching the *CBS Evening News.*

As we reached the customs building, we noticed that a border patrol van pulled up behind the building where the other green cars were parked.

The officers jumped out of the van and threw a handcuffed man against one of the parked cars. It looked like they were going to beat him. Two more border patrol officers pulled up in a car and jumped out to join them. One of the officers noticed we were watching. They straightened the man out and walked him inside—like gentlemen. They would have beat him. They would have beat him. But we were watching.

My fingers wanted to reach through the wire fence, not to touch it, not to feel it, but to break it down, to melt it down with what I did not understand. The burning was not there to be understood. Something was burning, the side of me that knew I was treated different, would always be treated different because I was born on a particular side of a fence, a fence that separated me from others, that separated me from a past, that separated me from the country of my genesis and glued me to the country I did not love because it demanded something of me I could not give. Something was burning now, and if I could have grasped the source of that rage and held it in my fist, I would have melted that fence. Someone built that fence; someone could tear it down. Maybe I could tear it down; maybe I was the one. Maybe then I would no longer be separated.

The first day in February, I was walking to a downtown Chevron station to pick up my car. On the corner of Prospect and Upson, a green car was parked—just sitting there. A part of my landscape. I was walking on the opposite side of the street. For some reason, I knew they were going to stop me. My heart clenched like a fist; the muscles in my back knotted up. *Maybe they'll leave me alone. I should have taken a shower this morning. I should have worn a nicer sweater. I should have put on a pair of socks, worn a nicer pair of shoes. I should have cut my hair; I should have shaved...*

The driver rolled down his window. I saw him from the corner of my eye. He called me over to him—*whistled me over*—much like he'd call a dog. I kept walking. He whistled me over again. *Here, boy.* I stopped for a second. Only a second. I kept walking. The border patrol officer and a policeman rushed out of the car and ran toward me. I was sure they were going to tackle me, drag me to the ground, handcuff me. They stopped in front of me.

"Can I see your driver's license?" the policeman asked.

"Since when do you need a driver's license to walk down the street?" Our eyes met. "Did I do something against the law?"

The policeman was annoyed. He wanted me to be passive, to say: "Yes, sir." He wanted me to approve of his job.

"Don't you know what we do?"

"Yes, I know what you do."

"Don't give me a hard time. I don't want trouble. I just want to see some identification."

I looked at him—looked, and saw what would not go away: neither him, nor his car, nor his job, nor what I knew, nor what I felt. He stared back. He hated me as much as I hated him. He saw the bulge of my cigarettes under my sweater and crumpled them.

I backed away from his touch. "I smoke. It's not good for me, but it's not against the law. Not yet, anyway. Don't touch me. I don't like that. Read me my rights, throw me in the can, or leave me alone." I smiled.

"No one's charging you with anything."

My eyes followed them as they walked back to their car. Now it was war, and *I had won this battle.* Had I won this battle? Had I won?

This spring morning, I sit at my desk, wait for the coffee to brew, and look out my window. This day, like every day, I look out my window. Across the street, a border patrol van stops and an officer gets out. So close I could touch him. On the freeway—this side of the river—a man is running. I put on my glasses. I am afraid he will be run over by the cars. I cheer for him. *Be careful. Don't get run over.* So close to the other side he can touch it. The border patrol officer gets out his walkie-talkie and runs toward the man who has disappeared from my view. I go and get my cup of coffee. I take a drink—slowly, it mixes with yesterday's tastes in my mouth. The officer in the green uniform comes back into view. He has the man with him. He puts him in the van. I can't see the color in their eyes. I see only the green. They drive away. There is no trace that says they've been there. The mountains watch the scene and say nothing. The mountains, ablaze in the spring light, have been watching—and guarding—and keeping silent longer than I have been alive. They will continue their vigil long after I am dead.

The green vans. They are taking someone away. They are taking. Green vans. This is my home, I tell myself. But I am not sure if I want this to be my home anymore. The thought crosses my mind that maybe the *Migra* will stop me again. I will let them arrest me. I will let them warehouse me. I will let them push me in front of a judge who will look at me like he has looked at the millions before me. I will be sent back to Mexico. I will let them treat me like I am illegal. But the thoughts pass. I am not brave enough to let them do that to me.

Today, the spring winds blow outside my window. The reflections in the pane, graffiti burning questions into the glass: *Sure you were born…Identification…Do you live?…*The winds will unsettle the desert—cover Sunset Heights with green dust. The vans will stay in my mind forever. I cannot banish them. I cannot banish their questions: *Where are you from?* I no longer know.

This is a true story.

Suggestions for Discussion

1. Discuss the incidents in this memoir that describe and explain the author's anger over the actions of the border patrol. Are the patrol's actions consistently racist?
2. Why does the writer dislike the color of the border patrol officers' uniforms? The color of their cars and vans?
3. Describe Sáenz's feelings about the landscape of the border country in which he lives. How do these passages serve to portray the writer?
4. In the next to the last scene of the memoir, the writer describes a confrontation with a member of the border patrol. He wonders whether he has won this conflict. Has he? Explain your response.

Suggestions for Writing

1. Write a personal essay describing an incident, or a series of incidents, in which you confronted authority. Try to record how you behaved, what you felt, what your opponent felt, and so forth.
2. Most rational people despise the persistence of racism in this country. Write an essay describing a racist incident you observed or a racist conversation you overheard or participated in. Try to summarize the feelings generated by the incident or conversation and how you responded.

RIGOBERTA MENCHÚ

Things Have Happened to Me as in a Movie

Rigoberta Menchú (b. 1962), a Quiché Indian, was born in Guatemala. She taught herself Spanish when she was twenty. A founder of the Committee for the Peasants' Unity, she has widely traveled as an ambassador of the Indian people. She won the Casa de las Américas Prize of Cuba for her book, *I, Rigoberta,* and the Nobel Peace Prize in 1992. In this short memoir, resulting from an interview with César Chelala and translated by Regina M. Kreger, the writer recalls details from the Guatemalan suppression of the Indian people that are almost too painful to read.

I am Rigoberta Menchú; I am a native of the Quiché people of Guatemala. My life has been a long one. Things have happened to me as in a movie. My parents were killed in the repression. I have hardly any relatives living, or if I have, I don't know about them. It has been my lot to live what has been the lot of many, many Guatemalans.

We were a very poor family. All their lives my parents worked cutting cotton, cutting coffee. We lived about four months of the year on the high plain of Guatemala, where my father had a small piece of land; but that only supported us a short time, and then we had to go down to the plantations to get food.

During the whole time my mother was pregnant with me, she was on the plantation cutting coffee and cotton. I was paid twenty cents, many years ago, when I started to work in my town in Guatemala. There, the poor, the children, didn't have the opportunity for school; we did not have the opportunity to achieve any other life but working for food and to help our parents buy medicine for our little brothers and sisters. Two of my brothers died on the plantation cutting coffee. One of them got sick, couldn't be cured, and died. The other died when the landowner ordered the cotton sprayed while we were in the field. My brother was poisoned, there was no way to cure him and he died on the plantation, where we buried him.

We didn't know why those things happened. It's a miracle we were saved several times. When we got sick our mother looked for plants to cure us. The natives in Guatemala depended very much on nature. My mother cured us many times with the leaves of plants, with roots. That is how we managed to grow up. At ten years old, I started to work more in collaboration with my community, where my father, a local, native Mayan leader, was known by all the Indians of the region.

Little by little, my father got us involved in the concerns of the community. And so we grew up with that consciousness. My father was a catechist, and in Guatemala, a catechist is a leader of the community, and what he does especially is preach the Gospel. We, his children, began to evolve in the Catholic religion, and became catechists.

Little by little, we grew up—and really you can't say we started fighting only a short time ago, because it has been twenty-two years since my father fought over the land. The landowners wanted to take away our land, our little bit of land, and so my father fought for it. So he went to speak with the mayors, and with the judges in various parts of Guatemala. Afterwards, my father joined INTA, the land reform institution in Guatemala. For many years, my father was tricked because he did not speak Spanish. None of us spoke Spanish. So they made my father travel all over Guatemala to sign papers, letters, telegrams, which meant that not only he, but the whole community, had to sacrifice to pay the travel expenses. All this created an awareness in us from a very young age.

In the last years, my father was imprisoned many times, the first of those in 1954. My father landed in jail when he was accused of causing unrest among the population. When our father was in jail, the army kicked us out of our houses. They burned our clay pots. In our community we don't use iron or steel; we use clay pots, which we make ourselves with earth. But the army broke everything, and it was really hard for us to understand this situation.

Then my father was sentenced to eighteen years in prison, but he didn't serve them because we were able to work with lawyers to get him released. After a year and two months, my father got out of prison and returned home with more courage to go on fighting and much angrier because of what had happened. When that was over my mother had to go right to work as a maid in the city of Santa Cruz del Quiché, and all of us children had to go down to work on the plantations.

A short time later, my father was tortured by the landowners' bodyguards. Some armed men came to my house and took my father away. We got the community together and found my father lying in the road, far away, about two kilometers from home. My father was badly beaten and barely alive. The priests of the region had to come out to take my father to the hospital. He had been in the hospital for six months when we heard he was going to be taken out and killed. The landowners had been discussing it loudly, and the information came to us by way of their servants, who are also natives, and with whom we were very close. And so we had to find another place for my father, a private clinic the priests found for him so he would heal. But my father could no longer do hard work like he did before. A little later my father dedicated himself exclusively to working for the community, traveling, living off the land.

Several years passed, and again, in the year 1977, my father was sentenced to death. He landed in jail again. When we went to see him in the Pantán jail, the military told us they didn't want us to see my father, because he had committed many crimes. My mother went to Santa Cruz to find lawyers, and from them we learned that my father was going to be executed. When the time of the execution came, many union workers, students, peasants and some priests demonstrated for my father's freedom. My father was freed, but before he left he was threatened; he was told that he was going to be killed anyway for being a communist. From that moment on, my father had to carry out his activities in secret. He had to change the rhythm of his life. He lived hidden in several houses in Quiché, and then he went to the capital city. And so he became a leader of struggle for the peasants. It was then that my father said, "We must fight as Christians," and from there came the idea, along with other catechists, of forming Christian organizations which would participate in the process.

For us it was always a mystery how my father could carry out all those activities, which were very important, despite being illiterate. He never learned to read or write in his life. All his children were persecuted because of his activities, and our poverty really didn't help us defend ourselves, because we were in very sad circumstances.

All my father's activities had created a resentment in us because we couldn't have our parents' affection, because there were a lot of us children and a bigger worry was how to survive. On top of all this were the problems of the land, which upset my father very much. Many years before, rocks had fallen from the mountain and we had to go down from where we lived. When we went down and cultivated new land, the landowners appeared with documents and they told us the land was theirs before we came. But we knew very well the land had no owner before we got there.

They couldn't catch my father, but in the year 1979, they kidnapped one of my little brothers. He was sixteen. We didn't know who did it. We only knew that they were five armed men, with their faces covered. Since my father couldn't go out, we went with my mother and members of the community to make a complaint to the army, but they said they didn't know anything about what had happened to my brother. We went to City Hall, we went to all the jails in Guatemala, but we didn't find him. After many trips all over my mother was very upset. It had taken a lot for my brother to survive, and so for my mother it was very hard to accept his disappearance.

At that time the army published a bulletin saying there was going to be a guerrilla council. They said they had some guerrillas in their custody and that they were going to punish them in public. My mother said, "I hope to God my son shows up. I hope to God my son is there. I want to know what has happened to him." So we went to see what was happening. We walked for one day and almost the whole night to get to the other town. There were hundreds of soldiers who had almost the whole town surrounded, and who had gathered the people together to witness what they were going to do. There were natives of other areas as well as natives of that town. After a while an army truck arrived with twenty people who had been tortured in different ways. Among them we recognized my brother, who, along with the other prisoners, had been tortured for fifteen days. When my mother saw my little brother she almost gave herself away, but we had to calm her down, telling her that if she gave herself away she was going to die right there for being family of a guerrilla. We were crying, but almost all the rest of the people were crying also at the sight of the tortured people. They had pulled out my little brother's fingernails, they had cut off parts of his ears and other parts of his body, his lips, and he was covered with scars and swollen all over. Among the prisoners was a woman and they had cut off parts of her breasts and other parts of her body.

An army captain gave us a very long speech, almost three hours, in which he constantly threatened the people, saying that if we got involved with communism the same things were going to happen to us. Then he explained to us one by one the various types of torture they had applied to the prisoners. After three hours, the officer ordered the troops to strip the prisoners, and said: "Part of the punishment is still to come." He ordered the prisoners tied to some posts. The people didn't know what to do and my mother was overcome with despair in those few moments. And none of us knew how we could bear the situation. The officer ordered the prisoners covered with gasoline and they set fire to them, one by one.

Suggestions for Discussion

1. Menchú's account of the life-history of her Indian family is not meant to represent an unusual case. How does the writer make it seem representative?
2. What examples best reveal the punishing poverty of the Indians? How do they respond?
3. What roles do the mother and father play in this memoir? What qualities do they possess that make them seem heroic?
4. What is the relation of the title to the memoir?

Suggestions for Writing

1. Write a brief profile of Menchú's father. Summarize and evaluate his efforts to help the Indians of Guatemala. Was his life's effort a failure? Explain.
2. Compare and contrast the soldiers in Menchú's memoir with the border patrol guards in Sáenz's prologue. What accounts for the significant differences between the two groups? What about Menchú's memoir makes your reading of it so painful?

VO THI TAM

From Vietnam, 1979

Vo Thi Tam escaped from South Vietnam after the Communist victory. Like thousands of other refugees she endured the hardships recounted in this memoir, which first appeared in *American Mosaic* (edited by Joan Morison and Charlotte Fox Zabrisky, 1980). Vo Thi

Tam's story reminds the reader that throughout the twentieth century hundreds of thousands of people from many lands have overcome terrible suffering and overwhelming odds in their search for freedom.

My husband was a former officer in the South Vietnamese air force. After the fall of that government in 1975, he and all the other officers were sent to a concentration camp for reeducation. When they let him out of the camp, they forced all of us to go to one of the "new economic zones," that are really just jungle. There was no organization, there was no housing, no utilities, no doctor, nothing. They gave us tools and a little food, and that was it. We just had to dig up the land and cultivate it. And the land was very bad.

It was impossible for us to live there, so we got together with some other families and bought a big fishing boat, about thirty-five feet long.

Altogether, there were thirty-seven of us that were to leave—seven men, eight women, and the rest children. I was five months pregnant.

After we bought the boat we had to hide it, and this is how: We just anchored it in a harbor in the Mekong Delta. It's very crowded there and very many people make their living aboard the boats by going fishing, you know. So we had to make ourselves like them. We took turns living and sleeping on the boat. We would maneuver the boat around the harbor, as if we were fishing or selling stuff, you know, so the Communist authorities could not suspect anything.

Besides the big boat, we had to buy a smaller boat in order to carry supplies to it. We had to buy gasoline and other stuff on the black market—everywhere there is a black market—and carry these supplies, little by little, on the little boat to the big boat. To do this we sold jewelry and radios and other things that we had left from the old days.

On the day we left we took the big boat out very early in the morning—all the women and children were in that boat and some of the men. My husband and the one other man remained in the small boat, and they were to rendezvous with us outside the harbor. Because if the harbor officials see too many people aboard, they might think there was something suspicious. I think they were suspicious anyway. As we went out, they stopped us and made us pay them ten taels of gold—that's a Vietnamese unit, a little heavier than an ounce. That was nearly all we had.

Anyway, the big boat passed through the harbor and went ahead to the rendezvous point where we were to meet my husband and the other man in the small boat. But there was no one there. We waited for two hours, but we did not see any sign of them. After a while we could see a Vietnamese navy boat approaching, and there was a discussion on board our boat and the end of it was the people on our boat decided to leave without my husband and the other man. [*Long pause.*]

When we reached the high seas, we discovered, unfortunately, that the water container was leaking and only a little bit of the water was left. So we had to ration the water from then on. We had brought some rice and other food that we could cook, but it was so wavy that we could not cook anything at all. So all we had was raw rice and a few lemons and very little water. After seven days we ran out of water, so all we had to drink was the sea water, plus lemon juice.

Everyone was very sick and, at one point, my mother and my little boy, four years old, were in agony, about to die. And the other people on the boat said that if they were agonizing like that, it would be better to throw them overboard so as to save them pain.

During this time we had seen several boats on the sea and had waved to them to help us, but they never stopped. But that morning, while we were discussing throwing my mother and son overboard, we could see another ship coming and we were very happy, thinking maybe it was people coming to save us. When the two boats were close together, the people came on board from there—it happened to be a Thai boat—and they said all of us had to go on the bigger boat. They made us all go there and then they began to search us—cutting off our blouses, our bras, looking everywhere. One woman, she had some rings she hid in her bra, and they undressed her and took out everything. My mother had a statue of our Lady, a very precious one, you know, that she had had all her life—she begged them just to leave the statue to her. But they didn't want to. They slapped her and grabbed the statue away.

Finally they pried up the planks of our boat, trying to see if there was any gold or jewelry hidden there. And when they had taken everything, they put us back on our boat and pushed us away.

They had taken all our maps and compasses, so we didn't even know which way to go. And because they had pried up the planks of our boat to look for jewelry, the water started getting in. We were very weak by then. But we had no pump, so we had to use empty cans to bail the water out, over and over again.

That same day we were boarded again by two other boats, and these, too, were pirates. They came aboard with hammers and knives and everything. But we could only beg them for mercy and try to explain by sign language that we'd been robbed before and we had nothing left. So those boats let us go and pointed the way to Malaysia for us.

That night at about 9:00 P.M. we arrived on the shore, and we were so happy finally to land somewhere that we knelt down on the beach and prayed, you know, to thank God.

While we were kneeling there, some people came out of the woods and began to throw rocks at us. They took a doctor who was with us and they beat him up and broke his glasses, so that from that time on he couldn't see anything at all. And they tied him up, his hands behind him like this [*demonstrates*], and they beat up the rest of the men, too. They searched us for anything precious that they could find, but there was nothing left except our few clothes and our documents. They took these and scattered them all over the beach.

Then five of the Malaysian men grabbed the doctor's wife, a young woman with three little children, and they took her back into the woods and raped her—all five of them. Later, they sent her back, completely naked, to the beach.

After this, the Malaysians forced us back into the boat and tried to push us out to sea. But the tide was out and the boat was so heavy with all of us on board that it just sank in the sand. So they left us for the night....

In the morning, the Malaysian military police came to look over the area, and they dispersed the crowd and protected us from them. They let us pick up our clothes and our papers from the beach and took us in a big truck to some kind of a warehouse in a small town not far away. They gave us water, some bread, and some fish, and then they carried us out to Bidong Island....

Perhaps in the beginning it was all right there, maybe for ten thousand people or so, but when we arrived there were already fifteen to seventeen thousand crowded onto thirty acres. There was no housing, no facilities, nothing. It was already full near the beach, so we had to go up the mountain and chop down trees to make room for ourselves and make some sort of a temporary shelter. There was an old well, but the water was very shallow. It was so scarce that all the refugees had to wait in a long line, day and night, to get our turn of the water. We would have a little can, like a small Coke can at the end of a long string, and fill that up. To fill about a gallon, it would take an hour, so we each had to just wait, taking our turn to get our Coke can of water. Sometimes one, two, or three in the morning we would get our water. I was pregnant, and my boys were only four and six, and my old mother with me was not well, but we all had to wait in line to get our water. That was just for cooking and drinking of course. We had to do our washing in the sea.

The Malaysian authorities did what they could, but they left most of the administration of the camp to the refugees themselves, and most of us were sick. There were, of course, no sanitary installations, and many people had diarrhea. It was very hard to stop sickness under those conditions. My little boys were sick and my mother could hardly walk. And since there was no man in our family, we had no one to chop the wood for our cooking, and it was very hard for us just to survive. When the monsoons came, the floor of our shelter was all mud. We had one blanket and a board to lie on, and that was all. The water would come down the mountain through our shelter, so we all got wet.

After four months in the camp it was time for my baby to be born. Fortunately, we had many doctors among us, because many of them had tried to escape from Vietnam, so we had medical care but no equipment. There was no bed there, no hospital, no nothing, just a wooden plank to lie down on and let the baby be born, that was all. Each mother had to supply a portion of boiling water for the doctor to use and bring it with her to the medical hut when it was time. It was a very difficult delivery. The baby came legs first. But, fortunately, there were no complications. After the delivery I had to get up and go back to my shelter to make room for the next woman.

When we left Vietnam we were hoping to come to the United States, because my sister and her husband were here already. They came in 1975 when the United States evacuated so many people. We had to wait in the camp a month and a half to be interviewed, and then very much longer for the papers to be processed. Altogether we were in the camp seven months.

All this time I didn't know what had happened to my husband, although I hoped that he had been able to escape some other way and was, perhaps, in another camp, and that when I came to the United States I would find him.

We flew out here by way of Tokyo and arrived the first week in July. It was like waking up after a bad nightmare. Like coming out of hell into paradise if only—. [*Breaks down, rushes from room.*]

Shortly after she arrived in this country, Vo Thi Tam learned that her husband had been captured on the day of their escape and was back in a "reeducation" camp in Vietnam.

Suggestions for Discussion

1. What impression of Vo Thi Tam develops as we read her narrative? Discuss the details that serve to create her self-portrait.
2. What conditions in Vietnam lead the family and the others in the group to attempt an escape? Discuss the horrors that the refugees are forced to face. How might you have acted under similar circumstances?
3. What is the effect on the reader of the interviewer's comments?

Suggestions for Writing

1. If you live in an area where Vietnamese or other refugees from oppression live, record and transcribe some interviews and discuss them in a brief research paper, with Vo Thi Tam's narrative serving as background. Think carefully of the questions you will need to ask to elicit meaningful responses. One of your questions might deal with the expectations of the

immigrant on arriving in the United States and whether those expectations have been realized.

2. Choose a different group of immigrants escaping oppression or terror, such as the Armenians from Turkey or Iran, the Nicaraguans, or the Guatemalans. Do library research to enable you to compare their experience with that of the Vietnamese. Write a paper discussing the similarities and differences of the experiences of the two groups.

ESSAYS

THOMAS JEFFERSON

The Declaration of Independence

The Continental Congress assembled in Philadelphia in 1776 delegated to Thomas Jefferson (1743–1826) the task of writing a declaration of independence from Great Britain, which the Congress amended and adopted on July 4. After the Revolution, Jefferson became Governor of Virginia and in 1801 the third President of the United States. He was the father of what is called "Jeffersonian democracy," which exceeded the democracy then advocated by either Washington or Jefferson's rival, Alexander Hamilton. After leaving the presidency, he founded the University of Virginia as a place where truth could assert itself in free competition with other ideas. In its theory as well as in its style, the Declaration is a typical eighteenth-century view of man's place in society, which included the right to overthrow a tyrannical ruler.

When in the course of human events, it becomes necessary for one people to dissolve the political bands which have connected them with another, and to assume among the powers of the earth, the separate and equal station to which the Laws of Nature and of Nature's God entitle them, a decent respect to the opinions of mankind requires that they should declare the causes which impel them to the separation.

We hold these truths to be self-evident, that all men are created equal, that they are endowed by their Creator with certain inalienable rights, that among these are life, liberty, and the pursuit of happiness. That to secure these rights, governments are instituted among men, deriving their just powers from the consent of the governed. That whenever any form of government becomes destructive of these ends, it is the right of the people to alter or to abolish it, and to institute new government, laying its foundation on such principles and organizing its powers in such form, as to them shall seem most likely to effect their safety and happiness. Prudence, indeed, will dictate that governments long established should not be changed for light and transient causes; and accordingly all experience hath shown, that mankind are more disposed to suffer, while evils are sufferable, than to right themselves by abolishing the forms to which they are accustomed. But when a long train of abuses and usurpations, pursuing invariably the same object, evinces a design to reduce them under absolute despotism, it is their right, it is their duty, to throw off such government, and to provide new guards for their future security. Such has been the patient sufferance of these Colonies; and such is now the necessity which constrains them to alter their former systems of government. The history of the present King of Great Britain is a history of repeated injuries and usurpations, all having in direct object the establishment of an absolute tyranny over these States. To prove this, let facts be submitted to a candid world.

He has refused his assent to laws, the most wholesome and necessary for the public good.

He has forbidden his Governors to pass laws of immediate and pressing importance, unless suspended in their operation till his assent should be obtained; and when so suspended, he has utterly neglected to attend to them.

He has refused to pass other laws for the accommodation of large districts of people, unless those people would relinquish the right of representation in the legislature, a right inestimable to them and formidable to tyrants only.

He has called together legislative bodies at places unusual, uncomfortable, and distant from the depository of their public records, for the sole purpose of fatiguing them into compliance with his measures.

He has dissolved representative houses repeatedly, for opposing with manly firmness his invasions on the rights of the people.

He has refused for a long time, after such dissolutions, to cause others to be elected; whereby the legislative powers, incapable of annihilation, have returned to the people at large for their exercise; the State remaining in the meantime exposed to all the dangers of invasion from without and convulsions within.

He has endeavoured to prevent the population of these states; for that purpose obstructing the laws for naturalization of foreigners; refusing to pass others to encourage their migration hither, and raising the conditions of new appropriations of lands.

He has obstructed the administration of justice, by refusing his assent to laws for establishing judiciary powers.

He has made judges dependent on his will alone, for the tenure of their offices, and the amount and payment of their salaries.

He has erected a multitude of new offices, and sent hither swarms of officers to harass our people, and eat out their substance.

He has kept among us, in times of peace, standing armies without the consent of our legislatures.

He has affected to render the military independent of and superior to the civil power.

He has combined with others to subject us to a jurisdiction foreign of our constitution, and unacknowledged by our laws; giving his assent to their acts of pretended legislation:

For quartering large bodies of armed troops among us:

For protecting them, by a mock trial, from punishment for any murders which they should commit on the inhabitants of these States:

For cutting off our trade with all parts of the world:

For imposing taxes on us without our consent:

For depriving us in many cases of the benefits of trial by jury:

For transporting us beyond seas to be tried for pretended offences:

For abolishing the free system of English laws in a neighbouring Province, establishing therein an arbitrary government, and enlarging its boundaries so as to render it at once an example and fit instrument for introducing the same absolute rule into these Colonies:

For taking away our Charters, abolishing our most valuable laws, and altering fundamentally the forms of our governments:

For suspending our own legislatures, and declaring themselves invested with power to legislate for us in all cases whatsoever.

He has abdicated government here, by declaring us out of his protection and waging war against us.

He has plundered our seas, ravaged our coasts, burnt our towns, and destroyed the lives of our people.

He is at this time transporting large armies of foreign mercenaries to complete the works of death, desolation, and tyranny, already begun with circumstances of cruelty and perfidy scarcely paralleled in the most barbarous ages, and totally unworthy the head of a civilized nation.

He has constrained our fellow citizens taken captive on the high seas to bear arms against their country, to become the executioners of their friends and brethren, or to fall themselves by their hands.

He has excited domestic insurrections amongst us, and has endeavoured to bring on the inhabitants of our frontiers, the merciless Indian savages, whose known rule of warfare, is an undistinguished destruction of all ages, sexes, and conditions.

In every stage of these oppressions we have petitioned for redress in the most humble terms: our repeated petitions have been answered only by repeated injury. A prince whose character is thus marked by every act which may define a tyrant is unfit to be the ruler of a free people.

Nor have we been wanting in attention to our British brethren. We have warned them from time to time of attempts by their legislature to extend an unwarrantable jurisdiction over us. We have reminded them of the circumstances of our emigration and settlement here. We have appealed to their native justice and magnanimity, and we have conjured them by the ties of our common kindred to disavow these usurpations, which would inevitably interrupt our connections and correspondence. They too have been deaf to the voice of justice and of consanguinity. We must, therefore, acquiesce in the necessity, which denounces our separation, and hold them, as we hold the rest of mankind, enemies in war, in peace friends.

We, therefore, the Representatives of the United States of America, in General Congress assembled, appealing to the Supreme Judge of the world for the rectitude of our intentions, do, in the name, and by authority of the good people of these Colonies, solemnly publish and declare, That these United Colonies are, and of right ought to be, Free and Independent States; that they are absolved from all allegiance to the British Crown, and that all political connection between them and the state of Great Britain, is and ought to be totally dissolved; and that as Free and Independent States, they have full power to levy war, conclude peace, contract alliances, establish commerce, and to do all other acts and things which Independent States may of right do. And for the support of this declaration, with a firm reliance on the protection of Divine Providence, we mutually pledge to each other our lives, our fortunes, and our sacred honor.

Suggestions for Discussion

1. What is the basis for Jefferson's belief that "all men are created equal"?
2. In the eighteenth century, the notion of the "divine right" of kings was still popular. How does Jefferson refute that notion?
3. Discuss the list of tyrannical actions which Jefferson attributes to the King of Great Britain. Account for the order in which he lists them.
4. This essay has been called a "model of clarity and precision." Explain your agreement with this statement. How does Jefferson balance strong feeling with logical argument?

Suggestion for Writing

Jefferson asserts that "all men are created equal," and yet he does not include black slaves as equals. In Jefferson's *Autobiography,* he wrote that a clause "reprobating the enslaving the inhabitants of Africa" was omitted in the final draft "in complaisance to South Carolina and Georgia." Was Jefferson merely opportunistic in agreeing to strike this clause? Write an essay in which you relate the ideas of the Declaration to the ideas in Lincoln's Gettysburg Address. Show how one set of ideas leads to the other.

The Declaration of the Rights of Man

Soon after the fall of the Bastille on July 14, 1789, a day celebrated in France as July 4th is celebrated in the United States, the French National Assembly was asked to provide a declaration that would correspond to the American Declaration of Independence. The Assembly appointed a committee of five to draft the document. After several weeks of debate and compromise, the completed declaration was approved and proclaimed on August 27, 1789. An analysis of the Declaration shows that while a number of phrases resemble the American model, it derived more particularly from the English Bill of Rights of 1689. Ironically, the basis for democratic government embodied in this document was to be subverted by a leader of the new republic who would declare himself Emperor.

The representatives of the French people, gathered in the National Assembly, believing that ignorance, neglect, and disdain of the rights of men are the sole causes of public misfortunes and of the corruption of governments, have resolved to set forth, in solemn declaration, the natural, inalienable, and sacred rights of men, in order that this Declaration, held always before the members of the body social, will forever remind them of their rights and duties; that the acts of legislative and executive power, always identifiable with the ends and purposes of the whole body politic, may be more fully respected; that the complaints of citizens, founded henceforth on simple and incontrovertible principles, may be turned always to the maintaining of the Constitution and to the happiness of all.

The National assembly therefore recognizes and declares, in the presence and under the auspices of the Supreme Being, the following rights of Man and of citizen:

1. Men are born and will remain free and endowed with equal rights. Social distinctions can be based only upon usefulness to the common weal.

2. The end and purpose of all political groups is the preservation of the natural and inalienable rights of Man. These rights are Liberty, the Possession of Property, Safety, and Resistance to Oppression.

3. The principle of all sovereignty will remain fundamentally in the State. No group and no individual can exercise authority which does not arise expressly from the State.

4. Liberty consists in being able to do anything which is not harmful to another or to others; therefore, the exercise of the natural rights of each

individual has only such limits as will assure to other members of society the enjoyment of the same rights. These limits can be determined only by the Law.

5. The Law has the right to forbid only such actions as are harmful to society. Anything not forbidden by the Law can never be forbidden; and none can be forced to do what the Law does not prescribe.

6. The Law is the expression of the will of the people. All citizens have the right and the duty to concur in the formation of the Law, either in person or through their representatives. Whether it punishes or whether it protects, the Law must be the same for all. All citizens, being equal in the eyes of the Law, are to be admitted equally to all distinctions, ranks, and public employment, according to their capacities, and without any other discrimination than that established by their individual abilities and virtues.

7. No individual can be accused, arrested, or detained except in cases determined by the Law, and according to the forms which the Law has prescribed. Those who instigate, expedite, execute, or cause to be executed any arbitrary or extralegal prescriptions must be punished; but every citizen called or seized through the power of the Law must instantly obey. He will render himself culpable by resisting.

8. The Law should establish only those penalties which are absolutely and evidently necessary, and none can be punished except through the power of the Law, as already established and proclaimed for the public good and legally applied.

9. Every individual being presumed innocent until he has been proved guilty, if it is considered necessary to arrest him, the Law must repress with severity any force which is not required to secure his person.

10. None is to be persecuted for his opinions, even his religious beliefs, provided that his expression of them does not interfere with the order established by the Law.

11. Free communication of thought and opinion is one of the most precious rights of Man; therefore, every citizen can speak, write, or publish freely, except that he will be required to answer for the abuse of such freedom in cases determined by the Law.

12. The guarantee of the rights of Man and of the citizen makes necessary a Public Force and Administration; this Force and Administration has therefore been established for the good of all, and not for the particular benefit of those to whom it has been entrusted.

13. For the maintaining of this Public Force and Administration, and for the expense of administering it, a common tax is required; it must be distributed equally among the people, in accordance with their ability to pay.

14. All citizens have the right and duty to establish, by themselves or by their representatives, the requirements of a common tax, to consent to it

freely, to indicate its use, and to determine its quota, its assessment, its collection, and its duration.

15. Society has the right and duty to demand from every public servant an accounting of his administration.

16. No society in which the guarantee of rights is not assured nor the distinction of legal powers determined can be said to have a constitution.

17. The possession of property being an inviolable and sacred right, none can be deprived of it, unless public necessity, legally proved, clearly requires the deprivation, and then only on the necessary condition of a previously established just reparation.

Suggestions for Discussion

1. What is the major purpose of setting forth the principles enunciated in this declaration?
2. The declaration refers to a Supreme Being. Why did not the writers of the declaration refer simply to God?
3. How do the seventeen "rights of the Man and of the citizen" define the relationship between the individual person and the State?
4. How does the declaration define the function of the Law and of the State?
5. How does the declaration propose to guarantee freedom of speech?
6. Can you explain why the declaration says that the possession of property is an "inviolable and sacred right"? How does this statement basically differ from modern revolutionary thought?
7. On what principles is this declaration based?

Suggestions for Writing

1. Write an essay about the similarities to and differences from this declaration with the American Declaration of Independence and with the Bill of Rights of the American Constitution.
2. Examine the English Bill of Rights of 1689 and write an essay in which you explain the close relationship between the French and English declarations.

SENECA FALLS CONVENTION

Declaration of Sentiments and Resolutions, 1848

On July 19–20, 1848, between one and two hundred delegates (women and men) representing suffragist, abolitionist, and temperance groups met in Seneca Falls, New York, at a convention to discuss women's rights. The Declaration of Sentiments and Resolutions was written by Elizabeth Cady Stanton and Lucretia Coffin Mott, assisted by the delegates present. The first major document that sought to define the issues and goals of the nineteenth-century women's movement, it was modeled after the Declaration of Independence in order to suggest the natural line of development from the American Revolution. Consequently, it stated women's demands for legal, political, economic, and social equality. The only resolution that created an objection was the one on women's suffrage, but after debate it too was included. Sixty-eight women and thirty-two men signed the declaration.

When, in the course of human events, it becomes necessary for one portion of the family of man to assume among the people of the earth a position different from that which they have hitherto occupied, but one to which the laws of nature and of nature's God entitle them, a decent respect to the opinions of mankind requires that they should declare the causes that impel them to such a course.

We hold these truths to be self-evident: that all men and women are created equal; that they are endowed by their Creator with certain inalienable rights; that among these are life, liberty, and the pursuit of happiness; that to secure these rights governments are instituted, deriving their just powers from the consent of the governed. Whenever any form of government becomes destructive of these ends, it is the right of those who suffer from it to refuse allegiance to it, and to insist upon the institution of a new government, laying its foundation on such principles, and organizing its powers in such form, as to them shall seem most likely to effect their safety and happiness. Prudence, indeed, will dictate that governments long established should not be changed for light and transient causes; and accordingly all experience hath shown that mankind are more disposed to suffer, while evils are sufferable, than to right themselves by abolishing the forms to which they were accustomed. But when a long train of abuses and usurpations, pursuing invariably the same object, evinces a design to reduce them under absolute despotism, it is their duty to throw off such government, and to provide new guards for their future security. Such has been the patient sufferance of the women under this government, and such is now the necessity which constrains them to demand the equal station to which they are entitled.

The history of mankind is a history of repeated injuries and usurpations on the part of man toward woman, having in direct object the establishment of an absolute tyranny over her. To prove this, let facts be submitted to a candid world.

He has never permitted her to exercise her inalienable right to the elective franchise.

He has compelled her to submit to laws, in the formation of which she had no voice.

He has withheld from her rights which are given to the most ignorant and degraded men—both natives and foreigners.

Having deprived her of this first right of a citizen, the elective franchise, thereby leaving her without representation in the halls of legislation, he has oppressed her on all sides.

He has made her, if married, in the eye of the law, civilly dead.

He has taken from her all right in property, even to the wages she earns.

He has made her, morally, an irresponsible being, as she can commit many crimes with impunity, provided they be done in the presence of her husband. In the covenant of marriage, she is compelled to promise obedience to her husband, he becoming to all intents and purposes, her master—the law giving him power to deprive her of her liberty, and to administer chastisement.

He has so framed the laws of divorce, as to what shall be the proper causes, and in case of separation, to whom the guardianship of the children shall be given, as to be wholly regardless of the happiness of women—the law, in all cases, going upon a false supposition of the supremacy of man, and giving all power into his hands.

After depriving her of all rights as a married woman, if single, and the owner of property, he has taxed her to support a government which recognizes her only when her property can be made profitable to it.

He has monopolized nearly all the profitable employments, and from those she is permitted to follow, she receives but a scanty remuneration. He closes against her all the avenues to wealth and distinction which he considers most honorable to himself. As a teacher of theology, medicine, or law, she is not known.

He has denied her the facilities for obtaining a thorough education, all colleges being closed against her.

He allows her in Church, as well as State, but a subordinate position, claiming Apostolic authority for her exclusion from the ministry, and, with some exceptions, from any public participation in the affairs of the Church.

He has created a false public sentiment by giving to the world a different code of morals for men and women, by which moral delinquencies which exclude women from society, are not only tolerated, but deemed of little account in man.

He has usurped the prerogative of Jehovah himself, claiming it as his right to assign for her a sphere of action, when that belongs to her conscience and to her God.

He has endeavored, in every way that he could, to destroy her confidence in her own powers, to lessen her self-respect, and to make her willing to lead a dependent and abject life.

Now, in view of this entire disfranchisement of one-half the people of this country, their social and religious degradation—in view of the unjust laws above mentioned, and because women do feel themselves aggrieved, oppressed, and fraudulently deprived of their most sacred rights, we insist that they have immediate admission to all the rights and privileges which belong to them as citizens of the United States.

In entering upon the great work before us, we anticipate no small amount of misconception, misrepresentation, and ridicule; but we shall use every instrumentality within our power to effect our object. We shall employ agents, circulate tracts, petition the State and National legislatures, and endeavor to enlist the pulpit and the press in our behalf. We hope this Convention will be followed by a series of Conventions embracing every part of the country.

Whereas, The great precept of nature is conceded to be, that "man shall pursue his own true and substantial happiness." Blackstone in his Commentaries remarks, that this law of Nature being coeval with mankind, and dictated by God himself, is of course superior in obligation to any other. It is binding over all the globe, in all countries and at all times; no human laws are of any validity if contrary to this, and such of them as are valid, derive all their force, and all their validity, and all their authority, mediately and immediately, from this original; therefore,

Resolved, That such laws as conflict, in any way, with the true and substantial happiness of woman, are contrary to the great precept of nature and of no validity, for this is "superior in obligation to any other."

Resolved, That all laws which prevent woman from occupying such a station in society as her conscience shall dictate, or which place her in a position inferior to that of man, are contrary to the great precept of nature, and therefore of no force or authority.

Resolved, That woman is man's equal—was intended to be so by the Creator, and the highest good of the race demands that she should be recognized as such.

Resolved, That the women of this country ought to be enlightened in regard to the laws under which they live, that they may no longer publish their degradation by declaring themselves satisfied with their present position, nor their ignorance, by asserting that they have all the rights they want.

Resolved, That inasmuch as man, while claiming for himself intellectual superiority, does accord to woman moral superiority, it is pre-eminently his duty to encourage her to speak and teach, as she has an opportunity, in all religious assemblies.

Resolved, That the same amount of virtue, delicacy, and refinement of behavior that is required of woman in the social state, should also be required of man, and the same transgressions should be visited with equal severity on both man and woman.

Resolved, That the objection of indelicacy and impropriety, which is so often brought against woman when she addresses a public audience, comes with a very ill-grace from those who encourage, by their attendance, her appearance on the stage, in the concert, or in feats of the circus.

Resolved, That woman has too long rested satisfied in the circumscribed limits which corrupt customs and a perverted application of the Scriptures have marked out for her, and that it is time she should move in the enlarged sphere which her great Creator has assigned her.

Resolved, That it is the duty of the women of this country to secure to themselves their sacred right to the elective franchise.

Resolved, That the equality of human rights results necessarily from the fact of the identity of the race in capabilities and responsibilities.

Resolved, therefore, That, being invested by the Creator with the same capabilities, and the same consciousness of responsibility for their exercise, it is demonstrably the right and duty of woman, equally with man, to promote every righteous cause by every righteous means; and especially in regard to the great subjects of morals and religion, it is self-evidently her right to participate with her brother in teaching them, both in private and in public, by writing and by speaking, by any instrumentalities proper to be used, and in any assemblies proper to be held; and this being a self-evident truth growing out of the divinely implanted principles of human nature, any custom or authority adverse to it, whether modern or wearing the hoary sanction of antiquity, is to be regarded as a self-evident falsehood, and at war with mankind.

Resolved, That the speedy success of our cause depends upon the zealous and untiring efforts of both men and women, for the overthrow of the monopoly of the pulpit, and for the securing to woman an equal participation with men in the various trades, professions, and commerce.

Suggestions for Discussion

1. Compare the Declaration of Independence with the Seneca Falls Declaration and discuss their parallel structure. Note particularly the basis, the "whereas" statement, for the resolution that follows.
2. Examine and discuss the preliminary list of grievances that lead to the need for the resolutions.
3. How might a contemporary declaration on the rights of women differ from this one? What other resolutions might appear at a similar convention today?
4. Why was there objection to women's suffrage?
5. The convention was attended by abolitionists and members of the temperance movement. How were these causes compatible with a convention on women's rights?

Suggestions for Writing

1. Write a paper comparing the Declaration of Independence with the Seneca Falls Declaration. What was missing from the first of these declarations?
2. Write a paper in which you discuss how a contemporary convention might stress different grievances. Be specific. Try to write some contemporary resolutions.

ABRAHAM LINCOLN

The Gettysburg Address

Abraham Lincoln (1809–1865), the sixteenth President of the United States, is generally regarded, along with Thomas Jefferson, as one of the greatest American prose stylists. On November 19, 1863, he traveled to Gettysburg in southern Pennsylvania to dedicate the cemetery for the soldiers killed there the previous July. The simple words he composed form the most famous speech ever delivered in America. A close reading reveals why it continues to hold meaning for Americans today.

Four score and seven years ago our fathers brought forth on this continent, a new nation, conceived in Liberty, and dedicated to the proposition that all men are created equal.

Now we are engaged in a great civil war, testing whether that nation, or any nation so conceived and so dedicated, can long endure. We are met on a great battlefield of that war. We have come to dedicate a portion of that field, as a final resting place for those who here gave their lives that that nation might live. It is altogether fitting and proper that we should do this.

But, in a larger sense, we can not dedicate—we can not consecrate—we can not hallow—this ground. The brave men, living and dead, who struggled here, have consecrated it, far above our poor power to add or detract. The world will little note nor long remember what we say here, but it can never forget what they did here. It is for us the living, rather, to be dedicated here to the unfinished work which they who fought here have thus far so nobly advanced. It is rather for us to be here dedicated to the great task remaining before us—that from these honored dead we take increased devotion to that cause for which they gave the last full measure of devotion—that we here highly resolve that these dead shall not have died in vain—that this nation, under God, shall have a new birth of freedom—and that government of the people, by the people, for the people, shall not perish from the earth.

Suggestions for Discussion

1. How is the proposition "that all men are created equal" related to the issues of the Civil War?
2. Why does Lincoln not simply begin his essay "Eighty-seven years ago"? What would he lose in tone if he had done so?
3. In paragraph three, Lincoln says "The world will little note, nor long remember what we say here." How do you account for the fact that he was wrong? Why did he make this statement? What function does it serve?
4. How does Lincoln use the verbs *dedicate, consecrate, hallow?* Could one easily change the order of these words?
5. How does Lincoln connect the first paragraph of his speech to the last?
6. What was the "unfinished work" of the soldiers who died at the Battle of Gettysburg?

Suggestion for Writing

Write an essay in which you relate the power of this speech to the simplicity of its language.

NICCOLÒ MACHIAVELLI

Of Cruelty and Clemency, and Whether It Is Better to Be Loved or Feared

Niccolò Machiavelli (1469–1527) was a Florentine statesman. His best-known work, *The Prince,* written in 1513, is an astute analysis of the contemporary political scene. The work was first translated into English in 1640. This selection from *The Prince,* translated by Luigi Ricci and revised by E. R. P. Vincent, explains by examples from history why the prince must rely on the fear he creates rather than the love he might generate. Machiavelli explains also why the prince, though causing fear, must avoid incurring hatred.

Proceeding to the other qualities before named, I say that every prince must desire to be considered merciful and not cruel. He must, however, take care not to misuse this mercifulness. Cesare Borgia was considered cruel, but his cruelty had brought order to the Romagna, united it, and reduced it to peace and fealty. If this is considered well, it will be seen that he was really much more merciful than the Florentine people, who, to avoid the name of cruelty, allowed Pistoia to be destroyed. A prince, therefore, must not mind incurring the charge of cruelty for the purpose of keeping his subjects united and faithful; for, with a very few examples, he will be more merciful than those who, from excess of tenderness, allow disorders to arise, from whence spring bloodshed and rapine; for these as a rule injure the whole community, while the executions carried out by the prince injure only individuals. And of all princes, it is impossible for a new prince to escape the reputation of cruelty, new states being always full of dangers. Wherefore Virgil through the mouth of Dido says:

> Res dura, et regni novitas me talia cogunt
> Moliri, et late fines custode tueri.*

*Our harsh situation and the newness of our kingdom compel me to contrive such measures and to guard our territory far and wide. (Dido offers this explanation to the newly landed Trojans of why her guards received them with hostile and suspicious measures.)

Nevertheless, he must be cautious in believing and acting, and must not be afraid of his own shadow, and must proceed in a temperate manner with prudence and humanity, so that too much confidence does not render him incautious, and too much diffidence does not render him intolerant.

From this arises the question whether it is better to be loved more than feared, or feared more than loved. The reply is, that one ought to be both feared and loved, but as it is difficult for the two to go together, it is much safer to be feared than loved, if one of the two has to be wanting. For it may be said of men in general that they are ungrateful, voluble dissemblers, anxious to avoid danger, and covetous of gain; as long as you benefit them, they are entirely yours; they offer you their blood, their goods, their life, and their children, as I have before said, when the necessity is remote; but when it approaches, they revolt. And the prince who has relied solely on their words, without making other preparations, is ruined; for the friendship which is gained by purchase and not through grandeur and nobility of spirit is bought but not secured, and at a pinch is not to be expended in your service. And men have less scruple in offending one who makes himself loved than one who makes himself feared; for love is held by a chain of obligation which, men being selfish, is broken whenever it serves their purpose; but fear is maintained by a dread of punishment which never fails.

Still, a prince should make himself feared in such a way that if he does not gain love, he at any rate avoids hatred; for fear and the absence of hatred may well go together, and will be always attained by one who abstains from interfering with the property of his citizens and subjects or with their women. And when he is obliged to take the life of anyone, let him do so when there is proper justification and manifest reason for it; but above all he must abstain from taking the property of others, for men forget more easily the death of their father than the loss of their patrimony. Then also pretexts for seizing property are never wanting, and one who begins to live by rapine will always find some reason for taking the goods of others, whereas causes for taking life are rarer and more fleeting.

But when the prince is with his army and has a large number of soldiers under his control, then it is extremely necessary that he should not mind being thought cruel; for without this reputation he could not keep an army united or disposed to any duty. Among the noteworthy actions of Hannibal is numbered this, that although he had an enormous army, composed of men of all nations and fighting in foreign countries, there never arose any dissension either among them or against the prince, either in good fortune or in bad. This could not be due to anything but his inhuman cruelty, which together with his infinite other virtues, made him always venerated and terrible in the sight of his soldiers, and without it his other virtues would not have sufficed to produce that effect. Thoughtless writers admire on the one hand his actions, and on the other blame the principal cause of them.

And that it is true that his other virtues would not have sufficed may be seen from the case of Scipio (famous not only in regard to his own times, but all times of which memory remains), whose armies rebelled against him in Spain, which arose from nothing but his excessive kindness, which allowed more licence to the soldiers than was consonant with military discipline. He was reproached with this in the senate by Fabius Maximus, who called him a corrupter of the Roman militia. Locri having been destroyed by one of Scipio's officers was not revenged by him, nor was the insolence of that officer punished, simply by reason of his easy nature; so much so, that some one wishing to excuse him in the senate, said that there were many men who knew rather how not to err, than how to correct the errors of others. This disposition would in time have tarnished the fame and glory of Scipio had he persevered in it under the empire, but living under the rule of the senate this harmful quality was not only concealed but became a glory to him.

I conclude, therefore, with regard to being feared and loved, that men love at their own free will, but fear at the will of the prince, and that a wise prince must rely on what is in his power and not on what is in the power of others, and he must only contrive to avoid incurring hatred, as has been explained.

Suggestions for Discussion

1. How does Machiavelli show that Cesare Borgia, known for his cruelty, was more merciful than the people of Florence?
2. Explain the use of the quotation from Virgil.
3. Explain Machiavelli's argument that the prince cannot rely on the love of his subjects.
4. What attitudes does Machiavelli express when he says that "men forget more easily the death of their father than the loss of their patrimony"?
5. Compare and contrast the actions of Scipio and Hannibal. How does Machiavelli explain their actions to prove his point about the need of the prince to inspire fear?

Suggestion for Writing

Write an essay in which you comment on the ideas in this selection which may be brilliant but not admirable. What aspects of life does the author ignore? Why? Why does this selection not express the concern for freedom and human dignity that characterizes most of the selections in this section?

MARTIN LUTHER KING, JR.

Letter from Birmingham Jail

Martin Luther King, Jr. (1929–1968), nearly thirty years after his death by assassination in Memphis, remains the most charismatic leader of the civil rights movement of the 1950s and 1960s. He led sit-ins and demonstrations throughout the South and was founder and president of the Southern Christian Leadership Conference, leader of the 1963 March on Washington, as well as pastor of a large Baptist congregation in Atlanta. King followed the principles of Gandhi and Thoreau in all of his public actions and writings. In 1964 he received the Nobel Peace Prize. His writings include *Strength to Love* (1963) and *Conscience for Change* (1967). The occasion for "Letter from Birmingham Jail" was provided by a public statement by eight Alabama clergymen calling on civil rights leaders to abandon the public demonstrations in Birmingham and press their claims for justice in the courts. The letter, revised and published in *Why We Can't Wait* (1964), is printed here in its original form. King began to write it on the margins of the newspaper in which the public statement by the eight Alabama clergymen appeared. That statement is also printed here.

Public Statement by Eight Alabama Clergymen

(April 12, 1963)

We the undersigned clergymen are among those who, in January, issued "An Appeal for Law and Order and Common Sense," in dealing with racial problems in Alabama. We expressed understanding that honest convictions in racial matters could properly be pursued in the courts, but urged that decisions of those courts should in the meantime be peacefully obeyed.

Since that time there had been some evidence of increased forbearance and a willingness to face facts. Responsible citizens have undertaken to work on various problems which cause racial friction and unrest. In Birmingham, recent public events have given indication that we all have opportunity for a new constructive and realistic approach to racial problems.

However, we are now confronted by a series of demonstrations by some of our Negro citizens, directed and led in part by outsiders. We recognize the natural impatience of people who feel that their hopes are slow in being realized. But we are convinced that these demonstrations are unwise and untimely.

We agree rather with certain local Negro leadership which has called for honest and open negotiation of racial issues in our area. And we believe this kind of facing of issues can best be accomplished by citizens of our own metropolitan area, white and Negro, meeting with their knowledge and experience of the local situation. All of us need to face that responsibility and find proper channels for its accomplishment.

Just as we formerly pointed out that "hatred and violence have no sanction in our religious and political traditions," we also point out that such actions as incite to hatred and violence, however technically peaceful those actions may be, have not contributed to the resolution of our local problems. We do not believe that these days of new hope are days when extreme measures are justified in Birmingham.

We commend the community as a whole, and the local news media and law enforcement officials in particular, on the calm manner in which these demonstrations have been handled. We urge the public to continue to show restraint should the demonstrations continue, and the law enforcement officials to remain calm and continue to protect our city from violence.

We further strongly urge our own Negro community to withdraw support from these demonstrations, and to unite locally in working peacefully for a better Birmingham. When rights are consistently denied, a cause should be pressed in the courts and in negotiations among local leaders, and not in the streets. We appeal to both our white and Negro citizenry to observe the principles of law and order and common sense.

Signed by:

C. C. J. CARPENTER, D.D., LL.D., *Bishop of Alabama*
JOSEPH A. DURICK, D.D., *Auxiliary Bishop, Diocese of Mobile, Birmingham*
RABBI MILTON L. GRAFMAN, *Temple Emanu-El, Birmingham, Alabama*
BISHOP PAUL HARDIN, *Bishop of the Alabama-West Florida Conference of the Methodist Church*
BISHOP NOLAN B. HARMON, *Bishop of the North Alabama Conference of the Methodist Church*
GEORGE M. MURRAY, D.D., LL.D., *Bishop Coadjutor, Episcopal Diocese of Alabama*
EDWARD V. RAMAGE, *Moderator, Synod of the Alabama Presbyterian Church in the United States*
EARL STALLINGS, *Pastor, First Baptist Church, Birmingham, Alabama*

Letter from Birmingham Jail

MARTIN LUTHER KING, JR.
Birmingham City Jail
April 16, 1963

Bishop C. C. J. Carpenter
Bishop Joseph A. Durick
Rabbi Milton L. Grafman
Bishop Paul Hardin
Bishop Nolan B. Harmon
The Rev. George M. Murray
The Rev. Edward V. Ramage
The Rev. Earl Stallings

My dear Fellow Clergymen,

While confined here in the Birmingham City Jail, I came across your recent statement calling our present activities "unwise and untimely." Seldom, if ever, do I pause to answer criticism of my work and ideas. If I sought to answer all of the criticisms that cross my desk, my secretaries would be engaged in little else in the course of the day and I would have no time for constructive work. But since I feel that you are men of genuine good will and your criticisms are sincerely set forth, I would like to answer your statement in what I hope will be patient and reasonable terms.

I think I should give the reason for my being in Birmingham, since you have been influenced by the argument of "outsiders coming in." I have the honor of serving as president of the Southern Christian Leadership Conference, an organization operating in every Southern state with headquarters in Atlanta, Georgia. We have some eighty-five affiliate organizations all across the South—one being the Alabama Christian Movement for Human Rights. Whenever necessary and possible we share staff, educational, and financial resources with our affiliates. Several months ago our local affiliate here in Birmingham invited us to be on call to engage in a nonviolent direct action program if such were deemed necessary. We readily consented and when the hour came we lived up to our promises. So I am here, along with several members of my staff, because we were invited here. I am here because I have basic organizational ties here. Beyond this, I am in Birmingham because injustice is here. Just as the eighth century prophets left their little villages and carried their "thus saith the Lord" far beyond the boundaries of their home town, and just as the Apostle Paul left his little village of Tarsus and carried the gospel of Jesus Christ to practically every hamlet and city of the Graeco-Roman world, I too am compelled to carry the gospel of freedom beyond my particular home town. Like Paul, I must constantly respond to the Macedonian call for aid.

Moreover, I am cognizant of the interrelatedness of all communities and states. I cannot sit idly by in Atlanta and not be concerned about what happens in Birmingham. Injustice anywhere is a threat to justice everywhere. We are caught in an inescapable network of mutuality tied in a single garment of destiny. Whatever affects one directly affects all indirectly. Never again can we afford to live with the narrow, provincial "outside agitator" idea. Anyone who lives inside the United States can never be considered an outsider anywhere in this country.

You deplore the demonstrations that are presently taking place in Birmingham. But I am sorry that your statement did not express a similar concern for the conditions that brought the demonstrations into being. I am sure that each of you would want to go beyond the superficial social analyst who looks merely at effects, and does not grapple with underlying causes. I would not hesitate to say that it is unfortunate that so-called demonstrations are taking place in Birmingham at this time, but I would say in more emphatic terms that it is even more unfortunate that the white power structure of this city left the Negro community with no other alternative.

In any nonviolent campaign there are four basic steps: (1) collection of the facts to determine whether injustices are alive; (2) negotiation; (3) self-purification; and (4) direct action. We have gone through all of these steps in Birmingham. There can be no gainsaying of the fact that racial injustice engulfs this community. Birmingham is probably the most thoroughly segregated city in the United States. Its ugly record of police brutality is known in every section of this country. Its unjust treatment of Negroes in the courts is a notorious reality. There have been more unsolved bombings of Negro homes and churches in Birmingham than any city in this nation. These are the hard, brutal, and unbelievable facts. On the basis of these conditions Negro leaders sought to negotiate with the city fathers. But the political leaders consistently refused to engage in good faith negotiation.

Then came the opportunity last September to talk with some of the leaders of the economic community. In these negotiating sessions certain promises were made by the merchants—such as the promise to remove the humiliating racial signs from the stores. On the basis of these promises Rev. Shuttlesworth and the leaders of the Alabama Christian Movement for Human Rights agreed to call a moratorium on any type of demonstrations. As the weeks and months unfolded we realized that we were the victims of a broken promise. The signs remained. As in so many experiences of the past we were confronted with blasted hopes, and the dark shadow of a deep disappointment settled upon us. So we had no alternative except that of preparing for direct action, whereby we would present our very bodies as a means of laying our case before the conscience of the local and national community. We were not unmindful of the difficulties involved. So we decided to go through a process of self-purification. We started having workshops on nonviolence and repeatedly asked ourselves the questions, "Are you able to accept blows without retaliating?" "Are you able to endure the ordeals of jail?"

We decided to set our direct action program around the Easter season, realizing that with the exception of Christmas, this was the largest shopping period of the year. Knowing that a strong economic withdrawal program would be the by-product of direct action, we felt that this was the best time to bring pressure on the merchants for the needed changes. Then it occurred to us that the March election was ahead, and so we speedily decided to postpone action until after election day. When we discovered that Mr. Connor was in the run-off, we decided again to postpone so that the demonstrations could not be used to cloud the issues. At this time we agreed to begin our nonviolent witness the day after the run-off.

This reveals that we did not move irresponsibly into direct action. We too wanted to see Mr. Connor defeated; so we went through postponement after postponement to aid in this community need. After this we felt that direct action could be delayed no longer.

You may well ask, "Why direct action? Why sit-ins, marches, etc.? Isn't negotiation a better path?" You are exactly right in your call for negotiation. Indeed, this is the purpose of direct action. Nonviolent direct action seeks to create such a crisis and establish such creative tension that a community that has constantly refused to negotiate is forced to confront the issue. It seeks so to dramatize the issue that it can no longer be ignored. I just referred to the creation of tension as a part of the work of the nonviolent resister. This may sound rather shocking. But I must confess that I am not afraid of the word tension. I have earnestly worked and preached against violent tension, but there is a type of constructive nonviolent tension that is necessary for growth. Just as Socrates felt that it was necessary to create a tension in the mind so that individuals could rise from the bondage of myths and half-truths to the unfettered realm of creative analysis and objective appraisal, we must see the need of having nonviolent gadflies to create the kind of tension in society that will help men rise from the dark depths of prejudice and racism to the majestic heights of understanding and brotherhood. So the purpose of the direct action is to create a situation so crisis-packed that it will inevitably open the door to negotiation. We, therefore, concur with you in your call for negotiation. Too long has our beloved Southland been bogged down in the tragic attempt to live in monologue rather than dialogue.

One of the basic points in your statement is that our acts are untimely. Some have asked, "Why didn't you give the new administration time to act?" The only answer that I can give to this inquiry is that the new administration must be prodded about as much as the outgoing one before it acts. We will be sadly mistaken if we feel that the election of Mr. Boutwell will bring the millennium to Birmingham. While Mr. Boutwell is much more articulate and gentle than Mr. Connor, they are both segregationists dedicated to the task of maintaining the status quo. The hope I see in Mr. Boutwell is that he will be reasonable enough to see the futility of massive resistance to desegregation. But he will not see this without pressure from the devotees of civil rights. My friends, I must say to you that we have not made a single gain in civil rights without determined legal and nonviolent pressure. History is the long and tragic story of the fact that privileged groups seldom give up their privileges voluntarily. Individuals may see the moral light and voluntarily give up their unjust posture; but as Reinhold Niebuhr has reminded us, groups are more immoral than individuals.

We know through painful experience that freedom is never voluntarily given by the oppressor; it must be demanded by the oppressed. Frankly I have never yet engaged in a direct action movement that was "well timed," according to the timetable of those who have not suffered unduly from the disease of segregation. For years now I have heard the word "Wait!" It rings in the ear of every Negro with a piercing familiarity. This "wait" has almost always meant "never." It has been a tranquilizing thalidomide, relieving the emotional stress for a moment, only to give birth to an ill-formed infant of frustration. We must come to see with the distinguished jurist of yesterday that "justice too long delayed is justice denied." We have waited for more than three hundred and forty years for our constitutional and God-given rights. The nations of Asia and Africa are moving with jet-like speed toward the goal of political independence, and we still creep at horse and buggy pace toward the gaining of a cup of coffee at a lunch counter.

I guess it is easy for those who have never felt the stinging darts of segregation to say wait. But when you have seen vicious mobs lynch your mothers and fathers at will and drown your sisters and brothers at whim; when you have seen hate filled policemen curse, kick, brutalize, and even kill your black brothers and sisters with impunity; when you see the vast majority of your twenty million Negro brothers smothering in an air-tight cage of poverty in the midst of an affluent society; when you suddenly find your tongue twisted and your speech stammering as you seek to explain to your six-year-old daughter why she can't go to the public amusement park that has just been advertised on television, and see tears welling up in her little eyes when she is told that Funtown is closed to colored children, and see the depressing clouds of inferiority begin to form in her little mental sky, and see her begin to distort her little personality by unconsciously developing a bitterness toward white people; when you have to concoct an answer for a five-year-old son asking in agonizing pathos: "Daddy, why do white people treat colored people so mean?"; when you take a cross country drive and find it necessary to sleep night after night in the uncomfortable corners of your automobile because no motel will accept you; when you are humiliated day in and day out by nagging signs reading "white" men and "colored"; when your first name becomes "nigger" and your middle name becomes "boy" (however old you are) and your last name becomes "John," and when your wife and mother are never given the respected title "Mrs."; when you are harried by day and haunted by night by the fact that you are a Negro, living constantly at tip-toe stance never quite knowing what to expect next, and plagued with inner fears and outer resentments; when you are forever fighting a degenerating sense of "nobodiness";—then you will understand why we find it difficult to wait. There comes a time when the cup of endurance runs over, and men are no longer willing to be plunged into an abyss of injustice where they experience the bleakness of corroding despair. I hope, sirs, you can understand our legitimate and unavoidable impatience.

You express a great deal of anxiety over our willingness to break laws. This is certainly a legitimate concern. Since we so diligently urge people to obey the Supreme Court's decision of 1954 outlawing segregation in the public schools, it is rather strange and paradoxical to find us consciously breaking laws. One may well ask, "How can you advocate breaking some laws and obeying others?" The answer is found in the fact that there are two types of laws. There are *just* laws and there are *unjust* laws. I would be the first to advocate obeying just laws. One has not only a legal but moral responsibility to obey just laws. Conversely, one has a moral responsibility to disobey unjust laws. I would agree with Saint Augustine that "An unjust law is no law at all."

Now what is the difference between the two? How does one determine when a law is just or unjust? A just law is a man-made code that squares with the moral law or the law of God. An unjust law is a code that is out of harmony with the moral law. To put it in the terms of Saint Thomas Aquinas, an unjust law is a human law that is not rooted in eternal and natural law. Any law that uplifts human personality is just. Any law that degrades human personality is unjust. All segregation statutes are unjust because segregation distorts the soul and damages the personality. It gives the segregator a false sense of superiority and the segregated a false sense of inferiority. To use the words of Martin Buber, the great Jewish philosopher, segregation substitutes an "I-it" relationship for the "I-thou" relationship, and ends up relegating persons to the status of things. So segregation is not only politically, economically, and sociologically unsound, but it is morally wrong and sinful. Paul Tillich has said that sin is separation. Isn't segregation an existential expression of man's tragic separation, an expression of his awful estrangement, his terrible sinfulness? So I can urge men to obey the 1954 decision of the Supreme Court because it is morally right, and I can urge them to disobey segregation ordinances because they are morally wrong.

Let us turn to a more concrete example of just and unjust laws. An unjust law is a code that a majority inflicts on a minority that is not binding on itself. This is *difference* made legal. On the other hand a just law is a code that a majority compels a minority to follow that it is willing to follow itself. This is *sameness* made legal.

Let me give another explanation. An unjust law is a code inflicted upon a minority which that minority had no part in enacting or creating because they did not have the unhampered right to vote. Who can say the legislature of Alabama which set up the segregation laws was democratically elected? Throughout the state of Alabama all types of conniving methods are used to prevent Negroes from becoming registered voters and there are some counties without a single Negro registered to vote despite the fact that the Negro constitutes a majority of the population. Can any law set up in such a state be considered democratically structured?

These are just a few examples of unjust and just laws. There are some instances when a law is just on its face but unjust in its application. For instance, I was arrested Friday on a charge of parading without a permit. Now there is nothing wrong with an ordinance which requires a permit for a parade, but when the ordinance is used to preserve segregation and to deny citizens the First Amendment privilege of peaceful assembly and peaceful protest, then it becomes unjust.

I hope you can see the distinction I am trying to point out. In no sense do I advocate evading or defying the law as the rabid segregationist would do. This would lead to anarchy. One who breaks an unjust law must do it *openly, lovingly* (not hatefully as the white mothers did in New Orleans when they were seen on television screaming "nigger, nigger, nigger") and with a willingness to accept the penalty. I submit that an individual who breaks a law that conscience tells him is unjust, and willingly accepts the penalty by staying in jail to arouse the conscience of the community over its injustice, is in reality expressing the very highest respect for law.

Of course there is nothing new about this kind of civil disobedience. It was seen sublimely in the refusal of Shadrach, Meshach, and Abednego to obey the laws of Nebuchadnezzar because a higher moral law was involved. It was practiced superbly by the early Christians who were willing to face hungry lions and the excruciating pain of chopping blocks, before submitting to certain unjust laws of the Roman Empire. To a degree academic freedom is a reality today because Socrates practiced civil disobedience.

We can never forget that everything Hitler did in Germany was "legal" and everything the Hungarian freedom fighters did in Hungary was "illegal." It was "illegal" to aid and comfort a Jew in Hitler's Germany. But I am sure that, if I had lived in Germany during that time, I would have aided and comforted my Jewish brothers even though it was illegal. If I lived in a communist country today where certain principles dear to the Christian faith are suppressed, I believe I would openly advocate disobeying those antireligious laws.

I must make two honest confessions to you, my Christian and Jewish brothers. First I must confess that over the last few years I have been gravely disappointed with the white moderate. I have almost reached the regrettable conclusion that the Negroes' great stumbling block in the stride toward freedom is not the White Citizens' "Counciler" or the Ku Klux Klanner, but the white moderate who is more devoted to "order" than to justice; who prefers a negative peace which is the absence of tension to a positive peace which is the presence of justice; who constantly says "I agree with you in the goal you seek, but I can't agree with your methods of direct action"; who paternalistically feels that he can set the timetable for another man's freedom; who lives by the myth of time and who constantly advises the Negro to wait until a "more convenient season." Shallow understanding from people of good will is more frustrating than absolute misunderstanding from people of ill will. Lukewarm acceptance is much more bewildering than outright rejection.

I had hoped that the white moderate would understand that law and order exist for the purpose of establishing justice, and that when they fail to do this they become the dangerously structured dams that block the flow of social progress. I had hoped that the white moderate would understand that the present tension in the South is merely a necessary phase of the transition from an obnoxious negative peace, where the Negro passively accepted his unjust plight, to a substance-filled positive peace, where all men will respect the dignity and worth of human personality. Actually, we who engage in nonviolent direct action are not the creators of tension. We merely bring to the surface the hidden tension that is already alive. We bring it out in the open where it can be seen and dealt with. Like a boil that can never be cured as long as it is covered up but must be opened with all its pus-flowing ugliness to the natural medicines of air and light, injustice must likewise be exposed, with all of the tension its exposing creates, to the light of human conscience and the air of national opinion before it can be cured.

In your statement you asserted that our actions, even though peaceful, must be condemned because they precipitate violence. But can this assertion be logically made? Isn't this like condemning the robbed man because his possession of money precipitated the evil act of robbery? Isn't this like condemning Socrates because his unswerving commitment to truth and his philosophical delvings precipitated the misguided popular mind to make him drink the hemlock? Isn't this like condemning Jesus because His unique God consciousness and never-ceasing devotion to His will precipitated the evil act of crucifixion? We must come to see, as federal courts have consistently affirmed, that it is immoral to urge an individual to withdraw his efforts to gain his basic constitutional rights because the quest precipitates violence. Society must protect the robbed and punish the robber.

I had also hoped that the white moderate would reject the myth of time. I received a letter this morning from a white brother in Texas which said: "All Christians know that the colored people will receive equal rights eventually, but is it possible that you are in too great of a religious hurry? It has taken Christianity almost 2,000 years to accomplish what it has. The teachings of Christ take time to come to earth." All that is said here grows out of a tragic misconception of time. It is the strangely irrational notion that there is something in the very flow of time that will inevitably cure all ills. Actually time is neutral. It can be used either destructively or constructively. I am coming to feel that the people of ill will have used time much more effectively than the people of good will. We will have to repent in this generation not merely for the vitriolic words and actions of the bad people, but for the appalling silence of the good people. We must come to see that human progress never rolls in on wheels of inevitability. It comes through the tireless efforts and persistent work of men willing to be co-workers with God, and without this hard work time itself becomes an ally of the forces of social stagnation.

We must use time creatively, and forever realize that the time is always ripe to do right. Now is the time to make real the promise of democracy, and transform our pending national elegy into a creative psalm of brotherhood. Now is the time to lift our national policy from the quicksand of racial injustice to the solid rock of human dignity.

You spoke of our activity in Birmingham as extreme. At first I was rather disappointed that fellow clergymen would see my nonviolent efforts as those of the extremist. I started thinking about the fact that I stand in the middle of two opposing forces in the Negro community. One is a force of complacency made up of Negroes who, as a result of long years of oppression, have been so completely drained of self-respect and a sense of "somebodiness" that they have adjusted to segregation, and of a few Negroes in the middle class who, because of a degree of academic and economic security, and because at points they profit by segregation, have unconsciously become insensitive to the problems of the masses. The other force is one of bitterness and hatred and comes perilously close to advocating violence. It is expressed in the various black nationalist groups that are springing up over the nation, the largest and best known being Elijah Muhammad's Muslim movement. This movement is nourished by the contemporary frustration over the continued existence of racial discrimination. It is made up of people who have lost faith in America, who have absolutely repudiated Christianity, and who have concluded that the white man is an incurable "devil." I have tried to stand between these two forces saying that we need not follow the "do-nothingism" of the complacent or the hatred and despair of the black nationalist. There is the more excellent way of love and nonviolent protest. I'm grateful to God that, through the Negro church, the dimension of nonviolence entered our struggle. If this philosophy had not emerged I am convinced that by now many streets of the South would be flowing with floods of blood. And I am further convinced that if our white brothers dismiss us as "rabble rousers" and "outside agitators"—those of us who are working through the channels of nonviolent direct action—and refuse to support our nonviolent efforts, millions of Negroes, out of frustration and despair, will seek solace and security in black nationalist ideologies, a development that will lead inevitably to a frightening racial nightmare.

Oppressed people cannot remain oppressed forever. The urge for freedom will eventually come. This is what has happened to the American Negro. Something within has reminded him of his birthright of freedom; something without has reminded him that he can gain it. Consciously and unconsciously, he has been swept in by what the Germans call the *Zeitgeist*, and with his black brothers of Africa, and his brown and yellow brothers of Asia, South America, and the Caribbean, he is moving with a sense of cosmic urgency toward the promised land of racial justice. Recognizing this vital urge that has engulfed the Negro community, one should readily understand public demonstrations. The Negro has many pent-up resentments and latent frustrations. He has to get them out. So let him march sometime; let him have his prayer pilgrimages to the city hall; understand why he must have sit-ins and freedom rides. If his repressed emotions do not come out in these nonviolent ways, they will come out in ominous expressions of violence. This is not a threat; it is a fact of history. So I have not said to my people, "Get rid of your discontent." But I have tried to say that this normal and healthy discontent can be channeled through the creative outlet of nonviolent direct action. Now this approach is being dismissed as extremist. I must admit that I was initially disappointed in being so categorized.

But as I continued to think about the matter I gradually gained a bit of satisfaction from being considered an extremist. Was not Jesus an extremist in love? "Love your enemies, bless them that curse you, pray for them that despitefully use you." Was not Amos an extremist for justice—"Let justice roll down like waters and righteousness like a mighty stream." Was not Paul an extremist for the gospel of Jesus Christ—"I bear in my body the marks of the Lord Jesus." Was not Martin Luther an extremist—"Here I stand; I can do none other so help me God." Was not John Bunyan an extremist—"I will stay in jail to the end of my days before I make a butchery of my conscience." Was not Abraham Lincoln an extremist—"This nation cannot survive half slave and half free." Was not Thomas Jefferson an extremist—"We hold these truths to be self evident that all men are created equal." So the question is not whether we will be extremist but what kind of extremist will we be. Will we be extremists for hate or will we be extremists for love? Will we be extremists for the preservation of injustice—or will we be extremists for the cause of justice? In that dramatic scene on Calvary's hill three men were crucified. We must never forget that all three were crucified for the same crime—the crime of extremism. Two were extremists for immorality, and thus fell below their environment. The other, Jesus Christ, was an extremist for love, truth, and goodness, and thereby rose above His environment. So, after all, maybe the South, the nation, and the world are in dire need of creative extremists.

I had hoped that the white moderate would see this. Maybe I was too optimistic. Maybe I expected too much. I guess I should have realized that few members of a race that has oppressed another race can understand or appreciate the deep groans and passionate yearnings of those that have been oppressed, and still fewer have the vision to see that injustice must be rooted out by strong, persistent, and determined action. I am thankful, however, that some of our white brothers have grasped the meaning of this social revolution and committed themselves to it. They are still all too small in quantity, but they are big in quality. Some like Ralph McGill, Lillian Smith, Harry Golden, and James Dabbs have written about our struggle in eloquent, prophetic, and understanding terms. Others have marched with us down nameless streets of the South. They have languished in filthy, roach-infested jails, suffering the abuse and brutality of angry policemen who see them as "dirty nigger lovers." They, unlike so many of their moderate brothers and sisters, have recognized the urgency of the moment and sensed the need for powerful "action" antidotes to combat the disease of segregation.

Let me rush on to mention my other disappointment. I have been so greatly disappointed with the white Church and its leadership. Of course there are some notable exceptions. I am not unmindful of the fact that each of you has taken some significant stands on this issue. I commend you, Rev. Stallings, for your Christian stand on this past Sunday, in welcoming Negroes to your worship service on a nonsegregated basis. I commend the Catholic leaders of this state for integrating Springhill College several years ago.

But despite these notable exceptions I must honestly reiterate that I have been disappointed with the Church. I do not say that as one of those negative critics who can always find something wrong with the Church. I say it as a minister of the gospel, who loves the Church; who was nurtured in its bosom; who has been sustained by its spiritual blessings and who will remain true to it as long as the cord of life shall lengthen.

I had the strange feeling when I was suddenly catapulted into the leadership of the bus protest in Montgomery several years ago that we would have the support of the white Church. I felt that the white ministers, priests, and rabbis of the South would be some of our strongest allies. Instead, some have been outright opponents, refusing to understand the freedom movement and misrepresenting its leaders; all too many others have been more cautious than courageous and have remained silent behind the anesthetizing security of stained glass windows.

In spite of my shattered dreams of the past, I came to Birmingham with the hope that the white religious leadership of the community would see the justice of our cause and, with deep moral concern, serve as the channel through which our just grievances could get to the power structure. I had hoped that each of you would understand. But again I have been disappointed.

I have heard numerous religious leaders of the South call upon their worshippers to comply with a desegregation decision because it is the law, but I have longed to hear white ministers say follow this decree because integration is morally right and the Negro is your brother. In the midst of blatant injustices inflicted upon the Negro, I have watched white churches stand on the sideline and merely mouth pious irrelevancies and sanctimonious trivialities. In the midst of a mighty struggle to rid our nation of racial and economic injustice, I have heard so many ministers say, "Those are social issues with which the Gospel has no real concern," and I have watched so many churches commit themselves to a completely otherworldly religion which made a strange distinction between body and soul, the sacred and the secular.

So here we are moving toward the exit of the twentieth century with a religious community largely adjusted to the status quo, standing as a tail light behind other community agencies rather than a headlight leading men to higher levels of justice.

I have travelled the length and breadth of Alabama, Mississippi, and all the other Southern states. On sweltering summer days and crisp autumn mornings I have looked at her beautiful churches with their spires pointing heavenward. I have beheld the impressive outlay of her massive religious education buildings. Over and over again I have found myself asking: "Who worships here? Who is their God? Where were their voices when the lips of Governor Barnett dripped with words of interposition and nullification? Where were they when Governor Wallace gave the clarion call for defiance and hatred? Where were their voices of support when tired, bruised, and weary Negro men and women decided to rise from the dark dungeons of complacency to the bright hills of creative protest?"

Yes, these questions are still in my mind. In deep disappointment, I have wept over the laxity of the Church. But be assured that my tears have been tears of love. There can be no deep disappointment where there is not deep love. Yes, I love the Church; I love her sacred walls. How could I do otherwise? I am in the rather unique position of being the son, the grandson, and the great grandson of preachers. Yes, I see the Church as the body of Christ. But, oh! How we have blemished and scarred that body through social neglect and fear of being nonconformists.

There was a time when the Church was very powerful. It was during that period when the early Christians rejoiced when they were deemed worthy to suffer for what they believed. In those days the Church was not merely a thermometer that recorded the ideas and principles of popular opinion; it was a thermostat that transformed the mores of society. Wherever the early Christians entered a town the power structure got disturbed and immediately sought to convict them for being "disturbers of the peace" and "outside agitators." But they went on with the conviction that they were a "colony of heaven" and had to obey God rather than man. They were small in number but big in commitment. They were too God-intoxicated to be "astronomically intimidated." They brought an end to such ancient evils as infanticide and gladiatorial contest.

Things are different now. The contemporary Church is so often a weak, ineffectual voice with an uncertain sound. It is so often the archsupporter of the status quo. Far from being disturbed by the presence of the Church, the power structure of the average community is consoled by the Church's silent and often vocal sanction of things as they are.

But the judgment of God is upon the Church as never before. If the Church of today does not recapture the sacrificial spirit of the early Church, it will lose its authentic ring, forfeit the loyalty of millions, and be dismissed as an irrelevant social club with no meaning for the twentieth century. I am meeting young people every day whose disappointment with the Church has risen to outright disgust.

Maybe again I have been too optimistic. Is organized religion too inextricably bound to the status quo to save our nation and the world? Maybe I must turn my faith to the inner spiritual Church, the church within the Church, as the true *ecclesia* and the hope of the world. But again I am thankful to God that some noble souls from the ranks of organized religion have broken loose from the paralyzing chains of conformity and joined us as active partners in the struggle for freedom. They have left their secure congregations and walked the streets of Albany, Georgia, with us. They have gone through the highways of the South on torturous rides for freedom. Yes, they have gone to jail with us. Some have been kicked out of their churches and lost the support of their bishops and fellow ministers. But they have gone with the faith that right defeated is stronger than evil triumphant. These men have been the leaven in the lump of the race. Their witness has been the spiritual salt that has preserved the true meaning of the Gospel in these troubled times. They have carved a tunnel of hope through the dark mountain of disappointment.

I hope the Church as a whole will meet the challenge of this decisive hour. But even if the Church does not come to the aid of justice, I have no despair about the future. I have no fear about the outcome of our struggle in Birmingham, even if our motives are presently misunderstood. We will reach the goal of freedom in Birmingham and all over the nation, because the goal of America is freedom. Abused and scorned though we may be, our destiny is tied up with the destiny of America. Before the pilgrims landed at Plymouth, we were here. Before the pen of Jefferson etched across the pages of history the majestic words of the Declaration of Independence, we were here. For more than two centuries our foreparents labored in this country without wages; they made cotton "king"; and they built the homes of their masters in the midst of brutal injustice and shameful humiliation—and yet out of a bottomless vitality they continued to thrive and develop. If the inexpressible cruelties of slavery could not stop us, the opposition we now face will surely fail. We will win our freedom because the sacred heritage of our nation and the eternal will of God are embodied in our echoing demands.

I must close now. But before closing I am impelled to mention one other point in your statement that troubled me profoundly. You warmly commended the Birmingham police force for keeping "order" and "preventing violence." I don't believe you would have so warmly commended the police force if you had seen its angry violent dogs literally biting six unarmed, nonviolent Negroes. I don't believe you would so quickly commend the policemen if you would observe their ugly and inhuman treatment of Negroes here in the city jail; if you would watch them push and curse old Negro women and young Negro girls; if you would see them slap and kick old Negro men and young Negro boys; if you will observe them, as they did on two occasions, refuse to give us food because we wanted to sing our grace together. I'm sorry that I can't join you in your praise for the police department.

It is true that they have been rather disciplined in their public handling of the demonstrators. In this sense they have been rather publicly "nonviolent." But for what purpose? To preserve the evil system of segregation. Over the last few years I have consistently preached that nonviolence demands that the means we use must be as pure as the ends we seek. So I have tried to make it clear that it is wrong to use immoral means to attain moral ends. But now I must affirm that it is just as wrong, or even more so, to use moral means to preserve immoral ends. Maybe Mr. Connor and his policemen have been rather publicly nonviolent, as Chief Pritchett was in Albany, Georgia, but they have used the moral means of nonviolence to maintain the immoral end of flagrant racial injustice. T. S. Eliot has said that there is no greater treason than to do the right deed for the wrong reason.

I wish you had commended the Negro sit-inners and demonstrators of Birmingham for their sublime courage, their willingness to suffer, and their amazing discipline in the midst of the most inhuman provocation. One day the South will recognize its real heroes. They will be the James Merediths, courageously and with a majestic sense of purpose, facing jeering and hostile mobs and the agonizing loneliness that characterizes the life of the pioneer. They will be old, oppressed, battered Negro women, symbolized in a seventy-two year old woman of Montgomery, Alabama, who rose up with a sense of dignity and with her people decided not to ride the segregated buses, and responded to one who inquired about her tiredness with ungrammatical profundity: "My feets is tired, but my soul is rested." They will be young high school and college students, young ministers of the gospel and a host of the elders, courageously and nonviolently sitting in at lunch counters and willingly going to jail for conscience sake. One day the South will know that when these disinherited children of God sat down at lunch counters they were in reality standing up for the best in the American dream and the most sacred values in our Judeo-Christian heritage, and thus carrying our whole nation back to great wells of democracy which were dug deep by the founding fathers in the formulation of the Constitution and the Declaration of Independence.

Never before have I written a letter this long (or should I say a book?). I'm afraid that it is much too long to take your precious time. I can assure you that it would have been much shorter if I had been writing from a comfortable desk, but what else is there to do when you are alone for days in the dull monotony of a narrow jail cell other than write long letters, think strange thoughts, and pray long prayers?

If I have said anything in this letter that is an overstatement of the truth and is indicative of an unreasonable impatience, I beg you to forgive me. If I have said anything in this letter that is an understatement of the truth and is indicative of my having a patience that makes me patient with anything less than brotherhood, I beg God to forgive me.

I hope this letter finds you strong in the faith. I also hope that circumstances will soon make it possible for me to meet each of you, not as an integrationist or a civil rights leader, but as a fellow clergyman and a Christian brother. Let us all hope that the dark clouds of racial prejudice will soon pass away and the deep fog of misunderstanding will be lifted from our fear-drenched communities and in some not too distant tomorrow the radiant stars of love and brotherhood will shine over our great nation with all of their scintillating beauty.

Yours for the cause of
Peace and Brotherhood
MARTIN LUTHER KING, JR.

Suggestions for Discussion

1. What is the rhetorical tone of King's letter? How does he achieve that tone? List and explain a half-dozen examples.
2. How does King deal with the eight clergymen's accusation that the demonstrators are "outsiders"?
3. In the letter King refers to a number of enemies of integration; for example, Eugene "Bull" Connor, Albert Bantwell, Ross R. Barnett, George C. Wallace, and Laurie Pritchett. Identify these people and explain their role in the fight against integration.
4. How does King answer the charge that his actions, though peaceful, are dangerous because they lead to violence?
5. What are King's objections to the white churches' response to the fight for integration? What are his objections to white moderates?

Suggestions for Writing

1. Write an essay in which you comment on King's statement: "I submit that an individual who breaks a law that conscience tells him is unjust, and willingly accepts the penalty by staying in jail to arouse the conscience of the community over its injustice, is in reality expressing the very highest respect for the law."
2. Write a paper in which you explain King's use of the examples of Nazi Germany and Communist-controlled Hungary to defend his fight for civil rights.
3. Write a paper in which you agree or disagree with King's assessment of white moderates. Give explicit examples to support your position.
4. King calls his movement a viable alternative to black complacency, or acceptance of the status quo, and to the militant opposition of the black nationalists. Write a paper evaluating his assessment.
5. Write a paper in which you evaluate the civil rights movement of King's day in terms of the present. To what extent did his movement succeed? Fail?

WILLIAM FAULKNER

Nobel Prize Award Speech

William Faulkner (1897–1962) lived most of his life in Oxford, Mississippi. After a year at the university of his native state, he joined the Royal Canadian Air Force, eager to participate in World War I. His novels set in his imaginary Yoknapatawpha County include *The Sound and the Fury* (1929), *Light in August* (1932), *Absalom, Absalom!* (1936), and *The Hamlet* (1940). In his speech accepting the Nobel Prize for Literature in 1949, Faulkner states his belief in the significance and dignity of humankind and the need for the writer to reassert the universal truths of "love and honor and pity and pride and compassion and sacrifice."

I feel that this award was not made to me as a man but to my work—a life's work in the agony and sweat of the human spirit, not for glory and least of all for profit, but to create out of the materials of the human spirit something which did not exist before. So this award is only mine in trust. It will not be difficult to find a dedication for the money part of it commensurate with the purpose and significance of its origin. But I would like to do the same with the acclaim too, by using this moment as a pinnacle from which I might be listened to by the young men and women already dedicated to the same anguish and travail, among whom is already that one who will some day stand here where I am standing.

Our tragedy today is a general and universal physical fear so long sustained by now that we can even bear it. There are no longer problems of the spirit. There is only the question: When will I be blown up? Because of this, the young man or woman writing today has forgotten the problems of the human heart in conflict with itself which alone can make good writing because only that is worth writing about, worth the agony and the sweat.

He must learn them again. He must teach himself that the basest of all things is to be afraid; and, teaching himself that, forget it forever, leaving no room in his workshop for anything but the old verities and truths of the heart, the old universal truths lacking which any story is ephemeral and doomed—love and honor and pity and pride and compassion and sacrifice. Until he does so, he labors under a curse. He writes not of love but of lust, of defeats in which nobody loses anything of value, of victories without hope and, worst of all, without pity or compassion. His griefs grieve on no universal bones, leaving no scars. He writes not of the heart but of the glands.

Until he relearns these things, he will write as though he stood alone and watched the end of man. I decline to accept the end of man. It is easy enough to say that man is immortal simply because he will endure; that when the last ding-dong of doom has clanged and faded from the last worthless rock hanging tideless in the last red and dying evening, that even then there will still be one more sound: that of his puny inexhaustible voice, still talking. I refuse to accept this. I believe that man will not merely endure: he will prevail. He is immortal, not because he alone among creatures has an inexhaustible voice but because he has a soul, a spirit capable of compassion and sacrifice and endurance. The poet's, the writer's, duty is to write about these things. It is his privilege to help man endure by lifting his heart, by reminding him of the courage and honor and hope and pride and compassion and pity and sacrifice which have been the glory of his past. The poet's voice need not merely be the record of man, it can be one of the props, the pillars to help him endure and prevail.

Suggestions for Discussion

1. Do you agree with Faulkner's optimistic statement about man's ability to "endure and prevail"? Explain.
2. Do you think Faulkner's speech too brief for a major occasion such as the Nobel Prize Awards? Explain your answer.
3. Discuss whether or not man still lives in that state of general and universal physical fear to which Faulkner refers.

Suggestions for Writing

1. Summarize your own opinions about man's ability to survive the challenges of the next hundred years.
2. Prepare a formal speech in which you accept an international prize for literature or some other accomplishment.

HARRIET JACOBS

The Women

Harriet Jacobs (1818–1896) describes the effects of Nat Turner's Rebellion in *Incidents in the Life of a Slave Girl* (1861). The following selection, from *Black Slave Narratives,* pinpoints with simple clarity the moral dilemmas that face a young female slave caught between her owner's desires and his wife's jealousy.

I would ten thousand times rather that my children should be the half-starved paupers of Ireland than to be the most pampered among the slaves of America. I would rather drudge out my life on a cotton plantation, till the grave opened to give me rest, than to live with an unprincipled master and a jealous mistress. The felon's home in a penitentiary is preferable. He may repent, and turn from the error of his ways, and so find peace, but it is not so with a favorite slave. She is not allowed to have any pride of character. It is deemed a crime in her to wish to be virtuous.

Mrs. Flint possessed the key to her husband's character before I was born. She might have used this knowledge to counsel and to screen the young and the innocent among her slaves; but for them she had no sympathy. They were the objects of her constant suspicion and malevolence. She watched her husband with unceasing vigilance; but he was well practiced in means to evade it. What he could not find opportunity to say in words he manifested in signs. He invented more than were ever thought of in a deaf and dumb asylum. I let them pass, as if I did not understand what he meant; and many were the curses and threats bestowed on me for my stupidity. One day he caught me teaching myself to write. He frowned, as if he was not well pleased; but I suppose he came to the conclusion that such an accomplishment might help to advance his favorite scheme. Before long, notes were often slipped into my hand. I would return them, saying, "I can't read them, sir." "Can't you?" he replied; "then I must read them to you." He always finished the reading by asking, "Do you understand?" Sometimes he would complain of the heat of the tea room, and order his supper to be placed on a small table in the piazza. He would seat himself there with a well-satisfied smile, and tell me to stand by and brush away the flies. He would eat very slowly, pausing between the mouthfuls. These intervals were employed in describing the happiness I was so foolishly throwing away, and in threatening me with the penalty that finally awaited my stubborn disobedience. He boasted much of the forbearance he had exercised toward me, and reminded me that there was a limit to his patience. When I succeeded in avoiding opportunities for him to talk to me at home, I was ordered to come to his office, to do some errand. When there, I was obliged to stand and listen to such language as he saw fit to address to me. Sometimes I so openly expressed my contempt for him that he would become violently enraged, and I wondered why he did not strike me. Circumstanced as he was, he probably thought it was better policy to be forebearing. But the state of things grew worse and worse daily. In desperation I told him that I must and would apply to my grandmother for protection. He threatened me with death, and worse than death, if I made my complaint to her. Strange to say, I did not despair. I was naturally of a buoyant disposition, and always I had a hope of somehow getting out of his clutches. Like many a poor, simple slave before me, I trusted that some threads of joy would yet be woven into my dark destiny.

I had entered my sixteenth year, and every day it became more apparent that my presence was intolerable to Mrs. Flint. Angry words frequently passed between her and her husband. He had never punished me himself, and he would not allow anybody else to punish me. In that respect, she was never satisfied; but, in her angry moods, no terms were too vile for her to bestow upon me. Yet I, whom she detested so bitterly, had far more pity for her than he had, whose duty it was to make her life happy. I never wronged her, or wished to wrong her; and one word of kindness from her would have brought me to her feet.

After repeated quarrels between the doctor and his wife, he announced his intention to take his youngest daughter, then four years old, to sleep in his apartment. It was necessary that a servant should sleep in the same room, to be on hand if the child stirred. I was selected for that office, and informed for what purpose that arrangement had been made. By managing to keep within sight of people, as much as possible, during the daytime, I had hitherto succeeded in eluding my master, though a razor was often held to my throat to force me to change this line of policy. At night I slept by the side of my great aunt, where I felt safe. He was too prudent to come into her room. She was an old woman, and had been in the family many years. Moreover, as a married man, and a professional man, he deemed it necessary to save appearances in some degree. But he resolved to remove the obstacle in the way of his scheme; and he thought he had planned it so that he should evade suspicion. He was well aware how much I prized my refuge by the side of my old aunt, and he determined to dispossess me of it. The first night the doctor had the little child in his room alone. The next morning, I was ordered to take my station as nurse the following night. A kind Providence interposed in my favor. During the day Mrs. Flint heard of this new arrangement, and a storm followed. I rejoiced to hear it rage.

After a while my mistress sent for me to come to her room. Her first question was, "Did you know you were to sleep in the doctor's room?"

"Yes, ma'am."

"Who told you?"

"My master."

"Will you answer truly all the questions I ask?"

"Yes, ma'am."

"Tell me, then, as you hope to be forgiven, are you innocent of what I have accused you?"

"I am."

She handed me a Bible, and said, "Lay your hand on your heart, kiss this holy book, and swear before God that you tell me the truth."

I took the oath she required, and I did it with a clear conscience.

"You have taken God's holy word to testify your innocence," said she. "If you have deceived me, beware! Now take this stool, sit down, look me directly in the face, and tell me all that has passed between your master and you."

I did as she ordered. As I went on with my account her color changed frequently, she wept, and sometimes groaned. She spoke in tones so sad, that I was touched by her grief. The tears came to my eyes; but I was soon convinced that her emotions arose from anger and wounded pride. She felt that her marriage vows were desecrated, her dignity insulted; but she had no compassion for the poor victim of her husband's perfidy. She pitied herself as a martyr; but she was incapable of feeling for the condition of shame and misery in which her unfortunate, helpless slave was placed.

Yet perhaps she had some touch of feeling for me; for when the conference was ended, she spoke kindly, and promised to protect me. I should have been much comforted by this assurance if I could have had confidence in it; but my experiences in slavery had filled me with distrust. She was not a very refined woman, and had not much control over her passions. I was an object of her jealousy, and, consequently, of her hatred; and I knew I could not expect kindness or confidence from her under the circumstances in which I was placed. I could not blame her. Slaveholders' wives feel as other women would under similar circumstances. The fire of her temper kindled from small sparks, and now the flame became so intense that the doctor was obliged to give up his intended arrangement.

I knew I had ignited the torch, and I expected to suffer for it afterward; but I felt too thankful to my mistress for the timely aid she rendered me to care much about that. She now took me to sleep in a room adjoining her own. There I was an object of her especial care, though not of her especial comfort, for she spent many a sleepless night to watch over me. Sometimes I woke up, and found her bending over me. At other times she whispered in my ear, as though it was her husband who was speaking to me, and listened to hear what I would answer. If she startled me, on such occasions, she would glide stealthily away; and the next morning she would tell me I had been talking in my sleep, and ask who I was talking to. At last I began to be fearful for my life. It had been often threatened; and you can imagine, better than I can describe, what an unpleasant sensation it must produce to wake up in the dead of night and find a jealous woman bending over you. Terrible as this experience was, I had fears that it would give place to one more terrible.

My mistress grew weary of her vigils; they did not prove satisfactory. She changed her tactics. She now tried the trick of accusing my master of crime, in my presence, and gave my name as the author of the accusation. To my utter astonishment, he replied, "I don't believe it; but if she did acknowledge it, you tortured her into exposing me." Tortured into exposing him! Truly, Satan had no difficulty in distinguishing the color of his soul! I understood his object in making this false representation. It was to show me that I gained nothing by seeking the protection of my mistress; that the power was still all in his own hands. I pitied Mrs. Flint. She was a second wife, many years the junior of her husband; and the hoary-headed miscreant was enough to try the patience of a wiser and better woman. She was completely foiled, and knew not how to proceed. She would gladly have had me flogged for my supposed false oath; but, as I have already stated, the doctor never allowed anyone to whip me. The old sinner was politic. The application of the lash might have led to remarks that would have exposed him in the eyes of his children and grandchildren. How often did I rejoice that I lived in a town where all the inhabitants knew each other! If I had been on a remote plantation, or lost among the multitude of a crowded city, I should not be a living woman at this day.

The secrets of slavery are concealed like those of the Inquisition. My master was, to my knowledge, the father of eleven slaves. But did the mothers dare to tell who was the father of their children? Did the other slaves dare to allude to it, except in whispers among themselves? No, indeed! They knew too well the terrible consequences.

My grandmother could not avoid seeing things which excited her suspicions. She was uneasy about me, and tried various ways to buy me; but the never-changing answer was always repeated: "Linda does not belong to *me.* She is my daughter's property, and I have no legal right to sell her." The conscientious man! He was too scrupulous to *sell* me; but he had no scruples whatever about committing a much greater wrong against the helpless young girl placed under his guardianship, as his daughter's property. Sometimes my persecutor would ask me whether I would like to be sold. I told him I would rather be sold to anybody than to lead such a life as I did. On such occasions he would assume the air of a very injured individual, and reproach me for my ingratitude. "Did I not take you into the house, and make you the companion of my own children?" he would say. "Have I ever treated you like a Negro? I have never allowed you to be punished, not even to please your mistress. And this is the recompense I get, you ungrateful girl!" I answered that he had reasons of his own for screening me from punishment, and that the course he pursued made my mistress hate me and persecute me. If I wept, he would say, "Poor child! Don't cry! don't cry! I will make peace for you with your mistress. Only let me arrange matters in my own way. Poor, foolish girl! you don't know what is for your own good. I would cherish you. I would make a lady of you. Now go, and think of all I have promised you."

I did think of it.

Reader, I draw no imaginary pictures of southern homes. I am telling you the plain truth. Yet when victims make their escape from this wild beast of Slavery, northerners consent to act the part of bloodhounds, and hunt the poor fugitive back into his den, "full of dead men's bones, and all uncleanness." Nay, more, they are not only willing, but proud, to give their daughters in marriage to slaveholders. The poor girls have romantic notions of a sunny clime, and of the flowering vines that all the year round shade a happy home. To what disappointments are they destined! The young wife soon learns that the husband in whose hands she has placed her happiness pays no regard to his marriage vows. Children of every shade of complexion play with her own fair babies, and too well she knows that they are born unto him of his own household. Jealousy and hatred enter the flowery home, and it is ravaged of its loveliness.

Southern women often marry a man knowing that he is the father of many little slaves. They do not trouble themselves about it. They regard such children as property, as marketable as the pigs on the plantation; and it is seldom that they do not make them aware of this by passing them into the slave-trader's hands as soon as possible, and thus getting them out of their sight. I am glad to say there are some honorable exceptions.

I have myself known two southern wives who exhorted their husbands to free those slaves toward whom they stood in a "parental relation"; and their request was granted. These husbands blushed before the superior nobleness of their wives' natures. Though they had only counseled them to do that which it was their duty to do, it commanded their respect, and rendered their conduct more exemplary. Concealment was at an end, and confidence took the place of distrust.

Though this bad institution deadens the moral sense, even in white women, to a fearful extent, it is not altogether extinct. I have heard southern ladies say of Mr. Such-a-one, "He not only thinks it no disgrace to be the father of those little niggers, but he is not ashamed to call himself their master. I declare, such things ought not to be tolerated in any decent society!"

Suggestions for Discussion

1. Discuss the effectiveness of the author's narrative method. Compare it with that used by Richard Wright in "The Ethics of Living Jim Crow."
2. How successfully does she communicate her desperation? How does she do so?

Suggestion for Writing

Write a newspaper editorial commenting on the events reported by Harriet Jacobs.

CHIEF JOSEPH

His Message of Surrender, 1876

Chief Joseph, one of the leaders of the Nez Percé tribes, fought against the destruction of his people in a manner that made him a hero (along with other chiefs, such as Tecumseh, Crazy Horse, and Sitting Bull) in the eyes of white settlers in Montana and Idaho. As part of an effort to drive the Plains Indians off their lands and onto reservations, the army commissioners decided that Joseph's Nez Percé should be moved to join others on the Lapwai Reservation in Montana. When Joseph resisted, a series of battles followed, and the Nez Percé attempted to cross the Bitterroot Mountains to Idaho. In the skirmishes that followed, most of the Nez Percé were killed. After four months of fighting and a journey of thirteen hundred miles, they were stopped in a battle a short distance from the Canadian border. Chief Joseph persuaded the approximately 120 remaining warriors to surrender and sent a message to the American officer in command. The following brief passage is an extract from a larger message and is taken from an article, "Chief Joseph, the Nez Percé," by C. E. S. Wood in the *Century Monthly Illustrated* magazine (May 1884).

Hear Me, My Warriors

Hear me, my warriors; my heart is sick and sad.
Our chiefs are killed,
The old men are all dead
It is cold, and we have no blankets;
The little children are freezing to death.
Hear me, my warriors; my heart is sick and sad.
From where the sun now stands I will fight no more forever!

Suggestions for Discussion

1. Although Chief Joseph's message is addressed to General Howard, it seems to have a larger audience. How do you imagine that wider audience reacted? The interpreter of the message is reported to have wept as he delivered it. The original message was not in the form of a poem.
2. Examine several history books that describe the destruction of the Plains Indians and give a full account of Chief Joseph's defeat. Organize a group discussion of the incident. Attempt to interpret the meaning of the episode in American history. How does this brief document relate to the theme of freedom and human dignity?

Suggestion for Writing

Find and read the lengthier message in an account of the Nez Percé. Then write a paper on the differences between it and the extract printed in this text.

CHIEF SEATTLE

Speech on the Signing of the Treaty of Port Elliott, 1855

Chief Seattle (1786–1866) of the Suquamish and Dewamish tribes was a significant figure among Native Americans of the Pacific Northwest. The city of Seattle was named in his honor. He was one of several chiefs in the Northwest who maintained peaceful relations with the continually encroaching white settlers. This speech, translated by a doctor named Henry Smith, acknowledges the defeat of the Native Americans and their willingness to live on a reservation in the state of Washington, provided that the American government agrees to treat them humanely and to respect the differences in their culture.

Yonder sky that has wept tears of compassion upon my people for centuries untold, and which to us appears changeless and eternal, may change. Today is fair. Tomorrow may be overcast with clouds. My words are like the stars that never change. Whatever Seattle says the great chief at Washington can rely upon with as much certainty as he can upon the return of the sun or the seasons. The White Chief says that Big Chief at Washington sends us greetings of friendship and goodwill. That is kind of him for we know he has little need of our friendship in return. His people are many. They are like the grass that covers vast prairies. My people are few. They resemble the scattering trees of a storm-swept plain. The great, and—I presume—good, White Chief sends us word that he wishes to buy our lands but is willing to allow us enough to live comfortably. This indeed appears just, even generous, for the Red Man no longer has rights that he need respect, and the offer may be wise also, as we are no longer in need of an extensive country.... I will not dwell on, nor mourn over, our untimely decay, nor reproach our paleface brothers with hastening it, as we too may have been somewhat to blame.

Youth is impulsive. When our young men grow angry at some real or imaginary wrong, and disfigure their faces with black paint, it denotes that their hearts are black, and then they are often cruel and relentless, and our old men and old women are unable to restrain them. Thus it has ever been. Thus it was when the white men first began to push our forefathers westward. But let us hope that the hostilities between us may never return. We would have everything to lose and nothing to gain. Revenge by young men is considered gain, even at the cost of their own lives, but old men who stay at home in times of war, and mothers who have sons to lose, know better.

Our good father at Washington—for I presume he is now our father as well as yours, since King George has moved his boundaries further north—our great good father, I say, sends us word that if we do as he desires he will protect us. His brave warriors will be to us a bristling wall of strength, and his wonderful ships of war will fill our harbors so that our ancient enemies far to the northward—the Hydas and Tsimpsians—will cease to frighten our women, children, and old men. Then in reality will he be our father and we his children. But can that ever be? Your God is not our God! Your God loves your people and hates mine. He folds his strong and protecting arms lovingly about the paleface and leads him by the hand as a father leads his infant son—but He has forsaken His red children—if they really are his. Our God, the Great Spirit, seems also to have forsaken us. Your God makes your people wax strong every day. Soon they will fill the land. Our people are ebbing away like a rapidly receding tide that will never return. The white man's God cannot love our people or He would protect them. They seem to be orphans who can look nowhere for help. How then can we be brothers? How can your God become our God and renew our prosperity and awaken in us dreams of returning greatness? If we have a common heavenly father He must be partial—for He came to his paleface children. We never saw Him. He gave you laws but He had no word for His red children whose teeming multitudes once filled this vast continent as stars fill the firmament. No; we are two distinct races with separate origins and separate destinies. There is little in common between us.

To us the ashes of our ancestors are sacred and their resting place is hallowed ground. You wander far from the graves of your ancestors and seemingly without regret. Your religion was written upon tables of stone by the iron finger of your God so that you could not forget. The Red Man could never comprehend nor remember it. Our religion is the traditions of our ancestors—the dreams of our old men, given them in solemn hours of night by the Great Spirit; and the visions of our sachems; and it is written in the hearts of our people.

Your dead cease to love you and the land of their nativity as soon as they pass the portals of the tomb and wander way beyond the stars. They are soon forgotten and never return. Our dead never forget the beautiful world that gave them being.

Day and night cannot dwell together. The Red Man has ever fled the approach of the White Man, as the morning mist flees before the morning sun. However, your proposition seems fair and I think that my people will accept it and will retire to the reservation you offer them. Then we will dwell apart in peace, for the words of the Great White Chief seem to be the words of nature speaking to my people out of dense darkness.

It matters little where we pass the remnant of our days. They will not be many. A few more moons; a few more winters—and not one of the descendants of the mighty hosts that once moved over this broad land or lived in happy homes, protected by the Great Spirit, will remain to mourn over the graves of a people once more powerful and hopeful than yours. But why should I mourn at the untimely fate of my people? Tribe follows tribe, and nation follows nation, like the waves of the sea. It is the order of nature, and regret is useless. Your time of decay may be distant, but it will surely come, for even the White Man whose God walked and talked with him as friend with friend, cannot be exempt from the common destiny. We may be brothers after all. We will see.

We will ponder your proposition, and when we decide we will let you know. But should we accept it, I here and now make this condition that we will not be denied the privilege without molestation of visiting at any time the tombs of our ancestors, friends and children. Every part of this soil is sacred in the estimation of my people. Every hillside, every valley, every plain and grove, has been hallowed by some sad or happy event in days long vanished.... The very dust upon which you now stand responds more lovingly to their footsteps than to yours, because it is rich with the blood of our ancestors and our bare feet are conscious of the sympathetic touch.... Even the little children who lived here and rejoiced here for a brief season will love these somber solitudes and at eventide they greet shadowy returning spirits. And when the last Red Man shall have perished, and the memory of my tribe shall have become a myth among the White Men, these shores will swarm with the invisible dead of my tribe, and when your children's children think themselves alone in the field, the store, the shop, upon the highway, or in the silence of the pathless woods, they will not be alone.... At night when the streets of your cities and villages are silent and you think them deserted, they will throng with the returning hosts that once filled and still love this beautiful land. The White Man will never be alone.

Let him be just and deal kindly with my people, for the dead are not powerless. Dead, did I say? There is no death, only a change of worlds.

Suggestions for Discussion

1. Discuss the figurative language that Chief Seattle uses in the speech. How are similes and metaphors used to characterize white settlers and Native Americans?
2. What is the tone of the speech? How does its tone fit Chief Seattle's purposes?
3. Experts have argued that this translation by Dr. Smith reflects a stereotypical picture of the Native American. What examples can you find in support of this claim? Why might this have occurred despite Dr. Smith's fluency in tribal languages?
4. Identify some ironic aspects of the speech. How might Americans of the mid-nineteenth century have responded to Chief Seattle's predictions?

Suggestions for Writing

1. Chief Seattle's speech refers to Native American enemies from whom he expects the government to protect his tribes. Write a short research paper in which you explain who those enemies were and the grounds for their enmity.

2. Write a paper comparing and contrasting the poetic nature of this speech with that of the Gettysburg Address. How do the two speeches reflect not only the differences between the two speakers and the occasions for their speeches, but cultural differences as well?
3. Chief Seattle converted to Christianity in the 1830s. Does this speech reflect his conversion? Write a paper in which you contrast the fact of his conversion with what he says about God in the speech.

GEORGE ORWELL

The Principles of Newspeak

George Orwell (1903–1950), pseudonym of Eric Arthur Blair, a British writer with socialist sympathies, wrote essays and novels based on his experiences as a British imperial policeman in Burma, as an impoverished writer in Paris and London, and as a volunteer in the republican army in the Spanish Civil War. He was for a few years the editor of the magazine of the British Labour Party. Although his essays and letters are considered masterpieces of prose style, he is probably best known for the satirical anticommunist fable *Animal Farm* (1945) and for the novel *1984* published in 1949. Orwell conceived a terrifying vision of a future where mechanized language and thought have become the tools of a totalitarian society. This essay, written as an appendix to *1984,* presents "Newspeak," the official language of Oceania, as the logical outcome and instrument of a repressive government. It also suggests the Newspeak has its basis in what Orwell considered our degradation of the English language.

Newspeak was the official language of Oceania and had been devised to meet the ideological needs of Ingsoc, or English Socialism. In the year 1984 there was not as yet anyone who used Newspeak as his sole means of communication, either in speech or writing. The leading articles in the *Times* were written in it, but this was a tour de force which could only be carried out by a specialist. It was expected that Newspeak would have finally superseded Oldspeak (or Standard English, as we should call it) by about the year 2050. Meanwhile it gained ground steadily, all Party members tending to use Newspeak words and grammatical constructions more and more in their everyday speech. The version in use in 1984, and embodied in the Ninth and Tenth Editions of the Newspeak dictionary, was a provisional one, and contained many superfluous words and archaic formations which were due to be suppressed later. It is with the final, perfected version, as embodied in the Eleventh Edition of the dictionary, that we are concerned here.

The purpose of Newspeak was not only to provide a medium of expression for the world-view and mental habits proper to the devotees of Ingsoc, but to make all other modes of thought impossible. It was intended that when Newspeak had been adopted once and for all and Oldspeak forgotten, a heretical thought—that is, a thought diverging from the principles of Ingsoc—should be literally unthinkable, at least so far as thought is dependent on words. Its vocabulary was so constructed as to give exact and often very subtle expression to every meaning that a Party member could properly wish to express, while excluding all other meanings and also the possibility of arriving at them by indirect methods. This was done partly by the invention of new words, but chiefly by eliminating undesirable words and by stripping such words as remained of unorthodox meanings, and so far as possible of all secondary meanings whatever. To give a single example. The word *free* still existed in Newspeak, but it could only be used in such statements as "This dog is free from lice" or "This field is free from weeds." It could not be used in its old sense of "politically free" or "intellectually free," since political and intellectual freedom no longer existed even as concepts, and were therefore of necessity nameless. Quite apart from the suppression of definitely heretical works, reduction of vocabulary was regarded as an end in itself, and no word that could be dispensed with was allowed to survive. Newspeak was designed not to extend but to *diminish* the range of thought, and this purpose was indirectly assisted by cutting the choice of words down to a minimum.

Newspeak was founded on the English language as we now know it, though many Newspeak sentences, even when not containing newly created words, would be barely intelligible to an English-speaker of our own day. Newspeak words were divided into three distinct classes, known as the A vocabulary, the B vocabulary (also called compound words), and the C vocabulary. It will be simpler to discuss each class separately, but the grammatical peculiarities of the language can be dealt with in the section devoted to the A vocabulary, since the same rules held good for all three categories.

The A vocabulary. The A vocabulary consisted of the words needed for the business of everyday life—for such things as eating, drinking, working, putting on one's clothes, going up and down stairs, riding in vehicles, gardening, cooking, and the like. It was composed almost entirely of words that we already possess—words like *hit, run, dog, tree, sugar, house, field*—but in comparison with the present-day English vocabulary, their number was extremely small, while their meanings were far more rigidly defined. All ambiguities and shades of meaning had been purged out of them. So far as it could be achieved, a Newspeak word of this class was simply a staccato sound expressing *one* clearly understood concept. It would have been quite impossible to use the A vocabulary for literary purposes or for political or philosophical discussion. It was intended only to express simple, purposive thoughts, usually involving concrete objects or physical actions.

The grammar of Newspeak had two outstanding peculiarities. The first of these was an almost complete interchangeability between different parts of speech. Any word in the language (in principle this applied even to very abstract words such as *if* or *when*) could be used either as verb, noun, adjective, or adverb. Between the verb and the noun form, when they were of the same root, there was never any variation, this rule of itself involving the destruction of many archaic forms. The word *thought,* for example, did not exist in Newspeak. Its place was taken by *think,* which did duty for both noun and verb. No etymological principle was involved here; in some cases it was the original noun that was chosen for retention, in other cases the verb. Even where a noun and a verb of kindred meaning were not etymologically connected, one or other of them was frequently suppressed. There was, for example, no such word as *cut,* its meaning being sufficiently covered by the noun-verb *knife.* Adjectives were formed by adding the suffix *-ful* to the noun-verb, and adverbs by adding *-wise.* Thus, for example, *speedful* meant "rapid" and *speedwise* meant "quickly." Certain of our present-day adjectives, such as *good, strong, big, black, soft,* were retained, but their total number was very small. There was little need for them, since almost any adjectival meaning could be arrived at by adding *-ful* to a noun-verb. None of the now-existing adverbs was retained, except for a very few already ending in *-wise;* the *-wise* termination was invariable. The word *well,* for example, was replaced by *goodwise.*

In addition, any word—this again applied in principle to every word in the language—could be negatived by adding the affix *un-*, or could be strengthened by the affix *plus-*, or, for still greater emphasis, *doubleplus-*. Thus, for example, *uncold* meant "warm," while *pluscold* and *doublepluscold* meant, respectively, "very cold" and "superlatively cold." It was also possible, as in present-day English, to modify the meaning of almost any word by prepositional affixes such as *ante-*, *post-*, *up-*, *down-*, etc. By such methods it was found possible to bring about an enormous diminution of vocabulary. Given, for instance, the word *good,* there was no need for such a word as bad, since the required meaning was equally well—indeed, better—expressed by *ungood.* All that was necessary, in any case where two words formed a natural pair of opposites, was to decide which of them to suppress. *Dark,* for example, could be replaced by *unlight,* or *light* by *undark,* according to preference.

The second distinguishing mark of Newspeak grammar was its regularity. Subject to a few exceptions which are mentioned below, all inflections followed the same rules. Thus, in all verbs the preterite and the past participle were the same and ended in *-ed.* The preterite of *steal* was *stealed,* the preterite of *think* was *thinked,* and so on throughout the language, all such forms as *swam, gave, brought, spoke, taken,* etc., being abolished. All plurals were made by adding *-s* or *-es* as the case might be. The plurals of *man, ox, life* were *mans, oxes, lifes.* Comparison of adjectives was invariably made by adding *-er, -est* (*good, gooder, goodest*), irregular forms and the *more, most* formation being suppressed.

The only classes of words that were still allowed to inflect irregularly were the pronouns, the relatives, the demonstrative adjectives, and the auxiliary verbs. All of these followed their ancient usage, except that *whom* had been scrapped as unnecessary, and the *shall, should* tenses had been dropped, all their uses being covered by *will* and *would.* There were also certain irregularities in word-formation arising out of the need for rapid and easy speech. A word which was difficult to utter, or was liable to be incorrectly heard, was held to be ipso facto a bad word; occasionally therefore, for the sake of euphony, extra letters were inserted into a word or an archaic formation was retained. But this need made itself felt chiefly in connection with the B vocabulary. *Why* so great an importance was attached to ease of pronunciation will be made clear later in this essay.

The B vocabulary. The B vocabulary consisted of words which had been deliberately constructed for political purposes: words, that is to say, which not only had in every case a political implication, but were intended to impose a desirable mental attitude upon the person using them. Without a full understanding of the principles of Ingsoc it was difficult to use these words correctly. In some cases they could be translated into Oldspeak, or even into words taken from the A vocabulary, but this usually demanded a long paraphrase and always involved the loss of certain overtones. The B words were a sort of verbal shorthand, often packing whole ranges of ideas into a few syllables, and at the same time more accurate and forcible than ordinary language.

The B words were in all cases compound words.* They consisted of two or more words, or portions of words, welded together in an easily pronounceable form. The resulting amalgam was always a noun-verb, and inflected according to the ordinary rules. To take a single example: the word *goodthink,* meaning, very roughly, "orthodoxy," or, if one chose to regard it as a verb, "to think in an orthodox manner." This inflected as

*Compound words, such as *speakwrite,* were of course to be found in the A vocabulary, but these were merely convenient abbreviations and had no special ideological color.

follows: noun-verb, *goodthink;* past tense and past participle, *goodthinked;* present participle, *goodthinking;* adjective, *goodthinkful;* adverb, *goodthinkwise;* verbal noun, *goodthinker.*

The B words were not constructed on any etymological plan. The words of which they were made up could be any parts of speech, and could be placed in any order and mutilated in any way which made them easy to pronounce while indicating their derivation. In the word *crimethink* (thoughtcrime), for instance, the *think* came second, whereas in *thinkpol* (Thought Police) it came first, and in the latter word police had lost its second syllable. Because of the greater difficulty in securing euphony, irregular formations were commoner in the B vocabulary than in the A vocabulary. For example, the adjectival forms of *Minitrue, Minipax,* and *Miniluv* were, respectively, *Minitruthful, Minipeaceful,* and *Minilovely,* simply because *-trueful, paxful,* and *loveful* were slightly awkward to pronounce. In principle, however, all B words could inflect, and all inflected in exactly the same way.

Some of the B words had highly subtilized meanings, barely intelligible to anyone who had not mastered the language as a whole. Consider, for example, such a typical sentence from a *Times* leading article as *Oldthinkers unbellyfeel Ingsoc.* The shortest rendering that one could make of this in Oldspeak would be: "Those whose ideas were formed before the Revolution cannot have a full emotional understanding of the principles of English Socialism." But this is not an adequate translation. To begin with, in order to grasp the full meaning of the Newspeak sentence quoted above, one would have to have a clear idea of what is meant by *Ingsoc.* And, in addition, only a person thoroughly grounded in Ingsoc could appreciate the full force of the word *bellyfeel,* which implied a blind, enthusiastic acceptance difficult to imagine today; or of the word *oldthink,* which was inextricably mixed up with the idea of wickedness and decadence. But the special function of certain Newspeak words, of which *oldthink* was one, was not so much to express meanings as to destroy them. These words, necessarily few in number, had had their meanings extended until they contained within themselves whole batteries of words which, as they were sufficiently covered by a single comprehensive term, could now be scrapped and forgotten. The greatest difficulty facing the compilers of the Newspeak dictionary was not to invent new words, but, having invented them, to make sure what they meant: to make sure, that is to say, what ranges of words they canceled by their existence.

As we have already seen in the case of the word *free,* words which had once borne a heretical meaning were sometimes retained for the sake of convenience, but only with the undesirable meanings purged out of them. Countless other words such as *honor, justice, morality, internationalism, democracy, science,* and *religion* had simply ceased to exist. A few blanket words covered them, and, in covering them, abolished them. All words grouping themselves round the concepts of liberty and equality, for instance, were contained in the single word *crimethink,* while all words grouping themselves round the concepts of objectivity and rationalism were contained in the single word *oldthink.* Greater precision would have been dangerous. What was required in a Party member was an outlook similar to that of the ancient Hebrew who knew, without knowing much else, that all nations other than his own worshipped "false gods." He did not need to know that these gods were called Baal, Osiris, Moloch, Ashtaroth, and the like; probably the less he knew about them the better for his orthodoxy. He knew Jehovah and the commandments of Jehovah; he knew, therefore, that all gods with other names or other attributes were false gods. In somewhat the same way, the Party member knew what constituted right conduct, and in exceedingly vague, generalized terms he knew what kinds of departure from it were possible. His sexual life, for example, was entirely regulated by the two Newspeak words *sexcrime* (sexual immorality) and *goodsex* (chastity). *Sexcrime* covered all sexual misdeeds whatever. It covered fornication, adultery, homosexuality, and other perversions, and in addition, normal intercourse practiced for its own sake. There was no need to enumerate them separately, since they were all equally culpable, and, in principle, all punishable by death. In the C vocabulary, which consisted of scientific and technical words, it might be necessary to give specialized names to certain sexual aberrations, but the ordinary citizen had no need of them. He knew what was meant by *goodsex*—that is to say, normal intercourse between man and wife, for the sole purpose of begetting children, and without physical pleasure on the part of the woman; all else was *sexcrime.* In Newspeak it was seldom possible to follow a heretical thought further than the perception that it *was* heretical; beyond that point the necessary words were nonexistent.

No word in the B vocabulary was ideologically neutral. A great many were euphemisms. Such words, for instance, as *joycamp* (forced-labor camp) or *Minipax* (Ministry of Peace, i.e., Ministry of War) meant almost the exact opposite of what they appeared to mean. Some words, on the other hand, displayed a frank and contemptuous understanding of the real nature of Oceanic society. An example was *prolefeed,* meaning the rubbishy entertainment and spurious news which the Party handed out to the masses. Other words, again, were ambivalent, having the connotation "good" when applied to the Party and "bad" when applied to its enemies. But in addition there were great numbers of words which at first sight appeared to be mere abbreviations and which derived their ideological color not from their meaning but from their structure.

So far as it could be contrived, everything that had or might have political significance of any kind was fitted into the B vocabulary. The name of every organization, or body of people, or doctrine, or country, or institution, or public building, was invariably cut down into the familiar shape; that is, a single easily pronounced word with the smallest number of syllables that would preserve the original derivation. In the Ministry of Truth, for example, the Records Department, in which Winston Smith worked, was called *Recdep,* the Fiction Department was called *Ficdep,* the Teleprograms Department was called *Teledep,* and so on. This was not done solely with the object of saving time. Even in the early decades of the twentieth century, telescoped words and phrases had been one of the characteristic features of political language; and it had been noticed that the tendency to use abbreviations of this kind was most marked in totalitarian countries and totalitarian organizations. Examples were such words as *Nazi, Gestapo, Comintern, Inprecorr, Agitprop.* In the beginning the practice had been adopted as it were instinctively, but in Newspeak it was used with a conscious purpose. It was perceived that in thus abbreviating a name one narrowed and subtly altered its meaning, by cutting out most of the associations that would otherwise cling to it. The words *Communist International,* for instance, call up a composite picture of universal human brotherhood, red flags, barricades, Karl Marx, and the Paris Commune. The word Comintern, on the other hand, suggests merely a tightly knit organization and a well-defined body of doctrine. It refers to something almost as easily recognized, and as limited in purpose, as a chair or a table. *Comintern* is a word that can be uttered almost without taking thought, whereas *Communist International* is a phrase over which one is obliged to linger at least momentarily. In the same way, the associations called up by a word like *Minitrue* are fewer and more controllable than those called up by *Ministry of Truth.* This accounted not only for the habit of abbreviating whenever possible, but also for the almost exaggerated care that was taken to make every word easily pronounceable.

In Newspeak, euphony outweighed every consideration other than exactitude of meaning. Regularity of grammar was always sacrificed to it when it seemed necessary. And rightly so, since what was required, above all for political purposes, were short clipped words of unmistakable meaning which could be uttered rapidly and which roused the minimum of echoes in the speaker's mind. The words of the B vocabulary even gained in force from the fact that nearly all of them were very much alike. Almost invariably these words—*goodthink, Minipax, prolefeed, sexcrime, joycamp, Ingsoc, bellyfeel, thinkpol,* and countless others—were words of two or three syllables, with the stress distributed equally between the first syllable and the last. The use of them encouraged a gabbling style of speech, at once staccato and monotonous. And this was exactly what was aimed at. The intention was to make speech, and especially speech on any subject not ideologically neutral, as nearly as possible independent of consciousness.

For that purpose of everyday life it was no doubt necessary, or sometimes necessary, to reflect before speaking, but a Party member called upon to make a political or ethical judgment should be able to spray forth the correct opinions as automatically as a machine gun spraying forth bullets. His training fitted him to do this, the language gave him an almost foolproof instrument, and the texture of the words, with their harsh sound and a certain willful ugliness which was in accord with the spirit of Ingsoc, assisted the process still further.

So did the fact of having very few words to choose from. Relative to our own, the Newspeak vocabulary was tiny, and new ways of reducing it were constantly being devised. Newspeak, indeed, differed from almost all other languages in that its vocabulary grew smaller instead of larger every year. Each reduction was a gain, since the smaller the area of choice, the smaller the temptation to take thought. Ultimately it was hoped to make articulate speech issue from the larynx without involving the higher brain centers at all. This aim was frankly admitted in the Newspeak word *duckspeak,* meaning "to quack like a duck." Like various other words in the B vocabulary, *duckspeak* was ambivalent in meaning. Provided that the opinions which were quacked out were orthodox ones, it implied nothing but praise, and when the *Times* referred to one of the orators of the Party as a *double-plusgood duckspeaker* it was paying a warm and valued compliment.

The C vocabulary. The C vocabulary was supplementary to the others and consisted entirely of scientific and technical terms. These resembled the scientific terms in use today, and were constructed from the same roots, but the usual care was taken to define them rigidly and strip them of undesirable meanings. They followed the same grammatical rules as the words in the other two vocabularies. Very few of the C words had any currency either in everyday speech or in political speech. Any scientific worker or technician could find all the words he needed in the list devoted to his own speciality, but he seldom had more than a smattering of the words occurring in the other lists. Only a very few words were common to all lists, and there was no vocabulary expressing the function of Science as a habit of mind, or a method of thought, irrespective of its particular branches. There was, indeed, no word for "Science," any meaning that it could possibly bear being already sufficiently covered by the word *Ingsoc.*

From the foregoing account it will be seen that in Newspeak the expression of unorthodox opinions, above a very low level, was well-nigh impossible. It was of course possible to utter heresies of a very crude kind, a species of blasphemy. It would have been possible, for example, to say *Big Brother is ungood.* But this statement, which to an orthodox ear merely conveyed a self-evident absurdity, could not have been sustained by reasoned argument, because the necessary words were not available. Ideas inimical to Ingsoc could only be entertained in a vague wordless form, and could only be named in very broad terms which lumped together and condemned whole groups of heresies without defining them in doing so. One could, in fact, only use Newspeak for unorthodox purposes by illegitimately translating some of the words back into Oldspeak. For example, *All mans are equal* was a possible Newspeak sentence, but only in the same sense in which *All men are redhaired* is a possible Oldspeak sentence. It did not contain a grammatical error, but it expressed a palpable untruth, i.e., that all men are of equal size, weight, or strength. The concept of political equality no longer existed, and the secondary meaning had accordingly been purged out of the word *equal.* In 1984, when Oldspeak was still the normal means of communication, the danger theoretically existed that in using Newspeak words one might remember their original meanings. In practice it was not difficult for any person well grounded in *doublethink* to avoid doing this, but within a couple of generations even the possibility of such a lapse would have vanished. A person growing up with Newspeak as his sole language would no more know that *equal* had once had the secondary meaning of "politically equal," or that *free* had once meant "intellectually free," than, for instance, a person who had never heard of chess would be aware of the secondary meanings attaching to *queen* and *rook.* There would be many crimes and errors which it would be beyond his power to commit, simply because they were nameless and therefore unimaginable. And it was to be foreseen that with the passage of time the distinguishing characteristics of Newspeak would become more and more pronounced—its words growing fewer and fewer, their meanings more and more rigid, and the chance of putting them to improper uses always diminishing.

When Oldspeak had been once and for all superseded, the last link with the past would have been severed. History had already been rewritten, but fragments of the literature of the past survived here and there, imperfectly censored, and so long as one retained one's knowledge of Oldspeak it was possible to read them. In the future such fragments, even if they chanced to survive, would be unintelligible and untranslatable. It was impossible to translate any passage of Oldspeak into Newspeak unless it either referred to some technical process or some very simple everyday action, or was already orthodox (*goodthinkful* would be the Newspeak expression) in tendency. In practice this meant that no book written before approximately 1960 could be translated as a whole. Prerevolutionary literature could only be subjected to ideological translation—that is, alteration in sense as well as language. Take for example the well-known passage from the Declaration of Independence:

> We hold these truths to be self-evident, that all men are created equal, that they are endowed by their Creator with certain inalienable rights, that among

> these are life, liberty and the pursuit of happiness. That to secure these rights, Governments are instituted among men, deriving their powers from the consent of the governed. That whenever any form of Government becomes destructive of those ends, it is the right of the People to alter or abolish it, and to institute new Government...

It would have been quite impossible to render this into Newspeak while keeping to the sense of the original. The nearest one could come to doing so would be to swallow the whole passage up in the single word *crimethink.* A full translation could only be an ideological translation, whereby Jefferson's words would be changed into a panegyric on absolute government.

A good deal of the literature of the past was, indeed, already being transformed in this way. Considerations of prestige made it desirable to preserve the memory of certain historical figures, while at the same time bringing their achievements into line with the philosophy of Ingsoc. Various writers, such as Shakespeare, Milton, Swift, Byron, Dickens, and some others were therefore in process of translation; when the task had been completed, their original writings, with all else that survived of the literature of the past, would be destroyed. These translations were a slow and difficult business, and it was not expected that they would be finished before the first or second decade of the twenty-first century. There were also large quantities of merely utilitarian literature—indispensable technical manuals and the like—that had to be treated in the same way. It was chiefly in order to allow time for the preliminary work of translation that the final adoption of Newspeak had been fixed for so late a date as 2050.

Suggestions for Discussion

1. Explain Orwell's statement that Newspeak was designed to "diminish the range of thought." How does he demonstrate this statement by the use of the word *free?*
2. Summarize the uses of the A Vocabulary. Contrast it with present-day English and discuss the former's use of the parts of speech. Why are verbs usually suppressed? Why were most existing adverbs abolished? Why were all noun plurals formed by adding *-s* or *-es?*
3. Define the B Vocabulary. What were its uses? Discuss the examples given, particularly the sentence, "Oldthinkers unbellyfeel Ingsoc."
4. What difficulties faced the compilers of the Newspeak dictionary?
5. What are the precedents for Newspeak word combinations such as *Recdep* and *Ficdep?* What comment on current standard English does Orwell make here?

6. How does the word *duckspeak* symbolize the purpose of Newspeak?
7. What are the uses of the C Vocabulary? Why did the word *science* cease to exist?
8. Discuss the sentences, "Big Brother is ungood" and "All mans are equal" as examples of Newspeak.
9. What is the Newspeak equivalent of the opening passage of the Declaration of Independence? Discuss Orwell's reasons for inventing this translation. Relate the translation to the entire essay.

Suggestions for Writing

1. Examine your local newspaper for examples of words that resemble Newspeak and write an essay discussing the reasons for your choice.
2. Write an essay explaining how Newspeak is an instrument of power. Why is it a necessary ideal of Oceania? Discuss some words or sentences from contemporary political speeches or essays that come close to Newspeak.

PLATO

The Crito

Translated by Benjamin Jowett, revised by Peter White

Plato (428–348 B.C.), born of a noble family, lived in Athens during troubled political times. After the defeat of Athens in the Peloponnesian War, an autocratic and repressive government replaced the democracy, and it, in turn, was succeeded by a regime more demagogic than democratic. Under this government in 399 B.C., Socrates was prosecuted, tried, and condemned to death for subversive activities. In the *Apology* and the *Crito* (neither of them typical Platonic dialogues), Plato undertook the task of rehabilitating Socrates' reputation. Although the historian Xenophon has provided a somewhat different version of Socrates' trial, Plato's portrait of Socrates explains why he regarded him as the best of men. The *Crito* (and the *Phaedo*) presents Socrates in prison as he awaits execution. Crito, a wealthy Athenian, whose primary loyalty in this case is to his friend rather than to the state, urges Socrates to accept his help in escaping. In the course of the dialogue, Socrates leads Crito to agree that a respect for the law and a belief in personal integrity demand that Socrates accept his execution with dignity. Toward the end of the *Crito,* Plato personifies the laws of Athens to explain Socrates' decision to obey them.

Plato's *Republic,* written later than the *Crito,* and additional dialogues in which he uses Socrates to argue his own position on ethics, politics, and other philosophical issues, are Plato's versions of Socrates' conversations. He uses Socrates, however, as teacher of the Socratic method of discourse, which Plato employed in his dialogues, and so it is not surprising that soon after his fortieth year, Plato founded the Academy, the first institute for the purpose of educating suitable rulers for Athens, a school that became a model for many that followed.

SOCRATES: Why have you come at this hour, Crito? It must be quite early?

CRITO: Yes, certainly.

SOCRATES: What is the exact time?

CRITO: The dawn is breaking.

SOCRATES: I wonder that the keeper of the prison would let you in.

CRITO: He knows me, because I often come, Socrates; moreover, I have done him a kindness.

SOCRATES: And are you only just arrived?

CRITO: I came some time ago.

SOCRATES: Then why did you sit and say nothing instead of at once awakening me?

CRITO: That I could never have done, Socrates. I only wish I were not so sleepless and distressed myself. I have been looking at you, wondering how you can sleep so comfortably, and I didn't wake you on purpose, so that you could go on sleeping in perfect comfort. All through your life, I have often thought you were favored with a good disposition, but I have never been so impressed as in the present misfortune, seeing how easily and tranquilly you bear it.

SOCRATES: Why, Crito, when a man has reached my age he ought not to be repining at the approach of death.

CRITO: And yet other old men find themselves in similar misfortunes, and age does not prevent them from repining.

SOCRATES: That is true. But you have not told me why you come at this early hour.

CRITO: I come with a message which is painful—not, I expect, to you, but painful and oppressive for me and all your friends, and I think it weighs most heavily of all on me.

SOCRATES: What? Has the ship come from Delos, on the arrival of which I am to die?*

CRITO: No, the ship has not actually arrived, but she will probably be here today, as persons who have come from Sunium tell me that they left her there; and therefore tomorrow, Socrates, will be the last day of your life.

SOCRATES: Very well, Crito; if such is the will of the gods, I am willing; but my belief is that there will be a day's delay.

CRITO: Why do you think so?

SOCRATES: I will tell you. I am to die on the day after the arrival of the ship.

CRITO: Yes; that is what the authorities say.

SOCRATES: But I do not think that the ship will be here until tomorrow; this I infer from a vision which I had last night, or rather only just now, when you fortunately allowed me to sleep.

CRITO: And what was the nature of the vision?

SOCRATES: There appeared to me the likeness of a woman, fair and comely, clothed in bright raiment, who called to me and said: O Socrates,

"The third day hence to fertile Phthia shalt thou come."†

CRITO: What a singular dream, Socrates!

SOCRATES: There can be no doubt about the meaning, Crito, I think.

CRITO: Yes; the meaning is only too clear. But, oh! my beloved Socrates, let me entreat you once more to take my advice and escape. For if you die, I shall not only lose a friend who can never be replaced, but there is another evil: people who do not know you and me will believe that I might have saved you if I had been willing to give money but that I did not care. Now, can there be a worse disgrace than this—that I should be thought to value money more than the life of a friend? For the many will not be persuaded that I wanted you to escape and that you refused.

SOCRATES: But why, my dear Crito, should we care about the opinion of the many? Good men, and they are the only persons who are worth considering, will think of these things truly as they occurred.

*Once every year Athens sent a state ship on a ceremonial pilgrimage to the island of Delos; no executions could be carried out between its departure and return.

†The apparition borrows the words in which Achilles contemplated a return from Troy to his home, *Iliad* 9.363.

CRITO: But you see, Socrates, that the opinion of the many must be regarded, for what is now happening shows that they can do the greatest evil to anyone who has lost their good opinion.

SOCRATES: I only wish it were so, Crito, and that the many could do the greatest evil; for then they would also be able to do the greatest good—and what a fine thing this would be! But in reality they can do neither; for they cannot make a man either wise or foolish, and whatever result they produce is the result of chance.

CRITO: Well, I will not dispute with you; but please tell me, Socrates, whether you are not acting out of regard to me and your other friends: Are you not afraid that, if you escape from prison, we may get into trouble with the informers for having stolen you away and lose either the whole or a great part of our property—or that even a worse evil may happen to us? Now, if you fear on our account, be at ease; for in order to save you, we ought surely to run this or even a greater risk; be persuaded, then, and do as I say.

SOCRATES: Yes, Crito, that is one fear which you mention, but by no means the only one.

CRITO: Fear not—there are persons who are willing to get you out of prison at no great cost; and as for the informers, they are far from being exorbitant in their demands—a little money will satisfy them. My means, which are certainly ample, are at your service; and if, out of solicitude about me, you hesitate to use mine, there are non-Athenians here who will give you the use of theirs; and one of them, Simmias the Theban, has brought a large sum of money for this very purpose; and Cebes and many others are prepared to spend their money in helping you to escape. Therefore do not hesitate to save yourself because you are worried about this, and do not say, as you did in the court, that you will have difficulty in knowing what to do with yourself anywhere else. For men will love you in other places to which you may go, and not in Athens only; there are friends of mine in Thessaly, if you would like to go to them, who will value and protect you, and no Thessalian will give you any trouble. Nor can I think that you are at all justified, Socrates, in betraying your own life when you might be saved. You are only working to bring about what your enemies, who want to destroy you, would and did in fact work to accomplish. And further, I should say that you are deserting your own children; for you might bring them up and educate them, instead of which you go away and leave them, and they will have to take their chances; and if they do not meet with the usual fate of orphans, there will be small thanks to you. No man should bring children into the world who is unwilling to persevere to the end in their nurture and education. But you appear to be choosing the easier part, not the better and manlier, which would have been more becoming in one who has professed a life-long concern for virtue, like yourself. And indeed, I am ashamed not only of you but of us, who are your friends, when I reflect that the whole business will be attributed entirely to our want of courage. The trial need never have come on or might have been managed differently. And now it may seem that we have made a ridiculous bungle of this last chance, thanks to our lack of toughness and courage, since we failed to save you and you failed to save yourself, even though it was possible and practicable if we were good for anything at all. So, Socrates, you must not let this turn into a disgrace as well as a tragedy for yourself and us. Make up your mind then, or rather have your mind already made up; for the time of deliberation is over, and there is only one thing to be done, which must be done this very night, and, if we delay at all, it will be no longer practicable or possible; I beseech you therefore, Socrates, be persuaded by me, and do not be contrary.

SOCRATES: My dear Crito, your solicitude is invaluable if it is rightly directed, but otherwise, the more intense, the more difficult it is to deal with. And so we should consider whether I ought to follow this course or not. You know it has always been true that I paid no heed to any consideration I was aware of except that argument which, on reflection, seemed best to me. I cannot throw over the arguments I used to make in times past just because this situation has arisen: they look the same to me as before, and I respect and honor them as much as ever. You must therefore understand that if, on the present occasion, we cannot make better arguments, I will not yield to you—not even if the power of the people conjures up the bugaboos of imprisonment and death and confiscation, as though we could be scared like little children. What will be the fairest way of considering the question? Shall I return to your old argument about the opinions of men? We were saying that some of them are to be regarded, and others not. Now were we right in maintaining this before I was condemned? And has the argument which was once good now proved to be talk for the sake of talking—mere childish nonsense? That is what I want to consider with your help, Crito: whether, under my present circumstances, the argument will appear to be in any way different or not, and whether we shall subscribe to it or let it go. That argument, which, as I believe, is maintained by many persons of authority, was to the effect, as I was saying, that the opinions of some men are to be regarded, and of other men not to be regarded. Now you, Crito, are not going to die tomorrow—at least, there is no human probability of this—and therefore you are disinterested and not liable to be deceived by the circumstances in which you are placed. Tell me, then, whether I am right in saying that some opinions, and the opinions of some men only, are to be valued and that other opinions, and the opinions of other men, are not to be valued. I ask you whether I was right in maintaining this?

CRITO: Certainly.

SOCRATES: The good opinions are to be regarded, and not the bad?

CRITO: Yes.

SOCRATES: And the opinions of the wise are good, and the opinions of the unwise are bad?

CRITO: Certainly.

SOCRATES: Now what was the argument about this: does the serious athlete attend to the praise and blame and opinion of every man or of one man only—his physician or trainer, whoever he may be?

CRITO: Of one man only.

SOCRATES: And he ought to fear the censure and welcome the praise of that one only, and not of the many?

CRITO: Clearly so.

SOCRATES: And he ought to act and train and eat and drink in the way which seems good to his single master, who has understanding, rather than according to the opinion of all other men put together?

CRITO: True.

SOCRATES: And if he disobeys and disregards the opinion and approval of the one, and regards the opinion of the many who have no understanding, will he not suffer harm?

CRITO: Certainly he will.

SOCRATES: And what will the harm be: where will it be localized, and what part of the disobedient person will it affect?

CRITO: Clearly, it will affect the body; that is what is destroyed.

SOCRATES: Very good, and is not this true, Crito, of other things, which we need not separately enumerate? In questions of just and unjust, fair and foul, good and evil, which are the subjects of our present consultation, ought we to follow the opinion of the many, and to fear them, or the opinion of the one man who has understanding? Ought we not to fear and reverence him more than all the rest of the world, and, if we desert him, shall we not ruin and mutilate that principle in us which is improved by justice and deteriorated by injustice—there is such a principle?

CRITO: Certainly there is, Socrates.

SOCRATES: Take a parallel instance: if, ignoring the advice of those who have understanding, we destroy that which is improved by health and is deteriorated by disease, would life be worth having? and that which has been destroyed is—the body?

CRITO: Yes.

SOCRATES: Would life be worth living with an evil and corrupted body?

CRITO: Certainly not.

SOCRATES: And will life be worth living if that faculty which injustice damages and justice improves is ruined? Do we suppose that principle—whatever it may be in man which has to do with justice and injustice—to be inferior to the body?

CRITO: Certainly not.

SOCRATES: More honorable than the body?

CRITO: Far more.

SOCRATES: Then, my friend, we must not regard what the many say of us but what he, the one man who has understanding of just and unjust, will say and what the truth will say. And therefore you begin in error when you advise that we should regard the opinion of the many about just and unjust, good and evil, honorable and dishonorable. "Well," someone will say, "but the many can kill us."

CRITO: That is plain, and a person might well say so. You are right, Socrates.

SOCRATES: But dear Crito, the argument which we have gone over still seems as valid as before. And I should like to know whether I may say the same of another proposition—that not life, but a good life, is to be chiefly valued?

CRITO: Yes, that also remains unshaken.

SOCRATES: And a good life is equivalent to an honorable and just one—that holds also?

CRITO: Yes, it does.

SOCRATES: From these premises I proceed to argue the question whether I am justified in trying to escape without the consent of the Athenians; and if I am clearly right in escaping, then I will make the attempt, but, if not, I will abstain. The other considerations which you mention—of money and loss of character and the duty of educating one's children—are, I fear, only the doctrines of the multitude, who, if they could, would restore people to life as readily as they put them to death—and with as little reason. But since we have been forced this far by the logic of our argument, the only question which remains to be considered is whether we shall do right in giving money and thanks to those who will rescue me, and in taking a direct role in the rescue ourselves, or whether in fact we will be doing wrong. And if it appears that we will be doing wrong, then neither death nor any other calamity that follows from staying and doing nothing must be judged more important than that.

CRITO: I think that you are right, Socrates. How then shall we proceed?

SOCRATES: Let us consider the matter together, and you, either refute me if you can, and I will be convinced, or else cease, my dear friend, from repeating to me that I ought to escape against the wishes of the Athenians. It is most important to me that I act with your assent and not against your will. And now please consider whether my starting point is adequately stated, and also try to answer my questions as you think best.

CRITO: I will.

SOCRATES: Are we to say that we are never intentionally to do wrong, or that in one way we ought and in another we ought not to do wrong? Or is doing wrong always evil and dishonorable, as we often concluded in times past? Or have all those past conclusions been thrown overboard during the last few days? And have we, at our age, been earnestly discoursing with one another all our life long only to discover that we are no better than children? Or, in spite of the opinion of the many, and in spite of consequences, whether better or worse, shall we insist on the truth of what was then said, that injustice is always an evil and a dishonor to him who acts unjustly? Shall we say so or not?

CRITO: Yes.

SOCRATES: Then we must do no wrong?

CRITO: Certainly not.

SOCRATES: Nor, when injured, injure in return, as the many imagine; for we must injure no one at all?

CRITO: Clearly not.

SOCRATES: Again, Crito, may we do evil?

CRITO: Surely not, Socrates.

SOCRATES: And what of doing evil in return for evil, which is the morality of the many—is that just or not?

CRITO: Not just.

SOCRATES: For doing evil to another is the same as injuring him?

CRITO: Very true.

SOCRATES: Then we ought not to retaliate or render evil for evil to anyone, whatever evil we may have suffered from him. But I would have you consider, Crito, whether you really mean what you are saying. For this opinion has never been held, and never will be held, by any considerable number of persons; and those who are agreed and those who are not agreed upon this point have no common ground and can only despise one another when they see how widely they differ. Tell me, then, whether you agree with and assent to my first principle, that neither injury nor retaliation nor warding off evil by evil is ever right. And shall that be the premise of our argument? Or do you decline and dissent from this? For so I have ever thought, and continue to think; but, if you are of another opinion, let me hear what you have to say. If, however, you remain of the same mind as formerly, I will proceed to the next step.

CRITO: You may proceed, for I have not changed my mind.

SOCRATES: The next thing I have to say, or, rather, my next question, is this: Ought a man to do what he admits to be right, or ought he to betray the right?

CRITO: He ought to do what he thinks right.

SOCRATES: In light of that, tell me whether or not there is some victim—a particularly undeserving victim—who is hurt if I go away without persuading the city. And do we abide by what we agree was just or not?

CRITO: I cannot answer your question, Socrates, because I do not see what you are getting at.

SOCRATES: Then consider the matter in this way: imagine that I am about to run away (you may call the proceeding by any name which you like), and the laws and the government come and interrogate me: "Tell us, Socrates," they say; "what are you up to? are you not going by an act of yours to destroy us—the laws, and the whole state—as far as in you lies? Do you imagine that a state can subsist and not be overthrown in which the decisions of law have no power but are set aside and trampled upon by individuals?" What will be our answer, Crito, to questions like these? Anyone, and especially a rhetorician, would have a good deal to say against abrogation of the law that requires a sentence to be carried out. He will argue that this law should not be set aside. Or shall we retort, "Yes; but the state has injured us and given an unjust sentence." Suppose I say that?

CRITO: Very good, Socrates.

SOCRATES: "And was that our agreement with you?" the laws would answer; "or were you to abide by the sentence of the state?" And if I were to express my astonishment at their talking this way, they would probably add: "Take control of your astonishment and answer, Socrates—you are in the habit of asking and answering questions. Tell us: What complaint have you to make against us which justifies you in attempting to destroy us and the state? In the first place, did we not bring you into existence? Your father married your mother by our aid and brought you into the world. Say whether you have any objection to urge against those of us who regulate marriage." None, I should reply. "Or against those of us who after birth regulate the nurture and education of children, in which you also were trained? Were not the laws, which have the charge of education, right in commanding your father to train you in music and athletics?" Right, I should reply. "Well then, since you were brought into the world and nurtured and educated by us, can you deny in the first place that you are our child and slave, as your fathers were before you? And if this is true, do you really think you have the same rights as we do and that you are entitled to do to us whatever we do to you? Would you have any right to strike or revile or do any other evil to your father or your master, if you had one, because you had been struck or reviled by him or received some other evil at his hands?—you would not say this? And because we think it right to destroy you, do you think that you have any right to destroy us in return, and your country, as far as in you lies? Will you, O professor of true virtue, pretend that you are justified in this? Has a philosopher like you failed to discover that our country is more to be valued and higher and holier far more than mother or father or any ancestor, and more to be regarded in the eyes of the gods and of men of understanding? Also to be soothed and gently and reverently entreated when angry, even more than a father, and either to be persuaded or, if not persuaded, to be obeyed? And when we are punished by her, whether with imprisonment or beatings, the punishment is to be endured in silence; and if she leads us to wounds or death in battle, there we follow as is right; neither may anyone yield or retreat or leave his rank, but whether in battle, or in a court of law, or in any other place, he must do what his city and his country order him, or he must change their view of what is just; and if he may do no violence to his father or mother, much less may he do violence to his country." What answer shall we make to this, Crito? Do the laws speak truly, or do they not?

CRITO: I think that they do.

SOCRATES: Then the laws will say, "Consider, Socrates, if we are speaking truly that in your present attempt you are going to do us an injury. For, having brought you into the world, and nurtured and educated you, and given you and every other citizen a share in every good which we had to give, we further proclaim to any Athenian, by the liberty which we allow him, that if he does not like us when he has come of age and has seen the ways of the city and made our acquaintance, he may go where he pleases and take his goods with him. None of us laws will stand in the way if any of you who are dissatisfied with us and the city want to go to a colony or to move anywhere else. None of us forbids anyone to go where he likes, taking his property with him. But he who has experience of the manner in which we order justice and administer the state, and still remains, has entered into an implied contract that he will do as we command him. And he who disobeys us is, as we maintain, thrice wrong: first, because in disobeying us he is disobeying his parents; secondly, because we are the authors of his education; thirdly, because he has made an agreement with us that he will duly obey our commands, but he neither obeys them nor convinces us that our commands are unjust. We show flexibility. We do not brutally demand his compliance but offer him the choice of obeying or persuading us; yet he does neither.

"These are the sorts of accusations to which, as we were saying, you, Socrates, will be exposed if you accomplish your intentions; you, above all other Athenians." Suppose now I ask, why I rather than anybody else? They might reasonably take me to task because I above all other men have acknowledged the agreement. "There is clear proof," they will say, "Socrates, that we and the city were not displeasing to you. Of all Athenians you have been the most constant resident in the city, which, as you never leave it, you may be supposed to love. For you never went out of the city either to see the games, except once, when you went to the Isthmus, or to any other place unless when you were on military service; nor did you travel as other men do. Nor had you any curiosity to know other states or their laws: your affections did not go beyond us and our state; we were your special favorites, and you acquiesced in our government of you; and here in this city you had your children, which is a proof of your satisfaction. Moreover, you might in the course of the trial, if you had liked, have fixed the penalty at banishment, and then you could have done with the city's consent what you now attempt against its will. But you pretended that you preferred death to exile and that you were not unwilling to die. And now you do not blush at the thought of your old arguments and pay no respect to us, the laws, of whom you are the destroyer, and are doing what only a miserable slave would do, running away and turning your back on the compacts and agreements by which you agreed to act as a citizen. And, first of all, answer this very question: Are we right in saying that by your actions if not in words you agreed to our terms of citizenship? Is that true or not?" How shall we answer, Crito? Must we not assent?

CRITO: We cannot help it, Socrates.

SOCRATES: Then will they not say: "You, Socrates, are breaking the covenants and agreements which you made with us. You were not compelled to agree, or tricked, or forced to make up your mind in a moment, but had a period of seventy years during which you were free to depart if you were dissatisfied with us and the agreements did not seem fair. You did not pick Sparta or Crete, whose fine government you take every opportunity to praise, or any other state of the Greek or non-Greek world. You spent less time out of Athens than men who are crippled or blind or otherwise handicapped. That shows how much more than other Athenians you valued the city and us too, its laws (for who would value a city without laws?). And will you not now abide by your agreements? You will if you listen to us, Socrates, and you will not make yourself ridiculous by leaving the city.

"For just consider: if you transgress and err in this sort of way, what good will you do either to yourself or to your friends? That your friends will be driven into exile and deprived of citizenship or will lose their property is tolerably certain. And you yourself, if you go to one of the neighboring cities, like Thebes or Megara (both being well-ordered states, of course), will come as an enemy of their government, and all patriotic citizens will eye you suspiciously as a subverter of the laws, and you will confirm in the minds of the judges the justice of their own condemnation of you. For he who is a corrupter of the laws is more than likely to be a corrupter of the young and foolish portion of mankind. Will you then flee from well-ordered cities and law-abiding men? And will life be worth living if you do that? Or will you approach them and discourse unashamedly about—about what, Socrates? Will you discourse as you did here, about how virtue and justice and institutions and laws are the best things among men? Don't you think that such behavior coming from Socrates will seem disgusting? Surely one must think so. But if you go away from well-governed states to Crito's friends in Thessaly, where there is great disorder and license, they will be charmed to hear the tale of your escape from prison, set off with ludicrous particulars of the manner in which you were wrapped in a goatskin or some other disguise and metamorphosed in the usual manner of runaways. But will there be no one to comment that in your old age, when in all probability you had only a little time left to live, you were not ashamed to violate the most sacred laws from the greedy desire of a little more life? Perhaps not, if you keep them in good temper; but if they are out of temper, you will hear many degrading things. You will live as the flatterer and slave of all men, achieving what else but the chance to feast in Thessaly, as though you had gone abroad in order to get a meal? And where will the old arguments be, about justice and virtue? Say that you wish to live for the sake of your children—you want to bring them up and educate them—will you take them into Thessaly and deprive them of Athenian citizenship? Is this the benefit which you will confer upon them? Or are you under the impression that they will be better cared for and educated here if you are still alive, although absent from them; for your friends will take care of them? Do you fancy that, if you move to Thessaly, they will take care of them but that, if you move into the other world, they will not take care of them? No, if those who call themselves friends are good for anything, they will—to be sure, they will.

"Listen, then, Socrates, to us who have brought you up. Think not of life and children first and of justice afterwards but of justice first, so that you may defend your conduct to the rulers of the world below. For neither will you nor any that belong to you be happier or holier or juster in this life, or happier in another, if you do as Crito bids. Now you depart in innocence, a sufferer and not a doer of evil; a victim, not of the laws but of men. But if you escape, returning evil for evil and injury for injury, breaking the covenants and agreements which you have made with us and wronging those you ought least of all to wrong—that is to say, yourself, your friends, your country, and us—we shall be angry with you while you live, and our brethren, the laws in the world below, will receive you in no kindly spirit; for they will know that you have done your best to destroy us. Listen, then, to us and not to Crito."

This, dear Crito, is the voice I seem to hear murmuring in my ears, like the sound of the flute in the ears of the mystic; that voice, I say, is humming in my ears and prevents me from hearing any other. You must realize that you will be wasting your time if you speak against the convictions I hold at the moment. But if you think you will get anywhere, go ahead.

CRITO: No, Socrates, I have nothing to say.

SOCRATES: Then be resigned, Crito, and let us follow this course, since this is the way the god points out.

Suggestions for Discussion

1. What arguments does Crito use to urge Socrates to escape? To what extent do you agree with his position? How does Socrates counter his arguments?
2. Why does Socrates say that one should only consider the opinion of good people?
3. What qualities of character does Plato create for both Crito and Socrates? Which of the two men is more like most of us?
4. Explain Socrates' use of the analogy of the athlete and his trainer and the parallel question of whether life is worth living in a corrupted body.
5. How does Socrates distinguish between the value of "life" and "a good life"?
6. Socrates persuades Crito that a good man should never intentionally commit a wrong act. How does he relate this assertion to the issue of whether he should attempt to escape from prison?

7. Why does Socrates summon up the laws of Athens to discuss his strict obedience to them? What arguments do they offer?
8. Why does Socrates say that he must listen to the voice of the god? How does he connect the laws of the state to the god?

Suggestions for Writing

1. Socrates' arguments for obeying the laws of the state have not always found universal agreement. In modern times, civil disobedience has moved men like Henry David Thoreau, Mahatma Gandhi, and Martin Luther King, Jr. A research paper of five pages could compare and contrast the writings of Thoreau, Gandhi, and King with this dialogue by Plato.
2. Have you ever broken the law or been tempted to do so? What reasons have restrained you or otherwise guided your behavior? Write a paper of 500 words in which you analyze your own motives as Socrates analyzes his.

MARY GORDON

A Moral Choice

Mary Gordon (b. 1949) was born on Long Island, New York, and educated at Barnard College and the University of Syracuse. She has taught English at Dutchess County Community College and at Amherst College and has published short stories, poems, and novels that have received critical and popular success, including *Final Payments* (1978); *The Company of Women* (1981); *Men and Angels* (1985); *The Other Side* (1989); a collection of stories, *Temporary Shelter* (1990); and a collection of three novellas, *The Rest of Life* (1993). A writer often identified as a Catholic, she frequently deals with theological themes. In this essay, she calls for clear definitions of the moral issues surrounding abortion and explains why she has taken a pro-choice position.

I am having lunch with six women. What is unusual is that four of them are in their seventies, two of them widowed, the other two living with husbands beside whom they've lived for decades. All of them have had children. Had they been men, they would have published books and hung their paintings on the walls of important galleries. But they are women of a certain generation, and their lives were shaped around their families and personal relations. They are women you go to for help and support. We begin talking about the latest legislative act that makes abortion more difficult for poor women to obtain. An extraordinary thing happens. Each of them talks about the illegal abortions she had during her young womanhood. Not one of them was spared the experience. Any of them could have died on the table of whatever person (not a doctor in any case) she was forced to approach, in secrecy and in terror, to end a pregnancy that she felt would blight her life.

I mention this incident for two reasons: first as a reminder that all kinds of women have always had abortions; second because it is essential that we remember that an abortion is performed on a living woman who has a life in which a terminated pregnancy is only a small part. Morally speaking, the decision to have an abortion doesn't take place in a vacuum. It is connected to other choices that a woman makes in the course of an adult life.

Anti-choice propagandists paint pictures of women who choose to have abortions as types of moral callousness, selfishness, or irresponsibility. The woman choosing to abort is the dressed-for-success yuppie who gets rid of her baby so that she won't miss her Caribbean vacation or her chance for promotion. Or she is the feckless, promiscuous ghetto teenager who couldn't bring herself to just say no to sex. A third, purportedly kinder, gentler picture has recently begun to be drawn. The woman in the abortion clinic is there because she is misinformed about the nature of the world. She is having an abortion because society does not provide for mothers and their children, and she mistakenly thinks that another mouth to feed will be the ruin of her family, not understanding that the temporary truth of family unhappiness doesn't stack up beside the eternal verity that abortion is murder. Or she is the dupe of her husband or boyfriend, who talks her into having an abortion because a child will be a drag on his lifestyle. None of these pictures created by the anti-choice movement assumes that the decision to have an abortion is made responsibly, in the context of a morally lived life, by a free and responsible moral agent.

The Ontology of the Fetus

How would a woman who habitually makes choices in moral terms come to the decision to have an abortion? The moral discussion of abortion centers on the issue of whether or not abortion is an act of murder. At first glance it would seem that the answer should follow directly upon two questions: Is the fetus human? and Is it alive? It would be absurd to deny that a fetus is alive or that it is human. What would our other options be—to say that it is inanimate or belongs to another species? But we habitually use the terms "human" and "live" to refer to parts of our body—"human hair," for example, or "live red-blood cells"—and we are clear in our understanding that the nature of these objects does not rank equally with an entire personal existence. It then seems important to consider whether the fetus, this alive human thing, is a *person,* to whom the term "murder" could sensibly be applied. How would anyone come to a decision about something so impalpable as personhood? Philosophers have struggled with the issue of personhood, but in language that is so abstract that it is unhelpful to ordinary people making decisions in the course of their lives. It might be more productive to begin thinking about the status of the fetus by examining the language and customs that surround it. This approach will encourage us to focus on the choosing, acting woman, rather than the act of abortion—as if the act were performed by abstract forces without bodies, histories, attachments.

This focus on the acting woman is useful because a pregnant woman has an identifiable, consistent ontology, and a fetus takes on different ontological identities over time. But common sense, experience, and linguistic usage point clearly to the fact that we habitually consider, for example, a seven-week-old fetus to be different from a seven-month-old one. We can tell this by the way we respond to the involuntary loss of one as against the other. We have different language for the experience of the involuntary expulsion of the fetus from the womb depending upon the point of gestation at which the experience occurs. If it occurs early in the pregnancy, we call it a miscarriage; if late, we call it a stillbirth.

We would have an extreme reaction to the reversal of those terms. If a woman referred to a miscarriage at seven weeks as a stillbirth, we would be alarmed. It would shock our sense of propriety; it would make us uneasy; we would find it disturbing, misplaced—as we do when a bag lady sits down in a restaurant and starts shouting, or an octogenarian arrives at our door in a sailor suit. In short, we would suspect that the speaker was mad. Similarly, if a doctor or a nurse referred to the loss of a seven-month-old fetus as a miscarriage, we would be shocked by that person's insensitivity: could she or he not understand that a fetus that age is not what it was months before?

Our ritual and religious practices underscore the fact that we make distinctions among fetuses. If a woman took the bloody matter—indistinguishable from a heavy period—of an early miscarriage and insisted upon putting it in a tiny coffin and marking its grave, we would have serious concerns about her mental health. By the same token, we would feel squeamish about flushing a seven-month-old fetus down the toilet—something we would quite normally do with an early miscarriage. There are no prayers for the matter of a miscarriage, nor do we feel there should be. Even a Catholic priest would not baptize the issue of an early miscarriage.

The difficulties stem, of course, from the odd situation of a fetus's ontology: a complicated, differentiated, and nuanced response is required when we are dealing with an entity that changes over time. Yet we are in the habit of making distinctions like this. At one point we know that a child is no longer a child but an adult. That this question is vexed and problematic is clear from our difficulty in determining who is a juvenile offender and who is an adult criminal and at what age sexual intercourse ceases to be known as statutory rape. So at what point, if any, do we on the pro-choice side say that the developing fetus is a person, with rights equal to its mother's?

The anti-choice people have one advantage over us; their monolithic position gives them unity on this question. For myself, I am made uneasy by third-trimester abortions, which take place when the fetus could live outside the mother's body, but I also know that these are extremely rare and often performed on very young girls who have had difficulty comprehending the realities of pregnancy. It seems to me that the question of late abortions should be decided case by case, and that fixation on this issue is a deflection from what is most important: keeping early abortions, which are in the majority by far, safe and legal. I am also politically realistic enough to suspect that bills restricting late abortions are not good-faith attempts to make distinctions about the nature of fetal life. They are, rather, the cynical embodiments of the hope among anti-choice partisans that technology will be on their side and that medical science's ability to create situations in which younger fetuses are viable outside their mothers' bodies will increase dramatically in the next few years. Ironically, medical science will probably make the issue of abortion a minor one in the near future. The RU-486 pill, which can induce abortion early on, exists, and whether or not it is legally available (it is not on the market here, because of pressure from anti-choice groups), women will begin to obtain it. If abortion can occur through chemical rather than physical means, in the privacy of one's home, most people not directly involved will lose interest in it. As abortion is transformed from a public into a private issue, it will cease to be perceived as political; it will be called personal instead.

An Equivocal Good

But because abortion will always deal with what it is to create and sustain life, it will always be a moral issue. And whether we like it or not, our moral thinking about abortion is rooted in the shifting soil of perception. In an age in which much of our perception is manipulated by media that specialize in the sound bite and the photo op, the anti-choice partisans have a twofold advantage over us on the pro-choice side. The pro-choice moral position is more complex, and the experience we defend is physically repellent to contemplate. None of us in the pro-choice movement would suggest that abortion is not a regrettable occurrence. Anti-choice proponents can offer pastel photographs of babies in buntings, their eyes peaceful in the camera's gaze. In answer, we can't offer the material of an early abortion, bloody, amorphous in a paper cup, to prove that what has just been removed from the woman's body is not a child, not in the same category of being as the adorable bundle in an adoptive mother's arms. It is not a pleasure to look at the physical evidence of abortion, and most of us don't get the opportunity to do so.

The theologian Daniel Maguire, uncomfortable with the fact that most theological arguments about the nature of abortion are made by men who have never been anywhere near an actual abortion, decided to visit a clinic and observe abortions being performed. He didn't find the experience easy, but he knew that before he could in good conscience make a moral judgment on abortion, he needed to experience through his senses what an aborted fetus is like: he needed to look at and touch the controversial entity. He held in his hand the bloody fetal stuff; the eight-week-old fetus fit in the palm of his hand, and it certainly bore no resemblance to either of his two children when he had held them moments after their birth. He knew at that point what women who have experienced early abortions and miscarriages know: that some event occurred, possibly even a dramatic one, but it was not the death of a child.

Because issues of pregnancy and birth are both physical and metaphorical, we must constantly step back and forth between ways of perceiving the world. When we speak of gestation, we are often talking in terms of potential, about events and objects to which we attach our hopes, fears, dreams, and ideals. A mother can speak to the fetus in her uterus and name it; she and her mate may decorate a nursery according to their vision of the good life; they may choose for an embryo a college, a profession, a dwelling. But those of us who are trying to think morally about pregnancy and birth must remember that these feelings are our own projections onto what is in reality an inappropriate object. However charmed we may be by an expectant father's buying a little football for something inside his wife's belly, we shouldn't make public policy based on such actions, nor should we force others to live their lives conforming to our fantasies.

As a society, we are making decisions that pit the complicated future of a complex adult against the fate of a mass of cells lacking cortical development. The moral pressure should be on distinguishing the true from the false, the real suffering of living persons from our individual and often idiosyncratic dreams and fears. We must make decisions on abortion based on an understanding of how people really do live. We must be able to say that poverty is worse than not being poor, that having dignified and meaningful work is better than working in conditions of degradation, that raising a child one loves and has desired is better than raising a child in resentment and rage, that it is better for a twelve-year-old not to endure the trauma of having a child when she is herself a child.

When we put these ideas against the ideas of "child" or "baby," we seem to be making a horrifying choice of life-style over life. But in fact we are telling the truth of what it means to bear a child, and what the experience of abortion really is. This is extremely difficult, for the object of the discussion is hidden, changing, potential. We make our decisions on the basis of approximate and inadequate language, often on the basis of fantasies and fears. It will always be crucial to try to separate genuine moral concern from phobia, punitiveness, superstition, anxiety, a desperate search for certainty in an uncertain world.

One of the certainties that is removed if we accept the consequences of the pro-choice position is the belief that the birth of a child is an unequivocal good. In real life we act knowing that the birth of a child is not always a good thing: people are sometimes depressed, angry, rejecting, at the birth of a child. But this is a difficult truth to tell; we don't like to say it, and one of the fears preyed on by anti-choice proponents is that if we cannot look at the birth of a child as an unequivocal good, then there is nothing to look toward. The desire for security of the imagination, for typological fixity, particularly in the area of "the good," is an understandable desire. It must seem to some anti-choice people that we on the pro-choice side are not only murdering innocent children but also murdering hope. Those of us who have experienced the birth of a desired child and felt the joy of that moment can be tempted into believing that it was the physical experience of the birth itself that was the joy. But it is crucial to remember that the birth of a child itself is a neutral occurrence emotionally: the charge it takes on is invested in it by the people experiencing or observing it.

The Fear of Sexual Autonomy

These uncertainties can lead to another set of fears, not only about abortion but about its implications. Many anti-choice people fear that to support abortion is to cast one's lot with the cold and technological rather than with the warm and natural, to head down the slippery slope toward a brave new world where handicapped children are left on mountains to starve and the old are put out in the snow. But if we look at the history of abortion, we don't see the embodiment of what the anti-choice proponents fear. On the contrary, excepting the grotesque counterexample of the People's Republic of China (which practices forced abortion), there seems to be a real link between repressive anti-abortion stances and repressive governments. Abortion was banned in Fascist Italy and Nazi Germany; it is illegal in South Africa and in Chile. It is paid for by the governments of Denmark, England, and the Netherlands, which have national health and welfare systems that foster the health and well-being of mothers, children, the old, and the handicapped.

Advocates of outlawing abortion often refer to women seeking abortion as self-indulgent and materialistic. In fact these accusations mask a discomfort with female sexuality, sexual pleasure, and sexual autonomy. It is possible for a woman to have a sexual life unriddled by fear only if she can be confident that she need not pay for a failure of technology or judgment (and who among us has never once been swept away in the heat of a sexual moment?) by taking upon herself the crushing burden of unchosen motherhood.

It is no accident, therefore, that the increased appeal of measures to restrict maternal conduct during pregnancy—and a new focus on the physical autonomy of the pregnant woman—have come into public discourse at precisely the time when women are achieving unprecendented levels of economic and political autonomy. What has surprised me is that some of this new anti-autonomy talk comes to us from the left. An example of this new discourse is an article by Christopher Hitchens that appeared in *The Nation* last April, in which the author asserts his discomfort with abortion. Hitchens's tone is impeccably British: arch, light, we're men of the left.

> Anyone who has ever seen a sonogram or has spent even an hour with a textbook on embryology knows that the emotions are not the deciding factor. In order to terminate a pregnancy, you have to still a heartbeat, switch off a developing brain, and whatever the method, break some bones and rupture some organs. As to whether this involves pain on the "Silent Scream" scale, I have no idea. The "right to life" leadership, again, has cheapened everything it touches.

"It is a pity," Hitchens goes on to say, "that...the majority of feminists and their allies have stuck to the dead ground of 'Me Decade' possessive individualism, an ideology that has more in common than it admits with the prehistoric right, which it claims to oppose but has in fact encouraged." Hitchens proposes, as an alternative, a program of social reform that would make contraception free and support a national adoption service. In his opinion, it would seem, women have abortions for only two reasons: because they are selfish or because they are poor. If the state will take care of the economic problems and the bureaucratic messiness around adoption, it remains only for the possessive individuals to get their act together and walk with their babies into the communal utopia of the future. Hitchens would allow victims of rape or incest to have free abortions, on the grounds that since they didn't choose to have sex, the women should not be forced to have the babies. This would seem to put the issue of volition in a wrong and telling place. To Hitchens's mind, it would appear, if a woman chooses to have sex, she can't choose whether or not to have a baby. The implications of this are clear. If a woman is consciously and volitionally sexual, she should be prepared to take her medicine. And what medicine must the consciously sexual male take? Does Hitchens really believe, or want us to believe, that every male who has unintentionally impregnated a woman will be involved in the lifelong responsibility for the upbringing of the engendered child? Can he honestly say that he has observed this behavior—or, indeed, would want to see it observed—in the world in which he lives?

Real Choices

It is essential for a moral decision about abortion to be made in an atmosphere of open, critical thinking. We on the pro-choice side must accept that there are indeed anti-choice activists who take their position in good faith. I believe, however, that they are people for whom childbirth is an emotionally overladen topic, people who are susceptible to unclear thinking because of their unrealistic hopes and fears. It is important for us in the pro-choice movement to be open in discussing those areas involving abortion which are nebulous and unclear. But we must not forget that there are some things that we know to be undeniably true. There are some undeniable bad consequences of a woman's being forced to bear a child against her will. First is the trauma of going through a pregnancy and giving birth to a child who is not desired, a trauma more long-lasting than that experienced by some (only some) women who experience an early abortion. The grief of giving up a child at its birth—and at nine months it is a child whom one has felt move inside one's body—is underestimated both by anti-choice partisans and by those for whom access to adoptable children is important. This grief should not be forced on any woman—or, indeed, encouraged by public policy.

We must be realistic about the impact on society of millions of unwanted children in an overpopulated world. Most of the time, human beings have sex not because they want to make babies. Yet throughout history sex has resulted in unwanted pregnancies. And women have always aborted. One thing that is not hidden, mysterious, or debatable is that making abortion illegal will result in the deaths of women, as it has always done. Is our historical memory so short that none of us remember aunts, sisters, friends, or mothers who were killed or rendered sterile by septic abortions? Does no one in the anti-choice movement remember stories or actual experiences of midnight drives to filthy rooms from which aborted women were sent out, bleeding, to their fate? Can anyone genuinely say that it would be a moral good for us as a society to return to those conditions?

Thinking about abortion, then, forces us to take moral positions as adults who understand the complexities of the world and the realities of human suffering, to make decisions based on how people actually live and choose, and not on our fears, prejudices, and anxieties about sex and society, life and death.

Suggestions for Discussion

1. What is the function of the personal episode the author uses in the opening paragraph of the essay?
2. What reasons for abortion do anti-choice people ascribe to those who want abortions? What are the author's responses to those reasons?
3. How does the author deal with the issue of whether a fetus is live and human? Is her discussion of this issue valid or persuasive? Do you agree with the distinctions she makes between the terms "miscarriage" and "stillbirth"?
4. What does Gordon mean by the term "the ontology of the fetus"? How does this term become crucial to her argument in favor of choice?
5. For the author, what are the real moral choices surrounding a woman's decision to have an abortion? How complex does she believe the issue to be?
6. Gordon objects to the positions of the political left and right on this issue. Explain.

Suggestions for Writing

1. Write a paper in which you argue for or against Gordon's position on abortion. Summarize her argument and try to agree or disagree with it by reference to the points she makes.
2. Look at the last three paragraphs of Gordon's essay. Do you agree or disagree with her conclusions? Write an essay in which you state your position clearly and concretely.

SHELBY STEELE

On Being Black and Middle Class

Shelby Steele was born in Cedar Rapids, Iowa, in 1946. He has degrees from Coe College, the Southern University of Illinois, and the University of Utah. A frequent contributor to the national debate on race relations, Steele won a National Book Critics Circle Award and created a stir of controversy for *The Content of Our Character: A New Vision of Race* (1990), in which he claims African-Americans suffer from self-doubt and need to move beyond the issues of race. He has been on the faculty of the department of English at California State University, San Jose, for many years but has been on a leave of absence while he prepares a book manuscript for publication. The following essay, which originally appeared in the journal *Commentary,* examines the tensions and dilemmas facing a successful member of the black middle class who wants to retain his ethnic heritage.

Not long ago a friend of mine, black like myself, said to me that the term "black middle class" was actually a contradiction in terms. Race, he insisted, blurred class distinctions among blacks. If you were black, you were just black and that was that. When I argued, he let his eyes roll at my naiveté. Then he went on. For us, as black professionals, it was an exercise in self-flattery, a pathetic pretension, to give meaning to such a distinction. Worse, the very idea of class threatened the unity that was vital to the black community as a whole. After all, since when had white America taken note of anything but color when it came to blacks? He then reminded me of an old Malcolm X line that had been popular in the sixties. Question: What is a black man with a Ph.D.? Answer: A nigger.

For many years I had been on my friend's side of this argument. Much of my conscious thinking on the old conundrum of race and class was shaped during my high school and college years in the race-charged sixties, when the fact of my race took on an almost religious significance. Progressively, from the mid-sixties on, more and more aspects of my life found their explanation, their justification, and their motivation in race. My youthful concerns about career, romance, money, values, and even styles of dress became a subject to consultation with various oracular sources of racial wisdom. And these ranged from a figure as ennobling as Martin

Luther King, Jr., to the underworld elegance of dress I found in jazz clubs on the South Side of Chicago. Everywhere there were signals, and in those days I considered myself so blessed with clarity and direction that I pitied my white classmates who found more embarrassment than guidance in the fact of *their* race. In 1968, inflated by my new power, I took a mischievous delight in calling them culturally disadvantaged.

But now, hearing my friend's comment was like hearing a priest from a church I'd grown disenchanted with. I understood him, but my faith was weak. What had sustained me in the sixties sounded monotonous and off the mark in the eighties. For me, race had lost much of its juju, its singular capacity to conjure meaning. And today, when I honestly look at my life and the lives of many other middle-class blacks I know, I can see that race never fully explained our situation in American society. Black though I may be, it is impossible for me to sit in my single-family house with two cars in the driveway and a swing set in the back yard and *not* see the role class has played in my life. And how can my friend, similarly raised and similarly situated, not see it?

Yet despite my certainty I felt a sharp tug of guilt as I tried to explain myself over my friend's skepticism. He is a man of many comedic facial expressions and, as I spoke, his brow lifted in extreme moral alarm as if I were uttering the unspeakable. His clear implication was that I was being elitist and possibly (dare he suggest?) anti-black—crimes for which there might well be no redemption. He pretended to fear for me. I chuckled along with him, but inwardly I did wonder at myself. Though I never doubted the validity of what I was saying, I felt guilty saying it. Why?

After he left (to retrieve his daughter from a dance lesson) I realized that the trap I felt myself in had a tiresome familiarity and, in a sort of slow-motion epiphany, I began to see its outline. It was like the suddenly sharp vision one has at the end of a burdensome marriage when all the long-repressed incompatibilities come undeniably to light.

What became clear to me is that people like myself, my friend, and middle-class blacks generally are caught in a very specific double bind that keeps two equally powerful elements of our identity at odds with each other. The middle-class values by which we were raised—the work ethic, the importance of education, the value of property ownership, of respectability, of "getting ahead," of stable family life, of initiative, of self-reliance, etc.—are, in themselves, raceless and even assimilationist. They urge us toward participation in the American mainstream, toward integration, toward a strong identification with the society—and toward the entire constellation of qualities that are implied in the word "individualism." These values are almost rules for how to prosper in a democratic, free-enterprise society that admires and rewards individual effort. They tell us to work hard for ourselves and our families and to seek our opportunities whenever they appear, inside or outside the confines of whatever ethnic group we may belong to.

But the particular pattern of racial identification that emerged in the sixties and that still prevails today urges middle-class blacks (and all blacks) in the opposite direction. This pattern asks us to see ourselves as an embattled minority, and it urges an adversarial stance toward the mainstream, an emphasis on ethnic consciousness over individualism. It is organized around an implied separatism.

The opposing thrust of these two parts of our identity results in the double bind of middle-class blacks. There is no forward movement on either plane that does not constitute backward movement on the other. This was the familiar trap I felt myself in while talking with my friend. As I spoke about class, his eyes reminded me that I was betraying race. Clearly, the two indispensable parts of my identity were a threat to each other.

Of course when you think about it, class and race are both similar in some ways and also naturally opposed. They are two forms of collective identity with boundaries that intersect. But whether they clash or peacefully coexist has much to do with how they are defined. Being both black and middle class becomes a double bind when class and race are defined in sharply antagonistic terms, so that one must be repressed to appease the other.

But what is the "substance" of these two identities, and how does each establish itself in an individual's overall identity? It seems to me that when we identify with any collective we are basically identifying with images that tell us what it means to be a member of that collective. Identity is not the same thing as the fact of membership in a collective; it is, rather, a form of self-definition, facilitated by images of what we wish our membership in the collective to mean. In this sense, the images we identify with may reflect the aspirations of the collective more than they reflect reality, and their content can vary with shifts in those aspirations.

But the process of identification is usually dialectical. It is just as necessary to say what we are *not* as it is to say what we are—so that finally identification comes about by embracing a polarity of positive and negative images. To identify as middle class, for example, I must have both positive and negative images of what being middle class entails; then I will know what I should and should not be doing in order to be middle class. The same goes for racial identity.

In the racially turbulent sixties the polarity of images that came to define racial identification was very antagonistic to the polarity that defined middle-class identification. One might say that the positive images of one lined up with the negative images of the other, so that to identify with both required either a contortionist's flexibility or a dangerous splitting of the self. The double bind of the black middle class was in place.

The black middle class has always defined its class identity by means of positive images gleaned from middle- and upper-class white society, and by means of negative images of lower-class blacks. This habit goes back to the institution of slavery itself, when "house" slaves both mimicked the whites they served and held themselves above the "field" slaves. But in the sixties the old bourgeois impulse to dissociate from the lower classes (the "we-they" distinction) backfired when racial identity suddenly called for the celebration of this same black lower class. One of the qualities of a double bind is that one feels it more than sees it, and I distinctly remember the tension and strange sense of dishonesty I felt in those days as I moved back and forth like a bigamist between the demands of class and race.

Though my father was born poor, he achieved middle-class standing through much hard work and sacrifice (one of his favorite words) and by identifying fully with solid middle-class values—mainly hard work, family life, property ownership, and education for his children (all four of whom have advanced degrees). In his mind these were not so much values as laws of nature. People who embodied them made up the positive images in his class polarity. The negative images came largely from the blacks he had left behind because they were "going nowhere."

No one in my family remembers how it happened, but as time went on, the negative images congealed into an imaginary character named Sam, who, from the extensive service we put him to, quickly grew to mythic proportions. In our family lore he was sometimes a trickster, sometimes a boob, but always possessed of a catalogue of sly faults that gave up graphic images of everything we should not be. On sacrifice: "Sam never thinks about tomorrow. He wants it now or he doesn't care about it." On work: "Sam doesn't favor it too much." On children: "Sam likes to have them but not to raise them." On money: "Sam drinks it up and pisses it out." On fidelity: "Sam has to have two or three women." On clothes: "Sam features loud clothes. He likes to see and be seen." And so on. Sam's persona amounted to a negative instruction manual in class identity.

I don't think that any of us believed Sam's faults were accurate representations of lower-class black life. He was an instrument of self-definition, not of sociological accuracy. It never occurred to us that he looked very much like the white racist stereotype of blacks, or that he might have been a manifestation of our own racial self-hatred. He simply gave us a counterpoint against which to express our aspirations. If self-hatred was a factor, it was not, for us, a matter of hating lower-class blacks but of hating what we did not want to be.

Still, hate or love aside, it is fundamentally true that my middle-class identity involved a dissociation from images of lower-class black life and a corresponding identification with values and patterns of responsibility that are common to the middle class everywhere. These values sent me a clear message: be both an individual and a responsible citizen; understand that the quality of your life will approximately reflect the quality of effort you put into it; know that individual responsibility is the basis of freedom and that the limitations imposed by fate (whether fair or unfair) are no excuse for passivity.

Whether I live up to these values or not, I know that my acceptance of them is the result of lifelong conditioning. I know also that I share this conditioning with middle-class people of all races and that I can no more easily be free of it than I can be free of my race. Whether all this got started because the black middle class modeled itself on the white middle class is no longer relevant. For the middle-class black, conditioned by these values from birth, the sense of meaning they provide is as immutable as the color of his skin.

I started the sixties in high school feeling that my class-conditioning was the surest way to overcome racial barriers. My racial identity was pretty much taken for granted. After all, it was obvious to the world that I was black. Yet I ended the sixties in graduate school a little embarrassed by my class background and with an almost desperate need to be "black." The tables had turned. I knew very clearly (though I struggled to repress it) that my aspirations and my sense of how to operate in the world came from my class background, yet "being black" required certain attitudes and stances that made me feel secretly a little duplicitous. The inner compatibility of class and race I had known in 1960 was gone.

For blacks, the decade between 1960 and 1969 saw racial identification undergo the same sort of transformation that national identity undergoes in times of war. It became more self-conscious, more narrowly focused, more prescribed, less tolerant of opposition. It spawned an implicit party line, which tended to disallow competing forms of identity. Race-as-identity was lifted from the relative slumber it knew in the fifties and pressed into service in a social and political war against oppression. It was redefined along sharp adversarial lines and directed toward the goal of mobilizing the great mass of black Americans in this warlike effort. It was imbued with a strong moral authority, useful for denouncing those who opposed it and for celebrating those who honored it as a positive achievement rather than as a mere birthright.

The form of racial identification that quickly evolved to meet this challenge presented blacks as a racial monolith, a singular people with a common experience of oppression. Differences within the race, no matter how ineradicable, had to be minimized. Class distinctions were one of the first such differences to be sacrificed, since they not only threatened racial unity but also seemed to stand in contradiction to the principle of equality which was the announced goal of the movement for racial progress. The discomfort

I felt in 1969, the vague but relentless sense of duplicity, was the result of a historical necessity that put my race and class at odds, that was asking me to cast aside the distinction of my class and identify with a monolithic view of my race.

If the form of this racial identity was the monolith, its substance was victimization. The civil rights movement and the more radical splinter groups of the late sixties were all dedicated to ending racial victimization, and the form of black identity that emerged to facilitate this goal made blackness and victimization virtually synonymous. Since it was our victimization more than any other variable that identified and unified us, moreover, it followed logically that the purest black was the poor black. It was images of him that clustered around the positive pole of the race polarity; all other blacks were, in effect, required to identify with him in order to confirm their own blackness.

Certainly there were more dimensions to the black experience than victimization, but no other had the same capacity to fire the indignation needed for war. So, again out of historical necessity, victimization became the overriding focus of racial identity. But this only deepened the double bind for middle-class blacks like me. When it came to class we were accustomed to defining ourselves against lower-class blacks and identifying with at least the values of middle-class whites; when it came to race we were now being asked to identify with images of lower-class blacks and to see whites, middle class or otherwise, as victimizers. Negative lining up with positive, we were called upon to reject what we had previously embraced and to embrace what we had previously rejected. To put it still more personally, the Sam figure I had been raised to define myself against had now become the "real" black I was expected to identify with.

The fact that the poor black's new status was only passively earned by the condition of his victimization, not by assertive, positive action, made little difference. Status was status apart from the means by which it was achieved, and along with it came a certain power—the power to define the terms of access to that status, to say who was black and who was not. If a lower-class black said you were not really "black"—a sellout, an Uncle Tom—the judgment was all the more devastating because it carried the authority of his status. And this judgment soon enough came to be accepted by many whites as well.

In graduate school I was once told by a white professor, "Well, but...you're not really black. I mean, you're not disadvantaged." In his mind my lack of victim status disqualified me from the race itself. More recently I was complimented by a black student for speaking reasonably correct English, "proper" English as he put it. "But I don't know if I really want to talk like that," he went on. "Why not?" I asked. "Because then I wouldn't be black no more," he replied without a pause.

To overcome his marginal status, the middle-class black had to identify with a degree of victimization that was beyond his actual experience. In college (and well beyond) we used to play a game called "nap matching." It was a game of one-upmanship, in which we sat around outdoing each other with stories of racial victimization, symbolically measured by the naps of our hair. Most of us were middle class and so had few personal stories to relate, but if we could not match naps with our own biographies, we would move on to those legendary tales of victimization that came to us from the public domain.

The single story that sat atop the pinnacle of racial victimization for us was that of Emmett Till, the Northern black teenager who, on a visit to the South in 1955, was killed and grotesquely mutilated for supposedly looking at or whistling at (we were never sure which, though we argued the point endlessly) a white woman. Oh, how we probed his story, finding in his youth and Northern upbringing the quintessential embodiment of black innocence, brought down by a white evil so portentous and apocalyptic, so gnarled and hideous, that it left us with a feeling not far from awe. By telling his story and others like it, we came to *feel* the immutability of our victimization, its utter indigenousness, as a thing on this earth like dirt or sand or water.

Of course, these sessions were a ritual of group identification, a means by which we, as middle-class blacks, could be at one with our race. But why were we, who had only a moderate experience of victimization (and that offset by opportunities our parents never had), so intent on assimilating or appropriating an identity that in so many ways contradicted our own? Because, I think, the sense of innocence that is always entailed in feeling victimized filled us with a corresponding feeling of entitlement, or even license, that helped us endure our vulnerability on a largely white college campus.

In my junior year in college I rode to a debate tournament with three white students and our faculty coach, an elderly English professor. The experience of being the lone black in a group of whites was so familiar to me that I thought nothing of it as our trip began. But then halfway through the trip the professor casually turned to me and, in an isn't-the-world-funny sort of tone, said that he had just refused to rent an apartment in a house he owned to a "very nice" black couple because their color would "offend" the white couple who lived downstairs. His eyebrows lifted helplessly over his hawkish nose, suggesting that he too, like me, was a victim of America's racial farce. His look assumed a kind of comradeship: he and I were above this grimy business of race, though for expediency we had occasionally to concede the world its madness.

My vulnerability in this situation came not so much from the professor's blindness to his own racism as from his assumption that I would participate in it, that I would conspire with him against my own race so that he might remain comfortably blind. Why did he think I would be amenable to this? I can only guess that he assumed my middle-class identity was so complete and all-encompassing that I would see his action as nothing more than a trifling concession to the folkways of our land, that I would in fact applaud his decision not to disturb propriety. Blind to both his own racism and to me—one blindness serving the other—he could not recognize that he was asking me to betray my race in the name of my class.

His blindness made me feel vulnerable because it threatened to expose my own repressed ambivalence. His comment pressured me to choose between my class identification, which had contributed to my being a college student and a member of the debating team, and my desperate desire to be "black." I could have one but not both; I was double-bound.

Because double binds are repressed there is always an element of terror in them: the terror of bringing to the conscious mind the buried duplicity, self-deception, and pretense involved in serving two masters. This terror is the stuff of vulnerability, and since vulnerability is one of the least tolerable of all human feelings, we usually transform it into an emotion that seems to restore the control of which it has robbed us; most often, that emotion is anger. And so, before the professor had even finished his little story, I had become a furnace of rage. The year was 1967, and I had been primed by endless hours of nap-matching to feel, at least consciously, completely at one with the victim-focused black identity. This identity gave me the license, and the impunity, to unleash upon this professor one of those volcanic eruptions of racial indignation familiar to us from the novels of Richard Wright. Like Cross Damon in *Outsider*, who kills in perfectly righteous anger, I tried to annihilate the man. I punished him not according to the measure of his crime but according to the measure of my vulnerability, a measure set by the cumulative tension of years of repressed terror. Soon I saw that terror in *his* face, as he stared hollow-eyed at the road ahead. My white friends in the back seat, knowing no conflict between their own class and race, were astonished that someone they had taken to be so much like themselves could harbor a rage that for all the world looked murderous.

Though my rage was triggered by the professor's comment, it was deepened and sustained by a complex of need, conflict, and repression in myself of which I had been wholly unaware. Out of my racial vulnerability I had developed the strong need of an identity with which to defend myself. The only such identity available was that of me as victim, him as victimizer. Once in the grip of this paradigm, I began to do far more damage to myself than he had done.

Seeing myself as a victim meant that I clung all the harder to my racial identity, which, in turn, meant that I suppressed my class identity. This cut me off from all the resources my class values might have offered me. In those values, for instance, I might have found the means to a more dispassionate response, the response less of a victim attacked by a victimizer than of an individual offended by a foolish old man. As an individual I might have reported this professor to the college dean. Or I might have calmly tried to reveal his blindness to him, and possibly won a convert. (The flagrancy of his remark suggested a hidden guilt and even self-recognition on which I might have capitalized. Doesn't confession usually signal a willingness to face oneself?) Or I might have simply chuckled and then let my silence serve as an answer to his provocation. Would not my composure, in any form it might take, deflect into his own heart the arrow he'd shot at me?

Instead, my anger, itself the hair-trigger expression of a long-repressed double bind, not only cut me off from the best of my own resources, it also distorted the nature of my true racial problem. The righteousness of this anger and easy catharsis it brought buoyed the delusion of my victimization and left me as blind as the professor himself.

As a middle-class black I have often felt myself *contriving* to be "black." And I have noticed this same contrivance in others—a certain stretching away from the natural flow of one's life to align oneself with a victim-focused black identity. Our particular needs are out of sync with the form of identity available to meet those needs. Middle-class blacks need to identify racially; it is better to think of ourselves as black and victimized than not black at all; so we contrive (more unconsciously than consciously) to fit ourselves into an identity that denies our class and fails to address the true source of our vulnerability.

For me this once meant spending inordinate amounts of time at black faculty meetings, though these meetings had little to do with my real racial anxieties or my professional life. I was new to the university, one of two blacks in an English department of over seventy, and I felt a little isolated and vulnerable, though I did not admit it to myself. But at these meetings we discussed the problems of black faculty and students within a framework of victimization. The real vulnerability we felt was covered over by all the adversarial drama the victim/victimized polarity inspired, and hence went unseen and unassuaged. And this, I think, explains our rather chronic ineffectiveness as a group. Since victimization was not our primary problem—the university had long ago opened its doors to us—we had to contrive to make it so, and there is not much energy in contrivance. What I got at these meetings was ultimately an object lesson in how fruitless struggle can be when it is not grounded in actual need.

At our black faculty meetings, the old equation of blackness with victimization was ever present—to be black was to be a victim; therefore, not to be a victim was not to be black. As we contrived to meet the terms of this formula there was an inevitable distortion of both ourselves and the larger university. Through the prism of victimization the university seemed more impenetrable than it actually was, and we more limited in our powers. We fell prey to the victim's myopia, making the university an institution from which we could seek redress but which we could never fully join. And this mind-set often led us to look more for compensations for our supposed victimization than for opportunities we could pursue as individuals.

The discomfort and vulnerability felt by middle-class blacks in the sixties, it could be argued, was a worthwhile price to pay considering the progress achieved during that time of racial confrontation. But what may have been tolerable then is intolerable now. Though changes in American society have made it an anachronism, the monolithic form of racial identification that came out of the sixties is still very much with us. It may be more loosely held, and its power to punish heretics has probably diminished, but it continues to catch middle-class blacks in a double bind, thus impeding not only their own advancement but even, I would contend, that of blacks as a group.

The victim-focused black identity encourages the individual to feel that his advancement depends almost entirely on that of the group. Thus he loses sight not only of his own possibilities but of the inextricable connection between individual effort and individual advancement. This is a profound emcumbrance today, when there is more opportunity for blacks than ever before, for it reimposes limitations that can have the same oppressive effect as those the society has only recently begun to remove.

It was the emphasis on mass action in the sixties that made the victim-focused black identity a necessity. But in the eighties and beyond, when racial advancement will come only through a multitude of individual advancements, this form of identity inadvertently adds itself to the forces that hold us back. Hard work, education, individual initiative, stable family life, property ownership—these have always been the means by which ethnic groups have moved ahead in America. Regardless of past or present victimization, these "laws" of advancement apply absolutely to black Americans also. There is no getting around this. What we need is a form of racial identity that energizes the individual by putting him in touch with both his possibilities and his responsibilities.

It has always annoyed me to hear from the mouths of certain arbiters of blackness that middle-class blacks should "reach back" and pull up those blacks less fortunate than they—as though middle-class status were an unearned and essentially passive condition in which one needed a large measure of noblesse oblige to occupy one's time. My own image is of reaching back from a moving train to lift on board those who have no tickets. A noble enough sentiment—but might it not be wiser to show them the entire structure of principles, effort, and sacrifice that puts one in a position to buy a ticket any time one likes? This, I think, is something members of the black middle class can realistically offer to other blacks. Their example is not only a testament to possibility but also a lesson in method. But they cannot lead by example until they are released from a black identity that regards that example as suspect, that sees them as "marginally" black, indeed that holds *them* back by catching them in a double bind.

To move beyond the victim-focused black identity we must learn to make a difficult but crucial distinction: between actual victimization, which we must resist with every resource, and identification with the victim's status. Until we do this we will continue to wrestle more with ourselves than with the new opportunities which so many paid so dearly to win.

Suggestions for Discussion

1. How has the author's personal history brought him into conflict with the political movement to overcome racism?
2. Steele identifies and explains what it means to be a member of the middle class. Discuss his definition.
3. What is the negative consequence, for Steele, of seeing himself as a victim of racism?
4. Discuss the episode related by Steele of his anger with a white professor as they travel to a debating match.

Suggestions for Writing

1. Write an essay in which you evaluate Steele's statement of his dilemma both as student and professor. Do you sympathize with him? Do you agree or disagree with his position? Explain your position.
2. Take the part of a white or black student, and write a paper in which you discuss the "double bind" Steele describes. Try to examine carefully your own relation with a member of the opposite race.
3. Write a paper in which you evaluate Steele's solution to what he sees as the problem of being a member of the black middle class.

PETER H. KING

Of Crumpled Wings and Little Girls

Peter H. King (b. 1955) was born in Fresno, California, and educated at California State University, San Luis Obispo. He has worked as a reporter for the *San Francisco Examiner* and the Associated Press. At present he is a columnist for the *Los Angeles Times.* In this brief essay he explores examples of the undesirable interruption of the traditional rhythms of childhood.

My daughter is seven years old. She does not fly airplanes. She does ride a bicycle. This won't land her in any record book. Still, for her it represents a sweet victory over gravity, fear and the sting of skinned knees. As she speeds along, yellow hair streaming from a pink crash helmet, her face invariably will light up with the most wonderful smile. To her it feels almost like flying.

As I write this now, I am thinking of another 7-year-old. I am thinking of Jessica Dubroff, the little California girl who crashed in her airplane Thursday in Cheyenne, Wyo. She was attempting to establish a record as a pilot prodigy. It was her father's idea. He died, too, along with a flight instructor.

The television footage shot just before the crash is haunting. Jessica's lopsided grin. The furtive glance she sneaked at the coming storm even as she told an interviewer she was not afraid. The last image of her scampering through a deluge toward the Cessna, a cellular telephone stuck in her ear. She was talking to her mother.

"Do you hear the rain?" she asked.

When the skies cut loose like that where I live, my daughter and her younger brother come running to their parents' bed. They tell us with wide eyes they are not afraid, just a little lonely or something. They are kids. When Jessica Dubroff heard the thunder, felt the rain, she ran into an airplane, took off into the storm and died. Seven years old.

While her death provoked much anger—what were the parents thinking of, letting her fly in that weather, letting her fly at all?—the intent here is not to join that outraged jury. Rather, it is to suggest that Jessica's tragedy presents an example, albeit the most extreme one imaginable, of something at work across this country. Somewhere, somehow, faith in the eternal rhythms of childhood has been lost.

Kids now are pushed into sports by the age of five. Barely out of diapers, they're shuttled to computer classes, karate lessons, enrolled in kindergarten prep schools. Summer vacation is dead, the victim of parental dread that time spent barefoot in pursuit of polliwogs or pop flies is time wasted. Gotta keep up, the parents preach, either explicitly or through their own manic example. Gotta get ahead.

The instinct is innocent enough. Children are an unfolding story; parents can't help feeling the urge to skip forward to the final chapter, to see how things work out. And who wants a child to achieve less than possible? Still, there seems an almost desperate edge to the pushing. Perhaps it is entwined with that watershed poll of a decade ago, the survey which found that, for the first time, most Americans no longer expect their children's future to be brighter than their own.

If tomorrow promises a fight for fewer and fewer crumbs, the thinking goes, today is not too soon to start sharpening children's elbows, padding their resumes, molding them into little adults. "As she flies," Jessica's father had said, "she is learning math, physics, navigation, geography and weather—plus she will have a lifetime ticket to a certain social strata she can use or not."

A lifetime ticket.

When my daughter started school, she was thrown into competition with older children who'd been redshirted by their parents in order to gain academic advantage. It was a tough time, and I turned to a woman I know as "Miss Pat." Pat Hedlund runs a Pasadena preschool where my daughter once did time. She knows children—and parents. With a patient smile, she gave me a passage from "Zorba the Greek" to ponder:

> I discovered a cocoon in the bark of a tree, just as the butterfly was making a hole in its case and preparing to come out. I waited a while, but it was too long appearing and I was impatient. I bent over it and breathed on it to warm it. I warmed it as quickly as I could and the miracle began to happen before my eyes, faster than life. The case opened, the butterfly started slowly crawling out and I shall never forget my horror when I saw how its wings were folded back and crumpled....
>
> I tried to help it with my breath. In vain. It needed to be hatched out patiently and the unfolding of the wings should be a gradual process in the sun. Now it was too late. My breath had forced the butterfly to appear, all crumpled, before its time. It struggled desperately and, a few seconds later, died in the palm of my hand.

This, so sadly, is the parting image of Jessica, a little girl lost amid an airplane's crumpled wings.

Suggestions for Discussion

1. This brief essay uses a tragic incident that occurred in the spring of 1996 to make a comment about American values. What is the author's comment?
2. Explain the relation of the passage from *Zorba the Greek* to the tragic plane accident.
3. Why does the author make it clear that his essay is not written in anger?

Suggestion for Writing

Write an essay in which you take a position on the statement that in this country "faith in the eternal rhythms of childhood has been lost."

FICTION

WILLIAM FAULKNER

Dry September

William Faulkner (1897–1962) lived most of his life in Oxford, Mississippi. After a year at the university of his native state, he joined the Royal Canadian Air Force, eager to participate in World War I. His novels set in his imaginary Yoknapatawpha County include *The Sound and the Fury* (1929), *Light in August* (1932), *Absalom, Absalom!* (1936), and *The Hamlet* (1940). This story, taken from the section of Faulkner's *Collected Stories* (1950) called "The Village," offers an acute social and psychological analysis of life in a small Southern town after World War I. Notice how Faulkner focuses on the gentle barber, the hysterical spinster, and the brutal ex-soldier to provide social commentary.

I

Through the bloody September twilight, aftermath of sixty-two rainless days, it had gone like a fire in dry grass—the rumor, the story, whatever it was. Something about Miss Minnie Cooper and a Negro. Attacked, insulted, frightened: none of them, gathered in the barber shop on that Saturday evening where the ceiling fan stirred, without freshening it, the vitiated air, sending back upon them, in recurrent surges of stale pomade and lotion, their own stale breath and odors, knew exactly what had happened.

"Except it wasn't Will Mayes," a barber said. He was a man of middle age; a thin, sand-colored man with a mild face, who was shaving a client. "I know Will Mayes. He's a good nigger. And I know Minnie Cooper, too."

"What do you know about her?" a second barber said.

"Who is she?" the client said. "A young girl?"

"No," the barber said. "She's about forty, I reckon. She ain't married. That's why I dont believe—"

"Believe, hell!" a hulking youth in a sweat-stained silk shirt said. "Wont you take a white woman's word before a nigger's?"

"I dont believe Will Mayes did it," the barber said. "I know Will Mayes."

"Maybe you know who did it, then. Maybe you already got him out of town, you damn niggerlover."

"I dont believe anybody did anything. I dont believe anything happened. I leave it to you fellows if them ladies that get old without getting married dont have notions that a man cant—"

"Then you are a hell of a white man," the client said. He moved under the cloth. The youth had sprung to his feet.

"You dont?" he said. "Do you accuse a white woman of lying?"

The barber held the razor poised above the half-risen client. He did not look around.

"It's this durn weather," another said. "It's enough to make a man do anything. Even to her."

Nobody laughed. The barber said in his mild, stubborn tone: "I aint accusing nobody of nothing. I just know and you fellows know how a woman that never—"

"You damn niggerlover!" the youth said.

"Shut up, Butch," another said. "We'll get the facts in plenty of time to act."

"Who is? Who's getting them?" the youth said. "Facts, hell! I—."

"You're a fine white man," the client said. "Aint you?" In his frothy beard he looked like a desert rat in the moving pictures. "You tell them, Jack," he said to the youth. "If there aint any white men in this town, you can count on me, even if I aint only a drummer and a stranger."

"That's right, boys," the barber said. "Find out the truth first. I know Will Mayes."

"Well, by God!" the youth shouted. "To think that a white man in this town—"

"Shut up, Butch," the second speaker said. "We got plenty of time."

The client sat up. He looked at the speaker. "Do you claim that anything excuses a nigger attacking a white woman? Do you mean to tell me you are a white man and you'll stand for it? You better go back North where you came from. The South dont want your kind here."

"North what?" the second said. "I was born and raised in this town."

"Well, by God!" the youth said. He looked about with a strained, baffled gaze, as if he was trying to remember what it was he wanted to say or to do. He drew his sleeve across his sweating face. "Damn if I'm going to let a white woman—"

"You tell them, Jack," the drummer said. "By God, if they—"

The screen door crashed open. A man stood in the floor, his feet apart and his heavy-set body poised easily. His white shirt was open at the throat; he wore a felt hat. His hot, bold glance swept the group. His name was McLendon. He had commanded troops at the front in France and had been decorated for valor.

"Well," he said, "are you going to sit there and let a black son rape a white woman on the streets of Jefferson?"

Butch sprang up again. The silk of his shirt clung flat to his heavy shoulders. At each armpit was a dark halfmoon. "That's what I been telling them! That's what I—"

"Did it really happen?" a third said. "This aint the first man scare she ever had, like Hawkshaw says. Wasn't there something about a man on the kitchen roof, watching her undress, about a year ago?"

"What?" the client said. "What's that?" The barber had been slowly forcing him back into the chair; he arrested himself reclining, his head lifted, the barber still pressing him down.

McLendon whirled on the third speaker. "Happen? What the hell difference does it make? Are you going to let the black sons get away with it until one really does it?"

"That's what I'm telling them!" Butch shouted. He cursed, long and steady, pointless.

"Here, here," a fourth said. "Not so loud. Dont talk so loud."

"Sure," McLendon said; "no talking necessary at all. I've done my talking. Who's with me?" He poised on the balls of his feet, roving his gaze.

The barber held the drummer's face down, the razor poised. "Find out the facts first, boys. I know Willy Mayes. It wasn't him. Let's get the sheriff and do this thing right."

McLendon whirled upon him his furious, rigid face. The barber did not look away. They looked like men of different races. The other barbers had ceased also above their prone clients. "You mean to tell me," McLendon said, "that you'd take a nigger's word before a white woman's? Why, you damn niggerloving—"

The third speaker rose and grasped McLendon's arm; he too had been a soldier. "Now, now. Let's figure this thing out. Who knows anything about what really happened?"

"Figure out hell!" McLendon jerked his arm free. "All that're with me get up from there. The ones that aint—" He roved his gaze, dragging his sleeve across his face.

Three men rose. The drummer in the chair sat up. "Here," he said, jerking at the cloth about his neck; "get this rag off me. I'm with him. I dont live here, but by God, if our mothers and wives and sisters—" He smeared the cloth over his face and flung it to the floor. McLendon stood in the floor and cursed the others. Another rose and moved toward him. The remainder sat uncomfortable, not looking at one another, then one by one they rose and joined him.

The barber picked the cloth from the floor. He began to fold it neatly. "Boys, dont do that. Will Mayes never done it. I know."

"Come on," McLendon said. He whirled. From his hip pocket protruded the butt of a heavy automatic pistol. They went out. The screen door crashed behind them reverberant in the dead air.

The barber wiped the razor carefully and swiftly, and put it away, and ran to the rear, and took his hat from the wall. "I'll be back as soon as I can," he said to the other barbers. "I cant let—" He went out, running. The two other barbers followed him to the door and caught it on the rebound, leaning out and looking up the street after him. The air was flat and dead. It had a metallic taste at the base of the tongue.

"What can he do?" the first said. The second one was saying "Jees Christ, Jees Christ" under his breath. "I'd just as lief be Will Mayes as Hawk, if he gets McLendon riled."

"Jees Christ, Jees Christ," the second whispered

"You reckon he really done it to her?" the first said.

II

She was thirty-eight or thirty-nine. She lived in a small frame house with her invalid mother and a thin, sallow, unflagging aunt, where each morning between ten and eleven she would appear on the porch in a lace-trimmed boudoir cap, to sit swinging in the porch swing until noon. After dinner she lay down for a while, until the afternoon began to cool. Then, in one of the three or four new voile dresses which she had each summer, she would go downtown to spend the afternoon in the stores with the other ladies, where they would handle the goods and haggle over the prices in cold, immediate voices, without any intention of buying.

She was of comfortable people—not the best in Jefferson, but good people enough—and she was still on the slender side of ordinary looking, with a bright, faintly haggard manner and dress. When she was young she had had a slender, nervous body and a sort of hard vivacity which had enabled her for a time to ride upon the crest of the town's social life as exemplified by the high school party and church social period of her contemporaries while still children enough to be unclassconscious.

She was the last to realize that she was losing ground; that those among whom she had been a little brighter and louder flame than any other were beginning to learn the pleasure of snobbery—male—and retaliation—female. That was when her face began to wear that bright, haggard look.

She still carried it to parties on shadowy porticoes and summer lawns, like a mask or a flag, with that bafflement of furious repudiation of truth in her eyes. One evening at a party she heard a boy and two girls, all schoolmates, talking. She never accepted another invitation.

She watched the girls with whom she had grown up as they married and got homes and children, but no man ever called on her steadily until the children of the other girls had been calling her "aunty" for several years, the while their mothers told them in bright voices about how popular Aunt Minnie had been as a girl. Then the town began to see her driving on Sunday afternoons with the cashier in the bank. He was a widower of about forty—a high-colored man, smelling always faintly of the barber shop or of whisky. He owned the first automobile in town, a red runabout; Minnie had the first motoring bonnet and veil the town ever saw. Then the town began to say: "Poor Minnie." "But she is old enough to take care of herself," others said. That was when she began to ask her old schoolmates that their children call her "cousin" instead of "aunty."

It was twelve years now since she had been relegated into adultery by public opinion, and eight years since the cashier had gone to a Memphis bank, returning for one day each Christmas, which he spent at an annual bachelors' party at a hunting club on the river. From behind their curtains the neighbors would see the party pass, and during the over-the-way Christmas day visiting they would tell her about him, about how well he looked, and how they heard that he was prospering in the city, watching with bright, secret eyes her haggard, bright face. Usually by that hour there would be the scent of whisky on her breath. It was supplied her by a youth, a clerk at the soda fountain: "Sure; I buy it for the old gal. I reckon she's entitled to a little fun."

Her mother kept to her room altogether now; the gaunt aunt ran the house. Against that background Minnie's bright dresses, her idle and empty days, had a quality of furious unreality. She went out in the evenings only with women now, neighbors, to the moving pictures. Each afternoon she dressed in one of the new dresses and went downtown alone, where her young "cousins" were already strolling in the late afternoons with their delicate, silken heads and thin, awkward arms and conscious hips, clinging to one another or shrieking and giggling with paired boys in the soda fountain when she passed and went on along the serried store fronts, in the doors of which the sitting and lounging men did not even follow her with their eyes any more.

III

The barber went swiftly up the street where the sparse lights, insect-swirled, glared in rigid and violent suspension in the lifeless air. The day had died in a pall of dust; above the darkened square, shrouded by the spent dust, the sky was as clear as the inside of a brass bell. Below the east was a rumor of the twice-waxed moon.

When he overtook them McLendon and three others were getting into a car parked in an alley. McLendon stooped his thick head, peering out beneath the top. "Changed your mind, did you?" he said. "Damn good thing; by God, tomorrow when this town hears about how you talked tonight—"

"Now, now," the other ex-soldier said. "Hawkshaw's all right. Come on, Hawk; jump in."

"Will Mayes never done it, boys," the barber said. "If anybody done it. Why, you all know well as I do there ain't any town where they got better niggers than us. And you know how a lady will kind of think things about men when there aint any reason to, and Miss Minnie anyway—"

"Sure, sure," the soldier said. "We're just going to talk to him a little; that's all."

"Talk hell!" Butch said. "When we're through with the—"

"Shut up, for God's sake!" the soldier said. "Do you want everybody in town—"

"Tell them, by God!" McLendon said. "Tell every one of the sons that'll let a white woman—"

"Let's go; let's go: here's the other car." The second car slid squealing out of a cloud of dust at the alley mouth. McLendon started his car and took the lead. Dust lay like fog in the street. The street lights hung nimbused as in water. They drove on out of town.

A rutted lane turned at right angles. Dust hung above it too, and above all the land. The dark bulk of the ice plant, where the Negro Mayes was night watchman, rose against the sky. "Better stop here, hadn't we?" the soldier said. McLendon did not reply. He hurled the car up and slammed to a stop, the headlights glaring on the blank wall.

"Listen here, boys," the barber said, "if he's here, dont that prove he never done it? Dont it? If it was him, he would run. Dont you see he would?" The second car came up and stopped. McLendon got down; Butch sprang down beside him. "Listen, boys," the barber said.

"Cut the lights off!" McLendon said. The breathless dark rushed down. There was no sound in it save their lungs as they sought air in the parched dust in which for two months they had lived; then the diminishing crunch of McLendon's and Butch's feet, and a moment later McLendon's voice:

"Will!... Will!"

Below the east the wan hemorrhage of the moon increased. It heaved above the ridge, silvering the air, the dust, so that they seemed to breathe, live, in a bowl of molten lead. There was no sound of nightbird nor insect, no sound save their breathing and a faint ticking of contracting metal about the cars. Where their bodies touched one another they seemed to sweat dryly, for no more moisture came. "Christ!" a voice said; "let's get out of here."

But they didn't move until vague noises began to grow out of the darkness ahead; then they got out and waited tensely in the breathless dark. There was another sound: a blow, a hissing expulsion of breath and McLendon cursing in undertone. They stood a moment longer, then they ran forward. They ran in a stumbling clump, as though they were fleeing something. "Kill him, kill the son," a voice whispered. McLendon flung them back.

"Not here," he said. "Get him into the car." "Kill him, kill the black son!" the voice murmured. They dragged the Negro to the car. The barber had waited beside the car. He could feel himself sweating and he knew he was going to be sick at the stomach.

"What is it, captains?" the Negro said. "I aint done nothing. 'Fore God, Mr. John." Someone produced handcuffs. They worked busily about the Negro as though he were a post, quiet, intent, getting in one another's way. He submitted to the handcuffs, looking swiftly and constantly from dim face to dim face. "Who's here, captains?" he said, leaning to peer into the faces until they could feel his breath and smell his sweaty reek. He spoke a name or two. "What you all say I done, Mr. John?"

McLendon jerked the car door open. "Get in!" he said.

The Negro did not move. "What you all going to do with me, Mr. John? I aint done nothing. White folks, captains, I aint done nothing: I swear 'fore God." He called another name.

"Get in!" McLendon said. He struck the Negro. The others expelled their breath in a dry hissing and struck him with random blows and he whirled and cursed them, and swept his manacled hands across their faces and slashed the barber upon the mouth, and the barber struck him also. "Get him in there," McLendon said. They pushed at him. He ceased struggling and got in and sat quietly as the others took their places. He sat between the barber and the soldier, drawing his limbs in so as not to touch them, his eyes going swiftly and constantly from face to face. Butch clung to the running board. The car moved on. The barber nursed his mouth with his handkerchief.

"What's the matter, Hawk?" the soldier said.

"Nothing," the barber said. They regained the highroad and turned away from town. The second car dropped back out of the dust. They went on, gaining speed; the final fringe of houses dropped behind.

"Goddamn, he stinks!" the soldier said.

"We'll fix that," the drummer in front beside McLendon said. On the running board Butch cursed into the hot rush of air. The barber leaned suddenly forward and touched McLendon's arm.

"Let me out, John," he said.

"Jump out, niggerlover," McLendon said without turning his head. He drove swiftly. Behind them the sourceless lights of the second car glared in the dust. Presently McLendon turned into a narrow road. It was rutted with disuse. It led back to an abandoned brick kiln—a series of reddish mounds and weed- and vine-choked vats without bottom. It had been used for pasture once, until one day the owner missed one of his mules. Although he prodded carefully in the vats with a long pole, he could not even find the bottom of them.

"John," the barber said.

"Jump out, then," McLendon said, hurling the car along the ruts. Beside the barber the Negro spoke:

"Mr. Henry."

The barber sat forward. The narrow tunnel of the road rushed up and past. Their motion was like an extinct furnace blast: cooler, but utterly dead. The car bounded from rut to rut.

"Mr. Henry," the Negro said.

The barber began to tug furiously at the door. "Look out, there!" the soldier said, but the barber had already kicked the door open and swung onto the running board. The soldier leaned across the Negro and grasped at him, but he had already jumped. The car went on without checking speed.

The impetus hurled him crashing through dust-sheathed weeds, into the ditch. Dust puffed about him, and in a thin, vicious crackling of sapless stems he lay choking and retching until the second car passed and died away. Then he rose and limped on until he reached the highroad and turned toward town, brushing at his clothes with his hands. The moon was higher, riding high and clear of the dust at last, and after a while the town began to glare beneath the dust. He went on, limping. Presently he heard cars and the glow of them grew in the dust behind him and he left the road and crouched again in the weeds until they passed. McLendon's car came last now. There were four people in it and Butch was not on the running board.

They went on; the dust swallowed them; the glare and the sound died away. The dust of them hung for a while, but soon the eternal dust absorbed it again. The barber climbed back onto the road and limped on toward town.

IV

As she dressed for supper on that Saturday evening, her own flesh felt like fever. Her hands trembled among the hooks and eyes, and her eyes had a feverish look, and her hair swirled crisp and crackling under the comb.

While she was still dressing the friends called for her and sat while she donned her sheerest underthings and stockings and a new voile dress. "Do you feel strong enough to go out?" they said, their eyes bright too, with a dark glitter. "When you have had time to get over the shock, you must tell us what happened. What he said and did; everything."

In the leafed darkness, as they walked toward the square, she began to breathe deeply, something like a swimmer preparing to dive, until she ceased trembling, the four of them walking slowly because of the terrible heat and out of solicitude for her. But as they neared the square she began to tremble again, walking with her head up, her hands clenched at her sides, their voices about her murmurous, also with that feverish, glittering quality of their eyes.

They entered the square, she in the center of the group, fragile in her fresh dress. She was trembling worse. She walked slower and slower, as children eat ice cream, her head up and her eyes bright in the haggard banner of her face, passing the hotel and the coatless drummers in chairs along the curb looking around at her: "That's the one: see? The one in pink in the middle." "Is that her? What did they do with the nigger? Did they—?" "Sure. He's all right." "All right, is he?" "Sure. He went on a little trip." Then the drug store, where even the young men lounging in the doorway tipped their hats and followed with their eyes the motions of her hips and legs when she passed.

They went on, passing the lifted hats of the gentlemen, the suddenly ceased voices, deferent, protective. "Do you see?" the friends said. Their voices sounded like long, hovering sighs of hissing exultation. "There's not a Negro on the square. Not one."

They reached the picture show. It was like a miniature fairyland with its lighted lobby and colored lithographs of life caught in its terrible and beautiful mutations. Her lips began to tingle. In the dark, when the picture began, it would be all right; she could hold back the laughing so it would not waste away so fast and so soon. So she hurried on before the turning faces, the undertones of low astonishment, and they took their accustomed places where she could see the aisle against the silver glare and the young men and girls coming in two and two against it.

The lights flicked away; the screen glowed silver, and soon life began to unfold, beautiful and passionate and sad, while still the young men and girls entered, scented and sibilant in the half dark, their paired backs in silhouette delicate and sleek, their slim, quick bodies awkward, divinely young, while beyond them the silver dream accumulated, inevitably on and on. She began to laugh. In trying to suppress it, it made more noise than ever; heads began to turn. Still laughing, her friends raised her and led her out, and she stood at the curb, laughing on a high, sustained note, until the taxi came up and they helped her in.

They removed the pink voile and the sheer underthings and the stockings, and put her to bed, and cracked ice for her temples, and sent for the doctor. He was hard to locate, so they ministered to her with hushed ejaculations, renewing the ice and fanning her. While the ice was fresh and cold she stopped laughing and lay still for a time, moaning only a little. But soon the laughing welled again and her voice rose screaming.

"Shhhhhhhhhhh! Shhhhhhhhhhhhh!" they said, freshening the ice-pack, smoothing her hair, examining it for gray; "poor girl!" Then to one another: "Do you suppose anything really happened?" their eyes darkly aglitter, secret and passionate. "Shhhhhhhhhh! Poor girl! Poor Minnie!"

V

It was midnight when McLendon drove up to his neat new house. It was trim and fresh as a birdcage and almost as small, with its clean, green-and-white paint. He locked the car and mounted the porch and entered. His wife rose from a chair beside the reading lamp. McLendon stopped in the floor and stared at her until she looked down.

"Look at that clock," he said, lifting his arm, pointing. She stood before him, her face lowered, a magazine in her hands. Her face was pale, strained, and weary-looking. "Haven't I told you about sitting up like this, waiting to see when I come in?"

"John," she said. She laid the magazine down. Poised on the balls of his feet, he glared at her with his hot eyes, his sweating face.

"Didn't I tell you?" He went toward her. She looked up then. He caught her shoulder. She stood passive, looking at him.

"Don't, John. I couldn't sleep… The heat; something. Please, John. You're hurting me."

"Didn't I tell you?" He released her and half struck, half flung her across the chair, and she lay there and watched him quietly as he left the room.

He went on through the house, ripping off his shirt, and on the dark, screened porch at the rear he stood and mopped his head and shoulders with the shirt and flung it away. He took the pistol from his hip and laid it on the table beside the bed, and sat on the bed and removed his shoes, and rose and slipped his trousers off. He was sweating again already, and he stooped and hunted furiously for the shirt. At last he found it and wiped his body again, and, with his body pressed against the dusty screen, he stood panting. There was no movement, no sound, not even an insect. The dark world seemed to lie stricken beneath the cold moon and the lidless stars.

Suggestions for Discussion

1. Faulkner tells this story of a lynching in five parts. Discuss the relation of the parts to each other.
2. What is the function of Hawkshaw? Why is it appropriate for the story to open in a barber shop? Explain the discussion between the barbers and the customers.
3. In what ways is John McLendon different from the other men? What explains his power over them?
4. Explain the significance of the scene in which Will Mayes hits Hawkshaw in the mouth.
5. How do you know that nothing has happened to Miss Minnie Cooper? What aspects of her character make clear that she has invented an affront?
6. Explain the title of the story. How does Faulkner use weather as a force in the story? What has weather to do with the lynching?

Suggestions for Writing

1. Write an essay in which you explain how this story is an eloquent attack on lynching. Does the author permit himself to comment on what has occurred?
2. Write an essay in which you explain how the characters in this story provide a comment on the relation between the races.

RAY BRADBURY

Perhaps We Are Going Away

Ray Bradbury (b. 1920), who lives in Southern California, is among the most popular and prolific of science fiction writers. He is particularly well known for *The Martian Chronicles* (1950), *The Illustrated Man* (1951), and *Dandelion Wine* (1957). In this brief and powerful story from *The Machineries of Joy* (1963), Bradbury imagines the sense of danger and of coming disaster that a young Indian boy feels as he gets his first glimpse of European soldiers in America.

It was a strange thing that could not be told. It touched along the hairs on his neck as he lay wakening. Eyes shut, he pressed his hands to the dirt.

Was the earth, shaking old fires under its crust, turning over in its sleep?

Were buffalo on the dust prairies, in the whistling grass, drumming the sod, moving this way like a dark weather?

No.

What? What, then?

He opened his eyes and was the boy Ho-Awi, of a tribe named for a bird, by the hills named for the shadows of owls, near the great ocean itself, on a day that was evil for no reason.

Ho-Awi stared at the tent flaps, which shivered like a great beast remembering winter.

Tell me, he thought, the terrible thing, where does it come from? Whom will it kill?

He lifted the flap and stepped out into his village.

He turned slowly, a boy with bones in his dark cheeks like the keels of small birds flying. His brown eyes saw god-filled, cloud-filled sky, his cupped ear heard thistles ticking the war drums, but still the greater mystery drew him to the edge of the village.

Here, legend said, the land went on like a tide to another sea. Between here and there was as much earth as there were stars across the night sky. Somewhere in all that land, storms of black buffalo harvested the grass. And here stood Ho-Awi, his stomach a fist, wondering, searching, waiting, afraid.

You too? said the shadow of a hawk.

Ho-Awi turned.

It was the shadow of his grandfather's hand that wrote on the wind.

No. The grandfather made the sign for silence. His tongue moved soft in a toothless mouth. His eyes were small creeks running behind the sunken flesh beds, the cracked sand washes of his face.

Now they stood on the edge of the day, drawn close by the unknown.

And Old Man did as the boy had done. His mummified ear turned, his nostril twitched. Old Man too ached for some answering growl from any direction that would tell them only a great timberfall of weather had dropped from a distant sky. But the wind gave no answer, spoke only to itself.

The Old Man made the sign which said they must go on the Great Hunt. This, said his hands like mouths, was a day for the rabbit young and the featherless old. Let no warrior come with them. The hare and the dying vulture must track together. For only the very young saw life ahead, and only the very old saw life behind; the others between were so busy with life they saw nothing.

The Old Man wheeled slowly in all directions.

Yes! He knew, he was certain, he was sure! To find this thing of darkness would take the innocence of the newborn and the innocence of the blind to see very clear.

Come! said the trembling fingers.

And snuffing rabbit and earthbound hawk shadowed out of the village into changing weather.

They searched the high hills to see if the stones lay atop each other, and they were so arranged. They scanned the prairies, but found only the winds which played there like tribal children all day. And found arrowheads from old wars.

No, the Old Man's hand drew on the sky, the men of this nation and that beyond smoke by the summer fires while the squaws cut wood. It is not arrows flying that we almost hear.

At last, when the sun sank into the nation of buffalo hunters, the Old Man looked up.

The birds, his hands cried suddenly, are flying south! Summer is over!

No, the boy's hands said, summer has just begun! I see no birds!

They are so high, said the Old Man's fingers, that only the blind can feel their passage. They shadow the heart more than the earth. I feel them pass south in my blood. Summer goes. We may go with it. Perhaps we are going away.

No! cried the boy aloud, suddenly afraid. Go where? Why? For what?

Who knows? said the Old Man, and perhaps we will not move. Still, even without moving, perhaps we are going away.

No! Go back! cried the boy, to the empty sky, the birds unseen, the unshadowed air. Summer, stay!

No use, said the Old One's single hand, moving by itself. Not you or me or our people can stay this weather. It is a season changed, come to live on the land for all time.

But from where does it come?

This way, said the Old Man at last.

And in the dusk they looked down at the great waters of the east that went over the edge of the world, where no one had ever gone.

There. The Old Man's hand clenched and thrust out. There *it* is.

Far ahead, a single light burned on the shore.

With the moon rising, the Old Man and the rabbit boy padded on the sands, heard strange voices in the sea, smelled wild burnings from the now suddenly close fire.

They crawled on their bellies. They lay looking in at the light.

And the more he looked, the colder Ho-Awi became, and he knew that all the Old Man had said was true.

For drawn to this fire built of sticks and moss, which flickered brightly in the soft evening wind which was cooler now, at the heart of summer, were such creatures as he had never seen.

These were men with faces like white-hot coals, with some eyes in these faces as blue as sky. All these men had glossy hair on their cheeks and chins, which grew to a point. One man stood with raised lightning in his hand and a great moon of sharp stuff on his head like the face of a fish. The others had bright round tinkling crusts of material cleaved to their chests which gonged slightly when they moved. As Ho-Awi watched, some men lifted the gonging bright things from their heads, unskinned the eye-blinding crab shells, the turtle casings from their chests, their arms, their legs, and tossed these discarded sheaths to the sand. Doing this, the creatures laughed, while out in the bay stood a black shape on the waters, a great dark canoe with things like torn clouds hung on poles over it.

After a long while of holding their breath, the Old Man and the boy went away.

From a hill, they watched the fire that was no bigger than a star now. You could wink it out with an eyelash. If you closed your eyes, it was destroyed.

Still, it remained.

Is this, asked the boy, the great happening?

The Old One's face was that of a fallen eagle, filled with dreadful years and unwanted wisdom. The eyes were resplendently bright, as if they welled with a rise of cold clear water in which all could be seen, like a river that drank the sky and earth and knew it, accepted silently and would not deny the accumulation of dust, time, shape, sound and destiny.

The Old Man nodded, once.

This was the terrible weather. This was how summer would end. This made the birds wheel south, shadowless, through a grieving land.

The worn hands stopped moving. The time of questions was done.

Far away, the fire leaped. One of the creatures moved. The bright stuff on his tortoise-shell body flashed. It was like an arrow cutting a wound in the night.

Then the boy vanished in darkness, following the eagle and the hawk that lived in the stone body of his grandfather.

Below, the sea reared up and poured another great salt wave in billions of pieces which crashed and hissed like knives swarming along the continental shores.

Suggestions for Discussion

1. Explain the power of this account of the advent of Western man in America.
2. Discuss Bradbury's characterizations. Are they as important to the story as the events that occur or the descriptions of the setting? Explain.

3. This story is extremely brief. Would you want it any longer? Explain.

Suggestions for Writing

1. Describe the first encounter between the Indians and the Europeans.
2. Write an essay in which you try to warn the Indians to be wary of the Europeans. Be as convincing as possible.

POETRY

WOLE SOYINKA

Telephone Conversation

Wole Soyinka (b. 1934) was born in Ake, Nigeria, a member of the Yoruba tribe. He was educated at the Universities of Ibadan and Leeds, has received numerous honorary degrees, and has taught in the United States, England, and Africa. In 1986 he won the Nobel Prize for Literature, honoring his publications in fiction, nonfiction prose, poetry, drama, and opera. His many works include *A Man Died: Prison Notes* (1972); *Myth, Literature and the African Novel* (1976); a collection of poetry, *Ogun Ahibimen* (1976); *another memoir, Ake: The Years of Childhood* (1982); the play, *Requiem for a Futurologist* (1985); and *Art, Dialogue and Outrage* (1988). He was Goldwyn Smith Professor of African Studies and Theatre at Cornell from 1988 to 1992. He is now in exile from Nigeria. "Telephone Conversation" details the painful and ludicrous niceties of racial discrimination.

The price seemed reasonable, location
Indifferent. The landlady swore she lived
Off premises. Nothing remained
But self-confession. "Madam," I warned,
"I hate a wasted journey—I am African."
Silence. Silenced transmission of
Pressurized good-breeding. Voice, when it came,
Lipstick coated, long gold-rolled
Cigarette-holder pipped. Caught I was, foully.
"HOW DARK?"... I had not misheard.... "ARE YOU LIGHT
OR VERY DARK?" Button B. Button A. Stench
Of rancid breath of public hide-and-speak.
Red booth. Red pillar-box. Red double-tiered
Omnibus squelching tar. It *was* real! Shamed
By ill-mannered silence, surrender
Pushed dumbfoundment to beg simplification.
Considerate she was, varying the emphasis—

"ARE YOU DARK? OR VERY LIGHT?" Revelation came.
"You mean—like plain or milk chocolate?"
Her assent was clinical, crushing in its light
Impersonality. Rapidly, wave-length adjusted,
I chose. "West African sepia"—and as afterthought,
"Down in my passport." Silence for spectroscopic
Flight of fancy, till truthfulness clanged her accent
Hard on the mouthpiece. "WHAT'S THAT?" conceding
"DON'T KNOW WHAT THAT IS." "Like brunette."
"THAT'S DARK, ISN'T IT?" "Not altogether.
Facially, I am brunette, but madam, you should see
The rest of me. Palm of my hand, soles of my feet
Are a peroxide blonde. Friction, caused—
Foolishly madam—by sitting down, has turned
My bottom raven black—One moment madam!"—sensing
Her receiver rearing on the thunderclap
About my ears—"Madam," I pleaded, "wouldn't you rather
See for yourself?"

Suggestions for Discussion

1. What tone does Soyinka give the poem? How is that tone revealed in the questions and answers of the telephone conversation?
2. Why does the prospective renter reveal that he is black? What does this tell us about the attitude of the landlady? The general relation of the two races?
3. Explain why the poet chooses to end the poem with a witty question.

Suggestions for Writing

1. Write a paper in which you relate the incident described in Soyinka's poem to a similar circumstance in the United States.
2. In a paper explain the decision by the prospective renter to remain polite instead of abruptly ending the telephone conversation. Which response is more effective? Why?

WILFRED OWEN

Dulce et Decorum Est

Wilfred Owen (1893–1918) was born in Shropshire, England, and educated at Birkenhead Institute. Among the most celebrated of the English war poets, he was killed in action in World War I. Another war poet, Siegfried Sassoon, collected Owen's poems, which were first published in 1920. Other collections followed as did critical studies and memoirs. "Dulce et Decorum Est" (taken from Horace's statement, "It is sweet and fitting to die for one's country") opposes vivid and devastating images of the casualties of war with statements of sentimental patriotism. It shows war as the ultimate insult to human dignity.

Bent double, like old beggars under sacks,
Knock-kneed, coughing like hags, we cursed through sludge,
Till on the haunting flares we turned our backs,
And towards our distant rest began to trudge.
Men marched asleep. Many had lost their boots,
But limped on, blood-shod. All went lame, all blind;
Drunk with fatigue; deaf even to the hoots
Of gas-shells dropping softly behind.

Gas! Gas! Quick, boys!—An ecstasy of fumbling,
Fitting the clumsy helmets just in time,
But someone still was yelling out and stumbling
And flound'ring like a man in fire or lime.—
Dim through the misty panes and thick green light,
As under a green sea, I saw him drowning.
In all my dreams before my helpless sight
He plunges at me, guttering, choking, drowning.

If in some smothering dreams, you too could pace
Behind the wagon that we flung him in,
And watch the white eyes writhing in his face,
His hanging face, like a devil's sick of sin,
If you could hear, at every jolt, the blood
Come gargling from the froth-corrupted lungs
Bitter as the cud

Of vile, incurable sores on innocent tongues,—
My friend, you would not tell with such high zest
To children ardent for some desperate glory,
The old lie: *Dulce et decorum est*
Pro patria mori.

Suggestions for Discussion

1. In the first two stanzas, Owen presents two connected scenes of war. How are these two stanzas related to the final one?
2. Discuss the use of irony in the poem. Show why Owen uses the quotation from Horace.
3. Examine the series of images that Owen uses to describe war. Do they progress through the poem? Show why one cannot interchange the first two stanzas.

Suggestion for Writing

Owen's picture of the destruction of lives constitutes a poetic statement against war. Does this poem lead you to a belief in pacifism? Are there "just" and "unjust" wars? Try to sort out your attitudes and write an essay explaining under what conditions, if any, you might be willing to fight for your country. Support your statements with detailed arguments.

W. H. AUDEN

The Unknown Citizen

Wystan Hugh Auden (1907–1973), educated at Oxford University, was early recognized as a leader of the poets of his generation. His volumes of poetry include *The Orators* (1932), *The Double Man* (1941), and *The Age of Anxiety* (1947), which won a Pulitzer Prize in 1948. Born in England, he came to the United States at the outbreak of World War II. His autobiography, *Certain World: A Commonplace Book*, published in 1970, traces his return from leftist agnostic to the Church of England. In 1967 he was made a fellow of Christ Church, Oxford. In the following poem, published in 1940, Auden comments satirically on the behavior of a good citizen in a totalitarian state that resembles not only fascist Italy and Nazi Germany but democratic America and Britain as well.

(To JS/07/M/378 This Marble Monument Is Erected by the State)

He was found by the Bureau of Statistics to be
One against whom there was no official complaint,
And all the reports on his conduct agree
That, in the modern sense of an old-fashioned word, he was a saint,
For in everything he did he served the Greater Community.
Except for the War till the day he retired
He worked in a factory and never got fired,
But satisfied his employers, Fudge Motors Inc.
Yet he wasn't a scab or odd in his views,
For his Union reports that he paid his dues,
(Our report on his Union shows it was sound)
And our Social Psychology workers found
That he was popular with his mates and liked to drink.
The Press are convinced that he bought a paper every day
And that his reactions to advertisements were normal in every way.
Policies taken out in his name prove that he was fully insured,
And his Health-card shows he was once in a hospital but left it cured,
Both Producers Research and High-Grade Living declare
He was fully sensible to the advantages of the Installment Plan
And had everything necessary to the Modern Man,
A phonograph, a radio, a car and a frigidaire.
Our researchers into Public Opinion are content
That he held the proper opinions for the time of year;
When there was peace, he was for peace; when there was war, he went.
He was married and added five children to the population,
Which our Eugenist says was the right number for a parent of his generation,
And our teachers report that he never interfered with their education.
Was he free? Was he Happy? The question is absurd:
Had anything been wrong, we should certainly have heard.

Suggestions for Discussion

1. Discuss reasons for the state to bother erecting such a monument.

2. Analyze the strengths and weaknesses of the society described by Auden.
3. Discuss Auden's use of irony in the poem. Find specific examples.

Suggestions for Writing

1. Write a sketch describing and evaluating a typical day in the life of the unknown citizen.
2. Provide an alternative inscription for the monument.

PATRICIA SMITH

Always in the Head

Patricia Smith (b. 1955) was born in Chicago, where she grew up. Smith now lives in Boston where she is arts critic for the *Boston Globe.* Her collections of poetry include *Life According to Motown* and *Big Towns, Big Talk* (1992). A popular performance poet, Smith is the undefeated champion of Chicago's Uptown Poetry Slam and frequently appears at such venues as New York City's Nuyorican Poets Cafe. The following poem demonstrates her absolute mastery of colloquial speech.

for DAMON, MESFEN
and all my young black brothers

"I seen it lots of times, I seen it, just from being
on the street when something was going down;
I seen kids get killed, a few, my buddy Jules
got bucked, this gang he was down with, I mean he
wasn't even down with them when they started
beefin' with this other gang, but one day, it was hot,
I remember it was real hot, somebody called Jules
and he opened the window and looked out and
they got him in the head; you know all the
time now you got to get 'em in the head,
gotta bust that brain, man, don't shoot
'em in the head most likely they won't die,

and if they don't die you might as well kill
yourself cause soon as they can stand up
they be stalkin' you big time, man, might as well
blow yourself away. Gotta bust that brain, man.
But you know what was funny, even the folks
Jules was down with didn't know who smoked him
cause they was beefin' with so many other gangs,
and then there was Billy, they jacked him big time,
took him out just for talkin' shit, acting like he was
down with brothers who didn't even know his ass,
cockin' them colors wrong, and I'm sorry for laughin',
I know the shit ain't funny, but I was still looking to
see my boys hangin' in the hood, jivin' and scopin'
the bitches, but then I saw them at the wake, laid out
man, lyin' stiff, skin two colors too light, wearin' wigs
to hold their heads on and they mamas clawin' at them
and screamin' out their heads for Jesus, then I knew
Jules and Billy wouldn't be hangin' no more, but after
awhile you just deal with dyin', you get cold with it.
It's like, 'Yo man, somebody got their cap peeled last night,
you know who it was? Man, not him man, that's foul,
he was down, man, you goin' to the wake? No man,
can't make it, got a game, gotta kick some ass on the court.'
You just take in the word, you know, about somebody dyin'
and you deal with it, can't let it twist you round and
mess your head up cause then you let your guard down
and like I said before then you might as well kill yourself.
Me? I ain't sweatin' bout dyin'. I'm kickin' the right colors,
got my brim twisted proper. Sometimes it's even fun
hangin' out at places most people are scared of,
like down at Dudley late at night, the game is not
knowin' if you gon be there when somethin' goes down
and somethin' always does. Somebody gets bucked and
hits the street and some folks will say, 'Oh man, that's
too bad,' but almost everyone else will say, 'Did you see
that guy get shot? That was live, man. Did you see how
he ran, how he fell, how he screamed like a girl?
They got him in the head, man, they *busted* that brain,
It was like the movies, man. He screamed like a fuckin' girl.'"

Tuesday, wind shakes the windows. No one is outside,
at least not that I can see, and my son pulls on
a second sweatshirt, a bulky goosedown coat. He is 15,
a year younger than Jules, a year older than the child

who saw Jules open the window
to answer to his name, to let in some air.

There are times I hate being a reporter.
I am afraid of the stories. The voices are too real,
the colors too strong.
I rewind the tape, open another computer file,
hear my son yell goodbye and slam the door
on his way out. I run to the window.
Yes, his head is covered.

Suggestions for Discussion

1. Who is the principal speaker in the poem? What are the speaker's attitudes toward the events being described?
2. Explain the social background—the setting—of the poem.
3. Explain the title of the poem.

Suggestions for Writing

1. Write an essay in which you explain the comments and actions of the poem's characters. Summarize your own attitude toward the actions taken by the characters in the poem.
2. Explain the brief dedication at the beginning of the poem.

JIM WONG-CHU

Equal Opportunity

Jim Wong-Chu (b. 1949) was born in Hong Kong, brought to Vancouver, British Columbia, when he was four and reared by relatives in various places in North America. He is a founding member of "Pender Guy," the Chinese-Canadian radio program, and of the Asian-Canadian Writers Workshop. He has published a book of poetry, *Chinatown Ghosts* (1987), and co-edited *Many-Mouthed Birds* (1991), an anthology of Chinese-Canadian writers of poetry and fiction. Wong-Chu lives in Vancouver, where he works for the Canadian postal service. Using irony, this poem conveys the prejudice against Asian immigrants common in the United States and Canada until recent years.

in early canada
when railways were highways

each stop brought new opportunities

there was a rule

the chinese could only ride
the last two cars
of the trains

that is

until a train derailed
killing all those
in front

(the chinese erected an altar and thanked buddha)

a new rule was made

the chinese must ride
the front two cars
of the trains

that is

until another accident
claimed everyone
in the back

(the chinese erected an altar and thanked buddha)

after much debate
common sense prevailed

the chinese are now allowed
to sit anywhere
on any train

Suggestions for Discussion

1. Who is the speaking in the poem? Describe the speaker's attitude toward the events described in the poem.
2. There is no punctuation in the poem. Explain why it is not needed.

Suggestions for Writing

1. Write an essay comparing and contrasting the social attitude of this poem with Patricia Smith's "Always in the Head."
2. Using the poems by Wong-Chu and Patricia Smith, write an essay in which you explain the use of wit in social commentary.

The Examined Life: Education

I knew right there in prison that reading had changed forever the course of my life.

—MALCOLM X, "A Homemade Education"

We survived. The depths had been icy and dark, but now a bright sun spoke to our souls. I was no longer simply a member of the proud graduating class of 1940; I was a proud member of the wonderful, beautiful Negro race.

—MAYA ANGELOU, "Graduation"

The education of humanists cannot be regarded as complete, or even adequate, without exposure in some depth to where things stand in the various branches of science, and particularly, as I have said, in the areas of our ignorance.

—LEWIS THOMAS, "Humanities and Science"

Education doesn't end until life ends, because you never know when you're going to understand something you hadn't understood before.

—FRANK CONROY, "Think About It"

I was happy. I fell asleep at once. I had prayed for everybody: my talking family, cousins far away, passersby, and all the lonesome Christians. I expected to be heard. My voice was certainly the loudest.

—GRACE PALEY, "The Loudest Voice"

PERSONAL REMINISCENCES

LINCOLN STEFFENS

I Go to College

Joseph Lincoln Steffens (1866–1936) was born in San Francisco and graduated from the University of California at Berkeley. After his return from three years of study in Europe, he became a well-known muckraker and journalist. As editor of *McClure's*, *American*, and *Everybody's* magazines, he exposed corruption in business and government. His collections of essays include *The Shame of the Cities* (1904) and *The Struggle for Self-Government* (1906). His *Autobiography* (1931) is a very personal account of the history not only of journalism in the United States but of the leftist movement as well. This selection from it recalls his carefree days as an undergraduate and the beginnings of his serious interest in learning, while it questions the connection between the search for knowledge and the baccalaureate degree.

Going to college is, to a boy, an adventure into a new world, and a very strange and complete world too. Part of his preparation for it is the stories he hears from those that have gone before; these feed his imagination, which cannot help trying to picture the college life. And the stories and the life are pretty much the same for any college. The University of California was a young, comparatively small institution when I was entered there in 1885 as a freshman. Berkeley, the beautiful, was not the developed villa community it is now; I used to shoot quail in the brush under the oaks along the edges of the college grounds. The quail and the brush are gone now, but the oaks are there and the same prospect down the hill over San Francisco Bay out through the Golden Gate between the low hills of the city and the high hills of Marin County. My class numbered about one hundred boys and girls, mostly boys, who came from all parts of the State and represented all sorts of people and occupations. There was, however, a significant uniformity of opinion and spirit among us, as there was, and still is, in other, older colleges. The American is molded to type early. And so are our college ways. We found already formed at Berkeley the typical undergraduate customs, rights, and privileged vices which we had to respect ourselves and defend against the faculty, regents, and the State government.

One evening, before I had matriculated, I was taken out by some upper classmen to teach the president a lesson. He had been the head of a private preparatory school and was trying to govern the private lives and the public morals of university "men" as he had those of his schoolboys. Fetching a long ladder, the upper classmen thrust it through a front window of Prexy's house and, to the chant of obscene songs, swung it back and forth, up and down, round and round, till everything breakable within sounded broken and the drunken indignation outside was satisfied or tired.

This turned out to be one of the last battles in the war for liberty against that president. He was allowed to resign soon thereafter and I noticed that not only the students but many of the faculty and regents rejoiced in his downfall and turned with us to face and fight the new president when, after a lot of politics, he was appointed and presented. We learned somehow a good deal about the considerations that governed our college government. They were not only academic. The government of a university was—like the State government and horse-racing and so many other things—not what I had been led to expect. And a college education wasn't, either, nor the student mind.

Years later, when I was a magazine editor, I proposed a series of articles to raise and answer the question: Is there any intellectual life in our colleges? My idea sprang from my remembered disappointment at what I found at Berkeley and some experiences I was having at the time with the faculties and undergraduates of the other colleges in the east. Berkeley, in my day, was an Athens compared with New Haven, for example, when I came to know Yale undergraduates.

My expectations of college life were raised too high by Nixon's Saturday nights. I thought, and he assumed, that at Berkeley I would be breathing in an atmosphere of thought, discussion, and some scholarship; working, reading, and studying for the answers to questions which would be threshed out in debate and conversation. There was nothing of the sort. I was primed with questions. My English friends never could agree on the answers to any of the many and various questions they disputed. They did not care; they enjoyed their talks and did not expect to settle anything. I was more earnest. I was not content to leave things all up in the air. Some of those questions were very present and personal to me, as some of those Englishmen meant them to be. William Owen was trying to convert me to the anarchistic communism in which he believed with all his sincere and beautiful being. I was considering his arguments. Another earnest man, who presented the case for the Roman Catholic Church, sent old Father Burchard and other Jesuits after me. Every conversation at Mr. Nixon's pointed some question, academic or scientific, and pointed them so sharp that they drove me to college with an intense desire to know. And as for communism or the Catholic Church, I was so torn that I could not answer myself. The Jesuits dropped me and so did Owen, in disgust, when I said I was going to wait for my answer till I had heard what the professors had to say and had learned what my university had to teach me upon the questions underlying the questions Oxford and Cambridge and Rome quarreled over and could not agree on. Berkeley would know.

There were no moot questions in Berkeley. There was work to do, knowledge and training to get, but not to answer questions. I found myself engaged, as my classmates were, in choosing courses. The choice was limited and, within the limits, had to be determined by the degree we were candidates for. My questions were philosophical, but I could not take philosophy, which fascinated me, till I had gone through a lot of higher mathematics which did not interest me at all. If I had been allowed to take philosophy, and so discovered the need and the relation of mathematics, I would have got the philosophy and I might have got the mathematics which I miss now more than I do the Hegelian metaphysics taught at Berkeley. Or, if the professor who put me off had taken the pains to show me the bearing of mathematical thought on theoretical logic, I would have undertaken the preparation intelligently. But no one ever developed for me the relation of any of my required subjects to those that attracted me; no one brought out for me the relation of anything I was studying to anything else, except, of course, to that wretched degree. Knowledge was absolute, not relative, and it was stored in compartments, categorical and independent. The relation of knowledge to life, even to student life, was ignored, and as for questions, the professors asked them, not the students; and the students, not the teachers, answered them—in examinations.

The unknown is the province of the student; it is the field for his life's adventure, and it is a wide field full of beckonings. Curiosity about it would drive a boy as well as a child to work through the known to get at the unknown. But it was not assumed that we had any curiosity or the potential love of skill, scholarship, and achievement or research. And so far as I can remember now, the professors' attitude was right for most of the students who had no intellectual curiosity. They wanted to be told not only what they had to learn, but what they had to want to learn—for the purpose of passing. That came out in the considerations which decided the choice among optional courses. Students selected subjects or teachers for a balance of easy and hard, to fit into their time and yet "get through." I was the only rebel of my kind, I think. The nearest to me in sympathy were the fellows who knew what they wanted to be: engineers, chemists, professional men, or statesmen. They grunted at some of the work required of them, studies that seemed useless to their future careers. They did not understand me very well, nor I them, because I preferred those very subjects which they called useless, highbrow, cultural. I did not tell them so; I did not realize it myself definitely; but I think now that I had had as a boy an exhausting experience of *being* something great. I did not want now to be but rather to know things.

And what I wanted to know was buried deep under all this "college stuff" which was called "shop." It had nothing to do with what really interested us in common. Having chosen our work and begun to do it as a duty, we turned to the socially important question: which fraternity to join. The upper classmen tried to force our answers. They laid aside their superiority to "rush" those of us whose antecedents were known and creditable. It was all snobbish, secret, and exclusive. I joined a fraternity out of curiosity: What were the secrets and the mystic rites? I went blindfold through the silly initiation to find that there were no secrets and no mysteries, only pretensions and bunk, which so disgusted me that I would not live at the clubhouse, preferring for a year the open doors of a boarding-house. The next great university question was as to athletics. My ex-athletes from Oxford and Cambridge, with their lung and other troubles, warned me; but it was a mistake that saved me. I went with the other freshmen to the campus to be tried out for football, baseball, running, jumping, etc. Caught by the college and class spirit, I hoped to give promise of some excellence. Baseball was impossible for me; I had been riding horses when the other boys were preparing for college on the diamond. I had learned to run at the military academy and in the first freshman tests I did one hundred yards enough under eleven seconds to be turned over to an athletic upper classman for instruction. Pointing up to Grizzly Peak, a high hill back of the college, he said: "All you need is wind and muscle. Climb that mountain every day for a year; then come back and we'll see."

I did not climb Grizzly Peak every day, but I went up so often that I was soon able to run up and back without a halt. At the end of the year I ran around the cinder track so long that my student instructor wearied of watching me, but, of course, I could not do a hundred yards much under twelve seconds. Muscle and wind I had, but all my physical reactions were so slow that I was of no social use in college athletics. I was out of the crowd as I had been as a boy.

I shone only in the military department. The commandant, a U.S. Army officer, seeing that I had had previous training, told me off to drill the awkward squad of my class, and when I had made of them the best-drilled company in college, he gave me the next freshman class to drill. In the following years I was always drillmaster of the freshmen and finally commanded the whole cadet corps. Thus I led my class in the most unpopular and meaningless of undergraduate activities. I despised it myself, prizing it only for the chances it gave me to swank and, once a week, to lord it over my fellow students, who nicknamed me the "D. S."—damn stinker.

My nickname was won not only as a disciplinarian, however; I rarely punished any one; I never abused my command. I could persuade the freshmen to drill by arguing that, since it was compulsory, they could have more fun doing it well than badly; and that it was the one exercise in which they could beat and shame the upper classmen whose carelessness was as affected as their superiority. That is to say, I engaged their enthusiasm. All other student enthusiasms, athletics, class and college politics, fashions, and traditions I laughed at and damned. I was a spoilsport. I was mean, as a horse is mean, because I was unhappy myself. I could be enthusiastic in a conversation about something we were learning, if it wasn't too cut and dried; we had such talks now and then at the clubhouse in my later years. But generally speaking we were discussing the news or some prank of our own.

One night, for example, we sallied forth to steal some chickens from Dr. Bonte, the popular treasurer of the university. I crawled into the coop and selected the chickens, wrung their necks, and passed them out with comments to the other fellows who held the bag.

"Here," I said, "is the rooster, Dr. Bonte himself; he's tough, but good enough for the freshmen. Next is a nice fat hen, old Mrs. Bonte. This one's a pullet, Miss Bonte," and so on, naming each of the Bonte girls, till we were interrupted.

There was a sound from the house, the lights flashed in the windows, and—some one was coming. The other fellows ran, and I—when I tore myself out—I ran too. Which was all right enough. But when I caught up with the other thieves I learned that they had left the sack of chickens behind! Our Sunday dinner was spoiled, we thought, but no: the next day the whole fraternity was invited to dinner at Dr. Bonte's on Sunday. We accepted with some suspicion, we went in some embarrassment, but we were well received and soon put at our ease by Dr. Bonte, who explained that some thieves had been frightened while robbing his roost. "They were not students, I take it," he said. "Students are not so easily frightened; they might have run away, but students would have taken the bag of chickens with them. I think they were niggers or Chinamen."

So seated hospitably at table we watched with deep interest the great platter of roasted chickens borne in and set down before Dr. Bonte, who rose, whetted his carving-knife, and turning first to me, said: "Well, Steffens, what will you have, a piece of this old cock, Dr. Bonte? Or is he too tough for any but a freshman? Perhaps you would prefer the old hen, Mrs. Bonte, or, say, one of the Bonte girls."

I couldn't speak. No one could; and no one laughed, least of all Dr. Bonte, who stood there, his knife and fork in the air, looking at me, at the others, and back at me. He wanted an answer; I must make my choice, but

I saw a gleam of malicious humor in his eye; so I recovered and I chose the prettiest of the girls, pointing to the tenderest of the pullets. Dr. Bonte laughed, gave me my choice, and we had a jolly, ample dinner.

We talked about that, we and the students generally and the faculty—we discussed that incident long enough and hard enough to have solved it, if it had been a metaphysical problem. We might have threshed out the psychology of thieves, or gamblers, but no. We liked to steal, but we didn't care to think about it, not as stealing. And some of us gambled. We had to get money for theaters, operas, and other expenses in the city. I had only my board, lodging, and clothes paid for by my father, and others had not even that. We played cards, therefore, among ourselves, poker and whist, so that a lucky few got each month about all the money all of the other hard-ups had, and so had all the fun. We played long, late, and hard, and for money, not sport. The strain was too great.

One night my roommate, sunk low in his chair, felt a light kick on one of his extended legs; a second later there were two kicks against his other leg. Keeping still and watching the hands shown down, he soon had the signal system of two men playing partners, the better hand staying in the game. We said nothing but, watching, saw that others cheated, too. We knew well an old professional gambler from the mining-camps who was then in San Francisco. We told him all about it.

"Sure," he said, "cheating will sneak into any game that's played long enough. That's why you boys oughtn't to gamble. But if you do, play the game that's played. Cards is like horse-racing. I never bet a cent except I know, and know how, the game is crooked."

Having advised against it, he took us around to the gambling-houses and the race course and showed us many of the tricks of his trade, how to spot and profit by them—if we must play. "Now you won't need never to be suckers," he said. "And ye needn't be crooks either," he added after a pause. But we had it in for our opponents. We learned several ways to cheat; we practiced them till we were cool and sure. After that our "luck" was phenomenal. We had money, more than we needed. In my last two years at the university I had a salary as military instructor at a preparatory school in the town, and my roommate, the adopted son of a rich goldminer, had a generous allowance. But we went on playing and cheating at cards for the excitement of it, we said, but really it was for the money. And afterward, when I was a student in Germany, I played on, fair but hard—and for money I did not need, till one night at the Café Bauer in Berlin, sitting in a poker game that had been running all night, an American who had long been playing in hard luck, lost a large amount, of which I carried away more than my share. The next day we read in the papers that when he got home he had shot himself. I have never gambled since—at cards.

I Become a Student

It is possible to get an education at a university. It has been done; not often, but the fact that a proportion, however small, of college students do get a start in interested, methodical study, proves my thesis, and the two personal experiences I have to offer illustrate it and show how to circumvent the faculty, the other students, and the whole college system of mind-fixing. My method might lose a boy his degree, but a degree is not worth so much as the capacity and the drive to learn, and the undergraduate desire for an empty baccalaureate is one of the holds the educational system has on students. Wise students some day will refuse to take degrees, as the best men (in England, for instance) give, but do not themselves accept, titles.

My method was hit on by accident and some instinct. I specialized. With several courses prescribed, I concentrated on the one or two that interested me most, and letting the others go, I worked intensively on my favorites. In my first two years, for example, I worked at English and political economy and read philosophy. At the beginning of my junior year I had several cinches in history. Now I liked history; I had neglected it partly because I rebelled at the way it was taught, as positive knowledge unrelated to politics, art, life, or anything else. The professors gave us chapters out of a few books to read, con, and be quizzed on. Blessed as I was with a "bad memory," I could not commit to it anything that I did not understand and intellectually need. The bare record of the story of man, with names, dates, and irrelative events, bored me. But I had discovered in my readings of literature, philosophy, and political economy that history had light to throw upon unhistorical questions. So I proposed in my junior and senior years to specialize in history, taking all the courses required and those also that I had flunked in. With this in mind I listened attentively to the first introductory talk of Professor William Cary Jones on American constitutional history. He was a dull lecturer, but I noticed that, after telling us what pages of what books we must be prepared in, he mumbled off some other references "for those that may care to dig deeper."

When the rest of the class rushed out into the sunshine, I went up to the professor and, to his surprise, asked for this memorandum. He gave it to me. Up in the library I ran through the required chapters in the two different books, and they differed on several points. Turning to the other authorities, I saw that they disagreed on the same facts and also on others. The librarian, appealed to, helped me search the book-shelves till the library closed, and then I called on Professor Jones for more references. He was astonished, invited me in, and began to approve my industry, which astonished me. I was not trying to be a good boy; I was better than that: I was a curious boy. He lent me a couple of his books, and I went off to my club to read them. They only deepened the mystery, clearing up the historical question, but leaving the answer to be dug for and written.

The historians did not know! History was not a science, but a field for research, a field for me, for any young man, to explore, to make discoveries in and write a scientific report about. I was fascinated. As I went on from chapter to chapter, day after day, finding frequently essential differences of opinion and of fact, I saw more and more work to do. In this course, American constitutional history, I hunted far enough to suspect that the Fathers of the Republic who wrote our sacred Constitution of the United States not only did not, but did not want to, establish a democratic government, and I dreamed for a while—as I used as a child to play I was Napoleon or a trapper—I promised myself to write a true history of the making of the American Constitution. I did not do it; that chapter has been done or well begun since by two men: Smith of the University of Washington and Beard (then) of Columbia (afterward forced out, perhaps for this very work). I found other events, men, and epochs waiting for students. In all my other courses, in ancient, in European, and in modern history, the disagreeing authorities carried me back to the need of a fresh search for (or of) the original documents or other clinching testimony. Of course I did well in my classes. The history professors soon knew me as a student and seldom put a question to me except when the class had flunked it. Then Professor Jones would say, "Well, Steffens, tell them about it."

Fine. But vanity wasn't my ruling passion then. What I had was a quickening sense that I was learning a method of studying history and that every chapter of it, from the beginning of the world to the end, is crying out to be rewritten. There was something for Youth to do; these superior old men had not done anything, finally.

Years afterward I came out of the graft prosecution office in San Francisco with Rudolph Spreckels, the banker and backer of the investigation. We were to go somewhere, quick, in his car, and we couldn't. The chauffeur was trying to repair something wrong. Mr. Spreckels smiled; he looked closely at the defective part, and to my silent, wondering inquiry he answered: "Always, when I see something badly done or not done at all, I see an opportunity to make a fortune. I never kick at bad work by my class: there's lots of it and we suffer from it. But our failures and neglects are chances for the young fellows coming along and looking for work."

Nothing is done. Everything in the world remains to be done or done over. "The greatest picture is not yet painted, the greatest play isn't written (not even by Shakespeare), the greatest poem is unsung. There isn't in all the world a perfect railroad, nor a good government, nor a sound law." Physics, mathematics, and especially the most advanced and exact of the sciences, are being fundamentally revised. Chemistry is just becoming a science; psychology, economics, and sociology are awaiting a Darwin, whose work in turn is awaiting an Einstein. If the rah-rah boys in our colleges could be told this, they might not all be such specialists in football, petting parties, and unearned degrees. They are not told it, however; they are told to learn what is known. This is nothing, philosophically speaking.

Somehow or other in my later years at Berkeley, two professors, Moses and Howison, representing opposite schools of thought, got into a controversy, probably about their classes. They brought together in the house of one of them a few of their picked students, with the evident intention of letting us show in conversation how much or how little we had understood of their respective teachings. I don't remember just what the subject was that they threw into the ring, but we wrestled with it till the professors could stand it no longer. Then they broke in, and while we sat silent and highly entertained, they went at each other hard and fast and long. It was after midnight when, the debate over, we went home. I asked the other fellows what they had got out of it, and their answers showed that they had seen nothing but a fine, fair fight. When I laughed, they asked me what I, the D.S., had seen that was so much more profound.

I said that I had seen two highly trained, well-educated Masters of Arts and Doctors of Philosophy disagreeing upon every essential point of thought and knowledge. They had all there was of the sciences; and yet they could not find any knowledge upon which they could base an acceptable conclusion. They had no test of knowledge; they didn't know what is and what is not. And they have no test of right and wrong; they have no basis for even an ethics.

Well, and what of it? They asked me that, and that I did not answer. I was stunned by the discovery that it was philosophically true, in a most literal sense, that nothing is known; that it is precisely the foundation that is lacking for science; that all we call knowledge rested upon assumptions which the scientists did not all accept; and that, likewise, there is no scientific reason for saying, for example, that stealing is wrong. In brief: there was no scientific basis for an ethics. No wonder men said one thing and did another; no wonder they could settle nothing either in life or in the academies.

I could hardly believe this. Maybe these professors, whom I greatly respected, did not know it all. I read the books over again with a fresh eye, with a real interest, and I could see that, as in history, so in other branches of knowledge, everything was in the air. And I was glad of it. Rebel though I was, I had got the religion of scholarship and science; I was in awe of the authorities in the academic world. It was a release to feel my worship cool and pass. But I could not be sure. I must go elsewhere, see and hear other professors, men these California professors quoted and looked up to as their high priests. I decided to go as a student to Europe when I was through Berkeley, and I would start with the German universities.

My father listened to my plan, and he was disappointed. He had hoped I would succeed him in his business; it was for that that he was staying in it. When I said that, whatever I might do, I would never go into business, he said, rather sadly, that he would sell out his interest and retire. And he did soon after our talk. But he wanted me to stay home and, to keep me, offered to buy an interest in a certain San Francisco daily paper. He had evidently had this in mind for some time. I had always done some writing, verse at the poetical age of puberty, then a novel which my mother alone treasured. Journalism was the business for a boy who liked to write, he thought, and he said I had often spoken of a newspaper as my ambition. No doubt I had in the intervals between my campaigns as Napoleon. But no more. I was now going to be a scientist, a philosopher. He sighed; he thought it over, and with the approval of my mother, who was for every sort of education, he gave his consent.

Suggestions for Discussion

1. The first part of this reminiscence tells us about Steffens's carefree days as a student at Berkeley in the late nineteenth century. How does he describe student life? What was the main interest of most students at the university?
2. Why did Steffens fail to get ahead in athletics while achieving great success as a drillmaster? Why did military drill appeal to him?
3. What was Steffens's attitude toward money while he was a student? Why did he gamble? Explain how he learned to be a successful gambler. Explain why he gave up gambling.
4. Why was Steffens disappointed in his fraternity?
5. Explain the significance of the incident of the stealing of Dr. Bonte's chickens. Why is it included in this section?
6. What is the major difference between the first and second parts of the reminiscence?
7. How does Steffens get interested in the study of history? What determines his decision to continue his education in Germany?
8. Why were most of the students whom Steffens knew attending Berkeley? Does he respect their reasons? What does he think is the real reason for education?
9. How would you describe Steffens during his student days? Was he likeable? Explain your answer.

Suggestions for Writing

1. Using Steffens as a model, write an essay in which you attempt to summarize most of your classmates' reasons for going to college. Try to develop a

questionnaire in which you sample opinion so that you have information to summarize. Write an opinion of the reasons you discover.

2. College life differs greatly from one institution to another. Write an essay in which you compare college life at your own college or university with that of another. You may wish to ask someone much older than yourself how his or her college life differed from yours. You may wish to contrast your own experiences with those of Steffens.

MALCOLM X

A Homemade Education

Malcolm X (1925–1965), who became a Muslim while serving a prison sentence, was an early minister of the Nation of Islam's mosque in New York. Before his assassination, he was a spiritual leader, writer, lecturer, and political activist who worked for worldwide African-American unity and equality. The following selection is taken from his powerful *Autobiography of Malcolm X* (1965).

It was because of my letters that I happened to stumble upon starting to acquire some kind of a homemade education.

I became increasingly frustrated at not being able to express what I wanted to convey in letters that I wrote, especially those to Mr. Elijah Muhammad. In the street, I had been the most articulate hustler out there—I had commanded attention when I said something. But now, trying to write simple English, I not only wasn't articulate, I wasn't even functional. How would I sound writing in slang, the way I would *say* it, something such as, "Look, daddy, let me pull your coat about a cat, Elijah Muhammad—"

Many who today hear me somewhere in person, or on television, or those who read something I've said, will think I went to school far beyond the eighth grade. This impression is due entirely to my prison studies.

It had really begun back in the Charlestown Prison, when Bimbi first made me feel envy of his stock of knowledge. Bimbi had always taken charge of any conversations he was in, and I had tried to emulate him. But every book I picked up had few sentences which didn't contain anywhere from one to nearly all of the words that might as well have been in Chinese.

When I just skipped those words, of course, I really ended up with little idea of what the book said. So I had come to the Norfolk Prison Colony still going through only book-reading motions. Pretty soon, I would have quit even these motions, unless I had received the motivation that I did.

I saw that the best thing I could do was get hold of a dictionary—to study, to learn some words. I was lucky enough to reason also that I should try to improve my penmanship. It was sad. I couldn't even write in a straight line. It was both ideas together that moved me to request a dictionary along with some tablets and pencils from the Norfolk Prison Colony school.

I spent two days just riffling uncertainly through the dictionary's pages. I'd never realized so many words existed! I didn't know *which* words I needed to learn. Finally, just to start some kind of action, I began copying.

In my slow, painstaking, ragged handwriting, I copied into my tablet everything printed on that first page, down to the punctuation marks.

I believe it took me a day. Then, aloud, I read back, to myself, everything I'd written on the tablet. Over and over, aloud, to myself, I read my own handwriting.

I woke up the next morning, thinking about those words—immensely proud to realize that not only had I written so much at one time, but I'd written words that I never knew were in the world. Moreover, with a little effort, I also could remember what many of these words meant. I reviewed the words whose meanings I didn't remember. Funny thing, from the dictionary first page right now, that "aardvark" springs to my mind. The dictionary had a picture of it, a long-tailed, long-eared, burrowing African mammal, which lives off termites caught by sticking out its tongue as an anteater does for ants.

I was so fascinated that I went on—I copied the dictionary's next page. And the same experience came when I studied that. With every succeeding page, I also learned of people and places and events from history. Actually the dictionary is like a miniature encyclopedia. Finally the dictionary's A section had filled a whole tablet—and I went on into the B's. That was the way I started copying what eventually became the entire dictionary. It went a lot faster after so much practice helped me to pick up handwriting speed. Between what I wrote in my tablet, and writing letters, during the rest of my time in prison I would guess I wrote a million words.

I suppose it was inevitable that as my word-base broadened, I could for the first time pick up a book and read and now begin to understand what the book was saying. Anyone who has read a great deal can imagine the new world that opened. Let me tell you something: from then until I left that prison, in every free moment I had, if I was not reading in the library, I was reading on my bunk. You couldn't have gotten me out of books with a wedge. Between Mr. Muhammad's teachings, my correspondence, my visitors—usually Ella and Reginald—and my reading of books, months passed without my even thinking about being imprisoned. In fact, up to then, I never had been so truly free in my life.

The Norfolk Prison Colony's library was in the school building. A variety of classes was taught there by instructors who came from such places as Harvard and Boston universities. The weekly debates between inmate teams were also held in the school building. You would be astonished to know how worked up convict debaters and audiences would get over subjects like "Should Babies Be Fed Milk?"

Available on the prison library's shelves were books on just about every general subject. Much of the big private collection that Parkhurst had willed to the prison was still in crates and boxes in the back of the library—thousands of old books. Some of them looked ancient: covers faded; old-time parchment-looking binding. Parkhurst, I've mentioned, seemed to have been principally interested in history and religion. He had the money and the special interest to have a lot of books that you wouldn't have in general circulation. Any college library would have been lucky to get that collection.

As you can imagine, especially in a prison where there was heavy emphasis on rehabilitation, an inmate was smiled upon if he demonstrated an unusually intense interest in books. There was a sizable number of well-read inmates, especially the popular debaters. Some were said by many to be practically walking encyclopedias. They were almost celebrities. No university would ask any student to devour literature as I did when this new world opened to me, of being able to read and *understand.*

I read more in my room than in the library itself. An inmate who was known to read a lot could check out more than the permitted maximum number of books. I preferred reading in the total isolation of my own room.

When I had progressed to really serious reading, every night at about ten P.M. I would be outraged with the "lights out." It always seemed to catch me right in the middle of something engrossing.

Fortunately, right outside my door was a corridor light that cast a glow into my room. The glow was enough to read by, once my eyes adjusted to it. So when "lights out" came, I would sit on the floor where I could continue reading in that glow.

At one-hour intervals the night guards paced past every room. Each time I heard the approaching footsteps, I jumped into bed and feigned sleep. And as soon as the guard passed, I got back out of bed onto the floor area of that light-glow, where I would read for another fifty-eight minutes—until the guard approached again. That went on until three or four every morning. Three or four hours of sleep a night was enough for me. Often in the years in the streets I had slept less than that.

The teachings of Mr. Muhammad stressed how history had been "whitened"—when white men had written history books, the black man simply had been left out. Mr. Muhammad couldn't have said anything that would have struck me much harder. I had never forgotten how when my class, me and all of those whites, had studied seventh-grade United States history back in Mason, the history of the Negro had been covered in one paragraph, and the teacher had gotten a big laugh with his joke, "Negroes' feet are so big that when they walk, they leave a hole in the ground."

This is one reason why Mr. Muhammad's teachings spread so swiftly all over the United States, among *all* Negroes, whether or not they became followers of Mr. Muhammad. The teachings ring true—to every Negro. You can hardly show me a black adult in America—or a white one, for that matter—who knows from the history books anything like the truth about the black man's role. In my own case, once I heard of the "glorious history of the black man," I took special pains to hunt in the library for books that would inform me on details about black history.

I can remember accurately the very first set of books that really impressed me. I have since bought that set of books and I have it at home for my children to read as they grow up. It's called *Wonders of the World.* It's full of pictures of archaeological finds, statues that depict, usually, non-European people.

I found books like Will Durant's *Story of Civilization.* I read H. G. Wells' *Outline of History. Souls of Black Folk* by W. E. B. Du Bois gave me a glimpse into the black people's history before they came to this country. Carter G. Woodson's *Negro History* opened my eyes about black empires before the black slave was brought to the United States, and the early Negro struggles for freedom.

J. A. Rogers' three volumes of *Sex and Race* told about race-mixing before Christ's time; about Aesop being a black man who told fables; about Egypt's Pharaohs; about the great Coptic Christian Empires; about Ethiopia, the earth's oldest continuous black civilization, as China is the oldest continuous civilization.

Mr. Muhammad's teaching about how the white man had been created led me to *Findings in Genetics* by Gregor Mendel. (The dictionary's G section was where I had learned what "genetics" meant.) I really studied this book by the Austrian monk. Reading it over and over, especially certain sections, helped me to understand that if you started with a black man, a white man could be produced; but starting with a white man, you never could produce a black man—because the white chromosome is recessive. And since no one disputes that there was but one Original Man, the conclusion is clear.

During the last year or so, in the *New York Times,* Arnold Toynbee used the word "bleached" in describing the white man. (His words were: "White [i.e., bleached] human beings of North European origin. . . .") Toynbee also referred to the European geographic area as only a peninsula of Asia. He said there is no such thing as Europe. And if you look at the globe, you will see for yourself that America is only an extension of Asia. (But at the same time Toynbee is among those who have helped to bleach history. He won't write that again. Every day now, the truth is coming to light.)

I never will forget how shocked I was when I began reading about slavery's total horror. It made such an impact upon me that it later became one of my favorite subjects when I became a minister of Mr. Muhammad's. The world's most monstrous crime, the sin and the blood on the white man's hands, are almost impossible to believe. Books like the one by Frederick Olmstead opened my eyes to the horrors suffered when the slave was landed in the United States. The European woman, Fannie Kimball, who had married a Southern white slaveowner, described how human beings were degraded. Of course I read *Uncle Tom's Cabin.* In fact, I believe that's the only novel I have ever read since I started serious reading.

Parkhurst's collection also contained some bound pamphlets of the Abolitionist Anti-Slavery Society of New England. I read descriptions of atrocities, saw those illustrations of black slave women tied up and flogged with whips; of black mothers watching their babies being dragged off, never to be seen by their mothers again; of dogs after slaves, and of the fugitive slave catchers, evil white men with whips and clubs and chains and guns. I read about the slave preacher Nat Turner, who put the fear of God into the white slavemaster. Nat Turner wasn't going around preaching pie-in-the-sky and "nonviolent" freedom for the black man. There in Virginia one night in 1831, Nat and seven other slaves started out at his master's home and through the night they went from one plantation "big house" to the next, killing, until by the next morning 57 white people were dead and Nat had about 70 slaves following him. White people, terrified for their lives, fled from their homes, locked themselves up in public buildings, hid in the woods, and some even left the state. A small army of soldiers took two months to catch and hang Nat Turner. Somewhere I have read where Nat Turner's example is said to have inspired John Brown to invade Virginia and attack Harper's Ferry nearly thirty years later, with thirteen white men and five Negroes.

I read Herodotus, "the father of History," or, rather, I read about him. And I read the histories of various nations, which opened my eyes gradually, then wider and wider, to how the whole world's white men had indeed acted like devils, pillaging and raping and bleeding and draining the whole world's non-white people. I remember, for instance, books such as Will Durant's *The Story of Oriental Civilization,* and Mahatma Gandhi's accounts of the struggle to drive the British out of India.

Book after book showed me how the white man had brought upon the world's black, brown, red, and yellow peoples every variety of the sufferings of exploitation. I saw how since the sixteenth century, the so-called "Christian trader" white man began to ply the seas in his lust for Asian and African empires, and plunder, and power. I read, I saw, how the white man never has gone among the non-white peoples bearing the Cross in the true manner and spirit of Christ's teachings—meek, humble, and Christlike.

I perceived, as I read, how the collective white man had been actually nothing but a piratical opportunist who used Faustian machinations to make his own Christianity his initial wedge in criminal conquests. First, always "religiously," he branded "heathen" and "pagan" labels upon ancient non-white cultures and civilizations. The stage thus set, he then turned upon his non-white victims his weapons of war.

I read how, entering India—half a *billion* deeply religious brown people—the British white man, by 1759, through promises, trickery and manipulations, controlled much of India through Great Britain's East India Company. The parasitical British administration kept tentacling out to half of the subcontinent. In 1857, some of the desperate people of India finally mutinied—and, excepting the African slave trade, nowhere has history recorded any more unnecessary bestial and ruthless human carnage than the British suppression of the non-white Indian people.

Over 115 million African blacks—close to the 1930s population of the United States—were murdered or enslaved during the slave trade. And I read how when the slave market was glutted, the cannibalistic white powers of Europe next carved up, as their colonies, the richest areas of the black continent. And Europe's chancelleries for the next century played a chess game of naked exploitation and power from Cape Horn to Cairo.

Ten guards and the warden couldn't have torn me out of those books. Not even Elijah Muhammad could have been more eloquent than those books were in providing indisputable proof that the collective white man had acted like a devil in virtually every contact he had with the world's collective non-white man. I listen today to the radio, and watch television, and read the headlines about the collective white man's fear and tension concerning China. When the white man professes ignorance about why the Chinese hate him so, my mind can't help flashing back to what I read, there in prison, about how the blood forebears of this same white man raped China at a time when China was trusting and helpless. Those original white "Christian traders" sent into China millions of pounds of opium. By 1839, so many of the Chinese were addicts that China's desperate government destroyed twenty thousand chests of opium. The first Opium War was promptly declared by the white man. Imagine! Declaring *war* upon someone who objects to being narcotized! The Chinese were severely beaten, with Chinese-invented gunpowder.

The Treaty of Nanking made China pay the British white man for the destroyed opium: forced open China's major ports to British trade; forced

China to abandon Hong Kong; fixed China's import tariffs so low that cheap British articles soon flooded in, maiming China's industrial development.

After a second Opium War, the Tientsin Treaties legalized the ravaging opium trade, legalized a British-French-American control of China's customs. China tried delaying that Treaty's ratification; Peking was looted and burned.

"Kill the foreign white devils!" was the 1901 Chinese war cry in the Boxer Rebellion. Losing again, this time the Chinese were driven from Peking's choicest areas. The vicious, arrogant white man put up the famous signs, "Chinese and dogs not allowed."

Red China after World War II closed its doors to the Western white world. Massive Chinese agricultural, scientific, and industrial efforts are described in a book that *Life* magazine recently published. Some observers inside Red China have reported that the world never has known such a hate-white campaign as is now going on in this non-white country where, present birthrates continuing, in fifty more years Chinese will be half the earth's population. And it seems that some Chinese chickens will soon come home to roost, with China's recent successful nuclear tests.

Let us face reality. We can see in the United Nations a new world order being shaped, along color lines—an alliance among the non-white nations. America's U.N. Ambassador Adlai Stevenson complained not long ago that in the United Nations "a skin game" was being played. He was right. He was facing reality. A "skin game" *is* being played. But Ambassador Stevenson sounded like Jesse James accusing the marshal of carrying a gun. Because who in the world's history ever has played a worse "skin game" than the white man?

Mr. Muhammad, to whom I was writing daily, had no idea of what a new world had opened up to me through my efforts to document his teachings in books.

When I discovered philosophy, I tried to touch all the landmarks of philosophical development. Gradually, I read most of the old philosophers, Occidental and Oriental. The Oriental philosophers were the ones I came to prefer; finally, my impression was that most Occidental philosophy had largely been borrowed from the Oriental thinkers. Socrates, for instance, traveled in Egypt. Some sources even say that Socrates was initiated into some of the Egyptian mysteries. Obviously Socrates got some of his wisdom among the East's wise men.

I have often reflected upon the new vistas that reading opened to me. I knew right there in prison that reading had changed forever the course of my life. As I see it today, the ability to read awoke inside me some long dormant craving to be mentally alive. I certainly wasn't seeking any degree, the way a college confers a status symbol upon its students. My homemade education gave me, with every additional book that I read, a little bit more sensitivity to the deafness, dumbness, and blindness that was afflicting the black race in America. Not long ago, an English writer telephoned me from London, asking questions. One was, "What's your alma mater?" I told him, "Books." You will never catch me with a free fifteen minutes in which I'm not studying something I feel might be able to help the black man.

Yesterday I spoke in London, and both ways on the plane across the Atlantic I was studying a document about how the United Nations proposes to insure the human rights of the oppressed minorities of the world. The American black man is the world's most shameful case of minority oppression. What makes the black man think of himself as only an internal United States issue is just a catch-phrase, two words, "civil rights." How is the black man going to get "civil rights" before first he wins his *human* rights? If the American black man will start thinking about his *human* rights, and then start thinking of himself as part of one of the world's great peoples, he will see he has a case for the United Nations.

I can't think of a better case! Four hundred years of black blood and sweat invested here in America, and the white man still has the black man begging for what every immigrant fresh off the ship can take for granted the minute he walks down the gangplank.

But I'm digressing. I told the Englishman that my alma mater was books, a good library. Every time I catch a plane, I have with me a book that I want to read—and that's a lot of books these days. If I weren't out here every day battling the white man, I could spend the rest of my life reading, just satisfying my curiosity—because you can hardly mention anything I'm not curious about. I don't think anybody ever got more out of going to prison than I did. In fact, prison enabled me to study far more intensively than I would have if my life had gone differently and I had attended some college. I imagine that one of the biggest troubles with colleges is there are too many distractions, too much panty-raiding, fraternities, and boola-boola and all of that. Where else but in a prison could I have attacked my ignorance by being able to study intensely sometimes as much as fifteen hours a day?

Suggestions for Discussion

1. Discuss the significance of the title "A Homemade Education."
2. Explain how Malcolm X used his dictionary to improve his education.
3. Discuss his observation that "the ability to read awoke inside me some long dormant craving to be mentally alive."
4. Comment on his assertion that his "alma mater was books."
5. What details help make clear his passion for learning?

Suggestions for Writing

1. Compare and contrast "A Homemade Education" with another section of Malcolm X's *Autobiography.*
2. Write about one or more books that have played an important role in shaping your thinking, attitudes, and behavior.

MAYA ANGELOU

Graduation

Maya Angelou (b. 1928) was born in Stamps, Arkansas, to a childhood of poverty and pain. She has been a dancer and an actress, a coordinator of the Southern Christian Leadership Conference, a television writer and producer, and a poet. She is best known for her autobiographical works, *I Know Why the Caged Bird Sings* (1970), from which "Graduation" is taken, and *The Heart of a Woman* (1981). Her poem, "On the Pulse of Morning," delivered at the first inauguration of President Bill Clinton, was published in 1993. In "Graduation" Angelou captures the pain of racial discrimination, but reaffirms the power of the black community to survive.

The children in Stamps trembled visibly with anticipation. Some adults were excited too, but to be certain the whole young population had come down with graduation epidemic. Large classes were graduating from both the grammar school and the high school. Even those who were years removed from their own day of glorious release were anxious to help with preparations as a kind of dry run. The junior students who were moving into the vacating classes' chairs were tradition-bound to show their talents for leadership and management. They strutted through the school and around the campus exerting pressure on the lower grades. Their authority was so new that occasionally if they pressed a little too hard it had to be overlooked. After all, next term was coming, and it never hurt a sixth-grader to have a play sister in the eighth grade, or a tenth-year student to be able to call a twelfth-grader Bubba. So all was endured in a spirit of shared understanding. But the graduating classes themselves were the nobility. Like travelers with exotic destinations on their minds, the graduates were remarkably forgetful. They came to school without their books, or tablets or even pencils. Volunteers fell over themselves to secure replacements for the missing equipment. When accepted, the willing workers might or might not be thanked, and it was of no importance to the pregraduation rites. Even teachers were respectful of the now quiet and aging seniors, and tended to speak to them, if not as equals, as beings only slightly lower than themselves. After tests were returned and grades given, the student body, which acted like an extended family, knew who did well, who excelled, and what piteous ones had failed.

Unlike the white high school, Lafayette County Training School distinguished itself by having neither lawn, nor hedges, nor tennis court, nor climbing ivy. Its two buildings (main classrooms, the grade school and home economics) were set on a dirt hill with no fence to limit either its boundaries or those of bordering farms. There was a large expanse to the left of the school which was used alternately as a baseball diamond or a basketball court. Rusty hoops on the swaying poles represented the permanent recreational equipment, although bats and balls could be borrowed from the P.E. teacher if the borrower was qualified and if the diamond wasn't occupied.

Over this rocky area relieved by a few shady tall persimmon trees the graduating class walked. The girls often held hands and no longer bothered to speak to the lower students. There was a sadness about them, as if this old world was not their home and they were bound for higher ground. The boys, on the other hand, had become more friendly, more outgoing. A decided change from the closed attitude they projected while studying for finals. Now they seemed not ready to give up the old school, the familiar paths and classrooms. Only a small percentage would be continuing on to college—one of the South's A & M (agricultural and mechanical) schools, which trained Negro youths to be carpenters, farmers, handymen, masons, maids, cooks and baby nurses. Their future rode heavily on their shoulders, and blinded them to the collective joy that had pervaded the lives of the boys and girls in the grammar school graduating class.

Parents who could afford it had ordered new shoes and ready-made clothes for themselves from Sears, Roebuck or Montgomery Ward. They also engaged the best seamstresses to make the floating graduating dresses and to cut down secondhand pants which would be pressed to a military slickness for the important event.

Oh, it was important, all right. Whitefolks would attend the ceremony, and two or three would speak of God and home, and the Southern way of life, and Mrs. Parsons, the principal's wife, would play the graduation march while the lower-grade graduates paraded down the aisles and took their seats below the platform. The high school seniors would wait in empty classrooms to make their dramatic entrance.

In the Store I was the person of the moment. The birthday girl. The center. Bailey had graduated the year before, although to do so he had had to forfeit all pleasures to make up for his time lost in Baton Rouge.

My class was wearing butter-yellow piqué dresses, and Momma launched out on mine. She smocked the yoke into tiny crisscrossing puckers, then shirred the rest of the bodice. Her dark fingers ducked in and out of the lemony cloth as she embroidered raised daisies around the hem. Before she considered herself finished she had added a crocheted cuff on the puff sleeves, and a pointy crocheted collar.

I was going to be lovely. A walking model of all the various styles of fine hand sewing and it didn't worry me that I was only twelve years old and merely graduating from the eighth grade. Besides, many teachers in Arkansas Negro schools had only that diploma and were licensed to impart wisdom.

The days had become longer and more noticeable. The faded beige of former times had been replaced with strong and sure colors. I began to see my classmates' clothes, their skin tones, and the dust that waved off pussy willows. Clouds that lazed across the sky were objects of great concern to me. Their shiftier shapes might have held a message that in my new happiness and with a little bit of time I'd soon decipher. During that period I looked at the arch of heaven so religiously my neck kept a steady ache. I had taken to smiling more often, and my jaws hurt from the unaccustomed activity. Between the two physical sore spots, I suppose I could have been uncomfortable, but that was not the case. As a member of the winning team (the graduating class of 1940) I had outdistanced unpleasant sensations by miles. I was headed for the freedom of open fields.

Youth and social approval allied themselves with me and we trammeled memories of slights and insults. The wind of our swift passage remodeled my features. Lost tears were pounded to mud and then to dust. Years of withdrawal were brushed aside and left behind, as hanging ropes of parasitic moss.

My work alone had awarded me a top place and I was going to be one of the first called in the graduating ceremonies. On the classroom blackboard, as well as on the bulletin board in the auditorium, there were blue stars and white stars and red stars. No absences, no tardinesses, and my academic work was among the best of the year. I could say the preamble to the Constitution even faster than Bailey. We timed ourselves often: "WethepeopleoftheUnitedStatesinordertoformamoreperfectunion..." I had memorized the Presidents of the United States from Washington to Roosevelt in chronological as well as alphabetical order.

My hair pleased me too. Gradually the black mass had lengthened and thickened, so that it kept at last to its braided pattern, and I didn't have to yank my scalp off when I tried to comb it.

Louise and I had rehearsed the exercises until we tired out ourselves. Henry Reed was class valedictorian. He was a small, very black boy with hooded eyes, a long, broad nose and an oddly shaped head. I had admired him for years because each term he and I vied for the best grades in our class. Most often he bested me, but instead of being disappointed I was pleased that we shared top places between us. Like many Southern Black children, he lived with his grandmother, who was as strict as Momma and as kind as she knew how to be. He was courteous, respectful, and soft-spoken to elders, but on the playground he chose to play the roughest games. I admired him. Anyone, I reckoned, sufficiently afraid or sufficiently dull could be polite. But to be able to operate at a top level with both adults and children was admirable.

His valedictory speech was entitled "To Be or Not to Be." The rigid tenth-grade teacher had helped him write it. He'd been working on the dramatic stresses for months.

The weeks until graduation were filled with heady activities. A group of small children were to be presented in a play about buttercups and daisies and bunny rabbits. They could be heard throughout the building practicing their hops and their little songs that sounded like silver bells. The older girls (nongraduates, of course) were assigned the task of making refreshments for the night's festivities. A tangy scent of ginger, cinnamon, nutmeg and chocolate wafted around the home economics building as the budding cooks made samples for themselves and their teachers.

In every corner of the workshop, axes and saws split fresh timber as the woodshop boys made sets and stage scenery. Only the graduates were left out of the general bustle. We were free to sit in the library at the back of the building or look in quite detachedly, naturally, on the measures being taken for our event.

Even the minister preached on graduation the Sunday before. His subject was, "Let your light so shine that men will see your good works and praise your Father, Who is in Heaven." Although the sermon was purported to be addressed to us, he used the occasion to speak to backsliders, gamblers, and general ne'er-do-wells. But since he had called our names at the beginning of the service we were mollified.

Among Negroes the tradition was to give presents to children going only from one grade to another. How much more important this was when the person was graduating at the top of the class. Uncle Willie and Momma had sent away for a Mickey Mouse watch like Bailey's. Louise gave me four embroidered handkerchiefs. (I gave her three crocheted doilies.) Mrs. Sneed, the minister's wife, made me an underskirt to wear for graduation, and nearly every customer gave me a nickel or maybe even a dime with the instruction "Keep on moving to higher ground," or some such encouragement.

Amazingly the great day finally dawned and I was out of bed before I knew it. I threw open the back door to see it more clearly, but Momma said, "Sister, come away from that door and put your robe on."

I hoped the memory of that morning would never leave me. Sunlight was itself still young, and the day had none of the insistence maturity would bring it in a few hours. In my robe and barefoot in the backyard, under cover of going to see about my new beans, I gave myself up to the gentle warmth and thanked God that no matter what evil I had done in my life He had allowed me to live to see this day. Somewhere in my fatalism I had expected to die, accidentally, and never have the chance to walk up the stairs in the auditorium and gracefully receive my hard-earned diploma. Out of God's merciful bosom I had won reprieve.

Bailey came out in his robe and gave me a box wrapped in Christmas paper. He said he had saved his money for months to pay for it. It felt like a box of chocolates, but I knew Bailey wouldn't save money to buy candy when we had all we could want under our noses.

He was as proud of the gift as I. It was a soft-leatherbound copy of a collection of poems by Edgar Allan Poe, or, as Bailey and I called him, "Eap." I turned to "Annabel Lee" and we walked up and down the garden rows, the cool dirt between our toes, reciting the beautifully sad lines.

Momma made a Sunday breakfast although it was only Friday. After we finished the blessing, I opened my eyes to find the watch on my plate. It was a dream of a day. Everything went smoothly and to my credit. I didn't have to be reminded or scolded for anything. Near evening I was too jittery to attend to chores, so Bailey volunteered to do all before his bath.

Days before, we had made a sign for the Store, and as we turned out the lights Momma hung the cardboard over the doorknob. It read clearly: CLOSED. GRADUATION.

My dress fitted perfectly and everyone said that I looked like a sunbeam in it. On the hill, going toward the school, Bailey walked behind with Uncle Willie, who muttered, "Go on, Ju." He wanted him to walk ahead with us because it embarrassed him to have to walk so slowly. Bailey said he'd let the ladies walk together, and the men would bring up the rear. We all laughed, nicely.

Little children dashed by out of the dark like fireflies. Their crepe-paper dresses and butterfly wings were not made for running and we heard more than one rip, dryly, and the regretful "uh uh" that followed.

The school blazed without gaiety. The windows seemed cold and unfriendly from the lower hill. A sense of ill-fated timing crept over me, and if Momma hadn't reached for my hand I would have drifted back to Bailey and Uncle Willie, and possibly beyond. She made a few slow jokes about my feet getting cold, and tugged me along to the now-strange building.

Around the front steps, assurance came back. There were my fellow "greats," the graduating class. Hair brushed back, legs oiled, new dresses and pressed pleats, fresh pocket handkerchiefs and little handbags, all homesewn. Oh, we were up to snuff, all right. I joined my comrades and didn't even see my family go in to find seats in the crowded auditorium.

The school band struck up a march and all classes filed in as had been rehearsed. We stood in front of our seats, as assigned, and on a signal from the choir director, we sat. No sooner had this been accomplished than the band started to play the national anthem. We rose again and sang the song, after which we recited the pledge of allegiance. We remained standing for a brief minute before the choir director and the principal signaled to us, rather desperately I thought, to take our seats. The command was so unusual that our carefully rehearsed and smooth-running machine was thrown off. For a full minute we fumbled for our chairs and bumped into each other awkwardly. Habits change or solidify under pressure, so in our state of nervous tension we had been ready to follow our usual assembly pattern: the American national anthem, then the pledge of allegiance, then the song every Black person I knew called the Negro National Anthem. All done in the same key, with the same passion and most often standing on the same foot.

Finding my seat at last, I was overcome with a presentiment of worse things to come. Something unrehearsed, unplanned, was going to happen, and we were going to be made to look bad. I distinctly remember being explicit in the choice of pronoun. It was "we," the graduating class, the unit, that concerned me then.

The principal welcomed "parents and friends" and asked the Baptist minister to lead us in prayer. His invocation was brief and punchy, and for a second I thought we were getting back on the high road to right action. When the principal came back to the dais, however, his voice had changed. Sounds always affected me profoundly and the principal's voice was one of my favorites. During assembly it melted and lowed weakly into the audience. It had not been in my plan to listen to him, but my curiosity was piqued and I straightened up to give him my attention.

He was talking about Booker T. Washington, our "late great leader," who said we can be as close as the fingers on the hand, etc.... Then he said a few vague things about friendship and the friendship of kindly people to those less fortunate than themselves. With that his voice nearly faded, thin, away. Like a river diminishing to a stream and then to a trickle. But he cleared his throat and said, "Our speaker tonight, who is also our friend, came from Texarkana to deliver the commencement address, but due to the irregularity of the train schedule, he's going to, as they say, 'speak and run.'" He said that we understood and wanted the man to know that we were most grateful for the time he was able to give us and then something about how we were willing always to adjust to another's program, and without more ado—"I give you Mr. Edward Donleavy."

Not one but two white men came through the door offstage. The shorter one walked to the speaker's platform, and the tall one moved over to the center seat and sat down. But that was our principal's seat, and already occupied. The dislodged gentleman bounced around for a long breath or two before the Baptist minister gave him his chair, then with more dignity than the situation deserved, the minister walked off the stage.

Donleavy looked at the audience once (on reflection, I'm sure that he wanted only to reassure himself that we were really there), adjusted his glasses and began to read from a sheaf of papers.

He was glad "to be here and to see the work going on just as it was in the other schools."

At the first "Amen" from the audience I willed the offender to immediate death by choking on the word. But Amens and Yes, sir's began to fall around the room like rain through a ragged umbrella.

He told us of the wonderful changes we children in Stamps had in store. The Central School (naturally, the white school was Central) had already been granted improvements that would be in use in the fall. A well-known artist was coming from Little Rock to teach art to them. They were going to have the newest microscopes and chemistry equipment for their laboratory. Mr. Donleavy didn't leave us long in the dark over who made these improvements available to Central High. Nor were we to be ignored in the general betterment scheme he had in mind.

He said that he had pointed out to people at a very high level that one of the first-line football tacklers at Arkansas Agricultural and Mechanical College had graduated from good old Lafayette County Training School. Here fewer Amen's were heard. Those few that did break through lay dully in the air with the heaviness of habit.

He went on to praise us. He went on to say how he had bragged that "one of the best basketball players at Fisk sank his first ball right here at Lafayette County Training School."

The white kids were going to have a chance to become Galileos and Madame Curies and Edisons and Gauguins, and our boys (the girls weren't even in on it) would try to be Jesse Owenses and Joe Louises.

Owens and the Brown Bomber were great heroes in our world, but what school official in the white-goddom of Little Rock had the right to decide that those two men must be our only heroes? Who decided that for Henry Reed to become a scientist he had to work like George Washington Carver, as a bootblack, to buy a lousy microscope? Bailey was obviously always going to be too small to be an athlete, so which concrete angel glued to what country seat had decided that if my brother wanted to become a lawyer he had to first pay penance for his skin by picking cotton and hoeing corn and studying correspondence books at night for twenty years?

The man's dead words fell like bricks around the auditorium and too many settled in my belly. Constrained by hard-learned manners I couldn't look behind me, but to my left and right the proud graduating class of 1940 had dropped their heads. Every girl in my row had found something new to do with her handkerchief. Some folded the tiny squares into love knots, some into triangles, but most were wadding them, then pressing them flat on their yellow laps.

On the dais, the ancient tragedy was being replayed. Professor Parsons sat, a sculptor's reject, rigid. His large, heavy body seemed devoid of will or willingness, and his eyes said he was no longer with us. The other teachers examined the flag (which was draped stage right) or their notes, or the windows which opened on our now-famous playing diamond.

Graduation, the hush-hush magic time of frills and gifts and congratulations and diplomas, was finished for me before my name was called. The accomplishment was nothing. The meticulous maps, drawn in three colors of ink, learning and spelling decasyllabic words, memorizing the whole of *The Rape of Lucrece*—it was for nothing. Donleavy had exposed us.

We were maids and farmers, handymen and washerwomen, and anything higher that we aspired to was farcical and presumptuous.

Then I wished that Gabriel Prosser and Nat Turner had killed all whitefolks in their beds and that Abraham Lincoln had been assassinated before the signing of the Emancipation Proclamation, and that Harriet Tubman had been killed by that blow on her head and Christopher Columbus had drowned in the *Santa María.*

It was awful to be Negro and have no control over my life. It was brutal to be young and already trained to sit quietly and listen to charges brought against my color with no chance of defense. We should all be dead. I thought I should like to see us all dead, one on top of the other. A pyramid of flesh with the whitefolks on the bottom, as the broad base, then the Indians with their silly tomahawks and teepees and wigwams and treaties, the Negroes with their mops and recipes and cotton sacks and spirituals sticking out of their mouths. The Dutch children should all stumble in their wooden shoes and break their necks. The French should choke to death on the Louisiana Purchase (1803) while silkworms ate all the Chinese with their stupid pigtails. As a species, we were an abomination. All of us.

Donleavy was running for election, and assured our parents that if he won we could count on having the only colored paved playing field in that part of Arkansas. Also—he never looked up to acknowledge the grunts of acceptance—also, we were bound to get some new equipment for the home economics building and the workshop.

He finished, and since there was no need to give any more than the most perfunctory thank-you's, he nodded to the men on the stage, and the tall white man who was never introduced joined him at the door. They left with the attitude that now they were off to something really important.

(The graduation ceremonies at Lafayette Country Training School had been a mere preliminary.)

The ugliness they left was palpable. An uninvited guest who wouldn't leave. The choir was summoned and sang a modern arrangement of "Onward, Christian Soldiers," with new words pertaining to graduates seeking their place in the world. But it didn't work. Elouise, the daughter of the Baptist minister, recited "Invictus," and I could have cried at the impertinence of "I am the master of my fate, I am the captain of my soul."

My name had lost its ring of familiarity and I had to be nudged to go and receive my diploma. All my preparations had fled. I neither marched up to the stage like a conquering Amazon, nor did I look in the audience for Bailey's nod of approval. Marguerite Johnson, I heard the name again, my honors were read, there were noises in the audience of appreciation, and I took my place on the stage as rehearsed.

I thought about colors I hated: ecru, puce, lavender, beige and black.

There was shuffling and rustling around me, then Henry Reed was giving his valedictory address, "To Be or Not to Be." Hadn't he heard the whitefolks? We couldn't *be,* so the question was a waste of time. Henry's voice came out clear and strong. I feared to look at him. Hadn't he got the message? There was no "nobler in the mind" for Negroes because the world didn't think we had minds, and they let us know it. "Outrageous fortune"? Now, that was a joke. When the ceremony was over I had to tell Henry Reed some things. That is, if I still cared. Not "rub," Henry, "erase." "Ah, there's the erase." Us.

Henry had been a good student in elocution. His voice rose on tides of promise and fell on waves of warnings. The English teacher had helped him to create a sermon winging through Hamlet's soliloquy. To be a man, a doer, a builder, a leader, or to be a tool, an unfunny joke, a crusher of funky toadstools. I marveled that Henry could go through with the speech as if we had a choice.

I had been listening and silently rebutting each sentence with my eyes closed; then there was a hush, which in an audience warns that something unplanned is happening. I looked up and saw Henry Reed, the conservative, the proper, the A student, turn his back to the audience and turn to us (the proud graduating class of 1940) and sing, nearly speaking,

> "Lift ev'ry voice and sing*
> Till earth and heaven ring
> Ring with the harmonies of Liberty..."

*"Lift Ev'ry Voice and Sing"—words by James Weldon Johnson and music by J. Rosamond Johnson. Copyright by Edward B. Marks Music Corporation. Used by permission.

It was the poem written by James Weldon Johnson. It was the music composed by J. Rosamond Johnson. It was the Negro national anthem. Out of habit we were singing it.

Our mothers and fathers stood in the dark hall and joined the hymn of encouragement. A kindergarten teacher led the small children onto the stage and the buttercups and daisies and bunny rabbits marked time and tried to follow:

> "Stony the road we trod
> Bitter the chastening rod
> Felt in the days when hope, unborn, had died.
> 'Yet with a steady beat
> Have not our weary feet
> Come to the place for which our fathers sighed?"

Every child I knew had learned that song with his ABC's and along with "Jesus Loves Me This I Know." But I personally had never heard it before. Never heard the words, despite the thousands of times I had sung them. Never thought they had anything to do with me.

On the other hand, the words of Patrick Henry had made such an impression on me that I had been able to stretch myself tall and trembling and say, "I know not what course others may take, but as for me, give me liberty or give me death."

And now I heard, really for the first time:

> "We have come over a way that with tears
> has been watered,
> We have come, treading our path through
> the blood of the slaughtered."

While echoes of the song shivered in the air, Henry Reed bowed his head, said "Thank you," and returned to his place in the line. The tears that slipped down many faces were not wiped away in shame.

We were on top again. As always, again. We survived. The depths had been icy and dark, but now a bright sun spoke to our souls. I was no longer simply a member of the proud graduating class of 1940; I was a proud member of the wonderful, beautiful Negro race.

Oh, Black known and unknown poets, how often have your auctioned pains sustained us? Who will compute the lonely nights made less lonely by your songs, or the empty pots made less tragic by your tales?

If we were a people much given to revealing secrets, we might raise monuments and sacrifice to the memories of our poets, but slavery cured us of that weakness. It may be enough, however, to have it said that we survive in exact relationship to the dedication of our poets (include preachers, musicians and blues singers).

Suggestions for Discussion

1. Describe the feeling that comes over the students and teachers at school at the prospect of graduation.
2. How does Angelou describe the feelings in her own family? How is she treated by her brother? Her grandmother?
3. How does the black community become involved in the graduation? What special meaning does it have for them?
4. When do you begin to understand that something will go wrong? What details help you to understand? How do you know that the disappointment will come about from racial causes?
5. Summarize Donleavy's speech. How does Angelou make us feel its condescension and contempt?
6. How does the black community respond? What is the meaning of this response to Angelou? Explain.

Suggestions for Writing

1. Write an essay in which you contrast Angelou and Charles in John Cheever's story "Expelled." Your paper should include an explanation of why school has such different significance for the two of them.
2. Angelou describes a situation once common in segregated Southern schools that were separate but "unequal." Since the 1960s that situation has presumably changed. Write a research paper of 1,000 words in which you report your findings about schools in the South since desegregation. What new problems may have replaced those that Angelou describes?

ESSAYS

LEWIS THOMAS

Humanities and Science

Lewis Thomas (1913–1993) was a physician whose medical career centered on the Sloan Kettering Cancer Care Center in New York, the city of his birth. He wrote for medical journals at the same time that he wrote popular essays to present science and the scientist's view of the world to the lay public. He won the National Book Award in 1974 for *The Lives of a Cell: Notes of a Biology Watcher.* Other collections include *More Notes of a Biology Watcher* (1979), *The Youngest Science: Notes of a Medicine-Watcher* (1983), *Late Night Thoughts on Listening to Mahler's Ninth* (1984), and *The Fragile Species* (1992). In the following essay, Dr. Thomas advocates open discussion of what science does not yet know or understand.

Lord Kelvin was one of the great British physicists of the late nineteenth century, an extraordinarily influential figure in his time, and in some ways a paradigm of conventional, established scientific leadership. He did a lot of good and useful things, but once or twice he, like Homer, nodded. The instances are worth recalling today, for we have nodders among our scientific eminences still, from time to time, needing to have their elbows shaken.

On one occasion, Kelvin made a speech on the overarching importance of numbers. He maintained that no observation of nature was worth paying serious attention to unless it could be stated in precisely quantitative terms. The numbers were the final and only test, not only of truth but about meaning as well. He said, "When you can measure what you are speaking about, and express it in numbers, you know something about it. But when you cannot—your knowledge is of a meagre and unsatisfactory kind."

But, as at least one subsequent event showed, Kelvin may have had things exactly the wrong way round. The task of converting observations into numbers is the hardest of all, the last task rather than the first thing to be done, and it can be done only when you have learned, beforehand, a great deal about the observations themselves. You can, to be sure, achieve a very deep understanding of nature by quantitative measurement, but you must know what you are talking about before you can begin applying the numbers for making predictions. In Kelvin's case, the problem at hand was the age of the earth and solar system. Using what was then known about the sources of energy and the loss of energy from the physics of that day, he calculated that neither the earth nor the sun were older than several hundred million years. This caused a considerable stir in biological and geological circles, especially among the evolutionists. Darwin himself was distressed by the numbers; the time was much too short for the theory of evolution. Kelvin's figures were described by Darwin as one of his "sorest troubles."

T. H. Huxley had long been aware of the risks involved in premature extrapolations from mathematical treatment of biological problems. He said, in an 1869 speech to the Geological Society concerning numbers, "This seems to be one of the many cases in which the admitted accuracy of mathematical processes is allowed to throw a wholly inadmissible appearance of authority over the results obtained by them.... As the grandest mill in the world will not extract wheat flour from peascods, so pages of formulas will not get a definite result out of loose data."

The trouble was that the world of physics had not moved fast enough to allow for Kelvin's assumptions. Nuclear fusion and fission had not yet been dreamed of, and the true age of the earth could not even be guessed from the data in hand. It was not yet the time for mathematics in this subject.

There have been other examples, since those days, of the folly of using numbers and calculations uncritically. Kelvin's own strong conviction that science could not be genuine science without measuring things was catching. People in other fields of endeavor, hankering to turn their disciplines into exact sciences, beset by what has since been called "physics envy," set about converting whatever they knew into numbers and thence into equations with predictive pretensions. We have it with us still, in economics, sociology, psychology, history, even, I fear, in English-literature criticism and linguistics, and it frequently works, when it works at all, with indifferent success. The risks of untoward social consequences in work of this kind are considerable. It is as important—and as hard—to learn *when* to use mathematics as *how* to use it, and this matter should remain high on the agenda of consideration for education in the social and behavioral sciences.

Of course, Kelvin's difficulty with the age of the earth was an exceptional, almost isolated instance of failure in quantitative measurement in the nineteenth-century physics. The instruments devised for approaching nature by way of physics became increasingly precise and powerful, carrying the field through electromagnetic theory, triumph after triumph, and setting the stage for the great revolution of twentieth-century physics.

There is no doubt about it: measurement works when the instruments work, and when you have a fairly clear idea of what it is that is being measured, and when you know what to do with the numbers when they tumble out. The system for gaining information and comprehension about nature works so well, indeed, that it carries another hazard: the risk of convincing yourself that you know everything.

Kelvin himself fell into this trap toward the end of the century. (I don't mean to keep picking on Kelvin, who was a very great scientist; it is just that he happened to say a couple of things I find useful for this discussion.) He stated, in a summary of the achievements of nineteenth-century physics, that it was an almost completed science; virtually everything that needed knowing about the material universe had been learned; there were still a few anomalies and inconsistencies in electromagnetic theory, a few loose ends to be tied up, but this would be done within the next several years. Physics, in these terms, was not a field any longer likely to attract, as it previously had, the brightest and most imaginative young brains. The most interesting part of the work had already been done. Then, within the next decade, came radiation, Planck, the quantum, Einstein, Rutherford, Bohr, and all the rest—quantum mechanics—and the whole field turned over and became a brand-new sort of human endeavor, still now, in the view of many physicists, almost a full century later, a field only at its beginnings.

But even today, despite the amazements that are turning up in physics each year, despite the jumps taken from the smallest parts of nature—particle physics—to the largest of all—the cosmos itself—the impression of science that the public gains is rather like the impression left in the nineteenth-century public mind by Kelvin. Science, in this view, is first of all a matter of simply getting all the numbers together. The numbers are sitting out there in nature, waiting to be found, sorted and totted up. If only they had enough robots and enough computers, the scientists could go off to the beach and wait for their papers to be written for them. Second of all, what we know about nature today is pretty much the whole story: we are very nearly home and dry. From here on, it is largely a problem of tying up loose ends, tidying nature up, getting the files in order. The only real surprises for the future—and it is about those that the public is becoming more concerned and apprehensive—are the technological applications that the scientists may be cooking up from today's knowledge.

I suggest that the scientific community is to blame. If there are disagreements between the world of the humanities and the scientific enterprise as to the place and importance of science in a liberal-arts education, and the role of science in twentieth-century culture, I believe that the scientists are themselves responsible for a general misunderstanding of what they are really up to.

Over the past half century, we have been teaching the sciences as though they were the same academic collection of cut-and-dried subjects as always, and—here is what has really gone wrong—as though they would always be the same. The teaching of today's biology, for example, is pretty much the same kind of exercise as the teaching of Latin was when I was in high school long ago. First of all, the fundamentals, the underlying laws, the essential grammar, and then the reading of texts. Once mastered, that is that: Latin is Latin and forever after will be Latin. And biology is precisely biology, a vast array of hard facts to be learned as fundamentals, followed by a reading of the texts.

Moreover, we have been teaching science as though its facts were somehow superior to the facts in all other scholarly disciplines, more fundamental, more solid, less subject to subjectivism, immutable. English literature is not just one way of thinking, it is all sorts of ways. Poetry is a moving target. The facts that underlie art, architecture, and music are not really hard facts, and you can change them any way you like by arguing about them, but science is treated as an altogether different kind of learning: an unambiguous, unalterable, and endlessly useful display of data needing only to be packaged and installed somewhere in one's temporal lobe in order to achieve a full understanding of the natural world.

And it is, of course, not like this at all. In real life, every field of science that I can think of is incomplete, and most of them—whatever the record of accomplishment over the past two hundred years—are still in the earliest stage of their starting point. In the fields I know best, among the life sciences, it is required that the most expert and sophisticated minds be capable of changing those minds, often with a great lurch, every few years. In some branches of biology the mind-changing is occurring with accelerating velocities. The next week's issue of any scientific journal can turn a whole field upside down, shaking out any number of immutable ideas and installing new bodies of dogma, and this is happening all the time. It is an almost everyday event in physics, in chemistry, in materials research, in neurobiology, in genetics, in immunology. The hard facts tend to soften overnight, melt away, and vanish under the pressure of new hard facts, and the interpretations of what appear to be the most solid aspects of nature are subject to change, now more than at any other time in history. The conclusions reached in science are always, when looked at closely, far more provisional and tentative than are most of the assumptions arrived at by our colleagues in the humanities.

The running battle now in progress between the sociobiologists and the antisociobiologists is a marvel for students to behold, close up. To observe, in open-mouthed astonishment, the polarized extremes, one group of highly intelligent, beautifully trained, knowledgeable, and imaginative scientists maintaining that all sorts of behavior, animal and human, are governed exclusively by genes, and another group of equally talented scientists saying precisely the opposite and asserting that all behavior is set and determined by the environment, or by culture, and both sides brawling in the pages of periodicals such as *The New York Review of Books,* is an educational experience that no college student should be allowed to miss. The essential lesson to be learned has nothing to do with the relative validity of the facts underlying the argument, it is the argument itself that is the education: we do not yet know enough to settle such questions.

It is true that at any given moment there is the appearance of satisfaction, even self-satisfaction, within every scientific discipline. On any Tuesday morning, if asked, a good working scientist will gladly tell you that the affairs of the field are nicely in order, that things are finally looking clear and making sense, and all is well. But come back again, on another Tuesday, and he may let you know that the roof has just fallen in on his life's work, that all the old ideas—last week's ideas in some cases—are no longer good ideas, that something strange has happened.

It is the very strangeness of nature that makes science engrossing. That ought to be at the center of science teaching. There are more than seven-times-seven types of ambiguity in science, awaiting analysis. The poetry of Wallace Stevens is crystal-clear alongside the genetic code.

I prefer to turn things around in order to make precisely the opposite case. Science, especially twentieth-century science, has provided us with a glimpse of something we never really knew before, the revelation of human ignorance. We have been used to the belief, down one century after another, that we more or less comprehend everything bar one or two mysteries like the mental processes of our gods. Every age, not just the eighteenth century, regarded itself as the Age of Reason, and we have never lacked for explanations of the world and its ways. Now, we are being brought up short, and this has been the work of science. We have a wilderness of mystery to make our way through in the centuries ahead, and we will need science for this but not science alone. Science will, in its own time, produce the data and some of the meaning in the data, but never the full meaning. For getting a full grasp, for perceiving real significance when significance is at hand, we shall need minds at work from all sorts of brains outside the fields of science, most of all the brains of poets, of course, but also those of artists, musicians, philosophers, historians, writers in general.

It is primarily because of this need that I would press for changes in the way science is taught. There is a need to teach the young people who will be doing the science themselves, but this will always be a small minority among us. There is a deeper need to teach science to those who will be needed for thinking about it, and this means pretty nearly everyone else, in hopes that a few of these people—a much smaller minority than the scientific community and probably a lot harder to find—will, in the thinking, be able to imagine new levels of meaning that are likely to be lost on the rest of us.

In addition, it is time to develop a new group of professional thinkers, perhaps a somewhat larger group than the working scientists, who can create a discipline of scientific criticism. We have had good luck so far in the emergence of a few people ranking as philosophers of science and historians and journalists of science, and I hope more of these will be coming along, but we have not yet seen a Ruskin or a Leavis or an Edmund Wilson. Science needs critics of this sort, but the public at large needs them more urgently.

I suggest that the introductory courses in science, at all levels from grade school through college, be radically revised. Leave the fundamentals, the so-called basics, aside for a while, and concentrate the attention of all students on the things that are *not* known. You cannot possibly teach quantum mechanics without mathematics, to be sure, but you can describe the strangeness of the world opened up by quantum theory. Let it be known, early on, that there are deep mysteries, and profound paradoxes, revealed in their distant outlines, by the quantum. Let it be known that these can be approached more closely, and puzzled over, once the language of mathematics has been sufficiently mastered.

Teach at the outset, before any of the fundamentals, the still imponderable puzzles of cosmology. Let it be known, as clearly as possible, by the youngest minds, that there are some things going on in the universe that lie beyond comprehension, and make it plain how little is known.

Do not teach that biology is a useful and perhaps profitable science; that can come later. Teach instead that there are structures squirming inside all our cells, providing all the energy for living, that are essentially foreign creatures, brought in for symbiotic living a billion or so years ago, the lineal descendants of bacteria. Teach that we do not have the ghost of an idea how they got there, where they came from, or how they evolved to their present structure and function. The details of oxidative phosphorylation and photosynthesis can come later.

Teach ecology early on. Let it be understood that the earth's life is a system of interliving, interdependent creatures, and that we do not understand at all how it works. The earth's environment, from the range of atmospheric gases to the chemical constituents of the sea, has been held in an almost unbelievably improbable state of regulated balance since life began, and the regulation of stability and balance is accomplished solely by the life itself, like the internal environment of an immense organism, and we do not know how *that* one works, even less what it means. Teach that.

Go easy, I suggest, on the promises sometimes freely offered by science. Technology relies and depends on science these days, more than ever before, but technology is nothing like the first justification for doing research, nor is it necessarily an essential product to be expected from science. Public decisions about what to have in the way of technology are totally different problems from decisions about science, and the two enterprises should not be tangled together. The central task of science is to arrive, stage by stage, at a clearer comprehension of nature, but this does not mean, as it is sometimes claimed to mean, a search for mastery over nature. Science may provide us, one day, with a better understanding of ourselves, but never, I hope, with a set of technologies for doing something or other to improve ourselves. I am made nervous by assertions that human consciousness will someday be unraveled by research, laid out for close scrutiny like the workings of a computer, and then, *and then!* I hope with some fervor that we can learn a lot more than we now know about the human mind, and I see no reason why this strange puzzle should remain forever and entirely beyond us. But I would be deeply disturbed by any prospect that we might use the new knowledge in order to begin doing something about it, to improve it, say. This is a different matter from searching for information to use against schizophrenia or dementia, where we are badly in need of technologies, indeed likely one day to be sunk without them. But the ordinary, everyday, more or less normal human mind is too marvelous an instrument ever to be tampered with by anyone, science or no science.

The education of humanists cannot be regarded as complete, or even adequate, without exposure in some depth to where things stand in the various branches of science, and particularly, as I have said, in the areas of our ignorance. This does not mean that I know how to go about doing it, nor am I unaware of the difficulties involved. Physics professors, most of them, look with revulsion on assignments to teach their subject to poets. Biologists, caught up by the enchantment of their new power, armed with flawless instruments to tell the nucleotide sequences of the entire human genome, nearly matching the physicists in the precision of their measurements of living processes, will resist the prospect of broad survey courses; each biology professor will demand that any student in his path must master every fine detail within that professor's research program. The liberal-arts faculties, for their part, will continue to view the scientists with suspicion and apprehension. "What do the scientists want?" asked a Cambridge professor in Francis Cornford's wonderful *Microcosmographia Academica.* "Everything that's going," was the quick answer. That was back in 1912, and universities haven't much changed.

The worst thing that has happened to science education is that the great fun has gone out of it. A very large number of good students look at it as slogging work to be got through on the way to medical school. Others look closely at the premedical students themselves, embattled and bleeding for grades and class standing, and are turned off. Very few see science as the high adventure it really is, the wildest of all explorations ever undertaken by human beings, the chance to catch close views of things never seen before, the shrewdest maneuver for discovering how the world works. Instead, they become baffled early on, and they are misled into thinking that bafflement is simply the result of not having learned all the facts. They are not told, as they should be told, that everyone else—from the professor in his endowed chair down to the platoons of postdoctoral students in the laboratory all night—is baffled as well. Every important scientific advance that has come in looking like an answer has turned, sooner or later—usually sooner—into a question. And the game is just beginning.

An appreciation of what is happening in science today, and of how great a distance lies ahead for exploring, ought to be one of the rewards of a liberal-arts education. It ought to be a good in itself, not something to be acquired on the way to a professional career but part of the cast of thought needed for getting into the kind of century that is now just down the road. Part of the intellectual equipment of an educated person, however his or her time is to be spent, ought to be a feel for the queernesses of nature, the inexplicable things.

And maybe, just maybe, a new set of courses dealing systematically with ignorance in science might take hold. The scientists might discover in it a new and subversive technique for catching the attention of students driven by curiosity, delighted and surprised to learn that science is exactly as Bush described it: an "endless frontier." The humanists, for their part, might take considerable satisfaction watching their scientific colleagues confess openly to not knowing everything about everything. And the poets, on whose shoulders the future rests, might, late nights, thinking things over, begin to see some meanings that elude the rest of us. It is worth a try.

Suggestions for Discussion

1. Summarize Thomas's complaints about "the impression of science that the public gains."
2. How would he have science taught?
3. What advantages might there be in "a new set of courses dealing systematically with ignorance in science"?

Suggestions for Writing

1. Discuss one or more unanswered questions that you have encountered in your study of science.
2. Tell about an experience in which you had to change your mind because of new information.

FRANK CONROY

Think About It

Frank Conroy (b. 1936), a jazz pianist and critic, is director of the Writers Workshop at the University of Iowa. His books include an autobiography, *Stop-Time* (1967); *Midair* (1986); *Game Day* (1990); and *Body and Soul* (1993). In the following essay he uses autobiographical material to comment on the importance of continuity in education.

When I was sixteen I worked selling hot dogs at a stand in the Fourteenth Street subway station in New York City, one level above the trains and one below the street, where the crowds continually flowed back and forth. I worked with three Puerto Rican men who could not speak English. I had no Spanish, and although we understood each other well with regard to the tasks at hand, sensing and adjusting to each other's body movements in the extremely confined space in which we operated, I felt isolated with no one to talk to. On my break I came out from behind the counter and passed the time with two old black men who ran a shoeshine stand in a dark corner of the corridor. It was a poor location, half hidden by columns, and they didn't have much business. I would sit with my back against the wall while they stood or moved around their ancient elevated stand, talking to each other or to me, but always staring into the distance as they did so.

As the weeks went by I realized that they never looked at anything in their immediate vicinity—not at me or their stand or anybody who might come within ten or fifteen feet. They did not look at approaching customers once they were inside the perimeter. Save for the instant it took to discern the color of the shoes, they did not even look at what they were doing while they worked, but rubbed in polish, brushed, and buffed by feel while looking over their shoulders, into the distance, as if awaiting the arrival of an important person. Of course there wasn't all that much distance in the underground station, but their behavior was so focused and consistent they seemed somehow to transcend the physical. A powerful mood was created, and I came almost to believe that these men could see through walls, through girders, and around corners to whatever hyperspace it was where whoever it was they were waiting and watching for would finally emerge. Their scattered talk was hip, elliptical, and hinted at mysteries beyond my white boy's ken, but it was the staring off, the long, steady staring off, that had me hypnotized. I left for a better job, with handshakes from both of them, without understanding what I had seen.

Perhaps ten years later, after playing jazz with black musicians in various Harlem clubs, hanging out uptown with a few young artists and intellectuals, I began to learn from them something of the extraordinarily varied and complex riffs and rituals embraced by different people to help themselves get through life in the ghetto. Fantasy of all kinds—from playful to dangerous—was in the very air of Harlem. It was the spice of uptown life.

Only then did I understand the two shoeshine men. They were trapped in a demeaning situation in a dark corner in an underground corridor in a filthy subway system. Their continuous staring off was a kind of statement, a kind of dance. Our bodies are here, went the statement, but our souls are receiving nourishment from distant sources only we can see. They were powerful magic dancers, sorcerers almost, and thirty-five years later I can still feel the pressure of their spell.

The light bulb may appear over your head, is what I'm saying, but it may be a while before it actually goes on. Early in my attempts to learn jazz piano, I used to listen to recordings of a fine player named Red Garland, whose music I admired. I couldn't quite figure out what he was doing with his left hand, however; the chords eluded me. I went uptown to an obscure club where he was playing with his trio, caught him on his break, and simply asked him. "Sixths," he said cheerfully. And then he went away.

I didn't know what to make of it. The basic jazz chord is the seventh, which comes in various configurations, but it is what it is. I was a self-taught pianist, pretty shaky on theory and harmony, and when he said sixths I kept trying to fix the information into what I already knew, and it didn't fit. But it stuck in my mind—a tantalizing mystery.

A couple of years later, when I began playing with a bass player, I discovered more or less by accident that if the bass played the root and I played a sixth based on the fifth note of the scale, a very interesting chord involving both instruments emerged. Ordinarily, I suppose I would have skipped over the matter and not paid much attention, but I remembered Garland's remark and so I stopped and spent a week or two working out the voicings, and greatly strengthened my foundations as a player. I had remembered what I hadn't understood, you might say, until my life caught up with the information and the light bulb went on.

I remember another, more complicated example from my sophomore year at the small liberal-arts college outside Philadelphia. I seemed never to be able to get up in time for breakfast in the dining hall. I would get coffee and a doughnut in the Coop instead—a basement area with about a dozen small tables where students could get something to eat at odd hours. Several mornings in a row I noticed a strange man sitting by himself with a cup of coffee. He was in his sixties, perhaps, and sat straight in his chair with very little extraneous movement. I guessed he was some sort of distinguished visitor to the college who had decided to put in some time at a student hangout. But no one ever sat with him. One morning I approached his table and asked if I could join him.

"Certainly," he said. "Please do." He had perhaps the clearest eyes I had ever seen, like blue ice, and to be held in their steady gaze was not, at first, an entirely comfortable experience. His eyes gave nothing away about himself while at the same time creating in me the eerie impression that he was looking directly into my soul. He asked a few quick questions, as if to put me at my ease, and we fell into conversation. He was William O. Douglas from the Supreme Court, and when he saw how startled I was he said, "Call me Bill. Now tell me what you're studying and why you get up so late in the morning." Thus began a series of talks that stretched over many weeks. The fact that I was an ignorant sophomore with literary pretensions who knew nothing about the law didn't seem to bother him. We talked about everything from Shakespeare to the possibility of life on other planets. One day I mentioned that I was going to have dinner with Judge Learned Hand. I explained that Hand was my girlfriend's grandfather. Douglas nodded, but I could tell he was surprised at the coincidence of my knowing the chief judge of the most important court in the country save the Supreme Court itself. After fifty years on the bench Judge Hand had become a famous man, both in and out of legal circles—a living legend, to his own dismay. "Tell him hello and give him my best regards," Douglas said.

Learned Hand, in his eighties, was a short, barrel-chested man with a large, square head, huge, thick, bristling eyebrows, and soft brown eyes. He radiated energy and would sometimes bark out remarks or questions in the living room as if he were in court. His humor was sharp, but often leavened with a touch of self-mockery. When something caught his funny bone he would burst out with explosive laughter—the laughter of a man who enjoyed laughing. He had a large repertoire of dramatic expressions involving the use of his eyebrows—very useful, he told me conspiratorially, when looking down on things from behind the bench. (The court stenographer could not record the movement of his eyebrows.) When I told him I'd been talking to William O. Douglas, they first shot up in exaggerated surprise, and then lowered and moved forward in a glower.

"*Justice* William O. Douglas, young man," he admonished. "Justice Douglas, if you please." About the Supreme Court in general, Hand insisted on a tone of profound respect. Little did I know that in private correspondence he had referred to the Court as "The Blessed Saints, Cherubim and Seraphim," "The Jolly Boys," "The Nine Tin Jesuses," "The Nine Blameless Ethiopians," and my particular favorite, "The Nine Blessed Chalices of the Sacred Effluvium."

Hand was badly stooped and had a lot of pain in his lower back. Martinis helped, but his strict Yankee wife approved of only one before dinner. It was my job to make the second and somehow slip it to him. If the pain was particularly acute he would get out of his chair and lie flat on the rug, still talking, and finish his point without missing a beat. He flattered me by asking for my impression of Justice Douglas, instructed me to convey his warmest regards, and then began talking about the Dennis case, which he described as a particularly tricky and difficult case involving the prosecution of eleven leaders of the Communist party. He had just started in on the First Amendment and free speech when we were called in to dinner.

William O. Douglas loved the outdoors with a passion, and we fell into the habit of having coffee in the Coop and then strolling under the trees down toward the duck pond. About the Dennis case, he said something to this effect: "Eleven Communists arrested by the government. Up to no good, said the government; dangerous people, violent overthrow, etc. First Amendment, said the defense, freedom of speech, etc." Douglas stopped walking. "Clear and present danger."

"What?" I asked. He often talked in a telegraphic manner, and one was expected to keep up with him. It was sometimes like listening to a man thinking out loud.

"Clear and present danger," he said. "That was the issue. Did they constitute a clear and present danger? I don't think so. I think everybody took the language pretty far in Dennis." He began walking, striding along quickly. Again, one was expected to keep up with him. "The FBI was all over them. Phones tapped, constant surveillance. How could it be clear and present danger with the FBI watching every move they made? That's a ginkgo." he said suddenly, pointing at a tree. "A beauty. You don't see those every day. Ask Hand about clear and present danger."

I was in fact reluctant to do so. Douglas's argument seemed to me to be crushing—the last word, really—and I didn't want to embarrass Judge Hand. But back in the living room, on the second martini, the old man asked about Douglas. I sort of scratched my nose and recapitulated the conversation by the ginkgo tree.

"What?" Hand shouted. "Speak up, sir, for heaven's sake."

"He said the FBI was watching them all the time so there couldn't be a clear and present danger," I blurted out, blushing as I said it.

A terrible silence filled the room. Hand's eyebrows writhed on his face like two huge caterpillars. He leaned forward in the wing chair, his face settling, finally, into a grim expression. "I am astonished," he said softly, his eyes holding mine, "at Justice Douglas's newfound faith in the Federal Bureau of Investigation." His big, granite head moved even closer to mine, until I could smell the martini. "I had understood him to consider it a politically corrupt, incompetent organization, directed by a power-crazed lunatic." I realized I had been holding my breath throughout all of this, and as I relaxed, I saw the faintest trace of a smile cross Hand's face. Things are sometimes more complicated than they first appear, his smile seemed to say. The old man leaned back. "The proximity of the danger is something to think about. Ask him about that. See what he says."

I chewed the matter over as I returned to campus. Hand had pointed out some of Douglas's language about the FBI from other sources that seemed to bear out his point. I thought about the words "clear and present danger," and the fact that if you looked at them closely they might not be as simple as they had first appeared. What degree of danger? Did the word "present" allude to the proximity of the danger, or just the fact that the danger was there at all—that it wasn't an anticipated danger? Were there other hidden factors these great men were weighing of which I was unaware?

But Douglas was gone, back to Washington. (The writer in me is tempted to create a scene here—to invent one for dramatic purposes—but of course I can't do that.) My brief time as a messenger boy was over, and I felt a certain frustration, as if, with a few more exchanges, the matter of *Dennis* v. *United States* might have been resolved to my satisfaction. They'd left me high and dry. But, of course, it is precisely because the matter did not resolve that has caused me to think about it, off and on, all these years. "The Constitution," Hand used to say to me flatly, "is a piece of paper. The Bill of Rights is a piece of paper." It was many years before I understood what he meant. Documents alone do not keep democracy alive, nor maintain the state of law. There is no particular safety in them. Living men and women, generation after generation, must continually remake democracy and the law, and that involves an ongoing state of tension between the past and the present which will never completely resolve.

Education doesn't end until life ends, because you never know when you're going to understand something you hadn't understood before. For me, the magic dance of the shoeshine men was the kind of experience in which understanding came with a kind of click, a resolving kind of click. The same with the experience at the piano. What happened with Justice Douglas and Judge Hand was different, and makes the point that understanding does not always mean resolution. Indeed, in our intellectual lives, our creative lives, it is perhaps those problems that will never resolve that rightly claim the lion's share of our energies. The physical body exists in a constant state of tension as it maintains homeostasis, and so too does the active mind embrace the tension of never being certain, never being absolutely sure, never being done, as it engages the world. That is our special fate, our inexpressibly valuable condition.

Suggestions for Discussion

1. Discuss the four examples Conroy uses to comment on the continuity of education in life.

2. Which of Conroy's experiences interests you most? Explain why.

Suggestions for Writing

1. Use an example from your own experience to show that you may not understand until later what or how much you have learned from the experience.
2. Describe an encounter with a colorful, interesting person.

MARGO KAUFMAN

Who's Educated? Who Knows?

Margo Kaufman, the New York journalist, explores what it means to be an educated person in the 1990s.

What is an educated person? Someone who watches public television voluntarily and cites *The Atlantic* magazine and *Harper's* instead of *People* and *Us?* Is it someone who breaks into Tennyson at odd moments or programs a computer in machine language?

Confucius believed that the educated person knows "the ordinances of Heaven," "the rules of propriety" and the "force of words." But some people envision a walking course catalogue. Dr. H. Keith H. Brodie, president of Duke University, suggested that the all-knowing should know "something of history and literature; of the rules and laws of the universe; of human laws, government and behavior, and something of art—how to understand and respect the play of imagination, and how to be enriched and kept whole by it."

Of course, while such a smartypants would do very well on a game show like "Jeopardy," he or she might be judged lacking by someone with different priorities—which is just about everyone, since in high-minded circles nobody agrees on what educated people should know.

This Is Serious!

There does seem to be consensus that this is no laughing matter; even the most amusing turn solemn if not downright ponderous when the subject is broached. Take Bertice Berry, a former university professor who is now a stand-up comic. "I'd have to include curriculums from a diverse group of people, whether they won the battle or not," Ms. Berry said. "Works of women, Native Americans, Hispanics and African-Americans. And they'd probably take precedence over the dead white men."

At least the well-schooled dead white men. "An educated person is often an idiot," said the comedian Jackie Mason. "Having a lot of information doesn't mean you know how to deal with the reality of making intelligent adjustments in terms of real life and society. An educated person should be the kind of person who understands how to deal with people, with his job and with his family." Not surprisingly, Mr. Mason says that by his standards he is "one of the most educated people who ever lived." But then, people often define education in self-flattering terms.

"It's someone who always wants to learn more," said the Pulitzer Prize–winning playwright Wendy Wasserstein. "Someone who questions. Someone who thinks he doesn't know anything yet." Does she consider herself educated? "I still need to learn more, too," Ms. Wasserstein said.

Marjorie David, a Los Angeles writer-producer who says she was over-educated at Harvard and Columbia, suggested this definition: "It's the ability to critically assess material. People who can't put information in a context respond to the most superficial things. When they watch TV and are told to buy soap they buy it. But an education teaches you to assess the soap pitch." And to be suspicious of any product described as "feminine" or "all natural" or pitched by an old coot who looks as if he stepped out of a Norman Rockwell painting.

John Callahan, the syndicated cartoonist whose latest collection is titled "Do What He Says! He's Crazy!!!" declared that an educated person "knows what a cat wants for dinner" and "can read George Bush's lips." Shari Pendleton, better known as Blaze on the television program "American Gladiators," felt that the educated man or woman combines the "insight of Dr. David Viscott," a radio psychologist, "the intelligence of a Nobel Peace Prize winner and the drive of Michael Jackson."

Pendleton, whose specialty is playing a female Little John in a high altitude, high-technology version of his encounter with Robin Hood on the log, said she "aspires to possess all these qualities."

English and Calculus?

Back in academia, Steven B. Simple, president of the University of Southern California, said that for an American, "To be educated means proficiency in English and the second major language of our time, calculus." Mastery of English entails not just reading billboards and making oneself understood in supermarkets, but having a full understanding of the literature past and present and the ability to communicate, to serve people."

As for calculus, a subject that has led many a math phobic to a university without distribution requirements, "it has become the *lingua franca* of science and technology," said Mr. Simple, a professor of electrical engineering. Fortunately, it is still not a big icebreaker at parties.

Hanna H. Gray, president of the University of Chicago, offered what could be a recipe for the arts. The main ingredients are "the capacity for independent thought, a sense of relationship between different options, a sense of history, respect for evidence and a sense of how to define and approach important questions."

L. Jay Oliva, president of New York University, seasoned the soup with "strength of character, ethical behavior, understanding one's role in society as an active participant and feeling that helping other people is one of the most instructive and beneficial things you can do."

Lloyd Richards, professor emeritus at the Yale School of Drama, threw in "wit, wisdom, tolerance and the ability and willingness to share."

Experts ascribe the variety of definitions to the complexity of the subject. "There's no way either temporally or spatially of limiting what it means to be educated," said George Rupp, president of Rice University. "Knowledge is continually escalating, and spatially we don't have any easy limits to set around what we need to know."

Mr. Rupp pointed out that 1,000 years ago, a person who grew up in Christian Europe needed to understand the traditions of biblical and Greek culture to be considered educated. "Today we ask, 'Do we have to know about Buddhism, the history of Japan prior to Westernization and all the ranges of experience the Chinese have?' And there are exactly the same kinds of questions in social sciences and natural sciences."

Luckily for those of us who never heard of Gondwanaland, fractals or semiotics, Samuel Johnson postulated that knowledge is of two kinds—that which you know and that which you know how to find.

More than 2,000 years ago, Plato wrote that "The sum and substance of education is the right training, which effectively leads the soul of the child at play onto the love of the calling in which he will have to be perfect when he is a man."

By this definition, Steve Smith, director of the Ringling Bros. and Barnum & Bailey Clown College, is a sage. "You need the vision to know the world doesn't revolve around your ego," Mr. Smith said, "and in our case, juggling, magic, pantomime and how to ride a unicycle."

Suggestions for Discussion

1. Analyze three or four of the definitions of an educated person introduced by Kaufman.

2. Discuss the distinction between having knowledge and knowing how to use it.

Suggestions for Writing

1. What does it mean to you to be an educated person? Give examples.
2. To what extent has the concept of an educated person changed in your lifetime?

HOWARD GARDNER

Human Intelligence Isn't What We Think It Is

Howard Gardner (b. 1943) is professor of education at Harvard University. His books include *Frames of Mind: The Theory of Multiple Intelligences* (1985), *The Unschooled Mind: How Children Think and How Schools Should Teach* (1991), *Creating Minds* (1993), *Changing the World* (1994), and *Leading Minds* (1995). In the following essay Gardner discusses the importance of recognizing and cultivating different kinds of intelligence.

"People Have Multiple Intelligences"

Intelligence is not an absolute such as height that can be measured simply, largely because people have multiple intelligences rather than one single intelligence.

In all, I have identified seven forms of intelligence. The two that are valued most highly in this society are linguistic and logical-mathematical intelligences. When people think of someone as smart, they are usually referring to those two, because individuals who possess linguistic and logical-mathematical abilities do well on tests that supposedly measure intelligence.

But there are five other kinds of intelligence that are every bit as important: Spatial, musical, bodily-kinesthetic and two forms of personal intelligence—interpersonal, knowing how to deal with others, and intrapersonal, knowledge of self. None of these ought to have a priority over others.

"Shifting Importance" of the Seven Varieties

The relative importance of these seven intelligences has shifted over time and varies from culture to culture. In a hunting society, for example, it is a lot more important to have extremely good control of your body and know your way around than to add or subtract quickly. In Japanese society, interpersonal intelligence—the ability to work well in groups and to arrive at joint decisions—is very important.

Historically, different systems of education have emphasized different blends of intelligence. In the old apprenticeship system, bodily, spatial and interpersonal abilities were valued. In old-fashioned religious schools, the focus was on linguistic and interpersonal abilities. The modern secular school emphasizes the linguistic and logical-mathematical, but in the school of the near future I think that linguistic will become much less crucial. For working with computers, logical-mathematical intelligence will be important for programing, and intrapersonal intelligence will be important for individual planning.

What I'm saying is that while both logical-mathematical and linguistic are important today, it won't always be that way. We need to be sensitive to the fact that blends of intelligences keep shifting so that in the future we don't get locked into a specific blend.

Secrets Unlocked by Biological Research

Research in biology has laid the foundation for the theory of multiple intelligences.

Studies show that when someone suffers damage to the nervous system through a stroke or tumor, all abilities do not break down equally. If you have an injury to areas of the left hemisphere of the brain, you will lose your language ability almost entirely, but that will not affect your musical, spatial or interpersonal skills to the same extent.

Conversely, you can have lesions in your right hemisphere that leave language capacity intact but that seriously compromise spatial, musical or interpersonal abilities. So we have a special capacity for language that is unconnected to our capacity for music or interpersonal skills, and vice versa.

I'm not suggesting that this analysis is the last word. I would like to think of it as the first word in a new way of looking at human abilities.

"America Wastes Potential!"

In America, we are wasting a lot of human potential by focusing on only linguistic and logical intelligence. If an individual doesn't happen to be good in these, he or she often gets thrown on society's scrap heap.

What happens is that a youngster takes an IQ test and doesn't do very well. He gets labeled as not very smart and the teacher treats him accordingly.

But there are many roles in society in which it is not important that a person have a high intelligence in language and logic so long as he or she can function at a basic level in these domains.

For example, somebody good at working with his hands and figuring out how machines function might find a responsible position in a science lab or working backstage in a theater. If kids with such abilities were encouraged—rather than discouraged because they can't figure out who wrote the *Iliad*—they could be extremely valuable to society.

IQ Tests "Have Destructive Social Effects"

I would like to get rid of intelligence and aptitude tests; they measure only two forms of intelligence and have destructive social effects. These tests have been successful because they serve as a good predictor of how people will do in school in the short run. But how much does doing well in school predict success outside of school? Very little.

Those of us who take a position against IQ tests have the burden of coming up with ways of assessing abilities that are not completely impractical. My notion is something between a report card and a test score.

I would assess intellectual propensities from an early age. I use the word *propensities* because I don't believe intelligences are fixed for many years. The earlier a strength is discovered, the more flexibility there is to develop it. Similarly, if a child has a low propensity, the earlier intervention begins, the easier it is to shore up the child. So early diagnosis is important.

Preschools Where "Children Can Do Exploring"

I would not assess abilities through traditional paper-and-pencil tests. Instead, we need learning environments—preschools—in which children can do a lot of exploring on their own or with help from adults.

All children play with blocks, for example, but what do they do with them? How complex are the structures they make? How well can they remember them? Can they revise them in various ways? All of these questions can be answered by adults observing and playing with the children.

The same environment could be equipped with musical materials, and, again, children could explore on their own and with adults. If we had such environments, with periodic monitoring we could develop very good profiles of a child's propensities. This would give parents and teachers a better way of thinking about children than one or two test scores. Instead of looking at a child and saying, "He's smart" or "He's dumb," people would talk in terms of a child's strengths and weaknesses. It is a much more realistic view.

But no theory is going to tell people what to do once a child's propensities are assessed. That decision would depend on the value of those around the child. Some people would say, "Let's go with the child's strengths for all they are worth." Others would say, "It's very important to be good in language, so even though this kid isn't good in it, we're going to work on it."

"The Challenge for Education"

As children mature, the assessments would continue in a different vein. By the age of 10 or 11, the monitoring would shift to "domains," where you might come up with analyses such as "this person has the talent to be a doctor."

While having a high intelligence in an area doesn't predict exactly what you are going to do, it predicts the direction you are likely to move in. If somebody has a very highly developed bodily intelligence, he or she could become an athlete, dancer or surgeon. If somebody has a highly developed spatial intelligence, he or she might be at home in architecture, engineering, sculpture or painting.

The challenge for the educational community is to figure out profiles of young people and then to help them find roles in which they can use their abilities in a productive way.

Recognizing the Diversity of Our Capabilities

The Suzuki method of teaching music, developed in Japan, shows what can be done to foster a specific intelligence when the effort is undertaken intensively at an early age and a lot of energy is put into it. This method creates an environment that is rich with music; mothers play with the youngsters for 2 hours a day from the time they reach age 2. Within a few years, all participants become decent musicians.

In theory, we could "Suzuki" everything. The more time and energy invested early in life on a particular intelligence, the more you can buoy it up. I am not advocating this approach, merely pointing out the possibilities. But before we can make these kinds of decisions, we have to take a first step—recognizing the diverse intelligences of which human beings are capable.

Suggestions for Discussion

1. Name the seven forms of intelligence identified by Gardner.
2. What suggestions does he make for replacing traditional intelligence and aptitude tests?
3. How might the development of intelligence be enhanced?

Suggestions for Writing

1. Write about your strongest intelligence. Give examples from your experience.
2. Rank your own intelligences from strongest to least strong.

HENRY LOUIS GATES, JR.

Talking Black

Henry Louis Gates, Jr. (b. 1950), is the W. E. B. Du Bois Professor of the Humanities at Harvard University. His seminal books include *Figures in Black* (1987), *The Signifying Monkey: A Theory of Afro-American Literary Criticism* (1988), *Loose Canons: Notes of the Culture Wars* (1992), and a memoir entitled *Colored People* (1994). In the following essay he explores the importance of "the language of black difference."

For a language acts in diverse ways, upon the spirit of a people; even as the spirit of a people acts with a creative and spiritualizing force upon a language.

—ALEXANDER CRUMMELL, 1860

A new vision began gradually to replace the dream of political power—a powerful movement, the rise of another ideal to guide the unguided, another pillar of fire by night after a clouded day. It was the ideal of "book-learning"; the curiosity, born of compulsory ignorance, to know and test the power of the cabalistic letters of the white man, the longing to know.

—W. E. B. DU BOIS, 1903

The knowledge which would teach the white world was Greek to his own flesh and blood... and he could not articulate the message of another people.

—W. E. B. DU BOIS, 1903

Alexander Crummell, a pioneering nineteenth-century Pan-Africanist, statesman, and missionary who spent the bulk of his creative years as an Anglican minister in Liberia, was also a pioneering intellectual and philosopher of language, founding the American Negro Academy in 1897 and serving as the intellectual godfather of W. E. B. Du Bois. For his first annual address as president of the academy, delivered on 28 December 1897, Crummell selected as his topic "The Attitude of the American Mind Toward the Negro Intellect." Given the occasion of the first annual meeting of the great intellectuals of the race, he could not have chosen a more timely or appropriate subject.

Crummell wished to attack, he said, "the denial of intellectuality in the Negro; the assertion that he was not a human being, that he did not belong to the human race." He argued that the desire "to becloud and stamp out the intellect of the Negro" led to the enactment of "laws and Statutes, closing the pages of every book printed to the eyes of Negroes; barring the doors of every school-room against them!" This, he concluded, "was the systematized method of the intellect of the South, to stamp out the brains of the Negro!"—a program that created an "almost Egyptian darkness [which] fell upon the mind of the race, throughout the whole land."

Crummell next shared with his audience a conversation between two Boston lawyers which he had overheard when he was "an errand boy in the Anti-slavery office in New York City" in 1833 or 1834:

> While at the Capitol they happened to dine in the company of the great John C. Calhoun, then senator from South Carolina. It was a period of great ferment upon the question of Slavery, States Rights, and Nullification; and consequently the Negro was the topic of conversation at the table. One of the utterances of Mr. Calhoun was to this effect—"That if he could find a Negro who knew the Greek syntax, he would then believe that the Negro was a human being and should be treated as a man."

"Just think of the crude asininity," Crummell concluded rather generously, "of even a great man!"

The salient sign of the black person's humanity—indeed, the only sign for Calhoun—would be the mastering of the very essence of Western civilization, of the very foundation of the complex fiction upon which white Western culture had been constructed. It is likely that "Greek syntax," for John C. Calhoun, was merely a hyperbolic figure of speech, a trope of virtual impossibility; he felt driven to the hyperbolic mode, perhaps, because of the long racist tradition in Western letters of demanding that black people *prove* their full humanity. We know this tradition all too well, dotted as it is with the names of great intellectual Western racialists, such as Francis Bacon, David Hume, Immanuel Kant, Thomas Jefferson, and G. W. F. Hegel. Whereas each of these figures demanded that blacks write poetry to prove their humanity, Calhoun—writing in a post-Phillis Wheatley era—took refuge in, yes, Greek syntax.

In typical African-American fashion, a brilliant black intellectual accepted Calhoun's bizarre challenge. The anecdote Crummell shared with his fellow black academicians turned out to be his shaping scene of instruction. For Crummell himself jumped on a boat, sailed to England, and matriculated at Queen's College, Cambridge, where he mastered (naturally enough) the intricacies of Greek syntax. Calhoun, we suspect, was not impressed.

Crummell never stopped believing that mastering the master's tongue was the sole path to civilization, intellectual freedom, and social equality for the black person. It was Western "culture," he insisted, that the black person "must claim as his rightful heritage, as a man—not stinted training, not a caste education, not," he concluded prophetically, "a Negro curriculum." As he argued so passionately in his speech of 1860, "The English Language in Liberia," the acquisition of the English language, along with Christianity, is the wonderful sign of God's providence encoded in the nightmare of African enslavement in the racist wilderness of the New World. English, for Crummell, was "the speech of Chaucer and Shakespeare, of Milton and Wordsworth, of Bacon and Burke, of Franklin and Webster," and its potential mastery was "this one item of compensation" that "the Almighty has bestowed upon us" in exchange for "the exile of our fathers from their African homes to America." In the English language are embodied "the noblest theories of liberty" and "the grandest ideas of humanity." If black people master the master's tongue, these great and grand ideas will become African ideas, because "ideas conserve men, and keep alive the vitality of nations."

In dark contrast to the splendors of the English language, Crummell set the African vernacular languages, which, he wrote, have "definite marks of inferiority connected with them all, which place them at the widest distances from civilized languages." Any effort to render the master's discourse in our own black tongue is an egregious error, for we cannot translate sublime utterances "in[to] broken English—a miserable caricature of their noble tongue." We must abandon forever both indigenous African vernacular languages and the neo-African vernacular languages that our people have produced in the New World:

> All low, inferior, and barbarous tongues are, doubtless, but the lees and dregs of noble languages, which have gradually, as the soul of a nation has died out, sunk down to degradation and ruin. We must not suffer this decay on these shores, in this nation. We have been made, providentially, the deposit of a noble trust; and we should be proud to show our appreciation of it. Having come to the heritage of this language we must cherish its spirit, as well as retain its letter. We must cultivate it among ourselves; we must strive to infuse its spirit among our reclaimed and aspiring natives.

I cite the examples of John C. Calhoun and Alexander Crummell as metaphors for the relation between the critic of black writing and the larger institution of literature. Learning the master's tongue, for our generation of critics, has been an act of empowerment, whether that tongue be New Criticism, humanism, structuralism, Marxism, poststructuralism, feminism, new historicism, or any other *-ism*. But even as Afro-American literature and criticism becomes institutionalized, our pressing question now becomes this: in what tongue shall we choose to speak, and write, our own criticisms? What are we now to do with the enabling masks of empowerment that we have donned as we have practiced one mode of "white" criticism or another?

The Afro-American literary tradition is distinctive in that it evolved in response to allegations that its authors did not, and could not, create literature, a capacity that was considered the signal measure of a race's innate "humanity." The African living in Europe or in the New World seems to have felt compelled to create a literature not only to demonstrate that blacks did indeed possess the intellectual ability to create a written art, but also to indict the several social and economic institutions that delimited the "humanity" of all black people in Western cultures.

So insistent did these racist allegations prove to be, at least from the eighteenth to the early twentieth century, that it is fair to describe the subtext of the history of black letters in terms of the urge to refute them. Even as late as 1911, when J. E. Casely-Hayford published *Ethiopia Unbound* (the "first" African novel), he felt it necessary to address this matter in the first two paragraphs of his text. "At the dawn of the twentieth century," the novel opens, "men of light and leading both in Europe and in America had not yet made up their minds as to what place to assign to the spiritual aspirations of the black man." Few literary traditions have begun with such a complex and curious relation to criticism: allegations of an absence led directly to a presence, a literature often inextricably bound in a dialogue with its harshest critics.

Black literature and its criticism, then, have been put to uses that were not primarily aesthetic: rather, they have formed part of a larger discourse on the nature of the black, and his or her role in the order of things. Even so, a sense of integrity has arisen in the Afro-American tradition, though it has less to do with the formal organicism of the New Critics than with an intuitive notion of "ringing true," or Houston Baker's concept of "sounding." (One of the most frequently used critical judgments in the African-American tradition is "That shit don't sound right," or, as Alice Walker puts it in *The Color Purple,* "Look like to me only a fool would want to talk in a way that feel peculiar to your mind.") That is the sense I am calling on here, understanding how problematic even this can be. Doubleness, alienation, equivocality: since the turn of the century at least, these have been recurrent tropes for the black tradition.

To be sure, this matter of the language of criticism and the integrity of its subject has a long and rather tortured history in all black letters. It was David Hume, after all, who called Francis Williams, the Jamaican poet of Latin verse, "a parrot who merely speaks a few words plainly." Phillis Wheatley, too, has long suffered from the spurious attacks of black and white critics alike for being the *rara avis* of a school of so-called mockingbird poets, whose use of European and American literary conventions has been considered a corruption of a "purer" black expression, found in forms such as the blues, signifying, spirituals, and Afro-American dance. Can we, as critics, escape a "mockingbird" posture?

Only recently have some scholars attempted to convince critics of black literature that we can. Perhaps predictably, a number of these attempts share a concern with that which has been most repressed in the received tradition of Afro-American criticism: close readings of the texts themselves. And so we are learning to read a black text within a black formal cultural matrix. That means reading a literary culture that remains, for the most part, intransigently oral. If the black literary imagination has a privileged medium, it is what Douglass called the "live, calm, grave, clear, pointed, warm, sweet, melodious and powerful human voice." And the salient contribution of black literature may lie in its resolute vocality. But there is no black voice; only voices, diverse and mutable. Familiarly, there's the strut, confidence laced with bitters—

> I am a Waiter's Waiter. I know all the moves, all the pretty, fine moves that big book will never teach you...I built the railroad with my moves. (James Alan McPherson, "Solo Song")

Or the boisterous revelator:

> When he was on, Reverend Jones preached his gospel hour in a Texas church that held no more than 250 people, but the way he had the old sisters banging on them bass drums and slapping them tambourines, you'd think that God's Own Philharmonic was carrying on inside that old church where the loud-speaks blasted Jones's message to the thousands who stood outside. At the conclusion of Reverend Jones's sermon, the church didn't need no fire, because it was being warmed by the spirit of the Lord. By the spirit of Jesus. (Ishmael Reed, *The Terrible Threes*)

Yet how tonally remote they are from this cento of Baldwin, a preacher's son for whom King Jamesian inversions were second nature:

> In the case of the Negro the past was taken from him whether he would or no; yet to forswear it was meaningless and availed him nothing, since his shameful history was carried, quite literally, on his brow. Shameful; for he was heathen as well as black and would never have discovered the healing blood of Christ had not we braved the jungles to bring him these glad tidings....
>
> Where the Negro face appears, a tension is created, the tension of a silence filled with things unutterable. ("Many Thousands Gone")

Baldwin wrote of "something ironic and violent and perpetually understated in Negro speech," and in this he was describing his own careful, ungentle cadences. Contrast, again, the homeliest intimacies of nuance that Morrison will unexpectedly produce:

> There is a loneliness that can be rocked. Arms crossed, knees drawn up; holding, holding on, this motion, unlike a ship's, smooths and contains the rockers. It's an inside kind—wrapped tight like skin. (*Beloved*)

There's no hidden continuity or coherence among them. History makes them like beads on a string: there's no necessary resemblance; but then again, no possible separation.

And so we've had to learn to "read black" as a textual effect because the existence of a black canon is a historically contingent phenomenon; it is not inherent in the nature of "blackness," not vouchsafed by the metaphysics of some racial essence. The black tradition exists only insofar as black artists enact it. Only because black writers have read and responded to other black writers with a sense of recognition and acknowledgment can we speak of a black literary inheritance, with all the burdens and privileges that has entailed. Race is a text (an array of discursive practices), not an essence. It must be *read* with painstaking care and suspicion, not imbibed.

The disjunction between the language of criticism and the language of its subject helps defamiliarize the texts of the black tradition: ironically, it is necessary to create distance between reader and texts in order to go beyond reflexive responses and achieve critical insight into and intimacy with their formal workings. I have done this to respect the integrity of these texts, by trying to avoid confusing my experiences as an Afro-American with the black act of language that defines a text. This is the challenge of the critic of black literature in the 1980s: not to shy away from white power—that is, a new critical vocabulary—but to translate it into the black idiom, *renaming* principles of criticism where appropriate, but especially naming indigenous black principles of criticism and applying them to our own texts. *Any* tool that enables the critic to explain the complex workings of the language of a text is appropriate here. For it is language, the black language of black texts, that expresses the distinctive quality of our literary tradition. Once it may have seemed that the only critical implements black critics needed were the pom-pom and the twirled baton; in fact, there is no deeper form of literary disrespect. We will not protect the integrity of our tradition by remaining afraid of, or naive about, literary analysis; rather, we will inflict upon it the violation of reflexive, stereotypical reading—or nonreading. We are the keepers of the black literary tradition. No matter what approach we adopt, we have more in common with each other than we do with any other critic of any other literature. We write for each other, and for our own contemporary writers. This relation is a critical trust.

It is also a *political* trust. How can the demonstration that our texts sustain ever closer and more sophisticated readings *not* be political at a time when all sorts of so-called canonical critics mediate their racism through calls for "purity" of "the tradition," demands as implicitly racist as anything the Southern Agrarians said? How can the deconstruction of the forms of racism itself not be political? How can the use of literary analysis to explicate the racist social text in which we still find ourselves be anything *but* political? To be political, however, does not mean that I have to write at the level of a Marvel comic book. My task, as I see it, is to help guarantee that black and so-called Third World literature is taught to black and Third World and white students by black and Third World and white professors in heretofore white mainstream departments of literature, and to train students to think, to read, and to write clearly, to expose false uses of language, fraudulent claims, and muddled arguments, propaganda, and vicious lies—from all of which our people have suffered just as surely as we have from an economic order in which we were zeroes and a metaphysical order in which we were absences. These are the "values" which should be transmitted through the languages of cultural and literary study.

In the December 1986 issue of the *Voice Literary Supplement,* in an essay entitled "Cult-Nats Meet Freaky-Deke," Greg Tate argued cogently and compellingly that "black aestheticians need to develop a coherent criticism to communicate the complexities of our culture. There's no periodical on black cultural phenomena equivalent to *The Village Voice* or *Artforum,* no publication that provides journalism on black visual art, philosophy, politics, economics, media, literature, linguistics, psychology, sexuality, spirituality, and pop culture. Though there are certainly black editors, journalists, and academics capable of producing such a journal, the disintegration of the black cultural nationalist movement and the brain-drain of black intellectuals to white institutions have destroyed the vociferous public dialogue that used to exist between them." While I would argue that *Sage, Callaloo,* and *Black American Literature Forum* are indeed fulfilling that function for academic critics, I am afraid that the truth of Tate's claim is irresistible.

But his most important contribution to the future of black criticism is to be found in his most damning allegation. "What's unfortunate," he writes, "is that while black artists have opened up the entire 'text of blackness' for fun and games, not many black critics have produced writing as fecund, eclectic, and freaky-deke as the art, let alone the culture, itself.... For those who prefer exegesis with a polemical bent, just imagine how critics as fluent in black and Western culture as the postliberated artists could strike terror into that bastion of white supremacist thinking, the Western art [and literary] world[s]." To which I can only say, "Amen, Amen."

Tate's challenge is a serious one because neither ideology nor criticism nor blackness can exist as entities of themselves, outside their forms or their texts. This is the central theme of Ralph Ellison's *Invisible Man* and Ishmael Reed's *Mumbo Jumbo,* for example. But how can we write or read the text of "Blackness"? What language(s) do black people use to represent their critical or ideological positions? In what forms of language do we speak or write? Can we derive a valid, integral "black" text of criticism or ideology from borrowed or appropriated forms? Can a black woman's text emerge authentically as borrowed, or "liberated," or revised, from the patriarchal forms of the slave narratives, on the one hand, or from the white matriarchal forms of the sentimental novel, on the other, as Harriet Jacobs and Harriet Wilson attempted to do in *Incidents in the Life of a Slave Girl* (1861) and *Our Nig* (1859)? Where lies the liberation in revision, the ideological integrity of defining freedom in the modes and forms of difference charted so cogently by so many poststructural critics of black literature?

For it is in these spaces of difference that black literature has dwelled. And while it is crucial to read these patterns of difference closely, we should understand as well that the quest was lost, in an important sense, before it had even begun, simply because the terms of our own self-representation have been provided by the master. It is not enough for us to show that refutation, negation, and revision exist, and to define them as satisfactory gestures of ideological independence. Our next concern will be to address the black political signified, that is, the cultural vision and the black critical language that underpin the search through literature and art for a profound reordering and humanizing of everyday existence. We encourage our writers and critics to undertake the fullest and most ironic exploration of the manner and matter, the content and form, the structure and sensibility so familiar and poignant to us in our most sublime form of art, black music, where ideology and art are one, whether we listen to Bessie Smith or to postmodern and poststructural John Coltrane.

Just as we encourage our writers to meet this challenge, we as critics can turn to our own peculiarly black structures of thought and feeling to develop our own language of criticism. We do so by drawing on the black vernacular, the language we use to speak to each other when no white people are around. Unless we look to the vernacular to ground our modes of reading, we will surely sink in the mire of Nella Larsen's quicksand, remain alienated in the isolation of Harriet Jacobs' garret, or masked in the received stereotype of the Black Other helping Huck to return to the raft, singing "China Gate" with Nat King Cole under the Da Nang moon, or reflecting our balded heads in the shining flash of Mr. T's signifying gold chains.

We can redefine reading itself from within our own black cultures, refusing to grant the racist premise that criticism is something that white people do, so that we are doomed to imitate our white colleagues, like reverse black minstrel critics done up in whiteface. We should not succumb, as did Alexander Crummell, to the tragic lure of white power, the mistake of accepting the empowering language of white criticism as "universal" or as our own language, the mistake of confusing its enabling mask with our own black faces. Each of us has, in some literal or figurative manner, boarded a ship and sailed to a metaphorical Cambridge, seeking to master the master's tools. (I myself, being quite literal-minded, booked passage some fourteen years ago on the *QE2.*) Now we can at last don the empowering mask of blackness and talk *that* talk, the language of black difference. While it is true that we must, as Du Bois said so long ago, "know and test the power of the cabalistic letters of the white man," we must also know and test the dark secrets of a black discursive universe that awaits its disclosure through the black arts of interpretation. The future of our language and literature may prove black indeed.

Suggestions for Discussion

1. To what extent do Gates's historical and biographical allusions add weight and substance to his argument?

2. Discuss the writer's assertion that to "read black" is now a political trust. Cite examples.
3. Analyze Gates's discussion of the opinions of Alexander Crummell.

Suggestions for Writing

1. Discuss the significance of the three epigraphs that preface the essay. In what ways does each contribute to your understanding and appreciation of the essay?
2. Write a short analytical essay explaining what Gates means by his title, "Talking Black."

HAROLD BRODKEY

Reading, the Most Dangerous Game

Harold Brodkey (1930–1996) wrote fiction and commentary for *The New Yorker.* His books include *First Love and Other Sorrows* (1988), *Stories in an Almost Classical Mode* (1989), *The Runaway Soul* (1991), and *Profane Friendship* (1994). In the following essay he explores the act of reading and advocates reading "seriously."

Reading is an intimate act, perhaps more intimate than any other human act. I say that because of the prolonged (or intense) exposure of one mind to another that is involved in it, and because it is the level of mind at which feelings and hopes are dealt in by consciousness and words.

Reading a good book is not much different from a love affair, from love, complete with shyness and odd assertions of power and of independence and with many sorts of incompleteness in the experience. One can marry the book: reread it, add it to one's life, live with it. Or it might be compared to pregnancy—serious reading even if you're reading trash: one is inside the experience and is about to be born; and one is carrying something, a sort of self inside oneself that one is about to give birth to, perhaps a monster. Of course, for men this is always verging on something else (part of which is a primitive rage with being masculine, a dismay felt toward women and the world, a reader's odd sense of women).

The act of reading as it really occurs is obscure: the decision to read a book in a real minute, how one selects the book, how one flirts with the choice, how one dawdles on the odd path of getting it read and then reread, the oddities of rereading, the extreme oddities of the procedures of continuing with or without interruptions to read, getting ready to read a middle chapter in its turn after going off for a while, then getting hold of the book physically, having it in one's hand, letting one's mind fill with thoughts in a sort of warm-up for the exercise of mind to come—one riffles through remembered scenes from this and other books, one diddles with half-memories of other pleasures and usefulnesses, one wonders if one can afford to read, one considers the limitations and possibilities of this book, one is humiliated in anticipation or superior or thrilled in anticipation, or nauseated in retrospect or as one reads. One has a sense of talk and of reviews and essays and of anticipation or dread and the will to be affected by the thing of reading, affected lightly or seriously. One settles one's body to some varying degree, and then one enters on the altered tempos of reading, the subjection to being played upon, one passes through phases, starting with reacting to or ignoring the cover of the book and the opening lines.

The piercing things, the stabbingly emotional stuff involved in reading, leads to envy, worse even than in sibling or neighborhood rivalry, and it leads to jealousy and possessiveness. If a book is not religious or trashy, the problem of salesmanship, always partly a con, arises in relation to it, to all the problems it presents. A good reader of Proust complains constantly as a man might complain of a wife or a woman of her husband. And Proust perhaps had such a marriage in mind with the reader. A good book, like pregnancy or a woman known to arouse love, or a man, is something you praise in the light of a general reluctance to risk the experience; and the quality of praise warns people against the book, warns them to take it seriously; you warn them about it, not wanting to be evangelical, a matchmaker or a malicious pimp for a troubled and troubling view of the world.

I can't imagine how a real text can be taught in a school. Even minor masterpieces, "Huckleberry Finn" or "The Catcher in the Rye," are too much for a classroom, too real an experience. No one *likes* a good book if they have actually read it. One is fanatically attached, restlessly attached, criminally attached, violently and criminally opposed, sickened, unable to bear it. In Europe, reading is known to be dangerous. Reading always leads to personal metamorphosis, sometimes irreversible, sometimes temporary, sometimes large-scale, sometimes less than that. A good book leads to alterations in one's sensibility and often becomes a premise in one's beliefs. One associates truth with texts, with impressive texts anyway; and when trashy books vanish from sight, it is because they lie too much and too badly and are not worth one's intimacy with them. Print has so much authority, however, that sometimes it is only at the beginning of an attempt at a second reading or at the end of it, and only then, if one is self-assured, that one can see whether a book was not really worth reading the first time; one tells by how alterable the truth in it seems in this more familiar light and how effective the book remains or, contrarily, how amazingly empty of meaning it now shows itself to be. It is a strange feeling to be a practiced enough reader and writer to see in some books that there is nothing there. It is eerie: why did the writer bother? What reward is there in being a fraud in one's language and in one's ideas? To believe they just didn't know is more unsettling than to doubt oneself or to claim to be superficial or prejudiced or to give up reading entirely, at least for a while.

Or, in our country, we deny what we see of this and even reverse it: fraud is presented as happiness; an empty book is said to be well constructed; a foolish argument is called innovative. This is a kind of bliss; but lying of that sort, when it is nearly universal, wrecks the possibility of our having a literary culture or even of our talking about books with each other with any real pleasure. It is like being phony yachtsmen who only know smooth water and who use their motors whenever they can. This guarantees an immense personal wretchedness, actually.

Of course, in Europe, cultural patterns exist which slow the rate of change in you as a reader (as well as supplying evidence to use in comprehending what happens and will happen to you if you change because of a book). Of course, such change is never entirely good or wise. In our country, we have nothing to hold us back from responding to any sort of idea. With us everything is for sale—everything is up for grabs, including ourselves—and we have very little tradition worth hanging onto except the antic.

The country is organized not by religion or political machinery but by what are seen as economic realities but which are fashions in making money and spending money. We are an army marching in the largest conceivable mass so entirely within cultural immediacy that it can be said this is new in the history in the world, emotionally new in that while this has been true of other cultures for brief periods in the past, it was never true as completely or for such a large part of the population or so continuously, with so few periods of stasis. We pretend to tradition but really, nothing prevents us changing.

And we do change. Divorce, born-again Christianity, the computer revolution, a return to the farm, a move to the city. In Boston, at college at Harvard, I first knew people who claimed to be cultivated to the degree they remained unchanged not only in spite of the reading they claimed to have done but with the help of it. They did not realize what an imbecile and provincial notion that was—it was simply untrue: you could see it, the untruth of it. A rule of thumb about culture is that personal or public yearning for a better time to come or one in the past and nostalgia of any sort are reliable signs of the counterfeit. The past is there to be studied in its reality, moment by moment, and the future can be discussed in its reality to come, which will be a reality moment by moment; but doing that means being honest just as doing it makes you too busy to yearn; and doing it shows you that nostalgia is a swindler's trick. A sense of the real is what is meant by good sense. And because of the nature of time and because of how relentlessly change occurs, good sense has to contain a good deal of the visionary as well as of ironic apology to cover the inevitable mistakes. And this is doubly so with us, in the United States. Reality here is special. And part of reality here or elsewhere is that novels, plays, essays, fact pieces, poems, through conversion or in the process of argument with them, change you or else—to use an idiom—you haven't listened.

If the reader is not at risk, he is not reading. And if the writer is not at risk, he is not writing. As a rule, a writer and a book or a poem are no good if the writer is essentially unchanged morally after having written it. If the work is really a holding operation, this will show in a closed or flat quality in the prose and in the scheme of the thing, a logiclessness, if you will pardon the neologism, in the writing. Writing always tends toward a kind of moral stance—this is because of the weight of logic and of truth in it—but judging the ways in which it is moral is hard for people who are not cultivated. Profoundly educated persons make the best judges.

The general risk in being a man or woman of cultivation is then very high, and this is so in any culture, and perhaps requires too much strength for even a small group to practice in ours. But should such a guerrilla group arise, it will have to say that cultivation and judgment issue from the mouths of books and can come from no other source. Over a period of centuries, ignorance has come, justifiably, to mean a state of booklessness. Movie-educated people are strained; they are decontextualized; they are cultivated in a lesser way. Television and contemporary music are haunted by the search for messiahs; the usual sign of mass inauthenticity is a false prophet (which usually means a war will shortly break out and be lost). The absence of good sense signals the decline of a people and of a civilization. Shrewdness without good sense is hell unleashed.

I would propose as a social cure that in fourth grade and in the first year at college, this society mandate that we undergo a year of reading with or without argument as the soul can bear, including argument with teachers and parents and local philosophers if there are any. Of course something like this happens anyway but we probably ought to institutionalize it in our faddish way.

After all, if you don't know what's in good books, how can your life not be utterly miserable all in all? Won't it fall apart with fearsome frequency?

The best of what this species knows is in books. Without their help, how can you manage?

If I intend for my life to matter to me, I had better read seriously, starting with newspapers and working up to philosophy and novels. And a book in what it teaches, and in what it does in comforting and amusing us, in what it does in granting asylum to us for a while, had better be roughly equivalent to, or greater in worth than, an event involving other people in reality that teaches us or that grants us asylum for a while in some similar way, or there is no reason to bother with it. And I am careful toward books that offer refuge to my ego or my bad conscience. A writer who is opposed to notions of value and instruction is telling you he or she does not want to have to display loyalty or insight or sensitivity—to prose or to people: that would limit his or her maneuverability; and someone who does not believe that loyalty or insight or sensitivity or meaning has any meaning is hardly worth knowing in books or on the page although such people are unavoidable in an active life.

The procedures of real reading, if I may call it that, are not essentially shrewd, although certain writers, Twain and Proust for instance, often do play to the practice of shrewdness in their readers.

But the disappearance from the immediate world of one's attention, that infidelity to one's alertness toward outside attack, and then the gullibility required for a prolonged act of attention to something not directly inferior to one's own methods and experiences, something that emanates from someone else, that and the risk of conversion, the certainty that if the book is good, one will take on ideas and theories, a sense of style, a sense of things different from those one had before—if you think of those, you can see the elements of middle-class leisure and freedom, or upper-class insolence and power, or lower-class rebelliousness and hiddenness and disloyalty to one's surroundings, that are required for real reading.

And you can also see what the real nature of literature is—it is a matter of one's attention being removed from the real world and regarding nature and the world verbally: it is a messy mathematics in its way; it is a kind of science dealing in images and language, and it has to be right in the things it says; it has to be right about things.

I learned very early that when you were infatuated with someone, you read the same books the other person read or you read the books that had shaped the other person or you committed an infidelity and read for yourself and it was the beginning of trouble. I think reading and writing are the most dangerous human things because they operate on and from that part of the mind in which judgments of reality are made; and because of the authority language has from when we learn to speak and use its power as a family matter, as an immediate matter, and from when we learn to read and see its modern, middle-class power as a public matter establishing our rank in the world.

When a book is technically uninteresting, when such a book is not a kind of comically enraged protest against the pretensions of false technique and ludicrously misconceived subject matter, it is bound to be a phony. The democratic subversion of objects, of techniques, can never without real dishonesty stray far from its ostensible purpose, which is the democratic necessity of making our lives interesting to us. Folk art is, inevitably, a kind of baby talk in relation to high art—and this is shaming, but so is much in life, including one's odor giving one's secrets away (showing one's nervousness or one's lechery), but it is better to do that than live messageless and without nerves or desire. The moral extravagance of reading—its spiritual element and its class element—is bound to reflect both an absence of humility and a new kind of humility and both in odd ways. Two of our most conceited writers, Gertrude Stein and Ernest Hemingway, overtly wrote baby talk. Nowadays the young like financial reporting as a window on the world, and television and the interview. They are pursuing fact in the plethora of baby talk, and they are trying to exercise judgment in the middle of the overenthusiastic marketing of trash.

American colleges have taught our intellectuals to read politically in order to enter and stay in a group or on a track. One reads skimmingly then, and one keeps placing the authority for what one reads outside oneself. But actually people cannot read in a two-souled way, shrewdly, and with a capacity to feel and learn. Learning involves fear and sometimes awe and just plain factually is not shrewd—it is supershrewd if you like, it is a very grand speculation indeed; and graduate school stuff won't open out into awe and discovery or recognition or personal knowledge of events but only onto academic hustling. I mean when you stop theorizing and think about what is really there. Do I need to go on? One of the primary rules of language is that there must be a good reason for the listener to attend to a second sentence after the first one; to supply a good reason is called "being interesting." Not to attend to the second sentence is called "not listening." The reasons to listen are always selfish, but that does not mean they are only selfish.

It is hard to listen. It is also hard to write well and to think. These ought not to be unfamiliar statements. This ought not to be news.

See you in the bookstore soon.

Suggestions for Discussion

1. Discuss the significance of Brodkey's title.
2. Explain Brodkey's belief that the United States is organized by "fashions in making money and spending money."
3. Discuss the difficulties a reader encounters in Brodkey's lengthy, complex, and energetic sentences.

Suggestions for Writing

1. Analyze the reading that you do on a regular basis.
2. Discuss Brodkey's observation that "shrewdness without good sense is hell unleashed."

LOREN EISELEY

The Hidden Teacher

Loren Eiseley (1907–1977) was an anthropologist and academic administrator at the University of Pennsylvania. His publications include *Darwin's Century* (1958), which won the National Phi Beta Kappa Science Award, *The Mind as Nature* (1962), *The Unexpected Universe* (1969), *The Invisible Pyramid* (1970), and his autobiography, *All the Strange Hours: The Excavation of a Life* (1975). In the following essay, he emphasizes the importance of continuing exploration and discovery.

Sometimes the best teacher teaches only once to a single child or a grownup past hope.

—ANONYMOUS

I

The putting of formidable riddles did not arise with today's philosophers. In fact, there is a sense in which the experimental method of science might be said merely to have widened the area of man's homelessness. Over two thousand years ago, a man named Job, crouching in the Judean desert, was moved to challenge what he felt to be the injustice of his God. The voice in the whirlwind, in turn, volleyed pitiless questions upon the supplicant—questions that have, in truth, precisely the ring of modern science. For the Lord asked of Job by whose wisdom the hawk soars, and who had fathered the rain, or entered the storehouses of the snow.

A youth standing by, one Elihu, also played a role in this drama, for he ventured diffidently to his protesting elder that it was not true that God failed to manifest Himself. He may speak in one way or another, though men do not perceive it. In consequence of this remark perhaps it would be well, whatever our individual beliefs, to consider what may be called the hidden teacher, lest we become too much concerned with the formalities of only one aspect of the education by which we learn.

We think we learn from teachers, and we sometimes do. But the teachers are not always to be found in school or in great laboratories. Sometimes what we learn depends upon our own powers of insight. Moreover, our teachers may be hidden, even the greatest teacher. And it was the young man Elihu who observed that if the old are not always wise, neither can the teacher's way be ordered by the young whom he would teach.

For example, I once received an unexpected lesson from a spider.

It happened far away on a rainy morning in the West. I had come up a long gulch looking for fossils, and there, just at eye level, lurked a huge yellow-and-black orb spider, whose web was moored to the tall spears of buffalo grass at the edge of the arroyo. It was her universe, and her senses did not extend beyond the lines and spokes of the great wheel she inhabited. Her extended claws could feel every vibration throughout that delicate structure. She knew the tug of wind, the fall of a raindrop, the flutter of a trapped moth's wing. Down one spoke of the web ran a stout ribbon of gossamer on which she could hurry out to investigate her prey.

Curious, I took a pencil from my pocket and touched a strand of the web. Immediately there was a response. The web, plucked by its menacing occupant, began to vibrate until it was a blur. Anything that had brushed claw or wing against that amazing snare would be thoroughly entrapped. As the vibrations slowed, I could see the owner fingering her guidelines for signs of struggle. A pencil point was an intrusion into this universe for which no precedent existed. Spider was circumscribed by spider ideas; its universe was spider universe. All outside was irrational, extraneous, at best raw material for spider. As I proceeded on my way along the gully, like a vast impossible shadow, I realized that in the world of spider I did not exist.

Moreover, I considered, as I tramped along, that to the phagocytes, the white blood cells, clambering even now with some kind of elementary intelligence amid the thin pipes and tubing of my body—creatures without whose ministrations I could not exist—the conscious "I" of which I was aware had no significance to these amoeboid beings. I was, instead, a kind of chemical web that brought meaningful messages to them, a natural environment seemingly immortal if they could have thought about it, since generations of them had lived and perished, and would continue to so live and die, in that odd fabric which contained my intelligence—a misty light that was beginning to seem floating and tenuous even to me.

I began to see that among the many universes in which the world of living creatures existed, some were large, some small, but that all, including man's, were in some way limited or finite. We were creatures of many different dimensions passing through each other's lives like ghosts through doors.

In the years since, my mind has many times returned to that far moment of my encounter with the orb spider. A message has arisen only now from the misty shreds of that webbed universe. What was it that had so troubled me about the incident? Was it that spidery indifference to the human triumph?

If so, that triumph was very real and could not be denied. I saw, had many times seen, both mentally and in the seams of exposed strata, the long backward stretch of time whose recovery is one of the great feats of modern science. I saw the drifting cells of the early seas from which all life, including our own, has arisen. The salt of those ancient seas is in our blood, its lime is in our bones. Every time we walk along a beach some ancient urge disturbs us so that we find ourselves shedding shoes and garments, or scavenging among seaweed and whitened timbers like the homesick refugees of a long war.

And war it has been indeed—the long war of life against its inhospitable environment, a war that has lasted for perhaps three billion years. It began with strange chemicals seething under a sky lacking in oxygen; it was waged through long ages until the first green plants learned to harness the light of the nearest star, our sun. The human brain, so frail, so perishable, so full of inexhaustible dreams and hungers, burns by the power of the leaf.

The hurrying blood cells charged with oxygen carry more of that element to the human brain than to any other part of the body. A few moments' loss of vital air and the phenomenon we know as consciousness goes down into the black night of inorganic things. The human body is a magical vessel, but its life is linked with an element it cannot produce. Only the green plant knows the secret of transforming the light that comes to us across the far reaches of space. There is no better illustration of the intricacy of man's relationship with other living things.

The student of fossil life would be forced to tell us that if we take the past into consideration the vast majority of earth's creatures—perhaps over 90 percent—have vanished. Forms that flourished for a far longer time than man has existed upon earth have become either extinct or so transformed that their descendants are scarcely recognizable. The specialized perish with the environment that created them, the tooth of the tiger fails at last, the lances of men strike down the last mammoth.

In three billion years of slow change and groping effort only one living creature has succeeded in escaping the trap of specialization that has led in time to so much death and wasted endeavor. It is man, but the word should be uttered softly, for his story is not yet done.

With the rise of the human brain, with the appearance of a creature whose upright body enabled two limbs to be freed for the exploration and manipulation of his environment, there had at last emerged a creature with a specialization—the brain—that, paradoxically, offered escape from specialization. Many animals driven into the nooks and crannies of nature have achieved momentary survival only at the cost of later extinction.

Was it this that troubled me and brought my mind back to a tiny universe among the grass blades, a spider's universe concerned with spider thought?

Perhaps.

The mind that once visualized animals on a cave wall is now engaged in a vast ramification of itself through time and space. Man has broken through the boundaries that control all other life. I saw, at last, the reason for my recollection of that great spider on the arroyo's rim, fingering its universe against the sky.

The spider was a symbol of man in miniature. The wheel of the web brought the analogy home clearly. Man, too, lies at the heart of a web, a web extending through the starry reaches of sidereal space, as well as backward into the dark realm of prehistory. His great eye upon Mount Palomar looks into a distance of millions of light-years, his radio ear hears the whisper of even more remote galaxies, he peers through the electron miscroscope upon the minute particles of his own being. It is a web no creature of earth has ever spun before. Like the orb spider, man lies at the heart of it, listening. Knowledge has given him the memory of earth's history beyond the time of his emergence. Like the spider's claw, a part of him touches a world he will never enter in the flesh. Even now, one can see him reaching forward into time with new machines, computing, analyzing, until elements of the shadowy future will also compose part of the invisible web he fingers.

Yet still my spider lingers in memory against the sunset sky. Spider thoughts in a spider universe—sensitive to raindrop and moth flutter, nothing beyond, nothing allowed for the unexpected, the inserted pencil from the world outside.

Is man at heart any different from the spider, I wonder: man thoughts, as limited as spider thoughts, contemplating now the nearest star with the threat of bringing with him the fungus rot from earth, wars, violence, the burden of a population he refuses to control, cherishing again his dream of the Adamic Eden he had pursued and lost in the green forests of America. Now it beckons again like a mirage from beyond the moon. Let man spin his web, I thought further; it is his nature. But I considered also the work of the phagocytes swarming in the rivers of my body, the unresting cells in their mortal universe. What is it we are a part of that we do not see, as the spider was not gifted to discern my face, or my little probe into her world?

We are too content with our sensory extensions, with the fulfillment of that Ice Age mind that began its journey amidst the cold of vast tundras and that pauses only briefly before its leap into space. It is no longer enough to see as a man sees—even to the ends of the universe. It is not enough to hold nuclear energy in one's hand like a spear, as a man would hold it, or to see the lightning, or times past, or time to come, as a man would see it. If we continue to do this, the great brain—the human brain—will be only a new version of the old trap, and nature is full of traps for the beast that cannot learn.

It is not sufficient any longer to listen at the end of a wire to the rustlings of galaxies; it is not enough even to examine the great coil of DNA in which is coded the very alphabet of life. These are our extended perceptions. But beyond lies the great darkness of the ultimate Dreamer, who dreamed the light and the galaxies. Before act was, or substance existed, imagination grew in the dark. Man partakes of that ultimate wonder and creativeness. As we turn from the galaxies to the swarming cells of our own being, which toil for something, some entity beyond their grasp, let us remember man, the self-fabricator who came across an ice age to look into the mirrors and the magic of science. Surely he did not come to see himself or his wild visage only. He came because he is at heart a listener and a searcher for some transcendent realm beyond himself. This he has worshiped by many names, even in the dismal caves of his beginning. Man, the self-fabricator, is so by reason of gifts he had no part in devising—and so he searches as the single living cell in the beginning must have sought the ghostly creature it was to serve.

II

The young man Elihu, Job's counselor and critic, spoke simply of the "Teacher," and it is of this teacher I speak when I refer to gifts man had no part in devising. Perhaps—though it is purely a matter of emotional reactions to words—it is easier for us today to speak of this teacher as "nature," that omnipresent all which contained both the spider and my invisible intrusion into her carefully planned universe. But nature does not simply represent reality. In the shapes of life, it prepares the future; it offers alternatives. Nature teaches, though what it teaches is often hidden and obscure, just as the voice from the spinning dust cloud belittled Job's thought but gave back no answers to its own formidable interrogation.

A few months ago I encountered an amazing little creature on a windy corner of my local shopping center. It seemed, at first glance, some long-limbed, feathery spider teetering rapidly down the edge of a store front.

Then it swung into the air and, as hesitantly as a spider on a thread, blew away into the parking lot. It returned in a moment on a gust of wind and ran toward me once more on its spindly legs with amazing rapidity.

With great difficulty I discovered the creature was actually a filamentous seed, seeking a hiding place and scurrying about with the uncanny surety of a conscious animal. In fact, it *did* escape me before I could secure it. Its flexible limbs were stiffer than milkweed down, and, propelled by the wind, it ran rapidly and evasively over the pavement. It was like a gnome scampering somewhere with a hidden packet—for all that I could tell, a totally new one: one of the jumbled alphabets of life.

A new one? So stable seem the years and all green leaves, a botanist might smile at my imaginings. Yet bear with me a moment. I would like to tell a tale, a genuine tale of childhood. Moreover, I was just old enough to know the average of my kind and to marvel at what I saw. And what I saw was straight from the hidden Teacher, whatever be his name.

It is told in the Orient of the Hindu god Krishna that his mother, wiping his mouth when he was a child, inadvertently peered in and beheld the universe, though the sight was mercifully and immediately veiled from her. In a sense, this is what happened to me. One day there arrived at our school a newcomer, who entered the grade above me. After some days this lad, whose look of sleepy-eyed arrogance is still before me as I write, was led into my mathematics classroom by the principal. Our class was informed severely that we should learn to work harder.

With this preliminary exhortation, great rows of figures were chalked upon the blackboard, such difficult mathematical problems as could be devised by adults. The class watched in helpless wonder. When the preparations had been completed, the young pupil sauntered forward and, with a glance of infinite boredom that swept from us to his fawning teachers, wrote the answers, as instantaneously as a modern computer, in their proper place upon the board. Then he strolled out with a carelessly exaggerated yawn.

Like some heavy-browed child at the wood's edge, clutching the last stone hand ax, I was witnessing the birth of a new type of humanity—one so beyond its teachers that it was being used for mean purposes while the intangible web of the universe in all its shimmering mathematical perfection glistened untaught in the mind of a chance little boy. The boy, by then grown self-centered and contemptuous, was being dragged from room to room to encourage us, the paleanthropes, to duplicate what, in reality, our teachers could not duplicate. He was too precious an object to be released upon the playground among us, and with reason. In a few months his parents took him away.

Long after, looking back from maturity, I realized that I had been exposed on that occasion, not to human teaching, but to the Teacher, toying with some sixteen billion nerve cells interlocked in ways past understanding.

Or, if we do not like the anthropomorphism implied in the word teacher, then nature, the old voice from the whirlwind fumbling for the light. At all events, I had been the fortunate witness to life's unbounded creativity—a creativity seemingly still as unbalanced and chance-filled as in that far era when a black-scaled creature had broken from an egg and the age of the giant reptiles, the creatures of the prime, had tentatively begun.

Because form cannot be long sustained in the living, we collapse inward with age. We die. Our bodies, which were the product of a kind of hidden teaching by an alphabet we are only beginning dimly to discern, are dismissed into their elements. What is carried onward, assuming we have descendants, is the little capsule of instructions such as I encountered hastening by me in the shape of a running seed. We have learned the first biological lesson: that in each generation life passes through the eye of a needle. It exists for a time molecularly and in no recognizable semblance to its adult condition. It *instructs* its way again into man or reptile. As the ages pass, so do variants of the code. Occasionally, a species vanishes on a wind as unreturning as that which took the pterodactyls.

Or the code changes by subtle degrees through the statistical altering of individuals; until I, as the fading Neanderthals must once have done, have looked with still-living eyes upon the creature whose genotype was quite possibly to replace me. The genetic alphabets, like genuine languages, ramify and evolve along unreturning pathways.

If nature's instructions are carried through the eye of a needle, through the molecular darkness of a minute world below the field of human vision and of time's decay, the same, it might be said, is true of those monumental structures known as civilizations. They are transmitted from one generation to another in invisible puffs of air known as words—words that can also be symbolically incised on clay. As the delicate printing on the mud at the water's edge retraces a visit of autumn birds long since departed, so the little scrabbled tablets in perished cities carry the seeds of human thought across the deserts of millennia. In this instance the teacher is the social brain, but it, too, must be compressed into minute hieroglyphs, and the minds that wrought the miracle efface themselves amidst the jostling torrent of messages, which, like the genetic code, are shuffled and reshuffled as they hurry through eternity. Like a mutation, an idea may be recorded in the wrong time, to lie latent like a recessive gene and spring once more to life in an auspicious era.

Occasionally, in the moments when an archaeologist lifts the slab over a tomb that houses a great secret, a few men gain a unique glimpse through that dark portal out of which all men living have emerged, and through which messages again must pass. Here the Mexican archaeologist Ruz Lhuillier speaks of his first penetration of the great tomb hidden beneath dripping stalactites at the pyramid of Palenque: "Out of the dark shadows, rose a fairy-tale vision, a weird ethereal spectacle from another world. It was like a magician's cave carved out of ice, with walls glittering and sparkling like snow crystals." After shining his torch over hieroglyphs and sculptured figures, the explorer remarked wonderingly: "We were the first people for more than a thousand years to look at it."

Or again, one may read the tale of an unknown pharaoh who had secretly arranged that a beloved woman of his household should be buried in the tomb of the god-king—an act of compassion carrying a personal message across the millennia in defiance of all precedent.

Up to this point we have been talking of the single hidden teacher, the taunting voice out of that old Biblical whirlwind which symbolizes nature. We have seen incredible organic remembrance passed through the needle's eye of a microcosmic world hidden completely beneath the observational powers of creatures preoccupied and ensorcelled by dissolution and decay. We have seen the human mind unconsciously seize upon the principles of that very code to pass its own societal memory forward into time. The individual, the momentary living cell of the society, vanishes, but the institutional structures stand, or if they change, do so in an invisible flux not too dissimilar from that persisting in the stream of genetic continuity.

Upon this world, life is still young, not truly old as stars are measured. Therefore it comes about that we minimize the role of the synapsid reptiles, our remote forerunners, and correspondingly exalt our own intellectual achievements. We refuse to consider that in the old eye of the hurricane we may be, and doubtless are, in aggregate, a slightly more diffuse and dangerous dragon of the primal morning that still enfolds us.

Note that I say "in aggregate." For it is just here, among men, that the role of messages, and, therefore, the role of the individual teacher—or, I should say now, the hidden teachers—began to be more plainly apparent and their instructions become more diverse. The dead pharaoh, though unintentionally, by a revealing act, had succeeded in conveying an impression of human tenderness that has outlasted the trappings of a vanished religion.

Like most modern educators I have listened to student demands to grade their teachers. I have heard the words repeated until they have become a slogan, that no man over thirty can teach the young of this generation. How would one grade a dead pharaoh, millennia gone, I wonder, one who did not intend to teach, but who, to a few perceptive minds, succeeded by the simple nobility of an act.

Many years ago, a student who was destined to become an internationally known anthropologist sat in a course in linguistics and heard his instructor, a man of no inconsiderable wisdom, describe some linguistic peculiarities of Hebrew words. At the time, the young student, at the urging of his family, was contemplating a career in theology. As the teacher warmed to his subject, the student, in the back row, ventured excitedly, "I believe I can understand that, sir. It is very similar to what exists in Mohegan."

The linguist paused and adjusted his glasses. "Young man," he said, "Mohegan is a dead language. Nothing has been recorded of it since the eighteenth century. Don't bluff."

"But sir," the young student countered hopefully, "It can't be dead so long as an old woman I know still speaks it. She is Pequot-Mohegan. I learned a bit of vocabulary from her and could speak with her myself. She took care of me when I was a child."

"Young man," said the austere, old-fashioned scholar, "be at my house for dinner at six this evening. You and I are going to look into this matter."

A few months later, under careful guidance, the young student published a paper upon Mohegan linguistics, the first of a long series of studies upon the forgotten languages and ethnology of the Indians of the northeastern forests. He had changed his vocation and turned to anthropology because of the attraction of a hidden teacher. But just who was the teacher? The young man himself, his instructor, or that solitary speaker of a dying tongue who had so yearned to hear her people's voice that she had softly babbled it to a child?

Later, this man was to become one of my professors. I absorbed much from him, though I hasten to make the reluctant confession that he was considerably beyond thirty. Most of what I learned was gathered over cups of coffee in a dingy campus restaurant. What we talked about were things some centuries older than either of us. Our common interest lay in snakes, scapulimancy, and other forgotten rites of benighted forest hunters.

I have always regarded this man as an extraordinary individual, in fact, a hidden teacher. But alas, it is all now so old-fashioned. We never protested the impracticality of his quaint subjects. We were all too ready to participate in them. He was an excellent canoeman, but he took me to places where I fully expected to drown before securing my degree. To this day, fragments of his unused wisdom remain stuffed in some back attic of my mind. Much of it I have never found the opportunity to employ, yet it has somehow colored my whole adult existence. I belong to that elderly professor in somewhat the same way that he, in turn, had become the wood child of a hidden forest mother.

There are, however, other teachers. For example, among the hunting peoples there were the animal counselors who appeared in prophetic dreams. Or, among the Greeks, the daemonic supernaturals who stood at the headboard while a man lay stark and listened—sometimes to dreadful things. "You are asleep," the messengers proclaimed over and over again, as though the man lay in a spell to hear his doom pronounced. "You, Achilles, you, son of Atreus. You are asleep, asleep," the hidden ones pronounced and vanished.

We of this modern time know other things of dreams, but we know also that they can be interior teachers and healers as well as the anticipators of disaster. It has been said that great art is the night thought of man. It may emerge without warning from the soundless depths of the unconscious, just as supernovas may blaze up suddenly in the farther reaches of void space. The critics, like astronomers, can afterward triangulate such worlds but not account for them.

A writer friend of mine with bitter memories of his youth, and estranged from his family, who, in the interim, had died, gave me this account of the matter in his middle years. He had been working, with an unusual degree of reluctance, upon a novel that contained certain autobiographical episodes. One night he dreamed; it was a very vivid and stunning dream in its detailed reality.

He found himself hurrying over creaking snow through the blackness of a winter night. He was ascending a familiar path through a long-vanished orchard. The path led to his childhood home. The house, as he drew near, appeared dark and uninhabited, but, impelled by the power of the dream, he stepped upon the porch and tried to peer through a dark window into his own old room.

"Suddenly," he told me, "I was drawn by a strange mixture of repulsion and desire to press my face against the glass. I knew intuitively they were all there waiting for me within, if I could but see them. My mother and my father. Those I had loved and those I hated. But the window was black to my gaze. I hesitated a moment and struck a match. For an instant in that freezing silence I saw my father's face glimmer wan and remote behind the glass. My mother's face was there, with the hard, distorted lines that marked her later years.

"A surge of fury overcame my cowardice. I cupped the match before me and stepped closer, closer toward that dreadful confrontation. As the match guttered down, my face was pressed almost to the glass. In some quick transformation, such as only a dream can effect, I saw that it was my own face into which I stared, just as it was reflected in the black glass. My father's haunted face was but my own. The hard lines upon my mother's aging countenance were slowly reshaping themselves upon my living face. The light burned out. I awoke sweating from the terrible psychological tension of that nightmare. I was in a far port in a distant land. It was dawn. I could hear the waves breaking on the reef."

"And how do you interpret the dream?" I asked, concealing a sympathetic shudder and sinking deeper into my chair.

"It taught me something," he said slowly, and with equal slowness a kind of beautiful transfiguration passed over his features. All the tired lines I had known so well seemed faintly to be subsiding.

"Did you ever dream it again?" I asked out of a comparable experience of my own.

"No, never," he said, and hesitated. "You see, I had learned it was just I, but more, much more, I had learned that I was they. It makes a difference. And at the last, late—much too late—it was all right. I understood. My line was dying, but I understood. I hope they understood, too." His voice trailed into silence.

"It is a thing to learn," I said. "You were seeking something and it came." He nodded, wordless. "Out of a tomb," he added after a silent moment, "my kind of tomb—the mind."

On the dark street, walking homeward, I considered my friend's experience. Man, I concluded, may have come to the end of that wild being who had mastered the fire and the lightning. He can create the web but not hold it together, not save himself except by transcending his own image. For at last, before the ultimate mystery, it is himself he shapes. Perhaps it is for this that the listening web lies open: that by knowledge we may grow beyond our past, our follies, and ever closer to what the Dreamer in the dark intended before the dust arose and walked. In the pages of an old book it has been written that we are in the hands of a Teacher, nor does it yet appear what man shall be.

Suggestions for Discussion

1. Discuss the rhetorical importance of the fourth paragraph, which introduces the "lesson from a spider."
2. In what sense is the "spider a symbol of man in miniature"?
3. Explain Eiseley's belief that man is "at heart a listener and a searcher."

Suggestions for Writing

1. Use your observations of the conduct of another creature to make generalizations about human behavior.
2. Speculate on Eiseley's notion that we are "a part of that we do not see."

AMOJA THREE RIVERS

Cultural Etiquette: A Guide

Amoja Three Rivers is a cofounder of the Accessible African History Project. In the following essay originally published in *Ms.* magazine in 1991, she discusses the serious task of dispelling racial myths and stereotypes through language.

Cultural Etiquette is intended for people of all "races," nationalities, and creeds, not necessarily just "white" people, because no one living in Western society is exempt from the influences of racism, racial stereotypes, race and cultural prejudices, and anti-Semitism. I include anti-Semitism in the discussion of racism because it is simply another manifestation of cultural and racial bigotry.

All people are people. It is ethnocentric to use a generic term such as "people" to refer only to white people and then racially label everyone else. This creates and reinforces the assumption that whites are the norm, the real people, and that all others are aberrations.

"Exotic," when applied to human beings, is ethnocentric and racist.

While it is true that most citizens of the U.S.A. are white, at least four fifths of the world's population consists of people of color. Therefore, it is statistically incorrect as well as ethnocentric to refer to us as minorities. The term "minority" is used to reinforce the idea of people of color as "other."

A cult is a particular system of religious worship. If the religious practices of the Yorubas constitute a cult, then so do those of the Methodists, Catholics, Episcopalians, and so forth.

A large radio/tape player is a boom-box, or a stereo or a box or a large metallic ham sandwich with speakers. It is not a "ghetto blaster."

Everybody can blush. Everybody can bruise. Everybody can tan and get sunburned. Everybody.

Judaism is no more patriarchal than any other patriarchal religion.

Koreans are not taking over. Neither are Jews. Neither are the Japanese. Neither are the West Indians. These are myths put out and maintained by the ones who really have.

All hair is "good" hair. Dreadlocks, locks, dreads, natty dreads, et cetera, is an ancient traditional way that African people sometimes wear their hair. It is not braided, it is "locked." Locking is the natural tendency of

African hair to knit and bond to itself. It locks by itself, we don't have to do anything to it to make it lock. It is permanent; once locked, it cannot come undone. It gets washed just as regularly as anyone else's hair. No, you may not touch it, don't ask.

One of the most effective and insidious aspects of racism is cultural genocide. Not only have African Americans been cut off from our African tribal roots, but because of generations of whites pitting African against Indian, and Indian against African, we have been cut off from our Native American roots as well. Consequently, most African Native Americans no longer have tribal affiliations, or know for certain what people they are from.

Columbus didn't discover diddly-squat.

Slavery is not a condition unique to African people. In fact, the word "slave" comes from the Slav people of Eastern Europe. Because so many Slavs were enslaved by other people (including Africans), their very name came to be synonymous with the condition.

Native Americans were also enslaved by Europeans. Because it is almost impossible to successfully enslave large numbers of people in their own land, most enslaved Native Americans from the continental U.S. were shipped to Bermuda, and the West Indies, where many intermarried with the Africans.

People do not have a hard time because of their race or cultural background. No one is attacked, abused, oppressed, pogromed, or enslaved because of their race, creed, or cultural background. People are attacked, abused, oppressed, pogromed, or enslaved because of racism and anti-Semitism. There is a subtle but important difference in the focus here. The first implies some inherent fault or shortcoming within the oppressed person or group. The second redirects the responsibility back to the real source of the problem.

Asians are not "mysterious," "fatalistic," or "inscrutable."

Native Americans are not stoic, mystical, or vanishing.

Latin people are no more hot-tempered, hot-blooded, or emotional than anyone else. We do not have flashing eyes, teeth, or daggers. We are lovers pretty much like other people. Very few of us deal with any kind of drugs.

Middle Easterners are not fanatics, terrorists, or all oil-rich.

Jewish people are not particularly rich, clannish, or expert in money matters.

Not all African Americans are poor, athletic, or ghetto-dwellers.

Most Asians in the U.S. are not scientists, mathematicians, geniuses, or wealthy.

Southerners are no less intelligent than anybody else.

It is not a compliment to tell someone: "I don't think of you as Jewish/Black/Asian/Latina/Middle Eastern/Native American." Or "I think of you as white."

Do not use a Jewish person or person of color to hear your confession of past racist transgressions. If you have offended a particular person, then apologize directly to that person.

Also don't assume that Jews and people of color necessarily want to hear about how prejudiced your Uncle Fred is, no matter how terrible you think he is.

If you are white and/or gentile, do not assume that the next Jewish person or person of color you see will feel like discussing this guide with you. Sometimes we get tired of teaching this subject.

If you are white, don't brag to a person of color about your overseas trip to our homeland. Especially when we cannot afford such a trip. Similarly, don't assume that we are overjoyed to see the expensive artifacts you bought.

Words like "gestapo," "concentration camp" and "Hitler" are only appropriate when used in reference to the Holocaust.

"Full-blood," "half-breed," "quarter-blood." Any inference that a person's "race" depends on blood is racist. Natives are singled out for this form of bigotry and are denied rights on that basis.

"Scalping": a custom also practiced by the French, the Dutch, and the English.

Do you have friends or acquaintances who are terrific except they're really racist? If you quietly accept that part of them, you are giving their racism tacit approval.

As an exercise, pretend you are from another planet and you want an example of a typical human being for your photo album. Having never heard of racism, you'd probably pick someone who represents the majority of the people on the planet—an Asian person.

How many is too many? We have heard well-meaning liberals say things like "This event is too white. We need more people of color." Well, how many do you need? Fifty? A hundred? Just what is your standard for personal racial comfort?

People of color and Jewish people have been so all their lives. Further, if we have been raised in a place where white gentiles predominate, then we have been subjected to racism/anti-Semitism all our lives. We are therefore experts on our own lives and conditions. If you do not understand or believe or agree with what someone is saying about their own oppression, do not automatically assume that they are wrong or paranoid or oversensitive.

It is not "racism in reverse" or "segregation" for Jews or people of color to come together in affinity groups for mutual support. Sometimes we need some time and space apart from the dominant group just to relax and be ourselves. If people coming together for group support makes you feel excluded, perhaps there's something missing in your own life or cultural connections.

The various cultures of people of color often seem very attractive to white people. (Yes, we are wonderful, we can't deny it.) But white people should not make a playground out of other people's cultures. We are not quaint. We are not exotic. We are not cool.

Don't forget that every white person alive today is also descended from tribal peoples. If you are white, don't neglect your own ancient traditions. They are as valid as anybody else's, and the ways of your own ancestors need to be honored and remembered.

"Race" is an arbitrary and meaningless concept. Races among humans don't exist. If there ever was any such thing as race, there has been so much constant crisscrossing of genes for the last 500,000 years that it would have lost all meaning anyway. There are no real divisions between us, only a continuum of variations that constantly change, as we come together and separate according to the movement of human populations.

Anyone who functions in what is referred to as the "civilized" world is a carrier of the disease of racism.

Does reading this guide make you uncomfortable? Angry? Confused? Are you taking it personally? Well, not to fret. Racism has created a big horrible mess, and racial healing can sometimes be painful. Just remember that Jews and people of color do not want or need anybody's guilt. We just want people to accept responsibility when it is appropriate, and actively work for change.

Suggestions for Discussion

1. Which of the writer's pithy observations strike you as particularly apt and on target? Which seem hyperbolic or unfair? Explain your choices.
2. Discuss how people might "accept responsibility" and "actively work for change." What might you do, as an individual? Give three or four specific examples.
3. Why might reading this guide make one uncomfortable?

Suggestions for Writing

1. Describe one or more examples of sexual, racial, or other stereotyping that you have experienced or observed.
2. Make your own list of ten or more words that might offend certain people.

JANE GALLOP

Feminist Accused of Sexual Harassment

Jane Gallop (b. 1952) is Distinguished Professor of English at the University of Wisconsin, Milwaukee. In addition to being the editor of *Pedagogy,* she is the author of *Around 1981* (1992) and *Feminist Accused of Sexual Harassment* (1997). In the following essay she writes firsthand about the campaign against sexual harassment by feminists.

Twenty-five years ago, I thought Women's Studies was hot. And I've been devoted to the feminist pursuit of knowledge since that time. After college, I went on to graduate school and wrote a feminist dissertation. In the late nineteen seventies I got a job teaching at a university, and I've been teaching women's studies courses ever since. In the eighties, I set up and ran a Women's Studies Program at a college which did not yet have one. For more than two decades, I've been pursuing the dream of Women's Studies, led by my desire for the community which turned me on as a student.

Nowadays, Women's Studies is a lot older and more established; it doesn't feel so much like a bold experiment. While it still is said in women's studies circles that feminist teachers and students ought to have a nonhierarchical relation, ought to work together as sister seekers of knowledge, in fact the relation between feminist teachers and students is not what it was when Women's Studies was young. Students and faculty are no longer discovering feminism together; today, faculty who have been feminists for decades generally teach it to students for whom it is new. We are no longer discovering books together; instead, feminist faculty teach feminist classics we've read half a dozen times to students who are reading them for the first time. Whatever lip service we still might give to an egalitarian classroom, we function as feminist authorities, trying to get our students to understand a feminism we have long known. In this context, relations between us are defined much more by our roles as teacher and student than by any commonality as feminists. These days, rather than playing with our pedagogical roles, we seem to be trapped in them, our ability to connect as women very much limited by them.

For about a decade now, students in my feminist seminars have been complaining, in their anonymous evaluations, that I am "authoritarian." They expect a feminist teacher to be different, but my authority *as a feminist* feels too much like the male professor's authority in other classrooms. This experience of the feminist teacher as authority seems to betray the very principles of feminist teaching. The students see it as my personal betrayal, but I see it as a loss that follows inevitably from the maturation of Women's Studies.

My students want a feminist education that feels like Women's Studies did to me in 1971. And so do I, deeply. I want it for them, and I want it still, again for myself. My commitment to feminist education is precisely my passion for that experience, my certainty of its extraordinary value. But the fact that I experienced that community and that my students *did not* seems to change everything, to keep us from getting together to the place we all want to be.

Not that it never works. Sometimes it does. Sometimes a class or some more informal gathering suddenly comes together, and I feel the electricity, the buzz of live knowledge, the excitement of women thinking freely together. I always try to get us to that place where learning is a wild dance. When we get there, my students love me, and I'm crazy for them, but when, as is more often the case, we don't get there, we are all disappointed. And then the students are likely to blame me, call me authoritarian. Ironically, it is *their* image of me as an authority, their belief that I control everything that happens in the class, that makes them assume that we didn't get to that place because I don't want to be there.

Not only have feminist students complained on course evaluations that I am authoritarian, a few years ago feminist graduate students filed formal complaints with the university office of affirmative action charging that I had sexually harassed them. In the context of feminism, these two apparently different kinds of complaints are saying the same thing: that I abuse my power, get off on my power at the students' expense, that I am just as bad as the men.

During the time I was being investigated by the affirmative action office, the women who had filed complaints called a meeting of all the graduate students in the department, a predominantly feminist group. The purpose of the meeting was to get the grad students to band together so they would be strong enough to curtail my power. Here was a feminist space defined by the identity of the student; not only was any commonality with feminist faculty denied, but faculty were actually seen as the oppressor. The meeting functioned in part as a sort of speak-out where students could share with each other the abuses they had suffered. And in that context, charges of sexual harassment mingled freely with complaints about other manifestations of power.

In the campus atmosphere stirred up against me, little distinction was made between sexual harassment (the criminal charge leveled against me) and authoritarianism (a complaint about my teaching style). In the eyes of the students banded together to resist me, they were virtually the same crime, the crime of having power over them.

Versed in contemporary feminist theory, one of the students states in her complaint against me: "It is at the level of the institutionally enforced power differential that I wish to locate my harassment charge." She found it humiliating that I had power over her and considered it a betrayal of feminism. Harassment for her, in fact, meant precisely experiencing what she calls "the power differential." Now that there are feminist faculty securely installed in the academy, students can experience their feminist teachers as having institutional power over them. And that makes it possible to imagine a feminist teacher as a sexual harasser.

Back when I was a student, although we admired the power of our feminist teachers, we did not feel divided from them because of it. We did not experience their power as power over us, but rather as power for us—power for women, power for feminism. Bad power was men's power, the power society granted them to exploit women, impose upon women, abuse women. But twenty years later, students could took at me and see me as just like the men, just as bad as the men. And therefore worse.

A campus activist against sexual harassment, a student from another department who had never even met me, was quite willing to comment on my case to a reporter: "Jane Gallop is as bad as—*no, worse than*—the men who do this kind of thing." A woman seen to be as bad as the men is inevitably, *because she is a woman,* considered to be worse than the men. Although several men in my department had been accused of sexual harassment before me, none of those cases prompted students to rally against the accused.

Feminists often condemn the woman who is like a man as a traitor to feminism, a traitor to her sex. But the condemnation of what feminists call "the male-identified woman" bears a quite uncanny resemblance to a larger social prejudice, the vilification of women who are like men. Feminism has taught us a lot about that sexist image, how it works to limit and constrain women, to keep us in line, but feminists are not themselves always immune to it.

And what it means for a woman to be "just like a man" always comes down to two things: sex and power.

1993: At the very moment I am under investigation, Michael Crichton writes *Disclosure,* the first popular novel about sexual harassment. This novel by a best-selling author, a book that almost immediately became a Hollywood movie, marks a turning point: Harassment has taken root in the culture's imagination. Sexual harassment moves from the news to the novel. And mainstream culture's first attempt to imagine harassment conjures up, not the classic scenario, but a male victim and a female predator.

Disclosure sports the epigraph, "Power is neither male nor female," and this view of power seems to be behind the choice to portray a role-reversal harassment. The epigraph is actually spoken within the novel. The woman lawyer who functions as the book's authority on harassment explains to the male victim: "The figures suggest that women executives harass men in the same proportion as men harass women. Because the fact is, harassment is a power issue. And power is neither male nor female. Whoever is behind the desk has the opportunity to abuse power. And women will take advantage as often as men." This sounds like the moral of a story about a female sexual harasser.

Crichton is a writer known for the extensive research behind his books, and this one is no exception: *Disclosure*'s understanding of harassment is very up-to-date. Explanations of sexual harassment are beginning to move away from the idea that gender is the key factor and toward a gender-neutral notion of power. While a number of feminists have embraced this move, I consider it to be a serious departure from feminism.

Sexual harassment was originally understood within a more general feminist analysis of sexism. Feminists saw that the specific power men exercise over individual women—as a boss or a teacher, say—is enormously magnified by widespread societal assumptions that men should dominate women. In a society which expects male sexuality to be aggressive and female sexuality submissive, a boss can sexually harass his female employee with a devastating combination of economic, psychological, and social coercion. The boss's pressure on his employee is backed not only by literal economic power and general psychological intimidation, but also by social expectations that relations between the sexes are supposed to be like this.

When we move beyond the gender configuration of the classic harassment scenario, some important things change. The link between sex and power is not always the same. Whereas male heterosexuality in our culture connotes power, both homosexuality and female sexuality tend to signify weakness and vulnerability. If we imagine a sexual harassment scenario where the victim is male or the culprit female, the abuse of power would not be reinforced by society's sexual expectations. Outside novelistic turnabouts (and Hollywood fantasies featuring Demi Moore), a woman is much more likely to undermine than to enhance her authority by bringing her sexuality into the professional domain.

Not unlike *Disclosure*, my accusers locate harassment "at the level of the institutionally enforced power differential." Both reflect a current trend in thinking about harassment which reduces power to mere institutional position and forgets the feminist insight that the most destructive abuses of power occur because of widespread, deeply rooted social and psychological reinforcement.

Troubled by this move to a gender-neutral understanding of sexual harassment, I take *Disclosure* to be a dramatic portrayal of its real danger. Rather than worrying about male exploitation and women's disadvantage, the novel's reader is confronted with the image of an evil woman; the reader identifies with and fears for the poor man she preys upon. Under the guise of despising sexual harassment, we find ourselves once again vilifying women who presume to be sexual and powerful like men are.

Embracing a gender-neutral formulation of harassment, we leave the concern with sexism behind only to find ourselves faced with something quite traditionally sexist, an image of a woman who is evil precisely because she is both sexual and powerful. Meredith Johnson, *Disclosure*'s villainess, is a single career woman who is sexy and sexually aggressive, professionally adept and successful. She corresponds to the pop cultural image of a liberated woman. Although feminists have condemned women who are just like men, the larger society tends to think of women who are like men as "feminists." We might see Meredith Johnson as the fantasy of a feminist sexual harasser.

Disclosure marks a real turning point in the response to sexual harassment—or maybe a turn of the screw. As outrage at sexual harassment becomes popular, a role-reversal fantasy allows a wide audience to embrace the feminist issue of sexual harassment and at the same time turn it against liberated women.

As the century draws to a close, it appears that the campaign against sexual harassment may in fact be *the* success story of twentieth-century feminism. At a moment when abortion rights are endangered, when affirmative action is becoming unfashionable, when everyone is jumping on the family values bandwagon, when few women want to be thought feminists, there is a broad-based consensus that sexual harassment is despicable and measures against it have become very popular.

Although feminists targeted sexual harassment in the nineteen seventies, outrage against it did not become popular until the nineties. The Hill-Thomas hearings in late 1991 are generally credited with producing this effect. Although I have my own suspicions about the way that a black man makes it easier for Americans to see male heterosexuality as a threat to the social order, my concern here is rather with the more general question of how sexual harassment is understood at the moment when the nation finally rallies against it.

While the battle against sexual harassment has been feminism's great victory, I'm afraid that's because it has been too easy to separate the issue from feminism. Feminists took up the issue because we saw it as a form of sex discrimination, but sexual harassment is increasingly understood as having no necessary link to either discrimination or gender.

In 1990, Billie Wright Dziech, a national authority on sexual harassment, predicts that "genuine change can occur only when sexual harassment is approached as a professional rather than a gender issue." Three years later, Crichton's *Disclosure* treats harassment in just that way: Gender doesn't matter; what matters is who is "behind the desk." That same year, a university official finds it possible that I could be guilty of sexual harassment without having discriminated against anyone. The university's lawyer comments that they must punish me as harshly as the men so that the university won't be accused of sex discrimination. By the end of that year, 1993, Dziech announces that the discussion of sexual harassment has entered a "new phase."

According to Dziech, the issue has moved beyond its feminist framework and taken on a life of its own: "Whatever the future of feminism, sexual harassment is a subject that now stands on its own." Although feminism brought the problem to public awareness, the larger public does not necessarily share the feminist assessment of the problem. Once separated from the issue of sex discrimination, harassment can be linked to other versions of socially undesirable sexuality.

As sexual harassment breaks loose from its feminist formulation, the crusade against it might even become, not just independent of feminism, but actually hostile to feminism. Dziech envisions one particularly chilling possibility: "Eventually the political right will embrace protections against sexual harassment as part of its agenda for a return to traditional values." A return to traditional values always implies women returning to our proper place. And then we might see not just the odd spectacle of a feminist accused of sexual harassment, but the more general prospect of feminists being so accused precisely *because* we are feminists. Once sexual harassment is detached from its feminist meaning, it becomes possible to imagine feminism itself accused as a form of sexual harassment.

Suggestions for Discussion

1. What does Gallop mean when she writes that her students "want a feminist education that feels like Women's Studies did to me in 1971"?
2. Why and how did students resist "the crime of having power over them"?
3. Discuss her analysis of Michael Crichton's novel *Disclosure.*

Suggestion for Writing

Write about a case of sexual harassment you have either heard or read about or experienced.

FICTION

JOHN CHEEVER

Expelled

John Cheever (1912–1982) was born in Massachusetts, where he was expelled from a prep school and thereby propelled into a literary career. He devoted himself primarily to writing novels and stories and was published often in *The New Yorker.* He won the Pulitzer Prize in 1979 for the collection *The Stories of John Cheever.* His best-known novels of suburban life are *The Wapshot Chronicle* (1957) and *The Wapshot Scandal* (1964). The prep school in the story "Expelled," which Cheever wrote at seventeen, exists to prepare the sons of the middle class for admission into acceptable Eastern colleges with little concern for aesthetic, moral, or intellectual values.

It didn't come all at once. It took a very long time. First I had a skirmish with the English department and then all the other departments. Pretty soon something had to be done. The first signs were cordialities on the part of the headmaster. He was never nice to anybody unless he was a football star, or hadn't paid his tuition, or was going to be expelled. That's how I knew.

He called me down to his office with the carved chairs arranged in a semicircle and the brocade curtains resting against the vacant windows. All about him were pictures of people who had got scholarships at Harvard. He asked me to sit down.

"Well, Charles," he said, "some of the teachers say you aren't getting very good marks."

"Yes," I said, "that's true." I didn't care about the marks.

"But Charles," he said, "you know the scholastic standard of this school is very high and we have to drop people when their work becomes unsatisfactory." I told him I knew that also. Then he said a lot of things about the traditions, and the elms, and the magnificent military heritage from our West Point founder.

It was very nice outside of his room. He had his window pushed open halfway and one could see the lawns pulling down to the road behind the trees and the bushes. The gravy-colored curtains were too heavy to move about in the wind, but some papers shifted around on his desk. In a little while I got up and walked out. He turned and started to work again. I went back to my next class.

The next day was very brilliant and the peach branches were full against the dry sky. I could hear people talking and a phonograph playing. The sounds came through the peach blossoms and crossed the room. I lay in bed and thought about a great many things. My dreams had been thick. I remembered two converging hills, some dry apple trees, and a broken blue egg cup. That is all I could remember.

I put on knickers and a soft sweater and headed toward school. My hands shook on the wheel. I was like that all over.

Through the cloudy trees I could see the protrusion of the new tower. It was going to be a beautiful new tower and it was going to cost a great deal of money. Some thought of buying new books for the library instead of putting up a tower, but no one would see the books. People would be able to see the tower five miles off when the leaves were off the trees. It would be done by fall.

When I went into the building the headmaster's secretary was standing in the corridor. She was a nice sort of person with brown funnels of hair furrowed about a round head. She smiled. I guess she must have known.

The Colonel

Every morning we went up into the black chapel. The brisk headmaster was there. Sometimes he had a member of the faculty with him. Sometimes it was a stranger.

He introduced the stranger, whose speech was always the same. In the spring life is like a baseball game. In the fall it is like football. That is what the speaker always said.

The hall is damp and ugly with skylights that rattle in the rain. The seats are hard and you have to hold a hymnbook in your lap. The hymnbook often slips off and that is embarrassing.

On Memorial Day they have the best speaker. They have a mayor or a Governor. Sometimes they have a Governor's second. There is very little preference.

The Governor will tell us what a magnificent country we have. He will tell us to beware of the Red menace. He will want to tell us that the goddam foreigners should have gone home a hell of a long time ago. That they should have stayed in their own goddam countries if they didn't like ours. He will not dare say this though.

If they have a mayor the speech will be longer. He will tell us that our country is beautiful and young and strong. That the War is over, but that if there is another war we must fight. He will tell us that war is a masculine trait that has brought present civilization to its fine condition. Then he will leave us and help stout women place lilacs on graves. He will tell them the same thing.

One Memorial Day they could not get a Governor or a mayor. There was a colonel in the same village who had been to war and who had a chest thick with medals. They asked him to speak. Of course he said he would like to speak.

He was a thin colonel with a soft nose that rested quietly on his face. He was nervous and pushed his wedding ring about his thin finger. When he was introduced he looked at the audience sitting in the uncomfortable chairs. There was silence and the dropping of hymnbooks like the water spouts in the aftermath of a heavy rain.

He spoke softly and quickly. He spoke of war and what he had seen. Then he had to stop. He stopped and looked at the boys. They were staring at their boots. He thought of the empty rooms in the other buildings. He thought of the rectangles of empty desks. He thought of the curtains on the stage and the four Windsor chairs behind him. Then he started to speak again.

He spoke as quickly as he could. He said war was bad. He said that there would never be another war. That he himself should stop it if he could. He swore. He looked at the young faces. They were all very clean. The boys' knees were crossed and their soft pants hung loosely. He thought of the empty desks and began to whimper.

The people sat very still. Some of them felt tight as though they wanted to giggle. Everybody looked serious as the clock struck. It was time for another class.

People began to talk about the colonel after lunch. They looked behind them. They were afraid he might hear them.

It took the school several weeks to get over all this. Nobody said anything, but the colonel was never asked again. If they could not get a Governor or a mayor they could get someone besides a colonel. They made sure of that.

Margaret Courtwright

Margaret Courtwright was very nice. She was slightly bald and pulled her pressed hair down across her forehead. People said that she was the best English teacher in this part of the country, and when boys came back from

Harvard they thanked her for the preparation she had given them. She did not like Edgar Guest, but she did like Carl Sandburg. She couldn't seem to understand the similarity. When I told her people laughed at Galsworthy she said that people used to laugh at Wordsworth. She did not believe people were still laughing at Wordsworth. That was what made her so nice.

She came from the West a long time ago. She taught school for so long that people ceased to consider her age. After having seen twenty-seven performances of "Hamlet" and after having taught it for sixteen years, she became a sort of immortal. Her interpretation was the one accepted on college-board papers. That helped everyone a great deal. No one had to get a new interpretation.

When she asked me for tea I sat in a walnut armchair with grapes carved on the head and traced and retraced the arms on the tea caddy. One time I read her one of my plays. She thought it was wonderful. She thought it was wonderful because she did not understand it and because it took two hours to read. When I had finished, she said, "You know that thing just took right hold of me. Really it just swept me right along. I think it's fine that you like to write. I once had a Japanese pupil who liked to write. He was an awfully nice chap until one summer he went down to Provincetown. When he came back he was saying that he could express a complete abstraction. Fancy...a complete abstraction. Well, I wouldn't hear of it and told him how absurd it all was and tried to start him off with Galsworthy again, but I guess he had gone just too far. In a little while he left for New York and then Paris. It was really too bad. One summer in Provincetown just ruined him. His marks fell down...he cut classes to go to symphony...." She went into the kitchen and got a tray of tarts.

The pastries were flaky and covered with a white coating that made them shine in the dead sunlight. I watched the red filling burst the thin shells and stain the triangles of bright damask. The tarts were good. I ate most of them.

She was afraid I would go the way of her Japanese pupil. She doubted anyone who disagreed with Heine on Shakespeare and Croce on expression.

One day she called me into her antiseptic office and spoke to me of reading Joyce. "You know, Charles," she said, "this sex reality can be quite as absurd as a hypercritical regard for such subjects. You know that, don't you? Of course, you do." Then she went out of the room. She had straight ankles and wore a gold band peppered with diamond chips on her ring finger. She seemed incapable of carrying the weight of the folds in her clothing. Her skirt was askew, either too long in front or hitching up on the side. Always one thing or the other.

When I left school she did not like it. She was afraid I might go too near Provincetown. She wished me good luck and moved the blotter back and forth on her desk. Then she returned to teaching "Hamlet."

Late in February Laura Driscoll got fired for telling her history pupils that Sacco and Vanzetti were innocent. In her farewell appearance the headmaster told everyone how sorry he was that she was going and made it all quite convincing. Then Laura stood up, told the headmaster that he was a damned liar, and waving her fan-spread fingers called the school a hell of a dump where everyone got into a rut.

Miss Courtwright sat closely in her chair and knew it was true. She didn't mind much. Professor Rogers with his anti-feminization movement bothered her a little, too. But she knew that she had been teaching school for a long time now and no movement was going to put her out of a job overnight—what with all the boys she had smuggled into Harvard and sixteen years of "Hamlet."

Laura Driscoll

History classes are always dead. This follows quite logically, for history is a dead subject. It has not the death of dead fruit or dead textiles or dead light. It has a different death. There is not the timeless quality of death about it. It is dead like scenery in the opera. It is on cracked canvas and the paint has faded and peeled and the lights are too bright. It is dead like old water in a zinc bathtub.

"We are going to study ancient history this year," the teacher will tell the pupils. "Yes, ancient history will be our field.

"Now of course, this class is not a class of children any longer. I expect the discipline to be the discipline of well-bred young people. We shall not have to waste any time on the scolding of younger children. No. We shall just be able to spend all our time on ancient history.

"Now about questions. I shall answer questions if they are important. If I do not think them important I shall not answer them, for the year is short, and we must cover a lot of ground in a short time. That is, if we all cooperate and behave and not ask too many questions we shall cover the subject and have enough time at the end of the year for review.

"You may be interested in the fact that a large percentage of this class was certified last year. I should like to have a larger number this year. Just think, boys: wouldn't it be fine if a very large number—a number larger than last year—was certified? Wouldn't that be fine? Well, there's no reason why we can't do it if we all cooperate and behave and don't ask too many questions.

"You must remember that I have twelve people to worry about and that you have only one. If each person will take care of his own work and pass in his notebook on time it will save me a lot of trouble. Time and trouble mean whether you get into college or not, and I want you all to get into college.

"If you will take care of your own little duties, doing what is assigned to you and doing it well, we shall all get along fine. You are a brilliant-looking group of young people, and I want to have you all certified. I want to get you into college with as little trouble as possible.

"Now about the books. . . ."

I do not know how long history classes have been like this. One time or another I suppose history was alive. That was before it died its horrible fly-dappled unquivering death.

Everyone seems to know that history is dead. No one is alarmed. The pupils and the teachers love dead history. They do not like it when it is alive. When Laura Driscoll dragged history into the classroom, squirming and smelling of something bitter, they fired Laura and strangled the history. It was too tumultuous. Too turbulent.

In history one's intellect is used for mechanical speculation on a probable century or background. One's memory is applied to a list of dead dates and names. When one begins to apply one's intellect to the mental scope of the period, to the emotional development of its inhabitants, one becomes dangerous. Laura Driscoll was terribly dangerous. That's why Laura was never a good history teacher.

She was not the first history teacher I had ever had. She is not the last I will have. But she is the only teacher I have ever had who could feel history with an emotional vibrance—or, if the person was too oblique, with a poetic understanding. She was five feet four inches tall, brown-haired, and bent-legged from horseback riding. All the boys thought Laura Driscoll was a swell teacher.

She was the only history teacher I have ever seen who was often ecstatical. She would stand by the boards and shout out her discoveries on the Egyptian cultures. She made the gargoylic churnings of Chartres in a heavy rain present an applicable meaning. She taught history as an interminable flood of events viewed through the distortion of our own immediacy. She taught history in the broad-handed rhythms of Hauptmann's drama, in the static melancholy of Egypt moving before its own shadow down the long sand, in the fluted symmetry of the Doric culture. She taught history as a hypothesis from which we could extract the evaluation of our own lives.

She was the only teacher who realized that, coming from the West, she had little business to be teaching these children of New England.

"I do not know what your reaction to the sea is," she would say. "For I have come from a land where there is no sea. My elements are the fields, the sun, the plastic cadence of the clouds and the cloudlessness. You have been brought up by the sea. You have been coached in the cadence of the breakers and the strength of the wind.

"My emotional viewpoints will differ from yours. Do not let me impose my perceptions upon you."

However, the college-board people didn't care about Chartres as long as you knew the date. They didn't care whether history was looked at from the mountains or the sea. Laura spent too much time on such trivia and all of her pupils didn't get into Harvard. In fact, very few of her pupils got into Harvard, and this didn't speak well for her.

While the other members of the faculty chattered over Hepplewhite legs and Duncan Phyfe embellishments, Laura was before five-handed Siva or the sexless compassion glorious in its faded polychrome. Laura didn't think much of America. Laura made this obvious and the faculty heard about it. The faculty all thought America was beautiful. They didn't like people to disagree.

However, the consummation did not occur until late in February. It was cold and clear and the snow was deep. Outside the windows there was the enormous roaring of broken ice. It was late in February that Laura Driscoll said Sacco and Vanzetti were undeserving of their treatment.

This got everyone all up in the air. Even the headmaster was disconcerted.

The faculty met.

The parents wrote letters.

Laura Driscoll was fired.

"Miss Driscoll," said the headmaster during her last chapel at the school, "has found it necessary to return to the West. In the few months that we have had her with us, she has been a staunch friend of the academy, a woman whom we all admire and love and who, we are sure, loves and admires the academy and its elms as we do. We are all sorry Miss Driscoll is leaving us...."

Then Laura got up, called him a damned liar, swore down the length of the platform and walked out of the building.

No one ever saw Laura Driscoll again. By the way everyone talked, no one wanted to. That was all late in February. By March the school was quiet again. The new history teacher taught dates. Everyone carefully forgot about Laura Driscoll.

"She was a nice girl," said the headmaster, "but she really wasn't made for teaching history.... No, she really wasn't a born history teacher."

Five Months Later

The spring of five months ago was the most beautiful spring I have ever lived in. The year before I had not known all about the trees and the heavy peach blossoms and the tea-colored brooks that shook down over the brown rocks. Five months ago it was spring and I was in school.

In school the white limbs beyond the study hall shook out a greenness, and the tennis courts became white and scalding. The air was empty and hard, and the vacant wind dragged shadows over the road. I knew all this only from the classrooms.

I knew about the trees from the window frames. I knew the rain only from the sounds on the roof. I was tired of seeing spring with walls and awnings to intercept the sweet sun and the hard fruit. I wanted to go outdoors and see the spring. I wanted to feel and taste the air and be among the shadows. That is perhaps why I left school.

In the spring I was glad to leave school. Everything outside was elegant and savage and fleshy. Everything inside was slow and cool and vacant. It seemed a shame to stay inside.

But in a little while the spring went. I was left outside and there was no spring. I did not want to go in again. I would not have gone in again for anything. I was sorry, but I was not sorry over the fact that I had gone out. I was sorry that the outside and the inside could not have been open to one another. I was sorry that there were roofs on the classrooms and trousers on the legs of the instructors to insulate their contacts. I was not sorry that I had left school. I was sorry that I left for the reasons that I did.

If I had left because I had to go to work or because I was sick it would not have been so bad. Leaving because you are angry and frustrated is different. It is not a good thing to do. It is bad for everyone.

Of course it was not the fault of the school. The headmaster and faculty were doing what they were supposed to do. It was just a preparatory school trying to please the colleges. A school that was doing everything the colleges asked it to do.

It was not the fault of the school at all. It was the fault of the system—the noneducational system, the college-preparatory system. That was what made the school so useless.

As a college-preparatory school it was a fine school. In five years they could make raw material look like college material. They could clothe it and breed it and make it say the right things when the colleges asked it to talk. That was its duty.

They weren't prepared to educate anybody. They were members of a college-preparatory system. No one around there wanted to be educated. No sir.

They presented the subjects the colleges required. They had math, English, history, languages, and music. They once had had an art department but it had been dropped. "We have enough to do," said the headmaster, "just to get all these people into college without trying to teach them art. Yes sir, we have quite enough to do as it is."

Of course there were literary appreciation and art appreciation and musical appreciation, but they didn't count for much. If you are young, there is very little in Thackeray that is parallel to your own world. Van Dyke's "Abbé Scaglia" and the fretwork of Mozart quartets are not for the focus of your ears and eyes. All the literature and art that holds a similarity to your life is forgotten. Some of it is even forbidden.

Our country is the best country in the world. We are swimming in prosperity and our President is the best president in the world. We have larger apples and better cotton and faster and more beautiful machines. This makes us the greatest country in the world. Unemployment is a myth. Dissatisfaction is a fable. In preparatory school America is beautiful. It is the gem of the ocean and it is too bad. It is bad because people believe it all. Because they become indifferent. Because they marry and reproduce and vote and they know nothing. Because the tempered newspaper keeps its eyes ceilingwards and does not see the dirty floor. Because all they know is the tempered newspaper.

But I will not say any more. I do not stand in a place where I can talk.

And now it is August. The orchards are stinking ripe. The tea-colored brooks run beneath the rocks. There is sediment on the stone and no wind in the willows. Everyone is preparing to go back to school. I have no school to go back to.

I am not sorry. I am not at all glad.

It is strange to be so very young and to have no place to report to at nine o'clock. That is what education has always been. It has been laced curtseys and perfumed punctualities.

But now it is nothing. It is symmetric with my life. I am lost in it. That is why I am not standing in a place where I can talk.

The school windows are being washed. The floors are thick with fresh oil.

Soon it will be time for the snow and the symphonies. It will be time for Brahms and the great dry winds.

Suggestions for Discussion

1. Why is Charles expelled from his school? How does he respond to his expulsion?
2. Explain the form the story takes as a series of short portraits. How do these portraits serve to express Charles's view of the school?
3. Compare Margaret Courtwright with Laura Driscoll. Which was the better teacher? Why?
4. How did the Colonel embarrass the school on Memorial Day? What is Charles's reaction to him? What does his reaction reveal about Charles?
5. Explain the function of the last section of the story.

Suggestion for Writing

What do you believe to be the primary purpose of education? Is it different from that described in the story? What do you expect from an education? Write an essay in which you explain your ideas.

GRACE PALEY

The Loudest Voice

Grace Paley (b. 1922) grew up in New York City and studied at Hunter College. Her works include *The Little Disturbances of Man* (1959), *Later the Same Day* (1985), and *New and Collected Poems* (1992). "The Loudest Voice" is a humorous look at the Christmas holidays in an ethnically diverse New York public school.

There is a certain place where dumb-waiters boom, doors slam, dishes crash; every window is a mother's mouth bidding the street shut up, go skate somewhere else, come home. My voice is the loudest.

There, my own mother is still as full of breathing as me and the grocer stands up to speak to her. "Mrs. Abramowitz," he says, "people should not be afraid of their children."

"Ah, Mr. Bialik," my mother replies, "if you say to her or her father 'Ssh,' they say, 'In the grave it will be quiet.' "

"From Coney Island to the cemetery," says my papa. "It's the same subway; it's the same fare."

I am right next to the pickle barrel. My pinky is making tiny whirlpools in the brine. I stop a moment to announce: "Campbell's Tomato Soup. Campbell's Vegetable Beef Soup. Campbell's S-c-otch Broth..."

"Be quiet," the grocer says, "the labels are coming off."

"Please, Shirley, be a little quiet," my mother begs me.

In that place the whole street groans: Be quiet! Be quiet! but steals from the happy chorus of my inside self not a tittle or a jot.

There, too, but just around the corner, is a red brick building that has been old for many years. Every morning the children stand before it in double lines which must be straight. They are not insulted. They are waiting anyway.

I am usually among them. I am, in fact, the first, since I begin with "A."

One cold morning the monitor tapped me on the shoulder. "Go to Room 409, Shirley Abramowitz," he said. I did as I was told. I went in a hurry up a down staircase to Room 409, which contained sixth-graders. I had to wait at the desk without wiggling until Mr. Hilton, their teacher, had time to speak.

After five minutes he said, "Shirley?"

"What?" I whispered.

He said, "My! My! Shirley Abramowitz! They told me you had a particularly loud, clear voice and read with lots of expression. Could that be true?"

"Oh yes," I whispered.

"In that case, don't be silly; I might very well be your teacher someday. Speak up, speak up."

"Yes," I shouted.

"More like it," he said. "Now, Shirley, can you put a ribbon in your hair or a bobby pin? It's too messy."

"Yes!" I bawled.

"Now, now, calm down." He turned to the class. "Children, not a sound. Open at page 39. Read till 52. When you finish, start again." He looked me over once more. "Now, Shirley, you know, I suppose, that Christmas is coming. We are preparing a beautiful play. Most of the parts have been given out. But I still need a child with a strong voice, lots of stamina. Do you know what stamina is? You do? Smart kid. You know, I heard you read 'The Lord is my shepherd' in Assembly yesterday. I was very impressed. Wonderful delivery. Mrs. Jordan, your teacher, speaks highly of you. Now listen to me, Shirley Abramowitz, if you want to take the part and be in the play, repeat after me, 'I swear to work harder than I ever did before.'"

I looked to heaven and said at once, "Oh, I swear." I kissed my pinky and looked at God.

"That is an actor's life, my dear," he explained. "Like a soldier's, never tardy or disobedient to his general, the director. Everything," he said, "absolutely everything will depend on you."

That afternoon, all over the building, children scraped and scrubbed the turkeys and the sheaves of corn off the schoolroom windows. Goodbye Thanksgiving. The next morning a monitor brought red paper and green paper from the office. We made new shapes and hung them on the walls and glued them to the doors.

The teachers became happier and happier. Their heads were ringing like the bells of childhood. My best friend Evie was prone to evil, but she did not get a single demerit for whispering. We learned "Holy Night" without an error. "How wonderful!" said Miss Glacé, the student teacher. "To think that some of you don't even speak the language!" We learned "Deck the Halls" and "Hark! The Herald Angels."... They weren't ashamed and we weren't embarrassed.

Oh, but when my mother heard about it all, she said to my father: "Misha, you don't know what's going on there. Cramer is the head of the Tickets Committee."

"Who?" asked my father. "Cramer? Oh yes, an active woman."

"Active? Active has to have a reason. Listen," she said sadly, "I'm surprised to see my neighbors making tra-la-la for Christmas."

My father couldn't think of what to say to that. Then he decided: "You're in America! Clara, you wanted to come here. In Palestine the Arabs would be eating you alive. Europe you had pogroms. Argentina is full of Indians. Here you got Christmas.... Some joke, ha?"

"Very funny, Misha. What is becoming of you? If we came to a new country a long time ago to run away from tyrants, and instead we fall into a creeping pogrom, that our children learn a lot of lies, so what's the joke? Ach, Misha, your idealism is going away."

"So is your sense of humor."

"That I never had, but idealism you had a lot of."

"I'm the same Misha Abramovitch, I didn't change an iota. Ask anyone."

"Only ask me," says my mama, may she rest in peace. "I got the answer."

Meanwhile the neighbors had to think of what to say too.

Marty's father said: "You know, he has a very important part, my boy."

"Mine also," said Mr. Sauerfeld.

"Not my boy!" said Mrs. Klieg. "I said to him no. The answer is no. When I say no! I mean no!"

The rabbi's wife said, "It's disgusting!" But no one listened to her. Under the narrow sky of God's great wisdom she wore a strawberry-blond wig.

Every day was noisy and full of experience. I was Right-hand Man. Mr. Hilton said: "How could I get along without you, Shirley?"

He said: "Your mother and father ought to get down on their knees every night and thank God for giving them a child like you."

He also said: "You're absolutely a pleasure to work with, my dear, dear child."

Sometimes he said: "For God's sakes, what did I do with the script? Shirley! Shirley! Find it."

Then I answered quietly: "Here it is, Mr. Hilton."

Once in a while, when he was very tired, he would cry out: "Shirley, I'm just tired of screaming at those kids. Will you tell Ira Pushkov not to come in till Lester points to that star the second time?"

Then I roared: "Ira Pushkov, what's the matter with you? Dope! Mr. Hilton told you five times already, don't come in till Lester points to that star the second time."

"Ach, Clara," my father asked, "what does she do there till six o'clock she can't even put the plates on the table?"

"Christmas," said my mother coldly.

"Ho! Ho!" my father said. "Christmas. What's the harm? After all, history teaches everyone. We learn from reading this is a holiday from pagan times also, candles, lights, even Chanukah. So we learn it's not altogether

Christian. So if they think it's a private holiday, they're only ignorant, not patriotic. What belongs to history, belongs to all men. You want to go back to the Middle Ages? Is it better to shave your head with a secondhand razor? Does it hurt Shirley to learn to speak up? It does not. So maybe someday she won't live between the kitchen and the shop. She's not a fool."

I thank you, Papa, for your kindness. It is true about me to this day. I am foolish but I am not a fool.

That night my father kissed me and said with great interest in my career, "Shirley, tomorrow's your big day. Congrats."

"Save it," my mother said. Then she shut all the windows in order to prevent tonsillitis.

In the morning it snowed. On the street corner a tree had been decorated for us by a kind city administration. In order to miss its chilly shadow our neighbors walked three blocks east to buy a loaf of bread. The butcher pulled down black window shades to keep the colored lights from shining on his chickens. Oh, not me. On the way to school, with both my hands I tossed it a kiss of tolerance. Poor thing, it was a stranger in Egypt.

I walked straight into the auditorium past the staring children. "Go ahead, Shirley!" said the monitors. Four boys, big for their age, had already started work as propmen and stagehands.

Mr. Hilton was very nervous. He was not even happy. Whatever he started to say ended in a sideward look of sadness. He sat slumped in the middle of the first row and asked me to help Miss Glacé. I did this, although she thought my voice too resonant and said, "Show-off!"

Parents began to arrive long before we were ready. They wanted to make a good impression. From among the yards of drapes I peeked out at the audience. I saw my embarrassed mother.

Ira, Lester, and Meyer were pasted to their beards by Miss Glacé. She almost forgot to thread the star on its wire, but I reminded her. I coughed a few times to clear my throat. Miss Glacé looked around and saw that everyone was in costume and on line waiting to play his part. She whispered, "All right…" Then:

Jackie Sauerfeld, the prettiest boy in first grade, parted the curtains with his skinny elbow and in a high voice sang out:

"Parents dear
We are here
To make a Christmas play in time.
It we give
In narrative
And illustrate with pantomime."

He disappeared.

My voice burst immediately from the wings to the great shock of Ira, Lester, and Meyer, who were waiting for it but were surprised all the same.

"I remember, I remember, the house where I was born..."

Miss Glacé yanked the curtain open and there it was, the house—an old hayloft, where Celia Kornbluh lay in the straw with Cindy Lou, her favorite doll. Ira, Lester, and Meyer moved slowly from the wings toward her, sometimes pointing to a moving star and sometimes ahead to Cindy Lou.

It was a long story and it was a sad story. I carefully pronounced all the words about my lonesome childhood, while little Eddie Braunstein wandered upstage and down with his shepherd's stick, looking for sheep. I brought up lonesomeness again, and not being understood at all except by some women everybody hated. Eddie was too small for that and Marty Groff took his place, wearing his father's prayer shawl. I announced twelve friends, and half the boys in the fourth grade gathered round Marty, who stood on an orange crate while my voice harangued. Sorrowful and loud, I declaimed about love and God and Man, but because of the terrible deceit of Abie Stock we came suddenly to a famous moment. Marty, whose remembering tongue I was, waited at the foot of the cross. He stared desperately at the audience. I groaned, "My God, my God why hast thou forsaken me?" The soldiers who were sheiks grabbed poor Marty to pin him up to die, but he wrenched free, turned again to the audience, and spread his arms aloft to show despair and the end. I murmured at the top of my voice, "The rest is silence, but as everyone in this room, in this city—in this world—now knows, I shall have life eternal."

That night Mrs. Kornbluh visited our kitchen for a glass of tea.

"How's the virgin?" asked my father with a look of concern.

"For a man with a daughter, you got a fresh mouth, Abramovitch."

"Here," said my father kindly, "have some lemon, it'll sweeten your disposition."

They debated a little in Yiddish, then fell in a puddle of Russian and Polish. What I understood next was my father, who said, "Still and all, it was certainly a beautiful affair, you have to admit, introducing us to the beliefs of a different culture."

"Well, yes," said Mrs. Kornbluh. "The only thing...you know Charlie Turner—that cute boy in Celia's class—a couple others? They got very small parts or no part at all. In very bad taste, it seemed to me. After all, it's their religion."

"Ach," explained my mother, "what could Mr. Hilton do? They got very small voices; after all, why should they holler? The English language they know from the beginning by heart. They're blond like angels. You think it's so important they should get in the play? Christmas...the whole piece of goods...they own it."

I listened and listened until I couldn't listen any more. Too sleepy, I climbed out of bed and kneeled. I made a little church of my hands and said, "Hear, O Israel..." Then I called out in Yiddish, "Please, good night, good night. Ssh." My father said, "Ssh yourself," and slammed the kitchen door.

I was happy. I fell asleep at once. I had prayed for everybody: my talking family, cousins far away, passersby, and all the lonesome Christians. I expected to be heard. My voice was certainly the loudest.

Suggestions for Discussion

1. Explain the significance of the title of the story.
2. Discuss Shirley's opportunity, her predicament, and the resolution of the story.
3. Discuss Paley's humorous, yet respectful interweaving of Jewish tradition and sensibility with the public school celebration of the Christmas season.

Suggestions for Writing

1. Write about several examples of Paley's humor.
2. Describe a situation in which you or someone you know encountered pressure to perform in public.

POETRY

LANGSTON HUGHES

Theme for English B

Langston Hughes (1902–1962), a prominent black poet, was born in Missouri and educated at Lincoln University in Pennsylvania. Often using dialect and jazz rhythms, his work expresses the concerns and feelings of American blacks. His collections of poetry include *The Weary Blues* (1926) and *Shakespeare in Harlem* (1940); his novels include *Not Without Laughter* (1930) and *The Best of Simple* (1950). In "Theme for English B" he clearly expresses the chasm between the races that exists even in the college classroom.

The instructor said,

Go home and write
a page tonight.
And let that page come out of you—
Then, it will be true.

I wonder if it's that simple?
I am twenty-two, colored, born in Winston-Salem.
I went to school there, then Durham, then here
to this college on the hill above Harlem.
I am the only colored student in my class.
The steps from the hill lead down into Harlem,
through a park, then I cross St. Nicholas,
Eighth Avenue, Seventh, and I come to the Y,
the Harlem Branch Y, where I take the elevator
up to my room, sit down, and write this page:

It's not easy to know what is true for you or me
at twenty-two, my age. But I guess I'm what
I feel and see and hear, Harlem, I hear you:
hear you, hear me—we two—you, me, talk on this page.
(I hear New York, too.) Me—who?

Well, I like to eat, sleep, drink, and be in love.
I like to work, read, learn, and understand life.
I like a pipe for a Christmas present,
or records—Bessie, bop, or Bach.
I guess being colored doesn't make me *not* like
the same things other folks like who are other races.
So will my page be colored that I write?
Being me, it will not be white.

But it will be
a part of you, instructor.
You are white—
yet a part of me, as I am a part of you.
That's American.
Sometimes perhaps you don't want to be a part of me.
Nor do I often want to be a part of you.
But we are, that's true!
As I learn from you,
I guess you learn from me—
Although you're older—and white—
and somewhat more free.

This is my page for English B.

Suggestions for Discussion

1. With what details does Hughes convey a strong sense of identity?
2. How does he reveal his feelings about composition, learning, Harlem, his racial background, and his instructor?

Suggestion for Writing

Write an essay in which you attempt to convey some of your feelings about your own background, your likes and dislikes. Try to focus on details as Hughes has done in his poem.

LAWRENCE RAAB

The Shakespeare Lesson

Lawrence Raab (b. 1949) is professor of English at Williams College. His collections of poetry include *Other Children* (1987) and *What We Don't Know About Each Other* (1993). "The Shakespeare Lesson," a poem dedicated to his colleague at Williams, John Reichert, explores a classroom discussion of the play *Antony and Cleopatra.*

For John Reichert

None of the students liked Cleopatra.
She was selfish, they said, and Antony
was a wimp—because he wouldn't decide
how he felt, because he ran away,
and couldn't even kill himself.

They were so impatient
with the languors of Egypt, the perfume
and the barges, those fond little games
he felt so close to.
Is there anyone you admire? he asked,

himself half in love with Cleopatra.
Caesar, one student answered,
because Caesar knew what he wanted.
The sun caught in the smudged-up
panes of glass; he fiddled with the lectern.

Could he tell them Caesar
was the wrong answer?
Antony, after all, had betrayed the man
his soldiers needed him to be.
And Cleopatra was foolish, unpredictable...

Could he ask them not to feel
so certain about what they felt?
He said it was complicated.
Why does it have to be complicated?
someone asked. Is that always good?

And shouldn't they have talked,
 figured out what they meant
to each other? Why does everybody
 always have to die?
Let's look at the last scene, he said,

and saw a stage crowded with bodies,
 saw her body displayed among the others.
How does it make you feel?
 he asked, although he did not know anymore
what he wanted them to say.

Suggestions for Discussion

1. What problems does the professor have teaching Shakespeare's play?
2. Discuss Raab's resolution of the tension and anxiety in the class.

Suggestions for Writing

1. Describe a class of your own in which students and teacher did not seem to communicate effectively. Analyze the problems and tell how professor and students handled the situation.
2. Describe a class in which you, the other students, and the professor worked together with unusual effectiveness.

THEODORE ROETHKE

Elegy for Jane: My Student, Thrown by a Horse

Theodore Roethke (1908–1963) was born in Michigan and educated at the University of Michigan and Harvard. His poetry celebrated human relationships, the land, and all growing things with wit, an inventive verse form, and, at times, an almost surrealist language. He taught poetry writing for many years at the University of Washington in Seattle, and he won the Pulitzer Prize for *The Waking* (1953). His other collections include *The Lost Son and Other Poems* (1949) and

The Far Field (1964). Essays and lectures are collected in *The Poet and His Craft* (1965). "Elegy for Jane" is a tender poem expressing grief at the death of one of his students. Like many other modern poems on death, it achieves its force through wit and understatement.

I remember the neckcurls, limp and damp as tendrils;
And her quick look, a sidelong pickerel smile;
And how, once startled into talk, the light syllables leaped for her,
And she balanced in the delight of her thought,
A wren, happy, tail into the wind,
Her song trembling the twigs and small branches.
The shade sang with her;
The leaves, their whispers turned to kissing;
And the mold sang in the bleached valleys under the rose.

Oh, when she was sad, she cast herself down into such a pure depth,
Even a father could not find her:
Scraping her cheek against straw;
Stirring the clearest water.

My sparrow, you are not here,
Waiting like a fern, making a spiny shadow.
The sides of wet stones cannot console me,
Nor the moss, wound with the last light.

If only I could nudge you from this sleep,
My maimed darling, my skittery pigeon.
Over this damp grave I speak the words of my love:
I, with no rights in this matter,
Neither father nor lover.

Suggestions for Discussion

1. What is the relation of the first two stanzas to the rest of the poem?
2. How does the poet remember his dead student? What is the effect of the details he recalls?
3. Why does he call his dead student "my maimed darling" or "my skittery pigeon"? How would you describe this language?
4. Discuss the feelings that the poem expresses. How do you relate these feelings to the poet's language?
5. Explain the last two lines of the poem.

Suggestion for Writing

This poem expresses the feelings of a teacher for a dead student. Does this expression of feeling come as a surprise to you? Write an essay in which you discuss, from your experience, the kinds of relationships that exist between teachers and students. Relate your comments to the feelings expressed in this poem.

MARIANNE MOORE

The Student

Marianne Moore (1887–1972) was born in Missouri. She graduated from Bryn Mawr College, and went on to teach at an Indian school, work in the New York Public Library, and edit *The Dial* (1925–1929). Her early poems were published in 1921, her *Collected Poems* in 1951. She also wrote *Predilections* (1955), a volume of critical essays, a poetic translation of La Fontaine's *Fables* (1954), and a collection of poetry, *Tell Me, Tell Me* (1967). The following poem, taken from *What Are Years?* (1941, 1969), analyzes and praises the student.

"In America," began
the lecturer, "everyone must have a
degree. The French do not think that
all can have it, they don't say everyone
   must go to college." We
do incline to feel
   that although it may be unnecessary

to know fifteen languages,
one degree is not too much. With us, a
school—like the singing tree of which
the leaves were mouths singing in concert—is
   both a tree of knowledge
and of liberty,—
   seen in the unanimity of college

mottoes, *lux et veritas,*
Christo et ecclesiae, sapiet
felici. It may be that we

have not knowledge, just opinions, that we
 are undergraduates,
not students; we know
 we have been told with smiles, by expatriates

of whom we had asked "When will
your experiment be finished?" "Science
is never finished." Secluded
from domestic strife, Jack Bookworm led a
 college life, says Goldsmith;
and here also as
 in France or Oxford, study is beset with

dangers,—with bookworms, mildews,
and complaisancies. But someone in New
England has known enough to say
the student is patience personified,
 is a variety
of hero, "patient
 of neglect and of reproach,"—who can "hold by

himself." You can't beat hens to
make them lay. Wolf's wool is the best of wool,
but it cannot be sheared because
the wolf will not comply. With knowledge as
 with the wolf's surliness,
the student studies
 voluntarily refusing to be less

than individual. He
"gives his opinion and then rests on it";
he renders service when there is
no reward, and is too reclusive for
 some things to seem to touch
him, not because he
 has no feeling but because he has so much.

Suggestions for Discussion

1. What significance do you find in quotations from Einstein, lines 23–24, and Emerson, lines 34–35?
2. Finally, what values does Moore find in the student?

Suggestion for Writing

Define the life of the student in your college.

RICHARD WILBUR

A Finished Man

The distinguished American poet Richard Wilbur served as Poet Laureate of the United States in 1987. Winner of the National Book Award, he also won the Pulitzer Prize for Poetry in 1957 and 1989. In addition to his translations of Molière's plays, Wilbur has published such collections of his own poetry as *The Poems of Richard Wilbur* (1987) and *New and Collected Poems* (1988).

Of the four louts who threw him off the dock,
Three are now dead, and so more faintly mock
The way he choked and splashed and was afraid.
His memory of the fourth begins to fade.

It was himself whom he could not forgive;
Yet it has been a comfort to outlive
That woman, stunned by his appalling gaffe,
Who with a napkin half suppressed her laugh,

Or that gray colleague, surely gone by now,
Who, turning toward the window, raised his brow,
Embarrassed to have caught him in a lie.
All witness darkens, eye by dimming eye.

Thus he can walk today with heart at ease
Through the old quad, escorted by trustees,
To dedicate the monumental gym
A grateful college means to name for him.

Seated, he feels the warm sun sculpt his cheek
As the young president gets up to speak.
If the dead die, if he can but forget,
If money talks, he may be perfect yet.

Suggestions for Discussion

1. What thoughts run through the mind of the distinguished alumnus?
2. What values does he represent? Are they all attractive?

Suggestion for Writing

Describe a college ceremony you have attended. Speculate on the motives of various participants, including yourself.

The Examined Life: Personal Values

Beyond this—that the interior landscape is a metaphorical representation of the exterior landscape, that the truth reveals itself most fully not in dogma but in the paradox, irony, and contradictions that distinguish compelling narratives—beyond this there are only failures of imagination: reductionism in science; fundamentalism in religion; fascism in politics.

—BARRY LOPEZ, "Landscape and Narrative"

I who am blind can give one hint to those who see—one admonition to those who would make full use of the gift of sight: Use your eyes as if tomorrow you would be stricken blind. And the same method can be applied to the other senses. Hear the music of voices, the song of a bird, the mighty strains of an orchestra, as if you would be stricken deaf tomorrow. Touch each object you want to touch as if tomorrow your tactile sense would fail. Smell the perfume of flowers, taste with relish each morsel, as if tomorrow you could never smell and taste again. Make the most of every sense; glory in all the facts of pleasure and beauty which the world reveals to you through the several means of contact which Nature provides. But of all the senses, I am sure that sight must be the most delightful.

—HELEN KELLER, "Three Days to See"

PERSONAL REMINISCENCES

NANCY MAIRS

On Being a Cripple

Nancy Mairs (b. 1943) was born in California and received degrees from Wheaton College and the University of Arizona, where she earned her M.F.A. and Ph.D. Her professional career has been spent as an editor, professor, and writer. She writes in a variety of genres, including essays, poetry, autobiography, and fiction. Her books include *In All the Rooms of the Yellow House* (1984), for which she received the Poetry Award from the Western States Arts Foundation, *Plaintext* (1986), *Remembering the Bone House* (1989), *Carnal Acts* (1990), *Ordinary Time* (1993), and *Voice Lessons* (1994). In the selection that follows she shares the experience of dealing with a chronic, crippling disease in the midst of the demanding richness of personal, family, and professional life.

To escape is nothing. Not to escape is nothing.

—LOUISE BOGAN

The other day I was thinking of writing an essay on being a cripple. I was thinking hard in one of the stalls of the women's room in my office building, as I was shoving my shirt into my jeans and tugging up my zipper. Preoccupied, I flushed, picked up my book bag, took my cane down from the hook, and unlatched the door. So many movements unbalanced me, and as I pulled the door open I fell over backward, landing fully clothed on the toilet seat with my legs splayed in front me: the old beetle-on-its-back routine. Saturday afternoon, the building deserted, I was free to laugh aloud as I wriggled back to my feet, my voice bouncing off the yellowish tiles from all directions. Had anyone been there with me, I'd have been still and faint and hot with chagrin. I decided that it was high time to write the essay.

First, the matter of semantics. I am a cripple. I choose this word to name me. I choose from among several possibilities, the most common of which are "handicapped" and "disabled." I made the choice a number of years ago, without thinking, unaware of my motives for doing so. Even now, I'm not sure what those motives are, but I recognize that they are complex and not entirely flattering. People—crippled or not—wince at the word "cripple," as they do not at "handicapped" or "disabled." Perhaps I want them to wince. I want them to see me as a tough customer, one to whom the fates/gods/viruses have not been kind, but who can face the brutal truth of her existence squarely. As a cripple, I swagger.

But, to be fair to myself, a certain amount of honesty underlies my choice. "Cripple" seems to me a clean word, straightforward and precise. It has an honorable history, having made its first appearance in the Lindisfarne Gospel in the tenth century. As a lover of words, I like the accuracy with which it describes my condition: I have lost the full use of my limbs. "Disabled," by contrast, suggests an incapacity, physical or mental. And I certainly don't like "handicapped," which implies that I have deliberately been put at a disadvantage, by whom I can't imagine (my God is not a Handicapper General), in order to equalize chances in the great race of life. These words seem to me to be moving away from my condition, to be widening the gap between word and reality. Most remote is the recently coined euphemism "differently abled," which partakes of the same semantic hopefulness that transformed countries from "undeveloped" to "underdeveloped," then to "less developed," and finally to "developing" nations. People have continued to starve in those countries during the shift. Some realities do not obey the dictates of language.

Mine is one of them. Whatever you call me, I remain crippled. But I don't care what you call me, so long as it isn't "differently abled," which strikes me as pure verbal garbage designed, by its ability to describe anyone, to describe no one. I subscribe to George Orwell's thesis that "the slovenliness of our language makes it easier for us to have foolish thoughts." And I refuse to participate in the degeneration of the language to the extent that I deny that I have lost anything in the course of this calamitous disease; I refuse to pretend that the only differences between you and me are the various ordinary ones that distinguish any one person from another. But call me "disabled" or "handicapped" if you like. I have long since grown accustomed to them; and if they are vague, at least they hint at the truth. Moreover, I use them myself. Society is no readier to accept crippledness than to accept death, war, sex, sweat, or wrinkles. I would never refer to another person as a cripple. It is the word I use to name only myself.

I haven't always been crippled, a fact for which I am soundly grateful. To be whole of limb is, I know from experience, infinitely more pleasant and useful than to be crippled; and if that knowledge leaves me open to bitterness at my loss, the physical soundness I once enjoyed (though I did not enjoy it half enough) is well worth the occasional stab of regret. Though never any good at sports, I was a normally active child and young adult. I climbed trees, played hopscotch, jumped rope, skated, swam, rode my bicycle, sailed. I despised team sports, spending some of the wretchedest afternoons of my life sweaty and humiliated, behind a field-hockey stick and under a basketball hoop. I tramped alone for miles along the bridle paths that webbed the woods behind the house I grew up in. I swayed through countless dim hours in the arms of one man or another under the scattered shot of light from mirrored balls, and gyrated through countless more as Tab Hunter and Johnny Mathis gave way to the Rolling Stones, Creedence Clearwater Revival, Cream. I walked down the aisle. I pushed baby carriages, changed tires in the rain, marched for peace.

When I was twenty-eight I started to trip and drop things. What at first seemed my natural clumsiness soon became too pronounced to shrug off. I consulted a neurologist, who told me that I had a brain tumor. A battery of tests, increasingly disagreeable, revealed no tumor. About a year and a half later I developed a blurred spot in one eye. I had, at last, the episodes "disseminated in space and time" requisite for a diagnosis: multiple sclerosis. I have never been sorry for the doctor's initial misdiagnosis, however. For almost a week, until the negative results of the tests were in, I thought that I was going to die right away. Every day for the past nearly ten years, then, has been a kind of gift. I accept all gifts.

Multiple sclerosis is a chronic degenerative disease of the central nervous system, in which the myelin that sheathes the nerves is somehow eaten away and scar tissue forms in its place, interrupting the nerves' signals. During its course, which is unpredictable and uncontrollable, one may lose vision, hearing, speech, the ability to walk, control of bladder and/or bowels, strength in any or all extremities, sensitivity to touch, vibration, and/or pain, potency, coordination of movements—the list of possibilities is lengthy and yes, horrifying. One may also lose one's sense of humor. That's the easiest to lose and the hardest to survive without.

In the past ten years, I have sustained some of these losses. Characteristic of MS are sudden attacks, called exacerbations, followed by remissions, and these I have not had. Instead, my disease has been slowly progressive. My left leg is now so weak that I walk with the aid of a brace and a cane; and for distances I use an Amigo, a variation on the electric wheelchair that looks rather like an electrified kiddie car. I no longer have much use of my left hand. Now my right side is weakening as well. I still have the blurred spot in my right eye. Overall, though, I've been lucky so far. My world has, of necessity, been circumscribed by my losses, but the terrain left me has been ample enough for me to continue many of the activities that absorb me: writing, teaching, raising children and cats and plants and snakes, reading, speaking publicly about MS and depression, even playing bridge with people patient and honorable enough to let me scatter cards every which way without sneaking a peek.

Lest I begin to sound like Pollyanna, however, let me say that I don't like having MS. I hate it. My life holds realities—harsh ones, some of them—that no right-minded human being ought to accept without grumbling. One of them is fatigue. I know of no one with MS who does not complain of bone-weariness; in a disease that presents an astonishing variety of symptoms, fatigue seems to be a common factor. I wake up in the morning feeling the way most people do at the end of a bad day, and I take it from there. As a result, I spend a lot of time *in extremis* and, impatient with limitation, I tend to ignore my fatigue until my body breaks down in some way and forces rest. Then I miss picnics, dinner parties, poetry readings, the brief visits of old friends from out of town. The offspring of a puritanical tradition of exceptional venerability, I cannot view these lapses without shame. My life often seems a series of small failures to do as I ought.

I lead, on the whole, an ordinary life, probably rather like the one I would have led had I not had MS. I am lucky that my predilections were already solitary, sedentary, and bookish—unlike the world-famous French cellist I have read about, or the young woman I talked with one long afternoon who wanted only to be a jockey. I had just begun graduate school when I found out something was wrong with me, and I have remained, interminably, a graduate student. Perhaps I would not have if I'd thought I had the stamina to return to a full-time job as a technical editor; but I've enjoyed my studies.

In addition to studying, I teach writing courses. I also teach medical students how to give neurological examinations. I pick up freelance editing jobs here and there. I have raised a foster son and sent him into the world, where he has made me two grandbabies, and I am still escorting my daughter and son through adolescence. I go to Mass every Saturday. I am a superb, if messy, cook. I am also an enthusiastic laundress, capable of sorting a hamper full of clothes into five subtly differentiated piles, but a terrible housekeeper. I can do italic writing and, in an emergency, bathe an oil-soaked cat. I play a fiendish game of Scrabble. When I have the time and the money, I like to sit on my front steps with my husband, drinking Amaretto and smoking a cigar, as we imagine our counterparts in Leningrad and make sure that the sun gets down once more behind the sharp childish scrawl of the Tucson Mountains.

This lively plenty has its bleak complement, of course, in all the things I can no longer do. I will never run again, except in dreams, and one day I may have to write that I will never walk again. I like to go camping, but I can't follow George and the children along the trails that wander out of a campsite through the desert or into the mountains. In fact, even on the level I've learned never to check the weather or try to hold a coherent conversation: I need all my attention for my wayward feet. Of late, I have begun to catch myself wondering how people can propel themselves without canes.

With only one usable hand, I have to select my clothing with care not so much for style as for ease of ingress and egress, and even so, dressing can be laborious. I can no longer do fine stitchery, pick up babies, play the piano, braid my hair. I am immobilized by acute attacks of depression, which may or may not be physiologically related to MS but are certainly its logical concomitant.

These two elements, the plenty and the privation, are never pure, nor are the delight and wretchedness that accompany them. Almost every pickle that I get into as a result of my weakness and clumsiness—and I get into plenty—is funny as well as maddening and sometimes painful. I recall one May afternoon when a friend and I were going out for a drink after finishing up at school. As we were climbing into opposite sides of my car, chatting, I tripped and fell, flat and hard, onto the asphalt parking lot, my abrupt departure interrupting him in mid-sentence. "Where'd you go?" he called as he came around the back of the car to find me hauling myself up by the door frame. "Are you all right?" Yes, I told him, I was fine, just a bit rattly, and we drove off to find a shady patio and some beer. When I got home an hour or so later, my daughter greeted me with "What have you done to yourself?" I looked down. One elbow of my white turtleneck with the green froggies, one knee of my white trousers, one white kneesock were blood-soaked. We peeled off the clothes and inspected the damage, which was nasty enough but not alarming. That part wasn't funny: The abrasions took a long time to heal, and one got a little infected. Even so, when I think of my friend talking earnestly, suddenly, to the hot thin air while I dropped from his view as though through a trap door, I find the image as silly as something from a Marx Brothers movie.

I may find it easier than other cripples to amuse myself because I live propped by the acceptance and the assistance and, sometimes, the amusement of those around me. Grocery clerks tear my checks out of my checkbook for me, and sales clerks find chairs to put into dressing rooms when I want to try on clothes. The people I work with make sure I teach at times when I am least likely to be fatigued, in places I can get to, with the materials I need. My students, with one anonymous exception (in an end-of-the-semester evaluation) have been unperturbed by my disability. Some even like it. One was immensely cheered by the information that I paint my own fingernails; she decided, she told me, that if I could go to such trouble over fine details, she could keep on writing essays. I suppose I became some sort of bright-fingered muse. She wrote good essays, too.

The most important struts in the framework of my existence, of course, are my husband and children. Dismayingly few marriages survive the MS test, and why should they? Most twenty-two- and nineteen-year-olds, like George and me, can vow in clear conscience, after a childhood of chickenpox and summer colds, to keep one another in sickness and in health so long as they both shall live. Not many are equipped for catastrophe: the dismay, the depression, the extra work, the boredom that a degenerative disease can insinuate into a relationship. And our society, with its emphasis on fun and its association of fun with physical performance, offers little encouragement for a whole spouse to stay with a crippled partner. Children experience similar stresses when faced with a crippled parent, and they are more helpless, since parents and children can't usually get divorced. They hate, of course, to be different from their peers, and the child whose mother is tacking down the aisle of a school auditorium packed with proud parents like a Cape Cod dinghy in a stiff breeze jolly well stands out in a crowd. Deprived of legal divorce, the child can at least deny the mother's disability, even her existence, forgetting to tell her about recitals and PTA meetings, refusing to accompany her to stores or church or the movies, never inviting friends to the house. Many do.

But I've been limping along for ten years now, and so far George and the children are still at my left elbow, holding tight. Anne and Matthew vacuum floors and dust furniture and haul trash and rake up dog droppings and button my cuffs and bake lasagne and Toll House cookies with just enough grumbling so I know that they don't have brain fever. And far from hiding me, they're forever dragging me by racks of fancy clothes or through teeming school corridors, or welcoming gaggles of friends while I'm wandering through the house in Anne's filmy pink babydoll pajamas. George generally calls before he brings someone home, but he does just as many dumb thankless chores as the children. And they all yell at me, laugh at some of my jokes, write me funny letters when we're apart—in short, treat me as an ordinary human being for whom they have some use. I think they like me. Unless they're faking....

Faking. There's the rub. Tugging at the fringes of my consciousness always is the terror that people are kind to me only because I'm a cripple. My mother almost shattered me once, with that instinct mothers have—blind, I think, in this case, but unerring nonetheless—for striking blows along the fault-lines of their children's hearts, by telling me, in an attack on my selfishness, "We all have to make allowances for you, of course, because of the way you are." From the distance of a couple of years, I have to admit that I haven't any idea just what she meant, and I'm not sure that she knew either. She was awfully angry. But at the time, as the words thudded home, I felt my worst fear, suddenly realized. I could bear being called selfish: I am. But I couldn't bear the corroboration that those around me were doing in fact what I'd always suspected them of doing, professing fondness while silently putting up with me because of the way I am. A cripple. I've been a little cracked ever since.

Along with this fear that people are secretly accepting shoddy goods comes a relentless pressure to please—to prove myself worth the burdens I impose, I guess, or to build a substantial account of goodwill against which I may write drafts in times of need. Part of the pressure arises from social expectations. In our society, anyone who deviates from the norm had better find some way to compensate. Like fat people, who are expected to be jolly, cripples must bear their lot meekly and cheerfully. A grumpy cripple isn't playing by the rules. And much of the pressure is self-generated. Early on I vowed that, if I had to have MS, by God I was going to do it well. This is a class act, ladies and gentlemen. No tears, no recriminations, no faint-heartedness.

One way and another, then, I wind up feeling like Tiny Tim, peering over the edge of the table at the Christmas goose, waving my crutch, piping down God's blessing on us all. Only sometimes I don't want to play Tiny Tim. I'd rather be Caliban, a most scurvy monster. Fortunately, at home no one much cares whether I'm a good cripple or a bad cripple as long as I make vichyssoise with fair regularity. One evening several years ago, Anne was reading at the dining-room table while I cooked dinner. As I opened a can of tomatoes, the can slipped in my left hand and juice spattered me and the counter with bloody spots. Fatigued and infuriated, I bellowed, "I'm so sick of being crippled!" Anne glanced at me over the top of her book. "There now," she said, "do you feel better?" "Yes," I said, "yes, I do." She went back to her reading. I felt better. That's about all the attention my scurviness ever gets.

Because I hate being crippled, I sometimes hate myself for being a cripple. Over the years I have come to expect—even accept—attacks of violent self-loathing. Luckily, in general our society no longer connects deformity and disease directly with evil (though a charismatic once told me that I have MS because a devil is in me) and so I'm allowed to move largely at will, even among small children. But I'm not sure that this revision of attitude has been particularly helpful. Physical imperfection, even freed of moral disapprobation, still defies and violates the ideal, especially for women, whose confinement in their bodies as objects of desire is far from over. Each age, of course, has its ideal, and I doubt that ours is any better or worse than any other. Today's ideal woman, who lives on the glossy pages of dozens of magazines, seems to be between the ages of eighteen and twenty-five; her hair has body, her teeth flash white, her breath smells minty, her underarms are dry; she has a career but is still a fabulous cook, especially of meals that take less than twenty minutes to prepare; she does not ordinarily appear to have a husband or children; she is trim and deeply tanned; she jogs, swims, plays tennis, rides a bicycle, sails, but does not bowl; she travels widely, even to out-of-the-way places like Finland and Samoa, always in the company of the ideal man, who possesses a nearly identical set of characteristics. There are a few exceptions. Though usually white and often blonde, she may be black, Hispanic, Asian, or Native American, so long as she is unusually sleek. She may be old, provided she is selling a laxative or is Lauren Bacall. If she is selling a detergent, she may be married and have a flock of strikingly messy children. But she is never a cripple.

Like many women I know, I have always had an uneasy relationship with my body. I was not a popular child, largely, I think now, because I was peculiar: intelligent, intense, moody, shy, given to unexpected actions and inexplicable notions and emotions. But as I entered adolescence, I believed myself unpopular because I was homely: my breasts too flat, my mouth too wide, my hips too narrow, my clothing never quite right in fit or style. I was not, in fact, particularly ugly, old photographs inform me, though I was well off the ideal; but I carried this sense of self-alienation with me into adulthood, where it regenerated in response to the depredations of MS. Even with my brace I walk with a limp so pronounced that, seeing myself on the videotape of a television program on the disabled, I couldn't believe that anything but an inchworm could make progress humping along like that. My shoulders droop and my pelvis thrusts forward as I try to balance myself upright, throwing my frame into a bony S. As a result of contractures, one shoulder is higher than the other and I carry one arm bent in front of me, the fingers curled into a claw. My left arm and leg have wasted into pipe-stems, and I try always to keep them covered. When I think about how my body must look to others, especially to men, to whom I have been trained to display myself, I feel ludicrous, even loathsome.

At my age, however, I don't spend much time thinking about my appearance. The burning egocentricity of adolescence, which assures one that all the world is looking all the time, has passed, thank God, and I'm generally too caught up in what I'm doing to step back, as I used to, and watch myself as though upon a stage. I'm also too old to believe in the accuracy of self-image. I know that I'm not a hideous crone, that in fact, when I'm rested, well dressed, and well made up, I look fine. The self-loathing I feel is neither physically nor intellectually substantial. What I hate is not me but a disease.

I am not a disease.

And a disease is not—at least not singlehandedly—going to determine who I am, though at first it seemed to be going to. Adjusting to a chronic incurable illness, I have moved through a process similar to that outlined by Elizabeth Kübler-Ross in *On Death and Dying.* The major difference—and it is far more significant than most people recognize—is that I can't be sure of the outcome, as the terminally ill cancer patient can. Research studies indicate that, with proper medical care, I may achieve a "normal" life span. And in our society, with its vision of death as the ultimate evil, worse even than decrepitude, the response to such news is, "Oh well, at least you're not going to *die.*" Are there worse things than dying? I think that there may be.

I think of two women I know, both with MS, both enough older than I to have served as models. One took to her bed several years ago and has been there ever since. Although she can sit in a high-backed wheelchair, because she is incontinent she refuses to go out at all, even though incontinence pants, which are readily available at any pharmacy, could protect her from embarrassment. Instead, she stays at home and insists that her husband, a small quiet man, a retired civil servant, stay there with her except for a quick weekly foray to the supermarket. The other woman, whose illness was diagnosed when she was eighteen, a nursing student engaged to a young doctor, finished her training, married her doctor, accompanied him to Germany when he was in the service, bore three sons and a daughter, now grown and gone. When she can, she travels with her husband; she plays bridge, embroiders, swims regularly; she works, like me, as a symptomatic-patient instructor of medical students in neurology. Guess which woman I hope to be.

At the beginning, I thought about having MS almost incessantly. And because of the unpredictable course of the disease, my thoughts were always terrified. Each night I'd get into bed wondering whether I'd get out again the next morning, whether I'd be able to see, to speak, to hold a pen between my fingers. Knowing that the day might come when I'd be physically incapable of killing myself, I thought perhaps I ought to do so right away, while I still had the strength. Gradually I came to understand that the Nancy who might one day lie inert under a bedsheet, arms and legs paralyzed, unable to feed or bathe herself, unable to reach out for a gun, a bottle of pills, was not the Nancy I was at present, and that I could not presume to make decisions for that future Nancy, who might well not want in the least to die. Now the only provision I've made for the future Nancy is that when the time comes—and it is likely to come in the form of pneumonia, friend to the weak and the old—I am not to be treated with machines and medications. If she is unable to communicate by then, I hope she will be satisfied with these terms.

Thinking all the time about having MS grew tiresome and intrusive, especially in the large and tragic mode in which I was accustomed to considering my plight. Months and even years went by without catastrophe (at least without one related to MS), and really I was awfully busy, what with George and children and snakes and students and poems, and I hadn't the time, let alone the inclination, to devote myself to being a disease. Too, the richer my life became, the funnier it seemed, as though there were some connection between largesse and laughter, and so my tragic stance began to waver until, even with the aid of a brace and cane, I couldn't hold it for very long at a time.

After several years I was satisfied with my adjustment. I had suffered my grief and fury and terror, I thought, but now I was at ease with my lot. Then one summer day I set out with George and the children across the desert for a vacation in California. Part way to Yuma I became aware that my right leg felt funny. "I think I've had an exacerbation," I told George. "What shall we do?" he asked. "I think we'd better get the hell to California," I said, "because I don't know whether I'll ever make it again." So we went on to San Diego and then to Orange, and up the Pacific Coast Highway to Santa Cruz, across to Yosemite, down to Sequoia and Joshua Tree, and so back over the desert to home. It was a fine two-week trip, filled with friends and fair weather, and I wouldn't have missed it for the world, though I did in fact make it back to California two years later. Nor would there have been any point in missing it, since in MS, once the symptoms have appeared, the neurological damage has been done, and there's no way to predict or prevent that damage.

The incident spoiled my self-satisfaction, however. It renewed my grief and fury and terror, and I learned that one never finishes adjusting to MS. I don't know now why I thought one would. One does not, after all, finish adjusting to life, and MS is simply a fact of my life—not my favorite fact, of course—but as ordinary as my nose and my tropical fish and my yellow Mazda station wagon. It may at any time get worse, but no amount of worry or anticipation can prepare me for a new loss. My life is a lesson in losses. I learn one at a time.

And I had best be patient in the learning, since I'll have to do it like it or not. As any rock fan knows, you can't always get what you want. Particularly when you have MS. You can't, for example, get cured. In recent years researchers and the organizations that fund research have started to pay MS some attention even though it isn't fatal; perhaps they have begun to see that life is something other than a quantitative phenomenon, that one may be very much alive for a very long time in a life that isn't worth living. The researchers have made some progress toward understanding the mechanism of the disease: It may well be an autoimmune reaction triggered by a slow-acting virus. But they are nowhere near its prevention, control, or cure. And most of us want to be cured. Some, unable to accept incurability, grasp at one treatment after another, no matter how bizarre: megavitamin therapy, gluten-free diet, injections of cobra venom, hypothermal suits, lymphocytopharesis, hyperbaric chambers. Many treatments are probably harmless enough, but none are curative.

The absence of a cure often makes MS patients bitter toward their doctors. Doctors are, after all, the priests of modern society, the new shamans, whose business is to heal, and many an MS patient roves from one to another, searching for the "good" doctor who will make him well. Doctors too think of themselves as healers, and for this reason many have trouble dealing with MS patients, whose disease in its intransigence defeats their aims and mocks their skills. Too few doctors, it is true, treat their patients as whole human beings, but the reverse is also true. I have always tried to be gentle with my doctors, who often have more at stake in terms of ego than I do. I may be frustrated, maddened, depressed by the incurability of my disease, but I am not diminished by it, and they are. When I push myself up from my seat in the waiting room and stumble toward them, I incarnate the limitation of their powers. The least I can do is refuse to press on their tenderest spots.

This gentleness is part of the reason that I'm not sorry to be a cripple. I didn't have it before. Perhaps I'd have developed it anyway—how could I know such a thing?—and I wish I had more of it, but I'm glad of what I have. It has opened and enriched my life enormously, this sense that my frailty and need must be mirrored in others, that in searching for and shaping a stable core in a life wrenched by change and loss, change and loss, I must recognize the same process, under individual conditions, in the lives around me. I do not deprecate such knowledge, however I've come by it.

All the same, if a cure were found, would I take it? In a minute. I may be a cripple, but I'm only occasionally a loony and never a saint. Anyway, in my brand of theology God doesn't give bonus points for a limp. I'd take a cure; I just don't need one. A friend who also has MS startled me once by asking, "Do you ever say to yourself, 'Why me, Lord?'" "No, Michael, I don't," I told him, "because whenever I try, the only response I can think of is 'Why not?'" If I could make a cosmic deal, who would I put in my place? What in my life would I give up in exchange for sound limbs and a thrilling rush of energy? No one. Nothing. I might as well do the job myself. Now that I'm getting the hang of it.

Suggestions for Discussion

1. Why does Mairs prefer the word "cripple" to "handicapped" or "disabled" to describe her condition?
2. How does she characterize the plenty, the privation of her life?
3. What does she mean by "I'd take a cure; I just don't need one"?

Suggestions for Writing

1. Mairs asserts that her multiple sclerosis is only one part of her multifaceted self: "What I hate is not me but a disease. I am not a disease." Write about how people tend instead to identify with things that have happened to them or with aspects of themselves. Use an example from your own experience to support this idea.
2. "My life is a lesson in losses. I learn one at a time." What does this convey about Mairs's attitude toward life? How would you handle a life-long "crisis"?
3. Examine the role of humor as a survival tool. Use examples from the essay and your own experience to explore the topic.

FRANCINE PROSE

Bad Behavior

Francine Prose (b. 1947) earned degrees from both Radcliffe College and Harvard University. She has taught creative writing at Harvard, the University of Arizona, the Breadloaf Writers Conference, and Warren Wilson College, where she is on the faculty of the M.F.A. program. Prose has written a number of novels, most recently *The Peaceable Kingdom* (1993) and *Dybbuk: A Story Made in Heaven* (1996), and contributes to a variety of periodicals. She has won the Jewish Book Council Award, the Mile Award, and the Edgar Lewis Wallant Award for her fiction. This article challenges us to examine our understanding of the nature of sexual harassment.

Five men and women from the university community were convened in a campus conference room to decide if my friend Stephen Dobyns—a distinguished poet and novelist and a tenured creative-writing professor—was guilty of sexual harassment and should be dismissed from his job. The tone was one of such civility and high moral seriousness that I could only assume I was the only person in the room tuned in to the disturbing static beneath all this calm inquiry: the only one hearing echoes of Victorian melodrama, of badly overacted student productions of Arthur Miller's play *The Crucible.*

Perhaps my alienation came from my peculiar role—as a character witness for the alleged sexual harasser. I think of myself as a feminist. I write about "women's issues." I teach in writing programs and am painfully aware of the pressures facing young (and older) female writers. I find myself more often than not taking the woman's side. I believed Anita Hill.

Two months before the hearing, at a graduate-student party, an argument erupted—and my friend splashed a drink in the face of a student who had heard him make a remark about her breasts. (Witnesses say he told another writer to "stop looking at her breasts.") The student filed a formal complaint, and two others have come forward to say that his harassment has destroyed their ability to function in the classroom and at the writing desk.

Clearly, my friend is guilty—but only of bad behavior. You don't go throwing drinks in a student's face and talking about her breasts. Since the drink-throwing incident, my friend has been sober and regularly attends A.A. meetings, but a drinking problem used to exaggerate his confrontational personality. He has spoken without considering the feelings of his audience; he sometimes connects with other men with fairly crude talk about sex. But that's not sexual harassment as I understand it.

No one suggests that he offered to trade good grades for sex. He is not accused of sleeping with or propositioning students—one says he tried to kiss her at a drunken party—or of the focused protected hectoring we might call "harassment." The allegations all concern language: specifically, what the committee calls "salty language" used outside the classroom at graduate-student parties. They involve attempts to be funny, and to provoke. There was one cruel remark about a professor who wasn't present, and the suggestion that another might benefit from a "salty" term for a satisfactory sexual encounter.

Is this sexual harassment? Not in any clear sense, but those clear borders have been smudged by university policies that refer to "a hostile workplace," to "patterns of intimidation." "Hostile" and "intimidation" are subjectively defined, as they were by the student who testified (hilariously, I thought, though, again, no one seemed to notice) that he felt intimidated by my friend's use of a "salty" phrase. He felt he was being asked to condone a locker-room atmosphere that might offend the women present.

There was much talk of protecting women from blunt mentions of sex. And the young women who testified were in obvious need of protection. They gulped, trembled and wept, describing how my friend yelled at them in class or failed to encourage their work. Victorian damsels in distress, they used 19th-century language: they had been "shattered" by his rude, "brutish" behavior. After testifying, they seemed radiant, exalted, a state of being that, like so much else, recalled *The Crucible,* which used the Salem witch trials as a metaphor for the Army-McCarthy hearings.

Are these the modern women feminists had in mind? Victorian girls, Puritan girls, crusading against dirty thoughts and loose speech? I thought of all the salty words I have used in class—words that could apparently cost me my job—and of my own experience with sexual harassment: the colleague who told me that his department only hired me because I was a woman; if they could have found a black woman, they would have hired her. Such words were more damaging than anything he could have said about my breasts. But no one could have accused him of harassment: he didn't make a pass at me or refer to a sexual act.

Finally, I thought of students, men and women whose lives were changed by studying with Dobyns, an excellent teacher who cares about writing, who takes women seriously and is interested in their work and not (like many male teachers who are not, strictly speaking, guilty of sexual harassment) annoyed by female intelligence and bored by the subject of female experience. But these facts were irrelevant to the discussion of whether or not my friend got drunk and said this or that dirty word.

Soon after the hearing, he was informed that he had been found guilty of making five sexually harassing remarks. The committee recommended that he be suspended from his job without pay for two years, banned from campus except to use the library, required to perform 200 hours of community service and to pay one of his accusers $600 to compensate for the wages she lost because of the mental suffering he caused her.

It's as if a nasty bubble of Puritanism has risen to the surface and burst. There's been a narrowing of parameters—not of what can be done, but of what can be *said* by writers whose subject (one might think) is language. In an effort to protect the delicate ears of the gentle sex, a career has been damaged with casual glee. Feminists, academics, intellectuals—those who stand to lose the most from restrictions on free expression—are ignoring the possible consequences of the precedent they are setting. They must be choosing not to imagine the terrible swift ease with which our right to free speech can simply crumble away, gathering momentum as the erosion process begins—until human rights and women's rights are subjects too salty to mention.

Suggestions for Discussion

1. Do you consider throwing a drink in a student's face and talking about her breasts simply an example of "bad behavior"?
2. The author refers to "university policies that refer to a 'hostile workplace,' to 'patterns of intimidation.'" In fact these policies are not peculiar to her institution but are outlined in Title 7 of the Equal Employment Opportunities Commission and were affirmed by the Supreme Court in 1986. Do you believe that they should be amended so as not to penalize individuals such as the professor described in this article?
3. The distinction between what is done and what is said is a critical one in terms of sexual harassment, according to Prose. Do you agree?

Suggestions for Writing

1. Describe an instance of sexual harassment you or someone you know has experienced.
2. Many people believe that, except in rare cases, the lines of sexual harassment are too blurred to be subject to legal action. Do you agree?
3. What has concern about sexual harassment done to relations between the sexes? Depict this in a story or essay.

ESSAYS

RICHARD RODRIGUEZ

Heading into Darkness Once Again

Richard Rodriguez (b. 1944) earned his B.A. at Stanford, his M.A. at Columbia, and has done further graduate work at Berkeley and the Warburg Institute, London. He has been a Fulbright Fellow, held an NEH Fellowship, and won the Commonwealth Gold Medal, the Christopher Medal for *Hunger of Memory: The Education of Richard Rodriguez* (1982), and the Anisfield-Wolf Award for Race Relations. In 1992 he published a biography of his father, *Days of Obligation: An Argument with My Mexican Father.* At present he is an editor at Pacific News Service. In the piece that follows he attempts to come to grips with the meaning of terrorism in our time.

SAN FRANCISCO

The stranger sitting on the airplane to Paris may be a terrorist. Or that woman in Tel Aviv who got off the bus, just as you boarded, she looks suspicious.

Whatever else the explosion of TWA Flight 800 will teach us, this much is certain: The terrorist roams freely through the American imagination now. Immediately after the disaster, President Bill Clinton urged the nation toward caution: "Do not jump to conclusions." But that is precisely what we did.

After the explosion in Oklahoma City. witnesses reported seeing "Arabic-looking men in jogging suits running from the scene." This time, within hours of the TWA catastrophe, a "terrorism expert" on CBS supposed that the culprits were either Islamic militants or crew-cut freemen.

At the mall and in offices, speculation from the beginning was that it was a bomb. (This is what a friend first said to me, when he told me the news: "A bomb has exploded on a jetliner headed to Paris.") Then someone said that someone else had heard it was a missile. TV stations reported the news—there had been a blip on a radar screen.

The rapidity with which the imagination inclined to such scenarios was striking. The assumption implied a child-like faith in the machine. It was as though we could not believe that a Boeing 747 could fall out of the sky for mechanical reasons. The explosion of an engine or a ruptured fuel line seemed a more remote possibility than a heat-seeking missile.

If we trusted the machine, there was also menacing suspicion that the machine was explosive and bombs were the size of lipstick.

And everyone had stories to tell about the machine that failed. One woman said she had inadvertently carried a stun gun in her purse onto a plane—did not discover it until she reached Amsterdam and then realized the X-ray machine at the airport hadn't detected it. Another man said that his girlfriend has a necklace with a bullet as its centerpiece. "She gets on airplanes all the time—no problem."

It was easier to talk about incompetent security personnel (underpaid, inattentive) than to doubt the X-ray machine. After all hadn't the machine also detected a "blip" colliding with Flight 800?

In the Joseph Conrad novel *The Secret Agent,* terrorists are an odd group of sociopaths who work out of basements. After Arnold Schwarzenegger, we imagine terrorists in suits, in skyscrapers, a worldwide network.

After the bloodshed and the broken bodies, the most hideous aspect of the terrorist act is its anonymity. The terrorist does not know the victim. The victim does not know the terrorist. If the terrorist is ever seen, it is usually behind disguises (false beards, jaunty hats) or hidden by ski masks.

Terrorism is random. It is an attack on "women and children"—by which we mean civilians going about their routine lives.

Terror is, by definition, "overwhelming fear." Living in London some years ago, during a vicious season of IRA bombings. I was impressed by the British determination to carry on. The only defense against terrorism is the assumption of normalcy.

The terrorist tries to break down civic life. In Sarajevo, the terrorist succeeded. The terrorist makes it necessary that inconvenience attaches to every act of the day. One must stand in line to go to a museum or a church, be body-searched when going into a store. That way one is never able to forget the terrorist's grievance.

The terrorist's ultimate target is the imagination; it is there, in our mind, that terror lives or dies.

In the old order, the pre-Newtonian universe, humans imagined the regular movement of the sun and the planets to be regulated by God. After Isaac Newton, the movement of the universe was assumed by many to follow a purely natural progress. God became the wild card, the unpredictable intruder into history. To this day, insurance companies refer to "an act of God" meaning the unexpected.

Now the terrorist plays the wild card. He governs the realm of the unexpected. We assume the Pratt & Whitney engines whirl as smoothly as Newton's planets; the terrorist is the unnatural intruder.

In the ancient past and the not-so-distant past, travel was a dangerous experience. Any voyage out implied dangers. Every age but ours has known that the journey is a risk. We alone assumed our destination.

Now the journey is not so certain anymore. We become like ancient people about to head into darkness.

This is what the terrible events of the week teach us. Before any official was willing to say the word "terrorism," before the FBI was willing to admit the TWA explosion deserved a criminal investigation, before any clandestine terrorist group claimed dubious "credit" for the tragedy, we assumed the bomb.

In that sense, terrorism is now part of our everyday life. The terrorist has won.

Suggestions for Discussion

1. Rodriguez identifies randomness and anonymity as the most hideous aspects of terrorism. Would you agree?
2. What does the author mean when he says that the terrorist's ultimate target is the imagination?
3. How has terrorism, as the author asserts, become part of our everyday life?

Suggestions for Writing

1. Imagine yourself a terrorist. Describe how you would go about making your presence felt.
2. Assume that you are a passenger on TWA Flight 800. Describe your thoughts.

RONALD DWORKIN

Life Is Sacred: That's the Easy Part

Ronald Dworkin (b. 1931), a native of Massachusetts, was educated at Harvard and Oxford universities. A legal authority, he taught for some years at Oxford and since 1975 has been at New York University. He holds honorary degrees from three universities, and he is a Fellow both of the British Academy and the American Academy of Arts and

Letters. His books include *Taking Rights Seriously* (1977), *A Matter of Principle* (1985), *Law's Empire* (1986), *Life's Dominion* (1993), and *The Rise of the Imperial Self: America's Culture Wars in Augustinian Perspective* (1996). In this article he articulates a common ground on which he believes that proponents of intensely held opposing positions on abortion and euthanasia can meet to listen to one another.

The fierce argument about abortion and euthanasia now raging in America is this century's Civil War. When Dr. David Gunn was shot and killed in front of a Florida abortion clinic last March, any hope that the abortion battle had finally become less savage died with him. The argument over euthanasia has been less violent but equally intense. When Nancy Cruzan was finally allowed to die in a Missouri hospital in 1991, after seven years in a persistent vegetative state, people called her parents murderers and her nurses wept over what was being done to her.

These terrible controversies have been far more polarized and bitter than they need and should have been, however, because most Americans have misunderstood what the arguments are *about.* According to the usual explanation, the abortion struggle is about whether a fetus, from the moment of conception, is already a person—already a creature whose interests other people must respect and whose rights government must protect. If that is the correct way to understand the debate, then of course accommodation is impossible; people who think that abortion violates a fetus's right to life can no more compromise than decent people can compromise over genocide.

But in fact, in spite of the scalding rhetoric, almost none of those who believe abortion may be objectionable on moral grounds actually believe that an early fetus is a person with rights and interests of its own. The vast majority of them think abortion morally permissible when necessary to save the mother's life, and only somewhat fewer that it is permissible in cases of rape and incest. Many of them also think that even when abortion is morally wrong, it is none of the law's business to prohibit it. None of this is compatible with thinking that a fetus has interests of its own. Doctors are not permitted to kill one innocent person to save the life of another one; a fetus should not be punished for a sexual crime of which it is wholly innocent, and it is certainly part of government's business to protect the rights and interests of persons too weak to protect themselves.

So conservative opinion cannot consistently be based on the idea that a fetus has interests of its own from the moment of conception. Neither can liberal and moderate opinion be based simply on rejecting that idea. Most liberals insist that abortion is always a morally grave decision, not to be taken for frivolous or capricious reasons, and this positive moral position must be based on more than the negative claim that a fetus has no interests or rights.

I suggest a different explanation of the controversy: We disagree about abortion not because some of us think, and others deny, that an immature fetus is already a person with interests of its own but, paradoxically, because of an ideal we share. We almost all accept, as the inarticulate assumption behind much of our experience and conviction, that human life in all its forms is *sacred*—that it has intrinsic and objective value quite apart from any value it might have to the person whose life it is. For some of us, this is a matter of religious faith; for others, of secular but deep philosophical belief. But though we agree that life is sacred, we disagree about the source and character of that sacred value and therefore about which decisions respect and which dishonor it. I can best explain what the idea that life has intrinsic and objective value means by turning to the other agonizing controversy I mentioned, at the far edge of life.

Should a doctor prescribe enough pills to allow a patient with leukemia to kill herself, as Dr. Timothy Quill of Rochester did in 1991? Should he ever try to kill a patient in agony and pleading to die by injecting her with potassium chloride, as Dr. Nigel Cox did in Britain last year? Many people concede that in such terrible circumstances death would actually be in the patient's best interests, but nevertheless insist that killing her or letting her die would be wrong because human life has an independent, sacred value and should be preserved for that reason.

There is nothing odd or unusual about the idea that it is wrong to destroy some creatures or things, not because they themselves have interests that would be violated but because of the intrinsic value they embody. We take that view, for example, of great paintings and also of distinct animal species, like the Siberian tiger that we work to save from extinction. Paintings and species do not have interests: if it nevertheless seems terrible to destroy them, because of their intrinsic value, it can also seem terrible to destroy a human life, which most people think even more precious, though that human life has not yet developed into a creature with interests either. So people can passionately oppose abortion for that reason even though they do not believe that a collection of growing cells just implanted in a womb already has interests of its own.

Once we identify that different basis for thinking abortion wrong, we see that it actually unites as well as divides our society, because almost everyone—conservatives, moderates and liberals on the issue of abortion—accepts both that the life of a human fetus embodies an intrinsic value and that a frivolous abortion is contemptuous of that important value. Americans disagree about when abortion is morally permissible, not because many of them reject the idea that human life is sacred but because they disagree about how best to respect that value when continuing a pregnancy would itself frustrate or damage human life in some other grave way: when a child would be born seriously deformed, for example, or when childbirth would frustrate a teenage mother's chances to make something of her own life, or when the economic burden of another child would mean more privation for other children already living in poverty.

In such cases, respect for the inherent value of a human life pulls in two directions, and some resolution of the tragic conflict is necessary. How each of us resolves it will depend on our deeper, essentially religious or philosophical convictions about which of the different sources of life's sacred value is most important. People who think that biological life—the gift of God or nature—is the transcendently important source of that sacred value will think that the death of any human creature, even one whose life in earnest has not yet begun, is always the worst possible insult to the sanctity of life. Those who think that frustrating people's struggle to make something of their own lives, once those lives are under way, is sometimes an even greater affront to the value of life than an early abortion might resolve the conflict in the other direction.

That view of how and why we disagree about abortion also explains why so many people think that even when early abortion is morally wrong, government has no business forbidding it. There is no contradiction in insisting that abortion sometimes dishonors a sacred value and that government must nevertheless allow women to decide for themselves when it does. On the contrary, that very distinction is at the heart of one of the most important liberties modern democracies have established, a liberty America leads the world in protecting—freedom of conscience and religion. Once we see the abortion argument in this light, we see that it is an essentially *religious* argument—not about who has rights and how government should protect these, but a very different, more abstract and spiritual argument about the meaning and character and value of human life itself. Government does have a responsibility to help people understand the gravity of these decisions about life and death, but it has no right to dictate which decision they must finally make.

The same is true of euthanasia. Of course, any legal regime that permits doctors to help patients die must be scrupulously careful to protect the patient's real, reflective wishes and to avoid patients or relatives making an unwitting choice for death when there is a genuine chance of medical recovery. But government can do people great harm by not allowing them to die when that is their settled wish and in their best interests, as they themselves have judged or would judge their interests when competent to do so.

In both cases, the crucial question is not whether to respect the sanctity of life, but which decision best respects it. People who dread being kept alive, permanently unconscious or sedated beyond sense, intubated and groomed and tended as vegetables, think this condition degrades rather than respects what has been intrinsically valuable in their own living. Others disagree: They believe, about euthanasia as about abortion, that mere biological life is so inherently precious that nothing can justify deliberately ending it. The disagreement, once again, is an essentially religious or spiritual one, and a decent government, committed to personal integrity and freedom, has no business imposing a decision. Dictating how people should see the meaning of their own lives and deaths is a crippling, humiliating form of tyranny.

If we change our collective view of these two great controversies, if we realize that we are arguing not about whether abortion and euthanasia are murder but about how best to honor a humane ideal we all share, then we can cure the bitterness in our national soul. Freedom of choice can be accepted by all sides with no sense of moral compromise, just as all religious groups and sects can accept, with no sense of compromise, freedom for other versions of spiritual truth, even those they think gravely mistaken. We might even hope for something more: a healing sense, after all the decades of hate, that what unites us is more important than our differences. It is inevitable that free people who really do believe that human life is sacred will disagree about how to live and die in the light of that conviction, because free people will insist on making that profound and self-defining decision for themselves.

Suggestions for Discussion

1. Discuss Dworkin's argument that the abortion debate is essentially a religious one.
2. The author believes that we share a humane ideal and that what divides us is how we would choose to enact that ideal. Explain why you agree or disagree.
3. Dworkin sets the resolution to the bitter debates over abortion and euthanasia within a framework of religious tolerance. Do you support this? Why or why not?
4. "[T]he crucial question is not whether to respect the sanctity of life, but which decision best respects it." Explain your reasons for agreeing or disagreeing with this statement.

Suggestions for Writing

1. Sometimes we find ourselves in situations in which there is nothing we can do, no way we can act, that does not call some principle we hold into question. Create a dialogue that depicts this.
2. Debate: "*Resolved:* The role of the government is to help us understand our decisions, not to make them for us."

ROLLO MAY

The Man Who Was Put in a Cage

Rollo May (1909–1994) was a practicing psychotherapist in New York. He was a member of the William Alanson White Institute of Psychiatry, Psychoanalysis, and Psychology. In addition he wrote many books, such as *Man's Search for Himself* (1953), *Power and Innocence* (1972), *The Courage to Create* (1975), *Freedom and Destiny* (1981), *The Discovery of Being: Writings in Existential Psychology* (1983), *Love and Will* (1986), and *The Ageless Spirit* (1992). In this parable from *Psychology and the Human Dilemma* (1966), the psychologist is impelled to act on the man's impassioned cry in the dream: When any man's freedom is taken away, the freedom of everyone is also taken away.

> *What a piece of work is man! how noble in reason! how infinite in faculty! in form and moving how express and admirable!... The paragon of animals!*
>
> —SHAKESPEARE, *Hamlet*

We have quite a few discrete pieces of information these days about what happens to a person when he is deprived of this or that element of freedom. We have our studies of sensory deprivation and of how a person reacts when put in different kinds of authoritarian atmosphere, and so on. But recently I have been wondering what pattern would emerge if we put these various pieces of knowledge together. In short, what would happen to a living, whole person if his total freedom—or as nearly total as we can imagine—were taken away? In the course of these reflections, a parable took form in my mind.

The story begins with a king who, while standing in reverie at the window of his palace one evening, happened to notice a man in the town square below. He was apparently an average man, walking home at night, who had taken the same route five nights a week for many years. The king followed this man in his imagination—pictured him arriving home, perfunctorily kissing his wife, eating his late meal, inquiring whether everything was all right with the children, reading the paper, going to bed, perhaps engaging in the sex relation with his wife or perhaps not, sleeping, and getting up and going off to work again the next day.

And a sudden curiosity seized the king, which for a moment banished his fatigue: "I wonder what would happen if a man were kept in a cage, like the animals at the zoo?" His curiosity was perhaps in some ways not unlike that of the first surgeons who wondered what it would be like to perform a lobotomy on the human brain.

So the next day the king called in a psychologist, told him of his idea, and invited him to observe the experiment. When the psychologist demurred saying, "It's an unthinkable thing to keep a man in a cage," the monarch replied that many rulers had in effect, if not literally, done so, from the time of the Romans through Genghis Khan down to Hitler and the totalitarian leaders; so why not find out scientifically what would happen? Furthermore, added the king, he had made up his mind to do it whether the psychologist took part or not; he had already gotten the Greater Social Research Foundation to give a large sum of money for the experiment, and why let that money go to waste? By this time the psychologist also was feeling within himself a great curiosity about what would happen if a man were kept in a cage.

And so the next day the king caused a cage to be brought from the zoo—a large cage that had been occupied by a lion when it was new, then later by a tiger; just recently it had been the home of a hyena who died the previous week. The cage was put in an inner private court in the palace grounds, and the average man whom the king had seen from the window was brought and placed therein. The psychologist, with his Rorschach and Wechsler-Bellevue tests in his brief case to administer at some appropriate moment, sat down outside the cage.

At first the man was simply bewildered, and he kept saying to the psychologist, "I have to catch the tram, I have to get to work, look what time it is, I'll be late for work!" but later on in the afternoon the man began soberly to realize what was up, and then he protested vehemently, "The king can't do this to me! It is unjust! It's against the law." His voice was strong, and his eyes full of anger. The psychologist liked the man for his anger, and he became vaguely aware that this was a mood he had encountered often in people he worked with in his clinic. "Yes," he realized, "this anger is the attitude of people who—like the healthy adolescents of any era—want to fight what's wrong, who protest directly against it. When people come to the clinic in this mood, it is good—they can be helped."

During the rest of the week the man continued his vehement protests. When the king walked by the cage, as he did every day, the man made his protests directly to the monarch.

But the king answered, "Look here, you are getting plenty of food, you have a good bed, and you don't have to work. We take good care of you; so why are you objecting?"

After some days had passed, the man's protests lessened and then ceased. He was silent in his cage, generally refusing to talk. But the psychologist could see hatred glowing in his eyes. When he did exchange a few words, they were short, definite words uttered in the strong, vibrant, but calm voice of the person who hates and knows whom he hates.

Whenever the king walked into the courtyard, there was a deep fire in the man's eyes. The psychologist thought, "This must be the way people act when they are first conquered." He remembered that he had also seen that expression of the eyes and heard that tone of voice in many patients at his clinic: the adolescent who had been unjustly accused at home or in school and could do nothing about it; the college student who was required by public and campus opinion to be a star on the gridiron, but was required by his professors to pass courses he could not prepare for if he were to be successful in football—and who was then expelled from college for the cheating that resulted. And the psychologist, looking at the active hatred in the man's eyes, thought, "It is still good; a person who has this fight in him can be helped."

Every day the king, as he walked through the courtyard, kept reminding the man in the cage that he was given food and shelter and taken good care of, so why did he not like it? And the psychologist noticed that, whereas at first the man had been entirely impervious to the king's statements, it now seemed more and more that he was pausing for a moment after the king's speech—for a second the hatred was postponed from returning to his eyes—as though he were asking himself if what the king said were possibly true.

And after a few weeks more, the man began to discuss with the psychologist how it was a useful thing that a man is given food and shelter; and how man had to live by his fate in any case, and the part of wisdom was to accept fate. He soon was developing an extensive theory about security and the acceptance of fate, which sounded to the psychologist very much like the philosophical theories that Rosenberg and others worked out for the fascists in Germany. He was very voluble during this period, talking at length, although the talk was mostly a monologue. The psychologist noticed that his voice was flat and hollow as he talked, like the voice of people in TV previews who make an effort to look you in the eye and try hard to sound sincere as they tell you that you should see the program they are advertising, or the announcers on the radio who are paid to persuade you that you should like high-brow music.

And the psychologist also noticed that now the corners of the man's mouth always turned down, as though he were in some gigantic pout. Then the psychologist suddenly remembered: this was like the middle-aged, middle-class people who came to his clinic, the respectable bourgeois people who went to church and lived morally but were always full of resentment, as though everything they did was conceived, born, and nursed in resentment. It reminded the psychologist of Nietzsche's saying that the middle class was consumed with resentment. He then for the first time began to be seriously worried about the man in the cage, for he knew that once resentment gets a firm start and becomes well rationalized and structuralized, it may become like cancer. When the person no longer knows whom he hates, he is much harder to help.

During this period the Greater Social Research Foundation had a board of trustees meeting, and they decided that since they were expending a fund to keep a man supported in a cage, it would look better if representatives of the Foundation at least visited the experiment. So a group of people, consisting of two professors and a few graduate students, came in one day to look at the man in the cage. One of the professors then proceeded to lecture to the group about the relation of the autonomic nervous system and the secretions of the ductless glands to human existence in a cage. But it occurred to the other professor that the verbal communications of the victim himself might just possibly be interesting, so he asked the man how he felt about living in a cage. The man was friendly toward the professors and students and explained to them that he had chosen this way of life, that there were great values in security and in being taken care of, that they would of course see how sensible this course was, and so on.

"How strange!" thought the psychologist, "and how pathetic; why is it he struggles so hard to get them to approve his way of life?"

In the succeeding days when the king walked through the courtyard, the man fawned upon him from behind the bars in his cage and thanked him for the food and shelter. But when the king was not in the yard and the man was not aware that the psychologist was present, his expression was quite different—sullen and morose. When his food was handed to him through the bars by the keeper, the man would often drop the dishes or dump over the water and then would be embarrassed because of his stupidity and clumsiness. His conversation became increasingly one-tracked; and instead of the involved philosophical theories about the value of being taken care of, he had gotten down to simple sentences such as "It is fate," which he would say over and over again, or he would just mumble to himself, "It is." The psychologist was surprised to find that the man should now be so clumsy as to drop his food, or so stupid as to talk in those barren sentences, for he knew from his tests that the man had originally been of good average intelligence. Then it dawned upon the psychologist that this was the kind of behavior he had observed in some anthropological studies among the Negroes in the South—people who had been forced to kiss the hand that fed and enslaved them, who could no longer either hate or rebel. The man in the cage took more and more to simply sitting all day long in the sun as it came through the bars, his only movement being to shift his position from time to time from morning through the afternoon.

It was hard to say just when the last phase set in. But the psychologist became aware that the man's face now seemed to have no particular expression; his smile was no longer fawning, but simply empty and meaningless, like the grimace a baby makes when there is gas on its stomach. The man ate his food and exchanged a few sentences with the psychologist from time to time; but his eyes were distant and vague, and though he looked at the psychologist, it seemed that he never really *saw* him.

And now the man, in his desultory conversations, never used the word "I" any more. He had accepted the cage. He had no anger, no hate, no rationalizations. But he was now insane.

The night the psychologist realized this, he sat in his apartment trying to write a concluding report. But it was very difficult for him to summon up words, for he felt within himself a great emptiness. He kept trying to reassure himself with the words, "They say that nothing is ever lost, that matter is merely changed to energy and back again." But he could not help feeling that something *had* been lost, that something had gone out of the universe in this experiment.

He finally went to bed with his report unfinished. But he could not sleep; there was a gnawing within him which, in less rational and scientific ages, would have been called a conscience. Why didn't I tell the king that this is the one experiment that no man can do—or at least why didn't I shout that I would have nothing to do with the whole bloody business? Of course, the king would have dismissed me, the foundations would never have granted me any more money, and at the clinic they would have said that I was not a real scientist. But maybe one could farm in the mountains and make a living, and maybe one could paint or write something that would make future men happier and more free....

But he realized that these musings were, at least at the moment, unrealistic, and he tried to pull himself back to reality. All he could get, however, was this feeling of emptiness within himself, and the words, "Something has been taken out of the universe, and there is left only a void."

Finally he dropped off to sleep. Some time later, in the small hours of the morning, he was awakened by a startling dream. A crowd of people had gathered, in the dream, in front of the cage in the courtyard, and the man in the cage—no longer inert and vacuous—was shouting through the bars of the cage in impassioned oratory. "It is not only I whose freedom is taken away!" he was crying. "When the king puts me or any man in a cage, the freedom of each of you is taken away also. The king must go!" The people began to chant, "The king must go!" and they seized and broke out the iron bars of the cage, and wielded them for weapons as they charged the palace.

The psychologist awoke, filled by the dream with a great feeling of hope and joy—an experience of hope and joy probably not unlike that experienced by the free men of England when they forced King John to sign the Magna Charta. But not for nothing had the psychologist had an orthodox analysis in the course of his training, and as he lay surrounded by this aura of happiness, a voice spoke within him: "Aha, you had this dream to make yourself feel better; it's just a wish fulfillment."

"The hell it is!" said the psychologist as he climbed out of bed. "Maybe some dreams are to be acted on."

Suggestions for Discussion

1. What possible implicit judgment of the average man is evident in the king's imaginative recreation of his life? What is the significance of the king's selection of an average man for his experiment?
2. Formulate a plausible explanation of the fact that the anger and subsequent hate manifested by the man in the cage signified that he could be helped.
3. Define the various phases of the victim's response to his imprisonment and account for each of them. Include an analysis of the changes in his conversations with the several observers. How did the analogies cited contribute to your understanding of his metamorphosis?
4. Account for the reactions of the psychologist after his realization that the man was no longer sane, especially his feeling of emptiness within himself, the sense that "there is left only a void." Account for his final postdream resolution.

Suggestions for Writing

1. What does the form of the parable contribute to May's thesis? Write a paragraph elaborating on May's thesis. What is lost when you state it directly?
2. Using a vital subject like freedom of choice or love or the dignity of man, write a parable of your own in which you place it in fresh perspective.
3. Read a work that depicts a human as prisoner and victim. Write an analysis of the effects of incarceration on the human spirit, paying special attention to what qualities and activities of the mind distinguish one person from another under such adverse circumstances.
4. Relate the opening lines from *Hamlet* to the parable. Or develop an essay on the most difficult or the most crucial choices you have ever made, or are currently contemplating, and the factors you regard as central in arriving at a resolution.

5. May attributes the man's capitulation largely to the fact of his security. Defend or criticize this thesis. What if the victim were not an average man but a bright member of a youth commune, a poet, or a mystic? Rewrite the parable using one of the latter or any other victim as your protagonist.

JONATHAN KOZOL

Distancing the Homeless

Jonathan Kozol (b. 1936) was educated at Harvard University and Oxford University, where he was a Rhodes scholar. He has devoted most of his professional life to the field of basic education and was for some years the Director of the National Literacy Coalition. He has taught at a number of universities and has lectured at over 400. Among other honors, he has received the National Book Award (1968) and fellowships from the Field, Ford, Rockefeller, and Guggenheim foundations. He is considered to be one of the nation's most serious and provocative social thinkers. Of his many books the most recent include *Rachel and Her Children* (1988), *Savage Inequalities* (1991), *The Issue Is Race* (1992), and *Amazing Grace: The Lives of Children and the Conscience of a Nation* (1996). In the following selection Kozol analyzes the causes of homelessness, most of which he regards our society as being unable to face.

It is commonly believed by many journalists and politicians that the homeless of America are, in large part, former patients of large mental hospitals who were deinstitutionalized in the 1970s—the consequence, it is sometimes said, of misguided liberal opinion, which favored the treatment of such persons in community-based centers. It is argued that this policy, and the subsequent failure of society to build such centers or to provide them in sufficient number, is the primary cause of homelessness in the United States.

Those who work among the homeless do not find that explanation satisfactory. While conceding that a certain number of the homeless are, or have been, mentally unwell, they believe that, in the case of most unsheltered people, the primary reason is economic rather than clinical. The cause of homelessness, they say with disarming logic, is the lack of homes and of income with which to rent or acquire them.

They point to the loss of traditional jobs in industry (two million every year since 1980) and to the fact that half of those who are laid off end up in work that pays a poverty-level wage. They point to the parallel growth of poverty in families with children, noting that children, who represent one-quarter of our population, make up 40 percent of the poor: since 1968, the number of children in poverty has grown by three million, while welfare benefits to families with children have declined by 35 percent.

And they note, too, that these developments have coincided with a time in which the shortage of low-income housing has intensified as the gentrification of our major cities has accelerated. Half a million units of low-income housing have been lost each year to condominium conversion as well as to arson, demolition, or abandonment. Between 1978 and 1980, median rents climbed 30 percent for people in the lowest income sector, driving many of these families into the streets. After 1980, rents rose at even faster rates. In Boston, between 1982 and 1984, over 80 percent of the housing units renting below three hundred dollars disappeared, while the number of units renting above six hundred dollars nearly tripled.

Hard numbers, in this instance, would appear to be of greater help than psychiatric labels in telling us why so many people become homeless. Eight million American families now pay half or more of their income for rent or a mortgage. Six million more, unable to pay rent at all, live doubled up with others. At the same time, federal support for low-income housing dropped from $30 billion (1980) to $9 billion (1986). Under Presidents Ford and Carter, five hundred thousand subsidized private housing units were constructed. By President Reagan's second term, the number had dropped to twenty-five thousand. "We're getting out of the housing business, period," said a deputy assistant secretary of the Department of Housing and Urban Development in 1985.

One year later, the *Washington Post* reported that the number of homeless families in Washington, D.C., had grown by 500 percent over the previous twelve months. In New York City, the waiting list for public housing now contains two hundred thousand names. The waiting is eighteen years.

Why, in the face of these statistics, are we impelled to find a psychiatric explanation for the growth of homelessness in the United States?

A misconception, once it is implanted in the popular imagination, is not easy to uproot, particularly when it serves a useful social role. The notion that the homeless are largely psychotics who belong in institutions, rather than victims of displacement at the hands of enterprising realtors, spares us from the need to offer realistic solutions to the fact of deep and widening extremes of wealth and poverty in the United States. It also enables us to tell ourselves that the despair of homeless people bears no intimate connection to the privileged existence we enjoy—when, for example, we rent or purchase one of those restored townhouses that once provided shelter for people now huddled in the street.

But there may be another reason to assign labels to the destitute. Terming economic victims "psychotic" or "disordered" helps to place them at a distance. It says that they aren't quite like us—and, more important, that we could not be like them. The plight of homeless families is a nightmare. It may not seem natural to try to banish human beings from our midst, but it *is* natural to try to banish nightmares from our minds.

So the rituals of clinical contamination proceed uninterrupted by the economic facts described above. Research that addresses homelessness as an *injustice* rather than as a medical *misfortune* does not win the funding of foundations. And the research which *is* funded, defining the narrowed borders of permissible debate, diverts our attention from the antecedent to the secondary cause of homelessness. Thus it is that perfectly ordinary women whom I know in New York City—people whose depression or anxiety is a realistic consequence of months and even years in crowded shelters or the streets—are interrogated by invasive research scholars in an effort to decode their poverty, to find clinical categories for their despair and terror, to identify the secret failing that lies hidden in their psyche.

Many pregnant women without homes are denied prenatal care because they constantly travel from one shelter to another. Many are anemic. Many are denied essential dietary supplements by recent federal cuts. As a consequence, some of their children do not live to see their second year of life. Do these mothers sometimes show signs of stress? Do they appear disorganized, depressed, disordered? Frequently. They are immobilized by pain, traumatized by fear. So it is no surprise that when researchers enter the scene to ask them how they "feel," the resulting reports tell us that the homeless are emotionally unwell. The reports do not tell us we have *made* these people ill. They do not tell us that illness is a natural response to intolerable conditions. Nor do they tell us of the strength and the resilience that so many of these people still retain despite the miseries they must endure. They set these men and women apart in capsules labeled "personality disorder" or "psychotic," where they no longer threaten our complacence.

I visited Haiti not many years ago, when the Duvalier family was still in power. If an American scholar were to have made a psychological study of the homeless families living in the streets of Port-au-Prince—sleeping amidst rotten garbage, bathing in open sewers—and if he were to return to the United States to tell us that the reasons for their destitution were "behavioral problems" or "a lack of mental health," we would be properly suspicious. Knowledgeable Haitians would not merely be suspicious. They would be enraged. Even to initiate such research when economic and political explanations present themselves so starkly would appear grotesque. It is no less so in the United States.

One of the more influential studies of this nature was carried out in 1985 by Ellen Bassuk, a psychiatrist at Harvard University. Drawing upon interviews with eight homeless parents, Dr. Bassuk contends, according to the *Boston Globe,* that "90 percent [of these people] have problems other than housing and poverty that are so acute they would be unable to live successfully on their own." She also precludes the possibility that illness, where it does exist, may be provoked by destitution. "Our data," she writes, "suggest that mental illness tends to precede homelessness." She concedes that living in the streets can make a homeless person's mental illness worse; but she insists upon the fact of prior illness.

The executive director of the Massachusetts Commission on Children and Youth believes that Dr. Bassuk's estimate is far too high. The staff of Massachusetts Human Services Secretary Phillip Johnston believes the appropriate number is closer to 10 percent.

In defending her research, Bassuk challenges such critics by claiming that they do not have data to refute her. This may be true. Advocates for the homeless do not receive funds to defend the sanity of the people they represent. In placing the burden of proof upon them, Dr. Bassuk has created an extraordinary dialectic: How does one prove that people aren't unwell? What homeless mother would consent to enter a procedure that might "prove" her mental health? What overburdened shelter operator would divert scarce funds to such an exercise? It is an unnatural, offensive, and dehumanizing challenge.

Dr. Bassuk's work, however, isn't the issue I want to raise here; the issue is the use or misuse of that work by critics of the poor. For example, in a widely syndicated essay published in 1986, the newspaper columnist Charles Krauthammer argued that the homeless are essentially a deranged segment of the population and that we must find the "political will" to isolate them from society. We must do this, he said, "whether they like it or not." Arguing even against the marginal benefits of homeless shelters, Krauthammer wrote: "There is a better alternative, however, though no one dares speak its name." Krauthammer dares: that better alternative, he said, is "asylum."

One of Mr. Krauthammer's colleagues at the *Washington Post,* the columnist George Will, perceives the homeless as a threat to public cleanliness and argues that they ought to be consigned to places where we need not see them. "It is," he says, "simply a matter of public hygiene" to put them out of sight. Another journalist, Charles Murray, writing from the vantage point of a social Darwinist, recommends the restoration of the almshouses of the 1800s. "Granted Dickensian horror stories about almshouses," he begins, there were nonetheless "good almshouses"; he proposes "a good correctional 'halfway house'" as a proper shelter for mother and child with no means of self-support.

In the face of such declarations, the voices of those who work with and know the poor are harder to hear.

Manhattan Borough President David Dinkins made the following observation on the basis of a study commissioned in 1986: "No facts support the belief that addiction or behavioral problems occur with more frequency in the homeless family population than in a similar socioeconomic population. Homeless families are not demographically different from other public assistance families when they enter the shelter system.... Family homelessness is typically a housing and income problem: the unavailability of affordable housing and the inadequacy of public assistance income."

In a "hypothetical world," write James Wright and Julie Lam of the University of Massachusetts, "where there were no alcoholics, no drug addicts, no mentally ill, no deinstitutionalization,...indeed, no personal social pathologies at all, there would still be a formidable homelessness problem, simply because at this stage in American history, there is not enough low-income housing" to accommodate the poor.

New York State's respected commissioner of social services, Cesar Perales, makes the point in fewer words: "Homelessness is less and less a result of personal failure, and more and more is caused by larger forces. There is no longer affordable housing in New York City for people of poor and modest means."

Even the words of medical practitioners who care for homeless people have been curiously ignored. A study published by the Massachusetts Medical Society, for instance, has noted that the most frequent illnesses among a sample of the homeless population, after alcohol and drug use, are trauma (31 percent), upper respiratory disorders (28 percent), limb disorders (19 percent), mental illness (16 percent), skin diseases (15 percent), hypertension (14 percent), and neurological illnesses (12 percent). (Excluded from this tabulation are lead poisoning, malnutrition, acute diarrhea, and other illnesses especially common among homeless infants and small children.) Why, we may ask, of all these calamities, does mental illness command so much political and press attention? The answer may be that the label of mental illness places the destitute outside the sphere of ordinary life. It personalizes an anguish that is public in its genesis; it individualizes a misery that is both general in cause and general in application.

The rate of tuberculosis among the homeless is believed to be ten times that of the general population. Asthma, I have learned in countless interviews, is one of the most common causes of discomfort in the shelters. Compulsive smoking, exacerbated by the crowding and the tension, is more common in the shelters than in any place that I have visited except prison. Infected and untreated sores, scabies, diarrhea, poorly set limbs, protruding elbows, awkwardly distorted wrists, bleeding gums, impacted teeth, and other untreated dental problems are so common among children in the shelters that one rapidly forgets their presence. Hunger and emaciation are everywhere. Children as well as adults can bring to mind the photographs of people found in camps for refugees of war in 1945. But these miseries bear no stigma, and mental illness does. It conveys a stigma in the Soviet Union. It conveys a stigma in the United States. In both nations the label is used, whether as a matter of deliberate policy or not, to isolate and treat as special cases those who, by deed or word or by sheer presence, represent a threat to national complacence. The two situations are obviously not identical, but they are enough alike to give Americans reason for concern.

Last summer, some twenty-eight thousand homeless people were afforded shelter by the city of New York. Of this number, twelve thousand were children and six thousand were parents living together in families. The average child was six years old, the average parent twenty-seven. A typical homeless family included a mother with two or three children, but in about one-fifth of these families two parents were present. Roughly ten thousand single persons, then, made up the remainder of the population of the city's shelters.

These proportions vary somewhat from one area of the nation to another. In all areas, however, families are the fastest-growing sector of the homeless population, and in the Northeast they are by far the largest sector already. In Massachusetts, three-fourths of the homeless now are families with children; in certain parts of Massachusetts—Attleboro and Northampton, for example—the proportion reaches 90 percent. Two-thirds of the homeless children studied recently in Boston were less than five years old.

Of an estimated two to three million homeless people nationwide, about 500,000 are dependent children, according to Robert Hayes, counsel to the National Coalition for the Homeless. Including their parents, at least 750,000 homeless people in America are family members.

What is to be made, then, of the supposition that the homeless are primarily the former residents of mental hospitals, persons who were carelessly released during the 1970s? Many of them are, to be sure. Among the older men and women in the streets and shelters, as many as one-third (some believe as many as one-half) may be chronically disturbed, and a number of these people were deinstitutionalized during the 1970s. But in a city like New York, where nearly half the homeless are small children with an average age of six, to operate on the basis of such a supposition makes no sense. Their parents, with an average age of twenty-seven, are not likely to have been hospitalized in the 1970s, either.

Nor is it easy to assume, as was once the case, that single men—those who come closer to fitting the stereotype of the homeless vagrant, the drifting alcoholic of an earlier age—are the former residents of mental hospitals. The age of homeless men has dropped in recent years; many of them are only twenty-one to twenty-eight years old. Fifty percent of homeless men in New York City shelters in 1984 were there for the first time. Most had previously had homes and jobs. Many had never before needed public aid.

A frequently cited set of figures tells us that in 1955, the average daily census of nonfederal psychiatric institutions was 677,000, and that by 1984, the number had dropped to 151,000. Subtract the second number from the first, conventional logic tells us, and we have an explanation for the homelessness of half a million people. A closer look at the same number offers us a different lesson.

The sharpest decline in the average daily census of these institutions occurred prior to 1978, and the largest part of that decline, in fact, appeared at least a decade earlier. From 677,000 in 1955, the census dropped to 378,000 in 1972. The 1974 census was 307,000. In 1976 it was 230,000; in 1977 it was 211,000; and in 1978 it was 190,000. In no year since 1978 has the average daily census dropped by more than 9,000 persons, and in the six-year period from 1978 to 1984, the total decline was 39,000 persons. Compared with a decline of 300,000 from 1955 to 1972, and of nearly 200,000 more from 1972 to 1978, the number is small. But the years since 1980 are the period in which the present homeless crisis surfaced. Only since 1983 have homeless individuals overflowed the shelters.

If the large numbers of the homeless lived in hospitals before they reappeared in subway stations and in public shelters, we need to ask where they were and what they had been doing from 1972 to 1980. Were they living under bridges? Were they waiting out the decade in the basements of deserted buildings?

No. The bulk of those who had been psychiatric patients and were released from hospitals during the 1960s and early 1970s had been living in the meantime in low-income housing, many in skid-row hotels or boarding houses. Such housing—commonly known as SRO (single-room occupancy) units—was drastically diminished by the gentrification of our cities that began in 1970. Almost 50 percent of SRO housing was replaced by luxury apartments or by office buildings between 1970 and 1980, and the remaining units have been disappearing at even faster rates. As recently as 1986, after New York City had issued a prohibition against conversion of such housing, a well-known developer hired a demolition team to destroy a building in Times Square that had previously been home to indigent people. The demolition took place in the middle of the night. In order to avoid imprisonment, the developer was allowed to make a philanthropic gift to homeless people as a token of atonement. This incident, bizarre as it appears, reminds us that the profit motive for displacement of the poor is very great in every major city. It also indicates a more realistic explanation for the growth of homelessness during the 1980s.

Even for those persons who are ill and were deinstitutionalized during the decades before 1980, the precipitating cause of homelessness in 1987 is not illness but loss of housing. SRO housing, unattractive as it may have been, offered low-cost sanctuaries for the homeless, providing a degree of safety and mutual support for those who lived within them. They were a demeaning version of the community health centers that society had promised; they were the de facto "halfway houses" of the 1970s. For these people too, then—at most half of the homeless single persons in America—the cause of homelessness is lack of housing.

A writer in the *New York Times* describes a homeless woman standing on a traffic island in Manhattan. "She was evicted from her small room in the hotel just across the street," and she is determined to get revenge. Until she does, "nothing will move her from that spot.... Her argumentativeness and her angry fixation on revenge, along with the apparent absence of hallucinations, mark her as a paranoid." Most physicians, I imagine, would be more reserved in passing judgment with so little evidence, but this author makes his diagnosis without hesitation. "The paranoids of the street," he says, "are among the most difficult to help."

Perhaps so. But does it depend on who is offering the help? Is anyone offering to help this woman get back her home? Is it crazy to seek vengeance for being thrown into the street? The absence of anger, some psychiatrists believe, might indicate much greater illness.

The same observer sees additional symptoms of pathology ("negative symptoms," he calls them) in the fact that many homeless persons demonstrate a "gross deterioration in their personal hygiene" and grooming, leading to "indifference" and "apathy." Having just identified one woman as unhealthy because she is so far from being "indifferent" as to seek revenge, he now sees apathy as evidence of illness; so consistency is not what we are looking for in this account. But how much less indifferent might the homeless be if those who decide their fate were less indifferent themselves? How might their grooming and hygiene be improved if they were permitted access to a public toilet?

In New York City, as in many cities, homeless people are denied the right to wash in public bathrooms, to store their few belongings in a public locker, or, in certain cases, to make use of public toilets altogether. Shaving, cleaning of clothes, and other forms of hygiene are prohibited in the men's room of Grand Central Station. The terminal's three hundred lockers, used in former times by homeless people to secure their goods, were removed in 1986 as "a threat to public safety," according to a study made by the New York City Council.

At one-thirty every morning, homeless people are ejected from the station. Many once attempted to take refuge on the ramp that leads to

Forty-second Street because it was protected from the street by wooden doors and thus provided some degree of warmth. But the station management responded to this challenge in two ways. The ramp was mopped with a strong mixture of ammonia to produce a noxious smell, and when the people sleeping there brought cardboard boxes and newspapers to protect them from the fumes, the entrance doors were chained wide open. Temperatures dropped some nights to ten degrees. Having driven these people to the streets, city officials subsequently determined that their willingness to risk exposure to cold weather could be taken as further evidence of mental illness.

At Pennsylvania Station in New York, homeless women are denied the use of toilets. Amtrak police come by and herd them off each hour on the hour. In June 1985, Amtrak officials issued this directive to police: "It is the policy of Amtrak to not allow the homeless and undesirables to remain.... Officers are encouraged to eject all undesirables.... Now is the time to train and educate them that their presence will not be tolerated as cold weather sets in." In an internal memo, according to CBS, an Amtrak official asked flatly: "Can't we get rid of this trash?"

I have spent many nights in conversation with the women who are huddled in the corridors and near the doorway of the public toilets in Penn Station. Many are young. Most are cogent. Few are dressed in the familiar rags suggested by the term *bag ladies.* Unable to bathe or use the toilets in the station, almost all are in conditions of intolerable physical distress. The sight of clusters of police officers, mostly male, guarding a toilet from use by homeless women speaks volumes about the public conscience of New York.

Where do these women defecate? How do they bathe? What will we do when, in her physical distress, a woman finally disrobes in public and begins to urinate right on the floor? "Gross deterioration," someone will call it, evidence of mental illness. In the course of an impromptu survey in the streets last September, Mayor Koch observed a homeless woman who had soiled her own clothes. Not only was the woman crazy, said the mayor, but those who differed with him on his diagnosis must be crazy, too. "I am the number one social worker in this town—with sanity," said he.

It may be that this woman was psychotic, but the mayor's comment says a great deal more about his sense of revulsion and the moral climate of a decade in which words like these may be applauded than about her mental state.

A young man who had lost his job, then his family, then his home, all in the summer of 1986, spoke with me for several hours in Grand Central Station on the weekend following Thanksgiving. "A year ago," he said, "I never thought that somebody like me would end up in a shelter. Nothing you've ever undergone prepares you. You walk into the place [a shelter on the Bowery]—the smell of sweat and urine hits you like a wall. Unwashed bodies and the look of absolute despair on many, many faces there would make you think you were in Dante's Hell.... What you fear is that you will be here forever. You do not know if it is ever going to end. You think to yourself: it is a dream and I will awake. Sometimes I think: it's an experiment. They are watching you to find out how much you can take.... I was a pretty stable man. Now I tremble when I meet somebody in the ordinary world. I'm trembling right now.... For me, the loss of work and loss of wife had left me rocking. Then the welfare regulations hit me. I began to feel that I would be reduced to trash.... Half the people that I know are suffering from chest infections and sleep deprivation. The lack of sleep leaves you debilitated, shaky. You exaggerate your fears. If a psychiatrist came along he'd say that I was crazy. But I was an ordinary man. There was nothing wrong with me. I lost my kids. I lost my home. Now would you say that I was crazy if I told you I was feeling sad?"

"If the plight of homeless adults is the shame of America," writes Fred Hechinger in the *New York Times*, "the lives of homeless children are the nation's crime."

In November 1984, a fact already known to advocates for the homeless was given brief attention by the press. Homeless families, the *New York Times* reported, "mostly mothers and young children, have been sleeping on chairs, counters, and floors of the city's emergency welfare offices." Reacting to such reports, the mayor declared: "The woman is sitting on a chair or on a floor. It is not because we didn't offer her a bed. We provide a shelter for every single person who knocks on our door." On the same day, however, the city reported that in the previous eleven weeks it had been unable to give shelter to 153 families, and in the subsequent year, 1985, the city later reported that about two thousand children slept in welfare offices because of lack of shelter space.

Some eight hundred homeless infants in New York City, reported the National Coalition for the Homeless, "routinely go without sufficient food, cribs, health care, and diapers." The lives of these children "are put at risk," while "high-risk pregnant women" are repeatedly forced to sleep in unsafe "barracks shelters" or welfare offices called Emergency Assistance Units (EAUs). "Coalition monitors, making sporadic random checks, found eight women in their *ninth* month of pregnancy sleeping in EAUs.... Two women denied shelter began having labor contractions at the EAU." In one instance, the Legal Aid Society was forced to go to court after a woman lost her child by miscarriage while lying on the floor of a communal bathroom in a shelter which the courts had already declared unfit to house pregnant women.

The coalition also reported numerous cases in which homeless mothers were obliged to choose between purchasing food or diapers for their infants. Federal guidelines issued in 1986 deepened the nutrition crisis faced by mothers in the welfare shelters by counting the high rent paid to the owners of the buildings as a part of family income, rendering their residents ineligible for food stamps. Families I interviewed who had received as much as $150 in food stamps monthly in June 1986 were cut back to $33 before Christmas.

"Now you're hearing all kinds of horror stories," said President Reagan, "about the people that are going to be thrown out in the snow to hunger and [to] die of cold and so forth.... We haven't cut a single budget." But in the four years leading up to 1985, according to the *New Republic*, Aid to Families with Dependent Children had been cut by $4.8 billion, child nutrition programs by $5.2 billion, food stamps by $6.8 billion. The federal government's authority to help low-income families with housing assistance was cut from $30 billion to $11 billion in Reagan's first term. In his fiscal 1986 budget, the president proposed to cut that by an additional 95 percent.

"If even one American child is forced to go to bed hungry at night," the president said on another occasion, "that is a national tragedy. We are too generous a people to allow this." But in the years since the president spoke these words, thousands of poor children in New York alone have gone to bed too sick to sleep and far too weak to rise the next morning to attend a public school. Thousands more have been unable to attend school at all because their homeless status compels them to move repeatedly from one temporary shelter to another. Even in the affluent suburbs outside New York City, hundreds of homeless children are obliged to ride as far as sixty miles twice a day in order to obtain an education in the public schools to which they were originally assigned before their families were displaced. Many of these children get to school too late to eat their breakfast; others are denied lunch at school because of federal cuts in feeding programs.

Many homeless children die—and others suffer brain damage—as a direct consequence of federal cutbacks in prenatal programs, maternal nutrition, and other feeding programs. The parents of one such child shared with me the story of the year in which their child was delivered, lived, and died. The child, weighing just over four pounds at birth, grew deaf and blind soon after, and for these reasons had to stay in the hospital for several months. When he was released on Christmas Eve of 1984, his mother and father had no home. He lived with his parents in the shelters, subways, streets, and welfare offices of New York City for four winter months, and was readmitted to the hospital in time to die in May 1985.

When we met and spoke the following year, the father told me that his wife had contemplated and even attempted suicide after the child's death, while he had entertained the thought of blowing up the welfare offices of New York City. I would tell him that to do so would be illegal and unwise. I would never tell him it was crazy.

"No one will be turned away," says the mayor of New York City, as hundreds of young mothers with their infants are turned from the doors of shelters season after season. That may sound to some like denial of reality. "Now you're hearing all these stories," says the president of the United States as he denies that anyone is cold or hungry or unhoused. On another occasion he says that the unsheltered "are homeless, you might say, by choice." That sounds every bit as self-deceiving.

The woman standing on the traffic island screaming for revenge until her room has been restored to her sounds relatively healthy by comparison. If three million homeless people did the same, and all at the same time, we might finally be forced to listen.

Suggestions for Discussion

1. What according to Kozol is the primary cause of homelessness?
2. Does the writer view homelessness as a "clinical misfortune," as the end product of social forces, or as the result of personal failure?
3. Why is mental illness a popular explanation for homelessness, according to the author?
4. What arguments does Kozol use to disprove the theory that mental illness is the primary source of homelessness?

Suggestions for Writing

1. For the homeless child, what do you imagine would be the most painful aspects of having no home? Have you ever experienced this? How did you deal with it?
2. Homelessness is a growing problem. How might it be curtailed or eliminated altogether?

MAY SARTON

The Rewards of Living a Solitary Life

May Sarton (1912–1995) was the author of over sixteen volumes of poetry, twenty-two novels, and a number of journals, the last of which was published the year of her death. Among her best-known pieces are *Faithful Are the Wounds* (1955), *Plant Dreaming Deep*

(1968), *Kinds of Love* (1970), and *Magnificent Spinster* (1985). The author finds here that a strong sense of self allows her to find happiness in a solitary life.

The other day an acquaintance of mine, a gregarious and charming man, told me he had found himself unexpectedly alone in New York for an hour or two between appointments. He went to the Whitney and spent the "empty" time looking at things in solitary bliss. For him it proved to be a shock nearly as great as falling in love to discover that he could enjoy himself so much alone.

What had he been afraid of, I asked myself? That, suddenly alone, he would discover that he bored himself, or that there was, quite simply, no self there to meet? But having taken the plunge, he is now on the brink of adventure; he is about to be launched into his own inner space, space as immense, unexplored, and sometimes frightening as outer space to the astronaut. His every perception will come to him with a new freshness and, for a time, seem startingly original. For anyone who can see things for himself with a naked eye becomes, for a moment or two, something of a genius. With another human being present vision becomes double vision, inevitably. We are busy wondering, what does my companion see or think of this, and what do I think of it? The original impact gets lost, or diffused.

"Music I heard with you was more than music." Exactly. And therefore music *itself* can only be heard alone. Solitude is the salt of personhood. It brings out the authentic flavor of every experience.

"Alone one is never lonely: the spirit adventures, walking/In a quiet garden, in a cool house, abiding single there."

Loneliness is most acutely felt with other people, for with others, even with a lover sometimes, we suffer from our differences of taste, temperament, mood. Human intercourse often demands that we soften the edge of perception, or withdraw at the very instant of personal truth for fear of hurting, or of being inappropriately present, which is to say naked, in a social situation. Alone we can afford to be wholly whatever we are, and to feel whatever we feel absolutely. That is a great luxury!

For me the most interesting thing about a solitary life, and mine has been that for the last twenty years, is that it becomes increasingly rewarding. When I can wake up and watch the sun rise over the ocean, as I do most days, and know that I have an entire day ahead, uninterrupted, in which to write a few pages, take a walk with my dog, lie down in the afternoon for a long think (why does one think better in a horizontal position?), read and listen to music, I am flooded with happiness.

I am lonely only when I am overtired, when I have worked too long without a break, when for the time being I feel empty and need filling up.

And I am lonely sometimes when I come back home after a lecture trip, when I have seen a lot of people and talked a lot, and am full to the brim with experience that needs to be sorted out.

Then for a little while the house feels huge and empty, and I wonder where my self is hiding. It has be recaptured slowly by watering the plants, perhaps, and looking again at each one as though it were a person, by feeding the two cats, by cooking a meal.

It takes a while, as I watch the surf blowing up in fountains at the end of the field, but the moment comes when the world falls away, and the self emerges again from the deep unconscious, bringing back all I have recently experienced to be explored and slowly understood, when I can converse again with my hidden powers, and so grow, and so be renewed, till death do us part.

Suggestions for Discussion

1. In asking herself what her friend had been afraid of when he finally found himself alone at a museum, Sarton speculates as to whether he was afraid he would be bored or whether there was no self to meet. How does the presence or absence of a self relate to her thesis?
2. Why does vision become double vision in the presence of another human being?
3. How does the author distinguish between loneliness and solitude? Why does she feel that loneliness is felt most acutely with other people?
4. What details does Sarton offer to explain her happiness in leading a solitary life? What role does the self play in her satisfaction?

Suggestions for Writing

1. Are you persuaded by Sarton of the joys of the solitary life?
2. Defend or challenge her position that loneliness is most acutely felt in the presence of other people.

HENRY DAVID THOREAU

Why I Went to the Woods

Henry David Thoreau (1817–1862) was a philosopher and poet-naturalist whose independent spirit led him to the famous experiment recorded in *Walden, or Life in the Woods* (1854). Thoreau's passion for freedom and his lifetime resistance to conformity in thought and manners are forcefully present in his famous essay, "On the Duty of Civil Disobedience." Thoreau states that he went to the woods in order to encounter only the essential facts of life and avoid all that is petty, trivial, and unnecessary.

I went to the woods because I wished to live deliberately, to front only the essential facts of life, and see if I could not learn what it had to teach, and not, when I came to die, discover that I had not lived. I did not wish to live what was not life, living is so dear; nor did I wish to practice resignation, unless it was quite necessary. I wanted to live deep and suck out all the marrow of life, to live so sturdily and Spartan-like as to put to rout all that was not life, to cut a broad swath and shave close, to drive life into a corner, and reduce it to its lowest terms, and, if it proved to be mean, why then to get the whole and genuine meanness of it, and publish its meanness to the world; or if it were sublime, to know it by experience, and be able to give a true account of it in my next excursion. For most men, it appears to me, are in a strange uncertainty about it, whether it is of the devil or of God, and have *somewhat hastily* concluded that it is the chief end of man here to "glorify God and enjoy him forever."

Still we live meanly, like ants; though the fable tells us that we were long ago changed into men; like pygmies we fight with cranes; it is error upon error, and clout upon clout, and our best virtue has for its occasion a superfluous and evitable wretchedness. Our life is frittered away by detail. An honest man has hardly need to count more than his ten fingers, or in extreme cases he may add his ten toes, and lump the rest. Simplicity, simplicity, simplicity! I say, let your affairs be as two or three, and not a hundred or a thousand; instead of a million count half a dozen, and keep your accounts on your thumb-nail. In the midst of this chopping sea of civilized life, such are the clouds and storms and quicksands and thousand-and-one items to be allowed for, that a man has to live, if he would not founder and go to the bottom and not make his port at all, by dead reckoning, and he must be a great calculator indeed who succeeds. Simplify, simplify. Instead of three meals a day, if it be necessary eat but one; instead of a hundred dishes, five; and reduce other things in proportion. Our life is like a German Confederacy, made of up petty states, with its boundary forever fluctuating, so that even a German cannot tell you how it is bounded at any moment. The nation itself, with all its so-called internal improvements, which, by the way are all external and superficial, is just such an unwieldy and overgrown establishment, cluttered with furniture and tripped up by its own traps, ruined by luxury and heedless expense, by want of calculation and a worthy aim, as the million households in the lands; and the only cure for it, as for them, is in a rigid economy, a stern and more than Spartan simplicity of life and elevation of purpose. It lives too fast. Men think that it is essential that the *Nation* have commerce, and export ice, and talk through a telegraph, and ride thirty miles an hour, without a doubt, whether *they* do or not; but whether we should live like baboons or like men, is a little uncertain. If we do not get our sleepers, and forge rails, and devote days and nights to the work, but go to tinkering upon our *lives* to improve *them,* who will build railroads? And if railroads are not built, how shall we get to heaven in season? But if we stay at home and mind our business, who will want railroads? We do not ride on the railroad; it rides upon us. Did you ever think what those sleepers are that underlie the railroad? Each one is a man, an Irishman, or a Yankee man. The rails are laid on them, and they are covered with sand, and the cars run smoothly over them. They are sound sleepers, I assure you. And every few years a new lot is laid down and run over; so that, if some have the pleasure of riding on a rail, others have the misfortune to be ridden upon. And when they run over a man that is walking in his sleep, a supernumerary sleeper in the wrong position, and wake him up, they suddenly stop the cars, and make a hue and cry about it, as if this were an exception. I am glad to know that it takes a gang of men for every five miles to keep the sleepers down and level in their beds as it is, for this is a sign that they may sometimes get up again.

Why should we live with such hurry and waste of life? We are determined to be starved before we are hungry. Men say that a stitch in time saves nine, and so they take a thousand stitches to-day to save nine tomorrow. As for *work,* we haven't any of any consequence. We have the Saint Vitus' dance, and cannot possibly keep our heads still. If I should only give a few pulls at the parish bell-rope, as for a fire, that is, without setting the bell, there is hardly a man on his farm in the outskirts of Concord, notwithstanding that press of engagements which was his excuse so many times this morning, nor a boy, nor a woman, I might almost say, but would foresake all and follow that sound, not mainly to save property from the flames, but, if we will confess the truth, much more to see it burn, since burn it must, and we, be it known, did not set it on fire—or to see it put out, and have a hand in it, if that is done as handsomely; yes, even if it were the parish church itself. Hardly a man takes a half-hour's nap after dinner, but when he wakes he holds up his head and asks, "What's the news?" as if the rest of mankind had stood his sentinels. Some give directions to be waked every half-hour, doubtless for no other purpose; and then, to pay for it, they tell what they have dreamed. After a night's sleep the news is as indispensable as the breakfast. "Pray tell me anything new that has happened to a man anywhere on this globe"—and he reads it over his coffee and rolls, that a man has had his eyes gouged out this morning on the Wachito River; never dreaming the while that he lives in the dark unfathomed mammoth cave of this world, and has but the rudiment of an eye himself.

For my part, I could easily do without the post-office. I think that there are very few important communications made through it. To speak critically, I never received more than one or two letters in my life—I wrote this some years ago—that were worth the postage. The penny-post is, commonly, an institution through which you seriously offer a man that penny for his thoughts which is so often safely offered in jest. And I am sure that I never read any memorable news in a newspaper. If we read of one man robbed, or murdered, or killed by accident, or one house burned, or one vessel wrecked, or one steamboat blown up, or one cow run over on the Western Railroad, or one mad dog killed, or one lot of grasshoppers in the winter—we never need read of another. One is enough. If you are acquainted with the principle, what do you care for a myriad instances and applications? To a philosopher all *news*, as it is called, is gossip, and they who edit and read it are old women over their tea. Yet not a few are greedy after this gossip. There was such a rush, as I hear, the other day at one of the offices to learn the foreign news by the last arrival, that several large squares of plate glass belonging to the establishment were broken by the pressure—news which I seriously think a ready wit might write a twelvemonth, or twelve years, beforehand with sufficient accuracy. As for Spain, for instance, if you know how to throw in Don Carlos and the Infanta, and Don Pedro and Seville and Granada, from time to time in the right proportions—they may have changed the names a little since I saw the papers—and serve up a bullfight when other entertainments fail, it will be true to the letter, and give us as good an idea of the exact state or ruin of things in Spain as the most succinct and lucid reports under this head in the newspapers; and as for England, almost the last significant scrap of news from that quarter was the revolution of 1649; and if you have learned the history of her crops for an average year, you never need attend to that thing again, unless your speculations are of a merely pecuniary character. If one may judge who rarely looks into the newspapers, nothing new does ever happen in foreign parts, a French revolution not excepted.

What news! how much more important to know what that is which was never old! "Kieou-he-yu (great dignitary of the state of Wei) sent a man to Khoung-tseu to know his news. Khoung-tseu caused the messenger to be seated near him, and questioned him in these terms: What is your master doing? The messenger answered with respect: My master desires to diminish the number of his faults, but he cannot come to the end of them. The messenger being gone, the philosopher remarked: What a worthy messenger! What a worthy messenger!" The preacher, instead of vexing the ears of drowsy farmers on their day of rest at the end of the week—for Sunday is the fit conclusion of an ill-spent week, and not the fresh and brave beginning of a new one—with this one other draggle-tail of a sermon, should shout with thundering voice, "Pause! Avast! Why so seeming fast, but deadly slow?"

Shams and delusions are esteemed for soundless truths, while reality is fabulous. If men would steadily observe realities only, and not allow themselves to be deluded, life, to compare it with such things as we know, would be like a fairy tale and the Arabian Nights' Entertainments. If we respected only what is inevitable and has a right to be, music and poetry would resound along the streets. When we are unhurried and wise, we perceive that only great and worthy things have any permanent and absolute existence, that petty fears and petty pleasures are but the shadow of the reality. This is always exhilarating and sublime. By closing the eyes and slumbering, and consenting to be deceived by shows, men establish and confirm their daily life of routine and habit everywhere, which still is built on purely illusory foundations. Children, who play life, discern its true law and relations more clearly than men, who fail to live it worthily, but who think that they are wiser by experience, that is, by failure. I have read in a Hindoo book, that "there was a king's son, who, being expelled in infancy from his native city, was brought up by a forester, and, growing up to maturity in that state, imagined himself to belong to the barbarous race with which he lived. One of his father's ministers having discovered him, revealed to him what he was, and the misconception of his character was removed, and he knew himself to be a prince. So soul," continues the Hindoo philosopher, "from the circumstances in which it is placed, mistakes its own character, until the truth is revealed to it by some holy teacher and then it knows itself to be *Brahme.*" I perceive that we inhabitants of New England live this mean life that we do because our vision does not penetrate the surface of things. We think that that *is* which *appears* to be. If a man should walk through this town and see only the reality, where, think you, would the "Milldam" go to? If he should give us an account of the realities he beheld there, we should not recognize the place in his description. Look at the meetinghouse, or a courthouse, or a jail, or a shop, or a dwelling-house, and say what that thing really is before a true gaze, and they would all go to pieces in your account of them. Men esteem truth remote, in the outskirts of the system, behind the farthest star, before Adam and after the last man. In eternity there is indeed something true and sublime. But all these times and places and occasions are now and here. God himself culminates in the present moment, and will never be more divine in the lapse of all the ages. And we are enabled to apprehend at all what is sublime and noble only by the perpetual instilling and drenching of the reality that surrounds us. The universe constantly and obediently answers to our conceptions; whether we travel fast or slow, the track is laid for us. Let us spend our lives in conceiving then. The poet or the artist never yet had so fair and noble a design but some of his posterity at least could accomplish it.

Let us spend one day as deliberately as Nature, and not be thrown off the track by every nutshell and mosquito's wing that falls on the rails. Let us rise early and fast, or breakfast, gently and without perturbation; let company come and let company go, let the bells ring and the children cry—determined to make a day of it. Why should we knock under and go with the stream? Let us not be upset and overwhelmed in that terrible rapid and whirlpool called a dinner, situated in the meridian shallows. Weather this danger and you are safe, for the rest of the way is downhill. With unrelaxed nerves, with morning vigor, sail by it, looking another way, tied to the mast like Ulysses. If the engine whistles, let it whistle till it is hoarse for its pains. If the bell rings, why should we run? We will consider what kind of music they are like. Let us settle ourselves and work and wedge our feet downward through the mud and slush of opinion, and prejudice, and tradition, and delusion, and appearance, that alluvion which covers the globe, through Paris and London, through New York and Boston and Concord, through Church and State, through poetry and philosophy and religion, till we come to a hard bottom and rocks in place, which we can call *reality,* and say, This is, and no mistake; and then begin, having a *point d'appui,* below freshet and frost and fire, a place where you might found a wall or a state, or set a lamppost safely, or perhaps a gauge, not a Nilometer, but a Realometer, that future ages might know how deep a freshet of shams and appearances had gathered from time to time. If you stand right fronting and face to face to a fact, you will see the sun glimmer on both its surfaces, as if it were a cimeter, and feel its sweet edge dividing you through the heart and marrow, and so you will happily conclude your mortal career. Be it life or death, we crave only reality. If we are really dying, let us hear the rattle in our throats and feel cold in the extremities; if we are alive, let us go about our business.

Time is but the stream I go afishing in. I drink at it; but while I drink I see the sandy bottom and detect how shallow it is. Its thin current slides away but eternity remains. I would drink deeper; fish in the sky, whose bottom is pebbly with stars. I cannot count one. I know not the first letter of the alphabet. I have always been regretting that I was not as wise as the day I was born. The intellect is a cleaver; it discerns and rifts its way into the secret of things. I do not wish to be any more busy with my hands than is necessary. My head is hands and feet. I feel all my best faculties concentrated in it. My instinct tells me that my head is an organ for burrowing, as some creatures use their snout and fore paws, and with it I would mine and burrow my way through these hills. I think that the richest vein is somewhere hereabouts; so by the divining-rod and thin rising vapors, I judge; and here I will begin to mine.

Suggestions for Discussion

1. Why did Thoreau go to the woods?
2. With what details does Thoreau support his statement that "we live meanly like ants"?
3. Interpret Thoreau's rhetorical question in the context of his philosophy: "If you are acquainted with the principle, what do you care for a myriad instances and applications"?
4. With what details does Thoreau illustrate his impatience with man's proclivity for being deluded?
5. How do Thoreau's rhetorical questions, metaphors, and allusions contribute to substance and tone?
6. What aspects of American life does Thoreau repudiate and why?
7. What does he affirm? Paraphrase his last two paragraphs.

Suggestions for Writing

1. Discuss what you have learned from your observations of nature.
2. Discuss: "Our life is frittered away by detail."
3. Comment on: "Shams and delusions are esteemed for soundless truths, while reality is fabulous."
4. What would Thoreau's impressions be of our current preoccupations?

BARRY LOPEZ

Landscape and Narrative

Barry Lopez (b. 1945) is an essayist, author, and short story writer. His essays, often about landscape and culture, appear frequently in *Harper's* and *Orion.* His recent collection, *Field Notes: The Grace Note of the Canyon Wren* (1994), is linked to two previous collections of stories, *Desert Notes* (1976) and *River Notes* (1979). His nonfiction book, *Arctic Dreams* (1987), won the National Book Award. In this piece, taken from *Crossing Open Ground* (1989), Lopez explores the relationship between telling stories and discovering the purpose of our lives.

One summer evening in a remote village in the Brooks Range of Alaska, I sat among a group of men listening to hunting stories about the trapping and pursuit of animals. I was particularly interested in several incidents involving wolverine, in part because a friend of mine was studying wolverine in Canada, among the Cree, but, too, because I find this animal such an intense creature. To hear about its life is to learn more about fierceness.

Wolverines are not intentionally secretive, hiding their lives from view, but they are seldom observed. The range of their known behavior is less than that of, say, bears or wolves. Still, that evening no gratuitous details were set out. This was somewhat odd, for wolverine easily excite the imagination; they can loom suddenly in the landscape with authority, with an aura larger than their compact physical dimensions, drawing one's immediate and complete attention. Wolverine also have a deserved reputation for resoluteness in the worst winters, for ferocious strength. But neither did these attributes induce the men to embellish.

I listened carefully to these stories, taking pleasure in the sharply observed detail surrounding the dramatic thread of events. The story I remember most vividly was about a man hunting a wolverine from a snow machine in the spring. He followed the animal's tracks for several miles over rolling tundra in a certain valley. Soon he caught sight ahead of a dark spot on the crest of a hill—the wolverine pausing to look back. The hunter was catching up, but each time he came over a rise the wolverine was looking back from the next rise, just out of range. The hunter topped one more rise and met the wolverine bounding toward him. Before he could pull his rifle from its scabbard the wolverine flew across the engine cowl and the windshield, hitting him square in the chest. The hunter scrambled his arms wildly, trying to get the wolverine out of his lap, and fell over as he did so. The wolverine jumped clear as the snow machine rolled over, and fixed the man with a stare. He had not bitten, not even scratched the man. Then the wolverine walked away. The man thought of reaching for the gun, but no, he did not.

The other stories were like this, not so much making a point as evoking something about contact with wild animals that would never be completely understood.

When the stories were over, four or five of us walked out of the home of our host. The surrounding land, in the persistent light of a far northern summer, was still visible for miles—the striated, pitched massifs of the Brooks Range; the shy, willow-lined banks of the John River flowing south from Anaktuvuk Pass; and the flat tundra plain, opening with great affirmation to the north. The landscape seemed alive because of the stories. It was precisely these ocherous tones, this kind of willow, exactly this austerity that had informed the wolverine narratives. I felt exhilaration, and a deeper confirmation of the stories. The mundane tasks which awaited me I anticipated now with pleasure. The stories had renewed in me a sense of the purpose of my life.

This feeling, an inexplicable renewal of enthusiasm after storytelling, is familiar to many people. It does not seem to matter greatly what the subject is, as long as the context is intimate and the story is told for its own sake, not forced to serve merely as the vehicle for an idea. The tone of the story need not be solemn. The darker aspects of life need not be ignored. But I think intimacy is indispensable—a feeling that derives from the listener's trust and a storyteller's certain knowledge of his subject and regard for his audience. This intimacy deepens if the storyteller tempers his authority with humility, or when terms of idiomatic expression, or at least the physical setting for the story, are shared.

I think of two landscapes—one outside the self, the other within. The external landscape is the one we see—not only the line and color of the land and its shading at different times of the day, but also its plants and animals in season, its weather, its geology, the record of its climate and evolution. If you walk up, say, a dry arroyo in the Sonoran Desert you will feel a mounding and rolling of sand and silt beneath your foot that is distinctive. You will anticipate the crumbling of the sedimentary earth in the arroyo bank as your hand reaches out, and in that tangible evidence you will sense a history of water in the region. Perhaps a black-throated sparrow lands in a paloverde bush—the resiliency of the twig under the bird, that precise shade of yellowish-green against the milk-blue sky, the fluttering whir of the arriving sparrow, are what I mean by "the landscape." Draw on the smell of creosote bush, or clack stones together in the dry air. Feel how light is the desiccated dropping of the kangaroo rat. Study an animal track obscured by the wind. These are all elements of the land, and what makes the landscape comprehensible are the relationships between them. One learns a landscape finally not by knowing the name or identity of everything in it, but by perceiving the relationships in it—like that between the sparrow and the twig. The difference between the relationships and the elements is the same as that between written history and a catalog of events.

The second landscape I think of is an interior one, a kind of projection within a person of a part of the exterior landscape. Relationships in the exterior landscape include those that are named and discernible, such as the nitrogen cycle, or a vertical sequence of Ordovician limestone, and others that are uncodified or ineffable, such as winter light falling on a particular kind of granite, or the effect of humidity on the frequency of a blackpoll warbler's burst of song. That these relationships have purpose and order, however inscrutable they may seem to us, is a tenet of evolution. Similarly, the speculations, intuitions, and formal ideas we refer to as "mind" are a set of relationships in the interior landscape with purpose and order; some of these are obvious, many impenetrably subtle. The shape and character of these relationships in a person's thinking, I believe, are deeply influenced by where on this earth one goes, what one touches, the patterns one observes in nature—the intricate history of one's life in the land, even a life in the city, where wind, the chirp of birds, the line of a falling leaf, are known. These thoughts are arranged, further, according to the thread of one's moral, intellectual, and spiritual development. The interior landscape responds to the character and subtlety of an exterior landscape; the shape of the individual mind is affected by land as it is by genes.

In stories like those I heard at Anaktuvuk Pass about wolverine, the relationship between separate elements in the land is set forth clearly. It is put in a simple framework of sequential incidents and apposite detail. If the exterior landscape is limned well, the listener often feels that he has heard something pleasing and authentic—trustworthy. We derive this sense of confidence I think not so much from verifiable truth as from an understanding that lying has played no role in the narrative. The storyteller is obligated to engage the reader with a precise vocabulary, to set forth a coherent and dramatic rendering of incidents—and to be ingenuous.

When one hears a story one takes pleasure in it for different reasons—for the euphony of its phrases, an aspect of the plot, or because one identifies with one of the characters. With certain stories certain individuals may experience a deeper, more profound sense of well-being. This latter phenomenon, in my understanding, rests at the heart of storytelling as an elevated experience among aboriginal peoples. It results from bringing two landscapes together. The exterior landscape is organized according to principles or laws or tendencies beyond human control. It is understood to contain an integrity that is beyond human analysis and unimpeachable. Insofar as the storyteller depicts various subtle and obvious relationships in the exterior landscape accurately in his story, and insofar as he orders them along traditional lines of meaning to create the narrative, the narrative will "ring true." The listener who "takes the story to heart" will feel a pervasive sense of congruence within himself and also with the world.

Among the Navajo and, as far as I know, many other native peoples, the land is thought to exhibit a sacred order. That order is the basis of ritual. The rituals themselves reveal the power in that order. Art, architecture, vocabulary, and costume, as well as ritual, are derived from the perceived natural order of the universe—from observations and meditations on the exterior landscape. An indigenous philosophy—metaphysics, ethics, epistemology, aesthetics, and logic—may also be derived from a people's continuous attentiveness to both the obvious (scientific) and ineffable (artistic) orders of the local landscape. Each individual, further, undertakes to order his interior landscape according to the exterior landscape. To succeed in this means to achieve a balanced state of mental health.

I think of the Navajo for a specific reason. Among the various sung ceremonies of this people—Enemyway, Coyoteway, Red Antway, Uglyway—is one called Beautyway. In the Navajo view, the elements of one's interior life—one's psychological makeup and moral bearing—are subject to a persistent principle of disarray. Beautyway is, in part, a spiritual invocation of the order of the exterior universe, that irreducible, holy complexity that manifests itself as all things changing through time (a Navajo definition of beauty, hózhǫ́ǫ́). The purpose of this invocation is to recreate in the individual who is the subject of the Beautyway ceremony that same order, to make the individual again a reflection of the myriad enduring relationships of the landscape.

I believe story functions in a similar way. A story draws on relationships in the exterior landscape and projects them onto the interior landscape. The purpose of storytelling is to achieve harmony between the two landscapes, to use all the elements of story—syntax, mood, figures of speech—in a harmonious way to reproduce the harmony of the land in the individual's interior. Inherent in story is the power to reorder a state of psychological confusion through contact with the pervasive truth of those relationships we call "the land."

These thoughts, of course, are susceptible to interpretation. I am convinced, however, that these observations can be applied to the kind of prose we call nonfiction as well as to traditional narrative forms such as the novel and the short story, and to some poems. Distinctions between fiction and nonfiction are sometimes obscured by arguments over what constitutes "the truth." In the aboriginal literature I am familiar with, the first distinction made among narratives is to separate the authentic from the inauthentic. Myth, which we tend to regard as fictitious or "merely metaphorical," is as authentic, as real, as the story of a wolverine in a man's lap. (A distinction is made, of course, about the elevated nature of myth—and frequently the circumstances of myth-telling are more rigorously prescribed than those for the telling of legends or vernacular stories—but all of these narratives are rooted in the local landscape. To violate *that* connection is to call the narrative itself into question.)

The power of narrative to nurture and heal, to repair a spirit in disarray, rests on two things: the skillful invocation of unimpeachable sources and a listener's knowledge that no hypocrisy or subterfuge is involved. This last simple fact is to me one of the most imposing aspects of the Holocene history of man.

We are more accustomed now to thinking of "the truth" as something that can be explicitly stated, rather than as something that can be evoked in a metaphorical way outside science and Occidental culture. Neither can truth be reduced to aphorism or formulas. It is something alive and unpronounceable. Story creates an atmosphere in which it becomes discernible as a pattern. For a storyteller to insist on relationships that do not exist is to lie. Lying is the opposite of story. (I do not mean to confuse ignorance with deception, or to imply that a storyteller can perceive all that is inherent in the land. Every storyteller falls short of a perfect limning of the landscape—perception and language both fail. But to make up something that is not there, something which can never be corroborated in the land, to knowingly set forth a false relationship, is to be lying, no longer telling a story.)

Because of the intricate, complex nature of the land, it is not always possible for a storyteller to grasp what is contained in a story. The intent of the storyteller, then, must be to evoke, honestly, some single aspect of all that the land contains. The storyteller knows that because different individuals grasp the story at different levels, the focus of his regard for truth must be at the primary one—with who was there, what happened, when, where, and why things occurred. The story will then possess similar truth at other levels—the integrity inherent at the primary level of meaning will be conveyed everywhere else. As long as the storyteller carefully describes the order before him, and uses his storytelling skill to heighten and emphasize certain relationships, it is even possible for the story to be more successful than the storyteller himself is able to imagine.

I would like to make a final point about the wolverine stories I heard at Anaktuvuk Pass. I wrote down the details afterward, concentrating especially on aspects of the biology and ecology of the animals. I sent the information on to my friend living with the Cree. When, many months later, I saw him, I asked whether the Cree had enjoyed these insights of the Nunamiut into the nature of the wolverine. What had they said?

"You know," he told me, "how they are. They said, 'That could happen.'"

In these uncomplicated words the Cree declared their own knowledge of the wolverine. They acknowledged that although they themselves had never seen the things the Nunamiut spoke of, they accepted them as accurate observations, because they did not consider story a context for misrepresentation. They also preserved their own dignity by not overstating their confidence in the Nunamiut, a distant and unknown people.

Whenever I think of this courtesy on the part of the Cree I think of the dignity that is ours when we cease to demand the truth and realize that the best we can have of those substantial truths that guide our lives is metaphorical—a story. And the most of it we are likely to discern comes only when we accord one another the respect the Cree showed the Nunamiut. Beyond this—that the interior landscape is a metaphorical representation of the exterior landscape, that the truth reveals itself most fully not in dogma but in the paradox, irony, and contradictions that distinguish compelling narratives—beyond this there are only failures of imagination: reductionism in science; fundamentalism in religion; fascism in politics.

Our national literatures should be important to us insofar as they sustain us with illumination and heal us. They can always do that so long as they are written with respect for both the source and the reader, and with an understanding of why the human heart and the land have been brought together so regularly in human history.

Suggestions for Discussion

1. What does Lopez consider to be the key elements of a story? What is necessary to make a story "renew in us a sense of the purpose of our lives"?
2. Lopez speaks of "two landscapes—one outside the self, the other within." How does he characterize these?
3. What role does ritual play in affirming the order inherent in both landscapes and in establishing their true relationship?

Suggestions for Writing

1. Go to a place that you find to be beautiful. Be attentive to both the "obvious (scientific) and ineffable (artistic) orders" of the landscape. Write about the relations that emerge from this exterior world and from your own inner space.

2. Lopez says, "Beyond this—that the interior landscape is a metaphorical representation of the exterior landscape, that the truth reveals itself most fully not in dogma but in the paradox, irony, and contradictions that distinguish compelling narratives—beyond this there are only failures of imagination: reductionism in science; fundamentalism in religion; racism in politics." Try to engage this argument in an essay.

HELEN KELLER

Three Days to See

Helen Keller (1880–1968) was deaf and blind from the age of nineteen months. Through her teacher, Annie Sullivan, she learned to communicate by using sign language and later through voice lessons. She graduated from Radcliffe College with honors and wrote a critically acclaimed autobiography, *Story of My Life* (1902). Other books are *Optimism* (1903), *The World I Live In* (1908), and *Out of the Dark* (1913). In this essay Keller movingly describes the delights she would experience were she to be given three days to see.

All of us have read thrilling stories in which the hero had only a limited and specified time to live. Sometimes it was as long as a year; sometimes as short as twenty-four hours. But always we were interested in discovering just how the doomed man chose to spend his last days or his last hours. I speak, of course, of free men who have a choice, not condemned criminals whose sphere of activities is strictly delimited.

Such stories set us thinking, wondering what we should do under similar circumstances. What events, what experiences, what associations should we crowd into those last hours as mortal beings? What happiness should we find in reviewing the past, what regrets?

Sometimes I have thought it would be an excellent rule to live each day as if we should die tomorrow. Such an attitude would emphasize sharply the values of life. We should live each day with a gentleness, a vigor, and a keenness of appreciation which are often lost when time stretches before us in the constant panorama of more days and months and years to come. There are those, of course, who would adopt the epicurean motto of "Eat, drink, and be merry," but most people would be chastened by the certainty of impending death.

In stories, the doomed hero is usually saved at the last minute by some stroke of fortune, but almost always his sense of values is changed. He becomes more appreciative of the meaning of life and its permanent spiritual values. It has often been noted that those who live, or have lived, in the shadow of death bring a mellow sweetness to everything they do.

Most of us, however, take life for granted. We know that one day we must die, but usually we picture that day as far in the future. When we are in buoyant health, death is all but unimaginable. We seldom think of it. The days stretch out in an endless vista. So we go about our petty tasks, hardly aware of our listless attitude toward life.

The same lethargy, I am afraid, characterizes the use of all our faculties and senses. Only the deaf appreciate hearing, only the blind realize the manifold blessings that lie in sight. Particularly does this observation apply to those who have lost sight and hearing in adult life. But those who have never suffered impairment of sight or hearing seldom make the fullest use of these blessed faculties. Their eyes and ears take in all sights and sounds hazily, without concentration and with little appreciation. It is the same old story of not being grateful for what we have until we lose it, of not being conscious of health until we are ill.

I have often thought it would be a blessing if each human being were stricken blind and deaf for a few days at some time during his early adult life. Darkness would make him more appreciative of sight; silence would teach him the joys of sound.

Now and then I have tested my seeing friends to discover what they see. Recently I was visited by a very good friend who had just returned from a long walk in the woods, and I asked her what she had observed. "Nothing in particular," she replied. I might have been incredulous had I not been accustomed to such responses, for long ago I became convinced that the seeing see little.

How was it possible, I asked myself, to walk for an hour through the woods and see nothing worthy of note? I who cannot see find hundreds of things to interest me through mere touch. I feel the delicate symmetry of a leaf. I pass my hands lovingly about the smooth skin of a silver birch, or the rough shaggy bark of a pine. In spring I touch the branches of trees hopefully in search of a bud, the first sign of awakening Nature after her winter's sleep. I feel the delightful, velvety texture of a flower, and discover its remarkable convolutions; and something of the miracle of Nature is revealed to me. Occasionally, if I am fortunate, I place my hand gently on a small tree and feel the happy quiver of a bird in full song. I am delighted to have the cool waters of a brook rush through my open fingers. To me a lush carpet of pine needles or spongy grass is more welcome than the most luxurious Persian rug. To me the pageant of seasons is a thrilling and unending drama, the action of which streams through my finger tips.

At times my heart cries out with longing to see all these things. If I can get so much pleasure from mere touch, how much more beauty must be revealed by sight. Yet, those who have eyes apparently see little. The panorama of color and action which fills the world is taken for granted. It is human, perhaps, to appreciate little that which we have and to long for that which we have not, but it is a great pity that in the world of light the gift of sight is used only as a mere convenience rather than as a means of adding fullness to life.

If I were the president of a university I should establish a compulsory course in "How to Use Your Eyes." The professor would try to show his pupils how they could add joy to their lives by really seeing what passes unnoticed before them. He would try to awake their dormant and sluggish faculties.

Perhaps I can best illustrate by imagining what I should most like to see if I were given the use of my eyes, say, for just three days. And while I am imagining, suppose you, too, set your mind to work on the problem of how you would use your own eyes if you had only three more days to see. If with the oncoming darkness of the third night you knew that the sun would never rise for you again, how would you spend those three precious intervening days? What would you most want to let your gaze rest upon?

I, naturally, should want most to see the things which have become dear to me through my years of darkness. You, too, would want to let your eyes rest long on the things that have become dear to you so that you could take the memory of them with you into the night that loomed before you.

If by some miracle I were granted three seeing days, to be followed by a relapse into darkness, I should divide the period into three parts.

On the first day, I should want to see the people whose kindness and gentleness and companionship have made my life worth living. First I should like to gaze long upon the face of my dear teacher, Mrs. Anne Sullivan Macy, who came to me when I was a child and opened the outer world to me. I should want not merely to see the outline of her face, so that I could cherish it in my memory, but to study that face and find in it the living evidence of the sympathetic tenderness and patience with which she accomplished the difficult task of my education. I should like to see in her eyes that strength of character which has enabled her to stand firm in the face of difficulties, and that compassion for all humanity which she has revealed to me so often.

I do not know what it is to see into the heart of a friend through that "window of the soul," the eye. I can only "see" through my finger tips the outline of a face. I can detect laughter, sorrow, and many other obvious emotions. I know my friends from the feel of their faces. But I cannot really picture their personalities by touch. I know their personalities, of course, through other means, through the thoughts they express to me, through whatever of their actions are revealed to me. But I am denied that deeper understanding of them which I am sure would come through sight of them, through watching their reactions to various expressed thoughts and circumstances, through noting the immediate and fleeting reactions of their eyes and countenance.

Friends who are near to me I know well, because through the months and years they reveal themselves to me in all their phases; but of casual friends I have only an incomplete impression, an impression gained from a handclasp, from spoken words which I take from their lips with my finger tips, or which they tap into the palm of my hand.

How much easier, how much more satisfying it is for you who can see to grasp quickly the essential qualities of another person by watching the subtleties of expression, the quiver of a muscle, the flutter of a hand. But does it ever occur to you to use your sight to see into the inner nature of a friend or acquaintance? Do not most of you seeing people grasp casually the outward features of a face and let it go at that?

For instance, can you describe accurately the faces of five good friends? Some of you can, but many cannot. As an experiment, I have questioned husbands of long standing about the color of their wives' eyes, and often they express embarrassed confusion and admit that they do not know. And, incidentally, it is a chronic complaint of wives that their husbands do not notice new dresses, new hats, and changes in household arrangements.

The eyes of seeing persons soon become accustomed to the routine of their surroundings, and they actually see only the startling and spectacular. But even in viewing the most spectacular sights the eyes are lazy. Court records reveal every day how inaccurately "eyewitnesses" see. A given event will be "seen" in several different ways by as many witnesses. Some see more than others, but few see everything that is within the range of their vision.

Oh, the things that I should see if I had the power of sight for just three days!

The first day would be a busy one. I should call to me all my dear friends and look long into their faces, imprinting upon my mind the outward evidences of the beauty that is within them. I should let my eyes rest, too, on the face of a baby, so that I could catch a vision of the eager, innocent beauty which precedes the individual's consciousness of the conflicts which life develops.

And I should like to look into the loyal, trusting eyes of my dogs—the grave, canny little Scottie, Darkie, and the stalwart, understanding Great Dane, Helga, whose warm, tender, and playful friendships are so comforting to me.

On that busy first day I should also view the small simple things of my home. I want to see the warm colors in the rugs under my feet, the pictures on the walls, the intimate trifles that transform a house into home. My eyes would rest respectfully on the books in raised type which I have read, but they would be more eagerly interested in the printed books which seeing people can read, for during the long night of my life the books I have read and those which have been read to me have built themselves into a great shining lighthouse, revealing to me the deepest channels of human life and the human spirit.

In the afternoon of that first seeing day, I should take a long walk in the woods and intoxicate my eyes on the beauties of the world of Nature, trying desperately to absorb in a few hours the vast splendor which is constantly unfolding itself to those who can see. On the way home from my woodland jaunt my path would lie near a farm so that I might see the patient horses plowing in the field (perhaps I should see only a tractor!) and the serene content of men living close to the soil. And I should pray for the glory of a colorful sunset.

When dusk had fallen, I should experience the double delight of being able to see by artificial light, which the genius of man has created to extend the power of his sight when Nature decrees darkness.

In the night of that first day of sight, I should not be able to sleep, so full would be my mind of the memories of the day.

The next day—the second day of sight—I should arise with the dawn and see the thrilling miracle by which night is transformed into day. I should behold with awe the magnificent panorama of light with which the sun awakens the sleeping earth.

This day I should devote to a hasty glimpse of the world, past and present. I should want to see the pageant of man's progress, the kaleidoscope of the ages. How can so much be compressed into one day? Through the museums, of course. Often I have visited the New York Museum of Natural History to touch with my hands many of the objects there exhibited, but I have longed to see with my eyes the condensed history of the earth and its inhabitants displayed there—animals and the races of men pictured in their native environment; gigantic carcasses of dinosaurs and mastodons which roamed the earth long before man appeared, with his tiny stature and powerful brain, to conquer the animal kingdom; realistic presentations of the processes of evolution in animals, in man, and in the implements which man has used to fashion for himself a secure home on this planet; and a thousand and one other aspects of natural history.

I wonder how many readers of this article have viewed this panorama of the face of living things as pictured in that inspiring museum. Many, of course, have not had the opportunity, but I am sure that many who *have* had the opportunity have not made use of it. There, indeed, is a place to use your eyes. You who see can spend many fruitful days there, but I, with my imaginary three days of sight, could only take a hasty glimpse, and pass on.

My next stop would be the Metropolitan Museum of Art, for just as the Museum of Natural History reveals the material aspects of the world, so does the Metropolitan show the myriad facets of the human spirit. Throughout the history of humanity the urge to artistic expression has been almost as powerful as the urge for food, shelter, and procreation. And here, in the vast chambers of the Metropolitan Museum, is unfolded before me the spirit of Egypt, Greece, and Rome, as expressed in their art. I know well through my hands the sculptured gods and goddesses of the ancient Nile-land. I have felt copies of Parthenon friezes, and I have sensed the rhythmic beauty of charging Athenian warriors. Apollos and Venuses and the Winged Victory of Samothrace are friends of my finger tips. The gnarled, bearded features of Homer are dear to me, for he, too, knew blindness.

My hands have lingered upon the living marble of Roman sculpture as well as that of later generations. I have passed my hands over a plaster cast of Michelangelo's inspiring and heroic Moses; I have sensed the power of Rodin; I have been awed by the devoted spirit of Gothic wood carving. These arts which can be touched have meaning for me, but even they were meant to be seen rather than felt, and I can only guess at the beauty which remains hidden from me. I can admire the simple lines of a Greek vase, but its figured decorations are lost to me.

So on this, my second day of sight, I should try to probe into the soul of man through his art. The things I knew through touch I should now see. More splendid still, the whole magnificent world of painting would be opened to me, from the Italian Primitives, with their serene religious devotion, to the Moderns, with their feverish visions. I should look deep into the canvases of Raphael, Leonardo da Vinci, Titian, Rembrandt. I should want to feast my eyes upon the warm colors of Veronese, study the mysteries of El Greco, catch a new vision of Nature from Corot. Oh, there is so much rich meaning and beauty in the art of the ages for you who have eyes to see!

Upon my short visit to this temple of art I should not be able to review a fraction of that great world of art which is open to you. I should be able to get only a superficial impression. Artists tell me that for a deep and true appreciation of art one must educate the eye. One must learn through experience to weigh the merits of line, of composition, of form and color. If I had eyes, how happily would I embark upon so fascinating a study! Yet I am told that, to many of you who have eyes to see, the world of art is a dark night, unexplored and unilluminated.

It would be with extreme reluctance that I should leave the Metropolitan Museum, which contains the key to beauty—a beauty so neglected. Seeing persons, however, do not need a Metropolitan to find this key to beauty. The same key lies waiting in smaller museums, and in books on the shelves of even small libraries. But naturally, in my limited time of imaginary sight, I should choose the place where the key unlocks the greatest treasures in the shortest time.

The evening of my second day of sight I should spend at a theater or at the movies. Even now I often attend theatrical performances of all sorts, but the action of the play must be spelled into my hand by a companion. But how I should like to see with my own eyes the fascinating figure of Hamlet, or the gusty Falstaff amid colorful Elizabethan trappings! How I should like to follow each movement of the graceful Hamlet, each strut of the hearty Falstaff! And since I could see only one play, I should be confronted by a many-horned dilemma, for there are scores of plays I should want to see. You who have eyes can see any you like. How many of you, I wonder, when you gaze at a play, a movie, or any spectacle, realize and give thanks for the miracle of sight which enables you to enjoy its color, grace, and movement?

I cannot enjoy the beauty of rhythmic movement except in a sphere restricted to the touch of my hands. I can envision only dimly the grace of a Pavlova, although I know something of the delight of rhythm, for often I can sense the beat of music as it vibrates through the floor. I can well imagine that cadenced motion must be one of the most pleasing sights in the world. I have been able to gather something of this by tracing with my fingers the lines in sculptured marble; if this static grace can be so lovely, how much more acute must be the thrill of seeing grace in motion.

One of my dearest memories is of the time when Joseph Jefferson allowed me to touch his face and hands as he went through some of the gestures and speeches of his beloved Rip Van Winkle. I was able to catch thus a meager glimpse of the world of drama, and I shall never forget the delight of that moment. But, oh, how much I must miss, and how much pleasure you seeing ones can derive from watching and hearing the interplay of speech and movement in the unfolding of a dramatic performance! If I could see only one play, I should know how to picture in my mind the action of a hundred plays which I have read or had transferred to me through the medium of the manual alphabet.

So, through the evening of my second imaginary day of sight, the great figures of dramatic literature would crowd sleep from my eyes.

The following morning, I should again greet the dawn, anxious to discover new delights, for I am sure that, for those who have eyes which really see, the dawn of each day must be a perpetually new revelation of beauty.

This, according to the terms of my imagined miracle, is to be my third and last day of sight. I shall have no time to waste in regrets or longings; there is too much to see. The first day I devoted to my friends, animate and inanimate. The second revealed to me the history of man and Nature. Today I shall spend in the workaday world of the present, amid the haunts of men going about the business of life. And where can one find so many activities and conditions of men as in New York? So the city becomes my destination.

I start from my home in the quiet little suburb of Forest Hills, Long Island. Here, surrounded by green lawns, trees, and flowers, are neat little houses, happy with the voices and movements of wives and children, havens of peaceful rest for men who toil in the city. I drive across the lacy structure of steel which spans the East River, and I get a new and startling vision of the power and ingenuity of the mind of man. Busy boats chug and scurry about the river—racy speed boats, stolid, snorting tugs. If I had long days of sight ahead, I should spend many of them watching the delightful activity upon the river.

I look ahead, and before me rise the fantastic towers of New York, a city that seems to have stepped from the pages of a fairy story. What an awe-inspiring sight, these glittering spires, these vast banks of stone and steel—structures such as the gods might build for themselves! This animated picture is a part of the lives of millions of people every day. How many, I wonder, give it so much as a second glance? Very few, I fear. Their eyes are blind to this magnificent sight because it is so familiar to them.

I hurry to the top of one of those gigantic structures, the Empire State Building, for there, a short time ago, I "saw" the city below through the eyes of my secretary. I am anxious to compare my fancy with reality. I am sure I should not be disappointed in the panorama spread out before me, for to me it would be a vision of another world.

Now I begin my rounds of the city. First, I stand at a busy corner, merely looking at people, trying by sight of them to understand something of their lives. I see smiles, and I am happy. I see serious determination, and I am proud. I see suffering, and I am compassionate.

I stroll down Fifth Avenue. I throw my eyes out of focus so that I see no particular object but only a seething kaleidoscope of color. I am certain that the colors of women's dresses moving in a throng must be a gorgeous spectacle of which I should never tire. But perhaps if I had sight I should be like most other women—too interested in styles and the cut of individual dresses to give much attention to the splendor of color in the mass. And I am convinced, too, that I should become an inveterate window shopper, for it must be a delight to the eye to view the myriad articles of beauty on display.

From Fifth Avenue, I make a tour of the city—to Park Avenue, to the slums, to factories, to parks where children play. I take a stay-at-home trip abroad by visiting the foreign quarters. Always my eyes are open wide to all the sights of both happiness and misery so that I may probe deep and add to my understanding of how people work and live. My heart is full of the images of people and things. My eye passes lightly over no single trifle; it strives to touch and hold closely each thing its gaze rests upon. Some sights are pleasant, filling the heart with happiness; but some are miserably pathetic. To these latter I do not shut my eyes, for they, too, are part of life. To close the eye on them is to close the heart and mind.

My third day of sight is drawing to an end. Perhaps there are many serious pursuits to which I should devote the few remaining hours, but I am afraid that on the evening of that last day I should again run away to the theater, to a hilariously funny play, so that I might appreciate the overtones of comedy in the human spirit.

At midnight my temporary respite from blindness would cease, and permanent night would close in on me again. Naturally in those three short days I should not have seen all I wanted to see. Only when darkness had again descended upon me should I realize how much I had left unseen. But my mind would be so crowded with glorious memories that I should have little time for regrets. Thereafter the touch of every object would bring a glowing memory of how that object looked.

Perhaps this short outline of how I should spend three days of sight does not agree with the program you would set for yourself if you knew that you were about to be stricken blind. I am, however, sure that if you actually faced that fate your eyes would open to things you had never seen before, storing up memories for the long night ahead. You would use your eyes as never before. Everything you saw would become dear to you. Your eyes would touch and embrace every object that came within your range of vision. Then, at last, you would really see, and a new world of beauty would open itself before you.

I who am blind can give one hint to those who see—one admonition to those who would make full use of the gift of sight: Use your eyes as if tomorrow you would be stricken blind. And the same method can be applied to the other senses. Hear the music of voices, the song of a bird, the mighty strains of an orchestra, as if you would be stricken deaf tomorrow. Touch each object you want to touch as if tomorrow your tactile sense would fail. Smell the perfume of flowers, taste with relish each morsel, as if tomorrow you could never smell and taste again. Make the most of every sense; glory in the facts of pleasure and beauty which the world reveals to you through the several means of contact which Nature provides. But of all the senses, I am sure that sight must be the most delightful.

Suggestions for Discussion

1. With what details does Keller suggest the manifold things she observes, feels, and touches after an hour's walk through the woods?

2. What were Keller's criteria for her choices for the first day of seeing? What does she feel she loses in her understanding of her friends because of her lack of sight?
3. What desires and curiosities would be satisfied on Keller's second day?
4. What aspects of the theater does Keller miss in not being able to see?
5. What are Keller's goals in her visit to New York City?
6. What is significant about her plan for the evening of the last day?
7. How would you sum up Keller's values as reflected in her priorities for the three days of seeing?

Suggestions for Writing

1. How would you live each day (or a particular day) if you were to die tomorrow?
2. Write an essay discussing some of the things you take for granted.
3. If you were creating a compulsory course on "How to Use Your Eyes," what assignments would you make?
4. Should you have only three more days to see, how would you spend them?

JAMAICA KINCAID

A Small Place

Jamaica Kincaid (b. 1949) was born and raised in St. John's, Antigua, and has been a staff writer for *The New Yorker* since 1976. Winner of the Zabel Award from the American Academy of Arts and Letters in 1983 for *At the Bottom of the River,* she has written a series of books on island life, particularly as experienced by a child. These include *A Small Place* (1988) from which the following selection is taken, *Annie John* (1985), *Annie, Gwen, Lilly, Pam, and Tulip* (1989), *Lucy* (1990), and *Autobiography of My Mother* (1995). She was also editor of *Best American Essays* (1995). Here we see her bitterness at the contrast between what she knows about life on Antigua and what she considers to be the fantasy world of the tourists who visit it.

If you go to Antigua as a tourist, this is what you will see. If you come by aeroplane, you will land at the V. C. Bird International Airport. Vere Cornwall (V. C.) Bird is the Prime Minister of Antigua. You may be the sort of tourist who would wonder why a Prime Minister would want an airport named after him—why not a school, why not a hospital, why not some great public monument? You are a tourist and you have not yet seen a school in Antigua, you have not yet seen the hospital in Antigua, you have not yet seen a public monument in Antigua. As your plane descends to land, you might say, What a beautiful island Antigua is—more beautiful than any of the other islands you have seen, and they were very beautiful, in their way, but they were much too green, much too lush with vegetation, which indicated to you, the tourist, that they got quite a bit of rainfall, and rain is the very thing that you, just now, do not want, for you are thinking of the hard and cold and dark and long days you spent working in North America (or, worse, Europe), earning some money so that you could stay in this place (Antigua) where the sun always shines and where the climate is deliciously hot and dry for the four to ten days you are going to be staying there; and since you are on your holiday, since you are a tourist, the thought of what it might be like for someone who had to live day in, day out in a place that suffers constantly from drought, and so has to watch carefully every drop of fresh water used (while at the same time surrounded by a sea and an ocean—the Caribbean Sea on one side, the Atlantic Ocean on the other), must never cross your mind.

You disembark from your plane. You go through customs. Since you are a tourist, a North American or European—to be frank, white—and not an Antiguan black returning to Antigua from Europe or North America with cardboard boxes of much needed cheap clothes and food for relatives, you move through customs swiftly, you move through customs with ease. Your bags are not searched. You emerge from customs into the hot, clean air: immediately you feel cleansed, immediately you feel blessed (which is to say special); you feel free. You see a man, a taxi driver; you ask him to take you to your destination; he quotes you a price. You immediately think that the price is in the local currency, for you are a tourist and you are familiar with these things (rates of exchange) and you feel even more free, for things seem so cheap, but then your driver ends by saying, "In U.S. currency." You may say, "Hmmmm, do you have a formal sheet that lists official prices and destinations?" Your driver obeys the law and shows you the sheet, and he apologises for the incredible mistake he has made in quoting you a price off the top of his head which is so vastly different (favouring him) from the one listed. You are driven to your hotel by this taxi driver in his taxi, a brand-new Japanese-made vehicle. The road on which you are travelling is a very bad road, very much in need of repair. You are feeling wonderful, so you say, "Oh, what a marvelous change these bad roads are from the splendid highways I am used to in North America." (Or, worse, Europe.) Your driver is reckless; he is a dangerous man who drives in the middle of the road when he thinks no other cars are coming in the opposite direction, passes other cars on blind curves that run uphill, drives at sixty miles an hour on narrow, curving roads when the road sign, a rusting, beat-up thing left over from colonial days, says 40 mph. This might frighten you (you are on your holiday; you are a tourist); this might excite you (you are on your holiday; you are a tourist), though if you are from New York and take taxis you are used to this style of driving: most of the taxi drivers in New York are from places in the world like this. You are looking out the window (because you want to get your money's worth); you notice that all the cars you see are brand-new, or almost brand-new, and that they are all Japanese-made. There are no American cars in Antigua—no new ones, at any rate; none that were manufactured in the last ten years. You continue to look at the cars and you say to yourself, Why, they look brand-new, but they have an awful sound, like an old car—a very old, dilapidated car. How to account for that? Well, possibly it's because they use leaded gasoline in these brand-new cars whose engines were built to use non-leaded gasoline, but you mustn't ask the person driving the car if this is so, because he or she has never heard of unleaded gasoline. You look closely at the car; you see that it's a model of a Japanese car that you might hesitate to buy; it's a model that's very expensive; it's a model that's quite impractical for a person who has to work as hard as you do and who watches every penny you earn so that you can afford this holiday you are on. How do they afford such a car? And do they live in a luxurious house to match such a car? Well, no. You will be surprised, then, to see that most likely the person driving this brand-new car filled with the wrong gas lives in a house that, in comparison, is far beneath the status of the car; and if you were to ask why you would be told that the banks are encouraged by the government to make loans available for cars, but loans for houses not so easily available; and if you ask again why, you will be told that the two main car dealerships in Antigua are owned in part or outright by ministers in government. Oh, but you are on holiday and the sight of these brand-new cars driven by people who may or may not have really passed their driving test (there was once a scandal about driving licenses for sale) would not really stir up these thoughts in you. You pass a building sitting in a sea of dust and you think, It's some latrines for people just passing by, but when you look again you see the building has written on it PIGOTT'S SCHOOL. You pass the hospital, the Holberton Hospital, and how wrong you are not to think about this, for though you are a tourist on your holiday, what if your heart should miss a few beats? What if a blood vessel in your neck should break? What if one of those people driving those brand-new cars filled with the wrong gas fails to pass safely while going uphill on a curve and you are in the car going in the opposite direction? Will you be comforted to know that the hospital is staffed with doctors that no actual Antiguan trusts; that Antiguans always say about the doctors, "I don't want them near me"; that Antiguans refer to them not as doctors but as "the three men" (there are three of them); that when the Minister of Health himself doesn't feel well he takes the first plane to New York to see a real doctor; that if any one of the ministers in government needs medical care he flies to New York to get it?

It's a good thing that you brought your own books with you, for you couldn't just go to the library and borrow some. Antigua used to have a splendid library, but in The Earthquake (everyone talks about it that way—The Earthquake; we Antiguans, for I am one, have a great sense of things, and the more meaningful the thing, the more meaningless we make it) the library building was damaged. This was in 1974, and soon after that a sign was placed on the front of the building saying, THIS BUILDING WAS DAMAGED IN THE EARTHQUAKE OF 1974. REPAIRS ARE PENDING, The sign hangs there, and hangs there more than a decade later, with its unfulfilled promise of repair, and you might see this as a sort of quaintness on the part of these islanders, these people descended from slaves—what a strange, unusual perception of time they have. REPAIRS ARE PENDING, and here it is many years later, but perhaps in a world that is twelve miles long and nine miles wide (the size of Antigua) twelve years and twelve minutes and twelve days are all the same. The library is one of those splendid old buildings from colonial times, and the sign telling of the repairs is a splendid old sign from colonial times. Not very long after The Earthquake Antigua got its independence from Britain, making Antigua a state in its own right, and Antiguans are so proud of this that each year, to mark the day, they go to church and thank God, a British God, for this. But you should not think of the confusion that must lie in all that and you must not think of the damaged library. You have brought your own books with you, and among them is one of those new books about economic history, one of those books explaining how the West (meaning Europe and North America after its conquest and settlement by Europeans) got rich: the West got rich not from the free (free—in this case meaning got-for-nothing) and then undervalued labour, for generations, of the people like me you see walking around you in Antigua but from the ingenuity of small shopkeepers in Sheffield and Yorkshire and Lancashire, or wherever; and what a great part the invention of the wristwatch played in it, for there was nothing noble-minded men could not do when they discovered they could slap time on their wrists just like that (isn't that the last straw; for not only did we have to suffer the unspeakableness of slavery, but the satisfaction to be had from "We made you bastards rich" is taken away, too), and so you needn't let that slightly funny feeling you have from time to time about exploitation, oppression, domination develop into full-fledged unease, discomfort; you could ruin your holiday. They are not responsible for what you have; you owe them nothing; in fact, you did them a big favour, and you can provide one hundred examples. For here you are now, passing by Government House. And here you are now, passing by the Prime Minister's Office and the Parliament Building, and overlooking these, with a splendid view of St. John's Harbour, the American Embassy. If it were not for you, they would not have Government House, and Prime Minister's Office, and Parliament Building and embassy of powerful country. Now you are passing a mansion, an extraordinary house painted the colour of old cow dung, with more aerials and antennas attached to it than you will see even at the American Embassy. The people who live in this house are a merchant family who came to Antigua from the Middle East less than twenty years ago. When this family first came to Antigua, they sold dry goods door to door from suitcases they carried on their backs. Now they own a lot of Antigua; they regularly lend money to the government, they build enormous (for Antigua), ugly (for Antigua), concrete buildings in Antigua's capital, St. John's, which the government then rents for huge sums of money; a member of their family is the Antiguan Ambassador to Syria; Antiguans hate them. Not far from this mansion is another mansion, the home of a drug smuggler. Everybody knows he's a drug smuggler, and if just as you were driving by he stepped out of his door your driver might point him out to you as the notorious person that he is, for this drug smuggler is so rich people say he buys cars in tens—ten of this one, ten of that one—and that he bought a house (another mansion) near Five Islands, contents included, with cash he carried in a suitcase: three hundred and fifty thousand American dollars, and, to the surprise of the seller of the house, lots of American dollars were left over. Overlooking the drug smuggler's mansion is yet another mansion, and leading up to it is the best paved road in all of Antigua—even better than the road that was paved for the Queen's visit in 1985 (when the Queen came, all the roads that she would travel on were paved anew, so that the Queen might have been left with the impression that riding in a car in Antigua was a pleasant experience). In this mansion lives a woman sophisticated people in Antigua call Evita. She is a notorious woman. She's young and beautiful and the girlfriend of somebody very high up in the government. Evita is notorious because her relationship with this high government official has made her the owner of boutiques and property and given her a say in cabinet meetings, and all sorts of other privileges such a relationship would bring a beautiful young woman.

Oh, but by now you are tired of all this looking, and you want to reach your destination—your hotel, your room. You long to refresh yourself; you long to eat some nice lobster, some nice local food. You take a bath, you brush your teeth. You get dressed again; as you get dressed, you look out the window. That water—have you ever seen anything like it? Far out, to the horizon, the colour of the water is navy-blue; nearer, the water is the colour of the North American sky. From there to the shore, the water is pale, silvery, clear, so clear that you can see its pinkish-white sand bottom. Oh, what beauty! Oh, what beauty! You have never seen anything like this. You are so excited. You breathe shallow. You breathe deep. You see a beautiful boy skimming the water, godlike, on a Windsurfer. You see an incredibly unattractive, fat, pastrylike-fleshed woman enjoying a walk on the beautiful sand, with a man, an incredibly unattractive, fat, pastrylike-fleshed man; you see the pleasure they're taking in their surroundings. Still standing, looking out the window, you see yourself lying on the beach, enjoying the amazing sun (a sun so powerful and yet so beautiful, the way it is always overhead as if on permanent guard, ready to stamp out any cloud that dares to darken and so empty rain on you and ruin your holiday; a sun that is your personal friend). You see yourself taking a walk on that beach, you see yourself meeting new people (only they are new in a very limited way, for they are people just like you). You see yourself eating some delicious, locally grown food. You see yourself, you see yourself... You must not wonder what exactly happened to the contents of your lavatory when you flushed it. You must not wonder where your bathwater went when you pulled out the stopper. You must not wonder what happened when you brushed your teeth. Oh, it might all end up in the water you are thinking of taking a swim in; the contents of your lavatory might, just might, graze gently against your ankle as you wade carefree in the water, for you see, in Antigua, there is no proper sewage-disposal system. But the Caribbean Sea is very big and the Atlantic Ocean is even bigger; it would amaze even you to know the number of black slaves this ocean has swallowed up. When you sit down to eat your delicious meal, it's better that you don't know that most of what you are eating came off a plane from Miami. And before it got on a plane in Miami, who knows where it came from? A good guess is that it came from a place like Antigua first, where it was grown dirt-cheap, went to Miami, and came back. There is a world of something in this, but I can't go into it right now.

The thing you have always suspected about yourself the minute you become a tourist is true: A tourist is an ugly human being. You are not an ugly person all the time; you are not an ugly person ordinarily; you are not an ugly person day to day. From day to day, you are a nice person. From day to day, all the people who are supposed to love you on the whole do. From day to day, as you walk down a busy street in the large and modern and prosperous city in which you work and live, dismayed, puzzled (a cliché, but only a cliché can explain you) at how alone you feel in this crowd, how awful it is to go unnoticed, how awful it is to go unloved, even as you are surrounded by more people than you could possibly get to know in a lifetime that lasted for millennia, and then out of the corner of your eye you see someone looking at you and absolute pleasure is written all over that person's face, and then you realize that you are not as revolting a presence as you think you are (for that look just told you so). And so, ordinarily, you are a nice person, an attractive person, a person capable of drawing to yourself the affection of other people (people just like you), a person at home in your own skin (sort of; I mean, in a way; I mean, your dismay and puzzlement are natural to you, because people like you just seem to be like that, and so many of the things people like you find admirable about yourselves—the things you think about, the things you think really define you—seem rooted in these feelings): a person at home in your own house (and all its nice house things), with its nice back yard (and its nice back-yard things), at home on your street, your church, in community activities, your job, at home with your family, your relatives, your friends—you are a whole person. But one day, when you are sitting somewhere, alone in that crowd, and that awful feeling of displacedness comes over you, and really, as an ordinary person you are not well equipped to look too far inward and set yourself aright, because being ordinary is already so taxing, and being ordinary takes all you have out of you, and though the words "I must get away" do not actually pass across your lips, you make a leap from being that nice blob just sitting like a boob in your amniotic sac of the modern experience to being a person visiting heaps of death and ruin and feeling alive and inspired at the sight of it; to being a person lying on some faraway beach, your stilled body stinking and glistening in the sand, looking like something first forgotten, then remembered, then not important enough to go back for; to being a person marveling at the harmony (ordinarily, what you would say is the backwardness) and the union these other people (and they are other people) have with nature. And you look at the things they can do with a piece of ordinary cloth, the things they fashion out of cheap, vulgarly colored (to you) twine, the way they squat down over a hole they have made in the ground, the hole itself is something to marvel at, and since you are being an ugly person this ugly but joyful thought will swell inside you: their ancestors were not clever in the way yours were and not ruthless in the way yours were, for then would it not be you who would be in harmony with nature and backwards in that charming way? An ugly thing, that is what you are when you become a tourist, an ugly, empty thing, a stupid thing, a piece of rubbish pausing here and there to gaze at this and taste that, and it will never occur to you that the people who inhabit the place in which you have just paused cannot stand you, that behind their closed doors they laugh at your strangeness (you do not look the way they look); the physical sight of you does not please them; you have bad manners (it is their custom to eat their food with their hands; you try eating their way, you look silly; you try eating the way you always eat, you look silly); they do not like the way you speak (you have an accent); they collapse helpless from laughter, mimicking the way they imagine you must look as you carry out some everyday bodily function. They do not like you. *They do not like me!* That thought never actually occurs to you. Still, you feel a little uneasy. Still, you feel a little foolish. Still, you feel a little out of place. But the banality of your own life is very real to you; it drove you to this extreme, spending your days and your nights in the company of people who despise you, people you do not like really, people you would not want to have as your actual neighbour. And so you must devote yourself to puzzling out how much of what you are told is really, really true (Is ground-up bottle glass in peanut sauce really a delicacy around here, or will it do just what you think ground-up bottle glass will do? Is this rare, multicoloured, snout-mouthed fish really an aphrodisiac, or will it cause you to fall asleep permanently?). Oh, the hard work all of this is, and is it any wonder, then, that on your return home you feel the need of a long rest, so that you can recover from your life as a tourist?

That the native does not like the tourist is not hard to explain. For every native of every place is a potential tourist, and every tourist is a native of somewhere. Every native everywhere lives a life of overwhelming and crushing banality and boredom and desperation and depression, and every deed, good and bad, is an attempt to forget this. Every native would like to find a way out, every native would like a rest, every native would like a tour. But some natives—most natives in the world—cannot go anywhere. They are too poor. They are too poor to go anywhere. They are too poor to escape the reality of their lives; and they are too poor to live properly in the place where they live, which is the very place you, the tourist, want to go—so when the natives see you, the tourist, they envy you, they envy your ability to leave your own banality and boredom, they envy your ability to turn their own banality and boredom into a source of pleasure for yourself.

Suggestions for Discussion

1. Kincaid describes the visitor to Antigua as "An ugly thing, that is what you are when you become a tourist, an ugly, empty thing, a stupid thing, a piece of rubbish pausing here and there to gaze at this and taste that...." What is the reason for her rage?
2. The author argues that people become tourists because their lives are filled with banality and boredom. Discuss why you agree or disagree.
3. There are many Antiguas: what the tourist sees; what the native sees; what we interpret; what they live; what we experience. What is the "real" Antigua? Is Antigua a puzzle to be solved? Explain.

Suggestions for Writing

1. Several people present at the same "event" might each experience it differently. Antigua is an "event" of this kind. Describe your hometown, or something that happened in it, from a series of perspectives.
2. What *is* the case and what may *seem* to be the case are often very different. From your own experience, describe a scene (such as a meal at home or an encounter with a stranger) in which this was the case.

SIDNEY PERKOWITZ

Connecting with E. M. Forster

Sydney Perkowitz is the Charles Howard Chandler Professor of Physics at Emory University. He is author of *Empire of Light: A History of Discovery in Science and Art* (1996) and a number of scientific texts on optics. In this article he explores the novelist E. M. Forster's concept of "connection" and its relation to life on the Internet.

As my jetliner rears back, I look up from E. M. Forster's *Howards End* to gaze at the concrete sprawl of airport momentarily filling my window. The rows of parked airplanes and automobiles make a fitting backdrop: In the period when Forster wrote *Howards End,* 1908 to 1910, he was already decrying the filthy, cluttered underside of life in the motorized age. Although he was not alone in despising the stink of gasoline and the frantic pace of vehicles, Forster had an unusual grasp of how technological advance promised to change social interaction—often for the worse.

Forster also had an uncanny ability to predict exactly how technology would develop. At the century's beginning the telephone was new and the computer not even invented, yet Forster anticipated their modern evolution, perhaps most explicitly with his short story "The Machine Stops." Today the Internet and its related technologies are as ubiquitous as the automobile, within easy reach even as I fly five miles up. They raise all sorts of questions about relationships, community, and sexuality—the very same questions that Forster was contemplating in these two works.

For those who have never read *Howards End* (or missed Emma Thompson in the 1992 film version), it is a book about human connection.

Margaret Schlegel—the older of the two cultivated, well-to-do sisters central to the story—becomes impassioned over the phrase "Only connect!" which carries two meanings. One is a call to unite the opposing elements within each person—what Margaret calls the beast and the monk, the prose and the passion—while the other is a call to put the greatest energy into personal relations. "Only connect!" is the book's epigraph, and whenever Forster speaks as narrator he emphasizes the value of personal relationships.

But Forster also realizes that the quality of personal connection depends on the quantity—often inversely. "The more people one knows the easier it becomes to replace them," Margaret sighs. "It's one of the curses of London." Too many connections, in other words, devalues each one in a kind of emotional inflation. For the Schlegel sisters, this is the constant danger of frenetic city life; for the characters of "The Machine Stops," it is the inevitable by-product of remote communication technology.

Written in 1909 partly as a rejoinder to H. G. Wells's glorification of science, "The Machine Stops" is set in the far future, when mankind has come to depend on a worldwide Machine for food and housing, communications and medical care. In return, humanity has abandoned the earth's surface for a life of isolation and immobility. Each person occupies a subterranean hexagonal cell where all bodily needs are met and where faith in the Machine is the chief spiritual prop. People rarely leave their rooms or meet face-to-face; instead they interact through a global web that is part of the Machine. Each cell contains a glowing blue "optic plate" and telephone apparatus, which carry image and sound among individuals and groups.

The story centers around Vashti, who believes in the Machine, and her grown son Kuno, who has serious doubts. Vashti, writes Forster, "knew several thousand people; in certain directions human intercourse had advanced enormously." Although clumsy public gatherings no longer occur, Vashti lectures about her specialty, "Music During the Australian Period," over the web, and her audience responds in the same way. Later she eats, talks to friends, and bathes, all within her room. She finally falls asleep there, but not before she kisses the new Bible, the Book of the Machine.

Kuno, in contrast, once made his way illegally to the surface, where he saw distant hills, grass and ferns, the sun and the night sky. The Machine dragged him back to its buried world, but he understands the difference between pseudo-experience and reality. "I see something like you in this plate," he tells his mother, "but I do not see you. I hear something like you through this telephone, but I do not hear you." Vashti also senses the lack. Gazing at her son's image in the plate, she thinks he looks sad but is unsure "...for the Machine did not transmit nuances of expression. It only gave a general idea...that was good enough for all practical purposes...."

The drama in the story comes as the Machine inexplicably begins to decay, at first producing minor quirks. The symphonies Vashti plays through the Machine develop strange sounds that become worse each time she summons the music. That troubles her, but she comes to accept the noise as part of the composition. A friend's meditations are interrupted by a slight jarring sound, but the friend cannot decide whether that exists in her cell or in her head. More serious problems ensue with food, air, and illumination, but Vashti—like almost everybody else—clings to the conviction that the machine will repair itself.

When the Machine's demise is nearly complete, Vashti's faith fails with it in a way that recalls Margaret Schlegel's speech about large numbers of people. For all the thousands Vashti "knows," she dies nearly alone in a mob of panicked strangers, frantically clawing upwards to the Earth's surface as the Machine finally stops. Her sole redemption comes from a moment of true human contact: She encounters Kuno to talk, touch, and kiss "not through the Machine" just before they perish with the rest of the masses. Forster leaves us amid that final failure of the race to "Only connect," sustained solely by the promise that the few who survive on the surface will rebuild, without the Machine.

Long after Forster imagined this dire scene, the technology of connectivity is here. The details differ slightly: Instead of sound and moving images, we exchange written messages and pictures over the Internet, which links computers globally through fiber-optic telephone lines. (I use "Internet" here as a generic term for the major computer webs—the Internet itself and its World Wide Web, and the commercial nets connected to it, such as America Online. These, by the way, can also carry real-time sight and sound, which will surely grow in use.) But the logic of network connectivity, whether one-to-one or one-to-many, remains unchanged, and so does the loss of personal dimensions. The images in Forster's world move and speak, but do not convey facial nuances. Except for the limited use of still images, our electronic messages omit physical attributes. Forster's imaginary system, and our real one, offer unprecedented breadth of connection—there are an estimated 10 to 30 million Internet users worldwide—but do not allow people to touch, or to read each other directly.

On the Internet, Forster's implied questions still beg for answers. Open a magazine or newspaper, and you're likely to find an article asking a simple question: Does the Internet break down isolation, or merely provide pale simulations of friendship and love that drive out the real things? At one extreme, a recent newspaper story announces "On-Line addiction: wire junkies are multiplying as more people withdraw into their private worlds," and describes Internet users who are "ensnared in a net of fiber optic lines...and loneliness." But some users tell a different story. Mary Furlong, the founder of a group called SeniorNet, says: "I see a lot of loneliness in the senior population and lack of mobility.... Going on-line allows you to be intellectually mobile and be socially mobile"—exactly what the optic plates of Forster's world offer its confined inhabitants. There are even indications that the lack of physical presence can be advantageous. A London-based group finds the Internet to be a "nonprejudicial medium," especially valuable for children with conditions like cerebral palsy that affect speech.

In Forster's story, the rise of the Machine came from a belief in progress, which had "come to mean the progress of the Machine." Today, the relentless march of constantly updated computers and infrastructure sweeps us along to use the new technology because it is there, even when it conflicts with existing ways of life. A case in point is occurring in Italy, where a real estate consortium has spent more than $2 million for an entire village, Colletta di Castelbianco, founded in the thirteenth or fourteenth century and long since abandoned. The developers will turn its medieval walls and arches into a "telematic" village, creating apartments outfitted with the latest communications equipment including high-speed access to the Internet. The idea is that businessmen can operate on a global scale while enjoying the beauties of the rugged Ligurian region. Even the village cafes will be linked to the Internet, with facilities for video conferencing.

In a nation that values its cappuccino accompanied by enthusiastic conversation, the project evokes mixed reviews. Paolo Ceccarelli, an architect who studies the impact of computers, believes the Italian way of life is unlikely to bring forth many devoted Internet afficionados. He is depressed by the disconnection he sees in the Internet village. Echoing Forster's themes, he contemplates businessmen "parking their BMWs...climbing the stairs to their hermetically-sealed apartments and plugging in their portables in unison, all blissfully unaware of each other's presence."

It's true that even in Forster's vision, traces of emotion and relationship elude the grip of the Machine. "Human passions still blundered up and down," Forster wrote, and it is clear that Vashti and Kuno share a mother-son link, although Kuno has been raised in a public nursery. Sexual love, however, has changed radically. Sitting passive and isolated, people no longer touch each other, and their physical attractiveness has diminished. Vashti is described as a "swaddled lump of flesh...five feet high, with a face as white as a fungus." The Machine controls procreation, sending citizens traveling for the specific purpose of propagating the race. In this world where people do not kiss, where sex happens on assignment, Kuno rails that the Machine "has blurred every human relation and narrowed down love to a carnal act."

Human passions still blunder around the Internet, too, where people have fallen in love and gone on to form complete relationships or marry.

But in an outcome that Forster did not consider, the Internet also adds the more or less artificial experiences of cybersex to the sexual repertoire. Sex over the 'net means incomplete involvement in different degrees, from exchanges among mutually responsive participants to the solitary viewing of pornography. Remote sex has its undeniable impact, and in a world dealing with the disease of AIDS, it may stand in for unsafe actual sex. But can it stand in emotionally for genuine sexual love? Responding to this concern, participants at a recent Vatican conference on "Computers and Feelings" declared that cybersex is "the end of love. It is empty loneliness." That judgment is based on a recognition that human experience is diminished as it is filtered through electronic channels.

Forster went further. Fearing that more technology meant less humanity, he utterly rejected the technical achievements of his time. In 1908, after hearing of the first successful airplane flight over a kilometer-long circuit, he wrote in his journal, "...if I live to be old, I shall see the sky as pestilential as the roads.... Science...is enslaving [man] to machines.... Such a soul as mine will be crushed out." But we have come to learn that instead of producing a monolithically "bad" or "good" effect, a rich technology usually generates a balance sheet of benefits and costs—many of them unpredictable, because people use technology in unexpected ways. Thomas Mann once said, "A great truth is a truth whose opposite is also a great truth." A significant technology also embraces opposites; if some of its applications constrain human potential, others enhance it.

The Internet, in fact, helps people find kindred spirits. Forster did not foresee this development, but his story hints at it, for Vashti could either talk to a friend through the Machine or address an audience. Now many Internet users coalesce into groups that share concerns and emotional affinities. People with unusual beliefs or lifestyles, with secrets they dare not tell family and friends, seek each other out in thousands of news groups, list servers, and chat rooms. These cater to a variety of interests, problems, and ways of life, including a range of strong political views; divorce, grief, and loneliness; and a spectrum of sexuality, from heterosexual to homosexual, lesbian, and bisexual orientations, with variations. Within these groups, the private and the hidden can be revealed and validated, anonymously if desired.

Forster himself grappled with the partial secret of his homosexuality, which colored his life and his writing. His biographer, P. N. Furbank, concludes that Forster knew he was homosexual by the age of 21. But while a gay lifestyle was then acceptable in some quarters, Forster did not feel he could openly declare his sexuality, or act on it freely. The tension remained until he tried to release it in a way that would reaffirm him as a writer. After the success of *Howards End* in 1910, he feared his creativity had dried up.

Yet in 1913, the idea for a novel about homosexual love came to him in a moment of revelation. That seemed to show a way out of his barren time, and he wrote *Maurice* enthusiastically and at great speed. When it was done in 1914, however, Forster saw that it could not appear "until my death or England's," and it remained unpublished until after he died.

It is only a speculation, but a revealing one, to imagine how Forster would have fared with access to a like-minded group on a net, where he could have expressed what he had to suppress in the real world. After all, as a student at Cambridge he had been elected to the exclusive intellectual society called the "Apostles," where, among other topics, homosexuality was discussed in a spirit of free and rational inquiry, providing a sense of liberation that Forster later came to value greatly. On-line access would have created the opportunity to circulate *Maurice* to a larger but still select group that would accept its theme—a form of publication that would have brought even greater fulfillment.

Yet time on-line would have been ill used for Forster the writer. Aimless chat is the insidious seduction of the Internet; it can replace inward contemplation and real experience. In the decade after *Maurice,* Forster looked both inward and outward. His internal life became more unified as he came to terms with his self-doubts, and his sexuality. His external life developed as he worked for the Red Cross in Alexandria during the war, returned to England, and left again for his second visit to India. He deepened old relationships, and formed new ones, in all three places. All this must have been necessary, in ways hardly discernible at the time, before Forster could break free of his unproductive period to complete *A Passage to India* in 1924—a ripening that came only through the slow refining of life-as-lived into understanding.

Forster probably would have sensed this—just as he understood technology's potential to both isolate and overwhelm the individual. In the world of the Machine, each person could call or be called through his blue plate; but each could also touch an isolation switch to stop all interchange. While it is not always so simple, we can make individual choices about how and when to use technology, And in allowing his future humans their privacy between bouts of communication, Forster drew a fine metaphor for both aspects of "Only connect!": the joining of beast with monk carried out in the mind's solitude, the essential reaching out to others that breaks isolation—and the combination of the two, through the internal distillation of felt experience.

Suggestions for Discussion

1. Describe Forster's Machine.

2. Discuss the connection between Forster's Machine and the Internet.

Suggestion for Writing

Write an essay about technology's potential to both isolate and overwhelm the individual.

FICTION

ANTON CHEKHOV

The Bet

Translated by Constance Garnett

Anton Chekhov (1860–1904), Russian short story writer and playwright, practiced medicine briefly before devoting himself to literature. Among his plays are *The Sea Gull* (1896), *Uncle Vanya* (1900), *The Three Sisters* (1901), and *The Cherry Orchard* (1904). His stories, translated by Constance Garnett, were published as *The Tales of Chekhov* (1916–1923). The drama of the lawyer's solitary existence constitutes the central action of the story; it culminates in his walking out of the lodge a few hours before fulfilling the conditions of the bet; and it reaches its highest point of intensity, and its resolution, in the letter that passionately expresses his nihilism and supreme contempt for his fellow men.

I

It was a dark autumn night. The old banker was pacing from corner to corner of his study, recalling to his mind the party he gave in the autumn fifteen years before. There were many clever people at the party and much interesting conversation. They talked among other things of capital punishment. The guests, among them not a few scholars and journalists, for the most part disapproved of capital punishment. They found it obsolete as a means of punishment, unfitted to a Christian State and immoral. Some of them thought that capital punishment should be replaced universally by life imprisonment.

"I don't agree with you," said the host. "I myself have experienced neither capital punishment nor life imprisonment, but if one may judge *a priori,* then in my opinion capital punishment is more moral and more humane than imprisonment. Execution kills instantly, life imprisonment kills by degrees. Who is the more humane executioner, one who kills you in a few seconds or one who draws the life out of you incessantly, for years?"

"They're both equally immoral," remarked one of the guests, "because their purpose is the same, to take away life. The State is not God. It has no right to take away that which it cannot give back, if it should so desire."

Among the company was a lawyer, a young man of about twenty-five. On being asked his opinion, he said:

"Capital punishment and life imprisonment are equally immoral; but if I were offered the choice between them, I would certainly choose the second. It's better to live somehow than not to live at all."

There ensued a lively discussion. The banker who was then younger and more nervous suddenly lost his temper, banged his fist on the table, and turning to the young lawyer, cried out:

"It's a lie. I bet you two millions you wouldn't stick in a cell even for five years."

"If you mean it seriously," replied the lawyer, "then I bet I'll stay not five but fifteen."

"Fifteen! Done!" cried the banker. "Gentlemen, I stake two millions."

"Agreed. You stake two millions, I my freedom," said the lawyer.

So this wild, ridiculous bet came to pass. The banker, who at that time had too many millions to count, spoiled and capricious, was beside himself with rapture. During supper he said to the lawyer jokingly:

"Come to your senses, young man, before it's too late. Two millions are nothing to me, but you stand to lose three or four of the best years of your life. I say three or four, because you'll never stick it out any longer. Don't forget either, you unhappy man, that voluntary is much heavier than enforced imprisonment. The idea that you have the right to free yourself at any moment will poison the whole of your life in the cell. I pity you."

And now the banker, pacing from corner to corner, recalled all this and asked himself:

"Why did I make this bet? What's the good? The lawyer loses fifteen years of his life and I throw away two millions. Will it convince people that capital punishment is worse or better than imprisonment for life? No, no! all stuff and rubbish. On my part, it was the caprice of a well-fed man; on the lawyer's, pure greed of gold."

He recollected further what happened after the evening party. It was decided that the lawyer must undergo his imprisonment under the strictest observation, in a garden wing of the banker's house. It was agreed that during the period he would be deprived of the right to cross the threshold, to see living people, to hear human voices, and to receive letters and newspapers. He was permitted to have a musical instrument, to read books, to write letters, to drink wine, and smoke tobacco. By the agreement he could communicate, but only in silence, with the outside world through a little window specially constructed for this purpose. Everything necessary, books, music, wine, he could receive in any quantity by sending a note through the window. The agreement provided for all the minutest details, which made the confinement strictly solitary, and it obliged the lawyer to remain exactly fifteen years from twelve o'clock of November 14th, 1870 to twelve o'clock of November 14th, 1885. The least attempt on his part to violate the conditions, to escape if only for two minutes before the time freed the banker from the obligation to pay him the two millions.

During the first year of imprisonment, the lawyer, as far as it was possible to judge from his short notes, suffered terribly from loneliness and boredom. From his wing day and night came the sound of the piano. He rejected wine and tobacco. "Wine," he wrote, "excites desires, and desires are the chief foes of a prisoner; besides, nothing is more boring than to drink good wine alone, and tobacco spoils the air in his room." During the first year the lawyer was sent books of a light character; novels with a complicated love interest, stories of crime and fantasy, comedies, and so on.

In the second year the piano was heard no longer and the lawyer asked only for classics. In the fifth year, music was heard again, and the prisoner asked for wine. Those who watched him said that during the whole of that year he was only eating, drinking, and lying on his bed. He yawned often and talked angrily to himself. Books he did not read. Sometimes at nights he would sit down to write. He would write for a long time and tear it all up in the morning. More than once he was heard to weep.

In the second half of the sixth year, the prisoner began zealously to study languages, philosophy, and history. He fell on these subjects so hungrily that the banker hardly had time to get books enough for him. In the space of four years about six hundred volumes were brought at his request. It was while that passion lasted that the banker received the following letter from the prisoner: "My dear gaoler, I am writing these lines in six languages. Show them to experts. Let them read them. If they do not find one single mistake, I beg you to give orders to have a gun fired off in the garden. By the noise I shall know that my efforts have not been in vain. The geniuses of all ages and countries speak in different languages; but in them all burns the same flame. Oh, if you knew my heavenly happiness now that I can understand them!" The prisoner's desire was fulfilled. Two shots were fired in the garden by the banker's order.

Later on, after the tenth year, the lawyer sat immovable before his table and read only the New Testament. The banker found it strange that a man who in four years had mastered six hundred erudite volumes, should have spent nearly a year in reading one book, easy to understand and by no means thick. The New Testament was then replaced by the history of religions and theology.

During the last two years of his confinement the prisoner read an extraordinary amount, quite haphazard. Now he would apply himself to the natural sciences, then he would read Byron or Shakespeare. Notes used to come from him in which he asked to be sent at the same time a book on chemistry, a text-book of medicine, a novel, and some treatise on philosophy or theology. He read as though he were swimming in the sea among broken pieces of wreckage, and in his desire to save his life was eagerly grasping one piece after another.

II

The banker recalled all this, and thought:

"To-morrow at twelve o'clock he receives his freedom. Under the agreement, I shall have to pay him two millions. If I pay, it's all over with me. I am ruined for ever...."

Fifteen years before he had too many millions to count, but now he was afraid to ask himself which he had more of, money or debts. Gambling on the Stock-Exchange, risky speculation, and the recklessness of which he could not rid himself even in old age, had gradually brought his business to decay; and the fearless, self-confident, proud man of business had become an ordinary banker, trembling at every rise and fall in the market.

"That cursed bet," murmured the old man clutching his head in despair.... "Why didn't the man die? He's only forty years old. He will take away my last farthing, marry, enjoy life, gamble on the Exchange, and I will look on like an envious beggar and hear the same words from him every day: 'I'm obliged to you for the happiness of my life. Let me help you.' No, it's too much! The only escape from bankruptcy and disgrace—is that the man should die."

The clock had just struck three. The banker was listening. In the house every one was asleep, and one could hear only the frozen trees whining outside the windows. Trying to make no sound, he took out of his safe the key of the door which had not been opened for fifteen years, put on his overcoat, and went out of the house. The garden was dark and cold. It was raining. A damp, penetrating wind howled in the garden and gave the trees no rest. Though he strained his eyes, the banker could see neither the ground, nor the white statues, nor the garden wing, nor the trees. Approaching the garden wing, he called the watchman twice. There was no answer. Evidently the watchman had taken shelter from the bad weather and was now asleep somewhere in the kitchen or the greenhouse.

"If I have the courage to fulfill my intention," thought the old man, "the suspicion will fall on the watchman first of all."

In the darkness he groped for the steps and the door and entered the hall of the garden-wing, then poked his way into a narrow passage and struck a match. Not a soul was there. Some one's bed, with no bedclothes on it, stood there, and an iron stove loomed dark in the corner. The seals on the door that led into the prisoner's room were unbroken.

When the match went out, the old man, trembling from agitation, peeped into the little window.

In the prisoner's room a candle was burning dimly. The prisoner himself sat by the table. Only his back, the hair on his head and his hands were visible. Open books were strewn about on the table, the two chairs, and on the carpet near the table.

Five minutes passed and the prisoner never once stirred. Fifteen years' confinement had taught him to sit motionless. The banker tapped on the window with his finger, but the prisoner made no movement in reply. Then the banker cautiously tore the seals from the door and put the key into the lock. The rusty lock gave a hoarse groan and the door creaked. The banker expected instantly to hear a cry of surprise and the sound of steps. Three minutes passed and it was as quiet inside as it had been before. He made up his mind to enter.

Before the table sat a man, unlike an ordinary human being. It was a skeleton, with tight-drawn skin, with long curly hair like a woman's, and a shaggy beard. The colour of his face was yellow, of an earthy shade; the cheeks were sunken, the back long and narrow, and the hand upon which he leaned his hairy head was so lean and skinny that it was painful to look upon. His hair was already silvering with grey, and no one who glanced at the senile emaciation of the face would have believed that he was only forty years old. On the table, before his bended head, lay a sheet of paper on which something was written in a tiny hand.

"Poor devil," thought the banker, "he's asleep and probably seeing millions in his dreams. I have only to take and throw this half-dead thing on the bed, smother him a moment with the pillow, and the most careful examination will find no trace of unnatural death. But, first, let us read what he has written here."

The banker took the sheet from the table and read:

"Tomorrow at twelve o'clock midnight, I shall obtain my freedom and the right to mix with people. But before I leave this room and see the sun I think it necessary to say a few words to you. On my own clear conscience and before God who sees me I declare to you that I despise freedom, life, health, and all that your books call the blessings of the world.

"For fifteen years I have diligently studied earthly life. True, I saw neither the earth nor the people, but in your books I drank fragrant wine, sang songs, hunted deer and wild boar in the forests, loved women.... And beautiful women, like clouds ethereal, created by the magic of your poets' genius, visited me by night, and whispered to me wonderful tales, which made my head drunken. In your books I climbed the summits of Elbruz and Mont Blanc and saw from there how the sun rose in the morning, and in the evening suffused the sky, the ocean and the mountain ridges with a purple gold. I saw from there how above me lightnings glimmered cleaving the clouds; I saw green forests, fields, rivers, lakes, cities; I heard sirens singing, and the playing of the pipes of Pan; I touched the wings of beautiful devils who came flying to me to speak of God.... In your books I cast myself into bottomless abysses, worked miracles, burned cities to the ground, preached new religions, conquered whole countries....

"Your books gave me wisdom. All that unwearying human thought created in the centuries is compressed to a little lump in my skull. I know that I am cleverer than you all.

"And I despise your books, despise all worldly blessings and wisdom. Everything is void, frail, visionary and delusive as a mirage. Though you be proud and wise and beautiful, yet will death wipe you from the face of the earth like the mice underground; and your posterity, your history, and the immorality of your men of genius will be as frozen slag, burnt down together with the terrestrial globe.

"You are mad, and gone the wrong way. You take falsehood for truth and ugliness for beauty. You would marvel if suddenly apple and orange trees should bear frogs and lizards instead of fruit, and if roses should begin to breathe the odour of a sweating horse. So do I marvel at you, who have bartered heaven for earth. I do not want to understand you.

"That I may show you in deed my contempt for that by which you live, I waive the two millions of which I once dreamed as of paradise, and which I now despise. That I may deprive myself of my right to them, I shall come out from here five minutes before the stipulated term, and thus shall violate the agreement."

When he had read, the banker put the sheet on the table, kissed the head of the strange man, and began to weep. He went out of the wing. Never at any other time, not even after his terrible losses on the Exchange, had he felt such contempt for himself as now. Coming home, he lay down on his bed, but agitation and tears kept him a long time from sleeping....

The next morning the poor watchman came running to him and told him that they had seen the man who lived in the wing climb through the window into the garden. He had gone to the gate and disappeared. The banker instantly went with his servants to the wing and established the escape of his prisoner. To avoid unnecessary rumours he took the paper with the renunciation from the table and, on his return, locked it in his safe.

Suggestions for Discussion

1. If you agree that "The Bet" is primarily the lawyer's story, why is our view of the lawyer filtered through the reminiscences and observations of the banker? Why are we permitted to see the lawyer directly only twice? What

artistic purposes are served by the use of hearsay and notes and letters, and by the sparseness and flatness of the account of the lawyer's years of confinement?

2. Trace the changes in the lawyer's activities as they mark the development and resolution of the action. What are the implications as to his ultimate fate?
3. How do the shifts in time contribute to suspense and tone?
4. Find examples of irony and paradox.
5. How do you reconcile the lawyer's nihilism with his lyrical assertion that he has known the beauty of earth and love, has seen nature in her glory and tempestuousness, and has achieved wisdom—"all that the unresting thought of man has created"? What evidence can you find that Chekhov's vision of life extends beyond negation of all values?

Suggestions for Writing

1. Chekhov has said, "When you depict sad or unlucky people and want to touch the reader's heart, try to be colder—it gives their grief, as it were, a background against which it stands out in greater relief.... You must be unconcerned when you write pathetic stories,...the more objective, the stronger will be the effect." Write an evaluation of Chekhov's theories in relation to the characters of the banker and the lawyer, the tone of the story, and its denouement.
2. Write a position paper on the lawyer's (banker's) "examined life."
3. Write your own preferred conclusion to "The Bet"; or describe the lawyer's next fifteen years; or recount a conversation in which the banker tells his story the next morning.

FREDERICK PHILIP GROVE

The First Day of an Immigrant

Frederick Philip Grove (1879–1948), who immigrated to Canada from Germany, is considered to be a forefather of the Canadian literary tradition. With the publication of his earliest book in English, *Over Prairie Trails* (1922), he was recognized as a significant talent.

He won the Lorne Pierce Medal (1934), was elected a Fellow of the Royal Society of Canada (1941), and was awarded the Governer General's Award for *In Search of Myself* (1946). His work captured the struggles incurred by early Canadian immigrants, whom he wrote about with power and intensity. Some of his more well-known works are *Settlers of the Marsh* (1925), *A Search for America* (1927), and *The Master of the Mill* (1944). In the following story we find Grove's protagonist, Niels, learning to function in his new and complicated world.

About six miles west of the little prairie town of Balfour, twelve miles south of another little town called Minor, hard on the bank of the Muddy River which gurgles darkly and sluggishly along, there lies a prosperous farm, a very symbol of harvest and ease. Far and wide the red hip-roof of its gigantic barn shows above the trees that fringe the river which hardly deserves that name, seeing that it is no more than a creek. The commodious, white-painted dwelling, with its roofed-over porch and its glassed-in veranda, however, reveals itself for a moment only as you pass the gate of the yard while driving along the east-west road that leads past it, a few hundred feet to the north; for the old, once primeval bush has been carefully preserved here to enclose and to shelter the homestead; and the tall trees, with their small leaves always aquiver, aspen leaves, while screening the yard from view, seem at the same time to invite you to enter and to linger.

The east-west road cuts right through the property, leaving the level fields, at least the greater part of them, three hundred and twenty acres, to the north, while the yard nestles to the south in a bend of the little river which, curiously, makes the impression as if it were introduced into this landscape for the sole purpose of enfolding this home of man. Beyond the river, there is the remainder of another quarter section the greater part of which serves as pasture. Huge, sleek, gaily coloured cows and frisky colts, accompanied by anxious mares, have at all times access to the black-bottomed water.

The gates to both sides of the road—the one leading to the yard, and the other, opposite it, to the field—stand open; and a black track leads across the grey-yellow highway from one to the other. There, humus from the field is ground together with the clay of the grade into an exceedingly fine and light dust, perfectly dry, which betrays that many loads have already passed from the field to the yard.

It is a beautiful, crisp, and sunny morning of that reminiscent revival of things past which we call the Indian summer. A far corner of the fields, to the north-west, is bustling with the threshing crews. Engine and separator fill the air with their pulsating hum; and the yellow chaff of the straw comes drifting over the stubble and crosses the road and enters even the yard, threading its way through the trees which, apart from the trembling leaves, stand motionless, and through the entrance that winds in a leisurely way through their aisles. Slowly the chaff filters down, like fine, dry, light snow.

Now and then a wagon, drawn by heavy horses and heavily laden with bags of grain, passes slowly over the road; and every now and then an empty wagon—empty except for a pile of bags on its floor—rattles out in the opposite direction, going to the scene of operations in the field. From the gate a diagonal trail leads through the stubble to the engine; it is cut a few inches deep into the soft soil and worn smooth and hard by many haulings.

That happens just now; let us jump on at the back and go with the driver, an elderly, bearded man of unmistakably Scottish cast: broad-shouldered and heavily set, his grave, though not unpleasant face dusted over with grime and chaff. The wagon, being without a load, rattles along; the horses trot.

Twice the driver has to get out of the trail in order to let a load pass on its way to the yard. To the left, the ground now slopes down a grassy slough in which here and there a clump of willows breaks the monotony of the prairie landscape; no doubt this slough holds water in spring; but at present it is perfectly dry. At its far end, beyond the threshing outfit, an enormous hay-stack rises on its sloping bank.

Now we are in the field of operations. All about, long rows of stooks dot the stubble, big stooks of heavy sheaves. Hay-racks drive from one to the other, one man walking alongside and picking up the sheaves with his fork, pitching them up to another who receives and piles them on the load. Here the work proceeds in a leisurely, unhurried way which contrasts strangely with the scene ahead. The horses do not need to be guided; they know their work; a word from the man on the load is enough to tell them what is wanted.

We have reached the vibrating machines now, joined by a huge, swinging belt. But our Scotsman has to wait a few minutes before he can drive up to the spout that delivers the grain, for another teamster is filling the last of his bags.

Two or three hay-racks, loaded high with sheaves, stand waiting alongside the engine that hums its harvest song. The drivers are lazily reclining on their loads while they wait for those who are ahead of them to finish. They do not even sit up when they move a place forward; the horses know as well as their drivers what is expected of them. Here, the air is thick with chaff and dust.

The few older men in the crew set the pace; the younger ones, some of them inclined to take things easy, have to follow. Those who are alongside the feeder platform, pitching the sheaves, do not make the impression of leisurely laziness.

The engineer, in a black, greasy pair of overalls, is busy with long-spouted oil-can and a huge handful of cottonwaste. The "separator-man" stands on top of his mighty machine, exchanging bantering talk with the pitching men.

"Let her come, Jim," he shouts to one of the men, a tall, good-looking youth who works with a sort of defiant composure, not exactly lazily but as if he were carefully calculating his speed to yield just a reasonable day's work and no more; a cynical smile plays in his young, unruffled face. "Let her come," the separator-man repeats. "Can't choke her up."

"Can't?" challenges Jim's partner, a swarthy, unmistakably foreign-looking man.

And from the opposite side of the feeder-platform another foreigner, a Swede, a giant of a man, six feet four inches tall and proportionately built, shouts over, "We'll see about that." He is alone on his load, for, as usual, the crew is short-handed; and he has volunteered to pitch and load by himself.

And this giant, the Swede, starts to work like one possessed, pitching down the sheaves as if his life depended on choking the machine. The Ruthenian, on the near side, follows his example; but Jim, a piece of straw in the corner of his smiling mouth, remains uninfected. He proceeds in his nonchalant way which is almost provoking, almost contemptuous.

All about, the drivers on their loads are sitting up; this is a sporting proposition; and as such it arouses a general interest. Even the Scotsman follows proceedings with a smile.

But apart from these, there has been another looker-on. The outfit stands a few hundred feet from the edge of the slough which stretches its broad trough of hay-land slantways across this end of the field; and there, among some willows, stands a medium-sized man, with a cardboard suit-case at his feet and a bundle hanging from the end of a stout cane that rests on his shoulder. He is neither slender nor stout, five feet and eleven inches tall, and dressed in a new suit of overalls, stiff with newness, his flaxen-haired head covered with a blue-denim cap that, on its band, displays the advertisement of a certain brand of lubricating oil. His clean-shaven face is broadened by a grin as he watches the frantic efforts of the two men on their respective loads. His is an almost ridiculous figure; for he looks so foreign and absurd, the more so as his effort to adapt himself to the ways of the country is obvious and unsuccessful.

But he watches idly for only a very few seconds. Then he drops bundle and cane and runs, circling the engine, to the side of the Swede. There he looks about for a moment, finds a spare fork sticking with its prongs in the loose soil under the feeder-platform, grabs it, vaults up on the load of the giant, and, without a word of explanation, begins to pitch as frantically as the other two. The loads seem to melt away from under their feet.

The grimy separator-man on top of his machine laughs and rubs his hands. His teeth look strangely white in his dust-blackened face; his tongue and gums, when they show, strangely pink, as in the face of a negro. "Let her come, boys," he shouts again, above the din of the machine, "Let her come. Can't choke her up, I tell you. She's a forty-two. But try!" From his words speaks that pride which the craftsman takes in his tools and his output. He looks strange as he stands there, in the dust-laden air, on the shaking machine; his very clothes seem to vibrate; and in them his limbs and his body; he looks like a figure drawn with a trembling hand.

A fixed, nearly apologetic grin does not leave the face of the unbidden helper. There is good-nature in this grin; but also embarrassment and the vacancy of noncomprehension.

The elderly Scotsman who came out a little while ago has meanwhile driven up to the grain-spout and is filling his bags. He keeps watching the newcomer, putting two and two together in his mind. And when his load is made up at last, he detaches himself from the group, casting a last, wondering look at the man who is pitching as if he were engaged on piece-work, for, when the Swede has finished his load, this stranger has simply taken his place on the next one that has come along.

Then the Scotsman threads once more the diagonal trail across the field, staying on it this time when he meets another wagon, for the man with the load, such is the rule, has the right-of-way; and finally, when he reaches the gate, he drives through it and across the road, and on into the welcome shade. For the length of a few rods the entrance leads through the gap between the huge, park-like trees, and then it widens out into the yard. Right in front stands the house, a large, comfortable, and easy-going affair with a look of relaxation about it, though, no doubt, at present nobody there has time to relax, for, red from the heat of the ranges, women are frantically preparing the noon-day meal for the many-mouthed, hungry monster, the crew. The huge and towering barn, painted red, occupies the west side of the yard; and beyond it, a smaller building—it, too, painted red—is the granary for which the load is bound.

In its dark interior a man is working, shovelling wheat to the back. He is tall, standing more than six feet high, broad-shouldered but lean, almost gaunt. His narrow face is divided by a grey moustache which, as he straightens his back, he rubs with the back of his hand in order to free it from the chaff that has collected in its hairs. He is covered all over with the dust of the grain.

When the wagon approaches, he looks out and asks, "How many, Jim?"

Jim is backing his load against the open door. "Twenty-four," he answers over his shoulder.

The man inside takes a pencil suspended by a string from a nail and makes note of the number on a piece of card-board tacked to the wall.

Thus he keeps track of the approximate number of bushels, counting two and a half to the bag.

Jim, having tied his lines to the seat, tilts the first of the bags, and the man inside receives it on his shoulder and empties it into the bin to the left. That bin is already filled to one third of its height.

Jim speaks. "Got a new hand, Dave?" he asks.

"Not that I know of," replies the man inside with a questioning inflection.

"Fellow came about an hour ago, climbed up on a load, and started to pitch. Good worker, too, it seems."

"That so?" Dave says. "I could use another man well enough. But I didn't know about him."

"Looks like a Swede."

"Better send him over."

So, when Jim, the Scotsman, returns to the field, he shouts to the stranger, above the din of machine and engine. "Hi, you!" And when the stranger turns, he adds, "Boss wants to see you," nodding his head backwards in the direction of the yard.

But the stranger merely grins vacantly and, with exaggerated motion, shrugs his shoulders.

The others all look at Jim and laugh. So he, shrugging his shoulders in turn, drives on and takes his place behind the wagon at the spout.

Two more hours pass by; and still the stranger goes on with his unbidden work. The sun, on his path, nears the noon. Meanwhile the stranger has been the partner of all the men who drive up on his side of the outfit: but only one of them has spoken to him, that giant of a Swede who was the first man whom he helped. This giant is clean-shaven and dressed with a striking neatness, yes, a rustic foppishness which shows through all the dust and chaff with which he is covered. He does not wear overalls but a flannel shirt and corduroy trousers tucked into high boots ornamented with a line of coloured stitching along their upper edge. Those of the others who address him call him Nelson.

"Aer du Svensk?" he has asked of the stranger. "Are you a Swede?"

"Yo," the stranger has replied in the affirmative.

And further questions have brought out the fact that he has just arrived from the east, on a through-ticket reading from Malmoe in Sweden to Balfour, Manitoba, Canada. "You'll find lots of Swedes up there," the agent had told him at home, at Karlskrona in Blekinge, whence he hails.

Nelson grins when he hears that tale. Three years ago, when he himself left Sweden, he was told the same thing; but when he arrived, he found that the Swedish settlement was small and considerably farther north. Thus he has become wise in the tricks of the steamship-agent's trade. "Did the boss hire you?" he asks, speaking Swedish, of course, while they proceed with the work in hand.

"No. I haven't seen anybody yet. But I do want work."

"Better see him at noon. What's your name?"

"Niels Lindstedt."

"Come with me when the whistle blows," says Nelson as he drives away.

The brief conversation has cheered Niels greatly.

"I am in luck," he thinks, "to meet a Swede right away, a friend to help me in getting started."

In Balfour, where he had landed very early in the morning, he had almost lost courage when he had found that nobody understood him. But at the hardware store a man—the same who had made him a present of the cap he was wearing—had made signs to him as if pitching sheaves, meanwhile talking to him, tentatively, in short monosyllables, apparently asking questions. Niels had understood this sign language sufficiently to know that he was trying to find out whether he wanted work in the harvest fields; and so he had nodded. Next the hardware dealer had made clear to him, again by signs, that his clothes were unsuitable for work; for he had been dressed in a black cloth suit, stiff and heavy, the kind that lasts the people at home a lifetime, so strong that even years of wearing do not flatten out the seams. He had shown him the way to a store where he had acquired what he needed, till he thought that now he looked exactly like a Canadian. Then he had once more returned to the hardware store, and the friendly man had put him on the road, pushing him by the shoulder and pointing and shouting directions till he had picked up his suitcase and the bundle with the clothes he had been wearing and had started out. When, after a few hundred yards, he had looked back, the hardware man had still been standing at the corner of his street and nodding and waving his arm, for him to go on and on, for many miles. And he had done so.

Most of the men with whom he has been working are foreigners themselves. Niels knows the English or Canadian type sufficiently already to recognize that. Some are Slavonic, some German; though they, too, seem to have Russian blood.

Niels exults in the work. After the enforced idleness of the passage across the ocean and the cramped trip in the train, it feels good to be at work in the open. He wonders whether he will be paid for what he does. He is hungry, for he has had no breakfast; and so he hopes he will get his dinner at least. Probably, he thinks, that will be all he is entitled to. He has heard, of course, of the fabulous wages paid to the workingman in America. But possibly that is no more than idle talk. As hunger and the consequent exhaustion lay hold of him, he begins to view things pessimistically.

The size of the field about him dazes him. The owner, he thinks, must be some nobleman. Will a field one tenth, one fiftieth of the size of this one some day be within his own reach, he wonders? The mere thought of it sends him once more into a fury of work; again he pitches the sheaves like one possessed.

Then, suddenly, startlingly, the noon whistle blows from the engine; and when he sees Nelson, the giant, just arriving on top of a load of sheaves, he runs over and helps him to unhitch his horses.

"Come on," says Nelson and starts off, running and galloping his horses, in order to snatch a ride on a hay-rack which is returning empty to the yard. The rack waits for them, and they climb on, Nelson leading his horses behind.

When the team is stabled in the huge barn where Niels looks about and marvels, the two go over to the granary and find Dave Porter, the boss. Dave looks Niels over and asks a few questions, Nelson interpreting for his new friend.

A few minutes later the newcomer is hired at current wages of four dollars a day till threshing is over; and if he cares to stay after that, at a dollar and fifty a day for plowing till it snows or freezes up. Niels gasps at the figures and has to recalculate them in Swedish money, multiplying them by four: sixteen and six Kroner a day! There must be a mistake, he thinks; he cannot have heard right. The wages must be for the week. But when Dave turns away and Niels asks Nelson, the giant laughs and says, "No. No mistake."

So they turn and walk over to the house for dinner.

Niels is quick to learn; and by the time he has had his dinner and gone over the yard with Nelson while they are waiting for the horses to finish theirs, he has picked up much of the new country's lore.

In the granary where they return Nelson shows him the figures jotted down on the piece of card-board which show that already the huge bins hold eight thousand bushels of oats, four thousand of barley, and three thousand of wheat. Niels is awed by the enormity of these quantities. There is a strange sort of exhilaration in them. He merely pronounces the figures and has to laugh; and something very like tears comes into his eyes. Nelson chimes in with his throaty bass. No, Niels does not feel sorry that he has come out into this west.

Yet, when the horses are taken out again and the two new friends once more find room on an empty hay-rack, to return to the field, there is a shadow on his consciousness. At dinner, in the house, he has become aware of a certain attitude towards himself, an attitude assumed by those who were unmistakably Canadian. After all, this is not home; it is a strange country; and he is among strange people who look down upon him as if he were something inferior, something not to be taken as fully human. He does not understand that, of course. He has heard Jim, the cynical, good-looking young fellow say something to a number of the men who, like Niels himself, were apparently recent immigrants. Jim had contemptuously addressed them as "You Galishans!" And it had been clear that they resented it. Niels does not quite see why they should; if they are Galicians, why should they mind being called by that name? But he also understands that what they really resent is the tone in which it was said.

He wonders as he looks about while the horses trot briskly over the stubble whether in a few years' time this country will seem like home to him, as apparently it does to Nelson, his newly-won friend.

And with that he turns his mind away from his critical thoughts and back to his dreams. He sees himself established on a small farm of his own, with a woman in the house; and he sees the two of them sitting by lamplight in a neat little living room of that house while from upstairs there sounds down to them the pitter-patter of little children's feet—his own little children's, romping before they crawl into their snug little beds.

That is his vision: the vision that has brought him into these broad plains. And that vision is destined to shape his whole life in the future.

Suggestions for Discussion

1. All the characters in the story are immigrants. How does this affect the way they treat Niels?
2. How does the author draw you into the "work" of the story, both literally and metaphorically?
3. Niels does not find what he has been told to expect, but nevertheless he keeps hoping while he continues to hold on to his dreams. What makes this possible?

Suggestions for Writing

1. Niels is the classic outsider, a "ridiculous figure...foreign and absurd." Describe an instance when you felt as he does, an outsider looking in.
2. The United States is a nation of immigrants. Interview a family member or friend who remembers his or her immigration experience.
3. This is a story about rural resettlement one hundred years ago. Write a story about urban resettlement in the 1990s.

POETRY

MATTHEW ARNOLD

Dover Beach

Matthew Arnold (1822–1888), son of the famous Headmaster of Rugby, Thomas Arnold, was first a poet but later abandoned poetry to become a lecturer, a critic of life and literature, and an inspector of schools. His *Collected Poems* appeared in 1869, *Essays in Criticism* in 1865 and 1888, *Culture and Anarchy* in 1869, *Friendship's Garland* in 1879, and *Mixed Essays* in 1879. In "Dover Beach," the speaker at a moment of emotional crisis, speaking to one he loves, raises the question of whether humans can find any peace or joy or release from pain in a world of conflict.

The sea is calm tonight.
The tide is full, the moon lies fair
Upon the straits; on the French coast the light
Gleams and is gone; the cliffs of England stand,
Glimmering and vast, out in the tranquil bay.
Come to the window, sweet is the night-air!
Only, from the long line of spray
Where the sea meets the moon-blanched land,
Listen! you hear the grating roar
Of pebbles which the waves draw back, and fling,
At their return, up the high strand,
Begin, and cease, and then again begin,
With tremulous cadence slow, and bring
The eternal note of sadness in.

Sophocles long ago
Heard it on the Aegean, and it brought
Into his mind the turbid ebb and flow
Of human misery; we
Find also in the sound a thought,
Hearing it by this distant northern sea.
The Sea of Faith
Was once, too, at the full, and round earth's shore

Lay like the folds of a bright girdle furled.
But now I only hear
Its melancholy, long, withdrawing roar,
Retreating, to the breath
Of the night-wind, down the vast edges drear
And naked shingles of the world.

Ah, love, let us be true
To one another! for the world, which seems
To lie before us like a land of dreams,
So various, so beautiful, so new,
Hath really neither joy, nor love, nor light,
Nor certitude, nor peace, nor help for pain;
And we are here as on a darkling plain
Swept with confused alarms of struggle and flight,
Where ignorant armies clash by night.

Suggestions for Discussion

1. How does the sea symbolize modern life?
2. What is the speaker seeking and what values does he affirm?

MARK LEVINE

About Face

(A Poem Called "Dover Beach")

Mark Levine, born in Toronto, was educated at Brown University and the University of Iowa, where he received his M.F.A. At present he teaches at the University of Montana. In addition to *Debt* (1993), from which "About Face" is taken, he has written *Capital,* and he was included in *Best Poems of 1991.* This poem uses the frame of Matthew Arnold's Victorian poem, "Dover Beach," to make a powerful commentary about the violence of our contemporary world.

It's dead out here. The sea is calm tonight.
Just me, the sand, the sand-like

things, wriggling like wet pockets.
I cover my eyes with some fingers; I have fingers
to spare. I open my mouth and hear the medicine
splashing on my tongue. The cliffs of England stand.

Behind enemy lines? Yes. Toujours. The Sea of Faith
was once, too, at the full. The barricades are stacked
like empty chairs after tonight's performance.
Is tonight's performance over?
I'm dragging bodies along as decoys, a dozen
well-dressed bodies, greasy, glazed with red sauce. Tonight's menu:
Peking duck. My stench is making me hungry.
Commander, may I have a body too?

Is someone quaking in my boots? To fear? Perchance, to flee.
Out here "advance" looks a lot like "retreat."
My wheels kick up sand as they spin.
Listen! you hear the grating.
My gears are caught. No use hurrying.
Time's nearly up. And I have
thoughts to collect, faces to grow.

My instructions read: "Come as you
were, leave as you are." Only, from the long
line of spray—
Commander, can you hear me?
I'm waiting for my answer.

Come to the window. Sweet is the night air.
My guests are here, clamoring to be let in.
I am here, clamoring to be let in.
In. Where is that? Come to the window.
Knocking twice, I greet myself at the door and am surprised.

Oh naked shingles of the world. My enemy's skin is bad
from eating boiled soap and scrubbing with potatoes.
My enemy's parts are detachable.
He is having a reaction to his medicine:
pain-free, confused. Am I

my enemy's enemy? My enemy's keeper? My
enemy? Ah, love, let us be true.
We're all a bit tired
to be killing so much, but we continue.
The tickets were bought through the mail long ago so why not.
No time to save face.

Action. Action.
A cardboard bomber flies by with its flaming nets.
We are here as on a darkling plain.
Make me an offer. I'm going fast.
The theater is so crowded no one can be sure
if the fire is in their hair
or in their wigs.

Suggestions for Discussion

1. Why does Levine choose to set what he has to say within the frame of Matthew Arnold's "Dover Beach"?
2. "Am I / my enemy's enemy? My enemy's keeper? My / enemy?..." Who or what is the enemy in the poem?
3. There is a sense in Levine's poem that the despair that undergirds Arnold's poem has evolved in our time into the enactment of a death and destruction that overflows everything. If this is the case, what has brought it about?
4. The author uses theatrical metaphors throughout his poem. Why? What do they help us to understand?

Suggestions for Writing

1. A poet works not by explication, but by exemplification. Create ten images, or verbal pictures, that show to your reader something you want to convey. Try not to use modifiers. Nouns and verbs are most powerful by themselves.
2. War is a common subject of poetry. So is love. Find two other poems, on either of these topics, that say different things about the subject.

MARIANNE MOORE

The Mind Is an Enchanting Thing

Marianne Moore (1887–1972) was born in Missouri. She graduated from Bryn Mawr College, and went on to teach at an Indian school, work in the New York Public Library, and edit *The Dial* (1925–1929). Her early poems were published in 1921, her *Collected Poems* in 1951. She is also the author of *Predilections* (1955), a volume of critical essays, a poetic translation of La Fontaine's *Fables* (1954), and a collection of poetry, *Tell Me, Tell Me* (1967). The symbols of enchantment are drawn from nature, science, and art.

is an enchanted thing
   like the glaze on a
katydid-wing
      subdivided by sun
      till the nettings are legion.
Like Gieseking playing Scarlatti;

like the apteryx-awl
   as a beak, or the
kiwi's rain-shawl
      of haired feathers, the mind
      feeling its way as though blind,
walks along with its eyes on the ground.

It has memory's ear
   that can hear without
having to hear.
      Like the gyroscope's fall,
      truly unequivocal
because trued by regnant certainty,

it is a power of
   strong enchantment. It
is like the dove-
      neck animated by
      sun; it is memory's eye;
it's conscientious inconsistency.

It tears off the veil; tears
   the temptation, the
mist the heart wears,
      from its eyes,—if the heart
      has a face; it takes apart
dejection. It's fire in the dove-neck's

iridescence; in the
   inconsistencies
of Scarlatti.
      Unconfusion submits
      its confusion to proof; it's
not a Herod's oath that cannot change.

Suggestions for Discussion

1. The symbols of the poem derive from nature, art, and science. Identify them.
2. How do the similes contribute to the theme of enchantment? What paradoxes do you find, and how do they underscore the central theme?

THEODORE ROETHKE

The Waking

Theodore Roethke (1908–1963), American poet, taught during the last years of his life at the University of Washington. *The Waking: Poems, 1933–1953* was the winner of the Pulitzer Prize for Poetry in 1953. He received the Bollingen Award for Poetry in 1958. A collected volume, *Words for the Wind,* appeared in 1958, and *The Far Field* was published posthumously in 1964. Among the many modes of learning, the poet learns "by going where I have to go."

I wake to sleep, and take my waking slow.
I feel my fate in what I cannot fear.
I learn by going where I have to go.

We think by feeling. What is there to know?
I hear my being dance from ear to ear.
I wake to sleep, and take my waking slow.

Of those so close beside me, which are you?
God bless the Ground! I shall walk softly there,
And learn by going where I have to go.

Light takes the Tree; but who can tell us how?
The lowly worm climbs up a winding stair;
I wake to sleep, and take my waking slow.

Great Nature has another thing to do
To you and me; so take the lively air,
And, lovely, learn by going where to go.

This shaking keeps me steady. I should know.
What falls away is always. And is near.
I wake to sleep, and take my waking slow.
I learn by going where I have to go.

Suggestions for Discussion

1. Relate the title to the substance of the poem.
2. What are the modes of learning? Cite specific passages.
3. How does the use of paradox contribute to tone and substance? Comment on the rhythm, rhyme scheme, repetition of refrain, imagery, and diction.

Suggestion for Writing

Examine your own processes of learning and comment on their relative effectiveness.

JORGE LUÍS BORGES

The Web

Translated from the Spanish by Alastair Reid

Jorge Luís Borges (1899–1986), Argentinian poet, short story writer, essayist, critic, and university professor, was regarded until his death in 1986 as the greatest living man of letters writing in Spanish. Best known for his esoteric short fiction, Borges received little recognition in America until the publication in 1968 of English translations of *Ficciónes, Labyrinths,* and *The Aleph.* In this poem, which appeared shortly after Borges's death, he reviews a number of the key experiences of his life, anticipates his death, and wonders when it will occur, a death he faces with "impatient hope."

Which of my cities
am I doomed to die in?
Geneva,
where revelation reached me
from Virgil and Tacitus

(certainly not from Calvin)?
Montevideo,
where Luis Melián Lafinur,
blind and heavy with years,
died among the archives
of that impartial
history of Uruguay
he never wrote?
Nara,
where in a Japanese inn
I slept on the floor
and dreamed the terrible
image of the Buddha
I had touched without seeing
but saw in my dream?
Buenos Aires,
where I verge on being a foreigner?
Austin, Texas,
where my mother and I
in the autumn of '61
discovered America?
What language
am I doomed to die in?
The Spanish my ancestors used
to call for the charge, or to play *truco?*
The English of the Bible
my grandmother read from
at the edges of the desert?
What time will it happen?
In the dove-colored twilight
when color drains away,
or in the twilight of the crow
when night abstracts and simplifies
all visible things?
Or at an inconsequential moment—
two in the afternoon?
These questions are
digressions that stem not from fear
but from impatient hope.
They form part of the fateful web
of cause and effect
that no man can foresee,
nor any god.

Suggestions for Discussion

1. Relate Borges's speculations to the title "The Web."
2. What is the nature of Borges's memories?
3. What personal values are expressed?

Suggestions for Writing

1. Drawing upon your observation and experience, discuss the "fateful web of cause and effect."
2. Relate a series of key experiences that has played a role in shaping your attitudes.

GLOSSARY

Abstraction, levels of Distinguished in two ways: in the range between the general and the specific and in the range between the abstract and the concrete.

A general word refers to a class, genus, or group; a specific word refers to a member of that group. *Ship* is a general word, but *ketch, schooner, liner,* and *tugboat* are specific. It must be remembered, however, that the terms *general* and *specific* are relative, not absolute. *Ketch,* for example, is more specific than *ship,* for a ketch is a kind of ship. But *ketch,* on the other hand, is more general than *Tahiti ketch,* for a Tahiti ketch is a kind of ketch.

The distinction between the abstract and the concrete also is relative. Ideas, qualities, and characteristics which do not exist by themselves may be called abstract; physical things such as *house, shoes,* and *horse* are concrete. Notice, however, that concrete words not only can range further into the specific (*bungalow, moccasin,* and *stallion*), but they also can range back toward the general (*domicile, clothing,* and *cattle*). In making these distinctions between the abstract and the concrete and between the general and the specific, there is no implication that good writing should be specific and concrete and that poor writing is general and abstract. Certainly most good writing is concrete and specific, but it is also general and abstract, constantly moving from the general to the specific and from the abstract to the concrete.

Allusion Reference to a familiar person, place, or thing, whether real or imaginary: Woodrow Wilson or Zeus, Siam or Atlantis, kangaroo or phoenix. The allusion is an economical way to evoke an atmosphere, a historical era, or an emotion.

Analogy In exposition, usually a comparison of some length in which the unknown is explained in terms of the known, the unfamiliar in terms of the familiar, the remote in terms of the immediate.

In argument, an analogy consists of a series of likenesses between two or more dissimilar things, demonstrating that they are either similar or identical in other respects also. The use of analogy in argument is open to criticism, for two things alike in many respects are not necessarily alike in all (for example, lampblack and diamonds are both pure carbon; they differ only in their crystal structure). Although analogy never *proves* anything, its dramatic quality, its assistance in establishing tone, its vividness make it one of the most valuable techniques of the writer.

Analysis A method of exposition by logical division, applicable to anything that can be divided into component parts: an object, such as an automobile or a watch; an institution, such as a college; or a process, such as mining coal or writing a poem. Parts or processes may be described technically and factually or impressionistically and selectively. In the latter method the parts are organized in relation to a single governing idea so that the mutually supporting function of each of the components in the total structure becomes clear to the reader. Parts may be explained in terms of their characteristic function. Analysis may also be concerned with the connection of events; given this condition or series of conditions, what effects will follow?

Argument Often contains the following parts: the *proposition,* that is, an assertion that leads to the issue; the *issue,* that is, the precise phase of the proposition which the writer is attempting to prove and the question on which the whole argument rests; the *evidence,* the facts and opinions which the author offers as testimony. One may order the evidence deductively by proceeding from certain premises to a *conclusion;* or *inductively* by generalizing from a number of instances and drawing a *conclusion.* Informal arguments frequently make greater use of the methods of exposition than they do of formal logic. See Deduction, Induction, Logic, and Analogy.

The attempt to distinguish between argument and persuasion is sometimes made by reference to means (Argument makes appeals to reason: persuasion, to emotions); sometimes to ends (Argument causes someone to change his mind; persuasion moves him to action). These distinctions, however, are more academic than functional, for in practice argument and persuasion are not discrete entities. Yet the proof in argument rests largely upon the objectivity of evidence; the proof in persuasion, upon the heightened use of language.

Assumption That part of an argument that is unstated because it is either taken for granted by the reader and writer or undetected by them. When the reader consciously disagrees with an assumption, the writer has misjudged his audience by assuming what the reader refuses to concede.

Attitude Toward subject, see Tone. Toward audience, see Audience.

Audience For the writer, his expected readers. When the audience is a general, unknown one, and the subject matter is closely related to the writer's opinions, preferences, attitudes, and tastes, then the writer's relationship to his audience is in a very real sense his relationship to himself. The writer who distrusts the intelligence of his audience or who adapts his material to what he assumes are the tastes and interests of his readers compromises his integrity.

On the other hand, if the audience is generally known (a college class, for example), and the subject matter is factual information, then the beginning writer may well consider the education, interests, and tastes of her audience. Unless she keeps a definite audience in mind, the beginner is apt to shift levels of usage, use inappropriate diction, and lose the reader by appealing to none of his interests.

"It is now necessary to warn the writer that his concern for the reader must be pure; he must sympathize with the reader's plight (most readers are in trouble about half the time) but never seek to know his wants. The whole duty of a writer is to please and satisfy himself, and the true writer always plays to an audience of one. Let him start sniffing the air, or glancing at the Trend Machine, and he is as good as dead although he may make a nice living." Strunk and White, *The Elements of Style* (Macmillan).

Cause and Effect A seemingly simple method of development in which either the cause of a particular effect or the effects of a particular cause are investigated. However, because of the philosophical difficulties surrounding causality, the writer should be cautious in ascribing causes. For the explanation of most processes, it is probably safer to proceed in a sequential order, using transitional words to indicate the order of the process.

Classification The division of a whole into the classes that compose it; or the placement of a subject into the whole of which it is a part. See Definition and Analysis.

Coherence Literally, a sticking together, therefore, the joining or linking of one point to another. It is the writer's obligation to make clear to the reader the relationship of sentence to sentence and paragraph to paragraph. Sometimes coherence is simply a matter of putting the parts in a sequence that is meaningful and relevant—logical sequence, chronological order, order of importance. Other times it is helpful to underscore the relationship. An elementary but highly useful method of underscoring relationships is the use of transitional words: *but, however, yet* inform the reader that what is to follow contrasts with what went before; *furthermore, moreover, in addition to* continue or expand what went before.

Another elementary way of achieving coherence is the enumeration of ideas—*first, second, third*—so as to remind the reader of the development. A more subtle transition can be gained by repeating at the beginning of a paragraph a key word or idea from the end of the preceding paragraph. Such a transition reminds the reader of what has gone before and simultaneously prepares her for what is to come.

Comparison and Contrast The presentation of a subject by indicating similarities between two or more things (comparison); by indicating differences (contrast). The basic elements in a comparative process, then, are (1) the terms of the comparison, or the various objects compared, and (2) the points of likeness or difference between the objects compared. Often comparison and contrast are used in definition and other methods of exposition.

Concreteness See Abstraction, Levels of.

Connotation All that the word suggests or implies in addition to its literal meaning. However, this definition is arbitrary and, from the standpoint of the writer, artificial, because the meaning of a word includes *all* that it suggests and implies.

Contrast See Comparison.

Coordination Elements of like importance in like grammatical construction. Less important elements should be placed in grammatically subordinate positions. See Parallelism and Subordination.

Deductive Reasoning In logic, the application of a generalization to a particular; by analogy, in rhetoric, that development which moves from the general to the specific.

Definition In logic, the placing of the word to be defined in a general class and then showing how it differs from other members of the class; in rhetoric, the meaningful extension (usually enriched by the use of detail, concrete illustration, anecdote, metaphor) of a logical definition in order to answer fully, clearly, and often implicitly the question, "What is ——?"

Denotation The literal meaning of a word. See Connotation.

Description That form of discourse whose primary purpose is to present factual information about an object or experience (objective description); or to report the impression or evaluation of an object or experience (subjective description). Most description combines the two purposes. *It was a frightening night.* (An evaluation with which others might disagree.) *The wind blew the shingles off the north side of the house and drove the rain under the door.* (Two facts about which there can be little disagreement.)

Diction Style as determined by choice of words. Good diction is characterized by accuracy and appropriateness to subject matter; weak diction, by the use of inappropriate, vague, or trite words. The relationship between the kinds of words a writer selects and his subject matter in large part determines tone. The deliberate use of inappropriate diction is a frequent device of satire.

Discourse, forms of Traditionally, exposition, argument, description, and narration. See entries under each. These four kinds of traditional discourse are rarely found in a pure form. Argument and exposition may be interfused in the most complex fashion. Exposition often employs narration and description for purposes of illustration. It is important to remember, however, that in an effective piece of writing the use of more than one form of discourse is never accidental. It always serves the author's central purpose.

Emphasis The arrangement of the elements of a composition so that the important meanings occur in structurally important parts of the composition. Repetition, order of increasing importance, exclamation points, rhetorical questions, and figures of speech are all devices to achieve emphasis.

Evidence That part of argument or persuasion that involves proof. It usually takes the form of facts, particulars deduced from general principles, or opinions of authorities.

Exposition That form of discourse which explains or informs. Most papers required of college students are expository. The *methods* of exposition presented in this text are identification, definition, classification, illustration, comparison and contrast, and analysis. See separate entries in glossary.

Figure of Speech A form of expression in which the meanings of words are extended beyond the literal. The common figures of speech are metaphor, simile, analogy.

Generalization A broad conception or principle derived from particulars. Often, simply a broad statement. See Abstraction.

Grammar A systematic description of a language.

Identification A process preliminary to definition of a subject. For the writer it is that vastly important period preliminary to writing when, wrestling with inchoate glimmerings, she begins to select and shape her materials. As a method of exposition, it brings the subject into focus by describing it.

Illustration A particular member of a class used to explain or dramatize a class, a type, a thing, a person, a method, an idea, or a condition. The idea explained may be either stated or implied. For purposes of illustration, the individual member of a class must be a fair representation of the distinctive qualities of the class. The use of illustrations, examples, and specific instances adds to the concreteness and vividness of writing. See Narration.

Image A word or statement which makes an appeal to the senses. Thus, there are visual images, auditory images, *etc.* As the most direct experience of the world is through the senses, writing which makes use of sense impressions (images) can be unusually effective.

Inductive Reasoning In logic, the formulation of a generalization after the observation of an adequate number of particular instances; by analogy, in rhetoric, that development which moves from the particular to the general.

Intention For the particular purpose or function of a single piece of writing, see Purpose. Intention determines the four forms of discourse. See Exposition, Argument, Description, Narration. These intentions may be explicitly or implicitly set forth by the writer.

Irony At its simplest, involves a discrepancy between literal and intended meaning; at its most complex, it involves an utterance more meaningful (and usually meaningful in a different way) to the listener than to the speaker. For example, Oedipus's remarks about discovering the murderer of the king are understood by the audience in a way Oedipus himself cannot understand them. The inability to grasp the full implications of his own remark is frequently feigned by the satirist.

Issue The limitation of a general proposition to the precise point on which the argument rests. Defeating the issue defeats the argument. Typically the main proposition of an argument will raise at least one issue for discussion and controversy.

Limitation of Subject Restriction of the subject to one that can be adequately developed with reference to audience and purpose.

Metaphor An implied comparison between two things that are seemingly different; a compressed analogy. Effectively used, metaphors increase clarity, interest, vividness, and concreteness.

Narration A form of discourse the purpose of which is to tell a story. If a story is significant in itself, the particulars appealing to the imagination, it is *narration.* If a story illustrates a point in exposition or argument, it may be called *illustrative narration.* If a story outlines a process step by step, the particulars appealing to the understanding, it is designated as *expository narration.*

Organization, methods of Vary with the form of discourse. Exposition uses in part, in whole, or in combination identification, definition, classification, illustration, comparison and contrast, and analysis. Argument and persuasion often use the method of organization of inductive or deductive reasoning, or analogy. Description is often organized either around a dominant impression or by means of a spatial arrangement. Narration, to give two examples, may be organized chronologically or in terms of point of view.

Paradox An assertion or sentiment seemingly self-contradictory, or opposed to common sense, which may yet be true.

Paragraph A division of writing that serves to discuss one topic or one aspect of a topic. The central thought is either implied or expressed in a topic sentence. Paragraphs have such a great variety of organization and function that it is almost impossible to generalize about them.

Parallelism Elements of similar rhetorical importance in similar grammatical patterns. See Coordination.

Parody Mimicking the language and style of another.

Perspective The vantage point chosen by the writer to achieve his purpose, his strategy. It is reflected in his close scrutiny of, or distance from, his subject; his objective representation or subjective interpretation of it. See Diction, Purpose, Tone.

Persuasion See Argument.

Point of View In description, the position from which the observer looks at the object described; in narration, the person who sees the action, who tells the story; in exposition, the grammatical person of the composition. First person or the more impersonal third person is commonly used.

Proposition See Argument.

Purpose What the writer wants to accomplish with a particular piece of writing.

Rhetoric The art of using language effectively.

Rhetorical Question A question asked in order to induce thought and to provide emphasis rather than to evoke an answer.

Rhythm In poetry and prose, patterned emphasis. Good prose is less regular in its rhythm than poetry.

Satire The attempt to effect reform by exposing an object to laughter. Satire makes frequent recourse to irony, wit, ridicule, parody. It is usually classified under such categories as the following: social satire, personal satire, literary satire.

Style "The essence of a sound style is that it cannot be reduced to rules—that it is a living and breathing thing, with something of the demoniacal in it—that it fits its proprietor tightly and yet ever so loosely, as his skin fits him. It is, in fact, quite as securely an integral part of him as that skin is...In brief, a style is always the outward and visible symbol of a man, and it cannot be anything else." H. L. Mencken, *On Style,* used with permission of Alfred A. Knopf, Inc.

"Young writers often suppose that style is a garnish for the meat of prose, a sauce by which a dull dish is made palatable. Style has no such separate entity; it is nondetachable, unfilterable. The beginner should approach style warily, realizing that it is himself he is approaching, no other; and he should begin by turning resolutely away from all devices that are popularly believed to indicate style—all mannerisms, tricks, adornments. The approach to style is by way of plainness, simplicity, orderliness, sincerity." E. B. White from *The Elements of Style* (Macmillan).

Subordination Less important rhetorical elements in grammatically subordinate positions. See Parallelism and Coordination.

Syllogism In formal logic, a deductive argument in three steps: a major premise, a minor premise, a conclusion. The major premise states a quality of a class (All men are mortal); the minor premise states that X is a member of the class (Socrates is a man); the conclusion states that the quality of a class is also a quality of a member of the class (Socrates is mortal). In rhetoric, the full syllogism is rarely used; instead, one of the premises is usually omitted. "You can rely on her; she is independent" is an abbreviated syllogism. Major premise: Independent people are reliable; minor premise: She is independent; conclusion: She is reliable. Constructing the full syllogism frequently reveals flaws in reasoning, such as the above, which has an error in the major premise.

Symbol A concrete image which suggests a meaning beyond itself.

Tone The manner in which the writer communicates his attitude toward the materials he is presenting. Diction is the most obvious means of establishing tone. See Diction.

Topic Sentence The thesis that the paragraph as a whole develops. Some paragraphs do not have topic sentences, but the thesis is implied.

Transition The linking together of sentences, paragraphs, and larger parts of the composition to achieve coherence. See Coherence.

Unity The relevance of selected material to the central theme of an essay. See Coherence.

AUTHOR/ ARTIST AND TITLE INDEX